Vasil Khachidze Tim Wang
Sohail Siddiqui Vincent Liu
Sergio Cappuccio Alicia Lim (Eds.)

Contemporary Research on E-business Technology and Strategy

International Conference, iCETS 2012
Tianjin, China, August 29-31, 2012
Revised Selected Papers

Springer

Volume Editors

Vasil Khachidze
CeBA Canada, Ottawa, ON, Canada
E-mail: vasil.khachidze@cebacanada.org

Tim Wang
ITSB, PWGSC, Ottawa, ON, Canada
E-mail: tim.wang@cebacanada.com

Sohail Siddiqui
Algonquin College, Woodroffe Campus, Ottawa, ON, Canada
E-mail: sohail.siddiqui@gmail.com

Vincent Liu
Macau University of Science and Technology, Taipa, Macau
E-mail: g.liuyide@gmail.com

Sergio Cappuccio
National Research Council, Ottawa, ON, Canada
E-mail: sergio.cappuccio@nrc-cnrc.gc.ca

Alicia Lim
Carleton University, Ottawa, ON, Canda
E-mail: alicia_lim@carleton.ca

ISSN 1865-0929 e-ISSN 1865-0937
ISBN 978-3-642-34446-6 e-ISBN 978-3-642-34447-3
DOI 10.1007/978-3-642-34447-3
Springer Heidelberg Dordrecht London New York

Library of Congress Control Number: 2012949846

CR Subject Classification (1998): K.6, K.4.4, H.4, H.3, J.1, H.2

Typesetting: Camera-ready by author, data conversion by Scientific Publishing Services, Chennai, India

Printed on acid-free paper

Springer is part of Springer Science+Business Media (www.springer.com)

Preface

The International Conference on E-business Technology and Strategy (iCETS) provides a peer-reviewed forum for academic researchers, enterprises and business analysts, and government leaders from across the globe to share contemporary research on developments in the fields of e-business technology, information management systems and business strategy. It seeks to promote effective and vibrant networking among researchers and practitioners from around the world who are concerned about the effective management of information technology in organizations.

This network of researchers views fostering the development of emerging scholars in the information technology and e-business fields as its primary task. Consequently, the conference is designed to provide a venue for researchers to obtain substantive and beneficial feedback on their work.

There were 231 contributions submitted to iCETS 2012. After in-depth discussions, 65 high-quality contributions were selected for publication in this volume. The authors are from Australia, Canada, China, Korea, Italy, Ghana, Georgia, Thailand, UK, among other countries.

We thank all the authors who submitted papers, the Program Committee members, and the external reviewers. We also thank all the local people who were instrumental in making this edition of iCETS another very successful event.

August 2012

Vasil Khachidze
Tim Wang
Sohail Siddiqui
Vincent Liu
Sergio Cappuccio
Alicia Lim

Organization

Conference Chairs

Khaled Hassanein	McMaster University, Canada
Zhiyong Feng	Tianjin University, China
Vasil Khachidze	CeBA Canada, Canada
Jianwu Dang	Tianjin University, China
Yanqing Duan	University of Bedfordshire Business School, UK
Ajith Abraham	Technical University of Ostrava, Czech Republic
Martin Zhao	Mercer University, USA
Kartlos Kachiashvili	Georgian Technical University, Georgia
Yi Pan	Georgia State University, USA
Carl Adams	University of Portsmouth, UK
Marc Adam	Karlsruhe Institute of Technology, Germany
Tim Wang	ITSB, PWGSC, Canada
Vincent Yide Liu	Macau University of Science and Technology, Macau

Advisory Board

AbdelKrim Hamou-Lhadj	IBM Canada, Canada
Ajith Abraham	Machine Intelligence Research (MIR) Labs, USA
Volker Gruhn	University of Leipzig, Germany
Esma Aïmeur	University of Montreal, Canada
Denghua Zhong	Tianjin University, China
George Giaglis	Athens University of Economics and Business, Greece
Carl Adams	University of Portsmouth, UK
Ljubo Vlacic	Griffith University, Australia
Martin Zhao	Mercer University, USA
Zhiyong Feng	Tianjin University, China
Sergio Cappuccio	National Research Council, Canada
Tim Wang	ITSB, PWGSC, Canada

Program Committee

Ajith Abraham	MIR Labs, USA
Ali Al Mazari	PSCJ, Alfaisal University, Kingdom of Saudi Arabia
Andreas Pashalidis	Katholieke Universiteit Leuven, Belgium
Christos Bouras	University of Patras, Greece
Carl Adams	University of Portsmouth, UK

Chunyang Ye	University of Toronto, Canada
Chen-Yuan Chen	National Pingtung University of Education, Taiwan
Christopher Westland	University of Illinois, USA
Chih-Ping Wei	National Taiwan University, Taiwan
Dimitris Karagiannis	University of Vienna, Austria
Dan Ma	Singapore Management University, Singapore
Esma Aïmeur	University of Montreal, Canada
Francesco Bolici	Università degli Studi di Cassino, Italy
George Giaglis	Athens University of Economics and Business, Greece
Haibin Zhu	Nipissing University, Canada
Hepu Deng	RMIT University, Australia
Hui Zhang	Tianjin University, China
Indranil Bose	University of Hong Kong, Hong Kong
Joseph Barjis	Delft University of Technology, The Netherlands
Jingsong Wang	Tianjin University of Technology, China
Jung-Ran Park	Drexel University, USA
Khalil Drira	French National Center for Scientific Research, France
Kartlos Kachiashvili	Georgian Technical University in Tbilisi, Georgia
Ljubo Vlacic	Griffith University, Australia
Morad Benyoucef	University of Ottawa, Canada
Minqiang Li	Tianjin University, China
Marc T.P. Adam	Karlsruhe Institute of Technology, Germany
Michael Weiss	Carleton University, Canada
Martin Zhao	Mercer University, USA
Peng Zhou	Ministry of Industry and Information Technology, China
Shuwu Zhang	Chinese Academy of Sciences, China
Sergio Cappuccio	National Research Council, Canada
Soon Ae Chun	City University of New York, USA
Stoyan Tanev	University of Southern Denmark, Denmark
Tao Xu	Civil Aviation University of China, China
Thomas Tran	University of Ottawa, Canada
Volker Gruhn	University of Leipzig, Germany
Wojciech Cellary	Poznan University of Economics, Poland
Xiaohui Zhao	Unitec Institute of Technology, New Zealand
Yiliu Tu	University of Calgary, Canada
Yanchen Li	Macau University of Science and Technology, Macau
Yanbo Han	Chinese Academy of Sciences, China
Yanqing Duan	University of Bedfordshire, UK
Yide Liu	Macau University of Science and Technology, Macau
Zhaohao Sun	University of Ballarat, Australia

Editorial Board

Conference Secretariat

Jia Sun	Tianjin University, China
Vasil Khachidze	JEBTS, CeBA Canada, Canada
Yuexian Hou	Tianjin University, China
Tim Wang	ITSB, PWGSC, Canada
Vincent Liu	Macau University of Science and Technology, Macau
Sohail Siddiqui	Department of National Defence, Canada
Hong Yu	CeBA Canada, Canada
Huili Dong	Tianjin University, China

Table of Contents

E-commerce: Consumer Online Shopping in Canada

Ayoub Yousefi* and Jie Tang

King's University College, University of Western Ontario
ayousefi@uwo.ca

Abstract. E-commerce has changed the way businesses are conducted and transformed the market structures around the world. As a result, new relations have been developed between consumers and suppliers of all goods and services. Online shopping, which is driven by advances in the Internet and ICT Infrastructure, has altered consumers' attitude and the consumer-supplier relationship. The development, in turn, has generated new questions for business leaders, governments, and the researchers of all fields, including business and economics.

This paper investigates the factors that form the base for the online shopping decision of consumers. The study uses "A Survey of Access to and the use of Information Communication Technology", 2nd edition by Statistics Canada in 2000. From the survey, 6,818 useful observations and 17 relevant variables are chosen. The study adopts the Probit model and Maximum Likelihood Estimation technique for regression analysis. The empirical results reveal that, in general, the Network and Online banking securities are the most effective determining factors for online shoppers. In addition, making the online shopping environment safer and more user-friendly renders mutual benefits for both consumers and vendors.

Keywords: E-commerce, online shopping, network security, online banking.

1 Introduction

E-commerce is defined as any transactions made over the Internet. Most often this involves the transfer of goods, services, or information (United Nations, 2002). The number of Internet users has been growing rapidly over time. In addition to facilitating interpersonal social media, the Internet has also been used to connect with customers, suppliers, distributors and other potential players in the business chain. These functions are becoming more significant in developing countries due to their greater and faster growth as compared to developed countries.

The Internet offers access to larger markets and brings about more cash flow, lower labour cost, and bigger profits. There are 327 million fixed Internet subscriptions all around the world, equivalent to 4.3% of the total population, and the number has

* Corresponding author.

V. Khachidze et al. (Eds.): iCETS 2012, CCIS 332, pp. 1–14, 2012.

doubled over the past 10 years (OECD, 2011). Information sharing over the Internet is the most affordable, efficient and up-to-date media compared to other, traditional methods. The emergence of E-commerce can be attributed to the development of Information and Communications Technology (ICT). As ICT spreads to all sectors of the economy, it facilitates innovations, the creation of new goods and services, and modes of operation. More than before, manufacturers, distributors, retailers, and even individuals are setting their businesses up over the Internet. They take full advantage of the very affordable communication apparatus to gain better access to customers and generate more sales. Consumers are also participating in E-commerce in huge number, due to its convenience and efficiency. By using e-commerce, consumers save significantly on their travelling time and other related costs. Moreover, the Internet has made shopping experiences smarter by allowing the customers to compare prices and qualities in a larger scale, as opposed to a few stores within a limited location. As a result, e-commerce can affect total output and boost economic growth. Furthermore, rapid access to the technological changes and the e-commerce can also improve multi-factor productivity (MFP) and enhance economic growth of the nations. Many economic studies focus on the effects of e-commerce on business productivity, and others focus on the challenges of e-commerce, especially in developing countries. In this paper, we will examine the consumer side of the e-commerce to find out the factors that influence the decision of individuals in making Internet purchases. The survey used in this paper includes questions such as "ever used Internet to shop online"; "ever used e-banking"; "ever provided credit card online"; "willing to provide credit card over the Internet"; "used the Internet to subscribe newsgroup or not"; etc. From such factors, we identify those which significantly influence customer's decision of shopping over the Internet. We interpret, "ever used e-banking" to reflect e-banking reliability, and "willing to provide credit card over the Internet" to reflect credit card security concerns which would make the consumers more reluctant to shop online. We also interpret "Subscribe to newsgroup" to capture the increased probability of shopping over the Internet by having more updated sales information through the e-mails. In addition, we examine the effects on consumers' online shopping decision of some socio-economic factors such as age, annual income, gender, and area of residence. This paper is organized as follows: Section 2 presents a brief review of the relevant literature on customers' online shopping decisions. Next, section 3 explains the methodology and the rationale for the application of the Probit model. Section 4 then provides the sources of the data and describes their main features, and section 5 discusses empirical results of the significance level of each factor related to the online shopping decision. Finally, section 6 offers the results of the study and some suggestions.

2 Literature Review

E-commerce has become a mainstream mode of business for both consumers and businesses in OECD countries. It has experienced continued growth even during the current economic downturn; albeit at lower levels than before, the growth of e-commerce remains at higher levels than its offline counterparts for the same period (OECE, 2010).

The volume of online sales is taken as an indicator of how firms are adopting e-commerce as their sales channel.

According to the United Nations (2011), the common fundamental e-commerce models are:

a) Business to Business, B2B.
b) Business to Consumer, B2C.
c) Consumer to Consumer, C2C, and
d) Information retrieval.

Recently, attention has been focused on e-commerce over the Internet with the rapid developments of information technology, especially Internet networks. International guidelines and measurement standards are strongly needed to help monitor the progress and predict the future of e-commerce. As a result, widely differing estimates of the size and impact of e-commerce are concluded across different countries. For instance, Wong and Lam (1999) collected sales data in both resident and non-resident buyers as indicators of e-commerce readiness in Singapore. They used major findings of the survey such as Access to Internet, Web presence, E-commerce (EC) transactions, and EC supporting services. Their measures were constrained by several difficulties such as Identification and classification of EC firms, fast growth and unpredictability of the sector, availability of information, etc. Nonetheless, the result showed that strong growth can be expected not only to continue, but also to accelerate. Other researchers investigated the significance of the value that e-commerce has brought to firms and to the economy as a whole. Elia et al. (2006) investigated in the area of Small and Medium sized manufacture Enterprises (SMEs). They found out that there is a positive relationship between increased adoption and cumulative benefits for SME manufacturers in Canada. The paper further identified different benefits that firms gain from the use of e-commerce. Lal K. (2002) suggests that SMEs face a crucial competitive advantage by accessing international markets at minimal cost. Gunasekaran et al. (2002) examine how e-commerce minimizes production cost by making sub-assemblers bid on the project. The greater saving on operational cost was more evident for service sectors such as banks, real estate and travel agencies. Most servicers are made possible on the Internet, reducing the need to visit the actual location. In another manufacturing context, e-commerce creates potential opportunities such as faster product design, speedier ordering of parts and components, reduced lead times and lower inventory costs (Turner 2000). E-commerce has especially been more important in developing countries, due to its greater adoption and the challenges in doing do. Widely adopting e-commerce, however, is not easy in most developing countries. Many internal and external barriers may hinder the diffusion of e-commerce. Huy & Filiatrault (2006) revealed the owner/manager characteristic, organizational, and environmental matters related to the adoption of e-commerce. Cultural barriers in some countries contribute to rejecting e-commerce as the platform where business is conducted (Bingi et al, 2000). In countries like Sri Lanka and India, consumers have strong preferences toward doing business face to face. Since e-commerce consists of online shopping and other online transactions, this raises an interesting question as to what makes the customer purchase online. In other words, what factors influence the customer's online shopping decision? Such factors can logically include variables such as income, education level, Internet security, and so on. Vellido et al (2002) reported that variables such as age, household income, and web-usage patterns do not predict Internet purchasing behaviour. Kuo and Russell (1999) suggested that education, convenience orientation, experience orientation, channel knowledge, perceived distribution utility, and perceived accessibility are strong predictors of online buying status. Other studies like that of Girard et al (2003) inferred that the shopping orientation and demographics have a differential role to play based on the type of product purchased on the Internet. The most influential of orientations that varied by the product types to determine customer's preference were convenience and recreational shopper. In addition, they found that gender, education, and household income are also strong influences on customers' preferences. Even though online shopping has many identifiable advantages over conventional shopping practices, some customers are still reluctant to shop online due to lack of trust for some businesses, especially the new ones. Trust is believed to be the most important long-term barrier for realizing the potential of e-commerce to consumers. Kraeuter (2002) described two types of uncertainty: system-dependent and transaction-specific uncertainty. System-dependent uncertainty refers to the uncertainty about potential technological sources of errors and security gaps; this is due to lack of legal norms also known as e-commerce ethics. Kracher and Corritore (2004) pointed out the examination of e-commerce ethics has lagged behind the development of e-commerce and its technologies. Customers with weaker tolerance for uncertainty would feel insecure to purchase over the Internet, because of the above-mentioned reason. Specifically, credit card fraud is still a major problem for Internet purchasing. The second type of uncertainty is transaction-specific uncertainty. From the perspective of the consumers, transaction-specific uncertainty primarily concerns the quality of the products and services that are offered on the web. The quality of products is difficult to assess in e-market by only looking at pictures. Many lingering problems that happen regarding Internet purchases involve disputes over the quality of the product and follow-up services. Van den Poel and Leunis (1999) concluded that non-store shopping is perceived to be more risky than in-store shopping because shoppers lack the opportunity to physically examine or test the products and they fear not getting what they wanted. This raises a question as to how sellers over the Internet could increase the quality of their products and services to gain more customer trust. Purohit and Srivastava (2001) promoted a set of characteristics such as warranty, seller's reputation, and customer's testimonials which could influence customer's perceptions of product quality. These features can be used by the sellers to signal quality and to reduce perceived risk on the part of customers. By evaluating the different attributes, customer can be more informed when making a purchasing decision. Most of the above factors have been examined by researchers for their usefulness to reduce the risks of purchasing online, namely perceived risks. Dowling (1985) found that warranty has no effect on reducing perceived risk while Van den Poel and Leunis (1999) found the opposite as warranty is a very important indicator of trust for online shoppers. In Lwin and Williams' (2006) findings, the use of warranties by leading web sites is an effective tool to differentiate from other products. As such, reputable websites should offer warranties to lower online customer's perceived risks of purchasing online, increase their perceptions of product quality, and heighten their determination of a purchasing decision. The so-called 'established web sites', by virtue of their record of past performance and quality are more likely to attract consumers to purchase from them. Prime examples are the phenomenally successful Amazon and eBay. Benyoucef and Li (2011), on the other hand, pointed out that the reputation systems that many websites currently enjoy lack a global dimension. They introduced a reputation system which can be offered by a third party who connects with other online communities to provide aggregate feedback to viewers on a broader base. Such reputation systems can better assist customers' decision making regarding online shopping. Apart from the warranty of a reputable website, another important factor which can potentially reduce risks is the seller's own reputation on the established websites. Regardless of how reputable the website is, if the seller's own reputation is not high enough by past customers' feedbacks, potential customers would be less willing to buy from these sellers than the ones having higher reputations. What do these findings signal to Internet sellers? Improving one's reputation and providing adequate warranty and after-sales service are the keys to attracting more cautious Internet buyers. Above all the existing barriers to online shopping, the remaining major concern is e-payment security. He and Duan (2009) analyzed the pros and cons of several e-payment methods in terms of security level and ease of use. The commonly used method is credit and / or debit card at present, in which the personal information provided with the credit card is poorly protected. There are other methods, including Electronic Cheque, Electronic Currency, Smart Card Payment and Centralized Account System. In this paper, He and Duan pointed out that the successful development and acceptance of online e-payment is not merely compromising simplicity to achieve high security standards, but indicates a full understanding of the needs of both consumers and merchants. As technology develops, a straightforward and reliable online e-payment environment can greatly reduce the uncertainty associated with online shopping.

3 Research Methodology

In light of the existing research, we propose the following hypothesis. Customers' shopping decisions on the Internet will be affected by such variables as listed below:

Previous experience of using internet banking (E-banking);
Experience of subscribing to newsgroup (Newsgroup);
Ability to use a computer (Ability);
Effect of the Internet on time spending (Time spent);
Perception of the trustworthiness of other people (Trustworthiness);
Willingness to provide credit card online (Willingness);
Concerned about security when banking/purchasing over the Internet (Security);

Annual personal income (INCM);
Working hours (WKWEHR);
Education level (EDUYR);
Age group (AGER10);
Resident's region (Ontario, British Columbia, Quebec, Atlantic Provinces, Prairie Region);
Gender (SEX)

Data was retrieved from "A survey of Access to and the use of Information Communication Technology", 2nd edition, by Statistics Canada (2000). The survey was designed to evaluate information access to and use of information communication technology in Canada. Topics include:

General use of technology and computers,
Technology in the workplace,
Development of computer skills,
Frequency of Internet and E-mail use,
Non-users and security and information on the Internet;
Many other areas were surveyed; however, these are less important to the subject of this study.

The target population of the respondents included all individuals aged 15 and over living in a private household in one of the ten provinces. The original survey includes many aspects related to online shopping. It analyzes the general use of technology and computers, work and education background, computer technology in the workplace, volunteer work, etc. Since the purpose of this paper is to test the significance of factors which influence customer's online shopping decisions, we have selected the survey questions which are deemed relevant to the objective of this study. As a result, 17 variables are selected to be used in this paper and after exclusion for some missing values, 6,818 observations were compiled for testing. A Probit model was adopted to test the hypothesis made in the study. For the estimation of the model we used the Maximum Likelihood method. In what follows we briefly describe the rationale for the use of the Probit Model:

If y is a binary (0, 1) variable, we can use the cumulative probability to define the distribution of y, $E(y) = \phi(X\beta)$, $P(y=1) = \phi(X\beta)$.

Let $\phi(X\beta)$ be the cumulative probability function of a standard normal distribution,

$$\phi(X\beta) = \int_{-\infty}^{X\beta} \frac{1}{\sqrt{2\pi}} \exp(-z^2/2)dz$$

$$L(\beta|y) = P(Y_1\ Y_{2\ldots} Y_n) = \prod P(Y=1) \prod P(Y=0)$$
$$= \phi(X\beta)^{n_1}(1-\phi(X\beta))^{n_2}$$

Then, a choice must be made over the binary feature of the dependent variable (Ever used Internet to purchase goods/services online). Almost 450 observations of the dependent variable were "NO" and only about 200 of them were "Yes". Because of this imbalance of the observations, Probit model seemed to be a better model than OLS or Logit model.

4 Source of Data and Summary Statistics

This section provides tables of summary statistics of the variables used in the paper. Table 1 shows the experience and perceptions about E-commerce when the survey was conducted in 2000. As online shopping was not widely adopted at the time, we can see all five questions have unbalanced answers towards rejecting E-commerce. However, shoppers' preferences have shown dramatic changes over time, as mentioned earlier. Perception of trustworthiness of other people was selected as a proxy of trusting online shopping, since there exists no better question capturing trust with respect to products purchased online. The Internet shoppers have shown continued concern about product quality. More than before, online shoppers use the warranty or the website rating as signals before making an order.

Table 1. Experience and Perceptions about E-commerce (in %)

	1	0	Mean
Ever use Internet to purchase goods/services	26.3	73.7	0.28
Willing to provide your credit card over Internet	33.1	66.9	0.33
Ever use Internet electronic banking	26.3	73.7	0.26
Internet to subscribe newsgroup/listsev (mailing list)	17.5	82.5	0.18
Note; 1=Yes;2=NO			
Perception of trustworthiness of other people	50	50	0.5

Note: 1=Most people can be trusted; 0=Can't be too careful

Table 2 shows general information about the respondents such as age, educational level, annual income, working hours, ability to use a computer, concern about security online, and the effect of time spent on shopping over the Internet. The average age was about 25-30 years old with an annual income of $30,000 to $39,000. Worth noting, 45% of the respondents were greatly concerned about security when banking or purchasing over the Internet; and 90% of them thought the Internet did not change their time spent on shopping. Most of the respondents were about the average level of income, educational level and working hours. Other variables, such as gender and resident region, were not included in the table. Male respondents accounted for 50%; 28% of the respondents lived in Ontario, 18.5% in Quebec, 12.9% in BC, and 18.9% in Atlantic region.

Table 2. General Information about Responderts (in %)

	1	2	3	4	5	6	7	8	9	10	11	12	Mean
Annual personal income		3.6	5.5	6.2	6	15.6	18.6	14	10	10.6	3	5	7.05

Note: 1=No income;...,7=$30,00-$39,000; 12=$100,000 or more

	1	6	7	8	9	10	11	12	13	Mean
Number of years of elementray school education completed successfully by the respondent	0.2	0	0.15	0.35	1.1	3.1	13.7	65.5	15.9	11.9

Note: 1=one to five years, ...13=Thirteen

	1	2	3	4	5	6	7	Mean
Age group	17	28.3	29.7	18.5	5.8	0.7	0	2.7

Note: 1=15 to 21;..., 7=75 years and over

	1	5	10	30	40	60	100	Mean
Number of hours worked in a week	0	0.2	10	4.3	30	5.3	0.1	40.11

Note: 1=one hour;...,120=120 hours and more

	1	2	3	4	5	Mean
Ability to use a computer	6.8	19.6	30.9	27.1	15.6	3.3

Note: 1=Poor,..., 5=Excellent

	1	2	3	4	5	Mean
Concerned about security when banking/purchasing over Internet	1	15.6	7.4	30.2	45.8	4.04

Note: 1=No opinion;..., 7=Greatly

	1	2	3	Mean
Effect of Internet on time spent: shopping	8.3	90.4	1.3	1.93

Note: 1=Decreased, 2=Stany the same; 3=Increase

5 Regression Result

Model 1. Model 1 includes all variables. As the regression result shows in Table 3, the E-banking and Willingness variables are significant at the 1% level of significance. They are all positively correlated with online shopping, and Willingness is the dominant variable among all others. A unit of change in Willingness will on average increase the possibility of shopping online by 1.47 units. Other factors such as Newsgroup, Ability of using computers, E-banking, Security, and Income are also significant at the 1% level of significance with large z-statistic values. Sex is also significant at the 5% level of significance. Therefore, being a male or female has much less effect than other significant factors affecting consumers' online shopping decisions. However, the shopping time spent on the Internet has a negative effect. The more time the consumer has to spend to put in an order online, the less likely he or she will be to shop online. Another factor that is negatively correlated with online shopping is education, as more educated people shop less online. Factors such as age, working hours, and area of residence appeared insignificant in affecting online shopping decision. In the next section, we look at each factor in more detail.

Willingness. The regression result of the willingness to use credit card online revealed significant value by the Z-statistics measure. This has also been shown empirically by the research of Kracher and Corritore (2004) and Kraeuter (2002). Results suggest that the more willingness customers have toward using credit card online, the more likely they will be to purchase online. This implies that e-commerce can increase further by improving the level of website security and lowering customers' worries. In today's world, with the growing inclusion of trusted third parties, such as Paypal, in e-commerce and the increasing sophistication of relevant technology, consumer's concerns about security of credit card numbers and personal information are likely to diminish in the near future.

Table 3. Regressions on probability of shopping over the Internet (E-commerce)

	Model 1			Model 2			Model 3		
Variable	Coefficient	z-Statistic	Prob.	Coefficient	z-Statistic	Prob.	Coefficient	z-Statistic	Prob.
C	-1.586504	-5.143683	0	-1.803508***	-6.129303	0	-2.076999***	-12.46603	0
ABILITY	0.183882***	9.953207	0	0.184586***	10.00939	0	0.183696***	10.00737	0
EBANKING	0.375765***	8.673971	0	0.374717***	8.656833	0	0.373135***	8.628216	0
INCM	0.02993***	3.140938	0.0017	0.029381***	3.33956	0.0008	0.031151***	4.130548	0
NEWSGROUP	0.369749***	7.530165	0	0.37239***	7.622393	0	0.377006***	7.757934	0
SECURITY	0.067462***	3.552783	0.0004	0.067685***	3.576014	0.0003	0.06696***	3.541213	0.0004
TIMESPENT	-0.232584***	-3.879199	0.0001	-0.232794***	-3.889779	0.0001	-0.232563***	-3.888764	0.0001
TRUSTWORTHINESS	0.038855	0.977481	0.3283	0.044425	1.131337	0.2579	0.039262	1.009587	0.3127
WILLINGNESS	**1.478446*** **	**34.72392**	**0**	**1.477269*** **	**34.83754**	**0**	**1.48031*** **	**35.11436**	**0**
SEX	0.064709	1.582947	0.1134	0.059499	1.482106	0.1383			
EDUYR	-0.039188*	-1.783553	0.0745	-0.024835	-1.173205	0.2407			
AGEGR10	-0.000255	-0.013326	0.9894	-0.001076	-0.056302	0.9551			
WKWEHR	-0.000915	-0.552186	0.5808						
ATLANTIC	-0.047434	-0.774168	0.4388						
BC	-0.054997	-0.812053	0.4168						
ONTARIO	0.053854	0.972362	0.3309						
QUEBEC	-0.071101	-1.121757	0.262						

*** Significance at 1% ** Significance at 5% * Significance at 10%

Total obs	6817	Total obs	6817	Total obs	6817
McFadden R-squared	0.321411	McFadden R-squared	0.32063	McFadden R-squared	0.320163
Log likelihood	-2750.141	Log likelihood	-2753.3	Log likelihood	-2755.2

E-Banking. The estimated regression result for E-banking was significant. People who have had a previous experience with E-banking are more likely to purchase online due to its convenience, despite the potential online banking risks. E-banking is considered an instrument for e-commerce. It not only can reduce costs of performing many types of transactions for firms, but also reduce the cost of transferring money or other financial activities for customers. Figure 1 shows the percentage of those who use the Internet to download games and use banking services. Internet banking seems to be utilized by a higher percentage than other Internet activities.

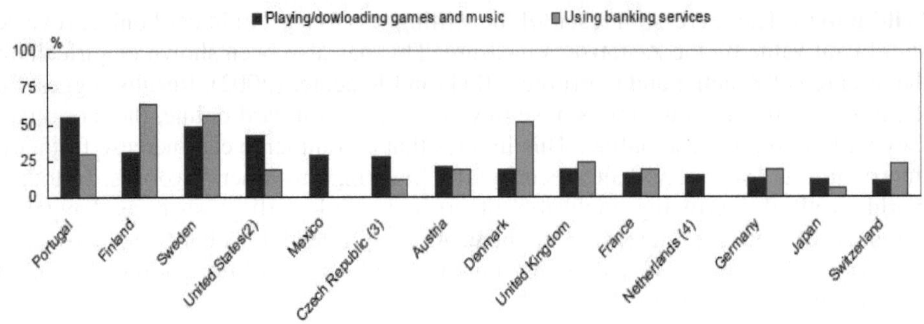

1. 2001 for France, Mexico, Netherlands, Portugal, Switzerland and the United States. Beginning of 2002 for Austria, Denmark, Finland, Germany, Sweden, the United Kingdom, and 2002 for Japan.
2. Playing games only instead of downloading games and music.
3. Banking services relate to year 2003 (Czech Statistical Office Survey).
4. Downloading music only instead of games and music.

Fig. 1. Internet use by type of activity, 2002 or latest available year: % of individuals using the Internet

Online banking has noticeably increased customers' satisfaction in that customers may access their accounts anywhere and anytime. By far, the major international online payment means are credit cards, which are also dominant in many national markets. In some countries, however, due to the potential high risks and fraud associated with credit cards, debit card payments via online banking are widely used as an alternative to credit cards. The worries associated with online payment fraud are widely monitored by banks and other service providers and as a result more and more online payment methods are emerging to attract more online shoppers.

Security. This variable is expected to reflect consumers' concern regarding the security of transactions on the Internet. The concern involves the security of the website that the customer visits. In most cases, vendors with online retail require personal information such as e-mail address to create an account. Kracher and Corritore (2004) analyzed the risk of losing personal information over the Internet when visiting online retail stores. Empirically, the chance of fraud occurring is greater than when shopping at a brick-and-mortar store. The speed and interconnectedness of the Internet makes it difficult to maintain consumers' privacy. As a result, the security issue remains one of the top concerns of online shoppers.

Newsgroup. As the regression results show, the Newsgroup factor plays an important role in Internet shopping. The purpose of shopping online for customers who live in a fast-paced world is primarily to increase savings. As discussed above, online shopping can save transportation time, money on banking transactions, and provide many other benefits. More than before, people have started to subscribe to different stores in order to receive deals which usually do not appear in store. Recently, this has evolved to a new level of online shopping. "The February 2011 survey found that US adult Internet users subscribe to an average of almost three daily or weekly shopping emails or newsletters, and 56% of Internet users subscribe to at least two of the emails." The idea of using online deals to attract customers is successfully explored by Groupon, a portmanteau derived from the words 'group' and 'coupon'. This is a deal-of-the-day website which features discount gift certificates usable at local or national companies. It became one of the biggest online trends offering subscribers daily deals that can be purchased in groups at discount rates. Groupon's success sets an example of effective Internet marketing. Email is a daily based activity conducted by individuals, and therefore there is a higher chance that customers will see the deals in their email more often than looking for them all over the Internet. Because of the considerably large amount of sales generated by the Internet marketing, many websites try to obtain emails using many different methods; an example of this is having pop-ups, which dims the website and pops out a window offering a special free service or deal and asks the customer to input an email address. This trend has noticeably spread to mobile devices lately. Presently, companies advertise through Short Message Service or other mobile services to generate a bigger customer pool. The findings suggest that e-mail subscription tends to cause customers to spend more.

Ability to Use a Computer. This variable appears to have a positive relationship with online shopping. It is not surprising to see that a person's ability to use a computer can increase the probability of purchasing online. The estimated coefficient of this variable is 0.18.

Income. Income also appears to be an influential factor for online shopping, but at a lower significance level compared to the previous four factors. As income increases by one unit, the probability of online shopping increases by 0.029 units. As expected, consumers with high income tend to shop more, whether in store or online, compared to lower income families. However, Pastore (2001) found that online shopping is more popular among less affluent families. The results seem counterintuitive and warrant further examination.

Model 2 and Model 3. Models 2 and 3 exclude some variables such as WKWEHR (working hours), age group, sex, education, and residence region. The regression results are similar to Model 1 in terms of significance. Willingness still has the strongest effect among other factors. Most of the other significant factors in Models 2 and 3 have increased slightly. That is, the significance levels remain almost the same, despite including fewer variables in the regression.

Regression Overall Results. All three models showed significant effects of E-banking, newsgroup, security, and willingness. Including more or fewer variables did not change the significance levels on the most influential factors. In response to the discovery that E-banking, newsgroup, security, and willingness have the strongest impact on consumers' shopping decisions over the Internet, e-marketers should focus on the influential factors associated with e-commerce and plan their marketing strategies accordingly.

Regression results also showed that gender, age group, educational level, working hours, rand esidence region do not influence online shopping decisions. Education shows a moderate negative effect in Model 1 and becomes insignificant in Model 2. This result, however, contradicts the finding of Girard et al (2003) that gender and education exert a strong influence on customers' preferences when after dividing shopping orientation into different groups and differentiated demographics. A survey conducted by Media Audit revealed that the Internet usage by less affluent, less educated minority groups, and homemakers rose sharply (Pastore 2001). Given that computers and the Internet are well diffused in Canada, as in most parts of the world, online shopping decisions are not expected to be determined by their education level. As the user groups of the Internet are getting younger, education level should not differentiate them with respect to making online shopping decisions. Trustworthiness showed no impact on online shopping decision making in all three models, which stands in contrast to our expectation. The literature review concluded that consumers are anxious about buying products over the Internet without first physically touching them. It was expected that there would be a significant positive correlation between online shopping decision and trustworthiness. Lack of trust has been shown to be a major barrier to online shopping for customers. Many e-commerce studies have discussed this matter at different levels. In online buying processes, consumers try to find confidence in the Internet products with adequate assuring indicators such as brand-names or warranties, to reduce their uncertainty about the product attributes that cannot be inspected prior to purchasing. Brand names usually carry more weight than other attributes in online shopping decisions. Most people tend to rely on brand names even when the products are listed on less reputable websites. Lwin and Williams (2006) suggest that a strong brand name conveys lower perceived purchasing risk, higher perceived product quality, and conjures higher willingness to purchase than a weak brand name. For many Internet vendors, however, building up a well-known brand name in a short period of time may not be an easy task to achieve. Finally, although gender appears to have no big impact on online shopping in this study, a report on Holiday Shopping (2001) showed that more females shop on the Internet and they are more price-oriented and more impulsive in shopping online than are males.

6 Conclusion

E-commerce and the Internet stimulate trade by lowing cost of transactions between distant markets. In addition, many intangible goods and services such as books and music, for example, can also be delivered to customers via the Internet; this traditionally was possible only through physical delivery. As societies embark on ever growing new technologies, e-services become even more popular than before. For businesses, the Internet has become a great platform to interact with customers, in pursuit of higher profits. As such, firms need to fully understand customers' concerns regarding online shopping and try to address them accordingly.

This study aims at identifying the factors that influence customers' online shopping decisions in Canada by using "A Survey of Access to and the use of Information Communication Technology, 2nd edition by Statistics Canada (2000)." The factor that has a significant impact on Internet shopping throughout each regression is customer's concern over e-commerce environment security. When e-banking is perceived to be more secure and products are more reliable, online shopping becomes more preferable to the modern consumer's lifestyle. Gender, education, age, working hours, and areas of living are shown to have no influence on preferences for online shopping, which may contradict the conclusions of Girard et al (2003). The results of this paper may be biased, due to the lack of questions in the survey directly related to our hypothesis. In summary, our study suggests that an environment that puts consumers at ease with the Internet and its security would promote online shopping and spur the growth of e-commerce. An integrated one-stop shopping experience, for instance, has shown to enhance much needed confidence, and simultaneously boost online shopping.

References

1. Bingi, P., Mir, A., Khamalah, J.: The challenges facing global e-commerce. Information System Management 17(4), 26–35 (2000)
2. Benyoucef, M., Li, H.: A System for Centralizing Online Reputation. Journal of Emerging Technologies in Web Intelligence 3(3) (August 2011)
3. Elia, E., Lefebvre, L.-A., Lefebvre, E'.: Focus of B-to-B e-commerce initiatives and related benefits in manufacturing small- and medium-sized enterprises (2006)
4. Gunasekaran, A., Marri, H.B., McGaughey, R.E., Nebhwani, M.D.: E-commerce and its impact on operations management. Int. J. Prod. Econ. 75, 185–197 (2002)
5. Girard, T., Korgaonkar, P., Silverblat, R.: Relationship of Type of Product, Shopping Orientations, and Demographics with Preference for shopping on the Internt. Journal of Business and Psychology 18(1), 101–120 (2003)
6. He, Q., Duan, Y.: Emerging Online E-Payment and Issues of Adoption. Encyclopedia of Information Science and Technology (2009)
7. Kracher, B., Corritore, C.L.: Is There a Special E-Commerce Ethics? Business Ethics Quarterly 14(1), 71–94 (2004)
8. Kraeuter, S.G.: The Role of Consumers' Trust in Online-Shopping. Journal of Business Ethics 39(1/2) (2002); Four Teenth Annual Conference of the European Business Ethics Network (EBEN), pp. 43–50 (August 2002)
9. Li, H., Kuo, C., Russell, M.G.: The Impact of Perceived Channel Utilities, Shopping Orientations, and Demographics on the Consumer's Online Buying Behavior. Journal of Comuter-Mediated Communications 5(2), 1–23 (1999)
10. Lal, K.: E-business and manufacturing sector: a study of small and medium-sized enterprises in India. Res. Policy 37, 1199–1211 (2002)
11. Lwin, M.O., Williams, J.D.: Promises, Promises: How Consumers Respond to Warranties in Internet Retailing. The Journal of Consumer Affairs 40(2), 236 (2006)
12. OECD, The economic and social role of Internet intermediaries 9 15 (April 2010)
13. Pastore, M.: Internet Use Continues to Pervade U.S Life (2001), `http://www.cyberatlas.Internet.com` (accessed on July 21)
14. Purohit, D., Srivastava, J.: Effect of Manufacturer Reputation, Retailer Reputation, and Product Warranty on Consumer Judgments of Product Quality: A Cue Diagnosticity Framework. Journal of Consumer Psychology 10(3), 123–134 (2001)
15. Statistics Canada. Wholesale Trade: The Year 2006 in Review (2006), `http://www.statcan.gc.ca/pub/11-621-m/11-621-m2007056-eng.html`

16. Statistics Canada. Electronic commerce and technology (2008)
17. `http://www.statcan.gc.ca/daily-quotidien/080424/dq080424a-eng.htm`
18. Turner, C.: The information E-conomy. Kogan Page, London (2000)
19. United Nations. Electronic Commerce,International Trade and Employment: Review of the Issue (April 8, 2002)
20. Van den Poel, D., Leunis, J.: The Impact of Prices, Branding and Money-Back Guarantee on Store Choice. In: Proceedings of the 8th International Conference on Research in the Distributive Trades, pp. B4.21–B4.29. Universita' Bocconi, Milan (1995); Vellido, A., Lisboa, P.J.G., Meeha, K.: Quantitative Characterization and Prediction for On-Line Purchasing Behavior: A Latent Variable Approach. International Journal of Electronics Commerce 4(4), 83–104 (2000)
21. Wong, J., Lam, E.: Measuring Electronic Commerce in Singapore: Methodological Issues and Survey Findings (1999)

Integrating Spatial Decision Support System with Graph Mining Technique

Abdul Halim Omar and Mohd Najib Mohd Salleh

Faculty of Computer Science and Information Technology, Universiti Tun Hussein Onn Malaysia, Batu Pahat, Johor, Malaysia
najib@uthm.edu.my

Abstract. Large scale crop productivity requires current and accurate information. The choice of a remotely spatial data source entails tradeoffs between cost and accuracy in a timely manner. A primary challenge to large-scale data integration is creating heterogeneous reliability data from different data sources to the same real-world entity. Spatial Decision Support System for agricultural sector can play an important role to facilitate users requiring a large amount of information that must be easily accessible. A fast developing trend in agro-pedagogical scenario analysis is the combination of multiple association data into coherent interaction networks to enable integrated scenario analysis. This paper explores data integration for spatial data sets using graph mining approach during the development of a prototype spatial DSS as a support tool for the farm manager. The results of mining spatial association rules could be implemented to explore alternative states of the environment and policy options to correlate key parameters conducted and better knowledge discovery.

Keywords: Spatial Decision Support System, scenario analysis, graph mining.

1 Introduction

In the agricultural sector, farm management and planning of large scale crop productivity requires current and accurate information. Land managers and decision makers are faced with daily problems related to growing development under a constant diminution of resources; they frequently encounter planning issues characterized by the complexity of interactions between environmental and socio-economic systems. This complexity is essentially related to the diversity of decision alternatives and their variability in space, diversity of criteria nature and the fact that decisions are often surrounded by uncertainty. In the past two decades, the remote and geographic information systems (GIS) were widely used as spatial information technologies to assist land managers in their daily work [7,8,18]. However, more technical expertise is required to improve the decision-making process. Indeed, in spite of their huge capacities in the acquisition and storage of spatial data, GIS have some limits when solving most real-world spatial decision problems. Therefore, the improvement of spatial

V. Khachidze et al. (Eds.): iCETS 2012, CCIS 332, pp. 15–24, 2012.

information in decision-making support is becoming a necessity under the multiple challenges facing decision makers who are supposed to present efficient solutions.

The effective process in decision making is becoming more and more indispensable in order to dynamically meet business and customer needs. In this setting, the integration of existing and multiple business processes in information systems aims to combine selected systems [3], so that they form unified views of interacting users with one single information system. For these reasons, the availability of powerful tools should help to afford a flexible problem-solving environment in which problems can be explored, understood and solved under multiple conflicting objectives. This is the principal aim of the present work, where we explore the effects of interfacing spatial analysis tools within the decision-making environment [4]. An integrated view can be created to facilitate information access and reuse through a single information access point. On the other hand, data from different complementing information systems is combined to gain a more comprehensive basis to satisfy needs. We review an application of graph mining which can find the deficiencies between user and system interaction and help to improve business process alignment. In this paper, we focus on the integration of information and highlight integration solutions that are provided by the database community. The relational information between entities and their attributes is important as it helps for new knowledge discovery. Mining relational knowledge in the business process not only requires relational data to be presented but also support for mining tasks effectively and efficiently [15,16]. We provide the semantic discovery that is needed in all integration examples given above and that will form a key factor for future integration solutions [5]. This paper is structured as follows: in Sec. 2, we describe the importance of data integration in agri-business domain applications. Sec. 3 presents our conceptual framework to address the integration using graph mining. In Sec. 4, we evaluate the performance of the framework and show the result from the experiment using real-world data sets. Sec. 5 presents discussion and concludes the paper.

2 Research Background

The contribution of agri-business to economic development, growth and exports has been important, and most recent literature has focused upon the challenges and solution to maintaining this important role. Some earlier studies on agriculture in regard to these challenges have provided a somewhat broad understanding of the issues [10, 13, 14]. In the studies, most researchers highlight key challenges to resource management, such as a lack of proper coordination amongst the country's development agencies, an inability of farmers to participate in mainstream agricultural development, under-utilization of available technical assistance and other incentives, and a lack of skilled and talented workers.

A large scale of crop planting decision-making involves multiple objectives and large heterogeneous data sets [4,5], many unknowns and uncertainties. The numerous constraints in land management are complex decision problems related to numerous actors and points of view. Therefore, more research and development efforts should be made to explore new tools to evaluate theoretical alternative scenarios for territory management projects and to improve interaction among the members of the project in agri-business.

The use of spatial information technologies affords large possibilities in formulating evaluation models inside the spatial decision support system (SDSS). The advantages of GIS improve the capacities as principal components in SDSS. Integration of multiple information systems generally aims at combining selected systems so that they form a unified entity and give users the illusion of interacting with one single information system. In this study, a business process of crop management and its attributes are represented in a graph showing the relationship between data objects and activities, which is important for discovering relational knowledge. Users are provided with a homogeneous logical view of data that is physically distributed over heterogeneous data sources. In general, information systems are not designed for integration. Thus, whenever integrated access to different source systems is desired, possible implicit spatial relationships may lead to more interesting patterns and rules [6,7]. Because of these relationships, all data in real world entities can be represented in the same abstraction principles and affect behavior of other entities in the neighborhood. This task can provide the resolution of schema and data conflicts regarding structure and semantics in the integration problem. The process of extracting spatial relationships provides interesting rules to the users. Well-known spatial relationships will generate high confidence rules; however, not all strong rules necessarily hold considerable information. The thousands of interesting and uninteresting rules can discourage users from interpreting them in order to find novel and expected knowledge [1].

3 Literature Review

To support effective decision making in business process, evaluation tools are needed to make informed long-term regional resource decisions and recognize research needs. These tools can help authorities involved in ecological restoration by identifying decision variables, developing problem solving heuristics, and evaluating the consequences of alternative policy actions. Spatial decision support systems (SDSS) for natural resource management are computer-based tools that tightly integrate decision theory models with ecological models and Geographic Information System analyses and mapping [12]. The information provided by SDSS gives decision makers increased ability to follow outcomes of interacting variables, improves the reproducibility of decisions, and documents the reason why a particular choice was made.

3.1 Spatial Decision Support System

A Spatial Decision Support System has the main characteristics of a DSS. In addition, it should be adapted to the specificity of spatial data. Densham et al. defined a SDSS as a geo-processing system designed to support the decision research process for complex spatial problems [9]. SDSS are also defined as a conceptual framework that assists decision makers in solving complex spatial problems. Hence, a SDSS has to provide input for spatial data and allow storage of complex structures common in spatial data. This kind of system should also include analytical techniques that are unique to spatial analysis and produce outputs in the form of maps, reports, charts and other spatial forms.

One of the most important characteristics of a SDSS is to support users while solving semi-structured or ill-structured spatial decision problems. According to Simon (1960), decision problems fall on a continuum, ranging from completely structured to unstructured decisions: the former occur when the decision-making problem can be structured either by the decision maker or on the basis of relevant theory, whereas the latter must be solved by the decision maker without any assistance from a computer.

3.2 Semantic Integration

The integration of heterogeneous, distributed information from the Web is a complicated task, especially the task of schema matching and integration. During the matching and integration process, the syntactic, semantic and structural heterogeneity between multiple information sources are investigated. In this paper, our main objective is to resolve semantic conflicts. The data, ontology and information integration communities face similar types of problems [12], and we leverage techniques developed by these communities.

In general, early integration approaches were based on a relational or functional data model and realized rather tightly-coupled solutions by providing one single global schema. To overcome their limitations concerning the aspects of abstraction, classification, and taxonomies, object-oriented integration approaches were adopted to perform structural homogenization and integration of data. With the advent of the internet and web technologies, the focus shifted from integrating purely well-structured data to also incorporating semi- and unstructured data while architecturally loosely-coupled mediator and agent systems became popular.

Frequent pattern and spatial association rule mining algorithm generates candidates and frequent sets [11,16]. The candidate generation in spatial data mining is not a problem because the number of predicates is much smaller than the number of items in transactional databases [15]. Moreover, the computational cost relies on the spatial join computation. Approaches that generate closed frequent sets compute the previous frequent sets and then verify if they are closed. Although they reduce the number of frequent sets, they do not warrant the elimination of well known patterns. In spatial association rule mining, it is more important to warrant that the resulting frequent sets are free of well known dependences, aiming to generate more interesting patterns than it is to reduce the number of frequent sets. Apriori [16] has been the basis for dozens of algorithms for mining spatial and non-spatial frequent sets, and association rules.

4 Research Methodology

The decision support framework for crop planting selection relates to land management and evaluations. Its first component is the analysis of the proposed scenarios and their respective effects on the physical environment. These analyses are supported by inputs from models that simulate each scenario, such as ecological and metrological models, urban growth models, and water-quality models. Tools provided in the second component evaluate effects on wildlife habitat and ecological communities caused by changes in the physical environment. The impact of the research project could be advantageously integrated into a GIS by means of appropriate integration models. The multiple actors implicated in such projects use their expertise and knowledge to affect priorities, defined also as scores, to spatial entities that are subject to an alteration by the project or that represent a potential area to improve the project. For instance, when it is a matter of choosing the best site for a culture, terrain slope is an important factor to consider in the study; thus, the agriculture engineer uses previous knowledge to determine a kind of a mathematical function relating slope to a suitability factor. This process corresponds to the elaboration of evaluation models whose formulation is necessary in the SDSS.

In this section, we study the ecological models that provide essential output for evaluating land suitability and management changes, allowing decisions to be made from multiple evaluations. Decision analysis provides tools for systematically formulating and evaluating multiple criteria and explaining why a particular decision was made [9,13]. Next, we apply an architectural perspective to create an overview of the different ways to address the integration problem. The presented classification is based on Anyanwu and Shiva's analysis [2] and distinguishes integration approaches according to the level of abstraction where integration is performed. Graph mining methods can be used to predict the information requirements of a user during the execution of activities in enterprise application.

4.1 Proposed Framework

In recent research, the idea of using semantic knowledge was introduced. One scholar proposed the idea of eliminating well-known patterns among target feature types and relevant feature types for data pre-processing.

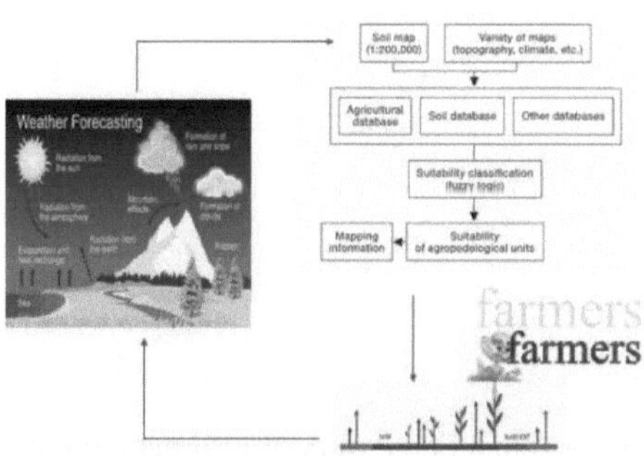

Fig. 1. Ecological and land management in crop plating selection

Figure 1 presents a procedural relationship between weather forecasting and land management conceptual framework. Conceptual models are an effective initial tool for group identification of resources and linkages to attributes in the agricultural environment. The criteria or performance are selected as measurable values of identified attributes and are used to evaluate the success of implemented plans. To evaluate the frequent pattern by eliminating the input space, notice that input space pruning reduces the frequent pattern independently of minimum support. Decision makers then determine the importance of each of these criteria and use this information to evaluate different alternatives. Decision models aid in weighing and evaluating alternatives and may also help decision makers pinpoint conflicts between objectives and conceptualize new alternatives that minimize these conflicts (Ozernoy, 1984). Once an alternative is selected and implemented, expected environmental change is compared to actual conditions through monitoring and directed experimentation, which may lead again to re-evaluations of criteria and implemented plans.

4.2 Data Integration

The integration problems of all information provide nearly the same view on a domain [17]. In the event the domain views of the sources differ, finding a common view becomes difficult. To overcome this problem, multi-ontology approaches as in Fig. 2 describe each data source with its own ontology; then, the local ontology must be mapped, either to a global ontology or between one another, to establish a common understanding. To find relevant documents is not an easy way to satisfy user preferences. In information retrieval, there are many aspects that must be considered to make sure it will work efficiently. Figure 2 is the conceptual framework of information extraction with regards to how information can be retrieved and clustered. It is just a general framework, and we focus on the clustering method in order to structure spatial data sets and cluster documents into relevant groups based on term frequency and concept.

There are four main steps to implement the task of data pre-processing for spatial association rule mining.

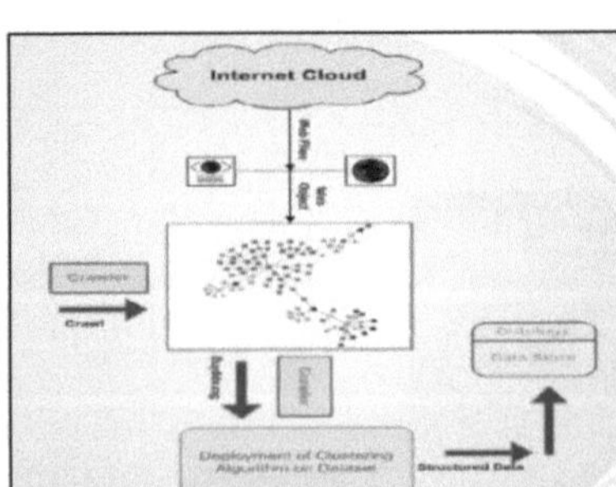

Fig. 2. Conceptual Framework of Information Extraction

Step 1: Internet Cloud

From the Internet cloud, where arbitrary data float and are presented in standards like HTML and XML, we retrieve all relevant information from both mark-up languages having their own rules to carry the data such as XML of Resource Description Framework (RDF). Therefore, in this step, mark-up languages are found and can be visited by the URL.

Step 2: Interconnection of Nodes

Tag data on HTML and XML can be retrieved by using Document Object Model (DOM). According to DOM, everything inside HTML document is a node. So the entire document is a document node; every HTML element is an element node; the text in the HTML elements are text nodes. These nodes constitute a graph that can be used for the deployment of web crawlers; for XML it is constructed in tree structure and it is therefore allows the web crawler to crawl all over the nodes.

Step 3: Scrapping Spatial Data Sets on the Web

Crawler will be deployed as an agent to scrap those data over the tags inside the web document and return a collection of data to be structured.

Step 4: Deploy Clustering Technique

When those spatial data sets have been scrapped, the clustering algorithm is deployed on that dataset to make it structured and unified for all users. Further, more structured data will be kept on the database by a named ontology database. This step will be further expounded in the discussion of clustering with frequent terms and frequent concepts. To map all data to one single domain model forces users to adapt to one single conceptualization of the world. This stands in contrast to the fact that receivers of integrated data widely differ in their conceptual interpretation of and preference for data. They are generally situated in different real-world contexts and have different conceptual models of the world in mind [10]. COIN [10] was one of the first research projects to consider the different contexts in which data providers and data receivers are situated.

In our own research, we continue the trend of taking into account user specific aspects in the process of semantic integration. We address the problem of how user-specific mental domain models and user-specific semantics of concepts can be reflected in the data integration process. We investigate how data — equipped with explicit and semantics — can be effectively pre-integrated on a conceptual level. That way, we aim to enable users to perform declarative data integration by conceptual modeling of their individual ways to perceive a domain of interest.

5 Experimental Results

We obtained crop management data sets from the proceedings of the National Conference on Agro-Environment, [14] which contains agricultural and agro-environment input. We converted the data into a graph transaction. The experimental results of finding frequent sub-graph in Figure 3 displays the number of discovered frequent sub-graphs on different values of the support threshold.

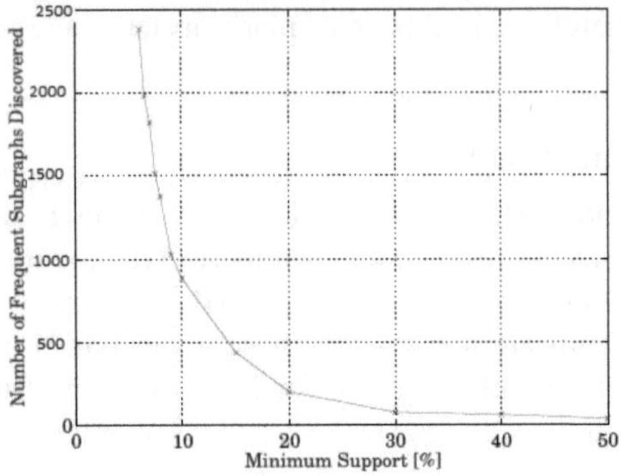

Fig. 3. Minimum support values and the number of discovered frequent sub-graph

To evaluate the frequent sub-graph reduction by different minimum support values, the number of frequent sub-graph increases exponentially. As we start with less minimum support (0% to 8%), the larger frequent sub-graph appeared, in which the edge and vertex labels have generally uniform distribution. In the next experiment, the integration of extracted knowledge from data sets is applied to the class label in classification. Figure 4 shows the ROC hulls for the splitting criteria on the given data sets. We use some of the common classification algorithm [2] such as neural network (NN) and different types of decision tree approaches, such as fuzzy DT and C4.5 to compare with SAR. Our experimental analysis of the performance evaluation of graph mining shows that there is a direct relationship between building the model and attribute size of the data sets. The experimental analysis also shows that spatial association Rule mining (SAR) has good classification accuracy compared to selected classifiers.

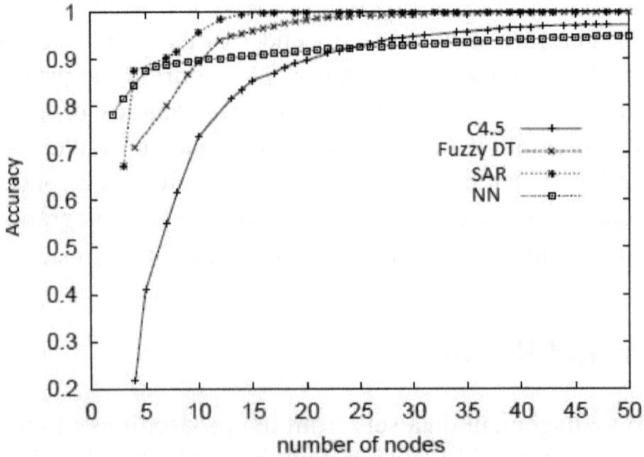

Fig. 4. ROC curve for crop management data sets

6 Discussion and Conclusion

The designed framework reduces the difficulties in linking and integrating spatial data drawn from separate sources. Analysis of the knowledge in various agricultural relations enables researchers to integrate graph mining with ontology reasoning in network data analysis. There is a growing need to provide unified access to these heterogeneous data sources. As the amount and complexity of structured data increases in an agricultural sector, large scale collaboration on sensor deployment and an increasing structured web are required. Furthermore, we investigate the incorporation of ancillary spatial data to improve the accuracy and specificity of land suitability classification from crop zoning and meteorological data used to modify the initial classification. Through this case study, we demonstrate how semantic graph mining can be applied to the analysis of land suitability and entities interactions analysis. The principal scope of the present work was the development of a methodological approach to improve the spatial decision-making process in land planning and natural resources management. We integrate tools elaborated in the field of advanced spatial analysis in a spatial decision support system. We showed how it is possible to interface these tools within the different stages of SDSS process. The developed methodology was applied to the problem of suitability assessment because many planning and resource management problems use this information support in negotiations between multiple actors and as a support for representing feasible solutions. The practical case study was based on an impact study where multiple environmental, technical and economic constraints are present. Combined with multi-thematic spatial data, these constraints were transformed into spatial evaluation database used as input for suitability computations models. These models are the principal component in the improvement of SDSS design and choice phases. Two major results have been obtained by the present research.

In this paper, we have addressed the problem of modeling structural relationships from relational databases for the purposes of graph mining. We explored alternative graph models and evaluated their space and time efficiency as well as their suitability and database independence; the architecture has been modularized. The significance of this work is the application of the results of this paper to large real-world activities data sets for mining patterns that could not be done otherwise.

Acknowledgement. The author would like to thank Universiti Tun Hussein Onn Malaysia for providing grant Vot0824 to support the research project.

References

1. Appice, A., Berandi, M., Ceci, M., Malerba, D.: Mining and Filtering Multi-level Spatial Association Rules with ARES. In: Hacid, M., Murray, N.V., Ras, Z.W., Tsumoto, L.S. (eds.) ISMIS 2005. LNCS (LNAI), vol. 3488, pp. 342–353. Springer, Heidelberg (2005)
2. Anyanwu, M.N., Shiva, S.G.: Comparative Analysis of Serial Decision Tree Classification Algorithms. International Journal of Computer Science and Security 3(3)

3. Lodhi, A., Kassem, G., Koeppen, V., Saake, G.: Investigation of Graph Mining for Business Processes. In: ICIIT. IEEE Computer Society, Lahore (2010)
4. Bayardo, R.J., et al.: Agent-Based Semantic Integration of Information in Open and Dynamic Environments. In: 1997 ACM SIGMOD International Conference on Management of Data (SIGMOD 1997), pp. 195–206. ACM, Tucson (1997)
5. Bogorny, V., Engel, P.M., Alavares, L.O.: Enchancing the process of Knowledge Discovery in Geographic Database using Geo-Ontologies. In: Nigro, H.O., Cisaro, S.E.G., Xodo, D.H. (eds.), IGI Global, New York, USA (2008)
6. Borges, J., Levene, M.: Data Mining of User Navigation Patterns. In: Masand, B., Spiliopoulou, M. (eds.) WebKDD 1999. LNCS (LNAI), vol. 1836, pp. 92–112. Springer, Heidelberg (2000)
7. Carver, S.J.: Integrating multicriteria evaluation with geographical information systems. International Journal of Geographical Information Systems 5, 321–339 (1991)
8. Carey, M.J., et al.: Towards Heterogeneous Multimedia Information Systems: The Garlic Approach. In: 5th International Workshop on Research Issues in Data Engineering-Distributed Object Management (RIDE-DOM 1995), Taipei, Taiwan, pp. 124–131 (1995)
9. Densham, P.J., Armstrong, M.P.: A heterogeneous processing approach to spatial decision support systems. In: Waugh, T.C., Healey, R.G. (eds.) Proceedings of the Sixth International Symposium on Spatial Data Handling Advances in GIS Research, pp. 29–45 (1994)
10. Goh, C.H., Madnick, S.E., Siegel, M.: Context Interchange: Overcoming the Challenges of Large-Scale Interoperable Database Systems in a Dynamic Environment. In: Third International Conference on Information and Knowledge Management (CIKM 1994), pp. 337–346. ACM, Gaithersburg (1994)
11. Laksmi, K., Meyyappan, T.: A Comparative Study of frequent Subgraph Mining Algorithms. International Journal of Information Technology Convergence and Services 2(2) (2012)
12. Mena, E., et al.: OBSERVER: An Approach for Query Processing in Global Information Systems based on Interoperation across Pre-existing Ontologies. In: First IFCIS International Conference on Cooperative Information Systems (CoopIS 1996), June 19–21, pp. 14–25. IEEE Computer Society, Brussels (1996)
13. Pereira, J.M.C., Dickstein, L.: A multiple criteria decision-making approach to GIS-based land suitability Evaluation. International Journal of Geographical Information Systems 7, 407–424 (1993)
14. Roslina, A., Abu Kasim, A.: Eliminating the Perspective Impacts of Global Warming on Malaysia Agricultural. In: 2nd Proceedings in National Conference on Agro-Environment, Malaysia, pp. 98–104 (2009)
15. Shenker, S., Chawla, S.: Spatial Databases: A tour. Upper Saddle, New York (2003)
16. Srikant, R., Agrawal, R.: Mining generalized Association Rules. In: Dayal, V., Gray, P.M.D., Nishio, S. (eds.) Proceedings of the 21th International Conference on Very Large Databases, pp. 403–419. Morgan Kaufmann, Zurich (1995)
17. Wache, H., et al.: Ontology-Based Integration of Information — A Survey of Existing Approaches. In: Stuckenschmidt, H. (ed.) Workshop on Ontologies and Information Sharing, IJCAI 2001, Seattle, USA, April 4-5, pp. 108–117 (2001)
18. Jankowski, P.: Integrating geographical information systems and multiple criteria decision-making methods. International Journal of Geographical Information Systems 9, 251–273 (1995)

Engaging Social Customers – Influencing New Marketing Strategies for Social Media Information Sources[*]

Barbara Gligorijevic[1,2,**] and Edwina Luck[1]

[1] Queensland University of Technology, Brisbane, Australia
[2] Queensland University of Technology, Kelvin Grove Campus, K Block, Office 414, 130 Victoria Road Park, Brisbane, Australia
{barbara.gligorijevic,e.luck}@qut.edu.au

Abstract. A global, online quantitative study among 300 consumers of digital technology products found the most reliable information sources were friends, family or word of mouth (WOM) from someone they knew, followed by expert product reviews, and product reviews written by other consumers. The most unreliable information sources were advertising or infomercials, automated recommendations based on purchasing patterns or retailers. While a very small number of consumers evaluated products online, rating of products and online discussions were more frequent activities. The most popular social media websites for reviews were Facebook, Twitter, Amazon and e-Bay, indicating the importance of WOM in social networks and online media spaces that feature product reviews as it is the most persuasive piece of information in both online and offline social networks. These results suggest that 'social customers' must be considered as an integral part of a marketing strategy.

Keywords: Social customer, information sources, word of mouth, social media, marketing strategy.

1 Introduction

The proliferation of social media websites where consumers are able to interact with brands, companies and other consumers has altered the marketing environment in which companies, marketers and advertisers operate. The Internet has spawned numerous online information sources while significantly transforming the ways in which consumers seek and find information to assist their purchases [1]. Through these changes in the Web 2.0 environment, we witness the emergence of the 'social customer', information search savvy consumers that use social connections like personal contacts or online networks to learn about products and brands. While companies are under a considerable amount of pressure to determine the best communication

[*] This research was carried out as part of the activities of, and funded by, Smart Services Cooperative Research Centre (CRC) through the Australian Government's CRC programme (Department of Innovation, Industry, Science and Research).

[**] Corresponding author.

V. Khachidze et al. (Eds.): iCETS 2012, CCIS 332, pp. 25–40, 2012.

channels for sending marketing messages to current or potential customers, the unleashed power of word of mouth information is dominating both offline and online conversations about brands, products and services [2]. The Web 2.0 environment and social media websites are fertile grounds for proliferation of electronic word of mouth [3], particularly in the case of digital technology products (computers, mobile phones, media players, home entertainment and others). This product category has a steady increase in global sales [4], a high penetration rate and short product usage life among consumers, resulting in periodic purchases of products more frequently than in other categories of durable goods. For this reason, consumers considering a purchase of digital technology products are more active and prominent users of user generated content such as product reviews, ratings and recommendations. As a result of the Web becoming the primary source of information [5], information searches on the Web [6] are rapidly shifting from websites where companies traditionally present commercial information to social networking spaces, where the consumers use information filtered by their peers or favoured networks that "[have] curated and surfaced" important information [7] that is also known in marketing as "word of mouth" information. According to studies conducted in this area, consumers are "turning to Web 2.0 for non- commercial, unbiased information" [8] and as such it represents an alternative source of information for consumers. As the social component of the Internet is accelerated in forums and through social networking services provided by some commercial entities (featuring consumer generated product reviews), it is apparent that this leads to the democratization of information, [9] allowing consumers to be heard by fellow customers and, more importantly, companies. This paper reports a fraction of the findings of a larger consumer behaviour study, conducted among consumers of digital technology products in Australia and internationally, regarding the use of information sources in the purchasing decision-making process. The following section details key literature.

2 Literature Review

Prevalent throughout the related literature are words such as 'engagement', 'participation', 'conversation' and 'dialogue' [10, 11], which encapsulate the meaning of the social customer within social media. The use of such terms can be attributed to the interactive nature of social media, which allows organizations and brands to actively engage consumers, and indeed, much of the literature suggests social media is vastly different from traditional media forms.

Another key difference relates to the real-time nature of social media, which has made communications more instantaneous, meaning that information is more readily shared. Evidently, scholars argue that firms can thereby more effectively engage users as information can be disseminated in a timely, efficient and direct manner [10]. However, it appears that this engagement occurs within social media sites by the users, rather than by the company. This true sense of the word 'community' has brought power to those who, in the past, may not have held that power. We term these people 'social customers'. Ward defines 'consumer socialization' as when individuals acquire skills, knowledge, and attitudes relevant to their purpose as being consumers [12]. The Internet and social networks have allowed the development of the social consumer because of this acquisition of new skills for the new world they inhabit. We have seen social consumers grow within their community with regards to engagement, participation, and dialogue. However, this is more so with co-creation of messages, sharing and the growth of the online community. Between hundreds of television channels, specialty magazines, and the Internet, it is no wonder why the marketing communication landscape can provide such a challenge for even the most experienced marketer to navigate. As Web 2.0 technologies have matured, we have witnessed leaps forward in communication as the Internet now stands apart from other media, such as television and radio, changing social networking communication from one-way offline communication into two-way digital communication [13]. While a review of the literature reveals clear and concise definition is lacking, scholars agree social media is an umbrella term for a range of communication tools [14]. Given this broad range of tools, there is no systematic way to effectively categorise social media tools, thereby making this research applicable. Electronic formats such as blogs, chat rooms, and social media sites including Facebook, Bebo and YouTube have made sharing information and opinions quicker and easier than ever before. More recently, Pinterest, Tumblr and Instagram have made sharing possible in different formats. Viral marketing, online word of mouth (eWOM) and other stealth marketing techniques are making their mark as the newest ways to spread marketing communication messages by breaking through traditional marketing clutter and providing consumers with information in non-traditional, yet more convenient ways. Numerous researches have been conducted to understand the reasons empowering eWOM. Bansal and Voyer [15] state that eWOM communication can aid consumers who may not understand the brand fully to get useful information from an experienced source. According to Hennig-Thurau et al. [16], the reasons why eWOM has become the hottest power is because online social networks are the most widely used of the existing eWOM formats, providing consumers with the opportunity to read others' consumption opinions and experiences, as well as to write contributions by themselves. In addition, eWOM communication articulated on online social networks can be expected to exert a stronger impact on consumers, due to the fact that online communication is easy to operate and requires less Internet-related knowledge on the part of the consumer to obtain information. Among these stealth marketing techniques, online social networks or virtual communities (VCs) stand out and have become a social phenomenon that have changed the way people communicate and relate to one another. VCs provide eWOM in archived threads that consumers can assess, and extend two-way communication exchanges between close relations to multiway exchanges among strangers across cyberspace. Online social networks facilitate peer-to-peer information exchange remarkably and allow consumers to transmit information as quickly and easily as possible to multiple recipients [17]. Moreover, eWOM plays an important role with opinion leaders, whose post-purchase opinion exerts a strong influence on information dissemination, product judgments, consumer satisfaction and repurchase intentions. It has been suggested that WOM and eWOM are more credible than marketer initiated communications, because the sources are unbiased. WOM effect has a vital influence on broadening consumers' knowledge fields and attitude changes, which extend to behaviour adjustments. As these virtual communities attract millions of users from all parts of the world, spreading both verbal and written materials to whom they are concerned, marketers nowadays should be well aware of the trend and be prepared to take advantage of it. Internet users go online to share their own experiences, opinions and consumer-related advice and information in the virtual world [16]. Hence, eWOM is regarded as a useful tool for customers' purchasing decisions and evaluation. As this trend is booming like never before, consumers are able to spread their messages about brands, products and companies, both negative and positive, to millions of other consumers all around the world with the click of a mouse. While previous studies report on significant effects and influence of WOM communication on consumers' judgments [18, 19, 20] across different communication platforms [21, 22] or correlations between customer (dis)satisfaction and posting of online reviews [23], yet another version of the eWOM, this study has taken a different approach. The study evaluated different information sources both online and offline and how reliable these sources were perceived by consumers in a specific marketing communication environment while numerous communication platforms and marcom vehicles were used throughout the purchasing decision making process. Within the current trend of multi–channels, screens and surfaces that provide cross-platform communication, continuous efforts are made to keep up with marketing opportunities. Nevertheless, in order to focus their efforts and develop proper marketing strategies, marketing professionals require precise and accurate indicators what consumers perceive as reliable sources of information and to what extent. The following section details this study's research questions.

3 Research Questions

The focus of the research included consumers of digital technology products such as personal computers, laptops, tablets, mobile phones, digital cameras, game consoles, or TV sets. This product category has a high penetration rate among consumers in all socio-economic groups. They are widely available in all markets and economies. The purchasing decision making process is very similar between early adopters / innovators and late adopters and laggards. The product specificities require some technical knowledge, and for this reason consumers are rarely engaged in impulse purchases but, rather, conduct comprehensive research prior to purchase. During this research process they are more likely to be under the influence of commercial information sources like advertising campaigns, product promotions and word of mouth information coming from peers in their social circles.

This survey was developed in order to better understand consumers' attitudes toward information sources with the following research questions utilised in this study, for which the methodology is further explained.

- How reliable do consumers (of digital technology products) perceive various information sources to be when considering a purchase?
- What is the consumers' attitude toward word of mouth information both offline and online, as opposed to commercial information?
- Do consumers participate in the spread of word of mouth information by displaying their satisfaction / dissatisfaction about purchased products and where?
- What is the dominant communication channel for the dissemination of word of mouth information about digital technology products?

4 Methodology of Research

This research was designed as a cross sectional quantitative study of 300 consumers of digital technology products carried out from September 2011 until March 2012. The study was conducted online with respondents coming from Australia (40 percent) and 30 other countries (60 percent), with 52.1 percent males and 47.8 percent females, and age groups up to 25 years 18.6 percent, 26 to 35 years 38.5 percent, 36 to 45 years 27.7 percent, 46 to 55 years 8.6 percent and 56 years and above 6.5 percent. The sample was recruited among international consumers invited to participate through e-mailing lists, forums and online advertising campaigns on Facebook. The invitation included a link to a self administrated questionnaire.

Table 1. Sample structure by age groups and gender in %

Up to 25	26 - 35	36 - 45	45 - 55	56 & above	Males	Females
18.6	38.5	27.7	8.7	6.5	52.2	47.8

The structured questionnaire with one open ended question had three major sections: the eligibility criteria section, which evaluated if the respondents were qualified to participate; the main questions investigating consumer's stance toward various information sources; and the demographic information section. In the eligibility section, the consumers were asked about past purchases in the last 18 months or a potential purchase of digital technology products in the near future. Based on their positive response they were accordingly invited to enter the survey. This criterion was imposed in order to select respondents that are able to recall the recent information searches during the purchasing process and how they evaluated the reliability of information sources in offline and online environments; in total there were twelve different categories of information sources. The listed information sources were: retailers or shop assistants, manufacturers, advertising or infomercials, magazines or news stories, online retailers, automated recommendations, detailed user generated product reviews, friends and family, short users' product recommendations, professional or experts product reviews, product ratings by users, and discussion forums. Further, the study explored the dominant methods of opinion sharing processes in the post-purchase stage among respondents, especially in the online environment through social media. It investigated the reasons for posting and sharing online opinions about digital technology products. Finally, in the open ended question the respondents were asked to list the web locations where they evaluated the purchased products. The format of the questions is further depicted in the findings section. For the purposes of this study the sampling technique of purposeful sampling [24] was utilised for the selection of eligible respondents with confirmed past purchases of digital technology products. Although in the past the online surveys were characterised to be of a skewed sample [25, 26, 27] due to the nature of this study and increased Internet usage penetration rates among general population it is safe to say that the data collection method and sample design allowed sample's diversity. Nevertheless the further limitations emerged from the size of the selected

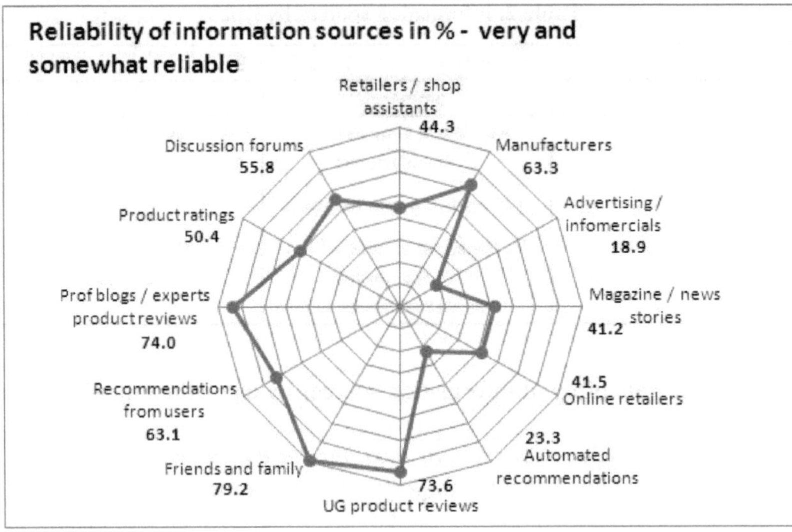

Fig. 1. Information sources reliability – very and somewhat reliable

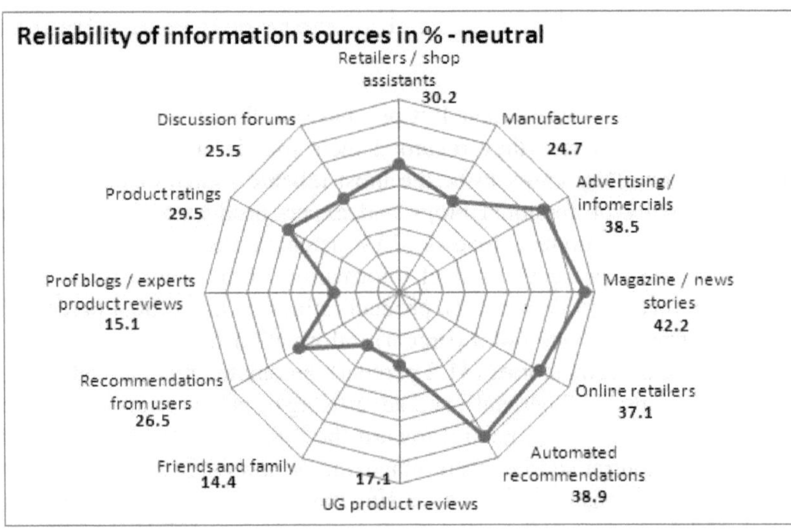

Fig. 2. Information sources reliability – neutral toward reliability of information sources

The least reliable information sources were considered to be advertising or infomercials (42.6 percent), automated recommendations based on purchasing patterns (37.9 percent), retailers' or shop assistants' advice (25.5 percent), product ratings by users (20.2 percent), information from online retailers (21.4 percent), discussion forums (18.7 percent), magazine and news stories (16.6 percent), product information from manufacturers (12 percent), professional blogs and expert product reviews (11 percent), short product recommendations from users (10.4 percent), detailed user generated product reviews (9.3 percent), and friends and family or word of mouth from someone they know with 6.4 percent.

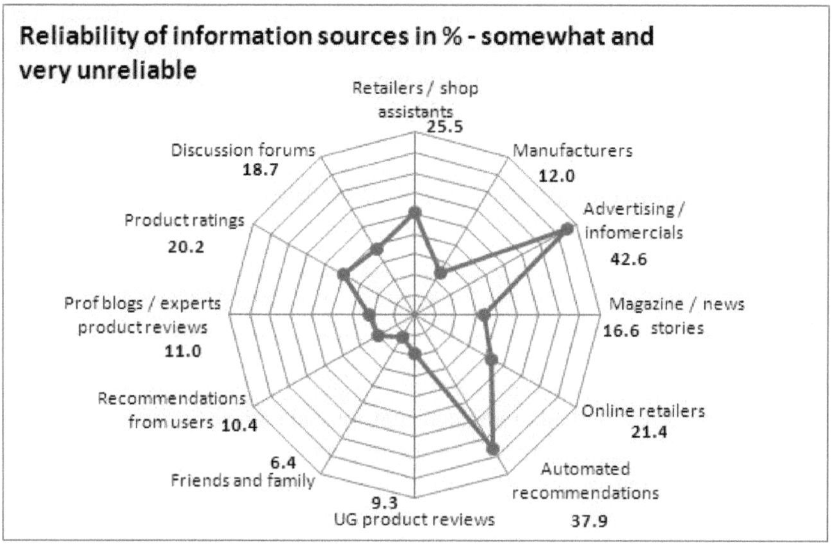

Fig. 3. Information sources reliability – somewhat and very unreliable

Discussion

Respondents found their friends and family and word of mouth from someone they know to be a very reliable source of information, but also consider experts or professionals that deliver product reviews and other fellow consumers posting product reviews to be trustworthy information sources. Manufacturers (or rather the products' related information they provided), were rated considerably high as reliable, contrary to advertising or infomercials, which were considered as very unreliable, thus indicating that advertising messages are considered to be created by advertisers and not as a part of the marketing communication campaigns for brands. Further, user created content in the form of user-generated product reviews, user recommendations, discussions in forums, or product ratings by consumers are noticeably highly evaluated as reliable – considerably more than automated product recommendations based on purchasing patterns of other consumers, or retailers' or shop assistants' advice. This signifies the trust levels toward reliability of information to be notably higher among fellow consumers than toward recommendations coming from commercial information sources. Additionally, these results signify that consumers perceive private, commercial and public information sources as very dissimilar. While private information sources in the form of word of mouth from someone they know had the strongest influence on their purchasing decisions as the most reliable, the least reliable were advertisements and infomercials that communicate commercial information. Furthermore, research outcomes postulate that customers do not conform to retailers' suggestions as strongly as to recommendations from other customers in the form of electronic word of mouth through user generated product reviews, recommendations and ratings, or discussions in online forums, demonstrating that these social media spaces are becoming crucially important for companies and brands when designing a marketing strategy. Hence, word of mouth information is considered among current or potential customers as more reliable and consequently more influential in the purchasing decision-making process. The following question examined the post-purchase behaviour of consumers and their participation rates in the dissemination of word of mouth information.

Question 2: "Do you usually share your satisfaction or dissatisfaction about the purchased product with others?"

5 point Likert scale	*Always*	*Often*	*Sometimes*	*Rarely*	*Never*

Findings

A large majority of respondents indicated that they always, often or sometimes share their satisfaction or dissatisfaction about the purchased product with their friends and colleagues 97.6 percent of the time. Sharing with their family or partner was 94.7 percent while 71.9 percent informed people in their offline social networks (school friends, acquaintances, club members). 51.6 percent told people in their online social network; 46.6 percent rated the product online; 44.4 percent told the retailer or sales personnel; 39 percent posted an online comment or discussion; 28.7 percent let the manufacturer know; 27.6 percent publicly expressed their opinion or experience on a blog; 25.8 percent wrote an online review; 25.8 percent did not tell anyone; 12.6 percent wrote a letter to an editor or expert.

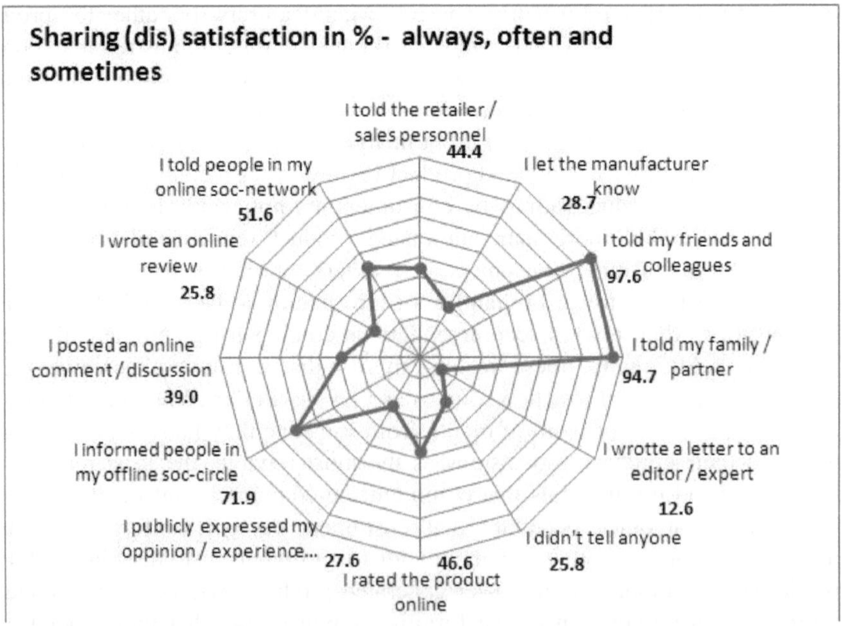

Fig. 4. Sharing of satisfaction or dissatisfaction – always, often and sometimes

Discussion

While respondents had a very high participation rate in the dissemination of word of mouth information about digital technology products in their offline social circles (friends and colleagues, family or partner) and to some extent in their online social circles, participation rate was lower in social media websites designed for posting product reviews, ratings or recommendations. Accordingly, regarding their satisfaction or dissatisfaction they informed the retailers or sales personnel, manufacturers and editors or experts at significantly lower rates. This leads to the conclusion that consumers do not expect to create any impact by providing an evaluation of products directly to retailers, manufacturers or publishers (editors/experts). On the other hand, informing their contacts about their satisfaction or dissatisfaction is expected to have more impact on brand image and companies' reputations. Moreover, these results reveal that the participation rate in dissemination of electronic word of mouth in social media websites that feature product reviews, ratings and recommendations is lower than in spreading of word of mouth information in social networks both offline and online. Correspondingly, consumers have reported significantly higher participation in posting short forms of product evolutions (product ratings) than longer forms (product reviews or blogs) or formal forms (informing the manufacturer, editor or expert). This indicates that the prolific customers who are writing product reviews or ratings have higher impact, through the dissemination of electronic word of mouth, on other customers who might be considering a product purchase. The following question explores the popular websites among respondents for dissemination of word of mouth information in the social media sphere.

Question 3 - open-ended: "Thinking about your last major purchase of digital technology product, which Websites did you use to express your review, opinion or comment?"

Findings

The highest number of respondents, among those that were evaluating products online, have indicated retailing websites Amazon (9 percent), eBay (7 percent), and Taobao[1] (2 percent) as the website where they have expressed their opinions about purchased digital technology products, followed by the online forum Whirlpool (5 percent), websites of digital technology products manufacturers Apple (3 percent) and Sony (1 percent), and Google product reviews (1 percent). The popular social networking websites for posting comments about products were reported to be Facebook (21 percent) and Twitter (7 percent).

[1] Taobao – the share of this website would be considerably higher if more respondents from China participated in this survey.

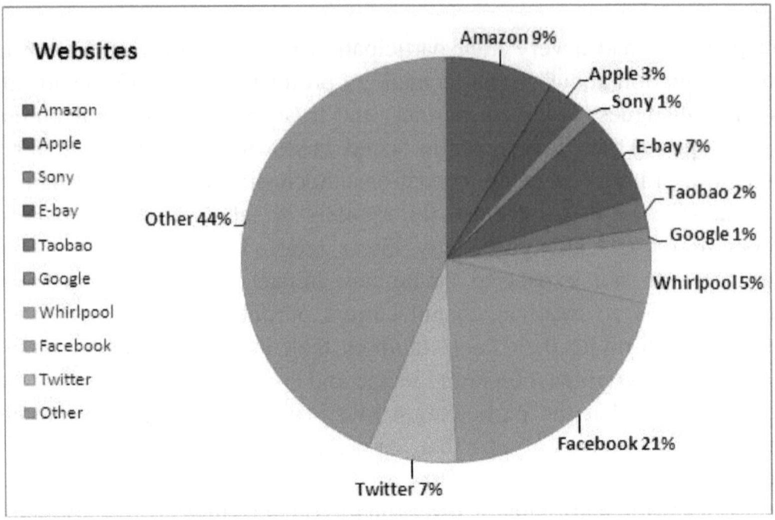

Fig. 5. Websites - posted product reviews on websites in %

Discussion

The attractiveness of retailing websites like Amazon, eBay and Taobao featuring customers' feedback and product reviews is implicit as these websites instigate this type of customers' participation, or in the case of Taobao provide incentives for customers. However, the highest number of respondents indicated Facebook as the website where, upon purchase, they have posted the product review, opinion or comment. Facebook contacts, also defined as "friends", were classified as a private information source - assuming that the majority of social connections were transferred from the offline environment to the online social networking website, and therefore these were considered as private information sources. This illustrates consumers' positive attitudes toward private information sources, both offline and online, and their higher participation rate in the dissemination of word of mouth.

6 Conclusions and Recommendations

Our study examined several aspects of consumer behaviour and attitudes toward information sources used throughout the purchasing decision making process in the category of digital technology products. The quantitative study was conducted among consumers in Australia (40 percent) and internationally (60 percent), with over 300 responses collected in an online survey using a structured questionnaire with an open ended question.

The results of the study show that word of mouth is the dominant form of information in both offline and online environments, and is the most influential through personal information sources (friends and family) and public sources (product reviews, ratings and recommendations posted online by other consumers). Commercial information sources (advertising and infomercials) are the least influential on consumers in their purchasing decision-making process. The perception of reliability of information sources among social customers when searching for information about digital technology products shows consumers' strong preference toward their personal contacts, i.e. friends and family or word of mouth from someone they know. Whereas online public information sources (user generated product reviews, ratings and recommendations, and professional blogs or experts' product reviews) were reported to be highly regarded by consumers as reliable and therefore influential, retailers and shop assistants were considerably less reliable and their influence was therefore not dominant in the purchasing decision-making process. Hence, marketing strategies that strongly rely on advertising online or offline, or advertising at the 'point of sale' will have less impact than brand presence in word of mouth communication. Further, we concluded that consumers' attitudes toward word of mouth information are very positive, contrary to product information coming from commercial sources. This sentiment was explicitly depicted in results of the survey that label the advertising and infomercials and automated recommendations based on purchasing patterns as the least reliable categories, followed by information from retailers (offline and online). Consumers have changed their window shopping practices from searching online commercial or retailing websites to looking for information from friends, family and peers – in social networks and social media spaces. This behavioural change is a strong sign for marketers that altering online marketing strategies from advertising to conversational or word of mouth marketing may lead to better return on marketing expenditures. Additionally, the posting of product reviews, product ratings or recommendations were the activities that had a lower participation rate than searching for the same type of information. We witnessed in the surveys' results dynamic activity in the dissemination of word of mouth among family or partners, friends and colleagues, offline social circles and online social networks. While the number of consumers who were actively posting product reviews was not very high, their impact is still strongly felt in the area of word of mouth activities acting as 'opinion leaders' in the domain of user generated content. For marketers, this indicates that the power of word of mouth is amplified in the case of prolific opinion leaders, as they are positing evaluations of the product in online spaces where social customers are looking for product related information. Hence, their opinions and attitudes are easily conveyed to fellow consumers with higher impact than that of online advertising. The findings of this research showed that the most popular social media websites for posting product related information as a form of electronic word of mouth were social networking websites Facebook and Twitter and the commercial retailing websites Amazon, eBay and Taobao. Popular manufacturing websites were Apple, Sony and Google product reviews, as well as Whirlpool forum. For marketers this indicates that although advertising is apparently not appealing to social customers, the social component of networking websites is abundant with word of mouth activities, which is potentially the strongest marketing tool in the online social media space. This study was conducted during the period of proliferation of social media websites harvesting user created content (Amazon product reviews, Tripadvisors travel reviews, Yelp local businesses) and rise of social networking websites like Facebook and Twitter as popular marcom and advertising spaces. The emergence of new information sources was a natural consequence of this process, while innovative formats of online publishing - the user created content of product reviews, ratings and recommendations, began to thrive in both corporate and independent social media websites. This research has established a guiding principle for marketers that has to be taken into consideration when developing online marketing strategies – social media spaces that foster consumer conversations and feature WOM information are more relevant to consumers that advertising messages. The most dominant form of communication in terms of reliability was reported to be WOM among friends and family and as such is unprecedented in influencing potential customers. Further, user created product reviews, ratings and recommendations have a reputation among consumers of being considerably reliable sources of eWOM. Additionally, it was discovered that a large majority of consumers were lurkers – mostly reading product reviews and posting to a lesser extent, as such they were susceptible to influence of those that are more active in posting eWOM acting as influencers in creating opinions about products or brands. Suggestions for marketers [29] would be to encourage current devoted customers to spark the WOM with new customers in those social media spaces that support this type of social interactions. Finally the most important social media spaces for expressing consumers (dis)satisfaction were Facebook, Twitter and Amazon – the online communities sprouting in these websites should be the focus of future marketing activities for engaging social customers by initiating interests and conversations through evaluation of products. These findings may be useful for marketing practitioners for planning of social media strategies indicating the most influential form of WOM, most thriving social media spaces for seeding of WOM information, and a suggestion that future forms of their marketing mix should include conversations with social customers. For further studies in the area of social media and information sources, these findings are bases upon which new studies can be developed. The recommendations for further research and limitations of the current study are described in the next section.

6.1 Limitations and Future Research

This study, with 300 responses and conducted in 32 countries, would provide a better diversity of feedback if the number of responses was higher. The data set with this type of limitation was not capable of conveying the cultural differences of word of mouth dissemination and reliability of information sources in developed, emerging and underdeveloped economies. In addition the list of information sources could have been different, exploring a wider list of commercial information sources and advertising models.

While this cross sectional study was conducted in 2011 and 2012 it could be easily replicated in the future and turned into a longitudinal study that would track trends and changes in the sphere of consumer behaviour. Additionally, by translating the questionnaire to other languages and conducting the research in non-English speaking countries the results would provide better geographical coverage. Furthermore it would be possible to compare results from countries with different levels of Internet penetration and usage of online retailing channels in order to investigate if and how 'window shopping' practices are altered by switching from traditional stores to online retailing and consequently the impact of electronic word of mouth in economies with a dominant traditional retailing model. Further it would be interesting to compare different types of information sources in online and offline environments and comparing different categories of word of mouth like: eWOM vs. face to face WOM, independent blogosphere vs. editorial content, television infomercials vs. Youtube corporate instructive videos, offline vs. online advertising, printed magazines vs. e-zines, corporate marcom content on websites of manufacturers vs. community blogs on these websites, Facebook fan clubs vs. brand followers on Twitter. As technology is exploding in the number of new applications and services linked to mobile communication, especially location-based services, our research has proven to be of great importance. We believe that this will create new opportunities for brands to build and develop relationships with consumers by providing high information value.

References

1. Kuruzovich, J., Ritu Agarwal, S.V., Gosain, S., Weitzman, S.: Marketspace or Market place? Online Information Search and Channel Outcomes in Auto Retailing. Information Systems Research 19(2), 182–201 (2008)
2. Kelsey group: Online Consumer Generated Reviews Have Big Impact on Offline Purchases. Study presented on Marketing Charts, http://www.marketingcharts.com
3. Davis, A., Khazanchi, D.: An Empirical Study of Online Word-of-Mouth as a Predictor for Multi-Product category e-commerce sales. Electronic Markets 18(2), 130–141 (2008)
4. CEA: Industry Sales Data (2012), http://ce.org/Research/Products-Services/Industry-Sales-Data.aspx
5. Spink, A., Wolfram, D., Jansen, M., Saracevic, T.: Spotting Fake Reviews Groups in Consumer Reviews. In: World Wide Web Conference. International World Wide Web Conference Committee, Lyon, France (2012)
6. Ondrusek, A.: The Attributes of Research on Enuser Online Searching behaviour: a Retrospective Views and Analysis. In: Library and Information Science Research, vol. 26(2), pp. 221–265. Elsevier, Science Direct (2004)
7. Ogneva, M.: Why your Company Needs to Embrace Social CRM. Mashable (2010), http://mashable.com/2010/05/21/social-crm/
8. Ng, S.: The Impact of Negative Word of Mouth in Web 2.0 on Brand Equity. In: Australian and New Zealand Marketing Academic Conference (2009)
9. Gligorijevic, B., Bruns, A.: Ratings and Recommendations Websites in the Travel and Tourism Industry. New Media Services Report. Smart Services CRC (2010)
10. Kaplan, A.M., Haenlein, M.: Users of the world, unite! The challenges and opportunities of Social Media. Business Horizons 53(1), 59–68 (2010)
11. Luck, E., Mathews, S.: What advertisers need to know about the Y Generation: An Australian perspective. Journal of Promotions Management, Special Issue 2(1-2), 134–147 (2009)
12. Ward, S.: Consumer socialization. Journal of Consumer Research 1(2), 1–16 (1974)
13. Riegner, C.: Word of mouth on the web: The impact of web 2.0 on consumer purchase decisions. Journal of Advertising Research 11, 436–447 (2007)
14. Taylor, M., Kent, M.L.: Toward a dialogic theory of public relations. Public Relations Review 28(1), 21–37 (2010)

15. Bansal, H., Voyer, P.: Word-of-mouth processes within a services purchase decision context. Journal of Service Research 3(2), 166–177 (2000)
16. Hennig-Thurau, T., Gwinner, K.P., Walsh, G.: Electronic word-of-mouth via consumer-opinion platforms: What motivates consumers to articulate themselves on the internet? Journal of Interactive Marketing 18(1), 38–52 (2004)
17. Sohn, D., Leckenby, J.D.: Product class knowledge as a moderator of consumer's electronic work-of-mouth behavior. Journal of Advertising Research 20, 7 (2005)
18. Bone, F.P.: Word-of-Mouth Effects on Short-term and Long-term Product Judgments. Journal of Business Research 32, 212–223 (1995)
19. East, R., Lomax, W.: Demographic bases of WOM. In: Australian and New Zealand Marketing Academic Conference (2010)
20. Liu, Y., Dong, D., Kandampully, J.: Online Information Services: The Impact on e-Word-of-Mouth. In: International Research Symposium in Service Management (2010)
21. Hennig-Thurau, T., Walsh, G.: Electronic Word of Mouth: Motives for and Consequences of Reading Customer Articulations on the Internet. International Journal of Electronic Commerce 8(2), 51–74 (2004)
22. Dwyer, P.: Measuring the value of electronic word of mouth and its impact in consumer communities. Journal of Interactive Marketing 21(2), 63–79 (2007)
23. Chen, Y., Fay, S., Wang, Q.: The Role of Marketing in Social Media: How Online Consumer Reviews Evolve. Journal of Interactive Marketing 25, 85–94 (2011)
24. Patton, M.: Qualitative research and evaluation methods. Sage, London (2002)
25. Coomber, R.: Using the Internet for survey research. Sociological Research Online 2(2) (1997), http://www.socresonline.org.uk/socresonline/2/2/2/html
26. Schmidt, W.C.: World Wide Web survey research: benefits, potential problems, and solutions. Behaviour Research, Methods, Instruments and Computers 29, 270–273 (1997)
27. Stanton, J.M.: An empirical assessment of data collection using the Internet. Personnel Psychology 51(3), 709–725 (1998)
28. Bethlehem, J.: Cross-sectional Research. In: Ader, H., Mellenbergh, G. (eds.) Research Methodology in the Social, Behavioural and Life Sciences, pp. 110–142. Sage, London (1999)
29. Bone, P.F.: Determinants of Word-of-Mouth Communications During Consumption. In: Sherry, J., Sternthal, B. (eds.) Advances in Consumer Research. Association for Consumer Research, Provo, UT 19, pp. 576–583 (1992)

Concept Based Orchestration of Web Services Using XOT*

Ho-Sang Jo[1], Jae-Dong Yang[2,**], and Wan Choi[3]

[1] Division of Electronics and Information Engineering,
Chonbuk National University, Jeonju, South Korea
[2] Division of Electronics and Information Engineering, Cloud Open R&D Center
Chonbuk National University, Jeonju, South Korea
[3] Cloud Computing Research Department
Electronics and Telecommunications Research Institute, Dae-jeon, South Korea
spooky0113@gmail.com, jdyang2000@naver.com, wchoi@etri.re.kr

Abstract. A web service is a well-known technique for implementing Service-Oriented Architecture (SOA) on the web. One of its major characteristics is that it realizes loose coupling between services, utilizing reusable services. In this paper, we propose a concept based orchestration technique enabling us to specify service orchestration procedures with concepts by using eXtended Object-based Thesaurus (XOT). XOT is a knowledge base that represents service categories as concepts encompassing reusable services and service composition patterns as their relationships. It drastically enhances reusability of services available on the web by allowing us to use the concepts in an orchestration procedure instead of actual service names. Each concept would later be substituted by appropriate service names or constituent concepts before the substitution, if it is composite one. To demonstrate its feasibility, we implement a broker for the concept based orchestration, X-OTMonto as the XOT manager and extended jUDDI as our service repository.

Keywords: web services, information retrieval, ontology.

1 Introduction

A web service is a way of implementing Service-Oriented Architecture (SOA) on the web, inherently designed to support interoperable service to service interaction over a network [1]. One of its major characteristics is that it realizes loose coupling between services by invoking each other based on SOAP (Simple Object Access Protocol). Each of the invoked services is stored into UDDI (Universal Description Discovery and Integration) after it is described by WSDL (Web Services Description Language). Since the loose coupling facilitates service composition, thereby maximizing the utilization of their reusability, the web service can be a basis for drastically reducing the

* This work was supported by the Industrial Strategic Technology Development Program (10039189, Development of SNS based on semi-automatically augmented ontology for facilitating knowledge service) funded by the Ministry of Knowledge Economy(MKE, Korea).
** Corresponding author.

V. Khachidze et al. (Eds.): iCETS 2012, CCIS 332, pp. 41–53, 2012.

cost of software development and maintenance. Especially when implementing composite services, effective discovery of interoperable services and dynamic composition of them could maximize the reusability of services [2],[3],[4].

To discover services relevant to users, UDDI and portal engines usually use keywords. Keyword based searching, however, has a serious limitation in expressing user requirements due to poor semantic expressiveness of WSDL. For example, since tModel in UDDI allows simple searching alone, depending on simple service names and description, it fails to support taxonomy based searching. Moreover, since the taxonomy based searching currently available also adopts simple ontology for classifying specific products according to UNSPSC or NAICS, irrelevant service retrieval is inevitable.

To compensate for this, Martin et al[5], Roman et al[6], and Akkiraju et al[7] describe the properties of services in terms of ontology such as OWL-S [8], WSMO [9] or WSDL-S [10], which make semantic queries and concept based match possible. For example, with OWL-S, encoding additional semantic information into UDDI enables us to retrieve services relevant but not exactly matched with searching keywords. Especially, with IOPE (Input, Output, Precondition, Effect) retrieval by using the process model of OWL-S, it even enables queries to specify a detailed process workflow pattern of services.

There are two general approaches to dynamic composition of discovered services: orchestration and choreography. Orchestration refers to an execution of specific services driven by a central broker with WS-BPEL (Web Services Business Process Execution Language) [11]. On the other hand, choreography relates to multi-party collaboration, involving externally observable interactions between services. It employs WS-CDL (Web Services Choreography Description Language) [12], somewhat like an extension of WSDL: WSDL describes web service interfaces, whereas WS-CDL specifies collaboration between web services. Since the orchestration is relatively effective in realizing mutual interaction between services and composing them, most researches related to service composition are based on the orchestration [13],[14],[15],[16],[17],[18],[19]. They include correlation mechanism based on process algebras [15], petri-net based model for service composition [16],[17] and automatic service composition based on state transition of services [18],[19]. However, the common problem among them is that they fail to provide flexible and adaptable methods of compatibility checking of output/input between constituent services when composing services.

This problem may be solved by exploiting ontology to specify the compatibility between domain specific terms. In other words, by inferring subsumption relationship specified in ontology, we can check the compatibility between parameters, i.e., output of a service and input of another service ready to receive the output. To be specific, Lécué, Silva, and Pires[20] develop a framework to support dynamic composition by semantic matchmaking with the ontology including hierarchical subsumption relationship between output/input parameters, and visualize possible composition relationships between services according to subsumption. Additionally, knowledge based composition of services using AI planning is proposed [21],[22] as well as a web service composition method to which conceptual modeling is applied [23],[24] .

However, the researches still show limitation in that they require a considerable amount of time to check the interoperability between services, due to the lack of pre-categorization of reusable services.

In this paper we propose a concept based orchestration technique based on eXtended Object-based Thesaurus (XOT), which makes it possible to dynamically specify adaptable orchestration of services. XOT is an ontology that contains relationships between concepts acting as categories where services participate as their instances. Besides usual relationships such as "subconcept-of" and "instance-of," it includes "followed_by" and "part_of", used to describe service composition patterns. Instead of actual services, a concept in XOT may be involved in an orchestration, just like a variable which could later be replaced by services or a set of constituent services if it is a composite one. The constituent services which constitute a composite service are related with it by "part_of" and in turn, the services may be related with each other by "followed_by", depending on the order of composition. Since they are the instances of their counterpart concepts, the same would be true in applying the relationships to the concepts. For example, suppose that the concept, train reservation is used in the specification of an orchestration. Then, a user may be guided to complete the orchestration procedure. In other words, by consulting XOT, our broker would capture that the train reservation consists of train reservation request and train reservation confirmation, together with the knowledge that the former should be subsequently followed by the latter. Based on this knowledge, it may recommend the user the corresponding instance or set of instances, which can replace each of the two concepts respectively. The orchestration procedure where concepts are completely replaced by actual services would be encoded into a set of the BPEL documents. Obviously, such an orchestration method could offer more chance for related services available on the web to be reused.

X-OTMonto, used as the management of XOT, is written in C++. The broker to perform the concept based orchestration is implemented with JSP and interacts with XOT through the JAVA API of X-OTMonto. Registry for discovering services is developed by extending jUDDI on the Eclipse platform.

This paper proceeds as follows: In Section 2, we explain XOT categorizing services with its concepts, together with their relationships. Section 3 investigates our method of concept based orchestration with XOT. We describe implementation detail in Section 4. Finally, conclusion and future works follow in Section 5.

2 XOT (eXtended Object-Based Thesaurus)

2.1 The Structure of XOT

XOT may be viewed as a structured set of concepts, each representing the category to which a set of services belong. By keeping track of various relationships between concepts, it enables us to discover relevant services needed for completing the orchestration procedure with BPEL.

Fig. 1 shows the concept hierarchy of XOT, where concepts represent the categories of services and relationships specify the composition pattern between concepts, such as "followed_by," "direct_followed_by" and "part_of." Each concept may take service IDs as its instances. Among the relationships, "part_of" is used to specify a composite service composition pattern in which more than two constituent services participate. For example, "MobileTrainReservation(MTR)" consists of "MobileTrainReservationRequest(MTRR)" and "MobileTrainReservationConfirma-tion(MTRC)," and MTRC, in turn, consists of "MobileMail" and "MobileMultimediaTransmission(MMT)." Note here that sub concepts inherit "part_of" from their super concepts, respectively.

The fact that MTRC follows MTRR in the composition may be represented by "direct_followed_by." Unlike "followed_by," it prohibits the orchestration broker from interposing other services between the two services it relates when composing them. On the contrary, in case of "MobileMail" using "followed_by," its service may firstly be composed with another service of some concept, i.e., a service of "MobilePhoneVibration."

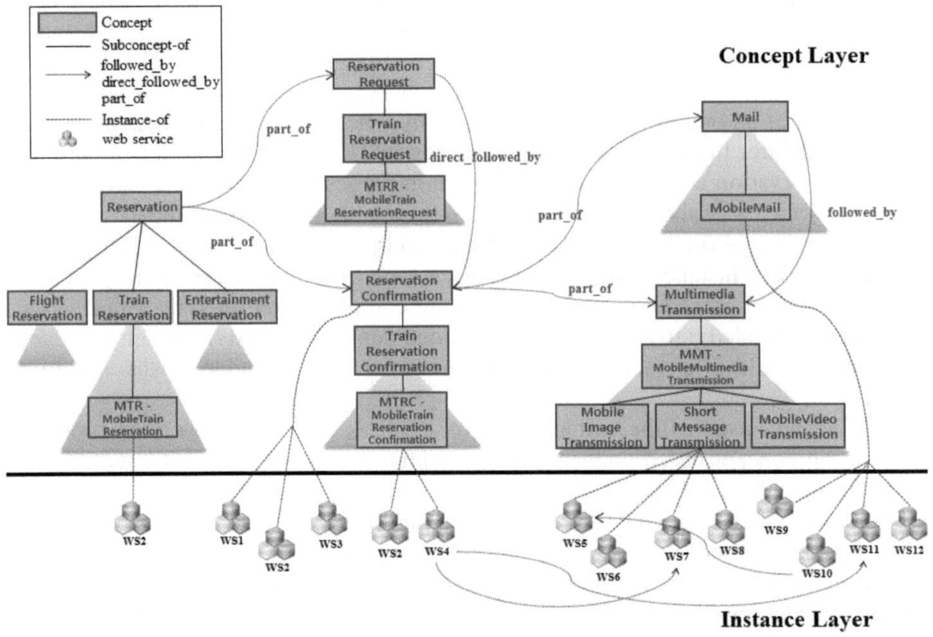

Fig. 1. Conceptual structure of XOT

2.2 Construction of Instances of the XOT Concepts

Generally, a service provider enrolls its service in UDDI after describing the service with WSDL. However, our system requires the additional task of categorizing the enrolled service to determine the XOT concept to which the service belongs as its instance, interrelating the service according to composition pattern relationships.

Fig. 2 shows the categorization that the broker performs by mapping a service name or indexing keywords on each of the XOT concepts. Clustering method or similarity calculation, explored by Liang et al, [25] may be applied to the categorization to enhance its precision. The clustering is made based on the annotation of services in WSDL that includes interfaces to define output/input parameters, service names or their functionality.

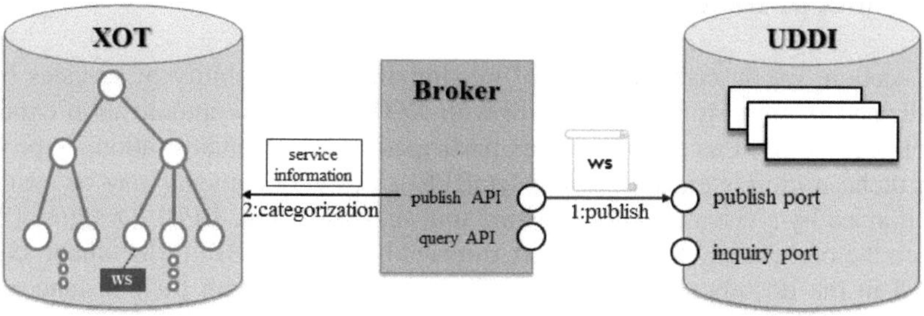

Fig. 2. Service enrollment and construction of XOT instance

As mentioned earlier, since a concept may have a composition pattern relationship with another concept, we need to examine which pair of their instances can have the relationship by checking the compatibility between their output/input parameters. For example, in Fig. 1, when new instance ws5 is inserted into "ShortMessage-Transmission," we need to check if it can be composed with each instance of "MobileMail," e.g., ws10, since its concept is related with "MobileMail" by "followed_by." To check if output/input parameters of the two service interfaces can be compatible with each other, we may adopt matchmaking algorithm [26] or similarity measure [27] based on the parameter domain ontology as depicted in Fig. 3. For example, if the output type of a service is text message and the input type of another service is message type, they would not be composed due to type mismatch between their output/input parameters. However, by the matchmaking algorithm exploiting subsumption hierarchy in the parameter domain ontology, we conceive that they are compatible since text message is the subtype of message.

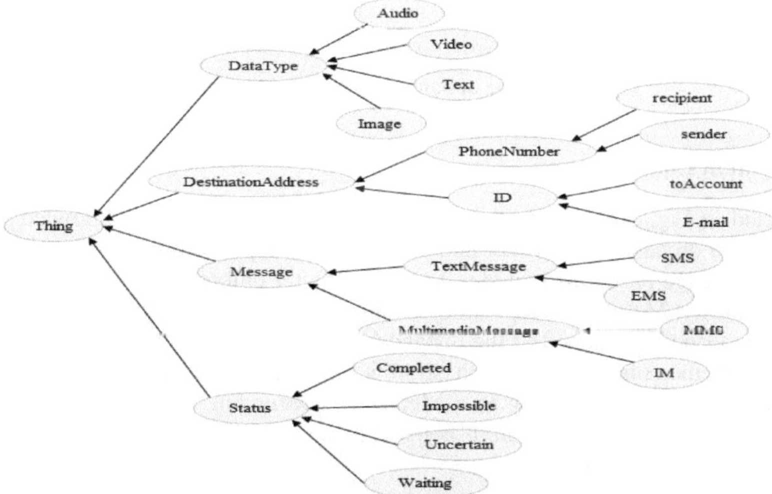

Fig. 3. Parameter domain ontology

3 Concept Based Orchestration with XOT

In this section, we describe the way of maximizing the reusability of services by conceptualizing the orchestration procedure with XOT. Such conceptualization entails that concepts can be used as service names participating in the orchestration. A procedure for the orchestration is encoded with MetaBPEL, whose documents may be easily generated if aided by a visualized composition tool such as Eclipse BPEL Designer [28].

When the orchestration is performed, directed by the MetaBPEL document, concepts included in the document can dynamically be instantiated with their instances, much like generating instances of classes in a java program. It may not only reduce trial errors, but also offload the burden of manual work when writing the BPEL documents.

Note that, if a composite concept for composite services is used in a MetaBPEL document, it should be replaced by the concepts for its constituent services prior to the replacement of the corresponding instances. The replacement is guided by the service composition pattern in XOT. For example, according to the pattern in Fig. 4, "Reservation" should firstly be replaced by "ReservationRequest" and "Reservation-Confirmation" before the replacement of the two concepts with their proper instances. Similarly, "ReservationConfirmation" may be replaced by "Mail" and "Multimedia-Transmission," before such replacement of instances.

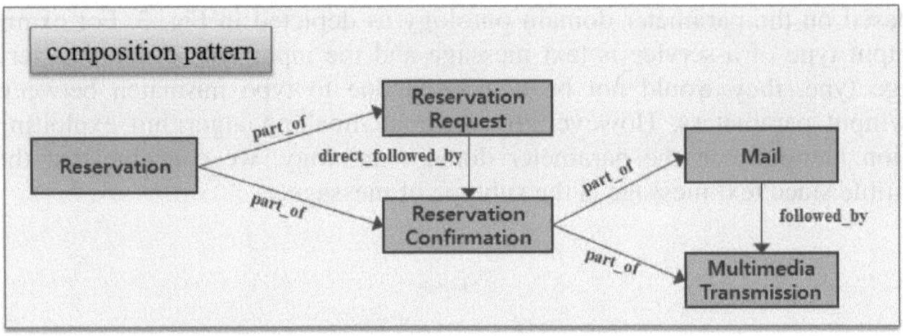

Fig. 4. Example of composition pattern of services

3.1 System Configuration

As depicted in Fig. 5, there are three parts in the proposed system: knowledge base, concept based orchestration broker and composition support tools.

The knowledge base part includes XOT, parameter ontology for checking parameter compatibility, MetaBPEL repository for storing MetaBPEL documents and jUDDI to discover services pertained as the instances of the XOT concepts.

The role of the concept based orchestration broker is to generate a set of executable BPEL documents corresponding to a MetaBPEL document, depending on user decision at each stage of orchestration. It is made by consulting the appropriate knowledge base: XOT coupled with jUDDI.

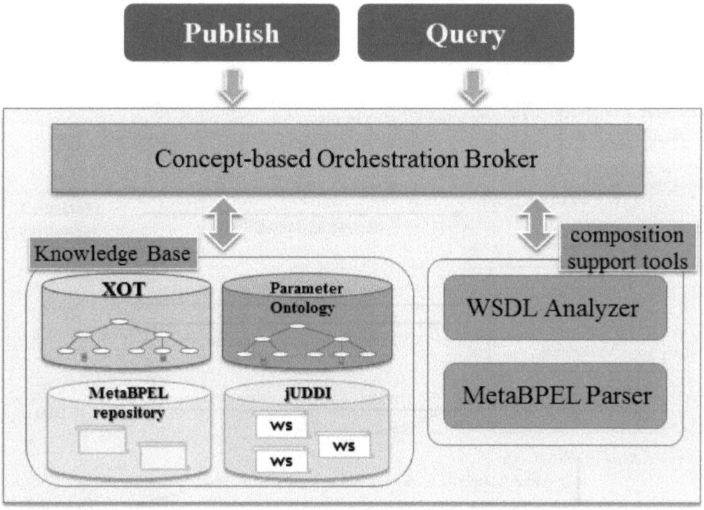

Fig. 5. Configuration of the proposed system

Composition support tools used by the broker are the WSDL analyzer for enrolling and indexing services, and the MetaBPEL parser for processing concepts in the context of the given MetaBPEL document.

3.2 Concept Based Orchestration

As a first step towards orchestration, our broker retrieves the MetaBPEL documents most relevant to the user request from the MetaBPEL repository. If such documents do not exist, he or she may write the needed MetaBPEL document in person. Secondly, the document is parsed by the MetaBPEL parser. Thirdly, to replace concepts in the document with the proper instance or a set of instances, the broker searches for the counterpart concepts in XOT, conceptually matching the concepts in accordance with the order in which they appear in the document. The candidate instances to replace each concept are suggested stepwise, waiting for user selection. Finally, a list of executable BPEL documents filled with pure instances is suggested to the user. Fig. 6 depicts the whole process of the orchestration.

Fig. 7 illustrates an example, which retrieves the corresponding concepts from XOT to be replaced by their instances. Firstly, suppose that "MTRR" appears in a MetaBPEL document as a result of the replacement of MTR by "part_of" (see Fig. 1) and that the broker extracts its instances, ws1, ws2, and ws3 from XOT and jUDDI. Secondly, by tracking "direct_followed_by", the broker shows the instances of the concept "MobileMail" which constitutes "MTRC" capable of being composed with each of ws1, ws2, and ws3; for example, it shows ws10 and ws11 connected to ws1. In the sequel, it captures the other constituent concept "MMT" and then suggests its instances according to the order "followed_by" directs. At each step, once users select one of the proper instances the broker suggests, it replaces the corresponding concept in the MetaBPEL document with the selected instance or a combination of selected instances accumulated so far, thereby generating executable BPEL documents as a result.

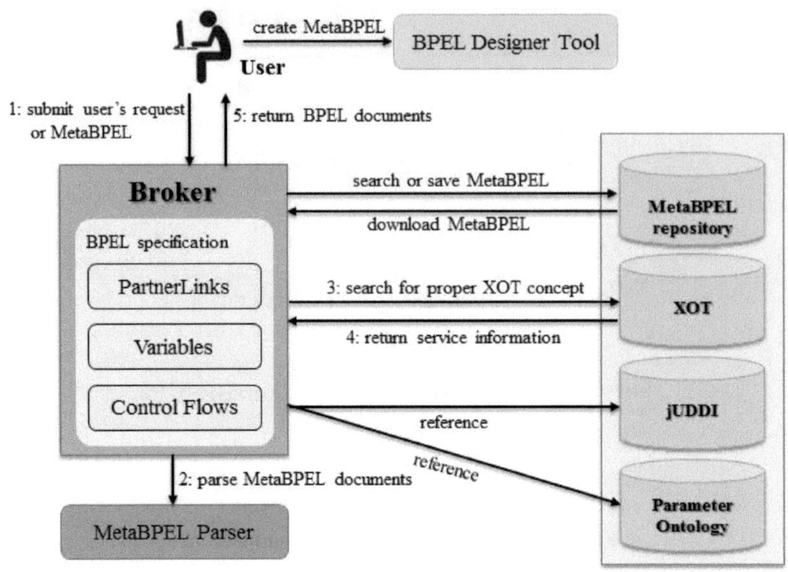

Fig. 6. Concept based orchestration

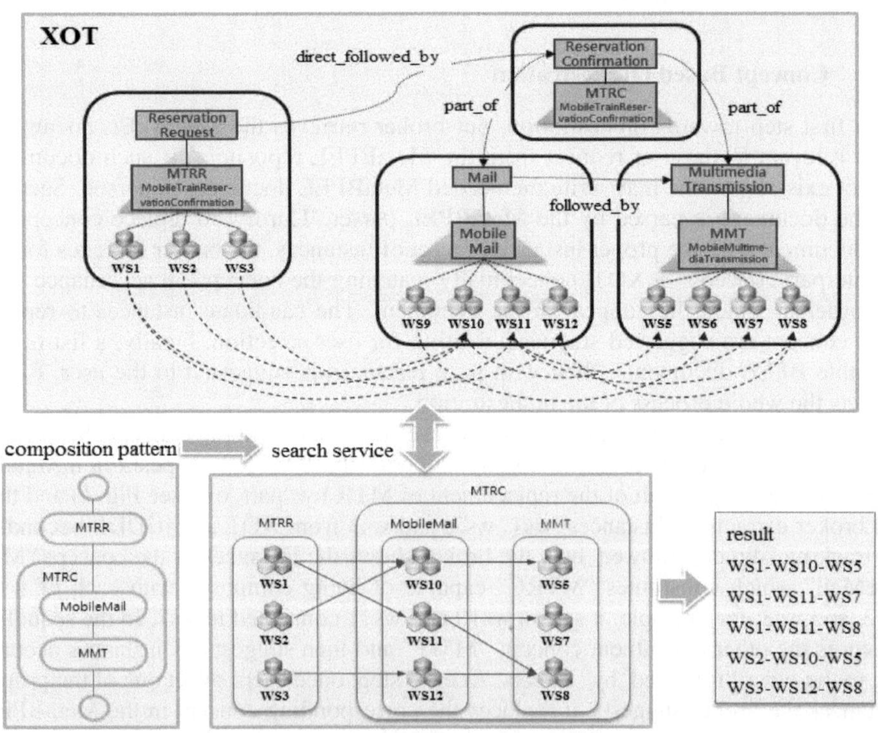

Fig. 7. Instantiating MetaBPEL document

4 Implementation

In this section, we develop a prototype of our concept based orchestration procedure exploiting XOT. This prototype shows how to handle the composite concept "TrainReservation" in Fig. 1 during the concept based orchestration.

To manage XOT, we implemented the XOT manager as shown in Fig. 8. To store and index WSDLs of instance services, jUDDI is constructed in Fig. 9. jUDDI collaborates with XOT to retrieve the instance services by service IDs, which replace the corresponding concepts.

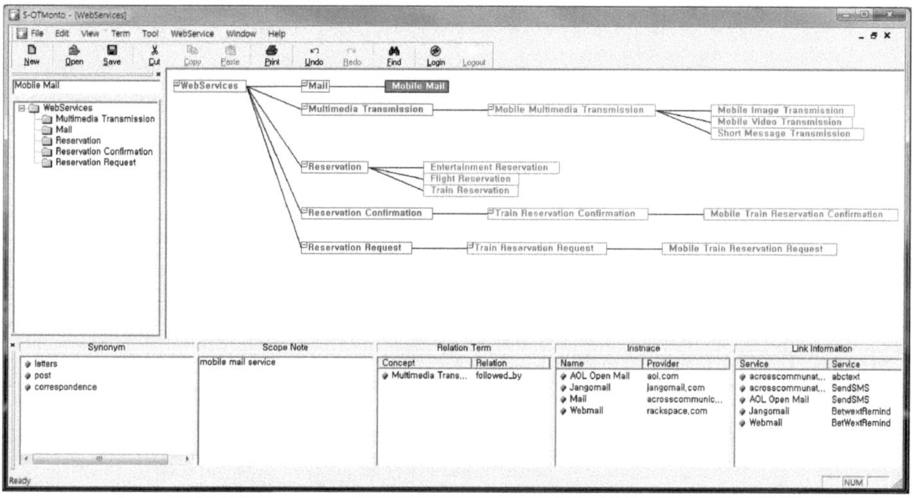

Fig. 8. Implementing the XOT manager

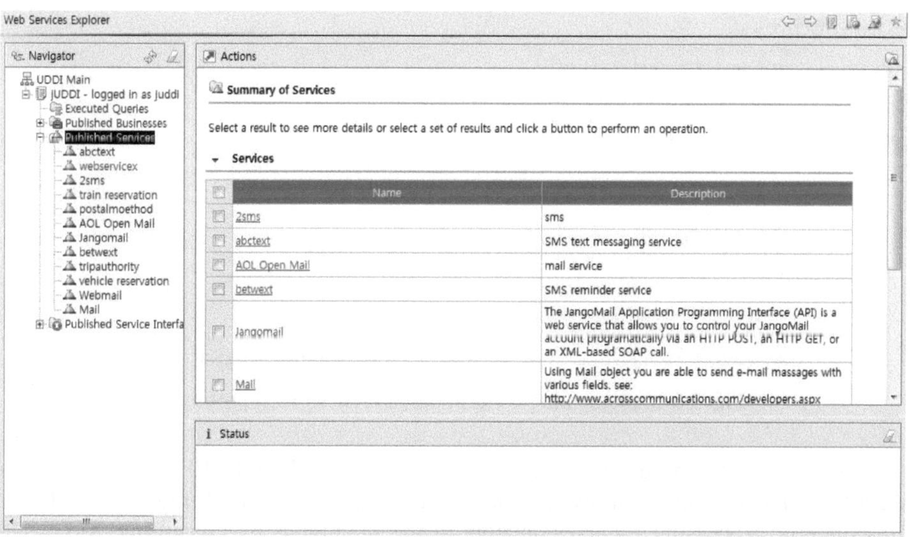

Fig. 9. Construction of jUDDI

```
Create procedure searchServices
   // return services which are the instances of concepts in XOT
  function getServices()
     index ← XOT index
     currentServiceConcept ← current concept in a MetaBPEL document
     beforeService ← service instance previously selected
     services ← Ø
     IF beforeServices is null THEN
        services ← index.instanceOfConcept(currentServiceConcept)
        RETURN services
     ELSE
        currentSList ← index.instanceOfConcept(currentServiceConcept)
        WHILE(each s in currentSList)
           IF s.enableComposite(beforeService) THEN
              services.add(s)
        ENDWHILE
        RETURN services
     ENDIF
```

Fig. 10. Procedure selecting, stepwise, searched instance services

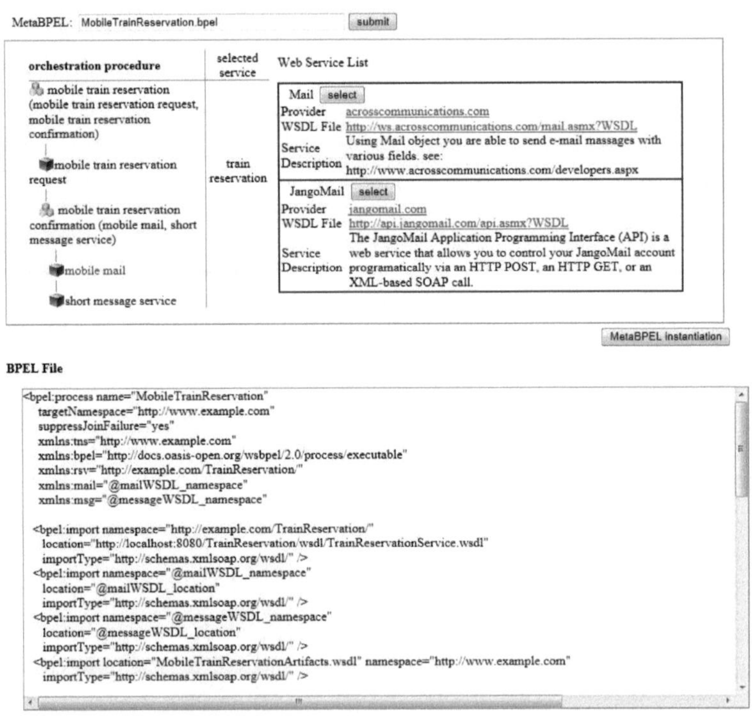

Fig. 11. Implementing concept based orchestration prototype

Assume now that a current concept is identified in a MetaBPEL document by the MetaBPEL parser. Fig. 10 shows our orchestration procedure, performed by the broker subsequently processing related concepts in the document by consulting XOT. This procedure uses the two functions: index.instanceOfConcept(currentServiceConcept) and s.enableComposite(beforeService). The former extracts services pertained as the instances of currentServiceConcept in jUDDI and the latter checks if the service 's' is interoperable with beforeService by consulting the corresponding composition pattern relationship.

Once users finish selecting the last service, the broker generates each of the executable BPEL documents satisfying the specification of the MetaBPEL document. Fig. 11 shows the prototype enabling the broker to generate the BPEL documents according to Fig. 10.

5 Conclusion and Future Work

In this paper, we proposed a new approach for performing a concept based orchestration of services with XOT and implemented its prototype to demonstrate its feasibility. Since concepts can be used in the MetaBPEL document as well as actual service names, it may allow more services to be involved in orchestration. This entails a considerable enhancement of the reusability of services available on the web. That is, if we systematically classify reusable services according to concepts in XOT and specify composition pattern between composite concepts, this approach would make it possible to recommend services beyond the extent of developer's knowledge for some orchestration. Extending their knowledge with XOT has the potential to be an effective strategy for maximizing the reusability of services.

In further research, we will semi-automate the specification of composition pattern relationships between concepts. Semantic web service technology based on the ontology such as OWL-S or WSMO leaves room for improvement in semi-automatic checking of the compatibility between output/input of services. Moreover, we would include other composition patterns into our ontology that must be specified when composing services - for example, we could include in XOT some relationships between constituent services parallel executed with each other.

References

1. Kreger, H.: IBM Software Group: Web Services Conceptual Architecture (WSCA 1.0) (May 2001), http://www.csd.uoc.gr/~hy565/newpage/docs/pdfs/papers/wsca.pdf
2. Rao, J., Su, X.: A Survey of Automated Web Service Composition Methods. In: Cardoso, J., Sheth, A.P. (eds.) SWSWPC 2004. LNCS, vol. 3387, pp. 43–54. Springer, Heidelberg (2005)
3. Erl, T.: Service-Oriented Architecture: Concepts, Technology, and Design. Prentice Hall PTR (2005)
4. Durvasula, S., et al.: SOA Practitioners' Guide Part 1 Why Services-Oriented Architecture? (2006), http://www.soablueprint.com/whitepapers/SOAPGPart1.pdf
5. Martin, D.L., et al.: Bringing Semantics to Web Services: The OWL-S Approach. In: Cardoso, J., Sheth, A.P. (eds.) SWSWPC 2004. LNCS, vol. 3387, pp. 26–42. Springer, Heidelberg (2005)

6. Roman, D., et al.: Web Service Modeling Ontology. Applied Ontology 1(1), 77–106 (2005)
7. Akkiraju, R., et al.: Web Service Semantics – WSDL-S. A joint UGA-IBM Technical Note, Version 1.0 (2005), http://lsdis.cs.uga.edu/library/download/WSDL-S-V1.pdf
8. OWL-S: Semantic Markup for Web Services, http://www.w3.org/Submission/OWL-S/
9. Web Services Modeling Ontology, http://www.wsmo.org/
10. WSDL-S, http://www.w3.org/Submission/WSDL-S/
11. WS-BPEL 2.0 Specification, http://docs.oasis-open.org/wsbpel/2.0/OS/wsbpel-v2.0-OS.html
12. Web Services Choreography Description Language Version 1.0, World Wide Web Consortium, http://www.w3.org/TR/ws-cdl-10/
13. Kovac, D., Trcek, D.: A Survey of Web services Orchestration and Choreography with Formal Models (2011), http://www.softec.si/pdf/kovac_damjan.survey.pdf
14. Urbieta, A., Barrutieta, G., Parra, J., Uribarren, A.: A survey of dynamic service composition approaches for ambient systems. In: The Ambi-Sys Workshop on Software Organisation and Monitoring of Ambient Systems, Canada, pp. 1–8 (2008)
15. Viroli, M.: A core calculus for correlation in orchestration languages. Journal of Logic and Algebraic Programming 70(1), 74–95 (2007)
16. Hamadi, R., Benatallah, B.: A Petri net-based model for web service composition. In: The 14th Australasian Database Conference, vol. 17, pp. 191–200 (2003)
17. Dong, W.L., Yu, H., Zhang, Y.B.: Testing BPEL-based Web Service Composition Using High-level Petri Nets. In: 10th IEEE International Enterprise Distributed Object Computing Conference (EDOC 2006), pp. 441–444 (2006)
18. Hwang, S.Y., Lim, E.P., Lee, C.H., Chen, C.H.: Dynamic Web Service Selection for Reliable Web Service Composition. IEEE Transactions on Services Computing 1(2), 104–116 (2008)
19. Bertoli, P., Pistore, M., Traverso, P.: Automated composition of Web services via planning in asynchronous domains. Artificial Intelligence 174(3-4), 316–361 (2010)
20. Lécué, F., Silva, E., Pires, L.F.: A framework for dynamic web services composition. In: 2nd ECOWS Workshop on Emerging Web Services Technology (WEWST 2007), Halle, Germany (2007)
21. Hatzi, O., Meditskos, G., Vrakas, D., Bassiliades, N., Anagnostopoulos, D., Vlahavas, I.: PORSCE II: Using Planning for Semantic Web Service Composition (2009), http://fire.dit.hua.gr/~raniah/documents/ickeps09.pdf
22. Li, X., Tang, X., Song, Z., Yuan, X.: Chen. D.: AFlow: An Automated Web Services Composition System Based on the AI Planning and Workflow. In: 2010 IEEE International Conference on Progress in Informatics and Computing (PIC), pp. 1067–1072 (2010)
23. Grossmann, G., Thiagarajan, R., Schrefl, M., Stumptner, M.: Conceptual Modeling Approaches for Dynamic Web Service Composition. In: Kaschek, R., Delcambre, L. (eds.) The Evolution of Conceptual Modeling. LNCS, vol. 6520, pp. 180–204. Springer, Heidelberg (2011)
24. Pahl, C., Gacitua-Decar, V., Wang, M., Bandara, K.Y.: Ontology-based composition and matching for dynamic service coordination. In: International Workshop on Ontology, Models, Conceptualization and Epistemology in Social, Artificial and Natural Systems, ONTOSE 2011, London, UK (2011)

25. Liang, Q., Li, P., Hung, P.C.K., Wu, X.: Clustering Web Services for Automatic Categorization. In: IEEE International Conference on Services Computing, SCC 2009, pp. 380–387 (2009)
26. Srinivasan, N., Paolucci, M., Sycara, K.: An Efficient Algorithm for OWL-S Based Semantic Search in UDDI. In: Cardoso, J., Sheth, A.P. (eds.) SWSWPC 2004. LNCS, vol. 3387, pp. 96–110. Springer, Heidelberg (2005)
27. Plebani, P., Pernici, B.: URBE: Web service retrieval based on similarity evaluation. IEEE Transactions on Knowledge and Data Engineering 21(11), 1629–1642 (2009)
28. Popovici, M., Muraru, M., Agache, A., Negreanu, L., Giumale, C., Dobre, C.: An Ontology-Based Dynamic Service Composition Framework for Intelligent Houses. In: 2011 10th International Symposium on Autonomous Decentralized Systems (ISADS), pp. 177–184 (2011)

Intellectual Property Rights in E-business Environment: Paradigm Shifts of Legal and Political Measures

Seyed Reza Eftekhari

Assistant Professor
Islamic Azad University – Gonabad Branch
Iran, IR
sreftekhari@gmail.com

Abstract. The function of conventional rules and policies in protecting IP rights in the WEB against piracy and misapplications has become the core element of legal discussions. It is a hardcore task for IP Regimes to insure the security of information, researches, formulas and secrets that are considered private property, and at the same time to refrain from any interference with public domains. The failure to protect intellectual works legally is proposed to deter innovation, evolution of scientific theory and investments in research tools. The fact that scientific works, research products, formulas and technological innovations that may form trade secrets and have valuable applications in the business world are available in different forms through world-wide web and as protectable properties poses the necessity of a paradigm shift in policies directed toward intellectual property protection. As a theoretical foundation of our subject matter, we propose a model for legal policies in relation to the protection of IP rights in a cyber framework along with the outline of so-called paradigm shift in scientific humanities.

Keywords: IP Rights, Patent Law, E-Business, Paradigm Shift, Legal Policy.

1 Introduction

Public policies directed toward protecting intellectual property rights are, historically, a function of general theory that indicates global turns in basic scientific areas. These universal turns or, as proposed by Kuhn, these "Paradigm shifts" against normal science patterns [1] covers the ideas and policies about IP rights and the philosophy of copyright law. The emergence of new products of knowledge and technology, and the idea that they are eligible to be patented as intellectual properties, has put forward new challenges against the existent legal approaches. Among these challenging topics are methods of doing business, especially in the context of computerized networks or methods of e-commerce. [2] We do not aim to offer an analysis of historical paradigm shifts in sciences, which traditionally covers the fast-developing idea of copy right law. Rather, this paper argues that the different perspectives that appeared in the eyes of thinkers and legislators respectively are the foundations upon which historical shifts were formed.

V. Khachidze et al. (Eds.): iCETS 2012, CCIS 332, pp. 54–61, 2012.

Viewing the history of copyright law in such a way indicates that "the history of intellectual property rights is a history of contestation. The inherent tensions in the idea of intellectual property recurrently resurface under philosophical, technological, or institutional pressure". [3] Historical phenomena have not undergone a linear path wherein every event is a stone upon which the next is shaped and prepares for the other. So are the scientific progresses, as they are comprised of historical discoveries. We argue that the IP concepts and co-related institutes have been formed according to a global paradigm shift. This paradigm shift is necessarily rooted in scientific humanities, firstly to fill the gap between the two conflicting areas, and secondly to bring to light the challenges faced by IP regimes in the virtual world. In this way the conventional methods of protecting IP rights will be revisited. Two kinds of serious challenges must be dealt with: the first includes challenges inside the e-business environment, including security issues, restrictions which might be imposed on the process of free use of patented material for noncommercial purposes, and the policies related to authorized domains; the second comprises concerns from outside, mainly regarding the systems of control and their effects on the afore-mentioned conflict.

Technological developments, along with political and social changes, were just influential in the development of the concept. Three remarkable shifts are noticed from a historical perspective. The role of global trends and international attempts to protect IP rights through these periods is very salient in the last century. These historical shifts are as follows. The first is "the resolution of the patent controversy of 1870-1875 in favor of intellectual property rights" [3], which might be considered the result of harsh legal and political debates among the devoted advocates of IP rights, urging policies adopted by states to protect them and their opponents in European countries. That is why some thinkers describe the traditional intellectual property law as an arcane and complex subject. [4]

The second shift discusses "the multilateral institutionalization of this resolution in the Paris and Berne Conventions" in the late 1800s. [3]

The third shift is "the recent multilateral intellectual property settlement in the World Trade Organization and the emerging contestation in its wake", in which such new areas of IP rights as patentable scientific products, research tools and e-worlds have come into the field. [3] The move toward redefinition of IP rights, along with introducing emerging patterns in protectable rights, disseminated the potential of a global attempt in redirecting IP rules. The last three decades witnessed ever-increasing quantities of potential subject matter for IP and the expansion of the boundaries of the IP institution as a result of new technological developments. [2]

2 Concept's Paradigm Shift

Generally speaking, the term "intellectual property" came into existence in the nineteenth century. [5] Before and after this time, how to define the concept of intellectual property was the dominant factor in professional debates. In earlier periods of legislating there might be a generally accepted idea that a protectable right to an artistic work or expression is alike to that of tangible things. Legal struggle to institutionalize IP rights through official processes of policy making has not been limited to answering the question of what is protectable as exclusive right and what is not. Institutionalizing intellectual property rights, especially those related to the scientific and technological domains, has created many dramatic debates among the proponents and opponents of the exclusive right over what is considered the achievements of human society in scientific areas and was therefore believed to be a shared and communal asset.

2.1 Historical Paradigm Shift in Conceptualizing IP Rights

Institutionalizing intellectual property rights in different subject matters has always been accompanied by shifting social and political trends, which have in turn produced a wide range of definitions of related concepts such as ownership and patentable objects. As Susan Sell [3] proposed, "the history of intellectual property protection reveals a complex yet identifiable relationship between three major factors. First, it reveals shifting conceptions of ownership, authorship and invention. These ideas denote what 'counts' as property, and who shall lay claim to it. Second, this history reflects changes in the organization of innovation and the production and distribution of technology. Third, it reflects institutional change with these shifting ideational and material forces".

The challenges over concepts have remained controversial to our times. In the last decades, these controversies placed the judiciary systems in a troubled situation to make decisions in many important cases regarding patents. Even in a developed system such as the U.S. patent circuit judges were said to have doubted their ability to adjudicate patent cases. [6] This is also the case with e-business patentable areas. The aforementioned concepts paradigm shift in IP rights concepts has its effects firstly on the judiciary system. Doubts about the domain of protectable rights and new-born subject matters are partly the results of theoretical arguments, and partly due to the different polices arisen from conceptualizing related items. This process of conceptualizing, along with the institutionalization of IP rights in legal procedures, from the early phases of authorship rules and industrial patents to the idea of e-business methods and protected computerized market values, comprises the long chain of challenging general policies. Recent speculations suggest that copyright discourse is the product of the conceptual world of authorship, and saturated with its terminology. [7] The process continues to cover such areas as e-business and technology-based methods of commerce.

2.2 Paradigm Shift in Protecting Policies

Public policies and the approach based on legal semiotics have followed a definite yet complex line to reach their current point. Three identifiable variables exert influence on the process of progressive copyright policies through history including legal theory, procedural adjudication and shifting concepts. Throughout the centuries, the power of state to enact proper rules and to enforce them through a constitutional framework was absent. 'The absence of an administrative agency overseeing a formal grant process means that it falls entirely to courts to both delineate and enforce a creator's entitlement during an infringement action'. [8] A new shift that has critically affected the current policies regarding IP rights is the approach that tries to forge connections between legal policies and development. It is because of this paradigm shift that 'one can now easily find patents on various methods in various disciplines, [2] including computerized programs and implemented business methods.

3 Policy Making, Paradigm Shifts and E-business

The title of this section refers to the progressing trend in policy making toward patenting methods, databases and areas of knowledge management related to the business world. Creating a safe and protected virtual environment, in which an enormous amount of data and private information and methods are manipulated, is the main concern of lawmakers worldwide. The latter decades of the twentieth century witnessed the huge expansion of e-environment and the dominant rise of communication technologies and computerized programs, especially in business domains. Knowledge management, trade, law and public policies focused most of their activities on virtual environment and internet.

As a matter of fact, the extension of IP rules to such areas as e-business and the variety of its subjects has some relation to social policy and legal definitions. E-business and e-commerce are inclusive of subject matters and activities with diverse natures that are strong and influential enough to provide a ground for a huge paradigm shift, or to change the view of legislators and prompt new theories about IP rights. As proposed by a scholar, today the changes in the societal perception of patentable subject matters are understood as fact. [2] As a result, such matters as the methods of conducting businesses have been titled under the intellectual property law, and their patents were issued under these and other relevant clauses. [2] In addition to attempts made by local legislators to legitimize different forms of protectable IP rights, they actually need to be reinforced, especially legal attempts concerning two categories of patents and copyrights which are most controversial. [9]

In the e-environment, computer programs and computerized business methods that concern internet-based activities are more and more likely to be eligible for patent protection under the current state of law in major patenting nations. [10] Presently, a great deal of business affairs are centralized in internet, consisting of methods, information, databases, technical data and knowledge management, urging the legislator body to protect them as private assets. As suggested by some scholars, 'the political and commercial world now seems quite willing to accept the notion that there is no point even thinking about a nascent idea or producing any new knowledge, if someone else might already be able to claim ownership of it'. [11] This means that partial knowledge can be definitely acclaimed as private property.

3.1 The Place of E-business

Copyrights law protects expressions and patent law protects ideas. This is common sense in IP law. When we are talking about e-business and its related subjects, however, it is the implementation of these ideas that matters, and not the idea itself.

Among the new subject matters that have been granted as patentable by legislators and achieved in the new era are methods of computerized tourism[1], advertising on the

[1] European Patent No. 846,301 (Issued June 10, 1998).

internet[2], running an automated restaurant business[3], treating cancer[4] and administrating mortgage[5]. Even activities in business such as methods of filling a patent application[6] [2] are subject to the rules.

Generally speaking, the approach to protect scientific products and internet-based knowledge and research tools has created harsh debates among the scholars and controversies about the nature of legal disciplines.

Two groups of arguments were proposed by thinkers rejecting the necessity of subjecting such items to the patent systems. These arguments focus primarily on areas that relate to scientific research, and then to internet-based activities and knowledge management.

Firstly, many scholars argue that the idea of protecting scientific products such as formulas, inventions, data bases and other technological information by putting them under patent rules and the exclusive right of their implementation is destructive and harmful to human progress. Robert Merton, as a sociologist of science, has suggested that patents undermine the communal values (societal assets) that promote normal science. [1] According to Vaver, IP rights law has not only put an end to innovation, but also has now become an end to itself. [11] Looking further, there is considerable doubts "whether copyrights and patents are necessary to encourage the production of creative works and inventions, or that the incremental gains in innovation outweigh the immense costs of an IP system." [9]

Secondly, there exists a well-known view that copyright law has brought about a kind of social conflict. Practically, this argument has been generalized to patent systems regarding subjects such as those mentioned above. The fundamental right of free access to knowledge [4] as public interest is undermined by copyright law, and the patent system conflicts with open sharing, which is considered the traditional norm in the scientific world. [1] A model to be discussed in the domain has included the United States Patent and Trademark Office decisions on some topics that identified four groups of business knowledge and methods and classified them under the U.S. Patent Classification System. [2] These patented areas cover different kinds of e-business and business knowledge, such as processing knowledge of customer affairs, data management regarding advertising and incentive programs, managerial acts for manipulating monetary transactions and human resource management.

3.2 E-business and Legal Theory

Theories about the nature and concepts of IP rights have always been influential in legal decisions made by the courts and shaping policies toward the end of protecting these rights. Due to e-dynamics and profound technological changes in the realm of business methods, intellectual property has become a core corporate asset. [5] Now the question poses itself of what is the view of local legal systems toward these dynamics in the IP domain.

---

[2] Japan Patent No. 2,756,483 (Issued March 13, 1998).
[3] Japan Patent No. 2,804,933 (Issued July 24, 1998).
[4] U.S. Patent No. 5,456,663 (Issued Oct. 10, 1995).
[5] U.S. Patent No. 5,876,648 (Issued March 2, 1999).
[6] U.S. Patent No. 6,049,811 (Issued April 11, 2000).

A look at the history of IP rights will show that the process of regulations has been a factor of the interaction of the three afore-mentioned categories: theory, concept, and policy. In this process there is always a comparison between two groups of subject matters considering the essential differences between the traditionally accepted subject matters and a business method. [2] Older principles, which have limited protection to concrete expressions, along with the emerging idea/expression dichotomy and other late nineteenth century decisions declaring that copyright protection did not extend to knowledge [7], are no longer the dominant view in the domain. The rise of new theories in the last decade and the practical processes tried by the courts in common law system led to the legitimacy of IP rights for the holders of computerized programs and the examiners of e-business methods.

However, the debate still exists in how legal theory and the nature of the subject may affect the area and change the concepts in the eye of policy makers. Presently, the legal and legislative question and disagreement is on the subject of how to justify such changes legally. [2] Future policies and approaches will show the extents to which the two above factors would generalize IP law policies. In fact, many leading scholars of intellectual property law are among the IP restrictors. They observe that goods held in common (public goods) are as much a part of the wealth of society as private goods. [12] In this way, in addition to the tangible properties that are subject to legal protection, the data, methods of conducting managerial and commercial affairs and information in the e-environment will also be entitled to IP rules.

3.3 Dealing with Emerging Challenges

Intellectual property law is currently under the pressure of legal and political challenges. The paradoxes and contradictions inherent in knowledge-as-property pattern [11] under IP regimes; the paradoxical nature of copyright law regarding the democratic paradigm directed toward democracy-enhancing mechanism [8]; pressure on World Intellectual Property Organization[7] (WIPO) to enact the draft of model Access to Knowledge Treaty [4] as a new international policy; the idea of the tragedy of common data which prescribes research data to be regulated under strong property rights policy [13]; the dilemma of piracy and concerns about the security of privacy in modern grid [14] and related policies, and many other challenges surround the extended world of business and scientific development.

The effects of legal and political policies on internet economy and on different levels of e-business and e-commerce are noticeable. Theoretically, patenting knowledge, information and methods related to internet economy and its managerial techniques does not stifle innovation and progress; rather it may boost them. Actually, the idea of internet economy faces some challenges, but a consensus is emerging that

[7] As noted by Kapzcynski, (2008) some reformist groups who attempt to promote a more open environment for innovation and knowledge mobilization 'have begun to seek to affiliate and make common cause under the rubric of "access to knowledge" (A2K). This has occurred most notably through a recent campaign to press the World Intellectual Property Organization to adopt a "development agenda".'

the information age and the Internet are exerting a transformative impact on society [12] and on the legal and political approaches, which will make IP rights law an ever-expanding domain.

With the idea of theoretical debates and policy-driven challenges in mind, we suggest that legal policies must act in three critical ways regarding internet-based businesses and such important subjects as knowledge management.

- Adopting protection policies, without noticing the two effective dimensions of conceptualization of the spiritual relation between intellectual properties and humans as well as society as a whole and of institutionalization of these concepts, is a failure.
- We need criminal policies against different kinds of piracy in the e-business world and other domains of intellectual property. Should these policies be accompanied by a global approach, they would be able to create a safe environment for computerized activities.
- Ethical issues are missing in the theoretical aspect in most of IP policies. How to introduce moral issues in the different levels of managing e-business is a universal concern. Moral and psychological safety of the e-business environment should be given priority in public policies.

4 Conclusion

Different policies for protecting intellectual property rights that are adopted under the pressure of legal and political approaches mostly focus on technological advances. As scientific theories propose, these policies have undergone historical paradigm shifts. This history of intellectual property law reveals two main streams of differentiation, including the critical changes in the conceptions of subjects related to IP such as ownership, authorship, and invention on one hand, and the changes in organizational structure of innovation [3] on the other.

Political attempts to institutionalize the main themes of the IP concepts have come to be successful throughout the centuries. In the historical process, three identifiable variables exert their influence on the progressive turn of copyright legalization and policies. They are legal theory, procedural adjudication and shifting concepts.

However, theoretical debates still exist regarding the nature and the extent of subject matters, especially in the three domains of scientific inventions, technological innovations, and knowledge assets. Toward the end of the twentieth century, the global trend toward defining and organizing the norms and standards of internet-based business and non-business activities urged legal bodies to impose regulations ranging from patent systems to the great task of revisiting traditional policies. Since internet data, which provide very useful tools and rich contributions to our collective pursuit of knowledge and justice [13], there should be proper legal and ethical standards to ensure the safety of these activities.

E-business has become a new and very extensive domain for knowledge-based and managerial activities such as methods of conducting business, especially in the context of computerized networks or as a method of e-commerce [2]. As such, e-business is considered one of the most important areas for exerting IP rules. We propose that this area must be protected through three kinds of legal policies, including institutionalization of the standards of e-business, ensuring the security of all activities in the e-environment by criminal measures, and disseminating ethical issues via the Internet and related environment, as human norms.

References

1. Lee, P.: Patents, Paradigm Shifts and Progress in Biomedical Science. The Yale Law Journal 114, 661–694 (2004)
2. Lee, N.: Patent Eligible Subject Matter Reconfiguration and The Emergence Proprietarian Norms: The Patent Eligibility of Business Methods. The Journal of Law and Technology IDEA 45(3), 321–359 (2005)
3. Sell, S.: "Intellectual Property and Public Policy in Historical Perspective: Contestation and Settlement" LOYOLA of Los Angeles Law Review. In: Digital Commons at Loyola Marymount University and Loyola Law School, vol. 38, Fall, pp. 267–322 (2004)
4. Kapczynski, A.: The Access to Knowledge Mobilization and the New Politics of Intellectual Property. The Yale Law Journal 117, 804–885 (2008)
5. Nguyen, X.-T., Maine, J.A.: The History of Intellectual Property Taxation: Promoting Innovation and Other Intellectual Property Goals? SMU Law Review 64, 101–161 (2011)
6. Lee, P.: Patent Law and the Two Cultures. The Yale Law Journal 120, 1–82 (2010)
7. Bracha, O.: The Ideology of Authorship Revisited: Authors, Markets, and Liberal Values in Early American Copyright. The Yale Law Journal 118, 186–271 (2008)
8. Balganesh, S.: Debunking Blackstonian Copyright. In: Reviewing 'Copyright's Paradox' by Neil Weinstock Netanel (2009); The Yale Law Journal 118, 1126–1179
9. Kinsella, N.S.: Against Intellectual Property. Journal of Libertarian Studies, Ludwig von Mises Institute 15(2), 1–53 (2001)
10. Lee, N.: Fragmented Infringement of Computer Program Patents in The Global Economy. The Intellectual Property Law Review IDEA 48(3), 345–379 (2008)
11. Singer, A.E., Singer, M.: Intellectual Property and Moral Imagination. Journal of Economic and Social Policy 7(1), 1–19 (2002), `http://epubs.scu.edu.au/jesp/vol7/iss1/1`
12. Schwartz, P.M., Treanor, W.M.: Eldred and Lochner: Copyright Term Extension and Intellectual Property as Constitutional Property. The Yale Law Journal, Schwartz FINAL 112, 2331–2414 (2003)
13. Yakowitz, J.: Tragedy of the Data Commons. Harvard Journal of Law and Technology 25(1), 1–66 (2011)
14. McNeil, S.K.: Privacy and the modern Grid. Harvard Journal of Law and Technology 25(1), 199–224 (2011)

A Multi-objective Programming for Web Services Composition

Shanshan Hao, Fuzan Chen*, Minqiang Li, and Jisong Kou

College of Management and Economics, Tianjin University
No. 92, Weijin Road, Nankai District, Tianjin, 300072, P. R. China
fzchen@tju.edu.cn

Abstract. Web service plays an important role in implementing Service Oriented Architecture (SOA). It is becoming vital to provide an efficient service composition mechanism with respect to user's requirements. Measuring the Quality of Service (QoS) can help to offer appropriate functions. However, most of the previous QoS-based researches were unable to guide a service selection to achieve a rapid and effective composition. To address this issue, firstly, we present a method to measure QoS in a composition. Secondly, QoS risk is defined as the variance between actual value and the expectation of QoS. Thirdly, we propose a multi-objective programming model, aimed at composite service plan optimization. Finally, genetic algorithm is used with synthetic data, and a weighted sum of risk values constitutes the fitness to lead the evolution of populations. Experimental results demonstrate that the presented model and algorithm provide effective and comprehensive information for decision makers to select appropriate web services for composition.

Keywords: Web service, Web service composition, QoS, Multi-objective programming, Genetic algorithm.

1 Introduction

In recent years, Web service has played an important role in implementing Service Oriented Architecture (SOA) for achieving dynamic business processes. With the increased number of web services advertised in public repository, it is becoming vital to provide an efficient web service composition mechanism with respect to user's requirements. To meet these requirements, a key step is measuring Quality of Service (QoS) to evaluate the nonfunctional performance of service composition, which can grant composition the appropriate functions.

Presently, there are many researches on how to choose a high-performance Web service composition based on QoS. QoS management systems have been established to measure and manage QoS characteristics [1-4]. There have been many approaches based on QoS computation and optimization to select Web service composition [5-8]. Structures of compositions have also been considered while computing QoS [9-12].

* Corresponding author.

V. Khachidze et al. (Eds.): iCETS 2012, CCIS 332, pp. 62–72, 2012.

However, the calculated QoS attributes are inadequate and previous research has mainly concentrated on calculating QoS. As a result, most of the existing studies failed to found a comprehensive system to measure the total QoS of a service composition. An efficient web service composition mechanism is therefore needed.

Our study aims to extend QoS characteristics and materialize the QoS-based method of selecting services. In the following section, we state the selection and composition technologies relevant to Web services. In the third section, we establish a system to measure the QoS of a composite service plan. In the fourth section, we define the QoS risk as the variance between actual value and the expectation of QoS and propose a multi-objective programming model to choose a composition with lowest risk. In the fifth section, the experiment of the model is stated and the results demonstrate that the presented model and algorithm provide effective information for decision makers to select appropriate web services for composition. Finally, in section 6 we conclude and indicate future work relating to our study.

2 Related Works

Until now, there have been many researches on technologies of selection and composition of Web services. On one hand, studies on the services selection developed from syntax to semantic, which means from Web Service Definition Language (WSDL) to Semantic Web Service (SWS). SWS extend WSDL with semantic descriptions. Service discovery and matching technologies based on semantics have been studied [11]. The description with semanteme can be recognized by machines, and supports the dynamic retrieval and fuzzy matching. Conversely, the technology of composition uses business process to achieve service composition. Business Process Execution Language (BPEL) describes services interaction as a business process or a workflow and uses service instances in a process.

Most methods mentioned above are essentially searching services based on key words of the QoS characteristics, which are described by specific languages. Both the languages and the searching processes must work under stringent specifications. BPEL only supports static composition and the structure of the composition cannot change once established. It lacks dynamic and automaticity. Furthermore, BPEL does not meet semantic-based fuzzy matching. With these defects, there are many further researches regarding how to combine and upgrade SWS and BPEL technologies [13,14]. Most methods achieve the dynamic and automaticity with large numbers of specific languages or specifications, which are complicated. In our study, the method we use to select service quantifies QoS and risk according to the description of QoS characteristics and the service execution history. Additionally, these descriptions are not directly used in the selection as key words, which allow for casual language and ignoring many specifications. As a result, the processes of selections and compositions are easier and the applicability of our method has been extended.

3 Problem Statement and Preliminaries

QoS measurement is vital to QoS management. After summarizing features of participants' actions in a service-oriented architecture and the previous study on QoS, we choose to calculate reliability, availability, expense cost, execution time and latency time.

A composite service is a complex service composed by relatively simple Web services from a large set of candidates. The following definition is given:

Definition 1 (Composite Service, CS): A composite service can be formally defined as CS= (SS, CF), and hereinto:

(1) SS is a set of Web services {S1, S2,..., Sm}, and Si is either an atomic service or another composite service. Logic control relations CF exist in Web services set SS.

(2) CF is a logic control relation set among Web services. For any two services Si and Sj in SS, there is a logic control relation of sequence, fork, iteration or parallel, which are shown in Figure 1.

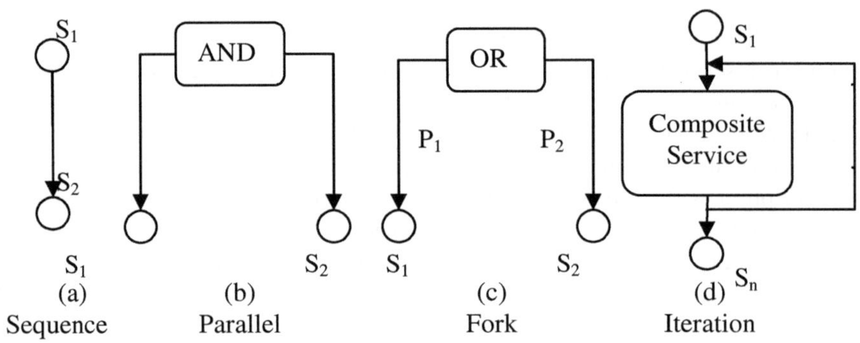

Fig. 1. Different logic control relations in composite services

The node *"OR"* means services following it are optional, and the execution possibilities of service S_1 and S_2 are P_1 and P_2, respectively.

Sub-QoSs of a composite service should be calculated in different categories. For different relations, the calculation methods are shown in Table 1.

Table 1. Calculations of QoS in different logic control relations

Sub-QoS	Sequence	Parallel	Fork	Iteration
Reliability,	min(q_1,q_2)	min(q_1,q_2)	min(q_1,q_2)	min(q_i)
expense cost	q_1+q_2	q_1+q_2	P_1q_1+P_2q_2	nq_{cs}
Execution time, latency time	q_1+q_2	max (q_1,q_2)	P_1q_1+P_2q_2	nq_{cs}

Herein, qi is the value of sub-QoS of service Si; P1 and P2 are the execution possibilities for service S1 and S2; n is the frequency of iterations. Availability of the QoS depends on whether or not the functions of services match the need. A service that is able to meet the needs of functions better has a higher value of availability.

Each service in composite services owns a few instances, and it can invoke an instance in an execution process. An example of a composite service is shown in Figure 2.

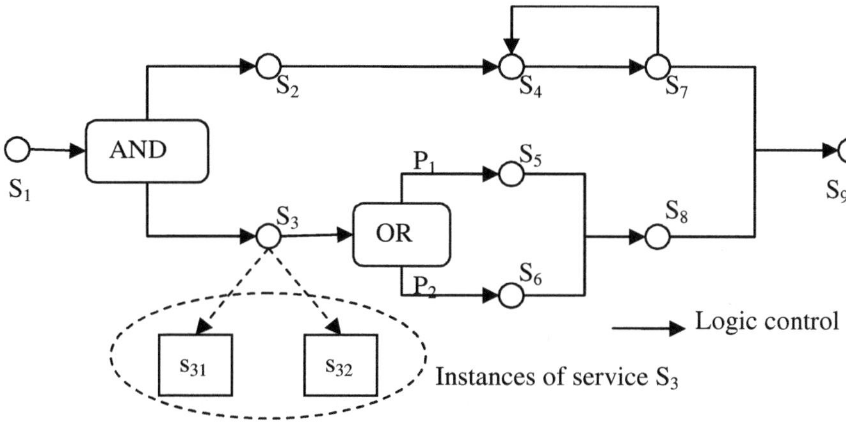

Fig. 2. An example of composite service. Nine atomic services are included in the CS. Service s_{61} and s_{62} are instances of S_6. Only one instance can be chosen for each service in an execution.

Definition 2 (Composite Service Plan, CSP): A composite service plan is a composite service which has been configured to a specific instance for every service in it. A CSP realizes the composite service and achieves functions needed by clients.

Different logic control relations produce different connections and dependences of the QoS. We calculate the QoS of a CSP with considerations of logic control relations and features of sub-QoSs.

4 Multi-objective Programming Model for Web Service Composition

We define QoS risk and present a multi-objective programming model in this section, aimed at selecting an optimal composition. Considering the measurement system of QoS, five criteria are chosen for programming, namely expense cost, execution time, latency time, reliability and availability,.

4.1 Risk of CSP

Some previous studies related risks to differences between results and expectations of actions. Harold Craig [15] treated risks as the change brought by the result of a decision. In Markowitz's Portfolio Selection model [16], investors tried to create a portfolio with the maximum expected return and minimum variance. Markowitz also pointed out that replacing "risk" with "variance of return" would result in little change of apparent meaning. After analyzing Markowitz's model, David R [17] noted that the model should gain a tradeoff between risk and return, and Michel [18] held that this tradeoff could be thought of as the difference between budgetary cost and unexpected cost. In his opinion, the model measured return by the average and measured risk by the variance between the average and the actual return.

In accordance with these discussions, the QoS risk is defined in our study as the variance between actual QoS values of a composition and expected values.

Definition 3 (Risk): Risk of a CSP can be formally defined as Risk= (CSP, D, R). D is a variance set {d1, d2, d3, d4, d5} And R is equal to the weighted sum of variances. The model presented below is based on this definition.

4.2 Multi-objective Programming Model

Five QoS criteria are related to risk. We use AHP to evaluate the impact weights of the five criteria. After calculation and normalizing, the weight vector is [0.2 0.2 0.089 0.511].

Based on this risk definition, risk is equal to the sum of variances of the criteria. Practically, it is better for expense cost to be less than expected rather than greater than expected, as it is with execution time and latency time. Conversely greater reliability than expected is better, and the availability exactly equal to the expectation is best. The objective functions are as follows:

$$min\ z_1 = 0.106d_1^+ + 0.106d_2^+ + 0.047d_3^+ + 0.270d_4^- + 0.471d_5\ . \quad (1)$$

$$max\ z_2 = 0.2d_1^- + 0.2d_2^- + 0.089d_3^- + 0.511d_4^+\ . \quad (2)$$

The final multi-objective programming model is shown below:

$$min\ p_1(z_1) + p_2(-z_2)$$

s.t.

$$f(x_{ijk}) - \hat{d}_k^+ + \hat{d}_k^- = x_k^* \quad (3)$$

$$d_k = \frac{100\hat{d}_k}{x_k^*} \quad (4)$$

$$\min\left(\sum_{j=1}^{10} x_{ij4} y_{ij}\right) - d_4^+ + d_4^- = x_4^* \tag{5}$$

$$d_5 = \sqrt{\sum_{i=1}^{n}\sum_{j=1}^{n}\left(x_{ij5} y_{ij} - x_{i5}^*\right)^2} = \sqrt{\sum_{i=1}^{n}\sum_{j=1}^{n}\left(d_{ij5} y_{ij}\right)^2} \tag{6}$$

$$y_{ij} = \begin{cases} 0 \\ 1 \end{cases} \tag{7}$$

$$\sum_{j=1}^{10} y_{ij} = 1 \tag{8}$$

$$a_k \le f(x_{ijk}) \le b_k \tag{9}$$

$$\sum_{j=1}^{10} x_{ij4} y_{ij} \ge c \tag{10}$$

$$Max\left(\left|\sum_{j=1}^{10} x_{ij5} y_{ij} - x_{i5}^*\right|\right) = Max\left(\left|\sum_{j=1}^{10} d_{ij5} y_{ij}\right|\right) \le \varepsilon \tag{11}$$

$$\hat{d}_k \ge 0 \ , \ d_k \ge 0, d_5 \ge 0; k = 1,2,3; i = 1,2,\cdots,n; j = 1,2,\cdots,n$$

Equations (3) to (8) indicate how to obtain the variances. In equation (3), constant x_k^* is the expectation value of criterion c_k of a whole CSP. Constant x_{ijk} represents the actual value of the criterion c_k of the candidate instance s_j for service S_i. Function $f(x_{ijk})$ calculates the actual values of the first three criteria of every CSP. The first three criteria should be normalized by unifying expectations with 100 in equation (4). Reliability of CSP is equal to the minimum of the chosen instances in equation (5). The variance of availability is calculated in Equation (6). Decision variable y_{ij} can only be 1 or 0, and $y_{ij} = 1$ means instance s_j is chosen for service S_i, as shown in equation (7). Equation (8) shows that only one instance can be chosen for a service.

Equations (9) to (11) are constraints. Constraint (9) and (10) provide the acceptable ranges of the first four criteria. Constraint (11) means that the largest variance of availability cannot be greater than the constant ε.

The advantage of the model is the division of variances into two categories. The objective function z1 guarantees the composition meet clients' needs, and z2 ensures that cost and time are less and reliability is greater. The method presents lowest risk, and improves the QoS performance of the composition as much as possible.

5 Experiments

In this section, we conduct a simulative experiment with the method above to test the feasibility of our model. The specific process is as follows.

5.1 Synthetic Dataset for Experiments

A CS with a specific structure is needed to perform the experiment. We suppose the structure of the composition is the same as that in Figure 3. There are ten services in the composition, and each of them has ten service instances.

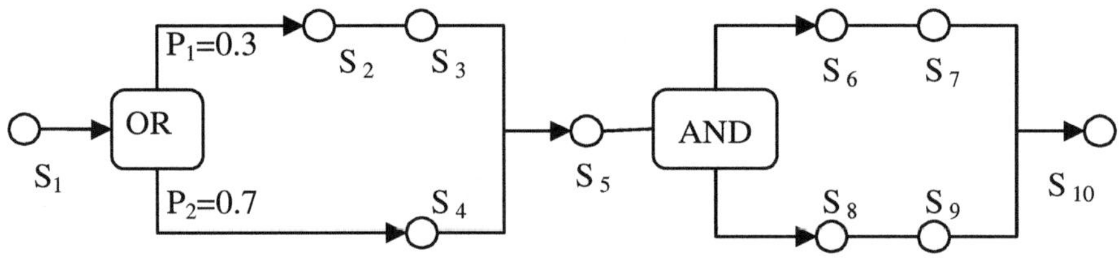

Fig. 3. The structure of the composite service

In the actual situation, we can obtain QoS data from the study of QoS. On account of limited resources, we use a synthetic dataset in the experiment. The synthetic dataset is the QoS data of all the instances for services in Figure 3.

5.2 Multi-objective Optimization Algorithm Design

We use the method of weight-sum to solve the model. According to importance degrees of Function z1 and z2, we set up the final objective function as follows:

$$Min\ z = 0.8z_1 - 0.2z_2$$

We design genetic algorithm to solve the proposed programming model.

(1) Encoding: We use real encoding. Each chromosome contains ten real numbers, indicating which instance is chosen for every service in the composition.
(2) Fitness: An individual is better if its object-value is less. The value of the final objective function will not be greater than 30. Therefore, fitness = 30 – object-value.
(3) Genetic operators: The roulette wheel strategy is used to replicate better individuals. We use single-point crossover to reproduce offspring chromosomes with a probability of 0.7. Additionally, mutation probability is 0.005.
(4) Individual retaining strategy: Roulette wheel rule has been slightly changed to retain population variety. CSP, which cannot meet all constraints, also has a lower fitness to be replicated with a lower probability.

The algorithm process is as follows:

Input: Population size, Max Generation, data sets
Output: the optimal individual, its object-value and fitness
Step 1: The initial population P_0, i=1, P_i=P_0;
Step 2: Use selection operator and individual retaining strategy to generate Q_1;
Step 3: For Q_1, randomly select 70% of the individuals and randomly select positions of each chromosome, crossing the rest of them, generating Q_2;
Step 4: For Q_2, randomly select gene bits with the probability of 0.005, changing them into another real number, generating Q_3;
Step 5: P_{i+1}= Q_3;
Step 6: i=i+1, determine whether it satisfies end condition or not, if not, return to step 2, or, output.

5.3 Results and Discussion

Let the population size be 80 and let the evolution iterate for 400 times. We choose one of our results as the example for discussion, which is shown in Figure 4.

Sub-figures in Figure 4 indicate the object-value of the 1st, 10th, 100th, 200th, 300th and 400th generations in this experiment. The minimum object-value appears in the 276th generation, which is -1.4828. The optimal individual is [8 2 9 1 3 6 9 7 3 1], which means that the 8th instance is chosen for the 1st service and so on.

Generally speaking, there will be a slight and small-range degeneration caused by the mutation in the evolution. However, the whole evolution still has a stable progress. Therefore, we have chosen better individuals to generate the offspring.

The fitness-values of generations are shown in Figure 5.

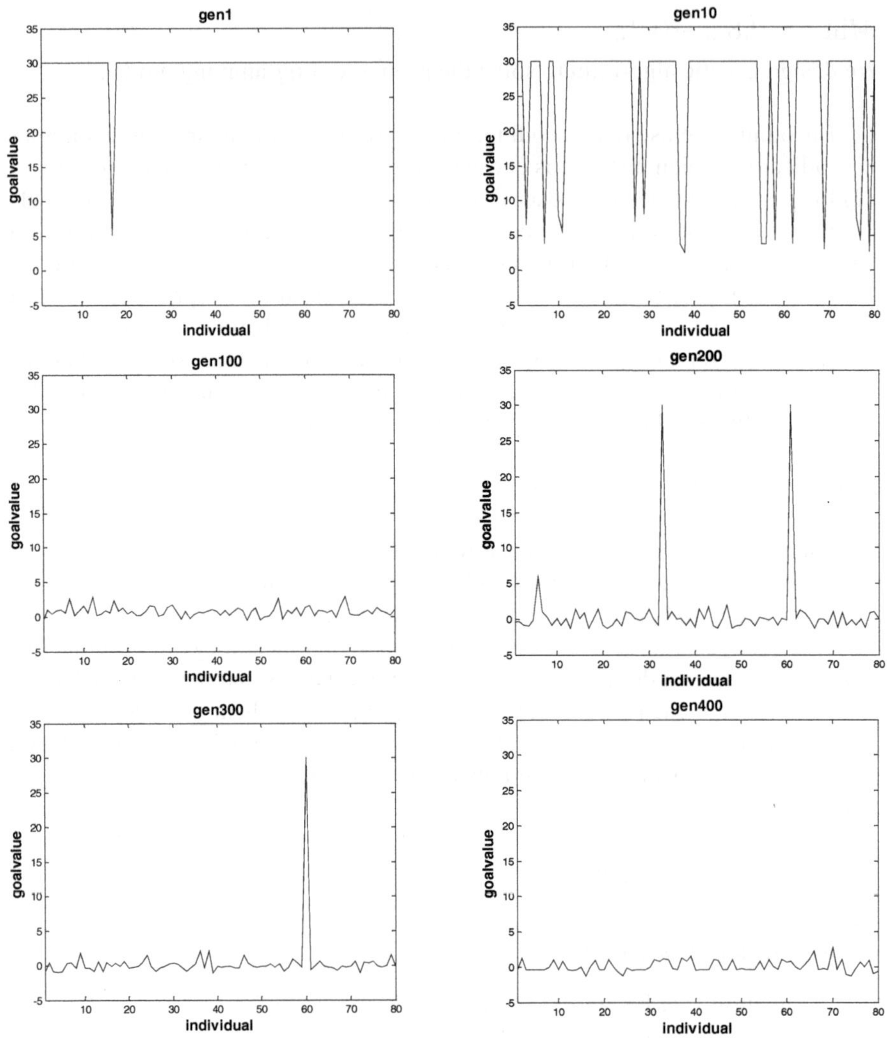

Fig. 4. Goal-value of several generations in one experiment

Figure 5 shows that we have chosen better individuals to generate the offspring.

In order to test the availability of our model, we have done experiments of changing the structure of the CS and the weights of functions z1 and z2. We compare the results of genetic algorithm to those of the ergodicity. The comparison is shown in Table 2.

Table 2 infers that results of genetic algorithm are all closed to the optimal values. Therefore, our model and algorithm provide effective information for selecting appropriate web services for compositions. Further, our method will take much less time than the global ergodicity and result in a satisfactory composition.

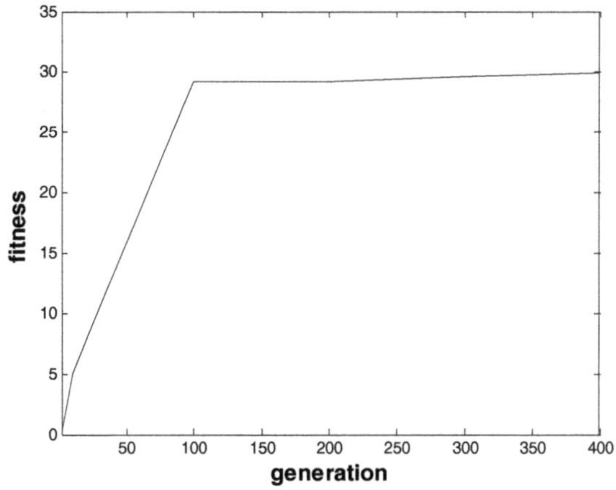

Fig. 5. Iteration of the fitness values

Table 2. Results of different experiments

	Original experiment	Change structure	Change weights
Results of genetic algorithm	-1.4828	-1.1505	-4.3974
Results of the ergodicity	-1.6724	-1.4208	-4.5308

6 Conclusions and Future Work

In this paper, we extended and summarized sub-QoSs. For a composite service, we calculated its QoS with consideration of QoS features and logic control relations in it.

We also defined the QoS risk and established a multi-objective programming model to guide how to choose Web service instances for a composite service plan. We used genetic algorithm to solve the model. Although it might not provide the lowest object-value, it results in a satisfactory composition in a relatively short time.

Additionally, we supposed that the chosen services satisfy dependence relations among them. In fact, these dependence relations may influence the value of QoS. Therefore, they may also change service selection. In summary, further studies will address how to precisely calculate the QoS of Web composite service within the dependence relations of different services; also, the creation of the best composition is another area for further work.

Acknowledgements. The work was supported by the National Science Fund for Distinguished Young Scholars of China (Grant No. 70925005) and the General Program of the National Science Foundation of China (No.71101103, No.61074152, No.71001076). This work was also supported by grants from the Research Fund for the Doctoral Program of Higher Education of China (20100032120086, 20100032110036, 20090032110065).

References

1. Yutu, L., et al.: QoS Computation and Policing in Dynamic Web Service Selection. In: 13th International World Wide Web Conference Proceedings, New York, pp. 798–805 (2004)
2. Lingshuang, S., Tian, L., Junfeng, Z., et al.: An extensible management framework for Web service QoS. Chinese Journal of Computers 31(8), 1458–1470 (2008) (in Chinese)
3. Soydan, B.A., Singh Munindar, P.: A DAML-based repository for QoS-aware semantic Web service selection. In: Proceedings of the IEEE International Conference on Web Services, California, USA, pp. 368–375 (2004)
4. Ran, S.: A Model for Web Services Discovery with QoS. ACM SIGecom Exchanges 4(1)
5. Liangzhao, Z., Boualem, B., Ngu, A.H., et al.: QoS-Aware Middleware for Web Services Composition. J. IEEE Transactions on Software Engineering 30(5), 311–327 (2004)
6. Liangzhao, Z., et al.: Quality Driven Web Services Composition. ACM Press (2003)
7. Zheyuan, J., et al.: An Optimization Model for Dynamic QoS-aware Web Services Selection and Composition. Chinese Journal of Computers 32(5), 1014–1024 (2009) (in Chinese)
8. Minghui, W., et al.: QoS-oriented Global Optimization Approach for Mass Web Services Composition. J. Computer Engineering and Application 46(15), 72–76 (2010) (in Chinese)
9. Jun, L., Jianzhong, Q., Shukuan, L.: Risk Prediction and Measurement for Software Based on Service Oriented Architecture. J. Communications in Computer and Information Science 35(Part 7), 515–522 (2009)
10. Kokash, N., D'Andrea, V.: Evaluating Quality of Web Services: A Risk-Driven Approach. In: Abramowicz, W. (ed.) BIS 2007. LNCS, vol. 4439, pp. 180–194. Springer, Heidelberg (2007)
11. Ping, S.: Optimal Selection of Composite Web Service based on QoS and Risk Evaluation. In: International Conference on E-Business and E -Government (ICEE 2011), Shanghai, China, pp. 2393–2396 (2011)
12. Hai, L., Weimin, Z., Kaijun, R.: A Risk-driven Selection Approach for Transactional Web Service Composition. In: Eighth International Conference on Grid and Cooperative Computing, Lanzhou, Gansu, pp. 391–397 (2009)
13. Yanlong, Z., Hongyi, S., Shouyi, Z.: A reflective framework to improve the adaptability of BPEL-based Web service composition. In: 2008 IEEE International Conference on Services Computing (SCC), Honolulu, HI, United states, pp. 343–350 (2008)
14. Palorno Duarte, M., Garca Dorringuez, A., Medina Bulo, I.: An architecture for dynamic invariant generation in WS-BPEL web service compositions. In: International Conference on e-Business (ICE-B 2008), Porto, Portugal, pp. 37–44 (2008)
15. Petersen, H.C., Lewis, W.C.: Managerial economics. Renmin University of China Press, Beijing (2009) (in Chinese)
16. Markowitz, H.: Portfolio Selection. The Journal of Finance 7(1), 77–91 (1952)
17. David, R.A., et al.: An introduction to management science: quantitative approaches to decision making. China Machine Press, Beijing (2009) (in Chinese)
18. Michel, C., Dan, G., Robert, M.: The essentials of risk management. China Finance and Economy Press, Beijing (2010) (in Chinese)

The Application of SOM and K-Means Algorithms in Public Security Performance Analysis and Forecasting

Yuanyuan Kou, Hongfei Cui, and Linying Xu*

School of Computer Science and Technology, Tianjin University,
300072 Tianjin, China
tjkouyy@126.com, hijack_go@163.com, linyingxu@tju.edu.cn

Abstract. As cluster analysis is the most commonly used Data Mining method in performance analysis and forecasting, this paper establishes an auxiliary model framework for the security system, using clustering techniques to analyze data. We compared the analysis results of SOM and k-means algorithms, testing for their strengths and weaknesses, combing these two algorithms, and finally proposing the two-stage clustering algorithm based on SOM and k-means algorithms. In this thesis, by clustering and analyzing the same or similar cases, combining with the recommendations of experts, and determining main factors affecting the performance among different regions, we provide references not only for the investigators who will analyze the cases, but also for the public security agencies in the performance prediction, police force forecast and later development of the public security warning system.

Keywords: data preprocessing, data warehouse, SOM, k-means, two-stage clustering algorithm.

1 Introduction

As an important method in data mining, clustering and analysis [1] can reasonably classify data. It divides the mining data into several classes according to some sort of similarity measure of the data properties. The data within the class has the greatest similarity, but data among different classes has the smallest. Important information hidden in the data can then be found.

There are a variety of cluster analysis methods. The two most commonly used methods are SOM algorithm and k-means algorithm. The SOM neural network [2] is an unsupervised learning mode. It can find the intrinsic characteristics of the large amount of data input by the self-organization of network structure, form the input data distribution topology on the output node weight vector space of network, reflect a certain distribution law of the input data and then cluster the input mode. The k-means

* Linying Xu: 1963- , Male, Professor, Microsoft .Net Research Lab, School of Computer Science and Technology, Tianjin University.

V. Khachidze et al. (Eds.): iCETS 2012, CCIS 332, pp. 73–84, 2012.

algorithm [3] is a typical distance-based clustering method, which uses the Euclidean Distance as the similarity evaluation. However, this algorithm requires pre-determined category centers, that is, initial values that determine the clustering effect. In this paper, these two algorithms were used in the performance prediction analysis of public security and compare the analysis of the results to the expert recommendation. Then, a combination algorithm based on SOM and k-means that is closer to the expert analysis was proposed. Experiments show that this new algorithm has better clustering results.

2 Establishing a Framework Model

Public Security Performance Appraisal System (PSPAS) is mainly used for the establishment of assessment library, the classification and extraction of data, assistant analysis of judgments, threshold warning, prediction of performance potential, indicator recommending and assessment functions of the intelligent inspector.

The data in PSPAS is limited to storage, query, retrieval and statistical analysis. In order to effectively use the index data to find useful knowledge hidden in these indexes, predict the performance, police force, and recommend indexes, this paper establishes an auxiliary model framework [4], shown in Fig. 1.

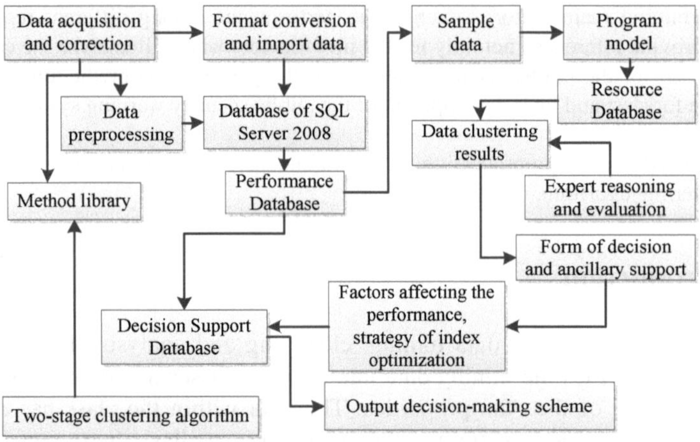

Fig. 1. The system processes the datasets extracted from the data warehouse with the combined algorithm, then compares the cluster result to schema in the resource database and combines the opinions of experts to discover the similarities of areas that have similar performance; finally, it forms the decision-making scheme

3 Data Preparation

The data of Public Security Performance Appraisal is incomplete and inconsistent. For analyzing data and mining useful knowledge conveniently, we must preprocess the data in the Performance Appraisal Database. The data pre-processing technique can improve the quality of the data, which can help to improve the accuracy and performance of the subsequent mining process.

3.1 Preprocessing Technique Based on the Data Warehouse

Generally, the data pre-processing has three steps: Data Cleaning, Data Integration and Data Reduction [5]. All phases of the process [6] are as follows:

Data Cleaning: fill in the vacancy values, smooth noisy data and remove outliers to resolve the problem of data inconsistency.

Data Integration: merge data stored in databases, data cube, and regular files into a consistent storage, such as data warehouse, which is a subject-oriented, integrated, time-varying and non-volatile collection of data that supports management decision-making.

Data Reduction: delete redundant data and cluster to convert the original large data sets to a smaller size, and maintain the integrity of the original datasets.

The entire process of the data pre-processing technique, concurrent with the whole process of building a data warehouse, [7] is shown in Fig. 2.

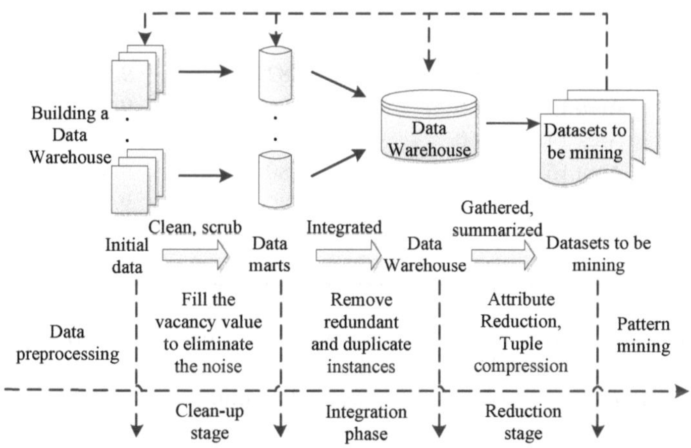

Fig. 2. Extract data from the original database, clean and scrub the extracted data to form data marts, then integrate the data marts to build data warehouse; finally, gather and summarize the data in the data warehouse, extract available datasets so that they can be mined for public security performance appraisal

As data pre-processing provides a reliable data support for performance analysis and assessment of the PSPAS, it will be helpful to identify potential and valuable information. Based on the data warehouse, data pre-processing technique forms available datasets for decision-makers to analyze and mine.

3.2 Data Preparation

Taking into account the confidentiality of the data, after consultation with the Public Security Bureau, we use data from the year 2010, which includes 18 counties in certain provinces, as shown in Table 1, and evaluate the construction of law enforcement standardization in these areas. Assessments include the results about the quality of assessment in criminal cases, public order cases and drug treatment cases.

Table 1. The sample data extracted from the minable data sets in data warehouse. Index 1 represents assessment results in criminal cases; Index 2 represents law and order assessment results; Index 3 represents drug cases quality test results.

No.	Area	Index 1	Index 2	Index 2
1	Area 1	19.82	19.88	9.83
2	Area 2	19.68	19.78	9.85
3	Area 3	19.56	19.80	9.69
4	Area 4	19.66	19.60	9.77
5	Area 5	19.72	19.80	9.85
6	Area 6	19.70	19.86	9.85
7	Area 7	19.70	19.78	9.79
8	Area 8	19.76	19.90	9.80
9	Area 9	19.72	19.82	9.81
10	Area 10	19.70	19.84	9.80
11	Area 11	19.78	19.90	9.72
12	Area 12	19.66	19.82	9.86
13	Area 13	19.66	19.86	9.83
14	Area 14	19.60	19.78	9.79
15	Area 15	19.68	19.80	9.89
16	Area 16	19.80	19.90	9.84
17	Area 17	19.72	19.86	9.77
18	Area 18	19.74	19.80	9.70

The sample data will be used in SOM, k-means and two-stage clustering algorithms later in this paper. For using the same data, it will be conductive not only to find the advantages and disadvantages by comparing SOM with k-means algorithm, but also to make more effective decisions for experts based on objective reality by adopting the two-stage clustering algorithm performance analysis and forecasting of the Public Security.

4 SOM Network Model and Algorithm Application

The self-organizing map (SOM) is an unsupervised learning algorithm of clustering and high-dimensional visualization, which is an artificial neural network developed by simulating the characteristics of the human brain handles signals. The model proposed by Teuvo Kohonen [8], a Professor in Finland in 1981, has now become the most widely used self-organizing neural network.

4.1 The Structure of the SOM Network

The SOM network is made up of input layer and competitive layer. The input layer is used for receiving the input mode and aggregating information to the competitive layer through weight vectors. The competitive layer is used for outputting results, the neurons of which are connected to each other. The arrangement of the competitive layer neurons takes many forms; one-dimensional linear, two-dimensional array and three-dimensional grid array [9], as shown in Fig. 3. The most typical structure is the two-dimensional array, which is more like the image of the cerebral cortex. According to the vector characteristics of the sample data, we will use three-dimensional grid array to analyze the data of the public security performance evaluation indicators in this paper.

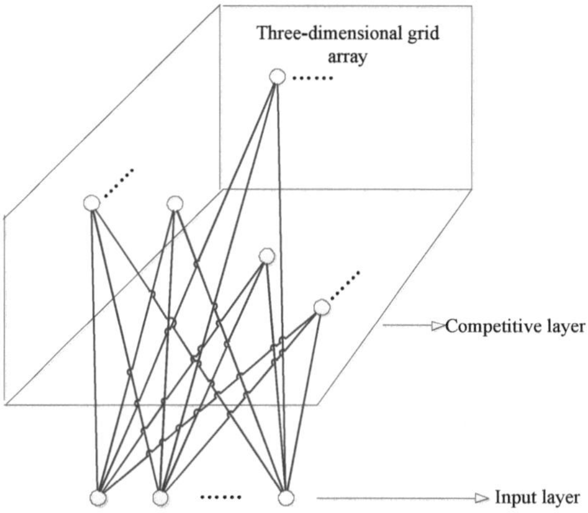

Fig. 3. The model used in this paper is the three-dimensional grid array, and the results will be displayed in three dimensions

The three-dimensional grid array is more conducive to analyzing the clustering and distribution of the assessment indicators from multiple angles, and provides an analytical basis for comprehensive analysis of correlation among indexes and optimization of indexes.

4.2 SOM Network Learning Algorithm

The SOM algorithm can find similarities between the input data automatically and configure the nearest similar input. Therefore, we can construct a very useful network which can choose to give a reaction for the input data.

The steps of SOM network learning algorithm are summarized as follows:

1) Set the initial value of the weights between the input layer and competitive layer using random numbers.

2) Input the input vector $X = [x_1, x_2, x_3, \ldots, x_n]^T$ to the input layer.

3) Calculate the Euclidean Distance [10] of weight vector and input vector between each neuron. The distance of the jth neuron and the input vector from the competitive layer is calculated by formula (1):

$$d_j = \sqrt{\sum_{i=1}^{n} (x_i - w_{ij})^2} . \tag{1}$$

In the formula above, w_{ij} is weight between the i neuron of the input layer and the j neuron of the competitive layer.

4) Calculate the distance between input vector and weight vector, then choose the shortest distance between the neurons; for example, if d_j is the shortest distance neuron, we will call it winning neuron noted as j^* and give the set of the adjacent neural.

5) Update the weight between the winning neuron and its adjacent neuron [11], calculated by formula (2):

$$\Delta w_{ij} = \eta h(j, j^*)(x_i - w_{ij}) . \tag{2}$$

In which η is a constant between 0 and 1, $h(j, j^*)$ is the neighborhood function, calculated by formula (3):

$$h(j, j^*) = \exp\left(-\frac{|j - j^*|^2}{\sigma^2}\right) . \tag{3}$$

In the formula, σ^2 gradually reduces with training, and the range of $h(j, j^*)$ narrows as learning progresses; the coarse adjustment gradually changes into micro adjustment. Therefore, the neighborhood function can play a role in producing efficient mapping.

6) Test whether the result of the operation meets the pre-set requirements; if it does, then the algorithm ends, otherwise, go back to step 2, and continue the next learning progress.

4.3 Experiments and Results Analysis

We will use the sample data provided by the data preprocessing for this test; for better analyzing and predicting the performance of all regions, competitive layer is in the form of a three-dimensional grid array in MATLAB. The test result is shown in Fig. 4.

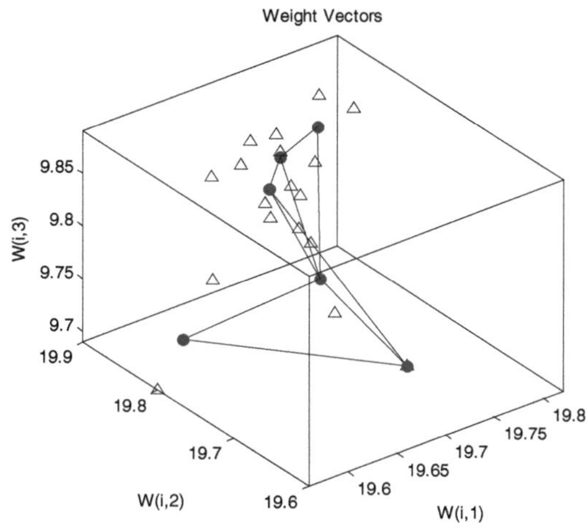

Fig. 4. The SOM clustering result displayed in three-dimensions. Triangles represent indexes; dots represented the cluster centers. There were six dots in the figure, and the index data were divided into six groups.

By the training of SOM network, the sample data were divided into six different groups; each group is displayed in Table 2.

Table 2. The results of SOM clustering. There were six groups, and every group has its own cluster centers.

Groups	Sample data	Cluster centers
1	1, 8, 11, 16, 17	(19.79, 19.89, 9.817)
2	4	(19.66, 19.60, 9.77)
3	2, 5, 7, 9	(19.69,19.80,9.864)
4	18	(19.76, 19.84, 9.708)
5	3, 14	(19.58, 19.79, 9.736)
6	6, 10, 12, 13, 15	(19.70, 19.83, 7.817)

Test results show that SOM algorithm can be an effective adaptive classification, but the selection of the learning speed and the training cycle has great influence on the training time. If there are a large amount of data and long training cycle, SOM network will have a great limitation on the training time.

5 K-Means Algorithm and Application

K-means algorithm, in which k is an input parameter and a collection of n objects is divided into k clusters, produces high similarity within the clustering results and low similarity between adjacent clusters.

Unlike the SOM algorithm, clusters of k-means are dense. It works better when distinction is significant between clusters. The time complexity of k-means algorithm is $O(nkt)$, in which k is the number of clusters, t is the number of iterations and n is the number of all samples. This algorithm has better scalability, high efficiency in dealing with large data, and always ends with local optimum.

5.1 K-Means Algorithm Principle

K-means algorithm steps [12] are summarized as follows:

1) Determine the input parameters k .

2) Randomly select k objects from the data sets; every object represents a cluster of initial mean or center.

3) Assign each object remained to the most similar clusters, according to the distance between the mean of each cluster, which are calculated by the Euclidean Distance as per formula (4):

$$\rho(A, B) = \sqrt{\sum_{i=1}^{n} (a_i - b_j)^2} \quad . \tag{4}$$

In the formula above, $\rho(A, B)$ is the distance between vector A and vector B in the n-dimensional space.

4) Calculate the new average of each cluster, repeating step 2 and step 3 until the average does not change.

The clustering results of k-means are greatly influenced by the choice of initial cluster centers, which, if selected improperly, may lead to clustering results falling into local optimal solution [13] and cannot get reasonable clustering results.

5.2 Experiments and Results Analysis

In this test, we select six points in the sample data randomly, shown in Table 3, and the clustering results are divided into six groups.

Table 3. These points selected from the sample data randomly. Index1 represents assessment results in criminal cases; Index 2 represents law and order assessment results; and Index 3 represents drug cases quality test results.

No.	Area	Index 1	Index 2	Index 3
2	Area 2	19.68	19.78	9.85
5	Area 5	19.72	19.80	9.85
9	Area 9	19.72	19.82	9.81
11	Area 11	19.78	19.90	9.72
14	Area 14	19.60	19.78	9.79
17	Area 17	19.72	19.86	9.77

Then, continue to enter the remained test data into MATLAB. Because the data is 18×3 matrix, the matrix row represents a point, and the clustering results will be displayed in a three-dimensional graphic. As shown in Fig. 5, different clusters are marked in different shapes and each cluster has its own center point.

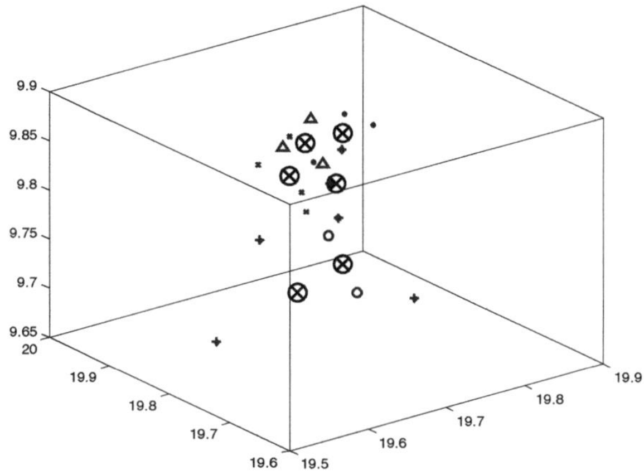

Fig. 5. The k-means clustering results displayed in three-dimensions. Every group has its own shapes, and ⊗ represents the cluster centers.

After k-means clustering, the sample data were divided into six different groups, each group shown in Table 4.

Table 4. The results of SOM clustering. There were six groups, and every group had its own cluster centers.

Groups	Sample data	Cluster centers
1	2, 12, 15	(19.6733, 19.8000, 9.8667)
2	5, 7, 9	(19.7133, 19.8000, 9.8167)
3	6, 10, 13, 17	(19.6950, 19.8550, 9.8125)
4	11, 18	(19.7600, 19.8500, 9.7100)
5	3, 4, 14	(19.6067, 19.7267, 9.7500)
6	1, 8, 16	(19.7933, 19.8933, 9.8233)

This test shows that k-means algorithm has a faster clustering speed. However, it is not suitable to discover clusters of large differences in size and it is sensitive to "noise" and "isolated points"; since such data have a greater impact on the average, its application has some limitations.

6 Two-Stage Clustering

K-means algorithm has the advantages of being simple, computes conveniently and quickly, but depends on the initial center, thus resulting in the clustering results potentially falling into the local minimum. This paper will combine the advantage of automatic clustering of SOM, and propose two-stage algorithm based on the SOM and k-means. To determine the clustering center more quickly, the input data will be clustered through SOM at first, the results of which will be used as the initial center vector in the k-means method. The experiments showed that the combination of these two algorithms can compensate for their defects, and better improve the clustering results.

6.1 Algorithm Characteristics

Characteristics of the two-stage clustering algorithm [14] are as follows:

1) Carries out the SOM algorithm and inputs the data to be clustered to the network, trains them, and then a set of weight vectors will be output. In this step, training time can be reduced by making SOM clustering not complete convergence; for instance, 200 cycles are enough for SOM.
2) Puts the weight vectors of the SOM clustering results as initial cluster centers. Initializes k-means algorithm, then clusters the data with k-means algorithm.

The combination algorithm does not only have the self-organization characteristics of the SOM network, but also has the high efficiency characteristics of the k-means algorithm. As a result, the long convergence time of the SOM network and the possibility of incorrectly selecting cluster centers of k-means will be compensated.

6.2 Experiments and Results Analysis

In this text, we use the cluster centers of training results by SOM as the initial center points. According to the results of the center points of the SOM, the initial cluster centers of k-means algorithm selected are shown in Table 5.

Table 5. These points were selected according to the training results by SOM. Index 1 represents assessment results in criminal cases; Index 2 represents law and order assessment results; and Index 3 represents drug cases quality test results.

No.	Area	Index 1	Index 2	Index 3
2	Area 2	19.68	19.78	9.85
3	Area 3	19.56	19.80	9.69
4	Area 4	19.66	19.60	9.77
8	Area 8	19.76	19.90	9.80
6	Area 6	19.70	19.86	9.85
18	Area 18	19.74	19.80	9.70

Enter the cluster centers listed above into MATLAB, and then use the k-means algorithm for subsequent processing. The clustering results are shown in Fig. 6.

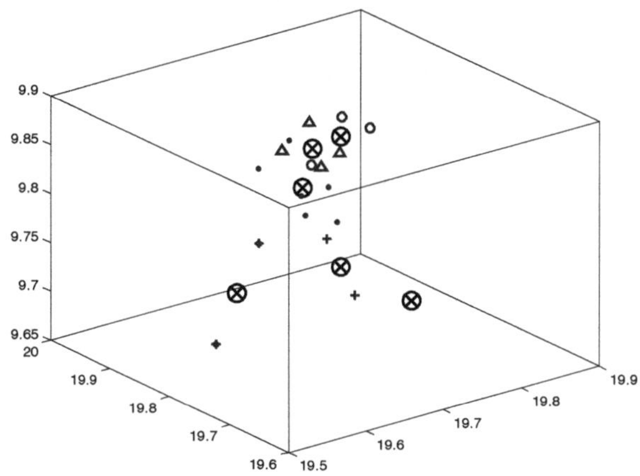

Fig. 6. The results of two-stage clustering. Different groups are marked with different shapes, and ⊗ represents the cluster centers.

The two-stage cluster test results shown in Table 6, which are used for comparative analysis of data in Table 2 and Table 4, combined with recommendations given by experts, allow us to determine that the SOM clustering is better, but time-consuming; k-means algorithm is fast, but the clustering results are influenced by the initial cluster centers; the two-stage clustering algorithm makes up for the shortcomings of the two methods above, and at the same time combines their advantages. The two-stage clustering algorithm not only had better results, but also improved the speed of calculation. Thus, it can be seen that the two-stage clustering algorithm is more conducive to the cluster analysis of sample data.

Table 6. The results of two-stage clustering. There were six groups, and every group had its own cluster centers.

Groups	Sample data	Cluster centers
1	2, 5, 12, 15	(19.6850, 19.8000, 9.8625)
2	3, 14	(19.5800, 19.7900, 9.7400)
3	4	(19.6600, 19.6000, 9.7700)
4	1, 8, 16	(19.7933, 19.8933, 9.8233)
5	6, 7, 9, 10, 13, 17	(19.7000, 19.8367, 9.8083)
6	1, 8, 16	(19.7600, 19.8500, 9.7100)

7 Summary

The data pre-processing technique provides strong guarantee for building data warehouse and prepares test data. Meanwhile, the auxiliary model framework established for the security system in this paper offers a good conception for developers and analysts; practice has proved that the model has a good reference value.

Through the comparative analysis of the SOM and k-means algorithm, we finally concluded that the two-stage clustering algorithm is suitable for clustering and analysis of indexes; the algorithm is strongly self-adaptive. In practical applications, identify the type and the center of the test data by SOM network, using the latter as the initial input of k-means. After inputting the appropriate initial value, we can then obtain satisfactory clustering results. Analysis of this study shows that this algorithm has better clustering results, and it can be better used in performance prediction of the PSPAS. Moreover, it can not only improve the relevance and effectiveness of the optimization index, but also provide technical support for the later forecast of police force, case analysis and dissemination of early warning information, etc.

References

1. Zong, Y.: Clustering quality improvement methods. Dalian University of Technology (2010)
2. Kaski, S., Kangas, J., Kohonen, T.: Bibliography of self-organizing maps (SOM) papers: 1981-1997. Neural Computing Surveys 1(3&4), 1–176 (1998)
3. Jain, A.K.: Data clustering: 50 years beyond K-means. Pattern Recognition Letters 31(8), 651–666 (2010)
4. Zhao, L.: Adopting the Data Ming Techniques in the Investigation. Computer Engineering and Science 6 (2006)
5. Han, J., Kamber, M.: Data Mining Concepts and Techniques, Fan, M., Meng, X (translate), pp. 30–53. Mechanical Industry Press, Beijing (2008)
6. Famili, F., Shen, W.M., Weber, R., Simoudis, E.: Data pre-processing and intelligent data analysis. International Journal on Intelligent Data Analysis 1(1) (1997)
7. Shen, R., Shi, X., Wu, Y.: Data Preprocessing Procedure Model based on Data Warehouse. Computer and Digital Engineering 33(009), 73–74 (2005)
8. Kaski, S., Lagus, K.: Comparing Self-Organizing Maps. In: Vorbrüggen, J.C., von Seelen, W., Sendhoff, B. (eds.) ICANN 1996. LNCS, vol. 1112, pp. 809–814. Springer, Heidelberg (1996)
9. Qin, A., Ceng, D., Wang, J.: Study on the Fault Diagnosis of Fan Based on SOM Neural Network. Wind Turbine Technology (001), 50–52 (2009)
10. Yang, L., Su, H., Zhang, Y., Chu, J.: A Method of Data Ming Based on SOM Clustering and Application. Computer Engineering and Science 29(8), 133–136 (2007)
11. Kohonen, T., Kaski, S., Lagus, K., Salojarvi, J., Honkela, J., Paatero, V., Saarela, A.: Self organization of a massive document collection. IEEE Transactions on Neural Networks 11(3), 574–585 (2000)
12. Wagstaff, K., Cardie, C., Rogers, S., Schrödl, S.: Constrained k-means clustering with background knowledge, pp. 577–584 (2001)
13. Yang, Z., Yang, Y.: Doucment Clustering Method Based on Hybird of SOM and k-means. Application Research of Computers 23(5), 73–79 (2006)
14. Krishna, K., Narasimha Murty, M.: Genetic K-means algorithm. IEEE Transactions on Systems, Man, and Cybernetics, Part B: Cybernetics 29(3), 433–439 (1999)

Semi-automatic Acquisition and Formal Representation of OpenAPI

Xiaocao Hu, Shizhan Chen, and Zhiyong Feng

School of Computer Science and Technology, Tianjin University
No. 92 Weijin Road, Tianjin, China
scsDobby@gmail.com, {shizhan,zyfeng}@tju.edu.cn

Abstract. The rapid development of OpenAPIs presents an urgent requirement for effective organization and management. Acquiring and normalizing OpenAPIs information becomes a crucial issue. This paper provides an Internet-oriented method for OpenAPIs acquisition, and gives different solutions for varied protocols based on formal representations of common OpenAPIs. For semi-structural protocol SOAP, OpenAPIs information is parsed automatically, and for unstructured protocol, such as AJAX and REST, after editing the regular expressions according to the styles of web pages, the interfaces information is acquired automatically as well. The experimental results of acquiring 13 OpenAPIs in 6 fields show that our methodology can obtain OpenAPIs correctly and represent them in formal formats; thus, this work lays the foundation of organization and management of OpenAPIs and (semi-) automatic mashup.

Keywords: OpenAPI, Mashup, OpenAPI organization.

1 Introduction

The term OpenAPI has been recently used by recent trends in Web 2.0. OpenAPI is a word used to describe sets of technologies that enable websites to interact with each other by using REST, SOAP, JavaScript and other web technologies. While its possibilities are not limited to web-based applications; it is becoming an increasing trend in Web 2.0 applications [1]. As more and more websites open their services, OpenAPIs have grown very large and diverse. In these circumstances, an independent third party can employ OpenAPIs in their own applications via invoking these OpenAPIs [2], or combine data and services through OpenAPIs as well as internal data sources to create mashups [3]. As mashups allow users to develop applications from a variety of OpenAPIs [4], the value of mashups is not in the data or service itself, but in a better user interface for the data, or in its ability to combine data from services in interesting or significant ways [5]. Since mashups allow the quick creation of custom applications and they are easy to create, even people who are technically less-savvy can create new mashups; mashups have been developed rapidly. While invoking OpenAPIs or composing them into new mashups, the key point is to find available ones with proper functionality from a large number of OpenAPIs. Thus, OpenAPIs presents an urgent requirement for organization and management.

V. Khachidze et al. (Eds.): iCETS 2012, CCIS 332, pp. 85–96, 2012.

ProgrammableWeb.com [6], an online social platform, provides services that allow users to publish different kinds of OpenAPIs, share interesting ideas and experience their own or third party mashups [7]. The site lists OpenAPIs and mashups by date of introduction and profiles them. It also categorizes OpenAPIs and mashups through a provided taxonomy and tags that users can associate with the entries [8]. Thus far, it has about 6,079 OpenAPIs and 6,646 mashups. OpenAPIs in ProgrammableWeb.com are described from two aspects, one being highlights information including summary, category, tags, protocols, data formats and API home, and the other being specifications information, which contains service endpoint, sign up and licensing, security, support and so on. Going to API home page for functional information is inconvenient to users who intend to learn the functionalities.

In order to construct a platform with functional information as well, acquiring and normalizing OpenAPIs information is necessary. In this paper, we first represent common OpenAPIs in formal specification, and then apply different methods to documentations which can be essential to OpenAPIs usability in terms of protocols. For OpenAPIs in unstructured protocol, such as AJAX [9] and REST [10], since their documentations are pages which have no structured format, we first edit regular expressions [11] based on the source codes of pages, and then acquire functional information automatically. For OpenAPIs in semi-structural protocol, such as SOAP [12], since their documentations are WSDL files which are based on XML, we can parse WSDL documentations automatically. The experimental results of acquisition of 13 OpenAPIs in 6 fields show that our methodology can obtain OpenAPIs correctly and represent them in formal formats; thus, this work lays the foundation of organization and management of OpenAPIs and (semi-)automatic mashup.

The rest of this paper is organized as follows: Section 2 represents common OpenAPIs in formal specification. Methodology will be presented in Section 3. Section 4 shows the sample acquisition and experimental results. The conclusion and future work are discussed in Section 5.

2 OpenAPI Model and Formal Representation

In this paper, we propose a common OpenAPIs model (Fig. 1) that is based on documentations and invocation of OpenAPIs. Since we focus on three protocols, OpenAPIs can be defined as follows:

Definition 1. OpenAPI model.

$$\text{OpenAPI} = \{\text{AjaxAPI}\} \cup \{\text{RestAPI}\} \cup \{\text{SoapAPI}\} \quad (1)$$

where AjaxAPI is short for OpenAPI in AJAX, ReseAPI refers to OpenAPI in REST, and SoapAPI is OpenAPI in SOAP.

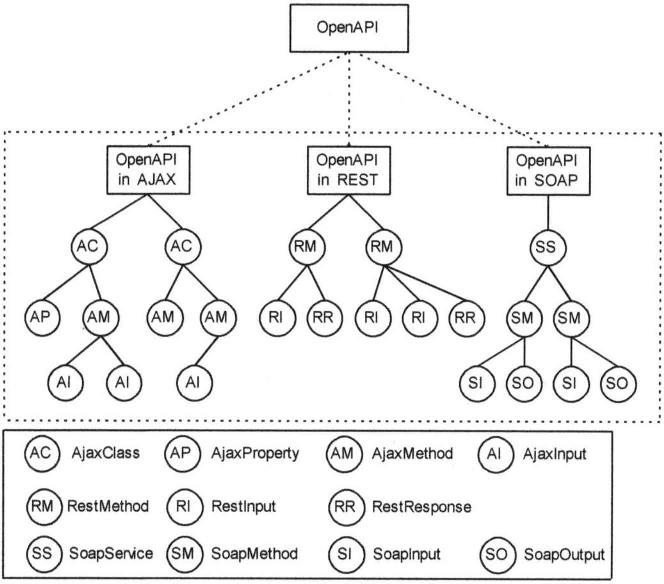

Fig. 1. Model of common OpenAPIs

In the model, AjaxAPIs are described in four levels: level one presents basic information, including name, description and so on, level two shows classes in the OpenAPI, level three describes properties and methods in the class, and level four denotes inputs required by the method. AjaxAPI is defined as follows:

Definition 2. AjaxAPI model.

$$\text{AjaxAPI} = (AN, AD, \{AjaxClass\}) . \tag{2}$$

$$\text{AjaxClass} = (ACN, ACD, \{AjaxProperty\}, \{AjaxMethod\}) . \tag{3}$$

$$\text{AjaxProperty} = (APN, APD) . \tag{4}$$

$$\text{AjaxMethod} = (AMN, AMD, AMRT, AMRD, \{AjaxInput\}) . \tag{5}$$

$$\text{AjaxInput} = (AIN, AID, AIT, AIR) \tag{6}$$

where AN is short for AjaxAPI name and AD refers to description of AjaxAPI. Ajax Class means class in AjaxAPI, ACN is name and ACD is description of AjaxClass. AjaxProperty means property in class, APN is name and APD is description of AjaxProperty. AjaxMethod is method in AjaxClass, AMN is name and AMD is description of AjaxMethod, AMRT is type and AMRD is description of result returned by

AjaxMethod. AjaxInput is input of AjaxMethod, AIN is name, AID is description and AIT is type of AjaxInput, and AIR denotes whether this input is optional.

RestAPIs are described in three levels: level one presents basic information as well as level one of OpenAPIs in AJAX; level two shows methods in the OpenAPI and level three describes inputs required by the method and responses returned by the same method. RestAPI is defined as follows:

Definition 3. RestAPI model.

$$\text{RestAPI} = (RN, RD, \{\text{Rest}Method\}) \ . \tag{7}$$

$$\text{RestMethod} = (RMN, RMD, CS, \{\text{Re}\,stInput\}, \{\text{Rest Re}\,sponse\}) \ . \tag{8}$$

$$\text{RestInput} = (RIN, RID, RIT, RIR) \ . \tag{9}$$

$$\text{RestResponse} = (RRN, RRD, RRT) \tag{10}$$

where RN is short for RestAPI name and RD refers to description of RestAPI. RestMethod means method in RestAPI, RMN is name, RMD is description, and CS is call string of RestMethod. RestInput is input of RestMethod, RIN is name, RID is description, RIT is type of RestInput and RIR denotes whether this input is optional. RestResponse means output of RestMethod, RRN is name, RRD is description and RRT is type of RestResponse.

SoapAPIs are described in four levels: level one presents basic information, level two shows services provided by the OpenAPI, level three describes operations in the service and level four denotes inputs and outputs of the method. SoapAPI is defined as follows:

Definition 4. SoapAPI model.

$$\text{SoapAPI} = (SN, SD, \{SoapService\}) \ . \tag{11}$$

$$SoapService = (SSN, SSD, SSNS, \{\text{Soap}Method\}) \ . \tag{12}$$

$$SoapMethod = (SMN, SMD, \{SoapInput\}, \{SoapOutput\}) \ . \tag{13}$$

$$SoapInput = (SIN, SIT) \ . \tag{14}$$

$$SoapOutput = (SON, SOT) \tag{15}$$

where SN is short for SoapAPI name and SD is description of SoapAPI. SoapService means service in SoapAPI, SSN is name, SSD is description and SSNS is name space of SoapService. SoapMethod means method in SoapService, SMN is name and SMD is description of SoapMethod. SoapInput means input of SoapMethod, SIN is name and SIT is type of SoapInput. SoapOutput means output of SoapMethod, SON is name and SOT is type of SoapOutput.

3 Semi-automatic Acquisition Based on Formal Representation

In the semi-automatic acquisition framework (Fig. 2), information of AjaxAPIs and RestAPIs are obtained from documentations in web page format. To ensure adequate accuracy, source codes of documentations are analyzed and regular expressions are edited based on source codes, then automatic acquisition is applied. Regular expressions that are utilized to parse certain information can be applied to parse information of the same type as well, since source codes of information of the same type have similar style in a certain OpenAPI. For example, regular expressions that are utilized to parse one class named A in a certain OpenAPI also can parse other classes in the same OpenAPI, since source code's style of A's information reveals styles of other classes' source codes. Information of SoapAPIs is acquired from WSDL documentations automatically.

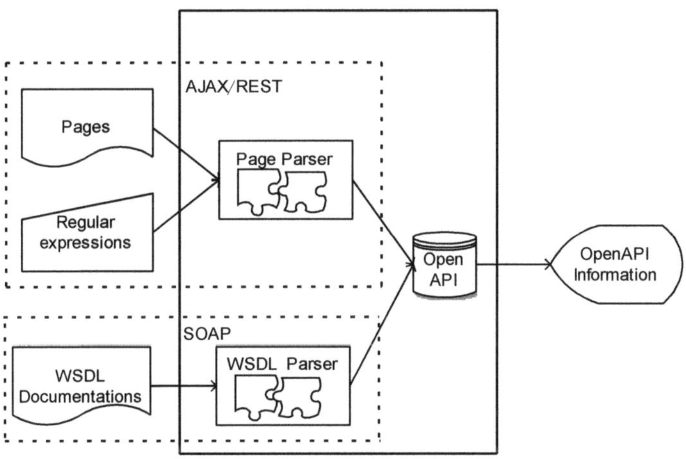

Fig. 2. Semi-automatic acquisition framework

3.1 Acquisition of AjaxAPIs and RestAPIs

The main principle of acquiring AjaxAPIs and RestAPIs (Fig. 3) is matching source codes of documentations with regular expressions, edited according to styles of source codes. Documentations may be home pages that list all classes or methods provided by the OpenAPI, and each class or method has a link that links to the detailed information of the class or method (Fig. 4). In this case, the first step is obtaining links through regular expressions, so as to acquire source codes of detailed documentations. For AjaxAPIs, varied regular expressions are applied to acquire source codes of a whole body information regarding AjaxClasses, AjaxProperties, AjaxMethods and AjaxInputs, and then these source codes are parsed into name and description of AjaxClasses,

AjaxProperties, AjaxMethods and AjaxInputs correspondingly through different regular expressions. For RestAPIs, varied regular expressions are utilized to acquire source codes of a whole body information regarding RestMethods, RestInputs and RestResponses, and then different regular expressions are applied to match source codes of information regarding RestMethods to obtain name, description and call string, parse source codes of information regarding RestInputs into name, description, type and option, and divide source codes of information regarding RestResponses into name, description and type.

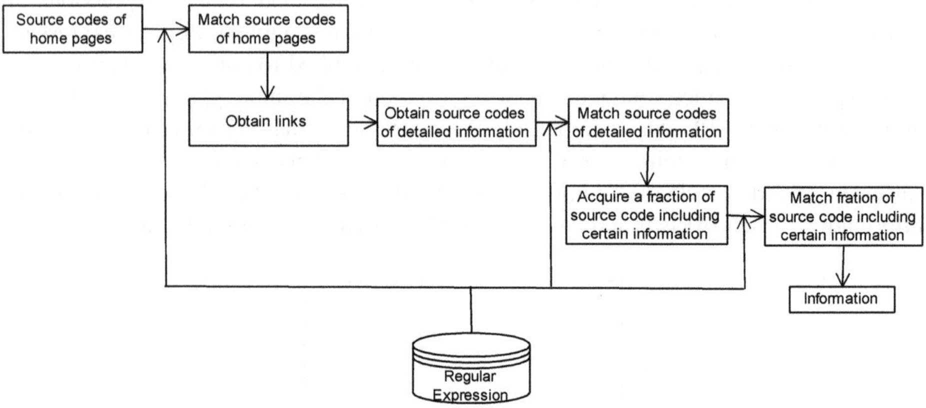

Fig. 3. Semi-automatic acquisition of AjaxAPIs and RestAPIs

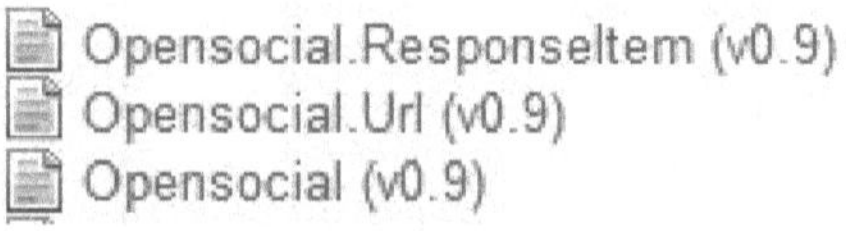

Fig. 4. Home page example

3.2 Acquisition of SoapAPIs

Acquiring information of SoapAPIs is parsing WSDL documentations. WSDL parser (Fig. 5) includes four modules. First, service extractor deals with the extraction of services that are provided by the SoapAPI and obtains name, description and name space of services. Second, operation extractor extracts methods that are exposed by services and acquires name and description of methods. Inputs and outputs of a method can be classified into simple data type and complex data type. If the data type is a primitive type, the tag is parsed and the corresponding name of the variable is acquired. If the data type is a not-primitive type or a user defined type, a hierarchy structure is obtained, representing composition relationships between non-primitive data types.

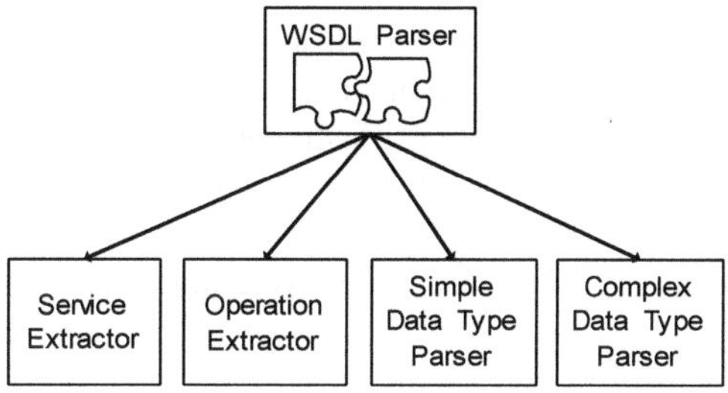

Fig. 5. WSDL parser

4 Experiment

4.1 Sample Acquisition

This section illustrates how semi-automatic acquisition works using a sample acquisition. Assume that information of OpenSocial is wanted. Therefore, documentations of OpenSocial can be accessed through the URL, http://docs.opensocial.org/display/OSD/0.9.

```
<div id="page-children" class="pageSectionBody">
    <span class="icon icon-page">Page:</span>
    <a href="/display/OSD/Errata+in+v0.9">Errata in v0.9</a>
    <br>
    <span class="icon icon-page">Page:</span>
    <a href="/display/OSD/Gadgets.flash+%28v0.9%29">Gadgets.flash (v0.9)</a>
    <br>
    .
    .
    .
    <span class="icon icon-page">Page:</span>
    <a href="/display/OSD/Osapi.Request+%28v0.9%29">Osapi.Request (v0.9)</a>
    <br>
</div>
```

Fig. 6. Source code that contains links pointing to detail documentations of classes

Since the first documentation lists all classes provided by OpenSocial, and each class has a link that points to the detailed documentation of the class (Fig. 4), links are obtained as the first step. Source code that contains links is shown in Fig. 6 and regular expressions numbered 1 and 2 in Table 1 are edited according to the style of the source code. As a result, 53 links which are exactly the same as the documentation displays are acquired. Note that, although 53 links are acquired, 47 links refer to classes, and the other 6 links refer to errata, JavaScript API reference, and so on.

As listing all processes of acquiring these 47 classes in OpenSocial is unrealistic, acquisition of AjaxClass is illustrated by acquiring a class named Gadgets.flash. Similarly, acquisition of AjaxMethod is illustrated by acquiring a method named gadgets.flash.embedFlash in class Gadgets.flash. In the documentation of class Gadgets.flash, source code that contains description is shown in Fig. 7 and regular expression numbered 3 in Table 1 is edited. Source codes that contain name and description of method gadgets.flash.embedFlash are shown in Fig. 8 and Fig. 9; regular expressions numbered 4 and 5 in Table 1 are edited correspondingly. Source code that contains returns of method gadgets.flash.embedFlash is shown in Fig. 10 and regular expressions numbered 6 and 8 in Table 1 are edited. Source code that contains inputs of method gadgets.flash.embedFlash is shown in Fig. 11, and regular expressions numbered 7 and 8 in Table 1 are edited. Regular expressions shown in Table 1 can also be applied to parse other classes, methods, inputs and returns in OpenSocial, since source codes of information of the same type have similar style in a certain OpenAPI.

```
<p>
    <b>gadgets.flash</b>
</p>
<p>Embeds Flash content in gadgets.</p>
```

Fig. 7. Source code that contains description of class Gadgets.flash

```
<h2>
    <a name="Gadgets.flash%28v0.9%29-gadgets.flash.embedFlash"></a>
    gadgets.flash.embedFlash
</h2>
```

Fig. 8. Source code that contains name of method gadgets.flash.embedFlash

```
<p>
    <b>Description</b><br/>
    Injects a Flash file into the DOM tree.
</p>
```

Fig. 9. Source code that contains description of method gadgets.flash.embedFlash

```
<p><b>Returns</b><br/>TypeDescription        |        </p>
|<div class="panel" style="border-width: 1px;"><div class="panelContent">
|<div class='table-wrap'>
|<table class='confluenceTable'><tbody>
|<tr>
<td class='confluenceTd'> Boolean </td>
<td class='confluenceTd'>        Whether the function call completes successfully </td>
</tr>
</tbody></table>
</div>
</div></div>
```

Fig. 10. Source code that contains returns of method gadgets.flash.embedFlash

```
<p><b>Parameters</b><br/>NameTypeDescription |  </p>
<div class="panel" style="border-width: 1px;">
    <div class="panelContent">
        <div class='table-wrap'>
            <table class='confluenceTable'><tbody>
                <tr>
                    <td class='confluenceTd'> swfUrl </td>
                    <td class='confluenceTd'>  String </td>
                    <td class='confluenceTd'>  SWF URL </td>
                </tr>
                .
                .
                .
                <tr>
                    <td class='confluenceTd'> opt_params </td>
                    <td class='confluenceTd'>  Object </td>
                    <td class='confluenceTd'>  An optional object that may contain any valid HTML
parameter; all attributes will be passed through to the Flash movie on creation </td>
                </tr>
            </tbody></table>
        </div>
</div></div>
```

Fig. 11. Source code that contains inputs of method gadgets.flash.embedFlash

```
1 OpenSocial
2     gadets.flash
3         gadets.flash.embedFlash
4             swfUrl
5             swfContainer
6             swfVersion
7             opt_params
```

Fig. 12. Hierarchical results of sample acquisition

Figure 12 shows the hierarchical results of the sample acquisition. Line 1 displays the OpenAPI, i.e. OpenSocial. Line 2 presents class gadets.flash, which is one of the classes provided by OpenSocial. Line 3 shows method gadets.flash.embedFlash which is a member of operations in class gadets.flash. Lines 4-7 list inputs of method gadets.flash.embedFlash. If we compare these results with original documentations, we can see that they are exactly the same.

Table 1. Regular expressions that are edited for acquisition of OpenSocial

Number	Regular Expression
1	<div id="page children" class="pageSectionBody">(.*?)</div>
2	<a href="(.*?)">(.*?)</a>
3	<p><b>(.*?)</b></p><p>(.*?)</p>
4	<h2>(.*?)</a>(.*?)</h2>
5	<p><b>Description</b> (.*?)</p>
6	<p><b>Returns</b>(.*?)</tbody>
7	<p><b>Parameters</b>(.*?)</tbody>
8	<td(.*?)>(.*?)</td>

Since acquisitions of OpenAPIs in REST are similar to the sample acquisition, regarding the former we will not go into detail. Acquisitions of OpenAPIs in SOAP start with addresses of WSDL documentations, and then execute automatically, so the demonstration of acquiring OpenAPIs in SOAP is left out.

4.2 Validation

Sample acquisitions have been achieved with results. Table 2 lists 13 OpenAPIs that cover 6 fields, which are classified by service contents. Tables 3-5 correspondingly present the results of acquiring OpenAPIs in AJAX, REST and SOAP. Compared with the original documentations, the acquisition results are the same. Table 6 shows the run time of each acquisition; since documentations are downloaded by the program in advance, run time ranges from 10ms to 715ms. Tables 3-6 show that our methodology can obtain information of OpenAPIs correctly at a high speed.

Table 2. List of experimental OpenAPIs

Protocol Field	AJAX	REST	SOAP
Map	Google Maps Virtual Earth		
Search	Google Search	Yahoo Search	
Social Network	OpenSocial	MySpace	
E-commerce		Amazon EBay Taobao	
Call		Twilio Skydeck	
News			YouTxt PostalMethods

Table 3. Statistics of acquiring OpenAPIs in AJAX

Information OpenAPI	AjaxClass	AjaxProperty	AjaxMethod	AjaxInput
Google Maps	93	161	338	256
Virtual Earth	36	146	176	342
Google Search	13	4	58	81
OpenSocial	47	170	179	192

Table 4. Statistics of acquiring OpenAPIs in REST

Information OpenAPI	RestMethod	RestInput	RestResponse
Yahoo Search	3	25	13
MySpace	12	100	19
Amazon	22	199	194
EBay	14	14	196
Taobao	107	1311	167
Twilio	36	74	352
Skydeck	3	24	32

Table 5. Statistics of acquiring OpenAPIs in SOAP

Information OpenAPI	SoapService	SoapMethod	SoapInput	SoapOutput
YouTxt	1	5	15	5
PostalMethods	1	14	84	81

Table 6. Run time of acquiring OpenAPIs

OpenAPI	Run time(ms)
Google Maps	319
Virtual Earth	201
Google Search	54
Open Social	100
Yahoo Search	258
MySpace	39
Amazon	715
EBay	176
Taobao	147
Twilio	20
Skydeck	10
YouTxt	655
PostalMethods	182

In fact, REST has increasingly displaced other design models such as SOAP and WSDL, as REST is less strongly typed than SOAP. Thus, not only is REST the dominant OpenAPI style by far, but interest in REST is growing rapidly, while interest in SOAP is declining. As a result, there are more OpenAPIs in REST than OpenAPIs in SOAP. For instance, ProgrammableWeb.com has 331 OpenAPIs in AJAX and 4,041 OpenAPIs in REST, while it contains only 1,222 OpenAPIs in SOAP. Therefore, we can conclude that semi-automatic acquisition of OpenAPIs in AJAX and REST is significant and our work is therefore valuable.

5 Conclusion and Future Work

As OpenAPIs develop rapidly, finding and learning the appropriate OpenAPI become very important issues. In this paper, we propose an Internet-oriented method for OpenAPIs acquisition. Our contributions and understanding can be summarized as follows:

- Semi-automatic acquisition lays the foundation of organization and management of OpenAPIs and (semi-)automatic mashup, and facilitates discovering and learning OpenAPIs.
- For common OpenAPIs, we first represent them in formal representation, and then apply different methods to documentations in terms of protocols. The experimental results of acquisition of 13 OpenAPIs in 6 fields show that our methodology can obtain OpenAPIs correctly and represent them in formal formats.

In the future, we will take more protocols or styles into account and acquire more OpenAPIs information. To this end, we plan to study characteristics of documentations of OpenAPIs in other protocols or styles and design varied strategies to deal with these documentations in terms of protocols or styles.

References

1. Wikipedia, http://en.wikipedia.org/wiki/Open_API
2. Sun, H., Zheng, Z., Chen, J., Pan, W., Liu, C., Ma, W.: Personalized Open API Recommendation in Clouds Via Item-based Collaborative Filtering. In: 4th IEEE International Conference on Utility and Cloud Computing, pp. 237–244. IEEE Press, New York (2011)
3. Weiss, M., Gangadharan, G.R.: Modeling the Mashup Ecosystem: Structure and Growth. R&D Management 40(1), 40–49 (2010)
4. Yu, J., Benatallah, B., Casati, F., Daniel, F.: Understanding Mashup Development. IEEE Internet Computing 12(5), 44–52 (2008)
5. Murgesan, S.: Understanding Web 2.0. IT Professional 9(4), 34–41 (2007)
6. ProgrammableWeb, http://www.programmableweb.com
7. Wang, J., Chen, H., Zhang, Y.: Mining User Behavior Pattern in Mashup Community. In: 10th IEEE International Conference on Information Reuse and Integration, pp. 126–131. IEEE Press, New York (2009)
8. Weiss, M., Sari, S.: Evolution of the Mashup Ecosystem by Copying. In: International Workshop on Web APIs and Services Mashups (2010)
9. Garret, J.J.: Ajax: A New Approach to Web Applications, http://www.adaptivepath.com/ideas/ajax-new-approach-web-applications
10. Fielding, R.T.: Architectural Styles and The Design of Network-based Software Architectures. PhD dissertation, University of California, Irvine (2000)
11. Friedl, J.: Mastering Regular Expressions. O'Reilly Media, Sebastopol (2006)
12. Wikipedia, http://en.wikipedia.org/wiki/SOAP

A Novel Subspace Classification Method for Large Datasets Based on Kernel-Based Fisher Discriminant Analysis

Yanlan Wang, Fuzan Chen*, Minqiang Li, and Jisong Kou

College of Management and Economics, Tianjin University
No. 92, Weijin Road, Nankai District, Tianjin, 300072, P. R. China
fzchen@tju.edu.cn

Abstract. With the rapid development of E-business and database, classification for high dimensions in large scale datasets becomes an important task of business intelligence. Recently, kernel-based methods have attracted more and more attention and have shown excellent performance in pattern recognition, machine learning and image classification etc. The common weakness of the kernel-based learning algorithms is that they cannot deal with a large dataset. In this paper, a novel classification method for large datasets named Sub-KFDA (Subspace classification based on Kernel Fisher Discriminant Analysis) is presented. A subspace mining approach based on frequent patterns and kernel-based fisher discriminant analysis is designed to decompose the initial large dataset classification problem into many small dataset classification problems. Experiment results on UCI datasets demonstrate that the proposed method has advantages in accuracy in comparison to other classification approaches.

Keywords: Classification, Subspaces, FDA, Frequent patterns.

1 Introduction

Classification for high dimensions in large scale datasets is an important task of business intelligence in the era of Information. Classification methods, such as Decision Tree (DT), Rule based learning algorithm (Rule), Association Classification methods (AC) and so forth have been widely applied in many classification fields and gained favorable results. However, they cannot deal well with this type of classification task. While dealing with high dimensional data, classifiers built by methods mentioned above become greatly complex. For example, trees constructed by DT method will face an extreme increase in depth and breadth; the Rule and AC method will face the problem of attributes combinatorial explosion. Conversely, when dealing with large datasets, all these classification methods will be confronted with a reduction in efficiency as they require more time to go through entire datasets.

To deal with high dimensional datasets, a general approach is to reduce the dimensionality of the input feature space by means of feature extraction methods, such as

* Corresponding author.

V. Khachidze et al. (Eds.): iCETS 2012, CCIS 332, pp. 97–108, 2012.

Principle Component Analysis (PCA) and Linear Discriminant Analysis (LDA). However, these linear transformation methods have their limitations. Recently, Kernel-based learning methods have attracted more and more attention and shown excellent performance in pattern recognition and machine learning [1][2]. Kernel-based learning machines, such as Support Vector Machine (SVM), kernel principle component methods (KPCA), and kernel Fisher discriminant analysis (KFDA) [2][3], are examples of widely and successfully applied kernel-based learning methods. Many researches show that these kernel-based methods can enhance the linear separation among data of different classes by applying nonlinear transformation techniques [2][3][4][5]. The kernel-based learning methods can efficiently map the input space into a high-dimensional feature space through kernel functions without knowing the details of corresponding transformation. In consequence, the kernel-based methods possess lower computational costs compared to other nonlinear transformation methods. However, the kernel-based learning algorithms still are unable to handle large scale datasets. For KPCA and KFDA, the efficiency of feature extraction closely depends on the number of training samples, and declines when the data scale increases [4]. Problems discussed above make it an urgent task to develop an effective classification method for these large scale datasets with high dimensionality.

Naturally, a smaller dataset classification problem is easier to solve than a large one; thus, if we can subdivide a large dataset into several blocks to turn the original large problem into many smaller problems, the large problem can be solved more easily. Based on this cognition, this paper proposes a novel classification method for large datasets with high dimensionality, named Sub-KFDA (Subspace classification based on Kernel Fisher Discriminant Analysis). It combines the effectiveness of a subspace mining method and a kernel-based feature extraction learning method. A sample subspace mining method is designed to decompose the initial large dataset into many smaller classification problems. A Kernel FDA method is conducted on each sample subspace to obtain the corresponding feature subspace described by the most discriminant vectors, which is expected to help achieve more accurate classification predictions. The experiment results on several UCI datasets demonstrate that the proposed method has advantages in accuracy, in comparison to other classification approaches.

The rest of this paper is organized as follows. Section 2 provides a brief review of the related work. Section 3 reports the basic ideas of Sub-KFDA method. Experimental results and performance study are given in Section 4, and Section 5 summarizes our research work.

2 Related Works

Compared to traditional classification algorithms, subspace classification methods have advantages in dealing with high dimensional problems in large scale datasets. At times, it is difficult to distinguish data of different classes in the entire high-dimensional feature space, while in a subspace comprised of a subset of the original feature set, interesting patterns can be easily discovered. Subspace classification methods are based on the hypothesis that individual classes lie in different vector subspaces [6]. In other words, the principle of subspace classification methods is finding potential patterns through datasets described by different subsets of the original feature set, instead of the entire input feature space. In the development process of subspace methods, three kinds of subspace classification methods can be categorized.

The first kind is not a subspace method in essence because it conducts classification tasks in the entire feature space, but it still has some resemblance to subspace methods and so we call it sample subspace method. Sample subspace methods use all the input features, but only a subset of the original data to build a classifier at a time, i.e., Bagging [7]. Bagging incorporates approaches of bootstrapping and classifier aggregation. Multiple training sub-datasets are generated by random sampling the original dataset with replacement, and each training sub-dataset is used to build a base classifier. All the base classifier's prediction results are aggregated by methods of majority vote or averaging to form the final classification result. Conversely, when it comes to a dataset with high dimensionality and the base classifier is a decision tree, the high dimensional problem remains unsolved.

The second kind can be referred to as feature subspace methods. This kind of subspace methods finds multiple feature subsets over the entire input feature space for the whole original dataset. Here, a subspace is the total dataset described by one of the feature subsets. The Random Subspace Method (RSM) [8] is an example of feature subspace methods. It takes advantage of bootstrapping and classifier aggregation, as in Bagging method. The difference is that RSM uses bootstrapping to randomly select a subset of the original features instead of a data subset to learn a subspace. The final prediction result for a new data sample is aggregated from the predicting results of all the generated feature subspaces. RSM can usually be computed more efficiently, since it is conducted on a smaller number of features [9].

The third kind is the subspace classification methods that generate classifiers on both subsets of the feature set and subsets of the original dataset. CLAFIC (CLAss Featuring Information Compression) [10], proposed by E. Oja in 1983, is one of the first subspace classification methods. In CLAFIC, each class corresponds to only one feature subspace, determined by PCA. Given a new data sample, CLAFIC classifies it into the class with the maximal projection of the feature vectors in the corresponding subspace. The drawbacks of the CLAFIC method include the following: (1) the method determining subspaces is unsupervised, since PCA extracts features without taking class information into consideration; (2) there is only one subspace for each class over the entirety of the input space. Another subspace method called random forest method (RF) [11] is a method with a collection of tree-structured classifiers that are built of both bootstrapping training data samples and random selecting feature vectors. RF has been empirically demonstrated to be able to outperform a single tree classifier such as CART and C4.5 [9]. RF, Bagging and RS can find more than one subspace for a specific class, but they still have defects. One defect lies in the fact that they select training data samples and/or features with randomization. This might cause some important feature combinations or interesting patterns to remain undiscovered. The other is that they can only apply unstable base learners to guarantee sufficient random subspaces. To overcome these weaknesses, Ting *et al.* propose a fundamentally different approach called Feating (Feature-Subspace Aggregating)[12]. Unlike generating subspaces randomly, Feating employs a complete enumeration of the feature space based on a user-specified number of features, and subdivides the original dataset into subspaces without duplication. A subspace in Feating comprises data samples covered by a same feature subset and the rest of the features in the original feature set. Feating can apply either unstable or stable base learners for prediction.

Methods mentioned above mostly acquire feature subspaces through feature selection technique, with the exception of CLAFIC. In fact, feature extraction is a more widely used technique for subspace mining, especially after the speedy development of kernel-based learning methods. As mentioned before, kernel-based learning methods can efficiently transform the input space nonlinearly into a higher dimensional feature space through a kernel function, and the extracted feature subset gained in the high space are proven able to enhance the linear separation among data of different classes. At present, many kernelized feature extraction algorithms have been proposed, such as KPCA proposed by Scholkopf in 1998 [13] and KFDA proposed by Mika in 1999 [3], and subspace classification methods based on these kernel algorithms have been studied in many articles and proven to occupy better classification accuracy than subspace methods based on normal feature extraction techniques [4][14][15][16].

In this paper, we propose a subspace classification method that takes advantages of both kernel-based learning method and frequent pattern discovery method to generate the subspaces we need. Kernel-based methods can extract the most discriminant feature vectors in the transformed high space, which can guarantee better prediction accuracy. The frequent pattern discovery method can help find subspaces of similarity data, where similarity is defined with same values on specific attributes. Frank, Hall and Pfahringer [17] demonstrate that a local model formed from instances similar to one we wish to classify will often be more accurate than a global model formed from all instances, which can be extended to infer that a subspace formed by similar data samples will hold higher classification accuracy. By combining these two techniques, our method is proven able to achieve better prediction accuracy than other kinds of classification methods. The proposed method belongs to the third kind of subspace methods, since we conduct classification on datasets consisting of only a part of the original data set and feature set.

3 Subspace Classification Based on KFDA

In this paper, we devise the Subspace classification based on Kernel Fisher Discriminant Analysis (Sub-KFDA) method, to solve the classification problem for large scale datasets with high dimensionality.

3.1 The Frame Diagram of Sub-KFDA Method

The Sub-KFDA method mainly comprises three parts. Firstly, an approach of subspace mining based on frequent patterns discovery is presented. Secondly, a feature extraction method based on a KFDA method for all subspaces gained in the first step is conducted. The final subspace set is confirmed after these two steps. Each subspace in the final subspace set is a subset of data described by only features extracted by KFDA method, and the subset data is a set of the original data matched by a specific frequent pattern. Thirdly, beginning the predicting part, a base learner is chosen to perform classification tasks on subspaces that are associated with those testing data only, and then an aggregation method is executed to aggregate all the subspace results into the final classification result.

3.2 The Subspace Mining Procedure Based on Frequent Patterns Discovery

In order to solve the large dataset classification problem, we suggest decomposing the initial large dataset into many small sample subspaces. Ting [12] and Frank [17] showed that a subspace formed from samples similar to one we wish to classify is often more accurate than the whole dataset (which they call a global model) formed from all samples. Considering this, the proposed subspace method here uses the subspaces spanned by samples covered by the same frequent pattern, which consists of a certain number of items as training datasets instead of using the whole original large dataset, as we believe that samples sharing the same attributes with equal values are of high similarities.

The idea of rule generation presented in MCAR algorithm [18] is employed on the frequent patterns discovery stage. MCAR takes advantage of vertical format representation and uses an efficient intersection method for discovering frequent patterns based on recursively intersecting frequent items of size n to find potential frequent items of size n+1 [18]. Moreover, the MCAR only requires a single scan over the whole training dataset. We appropriate the idea of intersection method based on vertical format representation from MCAR method, and modify it in some aspects to produce desired results. The following are key points of the subspace mining procedure based on frequent pattern discovery that we want to stress especially.

Firstly, considering that there are always many attributes in real datasets but not all attributes are actually necessary for analysis, we select only attributes ranked in the top N (if there are attributes more than N) according to the calculated Information Gain value to form the attribute subset for frequent patterns discovery. Another reason for this attributes selection is that we hope to accelerate the frequent patterns discovery and subspace mining procedure, as fewer attributes remained while at the same time obtain many candidate subspaces. Secondly, since the KFDA method requires sufficient training samples to guarantee high predicting accuracy, while an overlong frequent pattern may only cover a few training samples, we restrict the length of frequent patterns to M items in order to keep subspaces on a proper scale. We also define a minimum coverage threshold to identify whether the scale of a data subset covered by a frequent pattern is large enough to constitute a subspace. The main process of subspace mining based on frequent patterns discovery consists of the following four steps:

(1) for a candidate frequent pattern, if all the training samples it covers belong to an identical class, then mark the frequent pattern with the class label;
(2) or if the number of the covered training samples is less than a user-defined coverage threshold, then mark the frequent pattern with the most possible class labels of the covered samples;
(3) or if the length of the frequent pattern is less than M items, then add one item to it and restart from step (1);
(4) or if the frequent pattern has already reached the predefined maximal length M, then mark the frequent pattern with a subspace symbol and the training samples covered by the frequent pattern will form a sample subspace.

Finally, we have two kinds of frequent patterns. One is related directly to a specific class label and the other is associated with a sample subspace. Every sample subspace can be explained by the corresponding frequent pattern. In fact, the set of frequent patterns formed by every M attributes, including both kinds of frequent patterns, subdivides the original data space into non-overlapping subspaces.

3.3 The Subspace Mining Procedure Based on KFDA Method

After acquiring the sample subspaces, the next step is to perform feature extraction for each sample subspace to get the final subspace set. The Fisher Discriminant Analysis (FDA) method is a kind of supervised feature extraction method, as it takes class information into consideration in the training stage. The FDA method aims to find the most discriminative vectors to describe data, so as to achieve the purpose of dimension reduction. KFDA is a method of kernel-based FDA. KFDA is better than FDA with respect to discriminating data of different classes.

The KFDA method applied in Sub-KFDA is inherited from the two-phase KFD framework developed by Yang [2], which is defined as a KPCA plus a LDA (Linear Discriminant Analysis). The two-phase KFD method is distinguished from other Kernel-based FDA methods in that it takes advantages of two kinds of discriminant information: the regular discriminant vectors extracted from the range space and the irregular discriminant vectors extracted from the null space [2].

In this method, we firstly use the KPCA to map the input space $\boldsymbol{R}$ into a higher feature space $\boldsymbol{\Theta}$ via kernel function, then use LDA for further feature extraction in the KPCA-transformed feature space $\boldsymbol{\Theta}$. The kernel function applied in both the KPCA stage and LDA stage is the Gaussian kernel:

$$k(x, y) = \exp\left(-\frac{\| x - y \|^2}{2\sigma^2}\right) \quad (1)$$

In KPCA stage, the cumulative percentage is set to 100%, which means that all the projection vectors of positive eigenvalue ranked in a descending order will be selected until reaching the proportion. Then, the training data described by the projection vectors act as the input parameter to conduct LDA analysis. The final subspaces are described by features extracted from both the range space and the null space. In consequence, we obtain at most a total of two (c-1)-dimensional discriminant feature vectors, which is about twice more than other Kernel-based FDA method. c is the number of unique class labels in the training dataset. It is one of the internal causes explaining why the two-phase KFD method obtains better prediction results than others.

Yang et al. [2] also suggested a fusion strategy by introducing a fusion coefficient of regular discriminant information to fuse the two kinds of discriminant feature vectors in the decision level. In our method, we consider the irregular discriminant feature vectors to be as important as the regular discriminant feature vectors, and they are equally treated when used to project training samples.

3.4 Classification

To classify a test data, only subspaces of frequent patterns covering this test data sample will be selected to perform prediction task. Hence, one must find all the matched frequent patterns first. In this way, the useful subspaces are confirmed. For each subspace, first project the test data into the corresponding discriminant vector set. Then, the associated subspace and projected test data will act as training dataset and testing dataset respectively to have the base learner execute classification task.

We initialize a vector to store the predicted results for every test data, where every unit in the vector is related to a unique class label respectively. For each frequent pattern, if the matched frequent pattern is connected to a class label directly, then the count of this class unit in the vector will be increased by 1 immediately; otherwise, the corresponding class unit of the prediction result obtained by the base learner will be increased by 1. Finally, the class with majority vote in the unit will be selected as the final predicting result for the test data.

4 Analytical Results

Experiments are conducted on a total of 6 datasets from UCI repository machine learning databases [19] using a 10-fold cross validation. These datasets are selected because they are varying in data size and number of attributes, and can represent different situations. Table 1 gives the elementary information about these 6 datasets. The proposed Sub-KFDA method is implemented on MATLAB platform. Representative classification algorithms, such as Decision Tree algorithm (like J48), rule based classification method (like Jrip), K-Nearest Neighbor and Bagging are chosen to for comparison with the proposed algorithm in terms of classification accuracy. All the contrast experiments are conducted on Weka software.

Table 1. Datasets used in the experiments

ID	Dataset	Samples	Classes	Attributes
1	Nursery	12,960	5	8
2	Wave	5000	3	43
3	Satimage	6435	6	36
4	Segment	2310	7	18
5	Anneal	898	5	31
6	Dna	3186	3	61

4.1 Design of Basic Parameters in Experiments

All the datasets are discretized before the frequent pattern discovery process. Apart from the given training and testing datasets, every dataset is separated into 10 portions with 9 of them picked up at random to form the training dataset and the remaining one to form the testing dataset. The final prediction result is the average of the 10 experiments. Here, the number of attributes N selected to discover frequent patterns and subspaces is set to 10; the maximum length of frequent patterns M is set to 3 items for all the datasets except Nursery dataset, where M is set to 4 as the Nursery dataset is of much larger data scale, and we must control the subspaces in a smaller data scale from increasing the length of frequent patterns; the threshold of least covered samples to a frequent pattern is set to 15; the parameter of Gaussian kernel function σ is set as the 2-norm of the covariance of the training dataset.

We select two classification algorithms to perform independently as a base learner, the K-Nearest Neighbor algorithm (KNN) and the Minimum Centre Distance algorithm (MCD). The number of nearest neighbors in KNN algorithm is set to 5 in every dataset except the Nursery dataset, where the nearest neighbors is set to 10 to guarantee better classification accuracy, as Nursery dataset has a larger data scale. When classifying a new test data using the MCD method, the center point of each class is calculated first by the mean value of each extracted feature, and then test data is categorized into the class to which the nearest center point belongs. The Euclidean distance formula is selected to calculate the distance between the center point and the test data.

4.2 Analysis of Dimensionality Reduction Results

According to the main principle of the KFDA, all the samples are expected to have the greatest ratio of between-class distance and within-class distance after being projected onto the most discriminant vectors that the KFDA extracts in the high-dimensional feature space.

Fig. 1 shows the data distribution of a certain subset in experiments for 6 datasets respectively after being projected onto the discriminant vectors. As shown, data from Anneal and Nursery subspaces are projected onto a 2-dimensional space and data from Satimage and Segment subspaces are projected onto a 3-dimensional space, and data belonging to different classes have been separated dramatically.

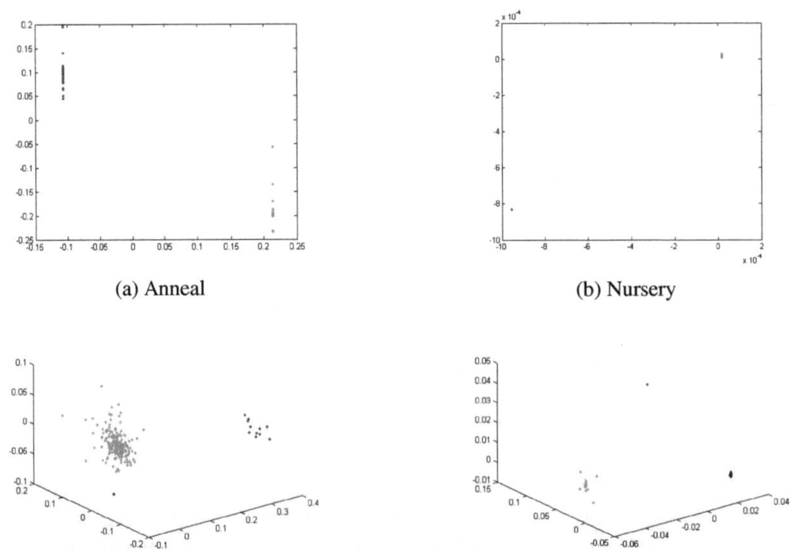

(a) Anneal (b) Nursery

(c) Satimage (d) Segment

Fig. 1. The data distribution of a certain subspace from datasets

Fig. 2 shows the statistical results of dimensionality and subspace distribution after feature extraction.

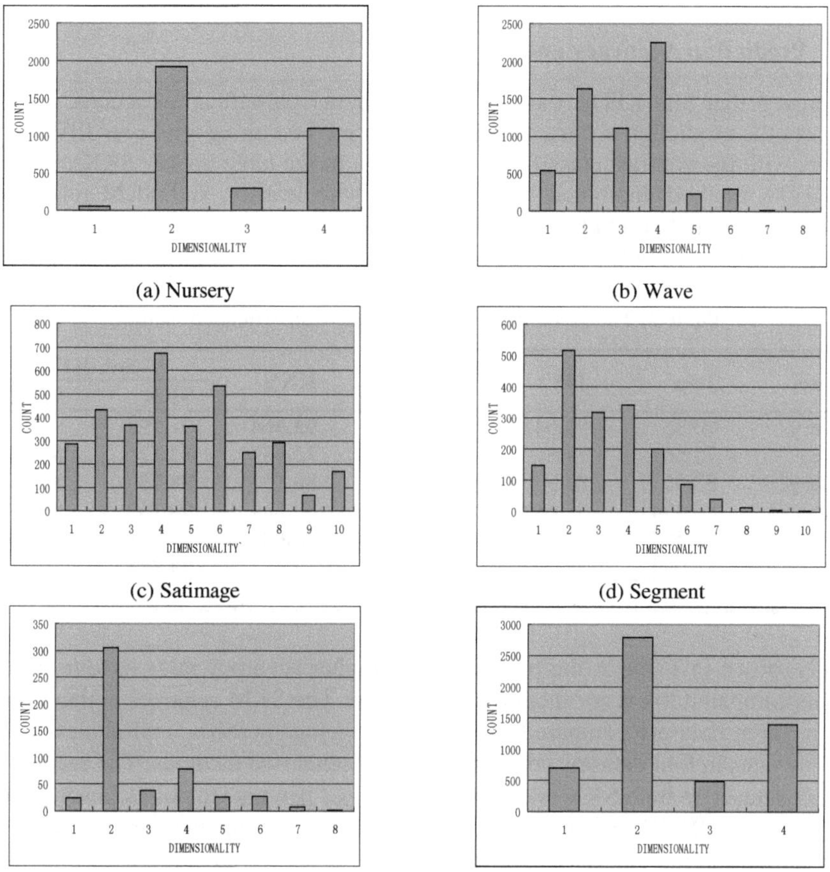

(a) Nursery (b) Wave

(c) Satimage (d) Segment

(e) Anneal (f) DNA

Fig. 2. The statistical results of dimensionality in all subspaces after feature extraction

The x-axis and y-axis are the dimensionality of a subspace and the number of subspaces belonging to different dimensional space, respectively. As shown in Figure 2, the dimensionality of major subspaces in almost all the datasets has been reduced to less than 4 feature vectors. As declared in section 3.3, the feature extraction method applied in the Sub-KFDA method extracts at most 2(c-1) discriminant features as the projection vectors, where c is the number of unique classes. Comparing the feature extraction results with the number of unique classes of datasets, we can observe that the final dimensionality of most subspaces is far less than the calculation of 2(c-1). For example, in the Anneal dataset, the number of unique classes is 5, and the dimensionality of most subspaces is 2, where 2 <<2(5-1). This is due to the method of subspace mining based on frequent pattern discovery, which gathers similar data samples only in each subspace so that there is less class diversity in a subspace. In conclusion, the proposed Sub-KFDA method can successfully achieve the goals of dimension reduction and data separation.

4.3 Prediction Accuracy and Precision

It is proven that Sub-KFDA can also achieve better classification accuracy. Table 2 compares the prediction accuracy of Sub-KFDA method along with two different base learners with the contrast classification methods. In the table below, SKK denotes the Sub-KFDA method combined with the KNN base learner, and SKM refers to the Sub-KFDA method combined with the MCD base learner. The highest accuracy rate for each dataset is in bold.

Table 2. The prediction accuracy of each classification method

Dataset	Jrip	J48	Bagging	KNN	Sub-KFDA	
					SKK	SKM
Nursery	90.857	92.641	93.071	**93.364**	91.597	91.481
Wave	75.56	74.8	77.84	75.98	**83.12**	**82.92**
Satimage	85.05	84.8	86.85	88.15	**88.75**	**88.55**
Segment	86.494	92.641	87.359	89.264	**94.762**	**95.152**
Anneal	98.552	98.552	**98.886**	**98.886**	97.774	97.33
DNA	94.044	94.357	93.825	79.812	**94.448**	93.417
Average	88.426	89.632	89.639	87.576	**91.742**	**91.475**

As is shown in Table 2, the SKK achieves higher accuracy rates in four out of six datasets compared to every other contrast method. The SKM achieves higher accuracy rates in three datasets compared to J48 and Bagging methods, and achieves higher accuracy rates in four datasets compared with the other two methods. The accuracies of Nursery dataset on both SKK and SKM are nearly 2 percentage points lower than Jrip, Bagging and KNN. We consider one possible reason to be that the number of attributes in this dataset is too small. Since our method is proposed to solve high dimensional problems, it may not be fitting to deal with the Nursery dataset. The accuracy of Anneal dataset is about 1 percentage point lower than the contrast methods; we consider the reason for this lie in the small scale of Anneal dataset,t since sufficient data samples are the basic requirement of KFDA method.

The average accuracy rate of all six datasets that SKK achieves is 2% higher than the highest average accuracy rate that the contrast methods achieve. Overall, results in Table 2 also show that both the performance at single dataset and the average performance of the SKK method are slightly better than the SKM method. In conclusion, the results demonstrate that the proposed method is very competitive in prediction accuracy, compared to traditional classification methods.

Table 3 gives the precision of each class for every dataset in 10-cross validation experiments. The precision values of Class 1 in Nursery dataset are zero. By digging into the dataset, we suppose one possible explanation is that the number of samples belonging to this class in the original dataset is too small, leading to two situations: one being that no samples are distributed into test datasets, the other that very few samples are in training dataset, thus resulting in wrong classification and low precision. In detail, the total number of samples in Nursery is 12,960, as can be seen in Table 1; however, the numbers of samples in class 1 of Nursery dataset are 2 samples, which comprise only 0.015% of the total dataset. After learning the distribution of the rest datasets, a common characteristic that classes with low precision share is that they own very few data samples. Beyond that, we can see that most classes in datasets have an acceptable precision value.

Table 3. The precision of each class in 6 datasets

Dataset	Sub-KFDA	Classes						
		1	2	3	4	5	6	7
Nursery	SKK	0	0.8871	0.9998	0.7158	0.8738	/	/
	SKM	0	0.8702	0.9998	0.7904	0.8814	/	/
Wave	SKK	0.8392	0.8541	0.8027	/	/	/	/
	SKM	0.8345	0.8425	0.8125	/	/	/	/
Satimage	SKK	0.9892	0.9643	0.9421	0.5403	0.8143	0.8979	/
	SKM	0.9783	0.9688	0.9244	0.5545	0.8608	0.8830	/
Segment	SKK	0.9779	1.0000	0.8768	0.9273	0.8748	0.9844	0.9855
	SKM	0.9779	1.0000	0.9012	0.9228	0.8745	0.9878	0.9886
Anneal	SKK	0.8889	0.9731	0.9945	0.8339	1.0	/	/
	SKM	0.9167	0.9620	0.9901	0.8339	1.0	/	/
DNA	SKK	0.9361	0.8790	0.9788	/	/	/	/
	SKM	0.9152	0.8438	0.9855	/	/	/	/

5 Conclusion

In this paper, we propose a novel classification method named Subspace classification method based on Kernel Fisher Discriminant Analysis (Sub-KFDA). The method takes advantage of frequent pattern discovery technique and kernel-based feature extraction technique to mine subspaces, and aims at dealing with the classification problem of large scale datasets with high dimensionality. In subspace mining progress, we first design a frequent pattern discovery method to mine subspaces of similar data samples, as we believe that subspaces that comprise data similar to test data can gain better prediction accuracy, and then adopt the KFDA method to conduct feature extraction. The Sub-KFDA method can combine with different base learners to conduct prediction task. Experiment results on UCI datasets prove that the proposed method has competitive performance in improving classification accuracy.

Acknowledgements. The work was supported by the National Science Fund for Distinguished Young Scholars of China (Grant No. 70925005) and the General Program of the National Science Foundation of China (No.71101103, No.61074152, No. 71001076). This work was also supported by grants from the Research Fund for the Doctoral Program of Higher Education of China (20100032120086, 20100032110036, and 20090032110065).

References

1. Müller, K.R., Mika, S., Rätsch, G., Tsuda, K., Schölkopf, B.: An Introduction to Kernel-Based Learning Algorithms. IEEE Trans. Neural Networks 12(2), 181–201 (2001)
2. Yang, J., Frangi, A.F., Yang, J., Zhang, D.: KPCA Plus LDA: A Complete Kernel Fisher Discriminant Framework for Feature Extraction and Recognition. IEEE Trans. Pattern Analysis and Machine Intelligence 27(2), 230–244 (2005)
3. Mika, S., Rätsch, G., Weston, J., Schölkopf, B., Müller, K.R.: Fisher discriminant analysis with kernels. In: Proc. IEEE Workshop Neural Networks, Signal Process. IX, pp. 41–48 (1999)
4. Xu, Y., Zhang, D., Jin, Z., et al.: A fast kernel-based nonlinear discriminant analysis for multi-class problems. Patterns Recognition 39, 1026–1033 (2006)
5. Cai, R., Hao, Z., Wen, W., Huang, H.: Kernel based gene expression pattern discovery and its application on cancer classification. Neurocomputing 73, 2562–2570 (2010)
6. Balachander, T., Kothari, R.: Introducing Locality and Softness in Subspace Classification. Pattern Analysis and Applications 2, 53–58 (1999)
7. Breiman, L.: Bagging predictors. Machine Learning 24(2), 123–140 (1996)
8. Ho, T.K.: The random subspace method for constructing decision forests. IEEE Trans. Pattern Anal. Mach. Intell. 20(8), 832–844 (1998)
9. Yan, R., Tesic, J., Smith, J.R.: Model-shared subspace boosting for multi-label classification. In: Proceedings of the 13th ACM SIGKDD International Conference on KDD, pp. 834–843. ACM, New York (2007)
10. Oja, E.: Subspace methods of pattern recognition. Research Studies Press (1973)
11. Breiman, L.: Random Forests. Machine Learning 45, 5–32 (2001)
12. Ting, K.M., Wells, J.R., Tan, S.C., et al.: Feating-subspace aggregating: ensembles for stable and unstable learners. Machine Learning 82, 375–397 (2011)
13. Schölkopf, B., Smola, A., Müller, K.R.: Nonlinear Component Analysis as a Kernel Eigenvalue Problem. Neural Computation 10, 1299–1319 (1998)
14. Balachander, T., Kothari, R.: Kernel based subspace pattern classification. In: Proceeding of International Joint Conference on Neural Networks, Washington, DC, USA, pp. 3119–3122 (1999)
15. Kitamura, T., Abe, S., Fukui, K.: Subspace Based Least Squares Support Vector Machines for Pattern Classification. In: Proceedings of International Joint Conference on Neural Networks, Atlanta, Georgia, USA, pp. 1640–1646 (2009)
16. Richman, M.B., Adrianto, I.: Classification and regionalization through kernel principal component analysis. Physics and Chemistry of the Earth 35, 316–328 (2010)
17. Frank, E., Hall, M., Pfahringer, B.: Locally weighted Naive Bayes. In: Proceedings of the 19th Conference on Uncertainty in Artificial Intelligence, pp. 249–256. Morgan Kaufmann, San Francisco (2003)
18. Thabtah, F., Cowling, P., Hammoud, S.: Improving rule sorting, predictive accuracy and training time in associative classification. Expert Systems with Applications 31, 414–426 (2006)
19. Murphy, P.M., Aha, D.W.: UCI Repository Machine Learning Databases. University of California, Irvine (1996)

Eliciting Security Requirements Method Based on Safety Knowledge Base

Xiaofei Yu, Xiaohong Li, and Qianqian Zhang

School of Computer Science and Technology, Tianjin University, Tianjin, China
{yuxiaofei,xiaohongli}@tju.edu.cn, qianqianzhangtju@gmail.com

Abstract. With the development of software technology, software security is receiving more and more attention. Security requirement is a key stage in the process of software development. In the present research, we propose a method to elicit security requirements; that is developed based on safety knowledge base. In the method, we perform analysis based on the asset, threat and Common Criteria security function components. Then, we summarize the relationship of the three. Based on this, we establish a safety knowledge base. Starting from the functional requirements of the application system, the system assets will be analyzed and matched automatically based on the established safety knowledge base, and finally we elicit the security requirements. The approach is very effective for the purpose of security requirement analysis, and elicits security requirements easily and efficiently. It will be very helpful for security software development.

Keywords: Security Requirements, Asset, Threat, Security Functional Component, Common Criteria.

1 Introduction

Software is facing an increasing number of security threats. Software security issues have become a focus for the public. However, the research of software security mostly focuses on the software implementation process. The security issues of the software requirements phase have been ignored for a long time. According to the statistics, many software security issues appear in the software requirements phase. Costs will be lowered if the security issues are solved as soon as possible in the process of software development. Therefore, security requirements engineering can greatly improve the security of software products and reduce the costs of software product development.

The eliciting of security requirements is very important in the requirement phase of software development. Because software security issues are unpredictable, eliciting security requirements becomes very difficult. So far, there have been many methods to elicit security requirements. Nancy R. Mead [1] has developed the SQUARE method in 2005 and security requirements engineering was divided into nine steps. This method has won the high recognition of the current security requirements engineering field. However, its implementation requires the guidance of security experts. Some researchers [2-7] proposed other security requirements engineering methods to extend

V. Khachidze et al. (Eds.): iCETS 2012, CCIS 332, pp. 109–121, 2012.

the Unified Modeling Language, such as Misuse case, and Abuse case. The main idea analyzes the threats and security vulnerability from the view of malicious attackers. Then it establishes the use case of security requirements. Dan Graham [8] introduced a method of eliciting requirements, called CLASP. This method analyzes the system security issues according to the interaction process between resources. Vivek Goel and Dianxiang Xu [9] proposed an aspect-oriented method to elicit requirements. In addition, there are goal-oriented engineering methods KAOS [10], TROPOS [11-13] and the model-based security risk assessment methodology CORAS [14].

There are still problems with the existing methods to elicit security requirements. Firstly, most of the methods depend on the capability and experience of security analysts Secondly, most of the methods tend to be very complex. It costs a great deal of time and effort to implement them.

This paper presents a method of eliciting security requirements based on safety knowledge base. We summarize and categorize the existing corresponding assets, threats, security functional components and other security information, and construct an informative software safety knowledge base. The knowledge base stores assets, threats, security function components and their relationships. We can elicit security requirements based on safety knowledge base. Firstly, starting with the system functional requirements, we analyze each functional use case to identify the critical assets. Secondly, we analyze the assets to obtain the relevant threats and security functional components based on the safety knowledge base. Finally, we refine and select the security functional components to achieve eliciting specific security requirements. The method of eliciting security requirements based on safety knowledge base can greatly reduce the cost of the security requirements analysis. It improves the developing efficiency of security software.

Section 2 of this paper introduces the method to elicit security requirements based on safety knowledge base; Section 3 uses the method to elicit security requirements for the specific application instance; Section 4 provides a summary and discusses future work.

2 Eliciting Security Requirements Method Based on Safety Knowledge Base

2.1 Concepts Related to Security Requirements

Currently, there is no unified definition on security requirement. From one perspective, security requirements are considered as functional requirements of a system, which are known as security function. The definition of security function is given by Common Criteria (CC) and it should refuse the access of some objects according to certain rules. Another view point is that security requirements are considered as non-functional requirements [20]. Sommerville and Kotonya [21] asserted that non-functional requirements should be defined as restrictions or limitations of system services. Haley et al. [22] defined security requirements as the restrictions of system functional requirements, able to reduce the scope of vulnerabilities that have existed among assets. Donald Firesmith [23-24] defined Security Requirement as a quality requirement.

Security requirement involves some basic concepts, including asset, threat, attack pattern and security goal. This paper provides the definitions based on the appropriate literature [16]. Asset is something of value that should be protected, including resources, datas, information, etc. Threat is a behavior to cause harm to an asset. Attack pattern is an abstraction mechanism [17]. It describes how an observed attack is executed. Security Goal is used to describe a target level of security protection that the assets need to achieve.

2.2 Eliciting Security Requirements Method

2.2.1 The Architecture of Eliciting Security Requirements

This paper presents a method of eliciting security requirements based on safety knowledge base (Fig. 1). Firstly, starting from the system functional requirements, we analyze each functional use case to identify the critical assets. Secondly, we analyze the assets to obtain the relevant threats and security functional components in support of safety knowledge base. Finally, we must refine and select the security functional components to achieve eliciting specific security requirements. Safety knowledge base is the summary of the security requirements knowledge. It establishes the mapping relation among assets, threats and security functional components.

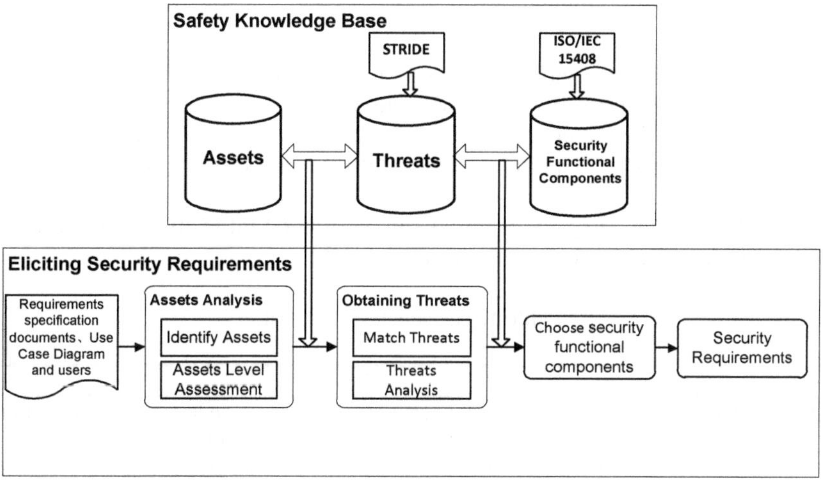

Fig. 1. Architecture of Eliciting Security Requirements

2.2.2 The Construction of Safety Knowledge Base

Safety knowledge base primarily stores three parts: the relevant assets, threats, and security functional components. By classifying assets, threats and security functional requirements respectively, we establish the hierarchical structure and construct the mapping relation among assets, threats and security functional components.

(1) Assets

Assets are the objects that need to be protected in the system. The assets are divided into three categories: role, data and resource. Resource can be divided into software and hardware resource. Data mainly includes users' data and system data. The role is the participant, including privileged user and ordinary user. Fig. 2 shows the classification of assets.

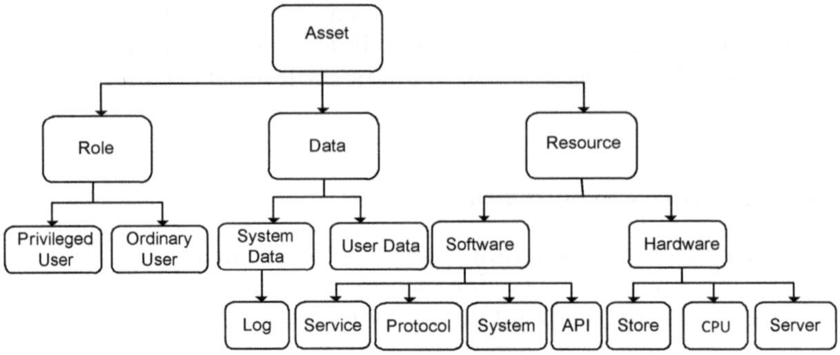

Fig. 2. Structure of Assets Classification

For each asset, we need to add a level property, which is used to describe the importance and value of the asset. Here with are three levels: high, medium and low. The asset's level is determined by the participants through their subjective evaluation according to actual requirements.

(2) Threats

Generally, threats can be divided into environmental threat and human threat. Environmental threat is caused by natural disasters or accident, such as power system interruption, or hardware damage. Human threat is caused by the participant of the system. According to the STRIDE threat model [18] proposed by Microsoft, threat is divided into five categories: Impersonation, Denial, Data tampering, Information leakage and DoS. Each category of threat can be divided into subclasses, called threat families. Specific descriptions are shown in Table 1.

Table 1. The subclass of threat

Threats Sorts	Threat Families
Impersonation	1. Obtaining legal certificate: access to the legal user's credentials by some means, thus carrying out impersonation; 2.Forging certificate: forging credentials by some technical means
Denial	1. Denial of behavior of the sender: senders denied the behaviors performed; 2. Denial of behavior of the receiver: receivers denied receiving message;
Data tampering	1. Data has been tampered during storing. 2. Data has been tampered during transmission.
Information leakage	1.The information has been leaked during storing; 2.The information has been leaked during transmission.
DoS	1.Resource consumption: service is unavailable through exhausting resources; 2. Utilizing the vulnerability: making use of the resource's own flaw results in unavailability of resource.

Attack Pattern

Each threat family consists of different kinds of attack patterns. Attack pattern describes the specific attack. CAPEC (Common Attack Pattern Enumeration and Classification) provides a detailed classification and description for attack pattern. Attack pattern includes the premise of attack, attack methods and attack consequences. For each attack pattern, we need to add a level, which is used to describe the degree of harm caused by the attack. The degree of damage is divided into the following four levels:

Damage Level I: The loss of important information data, system crash or system function failure, which cannot be recovered, and the value assignment of damage is 8–10.

Damage Level II: The loss of passwords and other important information, which leads to system function failure, it is difficult to recover, and the value assignment of damage is 5–8.

Damage Level III: Having a minor effect on system performance, it is easier to recover, and the value assignment of damage is 3–5.

Damage Level IV: Affects operation and can be very easily recovered, and the value assignment of damage is 0–3.

The Corresponding Relation of Assets and Threats

This paper gives the corresponding relation between assets and threats on the basis of their classification. For the role asset, there exists the threat of impersonation and denial. For the data asset, two types of threats were considered: data tampering and information leakage. For the resource asset, the threat of DoS is present. The corresponding relation of assets and threat is shown in Table 2:

Table 2. Corresponding relation of assets and threat

Asset Class	Threat Class
Role	Impersonation Denial
Data	Data tampering Information leakage
Resource	DoS

(3) Security Function Component

The security functional components which were offered by CC describe the security functional requirements. The security functional components are defined by CC in the form of ' class - subclass - component '. Components are the minimum optional security requirements set and the specific form of security requirements. CC contains in total 11 security functional classes, 66 security functional families and 135 security functional components.

Security Functional Class

Security functional components are divided into 11 classes in the CC: communication class (FCO), user data protection class (FDP), identification class (FIA), resource utilization class (FRU), security auditing class (FAU), password supporting class (FCS), privacy class (FPR), security management class (FMT), trusted path / channel class (FTP), assessment of objective security functional protection class (FPT) and assessment of objective access class (FTA). These 11 security functional classes are divided into the Basic Security Functional Class, the Assisted Security Functional Class and the Security Protection Functional Class (Fig. 3).

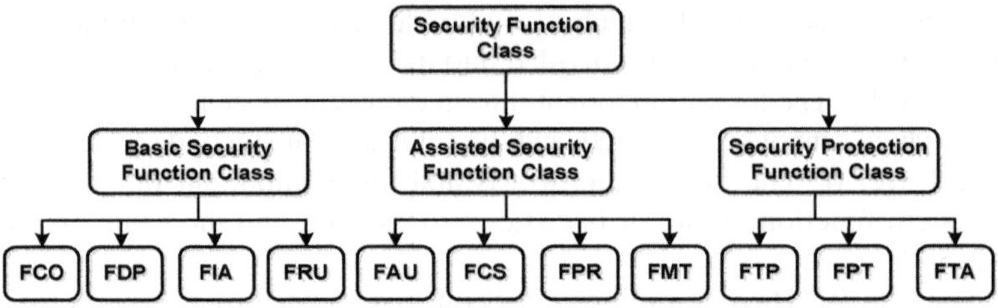

Fig. 3. Dividing of Security Function Class

The Basic Security Functional Class is relative to the five categories of threats (Table 3). It is used to mitigate the corresponding threat directly. FIA solves user identification, and mainly mitigates the impersonation threat. FCO mainly solves the role of denial during the communication process and mitigates denial threat. FDP primarily protects the integrity, confidentiality, and availability of user data. It also mitigates the threat of data tampering and information leaking. FRU is used to mitigate the threat of DoS.

Table 3. Corresponding relation of Threat class and Security function class

Threat Class	Security Function Class
Impersonation	FIA
Denial	FCO
Data Tampering	FDP
Information Leakage	
DoS	FRU

The Assisted Security Functional Class is used to assist Basic Security Functional Class to mitigate the threats. The Security Protection Functional Class serves to control the management and protection of security functions for the Basic Security Functional Class and Assisted Security Functional Class.

The Correspondence Relation of Threat and Security Functional Component
According to the existing relation between the threats and security functional components of the CC assessment and ST document, we combine the specific attack pattern to analyze the threats. It mitigates threats to use the related security functional components. Thus, we build the corresponding relation between the attack patterns and security functional components. For example, for Violent Attacks, the candidate security functional components to mitigate the threat are shown in Table 4.

Table 4. Corresponding relation of Violent Attacks and Security Function Components

Threat	Candidate Security Function Component
Violent Attacks	FIA_AFL authentication failure
	FIA_SOS verification of secrets
	FIA_UAU.7 protected authentication feedback

2.2.3 Specific Steps for Eliciting Security Requirements

Based on the safety knowledge base, specific steps to elicit security requirements are shown in Fig. 4.

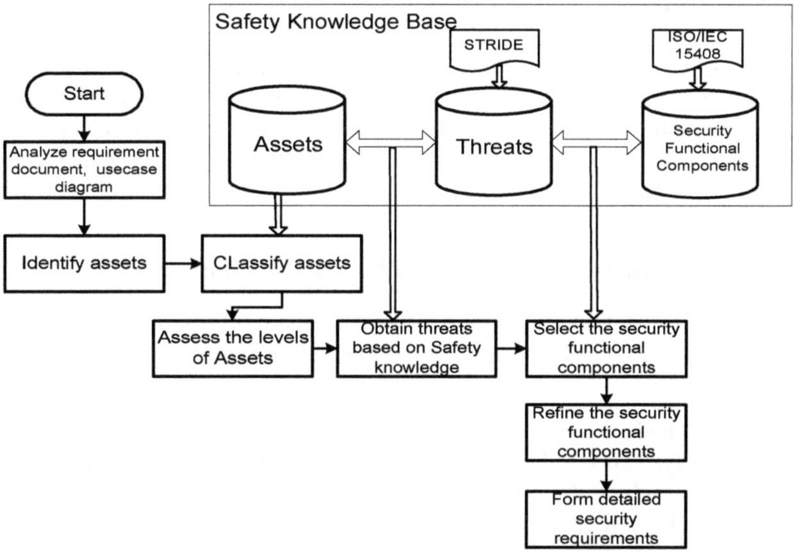

Fig. 4. Process of eliciting security requirements

1. Identify the Assets: Assets can be gained from the requirement specification document and the use case diagram. According to the system's functional requirements, analyze the system participants, functions, data information, hardware and software resources, etc. The assets may be abstract or specific, which is related to the actual functional requirements.

2. Classify Assets and Assess the Levels of Assets: We must classify assets based on safety knowledge base and make the level assessment for the assets. Highly valued assets to the system functions are assessed as high level; important assets which influence most of the system functions are assessed as medium-level; unimportant assets which influence less of the system functions are assessed as low-level. Priority should be given to the protection of high-level assets. For those assessed to be low-level, simple protection measures can be taken.

3. Obtain the Threat: Put the identified assets into the assets of safety knowledge base. We can obtain the relevant threats and attack patterns information automatically according to the mapping relation between specific assets and threats.

4. Select the Security Functional Components: We need to analyze and classify the threat based on safety knowledge base. Each attack pattern has one or more corresponding security functional components. We combine the level of assets with the damage level of the attack pattern and select the appropriate security functional components automatically.

5. Refine the Security Requirements: Finally, we combine the application requirements to refine the description of the security functional components, and then form detailed security requirements.

3 Case Study

In this section, we will apply the method of eliciting security requirements based on safety knowledge base to CA Access Control (CA Access Control for Windows r8 with patch NT-0604 CUMULATIVE RELEASE) [19]. We also compare the experimental results with the security requirements from the generated document of CA Access Control in CC Evaluation.

3.1 Eliciting Security Requirements of CA Access Control

CA Access Control System maintains user access to system resources. It contains four modules: Database, Request Management, Services and User Interfaces.

3.1.1 Asset Analysis

According to analysis of CA Access Control System and definition of the system asset, the assets mainly include three parts: users, access control lists and system resources. 'Users' refers to the visitors of the system and belong to the role class. Access control lists belong to the data class. They describe the rules for particular users to gain access to particular assets. System resources are the system information that users need to access, including data files, privilege programs, system processes, etc. These system resources belong to resource classes. Level assessment of the assets is shown in Table 5. The assessment is made based on the degree of importance of assets.

Table 5. Assets Information List

Name of Asset	Assets Category	Level of Assets
Users	Role	High
Access control lists	Data	Medium
System resources	Resources	High

3.1.2 Obtaining Threats

Input the assets into the safety knowledge base. Considering the corresponding relation between asset and threat, we can obtain the relevant threats. Considering which threats may occur (or cause great harm) and which are unlikely to happen (or cause less harm), we select the threats that correspond to assets. Assets access control lists are only stored in the database, and they will not appear in the transmission process. Thus, the threats of transmission data leakage and tampering will not be considered. The final threat list which corresponds to assets is shown in Table 6.

Table 6. Assets and Threats List

Name of Assets	Threats	Attack Patterns
Users	Obtain legal certificate	Violent attacks Certificate prediction Middleman attacks
	Denial of the behavior of the sender	---
Access control lists	Leakage of stored information	Bypass protection
	Tampering of stored information	Bypass protection Overload failure
System resources	Resource consumption	DoS

3.1.3 Security Functional Components

Considering the above threats and attack patterns, each attack pattern corresponds to one or more security functional components. The candidate security functional components can be obtained automatically based on the relationship between threat and security functional components in the safety knowledge base, which is shown in Table 7.

Table 7. Threats and Security Functional Components List

Threats name	Security functional components	Attack pattern	Level of Damage	Candidate security functional components
Obtain legal certificate	FDP_ATD.1	Violent attacks	8	FIA_AFL.1 FIA_SOS.1 FIA_UAU.7
		Certificate prediction	6	FIA_UAU.4 FIA_UAU.5
		Middleman attacks	6	FDP_ETC FDP_ITC
Denial of the sender	FCO_NRO.1 FCO_NRO.2	---	---	---
Tampering of stored information	FDP_ACC FDP_ACF	Overload failure Bypass protection	5 6	FDP_SDI FPT_SEP FMT_MOF
Resource consumption	FRU_RSA	DoS	4	FRU_RSA.1 FRU_RSA.2

3.1.4 Eliciting Security Requirements

Considering the level of assets and damage degree of attack pattern, we select the security functional components based on the above candidate security functional components. The final chosen security functional components are shown in Table 8.

Table 8. Security Functional Components List

NO.	Requirement	Requirement Name
1	FAU_GEN.1	Audit data generation
2	FAU_GEN.2	User identity association
3	FAU_SAR.1	Audit review
4	FAU_SAR.2	Restricted audit review
5	FAU_SAR.3	Selectable audit review
6	FAU_SEL.1	Selective audit
7	FAU_STG.1	Protected audit trail storage
8	FDP_ACC.1	Subset access control
9	FDP_ACF.1	Security attribute based access control
10	FIA_ATD.1	User attribute definition
11	FMT_MOF.1	Management of security functions behavior
12	FMT_MSA.1	Management of security attributes
13	FMT_MSA.3	Static attribute initialization
14	FMT_MTD.1	Management of TSF data
15	FMT_SMF.1	Specification of Management Functions
16	FMT_SMR.1	Security roles
17	FIA_AFL.1	authentication failure
18	FIA_SOS.1	verification of secrets
19	FTA_TSE.1	TOE session establishment
20	FMT_MSA.3	Static attribute initialization

Ultimately, refining the security functional components, we can create detailed descriptions of the security requirements, which will not be discussed in this paper.

3.2 Analysis of Results

Comparing the proposed method of eliciting security functional components in this paper with the security functional components of ST document [19], we find that the selected security functional components of the two are approximately the same. Fig. 5 shows the statistic of two methods eliciting security functional components for CA Access Control System.

The security functional classes of the two mainly focus on six categories: FAU, FDP, FMT, FTA, FIA and FPT. However, the specific selection of security functional components has differences in level as shown in table 9.

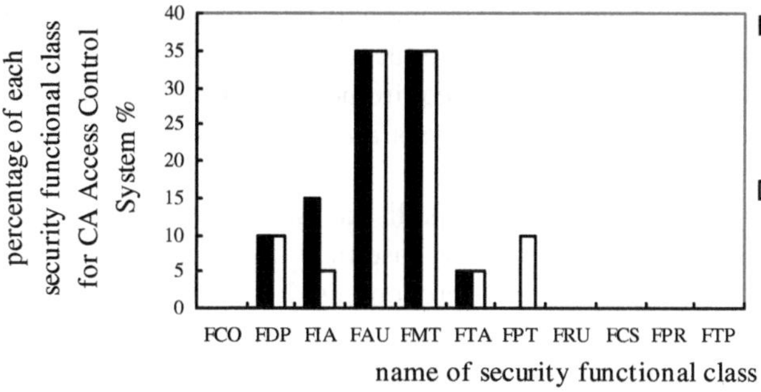

Fig. 5. The Statistic of each security functional class for CA Access Control System

Table 9. Selected Components of FIA Class

Class	the proposed method of eliciting security functional components in this paper	the security functional components of ST document [19]
FIA	FIA_ATD.1 FIA_AFL.1 FIA_SOS.1	FIA_ATD.1

This paper selects the FPT_SEP.2 component, while ST document [19] selects the FPT_SEP.1 component. FPT_SEP.2 and FPT_SEP.1 only have the distinction in the level of detail requirements. For the FIA Class, the method of this paper selects FIA_AFL.1, FIA_SOS.1 and FIA_ATD.1 components, while ST document only selects the FIA_ATD.1 component. FIA_AFL.1 and FIA_SOS.1 are mainly used to mitigate Violent Attacks. ST document did not consider these two threats. In addition, this paper elects the FPT_RVM.1 and FPT_SEP.1 to ensure that the security functions are not ignored, while the ST document use the self-defined security functional components FPT_RVM_EXP.1 and FPT_SEP_EXP.1. Overall, through the method proposed in this paper, the results of selecting the security functional components are basically the same with manual analysis. The selection of some security functional components is more detailed than ST document. The complete safety knowledge base will contribute to the comprehensive analysis of security requirements, and make the efficiency of implementation much better than the manual analysis.

4 Conclusions and Future Work

This paper includes two main aspects. 1. We construct an informative software safety knowledge base and conduct classification on existing assets, threats and security functional components. The knowledge base stores assets, threats, security function components and their relationship. 2. This paper presents a method to elicit security requirements based on safety knowledge base. The method introduces security functional components to describe security requirements according to Common Criteria (CC). It enables computers to deal with security requirements semi-automatically. It reduces the cost of the security requirements analysis and improves the developing efficiency of security software.

However, the method proposed in this paper still has some limitations. Some threats may not be considered. As safety knowledge base may involve a large number of concepts and elements, it requires further improvement. In the future, we must consider environmental threat and improper human error. Flaws of the software also cause system security issues, so we will consider the security vulnerabilities to describe threats.

Acknowledgments. We are grateful to the anonymous reviewers for their insightful comments and suggestions. This research was supported in part by National Natural Science Foundation of China (No.90718023, 91118003), Tianjin Research Program of Application Foundation and Advanced Technology (No.10JCZDJC15700), "985"funds of Tianjin University.

References

1. Nancy, R.M.: SQUARE Process. Software Engineering Institute. Carnegie Mellon University (2006)
2. Alexander: Misuse cases: Use cases with hostile intent. IEEE Software, 58–66 (2003)
3. McDermott, J., Fox, C.: Using abuse case models for security requirements analysis. In: Annual Computer Security Applications Conference, ACSAC 1999, pp. 55–64 (1999)
4. Seong, C.S., Jin, H.Y., Young, D.K., Jun, Y.C., Sang, J.L., Byung, K.K.: Building Security Requirements Using State Transition Diagram at Security Threat Location. In: Hao, Y., Liu, J., Wang, Y.-P., Cheung, Y.-M., Yin, H., Jiao, L., Ma, J., Jiao, Y.-C. (eds.) CIS 2005. LNCS (LNAI), vol. 3802, pp. 451–456. Springer, Heidelberg (2005)
5. Alfonso, R., Eduardo, F.M., Mario, P.: Capturing Security Requirements in Business Processes Through a UML 2.0 Activity Diagrams Profile. In: Roddick, J., Benjamins, V.R., Si-said Cherfi, S., Chiang, R., Claramunt, C., Elmasri, R.A., Grandi, F., Han, H., Hepp, M., Lytras, M.D., Mišić, V.B., Poels, G., Song, I.-Y., Trujillo, J., Vangenot, C. (eds.) ER Workshops 2006. LNCS, vol. 4231, pp. 32–42. Springer, Heidelberg (2006)
6. Jan, J.: UML Development of safety systems, pp. 37–55. Tsinghua University Press (2009) (in Chinese)
7. Choi, S., Kim, S., Lee, G.: Enhanced Misuse Case Model: A Security Requirement Analysis and Specification Model. In: Gavrilova, M.L., Gervasi, O., Kumar, V., Tan, C.J.K., Taniar, D., Laganá, A., Mun, Y., Choo, H. (eds.) ICCSA 2006. LNCS, vol. 3984, pp. 618–625. Springer, Heidelberg (2006)
8. Dan, G.: Introduction to the CLASP Process. Secure Software, Inc.
9. Xu, D.X., Goel, V., Nygard, K.: An Aspect-Oriented Approach to Security Requirements Analysis. In: Proceedings of the 30th Annual International Computer Software and Applications Conference (COMPSAC 2006), pp. 79–82 (2006)

10. Bertrand, P., Darimont, R., Delor, E., Massonet, P.: GRAIL/KAOS: an environment for goal driven requirements engineering. In: 20th International Conference on Software Engineering, ICSE 1998, pp. 612–613 (1998)
11. Bresciani, P., Perini, A., Giorgini, P., Giunchiglia, F., Mylopoulos, J.: Tropos: an agent-oriented software development methodology. Auton Agent Multi Agent Systems, 203–236 (2004)
12. Giorgini, P., Susi, A., Perini, A., Mylopoulos, J., Susi, A.: The tropos metamodel and its use. Inf. J. 29, 401–408 (2005)
13. Fuxman, A., Liu, L., Mylopoulos, J., Pistore, M., Roveri, M., Traverso, P.: Specifying and analyzing early requirements in tropos. Requir. Eng. J. 9(2), 132–150 (2004)
14. Braber, F., Hogganvik, I., Lund, M.S., Stølen, K., Vraalsen, F.: Model-based security analysis in seven steps—a guided tour to the CORAS method. BT Technol. J. 25(1), 101–117 (2007)
15. ISO/IEC JTC1/SC27, Information technology-Security techniques-Evaluation criteria for IT security, ISO/IEC 15408: 2005 (Common Criteria v3.0), ISO/IEC (2005)
16. Jin, Y., Liu, X., Zhang, J.: Research On Eliciting Security Requirement Methods. Computer Science (2011) (in Chinese)
17. Hon, J.Y., Zhang, Y.C., Kambayashi, Y.: Object-oriented Representation for XML Data. IEEE, Beijing (2001)
18. Michael, H., Steve, L.: The Security Development Lifecycle SDL: A Process for Developing Demonstrably More Secure Software. Publishing House of Electronics Industry (2008)
19. CA Access Control for Windows r8, `http://www.commoncriteriaportal.org/products/`.
20. Luo, B., Ding, E.: Requirements Engineering - Software Modeling and Analysis, pp. 13–21. Higher Education Press, Beijing (2009) (in Chinese)
21. Sommerville, K.: Integrating safety analysis and requirements engineering. In: Asia Pacific and International Computer Science Conference, pp. 259–271 (1997)
22. Haley, C.B., Laney, R.C., Nuseibeh, B.: Deriving Security Requirements from Crosscutting Threat Descriptions, pp. 112–121. ACM Press (2004)
23. Donald, F.: Specifying Reusable Security Requirements. Journal of Object Technology 3(1), 61–75 (2004)
24. Donald, G.F.: Engineering Security Requirements. Journal of Object Technology 2(1), 53–68 (2003)

Sale Channel Selection of Information Products in the Presence of Network Externality

Zhiyong Liu[1,2,*], Minqiang Li[1], and Jisong Kou[1]

[1] College of Management and Economics, Tianjin University, Tianjin 300072, China
[2] Business School, Tianjin University of Commerce, Tianjin 300134, China
Zy_liu1980@yahoo.com.cn, mqli@tju.edu.cn

Abstract. This paper analyzes the decision behaviors of the manufacturer, retailer, and consumers in the presence of network externality, and develops a sale channel model for maximizing the manufacturer's profit. Based on the comparison among different channels, it is shown that the manufacturer prefers versioning strategy with network externality when the consumer's valuation for information products is uniformly distributed, whereas one version strategy is more preferable without network externality. The best sale channel strategy is to distribute the high-quality version through the direct sale channel and the low-quality version through retailing channel when there is network externality.

Keywords: Information products, Sale channel model, Dual channel, Network externality.

1 Introduction

Network externality is defined as the phenomenon whereby the increased value of a product is affected by the number of those who consume similar or compatible products (Katz and Shapiro, 1985). The consumers can gain greater utility from a product by the sharing, accumulating, and communication of information, when there are more and more people using it. This is a typical characteristic of information products, such as social network sites (e.g. Facebook, Renren.com), software, and online games. Taking into consideration online games as an example, in addition to the inherent value of the game itself, the number of players is also an important factor of impacting the consumer's valuation for the product. In general, more players can attract new more consumers consuming the product (Meagher and Teo, 2005). The network externality, which exists in many information products, influences information products firms' decision in developing and selling new products.

Previous researches on information products generally assume that the consumer's willingness to pay and utility from consuming a product is relevant to quality and price (Bhargava 2001, Chen 2007)[2][5], but the number of consumers, i.e. the size of

* Corresponding author.

V. Khachidze et al. (Eds.): iCETS 2012, CCIS 332, pp. 122–134, 2012.

network, is another factor in the presence of network externality (Jing, 2000). Bundling, versioning and pricing strategies can be influenced by the network effect. For example, the mixed bundling strategy is the best choice for a firm without network externality; however, the pure bundling strategy is found to be better with network externality (Prasad 2010)[19]. Piracy, a serious threat to firms, can be moderately tolerated (Haruvy et al. 2004)[10], and even increase the firm's profit under some special conditions with network externality (Conner and Rumelt,1991)[7], especially if the low-quality version is illegally duplicated (Stephen,2003)[22]. Versioning is widely practiced in selling information products, and is more useful when there is network externality in the market (Baake 2001). Generally, the firm develops two versions of a product, and the low quality product is sold at a low price or even for free, in order to attract people who, in turn, could potentially purchase the higher-quality product, i.e. expand the size of its network, thereby earning the firm more profit than if it were to sell one single version (Ernan, 1998, Jing, 2003, 2007) [8,12,13]. In short, this stream of research shows that the quantity of consumers can be enlarged with network externality and the firm can benefit from the network effect.

Unlike the above research, this paper focuses primarily on the impact of the network effect on sale channel model of information products. It explores which of the three channel models, direct sale, retailing marketing or dual channel, is preferable for information products suppliers when network externality is considered.

Additional research has been conducted on the choice of sale channel of physical products. The supplier generally sells its product through retailers and distributors, and more suppliers are inclined toward direct sale due to the rapid adoption of e-commerce technology in business. Chiang (2003) analyzes the impact of direct sale model on the supplier and retailer's profit and shows that the direct channel can induce the retailer to lower the price, which, in turn, spurs demand in the retailing channel [6]. The supplier is more profitable, even if no sales occur in the direct channel. Yan (2008) draws a similar conclusion that although the direct sale channel can conflict with retailing marketing, it can promote the retailer to improve service quality and induce the supplier to lower its wholesale price, thereby increasing product sales, and thus improve profits [24]. Yan (2010) develops the brand differentiation and revenue-sharing strategy so as to eliminate channel conflict and coordinate the supply chain [25]. Cai (2010) studies more complex channel structures, and shows that the choice of channel model depends on product demand, channel operating cost and channel substitutability [4]. This type of research shows that the direct sale channel is gradually combined with the traditional retailing marketing channel in selling physical products (Tsay 2004, Yao 2005)[23,26]. However, when it comes to information products, one must consider which kind of channel model is most appropriate.

Khouja (2010) investigates the impact of digital distribution channel on the information goods industry, and shows that both direct channel and retailing marketing have their respective pros and cons. The dual distribution channel is the most profitable and suffers the least from piracy [16]. Guo (2011) established the conditions under which a publisher would sell only printed books (p-books), only e-books, and both. Choice of sale channels was determined by the reader acceptance of e-book, the wholesale price of the print-book, and the publisher's power of negotiation with bookstores [9].

Bonwoo (2011) analyzed several factors that affect an airline's decision to sell tickets[1] through an Online Travel Agency (OTA) platform or solely through their own websites, and found that airlines are less likely to use OTA platforms if they have many loyal consumers and the OTA platforms are highly competitive [3].

The previous researchers did not consider the impact of network externality on the selection of sale channels. However, inherent characteristics in many information products such as software play an important role in increasing the consumer's valuation for the product, and in attracting more and more people to consume. So how will one choose the appropriate sale channel for the information products firm under new considerations? The paper will extend this research based on network externality.

The rest of this paper is organized as follows. In section 2, we introduce the model and define network externality. Sections 3 and 4 consider the optimal pricing and versioning strategy in the presence of network externality when the product is sold via retailing channel and dual channel, respectively. In section 4, we derive the best sale channel model for the supplier. Finally, conclusions are presented in section 5.

2 Problem Specifications

When network externality effect is considered, the consumer purchases the product with quality x in a network size Q at a price p; he can obtain the net utility $(v+\gamma Q)x-p$, in which v denotes the consumer's valuation for the product with standard quality, vx is the product's "network-independent" or standalone value, and γQx is the "network-generated" value. Most models consider the network effects to be linear in the size of the user base[2] (Baake 2001, Jing 2003, 2007, Prasad 2010) [1,12,13,19]. Here, Q is the expected number of consumers who consume the product, and γ is the coefficient that denotes the degree of effect of network externalities on a consumer's valuation by consuming the product, also explained as the marginal value derived from network effect (Kim 2007) [17]. Particularly, $\gamma=0$ implies that there is no network externality; therefore, for a given product, large network size Q means that the consumer is more willing to buy the product with a higher price when network intensity is positive. In practice, the retailer often offers a low-quality version charged at a lower price in order to increase the network size, and in turn obtains more profit from a high-quality version because of the network externality effect.

The retailer offers two versions of information products with low-quality x_l at a price p_l and high-quality x_h at a price p_h ($x_l < x_h$). By offering the product, the retailer invokes retailing cost given by $bx_h^2/2$, where b is a retailer-specific cost coef-

---

[1] Presently, more and more tickets are offered in not paper format, but in digital form. These are easily distributed via multi-channel. However, in the strict sense, they do not belong to the category of information products, because they possess no duplicability.

[2] However, most researches neglect the situation that network-generated value relates to quality.

ficient. It should be noticed that the cost is only relevant to high-quality x_h. A high-quality information product can be easily degraded to a lower quality version by means of disabling a subset of functions, and the degradation cost is negligible.

v is assumed to have a distribution with a probability density function $f(\cdot)$ and a cumulative distribution function $F(\cdot)$. Denote v_1 to be the consumer indifference between purchasing x_l and making no purchase, and v_2 to be the consumer indifferent between purchasing x_h and x_l. We thus have $v_2 x_l + \gamma Q x_l - p_l = v_2 x_h + \gamma Q x_h - p_h$ and $v_1 x_l + \gamma Q x_l - p_l = 0$, where Q is the total expected sale of all products.

It is easily concluded that consumers are divided into two groups: those with valuation in $[v_2, 1]$ will purchase x_h, and those in $[v_1, v_2)$ will purchase x_l.

Define q_1 and q_2 as the quantity of consumers purchasing x_h and x_l, respectively. q_1 and q_2 are given by the following equations, in which Q is determined by the equation $Q = q_1 + q_2 = 1 - F(\frac{p_l}{x_l} - \gamma Q)$.

$$\begin{cases} q_1 = \mathrm{P}\{v \ge v_2\} = 1 - F\left(\dfrac{p_h - p_l}{x_h - x_l} - \gamma Q\right) \\ q_2 = \mathrm{P}\{v_1 \le v \le v_2\} = F\left(\dfrac{p_h - p_l}{x_h - x_l} - \gamma Q\right) - F\left(\dfrac{p_l}{x_l} - \gamma Q\right) \end{cases} \tag{1}$$

3 Retailing Channel Based on Fixed-Fee Policy

In the case of fixed-fee policy, the retailer is authorized to sell the product with quality x_h, charged with a fixed cost R. The fixed fee is independent of the sale volume. Once the retailer obtains the copyright from the supplier, he can produce different versions of information products by restricting its function, and the versioning cost is almost zero. For analytical convenience, the quality of high-quality version is assumed to be w times that of the low-quality version, i.e. $x_h = w x_l$, where $w \ge 1$. Our model is a Stackelberg game where the manufacturer is the leader and retailer is the follower, and they both have some information about the consumer demand, the distribution of WTP, the retailer's cost coefficient, etc.

The profit of supplier and retailer is written as Π_m and Π_r. $\Pi_m = R \cdot x_h - C$, $\Pi_r = q_1 \cdot p_h + q_2 \cdot p_l - b x_h^2 / 2 - R \cdot x_h$. For the product supplier, the fixed production cost C is sunk; hence, profit maximization is equivalent to revenue maximization.

It is assumed that v is uniformly distributed on $[0,1]$. The profit function based on fixed-fee policy can be solved by applying the first order optimal condition. Results are presented in Table 1.

Table 1. Solution under retailing marketing based on fixed-fee policy

	$\gamma < 0.5$ & $w \le \frac{2-3\gamma+\gamma^2}{\gamma+\gamma^2}$	$\gamma \ge 0.5$ or $w \ge \frac{2-3\gamma+\gamma^2}{\gamma+\gamma^2}$
The supplier's profit	$\frac{1}{4b(4\gamma-4+\gamma^2(w-1))^2}$	$\frac{(w(1+\gamma)^2-(1-\gamma)^2)^2}{64bw^2}$
The retailer's profit	$\frac{1}{8b(4\gamma-4+\gamma^2(w-1))^2}$	$\frac{(w(1+\gamma)^2-(1-\gamma)^2)^2}{128bw^2}$
The lower quality	$\frac{1}{8b(1-\gamma)+2b\gamma^2(1-w)}$	$\frac{(1+\gamma)^2w-(1-\gamma)^2}{8bw^2}$
The higher quality	$\frac{w}{8b(1-\gamma)+2b\gamma^2(1-w)}$	$\frac{(1+\gamma)^2w-(1-\gamma)^2}{8bw}$
The low-quality price	$\frac{2-(1+w)\gamma}{2bw(w\gamma^2-(\gamma+2)^2)^2}$	$\frac{\gamma((1+\gamma)^2w-(1-\gamma)^2)}{8bw^2}$
The high-quality price	$\frac{1-\gamma}{b(w\gamma^2-(\gamma+2)^2)^2}$	$\frac{(w(1+\gamma)+\gamma-1)\cdot((1+\gamma)^2w-(1-\gamma)^2)}{16bw^2}$
The quantity of consumer purchasing x_h	$\frac{2-\gamma}{4-4\gamma-\gamma^2(w-1)}$	$\frac{1+\gamma}{2}$
The quantity of consumer purchasing x_l	$\frac{\gamma w}{4-4\gamma-\gamma^2(w-1)}$	$\frac{1-\gamma}{2}$

3.1 The Impact of Network Externality on Profit

Based on above solution, the impact of network externality and quality difference between high-quality and low-quality versions on the supplier and retailer's profit is shown as Figure 1 and Figure 2 (setting $b=1$). The left graph and right graph in Figure 2 show the change of profit when quality difference value and network externality index are fixed to be $w=5$ and $\gamma=0.5$, respectively. It can be easily observed that the profit increases as network externality intensifies. Particularly, the supplier and retailer can maximize their profits as the quality difference approaches infinity, i.e. $w \to \infty$. This shows that versioning is a preferable strategy in the presence of network externality; furthermore, the bigger the difference in quality between two versions, the more profitable both supplier and retailer can be. Therefore, the firm should sell two versions of the product with greater vertical differentiation, rather than one single version.

When there is no network externality, the demand for low-quality version is almost zero, and therefore the firm should sell one single version without network externality.

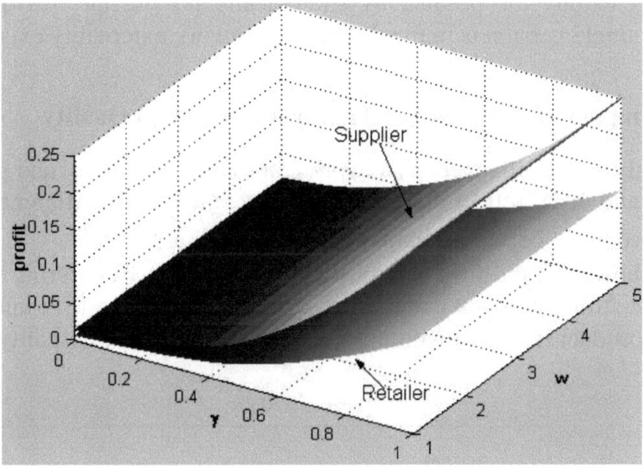

Fig. 1. The supplier and retailer's profit[3]

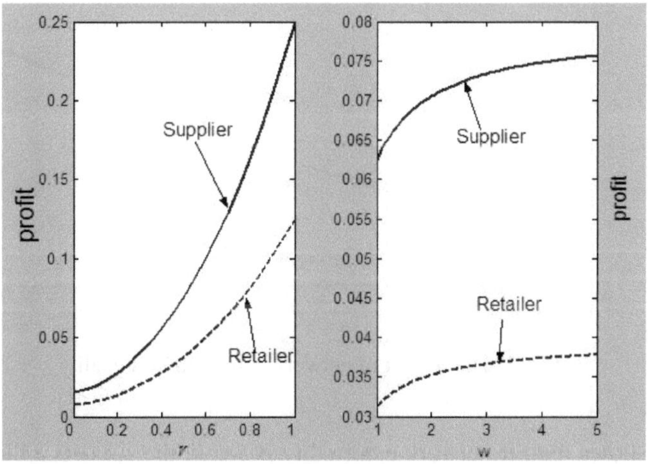

Fig. 2. The supplier and retailer's profit when setting $w = 5$ or $\gamma = 0.5$[4]

[3] In contrast with profit's change with γ, the profit increases moderately with w.

[4] When the parameters w and γ are assigned other values, the profit curve exhibits the same shape as the case when $w = 5$ or $\gamma = 0.5$.

Based on the analysis above, we can derive the optimal versioning strategy with network externality. The corollary 1 can be followed.

Corollary 1. When the sale cost is relevant with quality for an information products firm, network externality impacts the versioning strategy. The firm can be more profitable by offering two versions of products with great difference in quality, and attract all customers to buy the product by strategically pricing the low-quality product, whereas one single version is optimal when no network externality exists.

3.2 The Impact of Network Externality on Price and Quality

Next, we analyze the influence of network externality on quality and price, as shown in Figures 3 and 4. To reflect the change with γ, the quality difference between two versions of products, i.e. w, remains constant, equaling 5.

Figure 3 shows that the firm can attract the consumers by offering the low quality product if the strong network externality is present, while the firm must resort to the high quality product in order to attract consumers if network externality is weak.

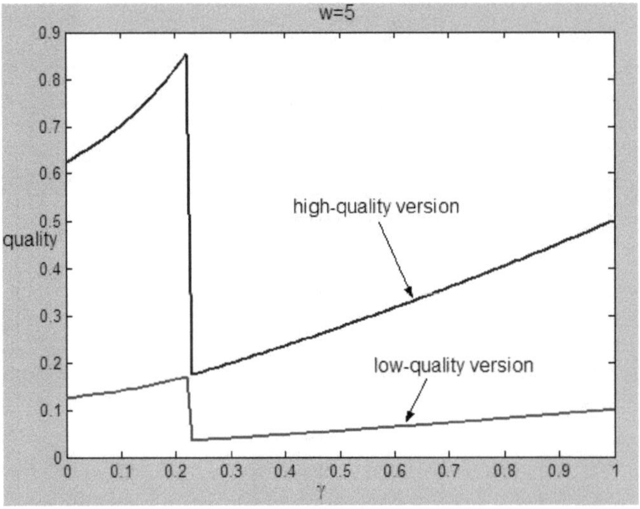

Fig. 3. The impact of network externality on quality

Figure 4 shows that, if network externality is weak, there exists a threshold γ^*, below which the optimal price of low-quality product decreases with network externality, and above which the optimal price increases with network externality. However, the optimal price of the high-quality product increases monotonically with network externality.

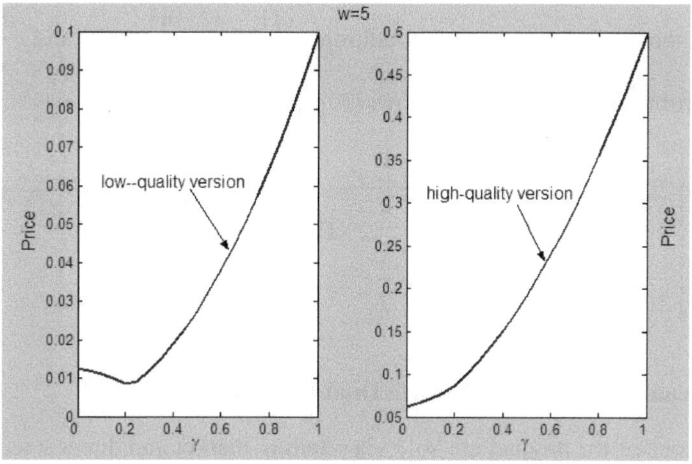

Fig. 4. The impact of network externality on price

4 Dual Channel Based on Fixed-Fee Policy

When the dual channel is used to sell information products, the supplier can distribute its product through both retailing market and direct sale. Two versions of the product (vertical differentiation) are offered, and the demand of high-quality and low-quality is denoted as q_1 and q_2, respectively.

It is assumed that when information products are sold via dual channel, the proportion of consumers who will prefer retailing market is θ. The supplier and retailer's sale cost coefficients are denoted as b_1 and b_2, respectively. Considering 3 types of sale mode, this section aims to determine the most preferable model for a supplier. Scenario 1 involves one single version via dual channel; Scenario 2 provides two versions via dual channel; Scenario 3 involves one version via direct sale, and another version via retailing.

4.1 Scenario 1: One Single Version via Dual Channel

One single-version product is sold via dual channel. It assumes that the price is decided by the retailer. The demand from the direct sale channel and retailing channel are given by $q_d = \dfrac{\theta(1-t)}{1-\gamma}$ and $q_r = \dfrac{(1-\theta)(1-t)}{1-\gamma}$, where $t = \dfrac{p}{x}$. The supplier and retailer's profit functions can be denoted as Π_m and Π_r, respectively, in which x and p are determined by the retailer, and R is determined by the supplier.

$$\begin{cases} \Pi_m = q_d \cdot p - b_1 x^2 / 2 + R \cdot x \\ \Pi_r = q_r \cdot p - b_2 x^2 / 2 - R \cdot x \end{cases} \tag{2}$$

Applying the first order optimal condition, $\frac{\partial \Pi_r}{\partial x}=0$, $\frac{\partial \Pi_r}{\partial p}=0$ and $\frac{\partial \Pi_m}{\partial R}=0$, the optimal profit can be derived as follows.

$$\Pi_m^* = \begin{cases} \dfrac{1}{32(2b_1+b_2)(1-\gamma)^2} & \gamma \le \dfrac{1}{2} \\ \dfrac{\gamma^2}{2(2b_1+b_2)} & \gamma > \dfrac{1}{2} \end{cases}, \quad \Pi_r^* = \begin{cases} \dfrac{b_1}{32(2b_1+b_2)^2(1-\gamma)^2} & \gamma \le \dfrac{1}{2} \\ \dfrac{b_1\gamma^2}{2(2b_1+b_2)^2} & \gamma > \dfrac{1}{2} \end{cases}$$

4.2 Scenario 2: Two Versions via Dual Channel

Two versions of the product are sold via retailing market and direct sale, in which the pricing decision of two versions of products is made by the retailer. The supplier and retailer's profit can be derived as follows. Based on equation 1, the demand of high-quality version, q_1, is $\frac{\gamma(1-t_l)}{1-\gamma}-\frac{t_h w-t_l}{w-1}+1$, and the demand of the low-quality version, q_2, is $\frac{t_h w-t_l}{w-1}-t_l$, where $t_h=\frac{p_h}{x_h}$, $t_l=\frac{p_l}{x_l}$. The supplier and retailer's profit functions can be denoted as per equation (3).

$$\begin{cases} \Pi_m = (1-\theta)(q_1 \cdot p_h + q_2 \cdot p_l) - b_1 x_h^2/2 + R \cdot x_h \\ \Pi_r = \theta(q_1 \cdot p_h + q_2 \cdot p_l) - b_2 x_h^2/2 - R \cdot x_h \end{cases} \tag{3}$$

The optimal profit can be derived as follows by applying the first order optimal condition.

$$\Pi_m^* = \begin{cases} \dfrac{1}{2(2b_1+b_2)(4\gamma-4+\gamma^2(w-1))^2} & \gamma<\dfrac{1}{2} \text{ and } 1<w\le \dfrac{2-3\gamma+\gamma^2}{\gamma+\gamma^2} \\ \dfrac{(\gamma^2(w-1)+2\gamma(w+1)+w-1)^2}{32w^2(2b_1+b_2)} & otherwise \end{cases},$$

$$\Pi_r^* = \begin{cases} \dfrac{b_1}{2(2b_1+b_2)^2(4\gamma-4+\gamma^2(w-1))^2} & \gamma<\dfrac{1}{2} \text{ and } 1<w\le \dfrac{2-3\gamma+\gamma^2}{\gamma+\gamma^2} \\ \dfrac{b_2(\gamma^2(w-1)+2\gamma(w+1)+w-1)^2}{32w^2(2b_1+b_2)^2} & otherwise \end{cases}$$

By comparing the profit of scenarios 1 and 2 and the case when the product is sold by the retailing channel, the corollary 2 can be derived.

Corollary 2. When the dual channel is applied, versioning is more profitable than no version strategy for suppliers, and the dual channel is inferior to retailing regardless of application of a versioning strategy.

4.3 Scenario 3: High-Quality via Direct Sale, Low-Quality via Retailing

The supplier sells its two versions of the product via dual channel, in which the high-quality version is distributed via the direct sale channel, and the low-quality version is distributed via the retailing channel.

$$\begin{cases} \Pi_m = -\dfrac{b_1 x_h^{\,2}}{2} + q_1 t_h x_h + R x_l \\ \Pi_r = -\dfrac{b_2 x_l^{\,2}}{2} + q_2 t_l x_l - R x_l \end{cases} \tag{4}$$

$$\Pi_m^* = \begin{cases} \dfrac{((w-1)w)^2}{2(2b_1 + b_2 w^2)(1-\gamma)^2 (3-4w+\gamma(2w-1))^2} & w \geq \dfrac{1-3\gamma+\gamma^2}{1-4\gamma+2\gamma^2} \text{ and } \gamma < \dfrac{2-\sqrt{2}}{2} \\ \dfrac{\left((w-1)(1+\gamma^2)+2\gamma(w+1)\right)^2}{32(2b_1 + b_2 w^2)} & \text{otherwise} \end{cases}$$

$$\Pi_r^* = \begin{cases} \dfrac{b_1 ((w-1)w)^2}{2(2b_1 + b_2 w^2)^2 (1-\gamma)^2 (3-4w+\gamma(2w-1))^2} & w \geq \dfrac{1-3\gamma+\gamma^2}{1-4\gamma+2\gamma^2} \text{ and } \gamma < \dfrac{2-\sqrt{2}}{2} \\ \dfrac{b_1 \left((w-1)(1+\gamma^2)+2\gamma(w+1)\right)^2}{32(2b_1 + b_2 w^2)^2} & \text{otherwise} \end{cases}$$

Comparing scenarios 2 and 3, the corollary 3 follows.

Corollary 3. When the supplier sells its product via the direct sale channel and the retailing market concurrently, the one single version model is inferior to versioning strategy. The dual channel is the best sale model, where the high-quality version is sold via the direct sale channel and the low-quality version is sold via the retailing channel.

5 Discussions and Conclusion

Based on the above analysis, network externality can influence the versioning strategy and sale channel model; therefore, information products firms should select the most profitable sale channel for selling products. As for versioning strategy, those products with less or no network externality should be sold in only one single version, whereas those with strong network externality should be offered in two versions. Similar conclusions to those of the present research are found in other studies (Jing 2003, 2007). As stated by Jing's research (Jing, 2007), the low-end product is used primarily to expand network size, and the high-end product is the primary source of profit [13]. However, Shivendu's research presented a different conclusion (Shivendu 2012), which showed that presence of network effect makes versioning strategy less likely to be optimal for the information products provider if there is a threat of piracy [21]. In his research, the market consists of two types of consumers: some high type consumers with a taste parameter and some low type consumers with a taste parameter. However, in this paper, we assume the consumers have no preference for the high-end version or low-end version, and they buy the product from which the maximum surplus can be derived.

Presently, in practice, the versioning strategy is often applied. Many information products firms, especially software vendors, generally offer a free product version in order to attract more consumers to the network, and then sell a high-quality version to pursue high returns from loyal consumers when the network size has expanded.

To expand the network size, information product content suppliers must always invest much in marketing. This implies a larger sale cost coefficient, i.e. b. It is difficult to achieve high market coverage for many software developers to bypass the retailer or intermediary. Meanwhile, the retailers generally focus on potential consumers in that they know more about the consumers' preference and attitude toward new products; therefore, in real practice, retailing channel is still a first priority in selling its product for the supplier. As depicted in Corollary 3, the supplier benefits mainly from direct channel while expanding the product network through a retailing channel. Network externality returns more profit for information products in specific sale channel models; however, generally the retailer is reluctant to sell only the low-quality version. Especially in the case of retailers with more power of negotiation with suppliers, they may require selling the high-quality products via retailing channel.

For analytic convenience, the paper simulates network externality in a simplified linear form, denoted by γQ. Most researches assume that the consumer's net utility is increasing linearly with the network size Q, however, a concave relationship would be more realistic. Additionally, it should be noted that there is difficulty in measuring network effect, and the issue of whether there is a better expression should be addressed. Do the conclusions derived still hold when other function forms are applied, especially if the two-sided network externality is considered (Rochet 2004) [20]? In addition, the consumer's valuation for the product is uniformly distributed, and therefore other distribution functions will probably draw different conclusions. These issues deserve extended research.

Acknowledgments. The work was supported by the National Science Fund for Distinguished Young Scholars of China (Grant No. 70925005).

References

1. Baake, P., Boom, A.: Vertical product differentiation, network externality, and compatibility decisions. International Journal of Industrial Organization 19, 267–284 (2001)
2. Bhargava, H.K., Choudhary, V.: Information goods and vertical differentiation. Journal of Management Information Systems 18(2), 89–106 (2001)
3. Bonwoo, K., Benny, M., Peter, O.: Online distribution of airline tickets: Should airlines adopt a single or a multi-channel approach? Tourism Management 32, 69–74 (2011)
4. Cai, G.: Channel selection and coordination in dual-channel supply chains. Journal of Retailing 86(1), 22–36 (2010)
5. Chen, Y., Seshadri, S.: Product Development and Pricing Strategy for Information Goods Under Heterogeneous Outside Opportunities. Information Systems Research 18(2), 150–172 (2007)
6. Chiang, W.K., Chhajed, D., Hess, J.D.: Direct marketing, indirect profits: a strategic analysis of dual-channel supply-chain design. Management Science 49(1), 1–20 (2003)
7. Conner, K.R., Rumelt, R.P.: Software piracy: An analysis of protection strategies. Management Science 37, 125–139 (1991)
8. Ernan, H., Prasad, A.: Optimal product strategies in the presence of network externalities. Information Economics and Policy 10, 489–499 (1998)
9. Guo, W.H., Cheng, T.C., Wang, S.Y.: Electronic books: To 'E' or not to 'E': A strategic analysis of distribution channel choices of publishers. International Journal of Production Economics 129(2), 338–346 (2011)
10. Haruvy, E., Mahajan, V., Prasad, A.: The effect of piracy on the market penetration of subscription software. Journal of Business 77, 81–107 (2004)
11. Jing, B.: Versioning information goods with network externality. In: Proceeding ICIS 2000 Proceedings of the Twenty First International Conference on Information Systems (2000)
12. Jing, B.: Market Segmentation for Information Goods with Network Externalities. Working paper, New York, p. 3 (2003)
13. Jing, B.: Network externalities and market segmentation in a monopoly. Economics Letters 95, 7–13 (2007)
14. Kacen, J., Hess, C.W.K.: Bricks or Clicks? Consumer attitudes toward traditional stores and online stores. Working paper, University of Illinois, Champaign, IL (2002)
15. Katz, M.L., Shapiro, C.: Network Externalities, Competition, and Compatibility. The American Economic Review 75(3), 424–440 (1985)
16. Khouja, M., Wang, Y.: The impact of digital channel distribution on the experience goods industry. European Journal of Operational Research 207(1), 481–491 (2010)
17. Kim, E., Lee, B.: An economic analysis of customer selection and leveraging strategies in a market where network externalities exist. Decision Support Systems 44, 124–134 (2007)
18. Meagher, K., Teo, E.G.S.: Two-part tariffs in the online gaming industry: The role of creative destruction and network externalities. Information Economics and Policy 17, 457–470 (2005)
19. Prasad, A., Venkatesh, R., Vijay, M.: Optimal Bundling of Technological Products with Network Externality. Management Science 56(12), 2224–2236 (2010)
20. Rochet, J.C., Tirole, J.: Two-sided markets: An overview. Working paper, IDEI University of Toulouse, France (2004)
21. Shivendu, S., Zhang, Z.: Versioning Strategy of Information Goods with Network Externality in the Presence of Piracy. In: 45th Hawaii International Conference on System Sciences (2012)

22. Stephen, P.K., Lampe, R.: Network externalities, price discrimination and profitable piracy. Information Economics and Policy 15(3), 271–290 (2003)
23. Tsay, A.A., Agrawal, N.: Channel Conflict and Coordination in the E-Commerce Age. Production and Operations Management 13(1), 93–110 (2004)
24. Yan, R.: Profit sharing and firm performance in the manufacturer-retailer dual-channel supply chain. Electronic Commerce Research 8(3), 155–172 (2008)
25. Yan, R.: Product brand differentiation and dual-channel store performances of a multi-channel retailer. European Journal of Marketing 44(5), 672–692 (2010)
26. Yao, D.Q., Liu, J.J.: Competitive pricing of mixed retail and e-tail distribution channels. Omega 33, 235–247 (2005)

Impact of IT Service Provider's Expertise and Customer's Sociability on Continuous Intention to Use

Jungwoo Lee, Yongki Park, and Junbeom Jang

Graduate School of Information, Yonsei University
Engineering Research Park B187N, 50 Yonsei-ro,
Seodaemun-gu, Seoul, 120-749, Republic of Korea
pykasd@gmail.com

Abstract. Relationship marketing, which focuses on the relationship with the customers, is considered important in the field of service marketing. This research explores the relations of customers' perceived expertise of service provider and customer's sociability, and how these factors are related to the intention to use. Relationship quality is set as a mediating variable. The relationship quality is measured by trust and commitment. Also, the relationship between trust and commitment is measured. The result of the analysis of survey data shows that, expertise and sociability factors have positive effects on relationship quality. Also, the two factors of relationship quality, trust and commitment, have positive effects on the intention to use. In addition, trust is positively related to commitment. In conclusion, service provider's expertise and customers' sociability are the factors of IT service's success.

Keywords: Provider expertise, Sociability, Marketing, Relationship marketing, IT service, Relationship quality, Continuous intention to use.

1 Introduction

Existing marketing for many and unspecified persons is successful as regards mass production activity, but reveals the critical point of fulfillment of individual desire. Firms come into request active attitude to recognize customer's potential requirements.

Particularly, development of information technology makes one-to-one marketing possible, taking advantage of customer information. Relationship marketing is to encourage customers to continue to use particular services, keeping relationships with customers in the long-term. Firms can reduce costs of customer acquisition and boost revenue [1], [2]. Relationship marketing has originally developed such that it focuses on the relationship between customer and salesperson in retail. With the development of information technology, its importance increased in the field of IT services.

When customers perceived service provider expertise highly, this led to a tendency to rely on the service provider [3]. Since highly sociable customers value social interaction, they can refer to the requirements of individuals and companies actively.

V. Khachidze et al. (Eds.): iCETS 2012, CCIS 332, pp. 135–146, 2012.

Depending on the service provider's intimation, difference in terms of implementation can be seen [4]. The implementation of deliverables in terms of degree of difference can be seen. A sense of closeness felt by the service provider produces definite results, reflecting external parts. Customers that have taken high quality outputs prefer to use existing services rather than service exchange.

In IT service, relationships with customers are the critical key to the success of the service [5]. In the case of IT outsourcing, the service provider must understand customer's task ideally and reflect the opinions and requirements that the customer needs. As the relationship extends between customers and the service provider, deduction and reflection show diversity [6].

This study developed a theoretical model from extant literature review concerning the provider's expertise and customer sociability onto continuous intention to use via relationship quality in IT service. Measures of these components were adopted from previous studies and were validated. Using these measures, an empirical test was conducted using 311 data solicited from employees of two electronic firms that experienced outsourcing from the global IT outsourcing company via partial least squares (PLS) modeling.

2 Literature Review and Hypotheses

2.1 Service Provider's Expertise

In business, expertise is a special knowledge of the service provider [7]. This knowledge is the ability to deliver the solution of needs to the customer and to provide customized service and high values. Thus, service providers should have a high level of expertise by holding accurate and up to date knowledge [8].

The service provider's knowledge effects the perception of the service provider's expertise by customers [8]. If the customer perceives highly the service provider's expertise, he or she relies on the service provider and uses the service continuously [3].

Highly perceived service provider's expertise positively impacts to trust [9]. Because service provider's expertise reflects the related competencies for service, when the customer perceives highly the provider's expertise, the customer can trust the service provider more and more [3]. The relationship between perceived service provider's expertise and commitment was revealed in Spake and Megehee's (2010) study. By applying them to IT services, we hypothesize the following.

H1: Perceived IT service provider's expertise is positively associated with trust.
H2: Perceived IT service provider's expertise is positively associated with commitment.

2.2 Sociability

Sociability is the tendency to prefer being with someone else rather than being alone [10]. Social benefits through social relations are the major result [11], and are a major factor in evaluating how successful services are as regards marketing [12].

Sociability shows differences in personality. Typically, people with high sociability are extroverts. Extroverts tend to communicate with other people consistently, considering the enjoyment of social activities as one of the factors of happiness. Contrastively, low-sociability people, introverts, prefer to be alone and without social activities [13]. They are characterized as quiet individuals who prefer private activity such as reading books. They show low preference for socializing with people, except with those they know intimately [14].

Depending on the nature of the individual differences, personality affects social relationship building because the extent of demands on social relationships appears differently [15]. As the customer's sociability is higher, extent of trust and commitment will be higher [4]. In other words, high-sociability customers have high expectations of the service provider and can build relationships in a short period of time. Based on these backgrounds, we hypothesized that customer sociability influences relationship quality (trust, commitment) with IT service provider.

H3: Customer's sociability is positively associated with trust.
H4: Customer's sociability is positively associated with commitment.

2.3 Relationship Quality

In relationship marketing research, relationship quality is defined as the level to which consumers rely on the service provider's integrity and have confidence in their future performance [16]. Constructs in relationship quality are high-level structures that make up different kinds of features, of which trust and commitment have been studied as the most important factors that describe relationship quality [17], [18], [19].

In the field of marketing research, trust is an essential component for successful partnership [20], [21]. High trust can help success in relationship marketing and lead to positive effects such as the word-of-mouth effect. In contrast, low trust brings about lethargic communication with others. Therefore, the trust that the customer places in the service provider is a main concern to marketers and managers in charge of relationships with customers [22].

Prior literature notes that commitment is defined as psychological attachment concerning the future welfare of the organization, and an enduring desire to maintain a valued relationship [14], [18], [19], [20], [21], [23], [24], [25]. Commitment is essential to maintaining a relationship and is core of relationships. Customer's commitment provokes service provider's positive attitude. It has an effect on repurchase intention in service.

Bove and Mitzifiris(2007) assert that trust is associated with commitment in relationships; Gabarino and Johnson(1999) noted that trust and commitment act as mediators for successful relationship exchange. In the case of the IT service sector, improvement of relationship quality has been recognized as an important issue in attracting new customers and retaining existing customers [6] [26]. In this article, we hypothesize as follows for analyzing the correlation between trust and commitment in IT service.

H5: Trust is positively associated with commitment.

2.4 Continuous Intention to Use

The continuous intention to use is an indicator of services that show whether a customer will use consistently. This is closely related with service provider's willpower to maintain the relationship with customers [27]. Service providers usually take actions that can be beneficial to the organization's performance; in some way, this action can bring about positive effects such as customer referrals, relational continuity, and customer satisfaction [25], [28].

Formulating trust between customers and service providers leads to word-of-mouth effect, and it becomes a criterion for continuous adoption decision [29], [30]. Also, service providers build economic processes that make possible increased productivity, and execute diverse strategies for customer's purchase. Through these efforts, customers trust that quality and pricing are adequate criteria to use the service continuously [31]. Formed commitment, according to trust, improves loyalty level [21]. Customer's commitment can be considered a critical factor in profits to a corporation. We hypothesize that both components (trust, commitment) and continuous intention to use a service enter into a relation.

H6: Trust is positively associated with continuous intention to use.
H7: Commitment is positively associated with continuous intention to use.

Through the above hypotheses, Fig. 1. presents a summary of all the hypothesized relationships between service provider's expertise, sociability and the mediation of relationship quality on continuous intention to use for IT service.

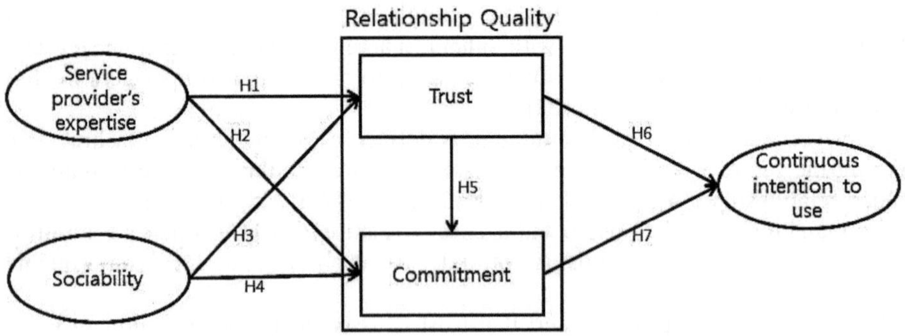

Fig. 1. Research Model

3 Research Method

3.1 Sample and Data Collection

The data were collected through questionnaires distributed to the electronic companies A and B, the latter having experienced outsourcing from the global IT outsourcing company A. The survey was conducted from December 2010 to February 2011. A total of 321 responses were received for a response rate of 49.4%. Eliminating outliers and unsuitable data, 311 data were analyzed. Of all the respondents who filled out the questionnaires, 36.0% were from R&D department, 34.1% purchasing/production/quality department, 10.3% marketing/sales department, 10% human resources/general affairs department, 7.1% planning/financial department and 2.6% IT/innovation department. Those who had work experience less than 5 years were 52.1%, 5-10 years 29.6%, and over 11 years 18.3%.

3.2 Operational Definition

The survey instruments are developed by identifying appropriate measurements from comprehensive literature review. Most of the survey instruments are adapted from the existing measures to the research context, and few are developed by converting appropriate definitions of the construct into a questionnaire format. Each item is then measured on a five-point Likert scale from 'strongly disagree' to 'strongly agree'. All the measures used in this study are shown in Table 1.

First, the service provider's expertise is the independent variable, defined to the level of customer's measurement concerning service provider's competence. Based on Spake and Megehee's study (2010), it was measured with three items. Another independent variable, customer's sociability is defined as tendency to affiliate with others and to prefer being with others over remaining alone; measurements were with five items from same researcher study. Second, relationship quality is based on Sharma and Patterson's study (1999); four items of trust and five items of commitment were used for measuring. Lastly, continuous intention to use is defined as continuous use of the services, and was measured with three items from Wang's study (2010). All measurements are explained Table 1.

4 Data Analysis and Results

This study uses Partial Least Squares (PLS) to examine the proposed model and its hypotheses. PLS is used because it requires minimal demands on sample size in order to validate a model compared to other SEM techniques, and it also places minimal restrictions on measurement scales and residual distributions [33]. Further, PLS is better suited for explaining complex relationships, as it avoids two serious problems: inadmissible solutions and factor indeterminacy [34].

Table 1. Measurement

Variable	Measurement		Literature
Service provider's expertise	EXP1 EXP2 EXP3	IT service provider possesses specialized knowledge IT service provider possesses extensive, broad knowledge IT service provider is experienced in solving problems like mine	[4]
Customer's sociability	SOC1 SOC2 SOC3 SOC4 SOC5	I like to be with other people I prefer working with others than working alone I enjoy social gatherings just to be with people I value having relationships with other people I generally view myself as a person who is interested in establishing relationships with others	
Trust	TRS1 TRS2 TRS3 TRS4	I have confidence in IT service provider. I trust whatever the IT service provider says is proper. IT service provider is trustworthy. IT service provider can be relied on to keep his/her promises.	[32]
Commitment	CMM1 CMM2 CMM3 CMM4 CMM5	I am very committed to the relationship with IT service provider The relationship between IT service providers to me is very important. I intend to maintain my relationship indefinitely. I make an effort to consider IT service provider. I should put maximum effort into maintaining my relationship with IT service provider.	
Continuous intention to use	CIU1 CIU2 CIU3	I intend to continue using IT service rather than discontinue using it. My intentions are to continue using IT service than use any alternative means. If I could, I would like to continue using IT service as much as possible.	[30]

4.1 Measurement Model

Internal consistency in this study is investigated by using Cronbach's α in order to assess the reliability of all the constructs. The constructs in the proposed model are above the 0.7 threshold, indicating a high reliability of items used for each construct. Cronbach's α ranges from 0.700 (Continuous intention to use) to 0.916 (Trust).

Convergent validity in this study is assessed by evaluating the composite reliability and the average variance extracted (AVE) from the measures. Table 4 shows that composite reliability values of the measures range from 0.833 to 0.943 and AVE ranges from 0.626 to 0.846. Both the composite reliability and AVE are above the threshold value of 0.7 and 0.5 respectively, meeting the criteria of convergent validity.

Discriminant validity is assessed by examining the square root of the average variance extracted as recommended by Fornell and Larcker [35]. Table 2 shows that the square root of AVE for each construct is greater than the correlations between it and all other constructs. Moreover, all the constructs are found to have a stronger correlation with their own measures than to those of others. This represents the appropriate assessment of discriminant validity.

4.2 Testing the Model

Fig. 2 represents the results obtained from PLS analysis. The Squared Multiple Correlation (similar to R^2 in regression analysis) of 0.463 indicates that the model explains a substantial amount of variance for continuous intention to use. As shown, the relationship between service provider's expertise and trust (β=0.588) is statistically significant ($p<0.01$), and also service provider's expertise is found to have a positive impact on commitment (β=0.308, $p<0.01$), supporting the H1 and H2.

Sociability is found to be statistically significant with all variables of relationship quality, trust (β=0.164, $p<0.05$) and commitment (β=0.358, $p<0.01$), thus supporting H3 and H4. Trust is found to have a statistically significant relationship with commitment (β=0.203, $p<0.01$), supporting H5.

The links between continuous intention to use and relationship quality, i.e. trust (β=0.261, $p<0.01$) and commitment (β=0.505, $p<0.01$), are statistically significant, offering evidence for H6 and H7. This shows that relationship quality has a great influence on continuous intention to use. This result was explained in Tab. 4 and Fig. 2.

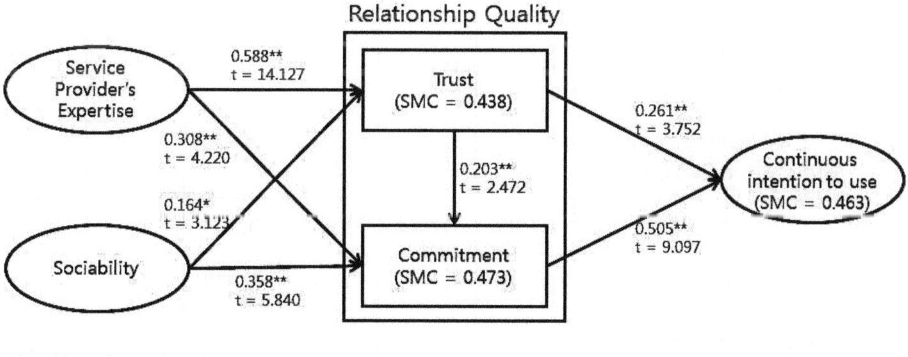

*p<0.05; **p<0.01; ***p<0.001

SMC = Squared Multiple Correlation

Fig. 2. Result of path analysis

Table 2. Measurement model evaluation

Constructor	Variance	Average	Standard Deviation (S.D.)	Factor Loading	Composite Reliability	Cronbach's α	Average Variance Extracted (AVE)
Service provider's expertise	EXP1 EXP2 EXP3	3.83 3.69 3.71	0.996 0.980 1.015	0.922 0.932 0.904	0.943	0.909	0.846
Customer's sociability	SOC1 SOC2 SOC3 SOC4 SOC5	4.04 3.99 4.09 4.21 4.01	0.737 0.797 0.816 0.742 0.795	0.885 0.841 0.878 0.860 0.822	0.933	0.910	0.735
Trust	TRS1 TRS2 TRS3 TRS4	3.69 3.77 3.82 3.78	0.930 0.914 0.949 0.982	0.883 0.841 0.932 0.916	0.941	0.916	0.799
Commitment	CMM1 CMM2 CMM3 CMM4 CMM5	3.56 3.75 3.71 3.86 3.62	1.042 1.008 0.974 0.936 0.928	0.836 0.876 0.885 0.824 0.880	0.934	0.912	0.740
Continuous Intention to use	CIU1 CIU2 CIU3	3.70 3.74 3.81	0.886 0.819 0.960	0.720 0.797 0.851	0.833	0.700	0.626

Table 3. Discriminant validity coefficients

	AVE	EXP	SOC	TRS	CMM	CIU
Service provider's expertise (EXP)	0.846	0.920				
Customer's Sociability (SOC)	0.735	0.342	0.857			
Trust (TRS)	0.799	0.644	0.365	0.894		
Commitment (CMM)	0.740	0.561	0.538	0.532	0860	
Continuous intention to use (CIU)	0.626	0.581	0.495	0.530	0.644	0.791

Table 4. Structural model results

Hypothesis	Path	Path coefficients (β)	t-value	Support
H1	EXP → TRS	0.588	14.127	Yes
H2	EXP → CMM	0.308	4.220	Yes
H3	SOC → TRS	0.164	3.123	Yes
H4	SOC → CMM	0.358	5.840	Yes
H5	TRS → CMM	0.203	2.472	Yes
H6	TRS → CIU	0.261	3.752	Yes
H7	CMM → CIU	0.505	9.097	Yes

5 Conclusion

This study examined the relative impact of perceived IT service provider's expertise and customer's sociability on relationship quality, and relationship quality on continuous intention to use. Relationship quality is measured in two dimensions (trust, commitment).

The result of data analysis showed that perceived service provider's expertise was positively associated with trust and commitment. Also, customer's sociability was positively associated with trust and commitment. Two elements of relationship quality (trust, commitment) were positively associated with continuous intention to use. Based on these results, academic and practical implications are derived. First, this study expands the breadth of the academic repertoire on the topic of service provider's expertise and customer sociability. Antecedent studies neglected expertise and sociability, and it is especially difficult to search both of the examined studies except relation between doctor and patient. Because this empirical study is an initial study about expertise and sociability, it has significant implications. This study suggests future research directions, and contributes to the development of related fields. Second, expertise is based on establishing a relationship with the customer. In the result of this study, if IT service provider's expertise is highly perceived by the customer, the relationship quality is improved. This substantiates the relationship between expertise and relationship quality [3], [8], [22], previously studied in different fields, in the field of IT service. In order to increase expertise, IT service providers must have current and specialized knowledge that are different from competitors, by extensive training. Based on this knowledge, the IT service provider supports customized service and the customer can highly perceive the service provider's expertise.

To provide new services to existing customers can generate additional profits. Third, the IT service provider should understand the customer's sociability. As a result, IT service provider's expertise and customer's sociability are factors influencing continued use of IT services. In general, if the customer has high sociability, they will require frequent social interaction and can form intimacy with the service provider. In order to increase the relationship quality, the IT service provider must understand and accept the customer's sociability.

This study provides suggestions for improvement in the IT service fields, but has some limitations. First, the sample is limited, because this study surveyed two electronic companies that have experienced outsourcing from IT outsourcing company A. In order to generalize this study, the survey must be conducted in a number of companies. Second, few studies deal with customer's sociability as the antecedent of relationship quality [4]. Study regarding the relation between customer's sociability and relationship quality will need to be conducted in various fields. Third, expertise and relationship quality and continuous intention to use can be affected by the size of service provider's firm. If the outsourcing firm is a major company, it is possible for the customer to think the company has high expertise.

References

1. Berry, L.: Relationship marketing of services—growing interest, emerging perspectives. Journal of the Academy of Marketing Science 23, 236–245 (1995)
2. Reichheld, F.F., Sasser Jr., W.E.: Zero defections: Quality comes to services. Harvard Business Review 68, 105–111 (1990)
3. Bendapudi, N., Berry, L.L.: Customers' motivations for maintaining relationships with service providers. Journal of Retailing 73, 15–37 (1997)
4. Spake, D.F., Megehee, C.M.: Consumer sociability and service provider expertise influence on service relationship success. Journal of Services Marketing 24, 314–324 (2010)
5. Chakrabarty, S., Whitten, D., Green, K.: Understanding Service Quality and Relationship Quality in is Outsourcing: Client Orientation & Promotion, Project Management Effectiveness, and the Task-Technology-Structure Fit. Journal of Computer Information Systems 48, 1–15 (2007)
6. Kettinger, W.J., Park, S.-H.S., Smith, J.: Understanding the consequences of information systems service quality on IS service reuse. Information & Management 46, 335–341 (2009)
7. French, J.R.P., Raven Jr., B.: The bases of social power. Studies in social power, pp. 150–167. Univer. Michigan, Oxford (1959)
8. Liu, A.H., Leach, M.P.: Developing Loyal Customers with a Value-adding Sales Force: Examining Customer Satisfaction and the Perceived Credibility of Consultative Salespeople. Journal of Personal Selling & Sales Management 21, 147 (2001)
9. Busch, P., Wilson, D.T.: An Experimental Analysis of a Salesman's Expert and Referent Bases of Social Power in the Buyer-Seller Dyad. Journal of Marketing Research 13, 3–11 (1976)
10. Cheek, J.M.: Shyness and sociability. Journal of Personality and Social Psychology 41, 330 (1981)
11. Gwinner, K., Gremler, D., Bitner, M.: Relational benefits in services industries: The customer's perspective. Journal of the Academy of Marketing Science 26, 101–114 (1998)

12. Hester, L., Koger, P., McCauley, C.: Individual differences in customer sociability. European Journal of Social Psychology 15, 453–456 (1985)
13. Hills, P.: Happiness, introversion–extraversion and happy introverts. Personality and Individual Differences 30, 595 (2001)
14. Spake, D.F., Beatty, S.E., Brockmand, B.K., Crutchfield, T.N.: Consumer confort in service relationships: measurement and importance. J. Serv. Res. 5, 316–332 (2003)
15. Young, L., Daniel, K.: Affectual trust in the workplace. International Journal of Human Resource Management 14, 139–155 (2003)
16. Crosby, L.A., Evans, K.R., Cowles, D.: Relationship Quality in Services Selling: An Interpersonal Influence Perspective. The Journal of Marketing 54, 68–81 (1990)
17. Hwang, S.A., Hwang, S.J.: The Influences of Employees' Customer Orientation and Relationship quality(satisfaction trust commitment) on Revisit Intention and Word of mouth Intention. Journal of Korea Service Management Society 6, 151–186 (2005)
18. Palmatier, R.W., Dant, R.P., Grewal, D., Evans, K.R.: Factors Influencing the Effectiveness of Relationship Marketing: A Meta-Analysis. The Journal of Marketing 70, 136–153 (2006)
19. Morgan, R.M., Shelby, D.H.: The Commitment-Trust Theory of Relationship Marketing. The Journal of Marketing 58, 20–38 (1994)
20. Garbarino, E., Johnson, M.S.: The Different Roles of Satisfaction, Trust, and Commitment in Customer Relationships. The Journal of Marketing 63, 70–87 (1999)
21. Bove, L., Mitzifiris, B.: Personality traits and the process of store loyalty in a transactional prone context. Journal of Services Marketing 21, 507–519 (2007)
22. Eisingerich, A.B., Bell, S.J.: Perceived service quality and customer trust - Does enhancing customers' service knowledge matter? J. Serv. Res. 10, 256–268 (2008)
23. Dwyer, F.R., Schurr, P.H., Oh, S.: Developing Buyer-Seller Relationships. The Journal of Marketing 51, 11–27 (1987)
24. Bitner, M.: Building service relationships: It's all about promises. Journal of the Academy of Marketing Science 23, 246–251 (1995)
25. Verhoef, P., Franses, P., Hoekstra, J.: The effect of relational constructs on customer referrals and number of services purchased from a multiservice provider: Does age of relationship matter? Journal of the Academy of Marketing Science 30, 202–216 (2002)
26. Carr, C.L.: Reciprocity: the Golden Rule of IS-User Service Relationship Quality and Cooperation. Communications of the ACM 49, 77–83 (2006)
27. Park, J.O., Hwang, Y.C.: The effects of service context factors on service quality, service value, customer satisfaction and repurchase intention. Journal of Korea Service Management Society 8, 79–110 (2007)
28. Kim, H.R., Seo, B.K., Kim, S.H.: The Impacts of Service scape on Trust, Customer Satisfaction and Reuse Intentions: The Case of Healthcare Services. Journal of Korea Service Management Society 11, 99–126 (2010)
29. Macintosh, G.: Customer orientation, relationship quality, and relational benefits to the firm. Journal of Services Marketing 21, 150–159 (2007)
30. Wang, S.C., Sy, E., Fang, K.: The post-adoption behavior of online knowledge community: decomposing customer value. Journal of Computer Information Systems 51, 60–70 (2010)
31. Grewal, D., Hardesty, D.M., Iyer, G.R.: The effects of buyer identification and purchase timing on consumers' perceptions of trust, price fairness, and repurchase intentions. Journal of Interactive Marketing 18, 87–100 (2004)

32. Sharma, N., Patterson, P.G.: The impact of communication effectiveness and service quality on relationship commitment in consumer, professional services. Journal of Services Marketing 13, 151–170 (1999)
33. Chin, W.W.: The partial least squares approach for structural equation modeling. In: Marcoulides, G.A. (ed.) Methodology for Business and Management, pp. 295–336. Lawrence Erlbaum Associates Publishers, Mahwah (1998)
34. Fornell, C., Bookstein, F.L.: Two Structural Equation Models: LISREL and PLS Applied to Consumer Exit-Voice Theory. Journal of Marketing Research 19, 440–452 (1982)
35. Fornell, C., Larcker, D.: Structural equation models with unobservable variables and measurement error: Algebra and statistics. Journal of Marketing Research 18, 382–388 (1981)

ASF: Improving Android Security with Layered Structure Instrumentation

Qianqian Zhang, Xiaohong Li, Xiaofei Yu, and Zhiyong Feng

School of Computer Science and Technology, Tianjin University, China
qianqianzhangtju@gmail.com,
{xiaohongli,yuxiaofei,zyfeng}@tju.edu.cn

Abstract. Due to the third-party applications that provide Smartphone users with functional extensions, more and more privacy leak events occur. While the existing security mechanism informs the user of the resources the application requires, it does not involve the usage of sensitive privacies. This paper presents Android Security Framework (ASF): a security framework for Android that guarantees the security of user privacy. In the framework layer, ASF is integrated for monitoring the operations that third-party applications perform on user privacies, and in the application layer, detectors inspect the safety of these operations based on ASF. Our security framework is implemented through layered structure, with minimal change to the existing Android code. A case study is presented as a preliminary validation of the security framework that helps users protect privacies.

Keywords: Smartphone, Android, security.

1 Introduction

With the development of mobile technology, smartphones can provide strong operation ability, network connection function and extensions of the third party applications. As regards Android's open-source feature, there are more and more third-party applications. Phone users are able to download and install many applications to extend functions and services. However, unlike Apple app store [1], there is no security evaluation mechanism available for Android [2], so it is highly possible for users to unknowingly download malware. These malwares access user privacies legally, but may send them out illegally via Internet or other media without the user's knowledge. In recent years, third party applications have triggered more and more security issues and made Android vulnerable to attacks.

The Android operating system is based on the Linux kernel, and extends process isolation strategy from Linux. It assigns a unique user ID for each application, and creates a sandbox to prevent the interference from other applications; this allows the system and applications to be isolated from each other. Meanwhile, Android deals with security issues by enforcing a permission-based security policy at each device and restricting the capability of installed applications with the use of permissions [3]. In addition, Android calls for a digital signature if an application is to be published.

V. Khachidze et al. (Eds.): iCETS 2012, CCIS 332, pp. 147–157, 2012.

However, like traditional Linux-based operating system, Android's critical processes and services run with the highest privileges (that is, as a root user). Thus, when the attacker detects the vulnerability of these processes and services, he can launch privilege escalation attacks. Meanwhile, Android's permissions mechanism is an "all-or-nothing" deal [2]. The user must grant the application all the permissions if he wants to install this application, or else the installation is cancelled. The permissions granted can not be revoked until the application is uninstalled.

Asaf Shabtai et al. [4] propose the use of Security-Enhanced Linux (SELinux) to strengthen mandatory access control of critical processes, which run with the highest privilege for Android. This kind of research focuses on the mechanism of Linux and is associated with traditional methods on PC.

Mohammad Nauma et al. propose an Android Permission Extension framework (APEX) [5], allowing the user to selectively consent to the permission requests or directly reject some permissions. Wook Shin et al. [6] deem that the permission mechanism lacks permission naming rules or restrictions, and described examples of how attackers take advantage of this flaw to obtain privileges ultimately. Considering the users' security requirements, Machigar Ongtang et al. focus on secure application interaction (Saint) [7], which is a modified infrastructure for addressing the current limitations of Android security though install time permission assignment policies and runtime inter-application communication policies. These policies in particular are context-sensitive.

On the basis of security mechanisms, some researches focus on the development of services and tools to analyze the security of third-party applications. For example, William Enck et al. propose Kirin security service [8], which performs lightweight certification of applications to mitigate malware at install time. Fuchs et al. [9] present a modular data flow analysis method, and develop a tool called ScanDroid that extracts the security description, and dynamically monitors whether the data stream in run-time meets the security description to complete the safety certification of the application. Enck et al. implement an information flow tracking and analysis system named Taintdroid [10], which monitors the behavior of the third-party applications and observes how these applications access and modify private resources to facilitate the analysis of applications by users or external security services.

Existent researches focus on permission assignment and security authentication of application. There are no new special methods or tools aimed at users' privacy protection. Just relying on the security mechanism of Android, the system neither monitors the usage of resources nor checks whether the users privacies have leaked out after assigning permissions to an application. In order to achieve comprehensive privacy protection, and ensure the legitimacy of third-party applications' operations on privacies, we extend the existing Android security mechanism, and specifically design a security framework in allusion to privacies. Privacies include the user's address book, geographical location, SMS, MMS, photos, videos and so on.

In this paper, all the monitored operations on privacies are performed by either root or normal user. In addition, this monitoring does not completely rely on whether the resource is protected by permission labels, so it is independent from the permission mechanism, to provide double protection. Our detection policies, unlike Hammad

Banuri et al. [2] using permission sequence, are behavior sequences. As a result, the detection range extends a great deal. Because the detection process is executed by the detectors in the application layer, each application is independent. The detectors can conduct fine-grained analysis without affecting the other applications' running speed.

Our main contributions include that Android Security Framework (ASF) can monitor and detect the third-party applications at the same time and a layered structure separates the two functions. In the framework layer, ASF monitors behaviors and manages all the detectors, which are responsible for detection in the application layer. We experiment on a third-party Android application that employs user privacies and raises their phone bills. The results indicate that ASF analyzes the applications with fine granularity and informs the users of the results in time, which guarantees the privacy security of phone users.

The rest of the paper is organized as follows. Section 2 describes the Android Security Framework (ASF). Section 3 represents the design of the security framework. Section 4 discusses the application sample and experiment results. Section 5 concludes the paper.

2 ASF Model

Android's software stack architecture is divided into three layers: operating system, middleware (runtime environment and core libraries, application framework) and the application. As shown in Figure 1, in the original Android system architecture, the components of applications only interact with the framework.

The middleware reference monitor provides mandatory access control (MAC) enforcement of how applications access components, with the assumption that all inter-application communication occurs through the described application-level ICC (the underlying UNIX system provides file and IPC isolation) [11].

Thus, the security framework is put in the initial position of the application framework interacting with the application. ASF consists of log-assist, hook-manager, and detector-manager. Our monitor task is realized through hook-manager and log-assist. The detector-manager helps detector to perform the detection task.

Android provides a lightweight log system, which is realized in the form of driver in the kernel. In user space, it provides interface to use this log system. If the protection level is low or the privacy is only read and not modified or sent out, the detector will inform users directly. The log-assist module can write the log system, which helps to reduce the hook-manager's workload.

The hook-manager module is responsible for intercepting all the applications' operations on privacies including networking, dialing, sending messages and so on. These services are either background or charges related. The protection level of this kind of operations on privacies is usually much higher, so the strength must be greater as well. Especially with respect to network, the problems are very complicated. The existing permission mechanism is coarse-grained.

The detector-manager provides the key APIs required by the upper detector applications marked with a red cross. Detector-manager communicates with hook-manager and log-assist to acquire all the applications' operations on the privacies. Regardless of protection level, the detector can react after implementing these APIs or reading logs.

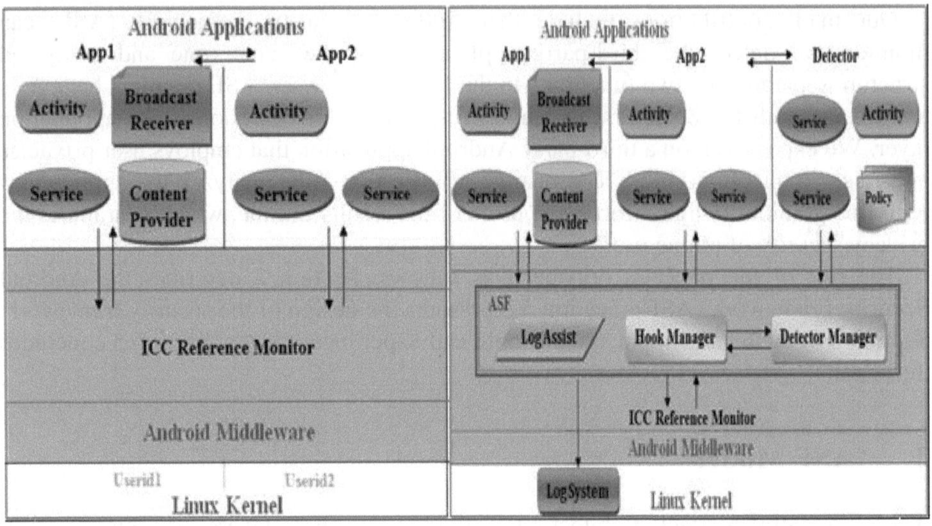

(A) (B)

Fig. 1. ASF model consists of *Log Assist, Hook Manager* and *Detector Manager. Detector* is developed based on ASF. They cooperate to monitor and detect operations of applications.

3 ASF Design

Behavior is an important feature of the application, and is the evidence to determine whether the application is malicious. Therefore, real-time, efficient and dynamic monitoring of the application behaviors is our primary goal. ASF improves Android security to a certain extent, especially when the applications operate on privacies. The privacies are classified into different categories. There are sensitive APIs and classes for each category, and so the policies to detect these behaviors about privacies are distinct as well.

3.1 Log Assist

Android provides a lightweight log system, which is realized in the form of driver in the kernel. In user space, it provides the interface to use this log system. Occasionally, third-party applications perform low protection level operations such as reading contacts but not modifying or sending out. In these cases, it is unnecessary to carry out the detection algorithm. It even impacts on user manipulation, thus the log-assist makes a difference in controlling these low-level protection operations.

The log-assist module can write the log system, which helps to reduce the hook-manager's workload. We choose chasses and interfaces related to low protection level privacies, and then use the class Log in the package android.util to write the log system. There are two arguments to be written. One is the TAG, the other is the message. The TAG is used to filter by the detector, and the message is the category adding operation name. These codes are integrated into the source code, so detector can read log information through command and inform users directly.

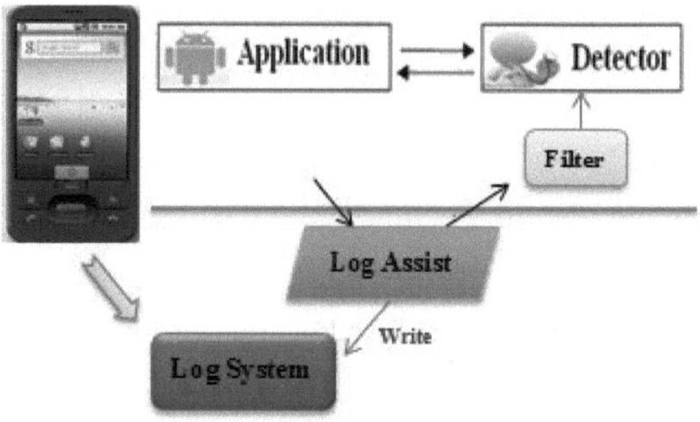

Fig. 2. Log *Assist* helps to write log information into *Log System*, and the *Filter* is responsible for filtering the log information from the *Log System*

3.2 Hook Manager

A hook-manager is deployed in the Android framework. This hook-manager supervises a series of hooks, integrating into the source code. Whenever the intent is sent, hooks capture it before reaching the target component. Thus, the hooks gain control firstly, and intercept all access to data and resources. Hook-manager is responsible to send these behaviors to detector-manager.

If an application wants to send SMS, it must request the permission "android.permission.SEND_SMS" with installation. As long as the user agrees to install this application, it is able to send SMS anytime, with or without the user's knowledge. Therefore, the privacies are probably sent out via SMS. This situation leads to increased charge for users as well.

To solve this problem, hooks are deployed in the classes of framework, as shown in Figure 3. Usually, programmers implement the function of sending SMS out through "SmsManager.getDefault().sendTextMessage(destinationAddress, scAddress, text, sentIntent, deliveryIntent);". The first three parameters are Sting type, and the last two parameters are PendingIntent type. The interface ISms and class IccSmsInterfaceManager are protected by Android, so programmers cannot find these interfaces and classes in SDK. The function of IccSmsInterfaceManager is modified to add three choices. The left choice represents the original implementation; the right skips the execution of sending SMS, and the middle turns to execute the capture and detection of the messages. The messages intercepted are delivered to the interfaces Detector_Manager supervises. Then, the detector takes charge of the analysis and decision.

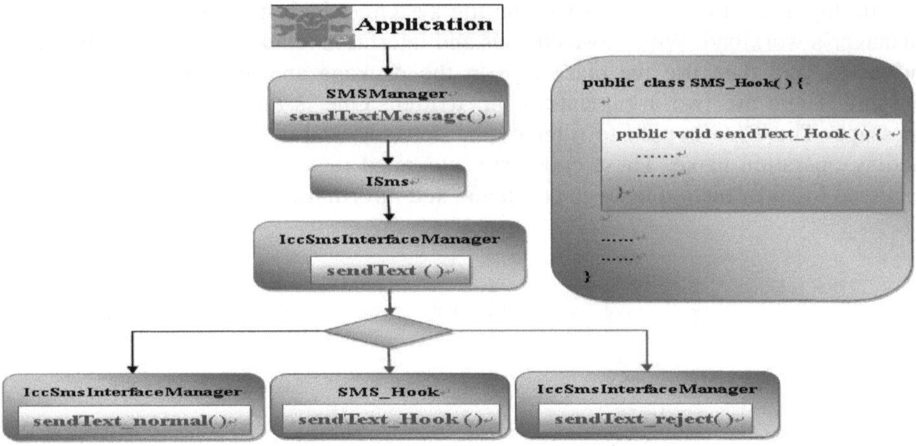

Fig. 3. Hook deployment. This example demonstrates the location of hooks and how to change the execution of functions in source code of Android framework.

3.3 Detector Manager and Detectors

Each time the hook intercepts messages or behaviors, it calls different detector interfaces. When the detectors implement these interfaces, they can acquire the messages and behavior sequences through binder mechanism. Android interface definition language (AIDL) is used to define detector interfaces. When using AIDL, we create a file named IDetectSMS.aidl, and declare several functions. Then, an interface named IDetectSMS is automatically generated, which extends android.os.IInterface. For example, when executing the parseUri() function, the hook named UriParseHook is invoked. Then, the function of UriParseHook calls several related interfaces, such as IDetectSMS interface, which are automatically generated by AIDL compiler.

As shown in Figure 4, a detector consists of a policy file and components. There are usually at least two kinds of components, e.g. activity and service. Activity component is in charge of UI display and interaction with users. Service component achieves detection algorithm in the background. The figure B reveals the ICC (inter-component-communication) of Android. The development of detector is the same as the third-party application. Through the ICC, the detector realizes the interaction between UI main thread and other threads achieving detection algorithm and background monitor.

On the one hand, detectors exploit the IPC though binder mechanism to obtain the behavior sequences from ASF, and match with the policy file. Here, BM algorithm is used. BM algorithm helps the sequence movement as large as possible [12]. Thus, detection speed and validity are guaranteed, because our behavior sequence is comprised of multiple words instead of single letters arranged randomly. Even if the movement is large enough, it is not easy to influence the match results.

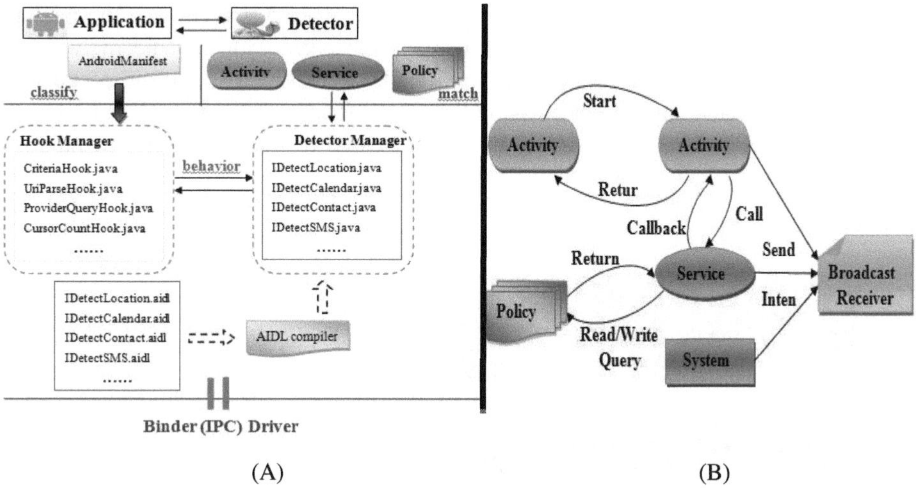

Fig. 4. Behavior detection through IPC. (A) describes the cooperation of *Hook Manager* and *Detector Manager* by binder mechanism. (B) portrays the ICC of Android. The four kinds of components constitute the *Detector* application.

On the other hand, another kind of detection is shown in Figure 3. Android ships with a debugging tool called the Dalvik Debug Monitor Server (DDMS). DDMS is integrated into Eclipse and is also shipped in the tools/ directory of the SDK. LogCat is integrated into DDMS, and outputs the messages that you print out using the Log class, along with other system messages. The detector can thus read the log information the log-assist writes, and then filter.

4 Application Study

This section represents how a third-party Android application steals user's contacts and increases user's mobile fees. This application is regarded as malware in most forums. Many users say their mobile charges have increased noticeably after installing this application. We try to prove that the ASF helps to inform the user of the operations the application is executing, and provide a detection result analysis. Then, the detector can assist users to uninstall the malwares in time. Our test platforms include Android SDK emulator and HTC Desire, running Android OS version 2.2, modified for ASF.

4.1 Experiment Setup

We install a sample malware on our HTC Desire running Android OS version 2.2 modified for ASF to prove that malwares can steal the users' privacies, and then a detector we developed is used to detect the behaviors of this sample malware.

According to its AndroidManifest.xml shown in Figure 5, we can see the package name of this malware. The right figure displays the permission list the malware requests. The permissions android.permission.READ_CONTACTS, android.permission.RECEIVE_SMS and android.permission.SEND_SMS are requested. When the user installs this application, the permissions are presented to the user. After installation, this application can receive and send SMS.

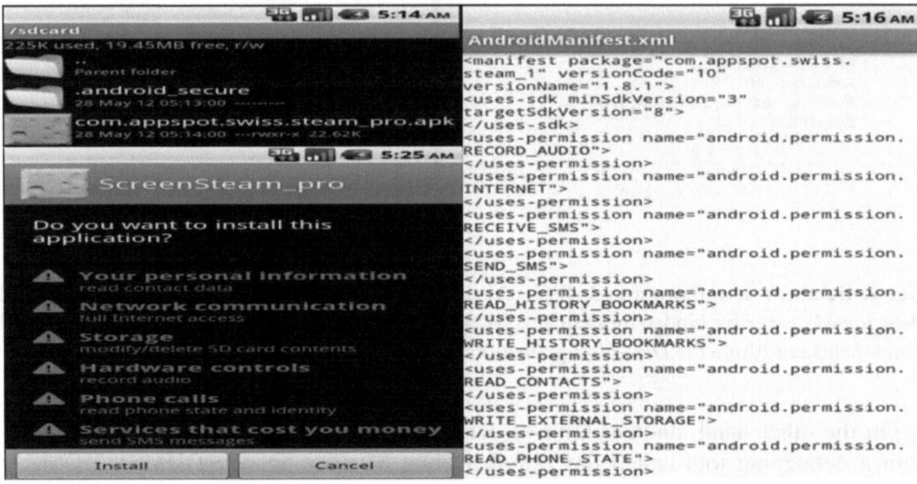

Fig. 5. The sample malware is a casual game. There are multifarious versions of this application in the Internet. The figure in the lower-left corner is a screenshot of the installation of this application; the right figure is a screenshot of its AndroidManifest.xml.

4.2 Findings

Since the malware was installed on the mobile phone, we recorded the charges for two months. The tester does not use this phone to call, access Internet or send messages. There are therefore only GPRS expenses before installing the application. The following graph reveals the change of phone charges. From the graph, we can see the expenses of messages and value-added service have emerged. Furthermore, the data traffic rose noticeably. The call charge is zero, as before.

We validate that this malware sends SMS successfully and there are no windows or notifications represented in the Smartphone. Therefore, users would know nothing about this operation. The right figure in table 1 shows the warning the detector provides. The user can see this screen before the SMS is sent out, and if he clicks the Stop button, detector points out the package name of this malware. The user can then uninstall the application. If he clicks the Ignore button, detector turns to background services.

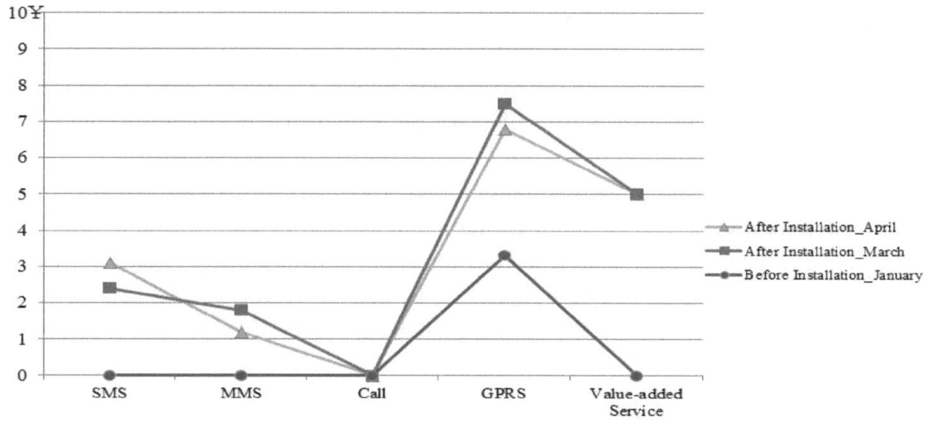

Fig. 6. Phone charges in RMB. The bottom blue line represents expenses before installing the application. The mobile phone is in the power-on state and its mobile networks and Wi-Fi are open all day. The other two lines show the expenses after installation.

Table 1. Behavior sequence of ample malware we acquire by our Hook_Manager. The detector is responsible for recording these sequences and generating detection warnings.

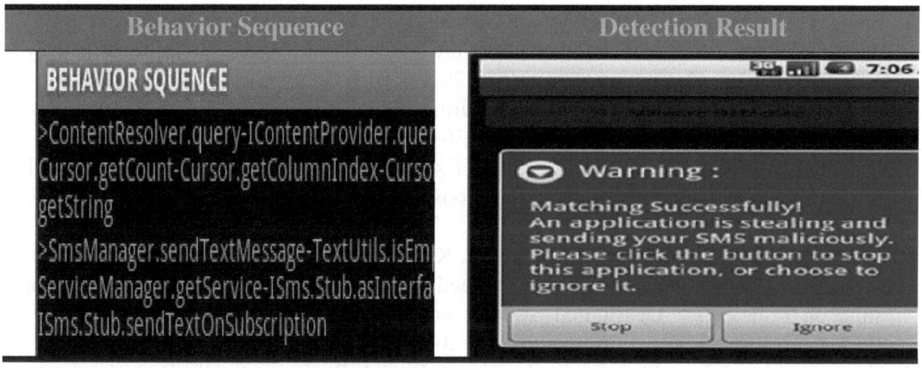

5 Conclusion and Future Work

Android is a completely open-source Smartphone platform. With the increase of its market share, the security of Android draws great attention. There are more and more third-party applications in Google Play. At the same time, many privacy leak events occur due to the extension of applications.

In this paper, we use layered structure, implementing ASF in the Android framework and detectors in the application layer. Experiment results demonstrate that ASF can improve the Android security to a certain extent, especially when the applications operate on privacies. The detector can inform the user in time to strengthen the control of the users' privacies.

Our planned future work includes implementing further enhancements to ASF and improvements of detection algorithm. One enhancement refers to monitoring extensive Android application interfaces as regards external storage, such as SD card. Another is a more detailed tracking of privacies to which the stolen information is sent to.

Acknowledgments. We are grateful to the anonymous reviewers for their insightful comments and suggestions. This research was supported in part by National Natural Science Foundation of China (No.90718023, 91118003), Tianjin Research Program of Application Foundation and Advanced Technology (No.10JCZDJC15700), "985" funds of Tianjin University.

References

1. Apple App Store Approval Process (March 5, 2007), `http://en.wikipedia.org/wiki/App.Store#Approvalprocess`
2. Banuri, H., Alam, M., Khan, S., Manzoor, J., Ali, B., Khan, Y., Yaseen, M., Tahir, M.N., Ali, T., Alam, Q., Zhang, X.: An Android runtime security policy enforcement framework. Journal of Personal and Ubiquitous Computing (July 2011), doi:10.1007/s00779-011-0437-6
3. Shin, W., Kiyomoto, S., Fukushima, K., Tanaka, T.: A Formal Model to Analyze the Permission Authorization and Enforcement in the Android Framework. In: International Symposium on Secure Computing, SecureCom 2010 (2010) (to appear)
4. Shabtai, A., Fledel, Y., Elovici, Y.: Securing Android-Powered Mobile Devices Using SELinux. IEEE Security and Privacy 8(3), 36–44 (2010)
5. Nauman, M., Khan, S., Zhang, X.: Apex: Extending Android Permission Model and Enforcement with User-defined Runtime Constraints. In: ASIACCS 2010, pp. 328–332. ACM (2010)
6. Shin, W., Kwak, S., Kiyomoto, S., Tanaka, K.F.A.T.: A Small but Non-negligible Flaw in the Android Permission Scheme. In: Proceedings of the 2010 IEEE International Symposium on Policies for Distributed Systems and Networks, POLICY 2010, pp. 107–110. IEEE Computer Society, Washington, DC (2010)
7. Ongtang, M., McLaughlin, S., Enck, W., McDaniel, P.: Semantically Rich Application-Centric Security in Android. In: Proceedings of the Annual Computer Security Applications Conference. IEEE (2009)
8. Enck, W., Ongtang, M., McDaniel, P.: On Lightweight Mobile Phone Application Certification. In: Proceedings of the 16th ACM Conference on Computer and Communications Security, pp. 235–245. ACM, New York (2009)
9. Fuchs, A.P., Chaudhuri, A., Foster, J.S.: "SCanDroid: Automated Security Certification of Android Applications", Android Applications. In: Submitted to IEEE S&P 2010: Proceedings of the 31st IEEE Symposium on Security and Privacy (2010)
10. Enck, W., Gilbert, P., Chun, B.-G., Cox, L.P., Jung, J., McDaniel, P., Sheth, A.N.: TaintDroid: An Information-Flow Tracking System for Realtime Privacy Monitoring on Smartphones. In: Proceedings of the 9th USENIX Conference on Operating Systems Design and Implementation, Vancouver, BC, Canada, October 04-06, pp. 1–6 (2010)

11. Enck, W., Ongtang, M., McDaniel, P.: Mitigating Android Software Misuse Before It Happens, Technical Report NAS-TR-0094-2008, Network and Security Research Center, Department of Computer Science and Engineering, Pennsylvania State University, University Park, PA, USA (November 2008)
12. Stanford Research, Xerox Palo Alto, A fast string searching algorithm. Communications of the ACM 20, 762–772 (1977)

A Threat Model-Driven Security Testing Approach for Web Application

Bobo Yan, Xiaohong Li, and Zhijie Du

College of Software, Tianjin University, China, TianJin University Tianjin, China
{bobo,xiaohongli,tjudzj}@tju.edu.cn

Abstract. Web applications have been playing a more and more essential role in daily life; hence, the problem of security is gaining more focus, and consequently a great deal of research on web application security testing has been developed. Among them, however, the most have been concentrated on the testing procedure arranged after the completion of the implementation process. In this paper, we propose a threat model-driven security testing approach for detecting threats, which consists of four activities: building threat tree, according to the attack pattern, against the threats web applications may confront; deriving a security testing sequence from thread model; deriving security testing data from UML sequence diagram parameters for extracting test inputs; generating executable security test case. Also, we proposed an algorithm for generating security testing sequences and conducted an empirical study to show the feasibility and effectiveness of our approach.

Keywords: Web application, Security testing, Threat Modeling, Attack pattern.

1 Introduction

Web applications are more widely used because they are open as well as easier to use and develop. However, web application security issues have become increasingly prominent. Therefore, it is very necessary to test web applications scientifically, efficiently and accurately.

With the adoption of model-based Language (UML) and the rise of model-driven techniques, formal verification techniques are gradually maturing, making model-based software testing methods and techniques has become a widespread concern [1,2,3,4,5]. Thus, new theoretical and commercial tools have appeared. Model-based testing can explicitly describe the expected behavior of an abstract model, then according to the model coverage criteria generate abstract test cases automatically, including input and expected output. The input part is instantiated to enter the system under test to test. Abstract processing is performed on the actual output of the test, then compared to the expected output, so that we can identify vulnerabilities of the system.

As presented by Utting and Legeard [6], the research on model-based testing has focused on test generation from intended behavior models, not from rigorous threat models. According to Marback et al [7] and Wang, Wong, and Xu [8], the existing

V. Khachidze et al. (Eds.): iCETS 2012, CCIS 332, pp. 158–168, 2012.

security testing techniques primarily use implicit threat models (e.g., thoughts in the security tester's mind) or informal threat descriptions (e.g., represented by attack trees). However, security testing with informal threat specifications (e.g., attack trees) has very limited ability to automate test generation or test execution. In [9], the author proposed the use of PrT network to model and verify Threat-driven security software. This method based on network structure is mainly used for the threats analysis, it can also verify whether the security nature of the system's behavior meets the security objectives. However, it does not build safety tests from the point of view of the threat. Kong, Xu, and Zeng [10] proposed a method to build a thread model based on UML design models (e.g., class diagrams, timing diagrams, state diagrams); this method does not focus on how to generate safety tests. Wang, Wong and Xu [11] presented a threat model-driven security testing method that can discover threatening behavior at run-time. In this approach, the UML sequence diagram is used to model threats in violation of security policy. Then, threat traces are extracted from the design level threat model. Each threat trace is a sequence of events that should not occur during system operation. In this paper, we use the threat tree to model web application threats, then generate test sequence by security test sequence generation algorithm.

In Automated Security Test Generation with Formal Threat Models [9], the threat tree is used for threat modeling; however, the generation of test data is based on the experience of the testers, or randomly generated invalid data from the blur tools. In this paper, we extract input data from the sequence diagram, and classify the input data by equivalent division and boundary value analysis. We can thus generate a data file, which will constitute our future test data.

The main contribution of this paper includes two aspects. First, our method uses threat tree based on attack patterns to build a rigorous threat model, which captures the different security vulnerabilities (e.g. spoofing, data tampering, information disclosure, denial of service and privilege escalation). Then, the safety test sequence is generated from the threat model through threat path generation algorithm. In fact, the safety test sequence is an abstract security test case. It is composed by the leaf nodes of threat tree and each leaf node has a corresponding event. Secondly, we extract the parameters of the event, which can receive messages in UML sequence diagram, and classify the input data by equivalent division and boundary value analysis. Thus, we are able to generate a data file, which will be our constitute test data. Then, the data file is loaded to the test sequence, so that it can instatiate the test sequence into security test cases. By running test cases, we verify whether the web application includes security vulnerabilities. In order to assess the proposed method, we use osCommerce as the experimental subject.

The remainder of this paper is organized as follows: Section 2 describes some concepts related to the modeling process, such as attack pattern, threaten tree, and web application security. Section 3 introduces safety test sequence generation process and algorithm. Section 4 describes how to generate safe test data, as well as how to convert the abstract security test sequence to executable security test cases. Section 5 presents a case study and Section 6 concludes the paper.

2 Modeling Process

2.1 Related Concepts

A. Web Application Threats

From an attacker's viewpoint, a Web application is an interesting target for several reasons. First, the quality of the source code related to security is often rather poor, as numerous bug reports show. Another factor is the applications' complex setup [12]. In recent years, web applications security issues were highlighted, thereby prompting a group of researchers to work on this problem. Among them, WASC (Web Application Security Consortium) is a typical representative. They carried out a detailed classification for web application threats [13]. Common web application vulnerabilities include: invalid input, broken access control, broken authentication and session management, cross-site scripting (XSS) Flaws, buffer overflow, injection flaws, improper error handling, denial of service, insecure configuration management.

In view of these threats faced by web applications, we use the current pandemic threat modeling approach to model threats. As is common knowledge, threat model has become a valuable web security testing practice, because threat model simulates the attack behavior from the attacker's viewpoint, and shows the process of how attackers penetrate the system. We can then test web applications comprehensively by using the product of the threat model. Thus, we can find web application vulnerabilities and then repair and update the web application.

In order to respond to web application security threats, researchers suggest that the attack pattern can describe threats comprehensively from the perspective of attackers. Also, attack pattern can better guide and assist developers and testers in their work.

B. Attack Pattern

The attack pattern is a blueprint for vulnerabilities. It is an abstract mechanism extracted from a large number of web application defects. Attack pattern express some frequent attack, and the corresponding mitigation program in a particular scene. Thus, we can identify the risk degree of defects that may occur in web applications, and determine which threats should have priority to mitigate, and which threats can be managed later.

However, these attack patterns are not formal or structured, and therefore they are difficult in terms of storage and processing by computers. In this paper, we use the XML Schema as attack model description language to define attack patterns. In XML files, the overall structure of the attack pattern description language is defined; along with data structure types of each element and the constraints that must be met. They describe the attack pattern ID, attack pattern description, attack pattern preconditions, and attack pattern post conditions, node collection and so on.

Naturally, in web application development threat modeling based on attack patterns can improve modeling accuracy and efficiency. Presently it is popular to use the threat tree for threat modeling.

C. Threat Tree

Threat tree is a set for web application. Any threat in this set is possibly a latent danger to influence the implement of functions and tasks for web application. The description of threat is based on attack model. The node of threat tree stands for the final threat target, which can be divided into several sub goals. The threat target is the goal the attacker wants to achieve by destroying the security of the computer system, such as obtaining confidential information, username and password and so on. Leaf node represents the aggressive behavior of an attacker who wants to achieve the ultimate threat goal. The intermediate nodes represent the subtasks and are between root node and leaf node. These subtasks are divided to realize the aims of the upper nodes and stand against the intermediate attack model. They can be further subdivided into several, lower level objectives. This is a progressive refinement process. Finally, the root node is realized in the form of sequence constituted by the sets of leaf nodes.

2.2 Thread Modeling

The threat modeling process abstractly describes how the attacker penetrates a web application. This process can be used for a variety of abstract levels or different web development phases, such as requirements analysis, design, implementation, and even the testing phase. In fact, thread model (TM) is a thread tree. The tree is composed of one or more AND / OR nodes; this means that Tree= (N), where N is a nonempty finite collection of AND/OR nodes. Nodes are divided into three kinds: root nodes, intermediate nodes and leaf nodes. The root node N_{root} shows the ultimate threat target that attackers want to achieve and can be decomposed into several sub goals. The intermediate node $N_{intermediate}$ comprises several sub targets that decompose from their parent node, representing intermediate attack mode that can reach the final threat target, and can be decomposed into a number of low level nodes. Leaf nodes N_{leaf} are specific goals, representing the specific attack mode that can reach the final threat target, with no decomposition. The three nodes satisfy $N_{root} \cup N_{intermediate} \cup N_{leaf} = N$ and $N_{root} \cap N_{intermediate} \cap N_{leaf} = \emptyset$.

AND type nodes represent all the child nodes of the parent node exist logical AND relationship. That is, if and only if all the AND type nodes are realized, their parent nodes are realized. Furthermore, the default implementation order of the child nodes is from left to right. OR type nodes represent all the child nodes of the parent node exist logical OR relationship. That is, when any one of the OR type nodes is realized, their parent nodes are realized.

Threat tree representation is shown in Figure 1.

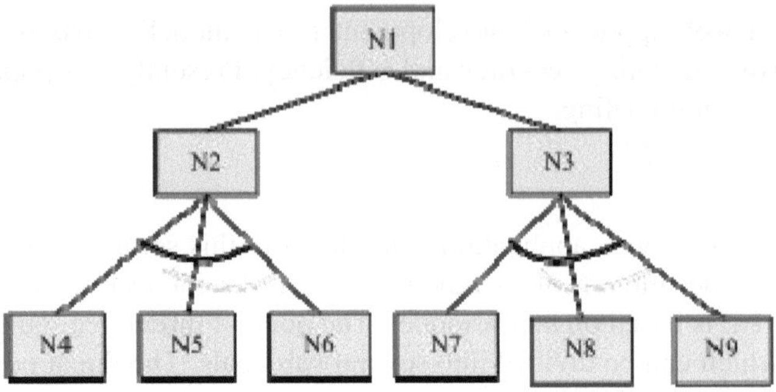

Fig. 1. Threat tree

Where N1 is the root node, N2 and N3 are intermediate nodes; N4, N5, N6, N7, N8, and N9 are leaf nodes. Also, N1 is an OR node, N2 and N3 are AND nodes.

The XML Schema is used as the description language to describe the threat tree. For example, the description of the node N1 is as follows:

```
<Node>
    <NodeID>1.N1</NodeID>
    <NodeDescription></NodeDescription>
    <NodeType>OR</NodeType>
    <NodeLocation>Root Node</NodeLocation>
      <ChildrenSet>
        <NodeID>1.1.N2</NodeID>
        <NodeID>1.2.N3</NodeID>
      </ChildrenSet>
</Node>
```

3 Test Sequence Generation

This paper uses XML as text representation of a threat model, so it can establish a corresponding relationship between XML elements and the threat tree models. After the analysis of the XML document, using the security test sequence generation algorithm automatically generates abstract security test sequence from the threat model. Security test sequence is an ordered set comprised by many associated leaf nodes. Recorded as Pa, $Pa = \{<N_i, N_j, \ldots, N_k> \mid N_i, N_j, \ldots, N_k \in N\}$.

The core code of safety test sequence generation algorithm is as follows:

Input: XML document of threat tree nodes, where N^{root} is the root node of the tree, n_{root} is the number of child nodes of the root node.

Output: a set of nodes, namely safety test sequence

Statement: Node C_i is the i-th child of the root; n_i is the number of child nodes of C_i; N_{and} represents the AND node; N_{or} represents the OR node; ao=1 represents AND type node; ao=0 represents OR type node,

```
PaGeneration( N^root, n_root){
 N^root.Pa ==null;
 For i from 1 to n_root
               // n_root is the root node has child nodes
  If (C_i.n_i == 0){ //if C_i is leaf node
   C_i.eventBinding();
     //binding the leaf node with the corresponding event
       C_i. specifyEventParameters();
    //binding the event with the corresponding parameters
      C_i.specifyEventParameterValue();
// binding event parameters with the test input data in
the database
      C_i.Pa= C_i;
    } Else
      PaGeneration(C_i,n_i);
// C_i is the i-th child node of the root, n_i
is the number of child nodes of Ci
  End For
  If (N^root .ao ==0){ // If the root node is OR node
    For i from 1 to n_root
      N^root.Pa= C_1.PaUC_2.Pa…UC_i.PaUC_nroot.Pa;
    End For
    Return N^root.Pa;
  } Else{ // If the root node is AND node
    For i from 1 to n_root
    N^root.Pa= C_1.Pa* C_2.Pa*… C_i.Pa* C_nroot.Pa;
    End For
    Return N^root.Pa;
 }
}
```

According to the security test sequence generation algorithm, security test sequences generated by the model shown in Figure 1 are N4, N5, N6 and N7, N8, N9.

4 Test Case Generation

Sequence diagram is to emphasize the message interaction diagram. The sequence diagram modeling can effectively extract the message parameters, as per our test data, A sequence diagram is one of the triples group (Obj, Msg, Event), and Obj is a set of objects in the sequence diagram; Msg is a set of messages in the sequence diagram; Event is a set of events sending and receiving messages in the sequence diagram. Any event can be expressed as a triples group (obj_{origin}, obj_{dest}, msg). obj_{origin} is the object sending a message, obj_{dest} is a received message object, and msg is message content that can be sent out or received.

Although the UML sequence diagram is used to describe interaction between two objects, in a different scene, the situation is not the same. One circumstance is the sequence diagram displays the interaction between objects that both are in a web application under test; another circumstance is the sequence diagram shows the interaction between an object in a web application under test and an object outside of the web application under test. [14] Generally, the trust values of web applications are higher than trust values of objects outside of web applications. In the latter, the interaction has crossed the trust boundary of the web application. Trust boundaries are potential targets and destinations whence an attacker can permeate the web application. Therefore, we must extract the message parameter from data files.

However, test data that is too large will produce serious test resource consumption, but an amount of data that is too small may result in incomplete coverage, resulting in omission test. Typically, the input data is divided into two categories; one category is effective input data, which can meet design needs and induce the system's normal operation. The other category is invalid input data; they require software to design error handling mechanisms for processing. In this paper, we use equivalence partitioning and boundary value analysis method to classify input data.

Due to the fact that test sequences generated in the third section are comprised by the leaf nodes, we will bind test the data with the event parameters of the leaf nodes, then we can generate a security test case.

5 Case Studies

5.1 Deployment of Case Studies

The object of experiments is an online shopping system based on the Web using the measured system osCommerce, PHP language and MySQL database to store data. The osCommerce system is an open source platform, and a primary choice of retailers who are willing to personally deploy the online shopping system. The experiment is conducted with two computers; one is a client machine, the other is a server. The operating system in server is Ubuntu10.10, and the operating system in client is Windows XP. We attempt to simulate the real environment when conducting of tests.

In experiment, we model seven threats: SQL injections, URL jump, unauthorized access, cross-site scripting, information disclosure, cookie validation error, and directory traversal.

5.2 Result Analysis of the Case Study

The purpose of the experiment is to verify that the security test cases can find threats existing in the web application. After testing, the experimental data are as follows:

Table 1. Execution results of the security test cases

Threat type ID	Threat type	The first experiment (directly modeling the threat model)				The second experiment (modeling based on attack patterns)			
			B	C	D	A	B	C	D
1	SQL injection	1	2	4	8	3	3	18	24
2	URL jump	1	1	2	2	3	3	6	6
3	Unauthorized access	1	1	4	6	3	3	20	22
4	Cross-site scripting	2	3	8	18	4	4	20	28
5	Information disclosure	1	1	2	5	2	2	6	10
6	Cookie validation error	1	1	2	4	2	2	4	6
7	Directory traversal	1	3	1	3	1	2	2	4
Total		8	12	23	56	18	19	76	100

A: The number of security test sequences that can find threads
B: The number of security test sequences
C: The number of security test cases that can find threads
D: The number of security test cases

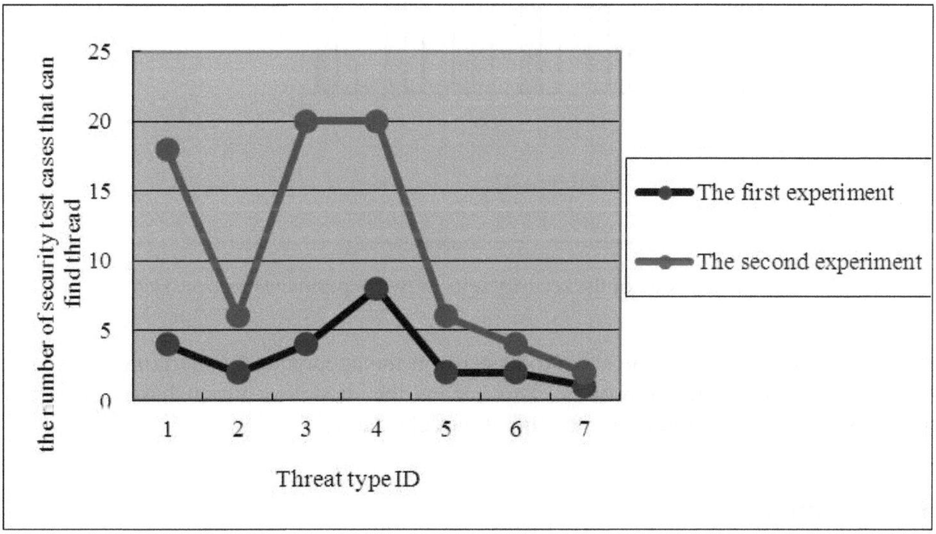

Fig. 2. The contrast between the numbers of security test cases that can find threads in two experiments respectively

Figure 2 shows that significant improvement on the number of security test cases was generated from the thread model in the second experiment.

After statistical calculation of the data in Table1, we can obtain the accuracy of test cases in the first experiment and second experiment.

Table 2. The accuracy of the security test case

Threat type ID	1	2	3	4	5	6	7
The first experiment	50%	100%	66.7%	44.4%	40%	50%	33.3%
The second experiment	75%	100%	90.9%	71.4%	60%	66.7%	50%

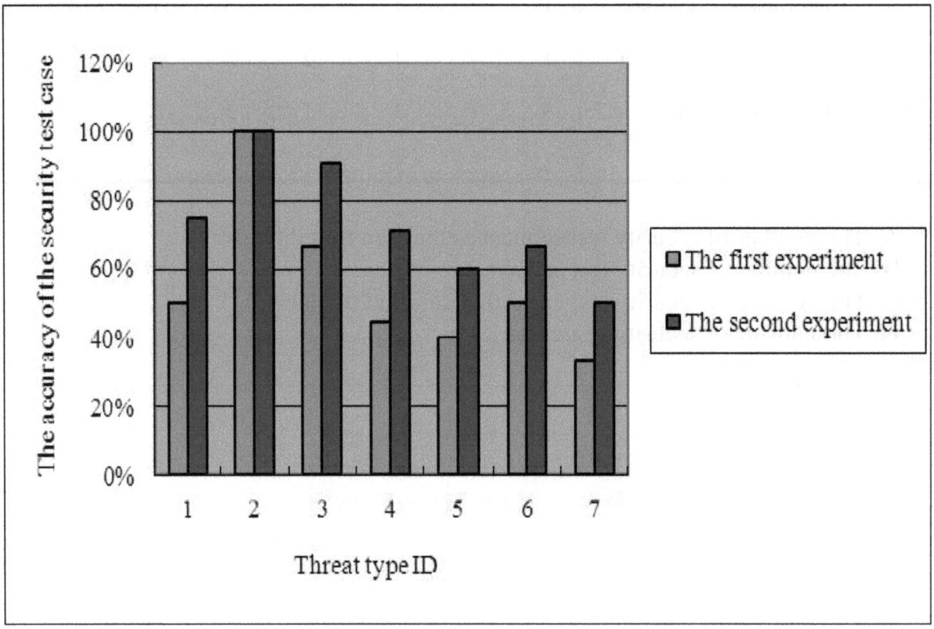

Fig. 3. Accuracy of the security tests in two experiments respectively

Figure 3 shows that in the second experiment the accuracy of generating safety test cases was significantly improved. This means the modeling threat based on attack patterns is better than modeling the threat model directly.

6 Conclusion

On the basis of attack pattern, this paper uses threat tree to model threat that may appear in web application, and gives abstract description of the method that attackers use to realize threat penetration. It then generates safety test sequences (that is, abstract test cases) based on test sequence generation algorithm. Safety test sequences are comprised of leaf nodes of the threat tree, and there is an event corresponding to each leaf node. Extract parameters of events that accept information in UML sequence diagram, and use them to form test data files, which are loaded in test sequences to obtain instantiated safety test cases. In this way, we can perform Web application test and detect security vulnerabilities in web applications. Experiments show that our method is quantifiable and reproducible, and it can effectively find the threats in Web applications.

Acknowledgements. We are grateful to the anonymous reviewers for their insightful comments and suggestions. This research was supported in part by National Natural Science Foundation of China (No.90718023, 91118003), Tianjin Research Program of Application Foundation and Advanced Technology (No.10JCZDJC15700), "985" funds of Tianjin University.

References

1. Pretschner, A., Ltzbeyer, H., Philipps, J.: Model Based Testing in Evolutionary Software Development. In: IEEE International Workshop on Rapid System Prototyping 2001, pp. 155–161 (2001)
2. Belinfante, A., Frantzen, L., Schallhart, C.: 14 Tools for Test Case Generation. In: Broy, M., Jonsson, B., Katoen, J.-P., Leucker, M., Pretschner, A. (eds.) Model-Based Testing of Reactive Systems. LNCS, vol. 3472, pp. 391–438. Springer, Heidelberg (2005)
3. Utting, M., Pretschner, A., Legeard, B.: A taxonomy of model-based testing, Technical report 04/2006, Department of Computer Science, The University of Waikato, New Zealand (April 2006)
4. Blackburn, M., Busser, R., Nauman, A.: Why model-based test automation is different and what you should know to get started. In: International Conference on Practical Software Quality and Testing (2004)
5. Tang, Y., Miao, H., Qian, Z.: Web Application Modeling and testing method Based on the functional components. Computer Science 36(7), 124–127+169 (2009) (in Chinese)
6. Utting, M., Legeard, B.: Practical Model-Based Testing: A Tools Approach. Morgan-Kaufmann (2006)
7. Marback, A., Do, H., He, K., Kondamarri, S., Xu, D.: Security test generation using threat trees. In: The Fourth International Workshop on the Automation of Software Test (AST 2009), Vancouver, Canada, May 18-19 (2009)
8. Wang, L., Wong, W., Xu, D.: A threat model driven approach for security testing. In: The 3rd International Workshop on Software Engineering for Secure Systems, SESS 2007 (May 2007)
9. Automated Security Test Generation with Formal Threat Models (2012)
10. Kong, J., Xu, D., Zeng, X.: UML-based Modeling and Analysis of Security Threats. International Journal of Software Engineering and Knowledge Engineering 20(6), 875–897 (2010)

11. Wang, L., Wong, W., Xu, D.: A threat model driven approach for security testing. In: The 3rd International Workshop on Software Engineering for Secure Systems (May 2007)
12. Holz, T., Marechal, S., Raynal, F.: New Threats and Attacks on the World Wide Web. IEEE Security and Privacy (2), 72–76 (2006)
13. Web Application Security Consortium: Threat Classification V2.0, `http://www.webappsec.org/`
14. Miao, H., Chen, S., Zeng, H.: Model-based web application testing. Journal of Computers 34(6) (June 2011) (in Chinese)

A Novel Architecture on FPGA for Face Detection Using Jumping Scanning Mechanism*

Chao Qin, Ming Che, and Weichao Li

School of Computer Science and Technology, Tianjin University, Tianjin, China
cheming@tju.edu.cn, {a52581120,ejliwei}@163.com

Abstract. Real-time face detection is important in human-computer interaction. A new FPGA-based parallel hardware architecture is proposed here. The Pareto Principle is used in the architecture to analyze the distribution of sub-window, showing that sub-windows with higher strong classifier information are concentrated and only a tiny part; the jumping scanning mechanism is designed to improve detection speed. In addition, sub-windows using line ram array effectively reduce the usage of on-chip memory, and achieve the same read speed of register array. The hardware architecture of face-detection is implemented and verified on Stratix IV; compared with the same computing resource, real-time face detection processing is realized at speed increased by 27%.

Keywords: FPGA, real-time face detection, jumping scanning strategy, AdaBoost.

1 Introduction

Face detection is the process of determining the locations and sizes of all possible human faces in a given image or a video sequence, regardless of position and condition. It is the essential first step in human-computer interaction, which is a challenging and active area. Because of high detection rate and fast processing, face detection proposed by Viola and Jones [1] based on statistic method is most popular among detection approaches. However, the algorithm must calculate every pixel in the given image and its scaled images and therefore requires considerable computational power, which is a bottleneck to the face detection in real time application of human-computer interaction.

In recent years, many hardware implements of the Viola and Jones [1] algorithm have been proposed. Ming Yang et al. [2], [3] used a complexity control scheme and scale integral image to achieve face detection in handheld camera, but the detection rate is decreased and the number of features is very small. Hung-Chih et al. [4] presented a novel fast E/W architecture on FPGA for face detection, which used a special RAM structure and a piped register module to increase the detection speed; however, they only used 52 features. Jin-Sung Kim et al. [5] proposed an architecture

* This work is supported partly by key projects in the science & technology pillar program of Tianjin, P.R. China. (No. 10ZCKFGX01100).

V. Khachidze et al. (Eds.): iCETS 2012, CCIS 332, pp. 169–175, 2012.

to reduce memory bandwidth and access time, but they did not mention the processing speed. Hybrid parallel execution and an image scaling method [7, 8] are used in the architecture to realize rapid and robust detection; however the detection rate and false positives are not mentioned. In previous works, they all have focused on utilizing hardware resources to construct the parallel structure to speed up the face detection speed; what they did not consider, however, is improving the speed by decreasing the number of sub-windows that need to be checked.

In this paper, a novel hardware architecture for the Viola and Jones method is proposed to realize real-time face detection by reducing the number of sub-windows. The sub-window that has higher strong classifier information content is only a small concentrated part, so only these sub-windows need to be calculated and the detection speed is thus improved. Line ram array is used in sub-window buffer to reduce the usage of on-chip memory, the read speed is the same as register array and the resource usage is less.

This paper is organized as follows. In Section 2, the algorithm of face detection based on AdaBoost is reviewed. Section 3 presents the proposed method. The performance of the proposed method is evaluated in Section 4 and Section 5 concludes this paper.

2 The Theory of Face Detection

The face detection algorithm proposed by Viola and Jones [1] uses a set of simple extracted Haar-Like features as weak classifiers to effectively distinguish face and non-face areas. It constructs a cascade structure of classifiers to achieve increased detection performance and reduce computation time. Details of the algorithm are described in the following paragraphs.

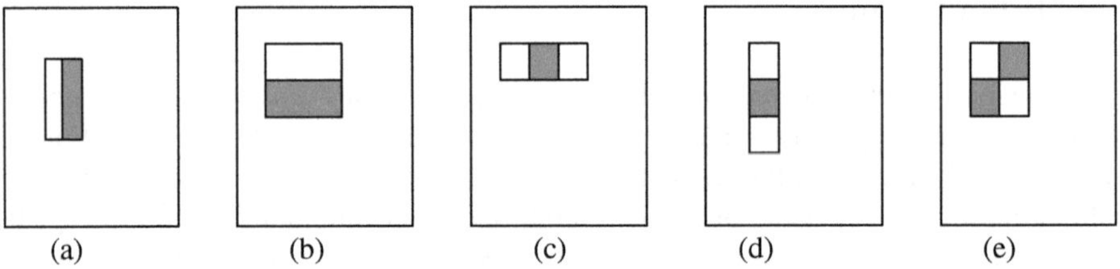

Fig. 1. Five kinds of Haar-Like features

A Haar-Like feature is composed of a group of rectangles. In the algorithm there are five kinds of features, as depicted in Fig. 1. The calculation is simple: The difference of the weighted sum of pixels in white rectangles subtracted from the weighted sum of pixels in the black rectangles is compared with the feature's threshold. If the difference is greater than the threshold, the feature result is the right value of the feature, otherwise the left value. To compute the features in linear time, an intermediate representation for the image, called the integral image, is introduced. The integral image at location (x, y) stores the sum of the pixels above and to the left of (x, y). Using integral image the pixel sum of rectangle can be immediately calculated with equation (1) where A, B, C, and D are the values of four integral images at corners, as per Figure 2.

$$Sum = A - B - C + D \quad (1)$$

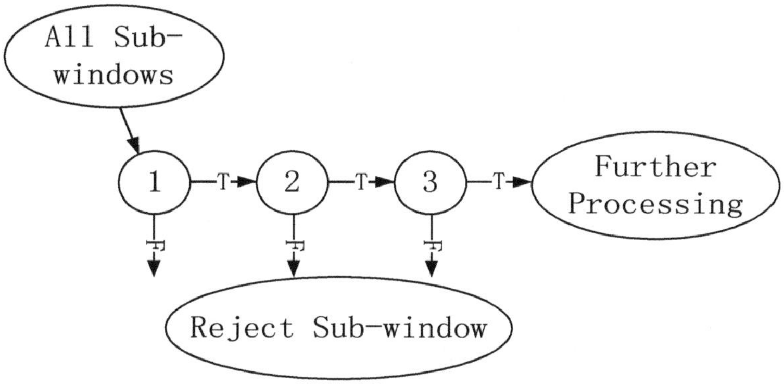

Fig. 2. The cascade structure

A cascade structure is used to make the detection faster. One stage in the cascade structure is a strong classifier, which is made by a number of Haar-Like features. The idea of cascade architecture is that the earlier stages that contain fewer features can reject many of the negative sub-windows while detecting all instances very quickly. The later stages that contain more features and compute slowly are evaluated only on the sub-windows that passed the previous stage. Thus, a large number of non-face sub-windows are discarded in first few levels and do not need to calculate the subsequent strong classifier, which will effectively decrease the number of features. Fig. 3 shows the cascade architecture consisting of n stages of classifiers.

3 Proposed Hardware Architecture

There are two reasons why the AdaBoost algorithm achieved in real-time requires many computing resources. On one hand, more than 2,000 weak classifiers are calculated to determine whether the sub-window contains a human face, and the cascade structure is used to reduce the amount of weak classifiers of non-face windows; on the other hand, hundreds of thousands of sub-windows are computed to determine the locations and sizes of all human faces, and jumping scanning mechanism is used to effectively reduce the number of sub-windows. Using the relationship between the strong classifier information contents of the adjacent windows, the jumping scanning mechanism is intended to skip the sub-windows that are likely non-face. In addition, compared with register array, window integral buffers using line ram arrays can achieve the same read speed and use fewer resources.

3.1 Jumping Scanning Mechanism

The Pareto principle states that, for many events, roughly 80% of the effects come from 20% of the causes. In other words, a few elements are important; the same is true in face detection. According to Viola and Jones [1], 80%-90% of all sub-windows are rejected after the first 2 strong classifiers, and the sub-windows that have higher strong classifier information content are only a small part. The strong classifier information contents of the adjacent windows are similar, and the sub-windows that have higher strong classifier information content are concentrated, as shown in Figure 4. Jumping scanning mechanism, which will mainly detect possible face areas, is adopted to skip a certain number of sub-windows when one sub-window has low strong classifier information content.

Assume T_n is a certain threshold of strong classifier information content, J means the skipped sub-window number, one window $w_{\{x, y\}}$ is rejected at the kth classifier. We denote it as $n(w_{\{x, y\}})=k$ (if $w_{\{x, y\}}$ passed all N stages, $n(w_{\{x, y\}})=N+1$). The jumping scanning mechanism is to use the current sub-window strong classifier information content to determine the next sub-window position, which may not be adjacent with the current sub-window. When current sub-window $n(w_{\{x, y\}})< T_n$, the next sub-window needed to compute is $w_{\{x, y+J\}}$, otherwise is $w_{\{x, y+1\}}$. Skipped sub-windows must be calculated again, to ensure all possible face areas are detected when current window $n(w_{\{x, y\}})>= T_n$, and the last computed window is $w_{\{x, y-J\}}$.

The detection rate may drop slightly if some face sub-windows are skipped erroneously. However, false positives will not increase the rate. The experimental results of the jumping scanning mechanism will be presented in Sec. 4.

3.2 Line Ram Array

In a weak classifier calculation, there are at least 8 pixels to be read each time. In order to improve detection speed, n weak classifiers are calculated at the same time, so at least 8*n pixels need to be read. Therefore, the window buffer is elaborately designed to meet the read speed requirement. One of the simplest ways is to set up multiple double interface rams, which will consume a large amount of on-chip memory because of redundant storage. Another way is register array, which can read and write very quickly and requires many logic resources because of random read.

Line ram array is the trade-off between multiple double interface rams and register array and will achieve the register array's read speed and use fewer resources. Assume sub-window size is m*m and a line ram size is m; we can use m line rams to construct the line ram array. To further reduce memory usage, weak classifiers are rearranged to ensure that the pixels of n weak classifiers that will be calculated at the same time are not in one row. Assume half of weak classifiers' pixels in three lines, and the rest in two lines; 2 line ram array can offer 2m/(2+3) weak classifiers' pixels.

4 System Design

The architecture we proposed is shown in Figure 3. Image Save module sends the data which obtained from camera to DDR2 and Image Scaler module. Image Scaler module, which uses [5] image scaling mode, scales the image data to every ratio image at the same time and sends the scaled data to face detectors. All scaled images are calculated in the face detectors module, which sends the detection result to Nios II processor. Nios II processor carries out similar sorting and merging of the face window.

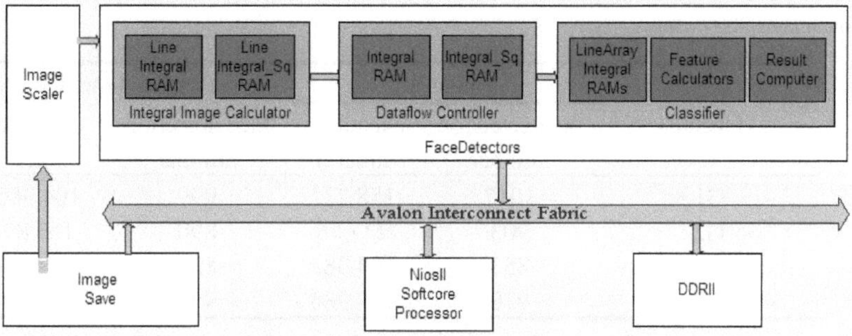

Fig. 3. System Architecture

The face detector module is composed of an integral image calculation module, a dataflow controller, and a classifier. The integral image and square integral image are calculated in integral image calculation module, and then sent to dataflow controller. Line integral ram and line integral_sq ram in the integral image calculation module are used to save one line of integral image and square integral image, which will be used to compute the next line. Dataflow controller provides data to the classifier and contains integral ram and integral_sq ram, which is used to save 22 lines of integral image and square integral image. The data of integral image and square integral image will be saved in the two rams and sent to classifier when in the top 20 lines. Jumping scanning mechanism is realized in this module.

Classifier module determines whether the window contains a face by computing weak classifiers. The module consists of line array buffer, feature calculator and result computer. Line array buffer uses two line array rams to ensure the computation of multiple classifiers at the same time. Feature calculator, which contains 6 pipelines, computes weak classifiers and sends the results i.e. features' left values or right values to result computer. Result computer adds the features' results in the same stage and compares with the stage threshold to judge whether the window may pass the current stage. If the window passes all stages, the window location and scale level are sent to Nios.

The weak classifiers and stage information implemented by OpenCV are used in this architecture and the jumping scanning mechanism is verified on PC. 800 pictures are randomly picked; assume 3 as the threshold of strong classifier information content. The 800 pictures are processed in OpenCV library function; we found that the number of continuous windows in which strong classifier information content is equal or greater than 3 is between 3 and 74. The number at 3, 4 and 5 is not great, so we choose 5 to be the skipped window number. Using the jumping scanning mechanism, the processing time is decreased by 27%, the total face number is only decreased by 1.9%, and the false detection rate is the same.

Table 1. Face detection number and execution time of the OpenCV and proposed method. Each group contains 200 pictures.

Group	OpenCV		Proposed method	
	face detection number	execution time(s)	face detection number	execution time(s)
G1	1017	158.272	999	104.3663
G2	903	237.56	890	165.898
G3	853	194.382	838	152.276
G4	978	178.384	954	137.804

5 Conclusion

The architecture proposed in this paper enhances the detection speed and reduces the memory usage of face detection. The jumping scanning mechanism is used to improve the operation speed while maintaining almost the same computing resources and detection rate. Memory usage is reduced by using a line ram array, which has the same read speed as the register array. Compared to the same calculation resource architecture, the detection speed is increased by 27%, realizing real-time face detection processing.

References

1. Viola, P., Jones, M.J.: Robust Real-Time Face Detection. International Journal of Computer Vision 57(2), 137–154 (2004)
2. Yang, M., Crenshaw, J., Augustine, B., Mareachen, R., Wu, Y.: Face detection for automatic exposure control in handheld camera. In: Fourth IEEE International Conference on Computer Vision Systems (2006)
3. Yang, M., Crenshaw, J., Augustine, B., Mareachen, R., Wu, Y.: AdaBoost-based face detection for embedded systems. Computer Vision and Image Understanding (2010)
4. Lai, H.-C., Savvides, M., Chen, T.: Proposed FPGA Hardware Architecture for High Frame Rate (>100fps) Face Detection Using Feature Cascade Classifiers. In: IEEE Conference on Biometrics: Theory, Applications and Systems (2007)
5. Kim, J.-S., Lee, H.J.: A Novel Architecture for Low Bandwidth and High Utilization in Face Detection with Haar-like Features (2011)
6. http://en.wikipedia.org/wiki/Pareto_principle
7. Hiromoto, M., Nakahara, K., Sugano, H.: A Specialized Processor Suitable for AdaBoost-Based Detection with Haar-like Features (2007)
8. Hiromoto, M., Nakahara, K., Sugano, H.: Partially Parallel Architecture for AdaBoost-Based Detection With Haar-Like Features. IEEE Transactions on Circuits and Systems for Video Technology 19(1) (January 2009)

On the Generalization of PAC-Bayes Bound for SVM Linear Classifier

Li Tang[1,2], Zheng Zhao[1], Xiujun Gong[1], and Huapeng Zeng[3]

[1] School of Computer Science and Technology, Tianjin University, Weijin Rd No. 92, Nankan, Tianjin, 300072, China
[2] Information Science and Technology Department,Tianjin University of Finance and Economics, Zhujiang Rd No. 25, Hexi, Tianjin, 300222, China
[3] Danfoss (Tianjin) Co., Ltd. , Tianjin, China
tangli0831@yeah.net, gongxj@tju.edu.cn, zenghuapeng@danfoss.com

Abstract. PAC-Bayes theorem has been considered as a framework for deriving some of the tightest generalization bounds both for linear classifiers and stochastic classifiers. However, the generalization capability of PAC-Bayes bound has not been explored extensively in practice. This paper applied the PAC-Bayes risk bound for linear SVM classifiers and compared the generalization of PAC-Bayes bound with the statistical indicators, including sensitivity, specificity and accuracy, for assessing model performances. A comprehensive experiment setup on five UCI datasets demonstrated that: sum of accuracy and bound is approximately equal to 1, and the bound has a high negative correlation with the accuracy and a certain negative correlation with specificity and sensitivity. The result calculated by PAC-Bayes bound and the N-fold Cross-Validation is highly consistent, and it shows that PAC-Bayes bound can reflect the generalization-risk bound perfectly.

Keywords: PAC-Bayes bound, generalization capability, linear classifier, SVM.

1 Introduction

With the development of E-business, there appears to be increasing sources of information. Machine learning plays an important role in handling mass data. In machine learning, there are two important problems, which are the learning ability of algorithms and assessment of the model performance, meanwhile Computational Learning Theory focuses on these two problem. PAC (Probably Approximately Correct) theory proposed by Valiant in 1984 [9], which derived "Computational Learning Theory", has advanced the framework of learning machine operation into computational complexity.

PAC, which is a basic theoretical framework for the study of learning and generalization, can be widely used for the learning problem of machine learning, and PAC learning gives the theoretical base for learning algorithms and performance guarantees for the train set.

V. Khachidze et al. (Eds.): iCETS 2012, CCIS 332, pp. 176–186, 2012.

The PAC-Bayesian theorem, initiated by McAllester [1], was improved by Langford [2]. PAC-Bayes bound, based on PAC learning and Bayes theorem, can be applied for the margin classifier [7] and linear classifier [8]. Ambroladze and Shawe-Talor gave the tighter PAC-Bayes bound and applied it to the SVM in 2006 [3], [6]. Experiments showed that the PAC-Bayes bound is a tighter risk bound for linear classifiers and stochastic classifiers, and also a better way for the analysis of the generalization performance of learning algorithms.

However, some problems still remain. First, on the test of generalization capabilities of PAC-Bayes bound, the statistical indicators, including sensitivity, specificity and accuracy, should be analyzed and validated, and the comparison between the bound and these indicators should been built.

Assessment of model performance is the important issue in machine learning. There are many ways to assess model performance, such as N-fold Cross-Validation, three-way data split [4] and PAC-Bayes bound. The typical method is cross-validation. The former two methods mainly depend on the experience and have no theoretical base. While PAC-Bayes bound provides the theoretical foundation for model performance assessments and parameter selection. However, there is no systematical comparison between N-fold Cross-Validation and PAC-Bayes bound on the assessment of model performance. We should realize the systematical experiments comparing with N-fold Cross-Validation and PAC-Bayes bound.

Our study made some achievements. In this paper, a large amount of data had been used to test the capabilities of generalization of PAC-Bayes bound and statistical indicators, including sensitivity, specificity and accuracy, which can evaluate the generalization performance. The statistical indicators are analyzed and compared with PAC-Bayes bound. We apply PAC-Bayes bound to the SVM and analyze its generalization capability by model accuracy. Second, the systematic experiments for model selection are built to compare the N-fold Cross-Validation and PAC-Bayes bound. The advantage and disadvantage of the two methods are summarized. The capabilities of model performance assessments by the two methods are tested by five datasets from UCI (University of California Irvine) Machine Learning Repository.

2 PAC-Bayes Bound

This section is devoted to a brief review of PAC-Bayes Theorem of Langford [2].

We assume a class C of classifiers with a prior distribution P over C and posterior distribution Q and a distribution D governing the generation of the input/output samples. We can define two error measures on the distribution of classifiers: the true error Q_D and the empirical error $\hat{Q}_S$. We use Q_D to denote the probability of misclassifying an instance x chosen from the distribution D with a classifier C chosen according to Q. Meanwhile, the empirical error $\hat{Q}_S$ means the probability of classifier c chosen according to Q misclassifying an instance x chosen from a sample S. We can derive the PAC-Bayes bound on the true error of the distribution of classifiers.

Theorem 2.1. For an arbitrary D, arbitrary prior P and confidence$\delta\in(0,1)$, then with probability at least 1-δ over the m training examples, all posteriors Q satisfy (1):

$$KL(\hat{Q}_S \| Q_D) \le \frac{KL(Q \| P) + \ln(\frac{m+1}{\delta})}{m} \qquad (1)$$

where KL is the Kullback-Leibler divergence between distributions Q and P with Q_D and $\hat{Q}s$ considered as distributions on {0,+1}.

If $\hat{Q}s$ is fixed, the left of inequality (1) is monotonically increasing depending on Q_D. Meanwhile, $\hat{Q}s$ and the right of inequality are fixed for a given learning algorithm and the training data set. Therefore, the inequality (1) gives the upper bound of the average true error rate Q_D, and Q_D is the absolute indicator of generalization performance of the algorithm. The theorem is of great significance for the analysis of learning algorithms.

The PAC-Bayes bound was developed for bounding the error of a linear classifier. Corollary 2.2 Linear classifiers performance may be bounded by (2).

$$KL(\hat{Q}_S(w,\mu) \| Q_D(w,\mu)) \le \frac{\frac{\mu^2}{2} + \ln(\frac{m+1}{\delta})}{m} \qquad (2)$$

δ is the confidence and m is the number of training examples. $Q_D(w,\mu)$ is to be a Gaussian distribution N(μ,1) for some μ>0 in the direction given by w at a distance μ from the origin. The bound holds with probability 1-δ over the random IID (Independent and Identically Distributed) selection of the training data.

In the right of inequality (1), the Kullback-Leibler divergence between the distribution Q and P of concept space is difficult to calculate. The reason is that the output of learning algorithms is a single classification function in general, and not the posterior distribution of the classification functions. Meanwhile the prior distribution of the classification function depends on the human subjective experience and knowledge. In the existing PAC-Bayes bound application for the linear classifier, it is assumed that the prior distribution and posterior distribution of the concept space are the multivariate normal distribution in the weight space. The diagonal elements of the covariance matrix are equal to one, and the other elements of the covariance matrix are equal to zero. Under this assumption, KL(Q||P) is replaced by $\mu^2/2$.

3 PAC-Bayes Bound Application for SVM

SVM (Support Vector Machine) is a machine-learning approach proposed by Vapnik [5] based on structural risk minimization principle of statistics learning theory.

The PAC-Bayes bound can be particularized for the case of linear classifiers in the following way. The m training patterns define a linear classifier that can be represented by the following equation [3]: $c(x)=\text{sign}(w^T\varphi(x))$, where $\varphi(x)$ is a nonlinear projection to a certain feature space where a linear classification actually takes place, and w is a vector that determines the separating plane from that feature space.

For any vector "w", we define a stochastic classifier in the following way: we choose the distribution $Q=Q(w,\mu)$ to be a spherical Gaussian with identity covariance matrix centered on the direction given by w at a distance μ from the origin. Moreover, we can choose the prior P(c) to be a spherical Gaussian with identity covariance matrix centered on the origin. The performance of classifiers can be bounded by the form in the formula (2). Here, $Q_D(w,\mu)$ is the true performance of the stochastic classifier, E_m is the average over the m training examples, $\gamma(x,y)$ is the normalized margin of the train patterns, and F(x) is the cumulative normal distribution.

$$\hat{Q}(w,\mu)_S = E_m[\tilde{F}(\mu\gamma(x,y))], \quad \tilde{F}(x) = 1 - F(x)$$

γ can be expressed this form:

$$\gamma(\mathbf{x},y) = \frac{y\mathbf{w}^T\phi(\mathbf{x})}{\|\phi(\mathbf{x})\|\|\mathbf{w}\|} \tag{3}$$

PAC-Bayes bound is applied for the linear SVM classifiers. The detailed process is as follows:

```
pseudo code for PAC-Bayes bound
begin
  define confidence delta = 0.1;
  define kl formula•
     KL = p*log(p/q) + (1-p)*log((1-p)/(1-q));
  read (test file) and read (train file);
  calculate the number of training sample;
  for(mu=0.01; mu<=100; mu=mu+0.1)
  {
    calculate KL;
    calculate random sample error rate (Qs);
    calculate PAC-Bayes bound by dichotomy;
    find mu that make PAC-Bayes bound minimal;
  }
  print the minimal bound and mu;
End.
```

4 Experiment and Results

4.1 Data Source

In this experiment, we apply five data sets, which are from UCI Machine Learning Repository, to compare the performance of our methods. The UCI Machine Learning Repository is a collection of databases, domain theories, and data generators that are used by the machine learning community for the empirical analysis of machine learning algorithms. LibSVM, which is a simple and easy-to-use support vector machines tool for classification and regression, and developed by Lin Chih-Jen, is used for the experiments.

Table 1. The UCI datasets

datasets	Class	Attribute	Data record
diabetes	2	8	768
German	2	24	1000
ionosphere	2	34	351
liver-disorders	2	6	345
Mushroom	2	112	8124

4.2 Test the Capabilities of Generalization of PAC-Bayes Bound with the Statistical Indicator

First, we use the statistical indicators to analyze the generalization. The statistical indicators are specificity, sensitivity and accuracy and their meaning is as follows.

Table 2. Statistical indicators

Classification		Condition	
		Positive	Negative
Test	Positive	True Positive	False Positive
outcome	Negative	False Negative	True Negative

Here, True Positive is written by TP, False Positive is written by FP, False Negative is written by FN, True Negative is written by TN.

Specificity = TN/(TN+FP), Sensitivity = TP/(TP+FN), Accuracy= True data/all data

Specificity and sensitivity are statistical measures of the performance of a binary classification test, also known in statistics as classification function. Specificity measures the proportion of negatives in a binary classification test which are correctly identified. Sensitivity measures the proportion of actual positives which are correctly identified.

The data set is divided into two parts by random: 20% and 80%, 40% and 60%. One part is the training data, the other part is the test data. We have developed two kinds of experiments to compare the data, which are the open test and close test. Open test means training of one part and testing of the other part. A close test means that training is one part and it will test itself.

Table 3. Experiment results of diabetes dataset

	close test				open test		
Data	Acc.	Spe.	Sen.	bound	Acc.	Spe.	Sen.
20%	78.43%	61.11%	87.88%	0.392	75.28%	49.07%	89.28%
40%	80.39%	63.16%	90.63%	0.321	75.32%	59.74%	83.12%
60%	78.79%	55.84%	90.26%	0.317	75.49%	49.12%	91.15%
80%	77.40%	54.67%	89.53%	0.319	78.43%	57.41%	89.90%
100%	77.08%	54.85%	89.00%	0.313			

Table 4. Experiment results of German dataset

	close test				open test		
Data	Acc.	Spe.	Sen.	bound	Acc.	Spe.	Sen.
20%	82.50%	97.99%	37.25%	0.325	73.13%	94.01%	26.91%
40%	78.25%	87.23%	58.73%	0.330	76.33%	85.45%	54.02%
60%	79.17%	90.61%	51.15%	0.300	74.75%	85.04%	52.38%
80%	77.00%	85.30%	58.63%	0.312	77.50%	87.92%	47.06%
100%	78.40%	88.29%	55.33%	0.289			

Table 5. Experiment results of ionosphere dataset

	close test				open test		
Data	Acc.	Spe.	Sen.	bound	Acc.	Spe.	Sen.
20%	92.86%	83.33%	100.00%	0.287	85.77%	58.33%	100.00%
40%	80.39%	63.16%	90.63%	0.321	84.36%	63.75%	96.95%
60%	87.20%	68.75%	98.47%	0.264	90.71%	71.74%	100.00%
80%	91.10%	75.00%	99.46%	0.196	77.14%	50.00%	97.50%
100%	89.74%	73.02%	99.11%	0.202			

Table 6. Experiment results of liver-disorders dataset

	close test				open test		
Data	Acc.	Spe.	Sen.	bound	Acc.	Spe.	Sen.
20%	71.01%	81.40%	53.85%	0.549	66.30%	82.80%	44.54%
40%	66.67%	88.61%	37.29%	0.525	59.90%	81.82%	29.07%
60%	70.53%	71.90%	68.60%	0.454	61.59%	60.76%	62.71%
80%	58.33%	47.13%	73.11%	0.555	53.62%	39.53%	76.92%
100%	65.51%	84.00%	40.00%	0.472			

Table 7. Experiment results of mushroom dataset

	close test				open test		
Data	Acc.	Spe.	Sen.	bound	Acc.	Spe.	Sen.
20%	90.29%	98.94%	80.95%	0.142	90.18%	98.60%	81.14%
40%	90.56%	99.16%	81.49%	0.126	89.43%	98.66%	79.38%
60%	90.07%	98.66%	80.71%	0.126	90.93%	99.16%	82.25%
80%	90.10%	98.84%	80.73%	0.122	90.11%	98.94%	80.56%
100%	90.20%	98.86%	80.90%	0.119			

In order to study the relationship between statistical indicators and the PAC-Bayes bound, we calculate the covariance and correlation coefficient between statistical indicators and bound with 20%, 40%, 60%, 80%, 100% data for each data set.

Table 8. Covariance and correlation coefficient with 100% data

dataset	Accuracy	Specificity	Sensitivity	bound
liver_disorders	65.51%	84.00%	40.00%	0.472
diabetes	77.08%	54.85%	89.00%	0.313
German	78.40%	88.29%	55.33%	0.289
ionosphere	89.74%	73.02%	99.11%	0.202
mushrooms	90.20%	98.86%	80.90%	0.119
covariance with bound	-0.010611072	-0.004980494	-0.018578083	
correlation coefficient with bound	-0.976132147	-0.280376118	-0.714716759	

Table 9. Covariance and correlation coefficient with 80% data

dataset	Accuracy	Specificity	Sensitivity	bound
liver_disorders	58.33%	47.13%	73.11%	0.555
diabetes	77.40%	54.67%	89.53%	0.319
German	77.00%	85.30%	58.63%	0.312
ionosphere	91.10%	75.00%	99.46%	0.196
mushrooms	90.10%	98.84%	80.73%	0.122
covariance with bound	-0.017113095	-0.023189026	-0.00797333	
correlation coefficient with bound	-0.981777546	-0.825872709	-0.388769758	

Table 10. Covariance and correlation coefficient with 60% data

dataset	Accuracy	Specificity	Sensitivity	bound
liver_disorders	70.53%	71.90%	68.60%	0.454
diabetes	78.79%	55.84%	90.26%	0.317
German	79.17%	90.61%	51.15%	0.300
ionosphere	87.20%	68.75%	98.47%	0.264
mushrooms	90.07%	98.66%	80.71%	0.126
covariance with bound	-0.006887858	-0.009211884	-0.00491714	
correlation coefficient with bound	-0.948433494	-0.566334711	-0.280819212	

Table 11. Covariance and correlation coefficient with 40% data

dataset	Accuracy	Specificity	Sensitivity	bound
liver_disorders	66.67%	88.61%	37.29%	0.525
diabetes	80.39%	63.16%	90.63%	0.321
German	78.25%	87.23%	58.73%	0.330
ionosphere	80.39%	63.16%	90.63%	0.321
mushrooms	90.56%	99.16%	81.49%	0.126
covariance with bound	-0.009550737	-0.003853519	-0.018054601	
correlation coefficient with bound	-0.99497368	-0.209886108	-0.688289622	

Table 12. Covariance and correlation coefficient with 20% data

dataset	Accuracy	Specificity	Sensitivity	bound
liver_disorders	71.01%	81.40%	53.85%	0.549
diabetes	78.43%	61.11%	87.88%	0.392
German	82.50%	97.99%	37.25%	0.325
ionosphere	92.86%	83.33%	100%	0.287
mushrooms	90.29%	98.94%	80.95%	0.142
covariance with bound	-0.009391997	-0.00974574	-0.011355576	
correlation coefficient with bound	-0.889375459	-0.532013455	-0.370620512	

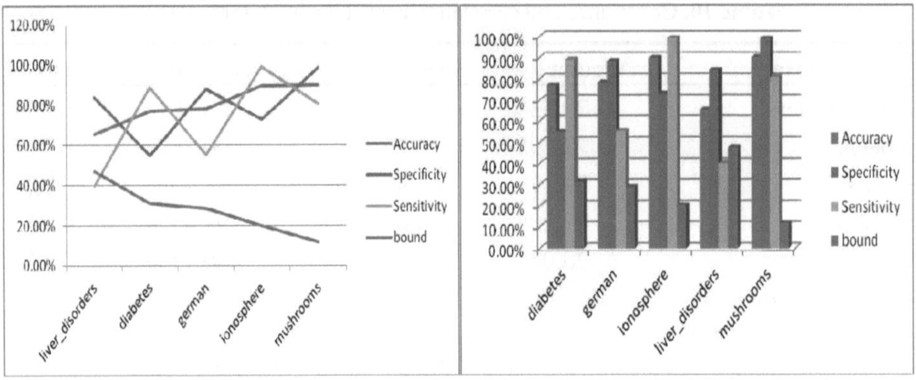

Fig. 1. Results of statistical indicators with 100% data of five datasets

By analyzing the results of experiment we can draw some conclusions: (1), the sum of accuracy and bound is approximately equal to 1, and it shows the bound can reflect generalization error perfectly. (2), the bound has a high negative correlation with the accuracy, that is to say, the accuracy of data is higher, and the bound is lower. (3), the bound also has a certain negative correlation with specificity and sensitivity, but the relationship between them cannot be found by calculating the correlation coefficient. Through the analysis of the data, we found that specificity is higher, and the bound is also lower. Whereas the sensitivity has no significant impact for small quantity of data, but can produce certain effect for the large data set. (4), accuracy of close test is higher than the open test, but only little difference.

4.3 Test the Capabilities of Model Performance Assessments

We compare the PAC-Bayes bound with the 5-fold Cross-Validation. Cross-Validation is a model evaluation method and it does not use the entire data set when training a learner. Some of the data is removed before training begins. When training is done, the data that was removed can be used to test the performance of the revised model on "new" data. This is the basic idea for a whole class of model evaluation methods called Cross-Validation. The data set is divided into “n” subsets, and the method is repeated “n” times. Each time, one of the n subsets is used as the test set and the other n-1 subsets are put together to form a training set. Then the average error across all n trials is computed. The advantage of this method is that it matters less how the data gets divided. Every data point gets to be in a test set exactly once, and gets to be in a training set n-1 times. The variance of the resulting estimate is reduced as n is increased. Normally, one performs 5 runs of 5-fold CV, averaging the results.

Table 13. 5-fold Cross-Validation and PAC-Bayes bound

dataset	Accuracy	Specificity	Sensitivity	bound
diabetes	76.82%	57.93%	87.28%	0.322
German	76.30%	87.58%	49.62%	0.299
ionosphere	84.64%	66.16%	99.38%	0.216
liver_disorders	56.52%	51.48%	65.29%	0.568
mushrooms	90.22%	95.36%	68.62%	0.103
covariance with bound	-0.0174738	-0.019891053	-0.006147845	
correlation coefficient with bound	-0.9945419	-0.76209998	-0.229377221	

The results show that the bound has a higher negative correlation with the accuracy calculated by Cross-Validation method and their sum is also equal to 1 approximately. The results of two methods are consistent, and bound can reflect the generalization error rate perfectly. Meanwhile the accuracy calculated by Cross-Validation method is more accurate than the accuracy directly calculated in the front experiments. The bound also has a high negative correlation with specificity.

By the experiments, we can analyze and compare the two model evaluation methods: N-fold Cross-Validation and PAC-Bayes bound.

The advantage of 5-fold Cross-Validation is that you can independently choose the times of trials, and the amount of data in each test set. The disadvantage of this method is that the training algorithm has to be rerun from scratch "n" times, which means it takes "n" times as much computation to make an evaluation. A variant of this method is to randomly divide the data into a test and training set "n" different times. It is involved in the high computational complexity. Meanwhile, this method is based on experience and lack of theoretical support.

N-fold Cross-Validation seems more extensive than the PAC-Bayes bound in practical applications. The reason is that the former is easier to understand by long-term experiments while the theoretical system of the latter is complex and it is the result of a series of theoretical reasoning and proving. Therefore, there are many experiments to do for the latter. After a long-term experiment, if it will be shown that the latter is more highlight than the former in the algorithm stability and performance guarantees, the latter may replace the former in some application of model assessment. Moreover, the complexity of PAC-Bayes bound algorithm should be much lower than the former.

5 Conclusion

We apply the PAC-Bayes risk bound for SVM linear classifiers and test the generalization capabilities of PAC-Bayes bound with the statistical indicators, including sensitivity, specificity and accuracy. The open tests and close tests are built and the covariance and correlation coefficient have been computed. We can draw the conclusion that the bound has the high negative correlation with the accuracy, and has some negative correlation with the specificity and sensitivity according the result of experiments. Meanwhile, the systematic experiments are built to compare the N-fold Cross-Validation and PAC-Bayes bound. The capabilities of model performance assessments by the two methods are tested by five UCI datasets. Finally, the advantage and disadvantage of the two methods is summarized.

Acknowledgments. This research is partly supported by the Natural Science Funding of China under grand number 61170177 and innovation funding of Tianjin University. We thank Professor Gong for give a direction when I was confused.

References

1. McAllester, D.A.: Some PAC-Bayesian Theorems. J. Machine Learning 37(3), 355–363 (1999)
2. Langford, J.: Tutorial on practical prediction theory for classification. Journal of Machine Learning Research 6, 273–306 (2005)
3. Ambroladze, A., Parrado-Hernandez, E., Shawe-Taylor, J.: Tighter PAC-Bayes Bounds. In: Proceedings of Neural Information Processing Systems, pp. 9–16 (2006)
4. Wei, C., Yu, E.C., Hwang, J.K., Sung, T.Y., Hsu, W.L.: Predicting RNA-binding sites of proteins using support vector machines and evolutionary information. J. BMC Bioinformatics, 20–23 (2008)
5. Vapnik, V.N.: The nature of statistical learning theory. Springer, Heidelberg (2000)
6. Shawe-Taylor, J.: PAC-Bayes Analysis of Classification, London (2007), `http://videolectures.net/aop07_shawe_taylor_pba/`
7. Marchand, M., Shah, M.: PAC-Bayes Learning of Conjunctions and Classification of Gene-Expression Data. In: Advances in Neural Information Processing Systems 2004, Vancouver, vol. 17, pp. 881–888 (2004)
8. Herbrich, R., Graepel, T.: A PAC-Bayesian Margin Bound for Linear Classifiers. IEEE Transactions on Information Theory 48(12), 3140–3150 (2002)
9. Valiant, L.: A theory of the learnable. J. Communications of the ACM 27, 1134–1142 (1984)

Optimality of Versioning for Information Products Using Niching SSGA

Haiyang Feng, Minqiang Li, and Fuzan Chen

School of Management, Tianjin University,
Tianjin 300072, P. R. China
{hyfeng,mqli,fzchen}@tju.edu.cn

Abstract. Information products are the most typical products in E-business, and versioning strategy is widely used in the information industry. This paper focuses on the numerical investigation of versioning strategy for information products under piecewise linear utility function and continuously distributed customers in the monopolist market. The utility function adopted in this paper is a piecewise linear function of the product quality that captures more exactly the valuation of customers on information products. Information products are differentiated along two quality dimensions in our model. Moreover, a Niching steady-state genetic algorithm (Niching SSGA) is introduced to obtain numerical solutions of the optimization problem that is analytically intractable. Numerical experiments verify that with piecewise linear utility function the monopolist has greater incentive to distribute more versions of different quality levels when customers become less tolerant to quality degradation, and the firm could obtain more profit from multi-version schemes.

Keywords: Versioning strategy, Niching steady-state genetic Algorithm, E-business, Information product.

1 Introduction

Information products, which are usually referred as "anything that can be digitized and transmitted based on the information and communication technologies (ICTs)", [1] are the most typical products in E-business. Information product providers use the versioning strategy to provide a product line to segments of customers. For instance, Microsoft Corporation always develops and distributes multiple versions of different quality levels for all its software products. Besides software products, versioning has also been commonly used to differentiate web services, movies, music, etc. Although Shapiro and Varian [2] conclude that versioning strategy is "the smart way to sell information", this strategy may sometimes bring significant negative effects. A lower quality version can cannibalize the market share of the higher quality version, and the versioning strategy may then become less profitable. Researchers have analyzed the optimality of versioning strategy under different conditions.

The earliest study on product-line design dates back to Mussa and Rosen [3]. They concluded that the monopolist would find it optimal to offer quality-differentiated

V. Khachidze et al. (Eds.): iCETS 2012, CCIS 332, pp. 187–198, 2012.

products, which is not always tenable in terms of information products. Moorthy [4] analyzed the optimality of product-line strategy with discrete customer distribution and concluded that customer self-selection would lead to "cannibalization" and internal competition of the product-line. Bhargava and Choudhary [5] extended prior researches by generalizing the customer distribution and marginal cost function, and found that the optimal solution for selling information products was to create a single version when utility function was a linearly multiplicative function of the product quality and customer preference. Versioning was an effective strategy to deter entry and gain more profit when there were competitors in the market [6]. In the presence of network externality, versioning had been justified to be profitable [7]. Bhargava and Choudhary [8] investigated a model with generalized customer valuation function and customer distribution and derived a simple rule for determining the optimality of versioning. The present paper focuses on the formulation of customer utility function with uniform customer distribution.

Utility function was always assumed to be a linear function of product quality in previous studies (see Mussa and Rosen [3], Bhargava and Choudhary [5], etc.). However, low-end customers may not be interested in high-level functionality, so utility obtained by the low-end customers from low-quality versions may be close or equal to that from high-quality versions. Meanwhile, high-end customers may have a zero willingness to pay (WTP) for a version with low quality level. In order to model these phenomena, Krishnan and Zhu [9] define saturation quality and reservation quality. Saturation quality is "the level of quality beyond which the customer's WTP for product quality tapers off." Reservation quality is "the level of quality below which a customer (segment) would not even consider buying the product."

The present paper considers the continuous market of customers who are quality sensitive. Moreover, we define a coefficient to measure customers' degree of intolerance to quality degradation. It is called the customer intolerance-coefficient and is equal to saturation quality divided by reservation quality. In this paper, it is numerically demonstrated that the monopolist has greater incentive to adopt a multi-version scheme when considering saturation and reservation effects, and with the increase of customer intolerance-coefficient, customers become less tolerant to quality degradation; thus, the cannibalization effect of lower quality versions to higher quality versions would be weaker, and the monopolist thus gets more profit with multi-version schemes.

Numerical investigation was commonly adopted when the model was analytically intractable in previous researches [6] [10]. In this paper, a novel Niching steady-state genetic algorithm [11] [12] is introduced to obtain the numerical solution of the optimization model, because it is difficult to obtain an analytical solution.

The rest of the paper is organized as follows. We formulate the general model in section 2. Section 3 introduces the Niching steady-state genetic algorithm adopted in this paper. Numerical experiments are reported and results are analyzed in section 4. Finally, section 5 concludes this study and points out further research directions.

2 Model Setup

Our investigation is limited to the domain of a monopoly. The monopolist attempts to adopt the versioning strategy to maximize total profit. This section describes how the product's quality, cost structure, customer demand, and utility function are modeled under two-dimensional product quality. Assumptions used in the model are firstly introduced.

Assumption 1: There is a monopolist and heterogeneous customers who are continuously distributed with their preference in the market. The monopolist offers one version or multiple versions of an information product to all customers for the pursuit of profit maximization.

Assumption 2: An individual customer typically demands at most one copy of a version of the product, the one that maximizes his/her surplus.

Assumption 3: The monopolist has already developed the highest-quality version, and the versioning strategy is implemented by quality degradation.

Assumption 4: Marginal cost of producing the information products is assumed to be zero, and fixed costs of developing the highest-quality version is assumed to be sunk. Meanwhile, quality degradation is costless.

Generally, all kinds of development and production costs are assumed to be zero in the model. However, the menu cost in the distribution process will be considered in section 4.2. Obviously, the cost structure greatly impacts the versioning decision of the firm, even in terms of information products. Bhargava and Choudhary [5] concluded that the versioning strategy was not optimal when the highest-quality version has the best cost-quality ratio. Lacourbe and Loch [10] verified that variable costs drive vertical differentiation. This paper focuses on customers' valuation function, and demonstrates that the versioning strategy could be profitable even under zero marginal cost.

In this paper, the quality of information products is denoted by a vector $\boldsymbol{q} = (q_1, q_2)$. q_1 and q_2 are both normalized to be in the closed interval $[0,1]$ ($q_1, q_2 \in [0,1]$). The highest-quality version that has already been developed is denoted by H whose quality is $\boldsymbol{q_H} = (q_{H1}, q_{H2})$ ($q_{H1} = q_{H2} = 1$). The firm can provide versions of any quality level in the two-dimensional space $Q = \{(q_1, q_2) \mid q_1, q_2 \in [0,1]\}$ without incurring any extra cost.

Linear utility function has been commonly adopted in previous researches, but it cannot describe some basic features of customer demand for information products. For example, the quality requirement of high-end customers is independent of price, and a high-end customer does not buy a low-quality version, even if it is priced very low or free. Low-end customers do not need high-quality functions of the information products, so they are reluctant to pay higher prices for higher-quality products. Thus, we adopt the formulation of utility function proposed by Krishnan and Zhu [9], and extend it to the context of continuous customer distribution.

In Krishnan and Zhu's design [9], saturation and reservation qualities were defined in the model of customer utility. A customer's marginal willingness to pay is zero when the quality of the information product is beyond his/her saturation quality. The utility derived by the customer from the version with quality level below reservation quality is zero. Customers' saturation quality in two dimensions are denoted as q_{1S} and q_{2S}, and reservation quality in two dimensions are referred to as q_{1R} and q_{2R}.

In this paper, θ_1 and θ_2 represent the customer's marginal valuations for the product along quality dimensions q_1 and q_2 respectively, and they are also normalized to be in the closed interval $[0,1]$. (θ_1,θ_2) is the customer type and indicates the customer's two-dimensional preference for quality. The customer type is continuously distributed for heterogeneous customers, and the customer market space is denoted by $M=\{(\theta_1,\theta_2)\mid\theta_1,\theta_2\in[0,1]\}$. It is assumed that customers with higher marginal WTP have higher saturation and reservation qualities. We further assume that the customer (θ_1,θ_2) has a saturation quality $q_{iS}=\theta_i$ $(i=1,2)$ and a reservation quality $q_{iR}=\beta\theta_i$ $(i=1,2,\ \beta\in(0,1))$. The parameter $\beta=q_{iR}/q_{iS}$ is the customer intolerance-coefficient. Naturally, a customer can tolerate a greater quality degradation when β is smaller. Thus, a new WTP function is described in Eq. (1).

$$W(q_1,q_2)=\begin{cases}0, & \text{if } q_i<q_{iR},\ i=1,2,\\ \sum_i\theta_i q_{iS}\dfrac{q_i-q_{iR}}{q_{iS}-q_{iR}}, & \text{if } q_i\in[q_{iR},q_{iS}],\ i=1,2,\\ \theta_i q_{iS}\dfrac{q_i-q_{iR}}{q_{iS}-q_{iR}}+\theta_j q_{jS}, & \text{if } q_i\in[q_{iR},q_{iS}],\ q_j\in(q_{jS},+\infty),\ i,j\in\{1,2\},\ i\neq j,\\ \sum_i\theta_i q_{iS}, & \text{if } q_i\in(q_{iS},+\infty),\ i=1,2.\end{cases}\tag{1}$$

WTP function (1) is a piecewise linear function of quality, as shown in Fig. 1.

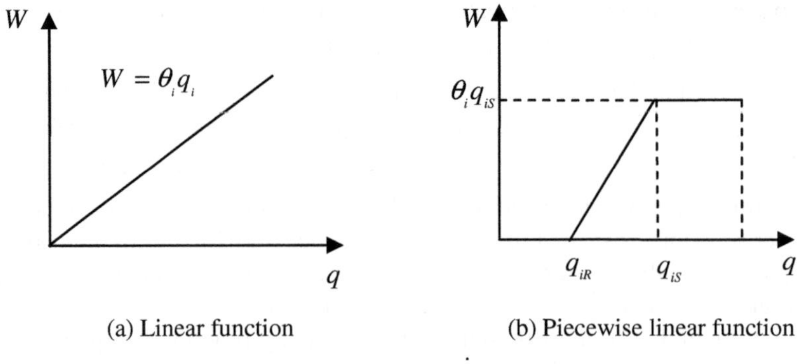

Fig. 1. Linear WTP function and piecewise linear WTP function ($i=1,2$)

The customer utility function is given in Eq. (2),

$$U(\theta_1,\theta_2;q_1,q_2;p)=W(\theta_1,\theta_2;q_1,q_2)-p,\tag{2}$$

where p is the price of the product (q_1,q_2).

In the following, we compare the profitability of one-version scheme, which only contains the highest-quality version H, with K-version scheme, which contains the highest-quality version H and multiple lower quality versions: $L_1,...,L_{K-1}$. Notations of price and quality of each version are shown in Table 1.

Table 1. Notations of price and quality of versions

Symbols	Explanation
p_H	Price of the highest-quality version H
p_{Lk}	Price of low-quality version L_k ($k=1,...,K-1$)
$\boldsymbol{q}_H=(q_{H1},q_{H2})$	Quality level of H, $(q_{H1},q_{H2})=(1,1)$
$\boldsymbol{q}_k=(q_{k1},q_{k2})$	Quality level of L_k, ($k=1,2,...,K-1$, $0\le q_{k1},q_{k2}\le 1$)

In the distribution process of an information product, menu cost is unavoidable. To some information products, their menu costs can be treated as sunk cost because it is invariant with the number of versions offered. However, menu cost of other information products will increase with the version number. For example, when a low-quality version is to be distributed, the monopolist may have to spend more money on advertising to introduce this low-quality version to its target customers. For those information products whose menu costs increase with the version number, the menu costs would have a nontrivial impact on versioning strategy. Therefore, we tend to analyze optimality of versioning either by considering the menu cost, or not, respectively. Menu cost is denoted by $c_d(K)$. Thus, the optimization problem for the versioning strategy is defined as:

$$\max_{p_{L1},...,p_{K-1},p_H;\boldsymbol{q}_1,...,\boldsymbol{q}_{K-1}} \pi_K = p_H n_H + \sum_{k=1}^{K-1} p_{Lk} n_{Lk} - c_d(K), \tag{3}$$

$$\text{s.t. } p_H > 0,$$

$$0 < p_{Lk} < p_H,\ k=1,2,...,K-1,$$

$$0 \le q_{ki} \le 1,\ k=1,2,...,K-1,\ i=1,2,$$

where n_H is the demand of the highest-quality version, and n_{Lk} is the number of customers who have purchased low-quality version L_k. As assumed in ***Assumption 2***, customers will purchase version a if its utility satisfies: $U_a \ge 0$, and $U_a \ge U_b$ ($a,b \in \{L_1,...,L_{K-1},H\}$, $a \ne b$).

Since model (3) is a nonlinear and multimodal optimization problem, the conventional analytical algorithms and standard heuristic algorithms do not efficiently obtain the optimal solutions; the Niching steady-state genetic algorithm (Niching SSGA) is employed to solve the optimization problem.

3 Niching Steady-State Genetic Algorithm

Solutions to the optimization problem are represented by chromosomes in GA. In order to obtain high-precision solutions, real coding is adopted to represent decision variables in problem (3), so a chromosome will be a vector of $3K-2$ (the number of price parameters is K, and the number of quality parameters is $2(K-1)$) dimensions. After defining the structure of individual strings, the evolution of the population can be conducted in a designed procedure.

At the beginning of the Niching SSGA, an initial generation of individuals that represent feasible solutions is produced randomly. After application of the genetic operators to the parents, good-quality offspring are born. The stronger individuals have a greater probability of survival in the competitive evolution. At the end of this simulated evolutionary process, near-optimal or optimal solutions can be derived.

```
Procedure Niching SSGA
T_max - number of generations
N - the population size
p_c - rates for crossover
q - the size for individual neighbor
initialize: P(0)
calculate: fitness(P(0))
for t=1 to T_max do
    four-tournament selection: A={a_1,a_2,a_3,a_4} ∈ P(t-1)
    uniform crossover: A'={a_1',a_2',a_3',a_4'} ← crossover(A)
    hill-climbing: A"={a_1",a_2",a_3",a_4"} ← hill-climbing(A')
    NNRC:
    for i=1 to 4 do
      calculate: dis(a_i", P(t-1))
      get: P'={b_1,b_2,...,b_q}, q nearest neighbor set
      find:
      b* = {b_j | fitness(b_j) ≤ fitness(b_k), b_j, b_k ∈ P'; j,k = 1,2,...,q; j ≠ k}
      if fitness(a_i" ≥ b*)
        replace: b* ← a_i"
      end if
    end for
    P(t) ← P(t-1)
```

Fig. 2. Procedure of the Niching steady-state GA

Before introducing genetic operators, we introduce the calculation of individuals' fitness. Assume that the total number of customers is 1,000,000, and the customer market space $M=\{(\theta_1,\theta_2) \mid \theta_1 \in [0,1], \theta_2 \in [0,1]\}$ is equally divided into 100×100

grids, then the customer number in each grid can be derived through the customer distribution function. There are 100 customers in each grid when customers are uniformly distributed. Moreover, we use the centre point of the grid to represent the types of all customers in this grid. For each set of decision variables, the profit gained by the firm is easy to obtain by examining the decision of customers in each grid. During the genetic evolutionary process, the profit is used to represent the fitness of an individual in the population. An individual that brings greater profit is more competitive in the evolutionary process.

The genetic algorithm is implemented in the steady-state scheme. In each generation, four individuals are selected by four-tournament selection to pair for crossover. After uniform crossover, four offspring are produced. Then, instead of mutation operation, a hill-climbing algorithm is exerted on each offspring to search for a better solution in its neighborhood. After this local search process in carried out, the four offspring are fine-tuned. Then, four chromosomes are selected from the population for replacement by the offspring. In order to locate and maintain multiple niches in a population, we adopt a novel replacement policy, which is called nearest neighbors replacement crowding (NNRC) [11] [12]. In the replacement process, the candidate individuals to be replaced are limited to offspring's q-nearest neighbors, and the one with the lowest fitness is to be replaced. In this study, Euclidean metric is used to measure the distance between two individuals. The NNRC makes the replacement policy totally local, and the competition among individuals is confined locally in different niches. Therefore, the diversity of the population can be preserved, which is critical to enhance the global search capability of the algorithm. The procedure of the Niching steady-state genetic algorithm (Niching SSGA) is presented in Fig. 2 and the procedure of the Hill-climbing algorithm is shown in Fig. 3.

```
Procedure Hill-climbing algorithm
  l - number of iterations
  σ(1) - initial standard deviation of
         Gaussian distribution
Δσ - decreased magnitude of σ in each iteration
n - number of parameters in the offspring a = {a(1),...,a(n)}
for i = 1 to l do
    for j = 1 to n do
      generate: ε ~ N(0, σ(i)^2)
      get: a' = {a(1),...,a(j) + ε,...,a(n)}
      if fitness(a' ≥ a)
        replace: u ← u'
      end if
    end for
    calculate: σ(i+1) = σ(i) − Δσ
end for
output a
```

Fig. 3. Procedure of the Hill-climbing algorithm

4 Numerical Results

In order to obtain a more accurate numerical solution, the Niching SSGA runs 30 times in each experiment, and the best solution is selected from the numerical results. It is assumed that the monopolist could offer at most five versions ($K \leq 5$). Major parameter settings of the genetic algorithms are recorded in Table 2.

Table 2. Parameter setting of the numerical method

Parameters	Value
Number of generation: $T_{\max}$	100
Population size: N	20
Crossover rate: p_c	0.8
Individual neighbor size: q	5
Iterations of hill-climbing: l	10
Initial standard deviation of Gaussian distribution: $\sigma(1)$	0.1
Decreased magnitude of σ in each iteration: $\Delta\sigma$	0.01

4.1 Optimal Versioning without Considering Menu Cost

By adopting the Niching SSGA described in section 3, this subsection tends to obtain the near-optimal solution of problem (3) numerically, with different customer intolerance-coefficient β . Menu cost is treated as sunk cost in this subsection: $c_d(K)=0$.

We first examine the optimal multi-version scheme under linear utility function: $U(\theta_1,\theta_2;q_1,q_2;p)=\theta_1q_1+\theta_2q_2-p$ as a benchmark case. As shown in Fig. 4(a), a three-version scheme is the most profitable scheme in this case. Then, we investigate the optimal multi-version scheme under piecewise linear utility function (2). It is illustrated in Fig. 4(b) that five-version schemes are more profitable than other schemes with different customer intolerance-coefficient β . Moreover, the profit increment is much more significant under the piecewise linear utility function, which means versioning strategy is more attractive.

Fig. 5 illustrates the maximal profit obtained in the optimal K -version scheme when $\beta \in \{0,0.1,...,0.9\}$. This experiment further verifies that the five-version scheme including the highest-quality version and 4 low-quality versions is always more profitable than other schemes with different customer intolerance-coefficient β . Meanwhile, with the increase of β , the monopolist can gain greater profit from the multi-version schemes. With the increase of parameter β , customers become less tolerant to quality degradation, so the low-quality version is less attractive to high-end consumers. Therefore, the cannibalization effect resulting from the offering of low-quality versions becomes weaker, thus multi-version schemes are preferable over a one-version scheme by the monopolist.

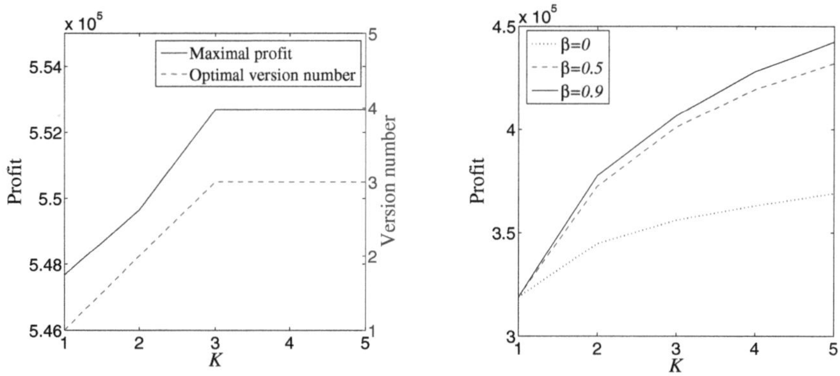

(a) Under linear utility function (b) Under piecewise linear utility function

Fig. 4. Maximal profit and optimal version number

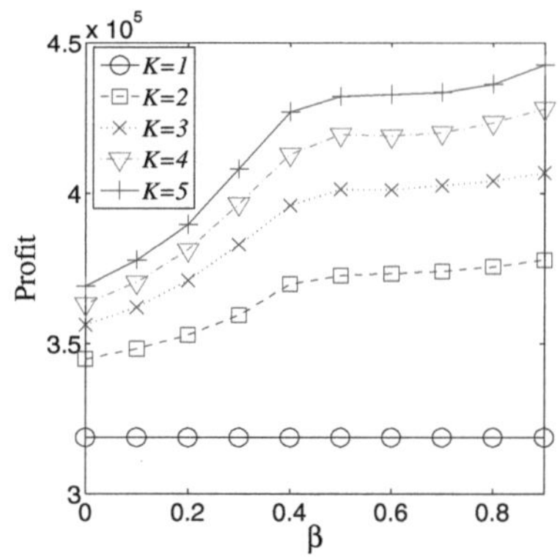

Fig. 5. Maximal profit in the optimal K -version scheme

From these numerical experiments, we can make the following observation.

Observation 1: As compared with the benchmark case, in which utility function is a linear function of product quality, the monopolist has greater incentive to adopt versioning strategy under piecewise linear utility function, and also to offer more versions. Moreover, with the increase of intolerance-coefficient β , multi-version schemes can bring greater profit to the monopolist.

4.2 Optimal Versioning Considering Menu Cost

It is assumed in this subsection that offering a low-quality version will lead to more menu cost in the distribution process. In this subsection, menu cost is given by $c_d(K) = \alpha m K^2$, where $m = 1000,000$ is the total number of customers and K , as defined in section 2, is the number of versions provided by the firm, and $\alpha > 0$ is an unrelated scalar parameter to represent the rate of increase of menu cost in total customer numbers.

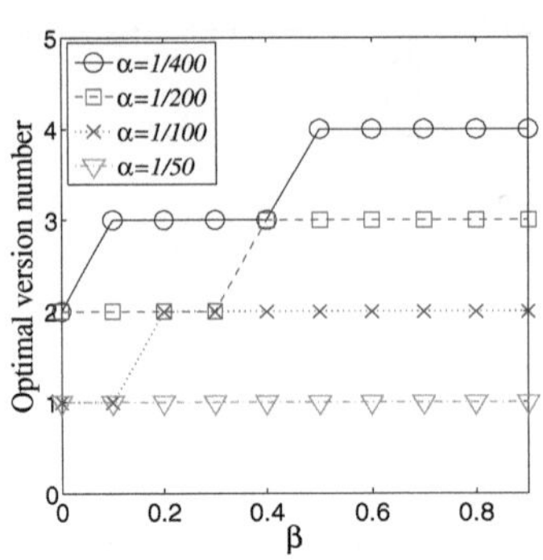

(a) Optimal version number

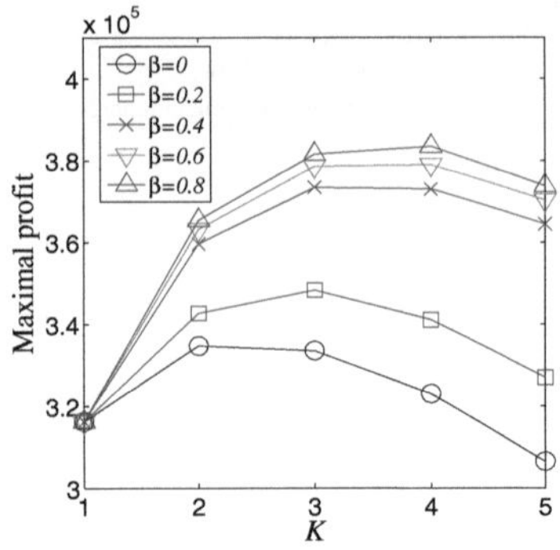

(b) Maximal profit ($\alpha = 1/400$)

Fig. 6. Optimal version number and maximal profit when menu cost is considered

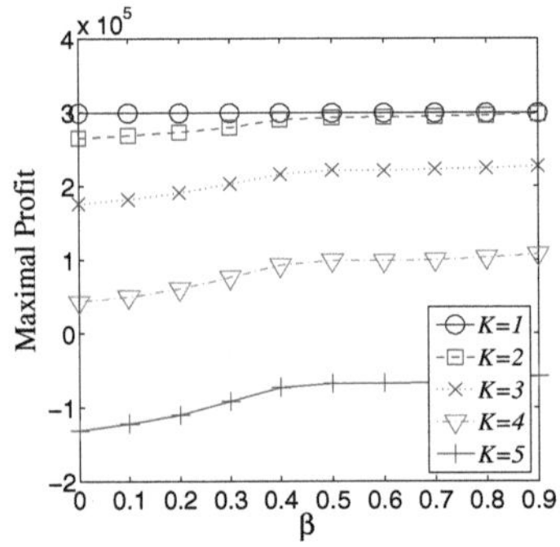

(a) $\alpha = 1/50$

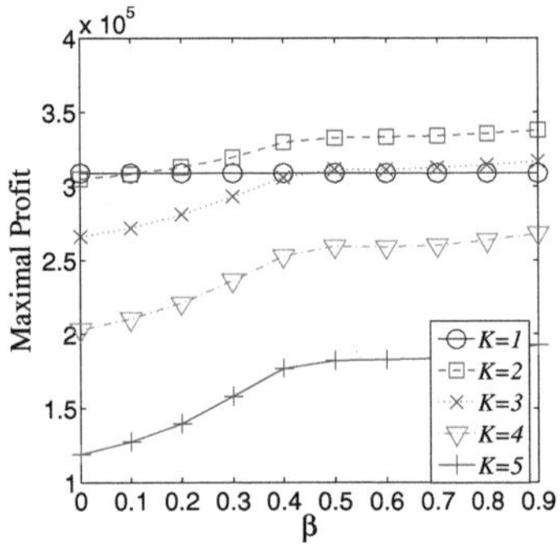

(b) $\alpha = 1/100$

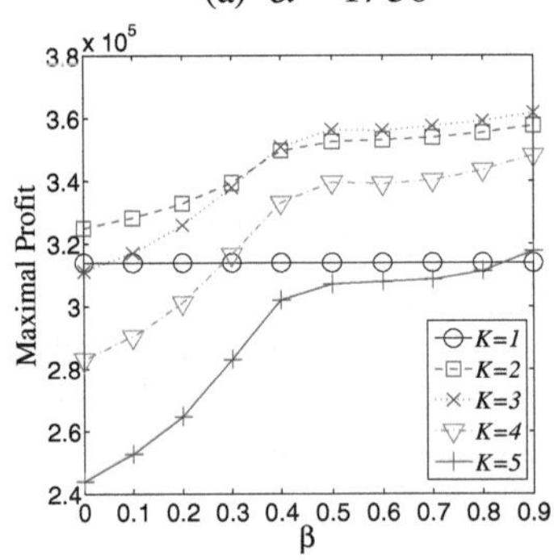

(c) $\alpha = 1/200$

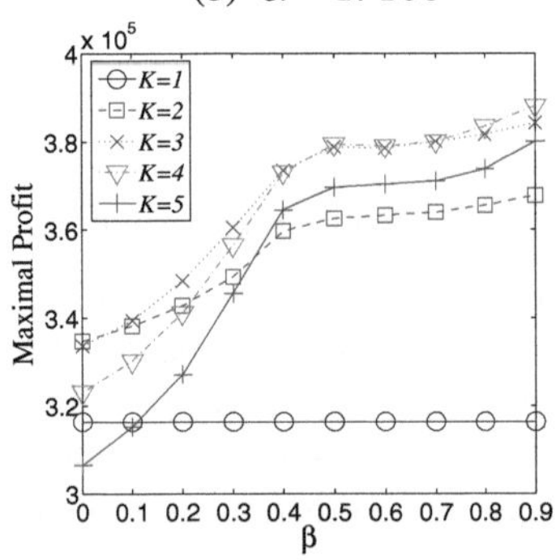

(d) $\alpha = 1/400$

Fig. 7. Maximal profit in the optimal K -version schemes

Fig. 6(a) shows the optimal number of versions against customer intolerance-coefficient β . Fig. 6(b) shows the change of maximal profit with respect to the number of versions offered by the firm. From this figure, it is clear that versioning is preferred better when β is bigger, and this is consistent with the conclusion obtained in subsection 4.1 in which menu cost was not considered. Moreover, the monopolist intends to offer more versions when α is smaller.

Fig. 7 illustrates the maximal profit gained by the monopolist in the optimal K-version schemes ($K = 1, 2, ..., 5$) when $\alpha \in \{1/50, 1/100, 1/200, 1/400\}$. As Fig. 7 shows, the one-version scheme becomes more attractive when α becomes bigger. When α is fixed, with the increase of parameter β , the profit increment is bigger if the firm chooses to offer more low-quality versions. Thus, we conclude the following.

Observation 2: If menu cost is considered, the most profitable scheme must contain fewer low-quality versions. In the case without considering menu costs, profit would increase monotonically with the number of versions provided (as shown in Fig. 5); however, in this case considering menu costs, profit would first increase and then decrease with it (as shown in Fig. 6 (b)).

4.3 Discussion and Managerial Insights

In this section, a Niching steady-state genetic algorithm has been adopted to compute the numerical solutions of the optimal versioning strategy of information product providers under a piecewise linear utility function with and without taking into consideration menu cost. In each generation of the Niching SSGA, a hill-climbing algorithm is designed to locally fine-tune an offspring. Numerical experiments demonstrate that the Niching SSGA works effectively and efficiently in the optimal versioning task of the information products.

It has been verified through numerical experiments that:

(1) When menu cost was not considered, the three-version scheme was the most profitable under linear utility function, while the five-version scheme was more profitable under piecewise linear utility function. Moreover, a multi-version scheme was more attractive under piecewise linear utility function.

(2) With the increase of customer intolerance-coefficient β , profit gained by the firm in the multi-version scheme would increase and would be invariable in the one-version scheme. Thus, multi-version schemes become preferable over one-version schemes for the firm, whether or not menu cost is considered, because an increase of β means customers are less tolerant to quality degradation; therefore, low-quality versions would cannibalize less market share of the highest-quality version. Furthermore, the most profitable scheme would contain more versions with the increase of β when considering menu cost.

(3) Since menu cost was defined as a quadratic function of version number, the most profitable scheme would contain fewer versions after considering menu cost. Maximal profit gained will first increase and then decrease with the version number. Moreover, if α , which measures the rate of increase of menu cost in total number of customers, becomes greater, the monopolist will prefer to offer fewer versions.

5 Conclusion

This paper investigates the optimality of versioning strategy under piecewise linear utility function. Numerical results verify that versioning is more attractive and the monopolist intends to offer more low-quality versions if the utility function changes from being linear in product quality to being piecewise linear, and when the customers become less tolerant to quality degradation, the cannibalization effect resulting from the offering of low-quality versions becomes weaker; thus the information product provider would have greater incentive to adopt a multi-version strategy. Furthermore, numerical experiments illustrate that a multi-version scheme is less attractive after considering menu cost. The main contribution of this paper resides in the following: (1) We adopt a Niching steady-state genetic algorithm for the optimal versioning of an information product. (2) A piecewise linear utility function is examined under continuous customer distribution and two-dimensional product quality; thus, some novel managerial insights are derived through numerical experiments.

Our model also has some limitations. Factors such as network externality and competition have heretofore not been considered. In further research, we will examine impacts of these factors on version strategy of information products in E-business, based on the numerical framework proposed in this paper.

Acknowledgments. This work was supported by the National Science Fund for Distinguished Young Scholars of China (Grant No. 70925005) and the General Program of the National Science Foundation of China (No.71101103, No.61074152, No.71001076). This work was also supported by grants from the Research Fund for the Doctoral Program of Higher Education of China (20100032120086, 20100032110036, 20090032110065).

References

1. Li, M., Feng, H., Chen, F.: Optimal versioning and pricing of information products with considering or not common valuation of customers. Comput. Ind. Eng. 63, 173–183 (2012)
2. Shapiro, C., Varian, H.R.: Versioning: The Smart Way to Sell Information. Har. Bus. Rev. 76, 106–114 (1998)
3. Mussa, M., Rosen, S.: Monopoly and product quality. J. Econ. Theory 18, 301–317 (1978)
4. Moorthy, K.S.: Market Segmentation, Self-Selection, and Product Line Design. Mark. Sci. 3, 288–307 (1984)
5. Bhargava, H.K., Choudhary, V.: Information Goods and Vertical Differentiation. J. Manage. Inform. Syst. 18, 89–106 (2001)
6. Chen, Y.-J., Seshadri, S.: Product Development and Pricing Strategy for Information Goods under Heterogeneous Outside Opportunities. Inform. Syst. Res. 18, 150–172 (2007)
7. Jing, B.: Network externalities and market segmentation in a monopoly. Econ. Lett. 95, 7–13 (2007)
8. Bhargava, H.K., Choudhary, V.: Research Note—When Is Versioning Optimal for Information Goods? Manage. Sci. 54, 1029–1035 (2008)
9. Krishnan, V., Zhu, W.: Designing a Family of Development-Intensive Products. Manage. Sci. 52, 813–825 (2006)
10. Lacourbe, P., Loch, C.H., Kavadias, S.: Product Positioning in a Two-Dimensional Market Space. Production and Operations Management 18, 315–332 (2009)
11. Li, M., Kou, J.: A novel type of niching methods based on steady-state genetic algorithm. Adv. in Nat. Comput. 36, 37–47 (2005)
12. Li, M., Lin, D., Kou, J.: An investigation on niching multiple species based on population replacement strategies for multimodal functions optimization. Soft Computing - A Fusion of Foundations, Methodologies and Applications 14, 49–69 (2010)

Incorporating Risk Attitude into the Iterated Prisoner's Dilemma: Application to E-business

Weijun Zeng, Minqiang Li, and Guofang Nan

College of Management and Economics, Tianjin University,
Tianjin 300072, China
weijunzeng2010@gmail.com, {mqli,gfnan}@tju.edu.cn

Abstract. The era of E-business has opened up new possibilities for the emergence of cooperation among enterprises. In this paper, the iterated prisoner's dilemma (IPD), which has been widely studied to understand how cooperative behaviors may survive among unrelated individuals when selfish actions can produce better short-term results, is investigated by considering players' risk attitudes. The risk of an IPD interaction is defined as the standard deviation of the one-move payoff. A two-population coevolutionary model is exploited to simulate the IPD games with two players having either identical or different risk attitudes. Results indicate that both risk-averse and profit-seeking players can cooperate well with their opponents in the noiseless and low-noise environments. In high-noise environments, however, risk-averse players perform better in comparison to the profit-seeking players. With respect to managerial meaning in the field of E-business economics, our results indicate that enterprises in competition should value long-term relationships with each other for the purpose of adapting to the fast changing market.

Keywords: E-business, cooperation, iterated prisoner's dilemma, risk attitude, coevolutionary model.

1 Introduction

E-business has become a major engine for global economics and trade [1]. The characteristics of E-business, including convenient online payments and high-speed internet-based connections, tend to lower barriers for enterprises to enter into both B2C and B2B commerce. Thus, competition among enterprises becomes intensified. On the other hand, the e-marketplace also provides consumers with an unprecedented ability to gather information and compare prices for individual preferences and satisfaction. In order to meet the requirements of customers with different preferences, differentiated-quality products are offered through innovative product-line design, where the collaboration among enterprises has become a main business strategy [2]. Cooperation seems to be the commonly adopted alternative for enterprises to gain sustained competitive advantage in creating value for final customers, especially in emerging and fast-growing industries. The compatibility of software products [3] and the technology-based alliance networks in the automotive industry [4] are examples of this trend.

V. Khachidze et al. (Eds.): iCETS 2012, CCIS 332, pp. 199–213, 2012.

To better understand how cooperation comes about, the IPD game, which has been widely used to model the evolution of cooperative behavior in a variety of fields [5], is investigated in this paper. As previous studies have shown, the emergence of cooperation in the IPD can be influenced by a number of factors. For example, by introducing an evolvable encounter length into the interactions of coevolving strategies within a population, Fogel [6] addressed the relationship between the mean length of encounter and the evolution of cooperation, and found that mutual cooperation was more likely to arise under long-term encounters. Weeks [7] argued that payoff values could also have a drastic impact on the emergence of cooperation, since they affect the evaluation of cooperative behaviors. Considering reputation-based games, Chong and Yao [8] showed that when coevolving strategies used reputation to estimate the behaviors of opponents prior to interactions and acted accordingly, the learning of cooperation was more likely.

In competition among enterprises, the enterprise's objective is to maximize payoff. However, steady cooperation with opponents may become important in the real world for the purpose of maintaining market shares and regular income [9]. When the IPD is used to model competition among two enterprises, the payoff of a player on each move (i.e., each one-shot PD game) will possibly change throughout the game process because the opponent's behavior is unknown in advance. However, the payoff would become stable if players have been engaged in a specific relationship. This fact provides a new perspective for studying cooperation and has not yet been completely addressed in previous research. In 1952, Markowitz [10] defined the variance of expected return as an indication of risk involved in financial prospects. Similarly, we attempt to define the risk in the IPD as the standard deviation of the one-move payoff, which indicates the riskiness involved in an IPD interaction. Based on this definition, a risk-averse player favors stability and tries to keep a steady interaction in the IPD, whereas a profit-seeking player tends to pursue the maximal payoff in each move.

A two-population coevolutionary learning framework (TPCL) is exploited to investigate the IPD interactions with two participants having either identical or different risk attitudes. The individuals in the two populations represent strategies for the two participants respectively. The learning process is driven through competitive coevolution in order to encourage an evolutionary "arms race", where improvement in the performance of a player can cause further improvement in that of the other player, and vice-versa. A modified niching method, namely q-NNR [11], is utilized for each population to promote the coevolution of multiple specialist strategies for each participant. Both the scenarios of noiseless and noisy IPD are considered.

The rest of this paper is organized as follows. Section 2 explains how we implement risk consideration in the IPD. Section 3 introduces the proposed TPCL learning model. The experimental studies are presented and discussed in Section 4; an economic interpretation of the relative results is also given in the E-business environment. Section 5 concludes this paper with remarks for future work.

2 Risk Consideration in the IPD

2.1 Motivation

Building long-term relationships with others is of paramount importance for an enterprise to gain sustained competitive advantage in the marketplace. Since the market environment is ever-changing, an enterprise needs to decide whether to change or to preserve the current relationship with particular partners for specific business goals.

The IPD game has been widely used to model long-term interactions between two individuals in economics [5]. It enables the investigation of how cooperative behavior survives when individuals' selfish actions produce better short-term results. Most studies of the IPD considered only the objective of maximizing players' payoffs. This study considers both maximizing payoffs and maintaining steady relationships in the IPD by incorporating risk attitude into the IPD game, where the risk involved in an IPD interaction is defined by the standard deviation of the one-move payoff.

2.2 Incorporating Risk Attitude into the IPD

In its basic form, the Prisoner's Dilemma (PD) is a two-player game, where each player can choose either to cooperate or to defect. The payoffs are determined by the payoff matrix illustrated in Fig.1, where the condition T>R>P>S is required.

		Player 2	
		Cooperate (C)	**Defect (D)**
Player 1	**Cooperate (C)**	(R,R)	(S,T)
	Defect (D)	(T,S)	(P,P)

Fig. 1. Payoff matrix of the Prisoner's Dilemma

As a result, defection is the best response to any action of an opponent, and both players will choose to defect. However, players would be better off if they cooperate with each other. A more interesting situation arises when the PD is played repeatedly (i.e. IPD). In this case, the payoffs should satisfy another condition 2R>T+S. Thus, each player has an opportunity to punish the other player for previous non-cooperative plays. Note that there are many possible values for T, R, P, and S that satisfy the above two conditions. We use T=5, R=3, P=1 and S=0 in our study [12-14].

In the following, we focus on incorporating risk attitude into the IPD game. Suppose that the one-move payoffs for the two players, i.e., Player 1 and Player 2, in an IPD game are $p_1 = (p_{11}, p_{12}, \dots p_{1l})$ and $p_2 = (p_{21}, p_{22}, \dots p_{2l})$, respectively, where l is the length of encounter and p_{ik} represents the payoff for player i on the kth move ($i = 1, 2$; $k = 1, 2, \dots, l$). Then the risk involved in this interaction for Player i can be measured as

$$r_i = \sqrt{\sum_{k=1}^{l} (p_{ik} - \overline{p}_i)^2} \qquad (1)$$

and his/her utility is expressed by

$$u_i = \frac{\overline{p}_i}{1 + \alpha_i \cdot r_i} \qquad (2)$$

where $\overline{p}_i = \sum_{k=1}^{l} p_{ik} / l$ and α_i represents the risk attitude of Player i ($i = 1, 2$). Here, if Player i is purely profit-seeking, then α_i is set to equal 0. Otherwise, $\alpha_i > 0$. The larger α_i is, the more risk-averse Player i should be.

Therefore, risk-averse players are more concerned with the preserved steady interaction with their opponents in the IPD, whereas profit-seeking players are active in profit maximization. Although both participants can benefit from mutual cooperation, profit-seeking players still exploit their opponents. However, such exploitation can only be a short-term behavior. Profit-seeking players prefer to retaliate against the opponents by defection, but risk-averse players may still cooperate after suffering a unilateral defection. However, if risk-averse players cannot be rewarded by cooperation in time, they tend to defect, and mutual cooperation may become more difficult or even impossible to reach, since risk-averse players would rather remain at the status quo.

The interactions will be more interesting if noise is considered [15]. This will also be discussed in our study. Here, noise is modeled as the mistake that a player makes. Given the probability of noise occurrence p_{noise}, a player, originally choosing Cooperation (or Defection) in a one-shot PD, will instead take Defection (or Cooperation) with a probability of p_{noise}.

3 Coevolutionary Model

In this section, we introduce the two-population coevolutionary learning model (TPCL) to study the IPD with two players having either identical or different risk attitudes. The strategy representation is explained in Section 3.1, while the procedure of coevolution is presented in Section 3.2.

3.1 Representation of Strategies

The encoding scheme uses a binary string to represent a complete IPD strategy that specifies the succeeding actions based on memory of the previous three moves, which has been commonly used in the learning model of the IPD [5]. Since each move has 4 possible outcomes, there are in total 4^3 possible histories of memory of length 3. Thus, a string has at least 64 bits in order to store an action for each possible history. Since there is no history of previous moves at the start of a game, additional bits, which carry the "pre-game" pseudo-history [14], are prefixed to the 64-bit string to specify a strategy's initial move. This method was widely used in previous research [16]. However, considering that people would often use first moves for exploration of the opponent's intention, we also specify the first three moves for each strategy. Thus, together, a 67-bit string represents a particular strategy. The first 64 are used for the history-based rules and the other 3 are used for exploration at the start of an IPD.

3.2 Procedure of Coevolution

The learning process in TPCL is driven through competitive coevolution to encourage an evolutionary "arms race" between the two players. Moreover, in order to overcome the pathologies of overspecialization in coevolutionary learning, a modified niching method, namely q-NNR [11], is utilized in both populations to promote the coevolution of multiple specialist strategies for each of the players. The end result is an IPD game with expert participants. Fig. 2 shows the basic procedure of coevolution. Details are described below.

3.2.1 Initialization

The terms "player α_1" and "player α_2" refer to the two participants in the IPD with risk attitudes α_1 and α_2 $(\alpha_1, \alpha_2 \geq 0)$ respectively. As illustrated in Fig. 2, coevolution starts with the random initialization of two populations of N strategies, i.e. POP_1 and POP_2, for player α_1 and player α_2 respectively. Then, each strategy s_{1i} ($i = 1, 2, \ldots, N$) in POP_1 competes with each strategy s_{2i} in POP_2 ($i = 1, 2, \ldots, N$) in an IPD game. After all of the cross-population competitions are finished, the fitness of a strategy is obtained by taking the average utility that it receives in all games it has played. Thus, strategies s_{1i} and s_{2i} are assessed respectively as follows:

$$F(s_{1i}) = u_1(s_{1i}) = \frac{1}{N}\sum_{j=1}^{N} \frac{\overline{p}(s_{1i}, s_{2j})}{1 + \alpha_1 \cdot r(s_{1i}, s_{2j})} \qquad (i = 1,2,\ldots,N) \tag{3}$$

$$F(s_{2i}) = u_2(s_{2i}) = \frac{1}{N}\sum_{j=1}^{N} \frac{\overline{p}(s_{2i}, s_{1j})}{1 + \alpha_2 \cdot r(s_{2i}, s_{1j})} \qquad (i = 1,2,\ldots,N) \tag{4}$$

where $\overline{p}(x, y)$ and $r(x, y)$ represent the average payoff per move and the risk respectively when the strategy x plays against the strategy y.

3.2.2 Genetic Operators: Crossover and Mutation

The strategies are evolved using a steady-state genetic algorithm and the genetic operators are identical for POP_1 and POP_2. For example, with the POP_1, two individuals (P_{11} and P_{12}) are randomly selected as parents from POP_1 to produce an offspring (O_1) in each generation by the following recombination:

$$O_1(i) = \begin{cases} P_{11}(i), & if \;\; p \leq p_c \\ P_{12}(i), & otherwise \end{cases} \qquad i = 1,2,\ldots,67 \tag{5}$$

where $p \in (0,1)$ is a randomly generated number for each bit of the offspring string, and p_c is the rate for crossover. Afterwards, the uniform bit-flip mutation is applied with a fixed probability p_m at each bit.

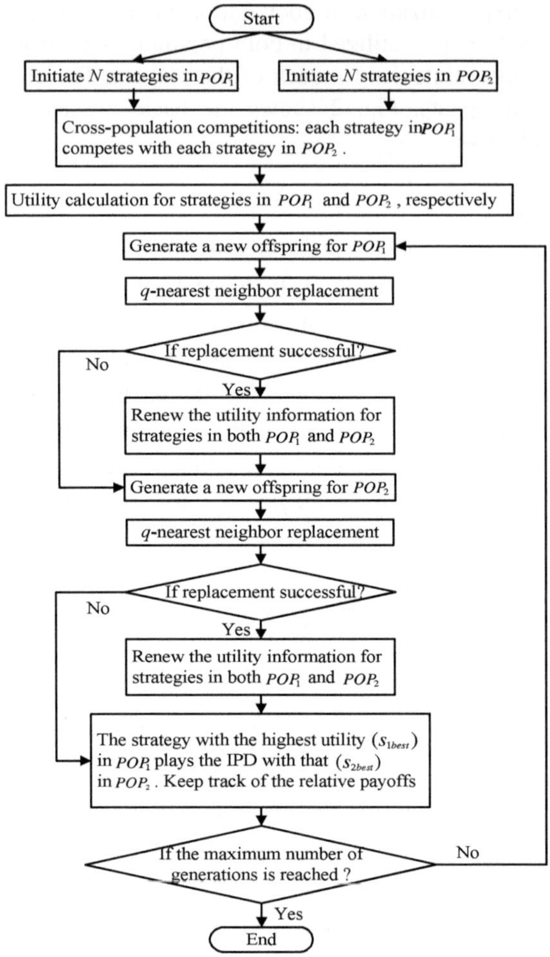

Fig. 2. The basic procedure of coevolution

3.2.3 *q*-Nearest Neighbor Replacement Policy

After the genetic operations, one strategy is selected from POP_1 for replacement by O_1 (This is also the case for POP_2). Here, we exploit a novel q-nearest neighbor replacement policy (q-NNR) [11], which is a niching method used to maintain multiple niches in a population: when an new offspring is inserted into the population, the candidate individuals to be replaced are limited to the offspring's q-nearest neighbors. Here, this method is used in order to promote the coevolution of multiple specialist strategies for each player in the IPD. After O_1 is generated, the similarity between O_1 and strategies s_{1i} ($i = 1,2,\ldots,N$) is calculated as:

$$d_{1i} = d(O_1, s_{1i}) = \sqrt{\sum_{j=1}^{67} [O_1(j) - s_{1i}(j)]^2} \qquad i = 1,2,\ldots,N \tag{6}$$

which is further sorted in descending order to get a list $\{ s'_{11}, s'_{12}, \ldots, s'_{1N} \}$, and the q strategies $\{ s'_{11}, s'_{12}, \ldots, s'_{1q} \}$ ranking highest are selected as the q-nearest neighbors of O_1 and their minimum utility is determined as $u_{1Min} = Min\,\{u(s'_{11}), u(s'_{12}), \ldots, u(s'_{1q})\}$. On the other hand, the utility of the offspring strategy $u_1(O_1)$ is calculated as follows:

$$u_1(O_1) = \sum_{j=1}^{N} \frac{\overline{p}(O_1, s_{2j})}{1 + \alpha_1 \cdot r(O_1, s_{2j})} \tag{7}$$

If $u_1(O_1) > u_{1Min}$, then the strategy with the minimum utility u_{1Min} in POP_1 will be replaced by O_1, and the utility information for strategies in both POP_1 and POP_2 is renewed accordingly.

The iteration of offspring generation, neighbor selection and replacement is repeated for POP_1 and POP_2 in rotation until the maximum number of generations is reached. Furthermore, after the neighbor replacements in POP_1 and POP_2 are finished in each generation, the best strategy with the highest utility (s_{1best}) for Player α_1 and that (s_{2best}) for Player α_2 are determined in order to play the IPD game. The relevant payoffs are recorded along with the coevolution.

4 Experimental Results

In this section, we conduct the IPD experiments by exploiting the TPCL model introduced in Section 3. The parameter setting is described in Section 4.1, while the computational results are presented in Section 4.2 and 4.3. An economic interpretation of the results in the E-business environment is given in Section 4.4.

4.1 Parameter Setting

Table 1 summarizes the parameters to be used in the experiments described below. 19 values are considered for α_1 and α_2, respectively, resulting in 190 different game scenarios. The length of encounter is set to be 53 (3 are exploration plays and the other 50 are history-based ones) to reduce computational expense. Note that the length of encounter is smaller than 150 that were used in most previous researches [13-15]. A longer encounter can better encourage cooperation; however, a length of about 20 would be sufficient for the emergence of cooperation as stated by Fogel [6]. Thus the game length of 53 is enough for our research purposes. The noise settings are based on the experimental work reported by Chong and Yao [15], and the parameters involved in the evolutionary process are selected based on Li and Kou's method [11]. Each of the following experiments is repeated for 20 independent runs.

Table 1. Parameter setting

Parameter	Value
Risk attitude (α_1, α_2)	({0,0.1,…,1.8}, {0,0.1,…,1.8})
Length of encounter (l)	50
Low noise (p_{noise})	0.001, 0.005
High noise (p_{noise})	0.05, 0.15
Population size (N)	50
Generations (G)	5000
Replacement parameter (q)	6
Crossover probability (p_c)	0.5
Mutation probability (p_m)	0.05

4.2 Evolution of Cooperation in Noiseless and Low-Noise Environments

Fig. 3 illustrates the average payoff per move for Player α_1 to play against Player α_2 ($\alpha_1, \alpha_2 \in \{0,0.1,0.2,...,1.8\}$) in the noiseless environment. The payoffs are taken from the final generation and averaged over 20 runs. It is seen that the payoffs are all close to 3, indicating that mutual cooperation is always achieved between the two players in the TPCL model. Fig. 4 plots the two players' average payoffs per move over 5,000 generations when $\alpha_1 = \alpha_2 \in \{0,0.2,0.4,...,1.6\}$. As has been shown by various studies on coevolutionary IPD strategy [6, 13, 15], the payoffs drop at first since the coevolving strategies tend towards mutual defection initially. However, the payoffs monotonously increased to 3 after a few dozen generations, and then the cooperation persisted between the two players in successive generations. Similar observations can be made for the other values of α_1 and α_2 as well. To our knowledge, no relevant studies have demonstrated such a high level of evolving cooperation. Fogel [6] investigated a population of coevolving strategies represented by finite-state machines and observed only the cyclic dynamics between cooperation and defection. Franken [13] showed that the fluctuation between cooperation and defection could be minimized if the binary representation of strategies was applied in the coevolution; however, the level of cooperation among the coevolving strategies was only 2.2, much lower than that in our experiments.

Observation on individual runs reveals that strategies for the two participants seem to reach an agreement when usage of the first three moves can lead to consecutive cooperation in the 50 history-based plays.

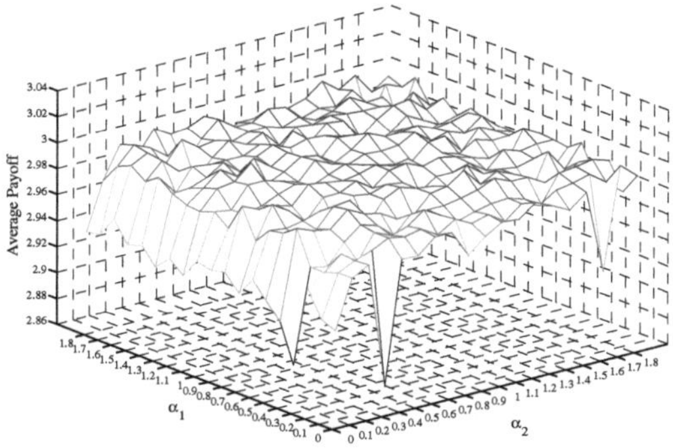

Fig. 3. Evolution of cooperation in the IPD in noiseless environment

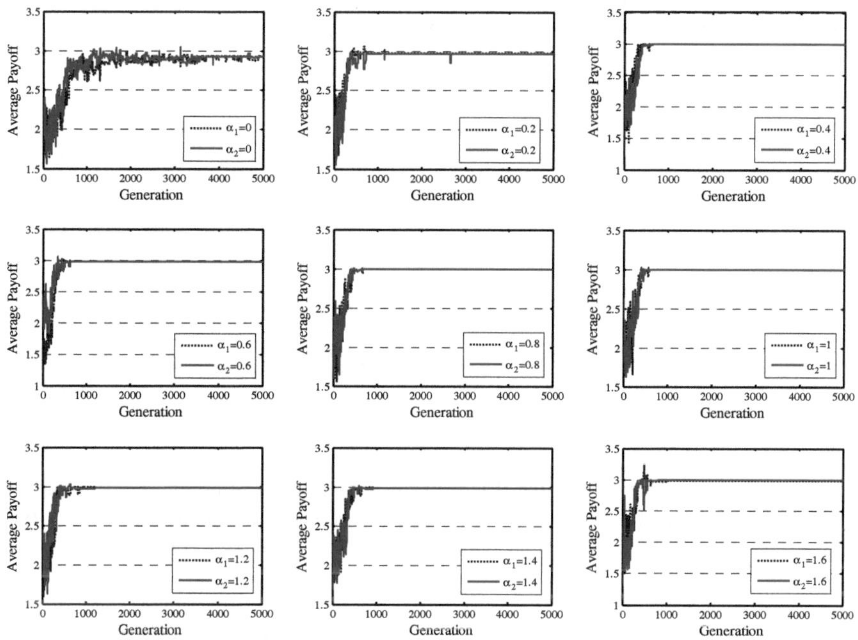

Fig. 4. The two participants' average payoffs per move over 5,000 generations when $\alpha_1 = \alpha_2 \in \{0, 0.2, 0.4, ..., 1.6\}$

For example, in an independent run in which $\alpha_1 = \alpha_2 = 0.2$, we observed that, from about generation 1,000, the best strategy s_{1best} for Player α_1 and that (s_{2best}) for Player α_2 both played "1-1-1" at the start of the IPD, resulting in a history of "111111" that decodes to 63. Furthermore, the bit positions 64 (63+1) of both s_{1best} and s_{2best} turned out to be "1" and thus the two strategies cooperated on the 4th move and then on the 5th move and so on to the 53rd move, leading to continuous mutual cooperative exchanges between the two players. It is noted that different runs might produce different usages for the first three interactions. However, s_{1best} and s_{2best} can still keep cooperating on the history-based plays. In the case in which $\alpha_1 \neq \alpha_2$, although the usages of the first three moves may differ between s_{1best} and s_{2best}, the continuous cooperative exchanges also emerge in the same way.

The local adaptation of strategies encourages this phenomenon. By adopting the rule of q-NNR in the TPCL, POP_1 and POP_2 are respectively evolved with multiple specialist strategies and thus behavioral diversity is successfully maintained in each of the populations. This is exactly the reason for the stable evolution of cooperation [17]. Noting that the resulting cooperative patterns between the two players depend completely on the usage of the first three moves in the interactions, we thus summarize the average values of bit positions 65, 66 and 67, respectively, for strategy s_{1best} in Table 2, where $\alpha_1, \alpha_2 \in \{0, 0.2, 0.4, ..., 1.6\}$. The results indicate that risk-averse players cooperate more than profit-seeking players on the first three moves. This explains the slight difference in the payoffs in Fig. 3.

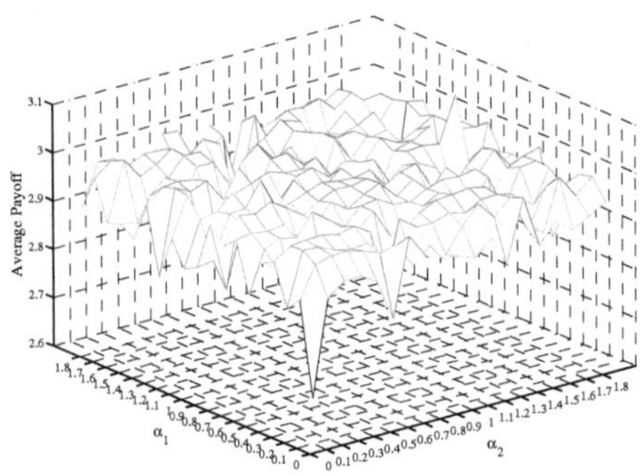

Fig. 5. Evolution of cooperation in the IPD in the low-noise environment with $p_{noise} = 0.001$

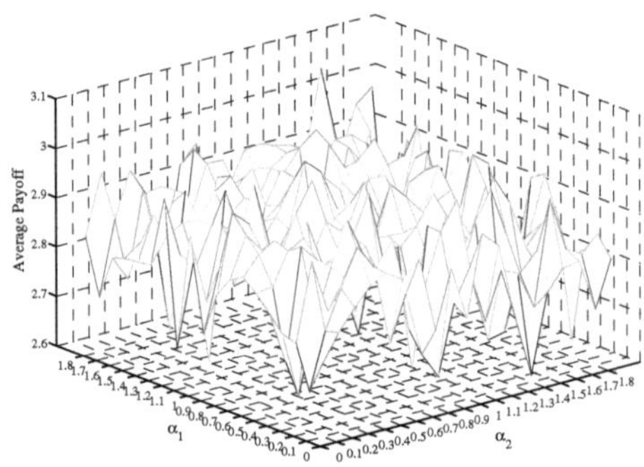

Fig. 6. Evolution of cooperation in the IPD in the low-noise environment with $p_{noise} = 0.005$

Figs. 5 and 6 depict the average payoffs per move for Player α_1 in the 190 different games with $p_{noise} = 0.001$ and $p_{noise} = 0.005$, respectively. The payoffs are again taken from the final generation and averaged over 20 runs. Compared with Fig. 3, it seems that the evolved cooperative patterns are not obviously affected by low noises. The payoff decreases slightly but still remains greater than 2.6 [6], indicating that mutual cooperation is still achieved between the two players in the low-noise environments.

Table 2. Average values of bit positions 65, 66, and 67, respectively, for strategy s_{1best}. Results are taken from the final generation and averaged over 20 runs. For brevity, only the cases in which $\alpha_1, \alpha_2 \in \{0, 0.2, 0.4, ..., 1.6\}$ are recorded

Bit			Player α_2								
			0	**0.2**	**0.4**	**0.6**	**0.8**	**1**	**1.2**	**1.4**	**1.6**
65	Player α_1	**0**	0.1	0.3	0.05	0.1	0.2	0.05	0.05	0.1	0.1
		0.2	0.5	0.65	0.7	0.7	0.75	0.65	0.7	0.6	0.9
		0.4	0.3	0.7	0.9	0.75	0.7	0.75	0.85	0.85	0.95
		0.6	0.45	0.7	0.75	0.85	0.85	0.7	0.8	0.75	0.85
		1.8	0.4	0.75	0.7	0.85	0.75	0.85	0.6	0.75	0.85
		1	0.35	0.65	0.75	0.7	0.85	0.85	0.9	0.85	0.68
		1.2	0.45	0.7	0.85	0.8	0.6	0.9	0.8	0.9	0.85
		1.4	0.45	0.6	0.85	0.75	0.75	0.85	0.85	0.85	0.95
		1.6	0.45	0.9	0.95	0.85	0.85	0.85	0.85	0.95	0.9
66	Player α_1	**0**	0.52	0.55	0.4	0.7	0.55	0.65	0.55	0.55	0.45
		0.2	0.7	0.75	0.9	0.8	0.85	0.8	0.9	0.7	0.95
		0.4	0.6	0.9	0.9	0.85	0.8	1	0.8	0.9	1
		0.6	0.8	0.8	0.85	0.9	0.9	0.8	0.9	0.9	0.9
		1.8	0.65	0.85	0.8	0.9	1	0.95	0.75	0.9	0.95
		1	0.75	0.85	1	0.8	0.95	0.92	1	0.85	0.85
		1.2	0.75	0.9	0.8	0.9	0.75	0.95	0.9	0.95	0.85
		1.4	0.7	0.7	0.9	0.9	0.9	0.9	0.95	0.95	1
		1.6	0.7	0.95	1	0.9	0.95	0.85	0.85	1	0.97
67	Player α_1	**0**	0.9	0.95	0.75	0.85	0.75	0.95	0.9	0.85	0.7
		0.2	0.8	0.87	0.95	0.9	0.95	0.9	0.95	0.95	1
		0.4	0.85	0.95	1	0.95	0.9	1	0.95	0.9	1
		0.6	0.8	0.95	0.95	0.95	1	1	0.95	0.95	1
		1.8	0.65	0.95	0.85	1	1	0.95	0.85	0.9	0.95
		1	0.95	0.9	1	0.95	0.95	0.97	0.95	0.9	0.95
		1.2	0.9	0.95	0.95	0.95	0.85	0.95	0.95	0.95	0.95
		1.4	0.75	0.95	0.9	0.9	0.95	0.9	0.95	0.9	1
		1.6	0.8	1	1	1	0.95	0.95	0.95	1	0.9

4.3 Impact of High Noise on Cooperation

Give $p_{noise} = 0.05$ and 0.15, we investigate the above-mentioned cooperative patterns' resistance to defection. Figs. 7 and 8 show the performances of Player α_1 in these two cases, respectively. Comparing these two figures with Figs. 3, 5 and 6, the payoff relatively drops, but consistently remains greater than 1.4 [6], which indicates that no games evolved to defection when simulated by the TPCL model. Table 3 summarizes the experimental results of the 20 independent runs for 10 different games, respectively. The results indicate that risk-averse players characterized with greater values for α_1 or α_2 could cooperate better with their opponents, and thus gained higher payoffs than profit-seeking players in the IPD with high noise. To verify this observation, Fig. 9 plots the payoff per move for Player α_1 ($\alpha_1 \in \{0,0.1,...,1.8\}$) when p_{noise} is set to be 0, 0.001, 0.005, 0.05, and 0.15, respectively, where the payoff is averaged from the 19 games the player participated (i.e., $\alpha_2 \in \{0,0.1,...,1.8\}$). In the noiseless and low-noise environments, there is no statistically significant difference in the performance between risk-averse (with large α_1) and profit-seeking (with small α_1) players. However, with increased noise in the IPD, risk-averse players do perform better than profit-seeking players, with a margin of about 0.3 in average payoff per move.

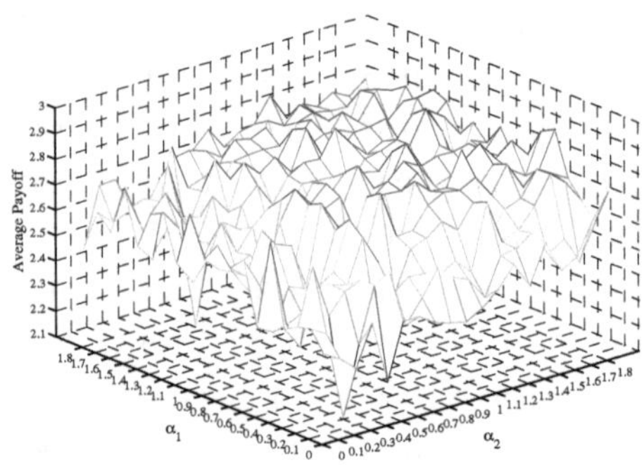

Fig. 7. Average performance of Player α_1 in the IPD with $p_{noise} = 0.05$

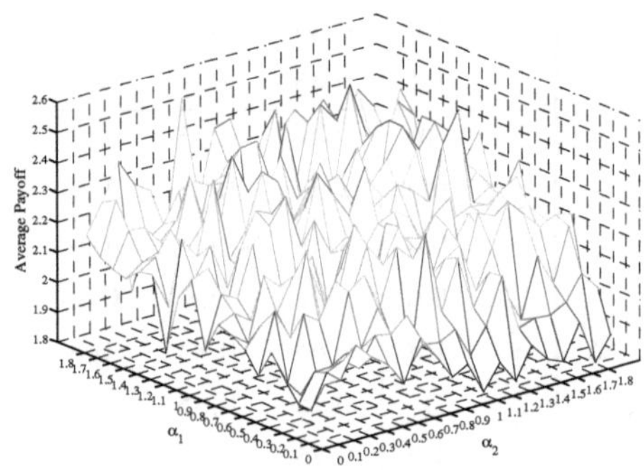

Fig. 8. Average performance of Player α_1 in the IPD with $p_{noise} = 0.15$

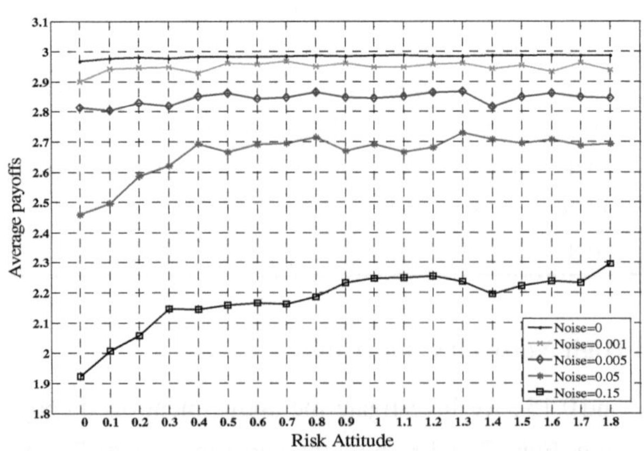

Fig. 9. Average payoff per move for Player α_1 for the 19 games in which he participated

Table 3. Comparison among games with different participants in the noisy environment with $p_{noise} = 0.05$ and $p_{noise} = 0.15$, respectively. "Average", "Max" and "Min" indicate the average, highest and lowest mean payoff per move for the two participants, respectively, taken from the 20 independent runs. NoR ≥ 2.6, $2 \leq$ NoR < 2.6, $1.4 <$ NoR < 2 and NoR ≤ 1.4 indicate the numbers of runs that ended with mutual cooperation, intermediate level of cooperation, low level of cooperation and mutual defection, respectively. The first value is given for the case with $p_{noise} = 0.05$ and the second $p_{noise} = 0.15$.

(α_1, α_2)	**Average**	**Max**	**Min**	NoR≥2.6	2≤NoR<2.6	1.4<NoR<2	NoR≤1.4
(0.0, 0.0)	2.415	2.764	1.707	(5, 0)	(13, 11)	(2, 9)	(0, 0)
(0.0, 0.1)	2.436	2.783	2.132	(4, 0)	(16, 7)	(0, 12)	(0, 1)
(0.2, 0.3)	2.573	2.764	1.962	(14, 0)	(5, 7)	(1, 13)	(0, 0)
(0.3, 0.5)	2.616	2.858	2.207	(12, 1)	(8, 18)	(0, 1)	(0, 0)
(0.5, 0.6)	2.708	2.962	2.377	(15, 3)	(5, 12)	(0, 5)	(0, 0)
(0.6, 0.8)	2.648	2.886	1.698	(14, 0)	(4, 19)	(2, 1)	(0, 0)
(0.8, 1.0)	2.663	2.943	2.037	(13, 4)	(7, 14)	(0, 2)	(0, 0)
(1.0, 1.4)	2.796	2.990	2.066	(19, 1)	(1, 17)	(0, 2)	(0, 0)
(1.4, 1.8)	2.755	2.971	2.386	(17, 2)	(3, 14)	(0, 4)	(0, 0)
(1.8, 1.8)	2.785849	2.962	2.443	(18, 2)	(2, 17)	(0, 1)	(0, 0)

4.4 Discussion

Most studies of the IPD have shown that cooperative behaviors can be learned from a set of random strategies using a coevolutionary algorithm; however, the evolution of cooperation would be unstable [6] and be destroyed by high levels of noise [15]. Nevertheless, it is observed in our experiment that, in the IPD games with risk-averse participants, cooperation can be always obtained and steadily sustained no matter whether in noiseless or noisy environments (in high-noise environment, an intermediate level of cooperation can be achieved). Note that the risk attitude defined by our study is associated with an individual's attitude towards his payoff variance in long-term interaction with his competitor, and a risk-averse player prefers to sustain a steady payoff. As to the managerial meaning in the field of E-business economics, our result suggests that, in the face of different competitive situations in the marketplace, an enterprise should manage to stabilize its payoff (thus reducing the risk in payoff) by steadily cooperating with the competitors.

In the era of E-business, enterprises are able to work together to supply high-quality products, services, or information in more efficient ways to satisfy different customers' demands. As they cooperate more routinely, the production and transaction costs will be significantly reduced, leading to greater revenue from the market for all enterprises. This benefits all cooperators by reducing the profit uncertainty (risk of payoff) that would otherwise be very high in the non-cooperative environment.

Long-term cooperation has become an essential part of E-business strategy. For instance, Ford, Daimler-Chrysler and General Motors have collaborated to develop "Covisint". This online marketplace enables them to directly purchase automotive parts and materials from their vast group of first tier suppliers (http://www clarity-consulting.com/optimizing_the_supply_chain.htm). The two largest video-streaming sites in China, Youku and Tudou, have signed a deal to merge, with the intention of leading the next phase of online video development in China (http://www.techinasia.com/youku-buys-tudou/). Following them, it is reported that Sohu, Tencent, and Qiyi will be teaming up to buy video rights together. The three will not actually be merging, it seems, but pooling their money together to buy video rights so that they can collectively afford to compete with Youku-Tudou (http://sg.finance.yahoo.com/news/sohu-tencent-qiyi-team-buy-041042519.html).

5 Conclusion

This paper addresses the problem of incorporating risk attitude into the IPD by simply defining the standard deviation of the one-move payoff as an indication of risk. A two-population coevolutionary learning model (TPCL) characterized with q-NNR is introduced to simulate the IPD game. Our experimental results show that, in both noiseless and low-noise environments, both risk-averse and profit-seeking players can cooperate well with their opponents by making an agreement on the usage of the first three moves that leads to consecutive cooperation in the history-based plays. However, in high-noise environments, risk-averse players cooperate better with their opponents and can thus gain higher payoffs than profit-seeking players in the IPD. Therefore, we conclude that introducing such a risk consideration indeed makes sense to the IPD.

There are several ways in which the work presented here can be extended. It will be interesting to examine the IPD game with intermediate levels of cooperation under the similar consideration of risk. Darwen and Yao reported [18] that full cooperative behaviors are more difficult to learn for the IPD with multiple choices as the degree of cooperation is usually stuck on some intermediate level for long periods. Herewith the question arises whether introducing such a risk consideration into the IPD with more choices would facilitate the stuck, or instead evoke full cooperation. One other approach that may be attempted is to change the profile of players in our learning model by adding famous man-made strategies [12] into the competition pool. Then, it would be interesting to see the difference in performances of risk-averse and profit-seeking players against those strategies. We leave these for future research.

Acknowledgments. The work was supported by the National Science Fund for Distinguished Young Scholars of China (Grant No. 70925005) and the General Program of the National Science Foundation of China (No.71101103, No.61074152, and No.71001076). This work was also supported by grants from the Research Fund for the Doctoral Program of Higher Education of China (20100032120086, 20100032110036, and 20090032110065).

References

1. Daniel, A.: The E-business Revolution: Living and Working in an Interconnected World. Prentice Hall, Upper Saddle River (2000)
2. Chakravarty, A.: Collaboration in E-Business: Technology and Strategy. International Series in Quantitative Marketing 16, 227–256 (2005)
3. Baake, P., Boom, A.: Vertical Product Differentiation, Network Externalities, and Compatibility Decisions. International Journal of Industrial Organization 19, 267–284 (2001)
4. Gulati, R., Gargiulo, M.: Where Do Interorganizational Networks Come From? American Journal of Sociology 104, 1439–1493 (1999)
5. Axelrod, R.: The Evolution of Cooperation. Basic Books, New York (1984)
6. Fogel, D.B.: On the Relationship between the Duration of an Encounter and the Evolution of Cooperation in the Iterated Prisoner's Dilemma. Evol. Comput. 3, 349–363 (1995)
7. Weeks, M.C.: Altered Payoff Values and the Effect on a Population of Iterated Prisoner's Dilemma Players. Master of Engineering Thesis, University of Louisville, Louisville, KY (1994)
8. Chong, S.Y., Yao, X.: Multiple Choices and Reputation in Multiagent Interactions. IEEE Trans. Evol. Comput. 11, 689–711 (2007)
9. Wilkinson, I., Young, L.: On cooperating Firms, Relations and Networks. Journal of Business Research 55, 123–132 (2002)
10. Markowitz, H.: Portfolio Selection. The Journal of Finance 7, 77–91 (1952)
11. Li, M., Kou, J.: A Novel Type of Niching Methods Based on Steady-State Genetic Algorithm. In: Wang, L., Chen, K., S. Ong, Y. (eds.) ICNC 2005. LNCS, vol. 3612, pp. 37–47. Springer, Heidelberg (2005)
12. Li, J., Hingston, P., Kendall, G.: Engineering Design of Strategies for Winning Iterated Prisoner's Dilemma Competitions. IEEE Transactions on Computational Intelligence and AI in Games 3, 348–360 (2011)
13. Franken, N., Engelbrecht, A.P.: Particle Swarm Optimization Approaches to Coevolve Strategies for the Iterated Prisoner's Dilemma. IEEE Trans. Evol. Comput. 9, 562–579 (2005)
14. Mittal, S., Deb, K.: Optimal Strategies of the Iterated Prisoner's Dilemma Problem for Multiple Conflicting Objectives. IEEE Trans. Evol. Comput. 13, 554–565 (2009)
15. Chong, S.Y., Yao, X.: Behavioral Diversity, Choices, and Noise in the Iterated Prisoner's Dilemma. IEEE Trans. Evol. Comput. 9, 540–551 (2005)
16. Darwen, P., Yao, X.: Speciation as Automatic Categorical Modularization. IEEE Trans. Evol. Comput. 1, 101–108 (1997)
17. Mcnamara, J.M., Barta, Z., Houston, A.I.: Variation in Behavior Promotes Cooperation in the Prisoner's Dilemma. Nature 428, 745–748 (2004)
18. Darwen, P., Yao, X.: Co-evolution in Iterated Prisoner's Dilemma with Intermediate Levels of Cooperation: Application to Missile Defense. Int. J. Comput. Intell. Appl. 2, 83–107 (2002)

Dynamic Neural Network Ensemble Construction for Classification

Jin Tian, Minqiang Li, and Fuzan Chen

School of Management, Tianjin University, Tianjin 300072, P.R. China
jtian_tju@yahoo.com.cn

Abstract. Neural network ensemble (NNE) receives increasing attention in recent research among the e-commerce community. In an NNE method, multiple component neural networks are trained and cooperate with each other to solve the same problem. This paper presents a dynamic ensemble construction approach based on a coevolution paradigm. The whole model is obtained by a specially designed cooperative coevolutionary algorithm. After the coevolution process, a further heuristic structure refining process on the ensemble size is conducted in order to find the appropriate ensemble size for different datasets. The dynamic ensemble size value is obtained by removing less-contribution component networks. Experimental results illustrate that the classification performance of the proposed algorithm is superior to the traditional ensemble methods on real-world datasets.

Keywords: neural network ensemble, cooperative coevolution, Pareto optimality, classification.

1 Introduction

Neural network ensemble (NNE) receives increasing attention in recent research among the e-commerce community, such as the e-commerce transaction anomaly classification [1] and the personal credit evaluation [2]. Early work on ensembles that are composed of a finite number of neural networks suggested that the consensus of an ensemble may outperform component networks, especially when the components are quite different [3].

Many in-depth researches on the ensemble have revealed its effectiveness in applications, and several ensemble approaches were investigated. Zhou and Jiang proposed a neural network ensemble algorithm, NeC4.5, based on C4.5 with the decision tree mechanism [4]. Garcı´a-Pedrajas and Fyfe used the immune network to evolve the NNE by incorporating the stimulation of antibodies in fitness evaluation, where the stimulation represented the interaction of antibodies in the antigen population [5]. Rosen proposed the decorrelation network training method for improving the quality of regression learning in NNEs that were composed through a linear combination of component networks [6]. In a previous work, we have designed a coevolutionary NNE method with a hybrid output combination in which the size of the ensemble was fixed [7].

V. Khachidze et al. (Eds.): iCETS 2012, CCIS 332, pp. 214–223, 2012.

Recently, some ensemble methods have been designed using the pruning or constructive mechanism, which make the NNE construction structured more dynamically. In this paper, we present a dynamic NNE construction method (DNNE) based on a specially designed cooperative coevolutionary algorithm (Co-CEA). Generally, the Co-CEA utilizes a divide-and-cooperative mechanism to evolve subpopulations with evolutionary algorithms in parallel [8], which can boost up the search process. A subpopulation is generated for every component and all the subpopulations are evolved simultaneously. In this mechanism, the fitness of an individual from a particular subpopulation is assessed by associating it with representatives from other subpopulations. The proposed algorithm uses multiobjective optimization and the emphasis is put not only on ensemble accuracy but also on diversity and cooperation. Furthermore, researchers have illuminated that some selected components could perform better than the original ensemble [9][10]. Thus, a further study on the ensemble size is conducted in order to find the appropriate ensemble size for different datasets. The dynamic ensemble size is obtained by removing less-contribution component networks.

The rest of the paper is organized as follows: section 2 presents the proposed algorithm in detail. Section 3 illustrates the experimental results of the proposed algorithm in comparison with other learning algorithms. Finally, Section 4 states the conclusions of the paper and future research lines.

2 DNNE

The proposed idea is that the NNE construction may benefit from encoding the different component networks into separate subpopulations, which are evolved concurrently. We adopt Radial Basis Function Neural Network (RBFNN) as the component network. For each component network, a matrix-form mixed encoding method is designed to generate the subpopulation of the RBFNN structure. The output weights between the hidden layer and the output layer of the RBFNN are calculated directly by the pseudo-inverse method [11]. The DNNE outputs the complete ensemble solution by integrating the best individuals from the subpopulations. Since the size of the ensemble is dynamic during the ensemble training process, the winner-takes-all rule is utilized to calculate the ensemble output combination. The dataset is divided into three sets: the training set, the validation set, and the testing set.

2.1 Multiobjective Optimization of Individuals

Supposing that the elite pool $\boldsymbol{\Theta}^* = \{\boldsymbol{E}_1^*, \boldsymbol{E}_2^*, \ldots, \boldsymbol{E}_M^*\}$, which is composed of the representatives in the subpopulations. M is the ensemble size. Individuals in one subpopulation are assigned fitness values in conjunction with individuals from other subpopulations. Two objectives are used in the proposed algorithm:

(1) Classification accuracy

This objective measures the contribution of individuals in subpopulations, and is calculated by the ensemble combination output. The winner-takes-all rule is adopted here. Since we chiefly treat the multi-class classification task, the label of a certain sample is determined by the maximum output in the ensemble components. That is, every component should give its maximum output among the component's multi-outputs, as well as the corresponding class label. The final decision of a certain sample is decided by the largest value of these maximum outputs. The corresponding class label is set to the sample.

The lth individual in the tth subpopulation, $\boldsymbol{C}_t^l$, gets its fitness value by calculating the combination output of the estimated ensemble structure $\boldsymbol{\Theta}_t^l = \{\boldsymbol{E}_1^*, \ldots, \boldsymbol{E}_{t-1}^*, \boldsymbol{C}_t^l, \boldsymbol{E}_{t+1}^* \ldots, \boldsymbol{E}_M^*\}$. This objective is represented as the ratio of correctly classified samples in the total validation set by the $\boldsymbol{\Theta}_t^l$:

$$f_1(\boldsymbol{C}_t^l) = \frac{N_{cr}(\boldsymbol{\Theta}_t^l)}{N_v} \tag{1}$$

where $N_{cr}(\boldsymbol{\Theta}_t^l)$ is the number of samples classified correctly on the validation set by the estimated network with hidden node structure $\boldsymbol{\Theta}_t^l$, and N_v is the size of the validation set.

(2) Diversity measure

The second objective aims to evaluate the diversity of the components. Yule's Q statistic is adopted to assess the similarity of two component networks' outputs [12].

In DNNE, computing the diversity of individual $\boldsymbol{C}_t^l$ is to measure the difference between $\boldsymbol{C}_t^l$ and the representatives in other subpopulations, $\boldsymbol{E}_1^*, \ldots, \boldsymbol{E}_{t-1}^*, \boldsymbol{E}_{t+1}^* \ldots, \boldsymbol{E}_M^*$. Q_{tj}^l is denoted as the Q values that assess the diversity between $\boldsymbol{C}_t^l$ and the representative $\boldsymbol{E}_j^*$, $j = 1, \ldots, M$. The average of these Qs is an explicit index that illuminates the diversity of $\boldsymbol{C}_t^l$:

$$\bar{Q}_t^l = \frac{\sum_{j=1,\ldots,M; j \neq t} Q_{tj}^l}{M-1} \tag{2}$$

In order to normalize this measure to vary from 0 to 1, the objective is modified as:

$$f_2(\boldsymbol{C}_t^l) = \frac{1 - \bar{Q}_t^l}{2} \tag{3}$$

The multiobjective algorithm is adopted to evaluate the fitness of individuals [13]. Since the objectives are in conflict with each other, there is usually not a solution that maximizes all objectives simultaneously. Multiobjective optimization with conflicting objectives aims to find a set of optimal solutions instead of one optimal solution.

2.2 Coevolution Process

In DNNE, a matrix-form mixed encoding genotype representation is designed. Each individual is encoded as $\boldsymbol{C}_t^l = [\boldsymbol{c}_t^l \quad \boldsymbol{\sigma}_t^l \quad \boldsymbol{b}_t^l]$ ($l = 1, 2, \ldots, L$, $t = 1, 2, \ldots, M$). $\boldsymbol{c}_t^l$ and

σ_t^l are the hidden nodes and the radius widths of C_t^l. b_t^l is the control vector and could be set as 0 or 1 which indicates that the corresponding hidden node is inactive or active. M is the ensemble size.

M training subsets are obtained by the bootstrap resampling method in the training set. Then, M initial networks are generated and L individuals are generated based on one initial component network to form one subpopulation with the control vectors initialized as 0 or 1 randomly.

The fitness of an individual is assessed by the multiobjective optimization that is fulfilled by Pareto ranking. Tournament selection and elitist selection [14] are utilized to select individuals for the next generation.

Uniform crossover is used to exchange information between two individuals that are picked randomly from the mating pool to produce offspring. A special designed mutation operator is utilized in the proposed algorithm, which makes the real-valued encoding part and the binary-valued encoding part mutate separately. A ratio, p_{ad}, has been introduced to decide whether the mutation occurs in the control bit or the real number part. For a hidden node c_t^{li} in C_t^l, a random number r_{ad} is generated. If $p_{ad} > r_{ad}$, the operation only inverts the control bit (if the original bit is 0, it is mutated to 1, and vice versa). If $p_{ad} \le r_{ad}$ and the corresponding control bit is 1, the mutation introduces variances to the real-valued genes:

$$c_t^{li\prime} = c_t^{li} + N(0,1) \times (c_t^{*,i} - c_t^{li}) \tag{4}$$

$$\sigma_t^{li\prime} = \sigma_t^{li} + N(0,1) \times (\sigma_t^{*,i} - \sigma_t^{li}) \tag{5}$$

where $c_t^{li\prime}$ and $\sigma_t^{li\prime}$ are the new values, c_t^{li} and σ_t^{li} are the current values, $c_t^{*,i}$ and $\sigma_t^{*,i}$ are the corresponding values of the hidden nodes in the elite pool. $N(0,1)$ is a random number which obeys the standard normal distribution.

2.3 Heuristic Structure Refining Process

Some experiments in early literature indicate that most ensemble methods perform better when the ensemble size is bigger than 10 or 15, and particularly perform best when the size is 25; however, the addition of new networks to the ensemble does not always increase the testing accuracies when the ensemble size increases [15]. Moreover, the pre-designed and fixed ensemble size M is usually not suitable for various datasets with different sizes of available samples. Thus the final representatives in the elite pool are further testified. In the heuristic structure refining process, we testify the ensemble component performance and further investigate the appropriate size of an ensemble for different datasets.

After the coevolution process, we have gained the M representatives from the subpopulations to compose the ensemble. The performances of the representatives are then evaluated by two objectives:

(1) Independence performance

This objective evaluates the components when they are required to complete the classification task independently with no information from other components. This objective is represented as the ratio of correctly classified samples in the validation set by the RBFNN:

$$Obj_1(\boldsymbol{E}_t^*) = \frac{N_{cr}(\boldsymbol{E}_t^*)}{N_v} \tag{6}$$

(2) Diversity of the component with other representatives

We adopt the Pairwise Failure Crediting (PFC) method [16] to get the diversity value.

$$Obj_2(\boldsymbol{E}_t^*) = PFC_t = \frac{\sum_{j=1,\ldots,M;j\neq t} h_{tj}}{M-1} \tag{7}$$

where h_{tj} is the diversity measure value of the component $\boldsymbol{E}_t^*$ and $\boldsymbol{E}_j^*$ based on Hamming distance.

The M components are evaluated by the two objectives and ranked by Pareto ranking. The less-contribution component is removed. The two processes, the coevolution process and the structure refining process, are operated in turn until the validation accuracy obtained by the whole ensemble is decreased. Finally, the representatives in the elite pool are output as the final estimation of the ensemble model.

3 Experimental Studies

Experiments were conducted on 12 datasets from the UCI Repository to evaluate the performance of the proposed method. These are real-world datasets that are different with respect to the number of available patterns (from 148 to 1,484), attributes (from 5 to 35), and classes (from 2 to 21). Each dataset was divided into three sets: 50% of the patterns were used for learning, 25% for validation, and the remaining 25% for testing. For each dataset, 30 runs of the algorithms were performed.

3.1 Experiment 1

The experiments were carried out to compare the performance of the DNNE against typical conventional training algorithms. The experiment parameters used in the DNNE algorithm were set as follows. The population size L was 50, the maximum generations G was 200, and the initial ensemble size M=25. The probability of crossover p_c was 0.8. The non-structure mutation rate p_m was 0.2, and the structure mutation rate p_{ad} was 0.6.

Firstly, the proposed algorithm is compared with the initial NNE which uses fixed ensemble size without the heuristic structure refining process. Table 1 shows the performance of the two algorithms, including the average testing accuracies, the average hidden node number of the component networks, Nc, and the reduced ensemble size.

Table 1. Performance of DNNE and Initial NNE

Dataset	Initial NNE (*M*=25)		DNNE (Dynamic *M*)		
	Test	*Nc*	Test	*Nc*	*M**
Breast	0.9623	10.34	0.9628	11.19	9.700
Heart	0.8221	18.92	0.8157	19.58	11.63
Hepa	0.8365	14.49	0.8365	15.07	10.67
Lymph	0.8189	6.592	0.8216	6.804	9.067
New-thy	0.9570	11.77	0.9564	12.86	8.133
Pima	0.7655	21.92	0.7670	22.78	18.43
Pri-tum	0.3909	32.27	0.3924	32.66	14.73
Soy	0.8962	23.10	0.8918	23.76	13.81
Vehicle	0.7497	48.77	0.7453	49.66	20.87
Votes	0.9502	13.00	0.9517	14.03	8.333
Wines	0.9636	7.637	0.9659	7.807	8.067
Yeast	0.6101	43.57	0.6029	43.71	13.67
Ave	0.8103	21.03	0.8092	21.66	12.26

The experimental results indicate that the NNE models with the reduced ensemble sizes achieve good performance on most datasets. Specifically, the dynamic value of *M* is above 15 only on two datasets, Pima and Vehicle, while the proposed algorithm yields ensemble models containing about 10 components on the other datasets. The experimental results reveal the dependence of *M* on the dataset size, and there exists a subset of key components in the ensemble that can perform as well as all components.

Secondly, the proposed algorithm is compared with the Standard Genetic Algorithm (SGA), which is used to train the single neural network. Table 2 shows the performance of the DNNE, including the average testing accuracies, the average hidden node number of the component networks, *Nc*, and the average generations of convergence.

Table 2. Performance of DNNE and SGA

Datasets	DNNE			SGA		
	Test	*Nc*	*G*	Test	*Nc*	*G*
Breast	0.9628	11.19	12.7	0.9559	18.07	118.8
Heart	0.8157	19.58	30.5	0.8068	18.93	102.8
Hepa	0.8365	15.07	25.63	0.8343	16.73	31.10
Lymph	0.8216	6.804	28.57	0.7705	15.10	161.0
New-thy	0.9564	12.86	15.67	0.9472	16.67	31.05
Pima	0.7670	22.78	31.04	0.7508	26.40	111.4
Pri-tumor	0.3924	32.66	27.4	0.3896	45.92	172.0
Soy	0.8918	23.76	8.281	0.7340	69.88	125.5
Vehicle	0.7453	49.66	46.07	0.6607	57.28	57.09
Votes	0.9517	14.03	22.3	0.9427	18.16	35.70
Wines	0.9659	7.807	19.28	0.9375	7.899	53.43
Yeast	0.6029	43.71	43.3	0.5749	52.42	141.6
Ave	0.8092	21.66	25.89	0.7754	30.29	95.12

Table 2 illustrates that the proposed algorithm is able to produce NNE models with higher learning accuracy, as compared to the SGA. Particularly, DNNE outperforms SGA on most datasets, especially on Heart, Lymph, Pri-tumor, Soy, Vehicle, Wines and Yeast. Moreover, the average generation for convergence in the DNNE is 25.89, which is much smaller than 95.12 in the SGA.

Thirdly, experiments were carried out to verify the performance of the proposed method and some conventional ensemble algorithms, such as AdaBoost (AB) [17], Bagging (BA) [18], Dagging (DA) [19], and MultiBoost (MB) [20]. Table 3 reports the average testing accuracies of the DNNE and these compared algorithms.

Table 3. Average testing accuracies of DNNE and other ensemble algorithms

Dataset	DNNE	AB	BA	DA	MB
Breast	0.9628	0.9597	0.9524	0.9559	0.9646
Heart	0.8157	0.8055	0.8016	0.8243	0.8278
Hepa	0.8365	0.8279	0.8588	0.8036	0.8511
Lymph	0.8216	0.8174	0.8239	0.7813	0.8122
New-thy	0.9564	0.9589	0.9676	0.8858	0.9664
Pima	0.7670	0.7510	0.7583	0.7332	0.7420
Pri-tumor	0.3924	0.2921	0.4271	0.4409	0.2921
Soy	0.8918	0.2811	0.8397	0.7827	0.2811
Vehicle	0.7453	0.6785	0.6623	0.6958	0.6734
Votes	0.9517	0.9473	0.9476	0.9264	0.9485
Wines	0.9659	0.9746	0.9668	0.9304	0.9738
Yeast	0.6029	0.4057	0.5958	0.4555	0.4057
Ave	0.8092	0.7250	0.8002	0.7680	0.7282

As shown in Table 3, the NNE models trained by DNNE obtain the best or near to the best prediction accuracies particularly on Breast, Lymph, Pima, Vehicle and Yeast, and on average as well. In total, the DNNE performs competitively on most datasets as compared with other ensemble algorithms. Fig.1. gives the testing performance of all algorithms over 30 runs in the point-and-figure plots on every dataset.

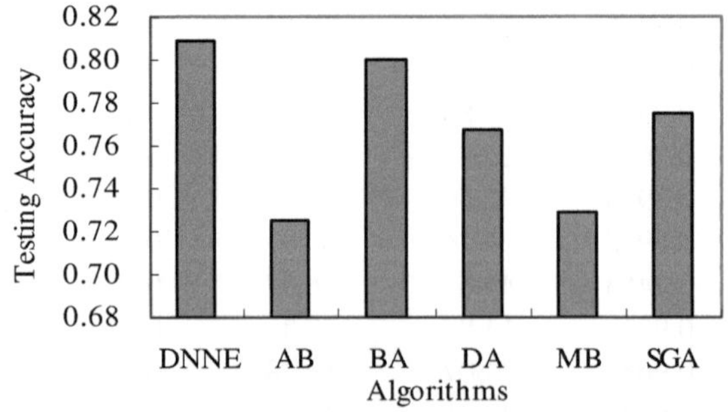

Fig. 1. The average testing accuracy of the six algorithms over 30 runs

3.2 Experiment 2

Bias-variance decomposition is often used in studying the performance of ensemble methods [21]. Here, we adopt the decomposition method proposed by Kohavi and Wolpert [22]. The bias and variance of the DNNE and the compared ensemble approaches are shown in Table 4 and Table 5, respectively.

Table 4. The bias of the DNNE and other ensemble algorithms

Dataset	DNNE	AB	BA	DA	MB	SGA
Breast	0.0289	0.0262	0.0331	0.0375	0.0318	0.0657
Heart	0.1464	0.1232	0.1256	0.1349	0.1218	0.1514
Hepa	0.1309	0.0861	0.0972	0.0665	0.0861	0.1529
Lymph	0.1728	0.1360	0.1366	0.1328	0.1351	0.2001
New-thy	0.0362	0.0481	0.0579	0.2842	0.1544	0.1141
Pima	0.1855	0.1447	0.1545	0.2522	0.1602	0.1844
Pri-tumor	0.4245	0.4958	0.4055	0.6418	0.4958	0.4261
Soy	0.1704	0.5141	0.1863	0.4465	0.5141	0.3910
Vehicle	0.1701	0.3491	0.1765	0.2406	0.3491	0.3083
Votes	0.0382	0.0149	0.0286	0.0397	0.0293	0.1008
Wines	0.0307	0.0477	0.0402	0.0591	0.0522	0.1001
Yeast	0.3082	0.5535	0.2874	0.5617	0.5535	0.3475
Ave	0.1536	0.2116	0.1441	0.2415	0.2236	0.2119

Table 5. The variance of the DNNE and other ensemble algorithms

Dataset	DNNE	AB	BA	DA	MB	SGA
Breast	0.0178	0.0171	0.0185	0.0037	0.0217	0.1360
Heart	0.0805	0.0920	0.1075	0.0773	0.0991	0.1462
Hepa	0.0674	0.0903	0.0440	0.0840	0.0841	0.1720
Lymph	0.1265	0.1381	0.1201	0.1338	0.1137	0.2216
New-thy	0.0179	0.0418	0.0574	0.0200	0.0620	0.2001
Pima	0.0881	0.0915	0.0852	0.0393	0.0850	0.1846
Pri-tum	0.2611	0.2363	0.2350	0.1071	0.2363	0.4368
Soy	0.2992	0.2113	0.1551	0.1126	0.2113	0.4507
Vehicle	0.1401	0.2293	0.1265	0.2134	0.2293	0.3304
Votes	0.0288	0.0156	0.0030	0.0147	0.0071	0.1750
Wines	0.0321	0.0737	0.0799	0.1159	0.0962	0.1870
Yeast	0.1523	0.0609	0.1337	0.0769	0.0609	0.3919
Ave	0.1093	0.1082	0.0972	0.0832	0.1089	0.2527

Note that since our priority is relative performance, as opposed to absolute performance, the bias/variance of the ensemble algorithms has been normalized according to that of SGA and the average results of the relative bias/variance on all datasets are shown in Fig. 2. In other words, the bias/variance of SGA is regarded as 1.0, and the reported bias/variance of the ensemble algorithms is in fact the ratio against the bias/variance of the SGA.

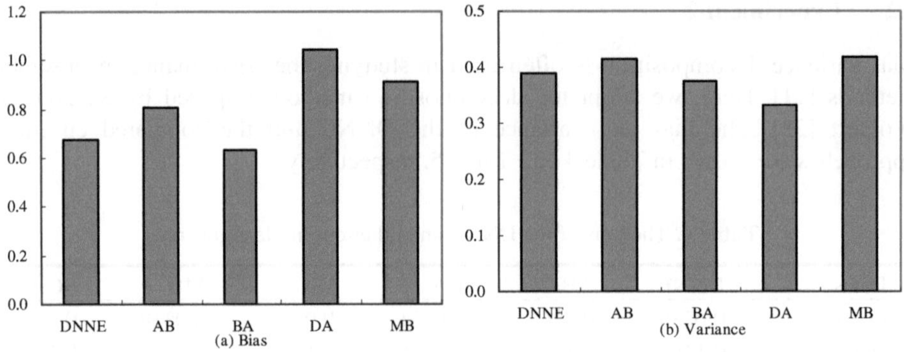

Fig. 2. Comparison of the average relative bias and variance of the ensemble algorithms

Although DNNE's ability of reducing the variance is not as good as those of some compared algorithms, such as BA, it can still effectively reduce the variance. Moreover, DNNE's ability to reduce the bias is better than that of other compared ensemble algorithms. This is partially due to its ability to significantly reduce both the bias and the variance.

4 Conclusion

This paper has presented a dynamic NNE approach based on coevolutionary algorithm. A component network of the ensemble in the proposed model corresponds to a separate subpopulation. The RBFNN is employed as the component network. The whole algorithm contains two processes: the coevolution process and the structure refining process. We conducted a study to determine the available ensemble size for different datasets. Experimental results illustrated that the classification performance of the proposed algorithm is superior to the traditional ensemble methods on real-world datasets.

There are two issues to be addressed in future research. One issue is the combination with the incremental learning methodology that has recently received greater attention. The other issue is further study on the dynamic refining of the coevolution subpopulations in order to introduce a more reliable NNE construction.

Acknowledgments. This work was supported by the National Science Fund for Distinguished Young Scholars of China (Grant No. 70925005) and the General Program of the National Science Foundation of China (Grant No. 71001076, No. 71101103). This work was also supported by grants from the Research Fund for the Doctoral Program of Higher Education of China (No. 20090032120073, No. 20090032110065).

References

[1] Yang, H., King, I.: Ensemble Learning for Imbalanced E-commerce Transaction Anomaly Classification. In: Leung, C.S., Lee, M., Chan, J.H. (eds.) ICONIP 2009, Part I. LNCS, vol. 5863, pp. 866–874. Springer, Heidelberg (2009)

[2] Wu, C., Xia, H.: Study of personal credit evaluation under C2C environment based on support vector machines ensemble. In: Proceedings on the 15th Annual Conference on Management Science and Engineering, September 10-12, pp. 25–31. IEEE Computing Society, Los Alamitos (2008)

[3] Krogh, J.V.: Neural Network Ensembles, Cross Validation, and Active Learning. Advances in Neural Information Processing Systems 7, 231–238 (1995)

[4] Zhou, Z.H., Jiang, Y.: NeC4.5: Neural Ensemble Based C4.5. IEEE Transactions on Knowledge and Data Engineering 16(6), 770–773 (2004)

[5] García-Pedrajas, N., Fyfe, C.: Immune Network Based Ensembles. Neurocomputing 70(7-9), 1155–1166 (2007)

[6] Rosen, B.E.: Ensemble Learning Using Decorrelated Neural Networks. Connections Science 8(3), 373–384 (1996)

[7] Tian, J., Li, M.Q., Chen, F.Z.: Coevolutionary learning of neural network ensemble for complex classification tasks. Pattern Recognition 45, 1373–1385 (2012)

[8] Zhao, Q.F., Higuchi, T.: Evolutionary Learning of Nearest Neighbor MLP. IEEE Transactions on Neural Networks 7, 762–767 (1996)

[9] Zhou, Z.H., Wu, J., Tang, W.: Ensembling Neural Networks: Many Could Be Better Than All. Artificial Intelligence 137(1-2), 239–263 (2002)

[10] Perrone, M.P., Cooper, L.N.: When Networks Disagree: Ensemble Method for Neural Networks. Artificial Neural Networks for Speech and Vision, 126–142 (1993)

[11] Casasent, D., Chen, X.W.: Radial Basis Function Neural Networks for Nonlinear Fisher Discrimination and Neyman-Pearson Classification. Neural Networks 16, 529–535 (2003)

[12] Kuncheva, L.I., Whitaker, C.J.: Measures of Diversity in Classifier Ensembles and Their Relationship with the Ensemble Accuracy. Machine Learning 51(2), 181–207 (2003)

[13] Ficici, S.G., Pollack, J.B.: Pareto Optimality in Coevolutionary Learning. In: Kelemen, J., Sosik, P. (eds.) ECAL 2001. LNCS (LNAI), vol. 2159, pp. 316–325. Springer, Heidelberg (2001)

[14] Li, M.Q., Kou, J.S., et al.: The Basic Theories and Applications in GA. Science Press, Beijing (2002)

[15] Opitz, D., Maclin, R.: Popular Ensemble Methods: An Empirical Study. Journal of Artificial Intelligence Research 11, 169–198 (1999)

[16] Chandra, A., Yao, X.: Ensemble Learning Using Multi-Objective Evolutionary Algorithms. Journal of Mathematical Modelling and Algorithms 5(4), 417–425 (2006)

[17] Freund, Y., Schapire, R.: Experiments with a New Boosting Algorithm. In: Thirteenth International Conference on Machine Learning, pp. 148–156 (1996)

[18] Breiman, L.: Bagging Predictors. Machine Learning 24(2), 123–140 (1996)

[19] Ting, K.M., Witten, I.H.: Stacking Bagged and Dagged Models. In: Fourteenth International Conference on Machine Learning, pp. 367–375 (1997)

[20] Webb, G.I.: Multiboosting: a Technique for Combining Boosting and Wagging. Machine Learning 40, 159–196 (2000)

[21] Domingos, P.: A Unified Bias-Variance Decomposition and Its Applications. In: International Conference on Machine Learning, pp. 231–238 (2000)

[22] Kohavi, R., Wolpert, D.H.: Bias Plus Variance Decomposition for Zero-One Loss Functions. In: International Conference on Machine Learning, pp. 275–283 (1996)

A Secure Data Exchange Protocol for the Internet of Things

Yaping Zhang[1], Lina Bo[2], and Qian Ma[2]

[1] School of Computer Software, Tianjin University, Tianjin, China
[2] School of Computer Science and Technology, Tianjin University, Tianjin, China
{tjuypzh99,bbln123}@126.com

Abstract. With the rapid development of the RFID systems in the Internet of Things, many significant security concerns have been raised. This paper proposes a new Secure Data Exchange Protocol. This protocol combines Hash and stream cipher encryption algorithms. The analysis shows that this protocol involves no computationally intensive cryptographic operations and relatively little storage.

Keywords: RFID, Hash algorithm, sequence encryption.

1 Introduction

The Internet of Things is a network, which uses information sensing devices such as radio frequency identification (RFID), infrared sensors, global positioning systems or laser scanners, to make any things connect to the Internet up to the information exchange and communication, in accordance with the agreed protocol in order to achieve intelligent identification, location, tracking, monitoring and management. Internet of Things is proposed based on the Internet, so it does not only have the traditional Internet security issues, but also has its own security particularity, such as large and complex network nodes, limited computing and storage capacity, relatively exposed environment and so on.

This paper is based on the RFID systems. RFID is a non-contact automatic identification technology, which can automatically identify the object by the radio frequency (RF) signal and access the relevant data. RFID systems typically consist of three parts, including RFID tags, RFID readers and the back server. The composition of RFID systems is shown in Fig 1.

The reader can read the information of the tags through radio frequency (RF) signal, while the back server communicates with the reader through a wired network. However, an unauthorized or illegal reader can also read and gather information from the tags within its scope; therefore, user privacy may be disclosed through stealing or modifying on the part of the attackers. Combined with the inherent vulnerability of wireless communications, RFID systems still face a variety of security challenges and threats.

V. Khachidze et al. (Eds.): iCETS 2012, CCIS 332, pp. 224–231, 2012.

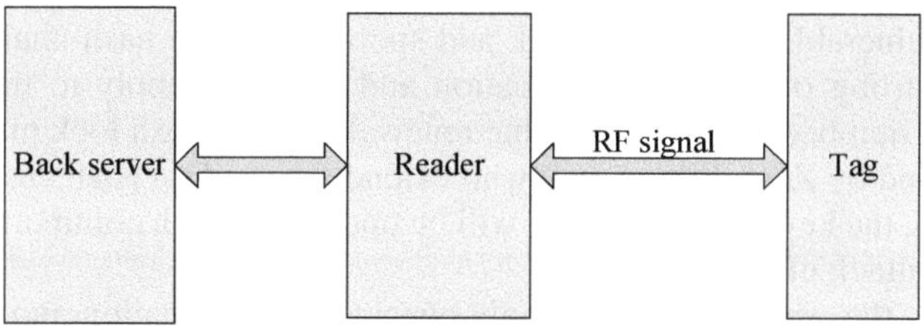

Fig. 1. The composition of RFID systems

Taking into account the particularity of the Internet of Things, to solve security issues in the communication process, this paper proposes a new protocol, Secure Data Exchange Protocol, which is based on the Hash algorithm and sequence encryption algorithm, in order to provide a more secure environment on the Internet of Things. This protocol can thus protect user privacy and prevent information leakage.

2 Related Studies

With the wide range of application of RFID systems, there have been a large number of studies on the security threats incurred by using tags. The protection of user privacy in RFID systems is very particular, because the RFID chip is low-cost and its storage and computing capacity are very limited. It cannot carry out complex calculations or store large amounts of data; therefore, although the traditional symmetric encryption algorithm and asymmetric encryption algorithm are relatively perfect, they are not applicable for the RFID systems. Currently, at home and abroad there are two research fields on the security technology of low-cost tags, including physical methods and security protocols.

Physical methods mainly consist of the KILL command mechanism, the SLEEP label, electrostatic shielding, and so on. Although they can provide some security guarantees, they will cause much waste so that they are not suitable for large-scale application. In terms of resistance to security and privacy threats, designing security protocols is more practical.

As regards security protocols, there are many published papers. The minimalist cryptography algorithm [1] proposed by A. Juels et al. needs only simple XOR logic within the tags. This algorithm has low requirements on the tags and is easy to operate, but its security level is not high enough. Re-encryption technology [9], encrypting the tag repeatedly, is another RFID security mechanism. Its encryption and decryption is completed by the reader, while the tag just as carriers has low technology requirements. However, it does not have an authentication process and there are tracking problems in the interval of every re-encryption. The application of hash-based method is most widely useful, because it is able to provide mutual authentication between the reader and the tag. In addition, hash functions are considered to be the basic components of lightweight cryptography, and it can be achieved in the RFID chips easily. Presently, there are many authentication protocols based on the hash functions, such as hash lock protocol [2], random hash lock protocol [3], hash chain protocol [4], key value renewal random hash lock protocol [5], and so on. However, it is difficult for them to resist all kinds of security threats fully and effectively. Hash lock protocol and random hash lock protocol are vulnerable to replay attack and spoofing, while hash chain protocol can only provide strong one-way authentication and does not apply to the systems that contain a large number of tags. Key value renewal random hash lock protocol is a new method proposed by Zeng Lihua et al. who extend the random hash chain mechanism. In this protocol, the key value of the tag will be updated in each communication process to prevent the attack effectively.

In summary, the various protocols only consider authentication and do not address the security issues in information transmission after the authentication. Therefore, this paper not only achieves mutual authentication between reader and tag, but also achieves sequence encryption for the information using the key stream generated by the linear feedback shift register to ensure information security in the transmission process. Finally, the paper forms a complete Secure Data Exchange Protocol that can be used in the RFID systems to provide privacy and information security.

3 Secure Data Exchange Protocol

This protocol takes into account the fact that some of the Internet of Things application environments use active tags, which have simple computing capacity. Additionally, it assumes that the transmission channel between the reader and the back server is safe; only the wireless communication between the reader and the tags need to be considered. Each tag stores its own ID and the initial key K, as well as some detailed data which have a fixed format. The database in back server stores all of the IDs and their corresponding initial keys K.

The Secure Data Exchange Protocol can be divided into three parts: identity authentication, information transmission and communication disconnection. Detailed description of each part is as follows:

3.1 Identity Authentication

Identity authentication mainly checks the readers and tags to confirm that both of them are legitimate and not attacker counterfeits or forges. It primarily uses the lightweight cryptography component -- hash function, which denotes one-way conversion. The hash function is able to convert data of arbitrary length to fixed length data, but it is difficult for other data to hash convert the same value. The unidirectivity of hash function can ensure its security.

3.2 Handshake Authentication Protocol

Information transmission primarily completes the data encryption and transmission. Encryption in this paper uses the sequence encryption based on linear feedback shift register. Each tag and the back server must install the linear feedback shift register with the same feedback function having high speed and simple structure. The structure of an n-stage linear feedback shift register [7] is shown in Fig 2. as shown below:

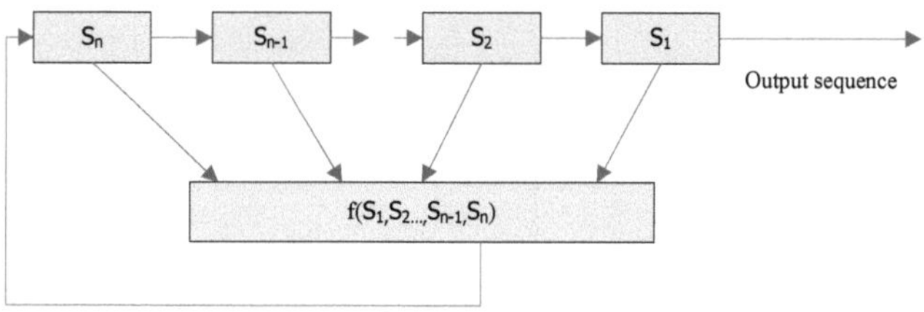

Fig. 2. Structure of an n-stage linear feedback shift register

Among them, S1, S2, …, Sn represent (0,1) storage units. At any time the value of S1, S2, …, Sn is named the state of the feedback shift register. The linear function f (S1, S2, …,Sn) is named the feedback function of the feedback shift register. After a shift pulse, each register bit will move to the right, so the rightmost one moves out as the output, while f(S1, S2, …,Sn) will feedback to the left. Therefore, through controlling shift pause, the register can generate a specified number of output sequences as the key stream.

The encryption of data uses sequence encryption methods that calculate the XOR between each bit of the data and the key stream generated by the linear feedback shift register. Then, the tag will take the hash value of the connection of the sender's ID and recipient's ID and the encrypted data as the authentication of the message to be sent. The specific format of the message is shown in Fig 3. below, and it is the eventual format of the information to be sent to the reader.

recipient's ID	Sender's ID	Encrypted information	authentication

Fig. 3. Specific format of the message

3.3 Communication Disconnection

The last process is communication disconnection. When the back server confirms that it has received the message correctly, it will send a message to the tag to stop communication. Otherwise, if the back server does not receive the message correctly, it will notify the tag to resend.

3.4 Detailed Process

The detailed process of the Secure Data Exchange Protocol is shown in Fig 4. below:

- Step 1: The reader sends a read command to pass a random number *s* to the tag.

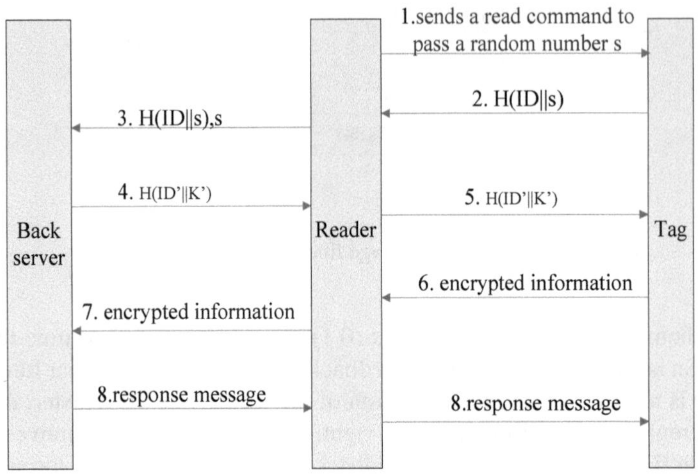

Fig. 4. Detailed process of the Secure Data Exchange Protocol

- Step 2: The tag combines its ID with the random number *s*, then takes hash value as H(ID||s) and returns it to the reader (note that the || represents combination and H(…) represents a hash function).
- Step 3: The reader passes H(ID||s) and the random number *s* to the back server.
- Step 4: For all the IDs in the back database, the back server will calculate H(ID||s), if there is an ID' that makes H(ID'||s) = H(ID||s) established, then the legitimacy of the tag is verified. Otherwise, the identity authentication fails and the communication will be stopped. After that, the sever will take hash value of ID' and the corresponding K' as H(ID'||K') and pass it to the tag through the reader.
- Step 5: To its own ID and the initial key K, the tag will take hash value H(ID||K). Then the tag determines, using the built-in comparator, whether the equation H(ID||K)= H(ID'||K') is established. If the equation is established, then the reader is legitimate. Otherwise, Step 4 is repeated.
- Step 6: At first, it is necessary to generate a new key stream to replace the initial key K. The initial state of the linear feedback shift register is set the same as the initial key K. Then, through controlling the shift pause, a new key stream K1 with a given amount of bits will be generated. Next, using the new key stream K1, the data is encrypted; in the other words, the XOR between each bit of the data and the key stream K1 is calculated. Then, the hash value of the first three parts is taken as the authentication of the message. Finally, the encrypted message is passed to the back server through the reader.
- Step 7: Back server takes hash value of the first three parts of the received message and determines if it is equal to the fourth part-the authentication in

order to verify whether the message has been modified in the transmission process. If not, the message has been received correctly, and according to the sender's ID the back server will receive the corresponding initial key K. As with the tag's operation, the back server will obtain a new key stream K1 through the linear feedback shift register with the initial state K to decrypt the message.

- Step 8: If the message is received correctly, the back server will send a message to the tag to disconnect the communication; at the same time, the tag and the back database should update the key value for the current state of the feedback shift register. If not correctly received, the server will send a message to notify the tag to resend.

4 Protocol Analysis

The protocol is analyzed from two aspects, including complexity and security.

4.1 Complexity Analysis

In terms of space complexity, each tag needs to store three sets of data, ID, K and data, while the back server needs to store two sets, ID and K. It can be seen that storage space and cost are both relatively minimal.

In terms of computation complexity, if only the successful situation is considered, the entire data exchange protocol needs hash operator (H), random number generation (R), concatenation operator (C), XOR operator (N) and so on. The specified situation is in Table 1:

Table 1. Computational Complexity

Stage	Computational complexity		
	Tag	Reader	Back Database
Identity authentication	C+H	R	$(\sum ID/2)(H+C)$
Information transmission	C+S+ N+H	–	H+C+S+N
Communication disconnection	–	–	–

From the above table, we can see that the calculation in the back server is more intensive, while the tag has relatively simple computations. For part of the active tags in the Internet of Things it is possible to complete these simple calculations, and we consider that the reader may share some calculations of other parts.

4.2 Security Analysis

In this protocol, all private information is encrypted by hash or sequence encryption. It is difficult for attackers or listeners to decrypt the original information from the intercepted data, thereby preventing the information from disclosing, and protecting the user's privacy.

This protocol firstly authenticates the identities of both parties before transmission, so that an unauthorized reader or a reader without back server is considered to be illegal and cannot read the data of the tags. If the tag is illegal, the back server will find it in time and stop the transmission. Thus, the attacker cannot impersonate or finagle.

This protocol implements the authentication of identity and information integrity in the process of the data exchange; therefore, it not only ensures the legitimacy of the two communication parties, but also guarantees the information has not been tampered during the transmission.

This protocol prevents the man-in-middle attack effectively. It is very difficult for the attacker as the man-in-middle to decrypt the stolen data to get the valid information. If the attacker tampers with the information, then both parties of communication will soon be aware and take appropriate action.

This protocol is a K value renewal data exchange protocol, as the value of K will be updated each transmission. Authentication and transmission use different keys, so that even though the attackers have passed through the authentication and intercepted the initial key, they are still unable to decrypt the message in the transmission.

5 Conclusion

With the wide range of application of RFID systems, the security issues it brings are more and more prominent. It is particularly important to protect user privacy and prevent information from being revealed. On the basis of previous research, integrating the authentication and information transmission, this paper puts forward a Secure Data Exchange protocol, which is supported by Hash algorithm and sequence encryption algorithm, based on the feedback shift register. The analysis shows that this protocol is simple and has both strong security and high practical value.

However, the paper also has some shortcomings and needs further improvements, as discussed below.

- First, the back server needs to manage the situation when the hash value occurs collision.
- Second, when updating the value of key it must be certain that the tag and the back server are synchronous. Otherwise, future communication will be affected.
- Finally, in this paper we only analyze the new proposed protocol, and there is no detailed comparison with other protocols.

References

1. Juels, A.: Minimalist cryptography for RFID tags. Sec. Commun. Netw., SCN (2004)
2. Sarma, S., Weis, S., Engels, D.: RFID Systems and Security and Privacy Implications. In: Kaliski Jr., B.S., Koç, Ç.K., Paar, C. (eds.) CHES 2002. LNCS, vol. 2523, pp. 454–469. Springer, Heidelberg (2003)
3. Weis, S.A., Sarma, S.E., Rivest, R.L., Engels, D.W.: Security and Privacy Aspects of Low-Cost Radio Frequency Identification Systems. In: Hutter, D., Müller, G., Stephan, W., Ullmann, M. (eds.) Security in Pervasive Computing. LNCS, vol. 2802, pp. 201–212. Springer, Heidelberg (2004)
4. Avoine, G., Oechslin, P.: A Scalable and Provably Secure Hash Based RFID Protocol. In: The 2nd IEEE Internationall Workshop on Pervasive Computing and Communication Security (PerSec), pp. 125–140 (2005)
5. Zeng, L., Xiong, Z., Zhang, T.: Key Value Renewal Random Hash Lock for Security and Privacy Enhancement of RFID. Computer Engineering 33, 151–153 (2007)
6. Chen, S., Chen, R., Ling, L.: An Improved Hash-Based RFID Two-Way Security Authentication Algorithm. Computer Systems & Applications 19, 67–70 (2010)
7. Zhao, L., Zhang, A.: The Study and Design of Stream Ciphers based on the Linear Feedback Shift Register. Southwest Jiaotong University, pp. 19–42 (2006)
8. Luo, Q., Zhang, J.: Status Quo and Development of Stream Cipher. Information and Electronic Engineering 4, 75–80 (2006)
9. Li, Z., Lu, G., Xin, Y.: Application of Re-encryption Technology in RFID Security. Computer Engineering 34, 160–162 (2008)

Enhancing Security of Online Payments: A Conceptual Model for a Robust E-Payment Protocol for E-Commerce

Augustine Takyi[1] and Patrick Ohemeng Gyaase[2]

[1] Computer Science Department
Sunyani Polytechnic, Sunyani
P.O. Box 206, Sunyani
augustinektakyi@yahoo.com
[2] Faculty of Information, Communication Sciences and Technology
Catholic University College of Ghana, Fiapre Sunyani
P.O. Box 363, Sunyani
kgyaase@gmail.com

Abstract. The rapid growth of the Internet and its adoption for commercial transactions is indisputable. However, the core security protocols of the Internet today are susceptible to security lapses, especially when it comes to online payment systems which are indispensable to the growth of e-commerce across the globe. This has led to the development of various online payment protocols to ensure the security of online transactions such as Secure Electronic Transaction and The Secure Socket Layer. In designing online payment protocols, there is often a trade-off between security and convenience. More and more participants of online transactions suffer in one way or another from fraudsters. Ghana is gaining notoriety in online fraud, and there is therefore a need to protect the interest of the participants in the areas of authentication, confidentiality, replay attacks as well as flexibility if e-commerce is to thrive in developing countries. This paper looks at some online payment protocols and develops a conceptual model of a protocol which requires live authentication from the cardholder. This ensures security, convenience, cardholder authentication, and verification of merchant; it is easy to implement without complications and to compare with other existing online payment protocols. Participants that are considered in this work are the Cardholder, Issuer, Merchant, and Acquirer.

Keywords: cardholder, issuer, merchant, authentication, non-repudiation, integrity.

1 Introduction

There is widespread usage of the Internet for commercial activities, but the core designs of Internet protocols make online transactions susceptible to risks. Extra measures are needed to minimize these risks. To effectively support e-commerce, e-payment systems must be secure, reliable and convenient with good authentication, privacy, integrity and non-repudiation. Online payment frauds cause millions of dollars in loss yearly, exposing the weakness in security of online payment systems[1].

V. Khachidze et al. (Eds.): iCETS 2012, CCIS 332, pp. 232–239, 2012.

In 2009, the United Kingdom reported $696 million losses due to card fraud while Australia recorded $US 144 million[2]. The statistics suggest that card-not present fraud, such as online payment fraud, is the most prevalent. Most proposed protocols to combat this are theoretically secure but their implementation has been unfeasible. [3] The confidence of online transaction participants therefore needs to be improved if the developing world is to benefit from the global adoption of e-commerce [4].

2 Online Payment Systems

Online payment transaction involves a complex set of practical and analytical challenges, including technological capabilities of service providers, commercial relationships, regulations and laws, security issues such as identification, authentication and verification with co-ordination among parties with different and competing interests[5].

2.1 Account-Based Online Payments

Credit Cards enable the holder to make credit purchases with a fixed limit.Credit cards were not specifically designed for online payment, hence the inherent risks associated with their use as such. [6] Authentication is done using the cardholder's name, credit card number and expiry dates. This information, if intercepted when provided for online transaction, could be used by fraudsters[7].

Debit Card: The value for online transaction is directly debited to the cardholder's bank account[6].

Mediating Systems: This System employs traditional payment means, with further layers. Using the service requires registration by providing credit card or bank account details as the source of payments. A very successful mediating service for online transactions is the PayPal payment system[5].

Mobile Payment Systems: Mobile payments are conducted through wireless devices. They may be used to conduct payments through a bank account or telephone bill[8].

Online Banking: A merchant redirects to the customer bank's web site to effect payment where customer payment details are automatically entered from the electronic bill and the payer only authorises.

2.2 Electronic Currency Systems

Smart Card Systems: Smart Cards are plastic cards with memory chips and embedded microprocessors which store more information than credit cards with inbuilt transaction processing capability[9] [7].

Online Cash Systems. Online cash systems such as Virtual BBVA (Spain) and similar systems in Italy, Austria and Australia [5] work via prepaid cards with different arrangements, but most require merchant subscriptions. Electronic tokens representing a certain value are exchanged in a similar way to cash.

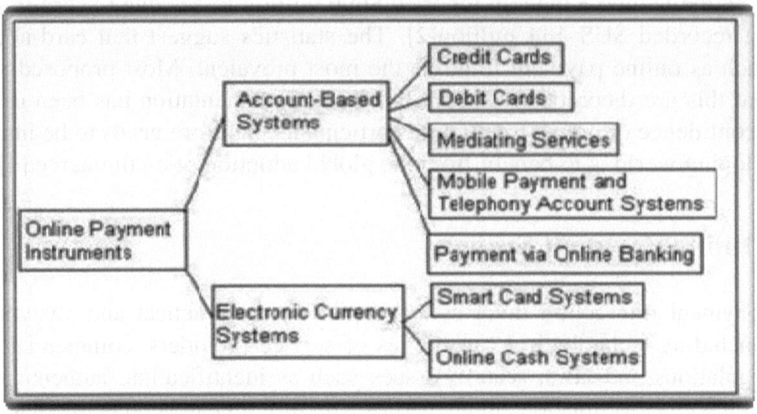

Fig. 1. Classification of on-line payment Systems for E-Commerce [10]

2.3 Online Card Processing

The five parties in e-payment environment are the Cardholder, Issuer Bank, Merchant, Acquirer Bank and Payment Gateway. The transactions between the banks are proven secured and reliable. The participants at risk are Cardholders and Merchants[7] [6].

Increasing globalization and the need to promote e-commerce in developing countries require a more secured, reliable and convenient e-payment protocol that is easy to deploy and convenient in application to all participants.

This paper presents a conceptual model for securing online transaction between parties with a balanced trade-off between Security and convenience.

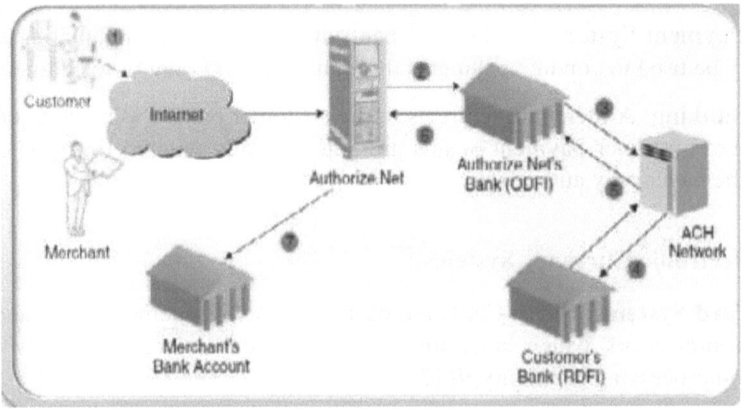

Fig. 2. Online Payment Process cycle [10] [6]

3 Electronic Payment Protocols

The success of e-commerce is based on standards, such as TCP/IP and HTTP, low-cost Internet access and protocols supporting online payments. E-payment protocols define e-commerce, distinguishing viable e-commerce sites from their information-only sites. An e-payment protocol does not move just data; it moves money.

i. iKP Family Protocols

The design; implementation and deployment iKP Secure Electronic Payment Protocol involves three parties: the buyer, the merchant and the acquirer gateway. The (i) is a variable representing the number of parties with public keys-pairs. [11] With 3KP all the parties possess public key-pairs.

ii. Secure Electronic Transaction (SET)

SET is an open encryption and security specification, designed to protect credit card transactions online and supported by companies such as VISA and MasterCard. [12] Designed for e-commerce, it provides confidentiality through encryption and data integrity with digital signature and authenticates both the cardholder and the Merchant. [12] SET also facilitates interoperability among software and network providers [13] [14]. SET requires a Public Key Infrastructure (PKI) which is a complete system for certificates. The certificates are issued by independent certificate authorities [14]. Replay attacks are a security concern to participants of SET protocol.

iii. One-Time Payment Scheme (CCT)

One-time credit card transaction number is designed to generate unique transaction numbers for single use in each transaction[12] [15], preventing replay attacks and eavesdropping. However, there Merchant verification concerns that could lead to fraud.

iv. Live Cardholder Authentication

This protocol authenticates the cardholder live, during the process of payment, combining both telephone banking and online banking together. The payment information are encrypted and forwarded through the Internet. The cardholder authentication is accomplished through a phone by the issuing bank requesting the customer for a PIN and the amount involved. Authentication is done using a combination of correct credit card details, i.e. phone number, PIN, and the transaction value. [16] The cardholder cannot authenticate the Merchant.

v. Secure Socket Layer (SSL)

The Secure Socket Layer protocol provides a private, encrypted session between the client and the server. The protocol and its related certificates are widely used in web browsers. The server authenticates itself to the client using the server certificate, but the authentication of the client to the server is optional[4] [17]. The information transmitted by the cardholder is encrypted with a sessional key generated through a handshake between the cardholder's browser and the merchant server. The absence of cardholder authentication and verification and cardholder authentication leaves room for fraud in the event of lost cards.

4 The Proposed Robust E-Payment Protocol (REPP)

Online payments have yet to gain wide usage in Ghana, due to security and high frequency of fraud in the online payment system[18]. To enable a roll-out of online payments, the indispensability of a more robust secure payment protocol that will withstand most common security threats cannot be over-emphasized. Such a protocol must be usable and convenient, giving the cardholder the options to make changes to or stop a transaction.

Cardholder authentication should be a key factor in deploying online payment protocol, as most of the existing protocol is silent with regards to the former. The merchant should also be verifiable, to enable the cardholder to feel secure and confident to do business with the merchant online. Furthermore, the ease of implementation for such protocol should be paramount.

The proposed Robust E-Payment Protocol (REPP) incorporates a solution to the above weaknesses identified in existing protocols, and if implemented can reduce fraud associated with e-payments in developing countries such as Ghana.

Robust Electronic Payment Protocol requires a merchant to register and obtain a certificate from a trusted Certificate Authority as indicated in **Step E** in the illustration below before operating online services. Hence, all merchants under the transaction of this protocol are trustworthy. Also, all data flow in the protocol is encrypted using SSL.

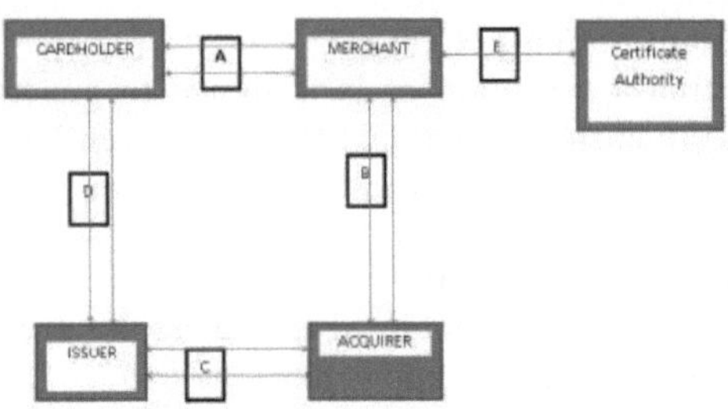

Fig. 3. A conceptual Model for Robust E-payment Protocol (REPP)

4.1 How the Protocol Works

- Purchase request: Cardholder makes an order at the merchant site (**Step A)**
- Authorization and Authentication Request: Merchant, through the Acquirer, validates whether the cardholder has enough funds **(Step B)**
- Authorization and Authentication: Acquirer forwards validation to Issuer **(Step C)**
- Authorization and Authentication: Issuer then confirms the purchase from the cardholder by prompting the cardholder to input his password
- Authorization and Authentication Response: Issuer then forwards the result to the Merchant through the Acquirer **(Steps, D, C, B, A)**
- Purchase response: Merchant Response **(Step A)**

Purchase Request

A cardholder initiates transaction by providing credit card details, which translates to a dual signature of the order and the payment details as shown below:

OI = k_m (OI).....i and PI = k_I (PI)......ii, Where OI = Order information, k_m = Merchant encryption key, PI = Payment Information, K_I = Issuer encryption key.

Equation (i) shows how order information is encrypted and forwarded to the merchant and (ii) shows how payment information is encrypted and forwarded to the issuer.

Both signatures are then forwarded to the merchant through Cipher text (SSL) which the merchant decrypts; the merchant then forwards the payment details to the Acquirer for onward transmission to the issuer.

Authorization and Authentication Request

The card issuer receives the payment request and decrypts it, identifies the cardholder and automatically rings the cardholder to authenticate the purchase. The cardholder then confirms by inputting a secret PIN through the phone. The issuer then forwards the authorization information to the merchant through SSL.

Purchase Response

The merchant, upon receiving the authorization through the payment gateway, then confirms the purchase to the cardholder or declines.

4.2 Comparative Analysis

SET improved upon the 3KP protocol by introducing dual signature, which prevented merchants from accessing the payment details hence making SET a bit more secure than 3KP. Nevertheless, the implementation of SET was still more complex than with the 3KP protocol, due to overhead costs in acquiring PKI.

The SSL protocol was easy to implement and more convenient to use, but absence of cardholder authentication and merchant verification made fraud rampant in the SSL protocol.

The live authentication payment protocol makes the merchant anonymous but provides live cardholder authentication.

One time transaction Number prevents replay attacks on the online payment system environment, but with no merchant verification and cardholder authentication.

The proposed REPP combines security, convenience and ease of use. The advantage of REPP over the protocols discussed is the option for the cardholder to terminate the transaction. Therefore, errors or fraud can easily be identified by the cardholder and the transaction can be terminated.

Table 1. Comparison of The proposed REPP with existing Protocol

Protocol	Security	Usability	Cardholder Authentication	Verification of Merchant	CardHolder Termination	Implementation
3KP	secured	Complex	good	yes	No	Complex
SET	secured	Complex	good	yes	No	Complex
SSL	secured	Convenient	seldom	No	No	Easy
CCT	secured	Convenient	seldom	No	No	Easy
LCA	secured	Convenient	good	No	No	Easy
REPP	secured	Convenient	good	yes	Yes	Easy

5 Conclusion

Though yet to be practically implemented, the proposed Robust Electronic Payment Protocol (REPP) theoretically compares very well with live cardholder authentication in terms of security, usability, cardholder authentication and implementation. However, the REPP verifies the merchant as much as SET does. The result therefore indicates that REPP is much more capable of minimizing fraud, convenient to use, and easy to implement in the real world. This proposed protocol could be an antidote to the recent fraudulent activities within the e-commerce environment. The proposed protocol would be implemented to test its robustness in a future work.

References

[1] http://travel.state.gov, http://travel.state.gov/travel/cis_pa_tw/cis/cis_1124.html (2010), http://travel.state.gov (accessed September 10, 2011)

[2] http://www.apca.com.au, http://www.apca.com.au/Public/apca01_live.nsf/ResourceLookup/Payment_Fraud_St (2009), http://www.apca.com.au (accessed November 5, 2010)

[3] Levi, A., Kroc, C.K.: CONSEPP:Conevient and Secure Electronic Payment Protocol Based on X9.59. In: 17th Annual Computer Security Applications Conference, New Orleans, Louisiana (2001)

[4] Hwang, J.-J., Yeh, T.-C., Li, J.-B.: Securing On-line Credit Card Payments Without Disclosing Information. Computer Standards and Interfaces, 119–129 (2003)

[5] Paunov, C., Vickery, G. http://www.oecd.org/dataoecd/37/19/36736056.pdf (April 18, 2006), http://www.oecd.org/dataoecd/37/19/36736056.pdf (accessed September 20, 2011)

[6] Sumanjeet, S.: Emergence of Payment Systems in the Age of Electronic Commerce: the State of Art. Global Journal of International Business Research, 17–36 (2009)

[7] Turban, E., Lee, J.K., King, D., Liang, T.P., Turban, D.: Electronic Commerce: Managerial Perspective 2010. Prentice Hall (2010)

[8] Xiao, H., Christianson, B., Zhang, Y.: A Purchase Protocol with Live Cardholder Authentication for Online Payment. In: The Fourth International Conference on Information Assurance and Security (2008)

[9] Bellare, M., Garay, J.A., Hauser, R., Herzberg, A., Krawczyk, H., Steiner, M., Tsudik, G., Herreweghen, E.V., Waidner: Design, Implementation and Deployment of the iKP Secure Electronic Payment System. IEEE Jurnal of Selected Areas in Communication 18(4) (April 2000)

[10] Hall, J., Kilbank, S., Barbeau, M., Kranakis, E.: WPP: A Secure Payment Protocol for Supporting Credit Card Transaction Over Wireless Network. In: IEEE International Conference on Telecommunications (ICT), Bucharest, Romania (2001)

[11] Fourati, A., Ayed, H.K.B., Kamoun, F., Benzekri, A.: A SET Base Approach to Secure the Payment in Mobile Commerce. In: 27th Annual IEEE Conference on Local Computer Networks, Tampa, Florida (2002)

[12] Ford, W.: Secure Electronic Commerce; Building the Infrastructure for Digital Signatures and Encryption, 2nd edn. Prentice Hall (2001)

[13] Paulson, L.C.: Verifying the SET Protocol: Overview. In: Abdallah, A.E., Ryan, P.Y.A., Schneider, S. (eds.) FASec 2002. LNCS, vol. 2629, pp. 4–14. Springer, Heidelberg (2003)

[14] Knospe, H., Schwiderski-Grosche, S.: Online Payment for Access to Heterogeneous Mobile Networks. In: IST Mobile and Wireless Telecommunication Summit, Thesaloniki, Greece (2002)

[15] Li, Y., Zhang, X.: Securing Credit Card Transaction with One-Time Payment Scheme. Electronic Commerce Research and Application, 413–426 (2005)

[16] Kaol, W.-C., Fang, C.-Y., Chen, Y.-Y., Shen, M.-H., Wong, J.: Integrating Flexible Electrophoretic and One-Time Password Generator in Smart Cards. IEEE (2008)

[17] Li, Y.: The Design of the Secure Payments Systems Based on SET Protocol. In: International Conference on Computer Science and Information Technology (2008)

[18] http://www.ibonus.net, http://www.ibonus.net/web/home/ (2011), http://www.ibonus.net (accessed September 11, 2011)

[19] MTN, http://www.mtn.com.gh/NewsArtDetails.aspx?AID=112&ID&CID=38&MID=11&FirstParentID=1 (2009), http://www.mtn.com.gh (accessed September 11, 2011)

[20] http://www.authorize.net, http://www.authorize.net/resources/howitworksdiagram/ (2011), http://www.authorize.net (accessed September 23, 2011)

[21] http://www.bog.gov.gh, http://www.bog.gov.gh/index1.php?linkid=183&adate=28/01/2008&archiveid=1102&page=1 (Febuary 2008), http://www.bog.gov.gh (accessed September 23, 2011)

An Improved Secure Communications Protocol

Yaping Zhang[1], Chunyan Li[2], Jingyuan Zhang[2], and Bing Sun[2]

[1] School of Computer Software, Tianjin University, Tianjin, China
[2] School of Computer Science and Technology, Tianjin University, Tianjin, China
{tjuypzh99,lichunyan}@126.com

Abstract. This paper proposes an improved security communication protocol SCP, which works at the application layer. In this protocol, third party authentication server is used to complete the server and client customer authentication. The hybrid encryption algorithm, which combines block encryption with stream encryption, is adopted to encrypt communication data. SCP provides pseudo-random number encryption, mutual identification authentication, and message integrity check service, and achieves a good network security transmission mechanism.

Keywords: SCP, Identification authentication, Hybrid encryption algorithm, security.

1 Introduction

Security communication protocol is very important in the Internet. SSL, the Internet protocol for session-based encryption and authentication, provides data integrity and privacy service. However, SSL adopts server authentication and optional client authentication to preclude eavesdropping, tampering, and message forgery in client-server applications. It will be benefit the Trade Company, and not the customer. SSL/TLS adopts a single encryption algorithm in the data encryption, and uses the same key in one session, but on the Internet the amount of data exchanged is so large that the attackers can acquire more cipher text easily, increasing the probability of decryption. For the analysis of the weakness of SSL and TLS protocols, a scheme is proposed to improve the security of SSL by modifying hand-shake protocol by Zhao and Liu [1]. Liu et al and Takamichi, Kiyomi, and Ryosuke [2] - [3] improve SSL/TLS protocol to protect the important network information such as E-commerce etc. SET, the secure electronic transaction, involves three parties, namely the cardholder, the merchant, and the payment gateway (essentially a bank). It assures the mutual authentication of the consumers and the trade company by third-party institution, uses digital signature to guarantee integrity, and uses certificates to verify dealers' identity [4]. However, SET is very complex; most customers shopping on the Internet do not use it in reality.

The security communication protocol (SCP) combines block encryption with stream encryption, achieving “one-time pad” incomputability, and takes into account high efficiency of block encryption. Its confidentiality is high.

V. Khachidze et al. (Eds.): iCETS 2012, CCIS 332, pp. 240–249, 2012.

2 SCP Overview

SCP consists of two sub-protocols, namely handshake authentication protocol and data transfer protocol. There are three entities in the process, which are communication client (CC), authentication server (AUS) and communication server (CS). Authentication server is used to complete mutual authentication with the client and server respectively, based on Digital Certificates. After authentication is completed, authentication server generates a temporary session key (Sk) and related session message summary (Sms). There are three stages to complete the communication process, as per Fig.1.

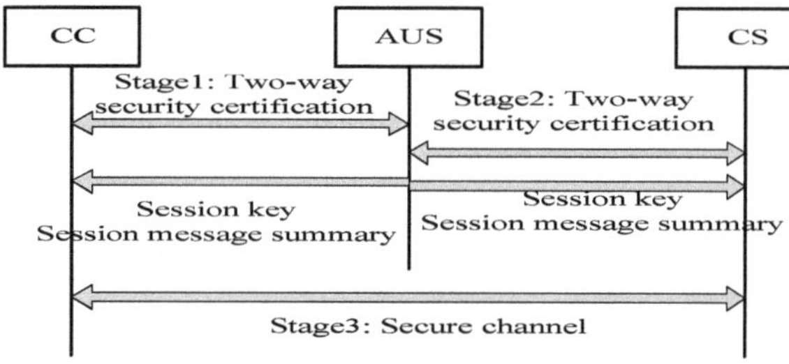

Fig. 1. Communication process

After handshake authentication protocol, the data transfer protocol adopts hybrid encryption algorithm to encrypt communication data, and ensures secure communication between two parties (the client and the server).

3 SCP Working Principles

3.1 Symbols

Symbols used in the protocol are shown as follows:

ID_{CC}: identity of the client;
ID_{CS}: identity of the Server;
KU_{CC}: public key of Client;
KR_{CC}: private key of Client;
KU_{CS}: public key of Server;
KR_{CS}: private key of Server;
KU_{AUS}: public key of AUS;
KR_{AUS}: private key of AUS;
E(X, K): encrypt X using K.

3.2 Handshake Authentication Protocol

The handshake authentication protocol is a key component of SCP, and operates before transmitting the truly effective data in order to complete the following tasks:

- Achieve mutual authentication between the client and authentication server;
- Achieve mutual authentication between authentication server and the server;
- Confirm session key and related session information;
- Maintain the freshness of session key.

The client certificate and server certificate, which are issued by AUS (or based on mechanism PKI to obtain other certificates), should be implanted into CC and CS, respectively, in advance. In addition, CC and CS can regularly request to update the certificates, and check the revocation list of certificates when necessary. According to the public key certificate, AUS gets KU_{CC} and KU_{CS}, and at the same time CC and CS get KU_{AUS}.

(1) Mutual Authentication between CC and AUS
The sequence diagram is shown in Fig.2.

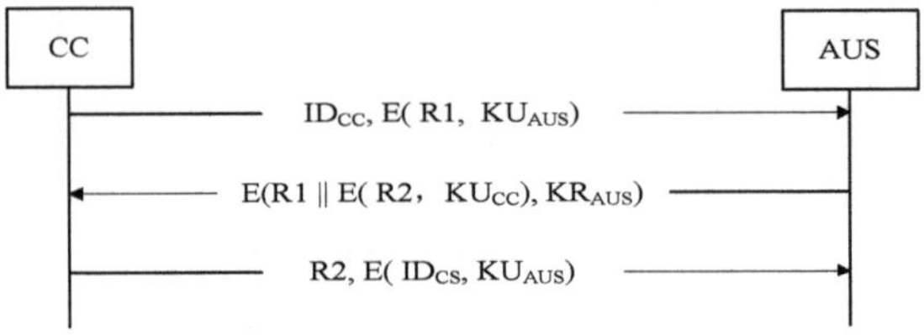

Fig. 2. Mutual authentication between client and authentication server

Step 1: CC→AUS. CC sends an authentication request to AUS, and generates a random number R1, then sends ciphertext E (R1, KU_{AUS}) and ID_{CC} to AUS.

Step 2: AUS→CC. AUS decrypts E (R1, KU_{AUS}) with KR_{AUS} to get R1, and generates a random number R2 which is encryted with KU_{CC}. AUS encrypts R1 and E (R2, KU_{CC}) using KR_{AUS}, then sends ciphertext E (R1|| E (R2, KU_{CC}), KR_{AUS}) to CC. CC examines whether R1 is the random number from step 1. If so, AUS is authenticated.

Step 3: CC→ AUS. CC decrypts E (R1|| E (R2, KU_{CC}), KR_{AUS}) with KU_{AUS} to get E (R2, KU_{CC}), then CC decrypts E (R2, KU_{CC}) using KR_{CC} to get R2. Afterward, R2 and E (ID_{CS}, KU_{AUS}) are sent to AUS. AUS judges whether R2 is the random number from previous selection. If so, CC is verified and there is no replay attack. If identity has not been confirmed, communications will be halted; conversely, AUS decrypts E (IDCS, KU_{AUS}) using KR_{AUS}, obtaining ID_{CS}, and connects to the server for authentication.

(2) Mutual Authentication between AS and CS
The sequence diagram is shown in Fig.3.

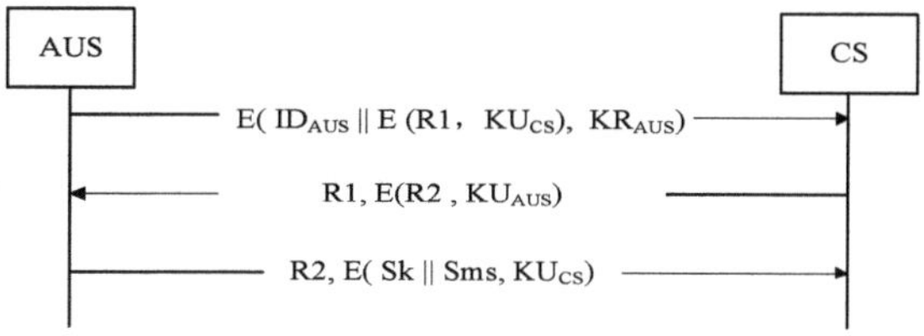

Fig. 3. Mutual authentication between authentication server and server

Step 1: AUS→CS. AUS sends a connection request to CS, and generates a random number R1. AUS encrypts ID_{AUS} and E (R1, KU_{CS}) with KR_{AUS}, then sends E (ID_{AUS}|| E (R1, KU_{CS}), KR_{AUS}) to CS.

Step 2: CS→AUS. CS decrypts E (ID_{AUS} || E (R1, KU_{CS}), KR_{AUS}) with KU_{AUS} and KR_{CS} to get R1, and generates a random number R2. CS encrypts R2 using KU_{AUS}, and then sends R1 and E (R2, KU_{AUS}) to AUS. AUS examines whether R1 is the random number from step 1. If so, CS is authenticated.

Step 3: AUS→CS. CS judges whether R2 is the random number from previous selection. If so, AUS is authenticated and there is no replay attack. If identity has not been confirmed, communications are halted; conversely, AUS can generate the session key (Sk). AUS encrypts Sk and session message summary (Sms), producing ciphertext E (Sk|| Sms, KU_{CS}), which is sent to CS, then sends E (Sk|| Sms, KU_{CC}) and E (Ks|| Sms, KU_{CS}) to CC. CC decrypts E (Sk|| Sms, KU_{CC}) with KR_{CC}, getting Sk and related Sms. Similarly, CS decrypts E (Ks|| Sms, KU_{CS}) with KR_{CS}, getting Sk and its Sms.

3.3 Data Transfer Protocol

The sequence diagram of data transmission is shown in Fig.4.

The initialization phase of data transfer protocol includes the following message.

(1) The Client_Hello message (CC→CS)

For communications to begin between a client and a server securely, the client must first send a Client_Hello message to the server. The message contains a hello request, E (Sk|| Sms, KU_{CS}), E (Sms, Sk) and the encryption algorithm supported by CC

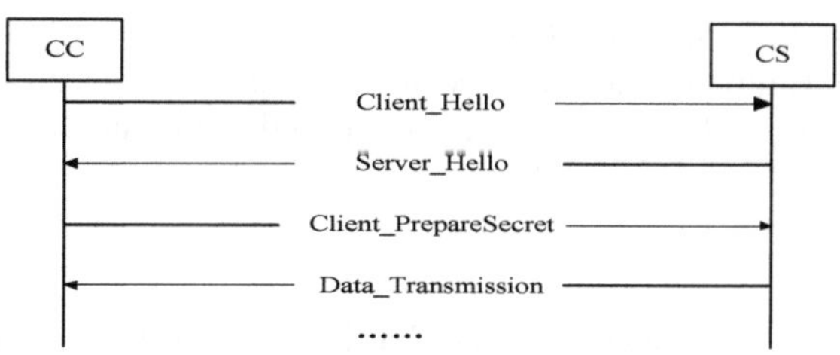

Fig. 4. Data transfer process

Function:

- CC sends E (Sk || Sms, KU_{CS}) to CS. Because CS has also received E (Sk || Sms, KU_{CS}) from AUS and E (Sms, Sk), it demonstrates that the client has received Sk from AUS.
- CC provides CS with the encryption algorithms (sequence encryption and block encryption which includes DES, AES and 3EDS, etc.) supported by CC. XML format [6] description of Client_Hello Message is shown in Fig.5.

```
<SCP>
  <Client_Hello>
    <Protocol_Version>1.0</Protocol_Version>
    <Client_Certificate>
       <Session>
         <Session_info> E(Ks||Sms, KUCS ) </Session_info>
         <Session_keyProv> E(Sms,Ks) </Session_keyProv>
       </Session>
    </Client_Certificate>
    <Client_Block Cipher>
      <Algotithm>AES</Algorithm>......
    </Client_Block Cipher>
    <Client_Stream Cipher>
      <Algotithm>RC4<Algotithm>......
    </Client_Stream Cipher>
  </Client_Hello>
</SCP>
```

Fig. 5. XML format of Client_Hello Message

(2) The Server_Hello message (CS→CC)
After the Client_Hello message has been sent out, the server can respond with a Server_Hello message. It shows CS has monitored the communication request from CC.

Function:

- CS checks E (Sk || Sms, KU_{CS}) from CC. If it is same as the message from AUS, CS decrypts E (Sms, Sk). If the result is Sms, CS can confirm the identity of CC.
- CS selects proper algorithms from the library supported by CC, and then returns a list of selected algorithms to prepare for data transfer protocol.

- CS provides a random number R as a parameter of generating initial key of communicating parties, then encrypts it with Sk. CS sends the ciphertext E(R, Sk) to CC.

Consequence. Communicating parties establish a secure data transmission pipe, and determine the required algorithms.

XML format description of Server_Hello Message is shown in Fig.6.

```
<SCP>
  <Server_Hello>
    <Server_Certificate>...... </Server_Certificate>
    <Server_Block Cipher>
      <Algotithm>...... </Algorithm>
    </Server_Block Cipher>
    <Server_Stream Cipher>
      <Algotithm>......<Algotithm>
    </Server_Stream Cipher>
    <Server_Random> E(R,Ks) </Server_Random>
  </Server_Hello>
</SCP>
```

Fig. 6. XML format of Server_Hello Message

(3) Client_Prepare Secret (CC→CS)

CC can send a Client_Prepare Secret message after a Server_Hello message is received by CS, which shows that CC has received the initial random number R and confirms the encryption algorithms. R is the input parameter of the random number generator and produces an initial key to encrypt data using mixed cryptogram arithmetic.

3.4 HyBrid Encryption Algorithm

Hybrid encryption algorithm combines block encryption with stream encryption [6].

Encryption:

Step 1: Break the plaintext M into blocks Mi (i=0, 1...) as input of block cipher encryption E_{block}.

Step 2: Put initial key K_{init} into random number generator of stream cipher encryption E_{stream}, and generate random key stream K_{stream}.

Step 3: Break K_{stream} into blocks K_i (i=0, 1...) as key input of E_{block}.

Step 4: According to block cipher encryption, encrypt every single M_i with K_i respectively, producing ciphertext C_i (i=0, 1...).

Step 5: Connect ciphertext block C_i to be a whole. Encryption process is finished.

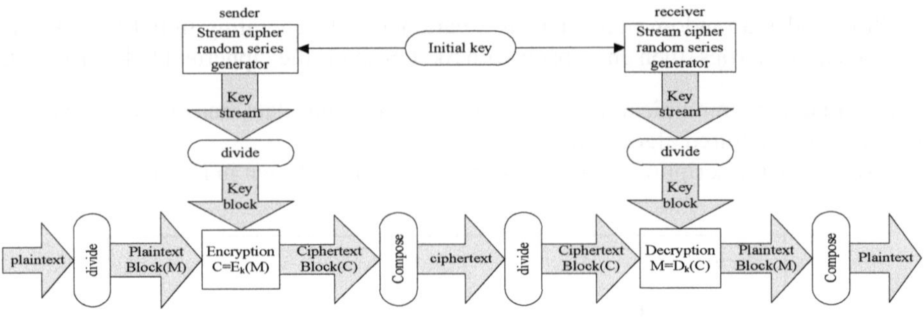

Fig. 7. Hybrid encryption algorithm model

Decryption is similar: we divide C into blocks C_i as input of block decryption D_{block}, then decryption is based on block decryption. The algorithm model is shown in Fig.7.

According to Shannon theory, Diffusion and Confusion are two basic elements of general encryption algorithm. Diffusion mechanism makes the statistical relation between plaintext and ciphertext as complex as possible to frustrate attempts of conjecturing the key; Confusion mechanism makes relations between statistical characteristics of ciphertext and makes the value of the encryption key as complex as possible to resisting declassification. Hybrid encryption algorithm achieves multiple diffusion and confusion mechanisms via the combination of block and stream encryption algorithms [7], and increases the difficulty of declassification in theory. It is theoretically incomputable, based on one-time pad of Shannon theory, and takes into consideration the high effectiveness of block cipher.

In the protocol, the client and server use the same initial key generator, and then input the random numbers respectively as initial keys which are chosen beginning with the data transmission, as per Fig.8.

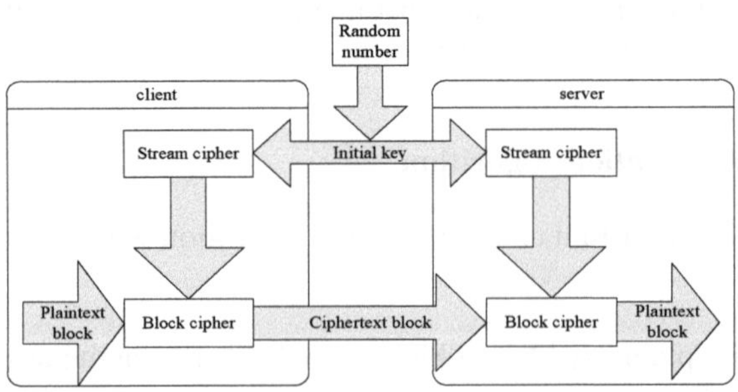

Fig. 8. Data transfer protocol encryption model

4 Security Analysis

SCP provides a higher level of security, analyzed from five aspects as follows[8].

4.1 Pseudo- Randomness of Key Stream

The key stream is produced by a stream cipher random series generator. To test the randomness of key stream, we adopt statistical methods and choose some random testing methods according to FIPS PUB 140-2 standard.

In this paper the Monobit Test is used to test pseudo-randomness. The random number generator produces 20,000 continuous "0" or "1", and 20,000 continuous numbers are added together to obtain a sum, which is defined as X. If 9725<X<10275, the random number generator passes this test. Passing the test, the random series generator has a well pseudo-randomness and can used in hybrid encryption algorithm.

4.2 Data Privacy Analysis

Privacy. Useful and real data will not leak to unauthorized users, even if it is intercepted. SCP adopts hybrid encryption arithmetic, in which the initial key of stream encryption has greater privacy. The initial key is produced by the random numbers chosen by the server. The ciphertext E(R, Ks) only appears twice on the Internet. Therefore, it can reduce the possibility of R being decrypted. The same initial key generator used by the client and server can produce better privacy in the random key.

4.3 Identity Authentication

Both communicating parties can establish their identities, and comfirm they are not the third parties who are pretending. The basis of information security begins when both communicating parties transmit effective data. SCP requires both communicating parties to provide certificates to verify their own identities, and the authentication server completes this process. Therefore, it can prevent hackers from impersonating one party to deceive the other party.

4.4 Data Integrity

Data cannot be changed, including addition, deletion, modification, forgery and so on, without the authorization features.

In the process of SCP data transmission, the message includes a field, that is, message digest. After receiving a message, the client can calculate the message digest independently, and compare with the received digest. If they are same, it shows that all the messages that the client has received are from the server and are therefore credible. Similarly, the server will also complete the process to verify all the messages that the server has received are from the client and credible.

According to message digest algorithm theory, message content is encrypted by Hash Algorithm; it is impossible to infer the integrated content computationally via the message digest and to construct a fake message of the known message digest. In summary, it is difficult to destroy the integrity.

4.5 Common Network Attacks

Man-in-the-Middle Attacks. In the process of authentication between the communicating parties, hackers as man-in-middle intercept the messages of client and server and send false messages to the client and server respectively [9]. In SCP protocol, handshake authentication protocol plays a very important role. In the second step "AUS→CC", hackers do not know KR_{AUS} of the message E (R1||E (R2, KU_{CC}), KR_{AUS}). It is therefore impossible to forge the message. This method also avoids man in middle attack.

Replay Attacks. Attackers intercept communication data and, after a while, send them again maliciously or fraudulently to reach illegal purpose. Replay attacks have been discussed in the previous section.

5 Conclusion

With the development of Internet and E-business, the security of on-line data transmission has been an important issue. After analyzing traditional security transmission technology on the Internet and cryptographic algorithm, we propose an improved secure communications protocol (SCP), within which three entities interact. Hybrid encryption algorithm is adopted, which implements staged diffusion technique and disturbance mechanism by combining block encryption and stream encryption. SCP guarantees information transmission between the client and server.

References

1. Zhao, H., Liu, R.: A Scheme to Improve Security of SSL. In: Pacific-Asia Conference on Circuit, Communication and System, PACCS 2009, pp. 401–404 (2009)
2. Liu, W., Ren, P., Zhang, Y., Duan, H.-X.: SSL-DP: A Rootkit of Network based SSL and TLS Traffic Decryptor. In: Proceeding-2nd Cybercrime and Trustworthy Computing Workshop, pp. 29–33 (2010)
3. Takamichi, S., Kiyomi, S., Ryosuke, H.: Authentication Binding Between SSL/TLS and HTTP. IEICE Transactions on Information and System E95-D(3), 797–803 (2012)
4. Brlek, S., Hamadou, S., Mullins, J.: A Flaw in the Electronic Commerce Protocol SET. Information Processing Letters 97, 104–108 (2006)
5. Zhang, X., Jiang, C., Huang, W., Meinel, C.: A XML Format Secure Protocol-OpenSSL. Computer Systems and Applications (2005)
6. Zhang, Y.-P., Sun, J., Zhang, X.: A Stream Cipher Algorithm Based on Conventional Encryption Techniques. Tianjin University (2004)

7. Luo, Q., Zhang, J.: The Status Quo and Development of Stream Cipher. Information and Electronic Engineering 4, 75–80 (2006)
8. Jing, X., Chaowen, C.: Analysis about the Security of SSL Protocol. Information Security 22, 19–21 (2006)
9. Rolf, O., Ralf, H., David, B.: SSL/TLS Session-aware User Authentication Revisited. Computer and Security 27, 64–70 (2008)

An Efficient Scheme for Implementation of SM2 Digital Signature over GF(p)

Yanhua Liu, Wei Guo, Ya Tan, Jizeng Wei, and Dazhi Sun

School of Computer Science and Technology, Tianjin University, Tianjin 300072, China
{yanhanliu,weiguo,tanya,jizengwei,sundazhi}@tju.edu.cn

Abstract. In this paper, we proposed an efficient implementation scheme for digital signature based on the cryptography algorithm SM2, which is established as the Elliptic Curve Cryptography (ECC) standard of China. Algorithm analysis reveals speed bottleneck lies in scalar multiplication, which is time consuming for the master processor to implement. Therefore, a configurable ECC coprocessor is employed in the scheme to improve the processing speed. In order to improve the efficiency of data transport within digital signature, a fine-grained programming and high Instruction Level Parallelism architecture is employed. To decrease intermediate registers, point doubling algorithm is optimized to reduce space complexity. The speed of critical steps within SM2 digital signature is improved significantly by the coprocessor. With these improvements, scalar multiplication can be achieved in 3 ms at 80 MHz for 192-bit ECC. The results show that our scheme is competitive for embedded platforms.

Keywords: SM2 digital signature, ECC, point doubling, scalar multiplication, coprocessor.

1 Introduction

The rapid progress in e-commerce on mobile handheld services has introduced new challenges to researchers working on digital signature of embedded platforms. ECC algorithms are considered better candidates for digital signature in the resource constraint environment because they require shorter key sizes to achieve the same security strength. Elliptic Curve Digital Signature Algorithm (ECDSA) has been widely used in various applications. The State Cryptography Administration of China also promulgated the digital signature of cryptography algorithm SM2, [1] which is an alternative to ECDSA, in December 2010.

Scalar multiplication is the core operation of SM2 digital signature. Scalar multiplication contains point doubling and addition, which are composed of basic modular arithmetic operations, such as modular multiplication, addition, and subtraction. Two new architectures are proposed by Miaoqing, Kris and Tarek [2] to achieve the critical operation Montgomery modular multiplication. To decrease data delay, these architectures precomputed partial results using two possible assumptions of input data. In order to speed up the elliptic curve point calculation, point addition and doubling algorithms are optimized by Dimitrios et al [3] to fit hardware implementation. While algorithmic-level improvements are continually proposed, efficient mapping and scheduling between hardware and software is becoming more and more

V. Khachidze et al. (Eds.): iCETS 2012, CCIS 332, pp. 250–258, 2012.

important. Sergey Morozov proposed system integration on an OMAP Platform for ECC in 2011 [4], distributing underlying field operations on the DSP and minimizing data exchange between ARM and DSP. To accelerate scalar multiplication over the general prime field, a high speed coprocessor based upon the Residue Number System is proposed by Guillermin [5], guaranteeing carry-free arithmetic and easy parallelism. And Raveen R. Goundar [6] also presented co-Z addition formulae for scalar multiplication on Weierstraβ elliptic curves to reduce time complexity and space complexity. However, to our knowledge, there is almost no relevant research work of software/hardware cooperative implementation for SM2 digital signature. As cryptography algorithm SM2 is an elliptic curve cryptography standard in China, which will be widely used for e-commerce in the future, it is very promising to research software/hardware cooperative implementation.

In this paper, an efficient implementation for SM2 digital signature scheme is presented.

- Point doubling algorithm is optimized to achieve an area-efficient architecture.
- Since digital signature scheme requires large computational resources, which strongly restricts software implementation, a software/hardware cooperative System-on-Chip (SoC) implementation scheme for SM2 digital signature is proposed.
- A TTA-like configurable ECC coprocessor is designed to exploit Instruction Level Parallelism and reduce redundant data transport.

The rest of the paper is organized as follows: in section 2, a brief algorithm analysis of SM2 digital signature and optimized point doubling algorithm are presented. An efficient scheme of SM2 digital signature for embedded platform is proposed in section 3. We then give performance evaluations in section 4. Finally, the conclusion of this work is summarized in section 5.

2 Algorithm Analysis and Optimization

2.1 SM2 Digital Signature

The digital signature of cryptography algorithm SM2 is based on ECC. The security of the protocol depends on the intractability of the Elliptic Curve Discrete Logarithm Problem (ECDLP). Meanwhile, the widely used ECDSA is also based on ECDLP. Acting as ECC standard of China, SM2 digital signature is an alternative of ECDSA, which will play an important role in e-commerce. A brief outline of SM2 digital signature is given below [1].

Assuming that user A signs the message M and generates signature according to the following steps of SM2 digital signature generation:

After receiving the signature, user B verifies signature (r, s) on the message M with public key P_A according to the following steps of SM2 signature verification:

2.2 An Optimized Algorithm of Point Doubling

Scalar multiplication dominates the performance of digital signature, and point doubling is the key component of scalar multiplication. In this section, an optimized point doubling algorithm is proposed.

Point doubling is programmable as a sequence of modular operations (multiplication, inversion, addition, and subtraction). Among these operations, modular inversion is most time consuming. A fast algorithm for point doubling is described in [8]. The algorithm adopts Jacobian coordinates to avoid the modular inversion in *Fp*. Based on this algorithm; we present a new alternative algorithm which is area efficient for hardware implementation. The algorithm is presented below:

Proposed Algorithm. Point doubling ($y^2 = x^3 - 3x + b$)

Input: Elliptic curve $y^2 = x^3 - 3x + b$, the point on the curve $P = (X_1, Y_1, Z_1) \in Fp$

Output: $Q = 2P = (X_3, Y_3, Z_3)$

1.	$U = Z_1^2$	$(U = Z_1^2)$
2.	$V = U^2$	$(V = Z_1^4)$
3.	$U = V + V$	$(U = 2Z_1^4)$
4.	$U = U + V$	$(U = 3Z_1^4)$
5.	$V = X_1^2$	$(V = X_1^2)$
6.	$W = V + V$	$(W = 2X_1^2)$
7.	$W = V + W$	$(W = 3X_1^2)$
8.	$V = U - V$	$(V = 3Z_1^4 - 3X_1^2)$
9.	$Y_3 = Y_1 + Y_1$	$(Y_3 = 2Y_1)$
10.	$Z_3 = Y_3 Z_1$	$(Z_3 = 2Y_1 Z_1)$
11.	$Y_3 = Y_3^2$	$(Y_3 = 4Y_1^2)$
12.	$W = Y_3 X_1$	$(W = 4X_1 Y_1^2)$
13.	$U = Y_1^2$	$(U = Y_1^2)$
14.	$Y_3 = Y_3 U$	$(Y_3 = 4Y_1^4)$
15.	$Y_3 = Y_3 + Y_3$	$(Y_3 = 8Y_1^4)$
16.	$X_3 = V^2$	$(X_3 = (3Z_1^4 - 3X_1^2)^2)$
17.	$U = W + W$	$(U = 8X_1 Y_1^2)$
18.	$X_3 = X_3 - U$	$(X_3 = (3Z_1^4 - 3X_1^2)^2 - 8X_1 Y_1^2)$
19.	$U = W - X_3$	$(U = 4X_1 Y_1^2 - X_3)$
20.	$U = VU$	$(U = (3Z_1^4 - 3X_1^2)(4X_1 Y_1^2 - X_3))$
21.	$Y_3 = U - Y_3$	$(Y_3 = (3Z_1^4 - 3X_1^2)(4X_1 Y_1^2 - X_3) - 8Y_1^4)$

Here I, M, and S are the cost of inversion, multiplication, and squaring, respectively. Typically, I $\approx$ 100M, M $\approx$ 0.8S [6]. The computational complexity of this algorithm is 4M+6S, as is that of Li et al [8]. However, the number of required intermediate variables is less than the number presented by Li et al [8]. So that space complexity is lower, which is critical for resource constraint embedded platform, and due to the reality that the cost of addition is negligible compared with multiplication, we apply addition in step3 and step4 of proposed algorithm instead of multiplication U=3*V. Furthermore, as the function units of modular multiplication can achieve modular squaring efficiently enough, a squarer circuit is omitted for area reduction reasons.

3 Implementation Scheme

Since SM2 digital signature requires large computational resources, which strongly restricts software implementation, hardware design can assist in achieving the critical steps within digital signature efficiently. A software/hardware cooperative SoC implementation scheme is proposed in this section.

To speed up scalar multiplication, a cryptographic processor is designed. Nevertheless, SM3 cryptographic hash algorithm contains a large amount of iterative and compressing operations. It is better to be implemented by master processor, to achieve a satisfactory balance between speed and area. Master processor is not good at modular reduction because a large amount of time is required for consuming mod operations, so we employed the coprocessor to overcome the limited processing capacity of master processor. As a result, in Fig.1 and Fig.2, the steps in black are implemented by the coprocessor, and the others by master processor on the SoC implementation platform.

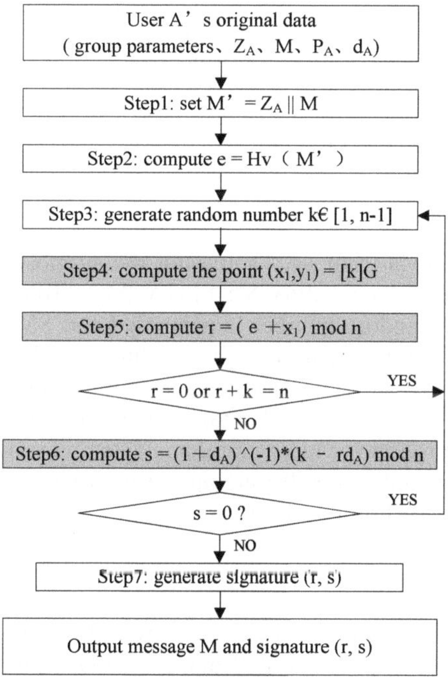

- ❖ Z_A denotes the ID information of user A
- ❖ M denotes the message
- ❖ P_A denotes the public key
- ❖ d_A denotes the secret key
- ❖ $M' = Z_A \| M$:generation a message which connects ID information Z_A with message M
- ❖ e denotes the hash value of message M'
- ❖ Hv denotes the hash function
- ❖ G denotes the base point
- ❖ [k]G denotes the scalar multiplication with scalar k and base point G
- ❖ r denotes part of SM2 digital signature
- ❖ s denotes the rest part of SM2 digital signature

Fig. 1. Flow of SM2 signature generation

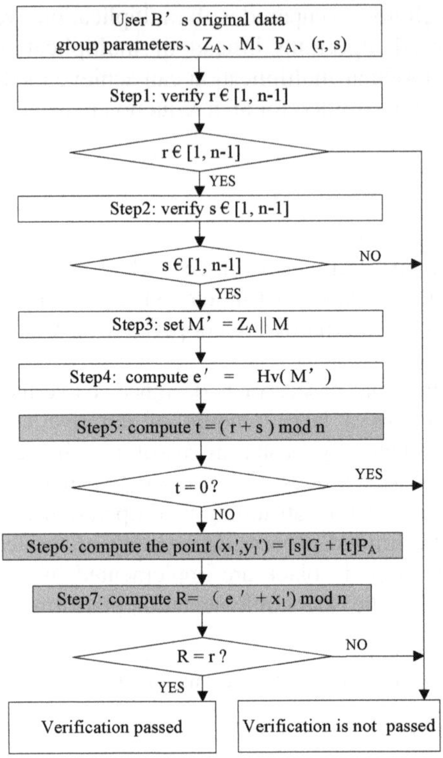

- ❖ Z_A denotes the ID information of user A
- ❖ M denotes the message
- ❖ P_A denotes the public key
- ❖ (r , s) denotes the digital signature which user B has received .
- ❖ M' = Z_A || M :generation a message which connects ID information Z_A with message M
- ❖ e' denotes the hash value of message M'
- ❖ Hv denotes the hash function
- ❖ G denotes the base point
- ❖ [s]G denotes the scalar multiplication with scalar s and base point G
- ❖ [t]P_A denotes the scalar multiplication with scalar t and point P_A (public key)
- ❖ [s]G+[t]P_A means calculate point [s]G and [t]P_A, then add the two point.

Fig. 2. Flow of SM2 signature verification

3.1 Implementation Platform

The block diagram of a SoC implementation platform for evaluating the proposed scheme is shown in Fig.3, which is implemented on Xilinx V5 FPGA. MicroBlaze CPU acts as master processor, within which a random number is generated and SM3 cryptographic hash algorithm is accomplished. In the meantime, it schedules the data stream in the evaluation platform. ECC coprocessor accomplishes scalar multiplication, which affects the overall performance. Meanwhile, it also takes charge of basic modular arithmetic operations and fast transmission for huge amounts of data is provided by DMA. TIMER and UART operate together for displaying the intermediate data to verify correctness and determine the speed bottleneck.

3.2 The Proposed ECC Cryptographic Processor

To speed up large operand operations, an ECC coprocessor based on Transport Triggered Architecture (TTA) for hardware implementation of scalar multiplication is proposed. TTA is a configurable architecture for special application, which is similar to VLIW to achieve Instruction Level Parallelism for programming. The most important feature of TTA is programming fine-grained data transports, which adds an extra level of control to the code generation.

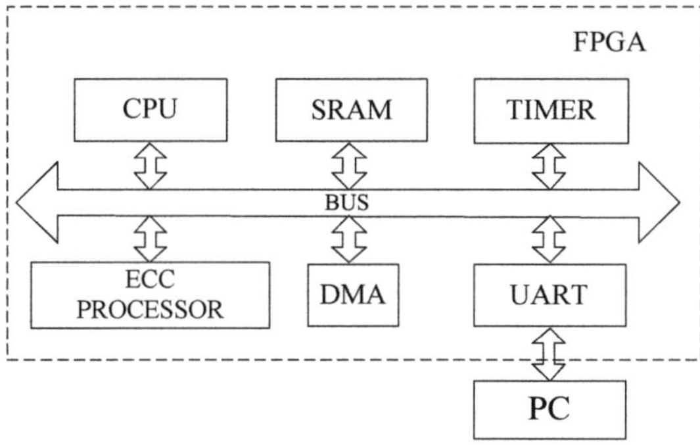

Fig. 3. Implementation platform for SM2 digital signature

As illustrated in Fig.4, this ECC cryptographic processor consists of three modules, including program flow control unit, function units and transport network. The processor's FUs are composed of Jump Unit (JMP), Arithmetic Logic Unit (ALU), Load and Store Unit (LDST), Large operand Addition/Subtraction Unit (LADSB), Multiplier Unit (LMUL) and Montgomery Multiplier Accumulators Unit (MMAU). The units of JMP and ALU implement operation jump, shifting and comparing. Data load and store is accomplished by LDST units. The LADSB unit supports addition and subtraction for large operand whose length more than bus width, while the LMUL and MMAU unit are used together to implement the FIOS Montgomery modular multiplication. The operation of outer loop in FIOS Montgomery modular multiplication is achieved by LMUL units and the inner loop operation by MMAU.

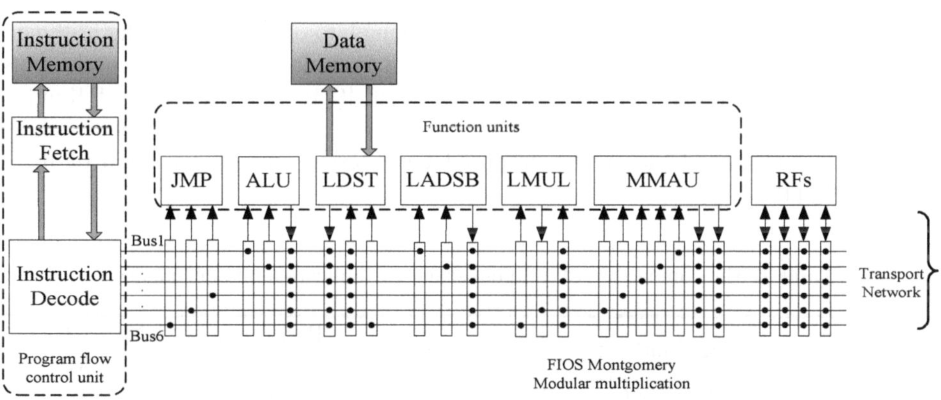

Fig. 4. A TTA-like ECC cryptographic processor

4 Implementation Results and Analysis

We have mapped our implementation platform for SM2 digital signature onto a Xilinx Virtex-5 XC5V-LX110T FPGA to obtain quantitative performance, for comparison purposes. The ECC coprocessor implementation can run at 80 MHz, occupies 13664 LUTs, and uses 14 DSP48E blocks as well as 16K RAM. FPGA design is highly adaptable and easily reprogrammable for varying prime field sizes, which makes it suitable for ECC, due to the large number of different secure curves, prime fields currently available. As scalar multiplication is time consuming for the master processor to implement, so an ECC coprocessor is design on FPGA to improve processing speed. Compared with other work, this work can achieve higher clock frequency and take less delay with smaller area cost. The result of the comparison is listed in Table 1. Our clock frequency is relatively faster, because a two-phase hybrid pipelining architecture, which includes transport pipelining and FU pipelining, is adopted to execute instruction. Sakiyama et al [9] propose a reconfigurable data path for RSA and ECC, but a 260 bit width data path is selected for 256-bit ECC, while the modular arithmetic units presented by McIvor, McLoone and McCanny [10] adopted 256-bit for large number processing. Kendall, Hamad and Daler [11] choose the large bit width for data path because routing signals requires many stages of generic bit-level FPGA switches. However, 32 bit data path is chosen in this work, which is another factor attributing to fast clock frequency. Since modular multiplication applied in the scheme is a key operation, it affects the overall performance of scalar multiplication. Sakiyama et al [9] adopted d-digit serial Montgomery modular multiplication and full word Montgomery modular multiplication is applied by McIvor et al [10], while Kendall et al [11] employed a regular (non-modular) multiplier coupled with modular reduction. Compared with these algorithms, FIOS Montgomery modular multiplication adopted in this work can offer less delay. So that execution time of scalar multiplication in this work is less compared with those designs [9], [10], and [11]. The area of the proposed design is relatively smaller, due to the fact that large operands of ECC can be efficiently converted into the 32-bit word length to operate in modular arithmetic units. While large operand is operated directly within modular arithmetic units in the works of Sakiyama et al and McIvor et al, [9-10] the area cost of Kendall et al.'s design [11] is increased to support the max key size 521 bit. Thus, taking these facts into consideration, the proposed coprocessor outperforms each of these designs [9], [10], [11].

Table 1. The comparison of different scalar multiplication implementations

Reference	Target Platform	Key size	Area	Performance [msec]	Max Clock Freq[MHZ]
[9]	XC3S5000	256	27,597 slices	17.7	40
[10]	XC2VP125	256	15,755 slices	3.86	40
[11]	XC2VP100-6	521	20,793 slices	7.24	50
This work	XC5V-LX110T	192	3,416 slices	3.0	80

To our knowledge, there is little relevant work about software/hardware cooperative implementation of SM2 digital signature. However, an efficient implementation of SM2 digital signature, which acts as the digital signature standard for e-commerce in China, is significant. Our scheme is implemented with the Micro Blaze as master processor and a TTA-like ECC coprocessor at 75 MHz. Peak performance of 311 times per second scalar multiplication for 192-bit ECC has been achieved, and the time needed for other critical steps is shown in Table 2. As SM3 cryptographic hash algorithm contains a large amount of iterative and compressing operations, it is better to implement it in the master processor to achieve a satisfactory balance between speed and area. Moreover, software implementation of hash algorithm costs only 0.128s. From Table 2, it can be seen that the main operation scalar multiplication is accelerated by coprocessor efficiently. Compared to software implementation scalar multiplication in the work of Haodong and Qun, [12] which costs 1.60s with an 8 MHz, 16-bit CPU for 160-bit ECC, the time of hardware implementation in this work just is 3.221 ms for 192-bit ECC. Modular reduction and inversion must be applied within SM2 digital signature during step 6 in the signature generation process. These are also performance critical operations. By taking advantage of ECC coprocessor, this operation can be achieved within 0.227 ms without any area cost, and the speed is significantly improved. This result shows that the scheme is an efficient solution to meet the requirement of SM2 digital signature on embedded platform.

Table 2. The performance of critical steps for SM2 digital signature

Function	Critical steps	Platform	Performance
Signature generation	Step2: $e = Hv(M')$	MicroBlaze	0.128s
	Step4: $(x_1, y_1) = [K]G$	ECC coprocessor	3.221ms
	Step5: $r = (e + x_1) \bmod n$	ECC coprocessor	0.173us
	Step6: $s = (1 + d_A)^{-1}(k - rd_A)$	ECC coprocessor	0.227ms
Signature verification	Step4: $e = Hv(M')$	MicroBlaze	0.128s
	Step5: $t = (r + s) \bmod n$	ECC coprocessor	0.106us
	Step6: $(x_1, y_1) = [s]G + [t]P_A$	ECC coprocessor	6.464ms
	Step7: $R = (e + x_1) \bmod n$	ECC coprocessor	0.173us

5 Conclusion

In this paper, an efficient software/hardware cooperative SoC implementation for SM2 digital signature scheme is presented. An optimized point doubling algorithm is applied to decrease hardware cost. A TTA-like ECC coprocessor is designed to accelerate key operation scalar multiplication. In comparison to other works, the ECC coprocessor can obtain a satisfactory balance between speed and area for scalar multiplication. Herewith, SM2 digital signature speeds up significantly, and the core operation scalar multiplication can be accomplished in 3 ms at 80 MHz with 3416 slices on Xilinx Virtex-5 FPGA. The results show that the proposed SM2 digital signature implementation meets the requirements of the embedded platform efficiently.

Acknowledgement. This work is supported in part by both the Natural Science Foundation of Tianjin (No. 11JCZDJC15800) and the National Natural Science Foundation of China (No. 61003306).

References

1. State Cryptography Administration of China: Public Key Cryptographic Algorithm SM2 Based on Elliptic Curves, http://www.oscca.gov.cn
2. Miaoqing, H., Kris, G., Tarek, E.G.: New Hardware Architectures for Montgomery Modular Multiplication Algorithm. IEEE Transactions on Computers 60(7) (2011)
3. Dimitrios, M.S., Apostolos, P.F., Harris, E.M., Athanasios, P.K., Thanos, S.: An RNS Implementation of an Fp Elliptic Curve Point Multiplier. IEEE Transactions on Circuits and Systems—I: Regular Papers 56(6), 1202–1213 (2009)
4. Sergey, M.: System Integration of Elliptic Curve Cryptography on an OMAP Platform. In: 2011 IEEE 9th Symposium Application Specific Processors (SASP), pp. 52–57. IEEE Computer Society, Los Alamitos (2011)
5. Guillermin, N.: A High Speed Coprocessor for Elliptic Curve Scalar Multiplications over Fp. In: Mangard, S., Standaert, F.-X. (eds.) CHES 2010. LNCS, vol. 6225, pp. 48–64. Springer, Heidelberg (2010)
6. Raveen, R.G., Marc, J., Atsuko, M., Matthieu, R., Alexandre, V.: Scalar Multiplication on Weierstrass Elliptic Curves from Co-Z Arithmetic. Journal of Cryptographic Engineering 1, 161–176 (2011)
7. State Cryptography Administration of China: SM3 Cryptographic Hash Algorithm, http://www.oscca.gov.cn
8. Li, M., Wu, D., Dai, K., Zou, X.C.: Research and Design of a High-Performance Scalable Public-Key Cipher Coprocessor. ACI'A Ele Ironica Sinica 3(3), 665–669 (2011)
9. Sakiyama, K., Mentens, N., Batina, L., Preneel, B., Verbauwhede, I.: Reconfigurable Modular Arithmetic Logic Unit for High-Performance Public-Key Cryptosystems. In: Bertels, K., Cardoso, J.M.P., Vassiliadis, S. (eds.) ARC 2006. LNCS, vol. 3985, pp. 347–357. Springer, Heidelberg (2006)
10. McIvor, C.J., McLoone, M., McCanny, J.V.: Hardware elliptic curve cryptographic processor over GF(p). IEEE Trans. Circuits Syst. I, Reg. Papers 53(9), 1946–1957 (2006)
11. Kendall, A., Hamad, A., Daler, R.: Flexible Hardware Processor for Elliptic Curve Cryptography Over NIST Prime Fields. IEEE Transactions on Very Large Scale Integration Systems 17(8) (2009)
12. Haodong, W., Qun, L.: Efficient Implementation of Public Key Cryptosystems on Mote Sensors. In: Ning, P., Qing, S., Li, N. (eds.) ICICS 2006. LNCS, vol. 4307, pp. 519–528. Springer, Heidelberg (2006)

A Browser Extension Vulnerability Detecting Approach Based on Behavior Monitoring and Analysis

Qin Wang, Xiaohong Li, and Bobo Yan

School of Computer Science and Technology, Tianjin University, China
{wangqin0612,xiaohongli,bobo}@tju.edu.cn

Abstract. Browser extension is a mechanism used to improve the performance and applicability of browsers by adding new personalization features. However, it may also introduce more security related vulnerabilities. Though the threats of malicious or vulnerable extensions have been addressed by several solutions, these solutions are still far from eliminating the threats, especially when the extensions' behavior sequences are unsafe. Using Firefox as an example, this paper provides an approach firstly to synthesize abstract behavioral models from XPCOM interfaces, invoking sequences of extensions obtained by the run-time interface invoking approach, which requires the preparatory implementation of a behavior monitoring system; secondly, it purposes to define the vulnerable behavior sequence patterns that are used to guide the testing process adopted on sequence matching methods for detecting the security and reliability vulnerability of extensions. The effectiveness and performance of our approach and detecting tool is provided with the support of experimental results.

Keywords: browser extension, behavior monitoring, behavior sequence, security.

1 Introduction

With the rapid development of network technology, various network applications have been greatly enriching the daily life of people. As the windows of these network applications, browsers have undoubtedly become an application people use most frequently, and, the extension mechanism [1] is supported by the major browsers, such as IE, Firefox, and Chrome. Also, new personalization features can be added to browsers within the extension mechanism, which are developed by third parties. As a result, users may add new features to fulfill their individualized functional requirements, by choosing to install appropriate extensions to browsers. However, the introduction of browser extension mechanisms makes the browser security problem even more critical.

Generally speaking, extensions apply for, and then are granted, high privilege to meet various functional requirements. However, with that high privilege, extensions can monitor and modify web content, change browser behavior and appearance by altering preferences, and access stored website passwords and cookie information. They can issue HTTP requests in the name of user, and open sockets to listen to connections or connect to remote servers. They can even access the local system and launch processes. All these

V. Khachidze et al. (Eds.): iCETS 2012, CCIS 332, pp. 259–270, 2012.

privileges, on the one hand, make it possible for extensions to greatly expand the functionalities of browsers; on the other hand, they also increase the attack surface for users' systems. Recently, a number of vulnerabilities [2] have been explored, which sounds the alarm to the indiscriminate use of browser extensions, and also provokes more researchers to focus on solving browser extensions security issues.

In Firefox extension system [1] [10], XULRunner [3] platform is responsible for the running of extensions, while through XULRunner, extensions can invoke many interfaces of cross platform component object model (XPCOM) to achieve a variety of required functions. Since the interfaces can be invoked, the extension can receive high privileges, leading to security problems. Mozilla adopted several measures to lessen the problem of Firefox extensions safety; including the following:

(1) Signature mechanism
In order to ensure that extensions are from the third-party developers claimed, and to maintain integrity during the transportation process, Mozilla provides signature mechanism, which makes it available to sign the extensions with the developers' names, which are used as data to be checked by users. However, signature mechanism makes limited contributions to solving the extension security issue.

(2) Review mechanism
In order to explore and prevent extension developers from submitting malicious or buggy extensions with security vulnerabilities, Mozilla adopts a series of review work on the newly released ones. However, Mozilla merely reviews the extensions' codes manually with the support of simple tools, which makes the review process to be accompanied with many human factors. Hence, review mechanism cannot provide adequate assurance to extension mechanism.

For the above, Firefox security mechanism does not perform well to solve the extension security problems.

Based on static information flow analysis [5], Sruthi Bandhakavi et al analyzed the Javascript code in the extensions statically, and developed a detecting tool called VEX [6], which was used to detect security vulnerabilities in Firefox extensions. With the help of VEX, they found hundreds of security vulnerabilities on buggy or malicious extensions. However, the majority of the task of detection was completed manually, which incurred a great workload and called for expert analysis. Furthermore, to limit abuse of priorities of extensions, Adam Barth proposed least privilege for Google Chrome [7] and redesigned the structure of extension system, which brought the extension priorities under control. Ter Louw et al enhanced web browser security by protecting browser code based integrity and user data confidentiality and integrity [8,9], and then proposed an extension isolation mechanism.

Though these approaches, together with the Firefox extension security mechanism, can protect the security of the browser in some aspects, threats of malicious and buggy extensions still exist. After a study on the 1448 XPCOM interfaces of Firefox 3.5[10], this paper classified each of them according to their functions, and divided these 57 classifications into 4 groups under the guide of security relation degree. Based on a large scale testing on extensions in Addons.mozilla.org and the statistical analysis of the results and using the instrument approach [11], which required coding hooks files and then planting them into the Firefox source code, we built a dynamic monitoring platform used to extract XPCOM interface invoking information of extensions on their runtime.

The instrumented browser, as a dynamic testing tool, can obtain not only the XPCOM interfaces invoking information, but also the interfaces invoking sequences of extensions. Thus, after a preliminary judgment on security, interface sequences extracted by the instrumented browser will be processed into a behavior sequences diagram with the instruction of interface classifications and the security related groups (the four groups represent security level).

The behavior sequences will be simplified as far as possible, and eventually be used as the inputs of vulnerable behavior sequence FSMs that were defined beforehand. All of the vulnerable behavior sequence FSMs and the matching algorithm constitute the sequence matching approach, which is used to detect vulnerabilities via extension behavior sequences. Still, it should be noted that, in order to improve the accuracy of detection and exclude false-positives, some manual review is necessary.

The remainder of this paper is organized as follows. Section 2 discusses related works, and Section 3 describes how to instrument the browser so as to introduce the browser extension behavior monitoring method. Section 4 further explains the approach of security judgment on behavior sequence. We describe our implementation, experiments and analysis of results in Sections 5, and conclude in Section 6.

2 Related Works

2.1 Static Analysis

Sruthi Bandhakavi proposed an approach that analyzes the JavaScript code via static information flow to detect the potential security flaws in browser extensions on the carrier VEX. However, this method cannot fully support the JavaScript features, such as Prototype and evaluation methods; that is to say, its applicability and detecting effects are not very satisfactory. In addition, this approach was based on information flows, which made it impossible to induct completely, leading a limited scope and a relatively low vulnerabilities discerning rate.

In contrast, our method provides dynamic information flow analysis based on instrumentation, which can lower the proportion of false consciousness and increase the vulnerabilities discerning rate, consequently increasing the coverage.

2.2 Instrumentation

University of California at Berkeley, united with Google, proposes a new browser extension mechanism [11]. It is a kind of instrumentation approach applied in Chrome browser. An extension in this mechanism is separated into three components running in different processes. These components communicate with each other through inter-process communication. Even in the event that an attacker compromises an extension, it will prevent the attacker from executing sensitive operations. The shortcoming of this mechanism is its runtime burden and ineffectiveness to indirect threat.

On the contrary, our system will test the extensions asynchronously, which does not present any workload to the browser, as our goal is to find malicious or buggy extensions and report them to Mozilla or the extension users. Additionally, our system is good at dealing with indirect threats.

2.3 Behavior Monitoring

Sabre [12] analyzes browser's behavior through monitoring data flow. It labels every JavaScript object with a tag to indicate its sensitivity. Its detecting method is that if a sensitive object is accessed insecurely, it will send a warning to the user. This method can detect attacks that steal sensitive information directly from browser; however, attacks that steal sensitive information using Trojan can circumvent it.

Similarly, SpyShield [13] is a tool that prevents sensitive information from leaking. It separates unauthorized add-ons from the browser. Then, all communication between extensions and the browser is managed according to the user's behavior. It cannot deal with a kind of malicious extension that imitates user's behavior or entices the user to do something dangerous.

With regard to the insufficiencies of the two systems mentioned above, our system can overcome them. Whether an attacker steals the user's critical data directly or with help of Trojan, its behaviors will be exposed to our system without distinction.

3 The Monitoring Approach of Browser Extension Behavior

Based on a study on XPCOM interfaces of Firefox 3.5, in order to reduce the security risks brought by malicious or vulnerable browser extensions, this paper classifies all of the XPCOM interfaces by their behavior types and subsequently defines all the classifications. With the support of the classifications and definitions, a Firefox extension behavior monitoring system is designed and implemented as the run-time dynamic extension behavior information extracting platform. For the outputs of the monitoring system, vulnerable behavior sequence definitions were processed beforehand and matching methods were used to further determine the security of under-tested extensions. The whole browser extension testing process is shown in Fig.1.

3.1 Browser Extension Behavior

Firefox exposes two types of interfaces to extensions: ① Javascript functions; XPCOM interfaces. From a security point of view, XPCOM interfaces were taken as the main focus of this paper for its great potential security risk inherited from its powerful functions.

In the evolution process of Firefox, a small part of XPCOM interfaces has been adjusted in some way, and the research work of this paper was conducted on Firefox 3.5. After a study on 1448 XPCOM interfaces of Firefox 3.5, according to the functions provided by the interfaces, we classified all them into 57 behavior categories, as listed in Table 1 in the behavior group column. Among these 57 categories, most are of

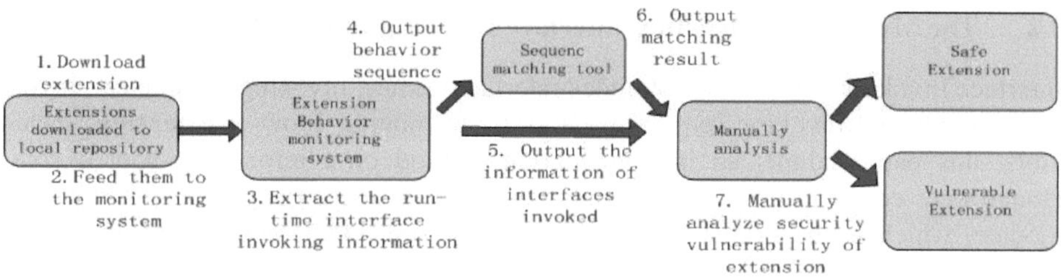

Fig. 1. Vulnerability detecting process

normal usage, but potential security risks may exist in others while they provide normal functions at the same time. For example, the interface behavior classification "Password" provides access functions to the password manager which is necessary for some kinds of browser extensions, but there is the possibility that sensitive information of users may be disclosed from it. According to the security related degree, the 57 classifications were divided into four groups with a unique security level for each. Detailed information is listed in Table 1.

Table 1. Security-related groups of XPCOM interface behavior

Security correlation	Behavior group of extension
Tight	Process launching, Thread management, Clipboard access (belonging to Accessibility), Arbitrary file access, Download, XPInstall, Network access via XPCOMAPI (belonging to Network access), Update, DOM injection (belonging to Doc handling)
Medium	Password, Login, Cookie, Preference, Profile, Network access (via XML HTTPRequest), Addons management
Loose	History, Bookmark, Dynamic code execution
None	Accessibility, Browser core, Auto complete, Log to console, Searching, Spell checking, DOM, Editor, Internationalization, Offline cache, XML parser, Network utilities, Parser, Channels, Protocol handlers, Sockets, Proxies, RSS/RDF, Data types and structures, Streams, Memory management, Component management, Additional XPCOM services, Javascript core, Javascript debugger, XPConnect, Authentication, Certification, Cryptograph, Additional security interfaces, Doc handling, Transaction management, Web worker, Window management, Print, Other tools, Storage, Images, ZIP/JAR process, JVM, Plugins

In short, through the study and analysis of XPCOM interfaces exposed to extensions from Firefox, this paper defined 57 Firefox extension behaviors based on their functional correlations, which could be used to guide security judgment in extension behavior monitoring process and, subsequently, the reduction process from extensions' XPCOM interface invoking sequences to behavior sequences.

3.2 The Method of Extracting Interface Invoking Information

Interface invoking information includes interface names, invoking parameters, invoking methods and invoking sequences. In order to monitor browser extensions' behaviors, this paper adopts an instrumentation method on Firefox core source code. Hooks were coded in C/C++ and planted into the JavaScript engine and XPConnect module, which is the bridge between JavaScript and XPCOM components used to obtain dynamic XPCOM interface invoking information. When the instrumented browser, with the under-testing extension installed, visits specified web pages, the hooks planted in will record the XPCOM interface invoking information dynamic, and complete the monitoring process.

After analyzing on JavaScript engine and XPConnect module source codes, to finish the browser instrumentation process, this paper selected certain positions to plant the hooks coded beforehand. Detailed information is listed in Table.2. XPConnect_FilterXPCOMRequest is primarily used to intercept XPCOM interfaces invoking information of extension and js_BuiltInFunctionCalled is primarily used to extract the JavaScript internal functions' invoking information of extensions, while the dom_AddEventListener is used to get the web page or Firefox window event listener adding behaviors if present.

Table 2. Hooks and their insert points

Hooks	Insert Points
js_hooks.c: XPConnect_FilterXPCOMRequest(...)	js/src/xpcconnect/src/xpcwrappednative.cpp: XPCWrappedNative::CallMethod(...) js/src/xpcconnect/src/qsgen.py
js_hooks.c: js_BuiltInFunctionCalled(...)	js/src/jsobj.cpp: obj_eval() js/src/jsinterp.cpp:js_InvokeConstructor() js/src/jsinterp.cpp:js_Interpret()
dom_hooks.c: dom_AddEventListener(...)	dom/src/base/nsDOMClassInfo.cpp: nsEventReceiverSH::AddEventListenerHelper() dom/src/base/nsDOMClassInfo.cpp: nsEventReceiverSH::RegisterCompileHandler() content/base/src/nsGenericElement.cpp: nsGenericElement::AddScriptEventListener()

According to each single piece of a XPCOM interface invoking information of under-testing extension and its security-related group information, preliminary judgment of extension security could be made in the monitoring process: if any vulnerability is found here, we can report the testing results immediately. Otherwise, we must simplify the XPCOM interface invoking sequences of every under-testing extension and reduce the XPCOM interface invoking sequences into behavior sequences, which can be used in the further detecting process (sequence matching, Section 4). In the following, the XPCOM interface invoking sequence simplification will be introduced.

3.3 The Simplification Process of Interface Invoking Sequence

After the dynamic XPCOM interface invoking sequences of under-testing extension were extracted, they would be processed according to the following steps:

① for the continuous duplicate XPCOM interfaces in the sequences, remove the continuous duplicate entries after every position where it first appeared for every time.

②for the de-duplicated XPCOM interface invoking sequences, according to the interface behavior classifications shown in Table 1, process the interface invoking sequences into behavior sequences further. The simplification process is shown below:

```
for each interface_name in the interface sequence
        look up the behavior group it belongs to;
        if  interface_name in a behavior group
                replace the current interface_name with the group_name;
                if next interface_name in the same group;
                        delete next interface_name;
                else  jump out of the loop;
```

Fig. 2. Simplification process

③transform the simplified extension behavior sequences into directed acyclic diagram:

```
for every node(group in sequence) adding to the graph
    if the next below the current node exists in current branch
        check the sequence below the next;
        if  same with previous
            ignore;
        else add a new branch from the latest matched previous node;
```

Fig. 3. Transformation process

After a three-step treatment, every XPCOM interface invoking sequence of its under-testing extension will be transformed into Multi-branching directed acyclic diagram, which can be taken as the behavior report of the under-testing extension. More importantly, every output diagram can be used to support the vulnerable behavior sequence matching approach, which is proposed to address the extension behavior sequence security problem in this paper. Moreover, the extension behavior sequence matching method will be introduced in Section 4.

4 Approach on Vulnerability Detection with Behavior Sequence

For every under-testing extension, finding no vulnerability in the monitoring system does not mean that there is no vulnerability at all. The safety of its behavior sequence is a critical factor to be considered. That is to say, we need to test the security of its behavior sequence. As described above, the behavior sequence of an extension can be extracted and simplified in the behavior monitoring system, which facilitates the behavior sequence testing process that adopted matching method where the behavior sequence of every under-testing extension will be matched to the pre-defined vulnerable behavior sequences.

4.1 Definitions of Vulnerable Behavior Sequences

Based on a large amount of experiments, and in light of the attacking patterns in existence and the unsafe behavior of vulnerable or malicious extensions, this paper extracts definitions of some vulnerable extension behavior sequences. We define some vulnerable sequences such as launching local process, of which FSM is shown in Fig. 4, ∈ represents null skip, and '?' represents any input of extension behavior.

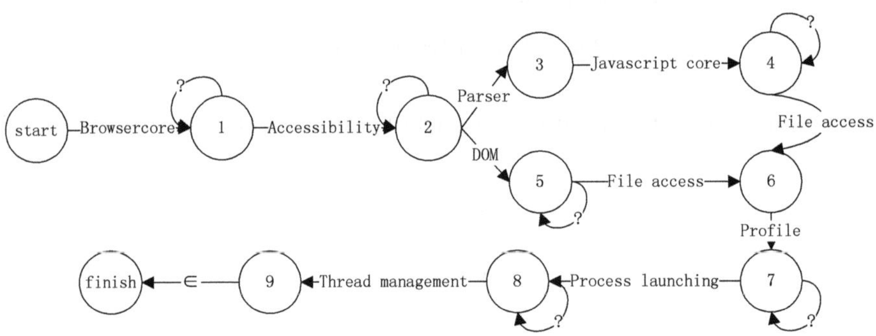

Fig. 4. FSM of local process launching sequence

4.2 Sequence Matching

The Directed acyclic sequence diagram obtained via the behavior monitoring system, whose process was described in Sec. 3.3, will be separated into every single trace thoroughly here. Taking every trace of the diagram of an under-testing extension as input of every FSM of vulnerable behavior sequence definition, whether there is a match determines whether there is a corresponding type of vulnerability. If a trace made a FSM of vulnerable sequence definition has skipped to the finish state, it means that the very type of vulnerability exists in the current extension that is being tested, and at that time the sequence matching approach would output the security risk report; when no FSMs have skipped to the finish state, the under-testing extension is considered to be safe.

Because of the accuracy issue of definitions regarding vulnerable behavior sequences, some manual review work may still be needed for excluding false-positives.

5 Implementation and Experiment

In order to verify the effectiveness of behavior monitoring and analyzing approach, this paper designed and implemented a Firefox extension monitoring prototype system on Firefox 3.5, in the Ubuntu 10.0.4 operating system. The prototype system diagram is shown in Fig. 5. The monitoring system downloads Firefox extensions from Addon.mozilla.com to the local repository, and every under-testing extension is installed to the instrumented browser in each testing procedure and uninstalled after the test. Every testing procedure tests only one local extension. During the run time of the extension, the instrumented browser will visit the specified web page, and user operations are simulated on the page. In the above process, XPCOM interfaces invoking information of the under-testing extension is recorded, and then transformed into behavior sequence diagram after preliminary analysis.

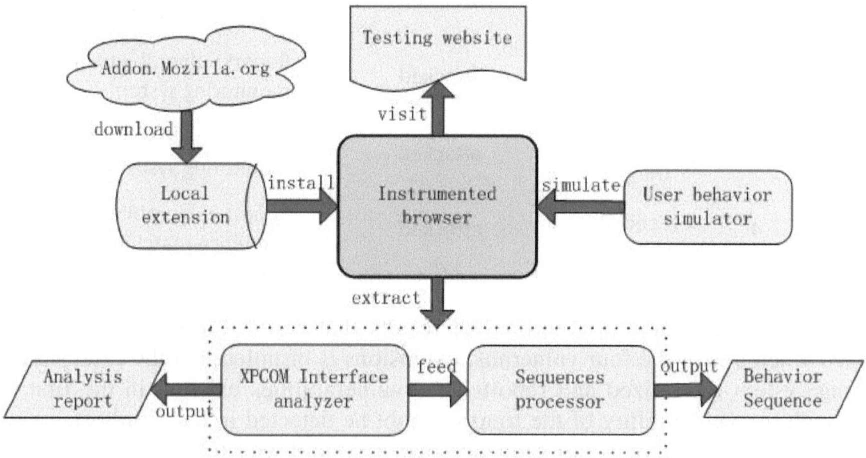

Fig. 5. Extension behavior monitoring system

This prototype monitoring system consists of four modules: instrumented browser, user behavior simulator, XPCOM interface analyzer and sequences processor.

Instrumented browser is the main module of this prototype system. It is implemented via coding hooks those are used to extract the XPCOM interface invoking information of the under-testing extension, and then planting the hooks to the appropriate points in JavaScript engine and XPConnect module of Firefox introduced in Table 1. User behavior simulator is responsible for simulating users' inputs from the keyboard and mouse while the instrumented browser is visiting the specified web page, which facilitates the dynamic XPCOM interface invoking information, including interface invoking sequence. XPCOM interface analyzer is used to record and preliminarily analyze the information obtained. It will provide an initial judgment according to the security-related groups of XPCOM interface behavior as shown in Table.1, and provides inputs for the sequence processor if necessary. The sequence processor is used for simplifying the XPCOM interface invoking sequence of an extension and transforming interface sequence into behavior sequence under the guidance of the simplification method provided in Sec. 3.3. The behavior sequence diagrams, as the outputs of sequence processor, are a critical basis of extension vulnerability detecting, processed as inputs of a simple sequence matching tool described in Sec. 4.

With the support of behavior monitoring system and sequence matching tool, we designed and completed experiments on the four vulnerable Firefox extensions [14 - 17] listed in Table 3. We constructed and restored an attack scene, conducted the experiments on native Firefox 3.5 and tested them with our vulnerability detecting approach. The results of our experiments are also listed in Table 3.

Table 3. Effectiveness testing results

Ex Num	Extension	Native Firefox	Detecting results
1	CoolPreview V2.7.2	attacked	Report vulnerability in monitoring system
2	Yoono V6.1.0	attacked	Report vulnerability in monitoring system
3	ScribeFire V3.4.1	attacked	Report vulnerability in monitoring system
4	Feed Sidebar V3.1	attacked	Report vulnerability in sequence matching tool

It can be seen from the experimental results that native Firefox 3.5 could be attacked when one of the four vulnerable extensions is installed, but the extension monitoring system recognized and reported the vulnerabilities existing in the first three. Although the vulnerability of the fourth cannot be detected in the monitoring system, it can be found in the behavior sequence matching tool with the local process launching FSM skipped to the finish state and reported.

The experimental results illustrate the effectiveness of the combination of behavior monitoring system and behavior sequence matching tool. That is to say, our browser extension vulnerability detecting approach based on behavior monitoring and analysis is effective; it is correct to focus on not only the single XPCOM interface invoked by an under-testing extension but also the XPCOM interface invoking sequence, when detecting the potential vulnerability of a browser extension.

6 Conclusion

This paper pursues further research on both browser extension mechanism and safety problems, in order to alleviate the safety problems. It puts forward a browser extension security vulnerability detection approach based on behavior monitoring analysis. Hence, under the guidance of the detecting method, the browser extension behavior monitoring system and the matching tool for testing the safety of under-testing extension sequence is designed and realized in this paper. It is used for real-time monitoring and extraction of extension behavior and analysis and deals with information invoking from XPCOM interfaces. The extension vulnerability report or extension behavior sequence diagram is used as the output of the monitoring system. Finally, vulnerability sequence matching method is used to provide further judgment on the safety of the extension behavior sequence. The experiment shows that the approach brings the browser some load, but it can be used as a kind of effective asynchronous detection means. It can judge the safety of extension and reduce the risk that browser extension mechanism brings to the users. Meanwhile, the results of the experiment have given direction for future research; namely, there needs to be more in-depth study on extension security vulnerability caused by illegal behavior sequence, more accurate definition of the vulnerable behavior sequence, and an enriched and complete vulnerability detecting approach.

References

1. Mozilla Foundation. Extensions (EB/OL) (April 04, 2011), `https://developer.mozilla.org/en/Extensions` (May 07, 2011)
2. Liverani, R.S.: Abusing Firefox Extensions (EB/OL) (August 14, 2009), `http://security-assessment.com/presentation/all/all/archive.html` (May 07, 2011)
3. Brent, S.: XULRunner: A New Approach for Developing Rich Internet Applications. IEEE Internet Computing 11(3), 67–73 (2007)
4. Verdurmen, J.: Firefox extension security. Raboud University, Netherlands (2008)
5. Amtoft, T., Banerjee, A.: Information Flow Analysis in Logical Form. In: Giacobazzi, R. (ed.) SAS 2004. LNCS, vol. 3148, pp. 100–115. Springer, Heidelberg (2004)
6. Bandhakavi, S.: VEX: Vetting Browser Extensions for Security Vulnerabilities (2010)
7. Barth, A., Felt, A.P., Saxena, P., Boodman, A.: Protecting browsers from extension vulnerabilities. In: Network and Distributed System Security Symposium (2010)
8. Louw, M.T., Lim, J., Venkatakrishnan, V.: Enhancing web browser security against malware extensions. Journal in Computer Virology 4, 179–195 (2008)
9. Ter Louw, M., Lim, J.S., Venkatakrishnan, V.N.: Extensible Web Browser Security. In: Hämmerli, B.M., Sommer, R. (eds.) DIMVA 2007. LNCS, vol. 4579, pp. 1–19. Springer, Heidelberg (2007)
10. Parrish R.: An introduction to XPCOM (EB/OL) (February 16, 2009) (May 07, 2011)
11. Barth, A., Felt, A.P., Saxena, P., Boodman, A.: Protecting browsers from extension vulnerabilities. In: Proceedings of the 17th Network and Distributed System Security Symposium, NDSS (2010)
12. Dhawan, M., Ganapathy, V.: Analyzing information flow in JavaScript-based browser extensions. In: Proceedings of the 25th Annual Computer Security Applications Conference (ACSAC), pp. 382–391 (2009)
13. Li, Z., Wang, X.-F., Choi, J.Y.: SpyShield: Preserving Privacy from Spy Add-Ons. In: Kruegel, C., Lippmann, R., Clark, A. (eds.) RAID 2007. LNCS, vol. 4637, pp. 296–316. Springer, Heidelberg (2007)

14. Security-Assessment.com. CoolPreviews Firefox Extension Privileged Code Injection (EB/OL) (August 25, 2009) (May 16, 2011)
15. Security-Assessment.com. Yoono Firefox Extension Privileged Code Injection (EB/OL) (January 13, 2010), http://www.security-assessment.com/files/documents/advisory/2010-01-13_Yoono_Firefox_Extension_Privileged_Code_Injection.pdf (May 16, 2011)
16. Security-Assessment.com. ScribeFire Firefox Extension Privileged Code Injection (EB/OL) (August 24, 2009), http://www.security-assessment.com/files/documents/advisory/2009-08-24_ScribeFire_Firefox_Extension_Privileged_Code_Injection.pdf (May 16, 2011)
17. Security-Assessment.com. Feed Sidebar Firefox Extension Privileged Code Injection (EB/OL) (August 24, 2009) (May 16, 2011)

Research on Location Selection Based on Genetic and Simulated Annealing Algorithm

Wenyuan Tao[1] and Jiayue Liu[2]

[1] School of Computer Software, Tianjin University, China
[2] School of Computer Science and Technology, Tianjin University, China
{taowenyuan,liujiayue}@tju.edu.cn

Abstract. When dealing with the problem of location selection, one must optimize multiple objective functions. The combination of genetic algorithms and simulated annealing algorithm can improve the solution efficiency and solve the premature convergence problem caused by the genetic algorithm. Using the logistics distribution system as an example, we established a terminal distribution model according to the characteristics and requirements. Based on the mathematic model and the analysis on influencing factors of the transportation costs, we conducted a study on the location selection of distribution center, and subsequently designed and implemented the corresponding genetic and simulated annealing algorithm, which could reduce delivery cost and optimize distribution models.

Keywords: genetic algorithms, simulated annealing algorithm, center of logistics distribution, location selection.

1 Introduction

Based on probability, genetic algorithm [1] is abstracted from the biological evolutionary and random iterative evolution. The basic idea is from Darwin's genetic theory, and proposed by Professor Holland in 1975. The genetic algorithm, a global optimization search method is of great practical value and provides a common framework for solving complex optimization problems. Genetic algorithm presents a solution to complex optimization problems and shows huge potential in many fields; it therefore attracts wide attention from scholars internationally. However, the genetic algorithm solution has its own shortcomings, such as poor local search ability and slow convergence.

Using genetic algorithm to solve practical problems will result in the convergence of local optimum solution of the objective function prematurely, that is, precocious phenomenon, which makes it difficult to obtain the global optimal solution. To solve these problems, some scholars have proposed a variety of hybrid algorithms. For example, the genetic climbing algorithm is recommended by Ackley; Mathefoud proposed genetic annealing algorithm; Miller put forward the optimization problem

V. Khachidze et al. (Eds.): iCETS 2012, CCIS 332, pp. 271–281, 2012.

for a NP-hard problem; however, these approaches cannot solve the location selection problem completely.

This paper is discusses genetic annealing algorithm, and studies how to use simulated annealing algorithm to improve the genetic algorithm. The simulated annealing algorithm [2] is an extension of the local search algorithm, which simulates the thermodynamic process of cooling high temperature metal, and is widely used in combinatorial optimization problems. Using the combination of genetic algorithms and simulated annealing algorithm can avoid the defects of the genetic algorithm. Moreover, adding a memory device to the combinational algorithm can optimize the allocation of resources when it is used for location selecting of the distribution center.

The location of the logistics distribution center [3] is directly related to distribution cost, and therefore reasonable planning on location selection can save the fixed cost and reduce the variable cost at the same time. Therefore, the research on location selection can help to improve delivery quality and promote the development of the logistics system. In this paper, the genetic annealing algorithm is applied to the study of the location problem, and on this basis, to present an improved method.

2 The Assumptions and Establishment of Mathematical Model

2.1 Assumption of Logistics Distribution Center Location Selection

This paper focuses on the location selection within a given area, on selecting a certain number of optional sites to build distribution centers in the region, in order to achieve various demands, and to minimize overall costs. In order to establish the mathematical model, the following assumptions are made:

1. Thc allocation of a ncw distribution center may only be carried out within a certain range;
2. Only single product logistics of the distribution center location problem are taken into account;
3. The model contains two transport stages: transportation from the supply point to the distribution centers and transportation from distribution centers to users;
4. The unit transportation fee between supply points and distribution centers, distribution centers and the user points, and unit management costs for the distribution center are known constants;
5. Transportation costs are proportional to the volume;
6. Transportation costs and distance present a linear relationship;
7. A distribution center can be delivered by more than one supply point; a user can be delivered by more than one distribution center;
8. The goods of each demand point are completely transported one time;
9. Total demand of the users within a region is a previously known constant.

2.2 The Mathematical Model of Logistics Distribution Center Location

To establish the model of the logistics distribution center location, the study of how to select the appropriate point from the existing alternative points as the distribution center is of great importance. Thus, the main factors to be taken into consideration are the total transportation costs, distribution costs in product distribution, variable costs of custody, average fixed costs, and basic investment costs of building a distribution center, etc. Based on the analysis of the main factors affecting these costs, cost expression can be derived, which could help to obtain minimal or near minimal fees.

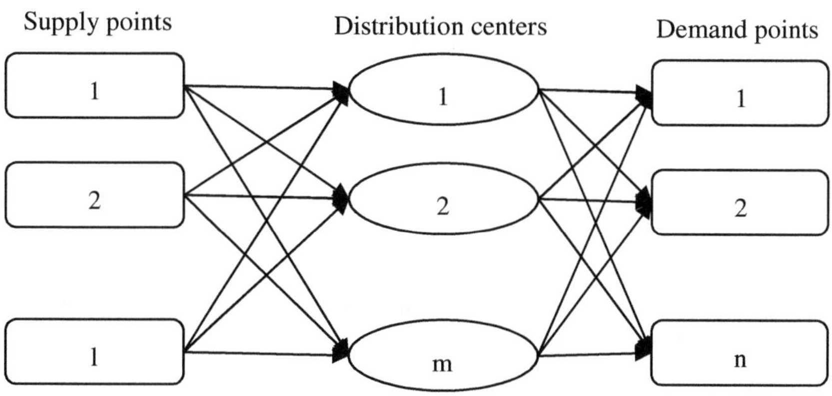

Fig. 1. The model of logistic distribution center location

1. Objective function

$$\text{Min } E=\sum_{k=1}^{l}\sum_{i=1}^{m}c_{ki}W_{ki}+\sum_{i=1}^{m}\sum_{j=1}^{n}h_{ij}X_{ij}+\sum_{i=1}^{m}Z_iF_i+\sum_{i=1}^{m}Z_iV_iW_i^{\theta} \tag{1}$$

2. Constraint condition

$$A_k-\sum_{i=1}^{m}W_{ki}\geq 0, k=1, 2,\ldots, l \tag{2}$$

$$M_i-\sum_{k=1}^{l}W_{ki}\geq 0, i=1, 2,\ldots, m \tag{3}$$

$$\sum_{i=1}^{m}X_{ij}-D_j\geq 0, j=1, 2,\ldots, n \tag{4}$$

$$\sum_{j=1}^{n} X_{ij} - \sum_{k=1}^{l} W_{ki} = 0, i=1, 2, \ldots, m \tag{5}$$

$W_{ki} \geq 0,\ X_{ij} \geq 0$

Indices:

- E - total cost;
- m - number of the distribution centers;
- l - number of the supply points;
- n - number of the demand points;
- Parameters
- W_{ki} - the amount transported from supply point k to distribution center i;
- X_{ij} - the amount transported from distribution center i to demand point j;
- $Zi = \begin{cases} 1, \text{the distribution center i is selected} \\ 0, \text{the distribution center i is not selected;} \end{cases}$
- F_i - the fixed cost of allocation distribution center i;
- c_{ki}-the unit cost of transportation from supply point k to distribution center i;
- h_{ij}-the unit cost of transportation from distribution center i to demand point j;
- A_k - the capacity of supply point k;
- M_i - the capacity of distribution center i;
- D_j - the demand of the demand point j;
- V_i - the variable cost coefficient of distribution center i;
- W_i - the flow of distribution center i;
- Index number $\theta = 1/2$.

3 The Implementation of Hybrid Genetic Annealing Algorithm

3.1 Basic Idea and Process of Genetic Algorithm

The genetic algorithm simulates biological evolution process, in which individual selection among the population, crossover and mutation operations are executed sequentially. By iteratively calculating the initial population, ultimately, the optimal solution or approximate solution could be obtained. Among the operations, selection reflects the natural law of survival of the fittest. By calculating the fitness function for each individual, the ones with high values of fitness function are recorded, which could improve the average fitness value. Crossover operation could help to avoid the loss of genes, and to improve the global convergence and computational efficiency, because the crossover operation allows the optimization process convergence to attain the global optimum quickly. The mutation operation assists the crossover operation to select a new individual by replacing allelic genes on individual chromosomes within the encoded string. When the three basic operations cooperate with each other, the genetic algorithm can achieve optimization process. The general process is shown in Fig. 2, and is followed by the detailed descriptions.

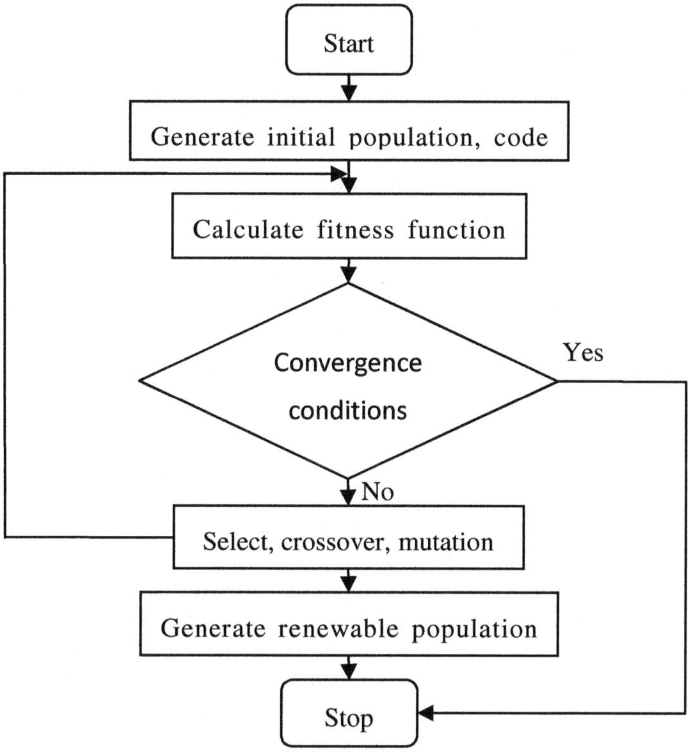

Fig. 2. Genetic algorithm process

1. The randomly generated initial population contains a certain number of chromosomes and each individual is expressed within the encoded string;
2. Calculate the fitness of each individual; determine whether to comply with the optimization criterion. If it meets the optimal solution, output the best individual and the optimal solution it represents, and then stop the calculation. Otherwise, continue to Step 3;
3. Select the renewable individuals according to the fitness; those with high fitness function values have higher probability of being selected, and the lower ones are likely to be eliminated;
4. Perform crossover and mutation operations to generate new individuals;
5. Produce a new generation of population. Go back to Step 2.

3.2 The Basic Idea and Process of Simulated Annealing Algorithm

The idea of simulated annealing algorithm is derived from the thermodynamic process of high temperature metal cooling. During the heating process, solid particles tend to be disordered and intrinsic energy consequently increases; when the temperature decreases, solid particles tend to regain order slowly. It reaches an equilibrium state at each temperature, and finally reaches the ground state at normal temperature, where the intrinsic energy is minimized. Theoretically, if the temperature setting was appropriate, the simulated annealing algorithm can converge to global optimal value with probability 1. When using solid annealing approach to simulate combination optimization problem, intrinsic energy E should be simulated as the objective function value f, while temperature T evolves into the control parameter t; consequently, simulated annealing algorithm for the solution of combinatorial optimization problems is completed: starting with the initial solution i and the initial control parameter t, repeat the "new solution - calculating the objective function - to accept or discard" iteration, and gradually decay value t. When the algorithm terminates, the solution is approximately optimal.

3.3 The Thought of Hybrid Genetic Annealing Algorithm

Analyzing genetic algorithms and simulated annealing algorithm, using the two algorithms in combination and retaining their preferable features can achieve improved genetic algorithm [4]. The improved algorithm uses the Metropolis [5] acceptance criteria to gain new solutions and accept deterioration with certain probability. It concurrently uses a group of parameters called cooling schedule to control the process, ensuring that the algorithm has the ability to jump out of local region, and outputs a global optimal solution or progressive global optimal solution.

Compared to the genetic algorithm, the hybrid algorithm has a larger range to select population. It highlights the characteristics of the simulated annealing algorithm. Meanwhile, by adjusting the temperature, the simulated annealing algorithm can accelerate the fitness function. When the temperature is high, the acceleration is not obvious. Conversely, the acceleration is very obvious when the temperature is low [6].

On thc basis of thc hybrid algorithm, this paper proposes the following improvements:

Memory Device

Adding the memory device to the genetic annealing algorithm to construct the algorithm with memory function, and using it to solve the problem of logistics distribution center selection can ensure the final solution obtained in a certain termination condition is at least the optimal one of all solutions in the search process. Adding the memory device is just adding a judge; it does not change the search direction of the algorithm. The memory device can be set with the variable i* and f*, where i* memorizes the current optimal solution and f* is its objective function value. Each time a new solution is to be accepted, compare the new objective function value with f*. If f is better than f*, replace i* and f* with i and f respectively; at the end of the algorithm, take i* and f* as the final solution and the final objective function respectively.

Improvement of the Initialization Method

Consider the formation of the initial population to suggest improvements to avoid small effective search space problems probably caused by small-scale chromosomes. The concrete action has three parts. Firstly, randomly generated chromosomes, then arrange them with the evaluation function value, and at last extract chromosomes as the initial population evenly spaced. The initial population obtained by this method is quite evenly distributed in the search space and can overcome the negative impact caused by the smaller group size, thereby effectively improving the search speed of the algorithm.

Improved genetic annealing algorithm processes are as follows:

Step 1: Given the population size maxpop, k=0; the initial temperature $t_k=t_0$, which generate an initial population pop (k); then the objective function value f(i) is calculated on the initial population, and the minimum chromosome i and corresponding function value f that produces the minimum value of the function $f_i(t_k)$ will be found and then be recorded as i*=i,f*=f; in the above, $f_i(t_k)$is the objective function value of state i at the temperature, i∈pop(k);

Step 2: If the stopping rules are met, the calculation will be stopped, and the optimized chromosome i* and f* will be outputted; otherwise, a random state j∈ N(i) which is a pro domain of every chromosome i∈pop(k) will be selected, and then be calculated to reject or accept according to the acceptance probability of simulated annealing algorithm:

$$A_{ij} = \min\left\{1, \exp\left[-\frac{f_j(t_k)-f_i(t_k)}{t_k}\right]\right\} \tag{6}$$

In the above, $f_i(t_k)$ and $f_j(t_k)$ are the objective values of state i and j respectively; furthermore, a new population newpop(k+1) will be elected after maxpop iterations.

$$\text{fitness}_j(t_k)=e^{-\frac{f_j(t_k)-f_i(t_k)}{t_k}} \tag{7}$$

Step 3: Calculate the fitness function (7). According to the probability distribution that is determined by the fitness function, select maxpop chromosomes from newpop(k+1) randomly to form a population newpop2(k+1);

Step 4: Making a crossover in accordance with the genetic algorithm, get crosspop(k+1), and then make a mutation to get mutpop(k+1);

Step 5: $t_{k+1} = d(t_k)$, k=k+1, pop(k)=mutpop(k), return to step 2.

The process is shown in Fig. 3.

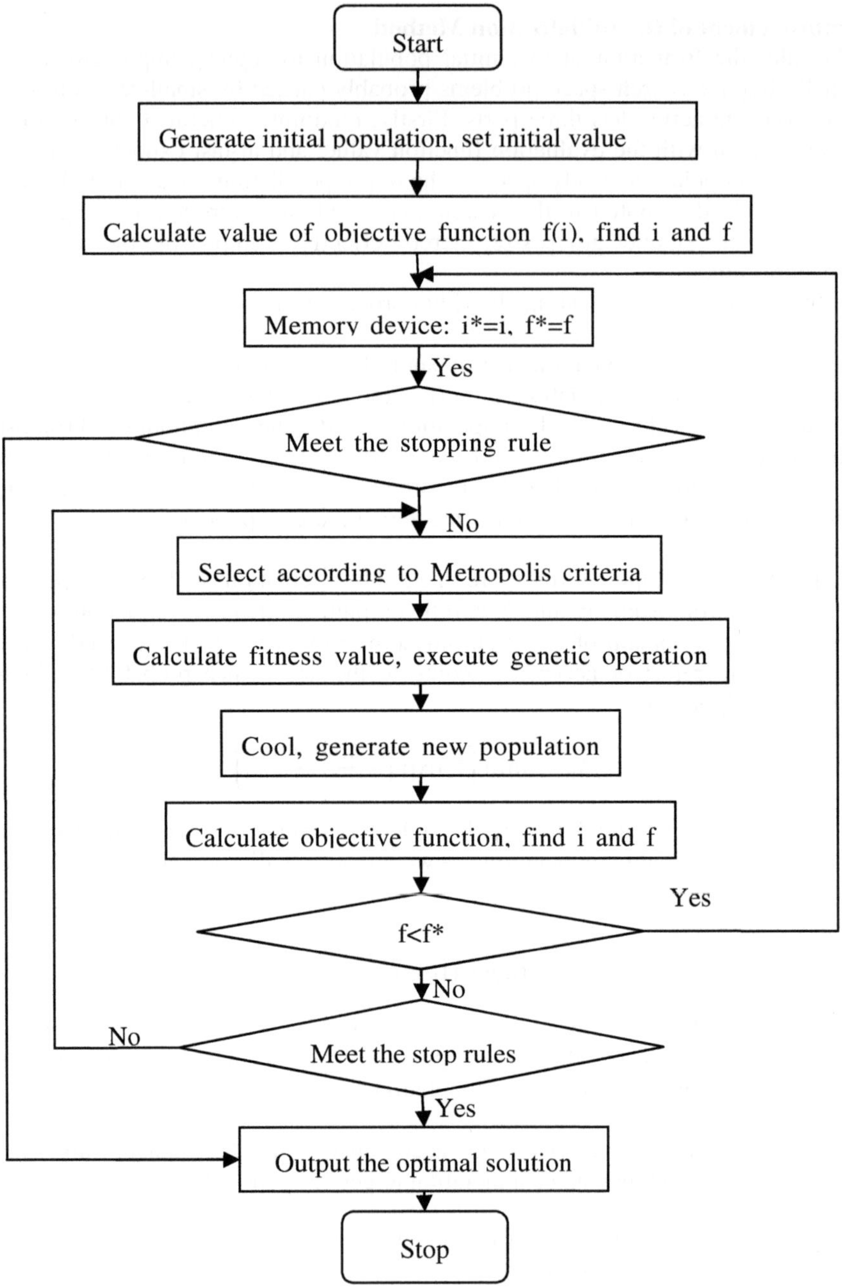

Fig. 3. Improved simulated annealing algorithm process

4 Application of the Genetic Annealing Algorithm in the Location of the Logistics Distribution Center

Assume that the supply points, distribution centers and the number of users, respectively, are 2, 4, 6; demand of each user is shown in Table 1; the unit cost of transportation of the supply point to the distribution center is in Table 2; the unit transportation cost of the distribution center to the users is shown in Table 3; the variable cost coefficient of distribution center i is shown in Table 4; fixed costs of distribution centers and capacity constraints are shown in Table 5.

Table 1. The demand of the users

User	1	2	3	4	6
Demand	12	10	10	15	10

Table 2. The unit transportation cost of the supply point to the distribution center

Supply Point	Distribution center			
	1	2	3	4
1	6	8	8	10
2	12	12	8	7

Table 3. The unit transportation cost of the distribution center to the users

Supply Point	Distribution center				
	1	2	3	4	6
1	5	10	4	9	10
2	12	15	10	10	8
3	15	11	10	5	5
4	10	10	4	5	6

Table 4. The variable cost coefficient of distribution center i

Distribution center	1	2	3	4
Variable cost	75	80	70	70

Table 5. Fixed costs of distribution centers and capacity constraints

Alternative point	1	2	3	4
Fixed cost	75	65	110	60
Capacity Constraints	30	20	40	20

To solve the problem, design chromosome coding according to the following method: chromosome encoding is divided into 3 parts, the first part has l*m bits (l and m represent the number of supply points and distribution centers respectively), and represents the delivery process, namely the quantity from the supply point to each distribution center; the second part has m bits (0 or 1), and represents whether the distribution center is selected; the third part has m*n bits (n means the number of demand points), and represents quantity transported from a distribution center to the users. The chromosome code is as follows:

s(1)	...	s(l*m)	1	1	0	1	r(1)	...	r(m*n)

Among them, from s(1) to s(l*m) respectively represents the quantity each supply point ships to the distribution center. The second part shows that the third distribution center is not selected. From r(1) to r(m*n) respectively represents the quantity each distribution center ships to each user.

To converge to the global optimum, genetic populations should have a certain size. However, in order to ensure computational efficiency, the population size should not be excessively large. General population scale values range from 10 to 100. Among the chromosomes meeting the conditions, two genes randomly exchange in the second part, and use the algorithm to adjust, making it a new chromosome that meets the requirements. Using the hybrid algorithm, the population size of each generation is 50; maximum generation as 1,500 with crossover rate 0.80; mutation rate is 0.05, the initial temperature is 10, and the attenuation coefficient is 0.85.Using the above steps of the algorithm on the computer, the optimal solution is that 1, 2, and 4 distribution centers are selected.

5 Conclusion

Combination of genetic algorithm and simulated annealing algorithm can amplify global search capability of genetic algorithm and local search capabilities of simulated annealing algorithm. On the basis of the hybrid genetic annealing algorithm, this paper proposes to add the memory device and improve the method of population initialization, and applies the improved method to the logistics distribution center location problem to obtain the most optimal solution. Finally, through an example, we verify that this hybrid algorithm can optimize the location problem.

References

1. Srinivas, N., Deb, K.: Multi-Objective function optimization using non-dominated sorting genetic algorithms. Evolutionary Computation 2(3), 221–248 (1995)
2. Kirkpatrick, S., Gelatt, C.D., Vecchi, M.P.: Optimization by simulated annealing. Science 220, 671–680 (1983)
3. Zhang, P., Wei, Q.: Logistics distribution center allocation model and elicitation algorithm. Traffic and Transportation Engineering 3(2), 65–68 (2003)

4. Lin, F.T., Kao, C.Y., Hsu, C.C.: Applying the genetic approach to simulated annealing in solving some NP hard. IEEE Trans. on SMC 23(6), 1752–1767 (1993)
5. Tian, Q., Pan, Q., Wang, F., Zhang, H.: Research on Learning Algorithm of BP Neural Network Based on the Metropolis Criterion. Techniques of Automation and Applications 22(5), 15 (2003)
6. Zhang, H., Wu, B., Yu, Z.: Research of New Genetic Algorithms Involving Mechanism of Simulated Annealing. Journal of University of Electronic of Science and Technology of China 32(1), 39–42 (2003)

Design and Implementation of Special Equipment Major Hazard Identification System

Jiang Liu[1], Manliang Chen[2], and Wenyi Xu[2]

[1] School of Computer Science and Technology, Tianjin University, Tianjin, China
[2] School of Computer Software, Tianjin University, Tianjin, China
{jiangliu,manliang99}@126.com, xwy_xfcl@sina.com

Abstract. By identifying a major hazard with the use of a large number of special equipment, the relevant departments can supervise the major hazard effectively. This paper introduces special equipment major hazard identification system. Based on B/S structure of the J2EE platform, the system uses a MVC design mode and technologies such as S2SH (Struts2, Spring, Hibernate) and web service. The functions of equipment information management, identification unit management and assessment data management have been implemented. Based on DW (Data Warehouse), OLAP (On-line Analytical Processing) technology can help the decision-maker to analyze the security situation of special equipment. Through the Microsoft SQL Server 2005 Analysis services tools, the multi-dimensional analysis of the data of special equipment major hazard identification are implemented by using OLAP.

Keywords: major hazard, S2SH, OLAP, Data Warehouse.

1 Introduction

Special equipment refers to life-threatening equipment, including boilers, pressure vessels (including gas cylinders, the same below), pressure piping, elevators, lifting machinery, the passenger tramway, large-scale recreational facilities, and factory dedicated motor vehicles [1]. Because of the particularity of special equipment, people must manage them scientifically and effectively in order to reduce the direct and indirect losses caused in the operation process. According to "Tianjin Special Equipment Security Situation Report In The First Half Of 2011" released by Tianjin Bureau of Quality and Technical Supervision, at the end of June 2011, there were 147,881 special equipment in Tianjin; 7,690 law enforcement officers have detected 3,445 special equipment enterprises and 31,773 special equipment [2]. Because of the huge number of devices, it is difficult to achieve timely supervision on each piece of equipment. People must determine which equipment has a higher potential safety hazard and supervise it primarily.

In 2000, People's Republic of China formally enacted mandatory national standards GB14218-2000 "Major hazard identification", Tianjin Bureau of Quality and Technical Supervision also released local standardsDB12/382－2008 "Special

V. Khachidze et al. (Eds.): iCETS 2012, CCIS 332, pp. 282–291, 2012.

equipment major hazard identification" in 2008. The special equipment major hazard is special equipment identification unit which may leads to serious casualties, property damage and environmental damage [3]. The identification of the major hazards from a large number of special equipment is conducive to maintaining social stability, the promotion of economic development and the protection of people's lives and property.

2 System Design

This paper introduces the "Special equipment major hazard identification system" based on Tianjin local standards DB12/382—2008 "Special equipment major hazard identification of special equipment". This system can exchange date with "Special equipment monitoring system" through web services. With the help of this system, people can scientifically and effectively identify the major hazards of special equipment.

2.1 System Architecture

The system architecture is shown in Figure 1.

All components of the system can be divided into presentation layer, business logic layer, data sharing layer, data access layer and data storage layer.

The presentation layer provides the system interface for the user. When the user sends a request to system, the system receives the request and displays the response to the user through the presentation layer. There are three types of users, including district-level supervisory users and municipal supervisory users and enterprise users. The system provides different user interfaces and system functions for different types of users.

The business logic layer achieves the business logic of the system, including corporate information management, device information management, identification unit management, assessment and identification, summary statistics , decision support and system maintenance module.

The data sharing layer and data access layer provide methods to operate data in the system. The business logic layer can exchange data with the data storage layer by calling web services or through direct access to data from Special equipment monitoring system. As the data source, identification system database will form the data warehouse for Special equipment major hazard identification system, through the process of abstract, transformation and ETL.

The data storage layer is located in the bottom of the system to manage data in the system, performing such functions as adding, updating, access and maintenance.

This system uses B/S (Browser/Server) architecture. Presentation layer runs on the client and business logic layer runs on the application server; data sharing layer, data access layer and data storage layer each run on the database server.

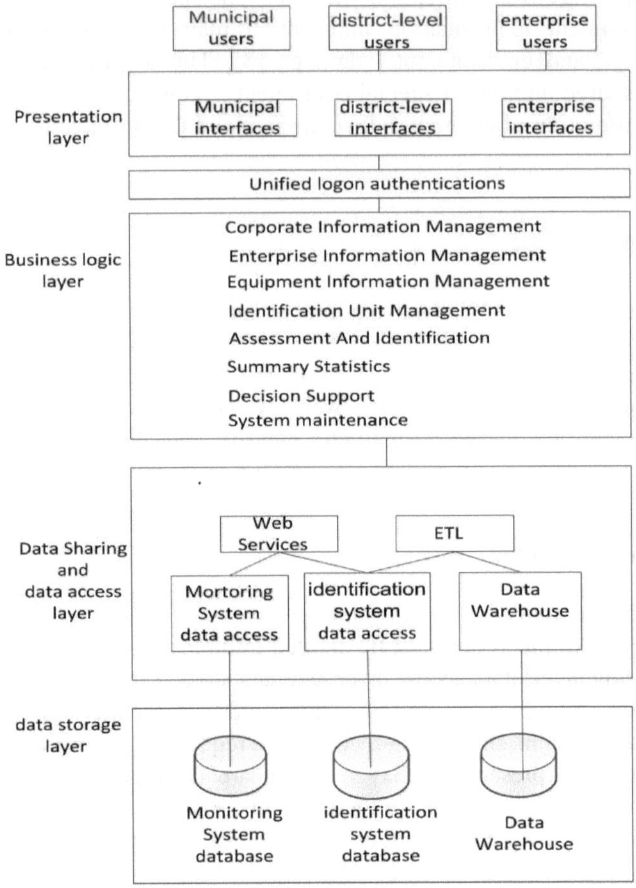

Fig. 1. System Architecture

2.2 System Functions

Special equipment major hazard identification system can provide services for a special equipment enterprise, the district-level supervisory organs and municipal supervisory organs at the same time. It identifies special equipment and provides statistical analysis services for decision makers. The system functions are shown in Figure 2.

(1) Basic information maintenance functions, including user information management, enterprise information management, special equipment information management.
(2) Special equipment major hazard identification functions, including identification unit management, identification unit assessment, assessment information query and statistical analysis of the assessment result. Identification unit management organizes and manages the major hazard of special equipment by unit. An

identification unit is a single special equipment, a special equipment cluster or a cylinder filling unit which is used for major hazard identification. The determination of different identification unit is different. Identification unit assessment function will calculate the identification index of identification unit according to user-entered information; the identification unit will then be assessed as major hazard special equipment if its identification index is more than 350. Statistical analysis of the assessment result function can display the distribution of major hazard for users in the forms of pie charts and histograms.

(3) Function of Decision Support, is materialized by using OLAP technique based on data warehouse, which analyzes Special equipment major hazard identification data. Obviously, it can bring a fresh perspective to decision-making and new information to enterprise or supervision institutions. We use Special equipment major hazard identification data as the OLAP data source to analyze Tianjin special

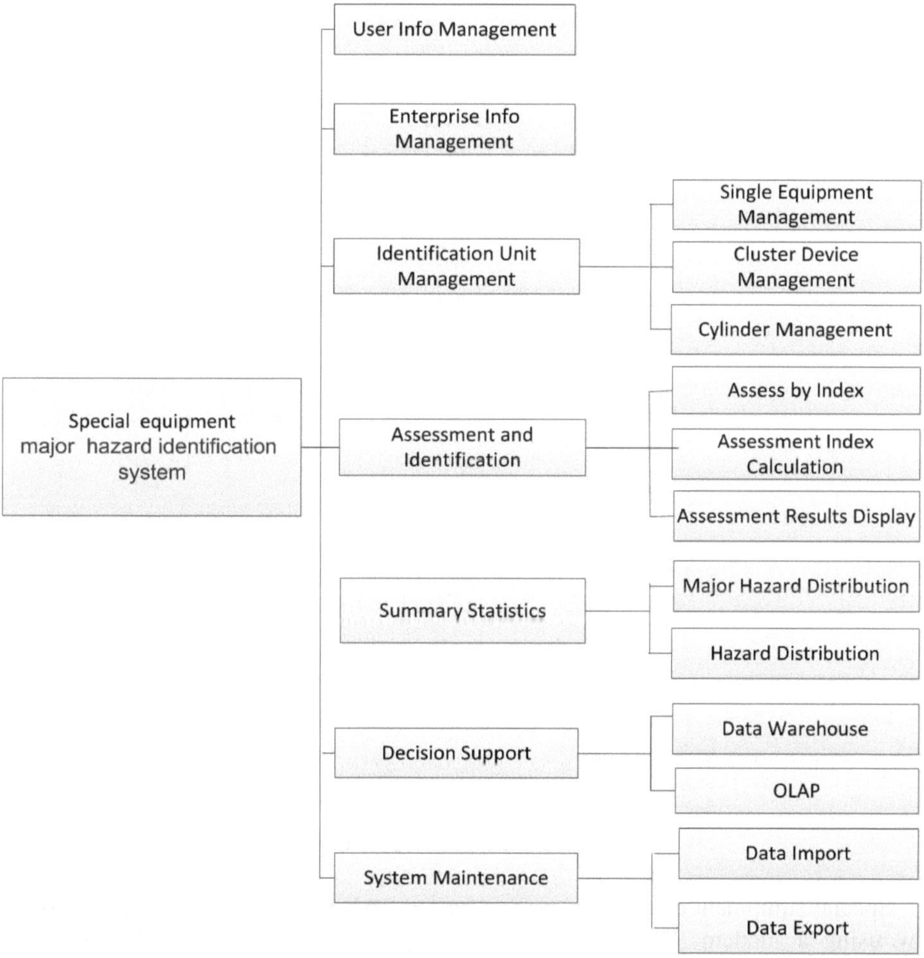

Fig. 2. System Functions

equipment security conditions. As a result, we produce many types of charts such as histograms, scatter plots, pivot tables, etc. which will provide the decision-making staff with more intuitive, multi-angle analysis, useful query of the city's various districts and counties as well as special equipment safety conditions for all enterprises. Finally, it will provide strong support for policy makers.

2.3 System Network Structure

The network structure of the system involves special equipment enterprise network, district-level supervisory network and municipal supervisory network. These networks communicate with each other via the Internet. The network structure is shown in Figure 3.

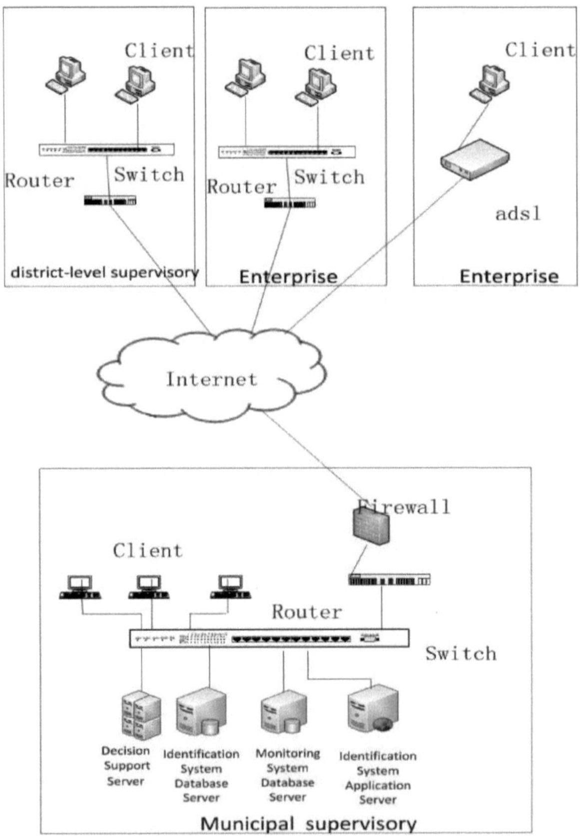

Fig. 3. The Network Structure

Special equipment enterprises can opt for the LAN by using a Router or the ADSL by using a modem. District-level supervisory organs and municipal supervisory organs can utilize the LAN with a Router.

All servers of the system are deployed in the network of municipal supervisory organs, including identification system database server, monitoring system database server, identification system application server and decision support server. Identification system database server is used to store and access data in the major hazard identification system of special equipment; monitoring system database server is used to store and access data in the special equipment monitoring system; identification system application server runs applications of the special equipment major hazard identification system; and decision support server stores and accesses the data warehouse of special equipment major hazard identification system.

District-level supervisory users, municipal supervisory users and enterprise users access servers from the client through their network.

3 System Implementation

3.1 Major Hazard Identification

According to the local standards of Tianjin Bureau Quality and Technical Supervision DB12/382-2008 "Special equipment major hazard identification", we can use the identification index method to identify major hazards for a special equipment unit. The identification index of special equipment identification unit H is displayed below.

$$H = \left[1 + \left(\sum_{i=1}^{5} K_i \right) / 5 \right] \cdot S \tag{1}$$

The parameters are as follows:

S: identification basic value;
K1: Factor of immediacy operation personnel death if an accident occurs;
K2: Factor of peripheral personnel death if an accident occurs;
K3: Factor of economic losses and environmental damage if an accident occurs;
K4: Factor of special equipment failure rate;
K5: Factor of the level of equipment security management.

When the identification index of special equipment identification unit H is greater than or equal to 350, the special equipment will be identified as a major hazard.

3.2 Web Service and Data Sharing

Tianjin Quality Management Institute has developed Special equipment monitoring system, which allows people to register special equipment into the system for centralized management. The monitoring system has been used for many years and has since accumulated large amounts of data. Special equipment major hazard identification system needs data from Special equipment monitoring system. In order to avoid duplication of entry and to ensure data consistency between different systems, identification system can exchange data with the monitoring system through web services.

A web service is a distributed computing model and external interface of a system for external application calls. A Web service is a universal model for building applications, which is based on common protocol and uses XML-based message processing as data communication. The data stored in the Special equipment monitoring system belongs to the internal data, and other systems therefore cannot directly access it. Considering data security issues, special equipment major hazard identification system performs data operations through interfaces provided by monitoring system web services. Once a web service is deployed, other applications can find and use it.

Web services chiefly have the following features:

(1) Operating system independence and programming language independence. Developers can use web services as long as they comply with the relevant protocol. Web services will provide strong support for the system and greatly improve the versatility of the system data.
(2) Software and data reuse. Web Service allows code reuse; furthermore, users can reuse the data related to the code. By using web service, the system can be more extensible, scalable and compatible.
(3) Easily debugged. Since the data is transmitted in ASCII text, it is easy for web service developers to debug during the development of web service. In addition, since there is no need to consider client compatibility issues, web service deployment is also very convenient.

Web services calling process between systems is shown in Figure 4.

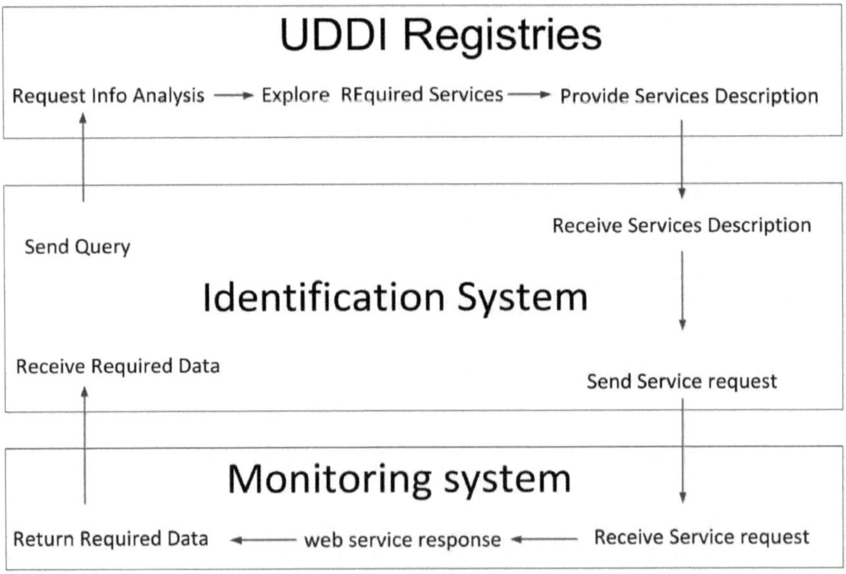

Fig. 4. Web Services Calling Process

Identification system will form SOAP (Simple Object Access Protocol) message according to query conditions, and send a request to UDDI (Universal Description Discovery and Integration) registries. The UDDI center will find the appropriate service description and send a service description message to identification system. Then, identification system will send a service request to monitoring system. Monitoring system will finish the query after receiving the request. Finally, results of the query will be sent to identification system in the form of SOAP message response.

3.3 Data Warehouse and OLAP

The concept of data warehouse was first proposed by William H. lnmon, who defined it as a data set that supports the process of management decisions [4]. Data Warehouse is data collection which is subject oriented, integrated, non-volatile and time variant.

On-Line Analytical Processing (OLAP) was first proposed by E.F. Codd, one of the masters of relational database techniques, in 1993. According to the definition in the OLAP committee's white paper, OLAP techniques can process the data stored in the data warehouse in parallel style, and can provide multidimensional views to the user. The user may be data analysis personnel or management personnel, for example, and must analyze the original data [5].

OLAP is based on Data warehouse. One of the key factors of OLAP's success is that OLAP technique can access correct, complete and integrated data. Data warehouse is not only a way of integrating data, but it also has the same characteristics that are the solid data foundation of OLAP analysis. As a way of data organization, data warehouse is the backstage foundation of OLAP analysis. OLAP techniques give data warehouse the ability to respond repeatedly and perform complex query analysis rapidly, allowing the data warehouse to be used in on-line analysis contexts. The quickness, analyzability and multi-dimensional properties of OLAP technique make it very suitable to be used in special equipment's major hazard identification.

In the data warehouse schema design structure, the common schema is divided into a star schema and snowflake schema, according to the relationship between fact tables and dimension tables. The star model is the most common structure of data warehouse design model, which is based on the fact tables as the core. In general, one case has high efficiency of query statistics, can optimize the data warehouse query response time and improve query performance. When one or more dimension tables are not directly connected to the fact table, but through other dimension tables connect to the facts on the table, the graphic resembles snow as the tables are connected together, thus it is called snowflake model. Snowflake model improves the flexibility of the data warehouse, but generally speaking, a snowflake model has query efficiency lower than the star schema.

To improve the query efficiency of the special equipment of major hazard data, use the star schema as the model structure of the data warehouse. The data warehouse data model is shown in Figure 5:

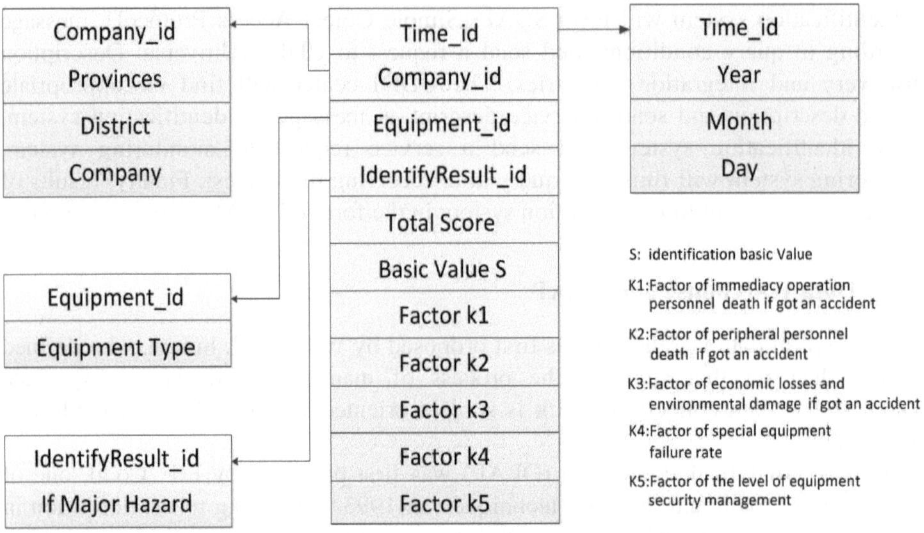

Fig. 5. Data Warehouse Model

The figure shows the special equipment major hazard data warehouse data model. This theme of the data warehouse includes one fact table and four dimension tables: the special equipment identification information fact table, the time dimension table, the geographical dimension table, special equipment type dimension table, and the identification results dimension table. The hierarchy of geographical dimension is as follows: company->district->province. The hierarchy of time dimension is as follows: day->month->year.

In our work, we use Microsoft SQL Server Analysis Services to analyze the cube data. The process is as follows: Firstly, we create the data source and view in SQL Server Business Intelligence. Secondly, we define dimensions and measures and create the cube. Thirdly, we deploy it on the Analysis Services in SQL Server. After the deployment process, we finish building the data warehouse. We can start to analyze the Major hazard identification data of special equipment using OLAP. As a result, we will have a grasp of security situation of the special equipment from various views.

3.4 The Architecture of S2SH

S2SH is lightweight j2ee open source architecture, which has advantages such as development of high efficiency. It meets the requirements change and it's also has high safety performance. S2SH uses the MVC design pattern, and divides the system into three layers, including presentation layer, business logic layer and data persistence layer. Clear division of labor at all levels makes sure the system is of "high cohesion, [and] low coupling."

Jsp and Struts2 act as the presentation layer of the system. Jsp is responsible for sending the request and receiving a response. As the control components in Struts2, Dispatch Filter receives the request and fills the request to the appropriate model components. Eventually, the request will be passed to Action, which is the core component of Struts2. Action will access the data persistence layer to interact with the database through the business logic layer. After all these processes, the result will be sent to "struts.xml" by Action and displayed by Jsp.

Hibernate is responsible for the data persistence layer of the system. By using ORM (Object Relational Mapping), Hibernate will operate database records in ways of persistent objects and provide data access methods to users. After the introduction of Hibernate, the system may be analyzed and designed in an object-oriented way.

Spring acts as a management container in the entire system. With the help of IOC (Inversion of Control), Spring can effectively manage the data persistence layer, the business logic layer and Action. By using AOP (Aspect-Oriented Programming) during transaction Management, the system can be more secure and more stable.

4 Conclusion

S2SH is a widely used lightweight web application framework. It has high efficiency and has high safety performance. The established special equipment major hazard identification system, based on S2SH, can capitalize upon the advantage of web applications, so that people can identify special equipment more effectively and scientifically.

The use of web service is conducive to the elimination of information silos, so as to achieve business collaboration. In the function of decision support, using OLAP techniques based on data warehouse provides strong support to the relevant departments' decision makers for management decisions. The creation of this system provides strong support for the government to prevent and reduce the occurrence of special equipment accidents. This system also provides guidance for the enterprise to monitor special equipment major hazards to ensure production safety.

References

1. State Council of the People's Republic of China. Order of the State Council of the People's Republic of China (549) Z (January 24, 2009)
2. Tianjin bureau of Quality and Technical Supervision, http://www.tjjj.gov.cn/html/business/tzsb/7501.html
3. Tianjin Bureau of Quality and Technical Supervision. Identification of major hazard special equipment Z (June 25, 2008)
4. Tan, X.: Data Warehouse and Its Potential in Weather Forecast. Journal of Applied Meteorological Science 17(3), 325–330 (2006)
5. He, Y., Zhang, J.: Data warehouse and OLAP practice tutorial, pp. 5–7. Tsinghua University Press, Beijing (2008) (in Chinese)ss

A Screening Method of Security Functional Components Based on Fuzzy

Yizhen Liu, Zhijie Du, Hong Shi, and Xiaohong Li

School of Computer Science and e Technology, TianJin University,
Tianjin 300072, China
liuyizhen_0822@163.com, {tjudzj,serena,xiaohongli}@tju.edu.cn

Abstract. Security requirement analysis based on Common Criteria (CC) plays an important role in security of software. However, there are no efficient methods for establishing a precise relationship between security requirement levels and CC security functional components. This paper presents a screening method based on fuzzy to solve this problem. We establish the screening mechanism of security functional components, acquire accurate membership values of security functional components in four security requirement levels and precisely determine security requirement levels to which these components belong. Finally, a specific example is given. Experimental results show that the method improves the accuracy of screening security functional components, and optimizes security requirement analysis process.

Keywords: Security Functional Component Screening, Fuzzy, Security Requirement Levels, Security Requirement Analysis, Common Criteria (ISO/IEC15408).

1 Introduction

Security issues based on the full life cycle has become the focus of the industry in software development. Security requirement analysis plays an important role in software project development.

In recent years, researchers have made significant progress in methods of security requirement analysis. Developed by Carnegie Mellon University in 2005, SQUARE [1] method divides security requirement engineering into nine steps. The method obtains higher recognition in security requirements engineering methods, but requires security experts' guidance and participation in its implementation process. Mellado proposed SREP [2] method in 2007, which adds CC to the safety life cycle model and use reusable security requirements. It is an asset-based and risk-driven security requirements method. The method proposed by Core security requirements artifacts [3] focuses on assets and possible hazards to assets in security requirements. Dan Grahan introduced a method of requirements elicitation known as CLASP [4]. The essence of this method is security analysis of a system based on the interaction between resources, but the process is quite complicated and needs experienced

V. Khachidze et al. (Eds.): iCETS 2012, CCIS 332, pp. 292–305, 2012.

security analysts to participate. There are goal-oriented methods of security requirements engineering, such as KAOS [5] and TROPOS [6-8].

Moreover, CC [9] as an international Common Criteria for IT security has also presented a security requirements engineering approach in its model and principles section. Starting from determining assets of a software system, we then analyze the security environment of the software based on assets. We then write security purposes corresponding to the security environment, and select security functional components and security assurance components [10] according to security purposes. Although CC has become the industry standard for IT security evaluation, it depends heavily on expert knowledge. The level driven security requirement analysis method based on CC [11] introduced a conception of security requirement level, provided a level dividing method and screening method of security functional components, and established a set of security requirements engineering methods. However, it used probabilistic statistical methods for screen security functional components, and the number of reference documents was insufficient. These two points cause thes accuracy of screening security functional components to decline, and lead to accuracy decline of security requirements analysis and loss of flexibility.

Based on these researches, we propose a screening mechanism for security functional components based on fuzzy theory, and obtain memberships of a component in four security requirements levels based on corresponding tone operator, then determine the security requirements levels of a component. Finally, we give an example to verify the validity of the method. The article is structured as follows: a screening mechanism of security functional components based on fuzzy; a screening method of security functional components based on fuzzy; a specific example of screening security functional components; conclusion.

2 A Screening Mechanism of Security Functional Components Based on Fuzzy

2.1 Definition of CC Security Functional Components

Common Criteria (CC) is an international security evaluation criteria. It was adopted as International Standard 15408 by ISO/IEC in 1999, and became internationally accepted as IT security evaluation criteria. Components are the specific forms and the minimum optional set of security requirements in CC. CC defines security functional components in the form of "Class–Family–Component". CC contains a total of 11 security functional classes, 65 security functional families and 134 security functional components. Sample class decomposition diagram is shown in Fig. 1. In accordance with CC, let E be the CC security functional requirements,

$$E=\{e_1,e_2,\cdots,e_{11}\}, \tag{1}$$

where $e_1\left(l\in[1,11]\right)$ is a security functional class. For each e_1,

$$e_l=\{e_{l1},e_{l2},\cdots,e_{lm}\}, \tag{2}$$

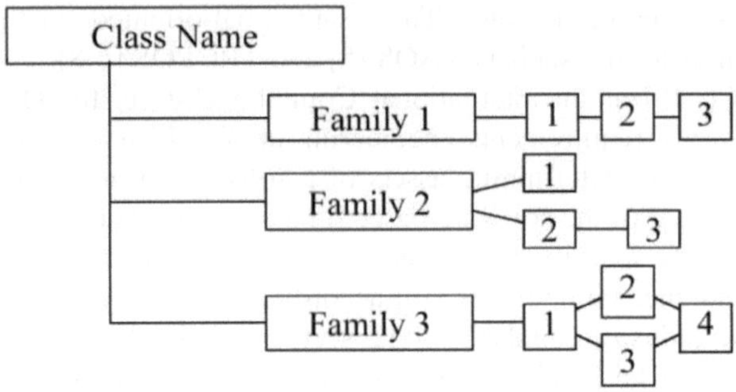

Fig. 1. Sample class decomposition diagram

where m is the number of families contained in e_1. For each security functional family $e_{ij}\ (i \in [1,11], j \in [1,m])$,

$$e_{ij} = \{e_{ij1}, e_{ij2}, \cdots, e_{ijn}\}, \tag{3}$$

where n is the number of components contained by e_{ij}. Every security functional component is defined as

$$e_{ijk} = \{Identification, Dependencies, Functional\ Elements\}, \tag{4}$$

where Identification provides descriptive information necessary to identify a component. Dependencies are the dependency relationship among components, and Functional Elements is a set of the smallest security functional requirements identified in the CC included in a component.

2.2 Security Requirement Level

Although security requirements analysis based on CC has gradually become the consensus of study, the security requirements analysis method proposed by CC depends highly on expert knowledge. In software engineering, we must select security functional components of different levels based on different security environments. To solve these two problems, the concept of security requirement level is introduced, that is, dividing levels for security requirement [15][16] and screening security functional components in accordance with levels of security requirements.

Security requirements levels are divided primarily based on loss severity caused by security problems, comprehensively into four levels: Even if systems of Level 1 produce security issues, they do not cause serious economic losses, such as personal websites; generally systems of Level 2 are common civilian systems, and security problems produced by them result in certain economic losses and business information leakage; systems of Level 3 involves systems regarding significant economic benefits or important information, and security issues produced by them cause serious losses such as bank information systems and population data systems; Systems of Level 4 are security critical systems, and security problems produced by them can cause very serious economic losses, national security information leakage and even life and health issues, such as air operations control systems and nuclear power plant remote control system.

To represent the relationship of security functional components and security requirement level, we add a "security requirement level" property to CC security functional components. Security functional component is defined as:

$$e_{ijk} = \{Identification, Dependencies, Functional\ Elements, SRLevel\}, \tag{5}$$

where SRLevel represents security requirement levels to which the component belongs, and contains values from 1 to 4.

2.3 The Screening Mechanism of Security Functional Components Based on Fuzzy

Based on the introduction of security requirement levels, this paper presents a screening mechanism of security functional components based on fuzzy, shown in Fig. 2. Performing level screening for CC security functional components in accordance with screening method of security functional components based on fuzzy, it can provide recommended components in different levels for systems in different security requirements levels. Then, in the security requirements analysis process, we can select security functional components at appropriate levels, according to the determined security requirement levels and the recommended components in different levels. This mechanism reduces the difficulty of using CC, and achieves the goal of partial automation in the process of software requirements analysis.

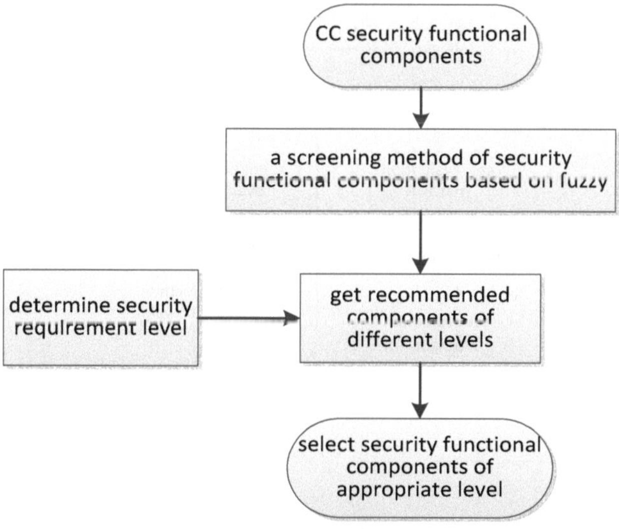

Fig. 2. Screening mechanism of security functional components based on fuzzy

3 A Screening Method of Security Functional Components Based on Fuzzy

In the screening mechanism, screening quality of functional components in each security requirement level directly affects the accuracy of software security requirements. In order to optimize security requirement analysis and improve accuracy of screening security functional components, this paper presents a screening method of security functional components based on fuzzy.

3.1 General Idea

This fuzzy screening method is based on fuzzy comprehensive evaluation model I [12], using model structure

$$A \circ R' = B = (b_1, b_2, \ldots, b_n) \tag{6}$$

to get the final comprehensive evaluation value B. In the formula above, R' is obtained by transforming evaluation matrix R using tone operator. R is obtained by single factor evaluation of factor set U judged on judgment set V. Values for elements in the evaluation matrix R are obtained by fuzzy statistical method. Fuzzy set

$$A = (a_1, \ldots, a_n) \tag{7}$$

represents weight distribution of various factors. We obtain comprehensive evaluation value B by the synthesis of A and R. Then the appropriate value of λ is determined using fuzzy cut set to screen out effective evaluation values. Finally, security requirement levels of security functional components are determined based on effective evaluation values. Flow chart of the screening method is shown in Fig.3.

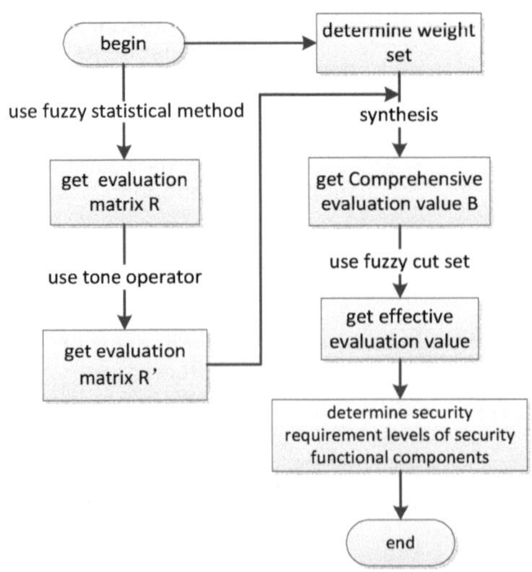

Fig. 3. Flow chart of the screening method of security functional components based on fuzzy

3.2 Specific Steps of the Screening Method

The specific steps of the screening method for security functional components are as follows:

1. Perform single factor judgment using fuzzy statistical methods to get evaluation matrix R .

Based on comprehensive evaluation model I shown above, we set the three elements of comprehensive evaluation as follows:

1)

$$\text{Factor set } U = \{\text{ST documents, PP documents, other analysis and reasoning}\}, \tag{8}$$

where the three factor indicators are expressed as x_1, x_2, x_3 respectively. PP documents and ST documents are the assessed and certified product documents given by Common Criteria Recognition Arrangement (CCRA) [13]. We can access 223 (127 available) PP documents and 1,711 ST documents in CCRA's official website. Other analysis and reasoning are obtained from analysis documents and reasoning summary of CC security functional components.

2) Judgment set $V = \{\text{Level1, Level2, Level3, Level4}\}$. (9)

3) Perform single factor evaluation to get evaluation matrix R :

$$R = \begin{bmatrix} r_{11} & r_{12} & r_{13} & r_{14} \\ r_{21} & r_{22} & r_{23} & r_{24} \\ r_{31} & r_{32} & r_{33} & r_{34} \end{bmatrix}, \tag{10}$$

where r_{1j}, r_{2j}, and $r_{3j}(j \in [1,4])$ are memberships of a security functional component in security requirements levels, and are obtained by fuzzy statistics for ST documents, PP documents, and other analysis and reasoning respectively. That is, there are times that the component appears in the elastic boundaries of the four levels in ST documents, PP documents and other analysis and reasoning respectively, using fuzzy statistical method, and then the times are divided by the respective number of documents to obtain membership values.

2. Get evaluation matrix R', using tone operator.

In natural language, there are some words expressing degree, such as "most", "highly", "very", "relatively", "some", "little". These words can be seen as tone operators. We use I to present fuzzy set of these words, and then: most I $\triangleq I^4$, highly I $\triangleq I^2$, very I $\triangleq I^{1.25}$, relatively I $\triangleq I^{0.75}$, some I $\triangleq I^{0.5}$. Tone operator is a transformation :

$$H_\lambda : \mathbb{F}(U) \to \mathbb{F}(U), \; H_\lambda I = I^\lambda. \tag{11}$$

In this paper, we use tone operator very I $\triangleq I^{1.25}$ to transform evaluation matrix R , and get

$$R'=H_{1.25}R \tag{12}$$

Elements in R′ express memberships that belong to a security functional component in four security requirements levels in "very" tone operator. We select tone operator "very" for two reasons: First, degree of membership expressed by "very" is what intend to find, and it means the membership of the component belongs to the four levels to a large extent. Second, the tone operator expands the distance among the original memberships, so that it can improve accuracy of screening components, when setting the same threshold in screening.

3. Determine A, the weight distribution of each factor.

Because different factors have different degrees of importance, they should be given weights. In this method, a_1, a_2 and a_3 are the three factors in A, and they indicate the weight of PP documents, ST documents and other analysis and reasoning respectively.

We determine the weight of each factor based on fuzzy scale binary comparison ordered matrix [17][18], and the fuzzy scale binary comparison ordered matrix is shown as follows:

$$M=\begin{bmatrix} m_{11} & m_{12} & \cdots & m_{1n} \\ m_{21} & m_{22} & \cdots & m_{2n} \\ & & \ddots & \\ m_{n1} & m_{n2} & \cdots & m_{nn} \end{bmatrix}=(m_{ij}) \tag{13}$$

,

where $m_{ij}=x_i/x_j$ indicates the fuzzy scale that represents the preferences between element x_i to element x_j in factor set U . Preferences are expressed in six levels: 0.5, 0.6, 0.7, 0.8, 0.9 and 1, which means equally preferred, moderately preferred, strongly preferred, very strongly preferred, extremely preferred and most preferred respectively. The formula for normalized weight a_i of element x_i is:

$$a_i=\frac{m_i}{\sum_{i=1}^{n} m_i}=\frac{\sum_{j=1}^{n} m_{ij}}{\sum_{i=1}^{n}\sum_{j=1}^{n} m_{ij}} \quad (i=1,2,\cdots,n). \tag{14}$$

4. Compute comprehensive evaluation value $B=(b_1,b_2,b_3,b_4)$, using formula (6).

The synthesis of each factor's weight distribution A and evaluation matrix R' is the comprehensive evaluation based on the factor set. Each element in B represents memberships of a security functional component on security requirements levels from Level 1 to Level 4 based on the "very" tone operator.

5. Determine security requirements levels that a component belongs to, using fuzzy cut set.

Fuzzy cut set is defined as: Let B $\in$ F(U), $\lambda \in [0,1]$, then cut set

$$B_\lambda = \{u \mid u \in U, B(u) \geq \lambda\}. \tag{15}$$

Because the comprehensive evaluation value is obtained based on "very" tone operator, $\lambda = 0.5$ and $B_{0.5}$ are appropriate to meet the actual need of obtaining memberships of a component on the four levels to a large extent. Thus, the levels corresponding to the elements greater than or equal to 0.5 are the security requirements levels to which a component belongs.

4 The Specific Example of Screening Security Functional Components

4.1 The Specific Example

To verify the effectiveness and validity of the fuzzy screening method, this paper gives a specific example of screening a security functional component and a screening result of a CC security functional class.

Using component FPT_RCV.1 in CC security functional class FPT class (TSF protection) as an example, we use the screening method of security functional components proposed in this paper to obtain memberships of this component in the four security requirements levels, Level 1, Level 2, Level 3 and Level 4, based on tone operator and to determine security requirements levels to which the component belongs.

1. Analyze the 1,711 ST documents given by CCRA, and use fuzzy statistical method to get fuzzy statistical probabilities of the component on the four levels. This is shown in Table 1.

Table 1. Fuzzy statistical results of FPT_RCV.1 in ST documents

	Level 1	Level 2	Level 3	Level 4
FPT_RCV.1	0.55	0.75	1	1

2. Analyze the 127 PP documents given by CCRA, and use fuzzy statistical method to get fuzzy statistical probabilities of the component on the four levels, shown in Table 2.

Table 2. Fuzzy statistical results of FPT_RCV.1 in PP documents

	Level 1	Level 2	Level 3	Level 4
FPT_RCV.1	0.45	0.70	1	1

3. Based on other analysis and reasoning and reference to Gollmann [14], perform fuzzy statistics to get the result in Table 3:

Table 3. Fuzzy statistical results of FPT_RCV.1 in other analysis and reasoning

	Level 1	Level 2	Level 3	Level 4
FPT_RCV.1	0.40	1	1	1

4. Perform single factor evaluation based on the above three factors to get evaluation matrix R:

$$R = \begin{bmatrix} r_{11} & r_{12} & r_{13} & r_{14} \\ r_{21} & r_{22} & r_{23} & r_{24} \\ r_{31} & r_{32} & r_{33} & r_{34} \end{bmatrix} = \begin{bmatrix} 0.55 & 0.75 & 1 & 1 \\ 0.45 & 0.70 & 1 & 1 \\ 0.40 & 1.00 & 1 & 1 \end{bmatrix} \tag{16}$$

5. Get evaluation matrix R', using "very" tone operator.

$$R' = H_{1.25} R = \begin{bmatrix} 0.47 & 0.70 & 1 & 1 \\ 0.37 & 0.64 & 1 & 1 \\ 0.32 & 1.00 & 1 & 1 \end{bmatrix}$$

6. Determine A, the weight distribution of each factor.

PP documents and ST documents are certified product documents given by CCRA; however, other analysis and reasoning are not sufficiently authoritative. Thus, the preferences of the first two are higher than the third one. PP is a security requirement that is independent at implementation and expresses a certain type of IT products; however, ST is a set of security requirements that is dependent on implementation. Therefore, the preference of ST documents is higher than PP documents in practical applications. So, the fuzzy scale binary comparison ordered matrix determined by the analysis above is:

$$M = \begin{bmatrix} m_{11} & m_{12} & m_{13} \\ m_{21} & m_{22} & m_{23} \\ m_{31} & m_{32} & m_{33} \end{bmatrix} = \begin{bmatrix} 0.5 & x_1/x_2 & x_1/x_3 \\ 1-x_1/x_2 & 0.5 & x_2/x_3 \\ 1-x_1/x_3 & 1-x_2/x_3 & 0.5 \end{bmatrix} = \begin{bmatrix} 0.5 & 0.7 & 0.9 \\ 0.3 & 0.5 & 0.8 \\ 0.1 & 0.2 & 0.5 \end{bmatrix}.$$

So, weight of ST documents: $a_1 = \frac{0.5+0.7+0.9}{3+1.5} = 0.467$,

weight of PP documents: $a_2 = \frac{0.3+0.5+0.8}{3+1.5} = 0.356$,

weight of other analysis and reasoning: $a_3 = \frac{0.1+0.2+0.5}{3+1.5} = 0.177$.

Then weights distribution $A = (a_1, a_2, a_3) = (0.467, 0.356, 0.177)$. Logical analysis and test statistics prove that the weight assignment is reasonable.

7. Get comprehensive evaluation value B.

$$B = A \circ R' = (0.467 \quad 0.356 \quad 0.177) \circ \begin{bmatrix} 0.47 & 0.70 & 1 & 1 \\ 0.37 & 0.64 & 1 & 1 \\ 0.32 & 1.00 & 1 & 1 \end{bmatrix}$$

$$= (0.40785 \quad 0.73174 \quad 1 \quad 1)$$

8. Determine security requirements levels to which the component belongs.

Using fuzzy cut set $B_{0.5}$, find level values corresponding to elements more than and equal to 0.5. Evidently, Level 1 is not within the valid range, and the component belongs to Level 2, Level 3, and Level 4.

In the same way, we obtain screening results of the 23 components in CC security functional class of FPT class (TSF protection). The correspondence relationship between security requirements levels and components in FPT class is shown in Table 4.

4.2 Results Comparison and Analysis

This screening method is compared with the method proposed by Liu [11]. Table 5 shows the different memberships on four levels for component FPT_RCV.1 in these two methods. In Liu's method [11], the probability of component FPT_RCV.1 belonging to the security requirement level Level 1 is 0.5, so it cannot be determined whether the component belongs to Level 1. However, we use this fuzzy screening method to get an accurate value 0.40785, which is obtained in "very" tone operator. Thus, we use fuzzy cut set and let $\lambda = 0.5$ to successfully resolve the confusion of fuzzy problem. As 0.40785 is less than 0.5, the component can be determined to not belong to Level 1. Moreover, FPT_RCV.1 represents the security requirement of "manual recovery", and allows TOE to provide the mechanism for returning to security state only by human intervention. Even if systems in Level 1 have security issues, they will not cause serious economic losses, and it is sometimes necessary to use automatic recovery instead of manual recovery. Therefore, the requirement for manual recovery can be ignored. The conclusion that FPT_RCV.1 does not belong to Level 1 is therefore more reasonable and accurate.

Table 4. The correspondence relationship between security requirement levels and components in FPTclass, using the screening method in this paper

Levels	Level 1	Level 2	Level 3	Level 4
Recommend Components		FPT_RCV.1 FPT_FLS.1 *FPT_TST.1*	*FPT_RCV.1* FPT_RCV.2 FPT_RCV.4 FPT_FLS.1 FPT_ITA.1 FPT_ITC.1 FPT_ITI.1 FPT_ITT.1 FPT_ITT.3 FPT_PHP.1 *FPT_PHP.3* FPT_RPL.1 FPT_SSP.1 FPT_STM.1 FPT_TDC.1 FPT_TRC.1 FPT_TST.1	FPT_RCV.3 *FPT_RCV.4* FPT_FLS.1 FPT_ITA.1 FPT_ITC.1 FPT_ITI.2 FPT_ITT.2 FPT_ITT.3 FPT_PHP.1 FPT_PHP.2 FPT_PHP.3 FPT_RPL.1 FPT_SSP.2 FPT_STM.1 FPT_TDC.1 FPT_TRC.1 FPT_TST.1

Table 5. Different memberships of four levels for component FPT_RCV.1 in these two methods

Component FPT_RCV.1	This screening method	The method in reference[11]
Level 1	0.40785	0.5
Level 2	0.73174	1
Level 3	1	1
Level 4	1	1

Table 6. The correspondence relationship between security requirement levels and components in FPTclass, using the screening method proposed by Liu [11]

Levels	Level 1	Level 2	Level 3	Level 4
Recommend Components	*FPT_RCV.1*	FPT_RCV.1 FPT_FLS.1 *FPT_ITA.1* *FPT_ITC.1* *FPT_ITI.1*	FPT_RCV.2 FPT_FLS.1 FPT_ITA.1 FPT_ITC.1 FPT_ITI.1 FPT_ITT.1 FPT_ITT.3 *FPT_PHP.1* FPT_RPL.1 FPT_SSP.1 FPT_STM.1 FPT_TDC.1 FPT_TRC.1 FPT_TST.1	FPT_RCV.3 FPT_FLS.1 FPT_ITA.1 FPT_ITC.1 FPT_ITI.2 FPT_ITT.2 FPT_ITT.3 FPT_PHP.1 FPT_PHP.2 FPT_PHP.3 FPT_RPL.1 FPT_SSP.2 FPT_STM.1 FPT_TDC.1 FPT_TRC.1 FPT_TST.1

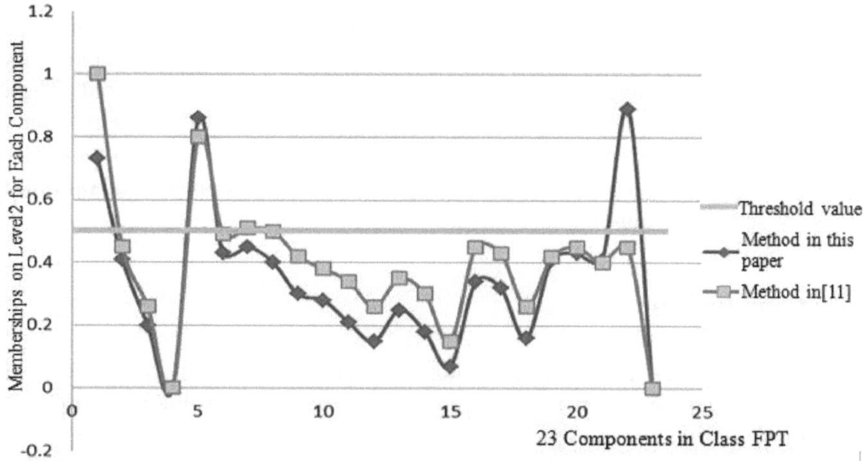

Fig. 4. The respective membership values of 23 components in FPT class on Level 2 using two methods separately. 1-23 components are FPT_RCV.1, FPT_RCV.2, FPT_RCV.3, FPT_RCV.4, FPT_FLS.1, FPT_ITA.1, FPT_ITC.1, FPT_ITI.1, FPT_ITI.2, FPT_ITT.1, FPT_ITT.2, FPT_ITT.3, FPT_PHP.1, FPT_PHP.2, FPT_PHP.3, FPT_RPL.1, FPT_SSP.1, FPT_SSP.2, FPT_STM.1, FPT_TDC.1, FPT_TRC.1, FPT_TST.1 and FPT_TEE respectively.

In addition, Table 6 shows the correspondence relationship between security requirements levels and components in FPT class, using the screening method presented by Liue [11]. The memberships of five components in italics on levels in Table 6, FPT_RCV.1, FPT_ITA.1, FPT_ITC.1, FPT_ITI.1 and FPT_PHP.1, obtained by using Liu's method, [11] are close to 0.5, so they cannot be determined to belong to these levels or not. However, we can acquire accurate memberships and determine the levels of these components using the screening method in this paper, as shown in Table 4. We add FPT_TST.1 in Level 2, add FPT_RCV.1 and FPT_PHP.3 in Level 3, and add FPT_RCV.4 in Level 4, using method in this paper.

Using these two methods separately, we obtain the respective membership values of 23 components in FPT class on Level 2, and the comparison is shown in Fig. 4. The red line expresses the membership values using the method in this paper, while the blue line designates the membership values using Liu's method [11], and the pink line shows the threshold value 0.5. From this scatter graph, we can infer that it is difficult to decide whether some components belong to Level 2, because their membership values in Level 2, which we acquire using Liu's method [11] are distributed around the threshold value. The differences between membership values and threshold value obtained by using the method in this paper increase more obviously than those obtained by using the method proposed by Liu [11]. Furthermore, we consider the fuzzy problem in this fuzzy screening method, and solve the problem of membership uncertainty and threshold selection using fuzzy theory, so that we can accurately determine whether components belong to the level.

The advantages of fuzzy screening method proposed in this paper compared with Liu's method [11] are: As designed by Liu [11], ST documents and PP documents are put together and are made probability statistics to get memberships. However, we not only make fuzzy statistics for ST documents and PP documents, but also refer to valuable analysis and reasoning and use fuzzy theory, so that this screening method greatly improves the accuracy of memberships and screening threshold. Therefore, experimental results show that the screening method of security functional components proposed in this paper is feasible, effective and reasonable. It also improves the accuracy of screening security functional components and optimizes the process of security requirements analysis.

5 Conclusion

This paper describes a screening method of security functional components on the basis of the screening mechanism based on fuzzy. It creates evaluation matrix, weight distribution matrix and comprehensive evaluation value, and uses them to obtain evaluation memberships of a component in security requirements levels based on the corresponding tone operator. Then, security requirements levels of each component are determined. Finally, we provide a specific example, which verifies the feasibility and effectiveness of the method. The comparison of experimental results with other methods reflects that this method improves the accuracy of screening security functional components, optimizes the security requirements analysis process and strengthens security of software.

Acknowledgments. We are grateful to the anonymous reviewers for their insightful comments and suggestions. This research was supported in part by National Natural Science Foundation of China (No.90718023, 91118003), Tianjin Research Program of Application Foundation and Advanced Technology (No.10JCZDJC15700), "985" funds of Tianjin University.

References

1. Mead, N.R.: SQUARE Process. Software Engineering Institute (January 2006)
2. Mellado, D., Fernandez-Medina, E., Piattini, M.: A common criteria based security requirements engineering process for the development of secure information systems. Computer Standards & Interfaces 29, 244–253 (2007)
3. Moffett, J.D., Haley, C.B., Nuseibeh, B.: Security Requirements Engineering: A Framework for Representation and Analysis. IEEE Transactions on Software Engineering (2008)
4. Gregoire, B., De Win, S., Joosen, W.: On the Secure Software Development Process: CLASP and SDL Compared. Software Engineering for Secure Systems (2007)
5. Bertrand, P., Darimont, R., Delor, E., Massonet, P., van Lamsweerde, A.: GRAIL/KAOS: an environment for goal driven requirements engineering. In: 20th International Conference on Software Engineering, ICSE 1998 (1998)
6. Bresciani, P., Perini, A., Giorgini, P., Giunchiglia, F., Mylopoulos, J.: Tropos: an agent-oriented software development methodology. Auton. Agent Multi Agent Syst. 8(3), 203–236 (2004)

7. Giorgini, P., Susi, A., Perini, A., Mylopoulos, J.: The tropos metamodel and its use. Inf. J. 29, 401–408 (2005)
8. Fuxman, A., Liu, L., Mylopoulos, J., Pistore, M., Roveri, M., Traverso, P.: Specifying and analyzing early requirements in tropos. Requir. Eng. J. 9(2), 132–150 (2004)
9. ISO/IEC JTC1/SC27, Information technology-Security techniques-Evaluation criteria for IT security, ISO/IEC 15408: 2009 (Common Criteria v3.1) (2009)
10. Mellado, D., Fernandez-Medina, E., Piattini, M.: A Comparison of the Common Criteria with Proposal of Information Systems Security Requirements. In: HASE 2004 (2004)
11. Liu, F.: Level driven security requirement analysis method based on CC. Tianjin University, Tianjin (2011)
12. Yang, L., Gao, Y.: Principle and application of fuzzy mathematics—3th version. South China University of Technology Press, Guangzhou (2001)
13. Common Criteria Portal (April 5, 2012), http://www.commoncriteriaportal.org/
14. Gollmann, D.: Computer Security. John Wiley & Sons Ltd. (1999)
15. GB/T 17859-1999, Computer information system security level dividing guidelines
16. GB/T 24856-2009, Information security technology–Technical requirements of security design for information system classified protection
17. Bai, X., Zhao, S.: Methods of determining weithts based on fuzzy analysis theory. Dongbei University of Finance and Economics, Jiangsu Statistics Journal (1998)
18. Lu, G., Chen, Z., He, X., Li, J.: A Method of Security Evaluation Based on Fuzzy Mathematics. In: ICACIA (2008)

An Assessment of the Use of Information Technology Tools and E-business by Informal Sector Entrepreneurs in Mauritius

Asrani Gopaul

Lecturer in Social Policy and International Social Work
University of Mauritius
as.gopaul@uom.ac.mu

Abstract. Globalization has long become a buzz word. Whereas globalization pundits and skeptics are both still fighting about the pro and cons of the global capitalist movement and struggle for power between rich and poor nations, colonized and post colonized nations, north and south, development has the tendency to forget that Internet and other e-knowledge enhancers are accelerating the process. Governments in once-poor neo colonized states in Africa and the world are now looking to the new E-economy as the solution to their poverty and other social problems. Access to the Internet can provide work for the poor, although knowledge pundits judge it to be the new form of slavery of the rich over the poor. Mauritius is no exception to the rule. Rapid international socio - conomic conditions and unemployment have accelerated the growth of the informal sector n Mauritius. Many unemployed people, chiefly from the manufacturing sector, have lost their employment and have now entered the informal sector, primarily as street vendors and household producers. Some have returned to agrarian works. However, a sector still lags behind in the use of internet and other E-tools: the informal sector. The informal sector represents a large share of business in African and other poor nations. Although if is difficult to express in exact figures the share of business dealings in the informal sector, mainly because of the lack of statistics and concrete definition, many barriers still exist in the informal sector that provoke business entrepreneurs to opt for informality. Barriers such as high taxes and neglect by relevant authorities tend to accentuate this informality dilemma. This research paper will demonstrate how people in the informal sector in Mauritius refuse to use internet and other tools in their daily business dealings.

Keywords: E business and informal sector, informality, barriers to formality and knowledge of IT among informal entrepreneurs, E business and social Justice.

1 Introduction

Economic performance cannot be measured without social justice Many empirical works have proven that the non-recognition of the informal sector is contrary to this

V. Khachidze et al. (Eds.): iCETS 2012, CCIS 332, pp. 306–315, 2012.

basic concept of social justice. (Unni, 2004; Verrick, 2006; Suprobo, Tarigan and Weis, 2007). The concept of the informal sector was launched by ILO in the 1980s (Bangasser, 2009). It was introduced on the international scene in 1972 by the International Labor Organization (ILO) in the Kenya Mission Report. It is very difficult to define the informal sector, and there is no universal definition when viewed at a micro level. It is very subjective, and the different elements that constitute the term itself vary from country to country. The concept of informality usually conveys a notion of illegality, poverty and refusal of authority. Some countries are now accepting it as the new avenue for employment creation, where the formal sector has become redundant. However, in many countries E-business is carried out at every level of the economy but still remains inaccessible for those in the informal sector. As in many parts of the world, the informal sector in Mauritius has never been clearly defined. It can be said that activities in the informal sector in Mauritius range from household production to street vending. Many reasons, such as refusal to pay high taxes and heavy unemployment linked to changing economic activities, contribute to inflate the number of people entering the sector (Gopaul, 2012). Recent financial crisis and relocation of capitalist-owned manufacturing industries have also contributed to the phenomenon. Government usually finds it difficult to control the informal sector, especially when the sector is equated with tax evasion and refusal to pay for relevant permits. The majority of actors in the informal sector usually cluster themselves in traditional methods for their daily business and, as we will see in this paper, some do not even know that they can make use of new tools such as e-business to maximize profit. Moreover, sometimes this lack of education causes the informal sector actors to become dependent on those that have access to e-business for daily business routines. According to Chen (2001), terms such as "E-business, E-commerce, E-innovation and E-tailing" involve electronic networks utilizing electronic data interchanges to improve business processes, operations and strategies. This entails that the buying, selling and any other services provided through such tools are considered under the term. Buying, selling and providing peripheral services are the daily routines of the informal sector workers. Thus, access to such tools and knowledge as e-business would be of great help in the promotion of social justice for all. This research will demonstrate how informal sector workers still lag behind in terms of the use of e-business, and the resulting denial of equity and social justice because relevant authorities are not taking the required steps to equalize the playing field.

2 Literature Review

The World Trade Organization defines E-commerce as the production, advertising, sales and distribution of products via telecommunications networks. For Clarkes (2005), E-business further includes detailed elements of electronic functions that support services for trading. Thus, internet-based technologies are used as an integral part of E-business for the carrying out of daily business activities. This further provides the opportunity to deduce that a minimum amount of educational background and knowledge are both necessary for the conduct of E-business. According to Davis et al

(1989), internet-based computer systems cannot improve business environments if they are not being fully utilized by all parties. According to Yasin and Yavas (2007), it took only five years for 100 million individuals to use the World Wide Web. Their literature review also proved that the most technologically advanced nations make use of these technologies on an extensive basis. Both authors agree on the fact that in Arab countries people prefer to make use of their personal network and personal contacts, rather than electronic media for carrying out business. Social capital that exists in developing countries has always been considered to be stronger than any modern technology tools. Daily business dealing in the informal sector relies heavily on social capital. This is also the case in Mauritius, as we will see in this research paper. Doolin et al (2005) explained that despite extensive use of e-commerce, growth has not been equitable across Europe. This phenomenon is replicable in developing countries. The use of information tools and e-business has always been very low among informal sector entrepreneurs. In fact, low-income countries, after severe plundering episodes from first world countries the during colonization periods and harsh detrimental Structural Adjustment Programmes periods of the 1970s and 1980s, still find it difficult to follow the trend set by developed nations. Access to modern business strategies, such as e-business and information tools that can help in the creation of wealth, tend to help the few capitalists that usually dominate the market. The reasons for this are mainly linked to a lack of education and sufficient access to information technology tools by low-class people. Literature on the use of e-business among informal sector entrepreneurs is very scarce. Other than some major work and initiatives carried out by civil society organizations like the SEWA (Self-Employed Women's Association) in India, it is very difficult to locate the phenomenon (ITC, 2003). According to Self-Employed Women's Association (SEWA), it is important for the informal entrepreneurs to access global markets in order to get out of the poverty trap (ITC, 2003). In India, the informal sector includes "*home-based workers, vendors, manual laborers and service providers; it accounts for up to 70% of gross domestic product and over 40% of exports; of the total workforce, 93% operate within the informal sector, and 60% of these are women" (ITC,2003).* The SEWA has eased access to e-business for poor informal sector entrepreneurs through access to a facilitation centre that is being run as a cooperative. Such organizations tend to help people with low educational background, who are on a majority in developing countries and tend to be found in the informal sector. The dilemma is that decision makers have an obligation to provide the space to enable every sector of the economy to profit from investment in technological advancements. They can prove to be a reliable tool in the fight against poverty. The informal sector, according to ILO, seems to be the neglected child of the economy. Those in the informal sector tend to suffer from their "informality": they do not have access to social protection, nor to basic amenities and, except for some civil society initiatives, they tend to be a niche for poverty cycle. Butcher and Sparks (2011) agree that considerable challenges are currently being faced by many small/medium firms. According to these authors, the difficulty lies in the barriers to the transfer of knowledge in different sectors and, in their case, the hospitality sector. This is also true for entrepreneurs in the informal sector, especially in developing countries. According to Palmer et al (2001), new internet technologies are not always readily accepted by target users, especially by small companies. This creates a very difficult situation for policy makers. Many scholars actually try to opine regarding the role of authorities in leveling the playing field for both formal and informal entrepreneurs; however, we cannot always blame only the authorities. Small firms, especially those in the informal sector, have developed many barriers to change. This paper will also try to locate and examine these artificial barriers. Thus, as we will see in this paper, barriers to the access of E-business by informal sector entrepreneurs in Mauritius create many unequal conditions for informal business owners, at times nearing exploitation and dependency on many other actors.

2.1 The Situation in Mauritius

Mauritius suffered the era of European colonization since the 16th Century, until achieving independence from the British in 1968. The island was an important stop for European nations on their way to the east for spices and other trade. The French brought slaves to work on sugar plantations until the abolition of slavery and the taking over of the island by the British in 1835. Following the abolition of slavery, Indian immigrants were massively imported to replace the slaves on the sugar plantations (Nave, 2000). Education became free in 1976 up to the secondary level and up to the tertiary level in 1988 (Bunwaree, 1994). Today, Mauritius is considered to be among the upper middle income countries (Hudson et al, 2008). The country is ranked first in Africa in term of governance according to the Mo Ibrahim Index. Although education has been free since 1976, and although Mauritius is considered to be an upper middle income country and, further, ranked 1st in Africa in many forums, the island still lags behind in the field of e-education. The high cost of information technology studies can be blamed for this situation. Though a number of incentives are provided by government to educate the population and bridge the gap in the present information and communication era, barriers still exist in the informal sector preventing informal entrepreneurs from benefitting from the electronic era. The main public body responsible for the development of business in Mauritius is the Board of Investment. According to the organization's website, the island is among the most competitive economies in Africa. However, a simple glance at the website of the board will reveal that the mission statement and strategic objectives of the organization do not have any focus for the development of the informal sector in Mauritius. Other organizations involved in the usage of ICT by small businesses in Mauritius are, namely, the SEHDA (Small Enterprise and Handicraft Development Authority) and the Ministry for Information Technology. However, like the Board of Investment, both these authorities do not have a clear-cut policy for the inclusiveness of informal sector entrepreneurs in their attempt to develop E-business among small firms. Martin and Matlay (2001) propose a Ladder Theory that can explain the resistance of adoption of electronic media in developing business by small firms in Mauritius. According to the authors there are different stages for firms in the adoption E-business, which they call "E Adoption". Mauritian small entrepreneurs may be considered to have halted at the first two stages, where firms are said to acquire only basic skills (e.g. e-mail, basic IT tools etc). As mentioned above, level of education and knowledge, coupled with the business culture in the informal sector, makes the low usage of E-business more evident in the informal sector, as we will see in this research paper. This also depends on requirements of the informal entrepreneur in terms of electronic media. In the next section, methodology will be explained.

3 Research Methodology

There is a shortage of qualitative research on the use of IT and E-business among informal sector entrepreneurs. The informal sector has always been considered a muddle, as no official statistics exist on the sector, especially in developing countries. The aim of the study was to evaluate the use of E-business among informal sector entrepreneurs in Mauritius.

3.1 Sample and Sampling Method

The sample consisted of 135 interviewees. The interviews were carried out on the place of work of the respondent. Observations were also made by the interviewer and any E-business/ IT tools seen on the site of work were noted. To eliminate any gender bias; the interviewees were divided into 65 men and 60 women. A convenient non-probability sampling method, where contact information of respondents was obtained through snowball effect as it is difficult to define the informal sector. Respondents were requested to direct us to other potential interviewees. They were contacted at their habitual place of work. Through snow balling, other informal sector entrepreneurs were contacted. Respondents were mostly household producers, informal taxi drivers, street vendors and small scale family business.

3.2 The Questionnaire

The questionnaire, a purely qualitative survey designed for the purpose of a long interview method, was designed and applied by an interviewer. Long interview, according to Mc Cracken (1989), differs from other types of interviews in that it is concerned with cultural categories and shared meanings rather than affective states of the individual respondent. Moreover, the long interview is designed to give the investigator a highly efficient and productive instrument of inquiry. Thus, this tool was deemed more appropriate for this research.

Questions inquired about:

- *(i)* *The knowledge of IT and E-business usage of the interviewee*
- *(ii)* *The background of the informal entrepreneur*
- *(iii)* *The characteristics of the trade being carried out*
- *(iv)* *The usage of E-business by their supplier, and resellers to whom their finished product was delivered*

(v) *Their daily activities with banking institutions and other electronic environments they might encounter during their trade.*

The questions were set in order to discover the daily reality of the informal entrepreneurs in terms of E-business and whether they were dependent on other users of E-business for their daily activities. A pilot questionnaire was tested initially and amendments were made. The first questionnaire was too time consuming and disturbed both the work and quality of responses. This was remedied by shortening the questionnaire into the above categories. The questionnaire was administered in Creole, the lingua Franca of the Mauritian population.

4 Analysis

The analysis was divided into two different sections:

(i) Observations on site of work; and
(ii) Questionnaire responses

(i) Analysis of Observational Facts on Site of Work

It could be induced from observation on site that very few (5 out of 135 respondents) made use of observable IT tools on their site of work. These were mainly in the form of advanced mobile phones with access to the Internet. However, they all agreed that the use was limited to only very basic applications. The fact that they were informal workers (this especially applies for those who work on the street; no access to WiFi or other medium of connection was used. It is a fact that WiFi is not available in Mauritius, even in the main urban centers, with the exception of areas near some large shopping centers, where informal workers do not have access). Informal taxi drivers also do not make use of E-tools that can be observed on their site of work. Household producers were dealing mainly in the production of low returning products, such as handicrafts, packed ready-to-eat snacks or foodstuffs, and backyard gardening. Some only had telephone lines, without proper connection to the Internet. The handicrafts and packed foodstuffs/ snack producers were primarily women. The household conditions and environments where the informal workers reside are not those that can be considered to belong to upper-class people. The street vendors were working on the street, at places where there were high volumes of traffic, but with poor sanitation and health and safety conditions. For example, in some places there were no water supply or toilet. From these observable facts, it can be deduced that informal workers are low income earners. Newspapers in Mauritius have reported that The Mauritius Revenue Authority was tracking very rich informal sector workers who were reluctant to pay taxes and were escaping the relevant authorities; they were not interviewed as they refused to give us an appointment. It was furthermore observed that women were allowed to work in more vulnerable places.

(ii) Analysis of the Interview Questionnaire

Answers obtained from the questionnaire were categorized into four different subcategories:

a. *Educational background and biographical data of respondent*
b. *Knowledge of respondent about E-business and IT tools relevant for business*
c. *Barriers to the use of E-business as demonstrated by the informal sector workers themselves*

a. Their dependency on others in their working environment, with whom they are dealing and who make use of E-Business Educational background and biographical data of respondent

b. The majority of the informal sector workers had not completed secondary school. Thus, they were poorly educated. In Mauritius, IT courses are offered only at the secondary level. The level of IT courses offered at primary schools is very basic. Government has put into place IT courses that are offered for the public at large. However, according to these people, their work load did not permit them to attend these courses. Thus, lack of proper education was a deterrent for these people to learn IT. Moreover, it was also a question of business culture: the business culture is not one that enables the sustainable use of E-business. The informal entrepreneurs were mostly between the ages of 24 to 56. It was only during the last decade that E-business and usage of IT has become a necessity for Mauritian business, irrespective of size and capital. However, apart from those who are very knowledgeable about IT applications and the usefulness of E-business in today's world, the majority agree that use of IT is beyond their ability. We must, however, point out that the majority (103 out of 135) agreed that knowledge of IT and E-business would have been very helpful and would have increased their profit by easing their access to bulk buying from other countries. This would have reduced their dependency on bulk sellers and consequently lead to more social equity. *Knowledge of respondent about E-business and IT tools relevant for business.*

As mentioned above, the majority of respondents agrees that they know about computers and that it would have been more profitable for them to make use of E-business; however, when the interviewer probed deeper, it was noticed that their knowledge about both IT tools and E-business was very limited. Thus, we can induce that the gap between those who have knowledge about IT/E-business tools and those who do not still remains a concern. Social justice may be a matter of concern here, as well as equitable social development. In the last ten years, the government has tried to provide access to IT for people at a grass-root level. However, the policies have been merely cosmetic in nature. The policies consisted of giving free access to the Internet at post offices; subsidized bank loans for purchase of computers and subsidized courses after working hours for computer training (payable by the purchase of access cards). However, the survey showed that very few of the respondents, 12 of 135, were aware of the courses and availability of access in post offices. They were aware of the loans for the purchase of computers through the development bank, but were reluctant to make use of these as since their work is in the informal sector they do not have a pay slip to produce. Moreover, the bank requests collateral in the form of a guarantor. 41 respondents (only 12 women) were aware that they could purchase and order their goods online, but this was a very complex situation for them. The dilemma remains in the fact that they were always troubled by authorities when trying to import goods by themselves. E-business could have been an alternative to going abroad and purchasing the goods (from China and Thailand primarily); however, lack of knowledge prevent them from doing so. They were dependent on gross resellers who make use of E-business. This had a considerable negative impact on their profit margin. Some flexibility by our regulators could have largely helped these entrepreneurs in their daily life. In the government programme it was announced that laptops would be given to every secondary school student, but in the last two years there has been no concrete action, again, to the detriment of fairness and social justice for these people.

c. *Barriers to the use of E-business as demonstrated by the informal sector workers themselves*

- The current barriers met by the informal business entrepreneurs to the use of E-business identified during the survey were as follows:Lack of education and adequate training proved to be the main barrier.
- Lack of knowledge of existing E-business practices was another main detrimental factor
- Some were already theoretically indebted to gross resellers; bargaining power of supplier tends to be high and the entrepreneurs thus find it difficult to stop trading with them. Without knowing it, they became dependent upon others who use E-business. Bulk buyers set the prices very high, and it was noticed that women paid higher prices than men. This could have been eliminated with equitable access to E-business.
- There was no access to WiFi or even internet at home. The cost of Internet access in Mauritius is very high (the lowest package being around 20 USD). The majority did not even have a PC at home.
- Insufficient access to credit and bank loans was another barrier;
- The informal sector workers had no access to suitable social protection for future contingency compared to formal workers. The government in Mauritius was setting up a social register but none of the informal entrepreneurs were aware of this.

The above barriers are results of poor socio-economic policy and planning by relevant authorities. Respondents were reluctant to talk about their monthly income. As a result, it was difficult to know whether income level affected access to information technology tools. However, it was recurrently mentioned that prices of hardware and access to internet were too high for them. Some pro-poor policies would have been most welcomed to remedy the situation.

d. *Dependency on others with whom they are dealing and who make use of E-business*

Interviewees were questioned about their sources of raw materials and sale of finished products. They mentioned that the finished products were either directly put on the local market for sale to clients, or sold to bulk buyers who export them (primarily local, crafted products). Some of them affirmed that the bulk buyers made use of E-business technology, such as internet, to export the finish product. When asked why they did not contact the client themselves, their answers referred to lack of education about E-business, absence of networking with potential international clients and turnover that was too low to cover costs. Some even mentioned that red-taping and complicated procedures deter their motivation to export their goods. Entrepreneurs meet with many difficulties to access cheaper raw materials. Again, bulk buyers have easy access through the Internet and E-business to international markets. This creates a situation of dependency, to the advantage of the bulk buyers.

5 Conclusion

As demonstrated in this paper, through this qualitative research we have been able to show how informal sector entrepreneurs suffer while conducting their business because of their inability to make use of information technology and E-business. The research, being qualitative in its approach, was able to provide some new insight into the use of information technology in the informal sector as compared to the formal sector. Based on the results obtained, some recommendations can be made: Relevant authorities must rethink their socio-economic objectives and planning in order to reduce the gap in the use of IT and E-business in Mauritius. As we have witnessed, informal sector entrepreneurs are becoming victims to their lack of education and knowledge about the field. Rethinking social policy, such as the restructuring of the education sector and minimizing barriers to formality, can also help in the long term. Cooperative movement can help the informal entrepreneur by providing training at grass-root level in E-business usage. Without the above alterations, social justice will only be a utopia. Furthermore, social development will not achieve its aim of being inclusive.

References

1. Bangasser, P.: The ILO and the informal sector: an institutional history. ILO Publications (2000) ISBN 92-2-112243-3
2. Bunwaree, S.: Mauritian Education in a Global context, editions de L'ocean Indien Mauritius (1994)
3. Butcher, K., Sparks, B.: Business improvement preferences for small/medium hospitality firms in Australia. International Journal of Contemporary Hospitality Management 23(3), 282–296 (2011)
4. Chen, B.: Do you have the right e-business structure? E-Business Advisor 19 (2001); quoted in Yasin, M.M., Yavas, U.: An analysis of E-business practices in the Arab culture: Current inhibitors and future strategies. Cross Cultural Management: An International Journal 14(1), 68–73 (2007)
5. Davis, F.D., Bagozzi, R.P., Warshaw, R.R.: User acceptance of computer technology: comparison of two theoretical models. Management Science 35(8) (1989)

6. Doolin, B., Dillon, S., Thompson, F., James, L.C.: Perceived risk, the Internet shopping experience and online purchasing behavior: a New Zealand perspective. Journal of Global Information Management 13(2), 982–1003 (2005)
7. Gopaul, A.: Globalisation and Development at Grassroot in Africa: The case of Women Street vendors and Household Producers in the Developing Island of Mauritius. In: IJSSM (2012)
8. Hudson, J., Kuhner, S., Lowe, S.: The short Guide to Social policy, p. 17. Policy Press
9. Mc Cracken, G.: The Long Interview. Qualitative Research Method Series, vol. 13. Sage Publications (1988)
10. Nave, A.: Marriage and the maintenance of ethnic group boundaries: the case of Mauritius. Ethnic and Racial Studies Journal 23(2), 329–352 (2000)
11. Palmer, W., Ellinger, E., Allaway, A., D'Souza, G.: A longitudinal examination of internet-based customer service system usage in small companies. Journal of Business & Industrial Marketing 27(1), 29–40 (2011)
12. Suprobo, T., Tarigan, U., Daniel, W.: Informal Sector in Indonesia and Social Security, Technical Report for the Government of Indonesia, Government of Indonesia (2007)
13. Unni, J.: Globalization and Securing Rights for Women informal workers in Asia. Journal of Human Development 5(3) (2004)
14. Verick, S.: The Impact of Globalization on the Informal Sector in Africa, Economic and Social Policy Division, United Nations Economic Cat Commission for Africa (2006)
15. Yasin, M., Yavas, U.: An analysis of E-business practices in the Arab culture: Current inhibitors and futurestrategies. Cross Cultural Management: An International Journal 14(1), 68–73 (2007)

Electronic sources

www.eregulations.mu/doingbiz.aspx board of investment acceded on 26 April 2012
www.webopedia.com/TERM/ E/ebusiness.html acceded on 20 may 2012
www.tradeforum.org/In-India-Integrating-the-Informal-Sector-into-the-Global-Economy ITC 2acceded 23 march 2012
http://www.rogerclarke.com/EC/ 2005 e business: a definition , acceded 26 april 2012

Secure Operation, Control, and Maintenance in Smart Grid Communications over Wireless Networks

Vincent Y. Liu[1] and Xiaobing Wang[2]

[1] Macau University of Science and Technology
ydliu@must.edu.mo
[2] Public Works and Government Service Canada
xiaobing.wang@pwgsc.gc.ca

Abstract. With advanced ubiquitous connectivity provided by wireless computing and mobile networks, the wireless smart grid can revolutionize the current electric power system. However, the use of wireless channels and ubiquitous technology introduce vulnerabilities that can be exploited to provide unauthorized access to the smart grid and impede operation. The harsh and complex electric-power-system environments also pose great challenges in security, privacy and reliability issues of wireless smart grid applications. The emerging wireless security threats are not covered by current smart grid security guidance, and thus regulations remain to be addressed. This paper presents a comprehensive survey of security for wireless smart grid with applications such as mobile ad hoc network, wireless sensor network (WSN), wireless mesh network and WiMAX. Also discussed are challenges in operating, controlling and maintaining secure communications within these networks.

1 Introduction

As a promising infrastructure that can enhance various aspects of modern electric power grids, smart grid can provide efficient, reliable and safe automation service with "smooth integration of renewable and alternative energy sources",[1] through highly interconnected and open information technology. With the help of Internet connection, power information (e.g., meter reading data) can be efficiently monitored and transferred. At the same time, power disturbances and outages (e.g., equipment failure and natural accidents) can be diagnosed and largely avoided.[1] Traditional electric-power-system communication systems are typically based on wired Internet connection. However, a wired communication system relies on copper or fiber-optic cable equipment between communication endpoints; these equipments are high in cost and lack support for long distance communication. Hence, there is an urgent need for wireless network technology to optimize the operation and management of the smart grid.

Driven by the rapid development of wireless technology and the adoption of mobile devices, services and networks, several wireless communication technologies

[1] D. Djenouri, "A Survey of Security Issues in Mobile Ad Hoc and Sensor Networks," *IEEE Communications Surveys & Tutorials*, vol.7, no. 4, 2005, pp. 2-28.

V. Khachidze et al. (Eds.): iCETS 2012, CCIS 332, pp. 316–324, 2012.

currently exist for smart grid systems and networks, such as WiMAX, wireless mesh networks, wireless sensor networks, and satellite communication. When compared to conventional wired communication networks, wireless network technologies have potential benefits, including rapid deployment, services, reliability, efficiency, self-healing, low cost, flexibility, remote controlling/monitoring and aggregated intelligence via power generation, delivery, and utilization [1]. There are two options for power grids to make use of wireless services: [2] (i) utilizing an existing infrastructure (e.g., public cellular infrastructure) of a public network, (ii) developing a private wireless network. The existing and potential services of wireless smart grid networks span a wide range, such as wireless automatic meter reading (WAMR), remote system monitoring and equipment fault diagnostics, etc [4].

Although wireless network technology brings significant advantages over traditional communication technologies in the harsh and complex electric-power-system environments, its open and interconnected features bring about major security challenges for the electric power system. Therefore, many new vulnerable areas are exposed as regards reliable delivery of power from the power plants to end users. For example, hackers may disrupt the grid at a later date from a remote location, leading to cascading-failure-induced disasters [2]; attackers may jeopardize the privacy of smart grid end users in wireless sensing networks; an infiltrator may also compromise selected nodes in a tactical delay-tolerant network and thus fail the critical mission of the supervisory control and data acquisition (SCADA) systems [5–6] There is an urgent need to protect the wireless smart grid from various security and privacy threats.

Current guidance for electric power system security does not cover threats to wireless network communication. Therefore, to ensure a secure, reliable and efficient high-capacity smart grid, the security of wireless network communication must be addressed. An important step toward realizing this target is the development of a unified framework for the identification of security properties that the wireless smart grid system and its applications must comprise. The purpose of the paper is to emphasize the role of wireless security issues for smart grid systems and networks. An extensive survey is provided to describe the characteristics of wireless network technology for smart grid systems in existence today. Potential wireless threats and their adverse impacts on smart grid operation are discussed. This paper provides such a framework, focusing on three representative applications for the operation, maintenance, and control of wireless smart grid applications.

The rest of the article is organized as follows: First, different wireless smart grid applications are presented, followed by a discussion on various known attacks as well as security requirements and services in securing group communication. Several proposals for security solutions over these different networks are then discussed.

2 Wireless Smart Grid Communication

Smart grid systems contain three major subsystems, namely power generation; power delivery; and power utilization. Within these major subsystems emerge seven specific

---

[2] V.C. Gungor, F.C. Lambert, "A Survey on Communication Networks for Electric System Automation," Computer Networks, vol. 50, no. 2, 2006, pp. 877–897.

domains:[3] power plant domain; substation domain; distribution domain; market domain; operation domain; service provider domain; and customer/end user domain.

Rapid advances in wireless networking have extended its application from wireless ad hoc networks and wireless sensor networks to emerging wireless networks including wireless mesh networks, delay-tolerant networks, vehicular networks, and satellite communication networks;[4] these technologies can be applied in each of the above-mentioned subsystems and domains and thereby enhance smart grid communication.

Table 1. Features and application of various wireless technologies for smart grid, including WiMAX, wireless sensor network (WSN), wireless mesh network (WMN) and wireless ad hoc network

Name	Features	Applications
WiMAX	Long distance support and large coverage area	Communication connections among power plants and substations
Wireless sensor network	Low cost, low power, greater fault tolerance, improved accuracy, and self configuration and organization	WAMR and Electric system monitoring
Wireless mesh network	Increased reliability, low installation costs and large coverage area	Customers (e.g. electric utility subscribers)
Wireless ad hoc network	Non-infrastructural; efficient data processing	Rescue operations

2.1 Wireless Applications in Smart Grid

With the advancement in communication technologies, wireless networks have facilitated many emerging applications. The characteristics of different wireless technologies are vastly different in terms of management, resources and routing. Table 1 illustrates the main features and application for various wireless technologies.

Wireless Ad Hoc Network for Smart Grid. A wireless ad hoc network is a collection of mobile nodes dynamically keeping the network connected without any predefined network infrastructure or centralized administration. Nodes belong to a single authority and communicate amongst each other using wireless radios, following a peer-to-peer network model of operation. Wireless ad hoc network is an emerging smart grid [9,10] and has been conceptualized mainly for the purpose of crisis solutions (e.g., in case of manmade or natural disaster). Examples include networks of power grid monitoring and data exchange between remote areas. In these networks, the nodes do not necessarily belong to a single authority. In addition, these networks could be larger, have a longer lifetime, and could be completely self-organizing, meaning that the network could be run solely by the operation of end-users [10].

[3] G. N. Ericsson, "Cyber Security and Power System Communication—Essential Parts of a Smart Grid Infrastructure," IEEE Transactions on Power Delivery, vol. 25, no. 3, 2010, pp. 1501 - 1507.

[4] W. Lou, K. Ren, "Security, Privacy, and Accountability in Wireless Access Networks," *IEEE Wireless Communications*, vol. 16, no. 4, 2009, pp. 80-87.

Wireless Sensor Networks for Smart Grid. Recently, WSNs have been widely recognized as a vital component of the next-generation electric power system. In contrast with wireless ad hoc networks, wireless sensor networks (WSNs) contain a large number of low cost, low power and multifunctional sensor nodes which can be an advantage for electric system automation applications, especially in urban areas [3]. These sensor nodes capitalize upon demographic, communication, situation or other data (physical environment, location data, distance, temperature, sound, air pressure, time, lighting levels, people nearby, customer preferences, customer emotional state, etc.), in addition to "mapping such physical characteristics of the environment to quantitative measurements" [3]. The collaborative and context-awareness nature of WSNs brings several advantages over traditional sensing, including greater fault tolerance, improved accuracy, larger coverage area and extraction of localized features. In the context of smart grid, the role of sensor node is to monitor the overall network and to communicate with the control center in the power utility (e.g., substation), in order to help operators decide the appropriate actions to pursue. The sensor node can communicate with the task manager via Internet or satellite. A typical application of WSN for smart grid is what is known as wireless automatic meter reading (WAMR) systems, which can determine the customer's real-time energy consumption accurately, as well as improve business performance and technical reliability of various electric utility operations. Besides, WAMR systems can remotely control flexible management systems (e.g., read data and get other important information from meters), and customers can download their archives and accomplish meter reading via a mobile device. WSN can also be used for remote system monitoring and equipment fault diagnostics and Electric System Monitoring.

WiMAX for Smart Grid. With WiMAX technology, the capacity of the wireless network backbone for smart grid can be increased by as much as 75 Mbps [3]. WiMAX supports long distance communication (up to 31 miles) connecting power plants, substations, end users and other utilities [3]. Compared to traditional point-to-multipoint networks, WiMAX offers a standardized communication technology for point-to-multipoint wireless networks (e.g., IEEE 802.16 standard) and supports non-line of sight communication. This enables collaboration between different substations without any performance degradation, which is another important concern for power plants. Recently, WiMAX technology also focuses on low latency handoff management [2–4], which is necessary for communications with high-speed, moving users (e.g., drivers or passengers in vehicular ad hoc networks).

Wireless Mesh Networks for Smart Grid. A wireless mesh network includes wireless routers and mobile wireless stations [4,5]. In the context of smart grid, a set of electric utility customers is clustered into wireless mesh domains, and each wireless mesh cluster is monitored by substations or power plants using WiMAX. In contrast to traditional wireless networks, nodes in the wireless mesh domain are dynamically self-organized to establish the network connectivity. This feature entails many advantages for power plants and substations, such as low-cost network maintenance, robustness, and reliable power service coverage. For example, by utilizing WMN technology, the network can extend the operation time for electric utilities, especially in the context of network element failure or network congestion.

2.2 Wireless Smart Grid Features

Based on the survey of different wireless applications for smart grid, we identify three common features of these wireless smart grid networks:

Non-infrastructural. Central servers, fixed routers or other specialized hardware are absent during wireless smart grid communication.

Multi-hop. Hosts in wireless smart grid networks are themselves the router in the lack of central routers, gateways and related equipment. Hence, data packets follow multi-hop routes and pass through different mobile nodes during the transition of energy information.

Autonomous Node Movement. Mobile nodes move autonomously and dynamically; it is difficult to track one particular node in the wireless smart grid network.

3 Threats to Wireless Smart Grid Communication

Wireless network technology is susceptible to smart grid communication. However, as we illustrated in the section "Wireless smart grid features", wireless channels can be easily attacked and made more vulnerable due to these common features. We divide threats that can affect security in wireless smart grid into two classes, attacks and misbehavior.

3.1 Attacks on Smart Grid

Attacks are any action that intentionally aims to cause damage to the wireless smart grid systems and network [4]. Here, we present some typical attacks [4]:

Attacks on Data Integrity and Confidentiality. This type of attack attempts to compromise the integrity or confidentiality of data transmitted through the wireless network.

Attacks on Power Consumption. The goal of this kind of attack is to exhaust the equipments' power supply, which is one of the most valuable assets in wireless communication. The worst case would cause a collapse of power grid communications.

Attacks on Service Availability and Bandwidth Consumption. These attacks can overwhelm the forwarding capability of nodes, and they can also consume sparsely available bandwidth. These attacks can result in a denial of service to legitimate members.

Attacks on Routing. These attacks focus on routing issues. They can change the routing information in the wireless network and result in unauthorized controlling of the network.

Attacks on Identity. These attacks focus on the authentication entity, and can obtain the vulnerable MAC and network addresses.

Attacks on Privacy. This type of attack violates anonymity and privacy during wireless communication. Electricity users could lose information regarding not only monthly energy usage status but also their activities (e.g., whether they are at home, at work, or traveling).

3.2 Misbehavior within Smart Grid

In contrast to attacks, misbehavior here means unauthorized behavior which can result in unintentional damage to the wireless smart grid systems and network. For instance, a node in the wireless smart grid network may refuse to transmit data packets for other remotes in order to save its resources, i.e., battery power. Actually, this is not an intentional attack but a kind of misbehavior. However, it also induces potential threats for quality and availability of service in the power grid.

3.3 Basic Security Requirements

In order to face these various challenges, previous research has provided several basic requirements for establishing a secure smart grid over the wireless network [2, 4-7, 11]:

Authentication. To ensure that the origin and destination of information are correctly identified, the injection of corrupted data by unauthorized entities must be prevented.

Confidentiality. Confidentiality is required for the prevention of passive attacks and unauthorized access to sensitive data, i.e., intellectual property.

Availability. Availability ensures the timely availability of wireless network services to authorized users.

Non-repudiation. Communication must be uncontested among users.

Early Detection. To prevent unwarranted communication delays, any manipulation of information must be detected as early as possible. Early detection can also eliminate or reduce false alarms.

As mentioned earlier, privacy is also a critical issue and can be attacked easily, especially in such contexts as bill payments, submission of service requests in case of emergency and checking energy usage from smart meters. However, it is not easy to describe the scope of smart grid privacy issues, as privacy problems can emerge not only in personal communications, but also in business transactions among power plants, substations and customers. Unfortunately, there has not been a well established standard for smart grid privacy issues. Here we deem the following privacy services indispensable:

Integrity. To ensure that the transmitted data is not illegally modified (e.g., changing, deleting, creating, delaying, or replaying data), the identity and content of the received data must be verified to match the original source.

Traceability. All actions performed on any information must be logged for a time period.

Access Control. The ability to limit and control access to information, devices or applications. Each instance of access must be verified to possess the appropriate permission.

4 Security Services for Wireless Smart Grid Communication

Security services for wireless smart grid communication must be able to integrate security maintenance (e.g., confidentiality and authentication), security operations (e.g., logging and availability), and other security control (e.g., access control and traceability) in a seamless fashion. While existing smart grid communication systems are now being refurbished or replaced with wireless networks or applications, information and device security issues must be taken into account. If a smart grid communication system is to be refurbished, the operational system aspect (which exists in power plant domain or substation domain) must be shielded from the administrative aspect to protect the operational aspect from digital attacks, theft, corruption, harm and destruction that are possible over the wireless connection. If a smart grid communication system is to be replaced, it is then a very good occasion to reconsider an overall wireless communication system structure, and then incorporate IT security on all power grid domains. The strategies to design a security service for smart grid are as follows.

4.1 Securing the Trust and Privacy Related Issues

As illustrated in the section "Wireless Applications in Smart Grid", power plants provide operation services such as switching operation, changing setups, recommendation of optimized operations, starting emergency procedure and performing system restorations, etc. [2]. Concurrently, substations have the responsibility of power system protection, load shedding, recovery from load shedding, shunt control and compensation control [2]. Numerous trust-related challenges will arise with the integration of wireless communication systems. This section surveys some securing services for trust-related issues.

Digital Signatures. References [9-10, 12] present discussions on the method to prevent attackers and unauthorized nodes; their solutions can be divided into two categories: digital signatures and certificated authority (CA). CA relies on a trusted certificate server in the wireless network, and the public key of the server is given to all valid end users before they need to access information.

Pros. The benefit of this method is that it can protect valuable data by excluding or even eliminate external attackers.

Cons. The trusted certificate server acts as required equipment and makes the wireless communication less flexible.

Trust Metric. Yi et al.[5] provide a trust metric named trust value to maintain protocol behavior. Different trust levels are defined and assigned to end users or nodes in the wireless network. The information of trust levels must be provided in order to transmit data through users of nodes.

Pros. This method does not rely on external device equipment, the authors have designed a protocol name Security-Aware Routing based on hierarchal trust values metric to maintain and control routes in the wireless network. The hierarchal key sharing mechanism can also be an advantage for the controlling of misbehavior activities.

Cons. The problem of this method is how trust values are defined, as there is no hierarchy in the general network.

4.2 Securing Communication and Device Related Issues

When wireless communicating across power utilities, organizations, and customers, the power plants are in charge of exchanging data with an independent system

---

[5] S. Yi et al., "Security-aware Ad-hoc Routing for Wireless Networks," *ACM Workshop on Mobile Ad Hoc Networks, Mobihoc*, 2001.

operator (e.g., peer transmission and distribution system operation) or regional transmission organization (e.g., substations, end users or other power plants), while substations are in charge of exchanging important information (e.g., protection data among substations) and alarms. During different communication processes, the lack of pervasive and effective communications and monitoring tools has led to the failure of smart grid. Network communication and safety-related factors have become the main causes of several major threats.

Neighbor Nodes Identification. As many attacks are from neighbor nodes in the wireless network context, reference [4, 14] present a three-round information exchange solution to ensure the neighbor relationship between two nodes. One well-behaving node can ignore the other once the exchange process fails. Hence, the neighbor detection attacks can be prevented.

Pros. The method can prevent rushing attacks from illegal nodes with higher power, as they cannot receive data packet from other nodes.

Cons. High overheads, especially when the mobility of nodes increases.

Secure Level Key Infrastructure. Huang et al.[6] proposed a secure level key infrastructure for the multicast context. This infrastructure includes an intrusion detection and deletion algorithm and a multicast protocol which divides a multicast routing tree into levels/branches. The detection algorithm can protect data and mitigate Dos-based flooding. At the same time, communication among nodes in different branches is protected by a level key--only the local level key is identified during movement of nodes. The infrastructure ensures communication between upstream nodes and downstream nodes, as it can re-encrypt the data packet with the level keys that downstream nodes share with parent nodes--this mechanism can reduce bandwidth and power consumption.

Pros. Low communication overheads.

Cons. Power consumption can be high when level changes are massive.

5 Conclusion

The number of applications of smart grid over wireless networks has been steadily increasing, such as wireless automatic meter reading (WAMR) and remote monitoring systems. However, since radio waves in wireless communication spread in the air, one common risk is that wireless channels are more insecure and susceptible to numerous attacks than wired networks [5]. Much existing work has attempted to incorporate security into smart grid.

To better understand securing service for smart grid over wireless networks, we have presented known threats that can disrupt wireless smart grid communication. We have discussed the features of wireless smart networks, and illustrated basic security services to complement these features and safeguard communications against these threats. We have demonstrated that several attacks or misbehaviors can be by the proper security services. We have also reviewed several existing works on operation, control, and maintenance in wireless smart grid communications.

---

[6] J.-H. Huang et al., "A Level Key Infrastructure for Secure and Efficient Group Communication in Wireless Sensor Networks," *Proc. 1st Int'l. Conf. on Security and Privacy for Emerging Areas in Commun. Net.*, Sep. 2005, pp. 249–60.

Although we attain security services for trust, communication and privacy issues, security for smart grid also requires management efforts with regards to policy. For example, a power plant could develop security policies and procedures for maintaining and controlling collaboration with substations and markets. However, today, there are no common rules or standards for data exchange or resource usage in wireless smart grid communication. We are studying this challenge in a case study of related companies in China.

Acknowledgments. This work was supported by Faculty Research Grant of Macau University of Science and Technology (Project No.: 0236).

References

1. Gungor, V.C., et al.: Opportunities and Challenges of Wireless Sensor Networks in Smart Grid. IEEE Transactions on Industrial Electronics 57(10), 3357–3564
2. Wei, D., et al.: Protecting Smart Grid Automation Systems Against Cyberattacks. IEEE Transactions on Smart Grid (accept June 05, 2011), doi:10.1109/TSG.2011.2159999
3. Djenouri, D.: A Survey of Security Issues in Mobile Ad Hoc and Sensor Networks. IEEE Communications Surveys & Tutorials 7(4), 2–28 (2005)
4. Gungor, V.C., Lambert, F.C.: A Survey on Communication Networks for Electric System Automation. Computer Networks 50(2), 877–897 (2006)
5. Metke, R., Ekl, R.L.: Security Technology for Smart Grid Networks. IEEE Transactions on Smart Grid 1(1), 99–107 (2010)
6. Sakarindr, P., Ansari, N.: Security Services in Group Communications over Wireless Infrastructure, Mobile Ad Hoc, and Wireless Sensor Networks. IEEE Wireless Communications 14(5), 8–20 (2007)
7. Ericsson, G.N.: Cyber Security and Power System Communication—Essential Parts of a Smart Grid Infrastructure. IEEE Transactions on Power Delivery 25(3), 1501–1507 (2010)
8. Lou, W., Ren, K.: Security, Privacy, and Accountability in Wireless Access Networks. IEEE Wireless Communications 16(4), 80–87 (2009)
9. Komninos, N., et al.: Authentication in A Layered Security Approach for Mobile Ad Hoc Networks. Computers Security 26(5), 373–380 (2007)
10. Komninos, N., et al.: Layered Security Design for Mobile Ad Hoc Networks. Computers Security 25(2), 121–130 (2006)
11. Sampigethaya, K.: Secure Operation, Control, and Maintenance of Future E-Enabled Airplanes. Proceedings of the IEEE 96(12), 1992–2007 (2008)
12. Castelluccia, C., Montenegro, G.: Protecting AODV Against Impersonation Attacks. ACM SIGMOBILE Mobile Computing and Communications Review 6(3), 108–109 (2002)
13. Yi, S., et al.: Security-aware Ad-hoc Routing for Wireless Networks. In: ACM Workshop on Mobile Ad Hoc Networks, Mobihoc (2001)
14. Hu, Y.-C., et al.: Rushing Attacks and Defense in Wireless Ad Hoc Network Routing Protocols. In: ACM Workshop on Wireless Security, San Diego, CA, USA (September 2003)
15. Huang, J.-H., et al.: A Level Key Infrastructure for Secure and Efficient Group Communication in Wireless Sensor Networks. In: Proc. 1st Int'l. Conf. on Security and Privacy for Emerging Areas in Commun. Net., pp. 249–260 (September 2005)

Eliminating False Matches Using Geometric Context

Muhua Zhang[1], Yuxiong Zhang[2], and Jianrong Wang[1]

[1] School of Computer Science and Technology, Tianjin University, Tianjin, China
[2] School of Computer Software, Tianjin University, Tianjin, China
{zhangmuhua1110,tjuzhangyuxiong}@163.com

Abstract. In this paper, we present a novel approach to encode strong geometric information with the final purpose of eliminating false matches. This approach aims to build an invariant coordinate as the spatial information representation of features set, which can improve accuracy of matches. Firstly, a set of reliable MSER pairs between two images are obtained by a MSER detector and matching. Secondly, all matched MSER pairs are fitted into elliptical regions to achieve rotation invariance, scale invariance, and affine invariance. Finally, for each elliptical region, we build an invariant coordinate system to represent spatial layout of features. We use Full-Geometry-Constraint (FGC) to eliminate false matches without rapidly decreasing on correct matches. The experimental evaluation results show that our method is robust against most geometric and photometric transformations including rotation, scale change, blur, viewpoint change, JPEG compression and illumination changes.

Keywords: image match, Maximally Stable Extremal Region, geometric context, invariant coordinate systems, geometric constraint.

1 Introduction

The visual problems of requiring a discriminative and accurate image match are challenging in computer vision and pattern recognition. There are many approaches that pursue more accurate correspondence between two sets of features, such as triangle-constraint [1], wide baseline matching [2], symmetry detection [3] and building panoramas [4]. To improve the quality of feature representation of an image, numerous feature extraction and description schemes have also been proposed, such as: (1) point-based descriptor, such as Harris corner detector [5], Hessian-Laplace detector [6], Hessian-Matrix based detector [7], SIFT [8], SURF [7]; and (2) region-based descriptor, such as IBR [9], Harris-Affine region [10], Hessian-Affine region [10], MSER [2] and salient region [11]. These different types, including point-based features and region-based features, solve different problems. The descriptor must be distinctive and robust to geometric and photometric deformations and noises.

Although the algorithm proposed for feature detection and description are sufficiently mature, the performance of finding correspondences between images and current similarity measurement approaches are still limited. The similarity

V. Khachidze et al. (Eds.): iCETS 2012, CCIS 332, pp. 325–334, 2012.

measurement of features is vital for image matching. At present, as asserted by X. Guo [1], the most widely used measurement is to adopt dot product between descriptors, and then compare the ratio between the first and the second nearest neighbors against a predefined threshold to decide whether they are matched (we denominate this as the baseline method, BLM). This measurement lost most geometric and photometric information, and the drawback is that it brings about a serious problem in that many false matches are wrongly regarded as correct matches.

To solve this problem, many approaches of similarity measurement have been proposed. Leordeanu and Herbert (2005) proposed a spectral technique [12] for correspondence problem, using pairwise constraints. This approach builds the adjacency matrix of a graph whose vertexes represent the potential correspondences. The weights on the edges represent pairwise agreements between potential correspondences. The author presented an efficient way of performing both supervised and unsupervised learning for graph matching.

RANSAC [13], proposed by Brown and Lowe (2003), is an iterative method to estimate parameters of a mathematical model from a set of observed data that contains outliers. It is a non-deterministic algorithm, in that it produces a reasonable result with only a certain probability. This method can be employed to estimate the homography between images, and filter out false matches according to the geometric constraint provided by the estimated homography.

The method called Circular Earth Mover's Distance (CEMD) [14] is developed by Rabin et al. (2008). They present an adaptation of the Earth Mover's Distance to one-dimensional circular histograms. This distance, which is called CEMD, is used to compare SIFT-like descriptors.

Jiang and Yu (2009) introduced a linear formulation [15] that simultaneously finds feature point correspondences and global geometrical transformation in a constrained solution space, which can accurately match features. This measurement improves matching accuracy, but at the cost of a reduced number of correct matches. Therefore, to boost the performance of finding correspondences, an effective technique for finding more good correspondences between two sets of features is imperative. To a certain degree, these measurements can improve matching accuracy.

In this paper, we aim to propose an effective similarity measurement approach, Full Geometry Constraint Measurement, for eliminating false matches. Our method concentrates on filtering false matches by introducing a novel measurement based on geometric context. It can be considered a process of geometric verification through building invariant coordinate systems. In the matching step, the geometric context is encoded to reinterpret features' layout to quarantine the matches that dissatisfy the right geometric relationship (see Fig. 1).

The rest of this paper is organized as follows. Full-Geometry-Constraint based on MSER, including MSER detectors, the method of encoding spatial information of matched features and matching strategy are detailed in Section 2. Section 3 provides discussion of scene disorder. In Section 4, we present a performance evaluation with a series of experiments.

(a) Matching result by BLM (b) Matching result by FGC

Fig. 1. Matching result comparison between baseline method and FGC method. Many false matches in (a) are eliminated in (b).

2 Full-Geometry-Constraint Based on MSER

In this section, we describe the flow of Full-Geometry-Constraint based on MSER, including MSER detector and the strategy of Encoding Spatial Information of matched features.

2.1 Maximally Stable Extremal Region

For obtaining a geometric invariant region, we select Maximally Stable Extremal Regions (MSER) as a basis of finding the geometric relationship between the original image and the matched image. We utilize MSERs, because in most cases MSER performs best among different schemes. Secondly, the advantage of MSER is its high efficiency, i.e. nearly linear complexity in terms of image pixels in extraction. An efficient (near linear complexity) and fast detection algorithm is presented in the original paper by Matas [2].

MSER was first proposed for wide baseline matching by Matas [2]. It has two desirable properties. For one, the set is closed under continuous (and thus perspective) transformation of image coordinates, and secondly, it is closed under monotonic transformation of image intensities [2]. As the most stable extremal region, MSER possesses the following characteristics:

- Invariance to affine transformation of image intensities.
- Covariance to adjacency preserving (continuous) transformation $T: \mathcal{D} \rightarrow \mathcal{D}$ on the image domain.
- Stability, as only extremal regions whose support is virtually unchanged over a range of thresholds is selected.
- Multi-scale detection. As no smoothing is involved, both very fine and very large structures are detected.
- The set of all extremal regions can be enumerated in $O(n \log(\log(n)))$, where n is the number of pixels in the image.

2.1.1 Maximally Stable Extremal Region Detector

MSERs are detected by analyzing the level set of a connected, weighted graph. It mainly comprises three steps: sorting pixels by intensity, merging connected components, and detecting extremal regions and confirming the maximally stable regions.

First, it proceeds by sorting the pixels by intensity. This would take $O(n)$ time, using BINSORT. After sorting, pixels are marked in the image, and the list of growing and merging connected components and their areas are maintained using the union-find algorithm. This would take $O(n\log(\log(n)))$ time. In practice, these steps are very fast. During this process, the area of each connected component as a function of intensity is stored to produce a data structure. A merge of two components is viewed as termination of existence of the smaller component and an insertion of all pixels of the smaller component into the larger one. In the extremal regions, the 'maximally stable' ones are those corresponding to thresholds where the relative area change as a function of relative change of threshold is at a local minimum, i.e. the MSER are the parts of the image where local binarization is stable over a large range of thresholds. The component tree is the set of all connected components of the thresholds of the image, ordered by inclusion. Efficient (quasi-linear regardless of the range of the weights) algorithms for computing it do exist, and thus this structure offers an easy way for implementing MSER.

More recently, Nister and Stewenius have proposed a truly (if the weights are small integers) worst-case $O(n)$ method in [16], which is also much faster in practice. This algorithm is similar to that of Ph. Salembier et al. [17]

2.1.2 Fitting Elliptical Region

Since original MSERs are those regions that have irregular shapes and are difficult to describe, it is necessary to construct shape descriptors for them. Usually, extremal regions are returned as a set of ellipsoids fitted to the actual regions.

Firstly, the fit is done by calculating the mean and variance of each maximally stable extremal region R:

$$\mu = \frac{1}{|\mathbf{R}|}\sum_{x\in\mathbf{R}}\mathbf{x}, \tag{1}$$

$$\mathbf{\Sigma} = \frac{1}{|\mathbf{R}|}\sum_{x\in\mathbf{R}}(\mathbf{x}-\mu)(\mathbf{x}-\mu)^T \tag{2}$$

Then the elliptical region is determined by the mean μ and the variance $\mathbf{\Sigma}$, i.e.

$$(\mathbf{x}-\mu)^T\mathbf{\Sigma}^{-1}(\mathbf{x}-\mu)=1, \tag{3}$$

where $\mathbf{x}=(x,y)^T$. Secondly, Matas et al. [26] proved that the covariance matrix $\mathbf{\Sigma}_1$ and covariance matrix $\mathbf{\Sigma}_2$, computed on original DR, and DR are related by affine transformation $\mathbf{y} = \mathbf{Ax}$. The equation can be stated as follows:

$$\mathbf{\Sigma}_1 = \frac{1}{|\mathbf{\Omega}_1|}\int_{\Omega_1}\mathbf{x}\mathbf{x}^T d\mathbf{\Omega}_1, \tag{4}$$

$$\Sigma_2 = \frac{1}{|\Omega_2|}\int_{\Omega_2} \mathbf{y}\mathbf{y}^T d\Omega_2 = \frac{1}{|\mathbf{A}||\Omega_2|}\int_{\Omega_1} \mathbf{A}\mathbf{x}\mathbf{x}^T\mathbf{A}^T |\mathbf{A}| d\Omega_1 = \mathbf{A}\Sigma_1\mathbf{A}^T, \quad (5)$$

Where $\mathbf{\Omega}_1$ and $\mathbf{\Omega}_2$ are regions defined by the first and second distinguished region. Also, if the DR is transformed by affine transformation matrix $\mathbf{A}$, the transformation between two ellipses is known:

$$\mathbf{y}^T\Sigma_2^{-1}\mathbf{y} = (\mathbf{A}\mathbf{x})^T(\mathbf{A}\Sigma_1\mathbf{A}^T)^{-1}(\mathbf{A}\mathbf{x}) = \mathbf{x}^T\mathbf{A}^T\mathbf{A}^{-T}\Sigma_1^{-1}\mathbf{A}^{-1}\mathbf{A}\mathbf{x} = \mathbf{x}^T\Sigma_1^{-1}\mathbf{x}. \quad (6)$$

After the fitting step, each detected elliptical region can be normalized into a circular region, from which a SIFT descriptor is computed. As is shown in Fig. 2, several matched elliptical region pairs are affine-covariant, so we can obtain the geometric relationship between the original image and the matched image from each pair of matched elliptical regions.

(a) image A

(b) image B

Fig. 2. Fitted ellipses from Maximally Stable Extremal Regions

2.2 Full-Geometry-Constraint

As shown in Fig. 2, we have determined the most stable MSER in reference image (image A) and its matching image (image B). For these corresponding MSER pairs, they contain geometrical transformation, including translation, scale transformation and affine transformation, so that we can obtain the geometrical relationship between image A and image B. In order to reinterpret features' positions based on these MSERs, and invariant coordinates system can be built through normalization of fitting ellipse of MSERs.

2.2.1 Normalization of Fitted Ellipse from MSER

Normalizing an ellipse to a circle is equal to finding a transformation equation. First, we describe the fitted ellipse by the mean μ and the variance $\mathbf{\Sigma}$ as $(\mathbf{x}-\mu)^T\mathbf{\Sigma}^{-1}(\mathbf{x}-\mu)=1$, where $\mathbf{x}=(x,y)^T$. To normalize the ellipse, $\mathbf{\Sigma}$ is decomposed by singular value decomposition as follows:

$$\mathbf{\Sigma}^{-1} = \mathbf{Q}\mathbf{\Lambda}\mathbf{Q}^{-1}, \quad (7)$$

where $\mathbf{Q}$ represents an orthogonal unitary matrix that is real-symmetric and $\mathbf{\Lambda}$ represents a diagonal matrix.

Second, we let $\mathbf{z} = \mathbf{Q}^T (\mathbf{x} - \mu)$ to obtain

$$\mathbf{z}^T \Lambda \mathbf{z} = 1, \tag{8}$$

where $\mathbf{z}$ represents the coordinate corresponding to the region normalized from $\mathbf{x}$. After finding the transformation equation $\mathbf{z} = \mathbf{Q}^T (\mathbf{x} - \mu)$, an invariant coordinate system can be built up.

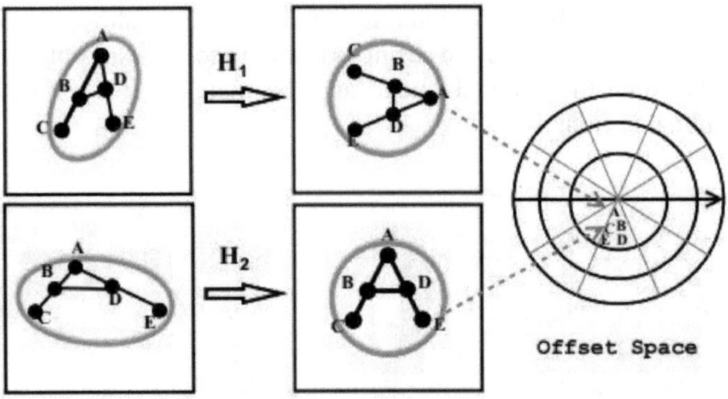

Fig. 3. Illustration of process design, including normalization of MSERs, building coordinate system and matching. Different alphabets (A, B, ...) represent different feature points.

2.2.2 Building Invariant Coordinate System

In this section, we propose a process of building an invariant coordinate system. As shown in Fig. 3, a normalized ellipse is obtained by transformation $\mathbf{z} = \mathbf{Q}^T (\mathbf{x} - \mu)$. It also means that the original image is changed to the transformed image by equivalent transformation.

The process of building invariant coordinate system mainly contains two steps. Firstly, we normalize the fitted ellipses of the selected MSER to circles. As stated in Section 2.1.2 and Section 2.2.1, the fitted ellipse is described with $(\mathbf{x} - \mu)^T \mathbf{Q} \Lambda \mathbf{Q}^{-1} (\mathbf{x} - \mu) = 1$, where $\mathbf{x}$ represents the coordinate in normalized space. Thus, a normalized space of the transformed image can be formed through normalizing the fitting ellipse. Secondly, every detected feature point is assigned to a coordinate. In the space of the transformed image, we regard the center of the normalized circle as original point O of the coordinate system. In order to compute conveniently, we select polar coordinates system regarding the long axis of fitted ellipse as polar axis, shown in Fig. 3. Therefore, the two essential elements of polar coordinate system, original point and polar axis, are established.

After building the invariant coordinate system, all matched feature points have their polar coordinates referenced to this coordinate system. Thus far, the spatial layout information of feature points can be encoded by computing their invariant coordinates.

2.2.3 Matching Scheme

In this section, we present the matching scheme in detail. We firstly select several matched MSER regions, which can be used to build the geometric relationship between the original image and the matched image. In order to obtain these matched MSER regions, the description and matching of MSER region are necessary. As described by Lowe [6], we use SIFT description method. After the step of matching MSERs, several matched MSERs adopted are ranked by

$$Score = \omega_1 * \min\{A_1, A_2\} + \omega_2 * \min\{1/F_1, 1/F_2\}, \tag{9}$$

Where A_1 and A_2 represent area of matched ellipses respectively. F_1 and F_2 represent flatness of matched ellipses respectively. ω_1 and ω_2 are predefined as weight coefficients. Eq. (9) indicates that we tend to select ellipses that are bigger and more rounded.

Once several matched MSER regions are obtained, invariant coordinate systems can be built up based on these MSER regions. In our scheme, to be more robust against noise and disorder (see Section 3), we build several coordinate systems with reference to their corresponding MSERs. The process of building invariant coordinates system is discussed in Section 2.2.2. For a geometric coordinate of one feature point, there are two essential elements, radius r and angle θ. First, we consider radius r: if the correspondences are correctly matched, their difference of radius is approximate to 0. Note that we regard the long axis of fitted ellipse as polar axis, as shown in Fig. 3. Therefore, if their matched coordinates are compared, there must be an augular offset between two true matched points. However, in the basis of the fact that similar scenes have similar geometric layout of feature points, the correct matched correspondences must have approximate augular offsets. As shown in Fig. 3, the whole augular space is split into several bins (the bin number is set as 36). Theoretically, for the most part, the augular offsets of correct matches should be located in the same or neighbor bin, which is named *Dominated Bin*. Thus, a few matches considered as "correct" matches in the baseline method are eliminated because they are not located in *Dominated Bin*. After computing their geometric relationship of candidate matched pairs, the candidate matches are accepted as final matches if they satisfy

$$\Delta r < \tau \text{ and } \Delta\theta \in [\theta_1, \theta_2], \tag{10}$$

Where Δr represents difference of radius and $\Delta\theta$ represents augular offset in built polar coordinate system. τ is predefined as the threshold and $[\theta_1, \theta_2]$ is *Dominated Bin*.

3 Discussion of Scene Disorder

As previously mentioned in Section 2.2.3, to be more robust against noise and disorder, we build several coordinate systems with reference to their corresponding MSERs in our scheme. Here, "disorder" means that there are multi-scenes or objects that have different locations with each other between two images. The number of coordinate systems has a great effect in the case that the objects or scenes are disordered between the original image and the matched image. If just a single-coordinate system was built up, our algorithm would fail to match multi-scenes that are disordered, as shown in Fig. 4 (a). Therefore, it is important for us to build a certain amount of coordinate systems to be robust against disorders. After the building up of multi-coordinate systems, different objects or scenes belong to different coordinate systems. Thus, our algorithm can match multi-scenes with disordered locations. Fig. 4 (b) demonstrates the above.

(a) Single-coordinate system (b) Multi-coordinate system

Fig. 4. Matching result comparison between different numbers of coordinate systems

4 Experiments

We detail experimental evaluation in this section. Our method is suitable for applying to almost all the local image features. In this work, we use the popular SIFT as an example.

Data Set. We evaluate our method with respect to several categories of images with different geometric and photometric transformations. There are 8 categories of images on INRIA dataset (Leuven, illumination change; UBC, JPEG compression; Bikes, blur; Trees, blur; Boat, scale change; Bark, scale change; Graffiti, viewpoint change; Wall, viewpoint change).

Comparison. We compare our baseline model method with the evaluation criteria based on precision (the ratio between the number of correct matches and the number of all matches) and correct-keep ratio (the ratio between the number of correct matches and the number of all correct matches). Note that the number of all correct matches is defined as number of matches if the distance between the accurate locations is less than 3 pixels in all matches. The distance between the accurate location can be computed by the provided homography for each pair of relative images. The comparison results are shown in Fig. 5. With respect to precision, all acquired from the FGC method are higher than those from the baseline method. Note that we do not draw the precision for the last pair of the Wall sequence, because it is undefined (0/0). Meanwhile, the numbers of correct matches still do not rapidly decrease. In our experiments, correct-keep ratio almost located in the range from 0.96 to 1.0, with the exception of the image sequences of Boat and Bark. Our method can noticeably eliminate false matches without rapidly decreasing on correct matches.

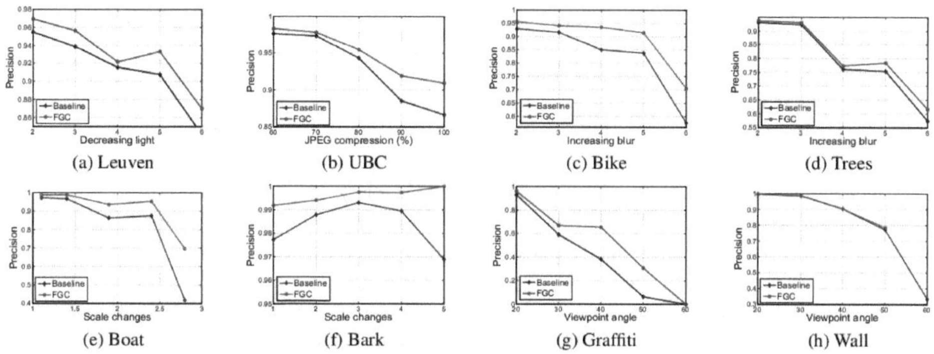

Fig. 5. Comparison results of precision for different categories from INRIA dataset

5 Conclusion

In this paper, we have proposed a novel algorithm for eliminating false matches, using geometric context based on MSER. This approach aims to build up an invariant coordinate, which can be regarded as the spatial information representation of features set. The proposed scheme contains three steps: (1) Reliable MSER pairs are obtained by MSER detector and matching; (2) Normalization of fitted ellipse from MSER; (3) Building invariant coordinate system. The experimental evaluation shows that our method is robust to most geometric and photometric transformations and scene disorders.

References

1. Guo, X., Cao, X.: Triangle-constraint for finding more good features. In: Int. Conf. Computer Vision Pattern Recognition, pp. 1393–1396. IEEE (2010)
2. Urban, M., Matas, J., Chum, O., Pajdla, T.: Robust wide baseline stereo from maximally stable extremal regions. In: British Machine Vision Conf., pp. 384–393 (2002)
3. Lee, S., Liu, Y.: Curved glide-reflection symmetry detection. In: Int. Conf. Computer Vision Pattern Recognition, pp. 1046–1053. IEEE (2009)
4. Brown, M., Lowe, D.: Recognising panoramas. In: Int. Conf. Comput. Vision, pp. 1218–1227 (2003)
5. Harris, C., Stephens, M.J.: A combined corner and edge detector. In: IEEE Alvey Vision Conference, vol. 20, pp. 147–151 (1988)
6. Mikolajczyk, K., Schmid, C.: A performance evaluation of local descriptors. IEEE Trans. Pattern Anal, Machine Intell. 27(10), 1615–1630 (2005)

7. Bay, H., Tuytelaars, T., Van Gool, L.: SURF: Speeded Up Robust Features. In: Leonardis, A., Bischof, H., Pinz, A. (eds.) ECCV 2006. LNCS, vol. 3951, pp. 404–417. Springer, Heidelberg (2006)
8. Lowe, D.: Distinctive image features from scale-invariant key-points. Int. J. of Computer Vision 60(2), 91–110 (2004)
9. Tuytelaars, T., Van Gool, L.: Matching widely separated views based on affine invariant regions. Int. J. of Computer Vision 59(1), 61–85 (2004)
10. Mikolajczyk, K., Schmid, C.: Scale and Affine invariant interest point detectors. Int. J. of Computer Vision 60(1), 63–86 (2004)
11. Kadir, T., Zisserman, A., Brady, M.: An Affine Invariant Salient Region Detector. In: Pajdla, T., Matas, J(G.) (eds.) ECCV 2004. LNCS, vol. 3021, pp. 228–241. Springer, Heidelberg (2004)
12. Leordeanu, M., Hebert, M.: A spectral technique for correspondence problems using pairwise constraints. IEEE Int. Conf. on Computer Vision 2, 1482–1489 (2005)
13. Fischler, M.A., Bolles, R.C.: Random Sample Consensus: A Paradigm for Model Fitting with Applications to Image Analysis and Automated Cartography. Comm. of the ACM 24(6), 381–395 (1981)
14. Rabin, J., Delon, J., Gousseau, Y.: Circular earth mover's distance for the comparison of local features. In: Int. Conf. Computer Vision Pattern Recognition, pp. 1–4 (2008)
15. Jiang, H., Yu, S.: Linear solution to scale and rotation invariant object matching. In: IEEE Conf. Comput. Vision Pattern Recog., pp. 2474–2481 (2009)
16. Nister, D., Stewenius, H.: Linear Time Maximally Stable Extremal Regions. In: Forsyth, D., Torr, P., Zisserman, A. (eds.) ECCV 2008, Part II. LNCS, vol. 5303, pp. 183–196. Springer, Heidelberg (2008)
17. Salembier, P., Oliveras, A., Garrido, L.: Anti-extensive Connected Operators for Image and Sequence Processing. IEEE Transactions on Image Processing 7(4), 555–570 (1998)

Online Service Quality in Social Commerce Websites

Jungwoo Lee, Myung Suk Cha*, and Cheulhyun Cho

Graduate School of Information, Yonsei University
Engineering Research Park B187N, 50 Yonsei-ro,
Seodaemun-gu, Seoul, 120-749, Republic of Korea
{jlee,dextercha,gochyun}@yonsei.ac.kr

Abstract. The popularity of SNS (Social Network Service), such as Facebook and Twitter, has created opportunities for new online business models (e-commerce). Among the new models, social commerce is a combination of two big digital trends: e-commerce and social media. In social commerce, social media assists customers with buying and selling products and services online, in the context of e-commerce. Social commerce is a more recent phenomenon and rapidly expanding in market; hence, it has not been studied as extensively. Therefore, the purpose of this study is to investigate the effects of service quality and recovery of social commerce websites on perceived value of consumer and consumer loyalty. The survey was conducted using the Parasuraman's E-S-Qual scale and E-RecS-Qual scale. In order to collect data, respondents were solicited by email, directing them to the survey site. A total of 137 data points were collected from people who frequently use social commerce websites. Then, multiple regression analysis was conducted using SPSS version 18.0. The research evidence suggests that the perceived value and customer loyalty are affected the most by online service recovery's 'responsiveness' factor in the social commerce website. On the other hand, 'efficiency' and 'system availability' factors of online service quality were found to be not significant enough to affect the perceived value of thc consumer. Furthermore, 'system availability' and 'compensation' factors of online service quality and recovery were also found to be not significant enough to affect customer loyalty. The findings of this study suggest that social commerce companies can make use of these findings by applying the associated principles in their marketing strategy. Also, the findings contribute to the extension of the literature in the application of the E-S-Qual and E-RecS-Qual scales to social commerce service quality and recovery.

Keywords: Social Commerce, Social Network Service, Service Quality, Service Recovery, Perceived Value, Customer Loyalty.

1 Introduction

The modern development and proliferation of the information communication technology (ICT) has allowed people to go online ubiquitously. According to the Korean

* Corresponding author.

V. Khachidze et al. (Eds.): iCETS 2012, CCIS 332, pp. 335–351, 2012.

government, the distribution rate of the Internet and computers was 81.8% and 81.9% per household, in the third quarter of 2011. With such exponential growth of distribution rate, the e-commerce (electronic commerce) market has grown accordingly. In addition, corporations are recognizing the internet as an important channel for providing products and services to their consumers. In 2011 the e-commerce market has grown 18.2% compared to the previous year, or approximately 244,000,000,000,000 won (equivalent to about 207,000,000 US dollars)[1].

Furthermore, the dispersion of mobile devices, such as smart phones and tablets, has made it easier for consumers to connect to the internet ubiquitously. Such changes in the ICT environment has also given rise to new online business models. Among these new business models, Social Commerce is the most recently developed. The word "Social Commerce" was first introduced by Yahoo's[1] "Pick List" service in the year 2005. Afterwards, the success of Groupon[2] in 2008 led to the dispersion of Social Commerce as a business model. In Korea, there are Big Three Social Commerce companies: Ticketmonster, Coupang and WeMakePrice. However, Groupon has entered the Korean market as of March of 2011 and Google[3] is conducting a beta test on their 'Google Offers' service, adding to the competition.

The distinction between traditional e-commerce and Social Commerce is that, while traditional e-commerce enhances the purchasing power of consumers and raises the discount rate by attracting as many consumers as possible, Social Commerce offers a high discount within a limited quantity and time to induce customers' purchasing needs. The broad definition of Social Commerce is a form of Internet-based "Social Media" that allows people to actively participate in the marketing and selling of products and services in online marketplaces and communities. In Korea, it is commonly defined as a group purchase via Social Network Service (SNS)[2]. Social Commerce has several advantages over other forms of online business models. First, for corporations, it is cost beneficial that SNS carries out the word-of-mouth role of marketing, without much effort on the part of corporations. Second, from the perspective of consumers, they can review feedback, such as price and quality information of the product or service, from other consumers. This allows consumers to make better decisions on purchasing products and services.

Currently, there is no definite way to classify the types of Social Commerce. However, Kim and Lee (2011) have identified six types of Social Commerce; (1) 'Flash

---

[1] Yahoo! Inc. is an internet corporation in the United States. It provides internet services, such as search engine, e-mail, advertising, online mapping and social media. It is one of the largest websites in the United States. It was founded by Jerry Yang and David Filo in January 1994 and was incorporated on March 1, 1995.

[2] Groupon Inc. is an e-commerce corporation in the United States, launched in November 2008. The company's business model features "Groupon" (a portmanteau derived from "group coupon") which becomes available for actual use if a certain number of people sign up for the offer. The company operates in North America, Europe, Asia and South America.

[3] Google Inc. is an internet corporation in the United States. It offers various internet & software services, such as search engine, e-mail, cloud computing, software and advertising technologies. The company was founded by Larry Page and Sergey Brin and incorporated on September 4, 1998.

Sale', (2) 'Group Purchase', (3) 'Social Shopping ', (4) 'Social Shopping Apps', (5) 'Purchase Sharing' and (6) 'Personal Shopper'[3, 4]. The 'Flash Sale' is a time-limited offer of high discounts. This system offers a win-win situation for both retailers and consumers by building brand loyalty and selling surplus stock within a short span of time for the retailers, and for consumers, offering high discount rates on a product or service. The 'Group Purchase' offers a product or service which becomes available only if a certain number of people sign up for the offer within the time-limit. 'Social Shopping' is where the consumers find online shopping sites with good deals, and share the information among consumers. 'Social Shopping Apps' include mobile applications where consumers can share their shopping experience within a built-in community. 'Purchase Sharing' analyzes the consumers' purchase record through credit card usage information and offers target marketing. Finally, the 'Personal Shopper' is a community based system where consumers can share feedback and information on specific deals, to make better decisions on purchases. In conclusion, these types of Social Commerce utilize the word-of-mouth marketing effect through the use of the Social Network.

Table 1. The Distinction between Traditional e-Commerce and Social Commerce

Factors	e-Commerce	Social Commerce
Core Concept	Opening and sharing of commerce platform	Joint system of commerce platform and SNS
Change Motive	Mash-up, Open API	SNS, Mobile, AR, LBS
Rationality Criteria	Collective Intelligence	Social Intelligence
Commerce Platform	Web	Social Web, On-line and Off-line
Transaction Mechanism	Monetary	Monetary, Word-of-Mouth
Principal Agent	Seller	Consumer

The topic of our study is important and timely given the growing importance of service quality in the success of Social Commerce online business models. The findings of our study will provide useful information that will guide Social Commerce corporations to evaluate their current service performance by analyzing their online service quality. However, our study is limited to the Korean Social Commerce market.

2 Literature Review

2.1 Online Service Quality

Service quality, in general, is defined as the difference between expected service and perceived service. [5-7] In principle, the online service quality is based on the traditional service quality concept. The traditional service quality refers to the quality of all *non-internet-based* consumer interactions and experiences with product or service providers [8]. Therefore, to measure the online service quality, it is important to consider the different characteristics of the Internet. Thus, over the years, some academic researchers have developed scales to measure online service quality.

In 2001, Yoo & Donthu (2001) developed a scale to measure online service quality, SITEQUAL. It is comprised of 4 dimensions and 9 items. The 4 dimensions are (1) ease of use, (2) aesthetic site quality, (3) processing speed and (4) security. However, SITEQUAL is criticized for not including all the perspectives of the purchasing process. Therefore, it cannot evaluate online service quality comprehensively [8, 9].

Wolfinbarger & Gilly (2003) focused on online retail businesses and created eTailQ. They developed a 14-item scale using focus groups, a sorting task, and an online-customer-panel survey. eTailQ has four dimensions: (1) customer service, (2) security/privacy, (3) website design and (4) fulfillment/reliability [10].

Barnes & Vidgen (2000; 2001a; 2001b; 2002), through their extensive research, have created another scale, WebQual. There are four versions of WebQual and the newest is WebQual 4.0. WebQual 4.0 is comprised of 3 dimensions: (1) usability, (2) information and (3) service interaction, including 22 items [11-14].

Bauer et al. (2006) developed their 25-item scale, the eTransQual, based on handling processes of e-commerce. It consists of 5 dimensions: (1) functionality/design, (2) enjoyment, (3) process, (4) reliability and (5) responsiveness [15].

The most recently created scale is the e-SELFQUAL by Ding et al. (2011). Their scale can be used to evaluate the relationships between online service quality and customer satisfaction, as well as loyalty in e-retailing. It is made of 4 dimensions and 11 items. The dimensions are (1) perceived control, (2) service convenience, (3) customer service and (4) service fulfillment.

Among these online service quality measurement scales, the most renowned is the E-S-QUAL. E-S-QUAL was created by Parasuraman et al. (2005) in 2005 as an extension of the service quality scale, SERVQUAL [8]. They defined online service quality as 'the extent to which a Web site facilitates efficient and effective shopping, purchasing, and delivery.' E-S-QUAL consists of four dimensions; (1) efficiency, (2) system availability, (3) fulfillment and (4) Privacy, with 22 items [8]. During the process of developing E-S-QUAL, a preliminary scale was developed and tested on consumers of amazon.com and walmart.com. As a result of this test, they have identified dimensions and items related to service recovery. Thus, they separated service recovery scale, the E-RecS-QUAL, consisting of 3 dimensions; (1) responsiveness, (2) compensation and (3) contact [8].

While these scales provide useful tools to evaluate web site quality, they do not measure the online service quality comprehensively. For example, SITEQUAL by Yoo & Donthu (2001) provides only the technical quality of a web site, rather than the service quality provided to consumers. Also, in the case of WebQual by Barnes & Vidgen (2000;2001a;2001b;2002), their scale does not capture all aspects of the purchasing process. Thus, the scale does not capture comprehensive online service quality [8]. On the other hand, E-S-QUAL and E-RecS-Qual by Parasuraman et al. (2005) captures pre- and post- online service aspects which comprehensively measures the online service quality. In addition, E-S-QUAL[4] has been extensively researched in various conceptual level and empirical level studies, including the works of Meng et al. (2009), Marimon et al. (2009), Boshoff (2007), Ingle & Connolly (2996), and Kim et al. (2006) [8, 16-21].

---

[4] Hereafter, E-S-QUAL and E-RecS-QUAL are referred to as just E-S-QUAL, as it is one model concept.

Table 2. Online Service Quality Measurement Scales

Authors	Scale	Dimensions
Yoo & Donthu (2001)	SITEQUAL	ease of use, aesthetic site quality, processing speed, security
Wolfinbarger & Gilly (2003)	eTailQ	customer service, security/privacy, website design, fulfillment/reliability
Barnes & Vidgen (2000; 2001a; 2001b; 2002)	WebQual 4.0	usability, information, service interaction
Parasuraman et al. (2005)	E-S-QUAL & E-RecS-QUAL	efficiency, system availability, fulfillment, privacy; responsiveness, compensation, contact
Bauer et al. (2006)	eTransQual	functionality/design, enjoyment, process, reliability, responsiveness
Ding et al. (2011)	e-SELFQUAL	perceived control, service convenience, customer service, service fulfillment.

Meng et al. (2009) and Eda et al. (2010) tested the validity and reliability of E-S-QUAL as a scale to measure the online service quality in different geographical and cultural settings. Meng et al. (2009) collected data from groups of Chinese and African Americans. Also, Eda et al. (2010) collected data from groups of Turkish nationals. The results showed that E-S-QUAL is highly valid and reliable in different geographic and cultural settings. Furthermore, Ingle & Connolly (2007) argued that E-S-QUAL is effective in diverse e-commerce settings. Thus, in this research E-S-QUAL scale is adopted to capture extensive online service attributes of Social Commerce websites.

2.2 Perceived Value

In general, the definition of perceived value is as a trade-off between total benefits received and total sacrifices. Carman (1978) established a model of values that influence lifestyle and consumption behaviors where an individual's lifestyle is directly influenced by his/her values. Thus, value acts as a standard when consumers purchase products or services [22]. Zeithaml (1988) defines perceived value as "the consumer's overall assessment of the utility of a product or service based on perceptions of what is received and what is given"[6]. She argued that some consumers perceive value when there is a low price and some perceive value when there is a balance between quality and price. In her results, different consumers weighed components of perceived value differently. She also found that some consumers obtained value from all relevant 'get' and 'give' components, leading to her definition of perceived value. On the other hand, Bolton & Drew (1991) argued the perception of value as a trade-off between only quality and price is too simplistic and needs more sophisticated measures to understand how consumers value products and services [23]. However, it is supported by many researchers, such as Dodds & Monroe (1985), Parasuraman et al. (1985), that willingness to buy (purchase intentions) is a key consequence of value perceptions. Thus, this study defines the perceived value as the trade-off of what consumer expects to receive for what is paid.

2.3 Loyalty

According to Bitner (1996) as the loyalty of consumers rises, the corporation can expect increase in purchase frequency and quantity, decrease in expense, and favorable word-of-mouth marketing effects. Therefore, consumer loyalty is a factor that promotes repetitive purchase by the consumers to enhance the benefit for the corporations [24]. Anderson & Srinivasan (2003) also defined consumer loyalty, in the context of e-commerce, as "the customer's favorable attitude toward an electronic business resulting in repeat buying behavior" [25]. They argued websites with high consumer loyalty will enjoy repetitive purchase of products and word-of-mouth marketing effects by the consumers, without much effort of marketing by the website. Also, Holland & Baker (2001) found through their research that consumers with high loyalty will bookmark certain websites and revisit them often. Furthermore, they will stay on the website for longer periods of time [26]. Thus, in this research, the loyalty to Social Commerce websites is defined as a favorable behavior and intention of consumers toward certain products and services of Social Commerce websites.

3 Online Research Method

3.1 Research Model

The purpose of this study is to analyze the Social Commerce website's online service quality and its effect on consumers' perceived value and loyalty. To achieve this, the E-S-QUAL scale, originally published by Parasuraman et al. (2005), was adopted. Also, to ensure the appropriateness of the scale in the environment of Social Commerce, experts were asked to review the validity of survey items. The expert group included professors and Ph.D candidates who have experience in online service quality researches. The sample group was selected based on their experiences of purchase from four major Social Commerce websites, 'Coupang,' 'Ticketmonster,' 'Groupon' and 'WeMakePrice,' in Korea. Before the survey was conducted, all samples were given an interview to describe their experience with these websites. The result showed many of the interviewees were not aware of or experienced a refund. This was due to the refund policy of the websites. The coupons or products consumers purchased were not allowed to be used after a certain period of time. Also, for some products or services, there were restrictions on the extension of the expiry date or refunds. Therefore, in this research the 'compensation' dimension was removed. The final research model is as shown in fig.1.

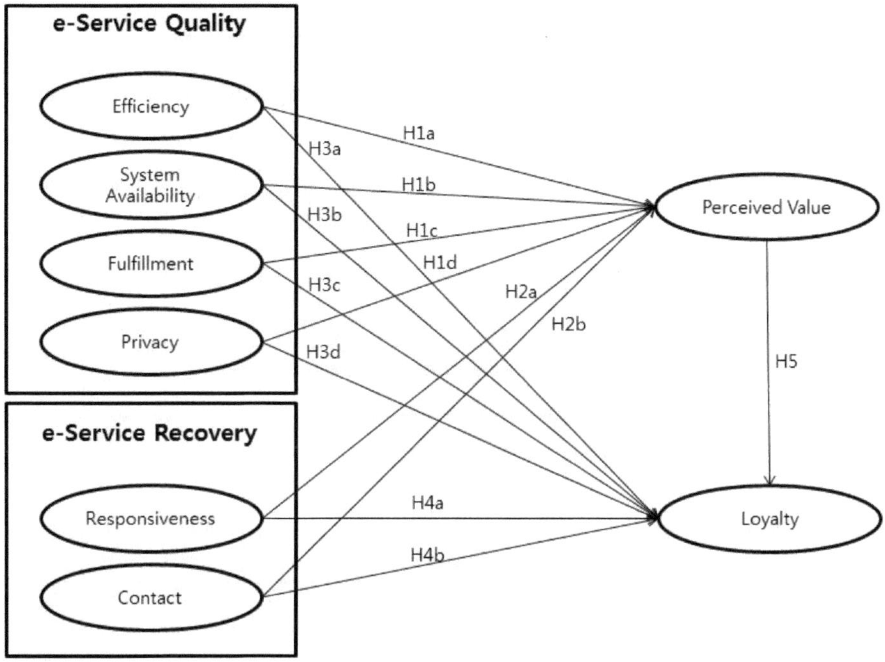

Fig. 1. Research Model

3.2 Operational Definition

In order to measure Social Commerce websites' online service quality and online service recovery, variables from E-S-QUAL and E-RecS-QUAL were used. Based on definitions proposed by Parasuraman et al. (2005), the operational definitions in this research are as follows: (1) 'efficiency' is defined as 'the ease and speed of accessing and using the Social Commerce website'; (2) 'fulfillment' is defined as 'the extent to which the Social Commerce website's promises about order delivery and item availability are fulfilled'; (3) 'system availability' is defined as 'the correct technical function of the Social Commerce website'; (4) 'privacy' is defined as 'the degree to which the Social Commerce website is safe and protects customer information'; (5) 'responsiveness' is defined as 'effective handling of problems and returns through the Social Commerce websites'; (6) 'contact' is defined as 'the availability of assistance through telephone or online representatives'; (7) 'perceived value' is defined as 'the trade-off of what consumer expects to receive for what is paid'; (8) 'loyalty' is defined as 'the favorable behavior and intention of consumers towards certain product and service of Social Commerce website.' Based on these definitions, the survey items were constructed.

Table 3. The Operational Definitions

Variables		Operational Definitions	References
Online Service Quality (E-S-QUAL)	Efficiency	the ease and speed of accessing and using the Social Commerce website	Parasuraman et al.(2005)
	Fulfillment	the extent to which the Social Commerce website's promises about order delivery and item availability are fulfilled	Parasuraman et al.(2005)
	System avail-ability	the correct technical function of the Social Commerce website	Parasuraman et al.(2005)
	Privacy	the degree to which the Social Commerce website is safe and protects customer in-formation	Parasuraman et al.(2005)
Online Service Recovery (E-RecS-QUAL)	Responsive-ness	effective handling of problems and returns through the Social Commerce websites	Parasuraman et al.(2005),
	Contact	the availability of assistance through tele-phone or online representatives	Parasuraman et al.(2005)
Perceived Value		the trade-off of what consumer expects to receive for what is paid	Parasuraman et al.(2005), Steenkamp et al.(2006)
Loyalty		the favorable behavior and intention of consumers towards certain product and service of Social Commerce website	Parasuraman et al.(2005), Anderson & Srinivasan(2003)

3.3 Research Hypothesis

3.3.1 Online Service Quality and Perceived Value

The concept of online service quality is derived from the traditional service quality concept to better fit the internet environment. Parasuraman et al. (2005) claim that the core concept of online and offline service quality is the same. Therefore, online service recovery's 'responsiveness' and 'contact' factors reflect the traditional service quality concept [8]. Bolton & Drew (1991) argued that perceived service value and perceived service quality are two different concepts. Thus, through their rigorous research, they have found that quality positively affects value. Rust, Zahorik and Keinngham (1996) also argued that the value of the service, quality and price have a high correlation. Therefore, if the service quality is highly evaluated, the service value also increases [23]. Hence, the following hypotheses were constructed:

H1a: Online service quality's 'efficiency' will have a positive influence on perceived value.
H1b: Online service quality's 'system availability' will have a positive influence on perceived value.

H1c: Online service quality's 'fulfillment' will have a positive influence on perceived value.

H1d: Online service quality's 'privacy' will have a positive influence on perceived value.

H2a: Online service recovery's 'responsiveness' will have a positive influence on perceived value.

H2b: Online service recovery's 'contact' will have a positive influence on perceived value.

3.3.2 Online Service Quality and Loyalty

The relationship between online service quality and loyalty has been extensively researched over the past years. Ostrowski et al. (1993) have focused their study on the commercial flight industry. Their results indicate consumers perceive value created by the service quality of the flight attendants, rather than the price aspects. Based on their findings, they argued the importance of service quality in building and maintaining consumer loyalty [27]. Maloles (1997) focused on the banking industry and found service quality and consumer satisfaction influence customer loyalty. Some researchers have studied in the context of the online environment and found that online service quality has an influence over loyalty [28, 29]. Therefore, in this research, the following hypotheses were constructed:

H3a: Online service quality's 'efficiency' will have a positive influence on loyalty.

H3b: Online service quality's 'system availability' will have a positive influence on loyalty.

H3c: Online service quality's 'fulfillment' will have a positive influence on loyalty.

H3d: Online service quality's 'privacy' will have a positive influence on loyalty.

H4a: Online service recovery's 'responsiveness' will have a positive influence on loyalty.

H4b: Online service recovery's 'contact' will have a positive influence on loyalty.

3.3.3 Perceived Value and Loyalty

The concept of perceived value inducing loyalty has been extensively studied over the past years. Bolton and Drew (1991) argued that perceived value maintains the seller and consumer relationship. This continuous relationship causes consumers to spread favorable word-of-mouth [23]. Cronin et al. (1997) also argued that they were able to explain the relationship better by adding the concept of value to the service in explaining consumer's purchase intentions [30]. Furthermore, Parasuraman et al. (2005) and Grewal (2000) argued that product quality and price can be imitated easily by competitors, whereas service quality, perceived value and loyalty are not easily imitated, thus substantially increasing corporate performance. In addition, they argued that perceived value has substantial influence on the loyalty of consumers. Therefore, in this research, the following hypothesis is constructed:

H5: Perceived value will have a positive influence on loyalty.

4 Results

4.1 Data Collection

The data collection was conducted through online surveys using Google Docs. The surveys were sent out to a random sample of internet users. A total of 150 surveys were collected. Among these, 13 respondents were discarded for the reason of no experience with Social Commerce websites and insufficient response. To analyze the general characteristics of the sample demographics, frequency analysis was carried out on variables such as gender and age. The results showed that 84 were male (61.3%) and 53 were female (38.7%), resulting in a slightly higher proportion of male respondents. 6 were 16-21 years of age (4.4%); 66 were 22-27 years of age (48.2%); 57 were 28-32 years of age (41.6%); 5 were 33-37 years of age (3.6%); and 3 aged 38 or older (2.2%). The devices used for connecting to the Social Commerce website were as follows; 89 people used PC (including laptops) (64.9%); 46 people used Smart Phones (33.6%); and 2 people used Smart Pads (1.5%). The answer with the highest frequency in the average usage rate was 'less than twice a week' (68.6%).

Table 4. Characteristics of the Sample Demographics

Classification		Frequency	Percentage (%)
Gender	Male	84	61.3
	Female	53	38.7
Age	16-21	6	4.4
	22-27	66	48.2
	28-32	57	41.6
	33-37	5	3.6
	38 or higher	3	2.2
Education	High school	2	1.5
	University	88	64.1
	Graduate School	47	34.4
Devices	PC(including laptops)	89	64.9
	Smart Phones	46	33.6
	Smart Pads	2	1.5
Mainly used Social Commerce website	Coupang	59	43.1
	Ticketmonster	50	36.5
	Groupon	14	10.2
	WeMakePrice	11	8.0
	Etc.	3	2.2
Frequency of usage (per week)	Less than twice	94	68.6
	3-6 times	28	20.4
	6-9 times	11	8.0
	9-12 times	2	1.5
	12 or more	2	1.5

4.2 Reliability and Validity Assessment

In order to test reliability and validity, the exploratory factor analysis (EFA) was conducted. Factor extractions were conducted through principle component analysis and rotation method of verimax. Tables 5 and 6 present the item loadings from the exploratory factor analysis (EFA). As the tables show, online service quality, online service recovery, perceived value and loyalty's factor loadings are above 0.5, and clearly tied into each factor. Thus, the result demonstrated the validity of all variables. In addition, Table 7 demonstrates the coefficient alpha values that range from 0.801 to 0.935, exceeding the conventional minimum of 0.7 [31] and high internal consistency, thus, the reliability of each dimension. In conclusion, these results show good support for the validity and reliability of the scales and factor structures.

Table 5. EFA Results of Online Service Quality and Online Service Recovery

Factors			Factor 1	Factor 2	Factor 3	Factor 4	Factor 5	Factor 6
Online Servicc Quality (E-S-QUAL)	Efficiency	EFF1	.793	-.010	.227	.058	-.129	.230
		EFF2	.768	.080	.076	.152	.235	.096
		EFF3	.765	.118	.034	.118	.135	.017
		EFF4	.683	.337	-.027	.163	.224	.-.012
		EFF5	.670	.249	-.127	.258	.291	.060
		EFF6	.613	.217	.250	-.120	-.028	.141
	System Availa-bility	AV1	.239	.792	.043	.005	.235	.114
		AV2	.087	.765	.230	.173	.-.034	.090
		AV3	.289	.728	.319	.254	.006	.073
		AV4	.356	.576	.255	.576	.119	.259
	Fulfillment	FULL1	.133	.192	.832	.054	.274	.049
		FULL2	.080	.159	.746	.111	.248	.160
		FULL3	.129	.146	.604	.182	.183	.257
		FULL4	.051	.369	.598	.237	.434	-.053
		FULL5	-.034	.219	.547	.267	.417	.099
	Privacy	PRI1	.203	.044	.249	.830	.113	.030
		PRI2	.207	.135	.157	.737	.147	.317
		PRI3	.081	.248	.117	.666	.327	.246

Table 5. (*continued*)

Factors			Factor 1	Factor 2	Factor 3	Factor 4	Factor 5	Factor 6
Online Service Recovery (E-RecS-QUAL)	Responsiveness	RES1	.213	.266	.209	.129	.805	.131
		RES2	.249	.141	.258	.138	.756	.204
		RES3	.021	.016	.276	.088	.743	.039
		RES4	.190	-.045	.398	.233	.637	.253
		RES5	.160	-.054	.492	.125	.574	.283
	Contact	CON1	.168	.193	.197	.234	.126	.790
		CON2	.168	.130	.200	.262	.147	.756
		CON3	.077	.453	-.005	.254	.401	.506

Table 6. EFA Results for Perceived Value and Loyalty

Factors		Factors 1	Factors 2
Perceived Value	VAL1	.857	.216
	VAL2	.748	.436
	VAL3	.711	.482
	VAL4	.654	.473
Loyalty	LO1	.367	.852
	LO2	.317	.832
	LO3	.334	.794
	LO4	.420	.789
	LO5	.397	.779

Table 7. Cronbach's Alpha of Factors

Factors		Cronbach's Alpha
Online Service Quality (E-S-QUAL)	Efficiency	.859
	System Availability	.841
	Fulfillment	.868
	Privacy	.824
Online Service Recovery (E-RecS-QUAL)	Responsiveness	.900
	Contact	.801
Perceived Value		.867
Loyalty		.935

4.3 Hypothesis Testing

For the purpose of hypothesis testing, multiple regression analysis was conducted. The result is shown in Table 8 and indicates 5 points.

First, the result indicates that, in the relationship between online service quality's independent variables and perceived value, the adjusted R^2 value is 0.446. Also, 'efficiency' and 'system availability' are found not to be significant at the significance level of 95%, hence H1a and H1b are rejected. On the other hand, the t-values of 'fulfillment' and 'privacy' are at 3.332 ($p<0.01$) and 4.007 ($p<0.01$). Therefore, online service quality's 'fulfillment' and 'privacy' factors have a positive influence on perceived value.

Second, in the relationship between online service recovery's independent variables and perceived value, the adjusted R^2 value is 0.435. Also, the t-values of 'responsiveness' and 'contact' are 6.524 ($p<0.01$) and 3.422 ($p<0.01$) respectively. This indicates that online service recovery's 'responsiveness' and 'contact' both have positive influences on perceived value. In addition, p-value of 'responsiveness' and 'contact' are 0.000 and 0.001 each, indicating considerably reliable results.

Third, in the relationship between online service quality's independent variables and loyalty, the adjusted R^2 value is 0.468. However, 'system availability' has a significance level at 5%, indicating 'system availability' does not have an influence over loyalty. On the contrary, 'efficiency,' 'fulfillment' and 'privacy' have t-values of 2.765 ($p<0.01$), 4.458 ($p<0.01$) and 4.868 ($p<0.01$), accordingly. Thus, 'efficiency,' 'fulfillment' and 'privacy' have positive influences on loyalty.

Table 8. Hypothesis Testing

Dependent Variable	Independent Variable		R^2	Adjusted R^2	F	β	t-value	p-value	Hypothesis	
Perceived Value	Online Service Quality (E-S-QUAL)	Efficiency	.463	.446	27.807	.141	1.802	.074	H1a	Rejected
		System Availability				.144	1.708	.090	H1b	Rejected
		Fulfillment				.272	3.332	.001	H1c	Accepted
		Privacy				.316	4.007	.000	H1d	Accepted
	Online Service Recovery (E-RecS-QUAL)	Responsive-ness	.443	.435	53.352	.493	6.524	.000	H2a	Accepted
		Contact				.259	3.422	.001	H2b	Accepted
Loyalty	Online Service Quality (E-S-QUAL)	Efficiency	.484	.468	30.302	.211	2.765	.007	H3a	Accepted
		System Availability				-.100	-1.212	.228	H3b	Rejected
		Fulfillment				.344	4.458	.000	H3c	Accepted
		Privacy				.389	4.868	.000	H3d	Accepted
	Online Service Recovery (E-RecS-QUAL)	Responsive-ness	.483	.475	62.599	.623	8.553	.000	H4a	Accepted
		Contact				.123	1.686	.094	H4b	Rejected
Loyalty	Perceived Value		.614	.611	214.388	.783	14.642	.000	H5	Accepted

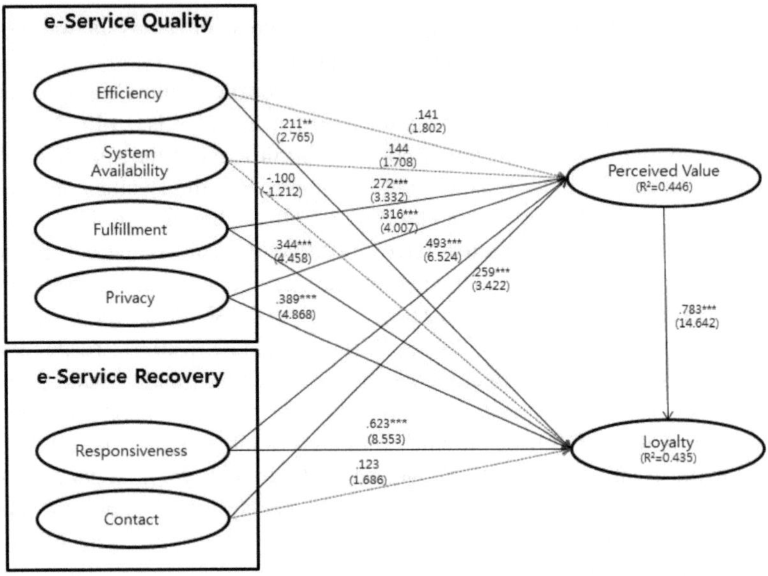

Fig. 2. The Result

Fourth, in the relationship between online service recovery's independent variables and loyalty, the adjusted R^2 value is 0.475. However, the 'contact' factor has a significance level of 5%, indicating rejection. On the contrary, 'responsiveness' has a t-value of 8.553 (p<0.01), and therefore has positive influence on loyalty.

Lastly, in the relationship between perceived value and loyalty, the adjusted R^2 valuc is 0.611 and the t-value is 14.643 (p<0.01). The result shows that the perceived value has a positive influence over loyalty.

5 Conclusion and Discussion

The purpose of this research was to examine the relationship among online service quality and recovery, perceived value and loyalty in the Social Commerce context. By adopting a reliable and valid measurement scale, the E-S-QUAL, we were able to conduct an empirical analysis. The result indicates that the factors of online service quality and recovery have positive influences on customers' perceived value and loyalty. Also, online service quality's 'efficiency' does not have a significant influence on perceived value, but has a significantly positive influence over loyalty. Furthermore, online service recovery's 'contact' does not have a great influence on loyalty, but has a positive influence over perceived value. It is also found that perceived value has a significant influence over loyalty.

We can derive the following major implications from this research. First, consumers' perceived value and loyalty are most influenced by online service recovery's 'responsiveness.' In other words, since the role of Social Commerce websites is providing a marketplace for sellers and consumers, they are required to respond to consumers' demand for cancelation or refund in a timely manner. Kim & Lee (2012) also indicated such needs in their studies on service quality of Social Commerce websites. Their results showed that factors regarding responsiveness were rated the lowest in consumer satisfaction[32]. Therefore, a system that can respond to customer complaints is necessary. Second, 'system availability' was not found to be significant in perceived value and loyalty. We can make an inference that problems faced by consumers are not directly related to the use of Social Commerce websites, but influenced by external factors. These external factors can be the consumer's environments, such as, the consumer's PC system and internet connectivity. Lastly, the existing studies on e-commerce websites and Social Commerce websites present marked differences. For example, studies on e-commerce websites have found that perceived value is not influenced by the 'privacy' factor [8, 16]. On the contrary, the studies on Social Commerce websites, including this research, have found the 'privacy' factor to influence perceived value. This coincides with the studies that state that 'privacy' is an important factor in Social Media. Since Social Commerce utilizes Social Media as a marketing tool, it is inevitable that 'privacy' is important factor for Social Commerce, as well.

The limitations of this research are as follows: First, the characteristic of Social Commerce service requires a group of people. Therefore, we must consider the social and cultural aspects of the service. However, in this research such aspects were neglected. Second, there are different types of Social Commerce services, such as flash sales, group purchase, social purchase and more. Third, this research was conducted in Korea and is based on the Korean Social Commerce market. Fourth, the 'compensation' factor of online service recovery was neglected. The consideration of these limitations in future study would contribute to a more comprehensive body of research.

References

1. Div, I.C. (ed.): StatisticsKorea: E-commerce and Cyber Shopping in 2011, Statistics Korea, p. 5 (2011)
2. Ryu, H.: The new change brought by mobile commerce. DIGIECO focus, KT Economics & Management Research Lab. (October 2010)
3. Kim, Y.: Social Commerce Market Status and Policy Issues. Broadcasting and Communications Policy 23, 41–63 (2011)
4. Lee, K., Noh, M.: A Study of Factors Influencing the Use of Social Commerce: Focusing Social Norm and Price Consciousness. Journal of Internet e-Commerce 11, 65–85 (2011)
5. Parasuraman, A., Zeithaml, V.A., Berry, L.L.: SERVQUAL: A Multiple-Item Scale for Measuring Consumer Perceptions of Service Quality. Journal of Retailing 64, 12–40 (1988)
6. Zeithaml, V.A.: Consumer Perceptions of Price, Quality, and Value: A Means-End Model and Synthesis of Evidence. The Journal of Marketing 52, 2–22 (1988)
7. Zeithaml, V.A., Parasuraman, A., Malhotra, A.: Service quality delivery through Web sites: A critical review of extant knowledge. Journal of the Academy of Marketing Science 30, 362–375 (2002)

8. Parasuraman, A., Zeithaml, V.A., Malhotra, A.: E-S-QUAL - A multiple-item scale for assessing electronic service quality. Journal of Service Research 7, 213–233 (2005)
9. Yoo, B., Donthu, N.: Developing a Scale to Measure the Perceived Quality of An Internet Shopping Site (SITEQUAL). Quarterly Journal of Electronic Commerce 2(1), 31–47 (2001)
10. Wolfinbarger, M., Gilly, M.C.: eTailQ: dimensionalizing, measuring and predicting etail quality. Journal of Retailing 79, 183–198 (2003)
11. Barnes, S.T., Vidgen, R.: WebQual: An Exploration of Web-site Quality. In: Proceedings of Eighth European Conference on Information System (EICS), pp. 298–305 (2000)
12. Barnes, S.T., Vidgen, R.: An Evaluation of Cyber-bookshops: The WebQual Method. International Journal of Electronic Commerce 6(1), 11–30 (2001)
13. Barnes, S.T., Vidgen, R.: Assessing the Quality of Auction Web Sites. In: Proceedings of the Hawaii International Conference on System Sciences (2001)
14. Barnes, S.T., Vidgen, R.: An Integrative Approach to the Assessment of e-Commerce Quality. Journal of Electronic Commerce Research 3(3), 114–127 (2002)
15. Bauer, H.H., Falk, T., Hammerschmidt, M.: eTransQual: A transaction process-based approach for capturing service quality in online shopping. Journal of Business Research 59, 866–875 (2006)
16. Mummalaneni, V., Juan, M.: An exploratory study of young Chinese customers' online shopping behaviors and service quality perceptions. Young Consumers 10, 157–169 (2009)
17. Boshoff, C.: A Psychometric Assessment of E-S-QUAL: a Scale to Measure Electronic Service Quality. Journal of Electronic Commerce Research 8, 101–114 (2007)
18. Ingle, S., Connolly, R.: Methodological and Research Issues Using E-S-QUAL to Measure Online Service Quality in Irish SMEs. Irish Journal of Management 27, 25–32 (2006)
19. Kim, M., Kim, J.-H., Lennon, S.J.: Online service attributes available on apparel retail web sites: an E-S-QUAL approach. Managing Service Quality 16, 51–77 (2006)
20. Meng, J., Mummalaneni, V.: Measurement Equivalency of Web Service Quality Instruments: A Test on Chinese and African American Consumers. Journal of International Consumer Marketing 22, 259–269 (2010)
21. Akinci, S., Atilgan-Inan, E., Aksoy, S.: Re-assessment of E-S-Qual and E-RecS-Qual in a pure service setting. Journal of Business Research 63, 232–240 (2010)
22. Carman, J.: Values and Consumption Pattern: A Closed Loop. Advanced in Consumer Research 5, 404–412 (1978)
23. Bolton, R.N., Drew, J.H.: A Multistage Model of Customers' Assessments of Service Quality and Value. Journal of Consumer Research 17, 375–384 (1991)
24. Bitner, M.J.: Evaluating Service Encounters: The Effects of Physical Surroundings and Employee Responses. The Journal of Marketing 54, 69–82 (1990)
25. Anderson, R.E., Srinivasan, S.S.: E-satisfaction and e-loyalty: a contingency framework. Psychology & Marketing 20, 123–138 (2003)
26. Holland, J., Menzel Baker, S.: Customer participation in creating site brand loyalty. Journal of Interactive Marketing 15, 34–45 (2001)
27. Ostrowski, P.L., O'Brien, T.V., Gordon, G.L.: Service quality and customer loyalty in the commercial airline industry. Journal of Travel Research 32, 16–24 (1993)
28. Ribbink, D., Riel, A.C.R.V., Lijander, V., Streukens, S.: Comfort your online customer: quality, trust and loyalty on the internet. Managing Service Quality 14 (2004)

29. Enzmann, M., Schneider, M.: Improving customer retention in e-commerce through a secure and privacy-enhanced loyalty system. Information Systems Frontiers 7, 359–370 (2005)
30. Cronin, J.J., Brady, M.K., Brand, R.R., Hightower Jr, R., Shemwell, D.J.: A cross-sectional test of the effect and conceptualization of service value. The Journal of Services Marketing 11, 375 (1997)
31. Nunnally, J.C.: Psychometric Theory. McGraw-Hill, New York (1967)
32. Jin, G.-S., Lee, J.-H.: Service Quality Factors Affecting Satisfaction and Repurchase Intention of Social Commerce. Journal of Contents 12, 311–321 (2012)

An Improved Algorithm for K-anonymity

Jing Zhang[1], Xiujun Gong[1], Zhipeng Han[1], and Siling Feng[2]

[1] School of Computer Science and Technology, Tianjin University, Weijin Rd No. 92, Tianjin, 300072, China
[2] College of Information Science & Technology, Hannan University Renmin Rd No. 58, Haikou, 570228, China
jing.zhang87@yahoo.cn, {gongxj,hanzhipeng}@tju.edu.cn, fengsiling2008@163.com

Abstract. K-anonymity is an important model that prevents joining attacks in privacy protecting. Many works have been conducted to achieve k-anonymity. OLA (Optimal Lattice Anonymization) is an efficient full-domain optimal algorithm among these works. The OLA algorithm uses a binary search to traverse the lattice and marks all the k-anonymous nodes, the process of which is time-consuming. In this paper, an improved algorithm based on OLA algorithm is proposed. We firstly computed the product of degree for each node in the lattice and selected the biggest one to judge whether it was k-anonymous; this changed the traversal sequence of binary search. Then, we introduced the conception of support from data mining, and augmented the structure of generalization hierarchy associated with the information of support. As a result there is no need to scan the entire data table repeatedly and we can find all k-anonymous nodes more efficiently.

Keywords: K-anonymity, OLA, Generalization Hierarchy, Degree, Privacy-protecting.

1 Introduction

1.1 Background

Presently, with the rapid growth of the information, more and more data is provided for people to share and use; at the same time, more and more attention has been paid to the privacy protection of released data. Thus, when releasing data we should both protect the privacy of the data and ensure data integrity as much as possible, then the data can be published. Protecting privacy while publishing microdata has long been recognized as a problem [1], [2]. Thereupon a method called K-anonymity was proposed. K-anonymity is a technique that prevents joining attacks by generalization or suppressing portions of the source data, so that no individual can be uniquely distinguished from a group of size k [3]. K-anonymity is simple and is easily implemented; it also can reduce information loss at the maximum extent while protecting personal privacy.

V. Khachidze et al. (Eds.): iCETS 2012, CCIS 332, pp. 352–360, 2012.

1.2 Related Works

There have been many works on computing k-anonymization, and three typical algorithms for k-anonymization are introduced [4].

The Datafly algorithm uses a heuristic to guide generalization once per attribute [5], [14]. The attribute with the most distinct values is generalized. Generalization continues by selecting a new attribute if the attribute does not satisfy k-anonymous; otherwise the algorithm runs to the end. The weakness of Datafly algorithm is that it does not necessarily provide k-minimal generalization, although it can be proved that its solutions always satisfy k-anonymity.

The Samarati algorithm conducts a binary search to find all nodes that satisfy k-anonymous [6], and then selects the nodes with the least steps as generalization nodes. Since there may be more than one such node, the algorithm selects one randomly or according to some criterion such as information loss metrics. However, the higher distance vector might have lower information loss, and the algorithm just selects the distance vector with the minimum height in lattice, which will not guarantee the result of the algorithm to always be globally optimal in this setting.

The Incognito algorithm traverses distance vectors in lattice through a bottom-up approach, combined with breadth-first strategy, to find all k-minimal distance vectors [8], [10]. After calculating the information loss according to a given information loss measurement, the algorithm selects the one with least loss to generalize. Since the Incognito traverses all the distance vectors in lattice, the result is globally optimal.

The OLA algorithm (Optimal Lattice Anonymization) [10], which is the foundation of our work, improves the Datafly algorithm and Incognito algorithm. It is an efficient full-domain optimal algorithm for k-anonymization. We will describe the OLA algorithm in detail in Sec. 2.2.

2 Materials and Methods

2.1 Basic Definitions

Quasi-Identifier Attribute. A quasi-identifier set is a minimal set of attributes in table T that can be joined with external information to de-identify individual records. For example, in Table 1, <Race,Date> is a quasi-identifier set.

Equivalence Classes. All the records that have the same values on the quasi-identifiers are called an equivalence class. For example, the set of the records {1, 3, 8} in Table 1 is an equivalence class. The sizes of equivalence class potentially change during de-identification.

Generalization Hierarchy. This refers to a set of nodes in a tree structure. All the values for each attribute can be found in the leaf nodes. The other nodes in the structure are the corresponding generalization values. Figure 1 and 2 are examples for attributes Race and Date.

Lattice. In Figure 3 there is an example for lattice. Every node in the lattice is a distance vector, the dimensionality of which is the number of quasi-identifier attributes, and the element is the height in the generalization hierarchy for each quasi-identifier attribute. The arrows represent the generalization relationships.

Generalization Strategy. A path from the lowest node to the top node in the lattice. For example, {[0,0],[0,1],[1,1],[1,2]} is a generalization strategy.

Information Loss Metrics. The generalization of a record into some generalized record has an associated cost in terms of information loss. There are several ways of defining that cost; e.g., the entropy measure [9], the tree measure [11], the Loss Metric (LM) [12], [13], the Ambiguity Metric (AM) [13], etc.

Table 1. An example of dataset including two quasi-identifier attributes

	Date	Race
1	01/01/08	Asian
2	01/02/08	Black
3	01/01/08	Asian
4	31/01/08	White
5	01/01/08	White
6	01/01/08	White
7	01/02/08	Black
8	01/01/08	Asian
9	31/01/08	Asian
10	01/01/08	White

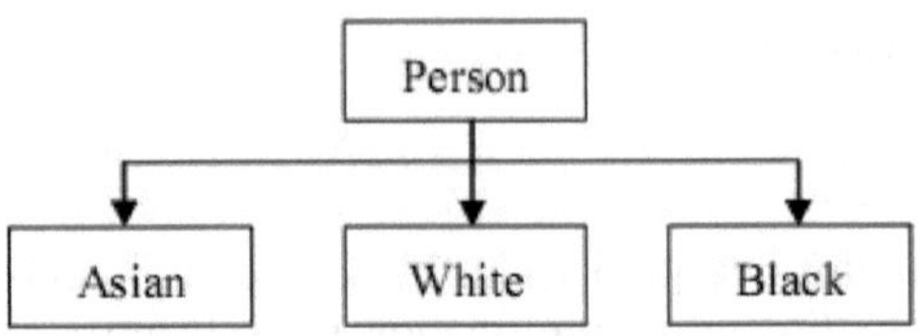

Fig. 1. Generalization hierarchy for Race

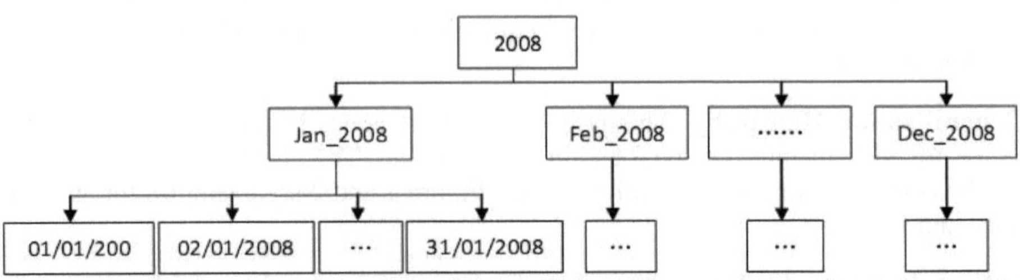

Fig. 2. Generalization hierarchy for Date

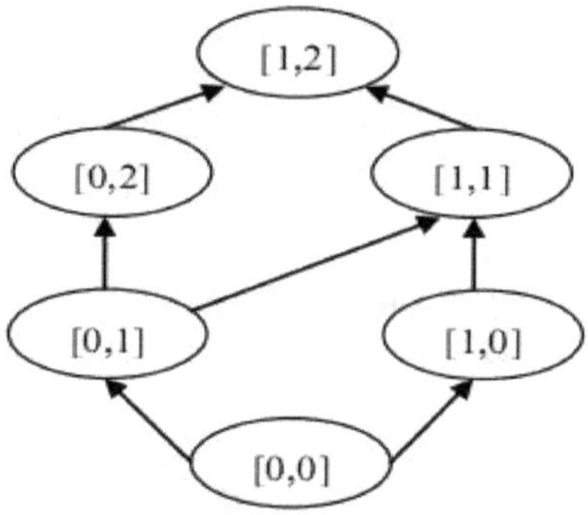

Fig. 3. A lattice for <Race,Date>

2.2 OLA (Optimal Lattice Anonymization) Algorithm

OLA is a full-domain optimal algorithm for de-identification. Usually, the generalization hierarchies for each quasi-identifier attribute have been given by the user (the owner of data) according to different anonymization requirements. These generalization hierarchies will form a lattice, in which there are many paths from the bottom node to the top node; each path is a generalization strategy.

The objective of OLA is to find the optimal node in the lattice. The optimal node is k-anonymous and has minimal information loss. First, for each generalization strategy, conduct a binary search to find all the k-anonymous nodes. There may be many k-anonymous nodes for each generalization strategy; only the k-anonymous node with the lowest height within the strategy is retained. For example, in Figure 3 both nodes <0,1> and <1,1> are k-anonymous, but they are both part of the same generalization strategy and <0,1> is below <1,1> in the lattice. This means that <0,1> will have less information loss on all the three metrics we considered. The node <0,1> is called a k-minimal node. These k-minimal nodes are then compared in terms of information loss, and the node with the smallest information loss is selected as the globally optimal solution. Because of the monotonicity property, the k-minimal node with the smallest information loss must also have the smallest information loss among all k-anonymous nodes in the lattice.

The most time-consuming computation in OLA is determining, for any node, whether it is a k-anonymous node. The most direct way is to read the source dataset into memory, then compute the size of the clusters in the source dataset according to generalization hierarchies and the height of generalization hierarchy in nodes of lattice, so that we can judge whether it is k-anonymous directly. Evidently, during information statistics there would be frequent reading and comparison string operations, which is time-consuming. We improve the algorithm with respect to this aspect and expect the improved algorithm would have better performance.

2.3 Our Improved Algorithm Based on OLA

To improve the efficiency, our algorithm changes the traversal sequence and devises a novel structure for the generalization hierarchy of quasi-identifier attributes to find all k-anonymous nodes.

Suppose Q is a generalized record; $<a_1,...,a_r>, a_j$ is a node in the generalization hierarchy for attribute j, for $1 \leq j \leq r$. The support of Q is defined as the set of records in the table that contain values in the leaf node associated with node a_j.

The conception of support was proposed for mining frequent itemsets for association rules in data mining [7], [11], [15], where k-frequent itemsets and k-anonymous nodes have much in common. In Table 2, we provide some examples of the supports of some generalized records.

Table 2. Supports of some generalized records

Generalized record	Support
01/01/08	{1,3,5,6,8,10}
01/02/08	{2,7}
31/01/08	{4,9}
Asian	{1,3,8,9}
White	{4,5,6,10}
Black	{2,7}
Jan_08	{1,3,4,5,6,8,9,10}
Feb_08	{2,7}
Person	{1,2,3,4,5,6,7,8,9,10}
2008	{1,2,3,4,5,6,7,8,9,10}

We can then describe our novel structure of the generalization hierarchy, and introduce how to efficiently find k-anonymous nodes in lattice using this structure.

2.3.1 Compute Supports Using New Structure

In order to find all k-anonymous nodes in lattice efficiently, we will augment the generalization hierarchy structures in a manner that will allow us to compute the support of any given nodes efficiently. To that end, we associate each leaf in the generalization hierarchy with a list that holds the indices of all records in the table that contain the value in that leaf. An example is shown in figure 4.

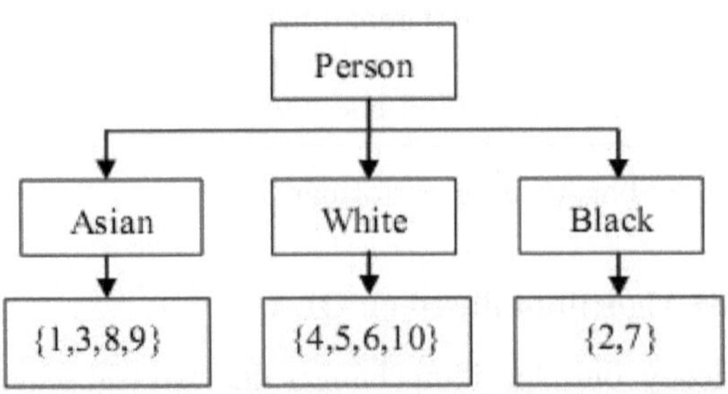

Fig. 4. New hierarchy for Race after augmenting

We will then introduce how to compute the supports for other nodes efficiently, based on this structure. If we wish to compute the support of the generalized record $< a_1,...,a_r >$, where a_j is a node in the generalization hierarchy for attribute j, then we must simply intersect the supports of each of the sets of records that are associated with the r nodes in the record. For example, if we wish to compute the support of the generalized record <Jan_08, White>, we firstly compute the support of node <Jan_08> and the support of <White>, and then intersect the two lists. The first list is {1,3,4,5,6,8,9,10} (it is the union of the supports of the node <01/01/08> and <31/01/08>), while the second list is {4,5,6,10}. The support of <Jan_08, White> is the corresponding intersection, {4, 5, 6, 10}. If k = 3, then the generalized record <Jan_08, White> is k-anonymous. We must judge all such generalized records corresponding to a node in lattice. If they are all k-anonymous, we can say this node in lattice is k-anonymous.

Computing the generalized record support in such a manner is much more efficient than traversing the complete database and inspecting each record. After making one pass over the entire database, the algorithm needs only to mine these compact generalization hierarchy structures instead of going again over the source data table.

The lattice is large if there are many quasi-identifier attributes. When finding k-anonymous nodes we need to traverse the lattice, and the OLA conducts a binary search and inspects all the nodes in each layer. Here we change the sequence of traversing lattice, and must therefore compute the product of degree for each node in the lattice.

2.3.2 Change the Sequence of Traversing Lattice

The out-degree for a node in lattice is the number of its parent nodes, and the number of its child nodes is the in-degree. The product of degree is the result of the product of in-degree and out-degree.

In the improved algorithm, we need to compute the product of degree for each node in lattice, and then sort all the nodes according to their products. The node whose product is the biggest will be selected, and then judged whether it is k-anonymous using the information of supports in front step.

The OLA algorithm marks quite a number of nodes when traversing lattice and the goal is to find the k-minimal node in each generalization strategy as quickly as possible. That is, we should mark as many of the nodes as possible when finding k-minimal nodes. Our algorithm also prunes the search space by implementing two basic ideas. The first idea is that if a node is k-anonymous, all of its ancestor nodes will also be k-anonymous. The second idea is that if a node is not k-anonymous, all of its descendant nodes will not be k-anonymous either. Unlike the OLA, we delete the nodes rather than marking nodes according to these two ideas, which can, to some extent, reduce the times of traversing lattice.

3 Results

The two data sets used in our experiment are shown in Table 3. Both of the Adult and CUP data sets have been used in many researches. The first column contains the name of data set and the source address. The second column contains quasi-identifier attributes in data sets and the corresponding height of generalization hierarchy

Table 3. Data sets used in our experiments

Data sets	Quasi-identifiers	Number of records
Adult From the UC Irvine machine learning data repository. ftp://ftp.ics.uci.edu/pub/machine-learning-databases/adult	• Age (3) • Profession (2) • Education (2) • Marital status (2) • Position (2) • Race (1) • Sex (1) • Country (3)	30,162
CUP From the Paralyzed Veterans Association on veterans with spinal cord injuries or disease. http://kdd.ics.uci.edu/databases/kddcup98/kddcup98.html	• ZIP code (5) • Age (4) • Gender (2) • Income (3)	63,441

we defined. The third column represents the size of the data set after removing the records with missing values.

Because we have improved the algorithm in terms of efficiency, there is no need to compare the information loss between our algorithm and the OLA. In fact, both of these algorithms cause the same rate of information loss, smaller than any other full-domain algorithms.

We compare our algorithm with the OLA algorithm and run these two algorithms on the above two data sets. Since both of the algorithms are full-domain optimal, we will evaluate them from two other aspects: one is the number of nodes computed when finding k-anonymous nodes; the other is runtime.

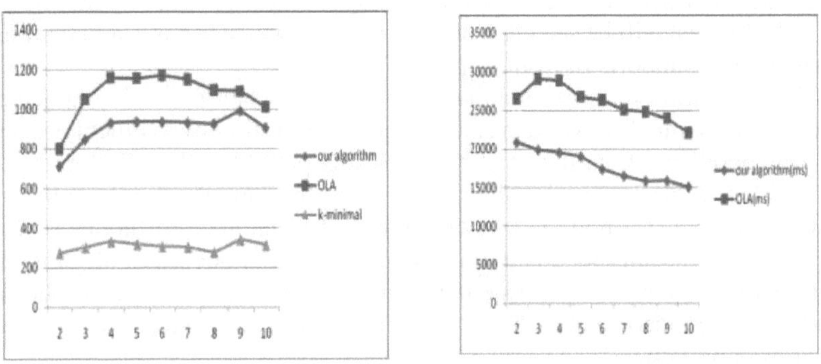

(a) (b)

Fig. 5. Results comparison under different k-Adult dataset: (a) the number of nodes computed; (b) runtime

The results are shown in figure 5 and figure 6. The left figure (a) is the number of nodes computed and k-minimal nodes under different values of k, and the right figure (b) displays the corresponding runtimes.

As shown, our algorithm can prune more nodes in lattice than OLA, and has a better performance in terms of runtime, which serves our original purpose. The comparison between the two data sets shows that the results are better on the Adult data set, because the nodes in lattice for Adult data set are much larger than CUP data set. Since our algorithm can prune much more nodes in lattice, the runtime of our algorithm is improved greatly on Adult data set, while on CUP data set there is little difference in runtime. The bottom line in the left figures is the number of k-minimal nodes, which is much smaller than computed nodes, i.e. there may be no need to compute all of the nodes. This is our focus for future work.

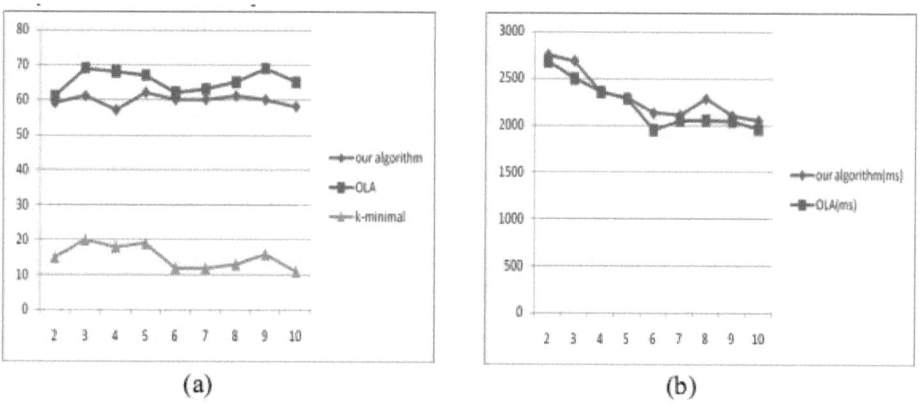

Fig. 6. Results comparison under different k-Cup dataset: (a) the number of nodes computed; (b) runtime

4 Conclusion

In this paper we described an improved full-domain optimal algorithm for k-anonymization. The improved algorithm computed the product of degree for each node, and started from the node whose product was largest to traverse the lattice. We also used a novel structure of generalization hierarchy to record the support of each generalized node in order to find k-anonymous nodes efficiently. Experiments showed that our improved algorithm can prune many nodes in lattice and provide much better performance in runtime.

Acknowledgments. This research is partly supported by the Natural Science Funding of China, under grant number 61170177 and innovation funding of Tianjin University.

References

1. Vaidya, J., Clifton, C.: Privacy-preserving data mining: Why, how, and when. IEEE Security & Privacy 2(6), 19–27 (2004)
2. Atzori, M., Bonchi, F., Giannotti, F., Pedreschi, D.: k-anonymous patterns. In: PADD 2005, pp. 10–21 (2005)

3. Sweeney, L.: k-anonymity: a model for protecting privacy. International Journal on Uncertainty, Fuzziness and Knowledge-based Systems 10(5), 557–570 (2002)
4. Li, J., Wang, H., Jin, H., Yong, J.: Current developments of k-anonymous data releasing. In: Proceedings of ehPASS 2006, Brisbane, Australia, pp. 109–121 (2006)
5. Sweeney, L.: Achieving k-Anonymity Privacy Protection Using Generalization and Suppression. International Journal on Uncertainty, Fuzziness and Knowledge-based Systems 10(5), 18 (2002)
6. Samarati, P.: Protecting Respondents' Identity in Microdata Release. IEEE Transactions on Knowledge and Data Engineering 13(6), 1010–1027 (2001)
7. Bayardo, B., Agrawal, R.: Data privacy through optimal k-anonymity. In: Proc. of the 21st Int'l Conference on Data Engineering, pp. 217–228. IEEE CS (2005)
8. LeFevre, K., DeWitt, D.J., Ramakrishnan, R.: Incognito: Efficient Full-domain k-anonymity. In: Proc. ACM Management of Data, Baltimore, Maryland, USA, pp. 49–60. ACM (2005)
9. Gionis, A., Tassa, T.: k-Anonymization with minimal loss of information. IEEE Trans. Knowl. Data Eng. 21(2), 206–219 (2009)
10. El Emam, K., Dankar, F., Issa, R.J., Jonker, E., Amyot, D., Cogo, E.: A globally optimal k-anonymity method for the de-identification of health data. J. Am. Med. Inform. Assoc. (Forthcoming 2009)
11. Aggarwal, G., Feder, T., Kenthapadi, K., Motwani, R., Panigrahy, R., Thomas, D., Zhu, A.: Anonymizing Tables. In: Eiter, T., Libkin, L. (eds.) ICDT 2005. LNCS, vol. 3363, pp. 246–258. Springer, Heidelberg (2005)
12. Iyengar, V.: Transforming data to satisfy privacy constraints. In: KDD 2002: Proceedings of the Eighth (2002)
13. Nergiz, M., Clifton, C.: Thoughts on k-anonymization. In: ACM SIGKDD International Conference on Knowledge Discovery and Data Mining, pp. 279–288 (2007)
14. Sweeney, L.: Guaranteeing anonymity when sharing medical data, the Datafly system. In: Proceedings, Journal of the American Medical Informatics Association. Hanley & Belfus, Inc., Washington, DC (1997)
15. Grahne, G., Zhu, J.: Fast algorithms for frequent itemset mining using fp-trees. IEEE Trans. Knowl. Data Eng. 17(10), 1347–1362 (2005)

Factors Affecting Emerging ICT Adoption in SMEs: An Actor Network Theory Analysis

Sunday Eze, Yanqing Duan, and Hsin Chen

Business School, University of Bedfordshire, LU1 3JU, Park Square, Luton, UK
{Sunday.Eze,Yanqing.Duan,Hsin.Chen}@beds.ac.uk

Abstract. The majority of ICT adoption studies regards ICT adoption as a one-off practice and focuses on factors influencing adoption at one particular decision point. Most studies appear to have ignored the fact that ICT adoption is a dynamic and ongoing process and that factors influencing its adoption should be accounted for, as the decision to adopt proceeds from one stage to another. This paper reports our research attempt to examine the dynamic process of ICT adoption in SMEs using Actor Network Theory (ANT). This study employs a qualitative approach to investigate how UK services SMEs are constantly engaging in ICT adoption, by focusing on the dynamic adoption process and critical factors. A framework was derived based on ANT with the empirical evidence collected. The findings suggest that using ANT to examine the process of emerging ICT adoption helps to unveil the recursive and dynamic nature of the process and the key factors at each stage. This paper presents and discusses the key findings on critical factors affecting the dynamic process of emerging ICTs adoption.

Keywords: ICT adoption, Emerging ICT, Service SMEs, Actor Network Theory.

1 Introduction

The success of business growth is not only enabled by ICT, but also dependent on the ability of organizations to constantly adopt and make the best use of emerging ICT for innovation and business performance. ICTs and their applications constantly create profound impacts through innovations and new advancements, yet most ICT adoption studies regard ICT adoption as a one-off practice and use the quantitative approach in identifying factors influencing adoption at one particular decision point. These studies appear to have ignored the fact that ICT adoption is a dynamic and ongoing process and factors influencing its adoption should be accounted for, as decisions to adopt are made and challenged along an adoption process. Traditional theories used to examine the adoption (e.g. Technology acceptance model (TAM), Diffusion of Innovation (DOI), etc.) are deterministic [1] and unable to reflect the level of complexities and diversities or capture the dynamic and evolutionary nature of ICT adoption and development. The majority of ICTs adoption research is based on the quantitative approach. For example, Williams et al. [2] revealed that the majority of studies (about

V. Khachidze et al. (Eds.): iCETS 2012, CCIS 332, pp. 361–377, 2012.

65%) employed a quantitative approach. Less than 25% of studies employed a qualitative approach. Approximately 9% of papers employed conceptual/theoretical/meta-analysis; clearly, the questionnaire survey was the dominant research method. For example, among the papers reviewed by Williams et al. [2], about 58% employed survey method, while 15% used case studies. Questionnaires are primarily employed to collect data on ICTs adoption and diffusion. Other methods, such as interviews, multi-method, mathematical model, field study, laboratory experiment, secondary data analysis, action research etc. were rarely used in ICTs adoption research. ICTs adoption studies mainly used the deductive approach involving theory confirmation and hypotheses testing.

Although this research design has certain advantages, it does have limitations. It regards ICTs adoption as a one-off action and focuses on fact affecting the decision making at one particular decision point. Theories and research methods used in this area should treat ICTs adoption as a dynamic and evolving process, instead of a static and one-off action. Therefore, this research aims to understand the critical factors affecting emerging ICT adoption from a dynamic process perspective, using Actor Network Theory. Emerging ICT, in its broad context, encompasses any new ICT development or improved ICT applications. Based on extensive literature review, Actor Network Theory (ANT) is employed as a theoretical lens to inform the study. Bearing in mind the current criticism and limitations on the dominant use of quantitative approaches in adoption research, this study used a qualitative approach. Unstructured and semi-structured interviews are used and deductive and inductive approaches are followed in data analysis. Thus far, 26 interviews have been conducted in two stages. A conceptual framework underpinned by ANT is developed to depict the dynamic process involving actors and associated critical success factors. In order to achieve the objective of the study, the paper examines ANT as a theoretical underpinning to support a framework for understanding both the dynamic and evolutionary nature of ICT adoption process in small service sector SMEs. Next, it presents the methods for data collection and analysis. The subsequent sections report the findings and discussion, implications, limitations and future research, and conclusion.

2 Theoretical Underpinning

Studies such as those of Bagozzi [3]and Vankatesh [4] have called on a new theoretical perspective that will boost our understanding of technology adoption and development [5] as well as how the technologies can be adopted, taking into account their broader context [6, 7]. Actor Network Theory (ANT) is one of the results of such inquiry. ANT was adopted for the purpose of understanding both the evolutionary and emergent nature of ICT. ANT attempts to address the role that technology plays in a social setting and the process by which technology bilaterally influences the social setting over time [8].The theory rejects the philosophies of both technological and social determinism [9, 10] for downplaying the ongoing and dynamic interaction between society and technology [11]. As such, the theory emphasizes that social and technological systems should not be studied in isolation. The strength of ANT in understanding ICT adoption lies in the study of both humans and technology [11]. ANT regards ICT, people, and any other element as actors, which are named "actants" [11], and defines an actor *as any element which bends, shapes around itself, makes other elements depend upon itself and translates their wills into the language of its own* [12P.286].This does not mean that ANT treats both human and non human as the same; rather, it examines technology/organization, people and others elements based on how strong their relationships are, and tracing such relationships is regarded as the basic tenet of ANT. Technology is unpredictable, and a single theory that assumes that this is possible cannot allow the researcher to trace the negotiation process that takes place during technology implementation [13, 14]. One of the key reasons for adopting ANT in this study is that "it is based on no stable theory" [15p.181]. As a result, a number of studies have drawn from different ANT constructs, which have helped them to unveil new ways of studying organization change and development processes. According to Van de Ven and Poole [16p.510], "It is the interplay between different perspectives that helps one gain a more comprehensive understanding of organizational life because any one theory perspective consistently offers only a single account of a complex phenomenon". ANT has many constructs and researchers always attempting to draw on these constructs to discover new ways of analyzing organization change and development processes. Key ANT concepts of inscription, translation, framing and stabilization are adopted for the study. These key concepts are explained below.

Inscription. Inscription is a process by which actors form values towards the technology or the extent to which the innovators determine or formulate what the technology or its functionalities are or should be [10]. Inscription is often influenced by organizations' beliefs, previous patterns of IT use and expectations over what the technology is about and can do [13, 17].

Translation. The process of aligning numerous interests and beliefs of different actors with that of the key actors within the network [18]. "Key Actors" are the competing actors that ensure that other actors support their claims in technology development and deployment [19]. It involves understanding how actors seek the interest of other human actors or convince others, directly or indirectly, in adopting new technologies [18].

Framing. According to Faraj et al.[10] new technologies undergo alteration or change because they either require advanced features, or improvement upon their existing features, especially when adopted by lead users. This often allows new or different ways of using these technologies to emerge. Such technology may not be successful if users do not believe the way they are designed and used [10]. Framing recognises that actors not only inscribe beliefs, interests and values regarding technology, but such values may be dissimilar and detached from one another [20]

Stabilization. Stabilization is where the relevant actors consider the problem to have been solved [21]. Stabilization of technology does not evidently mean that technology is not amendable. Indeed, technology and business processes might change or adjust over time or as Bijker, Hughes, and Pinch put it, "*closure by redefinition of a problem*" which leads to inscription again [21].

These four concepts of ANT described above were used in this research. ANT was also used in this research because traditional adoption theories have limitations in capturing the constant technology advancements as well as the dynamic and evolutionary nature of technology adoption. These theories do not challenge technology implementation. These theories have remained the theoretical foundation for many studies and theory such as Roger's diffusion of innovation accepts technology the way it is and relies heavily on early adopters or opinion leaders for its diffusion [22].These theories regard ICTs adoption as a one-off action. They are unable to reflect the dynamic and interplay aspects of adoption from a process point of view. Traditional adoption theories have permanent separation between the technology and the social world [14]. Theories and models that treat ICT adoption as a dynamic and evolving process, instead of a static and one-off action, are able to capture both the social and technology factors that motivate and/or inhibit technology adoption [18] at every stage of the adoption decision process.

3 Research Method

This study adopts a qualitative approach, in an attempt to understand and address factors influencing the dynamic process of emerging ICT adoption. The target sector for the empirical investigation is UK service SMEs. The UK service sector has expanded rapidly in recent years and represents about 20% of the national output [23]. The sector is essential in developing the economy, sustaining business competitiveness and supporting both the private and public sectors [23].The growing significance of services businesses suggests that the effort to improve all aspects of the economy is focused increasingly on the service sector.

3.1 Sampling

Since qualitative research emphasizes discovery and explanation of people's experiences [24], purposive sampling and snowball sampling were adopted. The logic behind purposive sampling is to purposefully select individuals randomly from a sample frame (crunch online data base and Luton business directory) to identify service SMEs that engaged in e-business practice during the 1st round of data collection. The purpose of this is to enable the researcher to make a reasonable comparison in relation to research objectives and not for statistical generalization [25]. Snowball sampling was used during the second round of the interview, which helped the researchers to gain access to key informants introduced by participants during the first round of the interviews.

3.2 Unstructured Interviews

The purpose of the 1st round of the unstructured interviews was three-fold. First, to understand the current state of emerging ICT adoption in small service SMEs in order to have a broad and unconstrained view; second, to test the applicability of the key ANT concepts: *inscription, translation, framing and stabilization*; third, to identify key actors involved in the adoption and the initial set of factors. The 1st round data helped to develop the initial framework and the semi-structured interview questions for the 2nd round of data collection. A formal letter was sent ahead of time detailing the purpose of the research and confidentiality issues. All the interviews lasted for about 45 minutes to 1 hour. In the first round, the interviewee sample was generated from online data base and 65 participates were contacted randomly, of which 11 participants agreed to be interviewed.

3.3 Semi-structured Interviews

In order to enhance the theoretical codes and identify factors to validate and confirm the outcome of the findings, in the second round of the interviews, 15 semi-structured interviews were conducted with a range of key human actors identified from the first round of interviewees involved. These included small business managers/customers, government agencies, consultants and IT vendors that the unstructured interview revealed. The initial framework for emerging ICT was introduced to guide conversation and subsequently allowed the participants to access their experiences while some degree of freedom is given to express their views during the semi- structured interviews. The framework was useful because it helped participants to articulate and interpret their experiences [24]. A comprehensive table of all actors interviewed is provided below.

Table 1. Sample, interview types and participants/actors

Sampling	Purposive											Snowball														
Interviews	1st round :unstructured											2nd round: semi-structured														
Participants	A1	A2	A3	A4	A5	A6	A7	A8	A9	A10	A11	A12	A13	A14	A15	A16	A17	A18	A19	A20	A21	A22	A23	A24	A25	A26
SME managers	■	■			■	■	■	■	■	■	■	■	■	■										■		
Government																			■	■	■		■		■	
Customers	■	■					■	■	■	■	■	■	■	■												
Consultants							■				■	■								■						■
IT experts			■	■									■		■	■	■	■	■	■						
Vendors							■	■			■															
Employees			■	■							■			■												

A1 to A 26= no of participants

4 Data Analysis

The study adopted a thematic data analysis technique. More specifically, hybrid approach was used, because codes were derived from theory in addition to those that emerged inductively from interview transcripts. This approach was useful because it allowed the application of theoretical codes to the raw data and also allowed themes to emerge inductively [26].The data analysis process is shown in detail in Figure 1. To ensure that the codes generated are applicable to the raw data, initial raw data was first coded into predefined and post defined categories, and reliability analysis was then conducted to ensure that the codes are applicable to subsequent raw data. Four colleagues were invited to conduct the data coding process by relating the quotes against the theoretical categories and the emerging categories.

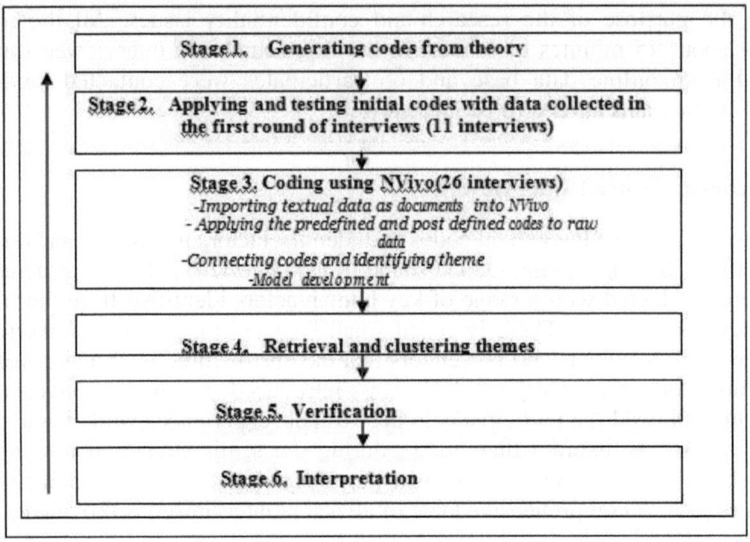

Fig. 1. Data analysis process

In stage three, all the transcribed data (unstructured and semi-structured interview data) were imported into NVivo. NVivo was further used to facilitate the analysis in stage 3, because of the volume of data involved. The data analysis was iterative in nature. Data was retrieved from NVivo in stage 4 and themes were conceptually clustered based on the related characteristics [27] of *inscription, translation, framing and Stabilization*. These codes depict the stages of the emerging ICT adoption process. A number of activities actors undertake in each stage drawn from interview transcripts aid in clustering the themes. Verification of the codes (factors) in stage 5 of the data analysis process provides further reliability and validity checks. Inter rater reliability analysis which involves percentage agreement was used. This approach was used because the data coded was nominal and required a presence or absence judgment by the judges [27]. The results of the reliability analysis are shown in Table 2.This surpassed the 70% benchmark suggested by Miles and Huberman [26] and Boyatzis [27].

Table 2. Reliability Analysis

Area	Number of Judges	Reliability	
		First- two judges	Second-two judges
Factors	4	0.84(84%)	0.89(89%)

5 Findings and Discussion

5.1 Establishing the Framework

It is crucial to first establish the conceptual framework, which helps account for the factors clustered within each stage of the adoption process and to support the claims that adoption of ICT is not a one off-action but rather a dynamic and ongoing process. The framework in Figure 2 provides a new lens to view ICT adoption and demonstrates the dynamic interaction of humans and technology in the network. It presents a number of actors involved in emerging ICT adoption and reveals that activities in the process are neither static nor a one-off action. Drawing on the interview transcripts, the findings suggest that actors in the adoption process are not viewed in isolation. Second, the perception of actors differs. Third, the position of actors changes over time. Finally, actors that challenge ICT adoption are both internal and external to small business managers (the key actors). As noted by one key actor, when roles are delegated for new ICT and finally introduced:

"...I bring it in the office and contact my customers in London, they will come and look at it and say that looks smaller or bigger. I will go back to the engineers and say... the process is fine but I will want a few adjustments... then they will make it again. I will go straight back to the customers and everybody is happy" (A10).

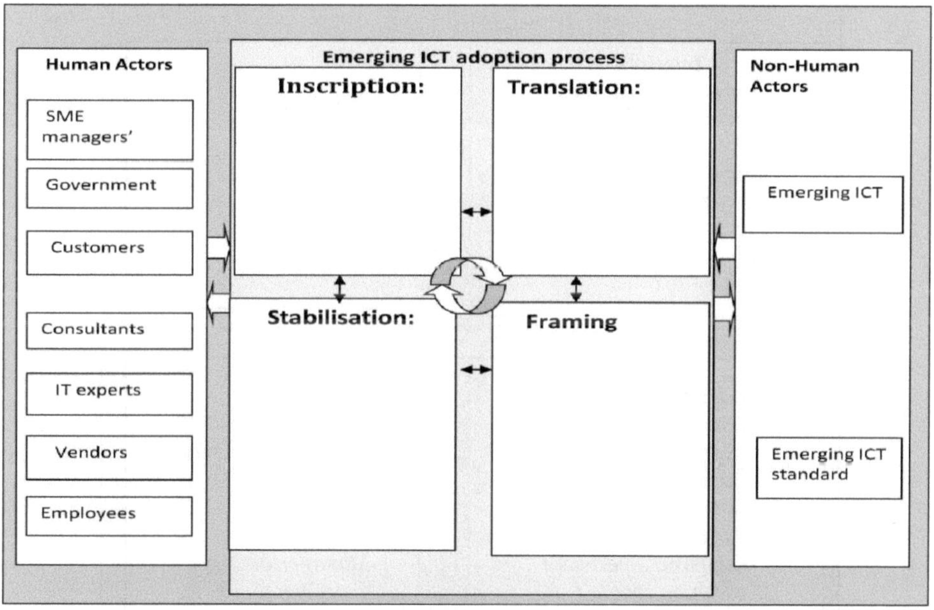

Fig. 2. Framework

In support of this another key actor notes:

> *"When you are an entrepreneur you need be able to do thing quickly fail, not necessary fail, but just understand your mistakes and then change them and continue to evolve. You must always have that mentality."(A6).*

Similar assertion was also made by one of the IT experts:

> *"...because technology advances with time and because of that every company want to keep up to date with their applications. For that reason you have to keep changing stuffs. That is one major thing that cannot be compromised" (A15).*

These statements demonstrate that emerging ICT involves the interplay among and between actors and is always an ongoing process. This implies that technology and people do not have inherently determinant boundaries; instead, they are integrated, which is only separated analytically.

5.2 Factors

Figure 4 depicts the factors influencing the dynamic process of ICT adoption. These factors have been identified as critical for informing emerging ICT adoption and development over time at every stage of the adoption process. Factors influencing emerging ICT adoption process are shown below:

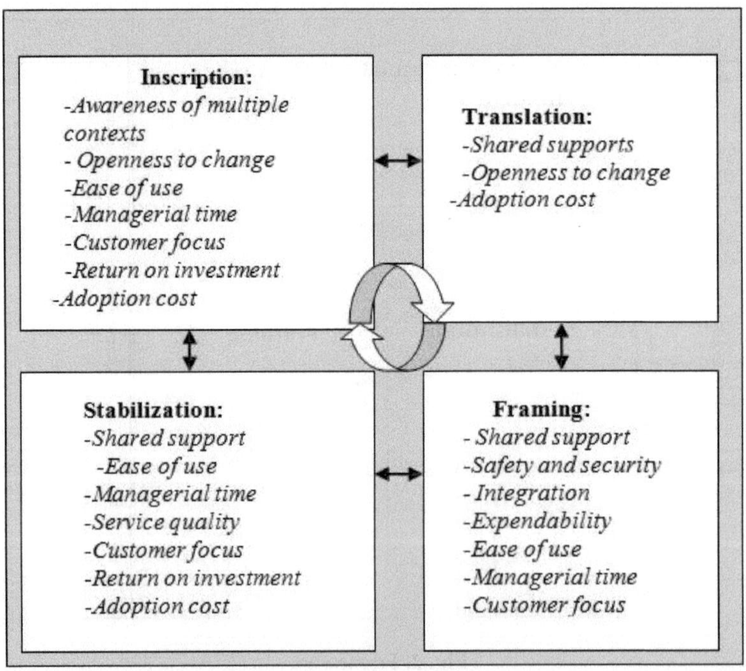

Fig. 3. Factors influencing emerging ICT adoption

Table 3 shows the factors and the stage(s) at which they influence emerging ICT adoption. These factors are now interpreted with supporting evidence.

Table 3. Factors affecting adoption

Factors	Stages			
	Inscription	Translation	Framing	Stabilization
Awareness of multiple context				
Openness to change				
Shared support				
Safety and security				
Integration				
Expandability				
Ease of use				
Managerial time				
Service quality				
Customer focus				
Return on investment				
Adoption cost				

5.2.1 Factors Affecting Adoption

Awareness of multiple contexts affects the **inscription stage.** A number of actors interviewed supported the statement that adoption and post-adoption development of any emerging ICT is an enormous task and organizations must face the challenges that come with it. Some interviewees note that this requires understanding of multiple situations that might affect adoption. As highlighted by one of the key actors: *"...we have to look at the bigger picture, how that technology is going to help the whole company" (A9).* Awareness of multiple contexts is the ability to take into account all options available and to ensure that the impending challenges are thoroughly evaluated. Teo et al., [28] note that internal organizational actors, external customers and suppliers who use the organizational products are the most important and should not be neglected. SMEs that address not just the multiple internal and external actors that may contribute to adoption failure, but give consideration to all emerging situations surrounding successful emerging ICT adoption, are more likely to engage in new ICT over time. Awareness of multiple contexts appears to be tightly linked to the inscription stage only.

Openness to change affects the **inscription and translation stage.** Most human actors note that recognizing all actors in emerging ICT and taking their ideas into consideration were essential for emerging ICT adoption success. This was highlighted across multiple cases: For example, one of the key actors points out that: *"as a CEO, you would have to encourage new ideas within the organization and what you should therefore do is you should be able to put a process or adopt a strategic role that will allow new ideas to flow..."(A12)*. Other actors (A10, A11) supported this assertion. Openness to change is the extent to which mangers recognize that diverse actors are the greatest resources businesses can ever have, and their opinions and ideas contribute immensely to organizations' success, which is what is inscribed into technology. According to Elie-Dit-Cosaque [29], openness to change fosters initiatives and freedom of actions and is related to greater performance. While observation shows that most key actors would be reluctant to simplify their duties [28], by encouraging others to participate in adoption decision making, the finding suggests that *recognizing* all actors and taking their ideas into consideration at the initial stages of adoption is what essentially triggers emerging ICT adoption often.

Shared supports affect adoption at the **translation, framing and stabilization stage.** Actors' perceptions about emerging ICT can be viewed differently, depending on the social setting and the knowledge of different actors. Key actors note that seeking for relevant people with the right skills, to realize the right ICT, is paramount. This was a point made by a number of key actors: *"because as I always say that the technical knowledge is new to me... if there is any special area, we have to consult all the relevant people who know the technology" (A14).* Shared support is defined as working together to a common purpose in order to achieve a shared goal. According to Macredie and Mijinyawa [30], it is a form of open participation involving various actors, including vendors and consultants who overcome problems posed by new technology [31]. Although achieving shared support at the translation stage is difficult and not guaranteed, Teo et al.[28] point out that such practice promotes open negotiations, stimulates further new ideas, innovative thinking, and continuous learning where the organization more or less depends on what they have learnt not just internally but also within their environment. Shared support was a factor recognized at the stages of translation, framing and stabilization. Evidence suggests that innovative key actors in most cases are responsible for generating ideas for emerging ICT. As a result, they constantly interact with others to ensure that meaning about the intended ICT is understandable by all parties. Key actors continually seek the support of those that agree with their own views and interest of regarding the new ICT and also ensure that implementation goals are achieved. The study suggests that shared support promotes mutual aid, instead of relying on their knowledge and assumptions.

Safety and security affects emerging ICT adoption at the **framing stage.** Participants stressed that if a new ICT is perceived to be unsafe, such as losing access to confidential information, the chance that it would be adopted is uncertain. This point was echoed by one of the key actors: *"Secure payment is a hard issue. Before you know there were several frauds, online security is a major issue... we adopt technology on a day to day [basis], whichever one is more secure we go over to that" (A9)*. Other human actors (A14) made similar assertions. The semi-structured interview findings also revealed that SMEs are eager to engage with emerging ICT if it is proven to keep track of not just the confidential information but also employee's safety.This assertion was highlighted by these actors (A1).Safety and security is tightly linked to the protection of information, people at work, and property from unanticipated conditions and is apparently a technology driven factor. While Yousafzai and Yani-De-Soriano [32] found that security is linked to distrust and skepticism about the ability of the application to work perfectly; the study suggests that security is not only vital when a business transaction moves beyond the boundaries of offline modes of conducting business, but extends to monitoring work and the safety of those at work. Safety and security, to a large extent, are still critical issues that greatly influence adoption of new ICT and this was visible at this stage.

Integration also affects **framing** stage only. Some actors interviewed widely perceived that businesses need to identify, and at the same time understand, opportunities offered by any new ICT. This requires learning to overcome failures by ensuring that they adopt and adapt the emerging ICT that is compatible with business arrangements. In support of this, one of the human actors notes that: *"Is all about how* [emerging ICT] *actually works with the rest of the other system in use...how it interfaces with the rest of the product?" (A12).* Similar assertions were made by other actors (A3, A13). Integration is defined as the capability of the emerging ICT to interface with existing applications without difficulty. According to Zhu et al. [33], connectivity eliminates incompatibility within the organization and can also restrict compatibility where new ICT is difficult to integrate with other applications. This happens when a firm's ICT application allows for connectivity among intra -inter-organizational systems functions, as well as compatibility that allow the exchange of information [34]. Similarly, the finding suggests that integration of ICT infrastructure remains a factor that triggers the introduction of emerging ICT. The non-integration nature of ICT infrastructure hampers business success and considering the nature of small businesses, key actors would not, in most cases, engage in any new application that will not meet their standards.

Expandability is another illustrative factor affecting **framing stage**. It was noted by some actors that some new ICT are modular in nature, while others are flexible and expandable. Most key actors' emphasize the need for expandable systems. According to one of them: *"...you know we got like 5 employees now... maybe in a couple of year's time, we will have 50 employees, is the system scalable? Also are the functionalities and the capabilities scalable?"(A5).* Similarly, another key actor (A13) also supported this. Expendability is the capacity of the emerging ICT to remain flexible, and continually accommodates new functionalities or features. ICT applications that are expendable serve as the basis on which other features can be developed easily. This creates a foundation for the strategic ICT capability of any business [34]. Expandability of ICT applications aids innovation of the business process and reduces the cost of developing or adopting entirely new systems. This happens when it is scalable and, most importantly, allows additional features when the need arises. Key actors would be most likely to engage with any emerging ICT if it demonstrates that it can accommodate new functions when the need arises.

Ease of use affects the **inscription, framing and stabilization stage.** Considering the nature of SME, it was not surprising that participants widely perceived that they struggle with new ICT as a result of limited knowledge and skills. As such, they always consider emerging ICTs that are simple. As noted: *"... we have embraced most of these technologies because we are much bigger, we are a big company but we had 25 people working for us and we were turning over a million. With that size, comes a lot of complications, headaches and now one person...can manage the entire task* *with these technologies" (A7).* Ease of use was a factor most actors considered at the stages of ***inscription, framing and stabilization***. The reason for this was that that the majority of key actors still lack ICT skills. As a result, they always ensure that they adopt and implement new ICT that is simple to use and adapts to the organization's arrangements. Ease of use is defined *as* the capacity of the emerging ICT to allow people with limited knowledge or limited ICT skills to accomplish complex tasks. It is also linked to the simplicity with which the new ICT is maintained in the near future. Empirical evidence from previous studies [35] has also shown that there is a positive correlation between ease of use and ICT adoption. Similar to our findings, if emerging ICT is highly exploitable regardless of the level of skill, it would mostly likely be adopted.

*Managerial tim*e affects the **inscription, framing and stabilization stages.** Key actors are often constrained by time as they try to meet their day to day business activities. Emerging ICT, in most cases, was considered if it saves times. This was echoed by a number of key actors. Among these actors is one who notes that adoption of new ICT is: "*... always based on a commercial decision whether that commercial decision is because it saves us time which ... saves us money"*. Managerial time, in this context, refers to the capability of the emerging ICT to serve and save time through an efficient means. Venkatesh and Davis [36] stress that time delay increases felt anger of not only the adopters but also the service customers and in turn has a negative impact on service quality. To act quickly during business operations is imperative for the improvement of business activities. Evidence suggests that the more the emerging ICT saves time and improves service delivery, the more it is likely to be accepted. Time was one of the factors that were highlighted and emphasize greatly emphasized. This factor was not only considered in ***inscription stage*** but was also visible at the ***framing*** and ***stabilization*** stages.

Service quality affects **stabilization stage** only. The finding reveals that key actors still face constant pressure, not just to survive and take advantage of every business opportunity, but also to be efficient and profitable. Actors widely perceived that emerging ICTs that are efficient and provide high quality of services may greatly trigger new ICT adoption. This was highlighted across multiple cases. For example, one actor notes that "*For us we really wanted an internet based solution because the services are good" (A2).* Drawing on a number of other key actors' views, service quality is linked to efficiency in terms of speed, improved services delivery at a reduced cost, and increased revenue. The sudden increase of service technology has incredibly changed the ways users interact with organizations to create service outcomes [37]. Service quality is defined in this context as the capability of the emerging ICT to deliver efficient results to the users. It also relates to the extent to which the emerging ICT is fast and helps improve service delivery, and in general, improves company's processes and profit. The study suggests that if the key actors' evaluation of the actual performance of the new system is less than its expected performance, it is likely that it would negatively affect adoption.

Customer focus affects **inscription, framing and stabilization.** We observed from our findings that customers still remain one of the building blocks of small businesses.

Customers were not only involved in the emerging ICT adoption decision, but most importantly, they determine whether the businesses flourish or not. Key actors widely perceived that they were concerned about their clients' satisfaction and retention, as they constitute an integral part of their decision making. This comment was widely mentioned: *"... [Technology] is actually quite expensive but we felt that it was worth us doing it in order to keep our clients..." (A5).*This was further supported by other human actors (A13, A5, A11). According to Moon [38], technology applications play a tremendous role in a number of stages in the buying process and customers heavily rely on them to deliver information about what to purchase, help find the items they are looking for, and provide follow up services. Customer focus was considered mostly at the ***inscription stage, framing stage and stabilization*** **stage** and was an integrated part of the adoption process. The finding also suggests that if new technology offers high quality services, it triggers the user from being mere prospects to adopters.

Return on investment affects **inscription stage** and most importantly the **stabilization stage**, where profits are expected from the investments made on the new ICT. The majority of actors interviewed clearly echoed that it is unlikely that any emerging ICT that does not generate return on investments and increase market share will be considered. There is no doubt that limited resources still hinder key actors from adopting new technology applications. As pointed out by one of the key actors: *"consequently it is unlikely that any SME will give consideration to any new or emerging ICT if it cannot be shown to produce a very quick ROI for the business" (A12).* The value small business managers attach to emerging ICT is directly linked to how much profit it can generate in return. Low and Johnson [39] contend that the inherent assumption of economic theories is that businesses are profit–driven. Return on investment is one of the significant factors that continually influence key actors' decisions to engage with new ICT. New ICT that does not assist continual improvements and allow firms to realize the potential productivity, market and values gains in a way that profits to the organization would be difficult to consider [40]. Similar to this, the finding also revealed that it is unlikely that any emerging ICT that does not generate return on investments and increase market share will be considered by key actors.

Adoption cost affects **inscription, framing** and **stabilization.** Participants widely perceived adoption cost as a key factor that determines if emerging ICT would be adopted or not. For example, one of the key actors notes: *"I feel the first time to develop student box...is the cost efficiency of the product" (A6).* Cost was not only associated with how cheap or inexpensive the emerging ICT is, but how the new ICT can assist in reducing the workforce and provide the services that other costly ICT applications offer. Cost, in most cases, was perceived as what triggers future adoption. Emerging ICT adoption is greatly determined by comparing the benefits and cost of using the emerging ICT. Cost, according to Wu and Ho [41] and Lacovou et al. [42], facilitates or inhibits adoption of new ICT. Several business organizations carry out cost–benefit analysis before adopting new technologies [31].Evidence suggests that adoption cost also facilitates future adoption and impacts greatly during evaluation and conceptualisation of the emerging ICT at inscription stage, but most importantly at the translation stage where prices in most cases are negotiated, and also at stabilization stage, especially when the need for new ICT emerges again. Observation reveals that adoption cost was quite visible at almost all the stages.

6 Implications

The conceptual framework developed for understanding factors influencing emerging ICT adoption has two important implications: The first implication is that the framework provides a basis for articulating and understanding factors and their influence at every stage of the adoption process. Researchers may find that the theoretical codes generated from ANT and the factors emerging within them are relevant in understanding emerging ICT adoption over time, as decisions are made and challenged along the adoption process. ANT and its strong explanatory power demonstrates that it is appropriate for exploring and understanding influencing factors and explaining their influence on emerging ICT adoption. Also, the hybrid approach to data analysis employed in this study demonstrated a number of ways theoretical driven codes and data driven codes were organized, analyzed and clustered in appropriate categories. We believed that this study has extended both the scope of ICT adoption models and data analysis approaches applicable for studying emerging ICT adoption. One of the practical implications of this paper is that the framework can be a reference point for practitioners who want to develop an in-depth understanding of these factors.

7 Limitations and Future Works

One of the limitations of this paper is that the scope of the factors presented is limited to the sectors concerned. There might be other factors that are prevalent to other industries or sectors. Secondly, qualitative research is interpretive in nature and the limitations in the sample used are common in qualitative research. The generalization of the findings and the framework remains to be established across a wider population. The study interviewed both end users of ICT and other actors, without focusing on a specific emerging ICT. While this may be criticized by other researchers who investigate a specific ICT in organizations, we believe that adoption is an ongoing action and managers do not rely on a single system, due to constant environmental changes; instead they rely on a number of technology applications, which constitute multiple types of emergingICT, to accomplish their tasks. Drawing on the first limitation, a further study may be essential to collect and collate a large number of data to test the reliability and validity of factors across wider populations.Such study can provide decision makers with useful benchmarks on these factors.

8 Conclusion

The paper presents our findings on factors affecting the dynamic process of emerging ICT adoption in SMEs based on ANT. A conceptual framework established in our study has been used to analyse the factors. First, we adopted a number of key concepts of ANT and stressed the need to use more explanatory theories and a qualitative approach to identify factors influencing emerging ICT adoption. The framework for emerging ICT was then established. This study identified 12 key factors that influence emerging ICT adoption in SMEs when different actors are involved in the adoption process. While these factors are critical as decisions to adopt are made and challenged along the adoption process, *shared support, ease of use, managerial time, customer focus,* and *adoption cost* affect three stages of the adoption process. In addition, *openness to change* and *return on investment* affects at least two stages while *awareness of multiple contexts, safety and security, integration, expandability and service quality* affect only one stage. The study recognized these factors as informing emerging ICT adoption.

References

1. Markus, M.L., Robey, D.: Information technology and organizational change: Causal structure in theory and research. Management Science 34(5), 583–598 (1998)
2. Williams, M., Dwivedi, Y.K., Lal, B., Schwarz, A.: Contemporary trends and issues in IT adoption and diffusion research. Journal of Information Technology 24, 1–10 (2009)
3. Bagozzi, R.P.: The legacy of the technology acceptance model and a proposal for a paradigm shift. Journal of the Association for Information Systems 8(4), 244–254 (2007)
4. Vankatesh, V., Davis, F., Morris, M.G.: Dead or alive? The development trajectory and future adoption research. Journal of Association for Information Systems 8(4), 267–286 (2007)
5. Lee, H., Oh, S.: A standards war waged by a developing country: Understanding international standard setting from the actor -network perspective. Strategic Information Systems 15, 177–195 (2006)
6. Silva, L.: Post -positivist review of technology acceptance model. Journal of the Association for Information Systems 8(4), 255–266 (2007)
7. Schwarz, A., Chin, W.: Looking forward: Toward an understanding of the nature and definition of IT acceptance. Journal of the Association for Information Systems 8(4), 230–243 (2007)
8. Mahring, M.H.J., Keil, M., Montealegre, R.: Trojan actor networks and swift translation: Bring actor-network theory to project escalation studies. Information Technology and People 17(2), 210–238 (2004)
9. Latour, B.: Science in Action. Harvard University Press, Cambridge (1987)
10. Faraj, S., Kwon, D., Watts, S.: Contested artifact: technological sense making, actor networks and the shaping of the web browser. Journal of Information, Technology and People 17(2), 186–209 (2004)
11. Hanseth, O.A., Berg, M.: Guest editor' Introduction: Actor network theory and information systems. What's so special? Information, Technology and People 17(2), 116–123 (2004)
12. Callon, M., Latour, B.: Unscrewing the big leviathan: How actors macro-structures reality and how sociologists help them to do so. In: Cetina, K.K., Cicourel, A.V. (eds.) Advances in Social Theory and Methodology: Toward Integration of Macro and Macro-Sociology. Routledge, London (1981)
13. Callon, M.: Techno-economic network and irreversibility. In: Law, J. (ed.) A Sociology of Monsters: Essays on Power. Routledge, London (1991)

14. Akrich, M., Callon, M., Latour, B.: The key to success in innovation part 1: The art of interessement. International Journal of Innovation Management 6(2), 187–206 (2002)
15. Callon, M.: Actor-network theory-The market test. In: Law, J., Hassard, J. (eds.) Actor Network Theory and After. Blackwell Publishing, Oxford (1999)
16. Van de Ven, Poole: Explaining development and change in organization. Academy of Management Review 20(3), 510–540 (1995)
17. Callon, M.: Techno-economic networks and irreversibility. In: Law, J. (ed.) A Sociology of Monster: Essays on Power, Technology and Domination, Routledge, London (1991)
18. Callon, M.: Some elements of sociology of translation: Domestication of the scallops and the fishermen of the Brieuc Bay. In: Law, J. (ed.) Power, Action and Belief: A New Sociology of Knowledge, Routledge, London (1986)
19. Sarker, S., Sarker, S., Sidorova, A.: Understanding business process change failure: An actor network perspective. Journal of Management Information Systems 23(1), 51–86 (2006)
20. Orlikowski, W.J., Gash, D.C.: Technological frame: Making sense of information technology in organization. ACM Transactions on Information Systems 12(2), 174–207 (1994)
21. Bijker, W.E., Hughes, T.P., Pinch, T. (eds.): The social construction of Technology Systems: New direction in the sociology and history of technology. Maple -Vail, Inc., USA (1989)
22. Andrade, A.D., Urquhart, C.: The affordances of actor network theory in ICT for development research. Information Technology and People 23(4), 352–374 (2010)
23. Department for business innovation and skills, `http://www.bis.gov.uk/assets/biscore/business-sectors/docs/10-798-professional-business-services-2020-vision-for-growth`
24. Schultze, U., Avital, M.: Designing interviews to generate rich data for information systems research. Information and Organization 21, 1–16 (2011)
25. Mason, J.: Qualitative researching. Sage Publication, London (1996)
26. Miles, M.B., Huberman, A.M.: Qualitative data analysis: An expanded sourcebook. Sage Publication Ltd., Thousand Oaks (1994)
27. Boyatzis, R.: Transforming qualitative information: Thematic analysis and code development. Sage Publication Ltd., London (1998)
28. Teo, T.H.S., Srrivastava, S.C., Ranganathan, C., Loo, J.W.K.: A framework for stakeholder oriented mindfulness: Case of RFID implementation at YCH Group. Singapore. European Journal of Information Systems 20, 201–220 (2011)
29. Elie-Dit-Cosaque, C., Pallud, J., Kalika, M.: The Influence of individual, contextual and social factors on perceived behavioral control of information technology: A field theory approach. Journal of Management Information Systems 28(3), 201–234 (2011)
30. Macredie, R.D., Mijinyawa, K.: A theory-grounded framework of open source software adoption in SMEs. European Journal of Information Systems 20, 237–250 (2011)
31. Khoumbati, K., Themistocleous, M., Irani, Z.: Evaluating the adoption of enterprise application integration in health care organization. Journal of Management Information Systems 22(4), 69–108 (2006)
32. Yousafzai, S., Yani-De-Soriano, M.: Understanding customer-specific factors underpinning internet banking adoption. International Journal of Bank Marketing 30, 60–81 (2012)
33. Zhu, K., Kraemer, K., Xu, S.: Electronic business adoption by Europe firms: A cross-country assessment of the facilitators and inhibitors. European Journal of Information Systems 12, 251–256 (2003)

34. Kim, G.S.B., Kim, K.K., Lee, H.G.: IT capabilities, process-oriented dynamic capabilities and firm financial performance. Journal of the Association for Information Systems 12(7), 487–517 (2011)
35. Moore, G., Benbasat, I.: Development of an Instrument to measure the perceptions of adoption in information technology innovation. Information Systems Research 2(3), 192–222 (1991)
36. Venkatesh, V., Davis, F.: A model of the antecedents of perceived ease of use: Development and test. Decision Science 27(3), 451–481 (1996)
37. Xu, J., Benbasat, I., Cenfetelli, R.: The effects of service and consumer product knowledge on online customer loyalty. Journal of the Association for Information Systems 12(11), 741–766 (2011)
38. Moon, Y.: Don't blame the computer when self -disclosure moderates the self-serving bias. Journal of Consumer Psychology 13(1/2), 125–137 (2003)
39. Low, B., Johnston, W.J.: The evolution of network position in emerging and converging technologies. Journal of Business and Industrial Marketing 24(4/5), 431–438 (2009)
40. Beaver, G.: Small business, entrepreneurship and enterprise development. Person Education Limited Harlow (2002)
41. Wu, W., Ho, C.: Technology adaptation:The case of implementing a collaborative product commerce systems to new product design. In: Proceedings of the 7th International Conference on Electronic Commerce, ICEC 2005 pp. 674–680 (2005)
42. Lacovou, A.L., Benbasat, I., Dexter, A.: Electronic data interchange and small organizations: Adoption and impact of technology. MIS Quarterly 19(4), 465–485 (1995)

A Probability Based Similarity Scoring for DNA Motifs Comparison

Bin Tian[1], Xiujun Gong[1], Wenjun Wu[1], and Siling Feng[2]

[1] School of Computer Science and Technology, Tianjin University, Weijin Rd No. 92, Tianjin, 300072, China

[2] College of Information Science & Technology, Hannan University, Renmin Rd No. 58, Haikou, 570228, China

{tianbin696,fengsiling2008}@163.com, gongxj@tju.edu.cn, wuwenjun1988@126.com

Abstract. Comparing putative motifs is an important trail for the clustering of redundant motifs and mapping motifs to transcription factors from previously characterized motif databases. Still, most existing methods computed similarity based on position independence assumption. Here, we propose a probability similarity scoring schema, incorporating both information content of positions and pairwise nucleotide dependencies within motifs using a novel feature extraction method. This paper describes the details of features extraction and demonstrates its ability to improve motifs comparison. Furthermore, we show the capability of our method in the identification of similar motifs in a simulated dataset and a real dataset. All discovered motifs are not only found in human tissue but also in relevant species, such as mouse and rat, which indicates that it is a possible approach for elucidating DNA motifs that employ cross-species sequence conservation.

Keywords: motifs comparison, position information content, pairwise nucleotide dependence, similarity measures.

1 Introduction

Identification of transcription-factor binding sites (TFBS) in promoter sequences is a crucial task for deciphering transcription regulation. These binding sites are often modeled using Position Weight Matrices (PWM), which are also called position frequency matrices, profiles, etc. [1]. Many computation tools have been proposed for the discovery of de novel motifs in promoter sequence from a set of related sequences, but none has surpassed others [2]. A proper solution is to combine multiple algorithms and collect results from them, resulting in a set of redundant motifs. Since methods may discover motifs similar to other putative motifs, or similar to known motifs from characterized libraries, it is important to cluster similar motifs or merge similar motifs. Therefore, appropriate tools for computing similarity of motifs are required.

Most existing similarity measures of pairwise motifs are calculated with position independence assumption, and the main difference among them is the similarity function of two columns. Previous approaches for quantifying motifs similarity include the

V. Khachidze et al. (Eds.): iCETS 2012, CCIS 332, pp. 378–389, 2012.

Pearson correlation coefficient (PCC) method [3,4] that is more effective than other methods, the average log-likelihood ratio method described by Wang and Stormo [5], the Kullback-Leibler distance used in many works [6,7], the Jensen Shannon divergence (JS) [8], and many other algorithms [9,10]. Furthermore, Habib and Kaplan showed that it is better to distinguish informative columns from non-informative columns when calculating the similarity of two motifs, and introduced a new tool, BLiCscore, that exceeds others [1]. Apart from measures based on computing column-by-column, Pape and Rahmann proposed a natural similarity measure based on the asymptotic covariance between the numbers of PWM hits incorporating both strands [11].

Osada and Zaslavsky showed that per-position information content and pairwise nucleotide dependencies can help to improve the discovery of transcription-factor binding sites [12]. It has also been observed that highly conserved positions within motifs are clustered together [13]; this occurs because transcription factors rarely bind to only a single position. As many tools utilize this information to discover TFBS, it is a possible approach for us to cluster redundant motifs using this information.

Since the amount of raw data is very large, feature extraction is an important aspect to clustering. Among many representatives of features, feature vector (FV) is one used by many applications. Likewise, we can transform a PWM into a feature vector combining statistical information of positions' information content and pairwise nucleotide dependencies. There are two advantages: the first is reducing the storage consumption and time consumption, the other is helping to reach good micro-clusters quickly and make it convenient to merge similar motifs within micro-clusters.

In this paper, we first design a method to extract features from PWMs. We try to consider the statistical information of position information content instead of per-position information content, and consider only the pairwise nucleotides that are adjacent in order to avoid complexity. We then try to cluster a simulated dataset based on both PWMs and feature vectors; results show that feature vectors help algorithms to improve the accuracies of clustering and reduce computation time. Furthermore, we derive a probability similarity measure based on Bayesian rules.

We compare our measure with three other methods based on FVs in a simulated dataset, and results show that our method can perform as well as others. We also try to cluster a real dataset using these algorithms and map these putative motifs to known motifs, and results show that these measures find many motifs that are found not only in human tissue but also in other species such as rat and mouse. This indicates that it is a possible approach for elucidating DNA motifs that employ cross-species sequence conservation.

2 Method

2.1 Data preparation

In this paper, experiments are performed in a simulated dataset and a real dataset. As regards the simulated dataset, we construct a set of motifs similar to given motif by using a simulation as follows: applying random shifts to PWMs to generate 9 simulated motifs for each given motif. We first randomly select two columns and exchange them to generate one type of motif, then select one or two columns randomly and remove them to generate another one; the latter is obtained by selecting one column and exchanging the frequencies of two nucleotides randomly. These simulated motifs from one given motif are thought to be from common source.

The known motifs that are given to generate simulated motifs are from Jaspar [14]. To make the distance between motifs as great as possible, we obtain 25 motifs from 25 different transcription factors: the set of TFs are AGL3, RUNX1, TFAP2A, Ar, br_Z1, CREB1, dl_1,NFIL3, En1, ELK1, Evi1, FOXF2, Gamyb, Gfi, Klf4, Foxq1, Foxd3, FOXI1, HLF, HMG-I/Y, HNF1A, Foxa2, ESR1, PPARG::RXRA and NFE2L2.

The real dataset is from human kidney tissue. The set of tissue-specific genes for kidney tissue is obtained by querying the tissue-specific gene expression database TiGER [15] and database TisGED [16] against the tissue specific names. The genes' promoter sequences are downloaded from DBTSS [17] and EPD [18], and the promoter regions with 1500bp (-499bp - +1000bp around Transcription Start Site (TSS)) are used for motifs searching.

To apply clustering on the real dataset from human tissue, we first search for putative motifs by using multiple motifs discovery tools. The algorithms used are AlignACE [19], Gibbs Motif Sampler [20], MEME [21] and BioProspector [22]. The lengths of candidate motifs are fixed to 8-23bp, and the expected numbers of motifs are set as 20, while other parameters are set to default settings. Finally, we obtain 1,337 motifs from these four motifs discovery tools for human kidney tissue.

Since the formats of motif outputs from different tools are diverse and inconvenient for motifs comparison, we transform all the outputs into the format of PWMs. We define a PWM as $M = \{f_{ib}, 0 < i \le l, b \in \{A, C, G, T\}\}$, where l is the length of a motif and f_{ib} represents the frequency of nucleotide b at position i. To avoid possible zero numbers, we get the estimated value of f_{ib} by using a Bayesian estimation approach [1].

2.2 Feature Extraction

Feature extraction techniques are widely employed to reduce the dimensionality of data and to enhance discriminatory information in pattern recognition, and many tools deal with feature extraction such as principal component analysis (PCA) and linear discriminant analysis (LDA) [23]. In fact, the design of a classifier becomes very simple if patterns from one class hold the same feature vector different from the feature vectors held by patterns from other classes [23]. As for different applications, there are many concrete measures for representing raw dataset. With respect to motifs clustering, we can explore the information that a PWM holds and construct a feature vector to model the motif.

In this section, we describe the construction of feature vectors for motifs. Given a PWM, we can summarize it by two aspects of information, the statistic information of positions' information content and pairwise nucleotide dependencies. The following sections present them respectively.

2.2.1 Statistical Information of Positions' Information Content

Information content (IC) of a position in a set of columns is referred to in many works and we introduce it briefly here. IC is an important concept based on the information-theoretic notion of entropy [12]. The information content of a position expresses the number of bits necessary to describe the position in a motif, and the higher the information content, the more conserved (or probably more important) the position [12]. We define the IC for position *i* within a motif as follows:

$$IC_i = 2 + \sum_b f_{ib} \log f_{ib} \tag{1}$$

Since the widths of motifs are diverse, it is important to transform ICs of motifs into a uniform vector, instead of using per-position IC directly. It is better not to make arbitrary decisions about the distribution of ICs within motif. However, we can divide the range of ICs into several regions and count the frequency of each part, just as is often done in image recognition, which performs well in some applications. Considering the range of motifs' lengths, the range of ICs can be divided into four regions as {[0.0-a], [a-b], [b-c], [c-2.0]}. One possible approach to the decision of these parameters is to define parameter b as the mean value of ICs and define a as upper quartile, and define c as lower quartile. To examine the performance of this approach, we compare it with other groups of parameters on a simulated dataset. To estimate the frequencies of ICs within four regions, we use a Bayesian estimation approach with a Dirichlet prior, whose parameters are (1,1,1,1). We define the vector for statistic information of positions' information content as $ICV = \{ICV_i, 1 \le i \le 4\}$.

2.2.2 Pairwise Nucleotide Dependencies

Whereas many methods assume that each base contributes independently to binding, it has been demonstrated that there are interdependent effects between bases [12]. There are many types of pairwise nucleotide dependencies, such as bases that are nearby whose distances can vary from zero to some instant number. Although it is better to consider all possible pairwise nucleotide dependencies, it is time-consuming and ineffective. In particular, we only consider pairwise nucleotides that are adjacent. Unlike Osada, Zaslavsky and Singh [12], we define pairwise nucleotide dependency as the probability that the two nucleotides occur concurrently. Given position-independent assumption, we define the probability of two nucleotides A and B occurring at the same time as $P(AB) = P(A)P(B)$. Following this, we calculate the probability of pairwise nucleotide dependency for a motif as:

$$P(AB) = \sum_{1 \le i \le l-1} \frac{f_{iA} * f_{(i+1)B}}{l-1} \tag{2}$$

Since the alphabet of DNA is composed of four nucleotides, there are 16 pairwise nucleotide dependencies such as {P(AA),P(AC),...,P(TG),P(TT)}. We define the vector for pairwise nucleotide dependencies as $PND = \{PND_i, 1 \le i \le 16\}$.

2.3 Probability Similarity Scoring Schema (PS^3) for Motifs Comparison

In this section, a novel motifs similarity scoring schema derived from Bayesian theory is described. Given two feature vectors (FVs) from two motifs, the aim is to define the similarity between them. We define the similarity of two motifs as the ratio of the probability of two motifs coming from a common source and the probability of these two motifs coming from independent sources, as:

$$PS^3(M_1,M_2)=\frac{P(M_1,M_2 \mid CS)}{P(M_1 \mid IS)P(M_2 \mid IS)} \tag{3}$$

Where CS and IS are abbreviations for common source and independent source, respectively. The probability of two motifs coming from common source can be derived as:

$$P(M_1,M_2 \mid CS)=\prod_{i=1,2} P(CS \mid M_i)=\prod_{i=1,2}\frac{P(M_i \mid CS)P(CS)}{P(M_i)} \tag{4}$$

Since motif modeled by a feature vector contains multiple items (an item is referred to as T), we can compute the probability of one motif coming from common source using Bayesian theory as follows:

$$\begin{aligned} P(M_i \mid CS) &= \sum_t P(M_i \mid CS,T=t)P(T=t \mid CS) \\ &= P(M_i)\sum_t \frac{P(T=t \mid M_i)P(T=t \mid CS)}{P(T=t)} \end{aligned} \tag{5}$$

In a similar way, the probability of one motif coming from an independent source can be derived as:

$$P(M_i \mid IS)=P(M_i)\sum_t \frac{P(T=t \mid M_i)P(T=t \mid IS)}{P(T=t)} \tag{6}$$

Since there is no knowledge for the prior distribution of a particular motif, we give the probability of common source and the probability of one motif uniform distribution. As there are only two motifs within a similarity scoring schema, it is possible to conclude that the probability of one item coming from an independent source and the probability of one item coming from a particular motif are the same. The probability of one item can be estimated from the background distribution. Because we transform a PWM of a motif into two feature vectors as described before, it is better to define the similarity scoring schema for two DNA motifs after taking the log as:

$$\begin{aligned} PS^3(M_1,M_2) &= \alpha \log \frac{P(ICV_1,ICV_2 \mid CS)}{P(ICV_1 \mid M_1)P(ICV_2 \mid M_2)} \\ &+ \beta \log \frac{P(PND_1,PND_2 \mid CS)}{P(PND_1 \mid M_1)P(PND_2 \mid M_2)} \end{aligned} \tag{7}$$

The parameters α and β can discriminate the contribution of statistical information of positions' information content and pairwise nucleotide dependencies. To determine the proper weights for these two aspects of information, we compare the results based on different groups of parameters.

2.4 Clustering

Differing from other works that merge similar motifs while clustering, we try to firstly cluster putative motifs into several micro-clusters and use other techniques to acquire the representatives for these micro-clusters. As there is no merging of similar motifs, and to reduce computation time, we define the similarity of two clusters as the similarity of two representatives from each one. However, the selection of representatives is a significant. There are many ways to deal with this issue, such as mean-value, median, mode, etc. However, these measures cannot be applied to our clustering procedure directly because of the complexity of motif. We choose a modified form from Mode, which is defined as the motif whose similarities with others within the same cluster are maximal.

There are many clustering techniques that can be applied, such as partitioning methods, hierarchical methods, density-based methods and so on [24]. Here, we only consider hierarchical agglomerative clustering algorithm, because of its simplicity. The algorithm computes the similarity between all pairs of clusters and merges the pair with the highest similarity score into a new cluster. One difficult issue with these algorithms is choosing one criterion that can help to decide when to stop clustering and get a proper number of clusters. Here, we consider one modified measure from within cluster similarity (WCs) [24], which is average within cluster similarity (AWCs).

$$AWCs(C) = \frac{1}{K}\sum_{k=1}^{K}\left(\frac{1}{\| C_k \|}\sum_{M_i, M_j \in C_k} sim(M_i, M_j)\right) \tag{8}$$

Where C ($C = \{C_k, 1 \le k \le K\}$) is the set of clusters and K is the number of clusters at current stage.

2.5 Criterion to Evaluate the Accuracies of Similarity Measures

To compare the accuracies of clustering based on different methods, we design accuracy value (AV) to score the performance of a method.

$$AV = P_{right} / (P_{right} + P_{wrong}) \tag{9}$$

Where P_{right} is the number of motif pairs that are classified into the same cluster and that are from the common source, while P_{wrong} is the number of motif pairs that are classified into the same cluster but are from different sources.

3 Results

3.1 Determination of Parameters

It is important in feature extraction to decide the parameters for the partition of ICs. To discriminate motifs, it is better to make the decision elaborately. One possible approach is to make the three partition points as upper quartile, mean value and down quartile. After analyzing the ICs of positions from the simulated dataset, we set it as {0.25, 0.50, 1.00}. To compare with other approaches, we also consider solutions that are listed as Figure 1 (a). The four algorithms used are PS^3, Euclidean Distance (ED), Pearson Correlation Coefficient (PCC) and Jensen Shannon divergence (JS). The results show that the average performance of the fourth group of solutions for the four methods is the best one, and it is actually a practical approach.

In addition to parameters for the partition of ICs, it is also important to determine the weights that combine the statistic information of positions' information content and pairwise nucleotide dependencies. Since we have no knowledge about the two aspects of information, the first possible solution is equal weight. However, this may not be the best approach, so we also consider other approaches as shown in Figure 1 (b). Results affirm that the sixth group of weights performs the best, and we can conduct experiments with default parameters equal to them.

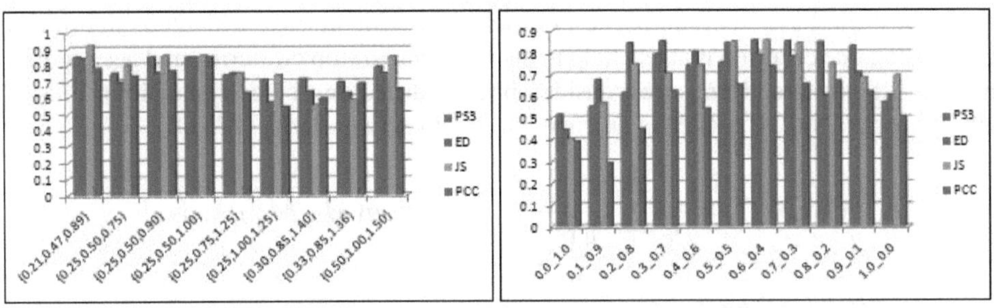

(a) (b)

Fig. 1. (a) The accuracies of different methods at different fractiles when the number of clusters comes to a predetermined value; (b) the accuracies of different methods at different groups of weights when the number of clusters comes to a predetermined value. Here, the predetermined value is 25.

3.2 Performance of Feature Vectors on Improving Motifs Comparison

Among many tools that can be used to score the similarity of motifs, we choose three methods for clustering based on both PWMs and feature vectors (FVs). We use a simulated dataset to test them. Results (Figure 2) prove that the FVs can vastly improve the performance of motifs comparison.

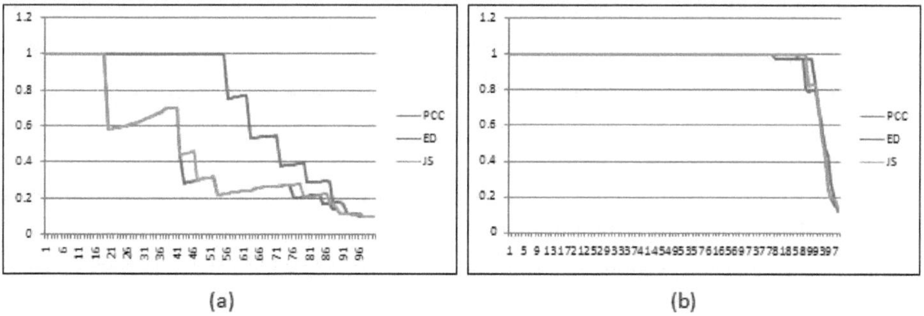

Fig. 2. (a) The accuracies of different methods for clustering based on PWMs; (b) the accuracies of different methods for clustering based on features vector (FVs). Here, the predetermined number of clusters is 10.

3.3 Decision of the Number of Clusters

Although it is difficult to determine the number of clusters, it is important for us to find a simple way to determine a proper number of clusters. Following methods described previously, we conduct experiments on both simulated dataset and real dataset using four methods. Results (Figure 3 (a)) show that the decisions of cluster number for different methods are basically consistent. Furthermore, results (Figure 3 (b)) indicate that the proper number of clusters for real dataset is between 17 and 20. In fact, we set the number as 18.

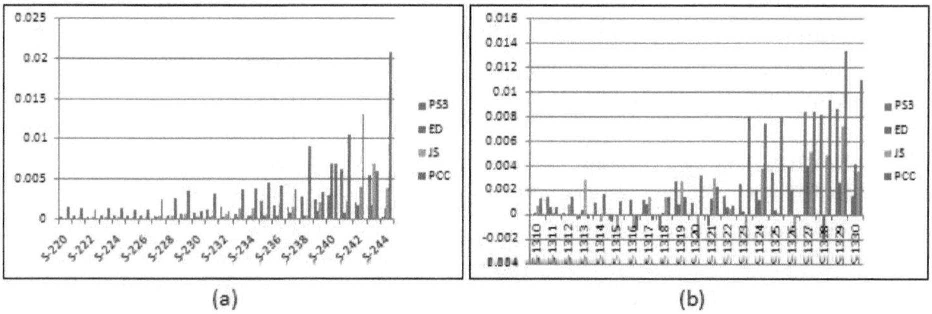

Fig. 3. The AWC values of different stages within clustering for different methods. (a) is an AWCs figure for simulated dataset; (b) is an AWCs figure for real dataset.

3.4 Results of Real Dataset from Human Kidney Tissue

We also conduct experiments on a real dataset from human kidney tissue. As described in previous section, the proper number of clusters is defined as 18. After clustering putative motifs from multiple tools' results, we try to map the result to known transcription-factors using STAMP tool [25] (http://www.benoslab.pitt.edu/stamp/). To display found TFs, the threshold for E-value is selected as smaller than 1.0e-5. Results (Table 1) show that our method finds most motifs found by other methods as well. Furthermore, PS^3 also finds some unique motifs mapped to known TFs.

There are 9 TFs from Jaspar mapped by putative motifs found by all four methods, br_Z1, HMG-I/Y, hb, Pax4, id1, AZF1, RAP1, btd and opa. After mapping to TRANSFAC [26] (7.0 - public), we find that there are counterparts in TRANSFAC for 7 TFs that are namely hb, Pax4, id1, AZF1, RAP1, btd and opa. Among them, Pax4 represents negative cell specificity in the kidney, liver, brain and testis, which appear mainly in human and rat. Id1 represents positive cell specificity in undifferentiated cells for both human and rat. Specially, HMG-I represents increased expression in various types of cancer within human tissue.

The TFs mapped by putative motifs found by PS^3 only are AP1, abi4, ARR1 and DAL81. From previous discussion, we conclude that it is a possible approach for elucidating DNA motifs that employ cross-species sequences conservation.

Table 1. Known transcription-factors mapped by putative motifs found by different methods

Matrix Id	Transcription-factor name	Methods
MA0010.1	br_Z1	PS3, ED, JS, PCC
MA0013.1	br_Z4	PCC
MA0039.1	Klf4	ED,JS, PCC
MA0041.1	Foxd3	ED, JS, PCC
MA0045.1	HMG-I/Y	PS3, ED, JS, PCC
MA0049.1	hb	PS3, ED, JS, PCC
MA0055.1	Myf	PCC
MA0068.1	Pax4	PS3, ED, JS, PCC
MA0073.1	RREB1	PS3, ED, PCC
MA0079.1	SP1	PS3, JS, PCC
MA0082.1	squamosa	ED, JS, PCC
MA0099.2	AP1	PS3
MA0120.1	id1	PS3, ED, JS, PCC
MA0123.1	abi4	PS3
MA0149.1	EWSR1-FLI1	PS3, ED, JS
MA0163.1	PLAG1	PCC
MA0274.1	ARR1	PS3
MA0277.1	AZF1	PS3, ED, JS, PCC
MA0287.1	CUP2	PCC
MA0290.1	DAL81	PS3
MA0323.1	IXR1	PCC
MA0359.1	RAP1	PS3, ED, JS, PCC
MA0361.1	RDS1	JS
MA0373.1	RPN4	PS3, ED, PCC
MA0375.1	RSC30	JS
MA0399.1	SUT1	JS
MA0429.1	YLL054C	JS
MA0443.1	btd	PS3, ED, JS, PCC
MA0456.1	opa	PS3, ED, JS, PCC

4 Conclusion and Discussion

Finding accurate and meaningful motifs is the foundation of analysis of tissue-specific genes and remains a considerable challenge. Although many tools deal with this issue, no one surpass others in all situations. A proper solution is to integrate the results from multiple algorithms by clustering redundant motifs and mapping motifs to known transcription-factors. Both these tasks involve motifs comparison. Most existing methods compute the similarity of motifs column-by-column, based on positions independent assumption.

In this paper, we present a novel probability similarity scoring schema (PS^3) based on feature extraction, which is derived from Bayesian theory. The extracted features reflect the statistic of positions' information content and pairwise nucleotide dependencies, which are main information regarding PWMs. The PS^3 discriminates two pairs of motifs while taking into account the probability that two motifs are from a common source and the probability that they are from independent sources. Results prove that our extracted features improve the performance of motifs comparison as compared to PWMs; the combination of PS^3 and extracted features performs as well as other measures and even exceeds others in some situations.

Feature extraction techniques play a vital role in classification, which can be applied to clustering. In this paper, we use simple methods to extract two aspects of features. Furthermore, we can consider other measures that help to extract features and reduce the dimensionality of data and enhance discriminatory information, such as PCA and LDA.

We use hierarchical agglomerative clustering to cluster similar motifs. As with other clustering techniques, it is important but difficult to decide the proper number of clusters. In this paper, the average within cluster similarity (AWCs) is derived to determine the proper number of clusters derived from within cluster similarity (WCs), and results prove the feasibility of AWCs. As for hierarchical agglomerative clustering, there is a vital disadvantage in that it is impossible to cancel previous clustering stages even if a better solution is found. To deal with this issue, we can consider the integration of hierarchical agglomerative clustering with iterative relocation methods [24].

In this paper, we select a representative of a cluster as the center of clusters, defined as before. However, there is one problem in this method: the selected representative may not contain the information from other similar motifs. A proper solution for this is to find the best alignment of two PWMs using similarity measures, and merge them after clustering motifs into micro-clusters.

Acknowledgements. This research is partly supported by the Natural Science Funding of China under grant number 61170177 and innovation funding of Tianjin University.

References

1. Habib, N., Kaplan, T., Margalit, H., Friedman, N.: A Novel Bayesian DNA Motif Comparison Method for Clustering and Retrieval. PLoS Comput. Biol. 4(2), e1000010 (2008), doi:10.1371/journal.pcbi.1000010

2. Tompa, M., Li, N., Bailey, T.L., Church, G.M., Moor, B.D., Eskin, E., Favorov, A.V., Frith, M.C., et al.: Accessing computational tools for the discovery of transcription factor binding sites. Nature Biotechnology 23(1) (January 2005), doi:10.1038/nbt1053
3. Hughes, J., Estep, P., Tavazoic, S., Church, G.: Computational identification of cis-regulatory elements associated with groups of functionally related genes in Saccharomyces cerevisiae. J. Mol. Biol. 296, 1205–1214 (2000)
4. Xie, X., Lu, J., Kulbokas, E., Golub, T.V., Lindblad-Toh, K., et al.: Systematic discovery of regulatory motifs in human promoters and 3' UTRs by comparison of several mammals. Nature 434, 338–345 (2005)
5. Wang, T., Stormo, G.D.: Combining phylogenetic data with co-regulated genes to identify regulatory motifs. Bioinformatics 19, 2369–2380 (2003)
6. Alerts, S., et al.: Computational detection of cis-regulatory modules. Bioinformatics 19(suppl. 2), ii5–ii14 (2003)
7. Roepcke, S., et al.: T-Reg Comparator: an analysis tool for the comparison of position weight matrics. Nucleic Acids Res. 33(suppl. 2), W438–W441 (2005)
8. Lin, J.: Divergence measures based on the Shannon entropy, pp. 145–151 (1991)
9. Tanaka, E., Bailey, T., Grant, C.E., Noble, W.S., Keich, U.: Improved similarity scores for comparing motifs. Bioinformatics 27(12), 1603–1609 (2011), doi:10.1093/bioinformatics/btr257
10. Schones, D.E., Sumazin, P., Zhang, M.Q.: Similarity of position frequency matrices for transcription factor binding sites. Bioinformatics 21(3), 307–313 (2005), doi:10.1093/bioinformatics/bth480
11. Pape, U.J., Rahmann, S., Vingron, M.: Natural similarity measures between position frequency matrices with an application to clustering. Bioinformatics 24(3), 350–357 (2008), doi:10.1093/bioinformatics/btm610
12. Osada, R., Zaslavsky, E., Singh, M.: Comparative analysis of methods for representing and searching for transcription factor binding sites. Bioinformatics 20(18), 3516–3525 (2004), doi:10.1093/bioinformatics/bth438
13. Kechris, K.J., Zwet, E.V., Bickel, P.J., Eisen, M.B.: Detecting DNA regulatory motifs by incorporating positional trends in information content. Genome Biology 5, R50 (2004)
14. Bryne, J.C., Valen, E., Tang, M.H.E., et al.: JASPAR, the open access database of transcription factor binding profiles: new content and tools in the 2008 update. Nucleic Acids Research 36, D102–D106 (2008) (database issue)
15. Liu, X., Yu, X.P., Donald, J.Z.: TiGER: A database for tissue-specific gene expression and regulation. Bioinformatics 9, 217 (2008)
16. Xiao, S.J., Zhang, C., Zhou, Q., Qi, Z.L.: TiSGeD: a database for tissue-specific genes. Bioinformatics 9, 217 (2008)
17. Suzuki, Y., Yamashita, R., Sugano, S., Nakai, K.: DBTSS, DataBase of Transcription Start Sites: progress report 2004. Nucleic Acids Res. 32, D78–D81 (2004) (database issue)
18. Schmid, C.D., Praz, V., Delorenzi, M., Perier, R., Bucher, P.: The Eukaryotic Promoter Database EPD. Nucleic Acids Res. 32, D82–D85 (2004) (database issue)
19. Hughes, J.D., Estep, P.W., Tavazole, S., Church, G.M.: Computational identification of cis-regulatory elements associated with functionally coherent groups of genes in Saccharomyces cerevisiae. J. Mol. Biol. 296, 1205–1214 (2000)
20. Thijs, G., et al.: A higher-order background model improves the detection of promoter regulatory elements by Gibbs sampling. Bioinformatics 17, 1113–1122 (2001)
21. Bailey, T.L., Elkan, C.: The value of prior knowledge in discovering motifs with MEME. In: Proceeding of the Third International Conference on Intelligent Systems for Molecular Biology, pp. 21–29. AAAI Press, Menlo Park (1995)

22. Liu, X., Brutlag, D.L., Liu, J.S.: BIOPROSPECTOR: Discovering Conserved DNA Motifs in Upstream Regulatory Regions of Co-Expressed Genes. In: Pacific Symposium on Biocomputing, vol. 6, pp. 127–138 (2001)
23. Li, H.F., Jiang, T., Zhang, K.S.: Efficient and Robust Feature Extraction by Maximum Margin Criterion. IEEE Transactions on Neural Networks 17(1) (2006)
24. Han, J.W., Kamber, M.: Data Ming Concepts and Techniques, 2nd edn. Morgan Kaufmann, San Francisco (1999)
25. Mahony, S., Benos, P.V.: STAMP: a web tool for exploring DNA-binding motif similarities. Nucleic Acids Res. 35, W253–W258 (2007) (web server issue), doi:10.1093/nar/gkm272
26. Wingender, E., Chen, X., Hehl, R., Karas, H., Liebich, I., Matys, V., Meinhardt, T., Prus, M., Reuter, I., Schacherer, F.: TRANSFAC: an integrated system for gene expression regulation. Nucleic Acids Res. 28(1) (2000)

Security Software Formal Modeling and Verification Method Based on UML and Z

Kunyu Cao*, Xiaohong Li, and Jinliang Xing

School of Computer Science and Technology, Tianjin University, Tianjin, China
{kunyucao,xiaohongli,jinliangxing}@tju.edu.cn

Abstract. With the continuous expansion of software application range and the frequent occurrence of software security accidents, software security has become the focus of attention. This paper proposes a security software formal modeling and verification method, which uses UML to organize the basic structure of software, and uses Z specification to supply security semantics for UML model in order to support formal model verification. This method can guarantee the security of software design, while reducing the complexity of formal modeling. On this basis, this paper also introduces a website register function as case study and discovers the security flaws in the system design; the effectiveness and practicality of this method is then demonstrated.

Keywords: software security, formal method, weakness detection, theorem proving.

1 Introduction

In software design process, the security flaws introduced by lack of security considerations are important factors causing rapid growth of software security issues. Microsoft's research report [1] pointed out that more than 50% of software security flaws stem from unsafe design, and will lead to higher repair costs in the later stages of software development. Therefore, the timely detection of defects in the earlier stages of software development is very necessary.

Modeling and verification is an important method to study the security of software design. However, due to the high level of difficulty and complexity of software modeling, there is not a standardized process to develop security software [2].

Software modeling can be divided into two major categories, formal and informal. Informal methods often cannot support model automatic verification effectively. Bau and Mitchell [3] proposed a conceptual framework that modeling system security from three aspects including system, threats and security attributes. Ali, El Kassas and Mahmoud [4] present a modeling method that combines SAM and threat modeling technique, but the formal refinement before model verification increases the complexity of the process.

---

* Corresponding author.

V. Khachidze et al. (Eds.): iCETS 2012, CCIS 332, pp. 390–401, 2012.

Formal methods can effectively support model verification methods such as belief logic [5], model checking [6] and theorem proving [7], but most of them face the restrictions of limited expression ability and higher modeling complexity. Yoo and Jee [8] introduced a formal integrated development and verification environment for safety-critical software, mainly used for requirements analysis and design of the reactor protection system. Khan and Zafar [9] modeled and verified security properties of a railway control system formally using Z [10] specification. Bartels and Glesner [11] presented a modeling and verification method for LLVM program based on CSP [12] [13], but CSP's limited expression ability cannot describe complex temporal behaviors.

To solve these problems, scholars have put forward a method of combining UML and formal language. Hei et al [14] proposed a method that transformed UML state diagrams into Petri net model, which verifies UML model indirectly through the verification of the Petri net model. Moebius, Stenzel and Reif [15] present a model-driven method that can generate a formal model for security verification from UML diagrams. These new ideas improved, to some extent, purely formal methods.

This Paper presents a security software formal modeling and verification method. Firstly, this method builds formal models containing semantics of software using UML and Z specification. After that, we formalize software weaknesses based on analysis and abstraction. Finally, this method verifies software design security by theorem proving, using Z-EVES tool.

Compared with other methods, this method has several advantages: 1) Combination of rigorous formal methods with UML fetch up the lack of security considerations of UML; 2) Using formal model as intermediate bridges the gap between high-level design model with specific code; 3) Using UML view as the modeling framework can reduce the system formal modeling complexity efficiently. 4) Application of theorem proving verification can effectively find weaknesses in software design in order to reduce hem in a timely manner. To the best of our knowledge, there exists no other approach that combines all of these benefits.

The rest of the paper is organized into four sections, where section 2 describes the construction of software formal modeling, section 3 describes software security verification, and section 4 demonstrates our method using a case study of website register system. Finally, section 5 provides concluding remarks.

2 Software Formal Modeling Method

2.1 Existing Problems

UML is used widely as an important software design modeling language in software development process. However, due to its lack of security considerations, although the software meets the functional requirements there are often some serious security flaws. In addition, UML has no rigorous mathematical support, resulting in uncertainty and ambiguity factors that hinder the efficiency of software development.

Formal method is an effective software modeling and security verification method. However, due to the high complexity of formal modeling, formal method cannot be applied to large-scale software development process.

In general, the use of only UML or formal method respectively cannot implements the goal of ensuring software security and decreasing procedure complexity.

2.2 The Proposed Method

To solve this problem, this paper proposes an integrated method that combines UML with formal language Z. This method extracts a software operating sequence from a UML sequence diagram and models it using Z, which can compensate for the disadvantages of the informality and lack of security expression ability of UML, while reducing the complexity of formal modeling. This paper has also modeled the weaknesses in Common Weakness Enumeration (CWE) to support design phase software security verification. The Method process is shown below.

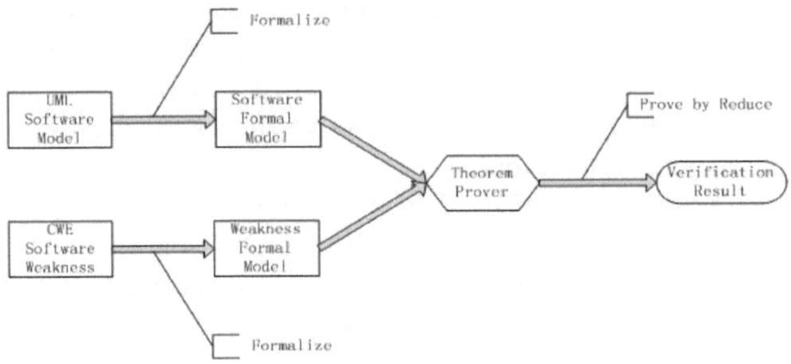

Fig. 1. An overview of proposed method

2.3 Software Modeling Framework

Based on the above method, the modeling framework is shown in Figure 2.

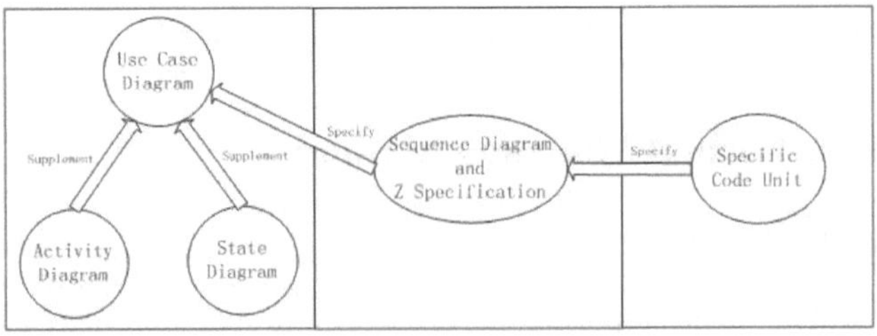

Fig. 2. Software Modeling Framework

The modeling process based on the definition of software life cycle is divided into three phases, namely requirements, design and implement phases. The requirements phase comprises the use of case diagram, activity diagram and state diagram, which describes software needs generally. The design phase is composed of sequence diagram and Z specification. The sequence diagram further refines each function module to describe the sequence of messages between function units. Then, using Z specification to provide more specific security semantics information for each system operation, the formal software behavior sequence is built in order to support the design stage software security verification. In coding phase, the constructed formal model can also help engineer more accurate and efficient implementation of software function.

2.4 Generation of the Formal Model

This paper use Z specification operation schema to model the software operation sequence extracted from UML sequence diagram. Each function in the sequence diagram can be described in an operation schema, in which the parameters and return value are represented by input and output. In schema declaration, the specific business logic of a function is defined as the rules of the predicate part of the schema. The Z specification template of functions is shown in Figure 3.

Operation_A
input?: seq Char
output!: seq Char

output! = input?

Fig. 3. Function Operation_A Formalization Template

The above Z specification shows that the parameters and return value of function Operation_A are all of string type. The predicate part of the specification indicates that the function is simply outputting the string without other process. For more complex functions, users only need to add the corresponding logical constraints in the predicate part.

The sequence diagram corresponds to the software function module which contains a group of software operations. After the formalization of each operation, there will be a formalized operation sequence of software function module. On this basis, section 3 will add formal security semantics for each operation, in order to support the software design phase security verification.

3 Software Security verification

3.1 Software Security Weakness Description

Software security weakness includes two basic elements: system behavior and security constraint. System behavior sequence consists of a series of system behaviors representing the software's actual actions. Security constraint is a specific system behavior sequence that security software should have. Once the system behaviors violate security constraint, which is lack certain safety-critical behaviors, there exists a security weakness. Their detailed definitions are as follows.

Definition 1: System behavior sequence (SBS)
SBSi = <SBi1, SBi2, SBi3, ..., SBin>, i = 1, 2, 3,..., Where SB is system behavior.

Definition 2: Security constraint (SC)
SCj = <CBj1, CBj2, CBj3,…, CBjn>, j = 1,2,3,…, Where CB is stands for constraint behavior.

Definition 3: Software security weakness (SSW)
SSWi = <CBi1, CBi2,…, CBij, ¬CBi(j+1), ¬CBi(j+2),…, ¬CBi(j+k), ¬CBi(j+k+1), … , CBin>, i, j, k = 1, 2, 3,…..

This paper formalizes software weaknesses based on these definitions. The formal definitions of system resource, event type, event, and security status are the basic elements of software weakness formalization process. System resources are the security-related elements of software in each system behavior, such as sensitive information input by a user. Each event has a certain event type associated with some resources; all system events constitute the system security status, which represents system behaviors. In the actual project, we must also define some variable types and built-in functions to assist modeling. For specific definitions, see Figures 4 and 5.

```
Resource ::= Resource1 | Resource2 | Resource3
EventType ::= Behovior1 | Behavior2 | Behavior3 | Behavior4 | Behavior5

 Event
|type : EventType
|resource : Reource
|

 SecurityStatus
|events : seq Event
|
```

Fig. 4. Formal Definitions of Event Type, Event and Security Status

```
Bool ::= True | False
[Char]
| md5 : seq Char → seq Char
```

Fig. 5. Formal Definitions of Auxiliary Types

Based on the previously described method and related definitions, software security flaws can be formalized for the Z specification model. The declaration part describes system resources, and the predicate part describes system behavior sequence, security constraints and the absent safety-critical behavior. Figure 6 shows the software weakness formalization template; it indicates that due to the lack of safety-critical behavior 3 between behavior 1 and behavior 2, there exists a security weakness.

$$\begin{array}{l}
\textit{Weakness} \\
\hline
\Delta SecurityStatus \\
resource?: Resource \\
\hline
\#\, events' \geqslant 2 \\
\exists n1, n3: \mathbb{Z} \mid 1 \leqslant n1 < n3 \leqslant \#\, events' \\
\quad \bullet\ (events'\ n1)\,.\,type = Behavior1 \\
\qquad \wedge\ (events'\ n1)\,.\,resource = resource? \\
\qquad \wedge\ (events'\ n3)\,.\,type = Behavior3 \\
\qquad \wedge\ (events'\ n3)\,.\,resource = resource? \\
\qquad \wedge\ \neg\,(\exists n2: \mathbb{Z} \mid n1 < n2 < n3 \\
\qquad\qquad \bullet\ ((events'\ n2)\,.\,type = Behavior2 \\
\qquad\qquad\quad \wedge\ (events'\ n2)\,.\,resource = resource?)) \\
\hline
\end{array}$$

Fig. 6. The Formalization Template of Software Security Weakness

3.2 Extension of Security Semantics

In order to support formal safety verification, this section adds some security-related semantics information for the software formal model. Specifically, system resources and system behaviors are introduced into the declaration part of function model and system events caused by the operation are added into the predicate part. The extension information does not belong to the business logic of this function; they represent the security-related system behaviors of the function operation. Such a function includes one or more system behaviors, and each sequence diagram corresponds to a system behavior sequence. Figure 7 presents the extended function Operation_A.

$$\begin{array}{l}
\textit{Operation_A} \\
\hline
input?: seq\ Char \\
output!: seq\ Char \\
\hline
output! = input? \\
\exists\, event: Event \\
\quad \bullet\ event\,.\,type = Behavior1 \\
\qquad \wedge\ event\,.\,resource = resource\ ? \\
\qquad \wedge\ events' = events \frown \langle\, event\, \rangle \\
\hline
\end{array}$$

Fig. 7. The Extended Function Operation_A Formal Model

3.3 Theorem Proving

In traditional software engineering, software security is entirely dependent on the ability and experience of security experts and engineers. This not only raises the threshold of safety design but also introduces some non-deterministic factors. Therefore, this paper validates software formal model using the theorem proving method based on the software formal model and weakness formal model; this method is shown in Figure 8.

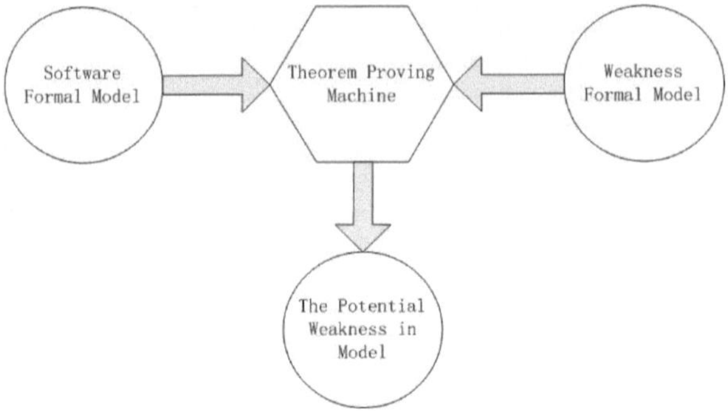

Fig. 8. Software Weakness Verification Schematic

This paper uses Z-EVES tool as a theorem proving machine to carry out proving by reduction. The input is the formal model of software and weaknesses, and to prepare corresponding weakness detection theorem, the proving result will show whether the software design contains any weakness. The weakness detection theorem is shown in Figure 9.

$$\textbf{theorem } \mathit{WeaknessDetection}$$
$$\mathit{SquenceDiagram} \Rightarrow \mathit{Weakness}\ [\mathit{resource}\ ? := \mathit{Resource}]$$

Fig. 9. Weakness Detection Theorem

4 Case Study: Website Registration

Website registration function is closely related to the security of users' sensitive information. Thus, this paper selected user registration function as a case to verify the effectiveness of the proposed method. The system sequence diagram (Figure 10) is obtained by reverse engineering of an actual website, the proving tool is Z-EVES 2.3.1 and the experiment platform is Windows 7.

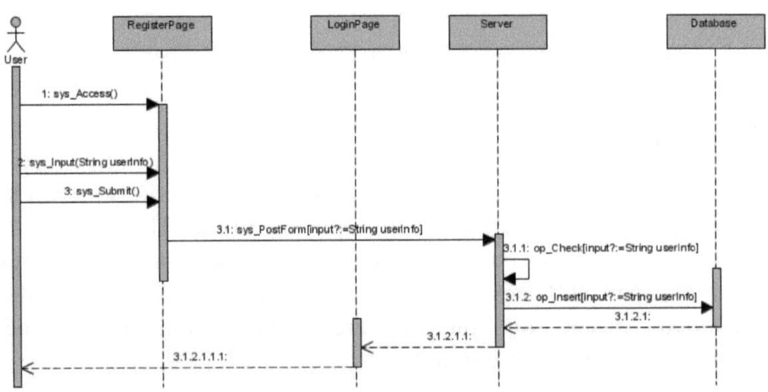

Fig. 10. Website Registration Module Sequence diagram

In this system, the system resource is user sensitive information, the event types include database operations, encryption operations and data transmission, and so on. There are also some auxiliary types and functions. Figure 11 shows the basic definitions of the formal model.

$$
\begin{aligned}
&Resource ::= UserInfo \\
&EventType ::= Query \\
&\quad\quad \mid KeyEncrypt \\
&\quad\quad \mid HashEncrypt \\
&\quad\quad \mid Store \\
&\quad\quad \mid Transmit \\
&\quad\quad \mid Validate \\
&\quad\quad \mid DeclareSensitive
\end{aligned}
$$

$$
\begin{aligned}
&Bool ::= True \mid False \\
&[Char] \\
&\quad MD5: \mathrm{seq}\ Char \rightarrow \mathrm{seq}\ Char \\
&\quad DES: \mathrm{seq}\ Char \rightarrow \mathrm{seq}\ Char \\
&\quad Check: \mathrm{seq}\ Char \rightarrow Bool \\
&\quad CheckValidation: \mathrm{seq}\ Char \rightarrow Bool \\
&\quad SQLInsert: \mathrm{seq}\ Char \rightarrow Bool
\end{aligned}
$$

Fig. 11. Registration Module Basic Definitions Formal Description

In accordance with the method of this article and the previous definition, the four system operations in sequence diagram can be modeled as shown in Figure 12. Figure 13 presents the system operation sequence.

$$
\begin{aligned}
&\underline{\quad sysInput \quad} \\
&\Delta SecurityStatus \\
&input?: \mathrm{seq}\ Char \\
&output!: \mathrm{seq}\ Char \\
&resource?: Resource \\
&\hline \\
&output! = input? \\
&\exists\, event: Event \\
&\quad \bullet\ event.type = DeclareSensitive \\
&\quad \wedge event.resource = resource? \\
&\quad \wedge events' = events \frown \langle event \rangle
\end{aligned}
$$

Fig. 12. Registration Module Basic Operations Formal Model

```
opCheck
ΔSecurityStatus
input?: seq Char
output!: seq Char
result!: Bool
resource?: Resource
────────────────
result! = Check input?
output! = input?
∃ event: Event
  • event.type = Query
    ∧ event.resource = resource?
    ∧ events' = events ⁀ ⟨event⟩
```

```
sysPostForm
ΔSecurityStatus
input?: seq Char
output!: seq Char
resource?: Resource

output! = input?
∃ event: Event
  • event.type = Transmit
    ∧ event.resource = resource?
    ∧ events' = events ⁀ ⟨event⟩
```

```
opInsert
ΔSecurityStatus
input?: seq Char
result!: Bool
resource?: Resource
────────────────
result! = SQLInsert input?
∃ event: Event
  • event.type = Store
    ∧ event.resource = resource?
    ∧ events' = events ⁀ ⟨event⟩
```

Fig. 12. (*Continued*)

$$
\begin{aligned}
&SD \mathrel{\widehat{=}} \\
&\quad InitSecurityStatus \mathbin{⨾} sysInput[resource? := UserInfo] \\
&\quad \mathbin{⨾} sysPostForm[resource? := UserInfo] \\
&\quad \mathbin{⨾} opCheck[resource? := UserInfo] \\
&\quad \mathbin{⨾} opInsert[resource? := UserInfo]
\end{aligned}
$$

Fig. 13. Registration Module Operation Sequence

The formal model above not only uses predefined functions describing the functional logic of each operation, but also describes the security-related system behaviors included in each operation. These behaviors compose a system behavior sequence <DeclareSensitive, Transmit, Query, Store>. By the sequence, it can that the system may contain weaknesses related to data transmission, database query and data storage. To verify the system's security, we can formalize the related weaknesses in three categories in CWE and prove each of them. Figure 14 presents three weakness examples that belong to different categories.

CWE89

$\Delta SecurityStatus$
$resource?: Resource$

$\# events' \geqslant 2$
$\exists n1, n3: \mathbb{Z} \mid 1 \leqslant n1 < n3 \leqslant \# events'$
$\quad \cdot\ (events'\ n1).type = DeclareSensitive$
$\quad \wedge\ (events'\ n1).resource = resource?$
$\quad \wedge\ (events'\ n3).type = Query$
$\quad \wedge\ (events'\ n3).resource = resource?$
$\quad \wedge \neg (\exists n2: \mathbb{Z} \mid n1 < n2 < n3$
$\qquad \cdot\ ((events'\ n2).type = Validate$
$\qquad \wedge\ (events'\ n2).resource = resource?))$

CWE319

$\Delta SecurityStatus$
$resource?: Resource$

$\# events' \geqslant 2$
$\exists n1, n3: \mathbb{Z} \mid 1 \leqslant n1 < n3 \leqslant \# events'$
$\quad \cdot\ (events'\ n1).type = DeclareSensitive$
$\quad \wedge\ (events'\ n1).resource = resource?$
$\quad \wedge\ (events'\ n3).type = Transmit$
$\quad \wedge\ (events'\ n3).resource = resource?$
$\quad \wedge \neg (\exists n2: \mathbb{Z} \mid n1 < n2 < n3$
$\qquad \cdot\ ((events'\ n2).type = KeyEncrypt$
$\qquad \wedge\ (events'\ n2).resource = resource?))$

CWE256

$\Delta SecurityStatus$
$resource?: Resource$

$\# events' \geqslant 2$
$\exists n1, n3: \mathbb{Z} \mid 1 \leqslant n1 < n3 \leqslant \# events'$
$\quad \cdot\ (events'\ n1).type = DeclareSensitive$
$\quad \wedge\ (events'\ n1).resource = resource?$
$\quad \wedge\ (events'\ n3).type = Store$
$\quad \wedge\ (events'\ n3).resource = resource?$
$\quad \wedge \neg (\exists n2: \mathbb{Z} \mid n1 < n2 < n3$
$\qquad \cdot\ ((events'\ n2).type = HashEncrypt$
$\qquad \wedge\ (events'\ n2).resource = resource?))$

Fig. 14. CWE Software Security Weakness Examples

The CWE89 signifies that, because there is no validation for user input before performing database query, the system may contain SQL injection weakness. CWE256 indicates that the system behavior sequence violates the constraint that sensitive information should be encrypted before inserting into the database, namely the weakness of sensitive information stored in clear text. Similar to the above, CWE319 is represented sensitive information transmitted in clear text.

Having verified the system according to the method described previously, the reasoning result of weakness CWE89 is shown in Figure 15.

Upon analyzing the proven result of CWE89, no value of n2 can be calculated;, in other words, due to the lack of security verification of user sensitive information before executing SQL query in the system, the software design contains SQL injection weakness. Similarly, the validation of CWE256 and CWE319 has obtained similar results; the design of system is unsafe and must be improved before implementation.

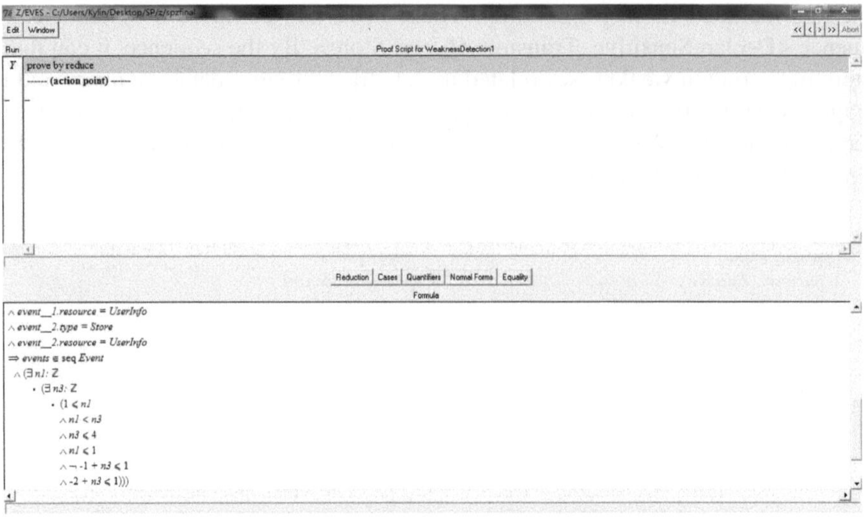

Fig. 15. CWE89 Theorem Proving Result

5 Conclusion and Future Work

This paper introduces a security software formal modeling and verification method, which is the composite application of UML and Z. This method uses two languages together to complete software and weakness formal modeling, and verification of the security of the software design model is performed by theorem proving. The results of the experiments show that this method is not only capable of detecting potential weakness efficiently, but can also reduce the complexity of formal modeling. In addition, our modeling method also helps with the transition of software design to code implementation.

Our future work will focus on two aspects: First, the research of software automatic modeling method to further reduce the requirement of expertise for formal modeling. The second aspect is the building of software security weakness repository to support security weakness automatic detection. These two aspects of research can effectively reduce the limitation of formal method and expand its application in software engineering practice.

Acknowledgements. We are grateful to the anonymous reviewers for their insightful comments and suggestions. This research was supported in part by National Natural Science Foundation of China (No.90718023, 91118003), Tianjin Research Program of Application Foundation and Advanced Technology (No.10JCZDJC15700), “985”funds of Tianjin University.

References

1. Michael, H., David, L.: Writing Secure Code, 2nd edn. Microsoft Press, Redmond (2003)
2. Xu, D.: Threat-Driven Modeling and Verification of Secure Software Using Aspect-Oriented Petri Nets. IEEE Transactions on Software Engineering 32(4), 265–278 (2006)
3. Bau, J., Mitchell, J.C.: Security Modeling and Analysis. IEEE Security & Privacy 9(3), 18–25 (2011)
4. Ali, Y., El Kassas, S., Mahmoud, M.: A Rigorous Methodology for Security Architecture Modeling and Verification. In: 42nd Hawaii International Conference on System Sciences, pp. 1–10 (2009)
5. Burrows, M., Abadi, M., Needham, R.: A Logic of Authentication. ACM Transactions on Computer Systems 8(1), 16–18 (1990)
6. Classen, A., Heymans, P., Schobbens, P.-Y., Legay, A.: Symbolic Model Checking of Software Product Lines. In: 33rd International Conference on Software Engineering. ACM Network, NY (2011)
7. Sutcliffe, G., Gables, C.: The 5th IJCAR Automated Theorem Proving System Competition. AI Communications 24(1), 75–89 (2011)
8. Yoo, J., Jee, E., Cha, S.: Formal Modeling and Verification of Safety-Critical Software. IEEE Software 26(3), 42–49 (2009)
9. Khan, S.A., Zafar, N.A.: Towards the Formalization of Railway Interlocking System using. Z- Notations IC4, 1–6 (2009)
10. Woodcock, J.C.P., Davies, J.: Using Z: Specification, Refinement and Proof. Prentice Hall International (1996)
11. Bartels, B., Glesner, S.: Formal Modeling and Verification of Low-Level Software Programs. In: 10th International Conference on Quality Software, pp. 200–207 (2010)
12. Sun, J., Liu, Y., Dong, J.S., Chen, C.: Integrating Specification and Programs for System Modeling and Verification. In: IEEE International Symposium on Theoretical Aspects of Software Engineering (2009)
13. Zhang, X., Liu, Y., Auguston, M.: Modeling and Analyzing Timed Security Protocols Using Extended Timed CSP. In: SSIRI 2010, pp. 217–226 (2010)
14. Hei, X., Chang, L., Ma, W., Gao, J., Xie, G.: Automatic Transformation from UML Statechart to Petri Nets for Safety Analysis and Verification. In: ICQR2MSE, pp. 948–951 (2011)
15. Moebius, N., Stenzel, K., Reif, W.: Generating Formal Specifications for Security-Critical Applications – A Model-Driven Approach. In: SESS 2009, pp. 68–74 (2009)

Research and Application of Warning and Intelligent Control System to Prevent Hollow Fiber Membrane Fouling

Tong Yun[1], Qu Ri[1], Xu Dan-yu[2], and Zheng Xian-qiang[2]

[1] The Academy of Computer Science and Technology, Tianjin University, Tianjin 30072, China
[2] Tianjin Academy of Environmental Science, Tianjin 300191, China

Abstract. According to the three-tier hardware architecture, BP neural network and fuzzy expert system we design a hollow fiber membrane fouling warning and intelligent control system, which can be realized on membrane fouling prediction, intelligent diagnosis and control. The system can effectively control the membrane systems with real-time operation; it can adjust system parameters with the water quality changes. It effectively inhibits membrane fouling, and reduces the off-line chemical cleaning of the membrane. With this, it can avoid physical and chemical damage, and extend membrane service life.

Keywords: hollow fiber membrane, membrane fouling, early warning, intelligent control, expert systems.

1 Introduction

The development of membrane separation technology promotes sewage treatment and reuse, among which is a hollow fiber device, which has the advantages of compact structure, convenience and flexibility of equipment control, and has been widely applied in the food and chemical industry, metallurgy, power generation and other industries for wastewater treatment [1],[2],[3]. However, the hollow fiber device can be affected by operation conditions, membrane material, water quality characteristics, etc. Thus, the core component-hollow fiber membrane is especially vulnerable to pollution in the process. The membrane pollution situation is usually judged by human experience, according to trans-membrane pressure differential and flux change [4]. Due to human factors, the parameter regulating process is very subjective, and membrane equipment parameter adjustments, which have low efficiency and precision, need repeated debugging. Once the membrane components require periodic gas water cleaning and chemical cleaning, the membrane filaments are subjected to a certain degree of pollution. Facts have proven that this general cleaning and recovery "end settlement" does not easily make the membrane filaments return completely to the initial state. Even if the membrane filaments return to the initial state, normal flux is difficult to maintain for a longer time. With the increase in the number of using and washing, the chemical effects of cleaning agents and residual membrane fouling

V. Khachidze et al. (Eds.): iCETS 2012, CCIS 332, pp. 402–413, 2012.

will directly affect the hollow fiber materials and structural properties, and the time to maintain normal flux will be shorter and shorter. In addition, due to lack of unified influent water quality standards for hollow fiber apparatus in the current, once paroxysmal water pollution appears, it is likely to subject membrane systems to severe pollution, and the latter will not return to normal standards. Finally, batched membrane module is scraped and leads to serious economic losses. In view of the above problems, this paper develops a decision-making method and system of intelligent diagnosis and early warning of membrane pollution for hollow fiber equipment, which can improve the accuracy and efficiency of membrane device parameters adjustment, so prolonging the chemical cleaning cycle and service life of membrane module, as well as saving operation costs so that the hollow fiber membrane devices have long-term and stable operation.

2 Hardware Architecture and Design of the Membrane Pollution Early Warning and Intelligent Control System

The hardware architecture of membrane pollution early warning and intelligent control system is shown in Figure 1, which contains three layers, "physics/ switch/ control". The first layer is the information monitoring layer for membrane module device (physical layer). It possesses the function of monitoring water quality parameters and controlling equipments. The second layer is the scene monitoring information layer (transit layer), or transfer layer, which is responsible for data communication forwarding, transferring bottom physical equipment information to the top control layer. The third layer is the remote sensing and control layer (control layer). It analyzes and handles the data transmission from transfer layer, and returns the resultant data to transit layer.

The structure design of this three-tier hardware makes each layer independent. The lower layer analyzes information through the interface provided by the upper layer. The upper layer gains and carries out the corresponding parameter from the upper layer. It guarantees the clarity of transfer process on information flow. The layered structure for implementation helps to regulate the details, make the whole engineering modular concrete, and reduce the complexity of system configuration. Therefore, it is convenient for further expansion and upgrade.

In the information monitoring layer of membrane module equipments (physical layer), the hollow fiber membrane system adopts PLC to realize data acquisition and control of intelligent instruments such as electromagnetic valve, pneumatic valve, flow meter, turbidity meter, and pH meter. Thus, it can access data information like operation parameters of water and membrane module. The on-site control network adopts EIA RS-232-C serial communication standard, using COM interface and DB-25 connector. On the transit layer, the site monitoring computer uses the on-site control network, and compiles information that the physical layer device collects to a standard format and writes into the on-site database; it communicates with the early warning server through the TCP protocol. At the same time, it accepts feedback control information from the warning center and controls the operation of membrane modules through the network intelligent instrumentation, PLC and other hardware devices with the on-site control network. At control layer, warning and intelligent control system runs on the warning center server; it accepts data from the transit layer, then intelligence analysis and real-time feedback. The system database contains all the database information the intelligent system needs, such as membrane historical data, forecast data of membrane fouling, membrane fouling diagnostic information, treatment options of membrane fouling, fault packet data, maintenance data, user information and so on. The system stores the data by RAID0+RAID1 technology, The RAID1 is used to ensure the availability and repair requirements of user data; RAID0 is used to ensure high-speed data storage requirements. The client, through TCP / IP protocol, remotely accesses the server warning center, and browses or monitors system under the authority, manual control and view the server operation information.

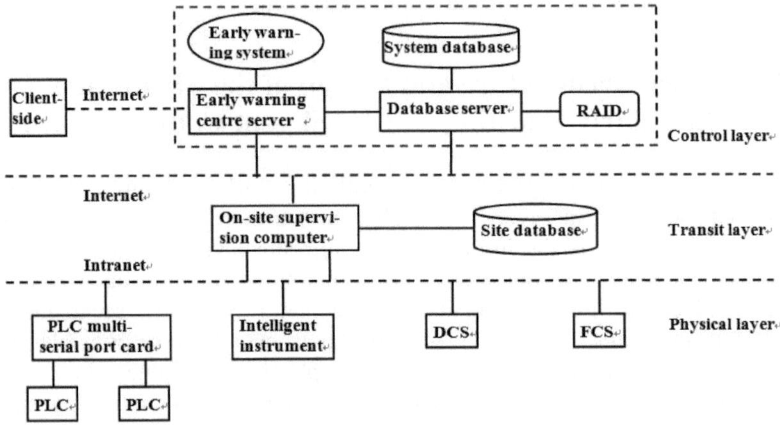

Fig. 1. The three-tier structure of hardware system

3 Software Design of the Membrane Fouling Early-Warning and Intelligent Control System

3.1 The Design of the Software System

The BP neural network, expert system and other artificial intelligent models [5],[6] are used in the software system to finish early-warning, evaluating, diagnosing and decision making on the information of wasted membrane. The system receives the membrane's equipment information and uses a series of logical methods and processes to obtain final treatment options and to achieve intelligent control. The processes are as follows:

1) Monitor the quality of the influent and effluent, the quantity of water of the membrane equipment and the operational parameter of the hollow-fiber membrane equipment;
2) According to the monitoring data, predict the trend, velocity and process of the membrane fouling;

3) According to the predicted result, evaluate the level of membrane fouling, analyze the doubtful factors of the early-warning, identify the warning situation and classify the early-warning;
4) Analyze the warning level, the predicted results and the information of the equipment at real time, then diagnose the possible factors that will pollute the membrane;
5) Identify the warning level and fouling factors and select the most suitable solution for membrane fouling in this situation;
6) Collect the data and information; control and ensure the hollow-fiber membrane equipment works safely through the information resource management module and human-computer interaction module.

3.2 Membrane Fouling Prediction and Evaluation

The assessment of membrane fouling prediction and classification of early warning is performed according to BP neural network [7]. Through the collection of water quality and device parameters, such as water quality, membrane flux decay rate V_J (equation **1**), trans-membrane pressure growth rate V_{TMP} (equation **2**), membrane injury L_S, and membrane fouling growth rate V_{MD}, the model forecasts the trend and evolution of the pollution.

$$V_J = \Delta Js/\Delta T = \Delta J_V/\Delta T = \Delta(\Delta p\varepsilon r^2/8\eta\iota l)/\Delta T \,. \qquad ((1)$$

$$V_{TMP} = \Delta TMP/\Delta T = \Delta([P_i + P_d]/2 - P_p)/\Delta T \qquad ((2)$$

Js is membrane flux; J_V is the flux of the filtration flow rate; ε is the porosity rate; r is the aperture; η is the viscosity; ι is the diffusion rate of twists and turns; l is the effective thickness; Δp represents change of pressure in the membrane, the pressure difference between upstream and downstream. TMP is trans-membrane pressure; P_i is water pressure; P_d is concentrated water pressure; P_p is the production of water pressure. T is the unit of time.

The membrane fouling evaluation and classified early-warning adopts neural network (BP model) to analyze the doubt factors of the early-warning, and to identify the warning situation and classify the early-warning. Based on the fouling velocity, trend and process of the membrane, the module evaluates the fouling level and the fouling state of the membrane. The module classifies different early-warning levels through the determinate membrane fouling reference frame, and sets early-warning signals. It also identifies membrane fouling early-warning levels. The content of the early-warning includes four parts: unhealthy state early-warning, fouling trend early-warning, fouling velocity early-warning and critical point early-warning. Early-warning levels are classified to blue, green, yellow, orange and red.

3.3 Membrane Fouling Diagnosis and Intelligent Decision-Making

The membrane fouling diagnosis and intelligent decision-making are achieved by expert system; through the analysis of the water quality parameters, trans-membrane pressure, membrane flux rate and other parameters, the intelligent control system can deduce the cause of the pollution and the pollution treatment program. The intelligent diagnosis' expert system consists of the database of membrane fouling diagnostic information, the inference engine, and the database of diagnostic strategy. The database of membrane diagnostic information contains the diagnostic information of membrane fouling classification; different kinds of membrane fouling have different rules. The system simulates experts' mode of thinking through the information in the database. The system contains proprietary diagnostic information database as the expert system's knowledge base. The inference engine matches the current water quality and quantity parameters, membrane status, and membrane fouling early-warning level to the rules in membrane diagnostic knowledge base repeatedly to obtain the appropriate conclusion to the final diagnostic information. The reasoning mode includes forward reasoning and backward reasoning. Forward reasoning can identify the fouling styles based on the monitoring parameters; backward reasoning can diagnose the controlling parameters of the membrane system and the quality of the influent and effluent, which cause the fouling of membrane based on the judged fouling styles. The database of diagnostic strategy contains the initial data that is used during the reasoning process, intermediate results and the final diagnostic results.

4 Performance Analysis of the Membrane Fouling Early-Warning and Intelligent Control System

4.1 Materials and Methods

The test equipment is the continuous micro-filtration pilot experiment system for capacity of $110\,m^3/d$. As Figure 2 shows, the equipment consists of the membrane fouling early-warning and intelligent control system and the micro-filtration membrane system. It includes four individual parts; we can conduct a study on the effluent under four different kinds of conditions at the same time. The experiment was conducted at the reused water workshop in Tianjin Rongcheng steel factory's sewage treatment plant. The membrane was an external pressure hollow-fiber membrane. Four membranes are divided into two groups; one group is controlled by manual work, and the other is controlled by the membrane fouling early-warning and intelligent control system. Study the effluent quality and operational process of two groups with the same influent quality.

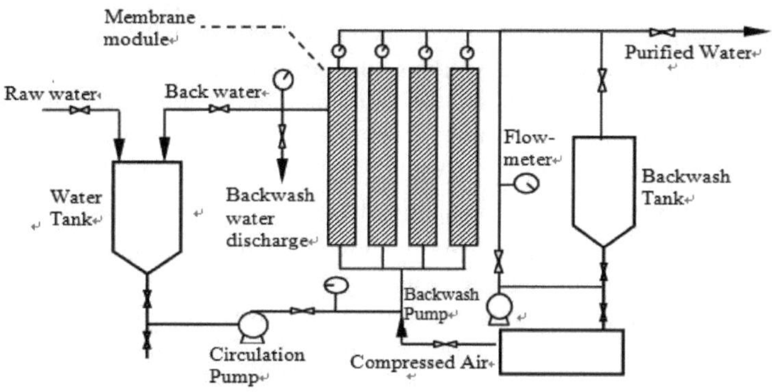

Fig. 2. Schematic of continuous micro-filtration

During the experiment, the system's pre-set parameters are as follows: water produce time 900s; backwash time 30s; recoil time 30s; sewage time 20s; a period of 980s; 88.16 times daily washing; pharmaceuticals for the 300ppm sodium hypochlorite (NaClO) and 500ppm hydrochloric acid (HCl); each membrane backwash water was $0.6 m^3/h$; daily consumption of each film is approximately the pharmaceutical 440L. During the tests, we have two conditions in the experiment: one is short-term mutant water quality, and the other is long-term stability water quality. The mutation changed in the short-term is manually controlled; the long-term condition is the normal ordinary municipal sewage. In the short term mutant water quality cases, we select the suspended solids (SS) as the main evaluation factors; in long-term stability water quality cases we select the suspended solids (SS) and chemical oxygen (COD) as the main factors of water quality assessment, which are the two most important factors leading to membrane fouling.

4.2 Results Analysis

4.2.1 Analysis of Predictive Accuracy

The prediction in the system includes water quality forecast, membrane flux decay rate forecast, growth rate of trans-membrane pressure forecast, and membrane injury forecast; we select the most important influence factors of membrane fouling (growth rate of the trans-membrane pressure) for analysis.

We calculate the growth rate of trans-membrane pressure's predicted values and measured values. We calculate the coefficient of determination (R2), the Mean Absolute Error (MAE), the Sum of Squares for Error (SSE), and the root mean square error (RMSE), and then analyze the prediction's accuracy and relevance. As Figure 3 shows, residuals in the data are between -0.27 to 0.23, the R2 is 0.81, the MAE is 0.1536, the SSE is 0.7185, and the RMSE is 0.1692. All the values show that the intelligent control system can be well predicted as regards the trans-membrane pressure growth. As shown, in 10 to 16 days, the system's prediction's values have large deviations from the actual values. The reason for this is that the water quality suddenly deteriorated, causing increased speed of TMP growth. In the experiment, with the operation of membrane systems, the growth rate of the trans-membrane pressure increased; at the beginning, the trans-membrane pressure's growth rate is 3.78kpa/d and in 50 days the values becomes 25.58kpa/d. The trans-membrane pressure (TMP) reaches the alarm value 0.1Mpa during the membrane system downtime. This causes increase of V_{TMP} due to the membrane system of the air-water backwashing, and chemical enhanced backwash cannot completely remove the contamination. With the increase of running time, the trans-membrane pressure increases and the degree of membrane fouling increases, which eventually leads to membrane system's trans-membrane pressure reaching the alarm value. At that point, the system stops running and it needs stop off-line cleaning, which is the only way to cause the membrane system to return to normal operation.

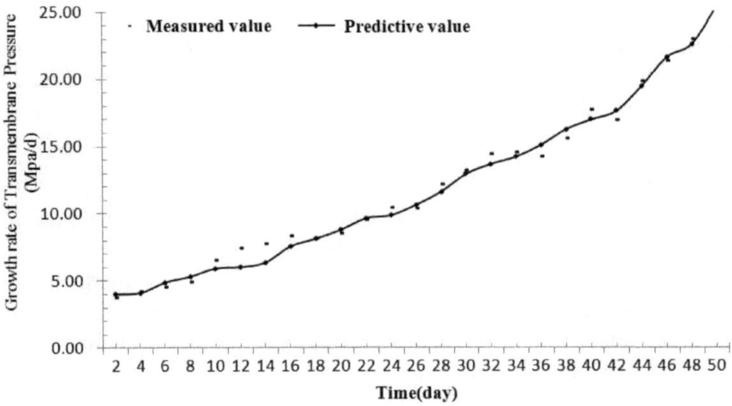

Fig. 3. Comparison chart of the predicted and actual values

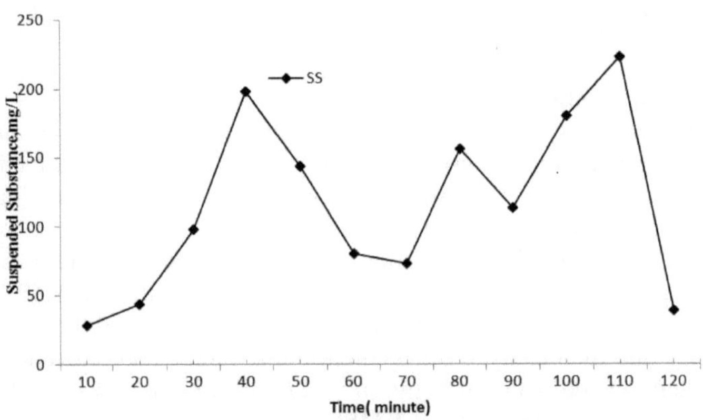

Fig. 4. SS values of influent water

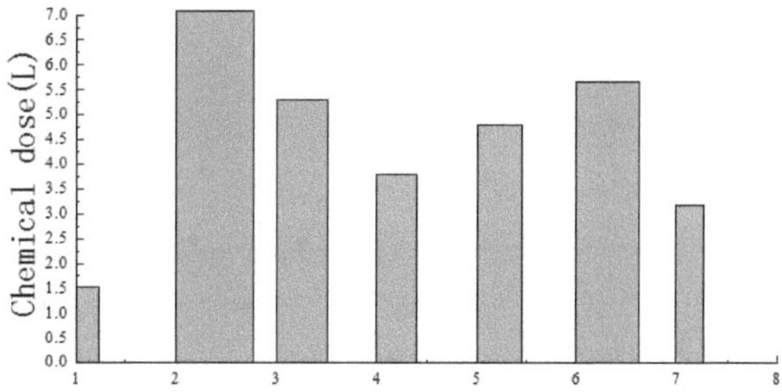

Fig. 5. Chemical dose and cleaning time chart

4.2.2 Sensitivity Analysis of the Regulation

The short-term mutant water quality is mainly used to test the system's control sensitivity. Adjust the water quality in the test, and simulate sudden pollution. As shown in Figure 4, we artificially adjust the SS value of the water in two hours. Under the control of the artificial membrane system in accordance with set parameters: a total of six anti-washing; the use of dose is 60L. Because the value of the influent SS is volatile and high, the water quality is poor and so the intelligent control system requires cleaning 7 times (Fig. 5). In the diagram, each vertical column represents the amount of each pharmaceutical film, and the width of each column used in cleaning time (minutes). In the first 20 minutes, the value of the influent SS is small and the membrane fouling rate is low; therefore, the membrane system cleaning time is short at this instance, and also entails less pharmaceutical use. Between 25 and 55 minutes, artificial adjustment caused the SS value to increase rapidly. The membrane fouling accelerated, indicating that membrane system needs real-time adjustment. Over an extended cleaning time, the dosage is increased to ensure that the intensity of membrane cleaning. Throughout the operation, changes in the intelligent control system based on water quality (SS value) adjust in real-time the backwash time, backwash frequency and dosing.

4.2.3 Run Stability Analysis

Long-term stability water quality is used primarily to test the system's control stability. On the 30d of the influent water quality monitoring, the suspended solids (SS) content is 15-55mg / L, and chemical oxygen (COD) content is 100-400mg / L. Figure 6 shows the influent suspended solids (SS); Figure 7 shows the chemical oxygen (COD).

In manual control the backwash time, backwash frequency and dosing are fixed variables. In the intelligent control system, according to the water quality changes, the system automatically adjusts the backwash frequency and backwash time. Upon water quality deterioration, the system increases drug dose, backwash frequency and duration. Conversely, when water quality is good, the system reduces cleaning time, as well as reduces the use of pharmaceutical.

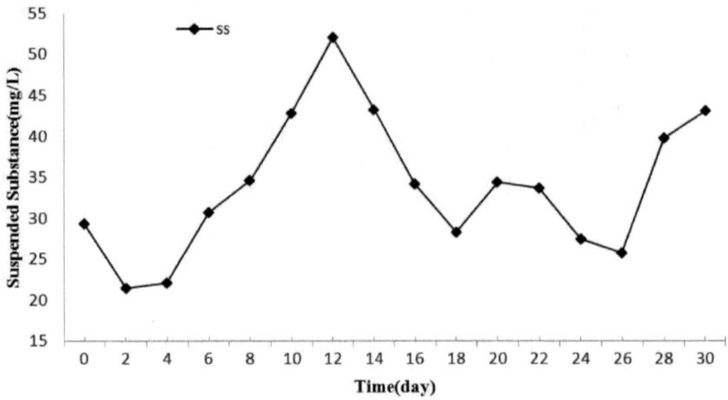

Fig. 6. The SS values of influent water

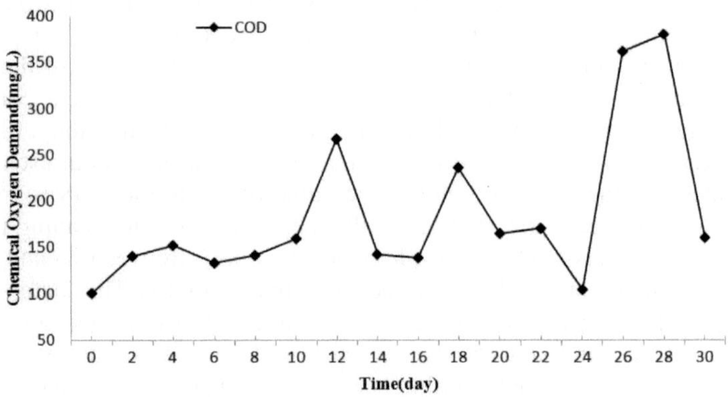

Fig. 7. The COD values of influent water

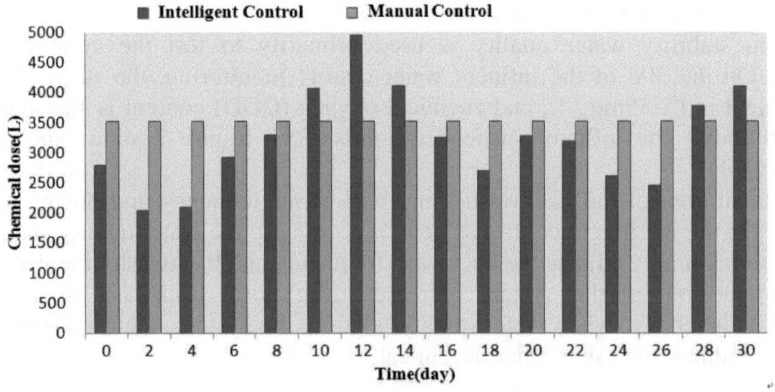

Fig. 8. The Chemical dose of intelligent control

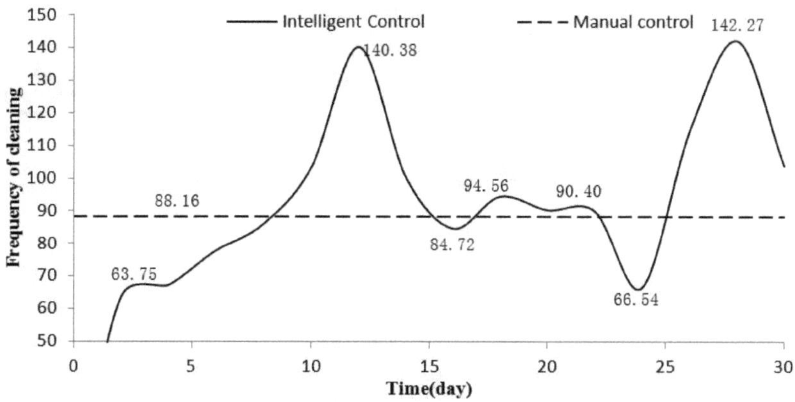

Fig. 9. The cleaning frequency of the intelligent control

As shown in Figure 9, the intelligent control system adjusts the backwash frequency and time with the water quality changes. In days 2 to 8, the water quality is better and the system is relatively less contaminated, and the intelligent system reduces backwash frequency and cleaning time as well as reduces the use of agents to prevent pharmaceutical waste. In days 10 to 15, the water quality conditions and the intelligent control system increase the daily backwash frequency and time in order to clean the membrane system better; the system increases the use of agents at this time. Statistics 30d pharmaceutical use, the system under manual control of pharmaceutical consumption is 28.16 m^3 , the system under the intelligent control for the pharmaceutical use of 25.81 m^3. In summary, compared to manual control, intelligent control provides more rational allocation of the backwash frequency and backwash time and rational and effective use of the pharmaceutical agents to avoid waste, while making the film a more effective cleaning system.

4.2.4 Economic Analysis

As Figure 10 shows, the purification period of CMF under manual control is 30 days. During the operational process, the influent pressure increases sharply, which indicates that numerous pollutants were settled on the surface of the micro-filtration membrane. At the 30th day, at operational period, influent pressure reached 0.1MPa, which is the warning signal. The purification period of CMF under the membrane fouling early-warning and intelligent control system increases to 40 days. The cleaning times reduce and the rate of influent pressure increases slowly. This indicates that, with the help of the membrane fouling early-warning and intelligent control system, we can control the pollutants' abortion on the surface of the membrane effectively; membrane fouling can be controlled well. As cleaning times lessen, so does damage to the membrane physical chemistry, thereby extending the lifetime of the membrane.

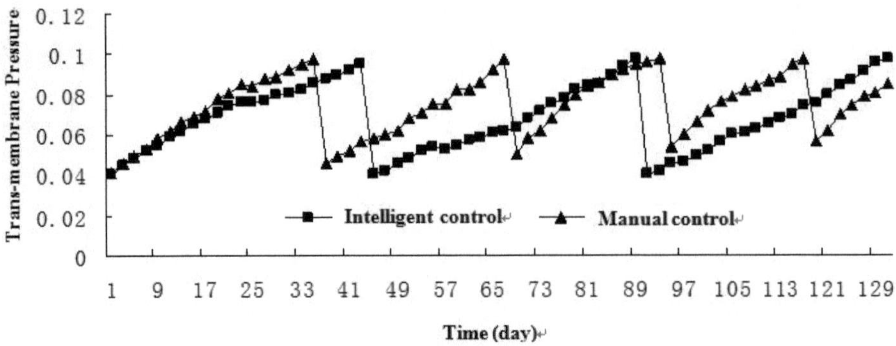

Fig. 10. Membrane systems cleaning

The two membrane systems within 60d statistical capacity of water, the flux decay rate, pharmaceutical consumption, cleaning time, water production, energy consumption, the results obtained are as follows: The manual control of membrane system produced a total of 3,312.56 m^3 water, the total cost is 2,020.67 yuan, and the average water production cost is 0.61 $Yuan / m^3$; the intelligent control membrane system's cumulative water production is 3,680.4 m^3, the total cost is 1,545.6 yuan, and the average water production cost is equal to 0.42 $Yuan / m^3$. Thus, with the use of intelligent control system, the system produced water per cubic meter to reduce production costs 0.19 Yuan, saving resources such as pharmaceutical and energy consumption, with some economic benefits.

5 Conclusions

1) Based on the three layers of the hardware architecture, integrating BP neural network, and fuzzy expert system, the warning and intelligent control system for hollow fiber membrane device was designed and developed. It can be used for membrane pollution forecast, diagnosis and control.
2) The system was used to control the treatment of wastewater by the micro-filtration membrane. The result shows that it can restrain membrane pollution problems, reduce the chemical and physical damage to membrane wires caused by cleaning many times, effectively extend membrane life, reduce the operating cost and improve economic benefits.

Acknowledgement. This work was financially supported by the National Natural Science Foundation of China under Grant No. 61170178.

References

1. Lv, X.: Study of continuous micro-filtration technology. Membrane Science and Technology 23(4), 20–23 (2003)
2. Yang, Z., Sun, Y., Pang, J.: Bio-augmentation Disposal of Car-Washing Wastewater with Membrane Bioreactor. Journal of Tianjin University (7), 640–643 (2005)
3. Sasson, M.B., Adin, A.: Fouling Mechanisms and Energy Appraisal in Micro-filtration Pretreated by Aluminum-based Electro-flocculation. Journal of Membrane Science 352(1), 86–94 (2010)
4. Al-Malack, M.H., Anderson, G.K.: Formation of Dynamic Membranes with Cross flow Micro-filtration. Journal of Membrane Science 112(1), 287–296 (1996)
5. Zhou, Z., Wang, Y.: The Simulating and Forecasting of Water Consumption Model Base on BP Neural Network in Irrigation Area. Journal of Agricultural Sciences (03) (2011)
6. Tao, W., Lu, Y.: The Integration of Expert Systems and Artificial Neural Networks in Decision Support Systems. Computer Simulation 15(3), 13–16 (1998)
7. Xiang, C.: Fault Diagnosis and Condition Monitor Based on Extensis. ChongQing University, ChongQing (2008)

Sharing and Building Management System Based on Handheld Mobile Devices

Yubao Li[1,2], Qing Xie[1], Guodong Liu[1], Zhenghua Shu[1], Dengji Zhao[1], and Bingxin Wang[1]

[1] Key Laboratory for Optoelectronics & Communication of Jiangxi Province, Jiangxi Science & Technology Normal University, Nanchang, Jiangxi, China
[2] Political Science and Public Management College, Wuhan University
xqwyy163@163.com

Abstract. In order to save resources and reduce redundant construction of the base station, the Ministry of Industry in 2008, the SASAC decided to vigorously promote the construction and sharing of telecommunications infrastructure. The sharing and building platforms have been developed and have achieved some results which were based on the policy and national conditions of China in Anhui, Jiangsu, Chongqing, Liaoning, Henan, and Hebei. However, the specific operation of the platform is just a software management system which based on the WEB. The function in terms of achieving a sharing telecommunications infrastructure is still insufficient to build a platform to provide a better basis.

Later, the continued improvement of the sharing and building system to better solve the problem of incomplete operator part of the telecommunications infrastructure is in order. This paper proposes a new route that combines the server and information collection terminal, such as WEB management systems and handheld mobile terminal equipment. WEB management system is responsible for managing the construction and sharing of basic information, so as to facilitate mutual sharing operators. Handheld mobile device receives the base station GPS location information, altitude, orientation, external photos, main base station internal equipment photos and furnishings orientation as well as other information through the WAP server, manual entry of 3G technology and automatic upload to the server. Therefore, a server and an information collection terminal combine to form a sharing platform with software and hardware as a whole; this is not only to provide for the sharing of the auxiliary equipment, but also to build a platform to provide more reliable and accurate parameter information.

Keywords: Sharing platform, handheld mobile devices, WEB software management systems, GPS geo-location information.

1 Introduction

In order to solve the duplication of investment and wasting of land resources, sharing and building platforms have been developed in Anhui, Jiangsu, Chongqing, Liaoning,

V. Khachidze et al. (Eds.): iCETS 2012, CCIS 332, pp. 414–421, 2012.

Henan, and Hebei. These systems include processing management, basic data management, data sharing and industry news and so on. They are not only to achieve the needs of sharing and building, namely comment and reply functions, approval for record, and implementation of on-line circulation archiving process, but also contribute to statistical analysis query and can generate statistical reports, monitoring indicators, and communication functions.

In China, the sharing and building platform is just in its preliminary stages of becoming established, just implemented the the management functions of the base station. The sharing system mostly processes the management systems, and its function is the same as the WEB management subsystem functions as discussed in this article in the software section.In other words, because it is not related to the base station of the investigation, design, and construction management, the system can only be a shared platform of the telecommunications infrastructure, not enough to build a sharing and building platform.

In the global arena, the sharing telecommunications infrastructure starts early and has many forms. Because of the different national conditions, the infrastructure is roughly divided into two categories, "passive" and active. In general, active infrastructure sharing scheme is more suitable for highly developed countries with small land area, such as Sweden. Passive infrastructure sharing is more flexible and generally more popular in large countries such as in India. The United States and Canada possess more sharing towers.

2 Concept

Because of insufficient overall planning of resourcing sharing system, and recurring investment problems, the network source utilization rate is low, partially causing the effect of low investment benefit. While the third generation mobile communications is coming,the restructuring of the telecommunications industry resultes in the changing of the competitive environment,a new round of investment has began from the three major telecom companies.The state departments issued "on promoting the sharing of telecom infrastructure of the emergency notice", will promote the sharing of telecom infrastructure work.

In order to realize the co-construction and share, we add an information acquisition terminal (Handheld mobile device) on the basis of the original. Handheld mobile device grasps information such as the base station of GPS (geographical positioning information), elevation, azimuth, exterior photos, base station apparatus, equipment photos, and display range into the WAP server and 3G technical manual and automatically uploads to the server. It forms the sharing platform with the software and hardware for integration. It does not only better to achieve the sharing auxiliary equipment, but also provides more reliable and accurate parameter information for the co-constructing and sharing of the perfect platform.

Handheld mobile equipment features wireless communication and Internet function, can realize the site survey base station, including GPS information, elevation information, and base station, and contains the following parameters:

- Camera: 300W pixels, that can shoot and record video, with 4X zoom;
- Electronic Compass: the plane electronic compass FNN-3200, specific parameters for: response rate of 3 times / sec; measurement accuracy of ± 1 ° ± 0.2 °; resolution; reproducibility of ± 0.4 °;
- Elevation: micro pressure elevation of BA5803 module, pressure measuring range: 10-1300mbar (1-130kpa): 0.1%FSO; pressure; pressure accuracy resolution: 0.012mbar; 10bar; overload pressure: year: -1mbar/ drift; temperature measurement range of 85 °C -40 °C: to; temperature resolution: < 0.01 °C temperature: 0.8 °C; accuracy; high resolution: operating temperature range: 10cm; to 85 °C -40 °C;
- Communication module: GSM communication module, 3G communication standard;
- Software module: B/S frame, picture and information by manual and automatic two way input, upload to server.
- Assembly performance: waterproof, dustproof, national standard.

3 System Platform Design

3.1 Specific Technique Route

Handheld mobile devices, the WAP (Wireless Application Protocol) sharing information acquisition and WEB management system and telecommunication infrastructure of geographic information system (GIS) effectively solve the problem with the operator of the telecommunication infrastructure.

Figure 1 shows the line of specific techniques: the four parts of the platform continuously improve and upgrade, augmenting the compatibility of the system. The system will therefore become a qualified product.

The system upgrades through its own system of hardware and software and the actual experience of the staff, so as to expand the platform to use, and realize the effective implementation of the project.

- By using the workflow, the system upgrade for telecommunications infrastructure sharing platform and station design management platform realizes co-construction and sharing.
- By Maya 3D modeling technology, the GIS system is perfected, meaningdisplay and infrastructure appearance and internal equipment are more intuitive;
- Through the improvement of WAP subsystem and base station , function is perfected, thus realizing the base station construction and management;
- The handheld terminal software is improved, making it more convenient to extract various sensor information, reduce the survey workload of personnel, and allowing the system to more easily penetrate into other provinces' markets.

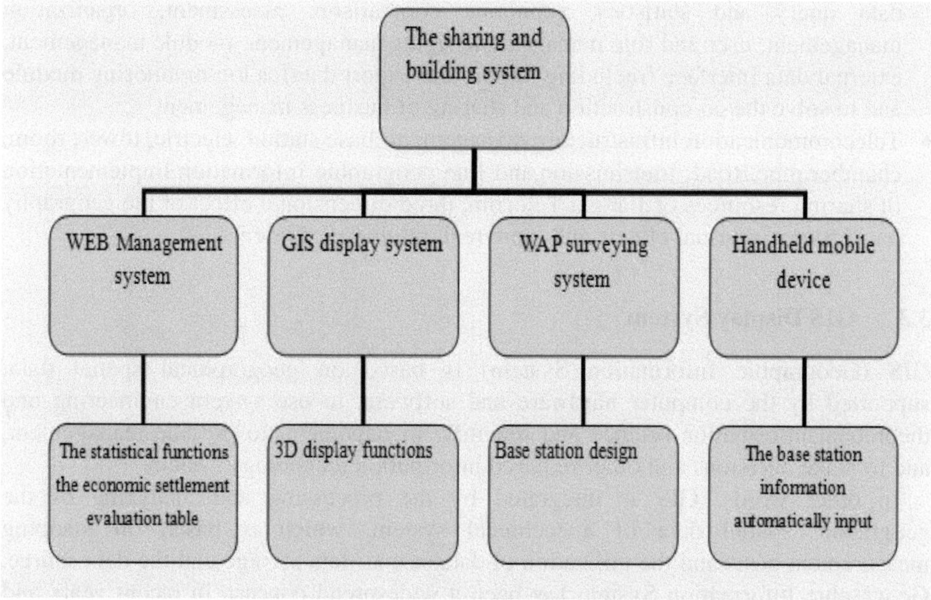

Fig. 1. Sharing and building system

3.2 WEB Technology and Platform Selection

Web management system is based on the Web building and sharing requirements, and takes into consideration the efficiency of the system, security, and technology maturity.The MS.NET framework is used to build the entire system, and the performance of the client page is processed through ASP. NET combination of HTML, CSS, and JAVASCRIPT.

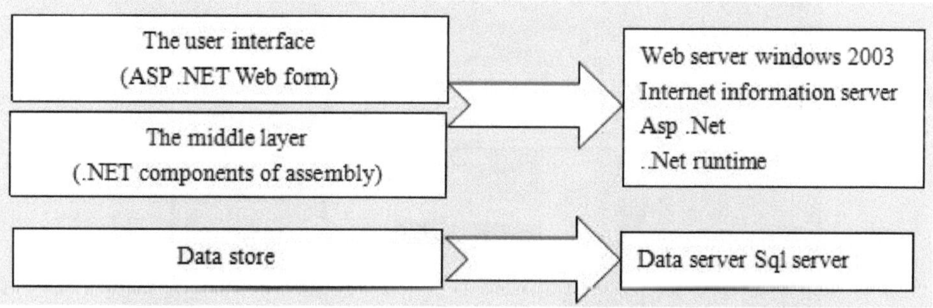

Fig. 2. The system architecture diagram

WEB Sharing Management System Includes the Following Features

- Information releasing platform:base station, electric, tower, room, chamber, pipe, rod Road, transmission line, the resident network, the basis of object management, data query and statistics, economic comparison, assessment, organization management, user and role management, rights management, module management, external data interface (including import and export data), a log monitoring module and to solve the co-construction and sharing of business management.

- Telecommunication infrastructure management :base station, electric, tower, room, chamber,pipe,Road, transmission,and line geographic information.Implementation of sharing resources of Jiangxi Telecom, three-dimensional effect of the geography background in visual effects and more real, intuitive experience.

3.3 GIS Display System

GIS (Geographic Information System) is based on geographical spatial data, supported by the computer hardware and software, to use system engineering and theoretical information science and scientific management, to provide management, and to make decisions and other required information technology system.

In other words, GIS is integrated by the processing and analyzing of the geographic spatial data of a technical system, which is based on mapping measurement basis and the utilization of database as data storage and the data source. Geographic Information System has been a widespread concern in recent years and has been a grounds for rapid development in terms of acquisition, storage, analysis and management of geospatial data, tools, techniques and disciplines.

In this system, we use the Google Earth platform and its satellite image data to realize the base station information as shown in the 3D scenes below. The platform not only provides more intuitive display through the base station location topography, but it also effectively helps policymakers decide the co-construction and sharing of the base station, to avoid duplication of field survey.

Fig. 3. GIS 3D scenes

3.4 WAP Surveying System

WAP (Wireless Application Protocol) is a global network communication protocol. It creates a standard for mobile Internet; its target is rich Internet information and advanced business using mobile phones and other wireless terminals. WAP just as universal platform, the Internet HTML online language information is converted to WML (Wireless Markup Language) to describe the information and display on the mobile phone screen.WAP requires only the mobile phone and WAP proxy server support, and does not require the existing mobile communication network protocol to make any changes, so it can be widely used in GSM, CDMA, TDMA, 3G and other networks.

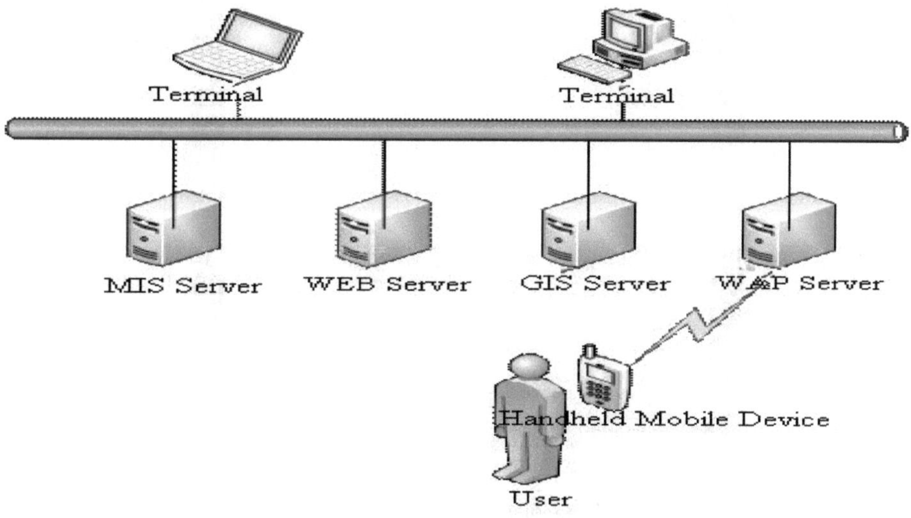

Fig. 4. WAP Platform structure diagram

There have been inputting the information more quickly through the improvement of WAP server software and a hand-held mobile terminal software, to achieve the various sensor parameter automatic input.It uses the ARM programming technology and views the system parameters in the port, it also automatically reads the related parameters and according to automatically upload to WAP server.

3.5 Handheld Mobile Device

The handheld terminal is similar to the mobile platform,and the interface is also similar to the general applications. We can directly enter the geographic information through the mobile phone platform, then the information is transmitted to the WAP server and overwrite existing information. The handheld mobile terminal bases on SoC on the core processor system, and the central processor uses the ARM architecture absolute mainstream. In addition to the core of the ARM architecture, it integrates the computing unit that is responsible for a variety of multimedia work in a chip, and software equipped on the windows phone system. The Fig.5. is the hand-held mobile terminal model.

Fig. 5. Handheld mobile device model

The following work together concurrently with in the handheld mobile device:

- Air pressure altitude sensor: prevents the GPS elevation information from jumping channels, provides accurate measurement of height information.
- Geomagnetic compass sensor: avoids dynamic GPS direction, realizes static pointing function.
- Use of 3G network technology: improves data upload speed to save time.

4 Summary

This paper introduces the present situation of telecom infrastructure management and the current situation of telecom infrastructure management system requirements, and solves the co-construction and sharing of business management needs. The business management system will process the daily management work on the network platform and realize the management of its business in optimum combination, as well as solve daily business management problems, improve business processing efficiency, change the current business processing mode, and further improve business management levels. The system provides a uniform standard for everyday business in management and build a flexible, efficient, safe and steady information systems business platform.

Telecom infrastructure geographic information system (GIS) allows the staff more macro visualization and micro management of infrastructure, and also creates organic links between the various kinds of telecom infrastructure.

References

1. Frisanco, T., Tafertshofer, P., Ang, R.: Infrastructure Sharing For Mobile Network Opterators. Digital Object Identifier 04, 129–136 (2008)
2. Recommendations on Growth of Telecom services in rural India: The Way Forward (TRAI) (October 2005)
3. High, the telecommunications infrastructure sharing policy studies, master's thesis of Beijing University of Posts and Telecommunications (2010)
4. Huang, H.: Chapter Yimin high, high, telecommunications infrastructure co-construction and sharing of telecommunication. Science 10, 76–80 (2009)
5. Wei, Z., Ma, K., Wen, Y.: Mobile communication base station sharing analysis of engineering application. The Telecommunications Technology 11, 58–64 (2010)

Social CRM for SMEs: Current Tools and Strategy

Sergio Cappuccio, Sagar Kulkarni, Muhammad Sohail,
Mustafa Haider, and Xiaobing Wang

Abstract. Social networking and other new technologies have given rise to the "social consumer," who now has the means to share reviews and opinions about virtually every kind of product and service. As a result, the days of the one-to-one relationship between companies and their customers are over. Now companies must contend with the huge and growing social web, where customer experiences and opinions are shared on a massive scale and corporate reputations can be ruined almost instantaneously. Navigating this new world requires a new way of approaching customer relationship management, commonly called social CRM. In addition to their traditional CRM tools and processes, companies must rethink their product, channel, and customer strategies in order to build an entirely new relationship with customers through greater transparency. This new relationship will have two goals: to develop the credibility needed in the social web and to use this web to boost sales. This effort will require a major shift in the corporate mind-set toward collaboration and transparency. But if it is done right, the resulting benefits in terms of reputation and a more valuable relationship with customers can be significant.

Keywords: Customer Relationship Management (CRM), Social CRM, Web 2.0, Small and Medium-Sized Enterprises (SMEs), E-Business, Social Network Tools, CRM Implementation.

1 Introduction

1.1 Background

Customer Relationship Management (CRM) is considered a tool to create competitive advantage. It has been recognized as a business strategy to enhance organization's ability to maintain effective relationships with the customers by using advanced information and communication technologies. Rapid development of CRM applications have seen the trend of more and more small and medium-sized enterprises (SMEs) seeking to implement CRM in order to survive and compete in the world of e-Business.

Social CRM is the merging of social networks with Customer Relationship Management to help businesses manage and build customer relationships using the information that customers freely share through their online profiles. Social CRM also includes using social networking resources to help improve customer dialogue. Canadian studies show that only 23% of SMEs have implemented a CRM solution (Croteau, 2003) and the following factors have been identified as barriers to the acquisition of a CRM solution:

V. Khachidze et al. (Eds.): iCETS 2012, CCIS 332, pp. 422–435, 2012.

- Lack of finances available for investment in capital
- Inadequate information technology resources
- The implementation of an effective CRM solution can be time-consuming

SMEs tend to use a variety of programs to accomplish their daily tasks.

In the past, SMEs were frequently placed in a challenging position: though they recognized the need for a powerful, efficient CRM solution, they were often financially incapable of investing in the types of programs that they required. As a result, they were forced to use multiple programs in order to accomplish the same tasks. Recently, however, additional products have been developed that are priced to support SMEs. With the plethora of choices that are now available, SMEs are able to carefully select the customer relationship management solution that is right for them. So what types of characteristics are these companies looking for in software?

1.2 Objective

This report aims to study the viability of using the online social network tools for SMEs to implement CRM. The study involves intensive review and induction of relevant theories on Social CRM, E-Business, SMEs and successful practice using social network tools for CRM in SME.

The report focuses on exploring how online social CRM serves as a compelling strategic choice for SMEs doing e-Business, which includes defining SMEs, identifying a set of benefits SMEs can reap from doing e-Business, and discussing strategies and impacts of CRM best practice on SMEs' generic competitive strategy derived from Porter's generic strategy framework.

1.3 Structure of the Report

The report is presented in the following five sections:

Social CRM Study. In this section three elements are defined - Social CRM, information on current technologies in Social CRM and the process model. At the end of the section, latest developments in social CRM are presented.

Online Social CRM for SME. In this section "need for online social CRM" is identified in terms of why it is important to take advantage of online social CRM.

Implementing Social CRM in SMEs. In this section we review social networking CRM tools for SMEs and discuss key issues in using such tools.

Case Study for a Canadian SME Using Social CRM. This section presents a case study of Tripadvisor.com as a social networking tool. We compare traditional CRM with Social online CRM and discuss best practices.

Conclusion. We conclude the report by providing a summary.

2 Traditional CRM vs. Social CRM

2.1 Definitions

CRM is the process of managing customer information and contact in such a way that encourages a mutually beneficial relationship between the corporation and the client.

This concept is a comprehensive approach that integrates every business process that touches customers, namely sales, marketing and customer service through integration of people, process and technology. It encompasses all aspects of the interaction between representatives of the company and the customer, some of which are included below:

- Customer service/help desk interaction
- Sales orders and leads
- Marketing
- Communication and information-sharing – both within and outside of the office
- Analytics and customer profitability

Proper usage of CRM will contribute to the creation and encouragement of a long-term relationship between the customer and the company. In financial terms, this translates to increased long-term profit, as a completely satisfied customer is more likely to return to that business to satisfy his or her needs for a longer period of time. Social CRM is a new concept that helps engage customers through the power of social media, chiefly Web 2.0 technologies (Blog, Facebook, Twitter, LinkedIn, etc.), in an effort to build organizational trust and brand loyalty and, ultimately, lead to continued business opportunities. For some authors social CRM is the next level in the CRM evolution (Muthupalaniappan, 2011). Adding a social media strategy to the existing CRM platform will help businesses tap into markets in an effective and efficient way. Social CRM also bolsters the sales and marketing force of a company with the power of social media and collaborative processes to close more deals. However, others prefer to define it as a new paradigm. Paul Greenberg, a writer for ZDNet.com provides a succinct definition: "CRM 2.0 is a philosophy and a business strategy, supported by a technology platform, business rules, processes and social characteristics, designed to engage the customer in a collaborative conversation in order to provide mutually beneficial value in a trusted and transparent business environment. It's the company's response to the customer's ownership of the conversation" (Greenberg, 2009). This new paradigm is not only supported by changes in technology but also by changes in society:

Search Engines. The exponential growth of reliance on Internet search which allows the retrieval of unstructured information ready to use in seconds has dramatically changed people's expectations regarding the amount of time they should wait to receive a response to their questions.

Telecom Networks and Smart Phones. In addition to the above, we saw significant advances in the use of mobile devices allowing the use of Internet and applications on the go. According to an early 2010 study by ComScore, over 45.5 million people in the United States owned smart phones out of a total 234 million subscribers and, according to Gartner in their November 2010 report, total smart phone sales doubled in one year and smart phones presently represent 19.3 percent of total mobile phone sales.

Gen Y Enters the Workforce. There are many studies regarding the impact of the first generation born and raised after the appearance of Internet but just regarding the numbers stated below (Table 1) it is easy to conclude that individuals of this generation, in addition to being 'technologically savvy', are not afraid of expressing their ideas through social media irrespective of corporate channels and rules.

Table 1. Gen Y use of technology

97%	own a computer
94%	own a cell phone
76%	use Instant Messaging.
15%	of IM users are logged on 24 hours a day/7 days a week
34%	use websites as their primary source of news
28%	author a blog and 44% read blogs
49%	download music using peer-to-peer file sharing
75%	of college students have a Facebook account
60%	own some type of portable music and/or video device such as an iPod

(Source: *Connecting to the Net Generation: What higher education professionals need to know abouttoday's students, by* Reynol Junco and Jeanna Mastrodicasa NASPA; 2007)

User Generated Content. During the last few years, users have spent more time on the web and shared more information with each other than before. In fact, people are regularly making their thoughts and opinions easily available to the world through the Internet. New forms of content generation, communication and collaboration have emerged on the web. For instance, user-generated content (UGC) allows Internet users to make comments in a large variety of forms, such as photos, videos, podcasts, ratings, reviews, articles and blogs. Roughly 75.2 million Internet users use UGC in the United States, but this figure is expected to increase up to 101 million in 2011. In 2007 approximately 60% of European online users used UGC (Carrera et al., 2008).

Examples of UGC activities in which people are engaging on the web include: reading or writing blogs, reading or writing customer reviews, taking part in social networking sites, listening to podcasts and setting up RSS feeds (Carrera et al., 2008). Unlike the early days of Internet when the websites only broadcasted one-way information, this new Internet trend is empowering users to create, edit and view information (Carrera et al., 2008).

Trust in "People Like Me". Edelman is an independent global Public Relation firm that publishes an annual report measuring the feelings of trust in businesses, governments, NGOs and media across 23 countries. The 2006 version says: "Person like yourself or your peer" is seen as the most credible spokesperson about a company and among the top three spokespeople in every country surveyed. This is partially attributed to corporate and banking scandals and the way that the government and traditional media react to them.

Social CRM is allowing companies to build upon the classic customer relationship management platforms and processes with Web 2.0 technologies in order to engage and involve the customer in a way that provides mutually beneficial value. In order to make this customer-centric ecosystem work, a company needs a centralized customer profile platform that can retrieve information from multiple data points, update the information in real time and also leverage appropriate customer interaction and Web 2.0 applications (Enrico, 2009).

2.2 Social Networks Used in CRM

Gaining the trust and loyalty of customers in a Web 2.0 world is among the toughest challenges faced by companies today. CRM helps engage a traditional customer who performs transactions with a company, understanding his needs better and serving him in a better way. But in today's world, a customer seeks out the larger community before engaging in any kind of relationship with an organization. The explosive growth of Facebook, Twitter, LinkedIn, and other social media platforms has given the customer the power to seek unlimited firsthand knowledge. This is where social CRM comes in. Gartner studies show an increasing percentage of customers using social media to gain knowledge of a company's offerings and its services. So it's critical to extend CRM capabilities to social media and vice versa to help engage the social customer of the present and the future.

While the list of social networking possibilities expands daily, it includes at least the following categories:

- Social networking: Facebook, Linkedin, Twitter, Digg, Ning
- Blogs
- Photo sharing
- Interactive applications (e.g. Mobile apps)
- Location based networks (e.g. Foursquare, Places)
- Aggregating channels (e.g. Comparison sites)
- Independent and sponsored sites, communities, review sites
- Webinars
- Discussion groups / user forums
- Company websites
- Search

2.3 Tools to Analyse Social Sites

There are a significant number of applications and services that make it possible to analyze and improve strategies in the use of social networks. Herewith are examples of such categories and tools:

- Analytics: Google Analytics Bit.ly
- Social media dashboards & monitoring: SproutSocial CoTweet HootSuite
- Twitter, Facebook & more: Tweetdeck Twitoaster
- Email marketing: MailChimp
- Blogs: WordPress
- Presentation, media & more: SlideShare
- Social optimization: Gigya

2.4 Social CRM Process Model

CRM comprises three phases: acquiring, enhancing, and retaining. Each phase supports increased intimacy and understanding between a company and its customers. These three phases are:

Acquiring new customers. The company acquires customers by promoting product and service leadership.

Enhancing the profitability of existing customers. The company enhances the relationship by encouraging excellence in cross selling and up selling, thereby deepening and broadening the relationship.

Retaining profitable customers for life. Retention focuses on service adaptability-delivering not what the market wants, but what customers want. (Kalakota et al 2000, P175).

Understanding the process of initiating and building fruitful business relationships is the key to social CRM. As a starting point, the following can be considered the stepping-stones in this strategy:

- Customers search for information on the Internet
- The customer's web click stream is analyzed
- The content behind the clicks is analyzed
- Conversation with the customer is converted into a collaborative experience
- The collaborative experience is transformed into a meaningful business relationship

Successful social CRM leverages the hub-and-spoke model, which pulls public social media sites (e.g., Facebook, Twitter, and LinkedIn) and niche sites (e.g., Flyertalk) to drive traffic to the company's own social media community. This involves building landing pages to meet the unique needs of identified segments, and integrating social information harvested from the community into the CRM system. Finally, the business may leverage insights from analyzing data contained in its CRM system to push out relevant topics and threads to the social media community.

3 Online Social CRM for SME

3.1 Canadian SME Current Status Analysis

In Canada, the term "SME" (for small and medium-sized enterprise) refers to all businesses with fewer than 500 employees, whereas firms with 500 or more employees are classified as "large" businesses. In addition, Industry Canada has used a definition based on the number of employees, which varies according to the sector — goods-producing firms are considered "small" if they have fewer than 100 employees, whereas for service-producing firms the cut-off point is 50 employees. Above that size, and up to 499 employees, a firm is considered medium-sized. The smallest of small businesses are called micro-enterprises, most often defined as having fewer than five employees. According to Stats Canada, by Dec 2010, of the 1 138 761 employer businesses, 2708 (about 0.2 percent) have 500 employees or more, 1 116 423 employer businesses (98 percent) have fewer than 100 employees, 75 percent have fewer than 10 employees and 55 percent have only 1 to 4 employees.

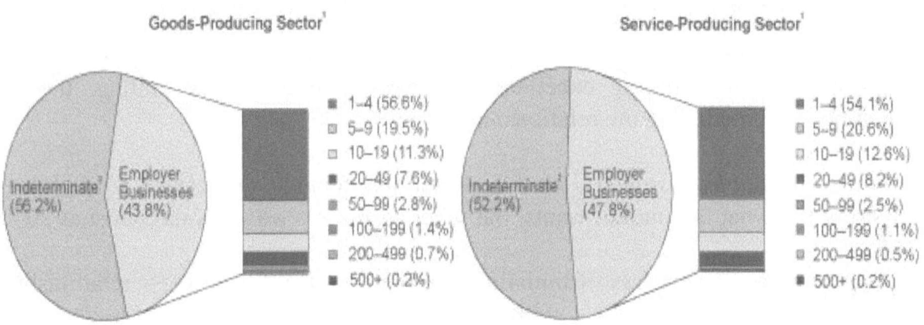

Source: Statistics Canada, Business Register, December 2010.

Fig. 1. Distribution of Business Locations in the Goods-Producing and Service-Producing Sectors by Firm Size (Number of Employees), December 2010

3.2 CRM in Canadian SMEs

One out of every four Canadian SMEs (23.9%) makes use of a CRM software package. CRM Systems are more prevalent among Canadian SMEs with 100 - 499 employees (51.6%).The equivalent figures are 30.8% for SMEs with 20 - 99 employees and 18.9% for companies with 5 - 19 employees. The survey indicates that 27.3% of Ontario companies have a CRM system, compared to 22.6% in British

Columbia, 22.3% in the Prairies, 22.2% in Quebec and 17.0% in the Atlantic. In relation to the industry sector, 49.9% of Canadian SMEs in the finance and insurance sector are equipped with CRM software packages. Although Canadian SMEs are increasingly making use of enterprise resource planning (ERP) software packages, the same cannot be said for CRM software packages.

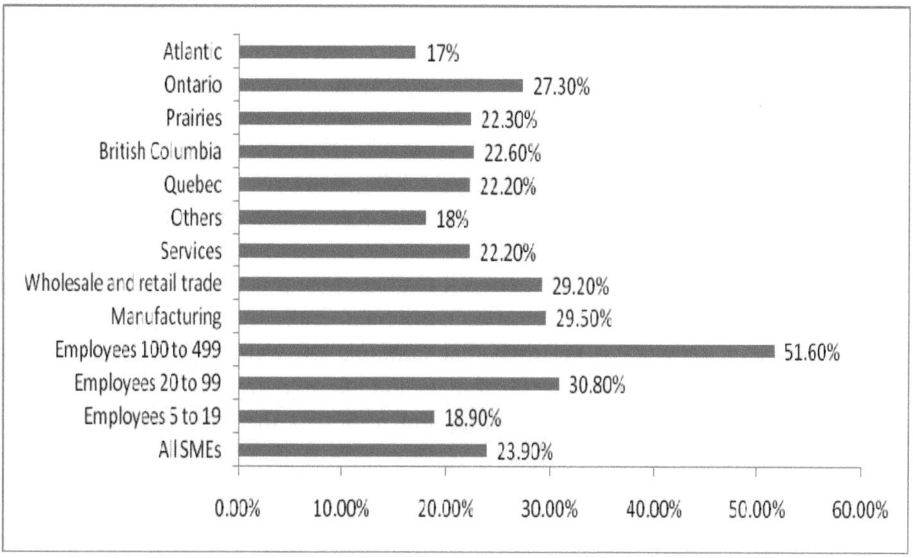

Fig. 2. Canadian SMEs making use of CRM systems.

Source: Croteau, A.-M.and Li, P.(2003), Critical success factors of CRM technological initiatives, *Canadian Journal of Administrative Sciences*, 20 (1), 21-34.

Uwizeyemungu, S.and Raymond, L.(2011), Information technology adoption and assimilation: Towards a research framework for service sector SMEs, *Journal of Service Science and Management*, 4 (2), 141-157.*Base: Canadian SMEs (n: 2,013)*

3.3 Benefits for SMEs in the Use of SCRM

The distinguishing characteristics of SMEs represent both advantages and disadvantages to SMEs regarding competitiveness and growth. For instance, compared with large firms, a relatively smaller customer base makes it possible for SMEs to react faster and more dynamically to customer needs, while a lack of financial resources and specialists will prevent SMEs from penetrating the global market. However, e-Business, referring to the conduct of business with the assistance of Internet and other information technologies, can effectively exploit advantages available to SMEs while offsetting drawbacks.

In general, SMEs can benefit from e-Business in the following aspects:

- Reduced cost
- New business opportunities
- Access to wider customer base locally and internationally

- Increased revenue from sales
- Access to timely information
- Increased speed to market

Among the potential benefits of migrating to the social CRM paradigm are the abilities to:

- Create unique customer experiences
- Be adaptable and responsive to the customer's voice and concerns
- Use market trends to develop the right products
- Predict the future trends and behaviour of customers
- Maximize the ROI of the traditional CRM platform
- Empower the sales force with real-time knowledge of customers and their behaviours
- Create a sales force social network to share best practices and knowledge on closing deals
- Create a knowledge network that contains the various conversations and collaborations between the customers and the organization
- Use the power of crowd sourcing and resources that are spread throughout the world
- Treat each customer uniquely

3.4 SCRM as an E-Business Strategic Imperative for SMEs

In order to optimally extract benefits from e-Business, the first and foremost thing for SMEs to do is to establish strategies that involve business goals and effective business models to achieve those goals. Three generic strategies, namely, overall cost leadership, differentiation and focus, have been introduced by M.E. Porter (1980). The framework that aims to outperform competitors can serve as a theoretical underpinning to later development of e-Business strategies for SMEs. It is, however, possible to argue that the above strategies are developed from the perspective of a product or service. This approach, according to the authors, can potentially improve a company's competition situation in the short term, but fail in supporting long-term growth. For instance, lowering prices would incur competitors' malicious revenge in form of price competition, resulting in the serious consequence of ultimate elimination of industry profits. Even an industry-unique product will only bring the company short-term competitive advantages since competitors are racing to come up with more innovative products. In short, this approach does not seem to work well in the e-Business world. Today customers are in control, as a result of the fact that it is easier than ever for them to comparison shop and, with a click of the mouse, to switch companies. As a result, the customer is becoming the most valuable but at the same time the scarcest asset of the company. Sustainable customer relationships are worth more than the company's products, stores, factories, web addresses, and even employees. In order to survive in the increasing competitive environment, a company's strategy should focus on how to find and retain the most profitable customers possible, instead of just providing superior products or service. (Kalakota et al 2000, P169).

Based on the above, companies that are not doing business in the way the customer wants are bound to be out of business. SMEs are operating in the contemporary world of sophisticated customers and intensifying competition against same-sized companies and large firms; therefore, the only way for SMEs to succeed is by focusing diligently on customer needs. This urgently requires SMEs to build e-Business models that are flexible, fast moving and customer focused. CRM, with best practices in transforming customer relationships into profitability and competitive advantage, is such an ideal e-Business model. The ultimate goal of CRM is to help SMEs to turn into customer-focused organizations that conduct business processes centered on customers.

3.5 Implementing Social CRM in SMEs

Based on our study above, in order to successfully implement social CRM system in SMEs, there are these key points SMEs must consider:

Develop a CRM Vision. One major determinant of successful CRM implementation is a unified understanding of a CRM vision throughout the entire enterprise, from top executives down to operational personnel.

As far as SMEs are concerned, a clear CRM vision should explain why the firm needs CRM in terms of how CRM enables and supports the company's corporate strategies such as overall cost leadership, differentiation, and focus. This vision will guide a SME through following processes of CRM planning. In short, the clearer the vision has formed and the more uniform the understanding of the CRM vision throughout the entire enterprise, the more smooth the subsequent CRM planning process will be.

Define CRM Requirements. To identify business requirements that are mostly efficient addressed by CRM tactics, one effective means proposed by Dyche (2002) is to map them to specific applicable CRM tactics. On the other hand this method also determines how effectively CRM capabilities can address certain business requirements.

Meet Business Objectives

Depending on the nature of the business, the objectives for SCRM could include the following:

- Greater number of website returning visitors
- E-commerce efficiency
- Increase in market share for core products
- Higher customer satisfaction ratings
- Intelligent marketing campaigns
- Increased service and require effectiveness

Improve: Be Ready to Hear What Customers Do Not Like about You. Social media is often a channel for anger against businesses and any company could become the next victim. One example of this is the case of Dave Carroll, a United Airlines passenger who, after a fruitless 9 months of negotiations with the airline for the breaking of a guitar during handling his baggage, wrote a song and created a music video about his experience. The YouTube video named 'United breaks Guitars' was posted on July 6, 2009 and garnered over half a million hits in 3 days-August 2009, and 11 million by now. In this context, SMEs need to develop a contingency plan to respond to complaints and be transparent about the efforts made to solve problems when they exist.

4 Case Study of a SME Using Social CRM: Tripadvisor.com as a SCRM Tool for SME

An example of sites that have a powerful impact on the SCRM strategy is TripAdvisor.com (Fig. 3).

This website assists users in gathering travel information, posting reviews and opinions of travel-related content and engaging in interactive travel forums. It is a pioneer of user-generated content. The website services are free to users, who provide most of the content, and the website is supported by an advertising business model.

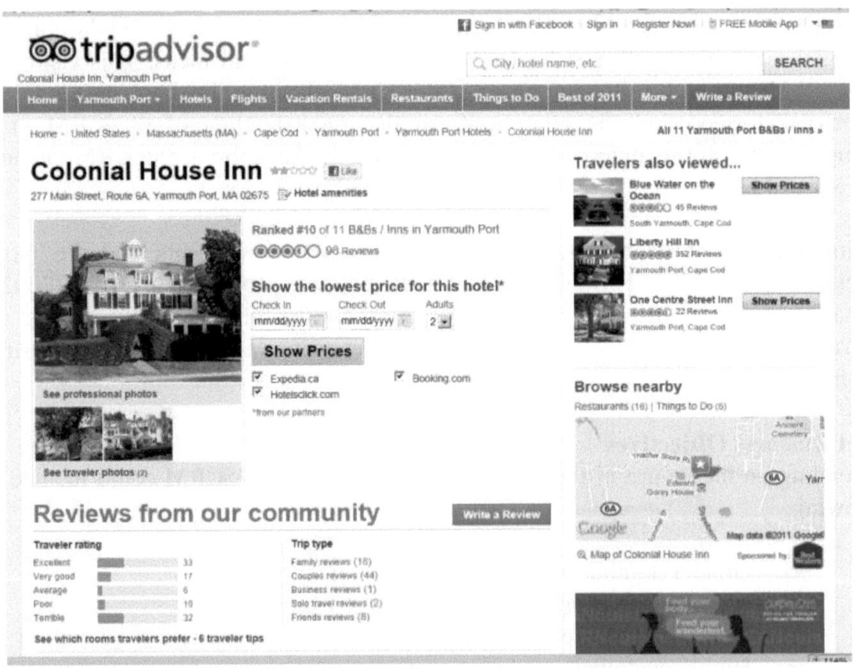

Fig. 3. Tripadvisor.com Website

As stated on its webpage, Tripadvisor is the largest travel community in the world and it attracts more than 65 million monthly visitors, 20 million members and over 50 million reviews and opinions.

Some features of TripAdvisor.com include the following:

- More than 50 million travel reviews and opinions from travelers around the world
- 1+ million businesses
- 93,000+ destinations
- 520,000+ hotels
- 155,000+ attractions
- 715,000+ restaurants
- 8,000,000+ candid traveler photos
- 98% of topics posted in forums are replied to within 24 hours

These figures reflect a significant power and have a consequential impact in the hospitality industry. Businesses operating in this industry must review their internal processes in order to be able to manage and respond to customers' demands. In the past, a bad experience of one customer had a very low impact on future sales or on the image of the company. One of the reasons for this was the inability to share that experience with other current or potential customers. In best cases, companies assigned a customer representative in charge of dealing with complaints with the objective of minimizing the damage.

Nowadays, not a single criticism could or should be ignored and the impact on internal processes is very important. For example, someone complaining about bad service affects the way staff is managed; bad reviews could mean changing supply management or may even be generated as a result of things that are not in direct control of management (e.g. noisy neighbourhood, poor transportation, etc).This process of reaction to customer criticism should be undertaken in addition to assigning resources to the complex task of responding to the reviews. In the case of hotels, the reviews are responded to in the name of the Manager or the owner and good judgement is required in order to balance respect toward the customer and openness to criticism. This also means dealing with false reviews or reviews made with pernicious intentions (e.g. looking for compensation). Some businesses, seeing the potential damage that this tool could cause to them, tried to resist this kind of sites but this is not a recommended action. On the contrary, businesses need to embrace these tools and try to profit from the opportunities that they offer.

5 Conclusion

Based on the research and the facts presented in this report, it is evident that Social CRM is becoming one of the most important tools for SMEs. Many SMEs are globally taking advantages of these sites and improving their performance, helping them to manage their customer relationships. Let us take a look at some of the major advantages and disadvantages of social networking sites as a CRM tool for SMEs:

Advantages

- Global reach with minimal efforts
- Instant feedback and improved communication
- Financial affordability due to lower costs compared to traditional CRM
- Continuous interaction with customers
- Provide excellent service to customers through web
- Minimal human resources to manage client relationships compared to traditional CRM

Disadvantages

- Need for resources in the area of IT
- IT security
- Feedback could be misleading
- Competitors may take advantage of anonymous postings
- Continuous monitoring of the websites required
- Requirements of additional funds to maintain website and web interaction with clients

In our opinion the advantages outweigh the disadvantages and hence it is important for SMEs to make social CRM a part of their business development and customer relationship. To improve the B2B and B2C relationship, both employees and customer feel that these are integral. Customers are becoming more and more aware of these tools and they want to take advantage of these tools. Therefore SMEs must capitalize upon these tools that are available to improve their CRM efforts and incorporate them into their business strategy. Social Media sites also give customers an opportunity to take a look at company's insight. This is extremely important for maintaining transparency while conducting business. Coleman Parkes Research, in a study released by Avanade in 2008 called "CRM and Social Media: Creating Deeper Customer Relationships" found that companies were seeing real world benefits even a mere three years into the usage of Social CRM. Some numbers about the benefits of Social CRM are listed below:

- 78% found that integrating CRM and social media led to improved feedback
- 75% found that it created a perception of the company as forward-looking
- 71% found that it led to a reduction in time needed for resolution of support issues
- 66% found it led to greater customer satisfaction
- 64% found it led to improved market reputation
- 40% found that they could see specific improvements and increases in sales

5.1 Bottom-Line

Social CRM is still maturing, but one thing is evident: it is becoming more and more popular and becoming the tool of choice for clients in today's IT age. SMEs can take advantage of these tools to improve their bottom-line. If it is not resource intensive, and if it is cost effective, the question is not "why should a company take advantage of it?" but rather "How fast can a company take advantage of it?"

References

1. Avanade: Coleman Parkes Research. CRM and Social Media: Creating Deeper Customer Relationships (2008)
2. CA Whitepaper, IT Strategic Planning for SMEs
3. http://www.cica.ca/research-and-guidance/it-advisorycommittee/publications/item36287.pdf
4. Carrera, P., et al.: MySpace, My Friends, My Customers. In: O'Connor, P., Höpken, W., Gretzel, U. (eds.) Information and Communication Technologies in Tourism 2008, pp. 94–105. Springer Wein, New York (2008)
5. Chess Media Group, Guide to Understanding Social CRM, http://www.e2conf.com/downloads/SocialCRM-whitepaper.pdf
6. Croteau: Critical Success Factors of CRM Technological Initiatives. Canadian Journal of Administrative Sciences 20(1), 21–34 (2003)
7. Dyché, J.: The CRM Handbook – A Business Guide to Customer Relationship Management. Addison-Wesley, Boston (2002)
8. Enrico, R.: CRM 2.0 – Where Web 2.0 meets CRM, CRM Today, http://www.crm2day.com/highlights/50455.php
9. Greenberg, P.: White paper: Social CRM Comes of Age, Oracle (2009), http://www.oracle.com/us/products/applications/crmondemand/036062.pdf
10. Industry Canada, The State of Entrepreneurship in Canada (2011), http://www.ic.gc.ca/eic/site/sbrp-rppe.nsf/vwapj/SEC-EEC_eng.pdf/$file/SEC-EEC_eng.pdf
11. Jantsch, J.: Let's Talk: Social Media for Small Business, http://www.ducttapemarketing.com/socialmediaforbusiness.pdf
12. Ravin, K., et al.: e-Business 2.0: roadmap for success. Addison-Wesley Pub. Co. (2000)
13. Muthupalaniappan, V.: Leveraging the Power of Web 2.0 to Engage the Social Customer. Destination CRM Magazine (November 2, 2011)

Research on Contingency Plan Simulation System Based on CAS Theory

Fei Chen[1], Wenjun Wang[1], Jieru Cheng[1], and Fei Wang[2]

[1] School of Computer Science and Technology, Tianjin University, Tianjin300072, China
[2] School of Computer Software, Tianjin University, Tianjin300072, China
qfnhm@126.com, wangfeiily@tju.edu.cn

Abstract. With the goal of multi-interaction, multi-layer, and other features of contingency plans, this paper focuses on the construction of a contingency plan simulation system. Based on multi-agent, this paper builds the main model for the contingency plan, formally specifies the resource agent, proposes a multi-agent reactive decision-making system, elaborates on each component's function in the reactive decision-making system, builds a multi-layer CAS simulation system modal on the basis of CAS and multi-agent based modeling techniques, and constructs a reasonable contingency plan simulation system.

Keywords: Contingency plan based on Multi-Agent, Reactive decision-making structure, Simulation.

1 Introduction

Contingency plans, also known as plans for possible major accident or disaster, are to ensure rapid, orderly and effective conduct of emergency and rescue operations, and reduce accident losses and pre-established plan [1]. Prior to sudden accident or events, determines who is responsible for doing what, when to do it, and the appropriate strategies and materials to prepare [2]. Success in emergency rescue depends not only on the plan itself, but is also closely associated with the decision makers of the command manipulation plan. The making of a controlled emergency plan, and decision-makers' capacity to optimize the integration of simulation and exercise of the contingency plans, plays an extremely important role in this session; it can be expected that event system simulation and further measure of the plan are reasonable for the purpose of a deeper level of correction, fulfilling the purpose of the contingency plans. A large number of emergency resources, major hazard, protection units, decision-making environment and a series of simulation elements must be considered in plans for the simulation modeling process; in order to address the needs of a large number of non-homogeneous analog elements, this paper introduces the Complex Adaption System (CAS) core theory to build the framework of the multi-level CAS simulation model. Complex Adaption System is proposed by the Santa Fe Institute; based on the Adaptive Agent (Agent) as the core, there is strong scientific guidance to solve the nonlinear,

V. Khachidze et al. (Eds.): iCETS 2012, CCIS 332, pp. 436–443, 2012.

multilevel nature, diversity, space-time cross-cutting and other features of the plan simulation system. CAS theory is applied to the simulation system of contingency plans in Multi-Agent-based modeling, the establishment of a multi-level CAS simulation system modeling framework. The following four sections provide greater detail.

2 State

CAS theory emphasizes individual adaptability of the main, by the adaptability of the main body of the complexity of the system as a whole. At present, CAS simulation technology has made outstanding achievements in the economic, social, military, biological fields and others. There are some mature applications of CAS theory , which are mainly in military large-scale simulations , such as the U.S. Navy Operations Command, MCCDC development of Marine Simulation System EINSTein that many combat model is based on, Weixin's CAWSOM based on the organization of complex adaptive main O_Agent war simulation model [3]. However, more mature framework in the field of emergency plan simulation platform should have many units, complex relationship, and frequent interaction. CAS theory does not focus on applications in the field of emergency plan simulation, so the significance of the build is strongly applied based on the framework of the simulation model of the CAS emergency simulation plans; this work is also particularly important and urgent. This article is primarily based on multi-agent contingency plans for modeling and emergency plan simulation system design.

3 Multi-Agent-Based simulation Model Design

The model based on multi-agent modeling, MABM (Multi-Agent based modeling), is a multi-agent model. It dominates the discrete decision-making process, the main technology for simulating the real world in a more natural fashion, to meet a higher level of complex mutual cooperation between the functions in the system business processes requirements. Reactive decision-making system based on MAS is built first.

3.1 Multi-agent Reactive Decision-Making System

MAS architecture of CAS research methods refers to MAS information and controls the Agent individuals and the distributed model of the behavior of decision-making power; the organic integration of command and control is to provide the Agent activities and interactive framework. Figure 1 presents the construction of Multi-Agent reactive decision-making system; the entities of the Agent in MAS are heterogeneous, and the system framework is based on modular bottom-up thinking. Multi-Agent Reactive decision-making system is a mental model system, relying on coherent information, rules, experiences, and situational awareness for decision-making, and using the continuous improvement of adaptive decision-making to accommodate emergency trends under the multi-scenario.

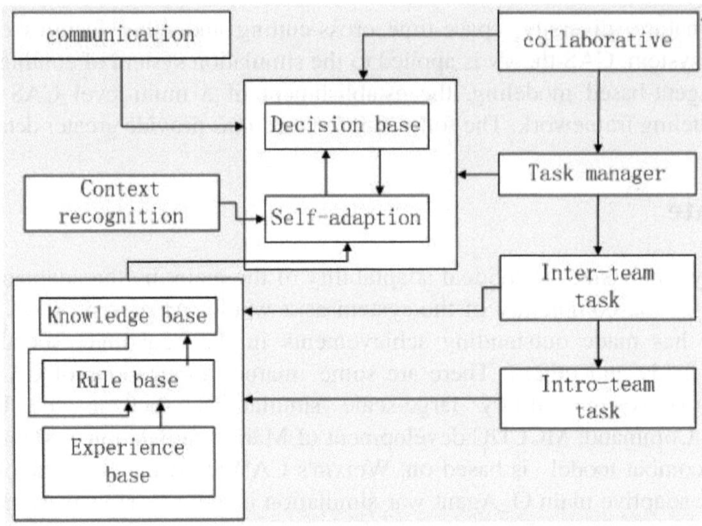

Fig. 1. Multi-Agent reactive decision-making system

The core of Multi-Agent Reactive decision-making system adapts to the three important components of the mechanism, the decision-making library system (Decision base), Adaptive (Self-Adaptation), and Knowledge (Knowledge base): Decision-making constantly updated Knowledge Base by Agent communicating with the outside world to get emergency scenarios or task flows that are between teams , and then make decisions. Self-Adaptation module, with the new scenario of the time of the linear relationship, in the perception of and access to knowledge of past decision-making to improve and complete charge, modified according to changing internal state goal motivations. The Knowledge Base contains predefined rules and communicates with updates and experiences of the experience library, which contains past emergency scenarios, case solutions and rules. The rule base comprises predefined rules of conduct of the individual agent. Agents receive knowledge and situational conditions from the emergency scene, then judge by decision-making library (decision base) and adaptive (Self-Adaptation), finally add knowledge and situational conditions to the rule base. Task Manager team and team task workflow management can be perceived between the team that has resources or demands resources to respond. The collaboration component is Agent team and external collaboration, including active and passive collaboration. Knowledge base and experience base in this reaction in the decision-making system, correspond with basic plan emergency knowledge and plans in order to deal with the emergencies rules below, to start building the knowledge base and experience in library decision-making based on Multi-Agent Based contingency plans model.

3.2 Contingency Plans for the Model Based on Agent

Contingency plans include subject, object, resources, case studies and process; the main body of the emergency plan includes the following: emergency lead agency (e.g. the Tianjin Emergency Office), a special command structure (e.g. Tianjin control of major animal epidemic diseases headquarters), executive agencies (e.g. Tianjin City rail transit emergency disposal of the command center), and lower regulatory agencies (e.g. Tianjin Tanggu emergency Management Office). The objects of the contingency plans include: various departments (e.g. the Tianjin Fire Station), subordinate agencies (e.g. the Nankai District Government), and regional agencies (e.g., Tianjin) [3]. Resources refer to the hardware resources in the event of an emergency call (e.g. fireside, medicines, etc.), software resources (including technological resources), and flexible resources. Emergency cases refer to unexpected events and expected events.

When modeling of the contingency plans, subject, object and resource are abstracted into the main agents, which respectively become Agent of the principal, object of Agent, resources Agent. Those main agents drive the entire simulation event based on a particular emergency case. Each Agent has communication, collaboration, and other functions. This paper focuses on discussion of resource Agent, the Agent-model abstraction for five-tuple. The Agent = {momentum (Situational), motivation (Motivation), doctrine (Doctrine to), behavior(Behavior), role (the Roles)}, physical resources Agent can be described as E_i[4]: $E_i := \{S_i, M_j, D_k, B_l, R_P\}$, i, j, k, l, $P \in [1,n]$. Among them: Si collection time T is time of all the attributes. Agent object in a scene S, S_i function on emergency scenarios, $f(S_i) = f(S(A_i, t_i))$. M_j is the goal of guiding agent behavior, on behalf of the state that the main want to reach. The target is the expected value of V (Expected Value), $M_j \in V$ is a collection of all task flow expectations [5]. D_k is a collection of rules; rules exist in the form of "if ... then" finite state automata. B_l is the action rule set. R_P is the role of the main in the system, and specifies the responsibilities and obligations in the principal business activities and associated power. The relationship between a main role which that is played (the Roles) and role (RoleLn) composition, ROLES = <Roles,RolcLn>. A subject in a system can play multiple roles or play more than one system's different roles [6]. In complex systems, the interactions between the main reaction of the subject and the main characteristics of the system, and between the subject and the environment, are achieved through message passing mechanism.

3.3 Multi-level CAS Model Framework for Simulation System

According to the theory of multi-agent modeling raised above Multi-Agent Reactive decision-making system, combined with SWARM and REPAST common CAS simulation platform architecture for Agent design patterns and modular thinking, build a multi-level CAS (MH-CAS-M, Multi-Hierarchical CAS model) simulation system modeling framework. Shown in Figure 2, MH-CAS-M framework includes four modules: the Agent module, GUI module, Function modules, and Reality module. MH-CAS-M retained REPAST as a procedural framework, and has good scalability.

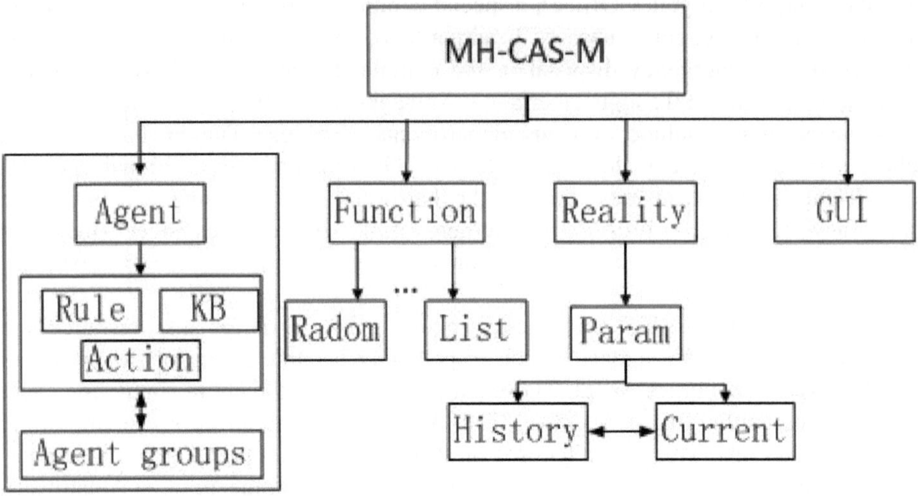

Fig. 2. Multi-level CAS model framework for simulation system

Agent module is used to describe the entities Agent situation, including the rule set and knowledge base, as well as an Action as an individual decision-making function [7]. Agent entities, which are inside and outside the state and their own decision-making, create a series of action instructions, sequencing of the behavior of entities of the Agent to the value of this function for the action sequence. Agent module can be extended for more than one Agent class agent groups, respectively. Figure 2 corresponds to the Agent, wherein heterogeneous interactions between the different types of Agent occur.

Function module is a set of auxiliary function modules of the MH-CAS-M framework, which contains the public functions of the system, such as a randomly generated function Random, the queue handler List (to choose the best Agent) and other functions. Reality module is the scenario module, used to describe entities Agent external scenarios, in which the current state preserves historical context. It includes historical scenarios (History), the current scenario (Current), and the initial parameter settings (the Param), such as the number of entities Agent, Reality or model, and data sources, including the GUI 2D and 3D model. GUI module, controlling the display class, is a module of the interaction between the model and researchers, which convert the simulation data into visual data. It can access and open source WORDWIND graphic displays [8] [9] [10].There are also some simple modules among several main modules, e.g. a communication module. Agent, in the framework of the group entity, can be a complex CAS system decomposed into a number of more simple, more manageable subsystems; each sub-group between the layer evolutes of the polymerization mode which is of the emergence of the CAS[9].

4 Emergency Plan Simulation System Design

The focus of the simulation system for contingency plans is a visualization of the simulation, which facilitates the variation of the abstract data through visual awareness for specific performance; simulation status value of the underlying database is constantly updated based on each entity Agent. The user can control the posture of the various entities Agent initialization property values. Entities are shown in Figure 3. The Agents model drawn from plans set simulation action; the behavior of these entities Agents is show by visualization of multi-angle. The simulation system consist of data layer, inference layer, application layer, visual layer architecture[10], which respectively correspond to the simulation model, the agent module, the Function module, the GUI module of the MH-CAS-M.

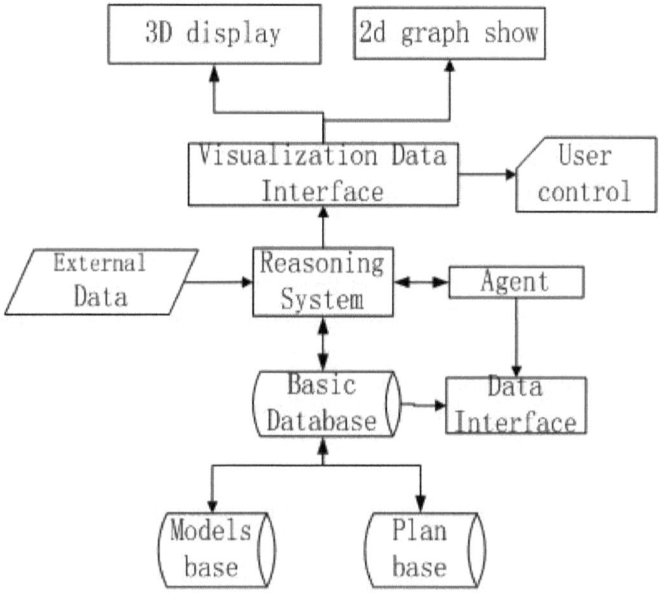

Fig. 3. Simulation system design

The underlying database contains the rule base, model base and plan library. The rule base is recognized by the conceptual world of justice and rules knowledge, and can also be added to the rule base Agent inspected after the actual event to judge doctrine. External database is Agent perceived data, and perceives the world in the perceived value of the collection. Contingency plans for the library contain the plan of the occurrence of the case and the expected case.

In Reasoning System [9], Agent is mainly based on the current scenario parameters and scene parameters, to make the reasoning of the next action, including the location of the transfer. Simulation system used in the visualization of open source World Wind (a visual globe developed by NASA Research) output of the dynamic trend of

Agent views the interaction between the state of each model in the 3D virtual geographic space and 2Dcurve of the underlying index, using the Matlab interface provided by REPAST output. 2D and 3D effects in the prototype system are shown in Figure 4.

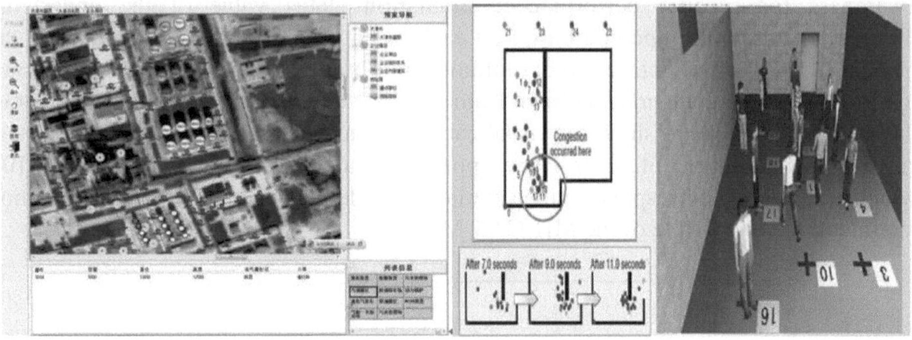

Fig. 4. Prototype system effect diagram

5 Summary and Outlook

The build of MH-CAS-M has high reusability, scalability, and clear structure. Reusability and scalability of the model lie in the fact that the model has completed many of the basic, public modeling works, and is based on a modular design. Each module is relatively independent and possesses clear functions; the development of new models based on the actual system features makes the appropriate modifications and additions. The emergency plan simulation system is also more reasonable and in the next research work will focus on the Agent-strong user-friendly, customizable and visual design with the goal of becoming more immersive. These will be the subjects of final research results, to be fully demonstrated.

References

1. 孙林. 基于 Agent 能源基础设施仿真模型设计与实现. 北京: 计算机应用 (2009)
2. 董存祥, 王文俊.杨鹏.应急预案体系本体模型 EPSOnto 及应用.计算机工程与应用, 235–238 (2009)
3. Ilachinski, A.: Artificial: Muktiagent-Based Simulation of Combat. World Scientific Publishing (2004)
4. Wang, R.: A Market-based Adaptation for Resolving Competing Needs for Scarce Resources. The Pennsylvania State University, IAT (2006)
5. Dudenhoeffer, D., Permann, M.R., Manic, M.C.: A Framework for Infrastructure Interdependency Modeling And Analysis. In: Proceedings of the 38th Conference on Winter Simulation, Monterey, California: [s.n], pp. 478–485 (2006)
6. Johnson, C.W.: Using Evacuation Simulations for Contingency Planning to Enhance the Security and Safety of the 2012 Olympic Venues. Safety Science 46, 302–322 (2008)

7. Eriksson, K., McConnell, A.: Contingency Planning For Crisis Management: Recipefor Success or Political Fantasy? Policy and Society 103, 11–22 (2011)
8. Jayaputera, G.T., Zaslavsky, A.B., Loke, S.W.: Enabling Run-Time Composition and Support for Heterogemeous Pervasive. Multi-Agent Systems. Journal of Systems and Software 80, 2039–2062 (2007)
9. Rosness, R.: A Contingency Model of Decision-Making Involing Risk of Accidental Loss. Safety Science, 807–812 (2009)
10. Palen, L., Liu, S., Citizen, B.: Communications in Crisis Anticipating a Future of ICT-Supported Public Participation. Emergency Action, 727–736 (2007)

MapCombine: A Lightweight Solution to Improve the Efficiency of Iterative MapReduce

Wei Xu, Xiujun Gong, and Xiaoyu Li

School of Computer Science and Technology,
Tianjin University,
Weijin Rd 92, Nankai, Tianjin, China 300072
{xuwaye,gongxj,lena}@tju.edu.cn

Abstract. MapReduce is a brilliant distributed computing strategy to process massive-scale data. However, for iterative applications, the general MapReduce needs to re-initialize runtime environment repetitively and re-load static data repetitively in every iteration. Thus, a great deal of CPU time and I/O bandwidth are wasted. This paper presents a lightweight solution to improve the efficiency of iterative MapReduce, which named MapCombine. The main contributions of MapCombine are as follows: (1) To avoid re-initialization of the runtime environment, a controller component is plugged into the general MapReduce model to schedule the iterations; (2) To process data without re-loading the static subset, we modify the general MapReduce model surrounding combine phase to cache the fixed data and 4e the workload before processing; (3) To make the communication between the controller and the combiners flexible with the consideration of fault tolerance and downtime recovery, we append an interaction layer to the MapReduce implementation architecture. We also show performance comparisons between MapCombine and Mahout for four clustering algorithms, and then conclude that the average speedup ratio provided by MapCombine is 1.14.

Keywords: Cloud Technologies, MapReduce, Data Mining, Iterative Algorithms.

1 Introduction

With the present increase in volume of data, massive-scale data mining becomes an impossible task by using a single machine in many domains such as astronomy, physics, bio-informatics and web-data analysis. To face this challenge, many new distributed computing strategies have been developed. MapReduce is a brilliant one of those strategies.

MapReduce is a programming model, and also an associated implementation for processing and generating large data sets [1]. The major advantages of MapReduce lie in its simple and efficient. From the perspective of its extraordinary simplicity, programmers only need to elaborately specify a map function and a reduce function in accordance with the MapReduce programming model. Then the program can be

V. Khachidze et al. (Eds.): iCETS 2012, CCIS 332, pp. 444–456, 2012.

executed in a distributed way on the MapReduce implementation automatically. Meanwhile, in the view of its excellent efficiency, the executable code is more transportable than the massive-scale data. By the concept of "moving computations to data" [2], MapReduce has shown improved quality on various data/compute intensive applications [3].

It seems that MapReduce has pointed out a bright road for data miners to transform large datasets into meaningful information. Unfortunately, however, there is always a disparity between the ideal and the reality. A number of data mining algorithms require "iterative computations", meaning that data are processed iteratively until the computation satisfies a convergence or a stopping condition [5]. Nevertheless, the general MapReduce computation model focuses on performing "single step computations" [4], that data through a map function processing and a reduce function processing, and then outputting the results.

For iterative applications, the general MapReduce computation model adopts the approach that creates a new job for each iteration. In this way, programmers must implement iterative programs by manually issuing multiple MapReduce jobs and orchestrating their execution using a driver program [5]. Not only the simplicity, but also the efficiency is hard to ensure. The general MapReduce computation model needs to re-initialize the distributed runtime environment in the beginning of each iteration, such that a great deal of CPU time is wasted. Moreover, for each iteration the static subset of the data needs to be re-loaded into memory thereby consuming a great deal of I/O bandwidth.

In response to those challenges, this paper presents a lightweight solution to improve the efficiency of iterative MapReduce, named MapCombine, by modifying the general MapReduce programming model and implementation based on Hadoop [6]. Firstly, to avoid the re-initialization of the runtime environment, a controller component is plugged into the general MapReduce model to schedule the iterations. In addition, to process data without re-loading the static subset, we modify the general MapReduce model surrounding combine phase to cache the fixed data and balance the nodes' workload before processing. Finally, to make the communication between the controller and the combiners flexible, we append an interaction layer to the general MapReduce implementation architecture. In particular, the interaction layer is also responsible for fault tolerance and downtime recovery. We also evaluate the performance of MapCombine and show comparisons with Mahout [7], a machine learning libraries based on Hadoop, for four clustering algorithms including Canopy, K-Means, Fuzzy K-Means, and Dirichlet.

This paper is organized as follows. In Section 2, the paper provides a brief overview of MapCombine, including framework, programming model, data stream and theoretical performance analysis. Section 3 introduces the details of map phase and combine phase of MapCombine. Section 4 describes the details of the new component, controller, including execution preparation, execution orchestrating and data further balancing. Section 5 presents the interaction layer and also the capability of downtime recovery. Next, Section 6 provides performance comparisons between MapCombine and Mahout for some clustering algorithms. To close, we summarize our related work, conclusions and the outline of future work.

2 System Overview

This section provides a brief overview of MapCombine, including framework, programming model, data stream, and theoretical performance analysis.

2.1 Framework

The whole MapCombine framework can be divided into two parts. One part is deployed on modified Hadoop implement. We modified the Hadoop mainly surrounding the combine phase. Mappers, combiners and reducers are all launched by the modified Hadoop. This part will undertake the major computation work. Thus, assigning more nodes to this part appears to be a wise choice. The other part contains controller and HBase. Controller interacts with the combiners through the HBase. The major job of this part is control and coordination, and therefore a small number of nodes should be assigned to this part, but the number must greater than two, for robustness.

2.2 Programming Model

Like the general MapReduce programming model proposed by Google, MapCombine also contains mapper, combiner and reducer. In addition, a new component named controller is plugged in. Programmers can design the distributed algorithm of MapCombine according to this line. Mappers receive the data records and transmit them to its local combiner. Combiners accept and process all of the data records transported by their local mappers. Controller merges the results produced by the combiners and interacts with the combiners for the next iteration. Reducer outputs the final results.

2.3 Data Stream

The data stream of MapCombine is shown in Figure 1. Each dotted line box refers to a node which is HDFS's DataNode and also modified Hadoop's TaskTracker. At first, data records are stored on HFDS. As the job begins, the split programs divide the input data into many splits. For example, node 1 stores four data records, A, B, C and D. The split programs divide them into two splits, one is A and B, the other one is C and D. Modified Hadoop creates one mapper for each split. Mapper1 is created for the first split, and Mapper2 for the second split. Depending on our "locality transmission" design, each mapper transmits its data records to the combiner, which runs on its local machine. For example, combiner1 gets A, B, C and D from mapper1 and mapper2. At this point, each combiner gets all the data records that HDFS has assigned to its node. The combiners can then process the data records iteratively under controller's guidance.

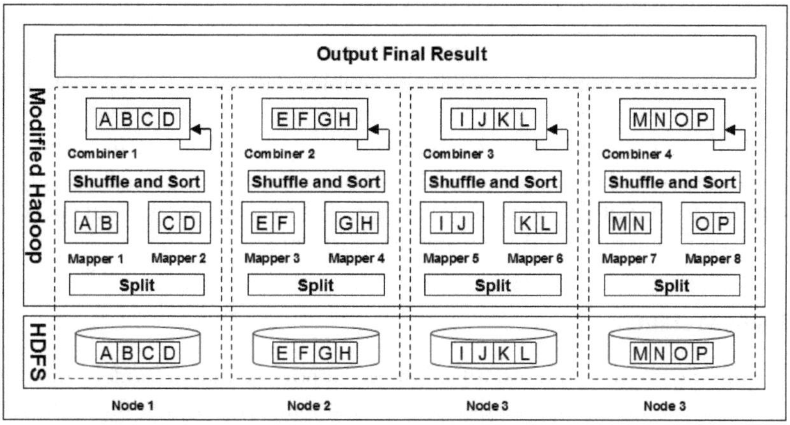

Fig. 1. The data stream of MapCombine

2.4 Theoretical Performance Analysis

As previously mentioned, a data mining job contains many iterations. Abstractly, every iteration can be divided into three phases. The first one is preparation phase, which initializes the distributed environment and accesses the input data records. The second is computation phase, by which the input data records are processed according to the distributed algorithm. The last phase is outputting phase. The results of current iteration are outputted to the distributed file system for the next iteration. Then, the next iteration continues these three phases until the results satisfy the stopping condition.

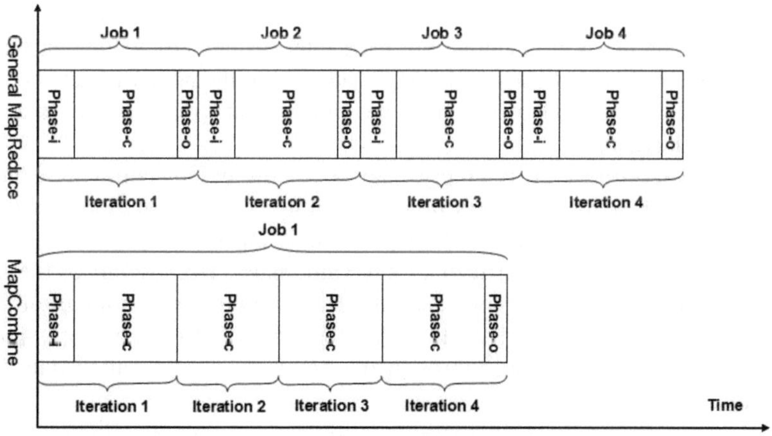

Fig. 2. The theoretical speedup ratio analysis

As shown in Figure 2, we use Phase-i, Phase-c and Phase-o to refer to these three phases. For the general MapReduce, all of the iterations contain Phase-i, Phase-c and Phase-o. On the other hand, MapCombine combines all jobs to a big one. The input data is stored in combiners' memory. The mining results of the previous iteration is transported from controller to all combiners. Thus, only the first iteration needs to initialize the distributed environment and access the input data. Likewise, only the last iteration needs to output the final results. Figure 2 shows the theoretical speedup ratio analysis between general MapReduce and MapCombine.

2.5 Light Weight

In MapCombine, a precondition of high-efficiency is that a node's memory has enough room for a mining application to hold the data records that the distributed file system assigns to this node's hard disk. Only under this precondition, will the JVM not report error. Therefore, we call MapCombine a light weight solution. Along with the increase of the memory size, the upper limit of MapCombine's capability is also increased.

3 MapCombine

This Section introduces the details of map phase and combine phase of MapCombine.

3.1 Locality Transmission

At first, data records are stored in HFDS. As the job begins, the split tasks divide the input data into many splits. One mapper is created for each split. In MapCombine programming model, the main duty of a mapper is to transmit its data to the combiner, which is running on its local machine. For each intermediate key/value pair outputted by a mapper, the intermediate key is the MAC address of the node (using other unique identification of a node is also possible); the intermediate value is the value of the inputted pair to the mapper.

In Hadoop, a tasktracker fills empty map task slots before combine/reduce task slots [6]. We modified the Hadoop's task scheduling code surrounding the combine phase. If a tasktracker completes all map tasks, it must create one but only one combine task to process the intermediate key/value pairs. Because all of the keys of intermediate pairs in a node are same and unique, a combiner will hold all of the data records that HDFS has assigned to its node. The course of data transmission from HDFS to combiner need not pass through the network. This is called data locality transmission.

3.2 Balanced Combiner

After the data transmission phase, all the data records have been received by the combiners. However, there is a small problem that some combiners have more data records than the others. This means that some combiners need longer time to process data records than the others in the computation phase. As the time cost by the parallel part is decided by the longest one, we need to assign the data records to the combiners as balanced as possible.

HDFS has a balance daemon that re-distributes blocks by moving them from over-utilized DataNodes to under-utilized DataNodes [6]. However, that makes the distributed file system balanced, in other words, that makes all jobs' data balanced but not a job's data balanced. The method MapCombine adopted to solve that problem is as follows: Every combine task will calculate how many data records it has and report the number to controller. Then, controller will compute an average and return it to the combiners. The above-average combiners will transmit the exceeding part to the interaction layer. The controller will transmit those records to the below-average combiners, in accordance with the shortage.

4 Controller

This section describes the details of the new component controller, such as execution preparation, execution orchestrating and data further balancing.

4.1 Execution Preparation

Controller is a program used to merge combiners' results and control the iterations. It is started after Hadoop and HBase, but before the job's jar. As a combiner starts, it will insert a field into HBase. The rowkey is its MAC address. Controller will monitor HBase and determine how many combiners are in the current job. Then, it will initialize the interaction layer by creating a data field and a flag field for each combiner. Before the first iteration, balancing the workload of all combiners is a priority of controller. As the phase has been introduced in foregoing paragraphs, it is unnecessary to repeat here.

4.2 Execution Orchestrating

After the initialization work, the data mining algorithms can be started. At the beginning of an iteration, all of the combiners will monitor controller's flag field. If the controller releases the signal of starting iteration, the combiners will access the controller's data field to obtain clustering centers or clustering model and then process their data. If a combiner finishes its work, the results will be inserted into that combiner's data field and a finishing signal will be inserted into that combiner's flag field. Then the combiner will monitor the controller's flag field for the next iteration. The controller monitors all combiners' flag fields. If all of the finishing signals have been delivered, the controller will obtain all results from the combiners' data fields. The controller then merges out the new clustering centers or clustering models and judges whether they satisfy a convergence or the stop condition. If not, the next iteration will be started.

It is worthwhile to note that data records are always stored on combiners' memory during the whole job. This avoids loading the static subset repeatedly. Also, only the control signals and the processing results need to be transmitted through the inter network. Transmission time and network load are no longer a trouble.

4.3 Further Balancing

As previously mentioned, a balance phase should be executed before the first iteration. The purpose is to make all combiners have the same quantity of data records. However, the same quantity of records does not equate to the same processing time. Some data records are more difficult to deal with than others. Therefore, at the end of each iteration, we design a further balancing phase. Every combiner will report the data processing time of current iteration to controller. Controller computes the average time. If the delta time between one combiner and the average cannot be tolerated, controller will transmit some data records from that combiner to others.

5 Interaction Layer

This section presents the interaction layer, and also the capability of fault recovery.

5.1 Interaction Layer

Interaction layer is designed for the communication between the combiners and the controller. It is based on HBase. HBase is a distributed column-oriented database built on top of HDFS. The interaction layer is like a warehouse. Data and flags are stored as cargoes. Each data or flag has a concerted rowkey as its label. The controller and the combiners collect data and flags according to the label.

It seems that a single node database is sufficient to support the interaction layer. As all intermediate results and all control flags are stored in the database. If the database fails, so does the whole job. Thus, using a distributed database is a better choice to ensure robustness. Robustness includes no data loss, and the job can continue running when a node of the distributed database fails. From the other point of view mentioned previously, the phase of balancing workload requires the transmission of a tiny percentage of the data. However, for a 20 Gigabyte data job, 5% of the data is 1 Gigabyte and all of the data flows are through the database. Therefore, another notable aspect is speed of data transmission.

HBase stands apart from distributed databases in not only the robustness for unpredictable fault and the transmission speed for parallel queries, but HBase is also based on HDFS, as Hadoop. This means that both Hadoop and Hbase can be deployed on the distributed file system we have set up, decreasing the time of building foundation. For another reason, HBase was once bundled as part of Hadoop, and it recently graduated from a Hadoop subproject to become an Apache top level project in May 2010. The common origins of HBase and Hadoop make it possible for a

Hadoop developer to handle HBase having spent a short amount of time studying. HBase is also an unstructured data oriented database that breaks through field format restriction and field length restriction. Flags, data records and even files can all be inserted into HBase.

5.2 Fault Recovery

A distributed computation implement often consists of many nodes. Although the probability of a single node failure is tiny, the probability of one node of a distributed implement failure is universal. In MapCombine, users need to set a maximum permissible time for combiners to process its data in one iteration. In the beginning of each iteration, the controller will wait for every combiner's intermediate results. If a combiner does not submit the results during the maximum permissible time, controller will judge that combiner node is failure. The controller will then kill the job. Fortunately, the intermediate results are reserved in HBase, and the job can be restarted from the latest success completed iteration.

6 Performance Evaluation

This section compares the performance of iterative data mining algorithms on MapCombine and Mahout. The algorithms include Canopy, K-Means, Fuzzy K-Means and Dirichlet Process.

6.1 Experimental Environment

The experimental environment comprised night machines. All machines use Intel E7210 2.40GHz processor, 4GB RAM and a 100 MB network connection. One of them is chosen as master node, and the others are used as slave nodes. All data mining applications are run respectively on two, four, six and eight slave nodes to collect the performance information.

Ubuntu 11.04 is installed on those nodes as their operating system. The versions of the implements are Hadoop 0.20.2, HBase 0.90.2 and Mahout 0.5. The experiments use US Census 1990 raw data set [9]. The data set includes 2.46 million records, and each record wtih125 attributes. The size of the data set is 823MB. Fifty is set as the number of iterations both for Mahout and MapCombine.

6.2 Experimental Algorithms

Canopy is a very fast and simple clustering algorithm. It is often used as an initial step for some other clustering algorithms. The experiments start with Canopy, as it can create initial centers and K value for other experiments. The parallel strategy of Mahout Canopy can be seen in Apache Mahout [7]. The parallel strategy of MapCombine Canopy is summarized as follows: (1) Map Tasks transmit all points to their local combine task. (2) The combine tasks perform canopy algorithm on their input points and output the canopy centers to the controller. (3) The controller clusters the canopy centers outputted by the combiners and then outputs the final canopy centers. (4) Finally, we start a MapReduce job to cluster the points into the final canopy centers.

K-Means is a simple, basic and well known clustering algorithm. K-Means requires a data miner to specify a K value. The parallel strategy of Mahout K-Means can again be seen in Apache Mahout [7]. The parallel strategy of MapCombine K-Means is summarized as follows: (1) Drive program chooses k points to be served as the initial clustering centers. (2) Map Tasks transmit all points to their local combine task. (3) Combine tasks get the clustering centers, compute the closest clustering center of each point and send the statistical results to controller. (4) Controller recomputes the new clustering centers. (5) Controller judges whether they satisfy a convergence; if not, go to (3) with the new clustering centers. (6) Finally, we start a MapReduce job to cluster the points into the final K-Means centers.

Fuzzy K-Means is an extension of K-Means clustering algorithm. It calculates the probability of belonging to every cluster for each point. A point can belong to more than one cluster. The interference of noise point is cut down. The parallel strategy of Mahout Fuzzy K-Means can be seen in Apache Mahout [7]. The parallel strategy of MapCombine Fuzzy K-Means is summarized as follows: (1) A Canopy job is run to get the original Fuzzy K-Means clusters. (2) Map Tasks transmit all points to their local combine task. (3) Combine tasks get the clustering centers, compute the probability of belonging to every cluster for each point and send the statistical results to controller. (4) Controller recomputes the new clustering centers. (5) Controller judges whether they satisfy a convergence; if not, go to (3) with the new clustering centers. (6) Finally, we start a MapReduce job to cluster the points into the final Fuzzy K-Means centers.

Dirichlet Process clustering algorithm uses probabilistic mixture models to cluster data points, and it can support irregular shape model clustering. The parallel strategy of Mahout Dirichlet Process clustering can be seen in Apache Mahout [7]. The parallel strategy of MapCombine Dirichlet Process clustering is summarized as follows: (1) Drive program creates the initial clustering models. (2) Map Tasks transmit all points to their local combine tasks. (3) Combine tasks get clustering models, assign each point to the probable cluster and send the statistical results to controller. (4) Controller recomputes the new clustering models. (5) Controller judges whether the maximum iteration limit is reached; if not, go to (3) with the new clustering models. (6) Finally, we start a MapReduce job to cluster the points into the final Dirichlet Process clustering models.

6.3 Experimental Analysis

The performance comparisons between Mahout and MapCombine are displayed in Figures 3 to 6. The average speedup ratios provided by MapCombine are as follows: (1) The average speedup ratio of Canopy is 1.09. (2) The average speedup ratio of K-Means is 1.20. (3) The average speedup ratio of Fuzzy K-Means is 1.09. (4) The average speedup ratio of Dirichlet Process is 1.16.

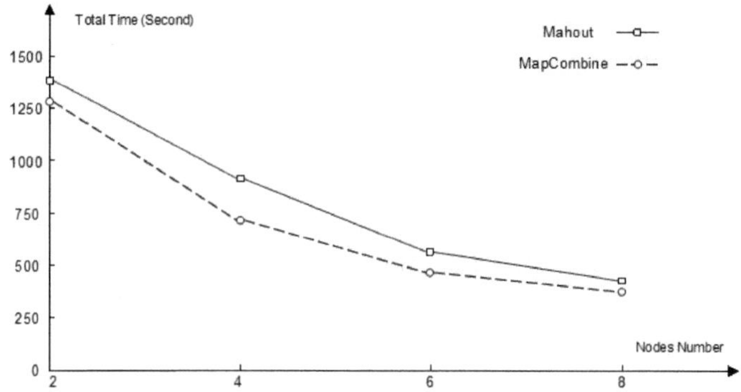

Fig. 3. The performance comparison of Canopy

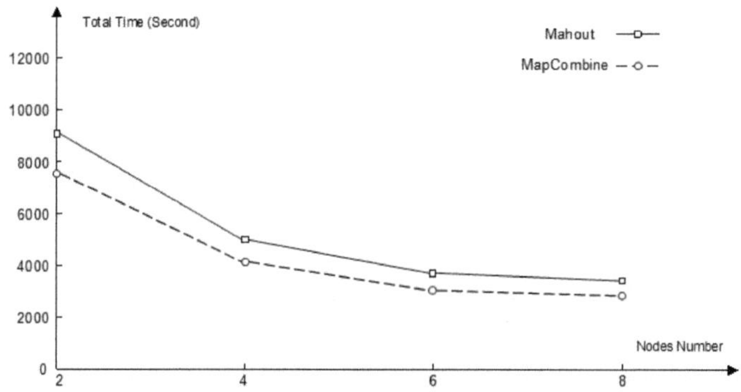

Fig. 4. The performance comparison of K-Means

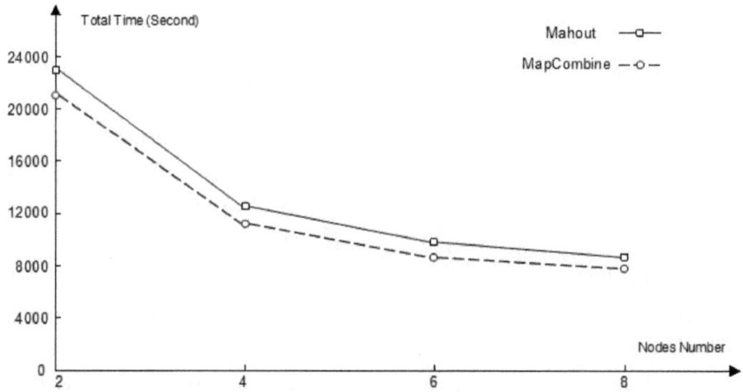

Fig. 5. The performance comparison of Fuzzy K-Means

The speedup ratio of Canopy and Fuzzy K-Means are lower, reflecting two different reasons. The Mahout Canopy uses only two jobs to cluster the data. There is less space to let MapCombine improve the efficiency. Thus, for a less iterative algorithm, the speedup ratio provided by MapCombine is limited. With regards to Fuzzy K-Means, MapCombine can save considerable time, but the running time for each iteration of Fuzzy K-Means is too long; the speedup ratio is not obvious. The running time for each iteration of Dirichlet Process is shorter; the speedup ratio is higher. K-Means possesses the shortest running time for each iteration, thus its speedup ratio is the highest. Therefore, the high speedup ratio provided by MapCombine usually appears in an application which iterations require a relatively short period of time.

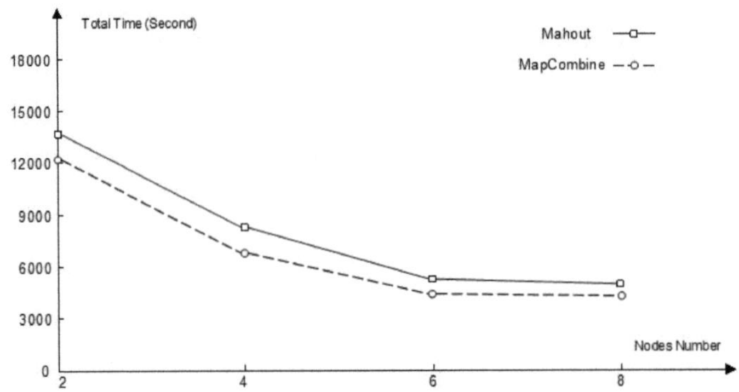

Fig. 6. The performance comparison of Dirichlet Process

7 Related Works

Distributed computation and data mining have both received much attention for several years. The MapReduce distributed computation model popularized by Google [10] has shown a brilliant strategy to process large datasets. Motivated by the Google MapReduce model, many MapReduce implementations and optimized MapReduce strategies have been presented.

Hadoop [6] is a well known open source MapReduce implementation based on HDFS [8]. It is widely used by industry and academe. Mahout [7] is a machine learning libraries on top of Hadoop, and this paper uses it for experimental contrast. Microsoft Dryad [11] is a MapReduce implement based on DAG (Directed Acyclic Graph) execution model. The derivative product DryadLINQ [12] integrates the Dryad with LINQ to enhance the ability to process structured data and iterative applications. To improve the efficiency of iterative MapReduce, there are also many optimized designs. Twister [4] is an in-memory MapReduce framework designed for iterative applications. The Mappers and Reducers of Twister cache the data in memory to avoid repeated data loading from disks. HaLoop [5] is a MapReduce implement that supports large-scale iterative data analysis applications. It designs several optimizations on top of Hadoop such as a loop-aware task scheduler, programming model extending and static data caching and indexing. Granules [13] is a streaming-based runtime for cloud computing with support for MapReduce. Granules allows complex distributed computational graphs with one or more feedback loops and provides rich life cycle support for iterative applications. Ericson and Pallickara [14] show its satisfactory performance for scientific applications, and there are also some researches that focus on the machine leaning ability of MapReduce [15] on top of work sets or GPU, such as Spark [16] and Mars [17].

8 Conclusions and Further Work

In this paper we described the detail of MapCombine, a lightweight solution to improve the efficiency of iterative MapReduce. To avoid the re-initialization of runtime environment and process data without re-loading the static subset, we purposed the following designs: (1) plugging a controller component into the general MapReduce model; (2) modifying the general MapReduce surrounding combine phase; (3) appending an interaction layer to the MapReduce implementation architecture. We also evaluated the performance comparisons between MapCombine and Mahout for four clustering algorithms. The average speedup ratio, which is 1.14, indicates that MapCombine performs well for iterative MapReduce applications.

Further, we plan to deploy and test more classes of data mining algorithms such as classification, pattern recognition and collaborative filtering, and we would like to set up an online data mining platform [18] to allow users to experience the efficiency of computing resources organized by MapCombine. Further reducing the I/O cost and network cost [19] are also valuable works.

Acknowledgements. This research is partly supported by the Natural Science Funding of China under grant number 61170177 and innovation funding of Tianjin University.

References

1. Dean, J., Ghemawat, S.: MapReduce: Simplified Data Processing on Large Clusters. In: Sixth Symposium on Operating System Design and Implementation, pp. 107–113. ACM Press, San Francisco (2004)
2. Fuggetta, A., Picco, G.P., Vigna, G.: Understanding Code Mobility. IEEE Transactions on Software Engineering 24, 342–361 (1998)
3. Ekanayake, J., Pallickara, S., Fox, G.: MapReduce for Data Intensive Scientific Analyses. In: Fourth IEEE International Conference on eScience, pp. 277–284. IEEE Press, Los Alamitos (2008)
4. Ekanayake, J., Li, H., Zhang, B.J., Gunarathne, T., Bae, S.H., Qiu, J., Fox, G.: Twister: A Runtime for Iterative MapReduce. In: First ACM HPDC International Workshop on MapReduce and its Applications, pp. 810–818. ACM Press, Chicago (2010)
5. Bu, Y., Howe, B., Balazinska, M., Ernst, M.: Haloop: Efficient Iterative Data Processing on Large Clusters. In: 36th International Conference on Very Large Data Bases, pp. 285–296. VLDB Endowment Press, Singapore (2010)

6. Apache Hadoop, http://hadoop.apache.org
7. Apache Mahout, http://mahout.apache.org
8. Ghemawat, S., Gobioff, H., Leung, S.T.: The Google File System. In: 9th Symposium on Operating Systems Principles, pp. 29–43. ACM Press, New York (2003)
9. UC Irvine Machine Learning Repository, http://archive.ics.uci.edu/ml/
10. Lammel, R.: Google's MapReduce programming model Revisited. Science of Computer Programming 70, 1–30 (2008)
11. Isard, M., Budiu, M., Yu, Y., Birrell, A., Fetterly, D.: Dryad: Distributed Data-Parallel Programs from Sequential Building Blocks. In: 2nd ACM SIGOPS/EuroSys European Conference on Computer Systems, pp. 59–72. ACM Press, Lisbon (2007)
12. Yu, Y., Isard, M., Fetterly, D., Budiu, M., Erlingsson, U., Gunda, P.K., Currey, J.: DryadLINQ: A System for General-Purpose Distributed Data-Parallel Computing Using A High-Level Language, pp. 1–14. ACM Press, San Diego (2008)
13. Pallickara, S., Ekanayake, J., Fox, G.: Granules: A Lightweight, Streaming Runtime for Cloud Computin With Support for Map-Reduce. In: IEEE International Symposium on Cluster Computing and the Grid Workshops, pp. 201–226. CRC Press, New Orleans (2009)
14. Ericson, K., Pallickara, S.: On the Performance of Distributed Clustering Algorithms in File and Streaming Processing Systems. In: Fourth IEEE International Conference on Date of Conference, pp. 33–40. IEEE Press, Melbourne (2011)
15. Chu, C., Kim, S., Lin, Y., Yu, Y., Bradski, G., Ng, A.: Map-Reduce for Machine learning on multicore. In: NIPS 2006, pp. 281–288. MIT Press, Cambridge (2007)
16. Zaharia, M., Chowdhury, M., Franklin, M., Shenker, S., Stoica, I.: Spark: cluster computing with working sets. Technical report, University of California Berkeley (2010)
17. He, B., Fang, W., Luo, Q., Govindaraju, N., Wang, T.: Mars: A Mapreduce Framework on Graphics Processors. J. Parallel and Distributed Computing 68, 1370–1380 (2008)
18. Boese, J.H., Andrzejak, A., Hoegqvist, M.: Beyond Online Aggregation: Parallel and Incremental Data Mining with Online Map-Reduce. In: 2010 Workshop on Massive Data Analytics over the Cloud, pp. 1–6. ACM Press, Raleigh (2010)
19. Cordeiro, R., Traina Jr., A.J.M., Lopez, J., Kang, U., Faloutsos, C.: Clustering Very Large Multi-Dimensional Datasets with Mapreduce. In: ACM SIGKDD Conference on Knowledge Discovery and Data Mining, pp. 690–698. ACM Press, San Diego (2011)

Centralization *vs.* Decentralization of Purchasing in the Public Sector: The Role of e-Procurement in the Italian Case

Renata Paola Dameri[1], Clara Benevolo[1], Cecilia Rossignoli[2], Francesca Ricciardi[3], and Marco De Marco[3]

[1] University of Genova, Italy
[2] University of Verona, Italy
[3] Catholic University of Milan, Italy
francesca.ricciardi@unicatt.it

Abstract. In this work, we sought to better understand the possible role of e-procurement in the evolving strategies of centralization (and decentralization) of public purchase centres. We conducted an explorative research study in the Italian context, where both centralization and decentralization of e-procurement have been experimented. The analysis of the Italian case highlighted an aspect that has been overlooked in literature so far: the strong and sudden centralization of purchasing caused by e-procurement adoption may present problems, especially in complex contexts with a past tradition of wide-spread de-centralized purchasing powers. The Italian case suggests that a possible solution may be the adoption of a hybrid model, where a centralized structure coordinates a network made of regional semi-centralized e-procurement centres, which, in turn, mediate with local contexts and involve or control the smallest agencies. The main features, strengths and weaknesses of this emerging organizational model for e-procurement agencies are discussed.

Keywords: e-procurement, eProcurement, public spending, purchase centre, centralization, decentralization.

1 Introduction

The performances of procurement processes in the public sector are becoming increasingly perceived as a critical aspect of government activities. From one perspective, in fact, public spending budgets are shrinking in many countries because of the economic crisis; conversely, the Public Administration (PA) must be prepared to meet a growing demand of services, both for structural reasons (e.g. population aging) and for emerging expectations due to increasing information flow and global competition.

In this scenario of very rapid and in-depth change of socio-economic conditions, e-procurement cannot be considered just a technical issue, of course. Similar to many other processes of ICT-enabled innovation, the introduction of e-procurement

V. Khachidze et al. (Eds.): iCETS 2012, CCIS 332, pp. 457–470, 2012.

involves significant changes at the organizational level, arouses power struggles, challenges well-established supply networks, and implies modifications in culture and habits. Moreover, since in the public sector it is the money of citizens that is to be spent, normative, ethic and participation issues are also strongly involved, and e-procurement proves to be, first of all, a political choice.

In this paper, we will focus on a specific issue in public procurement strategies, i.e. the dialectic between centralization and decentralization of purchasing centres. Our research question is then the following: *what is the possible role of e- procurement in the evolving strategies of centralization (and decentralization) of public purchase centres?*

Antecedents and consequences of purchasing centralization/decentralization are being investigated in regards to the private sector [1]; however, this issue is still quite under-investigated with respect to the public sector, where the implications of such choice are particularly important.

Then, in accordance with the mainstream methodological guidelines in Organization and Information Systems studies [2], we conduct an explorative qualitative research study, by collecting concepts and models from actors and by discussing them, in order to gain a better understanding of the topics raised by the research question.

The Italian case was deemed as very suitable to our goals, because (a) in Italy, government expenditure has been very high for a very long time (the national debt was 120% of GDP in 2011), and there is now an increasingly dramatic pressure to cut costs while improving the quality of purchasing; (b) the territorial organization of public bodies in Italy is complex and structured on several different levels, spanning from the central government to even very tiny local PA bodies; and (c) Italy has experimented both with centralization and decentralization of e-procurement processes. In fact, a centralized structure for e-procurement was built initially; then, a de-centralization of purchasing centres was authorized and implemented on a regional basis; and now, the trend is toward a hybrid model, where centralized or decentralized (e-)procurement processes are identified as preferable, depending on the nature of the purchased good or service, its economic value, the specific phase of the purchasing process, and the nature of the PA body involved. Italy is, then, an interesting case in order to better understand positive and negative aspects of both centralization and decentralization of public e-procurement.

In the next section, we will present a literature review with which we will seek to demonstrate that the issue of centralization versus decentralization in public sector e-procurement is still under-investigated. In the following section, we will provide details on our research methods and sources.

Thereafter is a descriptive explanation outlining the history of "the Italian way to e- procurement". The following section will include the main outcomes of our field research, describing the main features, strengths and weaknesses of the organizational model for e-procurement agencies stemming from the Italian experience.

Finally, in the Conclusion, a brief discussion on the research outcome will be provided, along with a synthetic description of further possible research activities.

2 Literature Review

2.1 Expected Positive Effects of e-Procurement

Literature provides us with several definitions of e-procurement, whereby different nuances of the term are highlighted; nevertheless, a quite inclusive definition may be the following, which states that e-procurement is "the use of integrated (commonly web- based) communication systems for the conduct of part or all of the purchasing process; a process that may incorporate stages from the initial need identification by users, through search, sourcing, negotiation, ordering, receipt and post-purchase review" [3].

The expected positive effects of e-procurement are numerous. We decided to classify them into the following categories:

1. Positive effects on transaction costs
2. Positive effects on purchase quality
3. Positive effects on inter-organizational interactions
4. Positive effects on internal organization.

In terms of transaction costs, e-procurement is expected to shorten procurement cycles, reduce inventory levels, reduce the costs of searching for appropriate goods and services, and obtain better prices [4] [5] [6].

As for purchase quality, e-procurement is expected to dramatically decrease wastages, to facilitate the adoption of proper quality standards and to prevent maverick buying [7] [8].

With respect to inter-organizational interactions, e-procurement is expected to result in better communication and collaboration between suppliers and buyers [9] [10].

Finally, with regards to internal organization, e-procurement is seen as a driver for business change, process quality improvement, enhanced operational efficiency and management effectiveness [11] [7].

According to Croom and Brandon, [4] efficiency improvements "arise through greater opportunity for lower prices from suppliers; from the reduction in process activity needed to complete the total 'requisition to payment' process; through the increased speed of the procurement process and better decision making as a result of improved management information" (p. 370). In particular, according to these authors, the primary typical efficiency improvements triggered by e-procurement include: (i) reduction in costs arising as a result of 'digitalizing' catalogues; (ii) fewer errors in order transmission; (iii) reductions in inventory, and (iv) reductions in suppliers' marketing costs.

2.2 Expected Positive Effects of e-Procurement in the Public Sector

If we concentrate on literature specifically focusing on e-procurement in the public sector, we can see that some further, "political" positive consequences of the adoption of e-procurement are expected that do not substitute those identified above, but must be added to and balanced with them:

5. Positive effects on democratic transparency
6. Positive effects on legality, integrity and compliance
7. Positive effects on competition fairness
8. Positive effects on the country's economic development.

As regards democratic transparency, Croom and Brandon-Jones [12] stress the importance of democratic control and respect for citizens' needs in public e-procurement initiatives. For a better understanding of these aspects, literature on e-procurement could be usefully linked, for example, to a focus on e-democracy and e- participation [13].

On the subject of legality, integrity and compliance, Engström et al. [14] highlight the importance of automatic reporting and of standardized, automated compliance to laws and norms, made possible by e-procurement.

Regarding competition fairness, Thai [15] reflects on the responsibility of governments in promoting fair and healthy economic behaviours, by leveraging their strength as buyers.

Finally, as for economic development, Thai [15] notes that the government's behavior as a purchaser can help local contractors and manufacturers. Coggburn [16] reminds us that there is a long tradition of public procurement seen as a vehicle for implementing various socioeconomic preference policies. Typical examples in the U.S. experience are the preferences for prison industry, minority-owned businesses, and for women-owned businesses.

Conversely, how can we concretely measure the performances of e- procurement initiatives? The cost savings are relatively easy to evaluate, but it is more difficult to measure improvements in quality, transparency, and effectiveness of public actions [17]. The creation of a shared framework to also evaluate the intangible and qualitative benefits of e-procurement [18], including constructs and metrics, would be an important goal for the scholarly community.

2.3 Literature on the Antecedents of Successful e-Procurement

Young literature on the "e-issues", such as e-commerce, e-participation or e-learning, usually starts by exploring the expected positive consequences of the adoption of the ICT-enabled innovation; only afterwards is scholarly attention caught by possible problems, unintended consequences, and potential failures. Literature on e-procurement is following the same path: in the first place, most scholarly writings have concentrated on the expected positive consequences of the adoption of this emerging ICT-enabled solution; some writings have then started to concentrate on factors that may hinder or, on the contrary, encourage the adoption of e-procurement; now, it is important to investigate what factors may positively or negatively influence the performances of e-procurement.

There is a certain consensus in literature on the fact that e-procurement implies changes in organizational structure, culture and mentality. Unless these changes are consistently implemented, any e-procurement innovation is likely to fail.

As for the organizational changes required by e-procurement adoption, it has been observed that e-procurement processes not only need the implementation of appropriate web sites [19] and efficient technological platforms to manage tenders, agreements and e-marketplaces, but they force an organization to rethink the administrative activity in public administration. In fact, all the procurement processes should be re-designed. Without such organizational redesign, e-procurement may produce some economic benefits, but it is not possible to reach the other (and perhaps more important) goals: administrative process quality, transparency, fair competition, efficiency and effectiveness of public services [20].

As for the cultural changes required by e-procurement adoption, it has been observed that suspicion, inertia and resistance against implementation are the stronger barriers to successful and profitable e-procurement implementation in the public sector [21] [22].

Albeit interesting, these are but generic statements. The amount of field research conducted on specific, measurable organizational and cultural variables influencing e-procurement performances is quite lacking. For example, Engström et al [14] assert that "to transform a procurement department into an e-procurement environment requires changes in buying behavior. It is a mistake to believe that the establishment of an e- procurement system can be comparable with the purchase of a new computer system. To succeed, significant planning must be done to find solutions that integrate strategy, technology, processes, and people. However, relatively little has been done with regards to empirical studies focusing on e-procurement implementation".

After analyzing the case of Sweden, Engström et al [14] identify the following important possible antecedents of successful public e-procurement: (i) a centrally standardized, highly usable e-procurement system, and (ii) effective education and training for the people involved in the procurement process.

An interesting suggestion with respect to possible antecedents of successful e-procurement comes from Johnson et al [23]. In a double survey, conducted in 1995 and in 2000 respectively, they compared and contrasted large public and private sector U.S. organizations in terms of organizational issues in the supply area. They found that there is a strong difference between private and public sector with regards to the centralization of purchase centres. Whilst among the organizations in the private sector as many as 22% of the surveyed companies relied on decentralized purchase centres, in the public sector this percentage was only 2%. In contrast, whilst in the public sector 52% of the surveyed bodies had centralized purchase structure, this percentage was only 27% in the private sector. Hybrid centralized-decentralized structures are present in similar percentages in the public and private sectors. In other words, there is a strong difference between the private and the public sector in the U.S. with regards to procurement centralization: public bodies display a much higher preference towards centralization. Why? The authors suppose that this choice is due to the specific challenges posed to the procurement function in PA bodies.

2.4 Literature on the Centralization-*vs*-Decentralization Strategies in Purchasing

Hardy and Williams [24] suggest that the adoption of e-procurement might lead to conflicts: in particular, regional policies of local purchases may clash with large national initiatives strongly oriented toward cost savings.

In other words, these authors imply that e-procurement innovation may impact on PA bodies' organizational structures, in particular as for the centralization and decentralization strategies.

This view is consistent with that of Mitchell [25], who says that e-procurement tends to change the relationships between buyers and suppliers. However, Engström et al [14] complain that "no study has been found focused specifically on public e-procurement's impact on the buying center, i.e., the members of the organization that influence the buying decision".

In a B2B setting, Osmonbekov, Bello, and Gilliland [8] suggested that the buying centre may decrease in size, include fewer hierarchical levels, and contain fewer functional areas when e-procurement is applied. Vagstad [26] found a correlation between the importance of local information and the preference for decentralized purchasing centres.

In summary, the analyzed literature suggests that the centralization-decentralization dynamics may be influenced by the adoption of e-procurement initiatives in the public sector, and may influence, in turn, the performances of such initiatives; however, the analysis of such reciprocal influences is still in its infancy.

We then decided to address the issue through an explorative field research, described below.

3 Research Method

As anticipated in the Introduction, we decided to conduct a qualitative research, in that the pioneering nature of our research question required an explorative study [2].

We chose to study the Italian public procurement centres using the method of purposeful sampling. The context of analysis was chosen taking into account the intensity criterion; in fact, the phenomenon under study, i.e. the public procurement centralization-decentralization dialectic, was important and highly visible in the chosen case.

As will be more thoroughly detailed below, each administrative Region in the Italian government structure has its own procurement centre; moreover, there is a central procurement centre, named Consip, which is in charge of negotiating and/or of providing national reference standards for a consistent amount of commodities and quasi-commodities.

In order to conduct our explorative research, we decided to interview managers from Consip and from a sample of the 20 Italian regional purchase centres. We chose 5 regional purchase centres where the implementation of e-procurement practices has a wide-spread reputation of being more mature. For each regional centre, we conducted a semi-structured interview, which was completed by follow-up phone calls and by the provision of documents such as annual reports and press releases (in Italian). The interviews were not recorded, in order to allow a friendlier and more natural approach, but we took notes and we enriched them with personal comments and fresh memories soon after the interviews.

We then conducted two semi-structured interviews to a Consip manager. The interviews lasted about 1 hour each. After this, we thoroughly studied the rich documentation provided by the Consip web site. This documentation includes reports, quantitative data, press releases, and also a rich and up-to-date review of the newspapers, which allows a good understanding of how the issues of public procurement are perceived in public opinion.

Finally, we studied the documentation provided by a University research centre of the post-graduate School of Management of the Politecnico of Milan, Italy. This research centre, named "Osservatorio eProcurement nella Pubblica Amministrazione" (i.e. Monitoring Centre on e-Procurement in the Public Administration), has been delivering a Report every year or two since 2006. These reports are very rich sources of information, including hundreds of thorough case-study analyses and quantitative surveys. Moreover, the reports have been presented in periodical Workshops, where PA managers, e-procurement solution vendors and scholars discuss cutting-edge issues as identified by the reports. All the reports, along with the audio-video recordings of the Workshops and/or the presentations of the speakers, are available online (http://www.osservatori.net/ and the entering the section "eprocurement_nella_pubblica_amministrazione").

We thoroughly studied this documentation, which proved very useful in order to triangulate the data coming from our interviews. Conversely, the last published Report of the Politecnico of Milan on e-Procurement dates back to 2010 [27], and then precedes the heating of the centralization-*vs*-decentralization debate, which occurred during the year 2011, following growing concerns for the Italian public expenditure sustainability. Our interviews and document analyses, on the contrary, allowed us to specifically focus on the centralization-vs.-decentralization issue, which is perceived as an emergent one by practitioners, and also by a certain part of the public.

We discussed our perceptions and interpretations of the analyzed conversations and documents until we reached a shared vision, which will be presented in the following paragraphs.

4 The Evolution of Public e-Procurement in Italy

4.1 The Centralization of e-Procurement Activities

Since the end of the 1990s, the Italian Government has started an innovation process aimed at introducing e-procurement processes in the public sector. The main goals of this innovation were to reduce expenses, to improve the transparency and fairness of purchasing, and to improve the efficiency of administrative processes in the Public Administration.

In this first phase, the role of the central Government was crucial. The Central Public Administration defined all the phases of the purchasing process and the operations to be automated, as well as the software applications to be used.

Moreover, the implementation of e-Procurement in the public sector required that laws and rules were defined, especially regarding the following: (i) the award of contracts concluded on behalf of the State, by regional or local authorities and other bodies governed by public law entities; (ii) the opening up of public procurement to competition; (iii) the verification of the suitability of tenderers, in open procedures, and of candidates, in restricted and negotiated procedures; and (iv) the electronic signature.

In the first phase of public e-procurement implementation, the central Government played the crucial role of regulator, both issuing its own laws and implementing European Directives. At present, all the rules regarding electronic activities of Italian Public Administration are collected in the "Codice dell'Amministrazione Digitale (CAD)", i.e. the Digital Administration Code. The latter is a set of rules governing the use of Information Technology in all the relations between the Italian Public Administration and citizens (D.Lgs. 07.03.2005, n° 82). In Europe, e-Procurement is ruled by Directive 2004/18/EC of the European Parliament and of the Council of 31 March 2004 on the coordination of procedures for the award of public works contracts, public supply contracts and public service contracts.

By these means, the Italian State defined its own e-Procurement reference model [28]. The reference model includes all the steps and activities needed to achieve the final signed contract, and namely:

1. The assessment of economic operators to be admitted to electronic tenders, auctions and markets, by checking their affordability and compliance to the law as for their commercial relations with public agencies;
2. the general framework of laws and rules to be applied to carry out all the procurement phases, complying with all the qualifications of a public tender such as trans- parency, accountability and so on;
3. the procedure to be followed for a regular award of a valid public contract;
4. the digital signature, for validating the contract.

To better support the launch of e-procurement and its first implementation, the Italian Government chose a centralized model and, in 1997, set up an ad-hoc public agency, called Consip, aimed at managing all the activities regarding public e- procurement. Consip SpA is a company belonging to the Italian Finance Ministry; its mission is to support e-Government initiatives and e-procurement in particular, with the mission of rationalizing public purchasing and improving contract transparency. Consip is in charge of the design and development of the new procurement processes and of the related ICT solutions. Its main mission is to implement the strategic directives of Italian Finance Ministry, by acquiring on the market the best technical solutions and competencies and by translating these ideas into ICT applications.

In order to implement public e-Procurement, Consip relies on the following: (1) framework agreements; (2) electronic auctions and tenders; and (3) e-marketplaces.

Through framework agreements, Consip intermediates the purchase of large amounts of a well defined good or service by all the public bodies, with the same prices and conditions drawn up in the contract. Consip is therefore responsible for awarding public contracts or framework agreements for all the public bodies. In view of the large volumes purchased, this technique helps to increase competition and streamlines public purchasing. Benefits are important especially for small public agencies that purchase small volumes and could only gain access to local markets with a lower degree of competition. Moreover, all the public bodies using framework agreements could save the cost to carry out the agreement by themselves.

Through electronic auctions and tenders, a public agency could award a public contract using the technical platform provided by Consip. This platform complies with the rules drawn up by the Italian laws and European directives about equal treatment and transparency in public purchasing. Therefore, the use of this platform grants the affordability of the technological instruments and prevents public bodies from the need to develop their own ICT solutions, saving time and money.

The e-Marketplace realized by Consip is called MEPA (Mercato Elettronico della Pubblica Amministrazione, i.e. Public Administration Electronic Market). MEPA is a comprehensive and integrated platform able to manage all the stages of public procurement: the selection and ranking of suppliers, the management of electronic catalogues, the request of quotation or request for orders, and the final contract award. On this e-marketplace, public bodies can meet several entities that have been previously determined to be qualified as suppliers and therefore compliant with the rules about public purchasing. The public bodies can then access a larger market and save money as a result of the higher competition between suppliers; they can streamline their procurement activities; and they can save time.

Because of the centralization of public e-procurement implemented by Consip, the Italian Government achieved good performances in a short time. The technological platform for e-procurement was made available for all the Italian public bodies, both the small and the large ones. This platform permitted the spread of e-procurement practices among all the public bodies through unifying, reliable and compliant methods and procedures. During the period 2004-2010, e-procurement in the Italian public sector increased from 76 million € to 6,000 million €. Among these, about 2,286 million € derive from transactions directly managed by Consip. Consip was credited with growing savings for the PA; the amount of estimated savings reached 5 billion Euros in 2011.

Qualitative benefits have also been achieved. The most important benefits are process streamlining, price savings and procurement time reduction. The quality of purchasing has increased, too, especially in correlation to the larger number of tenderers and therefore to the higher competition in the market of public procurement. Other benefits achieved involve document dematerialization and HR savings.

4.2 E-Procurement in the Italian Public Sector: The Decentralization Phase

Its successes notwithstanding, the strongly centralized Italian model for public e-procurement met some criticism. Indeed, Italian public bodies and agencies are very heterogeneous and widely spread throughout the country. The smallest bodies and local administrations had remained scarcely involved in the e-procurement "revolution" and Consip was often perceived as a distant actor. The Consip centralized platform was perceived as too generic to respond to the needs of so large a set of entities, with different expectations, schedules, and specific needs. Moreover, it was suggested that centralized solutions, like those developed by Consip, tend to incorporate best practices and then to maintain them for a long time, so slowing down further innovation and hindering the improved quality of continuous research. According to some sources, further, less readily confided reasons (linked to peripheral resistances to change and to vested interests threatened by the centralized purchase structure) created a political boost towards a reduction of Consip's role and power. For all these reasons, whilst Consip was praised for its performances, strong pressures were made to introduce a new, decentralized model.

In 2006, the Italian Government issued a law (Law n. 296) to rule the adoption of e-Procurement solutions at the regional level. The Italian state is made up of twenty Regions; they have administrative autonomy and they directly manage the Health Care System. The decentralization of purchasing centres to the regional level was mainly expected to overcome the scarce involvement in e-Procurement of small and local public agencies, registered in the first phase.

All the Regions now have the role of contracting authorities, that is, they can select and authorize suppliers, they can award public contracts and they can negotiate framework supply agreements to which all the public bodies and agencies in their own territory, including Health Care institutions, are compelled to make reference in their purchasing processes.

After the issue of Law 296/2006, each Region decided to develop its own organizational and technological solutions to build its regional procurement centre. This implies potentially positive effects, because it may allow a competition among emerging best practices, but it is also risky and costly.

In effect, the result was that the performances of the different Regional purchase centres were dramatically different. Italian public opinion today is increasingly astonished by the fact that the cost of the very same item (for example, a syringe, or a pair of latex gloves) may vary by as much as 200% or even more from region to region.

The lack of central coordination for the regional initiatives not only resulted in very poor performances in many regions, but also in the loss of opportunities that could have stemmed from cooperation and knowledge sharing.

The adoption of regional e-procurement, then, while enhancing transparency and potential comparability of purchasing performances, is paradoxically triggering a growing call for a renewed central coordination and evaluation of purchase processes.

For this reason, the Italian government created a network between Consip and the regional purchasing authorities, aimed at rationalizing the public spending and at creating positive synergies in the implementation and use of ICTs for public procurement.

Today, the PA bodies are bound to refer to Consip framework agreements for purchasing many commoditized and quasi-commoditized goods, such as desks, chairs, computers, etc. Due to economies of scale, purchasing through Consip can achieve savings of 70% or even more for this type of goods. Nevertheless, if a local PA body declares that it needs a certain specific kind of desk or chair or PC that is not included in those provided by Consip, they are allowed to negotiate directly with the suppliers. Moreover, there are many categories of goods and services that are not included in those managed by Consip, and there are many types of PA bodies (for example, schools) that are not bound to buy through the e-Procurement centres today.

Should the so-called "Consip approach" be strengthened and widened? The Spending Review, which is being conducted by the Italian government in these months, pushes toward this strategy; conversely, pressures are being exerted at regional and local levels, to maintain certain degrees of independence with respect to decentralized purchase decisions. In other words, the situation is highly dynamic and very suitable for qualitative research, since the different interests, opinions and behaviours of actors are highly visible in this phase.

In short, the introduction of e-Procurement in Italy, after the European directives, challenged the traditional, highly localized pulverization of purchase centres, because it requested the creation of a centralized, highly specialized procurement centre (Consip) and then of a network of purchase centres working at the regional level. The transparency and comparability of purchasing performances, made possible by technological innovations, caught growing attention among citizens, who are increasingly concerned about the economic crisis. The introduction of e-Procurement, then, far from being a mere technological innovation, has triggered in-depth organizational changes in public procurement, and has even made stronger political participation possible. This innovation process is far from its conclusion, but after our research we can seek to draw the emerging model for e-procurement that progressively stems from the Italian experience.

5 A Hybrid, Semi-centralized Model for Public e-Procurement

The situation of e-procurement in Italy seems to evolve towards a hybrid model, where a centralized structure coordinates a network made of 20 decentralized (or semi-centralized) agencies. This network carries on processes of purchase standardization, evaluation and control, increasingly enabled by ICTs.

In this model, the expected role of the centralized coordinating structure, i.e. Consip, consists in:

- developing technological platforms and tools for supporting all phases of procurement processes;
- collecting experiences and best practices, studying them and disseminating them (through the activity of the R&D Department);
- providing standards, recommendations and normative proposals;
- providing benchmarking for non-commodity spending;
- centrally managing the purchasing of all the commodities and quasi-commodities, at least in terms of cost negotiations and quality standards;

- promoting transparency, communication and citizen participation on procurement issues.

On the other side, the expected role of the semi-centralized agencies, i.e. the regional procurement centres, consists in:

- spreading the culture of e-procurement throughout their territories, involving also the smallest public bodies;
- supporting small bodies in implementing e-procurement practices;
- developing specific solutions to support particular needs in their environments;
- studying the impact of e-procurement on the quality of public services, considering also the specific needs of their own area;
- allowing bottom-up innovation, stimulated also by democratic competition and by citizen participation.

In this model, local PA bodies are encouraged to directly perform e-procurement processes, by exploiting the centralized and the regional platforms. The local e-procurement processes can be performed with different degrees of standardization and autonomy, depending on the nature of services/goods to be purchased, on costs, and on the specific nature of the purchasing PA body.

6 Conclusion

Our field research confirmed that the adoption of e-procurement in the public sector strongly pushes toward the centralization of purchasing structures, both for technological and for organizational reasons. This outcome is consistent with the (still rare) scholarly writings available on the issue.

Nevertheless, the analysis of the Italian case also highlighted an aspect that has been overlooked in literature so far: the strong and sudden centralization of purchasing caused by e-procurement adoption may present problems, especially in complex contexts wherein there has been a strong tradition of wide-spread decentralized purchasing powers.

The Italian case suggests that a possible solution may be the adoption of a hybrid model, where a centralized structure coordinates a network made of regional semi-centralized purchasing centres, which, in turn, mediate with local contexts and involve or control the smallest agencies.

The network of semi-centralized agencies may provide a possible antidote to the risks of rigidity and over-standardization inherent in a purely centralized model. Even more importantly, this network may play a pivotal role in promoting the necessary cultural change at the local level, and in managing and encouraging the transition towards e-procurement in small and very small local agencies.

The success of this hybrid model, on the other hand, implies strong coordination, clear definition of responsibilities, vision sharing and cooperation throughout the whole public procurement network – conditions that have been only partially achieved by the Italian e-procurement strategies so far.

In effect, Italy is presently a work-in-progress context, and therefore not very easy to analyze, but particularly interesting for theory building purposes.

Further research goals, stemming from our explorative work, may be the following:

1. To identify and thoroughly analyze e-procurement best practices with respect to critical aspects, for example, process redesign, requirements planning and involvement of small public bodies;
2. to draw quantitative scales for evaluating the performances of public procurement, not only in regards to the more immediate outcomes (cost savings), but also in terms of intangible benefits and concrete improvements in the final services provided to citizens;
3. to use the quantitative scales described above, in order to assess the impact of e-procurement on public procurement performances in different conditions, e.g. in case of different levels of centralization of the purchase centres, in case of different procurement processes involved in ICT-enabled innovation, in case of different types of purchased goods/services, etc.

Our research confirmed that public e-procurement is a very fertile field of study, involving technological, organizational and socio-political issues. We suggest that a stronger engagement of the scholarly community in these studies is highly advisable.

References

1. Dai, R., Narasimhan, S., Wu, D.J.: Buyer's Efficient E-Sourcing Structure: Centralize or Decentralize. Journal of Management Information Systems 22(2), 141–164 (2005)
2. Yin, R.: Case Study Research: Design and Methods. Sage Publications, Thousands Oaks (2003)
3. Croom, S., Brandon-Jones, A.: Impact of e-procurement: experiences from implementation in the UK public sector. Journal of Purchasing & Supply Management (13), 294–303 (2007)
4. Croom, S., Brandon-Jones, A.: Key issues in e-procurement: procurement implementation and operation in the public sector. Journal of Public Procurement 5(3), 367–387 (2005)
5. Davila, A., Gupta, M., Palmer, R.: Moving Procurement Systems to the Internet: The Adoption and Use of E-Procurement Technology Models. European Management Journal 21(1), 11–23 (2003)
6. Turban, E., King, D., Lee, J., Warkentin, M., Chung, H.: Electronic Commerce 2002: A Managerial Perspective. Pearson, NY (2002)
7. Dooley, K., Purchase, S.: Factors influencing e-procurement usage. Journal of Public Procurement 6(1/2), 28–45 (2006)
8. Osmonbekov, T., Bello, D., Gilliland, D.: Adoption of Electronic Commerce Tools in Business Procurement: Enhanced Buying Center Structure and Processes. Journal of Business and Industrial Marketing 17(2/3), 151–166 (2002)
9. Rossignoli, C., Carugati, A., Mola, L.: The strategic mediator: a paradoxical role for a collaborative e-marketplace. Electronic Market 19, 55–66 (2009)
10. Min, H., Galle, W.: E-Purchasing: Profiles of Adopters and Nonadopters. Industrial Marketing Management 32, 227–233 (2003)

11. Ash, C., Burn, J.: Assessing the benefits from e-business transformation through effective enterprise management. Journal of Information Systems 12, 297–308 (2003)
12. Croom, S., Brandon-Jones, A.: E-Procurement: Key Issues in E-Procurement Implementation and Operation in the Public Sector. In: Proceedings of the 13th International IPSERA Conference, Month and Dates, Catania, Italy (2004)
13. Ricciardi, F., Lombardi, P.: Widening the Disciplinary Scope of eParticipation. Reflections after a Research on Tourism and Cultural Heritage. In: Tambouris, E., Macintosh, A., Glassey, O. (eds.) ePart 2010. LNCS, vol. 6229, pp. 140–150. Springer, Heidelberg (2010)
14. Engström, A., Wallström, Å., Salehi-Sangari, E.: Implementation of Public e-Procurement in Swedish Government Entities. In: Proceedings of IMCSIT 2009 - International Multiconference on Computer Science and Information Technology 2009, pp. 315–319 (2009)
15. Thai, K.V.: Public Procurement Re-Examined. Journal of Public Procurement 1(1), 9–50 (2001)
16. Coggburn, J.: Exploring Differences in the American States' Procurement Practices. Journal of Public Procurement 3(1), 3–28 (2003)
17. Singer, M., Konstantinidis, G., Roubik, E., Beffermann, E.: Does e-Procurement save the state money? Journal of Public Procurement 9(1), 58–78 (2009)
18. Rendon, R.: Procurement process maturity: key to performance measurement. Journal of Public Procurement 8(2), 200–214 (2008)
19. Bruno, G., Esposito, E., Mastroianni, M., Vellutino, D.: Analysis of public e-procurement web site accessibility. Journal of Public Procurement 5(3), 344–366 (2005)
20. Reddick, C.: The growth of e-procurement in American state governments: a model and empirical evidence. Journal of Public Procurement 4(2), 151–176 (2004)
21. Vaidya, K., Sajeev, A., Callender, G.: Critical factors that influence e-procurement implementation success in the public sector. Journal of Public Procurement 6(1/2), 70–99 (2006)
22. Wirtz, B., Sebastian, L., Schierz, P.: An Empirical Analysis of the Acceptance of E-Procurement in the German Public Sector. International Journal of Public Administration 33(1), 26–42 (2010)
23. Johnson, P.F., Leenders, M.R., McCue, C.: A Comparison of Purchasing Organizational Roles and Responsibilities in the Public and Private Sectors. Journal of Public Procurement 3(1), 57–74 (2003)
24. Hardy, C.A., Williams, S.P.: E-government policy and practice: a theoretical and empirical exploration of public e-procurement. Government Information Quarterly (25), 155–180 (2008)
25. Mitchell, K.: Instituting e-procurement in the public sector. Public Management, 21–25 (November 2000)
26. Vagstad, S.: Centralized vs. decentralized procurement: Does dispersed information call for decentralized decision-making? International Journal of Industrial Organization 18(6), 949–963 (2000)
27. eProcurement: una concreta via verso innovazione, efficienza e trasparenza per la PA italiana, Osservatorio eProcurement nella Pubblica Amministrazione, Politecnico di Milano – Dipartimento di Ingegneria Gestionale. Available Online in Italian (2010), http://www.osservatori.net/eprocurement_nella_pubblica_amministrazione/rapporti
28. Alsac, U.: Use of e-procurement in Turkey's public health sector. Journal of Public Procurement 7(3), 333–361 (2007)

Consistent View Mapping of Large-Scale Ontology

Ruiguang Liu, Qingyi Meng, Zhiyong Feng, and Guozheng Rao

School of Computer Science and e Technology, TianJin University,
Tianjin 300072, China
{Lrg,zyfeng,rgz}@tju.edu.cn, goto4c00@yahoo.com.cn

Abstract. In the field of knowledge representation on large-scale ontology, there exists inevitable semantic inconsistency. The inconsistency in ontology is likely to preserve potential raw data. How to provide user the distinct personalized usage without any data lost and without inconsistency is a conundrum left to be solved. In this paper, an ontology view mapping mode is presented, which can create mapping from the original semantic dataset to the ontology views. It is processed through ontology parsing, reconstruction and consistency checking. The difficulties of semantic inconsistency and multi-culture expression conflict in large-scale ontology are smoothly solved by this model. As a result, original inconsistent ontology can be reused with several view mappings, without any inconsistency. The designed experiments verify our model and achieve the expected results.

Keywords: Ontology View, Ontology Inconsistency Detection, Ontology Modularization.

1 Introduction

With the development of Semantic Web and the rise of LOD (Linked Open Data), there are a large number of public ontologies, which are created by organizations and individuals, such as Linked Data, DBpedia etc. Because these ontologies have not been examined strictly, general inconsistency exists among them. In addition, due to the various backgrounds and professions of ontology writers, inconsistency in these ontologies is not only found in data conflict, but also represents the multi-culture expression. We want to create a solution to make full use of the inconsistent ontology, providing users personalized, diversified knowledge service while preserving all the data from original semantic dataset.

In order to achieve this aim, we focus the research on how to preserve the whole data from original large-scale ontology, while providing available inconsistent ontology view mappings to users. Our proposed model is combined with two main steps. First, dividing the original semantic dataset into consistent sub-ontologies, and then creating ontology view mappings with these sub-ontologies. In this way, the inconsistent data in large-scale ontology will be separated, avoiding inconsistency. Furthermore, inconsistency includes not only data structure conflict, but also the expressive difference. The problem is solved by dividing them into different view

V. Khachidze et al. (Eds.): iCETS 2012, CCIS 332, pp. 471–485, 2012.

mappings which separate the conflicts. This mapping model depends on our new ontology class sorting algorithm, creating personalized consistent view mappings with reconstructed sub-ontologies. All kinds of view mappings created will meet users' various demands, as distinct mapping provides users with optional ontology usage.

The structure of this paper is organized as follows: in Section 2, we summarize the previous achievements in ontology modularity and inconsistency detection. Section 3 defines the relative concepts used in the paper. Section 4 describes our system in detail. In Section 5, the experiments verify the expected results. Conclusions and directions for future work are given in Section 6.

2 Related Works

In this section, some critical technologies about ontology view mapping are discussed. We are most concerned with ontology modularization, and handling ontology inconsistency. For the reason that the achievements by the previous researchers are limited in their own fields respectively, they do little to consider combination with one another. We propose ontology view mapping model for large-scale ontology based on their works.

Many approaches aiming to solve problems in ontology modularization have been presented. The method by Stuchenschmidt & Klein [1] can partition large ontologies into smaller ones based on hierarchy, while taking into account the internal coherence of concepts. Kenneth Baclawski et al. have researched possible errors during ontology reasoning [2]. They presents a Tool known as ConsVISor to check formal ontologies, including both traditional data modeling languages and the more recent ontology languages. Peter Haase [3] et al. also present a model for inconsistency during ontology evolution, which will guarantee consistency of the ontology when changes occur. Achille Fokoue [4] proposes another method that can divide large ontology into small ones using ABox summary, while proving the availability and integrity. However, it depends upon the summary, not the whole data in original semantic dataset.

There are also some solutions for ontology inconsistency. Xi Deng [5] proposes a new approach to measuring inconsistencies in ontology with game theory. It can identify which axiom should be removed, to ensure the ontology consistent, meanwhile improving the quantity of inconsistent ontology diagnoses. Zhisheng Huang and F.van Harmelen et al. present a series of papers in this field. For inconsistency diagnoses, they present a framework to explain inconsistent information.[6] In order to solve inconsistent ontology reasoning, a prototype reasoner and pre-process algorithm are proposed.[7] As for the potential inconsistency in large-scale ontology, estimating inconsistent ontology, modifying it, inconsistency reasoning and multi-version reasoning are studied in detail . [8]

Referring to the previous works, we adopt some methods from ontology modularization and inconsistency detection. Reclassifying the original semantic dataset to obtain ontology view mappings, our model realizes the expected purpose of reusing original semantic dataset from different dimensions.

3 Ontology View Mapping System

3.1 Fundamental Definition

Some concepts and definitions should be defined at first, which are the prerequisites to illustrating this ontology view mapping system. The parameters that will be used in this paper are listed below.

O_{Raw} -The original semantic dataset to be parsed
O - Consistent sub-ontology set
C - Top class set belong for each created sub-ontology
O_t - The same classes belonging to several ontologies
V - Ontology view mapping set
$List_C$ - List of all the classes in original semantic dataset
$List_{Sorted}$ - The class list, sorted by weights in descending order
$List_{Deleted}$ - Already used classes in previous creation
C_T - The first class in current sorted class list

Assuming O_i , C_i are the elements belonging for O and C sets respectively, the fundamental sets O and C can be defined below.

Definition 1: The set of created sub-ontology of original semantic dataset O_{Raw} is defined as O, which can be expressed to $\mathrm{O} = \{\mathrm{O_i} | (\forall \mathrm{O_i} \subseteq \mathrm{O_{Raw}}) \wedge (\cup_{i=1}^{n} O_i = O_{Raw})\}$

Definition 2: If the set of top class belonging to each sub-ontology O_i, contained in O, is defined as C, which can be expressed to $\mathrm{C} = \{\mathrm{C_i} | \mathrm{C_i} \text{ is root class of } \mathrm{O_i}\}$ and $|\mathrm{O}| = |\mathrm{C}|$.

Set O and set C defined in Def.1 and Def.2 as the basic sets during sub-ontology creation. Based on them, there are some additional definitions, as follows.

Definition 3.1: If $(\mathrm{O_i} \in \mathrm{O}) \wedge (\mathrm{O_j} \in \mathrm{O}) \wedge (\mathrm{O_i} \neq \mathrm{O_j})$, O_t can be defined as $O_t = \{\mathrm{O}_t | (O_t = \phi) \vee (O_t = O_i \cap O_j)\}$.

Definition 3.2: If $(\mathrm{C_i} \in O_i) \wedge (\mathrm{C_j} \in O_j) \wedge (O_i \neq O_j)$, then defining $(\mathrm{C_i} \notin (\mathrm{O_i} \cap \mathrm{O_j})) \wedge (\mathrm{C_j} \notin (\mathrm{O_i} \cap \mathrm{O_j}))$.

Definition 3.3: If $\forall \mathrm{O_i} \in \mathrm{O}$, then O_i is consistent sub-ontology checked by reasoned.

The definitions above describe set of sub-ontology and the according set of top classes. The set of view mapping V needs them to be created. Fig.1 shows the routine of creation of Set V from original semantic dataset O_{Raw}.

Set V denotes that original semantic dataset is divided by different demands. Each view mapping V_i in set V is an abstract description on O_{Raw} from specific dimension, which also represents the distinct understanding about original semantic dataset. Especially, V is the set which contains the consistent view mappings of O_{Raw}, if the original semantic dataset O_{Raw} is inconsistent. The definition of set *V* is shown in Def. 4 below.

Definition 4: If there are N elements in set O, assuming set $K = \{k_j | (k_j \subseteq R^{+}) \wedge (k_j \leq N) \wedge (\sum k_j = N)\}$ •then defining $V = \{v_i | (\forall v_i = \cup_{i=1}^{k_j} O_i) \wedge (\cup_{i=1}^{m} v_i = O_{Raw})\}$

As defined in Def. 4, the union of all view mappings in set *V* must cover original semantic dataset O_{Raw} totally. Each V_i is non-fixed, because it can be composed by different consistent sub-ontology following user's requirement. So, the set *V* provide personalized view mappings, which not only contains all the data from original semantic dataset, but also meeting various requires for original semantic dataset O_{Raw}.

3.2 Ontology Views Creation

This system is designed to obtain the ontology view mapping set *V* defined in Def.4. The original semantic dataset O_{Raw} is to be processed by Processing System (short for PS below). Set *V* can be created with the processed results, sub-ontology set *O*. PS are composed of three parts, which are Parsing, then sorting and Reconstructing. The original semantic dataset O_{Raw} will be divided into some consistent sub-ontology in set *O*. Illustration of this system is shown in Fig.1.

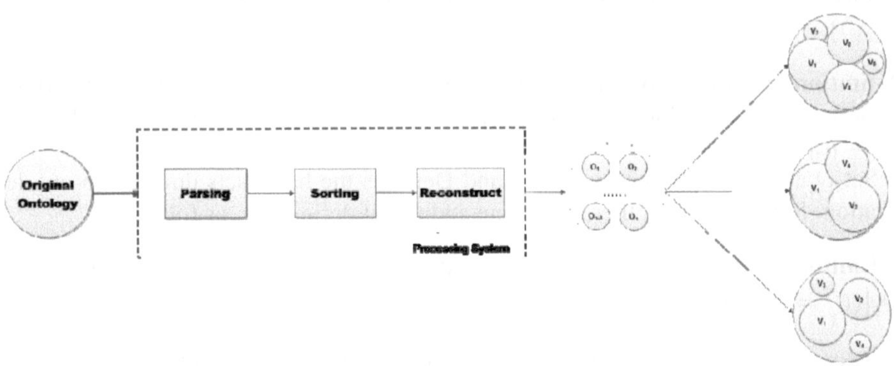

Fig. 1. Illustration of Ontology Mapping Creation

Parsing. This function includes ontology preprocessing and ontology parsing. PS applies JENA [9] development kits for data parsing. The aim of data preprocessing is to solve the difficulty of large-scale ontology reading. The parsing step will parse the classes, individuals and axioms mainly, then storing them in database. After this function, all the information of original semantic dataset O_{Raw} will be stored in database as triples, which provide the basic data for the following functions.

Sorting. In this function, PS will calculate weights of all the classes $List_C$ from O_{Raw} then sort them in descending order. In consideration of complex structures of classes in ontology, the results of reconstruction will be confusing and meaningless, if the

Sorting function is ignored. Therefore, this sorted classes $List_{Sorted}$ as the precondition for following process.

The sorting algorithm is designed to express relations among classes, including hierarchy depth, amount of individuals and the effects of being others' sub-class itself. Calculated weights of each class can reflect its relative importance among all the classes. Thus the reconstructed sub-ontologies, according to the sorted class list, are not only consistent ontology, but also express the structure of original semantic dataset.

After the completion of class sorting, there is probable that redundant data remain in database, especially on the condition of processing large-scale and inconsistent ontology. Without data cleaning, PS cannot guarantee the uniqueness of each triple. As a result, the following sub-ontology reconstruction will lead to unpredicted faults, and the view mapping will also not be created correctly. Therefore data cleaning should be executed before reconstruction. We can also ignore this step for small and consistent ontology.

Reconstruction. When the two functions above have been completed, $List_{Sorted}$ is obtained, and then sub-ontology will be created by reconstruction function for view mapping creation. $List_{Sorted}$ is dynamic, changing with the procedure of sub-ontology creation, and each sub-ontology, checked for inconsistency by Pellet[10] reasoner, is created from a root class C_T, which is currently the first element in $List_{Sorted}$. During the creation, there are two situations resulting in the finish of each sub-ontology creating procedure. One is that the inconsistency occurs, creating a consistent sub-ontology which cannot cover the corresponding whole hierarchy of original semantic dataset. Another situation is that there is no inconsistency in the procedure, leading to a creation of consistent sub-ontology that can cover its whole hierarchy of original semantic dataset. After each creation of sub-ontology, $List_{Sorted}$ needs to be refreshed, deleting the used classes in previous creation $List_{Deleted}$, and then resorting itself. The process of sub-ontology creation will finish until the $List_{Sorted}$ is empty.

Processed by PS, the original semantic dataset O_{Raw} is already divided into consistent sub-ontology set O. The creation of view mapping set V depends on the users, who can create various mappings meeting personalized needs.

3.2.1 Ontology Parsing

As the first step, the aim of this process is to parse original semantic dataset into triples. In this paper, we assume that ontology is composed by classes, individuals belonging for one class and all kinds of axioms. Procedure of parsing algorithm is shown in Algorithm 1.

Algorithm1. Ontology Parsing

```
  INPUT
    Pre-Processed Original Semantic Dataset O_Raw
  OUTPUT
    Class and individual triples stored in Database
procedure  - Parsing O_Raw and storage
```

```
 List classes in List_C
 //ListC={c|c is class in O_Raw}
repeat While (List_C is not NULL)
       If c is Resource Class
          Parsing Triples from c and storage
              If c has individuals
                        List instances I
             // I={i|i is individual of c}}
                Parsing Triples from i and storage
 end repeat
```

Firstly, all classes in O_{Raw} can be parsed with JENA development API. According to designed data analyzing routine, classes are classified into two kinds, *resource classes* and *anonymous classes*. This step focuses on parsing resource classes and individuals, then storing obtained triples in database according to hierarchy.

When the classes list, $List_C$, is created, parsing must traverse $List_C$. For each class, it should be judged whether it is *resource class* or *anonymous class*. If it is *anonymous* its triples are stored into database directly. As for the *resource class*, all its subclasses and individuals must be stored in order, while marked with its top class and direct parent class, preparing for the following steps. Axioms are also parsed into triples and stored separately. Taking into account the situations that ontologies are large-scale and inconsistent, parsed redundant data is inevitable. We leave the data cleaning step to the following procedure.

3.2.2 Sorting Calculation

When ontology parsing completes, PS should create sub-ontology. The meaning of sorting model has already been described above, thus only the illustration of sorting algorithm and its implementation are shown here. Taking into account thc structures of ontology, every ontology owns a class as root, from which traversing its whole hierarchy will begin.

For simplicity, Algorithm2 merely considers the influence of weights by classes and individuals, ignoring axioms and other limitations.

Algorithm2. Sorting Calculation

```
   INPUT
     i_base(constant parameter to indicate hierarchy• i_base
>1)
     SCW(subclass weights)  SCN(subclass number)
     INW(individual weights)   INN(individual number)
     i_deepest(constant parameter to indicate this current
class as other's subclass, i_deepest <1)
   OUTPUT
     Sorted Classes List List_Sorted
procedure - Create consistent sub-ontology based on List_C
   repeat While (C_root is not NULL)
```

Initial (level = 1 $Weight_C = 0$)
//initial parameters for every class CRoot
repeat If(C_{root} has n subclass)
$Weight_{level} = \sum_{k=1}^{n} i_{base}{}^{(level-1)}(SCW_i * SCN_i + INW_i * INN_i)$
//calculate current level weight
level++
end repeat
$Weight_C = \sum_{k=1}^{level} Weight_k$
//Sum all the Weight calculated previously
If(C_{Root} is subclass belonging for m classes)
Deepestlevel=max{$level_1, level_2 \ldots level_n$}
$Weight_C = Weight_C * i_{deepest}{}^{Deepestlevel}$
end repeat

Data of O_{Raw} has been obtained in the parsing function; PS can read needed data from database directly, including $List_C$. In order to achieve the results of designed sorting algorithm, every class in $List_C$ must be calculated as root class C_{Root}, traversing all its subclasses and corresponding individuals. In addition, the depth of subclass also impacts on weights of C_{Root}. Parameter i_{base} representing the depth of subclass is considered in algorithm2. The deeper the subclass is, the less the impact on C_{Root} i_{base} .

Another factor to be considered is that each class can be both parent class and subclass of others. The influence of being subclass should also be taken into account. In fact, C_{Root} could be subclass of several parents either directly or indirectly, while located at different depths. The $Weight_C$, result of previous calculation, should be multiplied with parameter $i_{deepest}{}^{Deepestlevel}$, which reflects the depth of subclass.

Each class in $List_C$ is needed to be calculated in terms of weights, according to sorting algorithm. Thereupon, the class weights list $List_{Sorted}$ could be generated through sorting results in descending order, which is indispensable for creation of sub-ontology, as it decides the creating scheme.

Here is a sample to illustrate the routine of sorting algorithm. In Figure 2, there is a simple ontology structure, which only shows the relationship between classes and individuals, excluding impact of various axioms and properties.

Assuming the ontology in Fig.3 is an original semantic dataset O_{Raw} , the classes from a_1 to d_1 are classes of O_{Raw} ,which are direct or indirect subclass of root class *Thing*. As expected in the designed Algorithm2, all the classes should be calculated weights. $List_C$={ a_1, a_2, b_1, b_2, b_3, c_1, c_2, c_3, d_1}, choose b_2 as the sample to illustrate while supposing the O_{Raw} data parsing has already been finished.

In the first step, some constant parameter should be initialized

$$i_{base} = 1.05 \; , i_{deepest} = 0.95 \; , SCW=5 \qquad INW=1$$

PS will judge whether b_2 owns subclass hierarchy at first. Its hierarchy contains classes { c_1, c_2, c_3, d_1}, while no individuals belong to b_2 itself. The process of b_2 weights calculation is shown below.

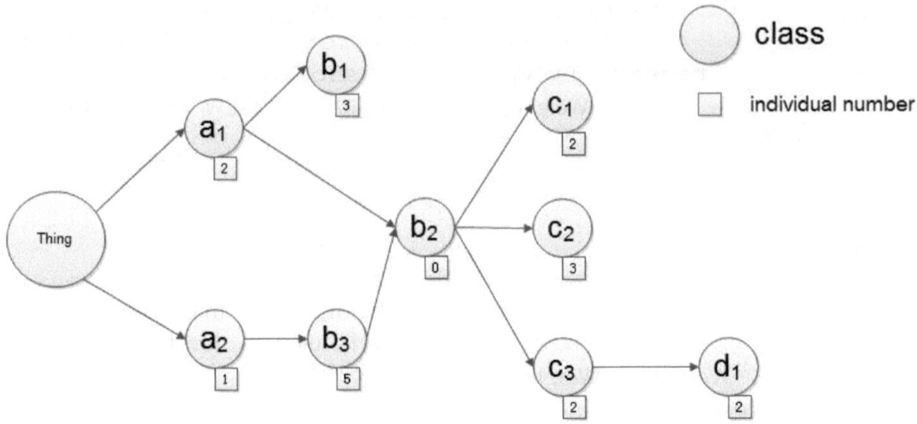

Fig. 2. Sample Sorting Algorithm

$\text{Weight} = \text{Weight}_{b2} + \text{Weight}_{c1} + \text{Weight}_{c2} + \text{Weight}_{c3} + \text{Weight}_{d1} = 1.05^{(1-1)}$ *(3*5+0*1)+ $1.05^{(2-1)}$ *(0*5+2*1)+ $1.05^{(2-1)}$ *(0*5+3*1)+ $1.05^{(2-1)}$ *(1*5+2*1)+ $1.05^{(3-1)}$ *(0*5+2*1)=29.805

At the time of obtaining weights of b_2, the result must be multiplied by the parameter $i_{deepest}^{Deepestlevel}$. This parameter is determined by the following steps. b_2 is the subclass of a_1,a_2 and b_3 at depths 2 , 3, 2 separately, assuming the root class is at depth 1 itself. Thus the *Deepestlevel*=max{2,3,2}=3. Finally, the weights of b_2 can be calculated as shown below.

$$\text{Weight}(b_2)=\text{Weight}*i_{deepest}^{(3-1)}=29.805*0.95^2=25.55$$

This result *Weight(b_2)* is the final weights of b_2, which is used to represent b_2 in the sorting list. The other remaining classes are also calculated in the same way. After that, $List_{Sorted}$ can be generated finally.

3.2.3 Sub-Ontology Creation

Sub-ontology creation is the third part of Processing System, which is used to create consistent sub-ontology by the order of $List_{Sorted}$. We choose Pellet as a consistency checker and reasoner in the procedure of creation, ensuring that each created sub-ontology is consistent.

Procedure of sub-ontology creation is shown in Fig.3.

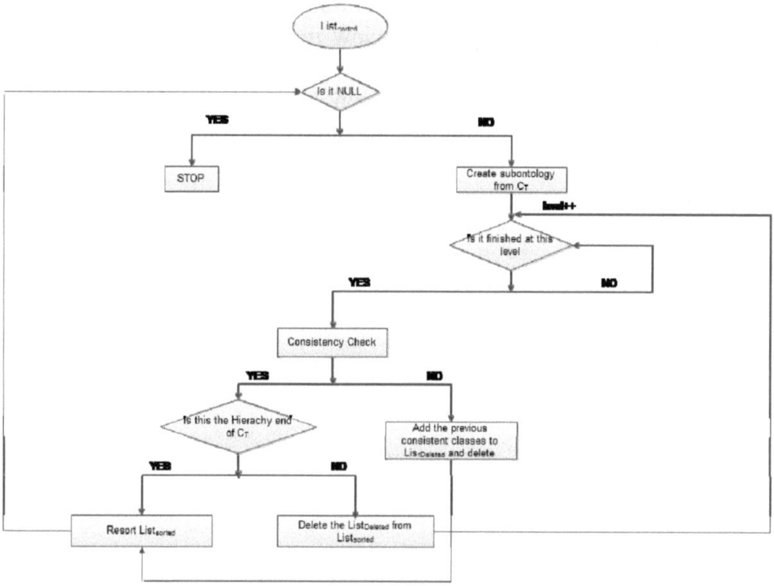

Fig. 3. Procedure of Consistent Sub-Ontology

This procedure of sub-ontology creation is the reverse routine of ontology parsing. Every sub-ontology is demanded to be created from a specific class, which is obtained from $List_{Sorted}$ dynamically.

As the top class in $List_{Sorted}$, C_T changes after creation of each consistent sub-ontology, ensure that there is no same sub-ontology in set O. Furthermore, inconsistency detection is deployed in the procedure of creation, which is throughout the whole reconstruction process. Creation will be controlled in two situations. On one hand, the creation will stop when inconsistency is detected a level, as the sub-ontology is created level by level. On the other hand, the procedure will not stop until all the subclass hierarchy is created, if there is no consistency in this creation. After each creation, we can obtain a consistent sub-ontology O_{New}, whose root class is C_T. All the classes used in O_{New} will be added into $List_{Deleted}$ each time, which will be deleted from $List_{Sorted}$. C_T will be regenerated after refreshing $List_{Sorted}$ following. The whole procedure will proceed until no classes are left in $List_{Sorted}$.

The number of sub-ontologies depends on whether the original semantic dataset O_{Raw} is consistent. Assuming there are N direct subclasses belonging to root class *Thing*, the amount of sub-ontology in set O will be more than N, if the original semantic dataset is inconsistent. On the contrary, the sub-ontologies are the ones whose C_T are the direct root classes of *Thing*, if there is no inconsistency in O_{Raw}.

3.2.4 Ontology View Mapping Creation

The ontology view mapping set V is the final target of this system. As the step after sub-ontology creation, several consistent sub-ontologies will be obtained in set O, whether or not O_{Raw} is consistent. Sub-ontology in O is consistent and contains corresponding information in O_{Raw}. The view mapping creation depends upon is the consistent sub-ontology in set O.

In order to meet various demands, different mapping should be created. So set V is uncertain, which is created dynamically to satisfy personalized need. This procedure is shown in Fig. 4.

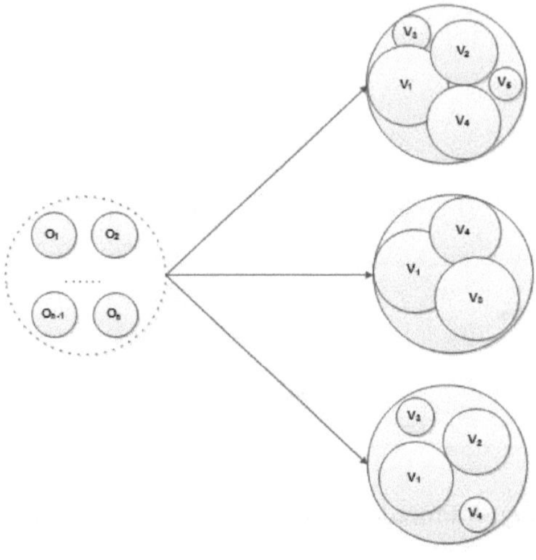

Fig. 4. Procedure of Consistent Sub-Ontology

For the distinct user demands, some different sub-ontology in set O could be composed to a view V_i. Every sub-ontology in O must be included in one view during each mapping creating procedure. Each view is a mapping that contains part of original semantic dataset data, satisfying with users' requirement. Additionally, there is no inconsistent data in view mapping at all, because sub-ontology in set O is checked for consistency during creation. Meanwhile the specific sub-ontologies, which are divided in the reconstruction step for the reason of inconsistency, cannot be contained in the same view. Quality of mappings is guaranteed in this way. As a result, various view mappings created under different user demands make up distinct view mapping sets V, each of them is a mapping from original semantic dataset at specific dimensions of needs.

If the original semantic dataset is consistent, the amount of set O is the same as that of top classes in original semantic dataset O_{Raw}, View mapping creation is non-flexible in this situation, because the optional sub-ontology for mapping creation is limited to a fixed number, amount of top classes. However, in the event that there is inconsistency in O_{Raw}, the amount of sub-ontology in O will be much more than the top class's number as described above. These created consistent sub-ontologies are the foundation of various view mappings, which are the purposes of this system.

4 Experiment

4.1 Experiment Design

The purpose of this experiment is to verify the proposed view mapping model with true semantic dataset. We selected two representative ontologies, *Zoo* and *Life*. There is inconsistency in *Zoo* to prove the results of processing inconsistent ontology, while *Life* is a consistent dataset that provides a comparison.

We also use some other systems to build our development environment, they are *JENA-2.6.4, Pellet-2.2.2 and JDK1.7* .

4.2 Experimental Procedure

This experiment is composed in two parts. In the first experiment, we testify to the correctness of our system by processing inconsistent ontology *Zoo*. In the second experiment, we choose a consistent ontology *Life* to provide the comparison results.

Experiment One: Creating ontology view mapping for inconsistent ontology *Zoo*

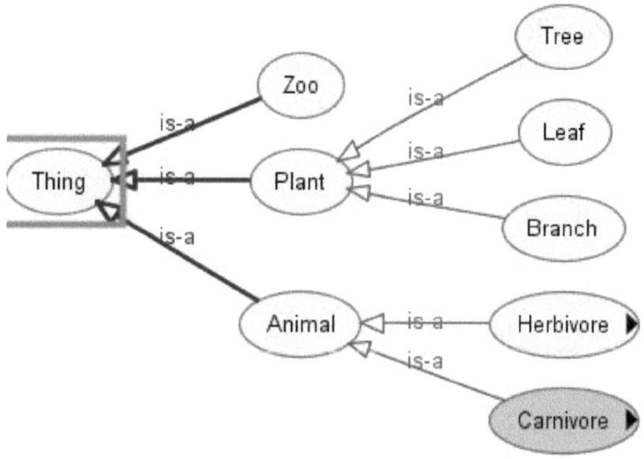

Fig. 5. Structure of ontology *Zoo*

As the parent of all classes, *Thing* owns 3 top sub-classes. They are *Plant, Zoo,* and *Animal*. The expected result of our system is that there are more than 3 consistent sub-ontologies being created in set *O*. After the process, set *O* of *Zoo* is O_{Zoo}=*{Plant, Animal, Carnivore, Zoo, Lion}*.

In the original semantic dataset *Zoo, Lion* and *Carnivore* belong to the direct or indirect subclass of *Animal* separately. They are created into two independent subclasses for the reason that there is inconsistency located in the *Animal* hierarchy. Finally, the ontology *Zoo* is divided into 5 consistent sub-ontologies.

1	http://www.owl-ontologies.com/animal.owl#Plant	<rdf:RDF xmlns:rdf="http://www.w3.org/1999/02...
2	http://www.owl-ontologies.com/animal.owl#Animal	<rdf:RDF xmlns:rdf="http://www.w3.org/1999/02...
3	http://www.owl-ontologies.com/animal.owl#Carnivore	<rdf:RDF xmlns:rdf="http://www.w3.org/1999/02...
4	http://www.owl-ontologies.com/animal.owl#Zoo	<rdf:RDF xmlns:rdf="http://www.w3.org/1999/02...
5	http://www.owl-ontologies.com/animal.owl#Lion	<rdf:RDF xmlns:rdf="http://www.w3.org/1999/02...

Fig. 6. Created subclasses of *Zoo*

In this situation, set *O* of *Zoo* contains 5 sub-ontologies. *Lion* and *Carnivore* cannot be included in the same view when creating view mappings, because they are separated for inconsistency in the *Animal* hierarchy during sub-ontology creation.

View mapping of *Zoo* depends on the user's demands. For example, if user is a geneticist, he can create mappings such as $V_{Zoo}=\{V_1, V_2, V_3\}$,which are $V_1=\{Plant\ U\ Animal\ U\ Zoo\}$, $V_2=\{Carnivore\}$ *and* $V_3=\{Lion\}$.

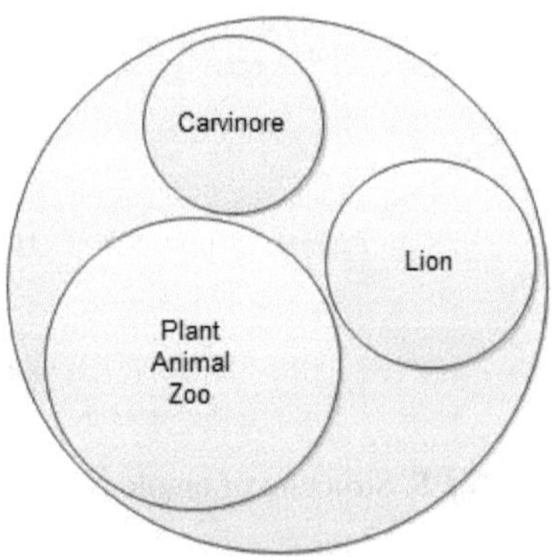

Fig. 7. One View Mapping Set of *Zoo*

Experiment Two: *Life*, a consistent ontology

This dataset is already verified as consistent ontology. There are 3 top subclasses of *Thing*, which namely *Entity, Obsolete, Nothing*. For the reason that the ontology is consistent, there are expected 3 sub-ontologies in set *O* of *Life*, each of them is created from top classes.

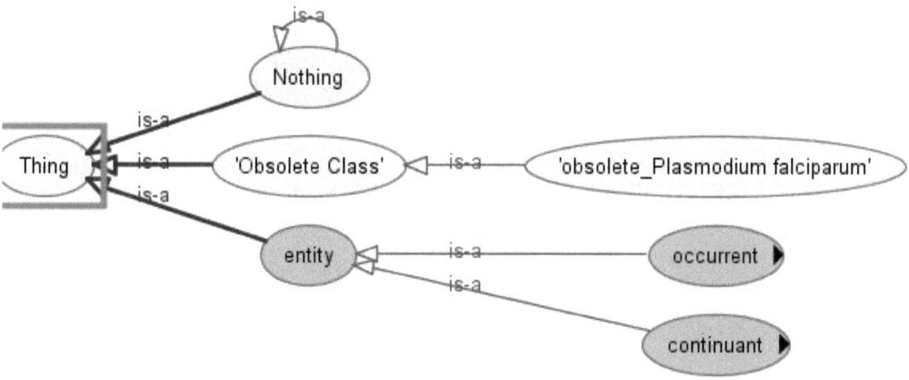

Fig. 8. Structure of ontology *Life*

1	http://www.ifomis.org/bfo/1.1#Entity	<rdf:RDF xmlns:obo="http://purl.obolibrary.or...
2	http://www.geneontology.org/formats/oboInOwl#Obsol...	<rdf:RDF xmlns:obo="http://purl.obolibrary.or...
3	http://www.w3.org/2002/07/owl#Nothing	<rdf:RDF xmlns:obo="http://purl.obolibrary.or...

Fig. 9. Created subclasses of *Life*

Entity has the most complicated structure and the maximum amount of data, the second one is *Obsolete*. *Nothing* is the subclass of all the other classes as defined in OWL. So the order of sub-ontology creation is also followed by this order, as order in $List_{Sorted}$.

The result is O_{Life}=*{Entity, Obsolete, Nothing}*, and the user can create view mapping such as $V_{Life}=\{V_1, V_2\}$, in which V_1=*{ Entity U Obsolete}* and V_2=*{Nothing}*. Referring to the result, there are no changes between view mapping set V_{Life} and original semantic dataset O_{Life}.

4.3 Conclusion of Experiment

From the results of experimental comparison between inconsistent ontology *Zoo* and consistent ontology *Life*, we can conclude that our system has solved the inconsistency in *Zoo* and provides the user personalized view mappings while preserving all the original data without any lost information. For the consistent ontology *Life*, there is hardly any impact, since our system is designed for inconsistent ontology processing. The experiment demonstrates the expected results.

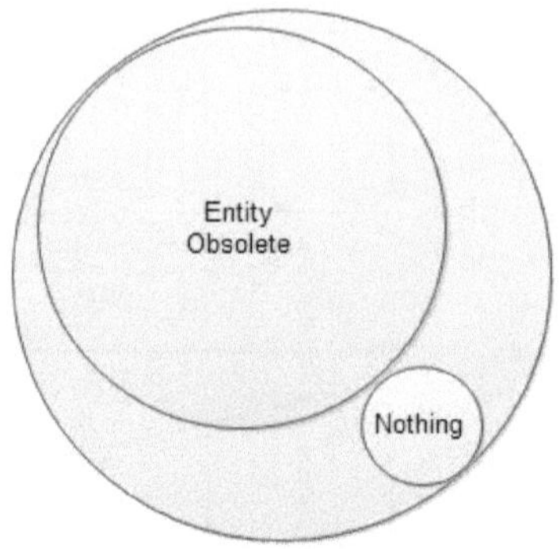

Fig. 10. One View Mapping Set of *Life*

5 Summary and Future Work

5.1 Summary

The view mapping model proposed in this paper has solved inconsistency in large-scale ontology, which is a new solution for inconsistent ontology while preserving all the data but dealing with inconsistency. Not only is the detection and location of inconsistency in semantic dataset solved, but this system also provides solution for personalized demands. It realizes the prospect of multi-dimensional mapping for inconsistent ontology. The designed experiment proves its correctness.

5.2 Future Work

In this paper, we present a model for inconsistent semantic dataset process and creating view mapping of it. However, there are still some imperfections left to be solved. In the sorting algorithm, we only consider classes and individuals, ignoring the impacts of axioms. We will improve this algorithm to reflect the ontology structure in a better way. Furthermore, we judge and acquire inconsistency merely in the process of sub-ontology creation, without marking and classifying different inconsistent information. The improvement on that is left for future consideration. As for the view mapping creation, we expected it can be created with users' background information and some other reference automatically, not only depending on users' creation by themselves.

Acknowledgements. This work is supported by the National Natural Science Foundation of China(No. 61070202, 61100049), Special Fund for Fast Sharing of Science Paper in Net Era by CSTD(No. 2011117).

References

1. Stuckenschmidt, H., Klein, M.: Structure-Based Partitioning of Large Concept Hierarchies. In: McIlraith, S.A., Plexousakis, D., van Harmelen, F. (eds.) ISWC 2004. LNCS, vol. 3298, pp. 289–303. Springer, Heidelberg (2004)
2. Baclawski, K., Kokar, M.M., Waldinger, R., Kogut, P.A.: Consistency Checking of Semantic Web Ontologies. In: Horrocks, I., Hendler, J. (eds.) ISWC 2002. LNCS, vol. 2342, pp. 454–459. Springer, Heidelberg (2002)
3. Haase, P., Stojanovic, L.: Consistent Evolution of OWL Ontologies. In: Gómez-Pérez, A., Euzenat, J. (eds.) ESWC 2005. LNCS, vol. 3532, pp. 182–197. Springer, Heidelberg (2005)
4. Fokoue, A., Kershenbaum, A., Ma, L., Schonberg, E., Srinivas, K.: The Summary Abox: Cutting Ontologies Down to Size. In: Cruz, I., Decker, S., Allemang, D., Preist, C., Schwabe, D., Mika, P., Uschold, M., Aroyo, L.M. (eds.) ISWC 2006. LNCS, vol. 4273, pp. 343–356. Springer, Heidelberg (2006)
5. Deng, X., Haarslev, V., Shiri, N.: Measuring Inconsistencies in Ontologies. In: Franconi, E., Kifer, M., May, W. (eds.) ESWC 2007. LNCS, vol. 4519, pp. 326–340. Springer, Heidelberg (2007)
6. Schlobach, S., Huang, Z.: Inconsistent Ontology Diagnosis: Framework and Prototype. EU-IST Integrated Project (IP) IST-2003-506826 SEKT
7. Huang, Z., van Harmelen, F., ten Teije, A.: Reasoning with Inconsistent Ontologies. In: International Joint Conference on Artificial Intelligence (2005)
8. Haase, P., van Harmelen, F., Huang, Z., Stuckenschmidt, H., Sure, Y.: A Framework for Handling Inconsistency in Changing Ontologies. In: Gil, Y., Motta, E., Benjamins, V.R., Musen, M.A. (eds.) ISWC 2005. LNCS, vol. 3729, pp. 353–367. Springer, Heidelberg (2005)
9. JENA (december 15, 2011), http://jena.apache.org/
10. Pellet (November 5, 2011), http://clarkparsia.com/pellet/

A Multi-objective Optimization Model for Information System Design

Yi Liu, Fuzan Chen*, Minqiang Li, and Jisong Kou

College of Management and Economics, Tianjin University
No. 92, Weijin Road, Nankai District, Tianjin, 300072, P.R. China
fzchen@tju.edu.cn

Abstract. In order to improve the quality of information system, components reuse has been widely developed both in academia and in industry. In this research, we focus on reusable information system development in which Component-Based Software System (CBSS) practices have grown rapidly. In CBSS development, system evolves using appropriate software components, selected based on customers' diversified requirements. However, few researches so far have drawn attention to measuring software quality concerning interactions of software components based on customers' satisfaction with the optimization models. In this paper, a multi-objective optimization model based on software quality, which consists of functionality and reliability, is presented for software components selection in the information system design. A Binary Particle Swarm Optimization (BPSO) algorithm is proposed to solve the optimization model. An illustrative example is used to demonstrate the feasibility and effectiveness of our proposed method.

Keywords: Component-based Software, Multi-objective Optimization, Software Quality, Binary Particle Swarm Optimization.

1 Introduction

Customers' requirements for information system have become increasingly diverse, whether in physical marketing or in E-business. In order to cope with the diversity, most information system/service providers have been primarily focused on information system design to satisfy the customers' demands by reusing system components or providing web service composition.

In past decades, information system/service providers presumed upon the customers' requirements to be constant and changeless in the software life cycle. However, customers change their minds frequently, and thus providers bear a heavy maintenance burden. The reusable idea is to perform system modularity, which encapsulates system functions into modules. Then, we can develop a system through the composition of system modules or sharing common system components. In the area of information system development, Component-Based Software System (CBSS)

* Corresponding author.

V. Khachidze et al. (Eds.): iCETS 2012, CCIS 332, pp. 486–495, 2012.

is the most popular methodology, in which system is consisted of software components. In previous studies, most articles attempted to improve software performance while considering the reduction of development cost [1-3]. Although all these objectives defined in these papers mirror customer satisfaction and conform to specific situations, customer satisfaction as an essential factor has not been addressed properly in the previous studies of optimization problems. Therefore, the greatest difference between our work and previous studies is that we apply customers' satisfaction in our optimization model for software components selection. The contribution of this paper is an approach that implements information system design based on customer satisfaction and analyzes the quality of component-based software. Furthermore, we propose a multi-objective optimization model for software components selection.

The rest of this paper is organized as follows. Section 2 gives an overview of current optimization approaches in component-based software development and describes related work in the area of customer satisfaction and software quality. Section 3 provides our improved multi-objective optimization model based on software functionality and software reliability. In Section 4, a BPSO approach to solving the optimization problem is proposed. In Section 5, an illustrative example and a discussion of the results are presented. Finally, conclusions and further work are described in Section 6.

2 Related Work

The methodology of component-based software development has been applied widely to improve the effectiveness of information systems. Component-based software system (CBSS) is well known as a methodology which focuses on the decomposition of a software system into functional components with well-defined interfaces [4].

There are a number of optimization approaches based on software performance using reusable software components. Jung et al. [1] aimed at improving the quality of Commercial Off-The-Shelf (COTS) software with a given quality level of each alternative. Tseng et al.[5] integrated Software Function (SF), Software Reliability (SR), Software Use (SU), Software Efficiency (SE),and Software Size (SS) into a single objective to measure the quality of software. Although these articles above were employed to meet customer satisfaction, none of these methods considered using customer satisfaction and software quality simultaneously in the optimization model.

The popular methods of calculating customer satisfaction are methods of expert estimation, making questionnaires [6-9] and regression analysis [10-12]. In this paper, we introduce Kano's model (Kano proposed it in 1984), [13] which classified the factors influencing customer satisfaction. Kano analyzed the relationship between overall satisfaction and the individual factors.

Many aspects of metrics, such as reliability, maintainability and portability, could measure software quality. Reliability, as a primary attribute of software quality, is usually used as an objective in software optimization models [5]. The most common approaches to measure reliability are based on Markov chains [12]and component failure data [14]. In our model, reliability is measured by CDG and SBRA algorithm, introduced by Yacoub et al. [15, 16].

The aim of this paper is to establish a novel reusable information system design model based on the tradeoff objectives between optimal software functionality and software reliability for maximum customer satisfaction. We attempt to describe the customers' requirements both in functional aspect and in non-functional aspect. We aim to balance software functionality and software reliability with optimizing the selection of software components.

3 Multi-objective Optimization Model

3.1 Software Functionality

In Kano's model, individual factors are grouped into three categories with different impacts on customer satisfaction, including basic factors, performance factors and excitement factors (see Fig. 1).

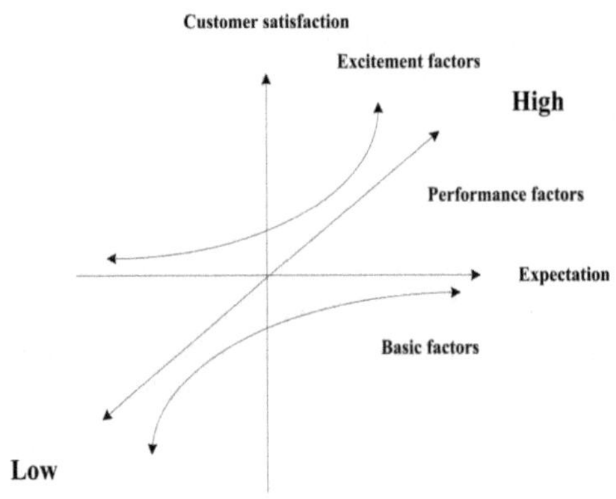

Fig. 1. Kano's model

Basic factors are minimized customers' requirements that cause dissatisfaction if they are not fulfilled, but do not lead to customer satisfaction if fulfilled. Performance factors lead to satisfaction if performance is high and to dissatisfaction if performance is low. Excitement factors are the factors that increase customer satisfaction if they are delivered but do not cause dissatisfaction if not delivered.

According to Kano's model above, we define three kinds of software components: basic components, performance components and excitement components. Software Functionality is based on the fulfillment of software functional requirements. We propose software functionality based on Kano's model for our optimization model, which is used to measure the functions of software components as well as how well customers are satisfied with them. The definition of the functions is based of Kano's model. We calculate the value of each kind of component function and sum it up as the total Software Functionality (*SF*).

$$SF = \sum_{i=1}^{f} \sum_{j=1}^{M_i} (k_{ij})^{m_{ij}} \tag{1}$$

where k_{ij} is the coefficient of the jth component in the ith kind of software components function, simulated from Kano's model. M_i is the number of the ith kind of software components. m_{ij} is a binary variable and means that if the jth component in the ith kind of software components is selected, m_{ij}=1; otherwise, m_{ij}=0. f represents how many kinds of software components we have defined. In this model, f is 3.

In software functionality model, the interaction of each kind of component can be expressed below:

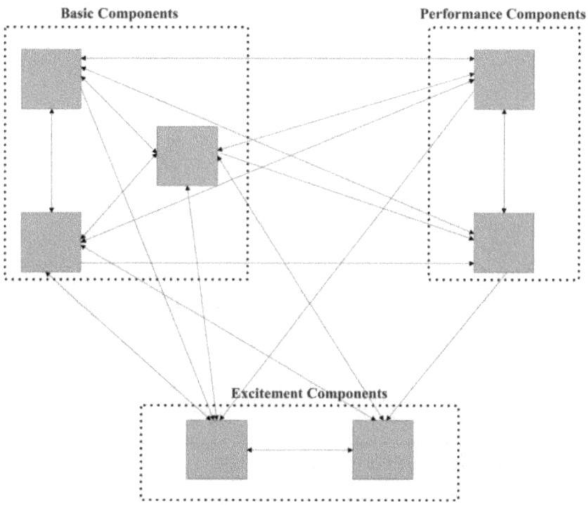

Fig. 2. Interactions of software components

3.2 Software Reliability

Yacoub et al.[15, 16] introduced CDG and SBRA for components reliability analysis. CDG is a directed graph that represents components, component reliabilities, connectors, connector (links and interface) reliabilities, and transition probabilities. After the construction of CDG, SBRA is applied for the estimation of software reliability. The SBRA algorithm is based on Depth First Search (DFS). After traversing CDG based on SBRA algorithm, we estimate the software reliability.

In contrast to SBRA algorithm, in our model, we separate the whole process of traversal graphing for calculating software reliability into several sub-processes; each sub-process representing the traversing of each component contains a note and its child notes. The traversal component may be regarded as the refreshment of every component's reliability. After that, every RC_i will be refreshed. In this way, we use the multiplication of the refreshed reliability of selected components to represent Software Reliability (SR).

$$\mathrm{SR} = \prod_{i=1}^{f} \prod_{j=1}^{M_i} f(R_{ij}) m_{ij} \tag{2}$$

where R_{ij} is the initial reliability of the jth component in the ith kind of software components. $f(R_{ij})$ is the refreshed reliability after the improved SBRA algorithm.

3.3 Multi-objective Optimization Model

The objectives of software functionality and software reliability under cost constraint above can be formulated as shown below :

$$Max \qquad \mathrm{SF} = \sum_{i=1}^{f} \sum_{j=1}^{M_i} (k_{ij})^{m_{ij}} \tag{1}$$

$$Max \qquad \mathrm{SR} = \prod_{i=1}^{f} \prod_{j=1}^{M_i} f(R_{ij}) m_{ij} \tag{2}$$

$$s.t. \qquad \sum_{i=1}^{f} \sum_{j=1}^{M_i} c_{ij} m_{ij} \le C \tag{3}$$

$$m_{ij} \in \{0,1\},\ i = 1,2,3;\ j = 1,\ldots,M_i;\ M_1 + M_2 + M_3 = M \tag{4}$$

Table 1. The notations above are explained as follows

M	the number of software components
M_i	the number of the ith kind of software components, i=1,2,3
f	the number of kinds of software components, In this model, f=3
C	the total cost constraint
c_{ij}	the fixed cost of the jth component in the ith kind of software components
k_{ij}	the coefficient of the jth component in the ith kind of software components function, i=1,2,3, j=1,…, M_i
m_{ij}	a binary variable, if the jth component in the ith kind of software components is selected, m_{ij}=1; otherwise, m_{ij}=0
R_{ij}	the initial reliability of the jth component in the ith kind of software components
$f(R_{ij})$	the refreshed reliability after the SBRA algorithm
RC_i	the reliability of component C_i
T_{ij}	the transition from component C_i to component C_j
RT_{ij}	the transition reliability of information sent from component C_i to component C_j
PT_{ij}	the transition probability from the current component C_i to next component C_j
$r_{i'j'}$	the number of degrees from the i'th component to the j'th component

The objective function (1) is formulated based on maximizing Software Functionality. The objective function (2) is formulated based on maximizing Software Reliability. Constraint (3) is cost upper bound. The money used to purchase software components for component composition should be below budget. Constraint (4) is the value threshold of each kind of software component.

4 Experimental and Analytical Results

4.1 An Illustrative Example

In our case, a total of nine software components available are considered, these are denoted as SC_1 to SC_9, respectively. We suppose SC_1-SC_3 belong to basic components, SC_4-SC_6 to performance components and SC_7-SC_9 are excitement components. To simplify, we consider only one specific scenario below, which describes transitions among software components in the application. Fig. 3 shows the nine components and their interactions. The links between components are directed edges. Every component as $<SC_i, RC_i>$ and every interaction between components as $<T_{ij},RT_{ij},PT_{ij}>$ in CDG have assigned values in Fig. 3.

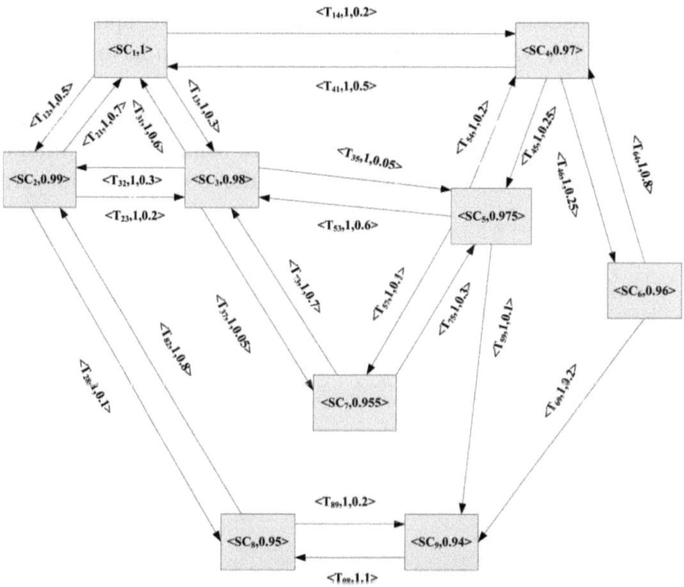

Fig. 3. CDG of the given example

In this part, we also encode the particle used in the BPSO algorithm. In the optimization model, every component is encoded into 0-1 variable.

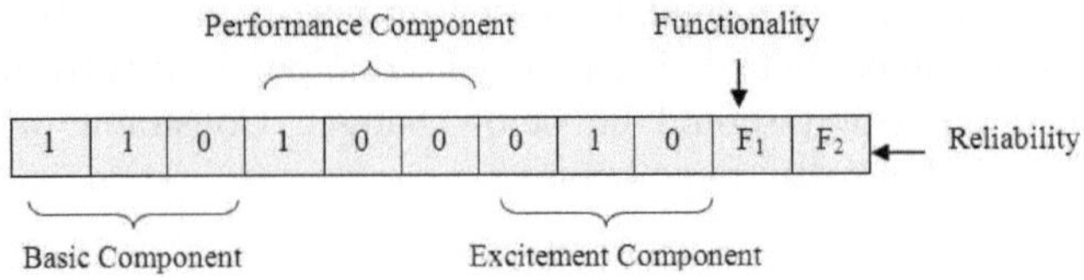

Fig. 4. Particle coding

As is shown in Fig. 4, every particle is encoded as $\overbrace{\left[1,1,1,0,0,\ldots\ldots,0,1,0,F_1,F_2\right]}^{M+2}$; the former M software components are valued 1 or 0 whether or not one of the components is selected. F_1 represents the first fitness value. In our model, it is equal to Software Functionality. F_2 represents the second fitness value as Software Reliability.

4.2 Experiments

In this section, we discuss the result of the multi-objective optimization model we have defined above. The values of objectives in this section have been normalized to eliminate effects of value's derivation. The value range ranges from 0 to 1, where 1 refers to a very high degree of software quality (functionality or reliability).We employ BPSO to solve the optimization model and select the maximum number of iteration as 200, population size as 50 and consider cost constraints limited to 12 (unit).

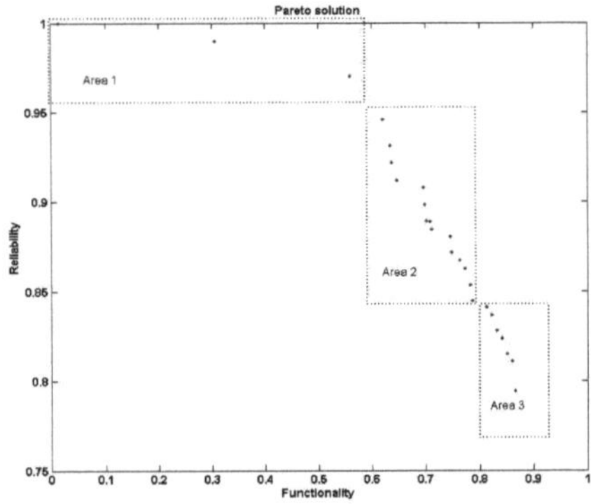

Fig. 5. Pareto solution of the tradeoff optimization model using BPSO algorithm

The Pareto solutions are shown in Fig. 5. The size of the Pareto-optical set under constraint is 25 solutions. It shows the results of solving the two objectives optimization model under cost constraints. The figure is in the form of Pareto-optimal points, for the tradeoff between software functionality and software reliability. Under the cost constraint, reliability can reach the maximum value of 1 when only SC_1 is selected, and functionality reaches its maximum at 0.8655 when SC_4 and SC_5 are not selected.

In order to better understand the Pareto solution in Fig. 5, we separate the Pareto-optimal points into three areas and analyze the numerical characteristics of each area in Table 2. SF represents software functionality, while SR represents software reliability.

Table 2. The numerical characteristics of the three areas

	Area 1		Area 2		Area 3	
	SF	SR	SF	SR	SF	SR
Mean	0.2928	0.9867	0.7098	0.8908	0.8401	0.8215
Median	0.3054	0.9900	0.7081	0.8892	0.8402	0.8239
Min	0.0137	0.9702	0.6211	0.8447	0.8122	0.7943
Max	0.5593	1.0000	0.7855	0.9459	0.8655	0.8412
Std	**0.2730**	0.0152	0.0560	0.0290	0.0196	0.0161

As shown in the table, there is a trend from Area 1 to Area 3 in that Functionality increases while Reliability decreases. As a result, Area 2 reaches a balance between Functionality and Reliability and can meet maximum customer satisfaction in these two objectives. The value in bold is an abnormal value among Stds due to the points in Area 1. The reason for this is that we have set large values to the coefficients of basic components. If one of them is not selected in component composition, there will be a heavy loss of customer satisfaction to Software Functionality. The three points in Area 1 are lack of basic components in each component composition.

According to the result above, we intend to give inferences and analyze the reason. Software Functionality and Software Reliability are a pair of tradeoff goals, so in the multi-objective optimization model, we get tradeoff Pareto solutions. The reason can be illustrated as we measure Software Functionality based on components selection; the more the components selected, the more the software functions fulfilled as well as the higher the degree of customer satisfaction. Meanwhile, we measure Software Reliability based on CDG. The reliability of the component-based software decreases as components increase.

5 Conclusion and Future Work

A new methodology of information system design based on reusable software components selection is proposed. Compared with previous methods, a novel way of software components classification, based on customers' satisfaction and multi-objective optimizations using Software Functionality and Reliability as the objectives, is proposed in this research. To obtain an optimal solution for selecting software components, the BPSO algorithm is introduced to solve the optimization problem. A simple example is used to illustrate the proposed methodology.

For better results, we should make the following improvements in future work: Firstly, sensitivity analysis of software components should be considered for identifying critical components in the next step. Secondly, as long as the presented cost estimation model has limitations, which did not take the costs of interfaces and transition between components into considerations, we should improve this cost model in the future. Thirdly, as we only measure reliability as one of software quality attributes representing software quality, we will attempt to add more quality attributes into the model in the future. However, our future research would focus on more complex real-world situations, developing effective information systems for enterprise application.

Acknowledgements. The work was supported by the National Science Fund for Distinguished Young Scholars of China (Grant No. 70925005) and the General Program of the National Science Foundation of China (No.71101103, No.61074152, No.71001076). This work was also supported by grants from the Research Fund for the Doctoral Program of Higher Education of China (20100032120086, 20100032110036, 20090032110065).

References

1. Jung, H.-W., Choi, B.: Optimization models for quality and cost of modular software systems. European Journal of Operational Research 112(3), 613–619 (1999)
2. Potena, P.: Composition and tradeoff of non-functional attributes in software systems: research directions. In: Proceedings of the 6th Joint Meeting on European Software Engineering Conference and the ACM SIGSOFT Symposium on the Foundations of Software Engineering: Companion Papers, Dubrovnik, Croatia, pp. 583–586 (2007)
3. Martens, A., Koziolek, H., Becker, S., Reussner, R.: Automatically improve software architecture models for performance, reliability, and cost using evolutionary algorithms. In: Proceedings of the First Joint WOSP/SIPEW International Conference on Performance Engineering, San Jose, California, USA, pp. 105–116 (2010)
4. Kwong, C.K., Mu, L.F., Tang, J.F., Luo, X.G.: Optimization of software components selection for component-based software system development. Computers & Industrial Engineering 58(4), 618–624 (2010)
5. Tseng, T.-L., Liang, W.-Y., Huang, C.-C., Chian, T.-Y.: Applying genetic algorithm for the development of the components-based embedded system. Computer Standards & Interfaces 27(6), 621–635 (2005)
6. Chikara, T., Takahashi, T.: Research of measuring the customer satisfaction for information systems. Computers & Industrial Engineering 33(3-4), 639–642 (1997)
7. Herrmann, A., Huber, F., Braunstein, C.: Market-driven product and service design: Bridging the gap between customer needs, quality management, and customer satisfaction. International Journal of Production Economics 66(1), 77–96 (2000)
8. Feciková, I.: An index method for measurement of customer satisfaction. The TQM Magazine 16(1), 57–66 (2004)
9. Sireli, Y., Kauffmann, P., Ozan, E.: Integration of Kano's model into QFD for multiple product design. IEEE Transactions on Engineering Management 54(2), 380–390 (2007)

10. Anderson, E.W., Fornell, C., Lehmann, D.R.: Customer satisfaction, market share, and profitability: findings from Sweden. The Journal of Marketing, 53–66 (1994)
11. Yadav, O.P., Goel, P.S.: Customer satisfaction driven quality improvement target planning for product development in automotive industry. International Journal of Production Economics 113(2), 997–1011 (2008)
12. Narayanan, S., Balasubramanian, S., Swaminathan, J.M.: Managing outsourced software projects: An analysis of project performance and customer satisfaction. Production and Operations Management 20(4), 508–521 (2011)
13. Kano, N., Seraku, N., Takahashi, F., Tsuji, S.: Attractive quality and must-be quality. The Journal of the Japanese Society for Quality Control 14(2), 39–48 (1984)
14. Grunske, L.: Identifying "good" architectural design alternatives with multi-objective optimization strategies. In: Proceedings of the 28th International Conference on Software Engineering, Shanghai, China, pp. 849–852 (2006)
15. Yacoub, S.M., Cukic, B., Ammar, H.H.: Scenario-based reliability analysis of component-based software. In: Proceedings of 10th International Symposium on Software Reliability Engineering, pp. 22–31. IEEE Computer Society, Boca Raton (1999)
16. Yacoub, S., Cukic, B., Ammar, H.H.: A scenario-based reliability analysis approach for component-based software. IEEE Transactions on Reliability 53(4), 465–480 (2004)

An Improved Method for the Feature Extraction of Chinese Text by Combining Rough Set Theory with Automatic Abstracting Technology

Min Shen, Baosen Dong, and Linying Xu*

School of Computer Science and Technology, Tianjin University,
300072 Tianjin, China
{shenminchina,venusforest2013}@gmail.com,
linyingxu@tju.edu.cn

Abstract. The Rough Set Theory can reduce features of Chinese text effectively [1], but it is often encountered that the reduction will need a very long time in the case of a large number of training sets [2]. To solve the problem, this article proposes a method of associating Rough Set Theory with Automatic Abstracting Technology (AAT). Firstly, by calculating the weight of each node-it consists of the Self-Frequency, Tree Frequency, Concept Generalization Degree and Concept Selection Degree -in the Concept Hierarchy Tree [3] which based on Tongyici Cilin semantic dictionary [4] [5], it can determine theme concepts of Chinese Text. Secondly, it will extract the topic sentences [6] by calculating the importance of sentences [7]. Finally, it reduces features of these topic sentences again by IQR (Improved Quick Reduct Algorithm), and constructs the vector. Then from the whole information retrieval system perspective, it is clear that this method can save time for Automatic Abstracting and reduction.

Keywords: Information Retrieval, Rough Set, Automatic Abstracting, Tongyici Cilin, IQR.

1 Introduction

Nowadays, when information has become explosive, information retrieval has become an effective method for information discovery and reasoning knowledge from large amounts of data. However, traditional information retrieval has drawbacks of trade-off of features, so in the rapid expansion of the information time, calculation is exponentially increasing. Automatic Classification and Automatic Abstracting as two key steps of Chinese information retrieval are both involved feature extraction [8]. Therefore, to reduce the computation time for Chinese information retrieval, the key is to reduce the time of feature extraction. Automatic Classification Technology based on Rough Set Theory proposed by Poland Warsaw Polytechnic University professor

* Linying Xu: 1963- , Male, Professor, Microsoft .Net Research Lab, School of Computer Science and Technology, Tianjin University.

V. Khachidze et al. (Eds.): iCETS 2012, CCIS 332, pp. 496–509, 2012.

Z. Pawlak, can be very good for the text feature reduction in the incomplete and imprecise condition [9], thereby reducing calculation time. But in larger training sets, there is also a problem with reduction time taking too long. Therefore, this paper presents an improved method, which processes from the perspective of the entire information retrieval. It firstly handles the Chinese text by Automatic Abstracting Technology based on concept, and then extracts the key features of the text data by IQR. Through the above operations it can provide the basis for subsequent processing in information retrieval. The text processing by Automatic Abstracting Technology is conceptually equivalent to the old text. On one hand, it can provide less processing set under the equivalent concepts for the IQR algorithm. On the other hand, provide a better reuse of module and data for the Automatic Abstracting processing module. So the entire time of information retrieval will be reduced.

Next is this paper's outline: First of all, this article defines some concepts. Secondly, it introduces the principles and theories used in this system, and through a number of examples to illustrate. Thirdly, it gives the results of the experiment and finally summarizes the advantages and the future works.

2 Concept Definition

2.1 Tolerance Relation

In order to define tolerance relation, we need to introduce the definition of knowledge system and incomplete knowledge system.

A knowledge system S can be defined as a four-tuple: $S = \langle U, A, V, f \rangle$

U is a collection of objects, namely domain. A is the set of object attributes. V is the range of the properties. f: $U \times A \rightarrow V$ is a function of property that $\forall u \in U, \forall a \in A$ have $f(u, a) \in V$.

In this knowledge system S, introducing an unknown or uncertain property $* \in V$, when the property (a) of an object (u) is uncertain, such as $f(u, a) = *$, this knowledge system is known as incomplete knowledge system.

Under the incomplete knowledge system, it is assumed that a subset of attributes $P \subseteq A$, tolerance relation $T(P)$ can be defined as follows:

$$T(P) = \{(x, y) | x \in U \wedge y \in U \wedge (\forall a \in P \Rightarrow f(x, a) = f(y, a) \vee f(x, a) = * \vee f(y, a) = *)\} \quad (1)$$

2.2 Importance of Attribute a for Attribute Set Q

Assumptions in the incomplete knowledge system: the decision attribute set $Q \subseteq A$ and condition attribute set $P \subseteq A$, then Q for P positive domain $POS_P(Q)$ and negative domain $NEG_P(Q)$ can be defined as follows:

$$POS_P(Q) = \bigcup_{X \in U/T} \underline{P}(X)$$

$$\mathrm{NEG_P(Q)} = \mathrm{U} - \bigcup_{\mathrm{X \in U/T}} \overline{\mathrm{P}}(\mathrm{X})$$

Among them, $\underline{P}(X)$ is lower approximation set of P for the subset (X) of objects. $\overline{P}(X)$ is upper approximation set. T is Tolerance Relation(formula (1)) and U/T is a partition for set of objects at T.

Upper approximation set and lower approximation set can be specifically defined as follows:

The condition attribute set $P \subseteq A$, subset $E \subseteq U$ of objects for P, $\overline{P}(E)$ and $\underline{P}(E)$ can be defined as the following formula:

$$\overline{\mathrm{P}}(\mathrm{E}) = \{\mathrm{x} \in \mathrm{E} | \mathrm{I_P(x)} \cap \mathrm{E} \neq \phi\}$$

$$\underline{\mathrm{P}}(\mathrm{E}) = \{\mathrm{x} \in \mathrm{E} | \mathrm{I_P(x)} \subseteq \mathrm{E}\}$$

$I_P(x)$ is Tolerance Class of object x for attribute set P.

Dependence degree of Q for P is defined as follows:

$$\delta_P(Q) = \frac{|POS_P(Q)|}{|U|}$$

Importance of attribute $a \in P$ for Q is defined as follows:

$$\delta_a(Q) = \delta_P(Q) - \delta_{P-\{a\}}(Q) \tag{2}$$

2.3 Self-frequency, Tree Frequency, Concept Generalization Degree, Concept Selection Degree

The number of occurrences of words directly meaning the concept of C is called the Self-Frequency of C. The total frequency of concept C in the concept hierarchy tree whose root node is concept of C is defined as Tree Frequency of C. The importance of the concept of C in its sub tree is called as Concept Generalization Degree of C. Based on the above three parameters, Concept Selection Degree of C can be defined and their formulas are as follows:

Assuming that, the collection of words whose semantic concept is C in the Chinese text as $\{W_1, W_2, W_3, \ldots\ldots, W_n\}$, then the formula of Self-Frequency of C as follows:

$$F_S(C) = \sum_{i=1}^{n} F(W_i) \tag{3}$$

Among them, $F(W_i)$ is the frequency of the word W_i appearing in the text.

Assuming the descendant collection of C is $\{W_1, W_2, W_3, \ldots\ldots, W_n\}$, then the formula of Tree Frequency of C as follows:

$$F_T(C) = F_S(C) + \sum_{i=1}^{n} \left(F_S(A_i) \times W_T^{Dep(C)-Dep(A_i)}\right) \tag{4}$$

Where: W_T is the conversion factor of each layer, $Dep(C)$ is the level of concept C in the concept hierarchy tree.

Assuming that, the descendant collection of C is $\{S_1, S_2, S_3, \ldots\ldots, S_n\}$, then the formula of Concept Generalization Degree of C as follows:

$$R(C) = 1 - \frac{\max_i F_T(S_i)}{\sum_{i=1}^{n} F_T(S_i)} \tag{5}$$

Then, the formula of Concept Selection Degree of C as follows:

$$Sel(C) = [\alpha \cdot \log_2(F_S(C) + 1) + \beta \cdot \log_2(F_T(C) + 1)] \times [\gamma \cdot R(C) + \delta] \tag{6}$$

Among them, α , β, γ, δ are weighting factors which are based on experience and experiment.

2.4 Importance of Paragraphs

Assuming that, theme concept set extracted from the above Concept Selection Degree is $\{T_1, T_2, T_3, \ldots\ldots, T_n\}$, and then the importance of the theme concept of T_i can be defined as follows:

$$I(T_i) = \lambda_{POS} \cdot \log_2 F_T(T_i) \tag{7}$$

Among them, $F_T(T_i)$ is Tree Frequency of T_i . λ_{POS} is weighting factor base on position, also called that the maximum weight of sentence position information contains T_i.

Assuming that, each paragraph is mapped into n-dimensional vector space of a node $P(T_1, W_1; T_2, W_2; \ldots\ldots; T_n, W_n)$, then the correlation degree of P_i and P_j is defined as follows:

$$Sim(P_i, P_j) = \cos\theta = \frac{\sum_{k=1}^{n} W_{ik} \times W_{jk}}{\sqrt{(\sum_{k=1}^{n} W_{ik}^2)(\sum_{k=1}^{n} W_{jk}^2)}} \tag{8}$$

After all correlation degrees are calculated, it needs to take the threshold value which is equal to the arithmetic mean of all paragraphs' to filter. The formula is as follows:

$$TV = \frac{\sum_{i=1}^{n} \sum_{j=i+1}^{n} Sim(P_i, P_j)}{n(n-1)/2}$$

Where: n is the number of paragraphs.

In summary, the formula of the Importance of Paragraphs can be defined as follows:

$$\lambda_{par}(i) = 1 + \frac{I_P(i)}{\sum_{k=1}^{n} I_P(k)} \tag{9}$$

Among them, $I_P(i) = \sum_{1 \le k \le n, k \ne i} A_P(i,k)$. $A_P(i,k)$ as follows:

$$A_P(i,k) = \begin{cases} 0, & Sim(P_i, P_j) < TV \\ 1, & Sim(P_i, P_j) \ge TV \end{cases}$$

2.5 Importance of Sentences

Assume that the vector space of sentence S is $S(T_1, W_1; T_2, W_2; \ldots\ldots; T_n, W_n)$, and then the importance of that sentence is the following formula:

$$W(S) = \lambda_{pos} \cdot \lambda_{par} \cdot \lambda_{cue} \frac{\sum_{i=1}^{n} W_i \times I(T_i)}{n} \tag{10}$$

Among them, λ_{pos} is the position weighting factor of S. λ_{par} is the importance of paragraph which contains sentence S. λ_{cue} is the weighting factor of cue words and tips. $I(T_i)$ is the formula (7).

2.6 Meet Degree of Meaning Blocks

Suppose that there are m Meaning Blocks in an article, denoted $S_1, S_2, S_3, \ldots\ldots, S_m$, and each Meaning Block has K_i paragraphs. Each paragraph's vector is $P(T_1, W_1; T_2, W_2; \ldots\ldots; T_n, W_n)$. Set up the center vector named $c(i)$ of Meaning Block i, and the formula as follows:

$$c(i) = \left(T_1, \sum_{j=1}^{K_i} W_{1,j}; T_2, \sum_{j=1}^{K_i} W_{2,j}; \ldots\ldots; T_n, \sum_{j=1}^{K_i} W_{n,j} \right) / K_i$$

Set Meaning Block S_i has K_i paragraphs, respectively, $P_{i,1}, P_{i,2}, \ldots\ldots, P_{i,K_i}$ and the Meet degree $J(S_i)$ of S_i is as following formula:

$$J(S_i) = \sum_{j=1}^{K_i} Sim\left(P_{i,j}, c(i)\right) \tag{11}$$

Among them, $Sim\left(P_{i,j}, c(i)\right)$ is correlation degree of P_i and $c(i)$.

3 Theories, Principles and Examples to Explain

3.1 Main Resources

This paper used the semantic dictionary which is finished by the Harbin Institute of Technology based on" Tongyici Cilin (extended version)". It defines the semantic encoding system. It can reflect the conceptual structure of the entries, as well as the relationship between the other entries by the word coding, such as synonymy, antonym and near-synonymy, contain, ownership and so on.

"Tongyici Cilin (extended version)" organized all the words according with the hierarchy of the tree, and the vocabulary is divided into large (12), medium (97) and small (1400) classes. Each small class has many words, these words are based on the distance and relevance of the meaning of a word is divided into a number of word groups. The words in each word group are further divided into a number of atomic groups where the meanings of words are same or similar or have great relevance.

Word coding levels refers to the Fig. 3-1-1 and specific coding reference Table 3-1-1.

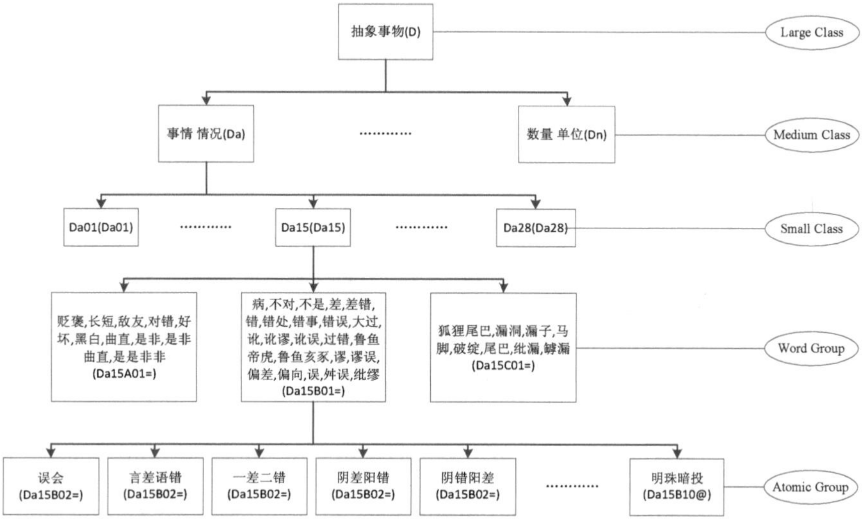

Fig. 3-1-1.

Table 3-1-1.

Bit of Encoding	1	2	3	4	5	6	7	8
Example	D	a	1	5	B	0	2	:-)\@
Class	Large Class	Medium Class	Small Class		Words Group	Atomic Group		
Level	1st	2th	3th		4th	5th		

In order to build the concept hierarchy tree, the article rearranging the semantic dictionary and stores information into database named Cilin.mdf. There are two main tables in this database. One is Cilin_BMSTree which stores data and structure of words in large, medium and small classes. Another is Cilin_SQunTree which stores data and structure of words in small classes, word groups, and atomic groups. The structure of table of Cilin_BMSTree and Cilin_SQunTree is shown in Table 3-1-2. After this treatment, it can provide greater convenience for the subsequent construction of concept hierarchy trees.

Table 3-1-2.

SN	Field	Desp	Type	Null	Mark
1	Id	Id	Int	No	Key Increment
2	ParentId	Id of Parent	Int	No	Foreign Key
3	ChineseName	Chinese Word	Varchar(200)	No	
4	Code	Coder	Varchar(20)	No	
5	OrderNum	SN	Int	No	
6	SumNum	Sum	Int	No	

3.2 Building the Concept Hierarchy Tree

Build the Concept Hierarchy Tree of Chinese Text

The article focuses on preprocessing the original Chinese text into an XML document with tags, and then divides the sentence into words with the N-Shortest Path algorithm, and does some optimizations for the division words [10]. After that it needs to query the database to get the encodings of division words. At last, it needs to build the concept hierarchy tree by combining with Cilin_BMSTree and Cilin_SQunTree. The construction algorithm is as follows:

- Initialize the table of WordTable, where each element (Word) is division word.
- Generate the new table of WordTable by deleting functional words, punctuations, numbers, and symbols.
- Get each encoding (KeyCode) of the element of WordTable by looking up the database, and add KeyCode and Word into the table of CodeTable. The adding process is as follows:
  - If CodeTable doesn't contain this node, initialize the node information which consists of KeyCode, Word, ParentId (value is -1), Self-Frequency (value is 1), and Tree Frequency (value is 1).
  - If CodeTable contains this node, update the node with Self-Frequency++ and Tree Frequency++.
- Add the parent node of node CodeTable into CodeTable by looking up the Cilin_SQunTree, and update the node of CodeTable with ParentId, and Initialize the node of parent node.
- If there are at least two parent nodes with a common parent node by looking up the Cilin_SQunTree, add this parent node of the parent nodes into CodeTable. Otherwise, end.
- If there is also a common parent node for above parent nodes by looking up the Cilin_BMSTree, add this parent node into CodeTable, until ParentId field of parent node in the Cilin_BMSTree table is equal to 0.
- Convert the nodes in CodeTable into Concept Hierarchy Tree. If the depth of the tree is 5, remove the root.

Concept Counting

Because the Concept Hierarchy Tree generated by the above algorithm is a collection of trees named forest, its traversal operation is starting from the leaf nodes, one by one to transfer the Self-Frequency of node. The algorithm is as follows:

- Each node in forest is added overlay mark IsAdded.
- Traverse the leaf node C and record the Self-Frequency of C as $\mathrm{SFrq}(\mathrm{C})$ one by one.
- Find the parent node of C:
  - If the field IsAdded of C is false, then it needs to set the field IsAdded of C to true and set the Self-Frequency of the parent node of C to plus $\mathrm{SFrq}(\mathrm{C})$.
  - Otherwise, continue to traverse the leaf nodes.

Calculation of Parameters

It should calculate Tree Frequency (formula 4), Concept Generalization Degree (formula 5) and Concept Selection Degree (formula 6) of each node in forest according to formulas in section of Concept Definition, and then determine the theme concept with threshold, recorded as $\mathrm{T}_1, \mathrm{T}_2, \ldots\ldots, \mathrm{T}_n$.

Examples

The words in WordTable are: 百合, 茶花, 奇花异草, 橙子, 苹果, 香蕉, 桔子.

According to the algorithm of Building the Concept Hierarchy Tree, it can generate the Concept Hierarchy Trees shown in Fig. 3-2-1. The number near the concept is the Self-Frequency of the concept (formula 3).

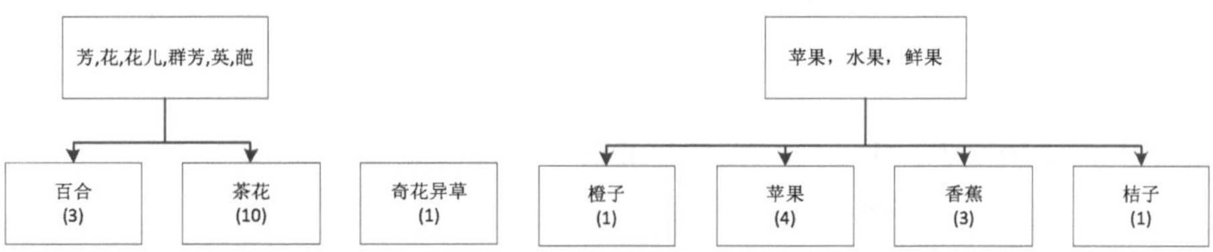

Fig. 3-2-1.

Self-Frequency of each concept as follows:

$\mathrm{F_S}(\text{百合}) = 3, \mathrm{F_S}(\text{茶花}) = 10, \mathrm{F_S}(\text{芳,花,花儿,群芳,英,葩}) = 0, \mathrm{F_S}(\text{奇花异草}) = 1,$
$\mathrm{F_S}(\text{橙子}) = 1, \mathrm{F_S}(\text{苹果}) = 4, \mathrm{F_S}(\text{香蕉}) = 3, \mathrm{F_S}(\text{桔子}) = 1, \mathrm{F_S}(\text{苹果,水果,鲜果}) = 0.$

Tree Frequency of each concept as follows:

$\mathrm{F_T}(\text{百合}) = \mathrm{F_S}(\text{百合}) + 0 = 3, \mathrm{F_T}(\text{茶花}) = \mathrm{F_S}(\text{茶花}) + 0 = 10,$
$\mathrm{F_T}(\text{芳,花,花儿,群芳,英,葩}) = \mathrm{F_S}(\text{芳,花,花儿,群芳,英,葩}) + 3 \times 0.9 + 10 \times 0.9 = 11.7$
$\mathrm{F_T}(\text{奇花异草}) = 1, \mathrm{F_T}(\text{橙子}) = 1, \mathrm{F_T}(\text{苹果}) = 4, \mathrm{F_T}(\text{香蕉}) = 3, \mathrm{F_T}(\text{桔子}) = 1,$
$\mathrm{F_T}(\text{苹果,水果,鲜果}) = \mathrm{F_S}(\text{苹果,水果,鲜果}) + 1 \times 0.9 + 4 \times 0.9 + 3 \times 0.9 + 1 \times 0.9 = 8.1$

Concept Generalization Degree of each concept as follows:

$$\mathrm{R}(百合) = 0, \mathrm{R}(茶花) = 0, \mathrm{R}(芳,花,花儿,群芳,英,葩) = 1 - \frac{10}{13} = \frac{3}{13},$$
$$\mathrm{R}(奇花异草) = 0, \mathrm{R}(橙子) = 0, \mathrm{R}(苹果) = 0, \mathrm{R}(香蕉) = 0, \mathrm{R}(桔子) = 0,$$
$$\mathrm{R}(苹果,水果,鲜果) = 1 - \frac{4}{9} = \frac{5}{9}.$$

Concept Selection Degree of each concept as follows: $\alpha = \beta = \gamma = \delta = 1$

$$\mathrm{Sel}(百合) = [\log_2(F_S(百合) + 1) + \log_2(F_T(百合) + 1)] \times [\mathrm{R}(百合) + 1] = 4,$$
$$\mathrm{Sel}(茶花) = 6.92 \bullet \mathrm{Sel}(芳,花,花儿,群芳,英,葩) = 4.51 \bullet \mathrm{Sel}(奇花异草) = 2,$$
$$\mathrm{Sel}(橙子) = 2, \mathrm{Sel}(苹果) = 4.64, \mathrm{Sel}(香蕉) = 4, \mathrm{Sel}(桔子) = 2,$$
$$\mathrm{Sel}(苹果,水果,鲜果) = 4.96.$$

By the above calculation it can select concepts: “茶花”,”苹果,水果,鲜果”.

3.3 Selection of Summary Sentences

Algorithm of Importance of Paragraphs

- Initialization matrix ($\mathrm{R}_{n\times n}$) of correlation degree between the paragraphs, where n is number of all paragraphs of Chinese text. $\mathrm{r}_{i,i} = 1, 1 \le i \le n$, $\mathrm{r}_{i,j} = 0, 1 \le i \le n, 1 \le j \le n, i \ne j$.
- Continue initializing $\mathrm{R}_{n\times n}$, where $\mathrm{r}_{i,j} = \mathrm{Sim}(\mathrm{P}_i, \mathrm{P}_j), 1 \le i \le n, 1 \le j \le n$.
- Calculate the threshold TV by the threshold calculation formula.
- Elements are lower than TV of $\mathrm{R}_{n\times n}$ are set to 0, while the value of greater than TV elements are set to 1. And then generate a new matrix $\mathrm{R}'_{n\times n}$.
- Iterate each row or column of matrix$\mathrm{R}'_{n\times n}$, and then calculate the importance of paragraphs $\lambda_{\mathrm{par}}(i), 1 \le i \le n$.

Algorithm of Initialization for Partitioning of Meaning Blocks

- Set threshold value for Partitioning of Meaning Blocks as T.
- Initialize the matrix $\mathrm{R}_{n\times n}$.
- Select the smallest one $\mathrm{r}_{i,i+1}$ as the first boundary of Meaning Blocks.
- Select the minimum from the rest of $\mathrm{r}_{i,j}$. If the distance (d) between the new boundary and other boundaries $d \ge 2$, and then choose the new boundary, otherwise do not choose.
- Repeat the above the step until the number of Meaning Blocks reaches the predetermined number of Meaning Block or the rest of $\mathrm{r}_{i,j} > T$.

Partitioning Algorithm of Meaning Blocks

- Divide the text into m Meaning Blocks by Algorithm of Initialization for Partitioning of Meaning Blocks and recoded as $\mathrm{L}_1, \mathrm{L}_2, \dots\dots, \mathrm{L}_m$.

- Calculate the individual Meet Degree ($J(L_i)$) of Meaning Block (L_i) and record sum of $J(L_i)$ as J.
- If it can increase the value of J to change the dividing line for any two adjacent Meaning block, and then adjust the boundary.
- Return above step, until it cannot make any adjustment.

Algorithm of Selection of Summary Sentences

- Extract the concepts of the sentence, and expressed as $S(T_1, W_1; T_2, W_2; \ldots\ldots; T_n, W_n)$, where W_i is the frequency of concept of T_i in the sentence.
- Calculate the Importance of Paragraphs by Algorithm of Importance of Paragraphs and recorded as $\lambda_{\text{par}}(i)$.
- Calculate the Importance of Sentences and recorded as $W(S_i)$.
- Divide paragraphs into Meaning Blocks by Partitioning Algorithm of Meaning Blocks.
- Decide the abstracting length of Meaning Blocks and then decide the abstracting length of paragraphs of Meaning Block according to user defined abstracting percentage.
- Pick out the sentences of each paragraph by the importance of sentences.

Examples

Assume that there are three paragraphs in the article and the vector of each paragraph as:

$P_1(T_1, W_1; T_2, W_2; \ldots\ldots; T_n, W_n) = \{2,2,2,2\}$,
$P_2(T_1, W_1; T_2, W_2; \ldots\ldots; T_n, W_n) = \{2,0,2,0\}$,
$P_3(T_1, W_1; T_2, W_2; \ldots\ldots; T_n, W_n) = \{0,1,1,2\}$.

- By Algorithm of Importance of Paragraphs available:

$$R_{3\times3} = \begin{pmatrix} 1 & 0.71 & 0.82 \\ 0.71 & 1 & 0.29 \\ 0.82 & 0.29 & 1 \end{pmatrix}, \text{TV}=0.61.\ R'_{3\times3} = \begin{pmatrix} 1 & 1 & 1 \\ 1 & 1 & 0 \\ 1 & 0 & 1 \end{pmatrix},$$

$I_P(1) = 2,\ I_P(2) = 1,\ I_P(3) = 1.$

$\lambda_{\text{par}}(1) = 1 + \frac{2}{4} = \frac{3}{2}$, $\lambda_{\text{par}}(2) = 1 + \frac{1}{4} = \frac{5}{4}$, $\lambda_{\text{par}}(3) = 1 + \frac{1}{4} = \frac{5}{4}$.

- Available by Partitioning Algorithm of Meaning Blocks:

Initialization for Partitioning of Meaning Blocks:

$L_1: 1,2$, $L_2: 3$. $c(1) = \{2,1,2,1\}$, $c(2) = \{0,1,1,2\}$.
$J(L_1) = \text{Sim}(P_1, c(1)) + \text{Sim}(P_2, c(1)) = 1.84$, $J(L_2) = 1$.
$J = 2.84$.

Adjust the boundary:

$L_1: 1$, $L_2: 2,3$. $c(1) = \{2,2,2,2\}$, $c(2) = \left\{1, \frac{1}{2}, \frac{3}{2}, 1\right\}$.
$J(L_1) = 1$, $J(L_2) = \text{Sim}(P_2, c(2)) + \text{Sim}(P_3, c(2)) = 2.44$.
$J = 3.44$.

Again adjust the boundary:

L_1: 1,2,3 . $c(1) = \left\{\frac{4}{3}, 1, \frac{5}{3}, \frac{4}{3}\right\}$.

$J(L_1) = \mathrm{Sim}(P_1, c(1)) + \mathrm{Sim}(P_2, c(1)) + \mathrm{Sim}(P_3, c(1)) = 2.57.$

$J = 2.57.$

From the above: Partitioning of Meaning Blocks is L_1: 1 ; L_2: 2,3.

3.4 Feature Reduction

The Auxiliary Algorithm

- There is a matrix $E_{n\times m}$, where n is the number of documents, m is the number of all the attributes. And the adjacent rows of $E_{n\times m}$ belong to the same category. The matrix is divided into different category matrix E_1, E_2, ……E_k, where *k* is the number of categories in the knowledge system.
- Calculate the Mathematical Expectation X and Sample Standard Deviation σ for each column vector of E_i, as a result there are two vectors: Mathematical Expectation with inner category ($\overline{X}$) and Sample Standard Deviation with inner category ($\overline{\sigma}$).
- Combine different Mathematical Expectation with categories ($\overline{X}$) into a matrix $M_{k\times m}$ and calculate the Sample Standard Deviation for each column vector of $M_{k\times m}$, resulting in one vector ($\overline{T}$): Sample Standard Deviation among categories.
- Find the maximum value of each column vector of $M_{k\times m}$, and take the corresponding value of σ , then constitute a vector $\overline{T}'$.
- Assuming that, the values of a property in the vectors $\overline{T}$ and $\overline{T}'$ are v and v'. The value of the threshold is θ. Then as follows:
  - If $v \geq \theta, v' < \theta$, put the property at the top and order properties in categories by the value of v.
  - If $v \geq \theta, v' \geq \theta$, put the property behind the above properties and order properties in categories by the value of $\frac{v}{v'}$.
  - If $v < \theta$, remove this property.
- Output the attribute set.

IQR

- $R = T = \Phi$.
- Get the attribute set C by the auxiliary algorithm.
- Get property (x) from (C − R) by order, such as: $x \in (C - R)$
  - If $\delta_{R\cup\{x\}}(D) > \delta_T(D)$ then $T = R\cup\{x\}$.
  - R=T.
  - If $\delta_R(D) = \delta_c(D)$ then break.
- Return R.

4 Experimental Results

4.1 Experimental Environment

The corpus is the 2011 CD-ROM version of the "People's Daily", including politics, economy, computer, sport, education and law, a total of 900 articles, each with 150 documents.

The development platform of the system is Windows 7, and the development tool is Visual Studio 2010, using the language of C Sharp. The source of dividing words is based on open source of ICTCLAS, and the related algorithm of Rough Set Theory is improved by the RSAS developed by the University of Edinburgh the Alexios Chouchoulas.

4.2 Experimental Results

In combination with Automatic Abstracting Technology and Rough Set Theory, the results of feature reduction for Chinese text are shown in Table 4-2-1. Reduction Degree is defined as follows:

Table 4-2-1.

Docs	Features (R)	Features with AAT (R_1)	Features with IQR	Features AAT and IQR (R_2)	RD1 $\log_{10}\left(\frac{R}{R_2}\right)$	RD2 $\log_{10}\left(\frac{R}{R_1}\right)$
6×5	4710	1210	4	4	3.07	0.59
6×10	6520	1701	5	5	3.12	0.58
6×20	8994	2780	8	8	3.05	0.51
6×50	13111	3503	13	13	3.00	0.57
6×100	17043	4309	15	15	3.06	0.60

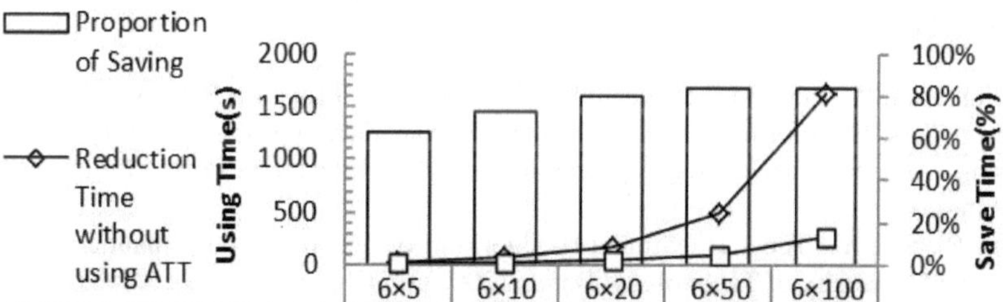

	6×5	6×10	6×20	6×50	6×100
Proportion of Saving	0.625	0.734	0.807	0.835	0.837
Reduction Time without using ATT	16	64	161	485	1624
Reduction Time with using ATT	6	17	31	80	264

Fig. 4-2-1.

$$\text{Reduction Degree} = \log_{10}\left(\frac{\text{the number of features before reducing}}{\text{the number of features after reducing}}\right)$$

The comparison between consumption time of using Automatic Abstracting Technology or not is shown in Fig. 4-2-1.

5 Summary and Feature Work

The system makes feature extracting and reduction for Chinese text by combining with Automatic Abstracting and Rough Set, be 3/4 faster than reduction only by simple Rough Set Theory. However, the system in the early processing with Automatic Abstracting Technology will greatly influence the follow-up process.

In the future, you can do something as follows:

i. During the process of building the Concept Hierarchy Tree, there is polysemy, which needs to be considered better semantic annotation system to make the concept more accurate.
ii. The setting of the threshold and the weighting factors: the system is based on experience or experiment to determine these values, which involves human intervention. There are substantial limitations on the future expansion, so that you can use an appropriate scheme of weighting for different types of articles by the use of machine learning method.
iii. Basic data sources: the system uses" Tongyici Cilin (extended version)" as semantic dictionary. Although it already contains many phrases, there will be some proper nouns, names, numbers, and special phrases not in the range. So in the future you can automatically or manually extend the dictionary.
iv. It is the Problem of Partitioning Algorithm of Meaning Blocks. The algorithm is basically using the method of enumeration. And the time consuming is too long, so in the future you can improve it by other algorithm.

References

1. Srinivasan, P., Ruiz, M.E.: Vocabulary Mining for Information Retrieval: Rough Sets and Fuzzy Sets. In: Information Processing and Management, pp. 15–38 (2001)
2. Jiang, M.: Natural language processing. Higher Education Press, Beijing (2006) (in Chinese)
3. Jin, B., Shi, Y., Teng, H.: Similarity algorithm of text based on semantic understanding. Dalian University of Technology, Dalian (2005) (in Chinese)
4. Wu, C., Zhang, Q., Miao, J.: Semantic comprehension of natural language processing and information retrieval model. Graduate School, Chinese Academy of Sciences (2008) (in Chinese)
5. Mei, J.: Tongyici Cilin. Shanghai Dictionary Publishing House, Shanghai (1985) (in Chinese)
6. Yang, X., Song, F., Zhong, Y.: Based on the selected to generate abstract method research and implementation of automatic abstract system. In: The Fourth National Computational Linguistics Conference Proceedings, pp. 313–318. Tsinghua University Press (1997) (in Chinese)

7. Mitra, M., Singhal, A., Buckley, C.: Automatic Text Summarization by Paragraph Extraction. In: Workshop on Intelligent Scalable Text Summarization, ACL/EACL 1997, Madrid, pp. 31–36 (1997)
8. Chen, W., Liu, T., Qin, B.: For bilingual sentence retrieval of Chinese sentence similarity computing. In: Joint Conference of the National Seventh Computer Linguistics, pp. 81–88. Tsinghua University Press, Beijing (2003) (in Chinese)
9. Chen, C., Yan, H.: Rough set theory in information retrieval. Guilin University of Technology (2011) (in Chinese)
10. Zong, C.: Statistical natural language processing. Tsinghua University Press, Beijing (2008) (in Chinese)

Neighborhood Covering Based Rule Learning Algorithms

Xiaoyun Zhang, Hong Shi, Xiaofei Yu, and TongChun Ni

Computer Science and Technology School, Tianjin University WeiJin Road, No. 92

Abstract. At present, Rough set theory has been extensively discussed and studied in machine learning and data mining. Pawlak rough set theory provides a solid theoretical basis for processing incomplete or inconsistent data described by nominal attributes. However, it fails to deal with real classification tasks, in which most of the sample sets are numerical data. Recently, neighborhood covering methods based on rough sets demonstrate promising views in classification rule learning. These methods apply to numerical or complex data. In this paper, we put forward new neighborhood covering rule learning algorithms. We redefine the neighborhood radius to generalize the model, experiments produce good results in reducing the rule number, and more powerful generalization ability is expected. In terms of rule learning strategy, we combine kernel covering method, create an optimization classification hyperplane, and solve quadratic programming problem to train support coverings, like support vectors in SVM. Experiments show good classification performance of our improved algorithm.

Keywords: Rough set, Neighborhood covering, covering reduction, neighborhood radius, Rule learning.

1 Introduction

Pawlak's rough set theory has become an important approach to deal with incomplete or inconsistent data, [3, 6, 14], especially with its fast development promoted by researchers in recent years. Rough set theory gradually finds its application in many fields, [11, 12, 13], such as fault diagnosis, financial analysis, biological and medical treatment, and so on.

Pawlak rough set gets the partition of the universe by a crisp equivalence relation, the classical rough set induced rule learning algorithm, through covering reduction, it only works in nominal applications. At the same time, the upper and lower approximations are too strictly defined to avoid the influence of noise.

Neighborhood rough sets[1, 7] are generalizations of rough sets which can be used in numerical or more complex rule learning tasks. In this article, we list the basic knowledge of covering in neighborhood rough sets and the covering reduction. We introduce algorithm NCR[5] (Neighborhood Covering Reduction), which computes the neighborhood of each sample to form a covering of the universe, such that the size of neighborhoods depends on the classification margin of samples[9]. This definition of neighborhood radius has disadvantages, and is sensitive to noisy data. Therefore, we try

V. Khachidze et al. (Eds.): iCETS 2012, CCIS 332, pp. 510–520, 2012.

some other ways to redefine the neighborhood radius; comparing experiments will reveal the results.

NCR methods obtain learning rules by relative covering reduction. Herewith, we introduce the idea of kernel covering methods[4] to develop a new algorithm, which reduces coverings from a new view by mapping the original covering space into kernel covering space. Our algorithm gets the support coverings through quadratic programming optimization method. Finally, we show some numerical experiments to evaluate the proposed new algorithm.

The rest of this work is organized as follows: In section 2 we introduce some basic information about covering methods in neighborhood rough sets and show some covering reduction techniques. Then we show the NCR (Neighborhood covering reduction) algorithm in section 3, analyze its weakness, and make several sensible changes. Section 4 shows experimental results on a serial of improved rule learning algorithms. Finally, we conclude in section 5.

2 Basic Covering Techniques of Neighborhood Rough Set

In this section, we introduce basic information about covering methods in neighborhood rough sets and show some covering reduction techniques.

Definition 1[9]. Let U be a nonempty and finite set of objects, where $U=\{x_1,x_2,...,x_n\}$ is called a universe of discourse. $C=\{X_1,X_2,...,X_n\}$ is a family of nonempty subsets of U, and $\bigcup_{i=1}^{k} X_i = U$. We say C is a covering of U, X_i is a covering element, and the ordered pair $\langle U,C\rangle$ is a covering approximation space.

Definition 2[2]. Let U be a nonempty and finite set of objects, where $U=\{x_1,x_2,...,x_n\}$ is called a universe of discourse. $C=\{X_1,X_2,...,X_n\}$ is a family of nonempty subsets of U, and $\bigcup_{i=1}^{k} X_i = U$. If $X_i \subseteq U$, $X_i \neq \varnothing$, and $X_i \cap X_j = \varnothing, (i \neq j)(i,j=1,2,...,k)$, we say C is a partition of U.

Comparing definition 1 and 2, we conclude that equivalence classes, generated from the partition of the universe, must have no intersection, whereas the covering of the universe allows the existence of overlap between each other. The concept of covering is considered as the extension of partition, and is more general. Therefore, covering methods are widely used to process heterogeneous data. As classical rough set uses partition to approximate subsets in nominal attribute space only, coverings based on neighborhood rough set have been developed to apply to numerical or more complex data.

Definition 3[7]. Let U be the universe of discourse, $\delta(x)$ is the neighborhood of x, where $\delta(x)=\{x_i:\Delta(x,x_i)\le\delta\}$, Δ is a distance function. Then $N=\{\delta(x_1),\delta(x_2),...,\delta(x_n)\}$ forms a covering of U, we call $\langle U,N\rangle$ a neighborhood covering approximation space. Let $X\subseteq U$ be a subset of the universe. The lower and upper approximations of X with respect to $\langle U,N\rangle$ are defined as

$$\underline{N}X=\{x\in U:\delta(x)\subseteq X\},$$

$$\overline{N}X=\{x\in U:\delta(x)\cap X\ne\varnothing\}.$$

As the elements of a covering overlap, some of them may be redundant for keeping the discernibility of the covering approximation space. In order to extract the essential information of the approximation space, it is expected to reduce the redundant elements of the covering.

Definition 4[5]. Let $\langle U,C\rangle$ be a covering approximation space, C' is a covering derived from C by reducing the redundant elements, and C' is irreducible. We say C' is a reduct of C, denoted by $reduct(C)$.

Definition 5[8]. Let $\langle U,C\rangle$ be a covering approximation space. $X\subseteq U$ and $X_i\in C$. If there exists $X_j\in C$, such that $X_i\subseteq X_j\subseteq X$, we say X_i is a relatively reducible element of C with respect to X; otherwise, X_i is relatively irreducible. If all the elements in C are relatively irreducible, we say C is relatively irreducible.

As per the two different definitions above, in covering reduction, the small coverings are selected to precisely approximate the original system with a finer granularity; while in relative covering reduction, the large coverings are preferred, as to obtain good generalization ability and less learning rules.

We have mentioned Δ is a distance function in Definition 3, without giving a concrete expression, now, supposing the sample sets are described by heterogeneous attributes, the distance function can be defined as follows:

Definition 6[10]. the distance function $HEMO$ is defined as:

$$HEMO(x,y)=\sqrt{\sum_{i=1}^{m}w_{a_i}\times d_{a_i}^2(x_{a_i},y_{a_i})}\quad,$$

Where m is the number of attributes, w_{a_i} is the weight of attribute a_i, $d_{a_i}(x,y)$ is the distance between samples x and y with respect to attribute a_i, defined as

$$d_{a_i}(x,y)=\begin{cases}1, & \text{if the attribute value of } x \text{ or } y \text{ is unkown,}\\ overlap_{a_i}(x,y), & \text{if } a_i \text{ is a nominal attribute,}\\ \mathrm{rn}\_diff_{a_i}(x,y), & \text{if } a_i \text{ is a numerical attribute.}\end{cases}$$

Where $overlap_{a_i}(x,y)=\begin{cases}0, \text{ if } x=y,\\ 1, \text{ otherwise.}\end{cases}$, and

$$rn\_diff_{a_i}(x,y)=\frac{|x-y|}{\max_{a_i}-\min_{a_i}}.$$

3 Improved Algorithms Based on NCR（Neighborhood Covering Reduction Algorithm）

3.1 Neighborhood Covering Reduction Based Rule Learning Algorithm NCR

NCR covering reduction procedures' main steps are:

(1) Compute the margins of training samples $m(x)$,

(2) generate neighborhood $\mathbb{N}(x)$ of the samples,

(3) determine the number of the samples covered by each covering in the neighborhood,

(4) select the neighborhood $\mathbb{N}(x)$ covering the largest number of samples,

(5) add a rule $[x, m(x), y]$ into the rule set, y is the decision of x,

(6) if a neighborhood is contained in another neighborhood, remove it.

(7) Sort the rules according to the size of the covering elements, in the descending order.

(8) Select the first several rules that producing the highest classification accuracy on training set or test set.

This algorithm greedily searches the largest neighborhood of samples in the forward search step and removes the rules covering the least samples to pruning rules. After training NCR gets the rule base, to make a decision in classification tasks, the algorithm computes the distances of a testing sample to each rule covering center in order; if the distance is less than the current neighborhood size $m(x)$, then the test sample is discriminated as the same class with the rule sample. If a sample is not covered by all the rule coverings, it is considered to belong to the nearest neighborhood.

3.2 Redefine the Neighborhood Radius

As per definition 3, δ is the size of the neighborhood, namely, the samples with their distance less than δ to the neighborhood center sample x constitute the neighborhood of x. Naturally, different definitions of the size δ will generate different neighborhoods.

NCR computes the margins of the training samples as in the following definition:

Let $\langle U, A, D \rangle$ be a neighborhood covering decision system, $x \in U$. $NM(x)$ is the nearest sample of x in the different class, $NH(x)$ is the nearest sample of x in the same class. Then the neighborhood radius of x is defined as:

$$m(x) = \Delta(x, NM(x)) - \Delta(x, NH(x))$$

Fig.1 gives a demonstration of the radius definition.

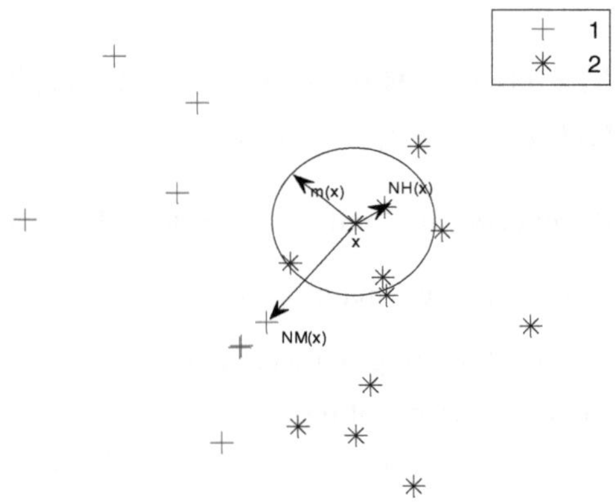

Fig. 1. Demonstration of the radius definition

We redefine the neighborhood radius as follows:

Definition 7. Let $\langle U, A, D \rangle$ be a neighborhood covering decision system, $x \in U$. $NM(x)$ is the nearest sample of x in the different class, $NH(x)$ is the nearest sample of $NM(x)$ in the same class with x. Then we get a new neighborhood radius of x, as shown in Fig. 2.

$$m(x) = \Delta(x, NM(x)) - \Delta(x, NH(x))$$

It is notable that different distance functions Δ will generate different neighborhoods, such as spherical neighborhood and quadrate neighborhood, so that the selection of Δ will influences the performance of rule learning algorithms; in response, we organize experiments on spherical neighborhood and quadrate neighborhood, generated by different Δ. We will discuss the experimental results in section 4.

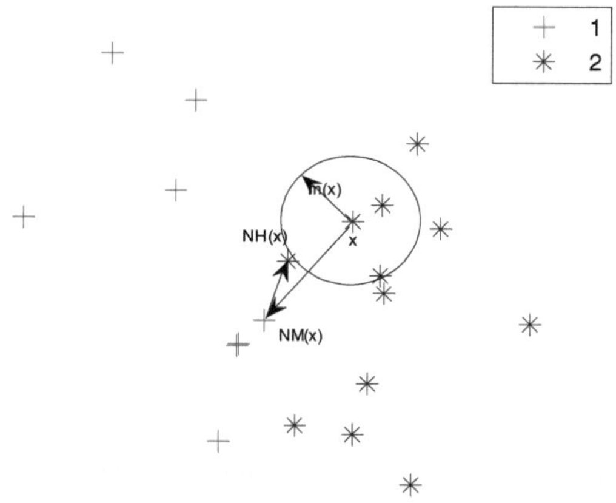

Fig. 2. A new defined neighborhood radius

3.3 Rule Learning with Kernel Covering Methods

NCR method calculates neighborhood size in original space, and uses the same way when making decisions; it compares the distance between the sample and a neighborhood with the size of the neighborhood, and then classifies the sample.

In our work, we combine kernel covering methods and map the original covering space into kernel covering space by Gaussian functions. Then the kernel coverings are considered the new training samples, replacing the original samples. We create an optimization classification hyperplane, like training support vectors in SVM, and introduce quadratic programming optimization method. At last the discriminant function will be used to classify new samples.

The discriminant function of hyperplane for binary classification problems is defined as

$$f(x) = \sum_{i=1}^{m} \alpha_i y_i K(a_i, x),$$

where m is the number of neighborhoods, α_i is undetermined correlation, a_i is the center of neighborhood, x is a testing sample, and y_i is the notion of categories. Set $y_i = 1$ in positive class, $y_i = -1$ in negative class. $K(a_i, x)$ is the Gaussian kernel distance from testing sample to the center of the neighborhood.

$$K(a_i, x) = \exp(-\frac{|a_i - x|^2}{d_i^2}) ,$$

where d_i is the neighborhood radius.

Here we solve the undetermined correlation α_i using the way to train support vectors in SVM, the quadratic programming optimization objective function is formulated as:

$$\max W(\alpha) = \sum_{i=1}^{m} \alpha_i - \frac{1}{2}\sum_{i,j=1}^{m} \alpha_i\alpha_j y_i y_j \left(K(a_i,a_j) + K(a_j,a_i)\right)/2$$

$$s.t. \quad \sum_{i=1}^{m} \alpha_i y_i = 0, \alpha_i \geq 0, i = 1,2,...,m$$

If $f(x) > 0$, then sample x belongs to the positive class. Otherwise, if $f(x) < 0$, x belongs to the negative class. We set the threshold ε, if $|f(x)| \leq \varepsilon$, then x cannot be recognized.

4 Experimental Analysis

In order to compare the proposed algorithms with the original algorithm, we organize experiments on six international standard UCI data sets. Detailed information is shown in Table 1. Among them, wine and iris are multiple-class (3) data, others are binary. samnum, atrmum, and labnum represent the number of samples, the number of attributes, and the number of classes, separately.

Table 1. Description of the testing data

dataset	*samnum*	*atrnum*	*labnum*
wine	178	13	3
iris	150	4	3
wdbc	569	30	2
german	1000	20	2
heart	270	13	2
crx	690	15	2

In fact, we improve algorithm NCR with respect to two main points, i.e. the definition of neighborhood radius and the rule learning strategy (including the decision strategy). Assembling these views, we test 3 different algorithms in our experiments: improving by redefining the neighborhood radius only (NCRr), improving with other rule learning strategy only (NCRc), improving with both the two updates (NCRrc).

We perform experiments using both the spherical neighborhood (Sn) and the quadrate neighborhood (Qn) with each dataset. Testing results are shown in Table 2. Each result includes the classification accuracy (acc), standard deviation(std), and rule numbers(rule).

Table 2. Comparing results of four methods with six datasets

		Sn			Qn		
		acc	std	rule	acc	std	rule
Wine	NCR	0.942	0.063	12.7	0.949	0.051	8.3
	NCRr	0.903	0.072	7.3	0.91	0.071	7.8
	NCRc	0.903	0.071	8.6	0.935	0.086	3.8
	NCRrc	0.875	0.097	6.4	0.966	0.048	4.5
Iris	NCR	0.98	0.045	7.4	0.94	0.073	9
	NCRr	0.993	0.021	6.8	0.98	0.032	6.2
	NCRc	0.973	0.034	4.1	0.973	0.047	4.5
	NCRrc	0.973	0.047	4.4	0.94	0.073	6.9
Wdbc	NCR	0.944	0.034	28	0.947	0.035	26.5
	NCRr	0.967	0.024	9	0.937	0.021	12.3
	NCRc	0.954	0.033	19.2	0.989	0.021	7.7
	NCRrc	0.958	0.03	11.7	0.965	0.022	10.5
German	NCR	0.669	0.026	16.2	0.675	0.043	100.2
	NCRr	0.7	0	1	0.709	0.009	22.5
	NCRc	0.585	0.114	12	0.665	0.064	65.1
	NCRrc	0.713	0.023	10.1	0.689	0.039	47.5
Heart	NCR	0.804	0.058	17.6	0.778	0.052	17
	NCRr	0.83	0.036	8.4	0.767	0.043	3.2
	NCRc	0.815	0.039	5.5	0.84	0.065	2.2
	NCRrc	0.811	0.044	6	0.821	0.08	3
Crx	NCR	0.843	0.149	54.5	0.848	0.166	71
	NCRr	0.883	0.096	32.3	0.849	0.161	38
	NCRc	0.875	0.103	35.1	0.867	0.13	33.2
	NCRrc	0.875	0.112	18.4	0.852	0.156	25.7

By comparative analysis, we can easily find that the rule numbers are significantly reduced with all the three improved algorithms, at almost each data point. NCRr performs better than NCR in classification accuracy; NCRc and NCRrc generally do the same as NCR in classification accuracy.

To visually display the performance of the improved algorithms, we show the experimental results on rule numbers and classification accuracy, in the case of the spherical neighborhood, and the quadrate neighborhood, separately.

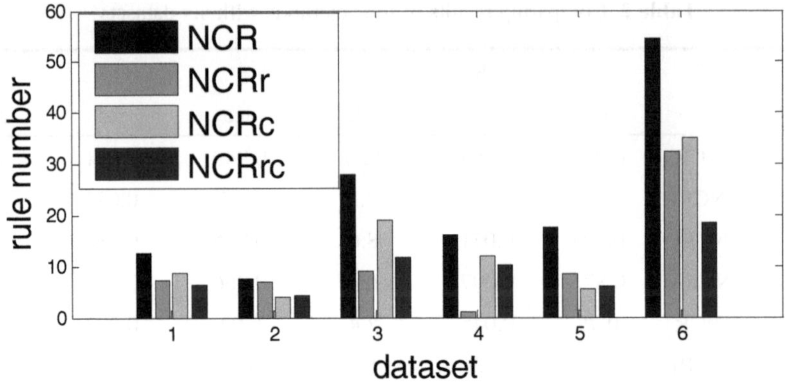

Fig. 3. Rule numbers of the 4 algorithms in spherical neighborhood

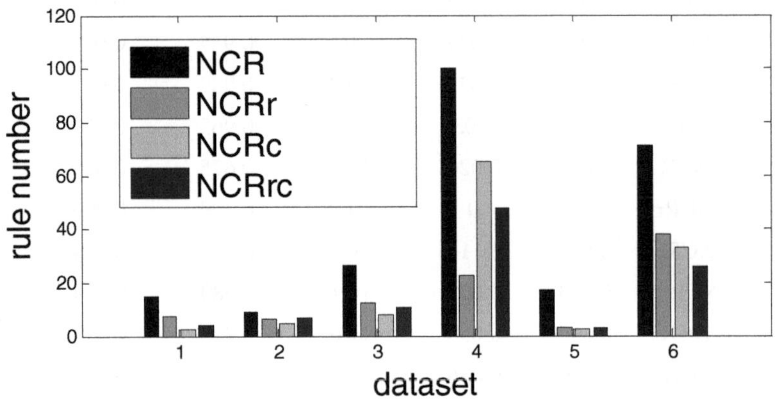

Fig. 4. Rule numbers of the 4 algorithms in quadrate neighborhood

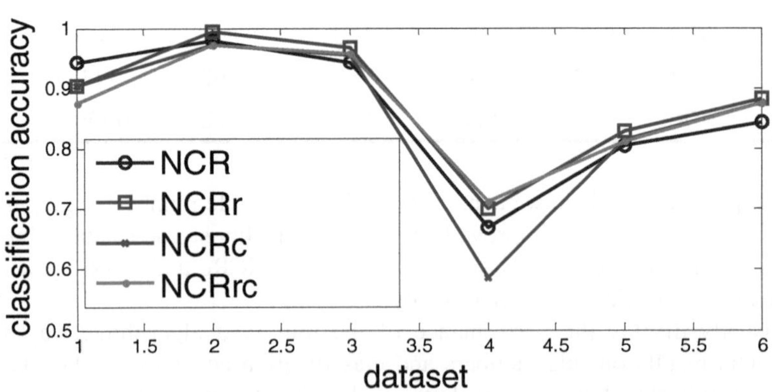

Fig. 5. Classification accuracy of the 4 algorithms in spherical neighborhood

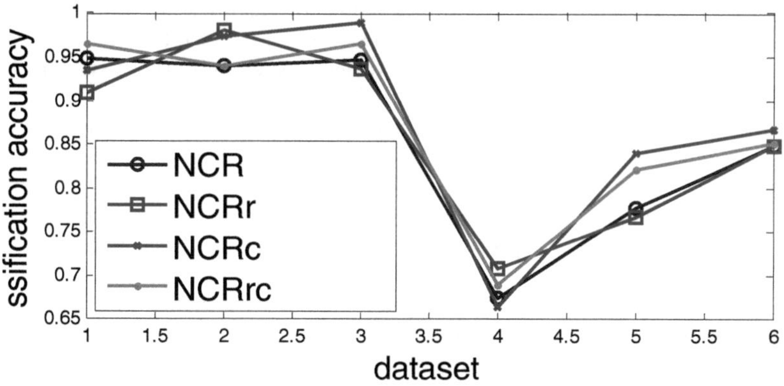

Fig. 6. Classification accuracy of the 4 algorithms in quadrate neighborhood

Evidently, our methods gain an overwhelming advantage in rule numbers both in spherical neighborhood and quadrate neighborhood. These results are expected in improving the generalization ability.

Generally speaking, as with algorithm (NCRr), improving by redefining the neighborhood radius only shows some advantages; the rest are similar to the original algorithm (NCR).

5 Conclusion

In this paper, we propose three improved algorithms based on NCR method. These algorithms are derived from two aspects, namely redefining the calculation methods of the neighborhood and updating rule learning mechanisms. Compared to NCR, our algorithms have reduced the rule numbers to a great extent, decreased the decision time and have improved the generalization power, while keeping the classification accuracy values. There is some space to develop, in that the training time increases for the introduction of the quadratic programming, and this is a direction for study in the future.

References

[1] Hu, Q., Yu, D., Xie, Z.: Neighborhood classifiers. Expert Systems with Applications 34, 866–876 (2008)

[2] He, Q., Xie, Z., Hu, Q., Wu, C.: Boundary instance selection based on neighborhood model. Neurocomputing 74(10), 1585–1594 (2011)

[3] Bhatt, R.B., Gopal, M.: Frct: fuzzy-rough classification trees. Pattern Analysis & Applications 11, 73–88 (2008)

[4] Wu, T., Zhang, L., Zhang, Y.: Kernel Covering Algorithm for Machine Learning. Chinese Journal of Computers 28(8), 1295–1301 (2005) (in Chinese)

[5] Du, Y., Hu, Q., Ma, P., et al.: Rule learning for classification based on neighborhood covering reduction. Information Sciences 181, 5457–5467 (2011)
[6] Qian, Y., Dang, C., Liang, J., et al.: Set-valued ordered information systems. Information Sciences 179, 2809–2832 (2009)
[7] Hu, Q., Pedrycz, W., Yu, D., Lang, J.: Selecting discrete and continuous features based on neighborhood decision error minimization. IEEE Transactions on Systems, Man, and Cybernetics – Part B: Cybernetics 40, 137–150 (2010)
[8] Hu, J., Wang, G.: Knowledge reduction of covering approximation space. Transactions on Computational Sciences, Special Issue on Cognitive Knowledge Representation, 69–80 (2009)
[9] Zhu, W., Wang, F.: Reduction and axiomization of covering generalized rough sets. Information Sciences 152, 217–230 (2003)
[10] Wilson, D.R., Martinez, T.R.: Improved heterogeneous distance functions. Journal of Artificial Intelligence Research 6, 1–34 (1997)
[11] Dubois, D., Prade, H.: Rough fuzzy sets and fuzzy rough sets. International Journal of General Systems 17, 191–209 (1990)
[12] Morsi, N.N., Yakout, M.M.: Axiomatics for fuzzy rough sets. Fuzzy Sets and Systems 100, 327–342 (1998)
[13] Radzikowska, A.M., Keree, E.E.: A comparative study of fuzzy rough sets. Fuzzy Sets and Systems 126, 137–155 (2002)
[14] Hong, T.P., Wang, T.T., Wang, S.L., et al.: Learning a coverage set of maximally general fuzzy rules by rough sets. Expert Systems with Applications 19, 97–103 (2000)

Facial Expression Pervasive Analysis Based on Haar-Like Features and SVM

Chao Xu, Caichao Dong*, Zhiyong Feng, and Tianyi Cao

School of Computer Science and Technology, Tianjin University,
Tianjin, P.R. of China
{xuchao,dongcc,zyfeng}@tju.edu.cn, caotianyi8@yahoo.com.cn

Abstract. The pervasiveness and applicability of computational models is important for facial expression analysis within different races. In this paper, an ingenious approach is proposed to verify the pervasiveness of facial expression model based on Haar-like features, Adaboost and SVM. The approach is constructed with three characteristics, including facial features extraction with Haar-like features, weak classifiers training with Adaboost, and facial expression recognition with SVM. The contribution is that the approach above can be applied to distinguish the differences of identified facial expression models within two human racial groups. Experiments are conducted on both eastern and western facial expressions recognition on the basis of a facial feature template being trained by western face databases. Results show that high accuracy rate is achieved from the same race template, while a general accuracy rate for the other senses. It is indicated that the approach improves the pervasiveness of facial expression model with high recognition accuracy and verifies the computational differences of facial expressions between different races.

Keywords: Expression Analysis, Haar-like Features, Adaboost, SVM.

1 Introduction

Facial expression recognition is more and more important in human-computer interaction and effective computing. Because facial expressions contain rich behavior information, human-computer interaction can be more effective if we are able to recognize facial expressions efficiently and effectively. A complete facial expression recognition system can be divided into three processes: the scan of facial expression image, facial expression feature extraction, and facial expression recognition. How to define facial expression features and extract complete, robust, compact and differentiated features from the collective of features is the key to improving facial expression recognition rate. In this paper, the training of feature model and facial expression recognition are conducted within different databases, and experimental results show that the proposed approach improves the pervasiveness of the facial expression model and verifies the computational differences of facial expression between races.

* Corresponding author.

V. Khachidze et al. (Eds.): iCETS 2012, CCIS 332, pp. 521–529, 2012.

Thus far, there are special research groups that conduct expert study relevant to this topic worldwide. Chen [1] reviewed the current research states of facial expression recognition; Lyons [2] obtained results on JAFFE (Japanese Female Facial Expression) by using PCA and LDA; Liu [3] recognized facial expressions by Gabor histogram feature and MVBoost; Wang [4] proposed a real-time facial expression classification method based on real Adaboost algorithm; Yao [5] presented a Gabor features dimension reduction method in facial expression recognition and achieved a high overall recognition rate. These methods have achieved high recognition rates and can complete some specific tasks.

Above methods trained the feature model and recognized facial expression in the same face database. They have achieved high recognition rates, but they have not gone deep into experiments within different face databases. On the basis of these works, experiments are conducted within different face databases to train a feature model and to recognize facial expression in this paper. Haar-like features [4, 5] can represent facial information and SVM [9] can keep higher recognition rates in small sample sets. The contribution in this paper is that Haar-like features are used to represent facial expressions, the feature template is trained in a western face database by Adaboost and facial expression is recognized in another face database by SVM. Results show that the feature template trained by western face database can recognize western facial expression with a high recognition rate and achieve a general recognition rate in eastern face database, which indicates that this approach has broader pervasiveness and verifies that difference does exist when recognizing facial expression within different races.

The rest of this paper is organized as follows: the relevant techniques and the overall model are introduced in section 2; experiments are designed and analyzed in section 3, and the conclusion of this paper is given in section 4.

2 Relevant Techniques and Overall Model

2.1 Haar-Like Feature and Integral Image

Haar-like feature consists of several rectangle regions and makes up a feature prototype. These regions have the same size and shape and are horizontally or vertically adjacent. Lienhar [7] extended Haar-like feature prototypes later and divided them into 3 categories: four edge features, eight line features and two center-surround features. In this paper, we employ those Haar-like feature templates used by Viola [6] (see Figure 1). The feature value of a feature prototype is the difference between the sum of the pixels within white regions and black regions.

Fig. 1. Haar-like features used in this paper

Viola first proposed the concept of integral image and applied it to compute Haar-like feature values. The value of the integral image at point (x, y) is the sum of all the pixels above and to the left:

$$ii(x, y) = \sum_{x' \le x} \sum_{y' \le y} I(x', y') \ . \tag{1}$$

where $I(x', y')$ is the image's pixel value at (x', y'), $ii(x, y)$ is the value of the integral image at (x, y). $ii(x, y)$ can also be computed by iterations:

$$\begin{aligned} ii(x, y) &= ii(x-1, y) + s(x, y) \\ s(x, y) &= s(x, y-1) + I(x, y) \end{aligned} \ . \tag{2}$$

where I(x, y) is the image's pixel value at (x, y), $s(x, y)$ is the sum of pixels from (x, 1) to (x, y) in the image.

An integral image is used to compute the sum of pixels from the starting point to various points in an image. The integral image matrix can be obtained by traversing the image once. The computation of Haar-like feature values is only related to the integral image and has nothing to do with the coordinates of the image. Whatever the feature size is, the calculation time of feature values is constant, and these computations are simple addition and subtraction, so the introduction of the integral image greatly reduces the calculation time.

78,460 Haar-like features can be obtained in a 20x20 image after Haar-like feature computations; it is very time-consuming to classify this large dimension feature vector directly, and some redundant dimensions will affect the recognition results, so it is necessary to reduce dimensions. Adaboost algorithm is used to extract some differentiated features in this paper.

2.2 Feature Extraction Using Adaboost Algorithm

Boosting algorithm, first proposed by Shapire, was improved upon by Freund, but the algorithms require some prior knowledge. Shapire and Freund proposed Adaboost [8] (Adaptive Boosting) algorithm in 1995, which is easier to apply because it does not require any prior knowledge.

The feature selection is performed by Adaboost. At first, each training sample is initialized with an equal weight. Then, weak classifiers are constructed using the individual Haar-like features. In each iteration, the single weak classifier with the minimum weighted error is selected to be linearly combined to form the final classifier with weight proportional to the minimum error. The samples are reweighted based upon the performance of the selected weak classifier, and the process is repeated.

Adaboost is not only a fast classifier, but also a good feature selection method. It can select some differentiated features from the feature space, compose feature subspace and construct feature template. The trained feature template is used to recognize facial expressions by SVM.

2.3 Facial Expression Recognition Using SVM

Support Vector Machine (SVM) [9] is a method which implements structural risk minimization, which converts practical problems to high dimension feature space by using nonlinear transformation. It solves nonlinear decision function in original space by constructing linear decision function in high dimension space. The complexity of SVM is unrelated to the sample dimension.

SVM is a typical binary classification that can solve problems of positive class or negative class. Facial expression recognition is a multi-class problem, and therefore must be converted to several binary classification problems. In this paper, one-to-one classification [10] is applied to solve this problem. If there are k categories, there will be k*(k-1)/2 classifiers. In the process of testing, each classifier votes for these categories and the category with the largest number of votes is the final recognition result.

2.4 The Overall Model

The overall model can be divided into two stages: off-line training by Adaboost and on-line recognition by SVM (see Figure 2).

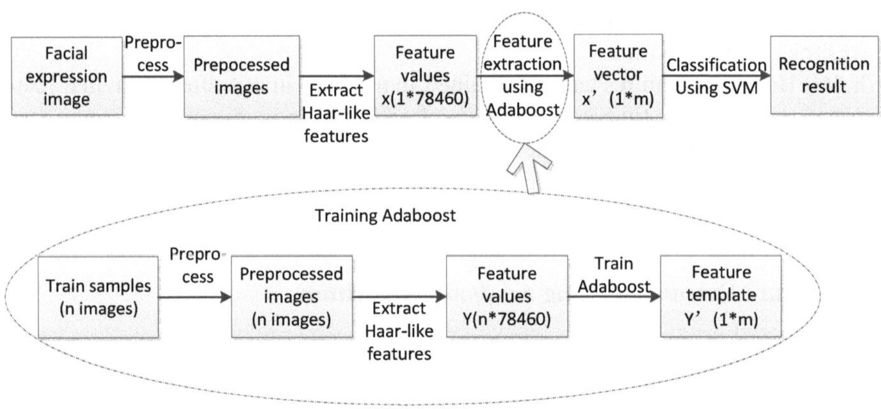

Fig. 2. The overall model

In the process of training, after selecting the training sample set and image preprocessing, we obtain Haar-like features and compute the corresponding feature values by integral image, then extract differentiated features using Adaboost and construct feature the subspace and feature template. The process of testing, firstly, involves scanning the facial expression image in the given image and computing Haar-like feature values using integral image, then mapping these feature values into feature subspace, and finally recognizing facial expression in subspace using feature template by SVM.

3 Experiments and Analysis

On the basis of these works in the references, training Adaboost algorithm and facial expression recognition are applied within different face databases in this paper. Haar-like feature values are computed in the MIT face database and feature extracted using Adaboost because of the high dimensionality and high redundancy of Haar-like features. Then, the feature subspace and feature template are constructed using these selected differentiated features. Facial expressions are recognized in western face database (Cohn-Kanade) and eastern face database (JAFFE) using the trained feature template by SVM. Results prove the effectiveness of the proposed approach, which improves the pervasiveness of facial expression model and verifies the computational differences of facial expression within different races.

3.1 Training Feature Template Using Adaboost

The key of the effectiveness of strong classifier is the extraction of Haar-like features, which dependents to a certain extent on the selection of training the sample set of Adaboost algorithm. Face database of MIT is used to train Adaboost algorithm, which contains 6,977 samples (2,429 positive samples and 6,977 negative samples). Some sample images are shown in Figure 3.

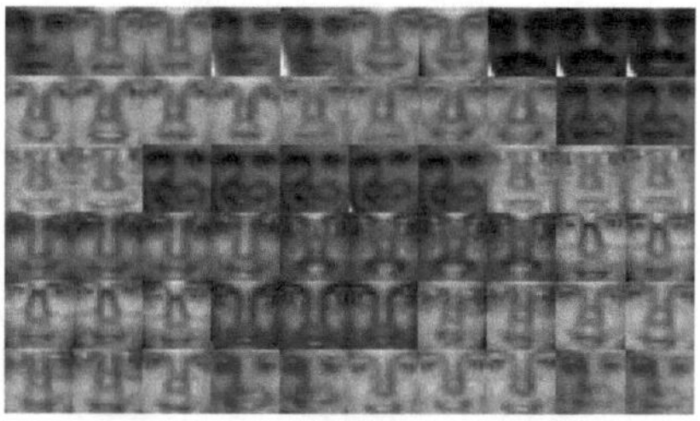

Fig. 3. Some samples in MIT

First, we select some samples in MIT to train Adaboost algorithm and extract features, and use these selected features to test the classification error among training samples (see Figure 4).

As we can see in Figure 4, with the increase in number of selected features, the training error decreases and finally converges to 0. Re-train Adaboost algorithm using MIT database and extract some Haar-like features, and construct feature template in differentiated feature subspace to recognize facial expression.

3.2 Facial Expression Recognition Using SVM

Cohn-Kanade [11] database and JAFFE [2, 4, 5] are used in the process of facial expression recognition. Facial expressions in Cohn-Kanade consist of 6 basic facial expressions (not including neutral), detecting the face region in the database image and resizing it first. Some typical facial expression examples in Cohn-Kanade are shown in Figure 5. JAFFE i.e. Japanese female facial expression database consists of 7 basic facial expressions (including neutral). Some typical facial expression examples in JAFFE are shown in Figure 6.

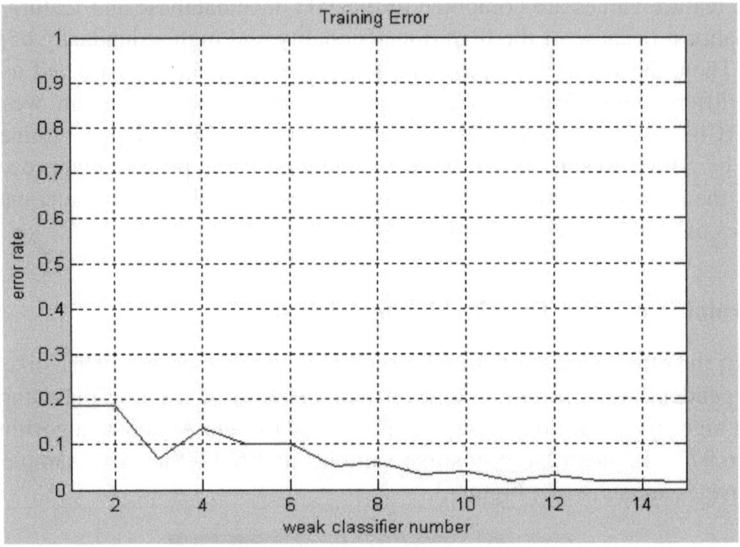

Fig. 4. Trend of training error

Fig. 5. Examples of facial expressions in Cohn-Kanade

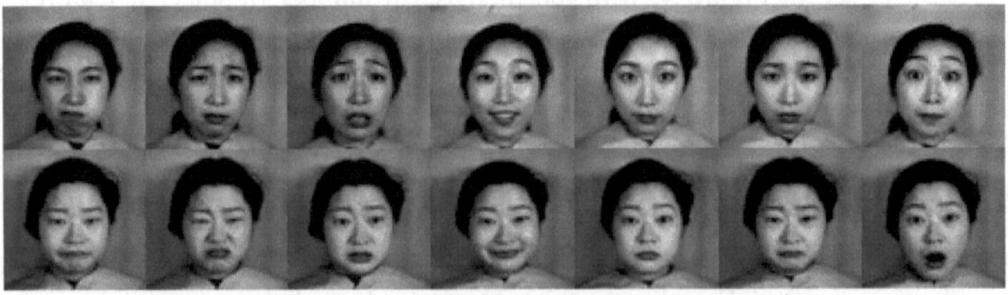

Fig. 6. Examples of facial expressions in JAFFE

900 images in Cohn-Kanade database and 210 images in JAFFE database are selected to recognize facial expression. The sample images are resized to 20x20 and 78,460 Haar-like features are obtained. Adaboost algorithm is used to extract some differentiated features to construct the feature template, which inputs vectors of facial expression recognition by using SVM.

Lyons [2] labeled 34 points on face images manually, and these points are convolved by a set of Gabor filters at 5 spatial frequencies and 8 orientations, then they classify these 1020-dimensional (5*8*34=1020) feature vectors by PCA and LDA and achieve recognition rate of 92%. Yao [5] makes use of Gabor feature and extracts features by using Adaboost which is trained in the same face database, and uses SVM to recognize facial expression and achieve an overall recognition rate of 97.1%. All these methods have used 10 fold cross-validations, used in this paper for easy comparison. The dataset is divided into 10 parts; the SVM is trained on the all of the data in the subspace and excludes one part out for testing. This process repeats 10 times. The highest overall recognition rate in the Cohn-Kanade database is 98.1%; experimental results are shown in Table 1.

Table 1. Experimental results in Cohn-Kanade database

Kernel function	Recognition rate (%)
Linear	90.9
Polynomial	97
RBF	98.1

The overall recognition rate in JAFFE database is 78.1%; performance comparison with other researchers is shown in Table 2.

Table 2. Performance comparison

	Recognition rate (%)	Training :testing	Test database	Train database
PCA+LDA[2]	92.0	9:1	JAFFE	JAFFE
Gabor+Adaboost+SVM[5]	97.1	9:1	JAFFE	JAFFE
Our approach	98.1	9:1	Cohn-Kanade	MIT
Our approach	78.1	9:1	JAFFE	MIT

Training Adaboost, feature extraction and facial expression recognition are conducted in the same face database in these referenced methods; the proposed approach in this paper conducts feature template training and facial expression recognition within different face databases. This approach trains Adaboost algorithm in a western face database, and the trained feature template is certainly close to the western facial expressions. An acceptable recognition rate is achieved when recognizing eastern facial expressions using the western feature template, which indicates that the proposed approach has broader pervasiveness in facial expression recognition. The feature template trained by a western face database is more likely to recognize western facial expressions and is not suitable to be used for recognizing eastern facial expressions, which verifies that difference does exist when recognizing facial expression within different races. Because satisfactory results on JAFFE have been achieved by using the referenced methods [2, 5], we do not duplicate the proposed approach to train Adaboost and to recognize facial expressions on the JAFFE database.

4 Conclusion

On the basis of referenced works, we proposed an approach constructed with three characteristics including, facial features extraction using Haar-like features, weak classifiers training with Adaboost, and facial expression recognition by SVM. The feature template trained using Adaboost algorithm on western face databases is applied to recognize another western face database and an eastern face database, respectively. Experimental results prove the effectiveness of the proposed approach: the feature template trained on western face database recognizes western facial expressions at a high recognition rate and recognizes eastern facial expressions at an acceptable recognition rate. Different face databases are used to train the feature template and recognize facial expression in this paper, thereby maintaining a high recognition rate and improving the pervasiveness of the facial expression model, and this also verifies that difference does exist when recognizing facial expression within different races.

References

1. Chen, L.X., Zhang, T., Gui, X.K., Yang, G.S.: Development of Research on Facial Expression Recognition. In: 2010 International Conference on Intelligent Control and Information Processing (ICICIP), pp. 451–454 (2010)
2. Lyons, M.J., Budynek, J., Akamatsu, S.: Automatic classification of single facial images. IEEE Transactions on Pattern Analysis and Machine Intelligence, 1357–1362 (1999)
3. Liu, X.M., Zhang, Y.J.: Facial Expression Recognition Based on Gabor Histogram Feature and MVBoost. Journal of Computer Research and Development 44, 1089–1096 (2007) (in Chinese)
4. Wang, Y.B., Ai, H.Z., Wu, B., Huang, C.: Real time facial expression recognition with AdaBoost. In: Proceedings of the 17th International Conference on Pattern Recognition, ICPR 2004, pp. 926–929 (2004)
5. Yao, W., Sun, Z.X., Zhang, Y.: Optimal Gabor Feature for Facial Expression Recognition. Journal of Computer-aided Design & Computer Graphics 20(1), 79–84 (2008) (in Chinese)
6. Viola, P., Jones, M.J.: Rapid object detection using a boosted cascade of simple features. In: CVPR 2001: Proceedings of the Conference on Computer Vision and Pattern Recognition, Los Alamitos, CA, USA, pp. 511–518 (2001)

7. Rainer, L., Jochen, M.: An Extended Set of Haar-like Features for Rapid Object Detection. In: Proceedings of ICIP (1), pp. 900–903 (2002)
8. Yoav, F., Robert, E.S.: A Desicion. Theoretic Generalization of On-Line Learning and an Application to Boosting. LNCS, vol. 904, pp. 23–37 (1995)
9. Chrisorpher, J.C.B.: A Tutorial on Support Vector Machines for Pattern Recognition. Data Mining and Knowledge Discoverry 2(2), 121–167 (1998)
10. Chang, C.C., Lin, C.J.: LIBSVM: a library for support vector machines (last updated May 20, 2011)
11. Kanade, C., et al.: Comprehensive database for facial expression analysis (2000)

Program Package for Decision Making

Kartlos J. Kachiashvili[1,2] and David I. Melikdzhanjan[3]

[1] Georgian Technical University, 77, Kostava Street, 0175, Tbilisi, Georgia
k.kachiashvili@gtu.edu.ge, kartlos55@yahoo.com
[2] Abdus Salam School of Mathematical Sciences of GC University, 68-B, New Muslim Town
Lahore, Pakistan
[3] I. Vekua Institute of Applied Mathematics of the Tbilisi State University, 2, University Street,
0186, Tbilisi, Georgia
davidmelikdzhanian@yahoo.com

Abstract. We offer an original, simple and convenient software package for testing statistical hypotheses concerning the parameters of probability distribution laws. The methods of statistical hypotheses testing allow us to solve problems from many spheres of human activity. Applications include engineering, physics, chemistry, medicine, biology, economics, defense, ecology, sociology and so on [see, for example, 1-6]. The problems arising in these areas include the fact that as a rule, the applications contain numerous parameters, i.e. the tasks are multivariate. The dimensionality of the tasks very often reaches up to several tens, even several hundreds. It is practically impossible to solve these tasks without special software. Despite the variety of statistical packages in which the methods of statistical hypotheses testing are realized, there is not known package realizing the methods similar to the ones realized in the offered package. In this package, in addition to well-known, classical methods of hypotheses testing, such as the Bayesian method with general and step loss functions; Sign Test; Mann-Whitney Test; Wilcoxon Test; Wilcoxon Signed-Rank Sum Test and the Wald sequential method [see for example, 7,8], entirely new, original methods, are realized. Among these are constrained Bayesian methods with restrictions on the probabilities of errors of the first or second types, quasi-optimum methods, and sequential analysis methods of Bayesian type for testing any number of hypotheses [9-13]. Simple, convenient and reliable methods of statistical hypotheses testing, based on different information distances (Euclidian and Makhalanobis) between them are also realized in the package.

The developed package is completely original and has no analogue. All algorithms, programs, texts, schedules, drawings, tables, registration etc. realized in the package belong to the authors.

Keywords: software, hypotheses testing, unconstrained Bayesian method, constrained Bayesian method, sequential method of Bayesian type, quasi-optimal method.

V. Khachidze et al. (Eds.): iCETS 2012, CCIS 332, pp. 530–540, 2012.

1 Introduction

The methods of statistical hypotheses testing allow us to solve problems from many spheres of human activity. Applications include engineering, physics, chemistry, medicine, biology, economics, defense, ecology, sociology and so on [see, for example, 1-6]. The problems arising in these areas include the fact that as a rule, the applications contain numerous parameters, i.e. the tasks are multivariate. The dimensionality of the tasks very often reaches up to several tens, and even several hundreds. It is practically impossible to solve these tasks without special software.

Today there are quite a number of available statistical software packages (both universal and specialized) with which the methods of statistical hypotheses testing are realized. Among these are **SPSS** (http://www.spss.com/), **SAS** (http://www.sas.com/), **BMDP** (http://www.statistical-solutions-software.com/products-page/bmdp-statistical-software/), **STATISTICA** (http://www.statsoft.com/products/), **STATGRAPHICS** (http://www.statgraphics.com/), **STADIA** (http:// www.sharewareconnection.com/software. php?list=Stadia+Survey), **SYSTAT** (http://www.systat. com/products.aspx), **Stata** (http://www.stata.com), **DataDesk** (http://www.datadesk.com), **Analyse-it** (http://www.analyse-it.com), **MINITAB** (http: //www. minitab.com/enUS/default.aspx), **SSP** (Smith's Statistical Package), **Statistical Software** (http://statpages.org/javasta2.html), **S-PLUS** (http://www.amazon.com), **MATLAB** (http://www.mathworks.com/testmeasurement/), **SOFA** (http://www.sofastatistics.com/home.php), **OpenStat** (http://www.statpages.org/miller/openstat/), **R** (http://www.r-project.org), **SDpro** and others [14-19].

Despite the variety of statistical packages in which the methods of statistical hypotheses testing are realized, we do not know of any package realizing the methods similar to those in the offered package. In the latter, in addition to well-known, classical methods of hypotheses testing such as the Bayesian method with general and step loss functions, Sign Test, Mann-Whitney Test, Wilcoxon Test, Wilcoxon Signed-Rank Sum Test and the Wald sequential method [see for example, 7,8], entirely new, original methods are realized. Among these are constrained Bayesian methods with restrictions on the probabilities of errors of the first or second types, quasi-optimum methods, and sequential analysis methods of Bayesian type for testing any number of hypotheses. Descriptions of these methods and the results of their investigation are given in the works of the authors [see for example, 9-13]. Simple, convenient and reliable methods of statistical hypotheses testing, based on different information distances (Euclidian and Makhalanobis) between them are also realized in the package. The set of the statistical methods of hypotheses testing realized in the package is given in Fig. 1.

The developed package is completely original and has no analogue. All algorithms, programs, texts, schedules, drawings, tables, registration etc. realized in the package belong to the authors.

2 Realization of Computations in the Package

The corresponding class of tasks (see Fig. 1) is chosen from the main menu of the package. Consider, for example, the sequence of actions for realization of constrained Bayesian tasks. After choosing the task "Constrained Bayesian task" in the opening page, in the window N, the dimension of the observation vector is entered, and in the window m the number of testing hypotheses plus one (for the observation vector) is entered, i.e. $m = S + 1$ (see Fig. 2). The observation vector is entered into the first column (x_j, $j = 1,...,N$) of the Table and the vectors of the numbers corresponding to tested hypotheses are entered in other columns (a_{ij}, $i = 1,...,S$). On the next page the corresponding constrained Bayesian task is chosen, the mode of uniformity of a priori probabilities of hypotheses is switched on or off, the type of the covariance matrix is chosen and the significance level of criterion is entered (see Fig. 3). On the next page the covariance matrix is entered (see Fig. 4). Once entered, the task is started for computation. The computation results are displayed in two windows on one page (see Fig. 5). The chosen parameters of the solved task are displayed in the first window, and the number of accepted hypotheses, the corresponding values of a risk function and the indefinite Lagrange multiplier are displayed in the second window.

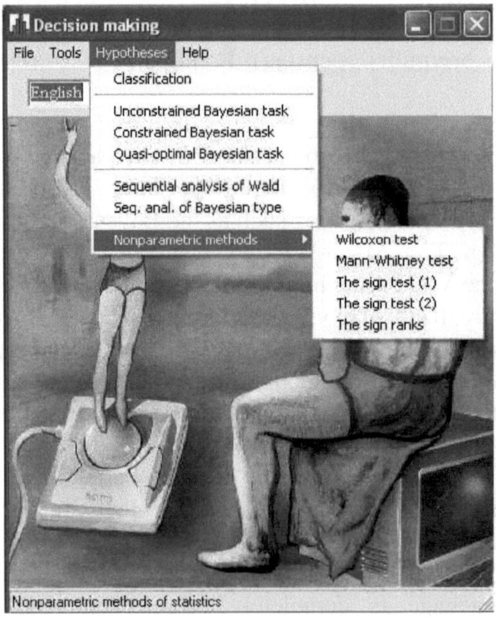

Fig. 1. Sections of the main menu of the package

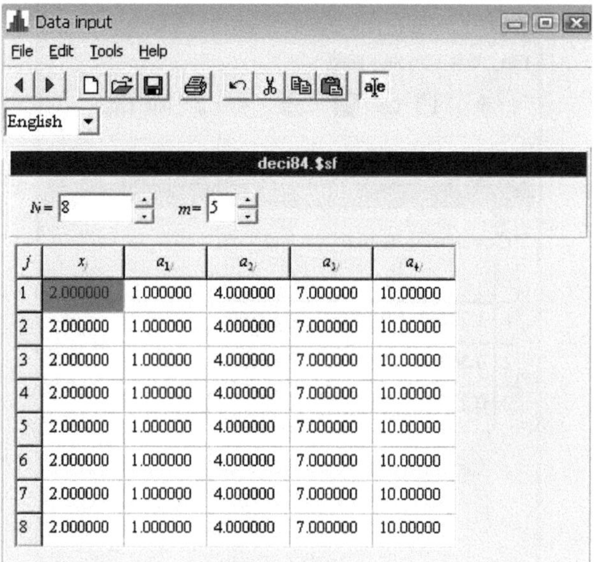

Fig. 2. The observation vector and the testing hypotheses

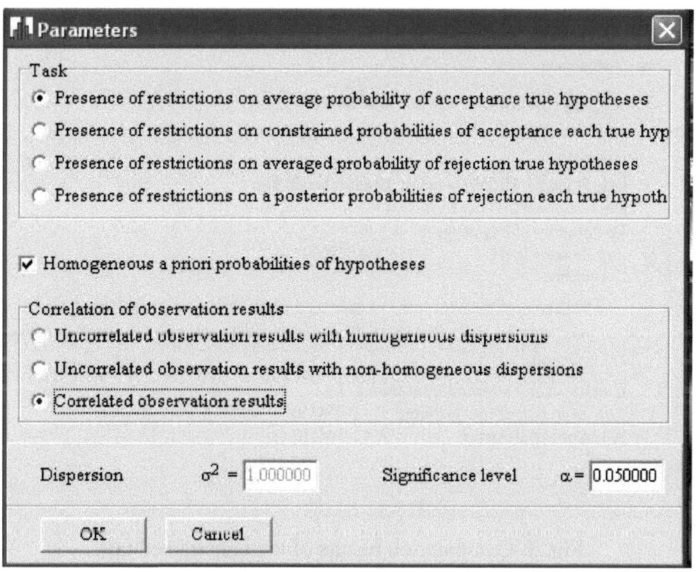

Fig. 3. Constrained Bayesian tasks

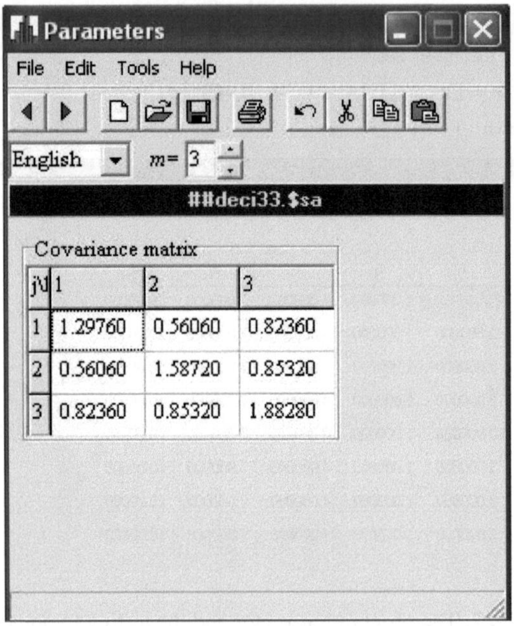

Fig. 4. Entering of covariance matrix

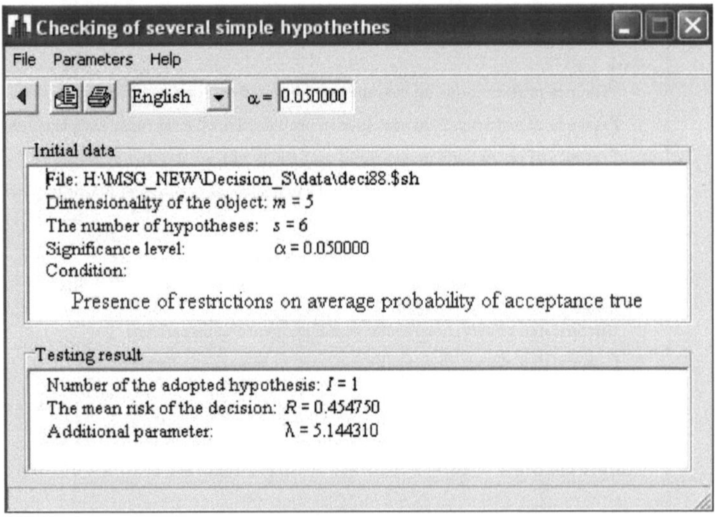

Fig. 5. Computation results of the constrained task

In the unconstrained Bayesian task for the arbitrary loss function, after the covariance matrix, the matrix of loss function is entered in addition. In unconstrained tasks of hypotheses testing, among the displayed computation results, naturally, there are no indefinite Lagrange multipliers.

In the sequential methods of Bayesian type, if on the basis of the entered observation result it is impossible to accept one of the tested hypotheses, by pressing a corresponding button, a window for entering a new observation result appears (see Fig. 6). After entering the new observation result, the sequential task runs etc. until the acceptance of one of the tested hypotheses. After acceptance of the hypothesis, in the window of the results, along with the accepted hypothesis, the number of observation results is displayed, on the basis of which the unequivocal decision is made.

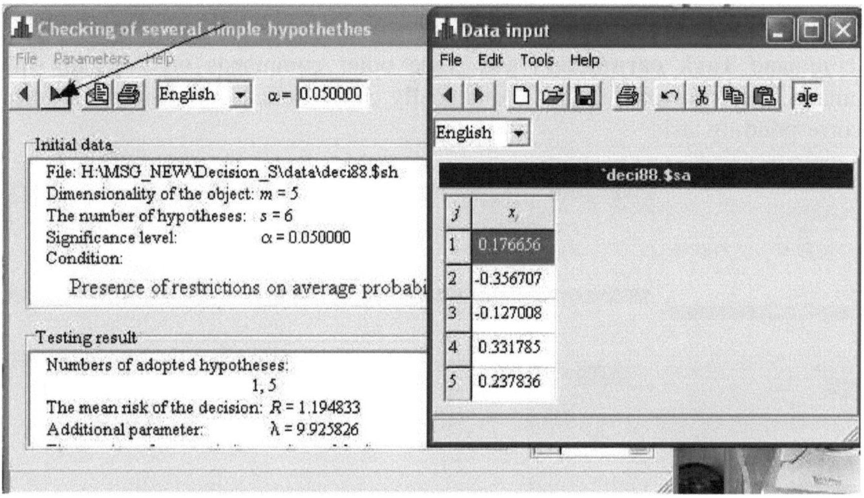

Fig. 6. Entering of repeated observations in sequential algorithms

3 Possibilities of Input-Output and Representation of Data in the Package

In addition to the above-listed functions, the package performs service functions of input-output, editing, graphic representation and visualization of the initial data and obtained results.

These possibilities are realized under the uniform scheme, which is used in all software packages created by the authors of the present work (see [19-21]).

The value of each parameter is changed by means of standard Windows components, in which it is possible to edit the text, to choose a line from the list, to set an indicator, etc.

When working with each form containing the main menu, the parameters are set by means of commands on the main menu from the groups **File**, **Tools** and **Hypotheses**. The most important parameters can also be specified by means of the components located on the **ToolBar**.

Parameters Used in All or Most Tasks of the Software:
Sizes of pages for printing out; they are changed by means of the command **File|Page setup**; *Working language*; (It can be chosen directly from the main form of the software (see Fig. 1), so at any stage of work (see, for example Fig.-s 2, 4, 5, 6))

Working directory is the directory where data files are looked up; it changes at each change of a folder in standard dialogue windows for opening and saving files.

Parameters Rarely Used or Are Used in a Few or Separate Tasks of the Software. These are upper bounds of sample sizes of different types. All of them are changed by means of the command **Tools|Boundaries** on the main menu of the main form of the software.

Specific parameters for separate tasks of the software are changed by means of the command **Task parameters** and some other commands on the main menu. Command **Task parameters** is automatically carried out before opening a form of the corresponding task.

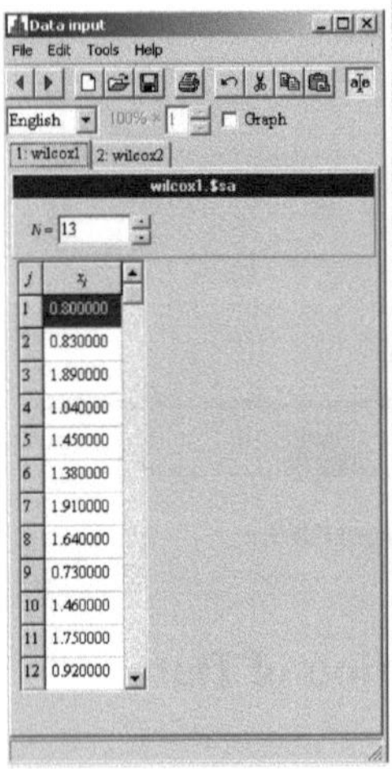

Fig. 7. Editing of the data in tables

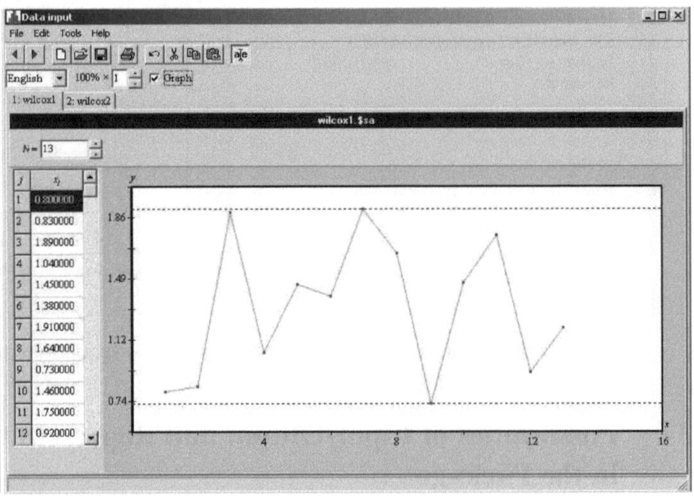

Fig. 8. Graphic representation of the data

Accomplishment of each task begins with the block of data input.

The entered data are represented in the form of tables. They form sequences of elements of the same type. There are the possibilities of entering the data that have not been recorded anywhere, reading the data from files and saving them in files by means of commands **File|New**, **File|Open**, **File|Save**, **File|Save as**, **File|Save all** standard for the text and graphic **Windows** editors.

The command of main menu **File|Send** performs entering the data in a text file. The command

File|Print performs printing of the table.

The data files have a relatively simple structure, the description of which can be found in **Help** files for the package, and they can be created outside of this package.

Graphic Representation of Data. For clear representation of data in the tasks from the group **Nonparametric methods.** There is a possibility of switching on *the graphic mode,* in which the edited data are represented in the form of a graph. In the graphic mode, the measured values can be edited by moving corresponding dots on the graph by the mouse.

Switching on/off the graphic mode, and the installation of the parameters determining a form of the graph, are carried out by means of the main menu command **Tools|Graph view**. When indicator **Draw broken line** is switched on, dots in the graph corresponding to edited data in the table cells are linked by a broken line. When indicator **Draw plot by wide lines** is switched on, these dots become large, and the line connecting them becomes thick. There is the possibility of increasing or reducing the scale of representation of the graph. If this scale is set to be greater than one, then scroll bars appear allowing movement throughout the graph (part of which remains beyond the assigned window).

It is also possible to switch on/off the graphic mode and to change the graph scale, by means of the components located on the **ToolBar** (see Figs. 7 and 8).

The results of computation are displayed on the screen in the form of text messages. Command **Print** carries out printing of the text and/or the graph.

Command **Send text** enters the text in the file, the name of which is determined by default or specified by the user. The user can choose one of the following types of files: file **LaTeX** (**.tex** file), a simple **text** file, or text file **MS DOS**. If the saved file already exists on a disk, the user can also establish the way of writing the text by means of indicator "**Preserve exist text**": add a new text to the existing one or remove the existing text from the file.

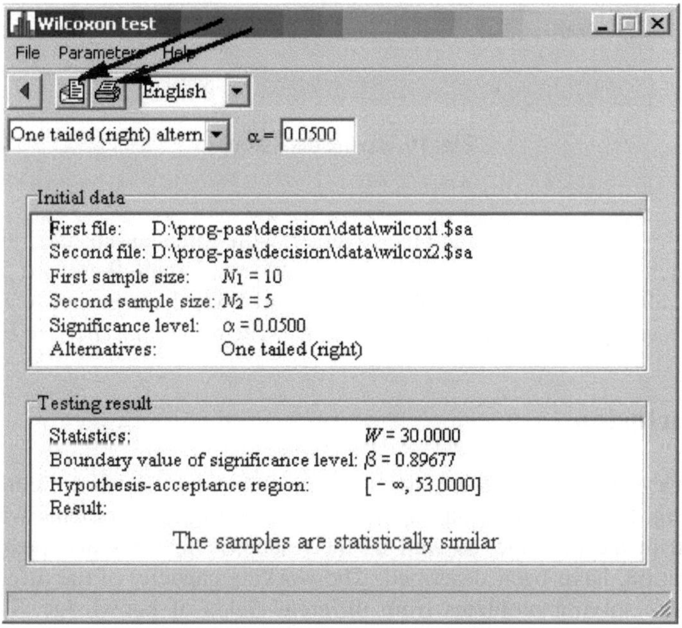

Fig. 9. Fast buttons of the **ToolBar**

It is also possible to separate the text displayed on the screen, and, by means of a combination of keys **Ctrl-C** and **Ctrl-V**, to move it to edited **Word** document or to a document of any other editor allowing to work with the text in **RTF** format.

The listed commands are called from the main menu or by means of fast buttons of the **ToolBar**, duplicating the corresponding items of the main menu (see Fig. 9).

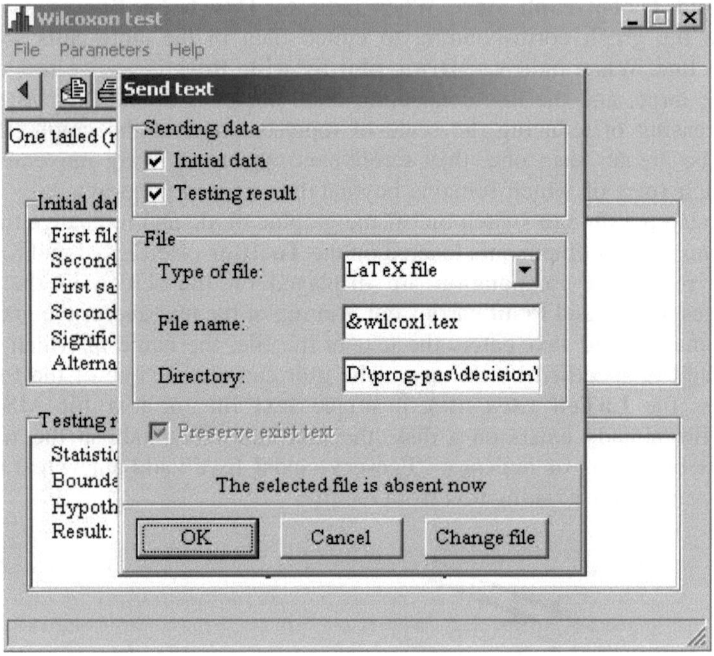

Fig. 10. Saving data groups

Usually the results of calculations, together with some initial data, are split into groups, which are displayed in different windows. When there are a few such groups, by calling the commands **Print** and **Send text**, the user can select which of the available groups he/she wants to print or to write down in a file (see Fig. 10).

4 Conclusion

In this work we offer software for making statistical decisions, convenient for understanding, familiarization and application. The original problems we developed and realized in the package, as well as their specific features and possibilities for their application, have been described. The working capacity of the offered package was tested for solving problems from different fields of knowledge. The obtained results justified the stability and reliability of the algorithms and the high quality of obtained results.

The package is realized in operational system **WINDOWS**. There is the possibility of choosing the language of dialogue with the package from the list of languages realized in it. Additionally, the user can, without special effort, add any language of his interest to the list of languages of dialogue with the package. For this purpose, unquestionably simple instructions are given in **Help**. It should be emphasized once again that the offered package is completely original, as all algorithms, programs, texts, graphs, figures, tables, legalization, etc. realized in this package are original; they belong to the authors and have no analogues.

References

[1] Weerahandi, S., Zidek, J.V.: Multi-Bayesian Statistical Decision theory. J. R. Statist. Soc. A 144(1), 85–93 (1981)

[2] Breusch, T.S.: Hypothesis Testing in Unidentified Models. The Review of Economic Studies 53(4), 635–651 (1986)

[3] Meng, C.Y.K.: A Bayesian Approach to the Multiplicity Problem for Significance Testing with Binomial Data. Biometrics 43, 301–311 (1987)

[4] Millard, S.P.: Proof of Safety as Proof of Hazard. Biometrics 43, 719–725 (1987)

[5] Kachiashvili, K.J., Melikdzhanian, D.I.: Identification of River Water Excessive Pollution Sources. International Journal of Information Technology & Decision Making 5(2), 397–417 (2006)

[6] Kachiashvili, K.J., Hashmi, M.A., Mueed, A.: The statistical risk analysis as the basis of the sustainable development. In: Proceedings of the 4th IEEE International Conference on Management of Innovation & Technology (ICMIT 2008), Bangkok, pp. 1210–1215 (2008)

[7] Hollander, M., Wolfe, D.: Nonparametric statistical methods. John Wiley and Sons, New York

[8] Wald, A.: Sequential Analysis. John Wiley and Sons, New York (1947)

[9] Kachiashvili, K.J., Mueed, A.: Conditional Bayesian Task of Testing Many Hypotheses, Statistics (2011), `http://dx.doi.org/10.1080/02331888.2011.602681`, doi:10.1080/02331888.2011.602681

[10] Kachiashvili, K.J., Hashmi, M.A., Mueed, A.: Sensitivity Analysis of Classical and Conditional Bayesian Problems of Many Hypotheses Testing. Communications in Statistics— Theory and Methods 41(4), 591–605 (2012)

[11] Kachiashvili, K.J.: Investigation and Computation of Unconditional and Conditional Bayesian Problems of Hypothesis Testing. ARPN Journal of Systems and Software 1(2), 47–59 (2011)

[12] Kachiashvili, K.J., Hashmi, M.A., Mueed, A.: Comparison Analysis of Unconditional and Conditional Bayesian Problems of Testing Many Hypotheses, Transactions. Automated Control Systems 1(10), 89–100 (2011)

[13] Kachiashvili, K.J., Hashmi, M.A.: About Using Sequential Analysis Approach for Testing Many Hypotheses. Bulletin of the Georgian Academy of Sciences 4(2), 20–25 (2010)

[14] Turin, I.N., Kulaichev, A.: The methods and facilities of data analysis in Windows environment. In: STADIA 6.0. Informatics and Computers, Moscow (1999)

[15] McDaniel, S., Hemedinger, C.: SAS for Dummies. John Wiley & Sons, New York (2007)

[16] Bühl, A., Zöfel, P.: SPSS Version 10. Einführung in die moderne datenanalyse unter Windows. Pearson Education Deuttschland GmbH (2001)

[17] Meyer, R.K., Krueger, D.D.: A Minitab Guide to Statistics. Prentice-Hall Publishing (2004)

[18] Dixon, W.J.: BMDP Statistical Software Manual. Edition User's Digest (1992)
[19] Kachiashvili, K.J., Melikdzhanian, D.I.: SDpro – The Software Package for Statistical Processing of Experimental Information. International Journal Information Technology & Decision Making 9(1), 1–30 (2010)
[20] Kachiashvili, K.J., Melikdzhanian, D.Y.: Software for Determination of Biological Age. Current Bioinformatics 4, 41–47 (2009)
[21] Kachiashvili, K.J., Melikdzhanian, D.Y.: Software Realization Problems of Mathe- matical Models of Pollutants Transport in Rivers. Advances in Engineering Software 40, 1063–1073 (2009)

Multi-Modal Fusion Emotion Recognition Based on HMM and ANN

Chao Xu, Tianyi Cao*, Zhiyong Feng, and Caichao Dong

School of Computer Science and Technology, Tianjin University, Tianjin, China
caotianyi8@yahoo.com.cn, {xuchao,zyfeng,dongcc}@tju.edu.cn

Abstract. Emotional states play an important role in Human-Computer Interaction. An emotion recognition framework is proposed to extract and fuse features from both video sequences and speech signals. This framework is constructed from two Hidden Markov Models (HMMs) represented to achieve emotional states with video and audio respectively; Artificial Neural Network (ANN) is applied as the whole fusion mechanism. Two important phases for HMMs are Facial Animation Parameters (FAPs) extraction from video sequences based on Active Appearance Model (AAM), and pitch and energy features extraction from speech signals. Experiments indicate that the proposed approach has better performance and robustness than methods using video or audio separately.

Keywords: Human-Computer Interaction, Emotion Recognition, Multi-modal Fusion, Artificial Neural Network, Hidden Markov Model, Active Appearance Model.

1 Introduction

Emotions play a significant role in human communication. Changes in a person's affective state have a great impact on perception and decision making. Emotion recognition brings affective dimensions into human-computer interaction. It enables computers to understand human non-verbal communication.

Psychological researchers have identified six basic emotions that people can recognize from facial expressions and speeches with high accuracy: happiness, anger, sadness, fear, disgust, and surprise [1]. Many researches on emotion recognition have been conducted on images that capture facial expression at its peak or video sequences of expression. Some researchers have been focused on recognizing affective states from speech signals.

In this work, we propose a multi-modal approach that fuses video and audio in recognizing human emotions. Affective features are extracted and fused from facial expression sequences and speech signals. Recognition results are acquired based on video and audio modalities.

---

* Corresponding author.

V. Khachidze et al. (Eds.): iCETS 2012, CCIS 332, pp. 541–550, 2012.

2 Related Works

Most studies on emotion recognition are based on six prototypical emotions proposed by Paul Ekman. Researchers extract affective features from video and audio and classify them into one of the six emotions.

Social psychological studies indicate that facial expressions form the major modality of human communications. Early methods use images of facial expression at its peak. Lyon, M. conducted Gabor filtering on face images for facial expression coding [2]. Franco, L. used face images in Yale database as training sets to recognize facial expressions [3].

However, experiments conducted by Basssili show that facial expressions in video sequences are recognized more accurately by humans than expressions in static images [4]. Ekman and Frieson developed Facial Action Coding System (FACS) to code the contraction of facial muscles [5]. Measuring units of FACS are action units (AUs), not muscles [6]. Some approaches detect and track facial feature points to extract expression features. Landabaso applied Facial Definition Parameters (FDPs) and Facial Animation Parameters (FAPs) to represent facial expressions [7]. FDPs and FAPs are low level features compliant with MPEG4 standards.

Many researchers recognize emotions from speech signals. Medan extracted pitch and energy of audio to recognize emotions [8]. Lin extracted 39 candidate voice features, including fundamental frequency, energy, formant frequencies, MFCCs and MBEs, and selected five of them as the best feature subset [9].

Emotion recognition is inherently an issue of multi-modal analysis. Three fusion strategies have been applied in multi-modal emotion recognition: feature-level fusion, modal-level fusion, and decision-level fusion. Song proposed tripled HMM to model expression features from upper face and lower face, and speech features [10]. Zeng presented Multi-stream Fused Hidden Markov Model (MFHMM), in which each group of features was modeled by a component HMM [11]. Zeng designed a voting method to fuse the recognition results [12]. De proposed a rule-based method that combines video and audio information to create a comprehensive output [13].

In this work, we propose an emotion recognition framework that extracts features from facial expression sequences and speech signals, and then fuses the features in decision level. In the phase of feature extraction, FAPs are extracted from video sequenced based on Active Appearance Model (AAM), and pitch and energy features are acquired from speech signals. In the phase of emotion classification, two HMMs are constructed to achieve affective states from video and audio respectively. Then, Artificial Neural Network (ANN) is applied as fusion mechanism for the whole model.

3 Feature Extraction

Feature extraction is a critical procedure of pattern recognition issue. The accuracy of affective features has a significant impact on the results of emotion recognition.

In this work, we extract facial expression features from video sequences and speech features from audio signals. In order to locate and track facial feature points, we construct AAM Model for facial images of different expressions. FAPs are calculated from motions of the key points as facial expression features. Pitch and energy features are calculated from audio signals as speech features.

3.1 Active Appearance Model

Active Appearance Model, first demonstrated by T. F. Cootes, is widely applied in detecting and tracking feature points of flexible objects, especially facial feature points. It combines shape and grey-level appearance information to build the model.

We build an Active Appearance Model for facial expression images. The training set should have images with different light intensity, postures, and facial expressions. Feature points should be previously located on each image. Figure 1 shows the 68 key points located on a facial image in Cohn-Kanade2010 facial expression database [14].

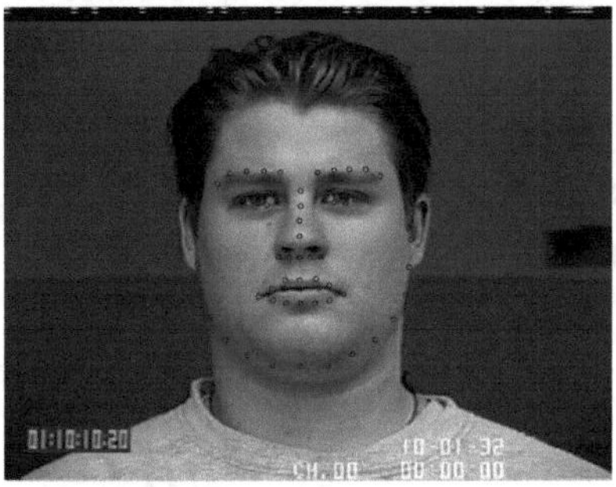

Fig. 1. Facial feature points

First, we model shape for training images. Suppose $\mathbf{x}_i$ represents the ith shape in the training set with n points. Set $\mathbf{x}_i = (x_{i0}, y_{i0}, x_{i1}, y_{i1} \ldots, x_{ik}, y_{ik}, \ldots, x_{i(n-1)}, y_{i(n-1)})$, $i = 1, 2, \ldots, n$, where m is the number of images. In order to compare equivalent points from different shapes, we align all the shapes in the training set by scaling, rotating and translating. A least-squares approach is used to align a pair of shapes. The mean shape of the aligned shapes is then acquired. Figure 2 shows feature points of all aligned shapes in IMM face database, where each color represents one feature point of all shapes. Locations of the shapes form Allowable Shape Domain. We conduct Principal Component Analysis (PCA) on the coordinates of the aligned shapes. The covariance matrix of the sample set is acquired, and the eigenvalues and eigenvectors of the matrix are calculated. The first t eigenvectors form the matrix $\mathbf{P}_s$, which indicates the statistics of aligned shapes. Any new shape can then be approximated by

$$\mathbf{x} = \bar{\mathbf{x}} + \mathbf{P}_s \mathbf{b}_s, \tag{1}$$

where $\bar{\mathbf{x}}$ is the mean shape, $\mathbf{P}_s$ is a set of orthogonal modes of variation, and $\mathbf{b}_s$ is a set of shape parameters.

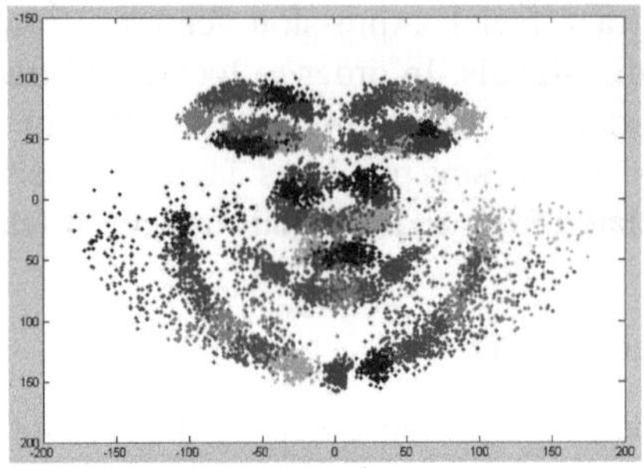

Fig. 2. Feature points of all aligned shapes

Second, we model grey-level appearance for training images. We apply Thin Plate Spline technique to warp each image, so that its key points match the mean shape. We then sample grey-level information $\mathbf{g}_m$ from the deformed patch. Analysis is conducted on normalized data. Any grey-level appearance can be approximated by

$$\mathbf{g} = \bar{\mathbf{g}} + \mathbf{P}_g \mathbf{b}_g , \tag{2}$$

where $\bar{\mathbf{g}}$ is the mean of normalized grey-level vectors. $\mathbf{P}_g$ is a set of orthogonal modes of variation, and $\mathbf{b}_g$ is a set of grey-level parameters.

Set a new vector $\mathbf{b} = \begin{pmatrix} \mathbf{b}_s \\ \mathbf{b}_g \end{pmatrix} = \begin{pmatrix} \mathbf{P}_s^T(\mathbf{x} - \bar{\mathbf{x}}) \\ \mathbf{P}_g^T(\mathbf{g} - \bar{\mathbf{g}}) \end{pmatrix}$. We conduct Principal Component Analysis on $\mathbf{b}$ and acquire $\mathbf{b} = \mathbf{Qc}$, where $\mathbf{Q} = \begin{pmatrix} \mathbf{Q}_s \\ \mathbf{Q}_g \end{pmatrix}$. Then (1), (2) are written as

$$\mathbf{x} = \bar{\mathbf{x}} + \mathbf{P_s Q}_s \mathbf{c} , \tag{3}$$

$$\mathbf{g} = \bar{\mathbf{g}} + \mathbf{P}_g \mathbf{Q}_g \mathbf{c} . \tag{4}$$

We can reconstruct an image by adjusting parameters in the model.

The model parameters have an important effect on image reconstruction. We construct an iterative method to calculate model parameters, resulting in the new image best approximating the original image.

3.2 Facial Animation Parameters

After detecting facial feature points from each image in video sequences by AAM, we track the motion of the points and calculate FAPs.

FAPs are defined in ISO MPEG-4 standard and they are closely related to facial actions, such as raising eyebrows and closing eyes. They represent basic facial actions and most natural expressions. As FAPs convey significant information about facial expressions, they are extracted from video sequences as expression features. FAPs used in this work include FAPs for the eyelid 19, 20, 21, 22, for the eyebrow 31, 32, 33, 34, 35, 36, 37, 38, 39, and for the lip 51, 52, 53, 54, 55, 56, 57, 58, 59, 60. Some of these are specified in Table 1.

Table 1. Facial Animation Parameters

FAP No.	FAP Name	FAP Description	FAP Units	FAP Motion Position
19	close_t_l_eyelid	Vertical displacement of top left eyelid	*ENS*	down
31	raise_l_i_eyebrow	Vertical displacement of left inner brow	*ENS*	up
51	lower_t_midlip_o	Vertical displacement of top middle lip	*MNS*	down

The values of FAPs are expressed in terms of Facial Animation Parameter Units (FAPUs). FAPUs allow FAPs on any facial model to be evaluated in a consistent way. FAPUs and their values are illustrated in Figure 3.

$$ENS = ENS0/1024$$
$$ES = ES0/1024$$
$$IRISD = IRISD0/1024$$
$$MNS = MNS0/1024$$
$$MW = MW0/1024$$

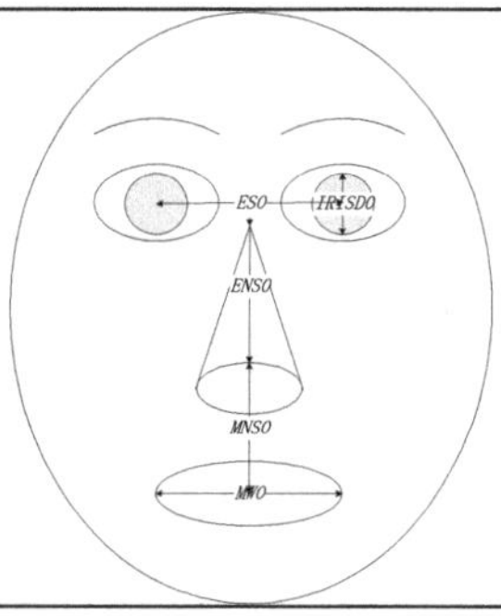

Fig. 3. Facial Animation Parameter Units

3.3 Audio Feature Extraction

Audio features for emotion recognition include energy and pitch. Both of them are prosodic features of voice. As the human voice keeps steady in a short time, we separate speech signals into frames (10-30 ms). All the features are calculated for each frame.

The mean energy in the frame and its first and second derivatives are used as energy features. The mean energy of the frame is computed as

$$E_n = \sum_{m=n-(N-1)}^{n} [\mathbf{x}(m)\boldsymbol{\omega}(n-m)]^2 , \tag{5}$$

where N is the length of a frame, and $\boldsymbol{\omega}(\cdot)$ is a window function.

The fundamental frequency and its first and second derivatives are used as pitch features. Fundamental frequency can be calculated by auto-correlation analysis. As auto-correlation function has maximums at fundamental cycles, we calculate the distance between a pair of adjacent maximums to estimate the fundamental frequency. Figure 4 shows the auto-correlation function, which has been filtered.

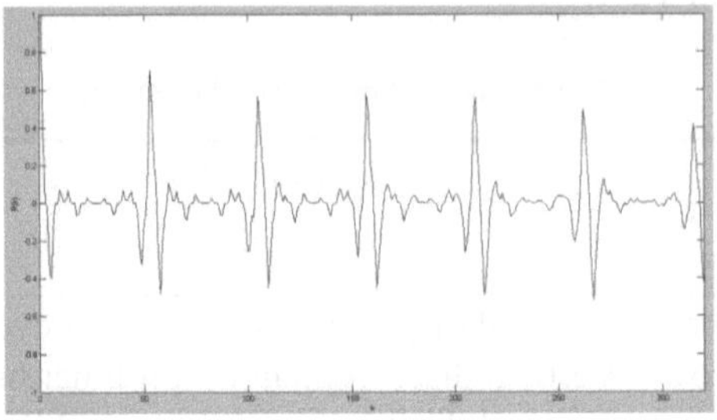

Fig. 4. Auto-correlation function of speech signals

Energy and pitch features extracted from speech signals of different affective states are distinct. Energy and pitch values of happiness, anger and surprise are relatively higher, while values of sadness are lower.

4 Emotion Classification

4.1 HMM Training on Visual and Acoustic Features

An HMM is a Markov Chain with finite unobservable states, each of which has a probability distribution associated with observations. An HMM is comprised of:

a) A set of states, $\mathbf{S} = \{S_i\}$, $1 \le i \le N$, where N is the number of states.

b) The initial state distribution, $\boldsymbol{\pi} = \{\pi_i\}$, $1 \le i \le N$.

c) The state transition probability matrix, $\mathbf{A} = \{a_{ij}\}$, $1 \le i \le N$, $1 \le j \le N$.

d) The state probability matrix, $\mathbf{B} = \{b_i(\mathbf{o}_k)\}$, where $\mathbf{o}_k$ represents the kth observation.

Thus, an HMM is defined as $\boldsymbol{\lambda} = (\boldsymbol{\pi}, \mathbf{A}, \mathbf{B})$.

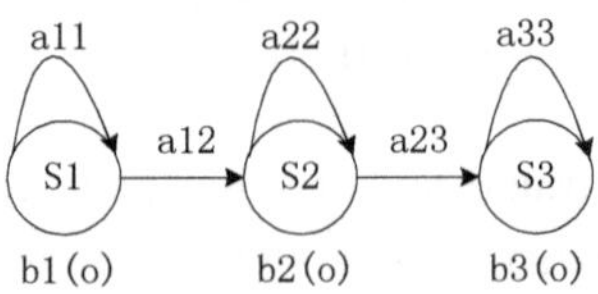

Fig. 5. Three-state left-to-right HMM

In this work, we have defined a three-state left-to right HMM, shown in Figure 5. We construct 12 HMMs respectively for 6 kinds of facial expressions and 6 kinds of acoustic emotions. The observation vectors of HMMs for video are FAPs, while the observations of HMMs for audio are vectors comprised of energy and pitch.

The training process for each HMM is shown in Figure 6. States are iteratively segmented by Viterbi method which calculates the maximum of the probability $P(\mathbf{O},\mathbf{Q}\mid\lambda)$ to find the optimal segmentation of $\mathbf{Q}$. On the other hand, mixture segmentation is conducted by K-Means Clustering.

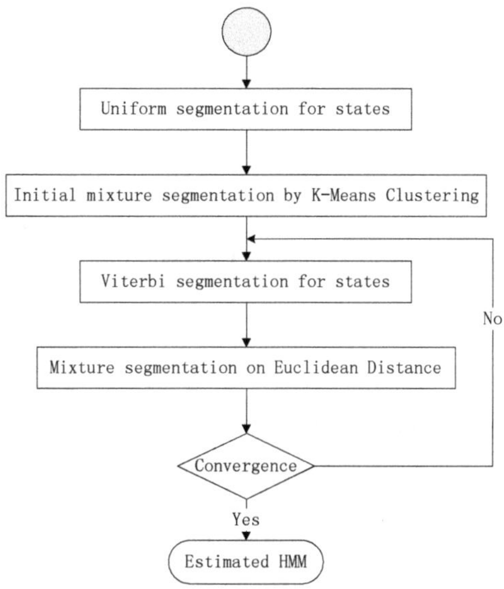

Fig. 6. Training process for HMMs

For a test feature vector sequence of video or speech, the probability of the observation sequence given an HMM $P(\mathbf{O},\mathbf{Q}\mid\boldsymbol{\lambda})$ is computed, where $\boldsymbol{\lambda}$ represents any HMM for video and audio. Thus, 12 probability values are acquired for each pair of facial expression sequence and speech signal.

4.2 Multi-modal Fusion Using ANN

Video and audio information are fused in the decision level by ANN. Multilayer Perceptron (MLP), a kind of ANN, is one of the most efficient classifiers. The learning process of MLP is based on Hebbian Learning Rule, i.e. samples of the training set are gradually input into the network, and the weight matrix of the network is adjusted based on the difference between the real output and the expected output. Figure 7 illustrates the model of MLP. The learning algorithm of MLP is as below. Firstly, initialize the network weights to small random values. Then, from the set of training input-output pairs, present an input pattern and calculate the network response. The desired network response is compared with the actual output. The weights of the network are updated by the errors computed above. The steps are repeated until the network reaches a predetermined level of accuracy.

In the training phase, the 12 HMM probability values of each pair of facial expression sequences and speech signals in the training set are used as the input of MLP, while the corresponding emotion is used as the desired network response. In the testing phase, the 12 HMM probability values acquired from the HMMs are given to the input layer of MLP and the output layer will show the recognition results of the fused facial expression sequences and speech signals.

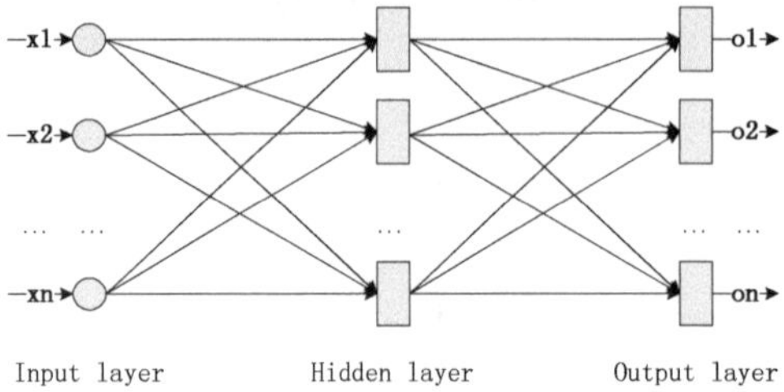

Fig. 7. Multilayer Perceptron

5 Experiments

5.1 Emotion Recognition Tests Based on Facial Expression Sequences

The experiment is conducted on Cohn-Kanade2010 facial expression database. It consists of video sequences of 123 subjects, each of which shows frontal face with different expressions and constant illumination. The number of available sequences of each expression is shown in Table 2.

Table 2. Number of video sequences of each expression

Anger	Contempt	Disgust	Fear	Happiness	Sadness	Surprise
45	18	59	25	69	28	83

In order to extract FAPs from each sequence, we build an Active Appearance Model for facial expression images. IMM face database is chosen as the training set for AAM. IMM database contains 240 images of 40 subjects, where each subject has 6 images with different light intensity, postures and facial expressions. 58 feature points are manually located on each image. Figure 8 illustrates the annotated key points on a video sequence of CK2010 database (three images of the sequence shown).

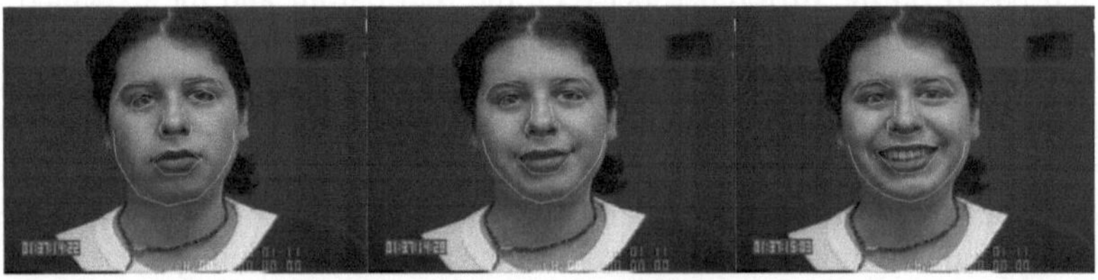

Fig. 8. Facial feature points locating and tracking (feature points linked by white lines)

FAPs extracted from video sequences are used as observations for the training of HMMs. The test is performed on Leave-One-Out method. All subjects in CK2010 database but one constitute the training set. Sequences of the remaining subject are recognized as one of the six basic emotions. The process is repeated for all the subjects, obtaining an average recognition rate of 84.7%. Table 3 displays the confusion table of facial expressions.

Table 3. Confusion Table of facial expressions

	Anger	Contempt	Disgust	Fear	Happiness	Sadness	Surprise	%
Anger	39	0	0	0	0	5	1	86.7
Contempt	0	15	3	0	0	0	0	83.3
Disgust	0	8	43	6	0	2	0	72.9
Fear	2	0	1	21	0	1	0	84.0
Happiness	0	2	0	0	64	0	3	92.8
Sadness	5	0	2	0	0	21	0	75.0
Surprise	3	1	0	0	5	0	74	89.2

5.2 Emotion Recognition Tests Based on Speech Signals

Berlin emotional speech database consists of 433 speeches, each of which lasts for 2-3 seconds. 10 subjects (5 males and 5 females) read 10 German sentences in six different emotions. Energy and pitch features are extracted as the observations of HMMs. Table 4 shows the recognition rates of four emotions. The recognition rate decreases with the increase of the number of emotions.

Table 4. Recognition rates of audio emotions

	Fear	Happiness	Sadness	Surprise
Rate (%)	78.6	83.9	90.5	81.2

5.3 Multi-modal Emotion Recognition Tests

The database for multi-modal recognition test consists of 240 pairs of facial expression sequences and speech signals, each of which are selected from CK2010 database and Berlin speech database. ANN is trained on HMM probabilities of the video-audio pairs. For a test sample, the HMM probabilities are given as the input of ANN, and the emotion recognition result will be shown in the output layer. The overall emotion recognition rate is 89.6%. It is shown that the recognition accuracy is improved by applying the multi-modal fusion approach.

6 Conclusion

Multi-modal emotion recognition is a challenging problem and an attractive research field. We construct a framework based on ANN, which has been successfully used in other multi-modal issues. We also make use of HMM, which is good at representing features of sequences. Experiments indicate that the multi-modal approach has higher accuracy than methods using only video or audio. Future works will be directed towards the improvement of feature extraction. More affective features, such as optical flow features and formant frequencies, will be extracted from video and audio respectively.

References

1. Ekman, P., Davidson, R.: The Nature of Emotion: Fundamental Questions. Oxford Univ. Press, New York (1994)
2. Lyons, M., Akamatsu, S.: Coding facial expressions with gabor wavelets. In: Third IEEE International Conference on Automatic Face and Gesture Recognition, pp. 200–205. IEEE Press (1998)
3. Franco, L., Treves, A.: A neural network facial expression recognition system using unsupervised local processing. In: Proceedings of the 2nd International Symposium on Image and Signal Processing and Analysis, pp. 628–632. IEEE Press (2001)
4. Bassili, J.: Emotion recognition: the role of facial movement and the relative importance of upper and lower areas of the face. Journal of Personality and Social Psychology 37(11), 2049–2058 (1979)
5. Ekman, P., Friesen, W.: Facial Action Coding System. Consulting Psychologists Press Inc., California (1978)
6. Tian, Y., Kanade, T., Cohn, J.: Recognizing action units for facial expression analysis. IEEE Transactions on Pattern Analysis and Machine Intelligence 23(2), 97–115 (2001)
7. Landabaso, J.L., Pardas, M., Bonafonte, A.: HMM recognition of expressions in unrestrained video intervals. In: Proceedings of IEEE Acoustics, Speech and Signal Processing, vol. 3, pp. III-197–III-200. IEEE Press (2003)
8. Medan, Y., Yair, E., Chazan, D.: Super resolution pitch determination of speech signals. IEEE Transactions on Signal Processing 39(1), 40–48 (1991)
9. Lin, Y., Wei, G.: Speech emotion recognition based on HMM and SVM. In: Proceedings of the Fourth International Conference on Machine Learning and Cybernetics, pp. 4898–4901 (2005)
10. Song, M., You, M., Li, N., Chen, C.: A robust multimodal approach for emotion recognition. Neurocomputing 71, 1913–1920 (2008)
11. Zeng, Z., Tu, J., Brian, M., Huang, T.S.: Audio-visual affective expression recognition through multistream fused HMM. IEEE Transactions on Multimedia 10(4), 570–577 (2008)
12. Zeng, Z., Tu, J., Liu, M., Zhang, T., Zhang, N., Zhang, Z., Huang, T.S., Roth, D., Levinson, S.: Bimodal HCI-related affect recognition. In: International Conference on Multimodal Interfaces, pp. 137–143 (2004)
13. De Silva, L.C.: Bimodal emotion recognition. In: Proceedings of the Fourth IEEE International Conference on Automatic Face and Gesture Recognition, pp. 332–335. IEEE Press (2000)
14. Lucey, P., Cohn, J.F., Kanade, T., Saragih, J., Ambadar, Z., Matthews, I.: The Extended Cohn-Kanade Dataset (CK+): A complete dataset for action unit and emotion-specified expression. In: Proceedings of IEEE Workshop on CVPR for Human Communicative Behavior Analysis, pp. 94–101. IEEE Press, San Francisco (2010)

Visual Modeling for Multi-level Parallel Computing Environment Based on DSL

Mengmeng Wang[1], Ce Yu[1,*], Jizhou Sun[1], Chao Sun[1], Zhou Jin[1], Gang Cheng[1], Xiaoqian Zhu[2], and Xiangfei Meng[2]

[1] School of Computer Science and Technology, Tianjin University
[2] National Supercomputer Center of China, Tianjin
Tianjin 300072, China
{mmwang,yuce,jzsun,schsch321}@tju.edu.cn

Abstract. As the increasingly high demands of computer processing power and speed, parallel computing has become an inevitable trend. With the development of technologies such as clusters and multi-core processors, there has achieved a very good support for parallel computing at the hardware level. But the inherent difficulty of parallel programs and programmers' habitual thinking for a serial program severely limits the popularization of parallel programs in a variety of areas of high-performance applications. In the system of PAVM, we have achieved the visual modeling of single-level parallel application, as well as the corresponding model verification and code generation work. Based on PAVM, this paper proposes a visual modeling methodology based on the hierarchical idea. A visual modeling system called M-PAVM is designed and implemented which supports three levels modeling for multi-core cluster environments. The hierarchical modeling scheme designed in this paper divides the process of parallel application modeling into three levels: task configuration, process task assignment and algorithm implementation. The first level is responsible for coarse-grained task division and for the mapping from tasks to computing nodes. The second level is used for designing the division, distribution and communication of subtasks, which is aimed at getting well-defined threads. And the last level is used for the design of algorithm and control logic in tasks, which is unrelated to the platform architecture. The application of gene matching in bioinformatics is presented to verify the system's effectiveness.

Keywords: multi-level parallel programming, hybrid parallel programming, visual modeling, DSL.

1 Introduction

With the development of multi-core processors [1], it has become the development trend of cluster systems that the computer architecture of each computing node will

* Corresponding author.

V. Khachidze et al. (Eds.): iCETS 2012, CCIS 332, pp. 551–560, 2012.

become multi-core processor. There are at least two levels of architectures in this kind of cluster system, namely the distributed memory architecture between computing nodes and the shared memory architecture inside computing nodes. This kind of cluster system is called multi-level hybrid parallel computing hardware environment.

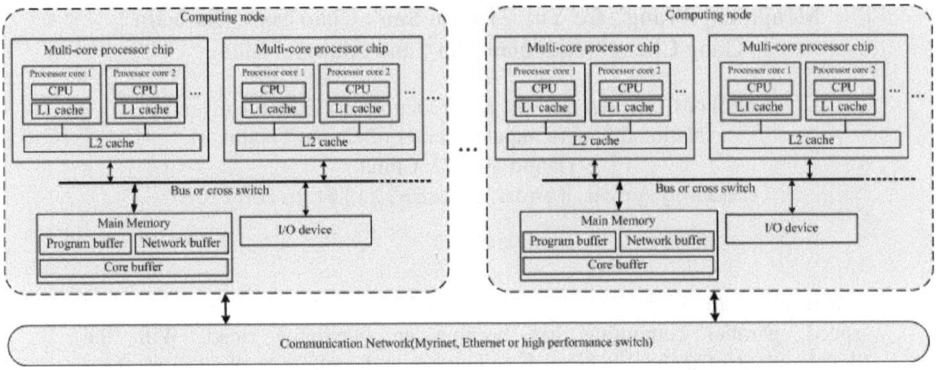

Fig. 1. The hardware architecture of multi-level parallel computing environment

The hardware architecture of multi-level parallel computing environment is shown in Figure 1. A hierarchical organizational structure and network interconnection is presented in the figure. Distributed internet architecture is applied between nodes with independent address space. Processor chips inside a node constitute a shared memory multiprocessor system. And a shared cache system on a chip is embedded inside of processor chip. In order to make full use of various levels of parallelism, the division and assignments of tasks in an application should be produced from outer to inner layer, and the computing synchronization and data sharing of tasks which are mapped inside and between computing nodes need to be implemented in different ways.

There exist many multi-level parallelization problems in the hardware environment of multi-level parallel computing, like the parallelism between computing nodes, between multi-processing chips inside the same computing node, and between the multi-processors inside the same chip. Such problems need to be solved by various programming models. Message passing programming model [2] and shared memory programming model [3] are used respectively between nodes and inside a node, which increases the difficulty of programming to a large extent.

To simplify the process of parallel programming and reduce the difficulty of parallel program development, specific design methods, programming models and tools for parallel programs in the hardware environment of multi-level hybrid parallel computing are required.

A visual modeling system called M-PAVM is introduced in this paper, which supports three levels modeling and is used for multi-core cluster environments. The hierarchical modeling scheme designed in this paper divides the process of parallel application modeling into three levels: task configuration, process task assignment and algorithm implementation. Programmers are able to design parallel programs at one or more levels; this also improves the reusability.

2 Related Works

The advantage of the visualization of parallel programming languages and development environments is that the program models are described in a graphical way, which is intuitive and allows programmers to develop programs without knowing the details. And the support for multi-level parallel programming environment provides reusability. In recent years, scholars have been making a large number of studies based on above issues and have achieved fruitful results.

CO_2P_3S [4] is a parallel programming environment based on design patterns and supporting parallel design patterns programming models. CO_2P_3S covers three levels of abstraction from low to high, namely original code, intermediate code and patterns. When designing parallel programs with CO_2P_3S, users should choose specific parallel pattern and define parameters at the pattern level first. And then intermediate codes of parallel framework and the pre-defined *hook* method will be produced by the code generator. The last step is to generate original codes in a particular language associated with a specific application and to run it in a specific parallel computing environment. CO_2P_3S implements the transformation and correspondence from high level abstract patterns to source code with the code generator. This idea has been adopted in a lot of visual development environments. The shortage of CO_2P_3S is that in distributed memory model, programmers must change the pattern to generate new codes through the distribution of shared memory, and from the users' view, remote exception management is needed for the distributed memory version of codes. Thus, there is still complexity in designing and developing parallel programs using CO_2P_3S.

Meander [5] is a kind of visual programming language and development environment orienting message-passing programming paradigm. Meander is implemented based on a fixed set of graphical nodes as basic elements and sequential code fragment in standard C as supplement. The advantage is that it is possible to describe the process topology by drawing a process diagram and to support the copy of process by defining templates. Meander supports hierarchical design, which allows users to encapsulate specific structural sub-graph of the detail graph in some node of the detail graph at higher level. When designing parallel programs with Meander, detail graph is needed to present the parallel control flow and to meet certain rules. Also the definition of the creation and communication of processes are required to be done at the same level. Although this approach simplifies the description of the program to a certain extent, but it will produce large and chaotic graphs for large scale programs, which makes it difficult to understand and maintain.

Parallel Application Visual Modeling (PAVM) [6] is a system that simplifies the development of parallel applications by providing a graphical user interface for visually modeling and generating corresponding source code framework according to the constructed model. Based on PAVM, this paper proposes a visual modeling methodology based on the hierarchical idea. The hierarchy modeling system is called M-PAVM, which supports three levels of abstraction when designing a parallel program in cluster environment.

M-PAVM is implemented based on DSL (Domain Specific Language) [7] [8], which is a tool developed by Microsoft to allow developers to design their own graphical tool.

3 Features of M-PAVM

3.1 The Idea of Hierarchic Modeling

The idea of hierarchic modeling in the visual modeling of multi-level parallel programs follows the design principles of partitioning and distributing tasks from top down level by level. The sets of modeling elements and construction methods of models at different levels of abstraction are provided correspondingly for models among process tasks and inside the process task. Specifically, coarse-grained task partitioning and mapping are provided at higher level of abstraction, and fine-grained task partitioning and mapping are provided at lower level of abstraction. When the task can no longer be partitioned, the algorithm description and design for the task is provided.

For model element instance that has been created in the model view of upper level, designers are able to design its implementation method in the model view of the next level in order to achieve the goal of refining the process of modeling level by level. The advantage of this approach is that the isolation of abstraction model and implementation model not only ensures that a change of model at certain modeling level will not affect other modeling levels, but also allows an abstract model has different implementation models, which is good to maintain, reuse and change the program model. At each level, the process of visual modeling follows the specifications based on model elements and construction rules.

3.2 Architecture of M-PAVM

M-PAVM divides the process of parallel application modeling into three levels: task configuration, process task assignment and algorithm implementation.

The first level is task configuration, whose role is to configure the multi-process execution environment for parallel programs based on the hardware architecture of multi-level parallel computing environment. At this level, static task models are created to implement the coarse-gained task division associated with the platform architecture and mapping from tasks to computing nodes. A series of process tasks or groups of process tasks are obtained when finishing modeling at this level.

The level of process task assignment is responsible for constructing the implementation model on corresponding computing nodes based on the task models created at the first level. Generally speaking, modeling at this level is the most complex and difficult. Two steps are proposed to complete the process of modeling: firstly certain method of division (data division or task division) is selected to divide the process task into a set of sub-tasks, and secondly each task or task group that can no longer be divided is mapped to the execution components of threads to form a good-encapsulated thread task.

Specific algorithm and control logic are designed at the last level, which is unrelated to the platform architecture.

3.3 The Level of Task Configuration

The entire task is divided preliminary according to the network topology among computing nodes, the distribution of resources and the characteristics of applications. The goal of coarse-grained division is to reduce the computing scale effectively through data division or task division, so as to reduce the computing time and improve the efficiency of execution. Generally, a simple dividing policy is enough to distribute the total amount of computation onto each computing node reasonably.

The level of task configuration includes two basic modeling elements: *Master* and *Worker*, and both of them have configurable properties. Table 1 shows the properties of these two modeling elements.

Table 1. Properties of *Master* and *Worker*

Name	Master	Worker
Graphical Symbol		
Property	Name	Name
	Host	Host
	Path	Path
		ProcessNum
	Parameter	Parameter
	Implementation	Implementation

- ➢ Name: the name of the process defined by user.
- ➢ Host: the computing node executed this process, which can be an IP address or the machine name (e.g. node01).
- ➢ Path: the path where the executable file of the process exists.
- ➢ ProcessNum: the number of processes executing the task. In a master-slave structure, the number of master is 1 as default.
- ➢ Parameter: parameters that passed to tasks.
- ➢ Implementation: a pointer to the process task implementation model. When this modeling element is double clicked, another edit view will be opened, and different *Worker* may point to the same implementation model.

3.4 The Level of Process Task Assignment

After configuring the execution environment for multi-processes, an important factor to ensure the high efficiency of each computing node is that process tasks should be divided further and distributed to the processor cores of corresponding computing node. Main work within a process typically includes: getting assigned tasks through communication, distributing tasks dynamically and broadcasting and moving intermediate data and results. Above functions can be modeled at the level of process task assignment.

Table 2 shows the modeling elements of this level. Most of these modeling elements support flexible property definition. *Name* is the unique handler identifying components. The property representing scale supports the reuse of components, for example, *Capacity* of ThreadPool specifies the maximum number of threads and *Scale* of ThreadGroup defines the number of threads in the current thread group. *PointerToImpleModel* points to the control flow model in the level of algorithm implementation. *CustomParameter* passes the parameters when assigning the tasks. *Scheduler* is a special component that belongs to the modeling system which doesn't have any editable properties and cannot be customized by users.

Table 2. Modeling elements the level of process task assignment

Name	Graphical symbol	Property
Subtask		TaskNumber, TaskScale, TaskBoundary, CustomParameter
Scheduler	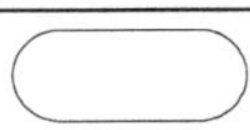	Identifier
ThreadPool	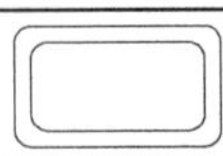	Name, Capacity, PointerToImpleModel, CustomParameter
ThreadGroup		Name, Scale, PointerToImpleModel, CustomParameter
FunctionCall	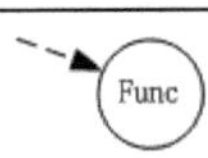	Name, CustomParameter

3.5 The Level of Algorithm Implementation

After the modeling at the level of task configuration and process task assignment, the last work that the programmers need to do is to construct concrete realization model which is responsible for the detailed computing and control logic.

At the level of algorithm implementation, specific symbols are used to describe the control flow of algorithms. Compared with the level of process task assignment, variables, functions and thread operations defined at this level are generally local.

In the system of M-PAVM, the modeling elements and rules of the level of algorithm implementation are just the same as those in the system of PAVM [6].

4 Implementation

M-PAVM is implemented with Microsoft Visual Studio DSL tools. Three types of models are registered in the guest operating system.

Figure 2 shows an example model at the level of task configuration. The arrow represents the assignment from master to worker. A multi-process execution environment with one master process and three worker processes is configured in this model.

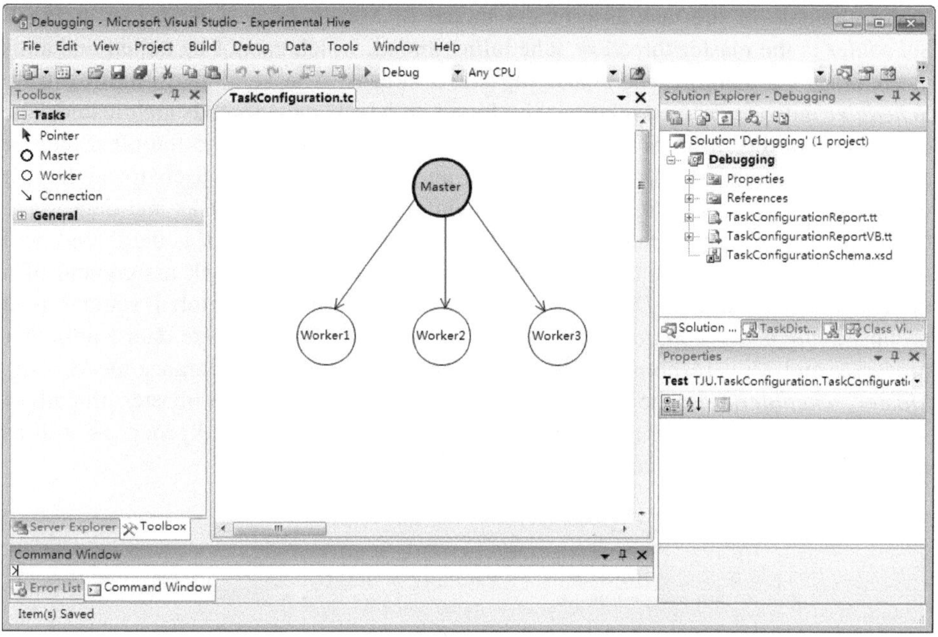

Fig. 2. An example model at the level of task configuration

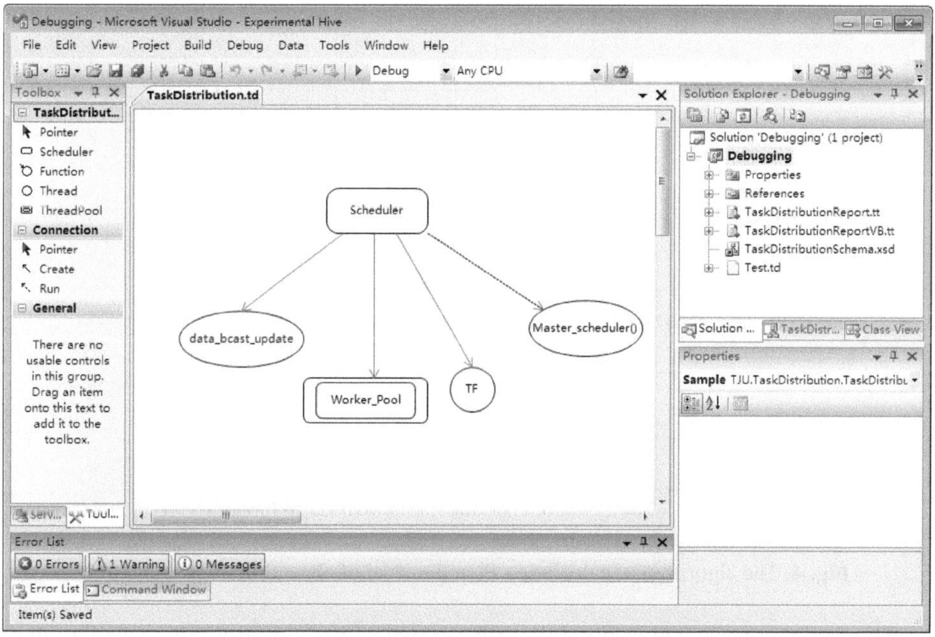

Fig. 3. The process task assignment of Master process

An example of the task assignment model of Master process is shown in Fig.3. *Scheduler* is the master thread or scheduling thread, which cannot be edited and aims at creating, maintaining and managing slave threads. The solid lines starting from *Scheduler* indicate derived relationship, based on which slave threads are created. The dash lines starting from *Scheduler* indicate calling relationship and the other side of the dash line is a master thread or function interface provided for users to implement the division, dynamic assignment and scheduling of computing tasks and data in the thread pool or among thread groups. In this example, *Worker_Pool* is the thread pool of the master process, each thread of which is responsible for task assignment of a certain worker process. *Data_bcast_update* and *TF* are both global static thread groups. *Data_bcast_update* is responsible for receiving intermediate data from other processes and *TF* is responsible for maintaining the thread fault tolerance mechanism. *Master_scheduler()* is the interface provided for users by the master thread or scheduling thread, aiming at scheduling the thread pool and thread group, as well as assigning and scheduling computing tasks and data dynamically.

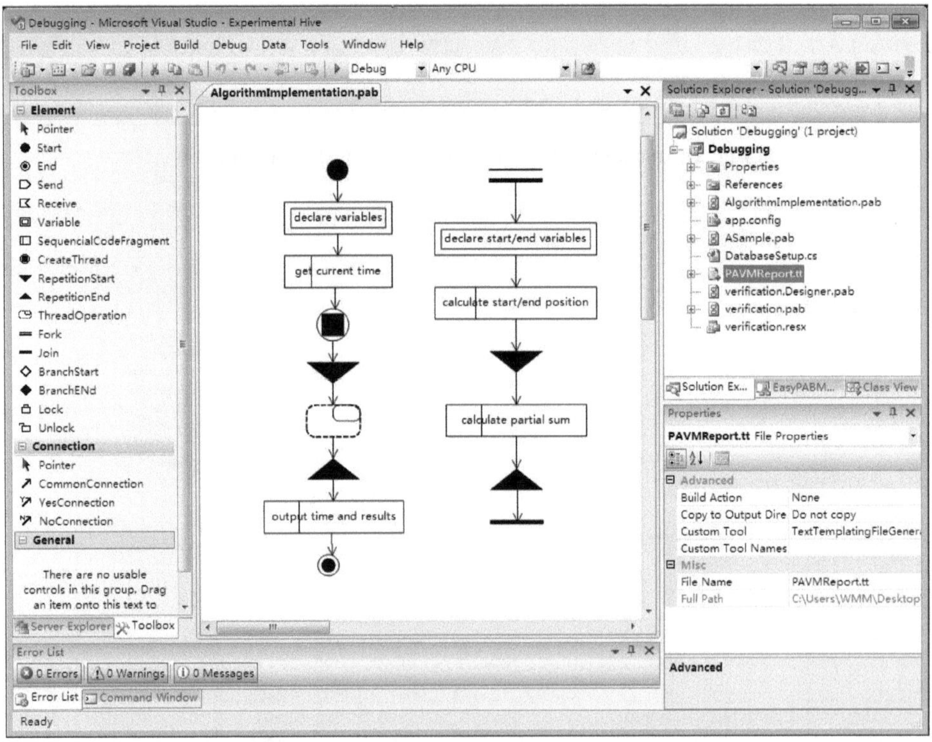

Fig. 4. The algorithm of calculating Pi at the level of algorithm implementation

The model constructed in Fig.4 describes a typical parallel program –calculating pi through the integral method. It is an example of modeling at the level of algorithm implementation.

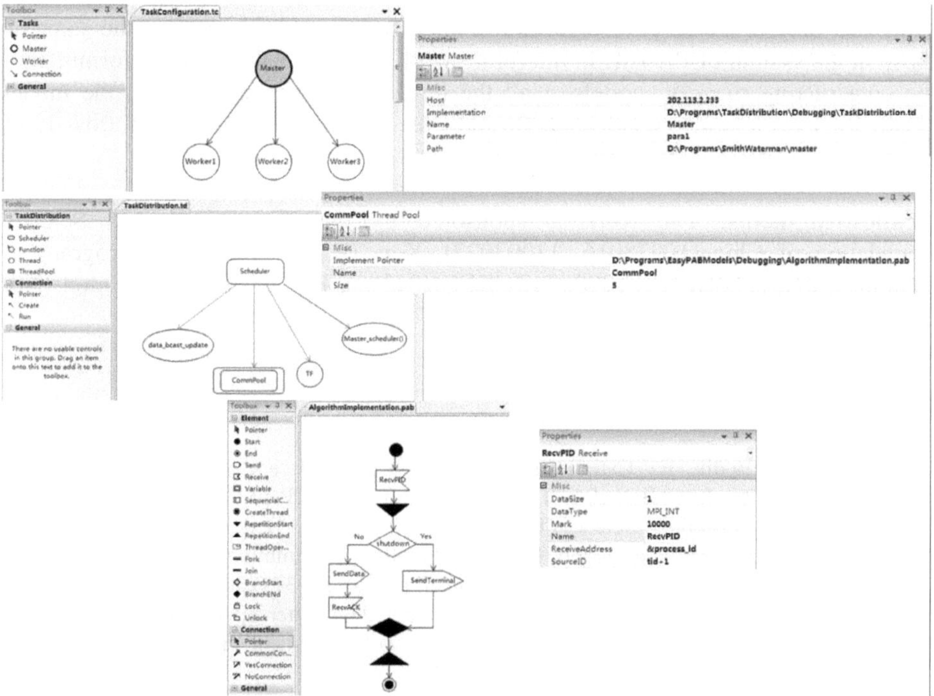

Fig. 5. A global view of modeling example constructed with the system of M-PAVM

Fig.5. is a global view of modeling example constructed with the system of M-PAVM. These models represent the parallel application searching for matching genes based on Smith-Waterman algorithm [9] in the field of bioinformatics. *Master* at the level of task configuration is implemented with the model constructed at the level of process task assignment. And the modeling element *CommPool* is implemented with the model at the level of algorithm implementation. The windows on the right side of Fig.6 are corresponding to the property configuration windows of modeling elements *Master*, *CommPool* and *RecvPID*.

5 Summary and Future Work

M-PAVM is a hierarchical modeling system based on the hardware architecture of multi-level parallel computing environment. With the help of M-PAVM, programmers are able to model parallel applications visually at three levels from top down, namely, the level of task configuration, process task assignment and algorithm implementation. M-PAVM provides reusable modules to developers and helps them reuse existing solutions for certain applications. M-PAVM is implemented with Microsoft Visual Studio DSL tools.

M-PAVM is still under development and there are a lot of improvements can be made. At all the three modeling levels, model verification and code generation are supported only at the level of algorithm implementation, which are just the same as those in the system of PAVM. In the future work, we will make effort in formulating the constructing rules of models at all the three levels, based on which the model verification work is also conducted. Besides, the automatic generation of cross-level code is also worth to be researched.

Acknowledgments. The work is sponsored by the National Natural Science Foundation of China(10978016, 11003027), Key Technologies R&D Program of Tianjin, China (11ZKFGX01000, 11ZCKFGX04200), FP7 of European Union (No. 287746).

References

1. Asanovic, K., Bodik, R., Catanzaro, B., et al.: The Landscape of Parallel Computing Research: A View from Berkeley. Technical Report No. UCB/EECS-2006-183. Electrical Engineering and Computer Sciences University of California at Berkeley (December 2006)
2. Bova, S.W., Breshears, C.P., Gabb, H., et al.: Parallel programming with message passing and directives. Computing in Science & Engineering 3(5), 22–37 (2001)
3. Giloi, W.K.: Parallel programming models and their interdependence with parallel architectures. In: Proceedings of Programming Models for Massively Parallel Computers, pp. 2–11 (1993)
4. Anvik, J., Schaeffer, J., Szafron, D., et al.: Asserting the utility of CO2P3S using the Cowichan problem set. Journal of Parallel and Distributed Computing 65(12), 1542–1557 (2005)
5. Giese, H., Wirtz, G.: Modular development of correct MEANDER programs. In: Proceedings of International Conference on Parallel and Distributed Processing Techniques and Applications, Las Vegas (1997)
6. Wang, M., Yu, C., Sun, J., et al.: Visual Modeling for Parallel Programming based on DSL. In: 3rd IEEE International Conference on Cloud Computing Technology and Science, CloudCom 2011, pp. 623–627 (2011)
7. Cook, S., Jones, G., Kent, S., Wills, A.C.: Domain-Specific Development with Visual Studio DSL Tools. Pearson Education, Inc., Boston (2007)
8. Visual Studio Visualization & Modeling SDK (DSL Tools), `http://social.msdn.microsoft.com/Forums/zh-CN/dslvsarchx/threads`
9. Smith, T.F., Waterman, M.S.: Identification of Common Molecular Subsequences. J. Mol. Biol. 147, 195–197 (1981)

A Framework for Multi-agent-Based Stock Market Simulation on Parallel Environment

Wang Chun-yu[1], Wu Hu-tong[1,*], Sun Chao, Sun Ji-zhou[1], Li Yue-lei[2], Wang Jian-jun[1], and Yu Ce[1]

[1] School of Computer Science and Technology, Tianjin University, Tianjin 300072, China
wht@tju.edu.cn
[2] School of Management, Tianjin University, Tianjin 300072, China

Abstract. Multi-agent-based modeling is an efficient way to simulate the stock market which can be regarded as a complex adaptive system. This paper introduces a framework to support massive amounts of agents in the stock market simulation on distributed parallel environment. The framework consists primarily of the market server and massive amounts of agents implemented base on Erlang language. It provides an interface for decision mechanism of agents and interface for auction rules of market server. The experiment is established in a distributed environment and presents a certain scalability of the framework.

Keywords: multi-agent-based modeling, simulation of stock market, parallel programming, Erlang.

1 Introduction

The simulation of stock market is an important method for the research on the behavior of the financial system. By comparing the data from the simulation market with that of real market, we can propose a more precise model of real market. The more accurately the simulation reflects the real one, the more accurately can we learn about the whole real market, and the more accurately is the decision made with the data from the simulation market.

A stock market is a complex adaptive system (CAS)[1]. Currently the most efficient way to simulate the CAS is agent-based modeling (ABM)[12], which focuses on individual activities, especially the interaction among individuals and the interaction between individuals and their environment[2]. Thus, we apply the idea of ABM to the stock market simulation model. In the simulation model, agents represent various investors in the real market, and they all have their own properties and decision mechanisms.[3] In the real world, all the investors operate concurrently, so we must make all the agents in the system run in parallel.

The system model consists primarily of market server, massive amount of agents and the messages passing among them. Considering the massive agents and messages,

[*] Corresponding author.

V. Khachidze et al. (Eds.): iCETS 2012, CCIS 332, pp. 561–570, 2012.

we implement the framework with Erlang, a message-passing oriented programming language which can easily create massive lightweight processes. [4]

The rest of this paper is organized as the follows. Section 2 describes the related works on ABM method and stock market simulation. In section 3, the paper presents the architecture of the framework in detail. The implementation of each module is presented in section 4 and experiment results are given in section 5. We conclude this paper with future works in section 6.

2 Related Works

Most platforms for financial simulation are based on the ABM method, such as Repast, Swam, ASM, etc.

Repast (Recursive Porous Agent Simulation Toolkit)[5] is a set of libraries that allows programmers to build simulation environments, create agents in social networks, collect data from simulations automatically, and build user interfaces easily.[7] Its features and design owe a lot to Swarm, one of the first agent-based modeling libraries. Both Repast and Swarm provide the interfaces and function libraries for easier programming in agent-based modeling.

While Repast and Swarm are designed as agent-based simulation platforms for social science applications, Artificial Stock Market (ASM) [2] is designed specifically for stock market simulation. ASM is a system with many trading strategies which are improved over time. It is one of the first agent-based models of a financial market, developed by W. Brain Arthur, John Holland et al at Santa Fe Institute in the early 1990s.[6]

Agents in these platforms or systems are trading in a sequential mode, while in the real market the investors are trading concurrently. To simulate the concurrent behavior of agents, Repast HPC implements the core Repast Simphony concepts (e.g. contexts and projections), modifying them to work in a parallel distributed environment.

In Repast HPC, message passing is implemented with MPI. As the messages and processes in MPI are of heavyweight, there may be a limit of the system performance and scalability. In this paper, we import Erlang, a language designed to deal with concurrent affairs. It is a message-passing oriented language, which can make the system high-efficient in communicating among processes. Besides, Erlang has its own process called Erlang Process, a much lighter process compared to the system process, and the processes are completely independent from each other. This feature makes it much easier to scale up an Erlang system. Therefore, we implement the framework with Erlang, and the details of the framework are described in the next section.

3 Framework Architecture

There are four modules in the framework: agent module, market module, socket layer and database module. The agent module communicates with the market module through the socket layer, so that the framework can support a distributed environment.

Orders and trading records are stored in the database, and the database module contains the database itself and all the operations on the database. The relation among all the modules is shown in Fig. **1**.

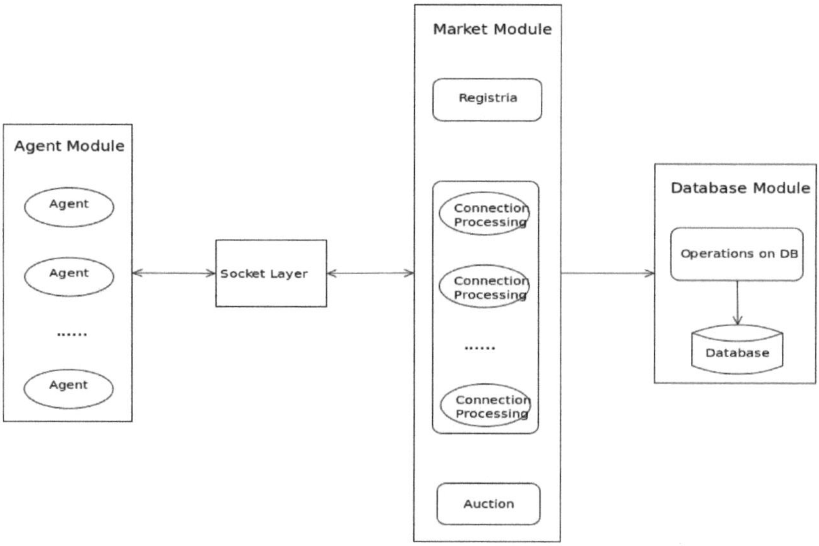

Fig. 1. Modules of the Framework

3.1 The Socket Layer

The socket layer integrates those operations related to socket programming, following the TCP network protocol. With socket programming, agents deployed to different nodes can communicate with each other and the market server. This module releases the agent module and market module from complex low-level communications between physical nodes, so that the two modules only need to focus on the functional operations of the framework.

A message in Erlang is a specific data structure called Erlang term, while messages transferred between sockets are of binary form. So every time a socket is created, a middle man process (such as MM_A and MM_B in Figure 2) is spawned to parse Erlang terms to binary code and vice versa. The middle man process also monitors the close of the socket and the exit of the Erlang process.

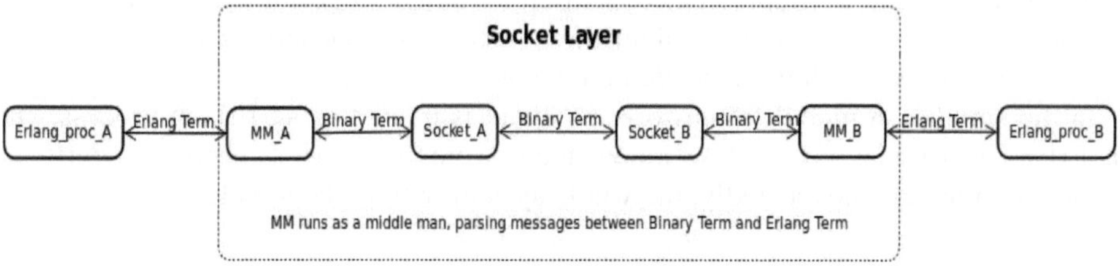

Fig. 2. Socket Layer

3.2 Agent Module

In agent module, the fundamental operations of agents are included. An agent first connects to the market server at certain host and port. After the connection is set up, the agent can get the pid of a middle man process (referred to MMpid in Figure 3), and then gets a unique ID number from the server to identify itself. The agent then begins its processing cycle: Continuously invoke an interface to make decisions about whether to sell or bid for stocks, then send orders generated in the decision process. The flow of an agent is shown in Figure 3:

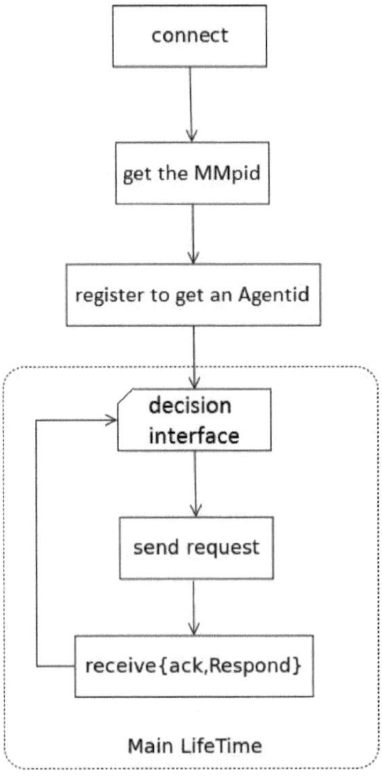

Fig. 3. Execution Flow of an Agent Process

The interface can be implemented with either simple algorithms just like random decision-making or complex algorithms such as Genetic Algorithm[8] and Neural_network Algorithm[8], depended on the users' specification.

In the simulation model framework, an agent is treated as an Erlang process, and an Erlang process is completely independent from the others. Therefore, once an agent is terminated unexpectedly, the whole system will not be affected.

3.3 Market Module

There are three sets of functions in the market module, which respectively deal with the connections from agents, registration of agents and the auction procedure. Details are shown in Figure 4 below.

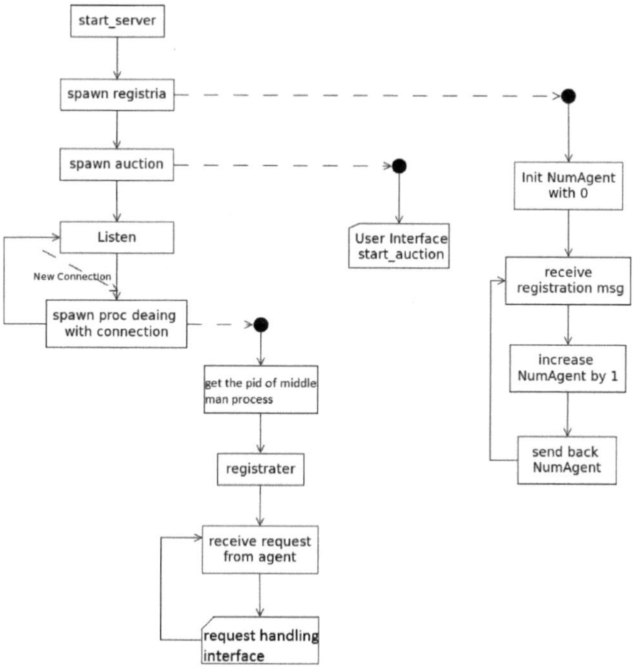

Fig. 4. Execution Flow of Market Server

➢ Connections Handling

Once an agent is successfully connected to the server, the server spawns a new Erlang process to handle this connection. The newly spawned process first gets the pid of a middle man process to communicate with sockets. Then it sends a registration message to the registrar process to get an identifier for the agent. After the registration, the process circularly invokes the request handling interface to deal with all the requests (mainly order submission at current stage).

The request handling interface greatly reduces the code's coupling, making it easier for users to modify the handling method or extend the server to deal with more types of requests. In the model system, as the most common request is order submission, we initialize the interface with a method of storing the orders into the database.

➢ Registrar

A registrar in the market server is treated as an Erlang process. The market server has only one registrar process to deal with the registration of all the agents. When the registrar process receives a registration request, it updates a global variable to get the next agent ID, and then sends the ID number back. If several processes request for registration at the exact same time, the registrar process ensures each process get the correct identifiers, due to the message processing mechanism of Erlang.

➢ Auction Procedure

The auction procedure is an Erlang process which fetches orders from database, then matches orders under a certain rule, generating a trading record, and finally writes the trading record back to the database. This procedure is repeated continuously, as is done in the real markets. The match rule is designed to be an interface for financial experts, because they may frequently modify the rule to do research work.

3.4 The Database Module

The database module consists of the database itself and all the operations on the database, such as creating tables, inserting or deleting items, etc.

Erlang has its own database, Mnesia, which gives a better support for fast key-value lookups, and many other features needed by a distributed, massively concurrent system. Erlang also provides open source drivers and APIs for some common database, such as MySQL, Berkeley DB, etc.[4]

As Mnesia is designed to store Erlang terms, it provides a good support for the data in an Erlang system. Therefore, we still choose Mnesia as the database, although the storage of Mnesia has an up-limit of 2GB, which can be ignored for the present stage. With the extension of the system, we may replace Mnesia with a more capable database, like MySQL. This change will not present much of a problem, as we have designed an interface containing all the operations on the database; therefore, we can manage the change by just modifying the interface instead of the market module.

4 Implementation

In this section, we present the implementation of the socket layer and market module in detail, while agent module and database module in brief.

➢ The Socket Layer

The middle man process is the most important in Socket layer, as it is treated as a message bridge between Erlang processes and sockets. The crucial codes of a middle man process are shown in Figure 5. In the codes, "Socket" and "ControlPid" respectively denote the identifier of the socket and Erlang process that indirectly communicate with each other through the middle man process. Messages with the head of "tcp" are from the socket. They are decoded to Erlang terms and then forwarded to the Erlang process the ContrlPid refers to. In a similar way, messages with the head of "send" are from the Erlang process and can be forwarded to the socket after encoded to binary form. If the middle man process receives messages with the head of "tcp_closed", it will send a message to inform the Erlang process of the close. When an exit signal of the Erlang process "EXIT" is trapped, the middle man process will directly close the socket.

The middle man process will continuously handle the messages from the Erlang process and sockets until either of them exit or close.

```
loop(Socket, ControlPid) ->
    receive
        %% if the MM receives the message of {tcp, Socket, Bin}
        {tcp, Socket, Bin} ->
            %% decode the Bin to Term
            Term = binary_to_term(Bin),
            %% send the message {chan, self(), Term} to the process identified by ControlPid
            ControlPid ! {chan, self(), Term},
            loop(Socket, ControlPid);
        {tcp_closed, Socket} ->
            ControlPid ! {chan_closed, self()};
        {send, Term} ->
            %% encode the Term to binary form, and then send it to the Socket
            gen_tcp:send(Socket, term_to_binary(Term)),
            loop(Socket, ControlPid);
        {'EXIT', ControlPid, Why} ->
            %% close the Socket
            gen_tcp:close(Socket);
        close ->
            gen_tcp:close(Socket);
        Other ->
            io:format("protocol error:~p~n", [Other]),
            loop(Socket, ControlPid)
    end.
```

Fig. 5. Key Code of a Middle Man Process

➢ Agent Module

In agent module, there are three simple functions and one interface to implement all the operations of agents. Function "connect (Host, Port, Service)" implements the connection and registration to the market server. "rpc (Dest, Request)" is invoked when agents send requests to the server. And "disconnect()" is called to disconnect the connection. The interface is the decision interface whose return value should either be {yes, order, OrderContent} or {no, no_orders}, respectively indicating the decision is to send OrderContent to the server or to do nothing.

➢ Market Module

The most crucial part of the market server is to handle multiple connections from agents, and the implementation is illustrated in Figure 6. After the server starts listen at a specific port, it will split to two parts, as is presented in segment 1. One of them (segment 2) deals with the new connections, and the other (segment 3) monitors the active connections. Every time there is a new connection, the listening function spawns a new process, denoted by "conProcess", to execute the function "handle_a_connection", add the new conProcess to a list containing all the live conProcesses, and then go on listening with the new list. When a connection is cut down, the conProcess related with it exits subsequently, and the monitor_connections function will trap the exit signal and delete the conProcess from the list.

➢ Database Module

In Mnesia, the tables attributes is defined in records, a data structure of Erlang. In the framework, there are 5 tables, whose definitions are described in Figure 7. In each record, the first element denotes the name of a table, and the second element included in the curly braces is the attributes of the table. The operations on the database are implemented with the BIFs (Build in Functions) of Mnesia.

```
%% segment 1

%% Listen at the port Port
Listen = gen_tcp:listen(Port),
%% spawn a new process to deal with new connections
spawn_link(fun(Listen) -> listening(Listen, [])),
%% a function in master process;
%% handle all the active connections
monitor_connections([]).


%% segment 2

%% ConnectionList contains all the alive conProcesses
listening(Listen,ConnectionList) ->
    %% accept a connection
    Socket = gen_tcp:accept(Listen),
    %% spawn a conProcess to execute the function 'handle_a_connection',
    %% the function will deal with the request from the Socket
    NewConnection = spwan_link(fun(Socket) -> handle_a_connection(Socket)),
    %% add the new conProcess to the ConnectionList
    NewConnectionList = [NewConnection|ConnectionList],
    listening(Listen,NewConnectionList).


%% segment 3

monitor_connections(ConnectionList) ->
    receive
        %% if receive the exit signal of Pid
        {'EXIT', Pid, _Why} ->
            %% delete the process from the ConnectionList
            NewConnectionList = lists:delete(Pid, ConnectionList),
            monitor_connections(NewConnectionList)
    end.
```

Fig. 6. Code Fragment to Handle Multiple Connections

```
%%
-record(id_table, {item,current_id}).
-record(sell_order_table,{orderid,agentid,stockid,amount,price,date,time,doneTag}).
-record(buy_order_table,{orderid,agentid,stockid,amount,price,date,time,doneTag}).
-record(trading_record_table,{tradingid,sell_orderid,buy_orderid,amount,price,date,time}).
-record(stock_table,{stockid,code,name}).
```

Fig. 7. Tables Definitions

5 Experiment

The experiment environment is set up with two physical nodes with erts-5.9 (Erlang Runtime System) installed. The memory of one node is 2GB, and the memory of the other is 4GB. To run the system, we implement the decision interface with a simple random algorithm, and the auction rule is such a simple mechanism that it just matches the two orders if the buy price is greater than or equal to the sell price.

There are two cases in the experiment.

In the first case, the market module and the database module are deployed to the node with a memory of 4GB, denoted by market node, and the agent module is deployed to the node with a memory of 2GB, denoted by agent node; the socket layer is deployed to both nodes. We specify the amount of agents running on the agent node with the argument AgentNum. With the increase of AgentNum, the maximum agentid, which denotes the actual amount of agents connected to the server, should increase correspondingly. Table 1 shows the correlation of AgentNum and the maximum agentid.

Table 1. Correlation of AgentNum and maximum agented

AgentNum	500	1000	1010	1020	1030	1500
MaxId	500	1000	1010	1019	1019	1019

The figures in Table 1 indicate that the amount of agents running on the agent node is up to 1019 when the argument AgentNum is set to a number much larger than 1019. The excess agents may be denied by the server for it is not capable to handle so many connections, or they are not started successfully due to the limited resources on agent node. We design a second case to find the possible reason.

In the second case, the deployment is similar to that of the first case unless that we deploy the agent module to both nodes. The argument AgentNum on each node is set to 1019. In such conditions, actual amount of agents connected to the server is 2038, which indicates that the problem is not caused by the market server.

Based on the result, we can derive that the amount of agents running on a node is limited by the memory resources of the node. Thus we can increase the amount of agents by adding physical nodes to the system. However, with the expansion of the system, the market server's capability to handle massive connections is a potential bottleneck, which will be addressed in future works.

6 Summary and Future Work

With the help of the framework, financial experts can focus on the core algorithms affecting the stock markets, and need not be concerned with the details in the scope of computer science, such as how the agents communicate with the market. As long as users fill the framework with the two algorithms: decision mechanism and auction rules, they can acquire an integrated system of stock market simulation.

As the framework gives a good support to parallel environment, it is assured that the massive agents can think and decide concurrently as the real investors do. Furthermore, with socket programming, distributed environment is also well supported, contributing to improving the scalability of the framework. With respect to the performance of the framework, it shows certain capability of fault tolerance and high efficiency in message passing, which are respectively due to the robust processes in Erlang and its message passing mechanism.

At the same time, the framework still has much room for improvement, especially in the market module. It is crucial to improve the capability of market server to handle thousands of connections. In the agent module, we can initialize all the agents with different parameters to create various agents, and provide the mechanism for agents to communicate with each other. Besides, the graphical user interface will be designed for visualization.

Acknowledgments. The work is sponsored by the National Natural Science Foundation of China (71131007, 61039001), Key Technologies R&D Program of Tianjin, China (11ZKFGX01000, 11ZCKFGX04200), and FP7 of European Union (No. 287746).

References

1. Nolfi, S.: Behaviour as a Complex Adaptive System: On the role of Self-Organization in the Development of Individual and Collective Behaviour. Complexus 2(3-4), 195–203 (2004)
2. Liao, S.-Y., Dai, J.-H.: Study on Complex Adaptive System and Agent-Based Modeling & Simulation. Journal of System Simulation 16(1), 113–117 (2004)
3. Johnson, P.E.: Agent-Based Modeling What I Learned From the Artificial Stock Market. Social Science Computer Review 20(2), 174–186 (2002)
4. Kluger, B.D., McBride, M.E.: Intraday Trading Patterns in an Intelligent Autonomous Agent-based Stock Market. Journal of Economic Behavior & Organization 79(3), 226–245 (2011)
5. Cesarini, F., Tbompson, S.: Programming Erlang, pp. 1-14, 323–327, 293–299. Southeast University Press, Nanjing (2010)
6. Tesfatsion, L.: General Software and Toolkits, Agent-Based Computational Economics (ACE) and Complex Adaptive Systems (CAS) (EB/OL) (April 26, 2012), `http://www2.econ.iastate.edu/tesfatsi/acecode.html`
7. Ehrentreich, N.: Technical trading in the Santa Fe Institute Artificial Stock Market revisited. Journal of Economic Behavior & Organization 61(4), 599–616 (2006)
8. Gilbert, N., Bankes, S.: Platforms and Methods for Agent-based Modeling. Proceedings of National Academy of Sciences of the United States of the America 99(3), 7197–7198 (2002)
9. Gilbert, N., Terna, P.: How to Build and Use Agent-based Models in Social Science. Mind & Society 1(1), 57–72 (2000)

Research on Police Performance Appraisal Early Warning Methods Based on Improved Decision Tree Algorithm

Yumei Cui, Jinduo Xu, and Linying Xu

School of Computer Science and Technology, Tianjin University, 92 Weijin Road, Nankai District, Tianjin, P.R. China
cuiandxu@126.com, {jinduoxu,linyingxu}@tju.edu.cn

Abstract. With the help of Police Performance Appraisal System, the working quality of the Public Security Organs of Tianjin has been improved. As a part of the system, Police Performance Appraisal Early Warning can accelerate feedback speed and improve the efficiency of the performance appraisal. This paper aims at proposing an improved decision tree classification algorithm based on ID3 algorithm to raise the accuracy of early warning. The attribute selection measure of the improved ID3 algorithm is determined by information gain, the attribute significance and the number of attribute values, which not only overcomes the disadvantage of the gain criterion tends to favor attributes with many values of ID3 algorithm, but also considers the dependence between the attributes. The datasets used by experiments come from the Police Performance Appraisal Early Warning System and the UCI Machine Learning Repository respectively. The comparative analysis of the experimental results shows that the improved ID3 algorithm is more accurate and stable.

Keywords: Early Warning, decision tree, classification, rough set, improved ID3 algorithm.

1 Introduction

The police performance is divided into individual performance and unit performance, and expects to improve the working quality of the public security organs. With the development of information technology, office automation, and e-government, vast amounts of data has been accumulated in the field of police performance appraisal. By analyzing and processing such a large number of historical data, performance appraisal early warning analysis can be achieved on all levels of Social Security Control Department, which can not only increase the speed of feedback and enhanced the effect of police performance appraisal, but also help to maintain social harmony and stability by improving the overall performance of Social Security Control Department.

In order to obtain the early warning level objectively, accurately, and quickly, it is a good choice to use the decision tree which has the high efficiency, the higher

V. Khachidze et al. (Eds.): iCETS 2012, CCIS 332, pp. 571–583, 2012.

accuracy and the intuitive classification rules[1][2]. Usually, the decision tree uses an ID3 algorithm. However, the ID3 algorithm has shortcoming of the gain, as criterion tends to favor attributes with many values [1], besides, the Performance Appraisal Early Warning System has its own specialty, such as the large number of performance indicators and the difference between the values of the performance indicators. So, the accuracy of early warning level obtained by using ID3 algorithm is unsatisfactory or even meaningless. In order to overcome the above disadvantages, an improved ID3 algorithm named SNID3 algorithm based on rough set theory is proposed in this paper. The attribute selection measure of the SNID3 algorithm is determined by information gain, the attribute significance and the number of attribute values. The SNID3 algorithm not only overcomes the disadvantage of ID3 algorithm mentioned above, but also considers the dependence between the attributes, so the SNID3 algorithm is more suitable for the Police Performance Appraisal Early Warning System than ID3 algorithm.

The rest of this paper is organized as follows: Section 2 introduces related work used in this paper. The SNID3 algorithm is descried in detail in Section 3. And then in Section 4, two kind of experimental datasets are chosen to compare the classification results of classical ID3 algorithm and SNID3 algorithm. Finally, conclusions are drawn and future research is outlined in section 5.

2 Related Work

SNID3 algorithm proposed in this paper is based on rough set theory, so the basic concepts of rough set theory [3] [4] are introduced at first. And then part of previous work about applying rough set theory in the decision tree classification method is introduced and analyzed.

2.1 Basic Concepts of Rough Set

1). knowledge expression system

The basic component of the information knowledge expression system is a collection of objects. In general, an information knowledge expression system is a 4-tuple$S = \langle U, V, A, f \rangle$, where U called the universe is a finite set of objects, $A = C \cup D$ is a finite set of attributes, subset C and D denote condition attribute set and decision attribute set, respectively. $V = \cup_{r \in R} V_r$ is a collection of attribute values, where V_r means the range of attribute $r \in R$, and, $f: U \times R \rightarrow V$ is called an information function, which specifies the attribute values of an object x in U.

For$\forall B \subseteq R$, an indiscernibility relation called $\mathrm{IND}(B)$ is defined as

$$\mathrm{IND}(B) = \{(x, y) | (x, y) \in U^2, \forall a \in B (a(x) = a(y))\} \tag{1}$$

For $\forall x \in U$, the equivalence class of x in B is defined as

$$[x]_B = \{y \in U: f(y, a) = f(x, a), \forall a \in B\} \tag{2}$$

2). Lower and upper approximation

Let $S = \langle U, V, A, f \rangle$ be an information knowledge expression system, every subset $X \subseteq U$ and indiscernibility relation B. The lower approximation of X (denoted by $B_{-}(X)$) and the upper approximation of X (denoted by $B^{-}(X)$) are defined as follows:

$$B_{-}(X) = \{x | (x \in U \wedge [x]_B \subseteq X)\} \quad (3)$$

$$B^{-}(X) = \{x | (x \in U \wedge [x]_B \cap X \neq \emptyset)\} \quad (4)$$

$B_{-}(X)$ is the set of all objects from U that can be certainly classified as elements of X according to the set of attributes B. $B^{-}(X)$ is the set of objects of U which can be possibly classified as elements of X based on the set of attributes.

3). Attribute significance

Suppose the set family $F = \{X1, X2, \dots, Xn\}$ ($U = \bigcup_{i=1}^{n} X_i$) is a kind of knowledge defined on the domain U. Let condition attribute subset $B \subseteq C$ and decision attribute D, the dependency of F on B is defined as

$$\gamma_B(F) = |POS_B(F)|/|U| \quad (5)$$

where $POS_B(F)$ is defined as

$$POS_B(F) = \bigcup_{i=1}^{n} B_{-}(X_i) \quad (6)$$

It is obvious that $0 \leq \gamma_B(Q) \leq 1$ and the higher the value of $\gamma_B(Q)$ the greater the dependency of B and F.

For $\forall a \in B$, the attribute significance of a on F is defined as

$$SGF(a, B, F) = \gamma_B(F) - \gamma_{B-\{a\}}(F) \quad (7)$$

It shows that the higher the value of $SGF(a, B, F)$ the greater the impact of attribute a between the condition attributes and decision attributes.

4). Attribute reduction and core

In most cases, the classification is determined by a few or even an attribute, rather than determined by the small differences of all the attributes in the relational database. The goal of attribute reduction is to find the necessary condition attributes form the condition attributes set. The found necessary condition attributes which must have the same classification with all condition attributes for decision attribute D are called the relative reduction and the minimum subset among it is called the core.

2.2 Decision Tree Based on Rough Set Theory

This paper aims at proposing an improved decision tree classification algorithm based on ID3 algorithm to raise the accuracy of the classification results that is accurate and meaningful early warning level. At present, a lot of people work on how to improve the accuracy of the classification result of decision tree. One of the common methods is to improve or redefine the attribute selection measures [5] [6] [7]. The other common method is to prune the decision tree [8] [9] [10]. Most of the works are trying to improve the decision tree algorithm based on knowledge of data mining and machine learning [11] [12]. Hu, Deng, and Sui [13] apply principal component analysis to solve the problem that the technologies in data mining are facing massive and multi-attribute data which affect the classification accuracy. Ding, Zheng, and Zang [6], as well as Wen [14], apply the attribute reduction method based on rough set theory to extract key attributes before constructing decision tree and takes attributes significance [6] or other factors [11] into account to reduce the attribute measure of multiple value attributes which can improve accuracy by overcoming the disadvantage of the gain criterion tends to favor attributes with many values of ID3 algorithm.

3 SNID3 Algorithm

3.1 Information Gain

The notation used here is as follows. Let D, the data partition, be a training set of class-labeled tuples. Suppose the class label attribute has m distinct values defining m distinct classes, C_i (for i =1, …, m). Let $C_{i,D}$ be the set of tuples of class C_i in D. Let |D| and $|C_{i,D}|$ denote the number of tuples in D and $C_{i,D}$, respectively [15].

The entropy of D (denoted as Info(D)) is defined by

$$\text{Info}(D) = -\sum_{i=1}^{m} |C_{i,D}|/|D| \log_2(|C_{i,D}|/|D|) \tag{8}$$

where $|C_{i,D}|/|D|$ is the probability that an arbitrary tuple in D belongs to class C_i. A log function to the base 2 is used, because the information is encoded in bits. Info(D) is just the average amount of information needed to identify the class label of a tuple in D.

Now, suppose we were to partition the tuples in D on some attribute A having v distinct values, $\{a_1, a_2, \dots, a_v\}$. Attribute A can be used to split D into v partitions or subsets, $\{D_1, D_2, \dots, D_v\}$, where D_j contains those tuples in D that have outcome a_j of A. $\text{Info}_A(D)$ is defined as

$$\text{Info}_A(D) = \sum_{j=1}^{v} |D_j|/|D| * \text{Info}(D_j) \tag{9}$$

$\text{Info}_A(D)$ is the expected information required to classify a tuple from D based on the partitioning by A. The smaller the expected information required, the greater the purity of the partitions.

Information gain is defined as

$$\text{Gain}(A) = \text{Info}(D) - \text{Info}_A(D) \tag{10}$$

3.2 Information Gain Adjusting by the Weight

The key part of decision tree algorithm is the attribute selection measure. ID3 uses information gain as its attribute selection measure [15]. However, pervious work has confirmed that this method has shortcoming of the gain criterion tends to favor attributes with many values and the dependence between attributes is not taken into account.

The idea of adjusting the information gain by the weight is motivated by the work of Chun Guan and Xiaoqin Zeng [7]. In this paper, the weight is calculated based on rough set theory so as to take the dependence between the attributes into account. The weight is corresponding to the attribute significance which is calculated based on the dataset. The idea of adjusting the information gain by the number of attribute values is motivated by the work of Dianhong Wang and Liangxiao Jiang [16]. The main idea of SNID3 algorithm is to adjust the information gain by the attribute significance and the number of attribute values.

For example, the attribute significance of attribute a is defined as:

$$\mathrm{SGF}(a, C, F) = \gamma_C(F) - \gamma_{C-\{a\}}(F) \tag{11}$$

where C is the set of condition attributes. Then the weight of a is defined as:

$$\mathrm{SN}(a) = \mathrm{SGF}(a, C, F)/N_a \tag{12}$$

in which N_a represents the number of attribute a values. Then the information gain adjusted by weight is defined as:

$$\mathrm{SNGain}(a) = \mathrm{SN}(a) * \mathrm{Gain}(a) \tag{13}$$

Notice here, the above formula is established when there is at least one attribute a that SN(a) is not zero, otherwise, SNGain(a) = Gain(a) is established. The attribute a with the highest SNGain(a) is chosen as the splitting attribute at node N.

3.3 SNID3 Algorithm: SNID3_Decision_Tree. Generate a Decision Tree from the Training Tuples of Data Partition S.

Input:

Data partition, S, which is a discrete set of training tuples and their associated class labels;

Condition attribute set C and decision attribute set D.

Output: A decision tree [15].

Method:

1). Create a node N;

2). If tuples in S are all of the same class, d_i then

3). Return N as a leaf node labeled with the class d_i;

4). If C is empty then

5). Return N as a leaf node labeled with the majority class in S;

6).Calculate the information gain and importance significance of condition attributes;

7). If all the importance significance of condition attributes are zero then

8). Set the attribute with max information gain as a;

9). Else calculate the improved information gain based on importance significance and set the attribute with max improved information gain as a;

10). Label node N with a;

11). for each outcome j of a

12). Let S_j be the set of data tuples in S satisfying outcome j;

13). If S_j is empty then

14). Attach a leaf labeled with the majority class in S to node N;

15). Else attach the node returned by SNID3_decision_tree (S_j, C) to node N;
Endfor

16). Return N;

3.4 The Application of SNID3 Algorithm

The SNID3 algorithm is proposed to apply in the Police Performance Appraisal Early Warning System. Notice that the performance indicators in the above system are so much that if the decision tree is constructed based on all the indicators, the efficiency and accuracy will be affected by those indicators useless to the results. In order to get a more effective and accurate decision tree, the performance indicators that have no impact to the results need to be removed. In this paper, the attribute reduction algorithm based on rough set theory is used to reduce the attributes.

The SNID3 algorithm can be extended to the systems with characteristics such as the large number of attributes, the big difference between the values of attributes and the importance significance of attributes to obtain more accurate and stable results.

4 Experimental Analysis

The experiments in this paper are conducted with the help of Weka, which is a popular suite of machine learning software written in Java, developed at the University of Waikato, New Zealand [17]. The secondary development based on Weka is necessary because of comparative analysis of the classification results between ID3 algorithm and SNID3 algorithm. MyEclipse7.5 is chosen as development tool. The source code of Weka is imported into MyEclipse7.5. And then add the implementation of SNID3 algorithm to the source code. Both of the classification results of ID3 algorithm and SNID3 algorithm can be obtained after running the program.

As part of the program, the attribute reduction and the calculation of attribute significance are simple implemented when programming. So there are some restrictions on the datasets applied to this program such as the program can only recognize the first character of the attribute's name and the values of attribute are limited in Integer. In order to verify SNID3 algorithm, the experimental datasets must be modified. The attribute's name can be identified by a character or a digital and the values of attribute whose type is nominal are converted to Integer.

Two kinds of datasets are chosen in this paper so as to make the experiments more persuasive. One kind of datasets comes from the Police Performance Appraisal Early Warning System. We conclude that SNID3 algorithm is more suitable to the system after comparing the classification results of ID3 algorithm and SNID3 algorithm. The other kind of datasets comes from UCI Machine Learning Repository. The ID3 algorithm and SNID3 algorithm are respectively tested based on four datasets from UCI. The results show that SNID3 algorithm is not only suitable for the Police Performance Appraisal Early Warning System, but also has extensibility.

4.1 Experiment on Dataset of the Police Performance Appraisal Early Warning System

1). Data preprocessing

The main function of the Police Performance Appraisal Early Warning System is to obtain early warning level according to work evaluation of the Public Security Organs of Tianjin, which is analyzed based on the values of the performance indicators. With the help of this system, it is convenient for the units to schedule their work effectively and problems can be detected early, which is helpful to prevent the occurrence of major accidents at work. The implementation of the early warning relies mainly on the theory of decision trees. The performance indicators are considered as condition attributes, and the early warning level is considered as decision attribute. One or several decision tree constructed based on history data is used to forecast the early warning level based on the current data.

In this part, data comes from the performance evaluation data of the Public Security Organs of Tianjin in 2010. The indicators belonging to pursuit-evasion are selected to facilitate doing experiments. At the same time, the values of the selected indicators in continuous ten months are chosen as dataset. The number of instances in the dataset is one hundred and eighty and the number of attributes is thirteen. Twelve of the attributes are condition attributes belonging to C, which is the set of condition attributes. C= {a, b, c, d, e, f, g, h, i, j, k, l} = {group categories, the number of city criminals captured by police of one unit, the average number of city criminals captured by one policeman, the number of other province criminals captured by police of one unit, the average number of other province criminals captured by one policeman, the number of other province criminals born in the city captured by police of one unit, the number of criminals on the Internet before October 31 last year captured by police of one unit, the number of criminals suspected "intentional homicide" cases captured by police of one unit, the number of criminals pursued by province captured by police of one unit, the number of criminals on the run for five years or more captured by police of one unit, the number of criminals classified as B level by Ministry of Public Security captured by police of one unit, the number of criminals classified as A level by Ministry of Public Security captured by police of one unit}. The last attribute is decision attribute belonging to D. D= {m} = {early warning level}.

The processing of the data is described below. Table 1 shows the data replaced all the attributes' name by letters. Table 2 represents the data discretized based on Table 1 with appropriate discretization method. Applying the attribute reduction algorithm based on dependency to the data in Table 2, the redundant attributes are removed and the rest of attributes are belonging to C'(C'= {e, f, g, h, j}). Removing the columns of attributes that is not in C' will get the data describing in Table 3.

Table 1. The data replaced all the attributes' names with letters

No	a	b	c	d	e	f	g	h	i	j	k	l	m
1	1	51	46.3	35	31.8	11	28	3	2	0	0	0	12.00
2	1	55	49	25	33.8	1	24	0	0	2	0	0	9.47
...	...	...	...	...	...	...	...	...	...	...	...	...	...
...	...	...	...	...	...	...	...	...	...	...	...	...	...
179	3	202	143	108	94	35	46	5	10	3	0	0	10.87
180	3	233	178	143	118	29	63	1	5	2	0	0	10.72

Table 2. The data discretized based on Table 1

No	a	b	c	d	e	f	g	h	i	j	k	l	m
1	1	0	0	0	0	3	1	2	1	0	0	0	2
2	1	0	0	0	0	0	1	0	0	2	0	0	0
...	...	...	...	...	...	...	...	...	...	...	...	...	...
...	...	...	...	...	...	...	...	...	...	...	...	...	...
179	3	2	2	2	2	5	3	3	3	3	0	0	1
180	3	3	3	3	3	5	4	1	2	2	0	0	1

Table 3. The data removed the columns of attributes that is not in C'

No	e	f	g	h	j	m
1	0	3	1	2	0	2
2	0	0	1	0	2	0
...	...	...	...	...	...	...
...	...	...	...	...	...	...
179	2	5	3	3	3	1
180	3	5	4	1	2	1

2). Data test

ROC curve [17]: In signal detection theory, a receiver operating characteristic (ROC), or simply ROC curve, is a graphical plot which illustrates the performance of a binary classifier system as its discrimination threshold is varied. It is created by plotting the fraction of true positives out of the positives (TPR = true positive rate) vs. the fraction of false positives out of the negatives (FPR = false positive rate), at various threshold settings. We evaluate the test performance according to whether the ROC curve rises rapidly towards the upper right-hand corner of the graph, or whether the value of area under the curve is large. For example, if the area is close to 1.0, it indicates that the test is good. If, however, the area is to 0.5, it shows that the test is bad [18].

The accuracy in Table 4 means the percentage of correctly classified instances. It has some disadvantages as a performance estimate, such as not chance corrected and not sensitive to class distribution. So in this paper, we chose the measure of ROC Area as a secondary consideration.

The data in Table 3 is tested by ID3 algorithm and SNID3 algorithm respectively. The accuracy and ROC Area are recorded when changing the test mode between 5-fold cross-validation, 10-fold cross-validation and 20-fold cross-validation. The experimental results are shown in Table 4.

Table 4. The experimental results based on data in Table 3

Test Mode	ID3-Accuracy	ID3-ROC Area	SNID3-Accuracy	SNID3-ROC Area
5-fold cross-validation	78.3333%	0.86	79.4444%	0.863
10-fold cross-validation	76.6667%	0.853	81.1111%	0.87
20-fold cross-validation	76.6667%	0.855	79.4444%	0.861

3). Result analysis

The Figure 1 is drawn based on the data in Table 4 showing the image of the experimental results. According to Figure 1, both accuracy and ROC Area of SNID3 algorithm are higher than ID3 algorithm in all three experiments. The most obvious contrast appears when the test mode is 10-fold cross-validation. Based on the above analysis, SNID3 algorithm is more suitable for the dataset of the Police Performance Appraisal Early Warning System, with which the results are more accurate and stable.

4.2 Experiment on Dataset of UCI

1). Data preprocessing

Datasets of Soybean (Small), Zoo, Pima Indians Diabetes and Ecoli are downloaded from the website of UCI Machine Learning Repository [19]. Then the Weka is used to adjust these datasets into ARFF data format and to construct decision tree based on these datasets. In the process, several points require special attention. We change the values of decision attribute in Soybean(Small) Dataset from {D1, D2, D3, D4} to {1, 2, 3, 4}, remove the column named animal name in Zoo Dataset, and discretize the data in Pima Indians Diabetes Dataset. Finally, the column named Sequence Name is removed and the date in Ecoli Dataset is discretized.

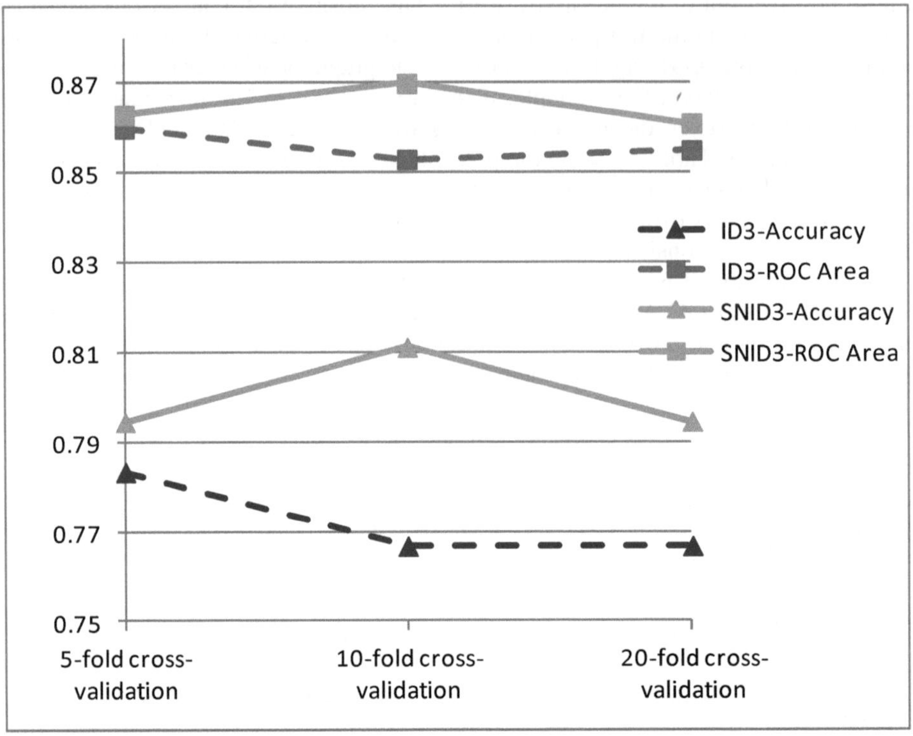

Fig. 1. The image of the experimental results drawn based on the data in Table 4

2). Data test
The above four datasets are tested by ID3 algorithm and SNID3 algorithm respectively. The accuracy and ROC Area are recorded when changing the test mode between 5-fold cross-validation, 10-fold cross-validation and 20-fold cross-validation. The experimental results show in Table 5.

3). Result analysis
We analyzed the result for each dataset separately and globally based on the experimental results shown in Table 5. For each dataset, we do three experiments. On the Soybean(Small) Dataset, there are two times the accuracy of SNID3 algorithm is higher than ID3 algorithm and one time opposite, there are two times the ROC Area of SNID3 algorithm is higher than ID3 algorithm and one time opposite. On the Zoo Dataset, both accuracy and ROC Area of SNID3 algorithm is lower than ID3 algorithm. On the Pima Indians Diabetes Dataset, both accuracy and ROC Area of SNID3 algorithm is higher than ID3 algorithm. On the Ecoli Dataset, there are two times the accuracy of SNID3 algorithm is higher than ID3 algorithm and one time opposite, there are three times the ROC Area of SNID3 algorithm is higher than ID3 algorithm.

Among all the twelve experiments, there are seven times the accuracy of SNID3 algorithm is higher than ID3 algorithm, one time is equal and four times are opposite, there are eight times the ROC Area of SNID3 is higher than ID3 algorithm and four times are opposite. The accuracy and ROC Area of ID3 algorithm are fluctuation while those of SNID3 algorithm are stable when the experimental dataset is tested with test mode of different folds of cross-validation which means the percentage of test set is different.

Table 5. The experimental results based on the selection datasets of UCI

Data Set	Test Mode	ID3-Accuracy	ID3-ROC Area	SNID3-Accuracy	SNID3-ROC Area
Soybean (Small)	5-fold cross-validation	89.3617%	0.942	97.8723%	0.983
Soybean (Small)	10-fold cross-validation	95.7447 %	0.977	97.8723%	0.983
Soybean (Small)	20-fold cross-validation	97.8723 %	0.986	97.8723%	0.983
Zoo	5-fold cross-validation	98.0198%	0.991	96.0396%	0.974
Zoo	10-fold cross-validation	98.0198%	0.991	96.0396 %	0.974
Zoo	20-fold cross-validation	97.0297%	0.986	96.0396 %	0.977
Pima Indians Diabetes	5-fold cross-validation	60.026%	0.618	61.9792%	0.648
Pima Indians Diabetes	10-fold cross-validation	58.0729%	0.605	62.6302%	0.661
Pima Indians Diabetes	20-fold cross-validation	57.6823%	0.614	63.4115%	0.684
Ecoli	5-fold cross-validation	66.9643%	0.834	68.75%	0.846
Ecoli	10-fold cross-validation	68.75%	0.839	70.2381%	0.848
Ecoli	20-fold cross-validation	69.3452%	0.849	69.0476%	0.851

Overall analysis, the SNID3 algorithm has a better accuracy and stability taking into accounts both accuracy and ROC Area on the selected four datasets.

5 Conclusion

In this paper, the SNID3 algorithm based on ID3 algorithm and rough set theory is proposed to use in the Police Performance Appraisal Early Warning System, with which the classification results are more accurate and stable. In order to overcome the disadvantage of the gain criterion tends to favor attributes with many values of ID3 algorithm, the attribute selection measure of the SNID3 algorithm is determined by information gain, the attribute significance and the number of attribute values. What is more, the measure is appropriate to consider the dependence between the attributes. Two kinds of experimental datasets are chosen in this paper. One kind of datasets comes from the Performance Appraisal Early Warning System. The other kind of datasets comes from the UCI Machine Learning Repository. These experimental datasets are tested by ID3 algorithm and SNID3 algorithm with test mode of 5-fold cross-validation, 10-fold cross-validation and 20-fold cross-validation respectively. The comparative analysis of the experimental results shows that SNID3 algorithm is more accurate and stable than ID3 algorithm. So the SNID3 algorithm is more suitable to the Police Performance Appraisal Early Warning System than the ID3 algorithm.

SNID3 algorithm is slightly inferior to the classic ID3 algorithm on the training time because of computing attribute significance additional. Therefore, it needs further research that how to reduce the calculation to improve the training time. It may be feasible to simplify the calculation of information gain through the use of mathematical knowledge [20]. Besides, the data of Police Performance Appraisal Early Warning System is not entirely discrete values and a part of continuous values need to be discretized. So the areas in continuous attributes with the simplest and the most reasonable discretization are worthy of further exploration and research.

References

1. Quinlan, J.R.: Induction of decision trees. Machine Learning 1(1), 81–106 (1986)
2. Quinlan, J.R.: C4.5: Programs for machine learning. Morgan Kaufmann Publishers, California (1993)
3. Pawlak, Z.: Information Systems Theoretical Foundations. Information Systems 6(3), 205–218 (1981)
4. Wang, G.: Rough Set Theory and Knowledge Acquisition. Xi'an Jiaotong University Press, Xi'an (2001) (in Chinese)
5. Wang, D., Jiang, L.: An Improved Attribute Selection Measure for Decision Tree Induction. In: Fourth International Conference on Fuzzy Systems and Knowledge Discovery, FSKD 2007, vol. 4, pp. 654–658 (2007)
6. Ding, B., Zheng, Y., Zang, S.: A New Decision Tree Algorithm Based on Rough Set Theory. In: Asia-Pacific Conference on Information Processing, APCIP 2009, vol. 2, pp. 326–329 (2009)
7. Guan, C., Zeng, X.: An Improved ID3 Based on Weighted Modified Information Gain. In: 2011 Seventh International Conference on Computational Intelligence and Security (CIS), pp. 1283–1285 (2011)
8. Rastogl, R., Shim, K.: PUBLIC: A Decision Tree Classifier that Integrates Building and Pruning. Data Mining and Knowledge Discovery 4, 315–344 (2000)
9. Chandra, B., Kothari, R., Paul, P.: A new node splitting measure for decision tree construction. Pattern Recognition 43, 2725–2731 (2010)
10. Wei, J., Wang, S., Yu, G., Gu, L., Wang, G., Yuan, X.: A novel method for pruning decision trees. In: 2009 International Conference on Machine Learning and Cybernetics, vol. 1, pp. 339–341 (2009)

11. Chen, J., Su, S., Xu, H.: Decision Tree Construction Algorithm Based on Multiscale Rough Set Model. In: 2011 International Conference on Computational and Information Sciences (ICCIS), pp. 247–250 (2011)
12. Takahashi, F., Abe, S.: Decision-tree-based multiclass support vector machines. In: Proceedings of the 9th International Conference on Neural Information Processing, ICONIP 2002, vol. 3, pp. 1418–1422 (2002)
13. Hu, J., Deng, J., Sui, M.: A New Approach for Decision Tree Based on Principal Component Analysis. In: International Conference on Computational Intelligence and Software Engineering, CiSE 2009, pp. 1–4 (2009)
14. Wen, W.: The Construction of Decision Tree Information Processing System Based on RoughSet Theory. In: 2010 Third International Symposium on Information Processing (ISIP), pp. 546–549 (2010)
15. Han, J., Kamber, M.: Data Mining: Concepts and Techniques, 2nd edn. Morgan Kaufmann (2005)
16. Wang, D., Jiang, L.: An Improved Attribute Selection Measure for Decision Tree Induction. In: Fourth International Conference on Fuzzy Systems and Knowledge Discovery, FSKD 2007, vol. 4, pp. 654–658 (2007)
17. Wikipedia, the free encyclopedia, http://en.wikipedia.org/wiki
18. OriginLab-Data Analysis and Graphing Software, http://www.originlab.com
19. Frank, A., Asuncion, A.: UCI Machine Learning Repository. University of California, School of Information and Computer Science, Irvine, CA (2010), http://archive.ics.uci.edu/ml
20. Chai, R., Wang, M.: A more efficient classification scheme for ID3. In: 2nd International Conference on Computer Engineering and Technology (ICCET), vol. 1, pp. V1-329–V1-332 (2010)

A GPU-Based Face Detection Algorithm for Low-Bandwidth Implementation

Feifei Li, Ming Che, and Chao Qin

School of Computer Science and Technology
Tianjin University
Tianjin China
{floria,cheming}@tju.edu.cn, a52581120@163.com

Abstract. As an indispensable prerequisite for safety monitoring and human-computer interaction, face detecting demands high real-time speed. A new parallel architecture of AdaBoost algorithm on GPU platform for detecting faces is proposed in this paper. Compared with the architectures ever been proposed before which don't fully develop the parallelism of the AdaBoost face detection algorithm, we put forward a method to compute several windows in a single thread and achieve the detection process in just one kernel, so as to increase the bandwidth between the host and the device. The experiments on the platform of GTX590 with resolution 640x480 images reach a detection speed of 25 FPS, which boosts the real-time performance validly.

Keywords: GPGPU, Parallel Computation, Face Detection, Real-time, Low-bandwidth.

1 Introduction

As one of the most important prerequisites of deeper research of human-machine interface, face detection technology calls for higher precision and more effective real-time speed. Compared with feature-based approaches to face detection, the appearance-based approach which generally relies on statistical learning seems to be more successful and robust and demands lower environmental requirements. Among these, the most widely used one is the AdaBoost face detection algorithm proposed by Viola and Jones in 2001[1]. In the algorithm, a window is used to scan an image, and the trained classifiers are computed in it to judge whether there is probably a face in the window or not.

As many classifiers are used for detecting, it is a computationally expensive task. Recently, to speed up the face detection process, people have improved the algorithm several times on CPU and reached basic real-time requirement [2[3]; however, the detection speed declines when the resolution of the image increases. Taking into consideration that it is difficult to speed up detection just on CPU, people set about developing the algorithm on CUDA,[4] released by NVIDIA which can achieve parallel computation based on hundreds of cores. The most critical demand is to fully

V. Khachidze et al. (Eds.): iCETS 2012, CCIS 332, pp. 584–591, 2012.

develop the algorithm's parallelism and design a suitable structure of threads to hide latency.

There are two usual strategies to apply AdaBoost on CUDA, namely image zoom and window zoom. Gao and Che, as well as Sharma, Thoa, and Yydyanathan [5][6] present a frame that is designed based on image zoom, which resizes an image into N layers from the original to a smaller one just as big as 20x20 scan-window. Then the scan-window on different locations of an image is disposed by one thread, and layers of the image are serially detected in different kernels. This method causes too many idle threads to hide transmission latency effectively especially when the image has been scaled smaller and it causes inadequate usage of resources. In accelerated face detection based on GPU and CUDA, [7] [8] [9] [10] the image size remains fixed and window scales up from 20x20 to about the same size of the image. Then the windows sliding by an image are parallel computed and the detection of different sizes of windows is carried out in different kernels. In that case, the thread number changes as the change of window size and the dimensions of grid and block are re-allocated for a new scale factor.

In this paper, we propose a novel algorithm based on scaling window which only launches one kernel in the detection process; as a result, bandwidth is effectively improved, and the waiting time of idle threads is decreased. In this method, each thread computes a series of scaled windows starting from the same pixel instead of a certain scale, and all threads are parallel computed.

2 Introduction of Algorithm and Detection Process

The AdaBoost face detection algorithm is based on the AdaBoost learning method to train a serial of critical features of faces through a number of samples. Then, a detection window scans in an image and features are computed and compared with thresholds to determine whether the window contains a potential face or not. The four features used in the method are shown in Figure 1, and each feature consists of two or three rectangles. Features are gained by subtracting the sum of the gray value of all pixels in black rectangle from the sum of the white one; the difference then characterizes features on different locations of a face.

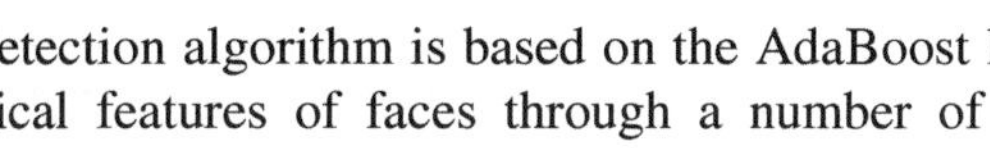

Fig. 1. Four kinds of features used in our method, containing two or three rectangles

To improve detection speed, thousands of weak classifiers, which are namely features, are combined in cascade structure to 22 stages of strong classifiers focusing attention on promising regions of the image. A window containing a potential face passes to the next stage and if not is rejected. Once it has passed all stages, the window is judged to contain a face. The cascade process is shown in figure 2. The later strong classifiers are more complex than the earlier ones; therefore, many non-face windows are rejected in the early process and much detection time is saved.

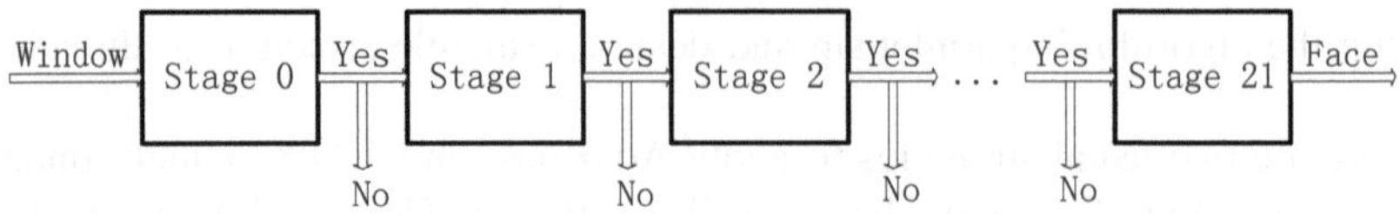

Fig. 2. Detection cascade process. The window containing a potential face is progressively retained.

Moreover, an intermediate image representation named integral image is introduced to compute features rapidly so that grayscale sum of any feature can be computed at any scale or location in constant time only through addition or subtraction of the values of the rectangular corners. The value of the integral image at location (x, y) contains the sum of all pixels above and at the left of the point. As a result, the sum of pixels within a rectangle can be computed just by four points' value. For example, the sum of all pixels in rectangle ABCD can be computed by the four points of A, B, C, and D. The formula is as follows:

$$Sum = ii(C) + ii(A) - ii(B) - ii(D)\,. \tag{1}$$

In order to achieve AdaBoost face detection algorithm on GPU, three parts of parallel structure can be designed, namely transforming a colorful image into a gray one, computing the integral image, and detecting faces. According to this, the computing tasks are allocated as follows:

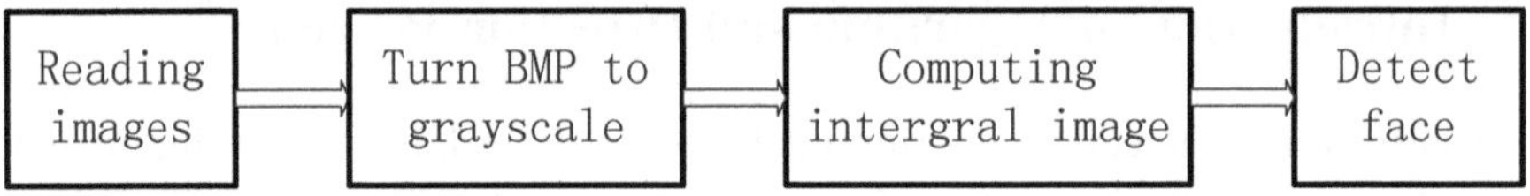

Fig. 3. The face detection process on GPU. After reading an image, turn a colorful image to grayscale and compute the integral image to prepare for following detection. Then, detect faces by computing features.

3 Structure Design of Face Detection Algorithm on GPU

3.1 Grayscale Images

Colorful images should be transformed to grayscale images before detecting, because the computation of features is based on a grayscale image. When a piece of the bitmap image is read in, it is stored as a sequence of three colors, blue and green and red. Formula (2) shows how to compute the grayscale value, in which u represents the brightness characterizing grayscale, and r, g, and b respectively represent red, green and blue:

$$u = 0.299 * r + 0.587 * g + 0.114 * b \tag{2}$$

As all pixels are independent, each pixel of a colorful image can be dealt with by one thread, so that all pixels can be parallel computed. To speed up the computation, the original image is copied from global memory to shared memory before computing. During computing, each thread is in charge of three consecutive bytes of a pixel, and then makes a calculation as per Formula (2). After computing, grayscale values are transmitted from shared memory to mapped memory at once.

As grayscale image is used frequently, we allocate a mapped memory on the host, which can be directly accessed by kernel in order to save time spent copying data between the device and the host.

3.2 Integral Image

The process of computing the integral image on GPU is divided into two steps: the first step is to compute the horizontal integral image, and the second step is to compute vertically on the basis of the former. Each step is dealt with in a kernel and the structure of both kernels is the same except for the dimensions of block and grid.

When computing horizontal integral image, there are numbers of rows in the horizontal direction and the integral of each row is gained respectively by using inclusive scan algorithm. Each row of the image is considered an array of one dimension sized N, to obtain the integral, log2n times of iteration of addition are needed, and the offset of addition begins from 1 and increases by double for one more time. Using an array of size 8 as an example, the process is shown in Figure 4:

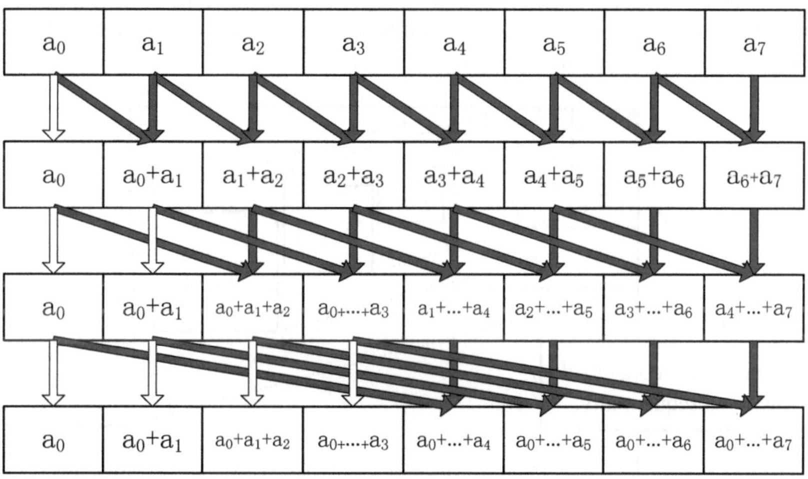

Fig. 4. The inclusive scan algorithm to gain integral image. An array of 8 elements needs 3 times operation of addition. At the first step, each two adjacent elements are added together and the results pass to the next level with a_0 directly passing to the corresponding position on the next level; at the second step, elements at intervals of 2 are added to the first two elements directly down; at the third step, elements at an interval of 4 are added up and the first four elements in the level are passed by directly. As the size of the array grows larger, the operations remain the same.

The block's number in a grid is designed to be equal to the width of the image and the threads' number in a block is equal to its length, so that one pixel can be dealt with by one thread. Before computing, image data are copied from global memory to shared memory and the size of shared memory in a block is allocated by twice the size of each row of the image, because raw data should be guarded against covering during iterative computation. After that, the final result of the integral image is bound with texture memory, which can accelerate access through caching.

3.3 Face Detection

To ensure all sizes of faces are gained, we scale up windows and slide them by a constant step in an image. As windows of different sizes at different locations can be used independently, they are all disposed in parallel. In general methods, when the size of windows or images is changed, the dimension of threads in a kernel should be changed appropriately, because one thread disposes just one window. Therefore, kernels are re-launched repeatedly to serially dispose multiple layers of the image or window. To decrease the time needed to launch kernels and transform information of classifiers repeatedly, we exploit new parallelism to compute all sizes of windows sequentially at the same location. Instead of scaling windows into different sizes before scanning, when the scan-window of 20x20 resolution slides by in an image, it is amplified by a scale factor step by step by taking the coordinate at the top left corner as the datum until the window size exceeds the image's boundary. Then, one thread disposes all windows of the same location and all threads run in parallel to finish all detecting tasks in an image. As a result, just one kernel is to be launched and the problem of uneven resource distribution among threads is reduced. The new parallel method is shown in Figure 5:

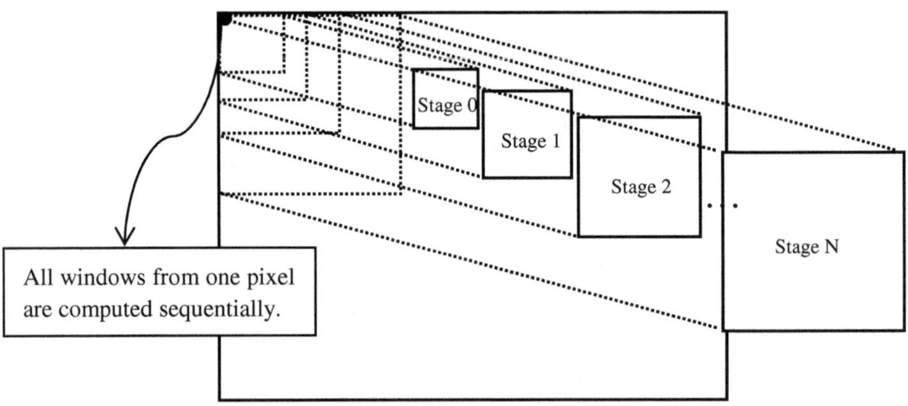

Fig. 5. Parallel method: all windows at the same position are dealt with a thread and windows at different positions are parallel computed

The number of threads is decided by the number of the smallest window sliding in the original image and the sliding step, which is ((image_width-window_size)/step+0.5)* ((image_height-window_size)/step+0.5). The thread corresponding to the first coordinate at the top left corner of the image should compute the most windows, because as the window moves right and down, bigger windows may exceed the image's boundary and are canceled.

As the capacity of shared memory is insufficient to store information of all stages of classifiers, classifiers are transmitted to share memory stage by stage. After sending data from one stage, all windows compute features of this stage. If the window passes the stage, it is signed by 1, if not, signed by 0. Then, only the windows with the signal of 1 need to detect the following stages of classifiers. The 22 stages of strong classifiers are sequentially transmitted and computed; after all stages are complete, the windows still signed by 1 are judged to contain a face. As a result, the terminal time of each thread is not simultaneous. Therefore, to avoid conflict to send results to global memory at the same time, we use the atomicAdd() primitive provided by CUDA to store results automatically.

4 Results

To show the availability of our structure of face detection algorithm on GPU, we realized our method and the other two main methods designed for GPU and compared their results. The platform we used is a combination of CPU and GPU; meanwhile, the CPU is Intel(R) Core(TM) i7-2600 with a main frequency of 3.4 GHz and the GPU is Gefore GTX590 with 512 processer cores. We detect faces on true color images with a resolution of 640x480 and there are one or more faces in the images. The classifiers we used is the free XML cascade classifiers from OpenCV library [11].

The first method is scaling the image down from the original using a scale factor of 1.2; a 20x20 window then scans in every layer of the image. Every thread works on one window in different layers at different locations, and the kernel is re-launched every time changes the scale factors of the window. The second method is scaling the window up from the side length of 20 to as long as the image's width and windows of different scaling factors scan in the image. As in the first method, each window is dealt with by one thread, and several kernels are launched to reset the dimensions of grid and block for different scaling factors. The third one is the method introduced in this paper; different sizes of windows at the same location are dealt with by one thread. In this method, just one kernel is launched. The results are shown in Figure 6:

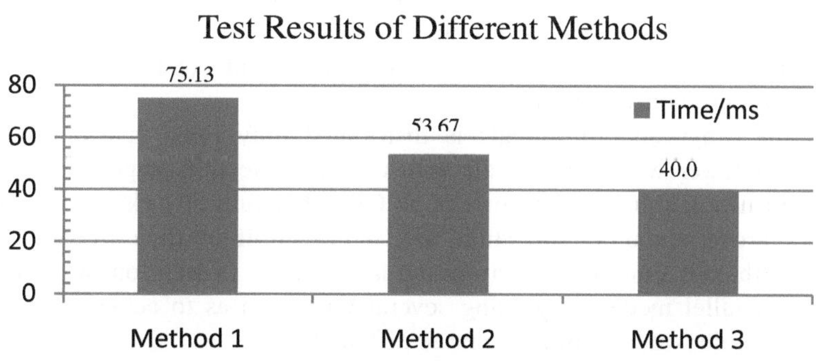

Fig. 6. The average time of three methods to detect faces for 640x480 images

In the figure above, we can see that our method only takes 40ms for one image and is thereby the least time-consuming of the three methods. The main reason for this is that the former two methods launch several kernels, improving bandwidth between the device and the host, while our method launches only one kernel to finish detecting. The other reason is that the division of tasks to one thread is uneven, so that transmission latency cannot be hidden effectively. Moreover, compared with the realization of AdaBoost algorithm only on CPU, our speedup ratio is nearly as high as 7.5.

In addition, we also experiment on GTX280 to represent the portability of the algorithm. In Figure 7, we can see that the total detection time on GTX590 is 1.6 times faster than on GTX280. With respect to hardware structure, GTX590 adopts a new architecture of Fermi, which not only increases core number, memory bandwidth and memory capacity, but also changes the framework of processors. Our algorithm produces a satisfying result on GTX590, which guarantees real-time requirement more effectively.

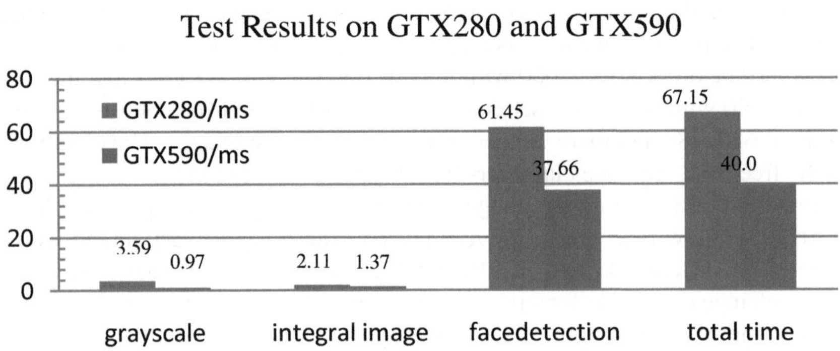

Fig. 7. The comparison of the test results on GTX280 and GTX590

5 Conclusion

In this paper, we put forward a new method to apply AdaBoost face detection algorithm on CUDA, and exploit the parallelism effectively to meet real-time requirements. Furthermore, experiment results show that our method is faster than other methods previously raised.

Since the dimension of threads is distributed only once, many windows are dropped and fewer windows are left with cascade detection stage by stage, which results in insufficient usage of resources on GPU. For future work, we would try our best to improve resource utilization and reduce waiting time by attempting to concentrate threads more effectively in the later stages. In addition, we will also try multi-core parallel methods by using several GPUs, so as to achieve simultaneous detection of more windows of the same or different sizes.

References

1. Viola, P., Jones, M.: Rapid Object Detection using a Boosted Cascade of Simple Features. In: Proceedings of the 2001 IEEE Computer Society Conference on Computer Vision and pattern Recognition, Kauai, Hawaii, USA, vol. 1, pp. 511–518 (2001)
2. Lienhart, R., Kuranov, A., Pisarevsky, V.: Empirical Analysis of Detection Cascades of Boosted Classifiers for Rapid Object Detection. In: Michaelis, B., Krell, G. (eds.) DAGM 2003. LNCS, vol. 2781, pp. 297–304. Springer, Heidelberg (2003)
3. Kasiński, A., Schmidt, A.: The Architecture and Performance of the Face and Eyes Detection System Based on the Haar Cascade Classifiers. In: Computer Science, Pattern Analysis and Applications, vol. 13, pp. 197–211. Springer (2010)
4. NVIDIA: NVIDIA CUDA C Best Programming Guide, Version 4.0 (2011)
5. Wei, G., Ming, C.: The face detection system based on GPU+CPU desktop cluster. In: Multimedia Technology (ICMT), Hangzhou, pp. 3735–3738 (2011)
6. Sharma, B., Thoa, R., Yydyanathan, N., Kale, A.: Towards a Robust, Real-time Face Processing System using CUDA-enabled GPUs. In: High Performance Computing (HiPC), Kochi, pp. 368–377 (2009)
7. Hefenbrock, D., Oberg, J.: Accelerating Viola-Jones Face Detection to FPGA-Level using GPUs. In: Proceeding FCCM 2010 Proceeding of the 2010 18th Annual International Symposium on Field-Programmable Custom Computing Machines, pp. 11–18. IEEE computer society, Washington, DC (2010)
8. Kong, J., Deng, Y.: GPU Accelerated Face Detection. In: Intellegent Control and Information Processing (ICICIP), Dalian, pp. 584–588 (2010)
9. Martínez-Zarzuela, M., Díaz-Pernas, F.J., Antón-Rodríguez, M., Perozo-Rondón, F., González-Ortega, D.: AdaBoost Face Detection on the GPU Using Haar-Like Features. In: Ferrández, J.M., Álvarez Sánchez, J.R., de la Paz, F., Toledo, F.J. (eds.) IWINAC 2011, Part II. LNCS, vol. 6687, pp. 333–342. Springer, Heidelberg (2011)
10. Krpec, J., Němec, M.: Face Detection CUDA Accelerating. In: The Fiffth International Conference on Advances in Computer-Human Interactions, Valencia, Spain, pp. 155–160 (2011)
11. OpenCV, `http://sourceforge.net/projects/opencvlibrary/`

Gaze Estimation Research with Single Camera*

Weichao Li, Ming Che, and Feifei Li

School of Computer Science and Technology
Tianjin University
Tianjin China
ejliwei@163.com, {cheming,floria}@tju.edu.cn

Abstract. Gaze estimation research has experienced significant progress in accuracy and tolerance of free head movement since reference light sources were introduced. The problem, however, is that it needs complex setup and restricted light environment to make sure there is no unexpected reflex light spot in the eye. This paper proposes a method that only needs one camera and no reference light source. The trade-off for minimizing the requirement is that only 3 out of 6 degrees-of-freedom of head movement is allowed. The 3D coordinates of feature points under restricted head movement can be determined. With these head movement information, we can compensate the results produced by homography between eye plane and screen plane. The model is simple and practical and the experimental data demonstrates that the RMS error is less than 1cm.

Keywords: gaze estimation, eye tracking, single camera, HCI.

1 Introduction

Gaze estimation is a technique that determines the gaze direction based on the photo or video of one's eye area. Gaze information is so important because it shows one's attention. Gaze estimation system can be utilized in many potential ways, such as human computer interactive (HCI) devices, medical diagnosis, space instruments, handicap assistance, etc. There are two ways to obtain the image, namely are intrusive and non-intrusive. The non-intrusive way requires less hardware set-up and gives the user a more comfortable experience, so it draws much more attention.

Based on the geometric model, estimation of the gaze direction requires coordinates of two points: the center of the pupil and center of the eyeball or corneal. The coordinates of the pupil center can be determined with 2 cameras by 3D reconstruction, but the center of eyeball or corneal is difficult to measure directly because it is invisible in the photo. The common solution is using reference light sources. With the first Purkinje images in the eye, the center of eye corneal can be determined according to the principles of reflection, such as the normal line of reflection passing through the center of the sphere. The set-up usually comes with 2 cameras and 2 light sources, [1][2][3] but it is also possible with one camera [4][5] when the eye-specific parameters are known, such as cornea curvature. There are also

* This work is supported partly by key projects in the science & technology pillar program of Tianjin, P.R. China. (No. 10ZCKFGX01100).

V. Khachidze et al. (Eds.): iCETS 2012, CCIS 332, pp. 592–599, 2012.

approaches using extra light sources not for the purpose of cornea center acquiring, such as the Cross-Ratio (CR) method, which employs 4 reference light sources[6][7]. By projecting a rectangular light pattern onto the cornea surface, the CR method estimates the point of gaze (POG) using invariant properties of projective geometry.

Reference light source has prevailed in major researches of recent years; however, it requires complex setup and a restricted light environment in order for the system to work. These requirements significantly limit the application of the system. This paper focuses on, in addition to introducing new equipment to allow more free head movement, exhausting the full potential of the minimum system to meet practical requirements. Some researchers have been working on this topic[8], but they usually require a non-moving head. With only one camera and no reference light source, this paper proposes a method that can tolerate 3 degrees-of-freedom head movement, which means the user can move the head along the x, y, and z axes, but rotation around the x, y, and z axes is not allowed. The whole theory is based on an assumption that pupil center and eye inner corner are coplanar (referred to as eye plane in the following passages) no matter where the user is looking. The screen and the eye plane can be related by a homography matrix if they do not move. When the head conducts restricted movement, the coordinates of feature points can be determined by 3D reconstruction process. With the coordinates of feature points, we can calculate the head movement compensation.

The remainder of this paper is organized as follows: section 2 introduces the POG estimation method, including homograph mapping and movement compensation; section 3 presents the experiment and data analysis; section 4 is the conclusion.

2 POG Estimation

2.1 Homography Mapping

In this section, the computing is based on the following assumptions:

1. We see the front of the eyeball as planar, not spherical, so that no matter where the user looks the pupil center and eye inner corner are always coplanar.
2. The head stays still.

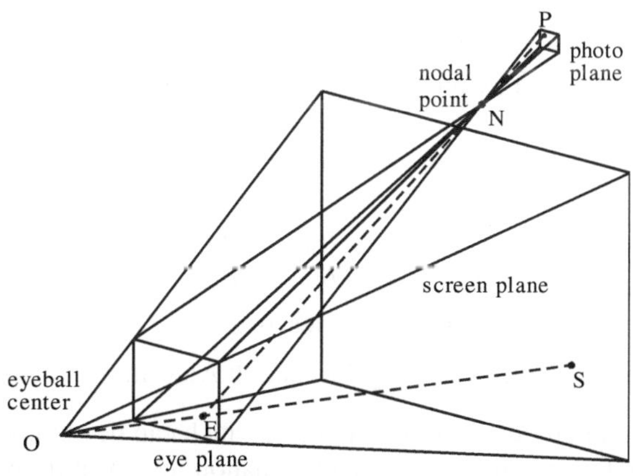

Fig. 1. Homography mapping between eye, screen and photo plane

We can establish the geometric model as shown in Fig.1, where 'S' is the point on screen at which the user is looking; 'N' is the nodal point of the camera; 'O' is the eyeball center; 'E' is the pupil center; and 'P' is the pupil center projection on the photo.

With equations (1) and (2), where $(x_S, y_S), (x_P, y_P), (x_E, y_E)$ represent the coordinates of point 'S', 'P', 'E' on plane screen, photo and eye, H_1 is the homography between eye and screen plane; H_2 is the homography between eye and photo plane; we can derive equation (3) where H is the homography between photo and screen plane. Now if we have H, the POG 'S' can be determined using the coordinates of point 'P' on the photo.

$$p_1 \begin{bmatrix} x_S \\ y_S \\ 1 \end{bmatrix} = H_1 \begin{bmatrix} x_E \\ y_E \\ 1 \end{bmatrix} \tag{1}$$

$$p_2 \begin{bmatrix} x_E \\ y_E \\ 1 \end{bmatrix} = H_2 \begin{bmatrix} x_P \\ y_P \\ 1 \end{bmatrix} \tag{2}$$

$$=> p \begin{bmatrix} x_S \\ y_S \\ 1 \end{bmatrix} = H \begin{bmatrix} x_P \\ y_P \\ 1 \end{bmatrix} \tag{3}$$

To determine the homography matrix H, we need several groups of coordinate data and we call this process 'calibration'. The user must look at some points on the screen and take face photos one at a time. The coordinates of feature points should then be precisely derived from every photo.

H is a 3X3 matrix, and there are 8 independent elements out of 9 because of the scale factor p. At least 4 groups of coordinates are needed to find H, but we use 9 groups to reduce the error with a method based on maximum likelihood criterion. Let $M_i = (x_{pi}, y_{pi})^T$, $m_i = (x_{si}, y_{si})^T$ be the coordinates on the photo and screen, i=1 to 9, and $h = (H_{11}, H_{12}, H_{13}, H_{21}, H_{22}, H_{23}, H_{31}, H_{32}, H_{33})^T$ be the 9 elements of H. Assuming the error is distributed with mean 0 and covariance matrix Λ_{m_i}, the maximum likelihood estimation of H is obtained by minimizing the following functional (4).

$$\sum_{i=1}^{9} (m_i - \hat{m}_i)^T \Lambda_{m_i}^{-1} (m_i - \hat{m}_i) \tag{4}$$

Where $\hat{m}_i = \frac{1}{H_{31}x_{pi} + H_{32}y_{pi} + H_{33}} \begin{bmatrix} H_{11}x_{pi} + H_{12}y_{pi} + H_{13} \\ H_{31}x_{pi} + H_{32}y_{pi} + H_{33} \end{bmatrix}$, $\Lambda_{m_i} = \sigma I$. In this case, the above problem becomes a nonlinear least-squares problem to minimize $\sum_{i=1}^{9} (m_i - \hat{m}_i)^T (m_i - \hat{m}_i)$. Here, Levenberg-Marquardt Algorithm is employed to solve the problem. The iteration requires an initial guess, which can be obtained as follows.

With the coordinates of 1 point and equation (3), we derive following two equations (5).

$$\begin{bmatrix} x_{pi} & y_{pi} & 1 & 0 & 0 & 0 & -x_{si}x_{pi} & -x_{si}y_{pi} & -x_{si} \\ 0 & 0 & 0 & x_{pi} & y_{pi} & 1 & -y_{si}x_{pi} & -y_{si}y_{pi} & -y_{si} \end{bmatrix} h = 0 \quad (5)$$

9 groups of coordinates make 18 equations with 9 unknown elements of h, and the equations can be written as $Lh = 0$. The initial values could use the right singular vector of L associated with the smallest singular value (or equivalently, the eigenvector of LTL associated with the smallest eigenvalue).[9]

2.2 Movement Compensation

If the head moves, the homography H we obtained from calibration will no longer be valid. Requiring the user to perform another calibration is, naturally, unrealistic. In this section, we will therefore introduce a method to compensate head movement without recalibration.

Several assumptions or restrictions should be noticed:

1. Only 3 out of 6 degrees-of-freedom head movement is allowed, which means the user can move the head along x, y, and z axes, but rotation around x, y, and z axes is not allowed.
2. We still see the front of the eyeball as planar and it is parallel with the photo plane.

Firstly, we must determine the coordinates of feature points in the world coordinates system (WCS). The parameters of the pinhole modeled camera can be described as per equation (6)

$$s\begin{bmatrix} u \\ v \\ 1 \end{bmatrix} = A[R \quad t]\begin{bmatrix} x \\ y \\ z \\ 1 \end{bmatrix} \quad (6)$$

where A is the camera's intrinsic matrix, and $[R \quad t]$ is the extrinsic parameters, which represents the rotation and translation that relates the world coordinate system to the camera coordinate system.

If we use the camera coordinate system as WCS, $[R \quad t]$ would be $\begin{bmatrix} 1 & 0 & 0 & 0 \\ 0 & 1 & 0 & 0 \\ 0 & 0 & 1 & 0 \end{bmatrix}$ which means no rotation and no translation. The equation will change to (7).

$$s\begin{bmatrix} u \\ v \\ 1 \end{bmatrix} = A\begin{bmatrix} x \\ y \\ z \end{bmatrix} \quad (7)$$

The intrinsic matrix $A = \begin{bmatrix} \alpha & 0 & u_0 \\ 0 & \beta & v_0 \\ 0 & 0 & 1 \end{bmatrix}$ can be estimated using the self-calibration method proposed by Zhang [9].

Let the inner corner points of two eyes be (x_l, y_l, z) and (x_r, y_r, z) in WCS, (u_l, v_l) and (u_r, v_r) on photo plane.

Substituting them into equation (7), we have equations (8) and (9).

$$\frac{\alpha}{z}(x_1 - x_2) = u_1 - u_2 \tag{8}$$

$$\frac{\beta}{z}(y_1 - y_2) = v_1 - v_2 \tag{9}$$

We already know the distance D between two eye inner corners in WCS.

$$D = \sqrt{(x_1 - x_2)^2 + (y_1 - y_2)^2} \tag{10}$$

With equations (8), (9) and (10), we find z and then both (x_l, y_l, z), (x_r, y_r, z) can be calculated.

Now consider the eye plane and photo plane as shown in Fig. 2. If the head moves along the x or y axis with the gaze direction remaining the same, vector $\overrightarrow{ab}$ will not change and it can be proved that $\overrightarrow{a'b'}$ will also not change. Therefore, if we make the eye inner corner the origin of the photo plane, the pupil center coordinates on the photo will not change. As a result, the POG estimation using pupil center coordinates as input will produce the same result 'A' as the head has not moved (see Fig. 3b). The compensation between actual POG 'B' and the imaginary POG 'A' is equal to the head movement, which can be derived from the eye corner coordinates. Of course, the unit of compensation should be translated to pixels on the screen.

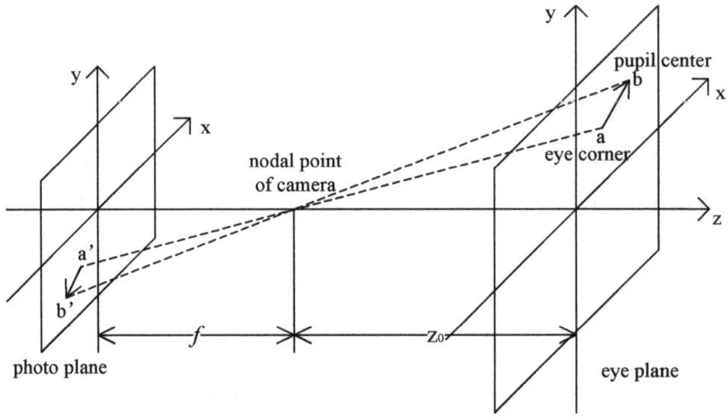

Fig. 2. Pupil-corner vector mapping

If the head moves along the z axis with the gaze direction remaining the same, it can be deducted that $\overrightarrow{a'b'} = \frac{z_0 + d}{f}\overrightarrow{ab}$, where d is the distance of head movement. We can estimate the imaginary POG 'A' as the head has not moved by using $\frac{z_0 + d}{z_0}\overrightarrow{a'b'}$ instead of $\overrightarrow{a'b'}$ (see Fig. 3c). The compensation between 'A' and 'C' is

$\left(\frac{x_p - x_{s\_A}}{z_0}(z - z_0), \frac{y_p - y_{s\_A}}{z_0}(z - z_0)\right)$, where (x_p, y_p, z) are the coordinates of the pupil center in WCS, and (x_{s_A}, y_{s_A}) is the imaginary POG 'A'.

Evidently, these two kinds of compensation can be added together to produce the final result if the head moves along the x, y, and z axes.

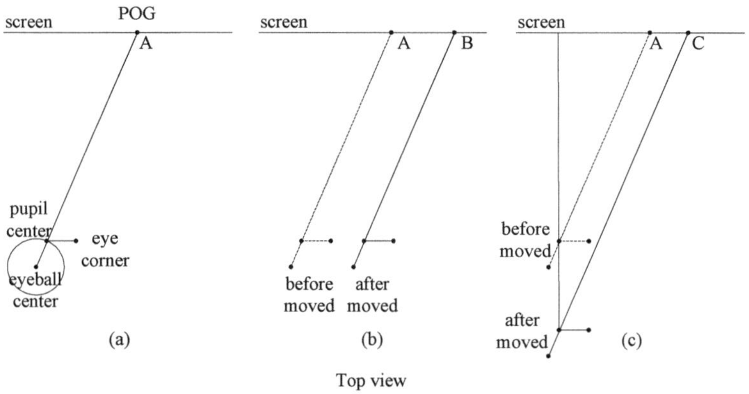

Fig. 3. Head movement compensation

3 Experimental Data

To verify the effectiveness of the system, we propose an experiment using a camera of 2048x1536 pixels and a 14-inch LCD display of 1280x800 pixels.

To preclude unnecessary error, we manually measured the feature points on the photo. After calibration process, the user performed 8 groups of tests (128 points total) with the head in 4 different positions. In each group, we tested 16 points well distributed on the screen. The result is shown in Fig.4 and the error is shown in Table 1.

Table 1. Gaze estimation result

	Head position	RMS error of X axis. pixel	RMS error of Y axis. pixel	RMS error of X axis. mm	RMS error of Y axis. mm
Group1	Did not move	28.66	30.22	6.83	7.21
Group2	Moved left	28.22	25.31	6.72	6.04
Group3	Moved right	37.00	26.75	8.82	6.39
Group4	Moved back	34.16	33.06	8.14	7.89

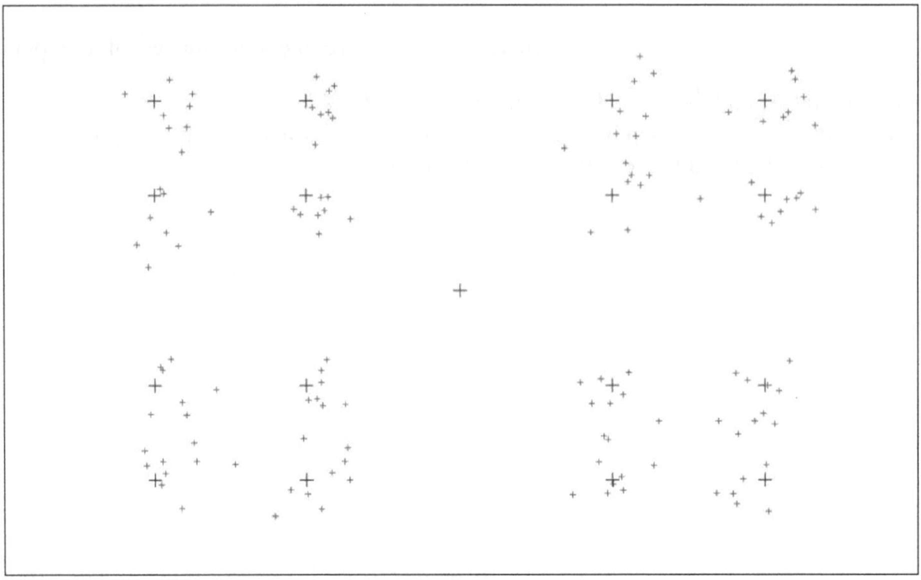

Fig. 4. Gaze estimation result

From the results, we can see that the RMS errors of 4 groups are close no matter where the head moves. Actually, the error comes mostly from the homography mapping rather than the head movement compensation. After all, the assumption that we see the front of eyeball as planar is quite significant. However, the result also shows that the RMS error is less than 1cm, which is practical for many applications of HCI devices.

4 Conclusion

In this paper, a method of gaze estimation based on homography mapping and head movement compensation is proposed. The method uses only one camera and no reference light source. Unlike most single camera methods, which require the user to stay still, this method allows 3 degrees-of-freedom head movement. The experimental results show that the RMS error is less than 1cm, which is acceptable for most HCI devices.

References

[1] Shih, S.W., Liu, J.: A novel approach to 3-D gaze tracking using stereo cameras. IEEE Transactions on Syst. Man and Cybern., Part B 34, 234–245 (2004)

[2] Model, D., Eizenman, M.: User-Calibration-Free Remote Gaze Estimation System. In: ETRA 2010: Proceedings of the 2010 Symposium on Eye-Tracking Research & Applications (2010)

[3] Guestrin, E.D., Eizenman, M.: Remote point-of-gaze estimation requiring a single-point calibration for application with infants. In: Proceedings of the 2008 Conference on Eye Tracking Research and Applications, p. 267 (2008)
[4] Villanueva, A., Cabeza, R.: A Novel Gaze Estimation System With One Calibration Point. IEEE Transactions on Systems, Man, and Cybernetics—Part B: Cybernetics 38(4) (August 2008)
[5] Morimoto, C.H., Amir, A., Flickner, M.: Detecting eye positionand gaze from a single camera and 2 light sources. In: Proceedings of the International Conference on Pattern Recognition (2002)
[6] Yoo, D.H., Chung, M.J.: A Novel Non-Intrusive Eye Gaze Estimation Using Cross-Ratio under Large Head Motion. Computer Vision and Image Understanding 98(1), 25–51 (2005)
[7] Hansen, D.W., Agustin, J.S., Villanueva, A.: Homography Normalization for Robust Gaze Estimation in Uncalibrated Setups. In: ETRA 2010 Proceedings of the 2010 Symposium on Eye-Tracking Research & Applications (2010)
[8] Shao, G., Che, M., Zhang, B., Cen, K., Gao, W.: A Novel Simple 2D Model of Eye Gaze Estimation. In: The 2nd International Conference on Intelligent Human-Machine Systems and Cybernetics (IHMSC 2010), pp. 300–304 (August 2010)
[9] Zhang, Z.: A flexible new technique for camera calibration. IEEE Transactions on Pattern Analysis and Machine Intelligence 22(11), 1330–1334 (2000)

An Improved Text Feature Selection Method for Transfer Learning

Jiang Liu[1], Hao Wang[1], and Jun Liu[2]

[1] School of Computer Science and Technology, Tianjin University, Tianjin, China
[2] School of Computer Software, Tianjin University, Tianjin, China
{jiangliu,liujun_0103}@126.com,
wwwmouse8888@sina.com

Abstract. Text classification is an important technology in text mining, and widely used in the real world. Two-class classification problem plays an important role in text classification. Many practical problems, including web page classification and spam filtering, are essentially two-class text classification problems. In this paper, we use two-class text classification problem as a baseline, and improve the traditional method for text feature selection so that the method can be more appropriate for transfer learning. We apply the improved method for text feature selection with a few new data and much old data. After the test, the updated method is proven to have effectively improved upon the classification precision and rate of recall.

Keywords: Text classification, Transfer learning, Feature selection, Two-class text classification.

1 Introduction

Text mining is a process of extracting implied, useful knowledge from the text corpus. This process is also called knowledge discovery in text database. [1]

Text classification is an important technology in text mining. Using a computer for text classification could be faster and more precise, and there have been many applications in real life. Two-class text classification plays an important role in text classification. Many practical problems, such as web page classification and spam filtering, are essentially two-class text classification problems. [3]

This paper use transfer learning theory on text classification, and then improves the traditional feature selection method in the text classification process in order to better adapt the process to transfer learning, with a few new data and much old data. The adapted method effectively improves the classification precision rate and recall rate.

2 Text Classification

Text classification is a process of labeling every document based on pre-defined classes. Text classification is a supervision learning process. It uses some labeled

V. Khachidze et al. (Eds.): iCETS 2012, CCIS 332, pp. 600–611, 2012.

documents as a training set, and determines a model which can represent the relation between text features and text classes, and then uses this model to judge the new documents. In fact, this process is essentially a pattern recognition process.

Text classification process is primarily composed of the following steps:

- Step 1: Obtain Training Documents. We either use the public dataset which is used frequently by researchers, or choose the training documents selected by experts for high quality.
- Step 2: Pretreatment of the information. Pretreatment work includes the removal of noise data, and stemming the English text. For Chinese text, there is the very important task of word segmentation. There are several effective tools for Chinese word segmentation, such as ICTCLAS, IKAnalyzer.
- Step 3: Feature selection. We use the words in the text as the text features.
- Step 4: Text Representation, Generally, the text is described by natural language which a computer is unable to understand. We therefore transfer the text to another form so that the computer can understand them. Presently, Vector Space Model (VSM) is a widely used method for text representation. [2]
- Step 5: Classification Algorithm Selection. In this step, we choose an algorithm to classify the text data, Such as Naïve Bayesian, KNN and so on.
- Step 6: Performance Evaluation: Commonly used evaluation indicators include the following: Precision, Recall, Macro Precision, Macro Recall and so on.

3 Transfer Learning

3.1 Introduction of Transfer Learning

Traditionally, machine learning methods are based on a strict assumption that the training data and the test data are Independent and identically distributed. However, this assumption cannot be guaranteed in reality. In order to classify the text on the web, we would collect data from the Internet, label these data, and train a classifier with these data. When using the classifier, however, we found that the data we used is outdated because web data are changing frequently.

The issue is then that of finding a way to improve machine learning by adding old labeled data. We can get a large number of old labeled data from relevant areas, although these data do not follow the same distribution in comparison to the test data. This type of training by using the data of relevant areas is called transfer learning. [4] In the 1990s, people began to focus on transfer learning, using existing knowledge to help machines acquire new knowledge.

There is no strict definition of transfer learning in the academic community. NIPS2005 gives a representative definition: transfer learning emphasizes the transfer of knowledge across domains, tasks, and distributions that are similar but not the same. [5]

The classification process of transfer learning is represented in Figure 1.

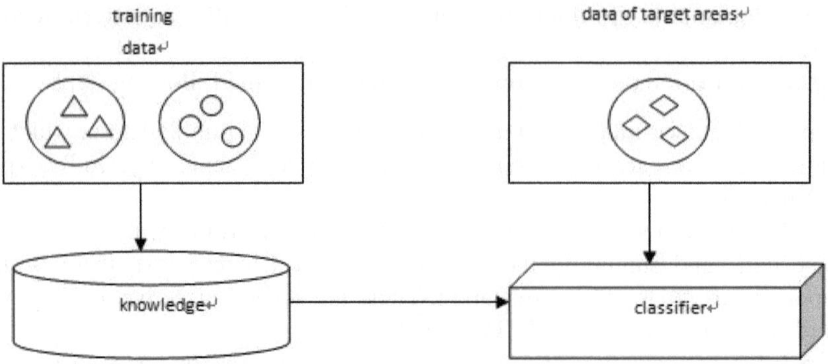

Fig. 1. The classification process of transfer learning

According to the data marked state, we can divide transfer learning into three categories: inductive transfer learning, transductive transfer learning and unsupervised transfer learning. In inductive transfer learning, parts of target data are labeled and source data may or may not be labeled. In transductive transfer learning, target data are not labeled, while source data are labeled. In unsupervised transfer learning, neither target data nor source data are labeled.

3.2 TrAdaboost Algorithm[5,9]

TrAdaboost algorithm is a sampling-based inductive transfer learning. It can sample data from other areas, and the sampled data obey the familiar distribution with target data. In TrAdaboost, we build the classifier using two kinds of data: identical distribution (new) data and different distribution data that is old data. The identical distribution data are labeled and adhere to the same distribution as test data, but are not substantive enough to be used in the training of an effective classifier. The different distribution data do not follow the same distribution as test data because they have been outdated; however we much different distribution data.

TrAdaboost Algorithm

Input: T=training set, T={ $T_d \cup T_s$ },

T_d =labeled different distributed data,

T_s =labeled identical distributed data,

S=unlabeled test data,

Learner= a weak learner, N=the maximum iterating times

For t=1,…,N

- **Step 1.** p^t is the weight distribution vector on T
- **Step 2.** Call Learner, the Input of Learner are T=training set, p^t, S=test set, the learner would return a classifier h_t:T_s (or{0,1}).
- **Step 3.** Calculate the error rate of h_t on T_s:

$$\varepsilon_t \leftarrow \sum_{i=n+1}^{n+m} \frac{w_i^t \times |h_t(x_i) - c(x_i)|}{\sum_{i=n+1}^{n+m} w_i^t}$$

- **Step 4.** $\beta \leftarrow \varepsilon_t/(1-\varepsilon_t)$, $\beta \leftarrow 1/(1+\sqrt{2\ln n/N})$ s.t. $\varepsilon_t < 1/2$
- **Step 5.** Update the weight vector:

$$w_i^{t+1} = \begin{cases} w_i^t \beta^{|h_t(x_i)-c(x_i)|}, 1 \le i \le n \\ w_i^t \beta_t^{-|h_t(x_i)-c(x_i)|}, n+1 \le i \le n+m \end{cases}$$

Output:

$$h_f(x) = \begin{cases} 1, \prod_{t=\lceil N/2 \rceil}^{N} \beta_t^{-h_t(x)} \ge \prod_{t=\lceil N/2 \rceil}^{N} \beta_t^{-\frac{1}{2}} \\ 0, else \end{cases}$$

---

4 Traditional Text Features Selection Methods

4.1 Document Frequency (DF) [6]

In this method, the evaluation function for the feature T is that: DF(T)=C(T)/N, while C(T) is the number of documents which contain the feature T, and N is the total number of documents. It is the simplest evaluation function. DF method is based on an assumption that the feature which has low frequency does not contain useful information. But this assumption is not comprehensive; at times low-frequency words contain important information while high-frequency words do not. Therefore, the performance of DF method is not considered good performance.

4.2 Information Gain (IG) [7]

Information Gain method is widely used in machine learning. In IG method, we evaluate one feature by its IG value. The IG value of feature t can be defined as:

$$\mathrm{IG}(t) = -\sum_{i=1}^{m} P(C_i)\log P(C_i) + P(t)\sum_{i=1}^{m} P(C_i \mid t)\log P(C_i \mid t) + P(\bar{t})\sum_{i=1}^{m} P(C_i \mid \bar{t})\log P(C_i \mid \bar{t}) \quad (1)$$

In formula (1), $P(C_i)$ represents the ratio of the number of the documents in class C_i to the total number of documents. $P(t)$ represents the proportion of the documents that contain the feature t in all documents. $P(C_i \mid t)$ represents the probability of the document that contains feature t belonging to class C_i. $P(\bar{t})$ represents the proportion of the documents that do not contain feature t in all documents. $P(C_i \mid \bar{t})$ represents the probability of the document that does not contain the feature t belonging to class C_i.

4.3 Mutual Information (MI)[8].

Mutual Information, which is a concept of information theory, is used to measure the interdependence of two signals in information. The evaluation of feature function is as below:

$$MI(t) = \sum_{i=1}^{m} P(C_i)\log\frac{P(t \mid C_i)}{P(t)} \quad (2)$$

In text classification, the mutual information of feature t and class C_i describes the interdependence of them. Feature t would have a high value of MI(t) if it has a high probability in one class and has low probability in other classes.

These methods attempt to find the relationship between the features and classes. The experiments show that each method has advantages and disadvantages; we cannot find a method that performs best in all data sets.

5 Method Improvements

Without considering different distribution of new data and old data in traditional text feature selection methods, features selected from old data cannot represent all information included in the new data well. If we represent and classify training data and test data on the basis of old data features, the result will certainly not be ideal. Features selected from new data could represent all information in the new data. However, a small number of new data maybe represent merely one aspect of information in test data, so we will not achieve very good results.

We could consider dividing the features selection process into two stages: In the first stage, phrases which are very representative in this field should be highly concerned. For example, phrases like "currency", "economy", "value", and so on should be selected in economic articles. These phrases contain strong economic information in both economic papers and economic commentaries. Features selected in this stage come chiefly from old data and some from new data, which depends on the proportion of new data in all data. Some features containing little class information are filtered out in the first stage. In the second stage, we determine which features are more suitable for new data and test data from the remaining features.

According to the above analysis, we must not just consider features which appear frequently and intensively in new data. Moreover, it is unreasonable to use all of the features directly for the text representation, either. Because old data accounts for most of the data, features selected would trend toward representing old data. In this paper, the trade-off of the old and new data is based on the following assumption:

A feature which appears frequently and is distributed similarly in the old and new data contains more category information. 'Distribution' here means the density at which features appear in the text. In the features selected in the first stage, we should use features that are distributed similarly in old and new data to represent the features of the text.

Features contain more information through the first selected stage. Similar distribution in the old and new data illustrates that these features can well represent the old and new data.

With this criterion, we must create a measure of the feature distribution in the old and new data. We need this measure to determine the degree of importance of the feature in category information. We can calculate with the following formula:

$$w(t,C_i) = f(t,C_i) * n(t,C_i) / N(C_i) \quad (3)$$

In formula (3), $f(t,C_i)$ means the number of times feature t appears in C_i. $C_i \in \{C_{same}, C_{dif}\}$ C_{same} represents the new data in test data, C_{dif} represents the old data in test data. $n(t,C_i)$ represents the $w_{same}(t,C_{same})$ number of text in C_i which contain feature t. $N(C_i)$ represents the total number of samples of C_i.

Based on the above formula, we can calculate feature *t* in the new data $w_{dif}(t, C_{dif})$ and appearances of feature *t* in old data. These two values represent the distribution of feature t in the old and new data. As the value of $w(t, C_i)$ becomes $w_{same}(t, C_{same})$ higher, feature *t* is $w_{dif}(t, C_{dif})$ more important in C_i. Features reserved ultimately are features which distribute similarly in the old and new data. Similar distribution requires that the values of and must be approximate. Then we can calculate the weights of feature *t* by the following formula:

$$W(t) = \max\{w_{same}(t, C_{same}), w_{dif}(t, C_{dif})\} / \min\{w_{same}(t, C_{same}), w_{dif}(t, C_{dif})\} \quad (4)$$

W(t) represents the final weights of feature *t*. If the weight is very close to 1, feature *t* is distributed similarly in the old data and new data.

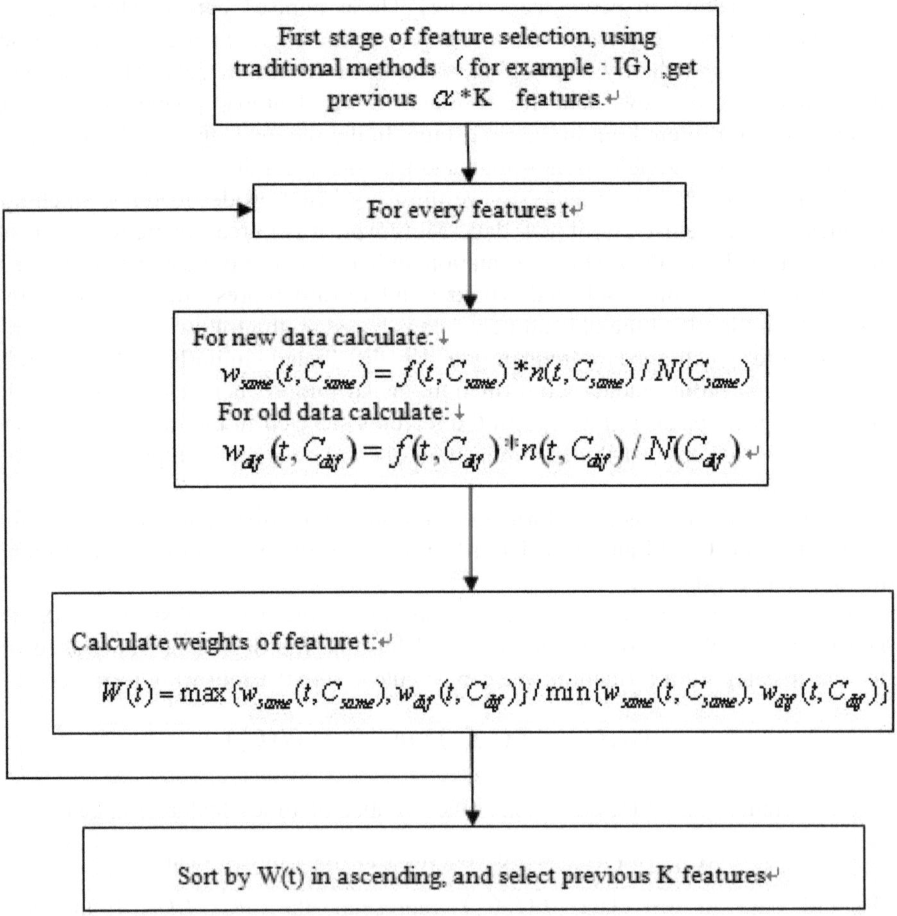

Fig. 2. Improved feature selection method

The method of feature selection in the first stage is identical to the traditional feature selection method. All of the old and new data are treated as training data. However, the number of selection should be greater than the final expected number. For instance, if we aim to have a final total of 1000 features, we should first select $1000*\alpha$ features. $\alpha>1$. The value of α can be adjusted according to the test case.

In the second stage, we perform a second selection on the $1000*\alpha$ features chosen in the first stage. According to the above formula, we could find $w_{dif}(t, C_{dif})$ and $w_{same}(t, C_{same})$, then calculate the value of weights by the following formula:

Sorting all features by W(t), we then select the desired features. Setting a threshold or determining the number of selected features, we obtain a number of features. Figure 2 displays the process of improved feature selection:

6 Experimental Results

Based on the Weka platform, this paper achieves Transfer learning and tests the effect of the improved feature selection method. During the experiment, we used a corpus of Fudan University and ICTCLAS segmentation tool from the Chinese Academy of Sciences. Firstly, we used TrAdaboost in the traditional feature selection methods to obtain experimental data. Then, we experiment again based on the improved feature extraction algorithm.

The following table shows the experimental results.

TP Rate: True Positive Rate (TPR). TP Rate represents the ratio of the number of positive instances recognized by the classifier to the total number of positive instances.

FP Rate: False Positive Rate (FPR). FP Rate represents the ratio of the number of negative instances which are thought to be positive ones by the classifier to the total number of negative instances.

Table 1. TrAdaboost classification results of the traditional feature selection method

	TP Rate	FP Rate	Precision	Recall	Class
	0.825	0.085	0.907	0.825	yes
	0.915	0.175	0.839	0.915	no
Weighted Avg.	0.87	0.13	0.873	0.87	

Table 1 shows the TrAdaboost classification results of the tradition feature selection method.

Correctly Classified Instances	*348*	*87%*
Incorrectly Classified Instances	*52*	*13%*

Table 2 shows the TrAdaboost classification results of the improved feature selection method; α value is 1.5.

Correctly Classified Instances	*356*	*89%*
Incorrectly Classified Instances	*44*	*11%*

Table 2. TrAdaboost classification results of the improved feature selection method; α = 1.5

	TP Rate	FP Rate	Precision	Recall	Class
	0.865	0.085	0.911	0.865	yes
	0.915	0.135	0.871	0.915	no
Weighted Avg.	0.89	0.11	0.891	0.89	

Table 3 is the result of α = 2

Correctly Classified Instances	*365*	*91.25%*
Incorrectly Classified Instances	*35*	*8.75%*

Table 3. TrAdaboost classification results of the improved feature selection method; α value is 2

	TP Rate	FP Rate	Precision	Recall	Class
	0.92	0.095	0.906	0.92	yes
	0.905	0.08	0.919	0.905	no
Weighted Avg.	0.913	0.088	0.913	0.913	

Table 4 is the result of α = 2.5

Correctly Classified Instances	*352*	*88%*
Incorrectly Classified Instances	*48*	*12%*

Table 4. TrAdaboost classification results of the improved feature selection method; α value is 2.5

	TP Rate	FP Rate	Precision	Recall	Class
	0.905	0.145	0.862	0.905	yes
	0.855	0.095	0.9	0.855	no
Weighted Avg.	0.88	0.12	0.881	0.88	

Table 5 is the result of α = 3

Correctly Classified Instances	*359*	*89.75%*
Incorrectly Classified Instances	*41*	*10.25%*

Table 5. TrAdaboost classification results of the improved feature selection method; α value is 3

	TP Rate	FP Rate	Precision	Recall	Class
	0.95	0.155	0.86	0.95	yes
	0.845	0.05	0.944	0.845	no
Weighted Avg.	0.898	0.103	0.902	0.898	

Table 6. TrAdaboost classification results of the improved feature selection method; α value is 4

	TP Rate	FP Rate	Precision	Recall	Class
	0.95	0.3	0.76	0.95	yes
	0.7	0.05	0.933	0.7	no
Weighted Avg.	0.825	0.175	0.847	0.825	

Table 6 is the result of α = 4

Correctly Classified Instances	*330*	*82.5%*
Incorrectly Classified Instances	*70*	*17.5%*

The purpose of the first stage of feature selection is to filter out those features that contain less of the category information. As the value becomes larger and larger, more and more features are selected in the second stage. In the second stage of feature selection, this article discusses the similarity in the distribution of features between the new data and old data.

As the distribution between new data and old data is more consistent, the feature ordering is closer to the top. With the increment of α, we can select features that contain more classification information and that are consistent with the distribution between new data and old data. These features are the features of the final selection in this article. As the increment of α keeps growing, many features pass through the first selection; these features contain less classification information and are consistent with the distribution between new data and old data. These features are not conducive to the text representation and would make the classification results worse.

The results show that we can produce the maximum correct classification rate when α value is 2. At the same time, we maximize the value of recall ratio and precision ratio.

7 Summary

This paper briefly introduces the basic concepts of text classification and the principal technologies currently used in text classification. It mainly discusses feature selection methods and studies the basic concepts of transfer learning. This paper also achieves transfer learning based on TrAdaboost algorithm and uses it in text classification. In order to improve the accuracy of text classification in transfer learning, this paper proposes a feature selection method based on two stages of selection and discusses the assessment of feature distribution after introducing the shortcomings of the existing feature selection algorithms in transfer learning.

The explanation of how to transfer learning for feature selection can be further deepened. The next step is to focus on looking for a more theoretical support for selection methods. This method should be able to find strong support in theory and analyze its efficiency and effectiveness.

References

1. Wang, L.K., Wang, H., Lu, Y.C.: The text mining and its Key Technologies and Methods. J. Computer Science 29, 12 (2002)
2. Salton, G.: A Vector Space Model for Automatic Indexing. J. Communication 18(11), 613–620 (1975)
3. Zhang, W.J.: Probability model in the text information retrieval. Journal of Intelligence 3, 107–110 (2005)

4. Chawla, N.V., Japkowicz, N., Kotcz, A.: Editorial: Special issue on learning from imbalanced data sets. Sigkdd Explorations Newsletters 6(1), 1–6 (2004)
5. Dai, W.Y.: Instance-based and Feature-based Transfer Learning. Dissertation. Shanghai Jiao Tong University, Shanghai (2008)
6. Yang, Y., Pederson, J.O.: Proceedings of the 14th International Conference on Machine learning, pp. 412–420. Morgan Kaufmann, Nashville (1997)
7. Mitchell, T.: Machine Learning. McCraw Hill (1996)
8. Kenneth, W.C., Patrick, H.: Word association norms, mutual information and lexicography. In: Proceedings of ACL27, pp. 76–83. Vancouver, Canada (1989)
9. Dai, W., Yang, Q., Xue, G.-R., Yu, Y.: Boosting for Transfer Learning. In: Proceedings of the 24th International Conference on Machine Learning, Corvallis, OR (2007)

Three-Dimensional Visual Simulation for Concrete Dam Construction Process

Jiang Liu[1], Chao Chang[2], and Ying Wei[2]

[1] School of Computer Science and Technology, Tianjin University, Tianjin, China
[2] School of Computer Software, Tianjin University, Tianjin, China
{jiangliu,chchpd,sheshilingdu}@126.com

Abstract. In order to facilitate concrete dam construction progress management, this paper puts forward a new visualization method based on Delta3D technology to simulate the process of concrete dam construction. Firstly, this paper models a three-dimensional concrete dam which will be cut into pieces. Secondly, it collects information regarding construction schedule and the actual construction progress. Finally, dynamically mapping the dam construction process in a virtual scene based on Delta3D.This method provides powerful analytical tools for project engineering construction and schedule control.

Keywords: concrete dam construction, three-dimensional visual simulation, progress simulation, Delta3D.

1 Introduction

As one of the key links in the construction of Water Conservancy and Hydropower project, Concrete Dam Construction is characterized by large-scale projects, a huge amount of resources invested and long construction periods. Therefore, the reasonable planning and effective management of the dam construction schedule are particularly important. However, with the traditional construction program it is difficult to produce an intuitive understanding, or detailing of form description and graphical presentation [1]; because of this, the dynamic changes over time are not accurately reflected.

In recent years, with the development of virtual reality technology and computer hardware technology, as well as the implementation of a large number of efficient graphical algorithms improving the speed and quality of rendering graphics, simulating the dynamic process of the concrete dam construction has become a reality. Through establishing the three-dimensional, dynamic, visualization of the virtual simulation environment, we use graphics to reflect the pouring appearance and simulate the results of the dam. This can take user into the space of three-dimensional project. Parties involved in project construction may do a series of work by this platform. For one, they have an intuitive understanding of the planned construction and the actual construction. Additionally, they may analyze the differences and the causes leading to discrepancies between original plans and actual construction.

V. Khachidze et al. (Eds.): iCETS 2012, CCIS 332, pp. 612–619, 2012.

Furthermore, they may also predict the development trend of dam construction and to realize a reasonable adjustment to the construction schedule. [2].

2 Current Status of the Research

Computer simulation technology provides a new approach to the study of water conservancy and hydropower construction. [3] Combining computer simulation technology with water conservancy hydropower construction and using methods such as construction process simulation, parametric analysis, and scheme optimization will greatly reduce the strength of the calculation of the technical staff and shorten the calculation time both for the construction options and mechanical support. At the same time, it improves the calculation.

In the 1970s computer simulation technology was used for water conservancy and hydropower projects. The construction of Austria's Schlegeis dam adopted deterministic digital simulation technology to select the best one from the cable machine pouring concrete program. D.H. Bassgen first proposed concrete pouring process simulation, based on concrete gravity dam construction at the 11th meeting of international dams in 1973[2]. In the case of meeting the actual existence conditions and construction standards of the pouring system, it simulated calculation for the pouring of the cable machine with computer simulation technology, thereby obtaining some characteristics of a cable machine, such as efficiency in simulation of pouring process, pouring strength and so on. Subsequently, computer simulation technology was gradually applied in water projects.

In China, the use of computer simulation technology in hydropower projects began in the 1980s. In 1984, technicians preliminarily verified the feasibility and effectiveness of computer simulation by using computer simulation to check and optimize their construction program on the Ertan Hydropower Station concrete dam arch curvature. In 1999, Architectural Engineering Institute of Tianjin University established a random factor analog system, and successfully simulated the impact of rainfall on the Long Tanya concrete hyperbolic arch dam during construction. In 1999, the dam pouring process computer simulation system was designed by the Three Gorges Development Corporation and Chengdu Survey and Design Institute. Then it was applied to the second phase of the Three Gorges project. The system helped the builder analyze the sensitivity factors of concrete construction, real-time control of the project's progress, and it dynamically displayed the pouring progress in three-dimensional scene. [2] At present, building a multi-object, multi-task, realistic three-dimensional virtual simulation system is still an anticipated important achievement for water conservancy and hydropower industry research.

3 Concrete Dam Model

3.1 Model of Data Analysis

The original data comes from a water diversion project in northwest China. It was a type of DEM called Contour Digital Elevation Model. Some useful information is produced; for example, it is a double curvature arch dam, its height H0 = 145 m, the top arc length S0 = 476 m, roof thickness t0 = 10 m, low thickness T0 = 42 m, the top arc of radius R0 = 525.6 m, half the central angle W0=52°34'10 ".

We adopt uniform quadratic curve arch model to analyze the data, based on the right hand coordinate system. [4]

The curve equation of dam in the xy plane is as follows:

$$x^2 = ay^2 + by \tag{1}$$

Through equation (1), the slope of the tangent could be obtained for any point (x,y)

$$\tan\phi = \frac{dy}{dx} = \frac{2x}{2ay+b} = \frac{2x}{\sqrt{4ax^2+b^2}} \tag{2}$$

The radius of curvature of any point is

$$R = \frac{\left[4x^2(1+a)+b^2\right]^{3/2}}{2b^2} \tag{3}$$

When x=0, from R=b/2= R_0, we can know that b=2 R_0, which is to say

$$R = R_0\left[(1+a)\left({}^{x}/{}_{R_0}\right)^2\right]^{3/2} \tag{4}$$

As regards the appropriate constraints for a value in the optimization of the dam body, we can control the variation of the radius of curvature in the horizontal direction. Through equation (1), we can also calculate the arc length from the crown to point x. The value of S is:

$$S = \int_0^x \sqrt{1+\left(\frac{dy}{dx}\right)^2}\, dx \tag{5}$$

When the model is being built, we can take *a* and ϕ for the design parameters to draw upstream coordinates (X_u, Y_u) and downstream coordinates (X_d, Y_d) in any elevation of the arch. The equation is as follows:

$$\begin{cases} X_u = x + \frac{t}{2}\sin\phi \\ Y_u = x - \frac{t}{2}\cos\phi \end{cases}, \quad \begin{cases} X_d = x - \frac{t}{2}\sin\phi \\ Y_d = x + \frac{t}{2}\cos\phi \end{cases} \tag{6}$$

t is the arch thickness. Experience has shown that the level of axial force of the arch along the horizontal direction changes little. However, its bending moment is generally greater than the arch bending moment, therefore the stress skewback is usually greater than the arch crown. The equation of arch dam thickness *t* on the transverse coordinates *x* is

$$\begin{cases} t_r = t_c + (t_{ar} - t_c)(x/x_{ar})^2 \\ t_l = t_c + (t_{al} - t_c)(x/x_{al})^2 \end{cases} \quad (7)$$

Right skewback thickness is 't_{ar}'; left skewback thickness is 't_{al}'; 't_c' refers to arch crown center thickness.

3.2 Model Building

Through the above analysis, we draw the three-dimensional model of the arch in AUTOCAD2004, combining CAD drawing functions. Presently, the gap between the CAD three-dimensional model and the real dam, in terms of appearance, is great. In order to make the model look more realistic, we used three-dimensional drawing software, such as 3DMAX. To draw, we imported the CAD model into 3DMAX environment to generate the body model. After that, the three-dimensional model was divided into segment and pouring block according to the schedule and engineering needs. Afterward, we superimposed the physical image data or artificial texture onto the three-dimensional model. The final state of the model is shown in Figure 1.

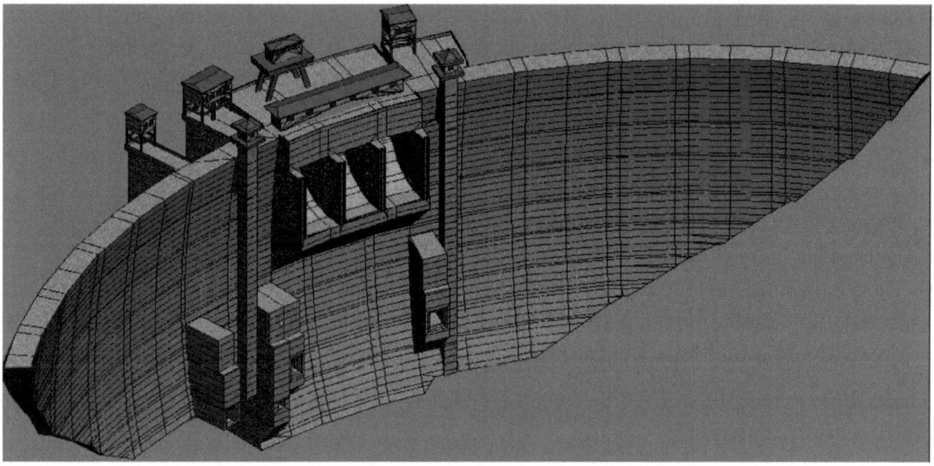

Fig. 1. The overall geometric model of the concrete dam

4 Dynamic Simulation of Construction Progress

4.1 Construction Progress Analysis

Based on experiences of water conservancy projects, the main pouring process has some restrictions; examples include supply of raw materials, the utilization of cable machine, and the installation time of the mental frame structure. In order to simplify the pouring process model for simulation of the concrete dam, we made the following assumption: there is an adequate supply of concrete raw materials; the utilization rate of cable machine is 100%; the metal frame and auxiliary design have the average installation time *t*, which add up to the pouring process.

In addition, the pouring process of the concrete dam can be used as a discrete event-driven model for analysis. In this paper, we adopt the time step method to analyze the model. [5] Therefore, the following seven points are the main properties of the dam blocks: dam section number, dam block number, dam block state, dam block elevation, dam block height, dam block length, dam block thickness, dam block size, pouring time.

During the simulation, the key point to be determined is the way in which the blocks of the dam are selected to be casted in the pouring progress. It is also the key problem of the dynamic simulation. There are often many dam blocks that can be poured at the same time. How to determine and choose upcoming pouring dam blocks is an important issue. There are many factors that affect this choice, such as the geometry of the dam blocks, interlayer intermittent time, adjacent to the dam block height, construction conditions, and special elevation section. Some of these factors are volatile. Therefore, the choice of the pouring dam blocks is complex while flexible. We use a control program, which combines computer dispatching with artificial adjustment parameters. Essentially, the choice of pouring dam blocks is made by scanning the top-level dam blocks one by one during the dam pouring process at each time period. Then, according to the construction specifications and restrictions, it is determined whether the dam blocks can be poured. Under normal circumstances, the pouring of dam blocks must observe the following three principles [5]:

- Lowest elevation principle: in order to prevent too large a height difference between dam blocks, the blocks of the dam with the lowest elevation will be set as highest priority to be casted in the next period.
- Balanced rising principle: for dam block interval is too long preferred
- Upstream dam surface priority over downstream dam surface principle: In order to avoid anti-elevation, upstream dam block pouring takes precedence over downstream dam block pouring.

These three principles reflect the basic characteristics of the controlling period in dam pouring construction.

4.2 Construction Process Simulation

In this paper, we use Delta3D engine and C++ language for three-dimensional simulation, and use MySQL to store and access the plan progress of the dam. Delta3D is a fully featured simulation engine which combines a series of excellent open source such as OSG, ODE, CAL3D, OpenGL, and so on. It provides a simple and feasible API. Its model uses dynamic loading algorithm, and supports a planet's terrain data. According to the construction schedule, we cut the dam model, write the appropriate information of dam blocks, and store them in the damblock table in database.

Table 1. Design of damblock table

Field	Field Type	Descriptionbe
SegmentID	int(10)	Not null, dam segment id
BlockID	int(10)	Not null, segment block id
State	bool	Not null, state of the block
ScheduleTime	date	Not null, store schedule time
RealTime	date	Not null, store real time
Altitude	float	Not null, altitude of the blocks
Height	float	Not null, height per block
Length	float	Not null, length per block
Thick	float	Not null, thickness per block

According the damblock table, we can write a class named DamBlock to set and operate dam information in program.

The following pseudo code implements the class

```
Class DamBlock{
      Public:
             DamBlock();
             void changeState();
             void compare();
             //other member function
        Private:
             int             segmentId;
             int               blockId;
             bool            state;
             float           altitude;
             float           height;
             float           length;
             float           thick;
             char            stime;
             char            rtime;
};
```

Finally, this paper designs an algorithm to sort the blocks, in order to decide which block should be serviced first.

According to the practical engineering experience, we create a decision-making mechanism, which is described by the following process.

- Get top level information of the dam, according with the blocks' state, segment id and block id.
- Find the maximum altitude, and then select a set of blocks that have altitude less than some value calculated by maximum altitude minus a constant.
- According to the real-time attributes, store a set of blocks by selecting lesser real-time.
- Allow blocks that have been stored to be seen in the scene through changing their state.

4.3 Simulation Results

Through changing the input of the time parameter, the user can obtain part of the model that has been poured. In addition, the user can roam the virtual environment by operating a mouse. The following figures illustrate the early phase, middle phase, and last phase of the concrete dam in 3D, respectively.

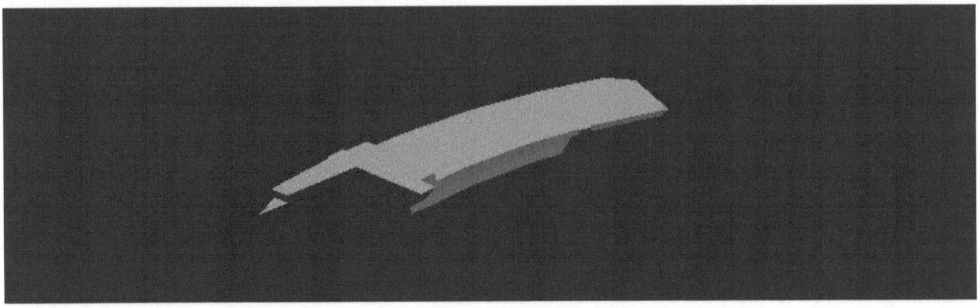

Fig. 2. Early stage of 3D image of concrete dam

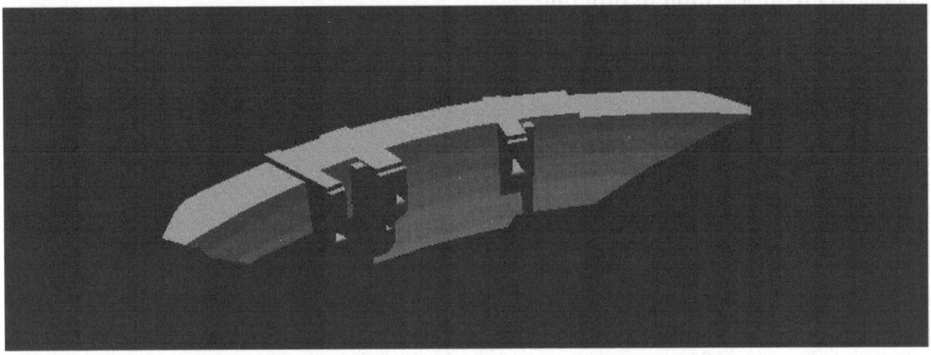

Fig. 3. Middle stage of 3D image of concrete dam

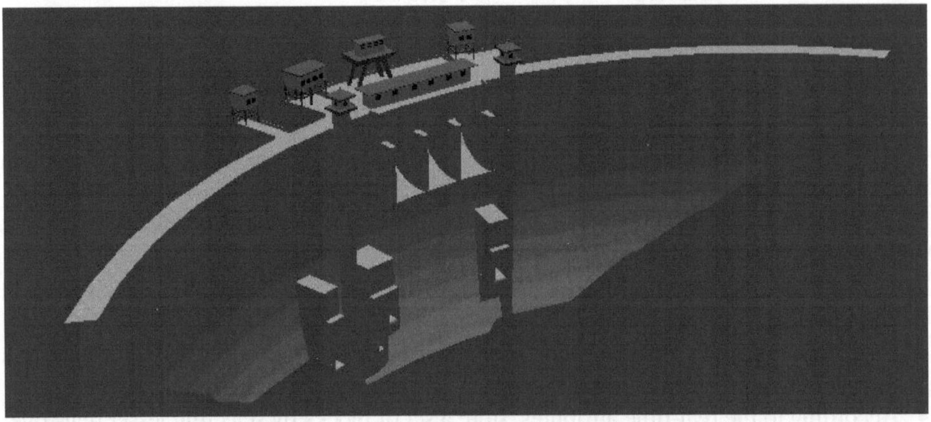

Fig. 4. Last stage of 3D image of concrete dam

5 Conclusion

This paper puts forward a method to build a three-dimensional model of concrete arch dams, and then using Delta3D simulates the process of construction; this method can be used in the actual water conservancy project.

This paper has some shortcomings; it is insufficient when roaming in the virtual environment. In addition, the virtual simulation should provide more professional guidance by combining with more of the parameters of the dam, such as temperature and stress, during the construction process.

References

1. Zhong, D., Liu, D., Zheng, J.: GIS-Based Three-Dimension Dynamic Visual Simulation for Concrete Dam Construction Process. System Engineering-Theory & Practice 5, 125–130 (2003) (in Chinese)
2. Song, Y., Zhong, D.: Study on Construction Schedule Management and Control Method for Hydraulic & Hydropower Engineering Based on Visual Simulation. System Engineering-Theory & Practice 8, 55–62 (2006) (in Chinese)
3. Zhang, Y., Sun, Y., Xia, S., Li, X.: Modeling and Rendering Method for Concrete Dams Construction Process. Journal of System Simulation 22(1), 231–235 (2010) (in Chinese)
4. Zhu, B.: Arch Dam Design and Research. China Water Power Press, Bei Jing (2002) (in Chinese)
5. Cheng, L.: Dynamic Three-Dimension Visual Simulation for Xiangjiaba Hydroplant Dam Concrete Construction. Dissertation, University of Wuhan (2004) (in Chinese)

Three-Dimensional Tongue Modeling Based on PCA for Visualized Pronunciation Feedback

Dian Huang[1], Hongcui Wang[1], Jianguo Wei[1], and Jianwu Dang[1,2]

[1] School of Computer Science and Technology, Tianjin University
92 Weijin Road, Nankai District, Tianjin 300072, China
[2] Japan Advanced Institute of Science and Technology
1-1, Asahidai, Nomi, Ishikawa 923-1211, Japan
huang_dian@163.com,
{laurelwind,jianguo.fr}@gmail.com,
jdang@jaist.ac.jp

Abstract. Pronunciation error feedback plays an important role in the CALL (Computer Assisted Language Learning) system. Accurate error feedback with detailed and appropriate guidance can make it easier for learners to correct their mistakes and to avoid similar mistakes in the future. In order to provide visualized pronunciation error feedback automatically and flexibly, in this paper, we proposed a three-dimensional tongue modeling method based on PCA. To do so, firstly, pronunciation data, which covers all 28 Japanese phonemes, was constructed from a three-dimensional physiological articulatory model. Then, the critical points of the three-dimensional tongue surface were picked and added to a sample matrix. Finally, the principal components were derived by PCA (Principal Component Analysis) method, and the tongue could then be reconstructed according to the analysis result. Based on the above work, we constructed a prototype of the feedback presentation system by combining the tongue with the palate and jaw.

Keywords: PCA, Three-Dimensional Tongue Model, Visual Error Feedback.

1 Introduction

Computer Assisted Language Learning (CALL) system is becoming increasingly popular, especially in the field of non-native language learning [1] [2]. As an essential module in a CALL system, error feedback progressively highlights its important role. Researches have shown that detailed and accurate error feedback is effective in correcting the errors addressed in the learning process [3]. Learners evaluate the learning effect only through listening by themselves if there is no feedback available. However this is a very difficult task for non-native language learners to accomplish well. A CALL system could contain language experts' judgments. Then, personalized and effective feedback can be provided, making learners aware of their study situation easily. Then, learners can accurately master the articulator placement and manner of articulation, and eventually, make non-native language learning more easy and efficient.

V. Khachidze et al. (Eds.): iCETS 2012, CCIS 332, pp. 620–627, 2012.

With the development of CALL system, the manifestation of the error feedback is also in progress and becoming more intuitive and easy to understand. In [4], when learners complete the learning process, the system presents feedback to users by automatically playing correct pronunciation. As presented by Kawai and Hirose [5], speech recognition technology is first used to check the length of learners' pronunciation, so that the suggestion of shortening or lengthening the pronunciation is given correspondingly. The method presented by Meng et al [6], uses zooming and highlighting the words that are confusing or difficult for learners, so as to prompt learners to pay more attention to those words. Tsubota, Dantsuji and Kawahara's system [7] identifies the aspects of English pronunciation with which the learners are experiencing difficulties, specifically searching for 10 areas predicted as being problematic for Japanese learners. After identifying the areas in which the students require more practice, the system then automatically provides feedback and practice in those areas in which errors were detected. LaRocca, Bellinger and Potter [8] present a system that detects spoken segmental errors and provides corrective feedback, such as articulatory information, in the form of a side view of a transparent head so that the student can see articulator placement. As presented by Eskenazi et al [9], a mid-sagittal two-dimensional model is used to present immediate corrective articulatory help for each type of phonetic or prosodic error that the student may make. In the system presented by Iribe et al [10], dynamic pronunciation posture is extracted, and when learners' pronunciation is incorrect, the system will give a demonstration of the articulator organs' movement for correct pronunciation, as well as demonstration of the wrong pronunciation made by the learners themselves.

Presently, for error feedback, multi-dimensional and accurate visualization has become the trend. Explicit guidance is more effective than implicit introduction alone [11]. In this paper, we attempt to establish a three-dimensional model that can provide intuitive, accurate description of articulator movements. The model can be adjusted to the corresponding parameters of the articulator organs, according to the learners' pronunciation errors, and then provide the targeted, personalized feedback guidance to help beginners learn the non-native language more efficiently and easily. At present, we have completed the accurate model description of articulator movements when a single phoneme is pronounced.

The rest of our paper is organized as follows: In Section 2, we present technical details of the model, and a feedback presentation system is shown in Section 3. Finally, in Section 4, we provide a summary.

2 Construction of Three-Dimensional Tongue Surface Model

Based on our previous research [12], the building process of the three-dimensional tongue surface model will be introduced in this section.

2.1 Pronunciation Sample Collection

In our system, we focused on the 28 Japanese phonemes, which are presented in Table 1. In order to model the entire pronunciation space, 20 groups of pronunciation data were collected for each phoneme, and then a total of 560 groups' pronunciation data were acquired.

Table 1. Japanese phonemes

Category	Phoneme	Number
Vowel	a i u e o	5
Consonant	k s t n h m y r w N g z d b p	15
	sy zy by py my ny ry sh	8

2.2 Data Acquisition and Sample Matrix Building

After acquiring pronunciation samples, we must learn key points of the tongue from all the pronunciation samples. In our model, the tongue back surface consists of an 11 × 5 mesh, shown in Fig. 1, and tongue front surface consists of a 7 × 5 mesh presented in Fig. 2. Furthermore, as mentioned before, the tongue can be represented by 75 points of which each is three-dimensional, so the tongue is 255-dimensional correspondingly. Moreover, as the length of each pronunciation ranges from 13 frames to 25 frames, our final matrix measures 10760 × 255.

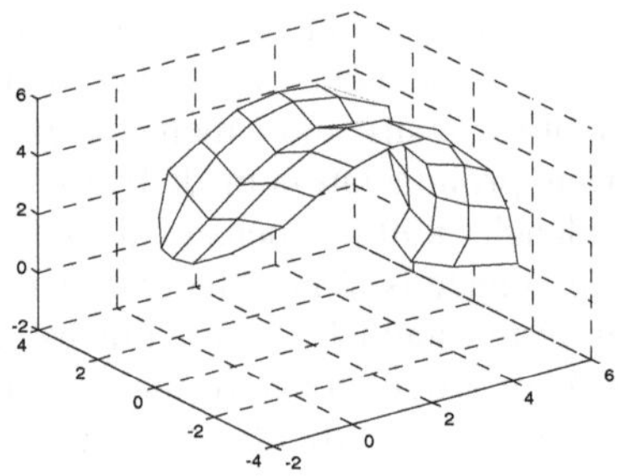

Fig. 1. The mesh of tongue back surface

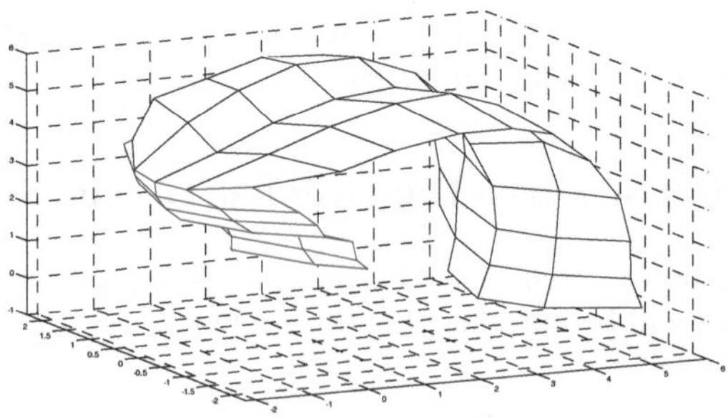

Fig. 2. The mesh of tongue surface where the red parts represent tongue front surface

2.3 Data Analysis and Reconstruction

Considering the high dimensionality, as well as the noisy and redundant data in the original matrix, the PCA (Principal Component Analysis) method is used in this paper to extract the principal components and reduce noise and redundancy.

By analyzing the sample matrix, the percentage of variance for each principal component and the cumulative variance of the first 8 principal components are shown in Fig. 3 and Fig. 4.

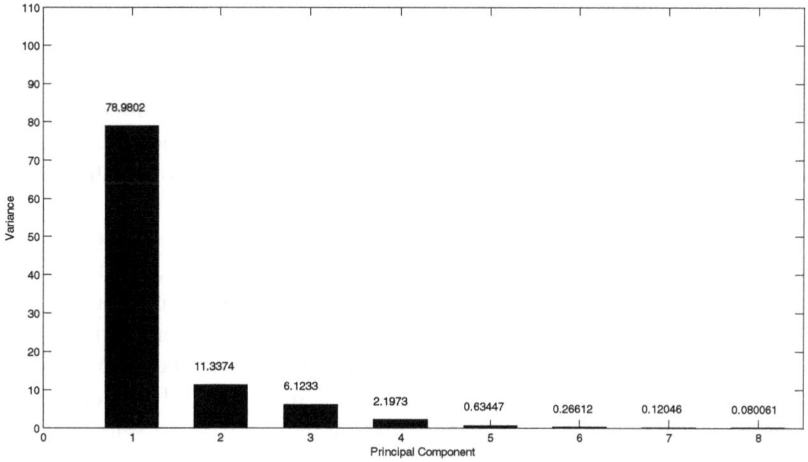

Fig. 3. The percentage of variance explained by each principal component

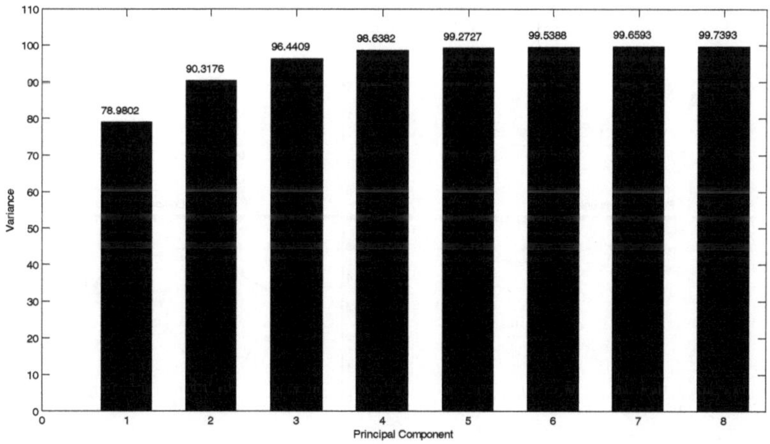

Fig. 4. The percentage of variance explained by principal components accumulatively

As show in Figure 3, the first principal component occupies nearly 79% of the variance, which means that the direction of tongue's movements in the pronunciation space is largely the same as the direction represented by the first principal component. Furthermore, as show in Figure 4, the first four principal components occupy 98.6% variance, meaning the first four principal components explain the most important information with respect to the tongue.

Based on the above observation, we decide to reconstruct the data through the first four principal components. The reconstruction method used here is introduced by Beautemps, Badin and Bailly [13]:

$$D = D_m + LF \cdot T. \tag{1}$$

In equation (1), D_m is the average of the original data in each dimension; T is the transformation matrix, and each column of T corresponds to the eigenvectors of the principal components; LF represents the load factor, and accomplishes the goal of weighting every eigenvector.

In order to view the meaning of each principal component represented more intuitively, we modify the multiple of each principal component, and then reconstruct the data. The different patterns of tongue are shown in Figure 5. It can be concluded that the first principal component relates to the tongue's movement back and forth; the second principal component relates to the tongue's movement up and down; the third principal component relates to the tongue tip's upward movement; and the fourth principal component corresponds to the tongue back's forward and backward movement.

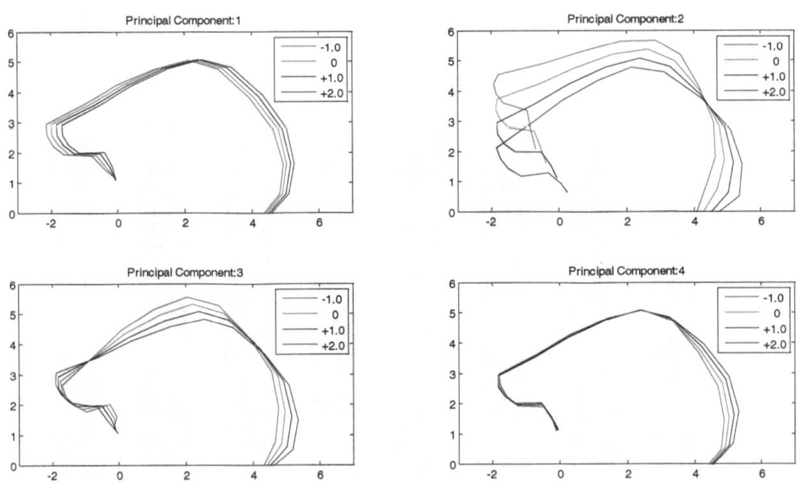

Fig. 5. The influence on mid-sagittal plane made by each principal component where +2.0 represents the increase of the corresponding feature factor to 2 times; +1.0 denotes remaining unchanged; 0 which means that the corresponding feature factor becomes 0, and -1.0 denotes the corresponding feature factor takes the opposite number of original

Moreover, in order to observe the effect of each principal component, we conduct another experiment on the width of tongue influenced by the principal components. The result illustrates that the third principal component has a significant impact on the width of tongue back and front surface, presented in Figure 6 and Figure 7. As the figures show, when the value of the feature vector of the third principal component is increased, the width of the tongue surface is also increased.

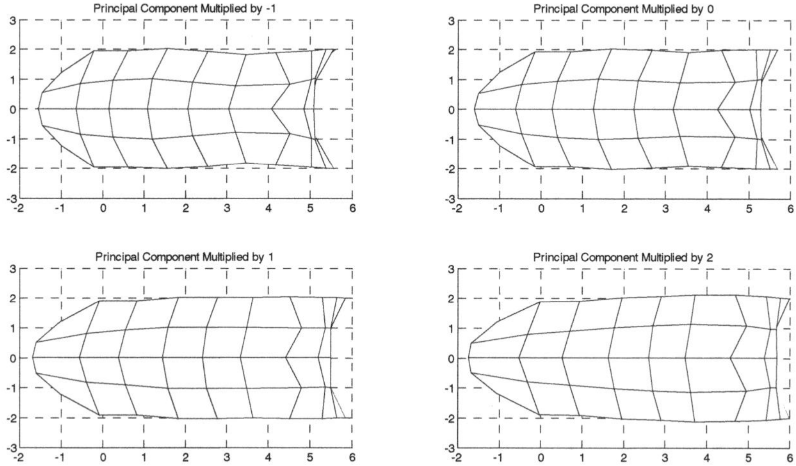

Fig. 6. The influence on the width of tongue back surface made by the third principal component. -1, 0, 1, +2 represent the multiple of the third principal component

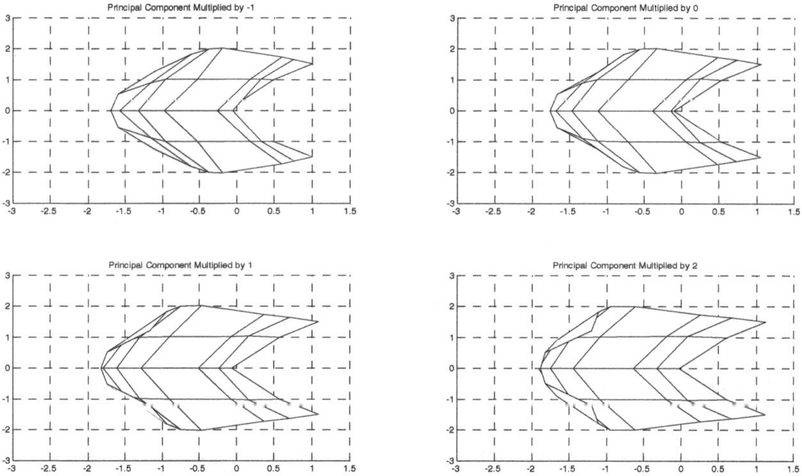

Fig. 7. The influence on the width of tongue front surface made by the third principal component. -1, 0, 1, +2 mean the multiple of the third principal component

3 Feedback Presentation System

Based on the above analysis of the tongue, we combine it with the movement of the palate and jaw organ. Figure 8 is an example of our feedback presentation system that can accurately describe the articulator trajectory.

When it is required to show the visualized pronunciation movement of a phoneme, the system will first judge whether the phoneme belongs to the 28 Japanese phonemes. If so, the movement will be presented; otherwise, a warning will be shown to remind users. Meanwhile, according to the analysis of the available data, we also studied the movement of the jaw. The control of the jaw is achieved through one point. When the tongue is moving in each frame, the system will calculate the start point and end point of jaw's movement simultaneously, so that the jaw can move along with the tongue.

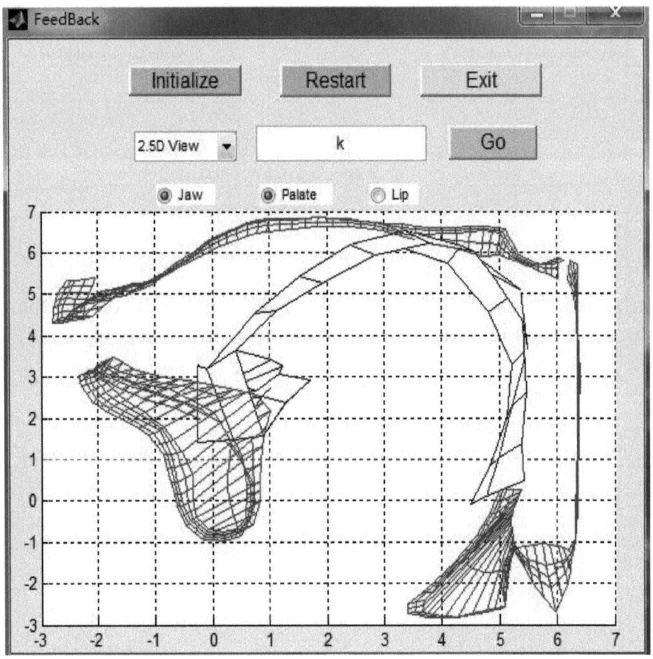

Fig. 8. The interface of our error feedback demonstration system

4 Summary

In this paper, we designed a three-dimensional surface tongue model based on PCA method. First of all, 560 groups' pronunciation data covering all 28 Japanese phonemes were collected and the length of each group ranges from 13 frames to 25 frames. Then, the key point data of the three-dimensional tongue was picked out, including 55 points for tongue back surface and 35 points for tongue front surface. 5 common points in the connection area were removed. Consequently, 75 points for the tongue surface as well as sample matrix were constructed correspondingly. Furthermore, using the PCA method, we obtain the principal components and reconstruct the data based on the result model. Based on the above analysis of tongue combined with the movement of the palate and jaw, a prototype of the feedback presentation system was constructed. It can accurately describe the articulator trajectory. Compared with a statistics-based feedback model, the three-dimensional model we designed is more accurate and intuitive. At the same time, compared with a physiology-based feedback model, our model has the advantages of small-computation and real-time. Our model can also be flexibly controlled, making it extensible for further realization of the pronunciation movement of words or sentences.

References

1. Luo, D., Qiao, Y., Minematsu, N., Yamauchi, Y., Hirose, K.: Regularized-MLLR speaker adaptation for computer-assisted language learning system. In: Interspeech, pp. 594–597 (2010)
2. Felps, D., Bortfeld, H., Gutierrez-Osuna, R.: Foreign accent conversion in computer assisted pronunciation training. Speech Communication 51(10), 920–932 (2009)
3. Neri, A., Cucchiarini, C., Strik, H.: ASR corrective feedback on pronunciation: does it really work? In: Proc. ISCA Interspeech, Pittsburgh, PA, pp. 1982–1985 (2006)
4. Williams, S.M., Nix, D., Fairweather, P.: Using Speech Recognition Technology to enhance Literacy Instruction for Emerging Readers. In: Fourth International Conference of the Learning Sciences, pp. 115–120. Erlbaum, Mahwah (2000)
5. Kawai, G., Hirose, K.: Teaching the pronunciation of Japanese double-mora phonemes using speech recognition technology. Speech Communication 30, 131–143 (2000)
6. Meng, H., Lo, W.K., Harrison, A.M., Lee, P., Wong, K.H., Leung, W.K., Meng, F.: Development of Automatic Speech Recognition and Synthesis Technologies to Support Chinese Learners of English: The CUHK Experience. In: Proc. of APSIPA (2010)
7. Tsubota, Y., Dantsuji, M., Kawahara, T.: An English pronunciation learning system for Japanese students based on diagnosis of critical pronunciation errors. ReCALL 16(1), 129–134 (2004)
8. LaRocca, S., Bellinger, S., Potter, T.: Voice-interactive German homework at the US Military Academy. In: Proc. ISCA ITRWINSTiL 2000, Dundee, Scotland, pp. 26–30 (2000)
9. Eskenazi, M., Kennedy, A., Ketchum, C., Olszewski, R., Pelton, G.: The Native Accent pronunciation tutor: measuring success in the real world. In: SLaTE Workshopon Speech and Language Technology in Education, pp. 124–127 (2007)
10. Iribe, Y., Manosavan, S., Katsurada, K., Hayashi, R., Zhu, C., Nitta, T.: Improvement of animated articulatory gesture extracted from speech for pronunciation training. In: ICASSP 2012, Kyoto, Japan (2012)
11. Ellis, N.C.: Implicit and Explicit Learning of Languages. Cambridge University Press (2000)
12. Fujita, S., Dang, J., Suzuki, N., Honda, K.: A computational tongue model and its clinical application. Oral Science International 5, 97–109 (2007)
13. Beautemps, D., Badin, P., Bailly, G.: Linear degrees of freedom in speech production: analysis of cineradio- and labio-film data and articulatory-acoustic modeling. Journal of the Acoustical Society of America 109(5), 2165–2218 (2001)

Comprehensive Mining on Medical Homepage Records Using Bayesian Network Approach

Zhipeng Han, Xiujun Gong, and Jing Zhang

School of Computer Science and Technology, Tianjin University, China
{hanzhipeng,gongxj}@tju.edu.cn,
jing.zhang87@yahoo.cn

Abstract. Hospitalizations today are confronted with increasing demand to ensure and improve the quality of care for patients. At present, many hospitals' clinical databases have accumulated large quantities of information about patients and their medical conditions. Potential knowledge within these data sets could provide new medical insight. We present a comprehensive analysis on medical records homepage, which is a Chinese standard representation for patient's records, using a Bayesian Network (BN) approach. For learning BN structure, we raise a Bayesian network searching algorithm medical-K2 by controlling random sequences of the nodes based on domain knowledge. In analysis and comparison, we develop a set of consistency checking mechanisms for the representations and describe the medical quality changes across different temporal periods and hospitals to find all possible factors for the quality of hospital care.

Keywords: Quality of Medical Care, Bayesian Network validation, Sub-graph Isomorphism.

1 Introduction

1.1 Background

Quality of Medical Care refers to using medical knowledge and related information under the existing conditions in medical services, improving patients' satisfaction and reducing the extent to which patients receive unexpected results [1], [2]. International quality indicator project (IQIP) was first used in America in 1985. IQIP is the most popular medical care quality management system, focusing on medical services within most hospitals in America [3]. In China, the majority of health care quality indicators used in hospitals is the evaluation of ISO9000 system [4]. In general, the current evaluation of the indicators of the quality of medical care does not form a complete system in China. Recently years, many studies have improved upon the quality of medical care, but most of the improvements depend heavily upon the context in which they are used and the ways that they are implemented. In our work, we propose a novel method for avoiding the defect mentioned above. We focus our research primarily on analyzing 13 medical care quality indicators with which the hospitals' manager and most patients are concerned.

V. Khachidze et al. (Eds.): iCETS 2012, CCIS 332, pp. 628–637, 2012.

1.2 Related Works

The International Quality Indicator Project (IQIP) was firstly applied in America in 1985. It is also the most popular quality-based medical management system in the world [10]. In China, most hospitals use medical indicators under the standard of ISO9000 system [11]. Generally, there are some problems with the system. Some of the indicators do not directly reflect the medical service result, and some indicators are not designed for medical quality. Furthermore, recent medical quality indicators do not form integrity measurement architecture.

The Bayesian network experiment contains two steps: learn the network structure and calculate the transfer probability tables (CPTs). There are few effective methods to build the network structure. The isomorphism graph problem is a NP problem. Many researches were devoted to the isomorphism graph problem, but all of the methods are unsuitable for our research while the attributes are known.

Early research in medical quality was mostly devoted to calculating the medical indicators. This cannot find the potential relationships that affect the indicators' results. They cannot reflect the dynamic changes over different periods. Taking the many factors above into account, we began our research. Herewith, firstly, we raise a Bayesian Network searching algorithm, medical-K2, and build Bayesian Network with medical-K2 on a dataset containing three hospitals' medical records concerning the 13 indicators we investigate. Then, we compare and analyze the common characteristics and the difference or changes between different hospitals within the same period, and different periods in the same hospital, based on the Bayesian Network result. Thirdly, we propose a new algorithm to finding the sub-graph isomorphism from a set of model graphs and develop a sub-graph query system. The main advantage of the proposed representation is that the node-to-node mapping information was known in our experiments.

2 Methods and Materials

2.1 Bayes Network

Bayesian Networks (BNs) are directed acyclic graphs (DAGs). The nodes in a BN represent the variables in the target domain. The links between nodes represent probabilistic dependencies among different variables. The node at the head of a link is called a child, and the node at the tail of a link is called a parent. Together, the graphical models represent the qualitative information in a domain, wherein domain variables are probabilistically dependent upon each other. The quantitative information of a BN is represented as the conditional probability distribution inside each node, which represents the probability of the variable under each configuration of its parent variables. Combining the qualitative and quantitative parts, a BN can define a factorized joint probability of variables $X_1, \ldots, X_i$ in the domain as per formula (1), where $\mathrm{Pa}(X_i)$ means the parents of variable X_i in the BN.

$$p(X_1, \dots, X_n) = \prod_i p(X_i | Pa(X_i)) \tag{1}$$

The dual nature of a Bayesian Network creates a natural division in learning a Bayesian Network as a two-stage process: first learn a network structure, and then learn the probability tables. Once a good network structure is identified, the conditional probability tables for each of the variables can be estimated.

2.2 Medical-K2 Algorithm

The K2 algorithm is implemented for local score metrics method, which uses a random order of the nodes at the beginning of the search. A node-ordering specifies an order of the nodes, with the understanding that no node can be an ancestor of a node that appears earlier in the order. As the amount of the nodes increases, the number of the network structures grows up to n!. Different node orders can construct different networks, and this also requires time and space. Fortunately, we have certain prior knowledge, which comes from medical expert's opinions, accumulated personal experiences and common sense. Such domain knowledge can be combined in the BN learning process to establish better structures. In light of the above parameters, combined with the essence of K2 algorithm, this paper proposed a more suitable algorithm for this research's needs: Medical-K2 algorithm. The detailed process is as follows:

1) First, Initialize the Matrix-k based prior knowledge.
2) Secondly, obtain a random sequence of n nodes.
3) Then, before determining the parent-child relationship between two nodes, we test the a priori knowledge of whether the relationship is forbidden. If not, judge if the edge can cause the network to obtain higher score, or else give up the edge.

The pseudo code of a greedy search algorithm for BN structure learning, BN learning with Medical-K2 is as follows:

```
Generate an initial DAG consistent with constraints as
the current DAG
Done = false
While ~Done
   Generate neighbors of the current DAG with adding
arc(N_i, N_j)
Filter out the N_i and N_j whether forbidden with the
matrix-k
Evaluate the remaining neighbor DAG
If the best score of the neighbor DAG is better than that
of the current DAG
    Set the DAG with the best score as the current DAG
Else
    Done = true
```

2.3 Isomorphism Sub-graph

In graph theory, an isomorphism of graphs *G* and *H* is a bijection between the vertex sets of *G* and *H*, $f: V(G) \rightarrow V(H)$ such that any two vertices μ and υ of *G* are adjacent in *G* if and only if $f(\mu)$ and $f(\nu)$ are adjacent in *H*. The isomorphic sub-graph of *G* and *H* stands the maximum isomorphism sub-graph of *G* and *H*.

A procedure for determining two graphs' maximum isomorphic sub-graph is helpful for our research as the maximum isomorphic sub-graph reflects the common characteristics of the dataset. No efficient deterministic algorithm is known for determining whether two given finite graphs, G_1 and G_2, are isomorphic [5]. A closely related but inherently more difficult problem is the sub-graph isomorphism problem; namely, given two finite graphs, G_1 and G_2, determine G_1 and G_2's maximum isomorphic sub graph. A sub-graph isomorphism indicates the potential relationships in the dataset. The emphasis is on the power of the algorithm for solving practical problems, rather than on the theoretical niceties of the algorithm [6]. Since we are dealing exclusively with finite graphs, a deterministic isomorphism algorithm based on reordering the nodes is easily given. Thus, we need only to test the edges in the edge set for each graph.

2.4 Data Source

The data of our experiment for mining was collected from three hospitals' medical databases, unified to the "Medical record homepage" format, which is a Chinese standard representation for patients' recorders. The attributes of the record are formally expressed as formula (2). The meanings are as follows. P_i: Patients' personal information. H_i: Hospital information. C_i: Clinical information. $D_i = [d_1, \ldots, d_{10}]$: Diagnosis information. O_i: Operation information.

$$R_i = \{P_i, H_i, C_i, D_i, O_i\} \tag{2}$$

Before the experiment, the dataset must remove the privacy data of the patients, as well as reduce redundant diagnoses and operation information. The processed dataset record is shown as formula (3).

$$X_i = \{P_{sai}, H_i, C_i, D_{mi}, o_i\} \tag{3}$$

P_{sai} contains the patient's sex and age information, and D_{mi} is also subset of D_i which only contains the main diagnosis, o_i stands for $|O_i|$. The amounts of processed data for our experiment are shown in Table 1.

Table 1. The data from three hospitals

Hospital\year	2009	2008	2007	2006	2005	2004
B	52496	56060	20318			
S	13698	14153	12919	11126	9685	12126
R	29172	24638	23321	19918	18687	8952

3 Results and Discussion

In this section, we describe experiments on testing the effect of the medical-k2 algorithm on the BN structure learning process, with the dataset collected from three Tianjin hospitals' medical records. We mainly focus on 13 indicators. The 13 indicators are as follows: Patient geographical distribution; Patient department distribution; Disease distribution; Hospitalization costs statistics; Drugs statistics; Patient statistics; Mortality rate; Blood transfusion statistics; Time before and after operation in hospital; Top 50 diseases; Re-admission to hospital; Re-admission to ICU; Auto discharged.

The experiments were run on the processed records, which contain the necessary attributes for the indicators. They include patients' basic information, hospitalization information, clinical information, the main diagnosis information and operation information. As we build Bayesian Network on each dataset, refer to Table 1. For every dataset we set each attribute as the start node, and the networks can be expressed as its adjacency matrix. To avoid random factors, we express the Bayesian Network results with the average matrix M. $\mathrm{M} = \sum_1^k M_i$ where M_i means the adjacency matrix of *i*th BN. The M is found as in the following Figures 1-3, each for a hospital's result. According to the picture, we concluded that the medical-k2 could filter the potential relationships among the processed records.

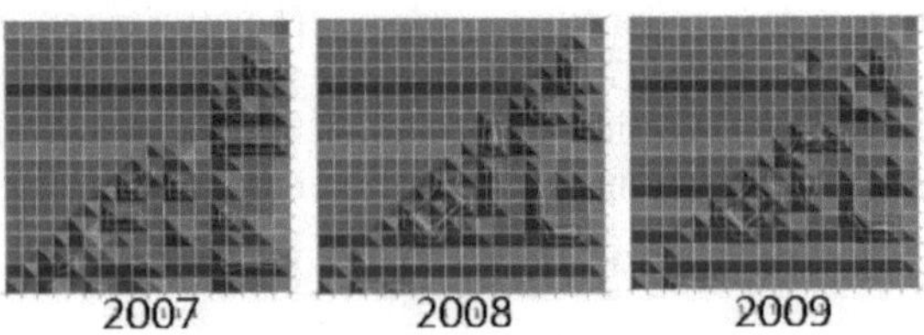

Fig. 1. The Matrix of Hospital B

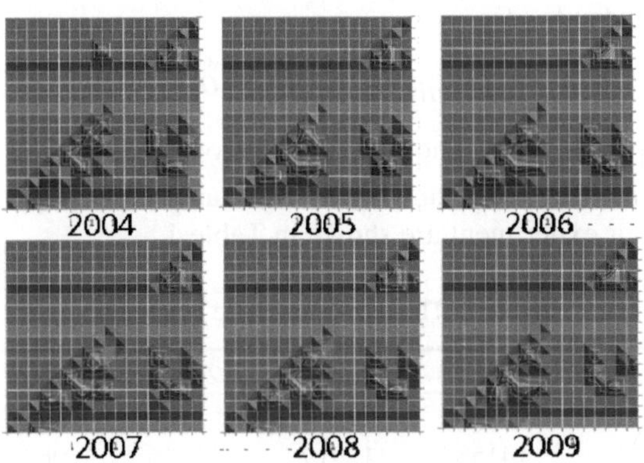

Fig. 2. The Matrix of Hospital S

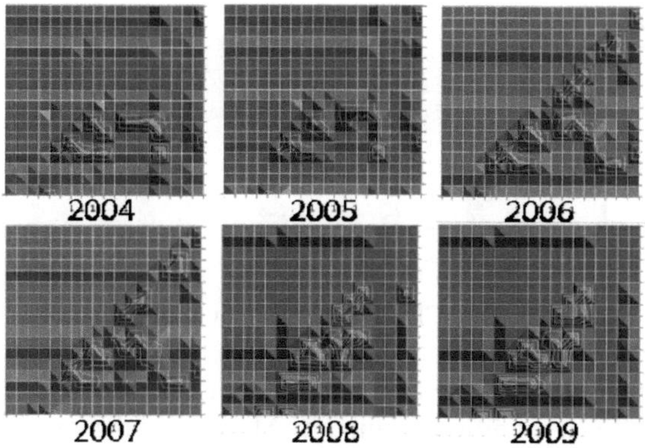

Fig. 3. The Matrix of Hospital R

Suppose the medical dataset record $X_i = (x_1, x_2, \dots, x_n)$ is a DAG model. The existing arc between N_i and N_j denotes the relationship between the attribute x_i and x_j. From the result, we found some arcs occur more than others. Through analysis of the top occurring arcs, we found the transformation of the dataset between different years for the same hospital and the difference between three hospitals at the same time. As mentioned above, the occurrence of the edge reflects the proximity of the attributes. Figure 4 shows the top 15 occurrences of the edge of the Hospital S in 2008 and 2009. From the top 15 links we found that the arcs (icd10, operationtime), (liveinhospitalfee, operationtime) and (job, inhospitaltime) in 2008 disappeared in 2009. We can gain hypothesis that the percentage of some kinds of diseases changed and then we will verify.

Hospital S_2008

```
(icd10,leavesection):13.0
(liveinhospitalfee,westernmedicinefee):13.0
(inhospitaltime,liveinhospitalfee):13.0
(ageperiod,job):12.0
(inhospitaltime,TimeAfterOperation):12.0
(operationtime,TimeAfterOperation):12.0
(TimeBeforeOperation,TimeAfterOperation):12.0
(operationtime,TimeBeforeOperation):11.0
(icd10,operationtime):10.0
(liveinhospitalfee,operationtime):10.0
(ageperiod,inhospitaltime):9.0
(sex,ageperiod):9.0
(job,inhospitaltime):9.0
(leavesection,leavesituation):9.0
(inhospitaltime,chinesemedicinefee):8.0
```

Hospital S_2009

```
(icd10,leavesection):13.0
(liveinhospitalfee,westernmedicinefee):13.0
(inhospitaltime,liveinhospitalfee):13.0
(ageperiod,job):12.0
(inhospitaltime,TimeAfterOperation):12.0
(operationtime,TimeAfterOperation):12.0
(operationtime,TimeBeforeOperation):12.0
(leavesection,leavesituation):12.0
(TimeBeforeOperation,TimeAfterOperation):12.0
(sex,ageperiod):10.0
(inhospitaltime,westernmedicinefee):10.0
(ageperiod,inhospitaltime):9.0
(inhospitaltime,chinesemedicinefee):9.0
(operationtime,leavesituation):9.0
(job,icd10):8.0
```

Fig. 4. Check top 15 occurring links in BN learning with medical K2 searching algorithm in Hospital S in 2008 and 2009

With our assumption, we check the top diseases in hospital S and statistics of the operation times. The result is shown in Fig. 5.

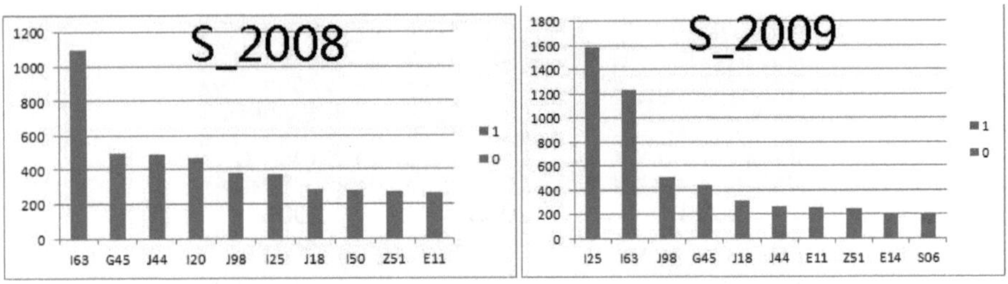

Fig. 5. The ICD-10 and the amount of patients

It can be seen that in 2009, the amount of the disease I25 (Chronic ischemic heart disease) increased by a significant amount. Moreover, the operation times for the disease S06 (Intracranial injury) is almost half of the patients that have undergone operation2 times.

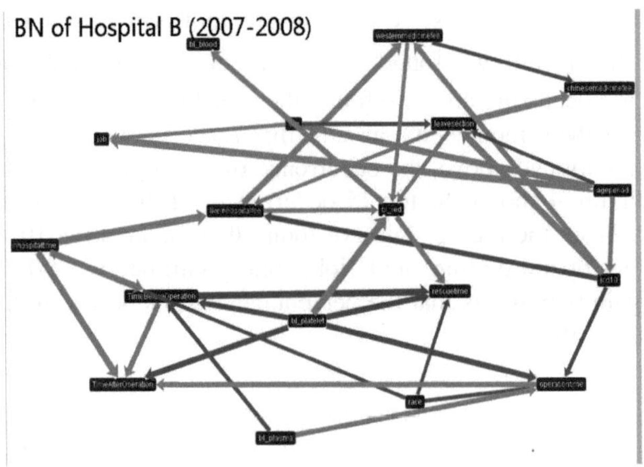

Fig. 6. The comparison of BNs for Hospital B in 2007 and 2008. The red indicates the relationships in 2007 that disappear in 2008. The grey indicates the relationships that appear in 2008. The width of the arrows denotes the interdependence of the attribute.

In Fig.6 above we see the nodes "TimeBeforeOperation" and "bl_platelet" have the greatest degree among the nodes that only take the red edges into account. We then checked the dataset of 2007 and 2008 for Hospital B. The main cause of this change was the increased number of accidents in 2008. We only take the nodes whose proximity up the threshold we set into account.

Tests have proven that our method can find obvious indicators changes and that the data records' characteristics cause these changes. The very small changes were embodied in the strength of the edges and the large changes were in the occurrence or disappearance of the edges.

4 The Isomorphism Sub-graph

In our research, as the nodes stand the attributes of medical record homepage, the set of nodes is limited. The arcs in Fig. 7 (a, b, c) denote the dependence between the nodes. The weights of the arcs represent the strength of the relationships between the attributes in the medical record homepage. In order to provide a better view of the results, we set a threshold for the arcs. Only the strongest relationships in our dataset were shown in the below figures.

The BNs of Hospital S between 2007 and 2009 and the isomorphic sub-graph are shown in Fig. 7.

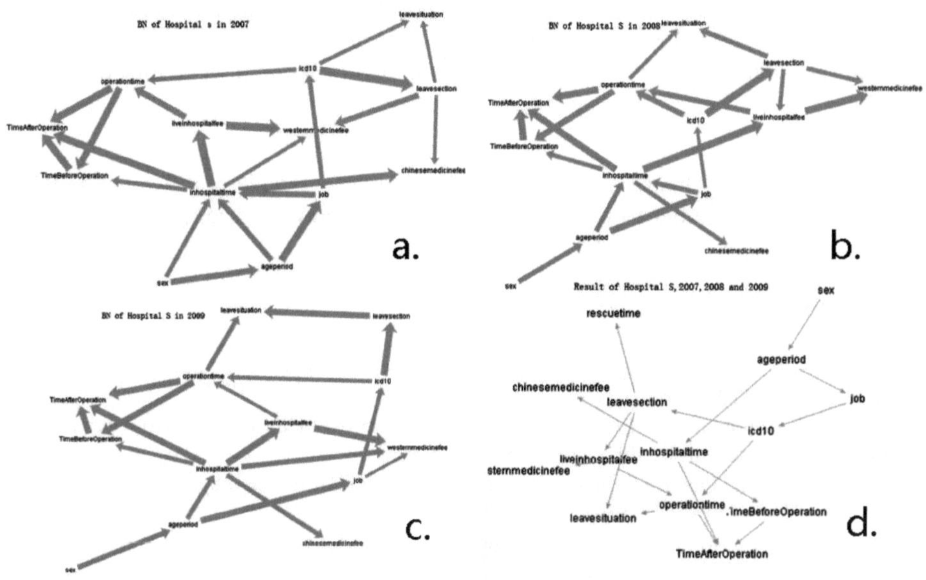

Fig. 7. The BNs for Hospital B of 2007(a), 2008(b) and 2009(c). Quarter 'd.' represents the maximum isomorphic sub-graph of the three years' BNs.

From Fig. 7 we determine that leave section is related with leave situation, live-in hospital fee and rescue time. The relationship with icd10 is meaningless. Along with this information, we check the strength of changes in different years. The arcs in the isomorphism sub-graph reflect the main characteristics in the dataset. Through analysis of the relationships occurring in the isomorphism, we can provide general information regarding the medical records. The results of the research are provided as feedback to the hospitals' specialists for further analysis.

As a result of our research, we also provide high-probability assumptions to the 3 hospitals, which confirmed and proved the effectiveness of our research.

5 Conclusion

In many hospitals, medical care is fragmented, and wrong policies may lead to worse outcomes. We provide the result of the experiment and make some assumptions about the medical to the hospital. We use the method of Bayesian Network analyzing the medical data, aiming at improving the quality of medical care. Identifying the possible direct dependency relationships among variables is an important task in exploratory data analysis. BNs are a good tool for this purpose. There are several advantages in BN-based data analysis: 1) easy to combine prior knowledge; 2) easy to interpret; and 3) easy to deal with missing and noise data. In this paper, we combine prior knowledge with BNs in the searching phase to retrain the BN learning process. As for analyzing the BNs, we provide an isomorphism sub-graph finding method. In the BNs learning and the BNs results comparison steps, we use prior knowledge as much as possible to improve the performance of our system, and this method is effective.

Acknowledgement. This research is partly supported by the Natural Science Fund of China under grant number 61170177 and innovation funding of Tianjin University.

References

1. Kizer, K.W.: The National Quality Forum seeks to improve health care. Academic Medicine 75, 320 (2000)
2. Walshe, K., Freeman, T.: Effectiveness of quality improvement: learning from evaluations. Quality and Safety in Health Care 11, 85–87 (2002)
3. Matthes, N.: The Quality Indicator Projects and its Clinical Indicators
4. 朱士俊: 医疗质量管理发展现状及展望. 解放军医院管理杂志 10, 204–206 (2003)
5. Corneil, D.G., Gotlieb, C.C.: An efficient algorithm for graph isomorphism. Journal of the ACM (JACM) 17, 51–64 (1970)
6. Körner, J., Malvenuto, C., Simonyi, G.: Graph-different permutations. Arxiv preprint arXiv:0709.4387 (2007)
7. Li, G., Leong, T.: Biomedical Knowledge Discovery with Topological Constraints Modeling in Bayesian Networks: A Preliminary Report. Studies in Health Technology and Informatics 129, 560 (2007)
8. Cooper, G.F., Herskovits, E.: A Bayesian method for the induction of probabilistic networks from data. Machine Learning 9, 309–347 (1992)
9. Friedman, N., Koller, D.: Being Bayesian about network structure. A Bayesian approach to structure discovery in Bayesian networks. Machine Learning 50, 95–125 (2003)
10. Thomson, R., Taber, S., Lally, J., Kazandjian, V.: UK Quality Indicator Project®(UK QIP) and the UK independent health care sector: a new development. International Journal for Quality in Health Care 56, i51–i56 (2004)
11. Hou, Q., Zhong, Q., Yang, J., Wang, C., Meng, Q., Gao, X.: Application of ISO9000: 2000 in Hospital Infection Quality Management. Chinese Journal of Nosocomiology 9 (2009)

12. Bobbio, A., Portinale, L., Minichino, M., Ciancamerla, E.: Improving the analysis of dependable systems by mapping fault trees into Bayesian networks. Reliability Engineering & System Safety 71, 249–260 (2001)
13. Beinlich, I.A., Suermondt, H.J., Chavez, R.M., Cooper, G.F.: The ALARM Monitoring System: A Case Study with two Probabilistic Inference Techniques for Belief Networks
14. Ullmann, J.R.: An Algorithm for Subgraph Isomorphism. J. ACM. 23, 31–42 (1976)
15. Körner, J., Malvenuto, C., Simonyi, G.: Graph-different permutations. Arxiv preprint arXiv:0709.4387 (2007)
16. Bouckaert, R.R.: Bayesian network classifiers in weka (2004)
17. Cheng, J., Greiner, R.: Learning Bayesian Belief Network Classifiers: Algorithms and System. In: Stroulia, E., Matwin, S. (eds.) Canadian AI 2001. LNCS (LNAI), vol. 2056, pp. 141–151. Springer, Heidelberg (2001)
18. Daly, B.J., Douglas, S.L., Kelley, C.G., O'toole, E., Montenegro, H.: Trial of a Disease Management Program to Reduce Hospital Readmissions of the Chronically Critically Ill*. Chest 128, 507–517 (2005)
19. Cheng, J., Bell, D.A., Liu, W.: An algorithm for Bayesian belief network construction from data, pp. 83–90. Citeseer (1997)
20. Singh, M., Valtorta, M.: An algorithm for the construction of Bayesian network structures from data, pp. 259–265. Citeseer (1993)

A Hybrid Recommendation Model for HTML5 Mobile Web Applications

Bo Chen[1,2], Hui He[3], and Ying Zhang[3]

[1] Beijing University of Posts and Telecommunications, Beijing, 100876, P.R. China
[2] Postdoctoral Workstation, China United Network Communications Group Co., Ltd. Beijing, 100033, P.R. China
[3] School of Control & Computer Engineering,
North China Electric Power University, Beijing, 100026, P.R. China
{chb615,hh1012,dearzppzpp}@gmail.com

Abstract. In Recent years, the HTML5 Web technologies have become more and more popular. HTML5 provides a variety of new features and APIs that can be used by the applications running in terminals' browsers, especially on mobile devices. This new kind of application is called HTML5 Mobile Web Applications (Web Apps hereafter). Web Apps are written in simple Web languages such as HTML, CSS and JavaScript, which are transparent to the Web App Store or the Web Platform. As a result, the functions of a Web App can be easily analyzed. Based on this special characteristic, we propose a three- level hybrid recommendation model that can combine the Web Apps' implicit features (i.e. functions) as well as traditional explicit features (e.g., user ratings, user review) to build a probabilistic model between the user layer and the application layer. Consequently, this model can be used to recommend which applications are best suited for a user, as well as which users would be the potential consumers of an application.

Keywords: HTML5, Mobile Terminal, Web Apps, Recommendation, Probabilistic Model.

1 Introduction

HTML (HyperText Markup Language) is the "main markup language for displaying web pages and other information that can be displayed in a web browser" [1]. In late 1991, Tim Berners-Lee published a document named "HTML Tags", which has been viewed as the first publicly available description of HTML [2]. Although this document contains only 18 elements comprising the initial, relatively simple design of HTML, it laid the foundation of the web. After that, in 1995, the IETF's HTML Working Group published "HTML 2.0" specification [3], which is the first official standardized HTML specification. The most significant improvement is that HTML 2.0 began to support the image tag. Since 1996, the HTML specifications have been maintained by the World Wide Web Consortium (W3C). In early 1997, HTML 3.2 [4], the first version developed and standardized by W3C, was published as a W3C

V. Khachidze et al. (Eds.): iCETS 2012, CCIS 332, pp. 638–647, 2012.

Recommendation. HTML 3.2 dropped math formulae entirely, reconciled overlap among various proprietary extensions, and adopted most of Netscape's visual markup tags. At the end of 1997, W3C published HTML 4.0 [5] as a formal Recommendation. It adopted many browser-specific element types and attributes. Subsequently, an updated version 4.01 [6] was published as a W3C Recommendation at the end of 1999. At that point, HTML became mature and strong enough to be to be considered as the primary markup language on the internet. Until now, HTML 4.01 is still the latest and most widely deployed formal HTML standard.

In 2008, nearly a decade after the publication of the last version, W3C, together with the Web Hypertext Application Technology Working Group (WHATWG), delivered the first working draft [7]. This is a revolutionary update compared with the previous versions. Since then, HTML is not only a web information display language with rich media and rich content features, but also a set of rich web application technologies with many new features. W3C had announced that its vision for the decade is to build a HTML5-based open web platform [8].

2 The Technical Framework of Mobile Web APPs

In May 2011, W3C advanced HTML5 to "Last Call" status. In 2012, this specification will be transferred into the "Candidate Recommendation" status. It is expected that in 2014, HTML5 will become a formal W3C Recommendation. [9]

In general, when talking about HTML5, we refer to the broad HTML5 technique family consisting of the HTML5 specification, CSS 3 and a serial of JavaScript APIs. W3C has declared 8 major characteristics of the HTML5 techniques, as illustrated below:

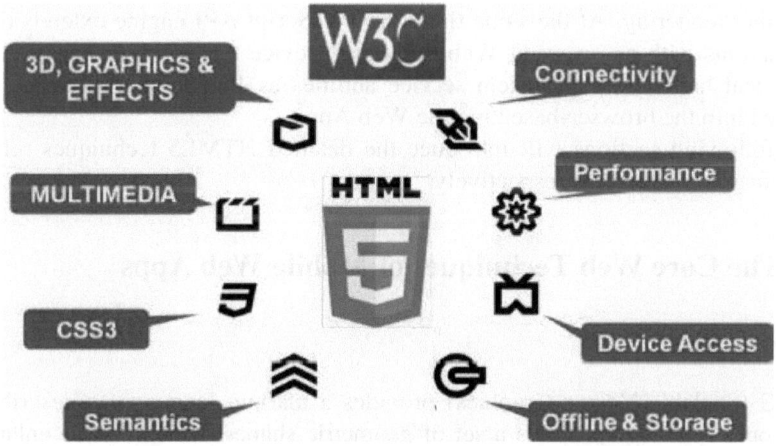

Fig. 1. Major Characteristics of HTML5 Techniques

Form a technical point of view, the HTML5 Web platform techniques can be categorized into a few areas, including Graphics; Multimedia; Device Adaptation; Forms;

User Interactions; Data storage; Hardware Integration; Network; Communication; and Packaging etc. [10].These techniques compose an entire architecture of the browser-based HTML5 mobile web platform.

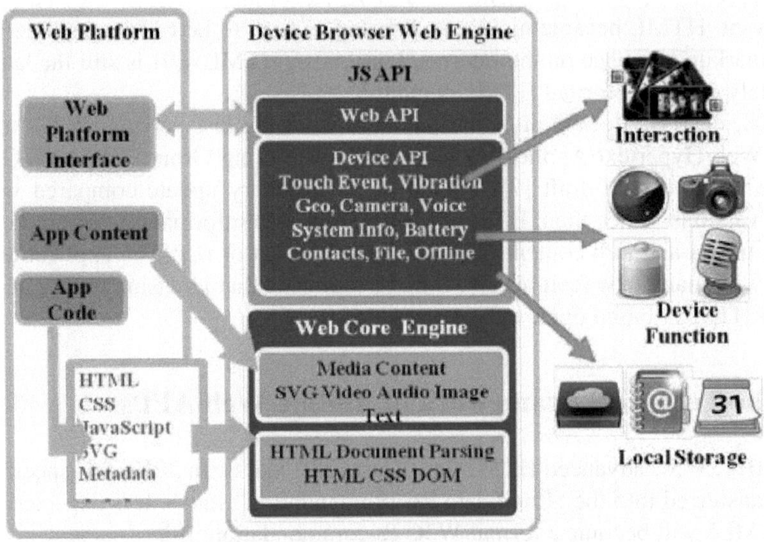

Fig. 2. The Browser Web Runtime Architecture of Mobile Web Apps

In the architecture of the browser-based web runtime of mobile web apps, the core component consists of the Web Core engine and the JavaScript API engine. The Web Core engine handles the parsing of HTML and CSS scripts, as well as media content display and rendering. At the same time, the JavaScript API engine extends the core web functions with a variety of Web APIs and Device APIs, which encapsulate the device local hardware and system service abilities as JavaScript interfaces, can be integrated into the browser-based mobile Web Apps.

The following sections will introduce the detailed HTML5 techniques related to the two major components respectively.

3 The Core Web Techniques of Mobile Web Apps

3.1 Graphics

2D SVG (Scalable Vector Graphics) provides a markup language to describe two-dimensional vector graphics as a set of geometric shapes, which can be enlarged or reduced at the user's request. In addition, SVG graphics can also be easily animated. Therefore, they are well-suited for creating advanced and slick user interfaces within the limited screen spaces on mobile devices.

2D Programmatic API: The <canvas> element added in HTML5 provides a less memory intensive programmatic API, which can be used for graphic rendering and image processing.

CSS (Cascading Style Sheets) Style: CSS3 is a set of specifications, which provide a various of graphic effects including rounded corners, complex background images, shadow effects, rotated content, animations, and even 3D effects. CSS3 can be used to style both SVG and HTML.

Downloadable Fonts: The set of fonts distributed in mobile devices are generally limited. According to the fonts that are needed to render the interface, WOFF (Web Open Font Format) enables automatically downloading the required fonts through style sheets.

3.2 Multimedia

Media Play: HTML5 adds two new multimedia tags, namely <video> and <audio> respectively. By using these tags, Web developers can embed and interact with video and audio content on Web pages.

3.3 Device Adaptation

Mobile devices differ from each other widely in term of screen size, resolution, type of keyboard, media recording capabilities, etc.

Device Information: According to the device information databases stored on the server-side, the Device Description Repository API allows Web developers to retrieve the characteristic data of the devices that are accessing their pages.

Device Adaptation: CSS Media Queries enables adapting the layout and behavior of a Web page based on the characteristics of the device, while CSS Device Adaptation defines a set of CSS directives to determine the size on which this layout should be based.

3.4 Forms

Due to limited text keyboards on mobile devices, to build convenient user input interface is critical for the user experience of web applications on these devices. HTML5 provides the ability to build rich forms to improve the user inputting experiences.

Date and Time Entities: can let the user to use a native calendar control.

Customized Entities: To type some common but complicated data (e.g. Email address, telephone number, web URL, etc), web developers can utilize the input type (e.g. *email, tel, url* etc.) to provide customized user input ways to make things easier.

For example, when a user is typing in an email form control, the web application could match the inputted characters with the session history and/or contact books to provide candidate email entities for the user to choose directly without typing the whole strings.

Input Pattern: The *pattern* attribute limits the string types that are acceptable in a text control. It can be used to improve the efficiency of both user input and background validations.

Input Hint: In complement to the *pattern* attribute, the *placeholder* attribute displays hints about what type of strings are expected in a text control while the user is typing in it.

Predefined Values: By utilizing the new *<datalist>* element, web developers can create free-text input controls with pre-defined values from which the user can select.

3.5 Packaging

There are two important aspects of the user experiences of Web applications: one is the permanent availability even in off-line situation on mobile devices, the other is a common form in which applications can be shared and distributed.

HTML5's Application Cache: this enables the browser keeping the manifest file and other major resources of a Web application in its cache. Therefore, even in off-line situation, at least the major functions of this application are still available in the local browser.

W3C Widgets Family: this series of specifications define a framework for distributing Web applications as Zip files. In each Web application's zip package, there is a configuration file, which is the basis of this application and defines additional features such as its signature, access to APIs, network usage, etc.

4 The Device API Extension of Mobile Web Apps

4.1 User Interactions

Touch-Based: Currently, touch-based input is the primary user interaction mode in the vast majority of mobile devices. W3C's Touch Events specification defines a set of low-level events that represent one or more points of contact with a touch-sensitive surface, and changes of those points with respect to the surface and any DOM elements displayed upon it (e.g. for touch screens) or associated with it (e.g. for drawing tablets without displays). [11]

Vibration: Haptic feedback (e.g. vibration) is another frequently-used form of interactions on mobile devices. W3C's Vibration API specification defines an API to access to the vibration mechanism on devices. [12]

Notification: Mobile device has become part of people's daily life as users rely on the device to remind or notify them of events. W3C's Web Notifications specification defines an API for displaying web notifications to users. [13]

4.2 Multimedia

Media Capture: While the new HTML5 audio and video tags allow one to play multimedia content, the HTML Media Capture specification defines a markup-based mechanism to access to media capture capabilities of the hosting device. [14]

Media Manipulation: Beyond recording, currently there are two additional APIs providing multimedia manipulation capabilities. [15] The Canvas 2D Context API enables modifying images and possibly videos. The Web Audio API defines a high-level JavaScript API for processing and synthesizing audio in web applications. [16]

4.3 Data Storage

The ability to save state, export content, and integrate data from other files and services on the system is a critical component of many web applications.

Simple Data Storage: the Web Storage specification offers two basic mechanisms, localStorage and sessionStorage, for storing structured data as key-value pairs in Web clients. [17]

File System Data: A few APIs are provided for the web applications to interact with a device filesystem: the FileSystems API gives access to general file operations and directory management, the File Reader API and File Writer API enable loading and modifying the content of a file respectively. [18]

Database Query: The Indexed Database API defines a database of values and hierarchical objects and performs advanced key-value data management. [19]

4.4 Hardware Integration

More and more hardware sensors are integrated into mobile devices, such as GPS, accelerometer, ambient light detector, microphone, camera, thermometer, etc.

Geolocation: The Geolocation API provides a common scripted access to geographical location information of the hosting device, which is agnostic of the underlying location information sources (GPS, WIFI networks identification, triangulation in cellular networks, etc.). [20]

Device Orientation: The Device Orientation Event Specification defines several new DOM events that provide access to the physical orientation and acceleration data of the hosting device. [21]

Camera/Microphone: see the previous multimedia section.

4.5 Network

XMLHttpRequest: It is a widely deployed API for loading content from Web servers using the HTTP and HTTPs protocol. The W3C XMLHttpRequest specification provides additional abilities including making requests on servers in a different domain, programmatic feedback on the progress of the network operations, and more efficient handling of binary content. [22]

CORS: To prevent user's credential and private data from being stolen and abused by other Web site, browsers generally do not allow one application to make requests across different domains from a single Web page. By using the Cross-Origin Resource Sharing (CORS) mechanism, Web applications can cooperate much widely between each other. [23]

Server-Sent Events: While XMLHttpRequest is useful for client-initiated network requests, to make better use of server-initiated requests on mobile devices, the Server-Sent Events API allows opening an HTTP connection for receiving push notifications from a server in the form of DOM events. Furthermore, this API can be extended to work with other push notification schemes such as Push SMS. [24]

Network-Information API: This API provides some network characteristics, such as the connection type, rough bandwidth and etc. [25]

4.6 Communication

Several specifications are designed to enable communications between users, between devices and also between applications

In-App: The postMessage API of HTML5 Web Messaging allows for Web Applications to communicate between each other.[26]

P2P: The Web Real-Time Communications specification defines a set of APIs to represent audio and video streaming media, and provide Peer-to-peer (P2P) connection across devices, and real-time communication between users.[27]

5 The Hybrid Recommendation Model

Currently, the most popular application style is the native apps running on smart phone operating systems (e.g. iOS and Android). These applications are written in professional programming languages, such as Object-C or Java. The app packages stored on the App Store are compiled binary files; their abilities and functions are unreadable by the App Store. Therefore, in the current App Store, when constructing some recommendation model to analyze app-user relationships, we mostly utilize some explicit features such as the users' ratings and feedback. [28]

While in the case of HTML5-based Mobile Web Apps, because they are written using HTML, CSS, and JavaScript languages and are deployed directly on the web platform, their script codes can be parsed directly. Therefore, it is possible to utilize the implicit and more essential features, i.e. the application's functions, which can be indicated by the APIs and HTML5 features used in its scripts.

These implicit features reflect the actual characteristics of an application. Furthermore, these features are evidently the basic factors that connect the users' preferences and applications. Therefore, the recommendation model built on these kinds of features can simulate users' preferences more truly.

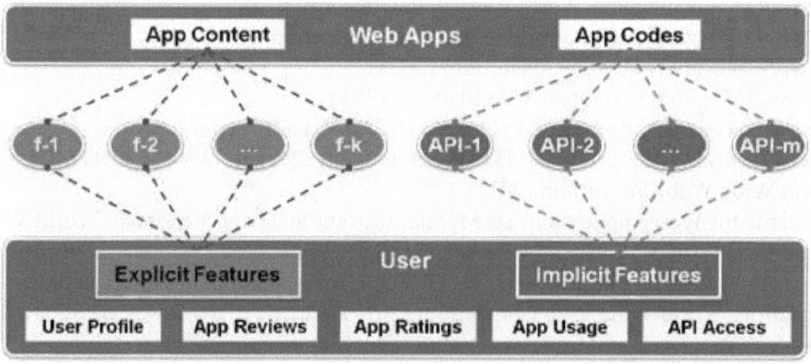

Fig. 3. The Hybrid Recommendation Model for Mobile Web Apps

As a result, we propose the following hybrid probabilistic model, which can utilize either the common explicit user feedback features, or the implicit application functions, illustrated as Figure 3.

In this model, both the explicit features and the application's implicit functions (represented as the APIs used in its scripts) can be treated equally in the probabilistic model:

For users to find the appropriate apps, we use

$$P(app|user) = P(app|f)*P(f|user) \quad (1)$$

For apps to find the potential users, we use

$$P(user|app) = P(user|f)*P(f|app) \quad (2)$$

Wherein, in the model construction stage, the *P(app|user)* and *P(user|app)* can be estimated by several approaches, such as

- simply using the user's rating level to normalize into the [0,1] interval;
- using some text sentiment analysis techniques, such as described by He and Chen [28], to evaluate these values from the user's review feedbacks.

Once these two kinds of probabilistic models are estimated, using some Maximum Likelihood training method, we can adjust the four probabilistic factors *P(app|f)*, *P(f|user)*, *P(user|f)*, *P(f|app)*.

While at the prediction stage, using the four factors mentioned above, we can make two kinds of recommendations as represented in formulations **(1)** and **(2)**.

References

1. HTML, Wikipedia, http://en.wikipedia.org/wiki/HTML
2. First Mention of HTML Tags on The WWW-Talk Mailing List. World Wide Web Consortium (1991)
3. Tim, B.L., Dan, C.: RFC 1866: Hypertext Markup Language – 2.0 – Acknowledgments. Internet Engineering Task Force (1995)
4. HTML 3.2 Reference Specification. World Wide Web Consortium (1997)
5. HTML 4.0 Specification. World Wide Web Consortium (1997)
6. HTML 4.01 Specification. World Wide Web Consortium (1999)
7. HTML5. World Wide Web Consortium (2008)
8. Hégaret, P.L.: The Next Open Web Platform (2011), http://www.w3.org/2011/Talks/0216-html5-plh/
9. W3C Confirms May 2011 for HTML5 Last Call, Targets 2014 for HTML5 Standard. World Wide Web Consortium (2011)
10. Standards for Web Applications on Mobile: Current State and Roadmap. World Wide Web Consortium (2012), http://www.w3.org/2012/02/mobile-web-app-state/
11. Brubeck, M., Moon, S., Schepers, D.: Touch Events version 1. W3C Candidate Recommendation. World Wide Web Consortium (2011), http://www.w3.org/TR/touch-events/
12. Kostiainen, A.: Vibration API. W3C Candidate Recommendation. World Wide Web Consortium (2012), http://www.w3.org/TR/vibration/
13. Kesteren, A., Gregg, J.: Web Notifications. W3C Working Draft. World Wide Web Consortium (2012), http://www.w3.org/TR/notifications/
14. Kostiainen, A., Oksanen, I., Hazaël-Massieux, D.: HTML Media Capture. W3C Working Draft. World Wide Web Consortium (2012), http://www.w3.org/TR/html-media-capture/
15. Hickson, I.: HTML Canvas 2D Context. W3C Working Draft. World Wide Web Consortium (2012), http://www.w3.org/TR/2dcontext/
16. Rogers, C.: Web Audio API. W3C Working Draft. World Wide Web Consortium (2012), http://www.w3.org/TR/webaudio/
17. Hickson, I.: Web Storage. W3C Candidate Recommendation. World Wide Web Consortium (2012), http://www.w3.org/TR/webstorage/
18. Uhrhane, E.: File API: Directories and System. W3C Working Draft. World Wide Web Consortium (2012), http://www.w3.org/TR/file-system-api/
19. Mehta, N., Sicking, J., Graff, E., Popescu, A., Orlow, J.: Indexed Database API. W3C Working Draft. World Wide Web Consortium (2012), http://www.w3.org/TR/IndexedDB/
20. Popescu, A.: Geolocation API Specification. W3C Proposed Recommendation. World Wide Web Consortium (2012), http://www.w3.org/TR/geolocation-API/

21. Block, S., Popescu, A.: Device Orientation Event Specification. W3C Working Draft. World Wide Web Consortium (2012), http://www.w3.org/TR/orientation-event/
22. Kesteren, A.: XMLHttpRequest. W3C Editor's Draft. World Wide Web Consortium (2012), http://dvcs.w3.org/hg/xhr/raw-file/tip/Overview.html
23. Kesteren, A.: Cross-Origin Resource Sharing. W3C Editor's Draft. World Wide Web Consortium (2012), http://dvcs.w3.org/hg/cors/raw-file/tip/Overview.html
24. Hickson, I.: Server-Sent Events. W3C Working Draft. World Wide Web Consortium (2012), http://www.w3.org/TR/eventsource/
25. Chitturi, S., Berjon, R.: The Network Information API. W3C Working Draft. World Wide Web Consortium (2012), http://www.w3.org/TR/netinfo-api/
26. Hickson, I.: HTML5 Web Messaging. W3C Candidate Recommendation. World Wide Web Consortium (2012), http://www.w3.org/TR/webmessaging/
27. Bergkvist, A., Burnett, D., Jennings, C., Narayanan, A.: WebRTC 1.0: Real-time Communication Between Browsers. W3C Working Draft. World Wide Web Consortium (2012), http://www.w3.org/TR/webrtc/
28. He, H., Chen, B.: A Smart Sentiment Analysis System in Word, Sentence and Text Level. Advanced Engineering Forum 1, 338–342 (2011)

A Distributed Ontology Repository Management Approach Based on Semantic Wiki

Guozheng Rao, Zhiyong Feng, Xin Wang, and Ruiguang Liu

School of Computer Science and Technology, TianJin University,
Tianjin 300072, China
{rgz,zyfeng,wangx}@tju.edu.cn,
tiduslrg@gmail.com

Abstract. As the foundation of Semantic Web, the size of ontologies on the Web has developed into tens of billions. Furthermore, the creation process of the repository takes place through open collaboration. However, the problem of inconsistent repository is made even worse because of openness and collaboration. Semantic wiki provides a new approach to build large-scale, unified semantic knowledge base. This paper focuses on the relevant problems, technologies and applications of semantic wiki based ontology repository with the combination of semantic wiki technologies and distributed ontology repository. A distributed ontology repository management approach and platform based on semantic wiki is presented. The platform is divided into three layers, including distributed ontology management layer, business logic layer, and application performance layer. Self-maintenance and optimization of distributed ontology repository is implemented by the management module with technology of ontology reasoning, ontology view extraction and ontology segmentation. The unified interface of the repository to provide knowledge storage and query services to application of semantic web is provided through knowledge bus mechanism with distributed ontology encapsulated. In the business logic layer, the operations of wiki and ontology are mapped to manage the wiki pages and ontology resources through mapping the wiki entries and ontology resources. In the application performance layer, a friendly interface is provided to build repository through combining the entry information display and the semantic information extraction.

Keywords: Distributed Ontology, Ontology Inconsistency, Semantic Wiki.

1 Introduction

As the foundation of Semantic Web, the size of ontologies on the Web has developed into tens of billions. However, Current ontology-engineering practices insufficiently address at least five fundamental aspects of building and committing to ontology: (1) Ontology engineering lag versus conceptual dynamics; (2) Resource consumption; (3) Communication between creators and users; (4) Incentive conflicts and network externalities; (5) Intellectual property rights [1]. Furthermore, the problems existing in current ontology engineering are as follows:

V. Khachidze et al. (Eds.): iCETS 2012, CCIS 332, pp. 648–657, 2012.

1) Ontology engineering is a tremendous task which needs iterative development. Furthermore, ontologies are complex and difficult to build and understand; this hinders their wide-spread adoption. The cost of building ontologies is still not accepted.
2) There are high barriers against lay users preventing the suggestion of new concepts. Most methodologies rely too much on experts' domain knowledge to carry on distributed developing.
3) Relevant research and technology is still unripe.
4) Most current methodologies are suitable for special applications [2].
5) Strategy for identifying concepts is "top-down" or "middle-out" in most of the current ontology engineering methodologies.

The rest of this paper is organized as follows. Related works are discussed in section 2. A distributed ontology repository management approach is presented in Section 3. Finally, discussion and conclusion are provided in the last section of the paper.

2 Related Works

Semantic Wikis try to combine Semantic Web standards such as RDF/S or OWL with the Wiki paradigm [3]. On the one hand, it is intended to annotate structure in the Wiki by providing metadata for existing features such as links and pages. On the other hand, one can strive to completely represent the Wiki content using instances of the respective ontology language [4]. COW, Combining Ontologies with Wikis, is an approach to building a Semantic Wiki, by bringing together two different concepts: easy content evolution with the help of Wikis, and formal knowledge representation using ontologies. IkeWiki [5] is a prototype Wiki system currently being developed at Salzburg Research. Kaukolu is built on JSPWiki and Sesame. Since Kaukolu is built on top of JSPWiki, it includes standard Wiki features such as file attachments, access control, plug-in support, and support for multiple back-ends. Maknaaims provides an easy and user-friendly user interface and powerful Semantic Web technologies in the backend. The engine implementation is based on JSPWiki and the Jena. OntoWiki [6] aims at providing support for agile, distributed knowledge engineering scenarios. It facilitates the visual presentation of a knowledge base as an information map, with different views on instance data. It enables intuitive authoring of semantic content, with an online editing mode for editing RDF content, similar to WYSIWYG for text documents. It fosters social collaboration aspects by keeping track of changes, allowing comments and discussing every single part of a knowledge base, enabling rating and measuring the popularity of content. OntoWiki enhances browsing and retrieval by offering semantic enhanced search strategies.

OpenRecord is similar to a Wiki, but with some database features added in. In OpenRecord the content is organized as a database of items or records. Each page on an OpenRecord site can query the database to get some set of items, and those items can be displayed in an editable table, in an outline format, or in other formats. In time, OpenRecord could grow to incorporate simple spreadsheet features, as well as interactive charting and graphing features, and OLAP and pivot table features. OpenRecord is still at an early stage of development.

Platypus Wiki [7] offers a simple user interface to create Wiki pages including metadata. It uses RDF, RDF Schema and OWL to manage the metadata and create ontologies. All pages are stored in an HTML file with metadata in RDF.

Semantic MediaWiki is an extension of MediaWiki – a widely used Wiki-engine that also powers Wikipedia. In Semantic MediaWiki, each article (Wiki page) describes a concept. Semantic statements can be made, by freely assigning link types to hyperlinks. Additionally, attributes of any concept can be specified in syntax similar to the link syntax. Instead of referring to another concept, they simply refer to a value.

SemperWiki is a cross-breed between Semantic Wikis and personal Wikis and serves as a personal information management system. It combines ease of use, one of the characteristics of Personal Wikis, with the improved retrieval and navigation functionalities of Semantic Wikis. It can be used as a stand-alone semantic information system or as a user interface of a Semantic Desktop system.

SweetWiki relies on the CORESE semantic search engine for querying and reasoning and on SEWESE, and its associated web server extension that provides API and JSP tags to implement ontology-based interfaces and a set of generic functionalities e.g. security management, ontology editors, web application life cycle.

WikSAR (Semantic Authoring and Retrieval within a Wiki) facilitates semantic authoring and provides the user with context-aware navigation, interactive graph visualization of the emerging ontology, as well as semantic retrieval. Embedding queries into Wiki pages creates views on the information space. Desktop integration includes accessing dates (e.g., reminders) entered in the Wiki via local calendar applications, maintaining bookmarks, and collecting web quotes within the Wiki.

[10] Making the Semantic Web a reality demands more and better ontologies. It proposes that building ontologies is inherently a social process constrained by technical, social, economic, and legal bottlenecks. Lee et al [8] show that standard Wiki technology can be easily used as an ontology development environment, reducing entry barriers for the participation of users in the creation and maintenance of ontologies, and describe challenges for building OntoWiki prototypes. Kawamoto et al [9] present an approach to enriching tags with semantics in order to integrate folksonomies and the Semantic Web. They also use online lexical resources, ontologies and Semantic Web resources for amending the tags. Martin Hepp (2005) focuses on using existing resources and ontologies to map tags into concepts, properties or instances and determine the relations between these mapped tags. Specia and Motta [11] Integrate folksonomies with the semantic web. Putting the community in the center of the ontology engineering process has already been proposed by Van Damme et al [12], and other work on collaborative ontology engineering. The authors are generating a community-driven ontology based on ontology maturing process.

Most of these projects have the following characteristics: Marked the link, context-sensitive expression, enhanced navigation, semantic search, and support reasoning. But Most of these functions focus on the perspective of application of Semantic Web.

3 A Distributed Ontology Repository Management Approach

Wiki is a management platform initially for special domain community to share and exchange information and knowledge. Wiki became a collaborative knowledge management platform because of its friendly and simple user interface. In this paper, a bottom-up ontology engineering methodology is proposed. Design mechanism of wiki is adopted to realize the ontologies. All web users can set up and maintain the ontologies. The characteristics of methodology are presented as follows:

(1) Collaboration rather than mapping

A user or an organization may build different ontologies based on corresponding requirements. The ontologies in the same domain may be heterogeneous. Many ontology mapping and matching approaches are suggested to solve this problem, but the results are not satisfactory. Each person can contribute to both the concept and attributes in System. The users who have common interest in a domain can take part in the same community. A community maintains a view of their domain ontologies. The user of this community can modify the ontologies. What is more, a user can attend several communities based on his own interest.

(2) Version control

The events of maintaining the ontology will be recorded by log ontology which will well support the evolution of the system. The version control system should provide each version for the review. Users can compare the differences and similarities of two versions, and then they can effectively control and manage the ontologies. At the same time, the reasoning of log ontology can support the evolution of the system.

(3) Access control

A large number of versions will destroy the system because of different backgrounds and research fields of the creator. The managers will fix the content such that it may not be changed.

(4) Formatting rules

Wiki Ontology should provide special syntax (such as the definition of attributes) for users so that they can easily maintain the ontologies and achieve the formatted output. An easy and friendly user interface is needed.

(5) Growth

Potential for growth. A concept can be not yet in existence (i.e. emerging concepts, such as SARS); by clicking on its name (hyperlinks), one can create the concept.

Revision history. The history of maintaining the ontology will be recorded by log ontology record. Various versions and views may be accessed.

(6) Open

The members of the community can create, modify, and delete concepts and attributes, but the community should retain control over its own edition ontology evolution. Ontology system changes can be observed by visitors.

(7) Reusability

Some APIs and web services should be disseminated to others for free. An incentive mechanism should be used to attract more people to contribute to the system.

(8) Multi-level indexing storage

In order to improve properties of access, storage and query, the multi-level indexing storage method is discussed. The users can get multi-level ontology expediently which raises the rate of ontology reuse.

A semantic wiki system is designed to meet the above requirements (Fig. 1), which consists of semantic wiki platform, data interfaces and data tiers. Distributed ontologies repository is the core component.

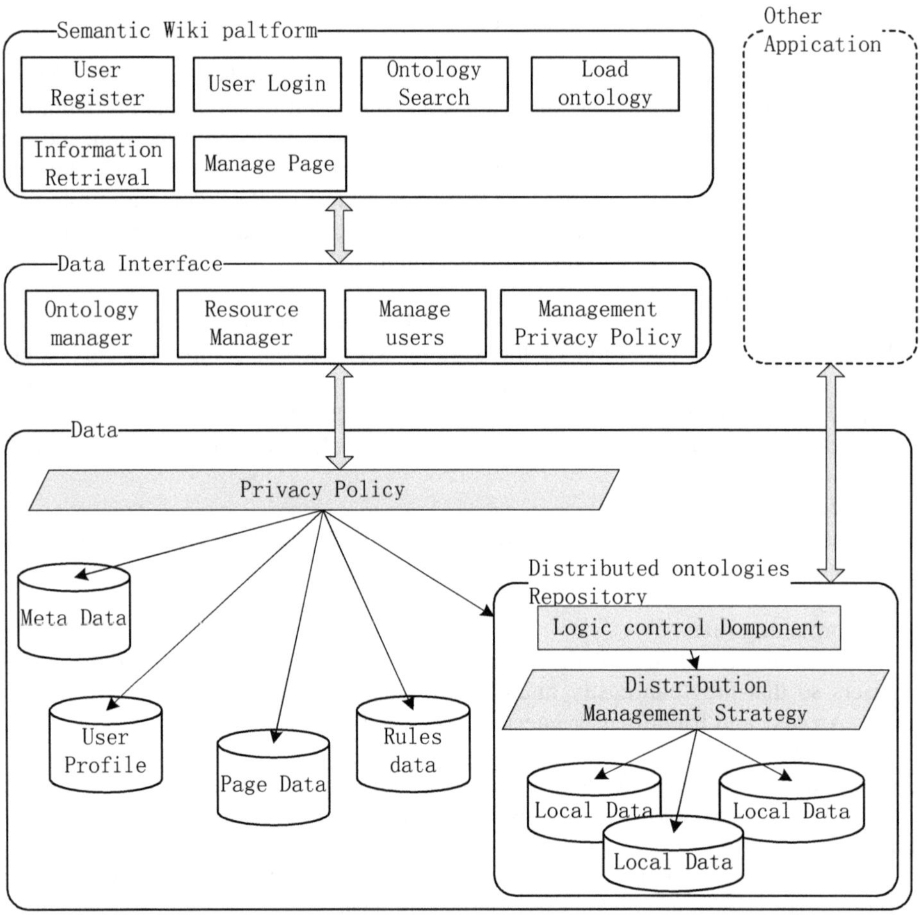

Fig. 1. Architecture of Semantic Wiki

3.1 Architecture of Distributed Ontologies Management

A web-based distributed ontology management system is designed for requirements. The ontology data is stored in multiple servers. Its architecture is shown in Fig. 2.

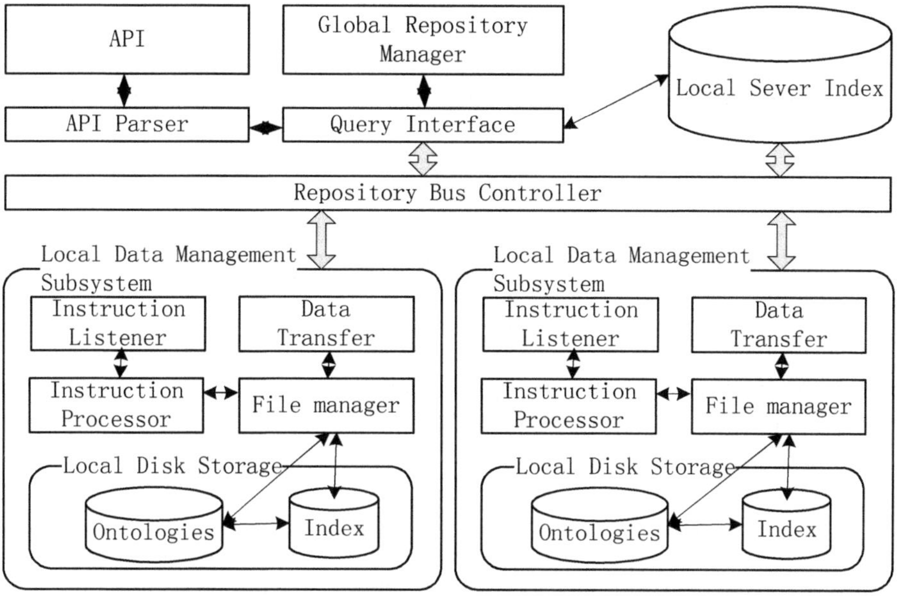

Fig. 2. Architecture of distributed ontologies management

The components are integrated by the repository bus controller and a standard set of knowledge instructions. The API component is provided to the users o develop their own program based on this system. The Local data management subsystem is managed by the global repository manager through the local server index.

There are five components in the local data management subsystem, namely, local disk storage, file manager, data transfer, instruction processor and listener. The local disk storage is the disk partition storing the ontology files and its index. Data is read and written through the file manager. It also receives and processes the instruction and provides data to the data transfer. Data transfer is the standard interface for the repository bus controller. The instructions from the bus are received by listener. They are then transferred to the instruction processor after pre-process. The global repository manager is located in the main server. It maintains the ontology repository through the local server index, which stores the information such as address, ontology list and state of the local server. The multicast and broadcast instructions are sent to the local server index and the repository bus controller by the query interface. API Parser is an adapter that translates the variety of API requests to the core basic query commands. The global repository manager is the core component. It keeps running in the backend of the main server. The ontology repository reasoning and evolutionary algorithms are implemented in it. The knowledge structure and storage is continually optimized through ontology consistent view extraction, ontology integration, ontology segment, and load balancing.

3.2 Design of Ontology Repository Interface

API is a unified interface layer of the web-based distributed ontology repository. The semantic web application service is provided for the developers with the API expediently. The API should interoperate with the past API. For the developers, a great global ontology is provided by the system. They can freely access the ontology through the API library without concern with implementation.

However, the distributed ontologies repository is different from a simple ontology. To operate the entire repository by loading it into memory is impossible, so ontology integration and ontology extraction algorithm are required. The semantic reasoning scope of ontology knowledge is limited in combining the context of the knowledge application. Users can extract a consistent local ontology view (segment) for the requirement application; furthermore, they can deal with multi-ontology reasoning view in a number of local ontologies.

3.3 Key Algorithms of Semantic Web Repository Management

Tableau algorithm based on description logic can determine satisfiability and consistency of a concept in ontology. In this system, we put forward aiming at the problems of considerable quality discrepancy and semantic inconsistency, and then a multi-view ontology knowledge organization model will be built up. The algorithm of maximal consistent ontology view extraction is presented as follows.

Definition 1. (subset covering) $\bigcup_{i=1}^{N} SO_i$ is a subset covering of O, when the conditions as follow is satisfied.

(1) $\forall SO_i, SO_j, i \neq j, 1 < i, j < N, SO_i, SO_i \subseteq O, SO_i \cap SO_i \neq \varnothing$

(2) $\bigcup_{i=1}^{N} SO_i = O$

Definition 2. (max consistent subset covering) $\bigcup_{i=1}^{N} SO_i$ is the max consistent subset covering of O, when the conditions as follow is satisfied.

(1) $\forall SO_i, SO_j, i \neq j, 1 < i, j < N, SO_i, SO_i \subseteq O, SO_i \cap SO_i \neq \varnothing$

(2) $\bigcup_{i=1}^{N} SO_i = O$

(3) SO_i, SO_j is consistent ontology.

(4) x is concept of ontology O , $x \in O$ $\forall SO_k \in \{SO_1, SO_2, \cdots, SO_N\}, x \notin SO_k$, $SO_k^{'} = x \bigcup SO_k$, if $SO_k^{'}$ is inconsistent, then $SO_k^{'}$ is the max consistent subset.

Definition 3. (ontology view) VO is an ontology view of $\bigcup_{i=1}^{N} SO_i$ when the conditions as follow are satisfied.

(1) $\bigcup_{i=1}^{N} SO_i$ is the max consistent subset covering of O

(2) $VO \in \left\{ 2^{\bigcup_{i=1}^{N} SO_i} \right\}$

Algorithm 1. Find max consistent subset covering with key words given by users:

Input: key words given by user, $KW = \{w_1, w_2, \cdots, w_n\}, n \in N$.

Output: ontology view of the user VO

Steps:

(1)Let $w_1 \succ w_2 \succ \cdots \succ w_n$ (since $w_i \succ w_j$ means w_i is more important than w_j, so w_1 is the most important key word in KW)

(2) Loop 1:
Let $C = \varnothing$
Search the concept c_i is similar to w_i
If the similarity is too low (It is less than the value given (e.g. 0.5))), break
$C = C \cup c_i$
End loop 1

(3) Loop 2:
If $O = \varnothing$
then, break
ELSE
Let $c_1 \succ c_2 \succ \cdots \succ c_m, c_j \in C, 1 < j < m$
Locate c_1 in O,
Find the max consistent subset SO_1 and $c_1 \in SO_1$
$O = O - SO_1$, $C = C - c_1$

(4) Loop 3
If $C = \varnothing$
then, break
ELSE
Find $c_j \in C$ and $c_j \notin SO_1$

(5)END Loop3

(6)END Loop 2

(7) $VO = \bigcup_{i=1}^{M} SO_i$

Ontology view of the user, VO is consistent ontology set, so it can be reasoned by the classic semantic web reasoning engine, just like RACER, Jess and Jena.

Ontology repository in the semantic Web is very large. Any application will not need all the ontology to reason; therefore the way to find the most relevant ontology set is the key issue. To address this issue, ontology similarity algorithm is designed to find the most relevant ontology set.

3.4 Similarity between Concept and Ontology

Given ontologies set $\Omega = \{o_1, o_2, ..., o_n\}$ and concepts of the ontology c. Then, the weight of the correlation between concept c and ontologies $o_1, o_2, ..., o_n$ can be defined $w_1, w_2, ..., w_n$. The concepts set [c] associated with c can be inferred based on the inference rules. The weight of each element in c is valued in each dimension of the vector space. At last, ontology similarity can be calculated with the cosine of the angle between vectors of two ontologies. The formula is listed as follows:

$$w_{i,j} = \log(f(c_i, o_j) + 1) \times \log(\frac{n}{n'} + 1) \tag{1}$$

$$Sim(c_i, O) = \frac{\sum_{i=1}^{\|[c]\|} w_{i,j} \times w_{i,k}}{\sqrt{\sum_{i=1}^{\|[c]\|} w_{i,j}^2 \times \sum_{i=1}^{\|[c]\|} w_{i,k}^2}} \tag{2}$$

$w_{i,j}$ is the vector value of the i dimension of o_j in the concepts set [c], the weight of concept c_i in the ontology o_j. In formula (1) n is the number of ontologies in the ontologies set, and n' is the number of ontologies including concepts c; moreover, $f(c_i, o_j)$ is occurrence frequency that concept c_i is included in ontology o_j in the body. Formula (2) is used to calculate the cosine of the angle between the two dimensional vectors.

4 Conclusion

In this paper, we propose a bottom-up ontology engineering methodology. Design mechanism of wiki is adopted to realize the ontologies. All web users can set up and maintain the ontologies. The users who have the same interest in a domain can take part in the same community, but the community should retain control over its own edition ontology evolution. The events of maintaining the ontology will be recorded by log ontology which will well support the evolution of ontologies. Furthermore, in order to improve properties of access, storage and query, the multi-level indexing storage method is discussed. Users can get multi-level ontology expediently, raising the rate of ontology reuse. The system should enable high interoperability between similar ontology-based systems in the future since most of the intending information system should base on ontologies. In summary, our approach aims at providing new approaches to the organization and processing of large-scale open ontology knowledge and new user-centered ways of acquiring ontology knowledge, which will help promote the knowledge sharing and application of large-scale ontologies on the Web.

Acknowledgements. This work is supported by the National Natural Science Foundation of China (No. 61070202, 61100049), Special Fund for Fast Sharing of Science Paper in Net Era by CSTD (No. 2011117).

References

1. Hepp, M.: Possible Ontologies: How Reality Constrains the Development of Relevant Ontologies. IEEE Internet Computing 11(1), 90–96 (2007)
2. Hendler, J., Berners-Lee, T.: From the semantic web to social machines: A research challenge for AI on the World Wide Web. Artificial Intelligence 174(2), 156–161 (2010)
3. Happel, H.-J., Maalej, W., Panagiotou, D.: D7: Report describing state-of-the art in SE Knowledge Desktop. Project Deliverable. IST-Project TEAM 35111. Technical report (2007), `http://www.team-project.eu/documents/`
4. Hammouda, K., Kamel, M.: Phrase-based document similarity based on an index graph model. In: IEEE International Conference on Data Mining, pp. 203–210. IEEE Press, Maebashi (2003)
5. Komondoor, R., Horwitz, S.: Using Slicing to Identify Duplication in Source Code. In: Cousot, P. (ed.) SAS 2001. LNCS, vol. 2126, pp. 40–56. Springer, Heidelberg (2001)
6. Anyanwu, K., Maduko, A., Sheth, A.: Ranking Complex Relationship Search Results on the Semantic Web. In: Proceedings of the 14th International Conference on World Wide Web, pp. 117–127. ACM Press, New York (2005)
7. Brunkhorst, I., Chirita, P., Co-stache, S., Gaugaz, J., Ioannou, E., Iofciu, T., Minack, E., Nejdl, W., Paiu, R.: The Beagle++ Toolbox: Towards an Extendable Desktop Search Architecture. In: Proceedings of the 2nd Semantic Desktop Workshop held at the 5th International Semantic Web Conference, Athens, GA, United States (2006)
8. Lee, J., Park, J.-H., Park, M.-J., Chung, C.-W., Min, J.-K.: An intelligent query processing for distributed ontologies. Journal of Systems and Software 83(1), 85–95 (2010)
9. Kawamoto, K., Mase, M., Kitamura, Y., Tijerino, Y.: Semantic Wiki Where Human and Agents Collaborate. In: Proceedings of the 2008 IEEE/WIC/ACM International Conference on Web Intelligence and Intelligent Agent Technology, pp. 147–151. IEEE Computer Society, Washington (2008)
10. Hepp, M., Bachlechner, D., Siorpaes, K.: OntoWiki: Community-driven Ontology Engineering and Ontology Usage based on Wikis. In: Proceedings of the 2005 International Symposium on Wikis (WikiSym 2005), San Diego, California, USA (2005)
11. Specia, L., Motta, E.: Integrating Folksonomies with the Semantic Web. In: Franconi, E., Kifer, M., May, W. (eds.) ESWC 2007. LNCS, vol. 4519, pp. 624–639. Springer, Heidelberg (2007)
12. Van Damme, C., Hepp, M., Siorpaes, K.: Folks Ontology: An Integrated Approach for Turning Folksonomies into Ontologies. In: Proceedings of the ESWC 2007 Workshop "Bridging the Gap between Semantic Web and Web 2.0", Innsbruck, Austria, pp. 71–84 (2007)

Thai Immigrant Entrepreneurs in New Zealand

Pusanisa Thechatakerng

Maejo Unversity, Chiangmai 50290 Thailand
thepusanisa@yahoo.com

Abstract. Entrepreneurship is recognized as an important opportunity for job growth and economic development. In addition, entrepreneurship can be a way to improve the economic position of immigrants. Thus, immigrant entrepreneurs are driving the new economy. For immigrants from Thailand, the number of Thai restaurants and Thai businesses in New Zealand are increasing steadily. With these phenomena, this study tries to examine the following questions: a) What are the demographical characteristics of the Thai immigrant groups? b) Which factors influence an individual's decision to become an entrepreneur? c) How is the business performance of the immigrant entrepreneurs? d) Finally, what is the degree of satisfaction of Thai immigrant entrepreneurs in New Zealand? As an exploratory research, 4 immigrant entrepreneurs were interviewed in Wellington. The results show the various characteristics of entrepreneurs; for example, immigrant entrepreneurs are of various ages, from 26 to 62; some are married, some single; they tend to be educated persons, and they practice Buddhism. The important factors influencing immigrants to be entrepreneurs are freedom and time management. The result also shows positive signs regarding their businesses' performance.

Keywords: Immigrant, Entrepreneur, Thai, New Zealand.

1 Problem Statement and Objectives

1.1 Problem Statement

Entrepreneurship is recognized as an important opportunity for job growth and economic development (Thechatakerng, 2009; Jansen et al. 2004; Van Stel and Carree, 2002). In addition, entrepreneurship can be a way to improve the economic position of immigrants (Mancilla et al, 2010), and their rate of entrepreneurship has risen steadily in the last decade. Thus, immigrant entrepreneurs are driving the new economy (John Wiley & Sons, 2009). The rate of entrepreneurship shows considerable variation. This is especially true among immigrant populations. Many immigrants in New Zealand are of Chinese, Greek, Italian and Lebanese origin (Collins, 2008; Lee, 2008); predominantly in some decades, Korean, Indian, Thai, Malaysian, Sri Lankan and other "minority" groups have been engaged in immigrant entrepreneurship (Lever-Tracy et al., 1991; Collins et al., 1995: 84-90). In New Zealand, Thai immigrants constitute one of eight largest

V. Khachidze et al. (Eds.): iCETS 2012, CCIS 332, pp. 658–670, 2012.

Asian ethnic groups (Statistics New Zealand, 2012). These immigrants belong to either the first generation (if they themselves have been born elsewhere) or the second generation (if at least one of their parents has been born elsewhere).

For immigrants from Thailand, the rate of immigration is increasing; this can be observed from the number of Thai restaurants and Thai businesses in New Zealand. Moreover, the Thai population has increased from 393 in 1986 to 4,554 in 2001 (Lee, 2008) and has increased to 6,057 in 2006 (Statistics New Zealand, 2012). Immigration from Thailand has a history of more than three decades, and yet these immigrants often find themselves in marginal economic positions (Hart, 2011; Hold, 2011; Zotan et al., 2009; Lee, 2008 Rath, 2006; Mendez & Wanatabe, 2005). Therefore, the study obtains some perspective on immigrant entrepreneurs. With this view, we focus on demographical determinants such as gender, age, education, household composition, degree of urbanization, and others in characteristics of enterprises. Beyond these, we focus on only legal immigrants, andimmigrant entrepreneurs who run their restaurants in the first generation.

1.2 Study Objectives

We attempt to explore various determinants of entrepreneurship related to economical, psychological, sociological and demographical aspects of entrepreneurship. Additionally, this paper illustrates that the demographical work of a population is an important determinant of entrepreneurship. Therefore, we focus on demographical variables as possible determinants of immigrant entrepreneurship.

This paper, then, tries to examine the following research questions:

1. What are the demographical characteristics of the Thai immigrant groups?
2. Which factors influence an individual's decision to become an entrepreneur?
3. How is the businesses performance of immigrant entrepreneurs?

2 Literature Review

Since then, the number of immigrants has increased, and the presence of Thai immigrant entrepreneurs in New Zealand restaurant businesses has also enlarged (Lee, 2008). We therefore consider existing theories explaining immigrant entrepreneurs, namely *Middleman minority theory, the Blocked mobility theory, Ethnic enclave economy theory,* and *Interactive Theory.*

Middleman minority theory explains the phenomenon of ethnic businesses. This concept refers to the minority groups that have played an intermediary economic role between producers of the dominant group and minority customers in different societies (Min & Bozorgmehr, 2003; De Raijman, 1996).*The Blocked mobility theory* focuses on immigrants' disadvantage in the general labor market. Min and Bozorgmehr (2003) argued that immigrants experience disadvantages related to employment in the primary labor market as compared to native born workers. Certainly, the language barrier is the most visible disadvantage to some immigrant groups. There are also other labor force disadvantages such as physical disability, ethno-racial discrimination, unrecognized educational credentials, exclusion from referral networks, undocumented status, and little to no work experience (Valenzuela, 2000; De Raijiman, 1996). Entrepreneurship, then, is the alternative means of economic advancement for marginalized groups (Middleton, 2005; Hiebert, 2003; Min & Bozorgmehr, 2003).*Ethnic enclave economy theory* proposes an alternative labor market for immigrants who would otherwise be channeled into peripheral sectors (Lee, 2003). It denotes that most immigrants cannot escape from the bottom of the general labor market without the ethnic enclave economy. The term "ethnic enclave" refers to an "immigrant enclave" whereby immigrant workers are employed in the enterprises owned by members of the same ethnicity (Lee, 2003). Therefore, the enclave theory concentrates on geographically self–contained ethnic communities within metropolitan areas (Butler & Greene, 1997). That is to say, immigrants of the same ethnicity gather around certain locations for their residence, and some run businesses targeting customers from the same ethnic group. However, it is worth noting that every immigrant group does not make up an ethnic enclave economy. In order for an enclave economy to emerge, immigrants must have three prerequisites: entrepreneurial skills, capital, and a supply of ethnic labor (Le, 2000; Logan et al., 1994, Portes and Manning, 1986).

Interactive Theory approach, the last important theory, suggests that ethnic business proliferates in industries wherein there is found congruence between the demands of the economic environment and the informal resources of the ethnic population (Waldinger, 1986). The most obvious example is a kind of business, related to jobs abandoned by native workers in the mainstream economy, or a particular mainstream need which is unattractive to native business (Agrawal & Chavan, 1997). For immigrants' entrepreneurial behaviour, social human networks contribute significantly to immigrant entrepreneurship according to this theory (Mitchell, 2003). For example, new immigrants can have access to employment opportunities in businesses that are run by owners of the same ethnicity, rather than to mainstream employment opportunities. They also learn business skills there, and this leads them to become independent entrepreneurs in the future. With all theories explained above, ́the literature review would focus as follows on *Immigrant entrepreneurs.* In this study, entrepreneurship is defined as business ownership, where business refers to businesses with and without employees and includes sole proprietors and partnerships as well as private and public limited enterprises. Rate of entrepreneurship is defined as the number of entrepreneurs, which will be based upon the number from a database by Population Statistics (Chou, 2000, p. 22) and 2001 census data (Statistics NZ, 2002), New Zealand. *Demography and immigrant entrepreneurship* focuses on *Entrepreneurship,* which we center in factors influencing an individual's decision to become an entrepreneur, e.g. psychological determinants (motives and character traits of entrepreneurs), sociological determinants (on the collective background of entrepreneurs), economical determinants (on the impact of economic climate and technological developments) and demographical determinants of entrepreneurship (Jansen et al., 2003; Verheul et al., 2001). Existing literature expresses the framework of demography and immigrant entrepreneurs which are applicable to this study; we then adopt and utilize this framework in order to clarify Thai entrepreneurs in the study.

3 Methodology

3.1 Sampling

As part of the exploratory study, the objective of the interviews is clarification for immigrant entrepreneurs' contingency effects. A small sample is sufficient to meet this objective. The sampling implied the interviews of 4 entrepreneurs from the Thai immigrant group. Interviews were limited to entrepreneurs from a single sector of industry, i.e. Thai restaurants. The restaurant sector was selected because the share of immigrant entrepreneurs is high and it is simple to sample entrepreneurs from this sector. A two-step sampling procedure was applied. In the first step, the high density immigrants area is selected; in this study, we select Thai restaurants located at the city centre. Next, restaurants that appear to be owned by individuals from a Thai immigrant group are visited. The owner is then invited to participate in the study. Interview form is used as a tool to collect data in the study.

3.2 Validity

Several validity issues are inherent within this paper. The first issue is in the small sample size used. We sample only the owners of Thai restaurants in the city centre, of which the restaurants are suggested through public media. This may limit the generalizability of the findings.

3.3 Methods of data analysis

One possible data source is documentary analysis, which provides more information about immigrant entrepreneurs in New Zealand; we focus only in Wellington, the capital city of new Zealand. The source of documentary review comes from reports from a database by Population Statistics (Chou, 2000, p. 22) and 2001 census data (Statistics NZ, 2002), New Zealand and similar research contexts from developed countries.

4 Results

The results found in this section demonstrate the demographical characteristics of the Thai immigrant entrepreneurs, factors influencing an individual's decision to become an entrepreneur, and businesses performance of entrepreneurs.

4.1 Social Characteristics & Back ground of Immigrant Entrepreneurs and Businesses

Characteristics & Back ground

4.1.1 Characteristics and Back ground of Immigrant Entrepreneurs

a. Characteristics of Immigrant Entrepreneurs

Immigrant entrepreneurs are various ages; the youngest one is 26 year old, and maintains single status. His view is open, much like as occidental people, perhaps due to his western background. His education background is from New Zealand, Master of Entrepreneurship. His worldview is unlike those of oriental origin (Thechatakerng & Rialp, 2005). He now has his own house in Wellington. The next is 31 years old, a married Buddhist entrepreneur, with 1 child and his own house. He dropped out from high school, and now runs his own Thai restaurant. The 3rd entrepreneur is 42 years of age, a Buddhist who stays with his girlfriend with 3 children at his own house. The eldest immigrant entrepreneur is the age of 62; she married a New Zealand citizen, and then she immigrated to Wellington to stay with her family with 4 children in her own home. In summary, each of the target entrepreneurs has his or her own house in Wellington. They are generally married, Buddhists with children.

Table 1. Characteristics & Back ground of Immigrant Entrepreneurs

Name	Age	Education	Status	Children	Religion	Living
Mr. T	26	Master of Entrepreneurship	Single	-	Free thinker	Own home
Mr. VP	31	High school	Married	1	Buddhism	Own home
Mrs. E	62	Master of Business Administration	Married	4	Buddhism	Own home
Mr. A	42	Vocational	-	3	Buddhism	Own home

b. Reason for Coming to Wellington as Opposed to Other Areas

Mr. T, the youngest entrepreneur, is a new dynamic entrepreneur. He told us that "When I graduated [with a] BA from Victoria University here, I saw an opportunity at that time in 2006 there was a few Thai restaurants in Wellington, in comparison with other places such as Auckland where there were so many Thai restaurants have already established". He continued that "the cost of living here is lower than other places. I like this place, there is not much habitant only 600,000 people and there are only 200 Thai people here, I only roughly estimated". Mr. VP came with his grandmother who lives here and did not move elsewhere. For Mr. A, he came to work here and he like this city. He explained "I like Wellington, it's quite calm and the weather is so good. The eldest entrepreneur, Mrs. E, first came here as a Columbia student at Victoria University by a scholarship that was provided only in Wellington. She explained that "Later, I married with a New Zealand guy and worked here as [an] English teacher at school for 5 years. After that I worked for Thai embassy for 11 years". Thus, some reasons for immigration include education, relatives and marriage with local people. In short, "opportunity" for better life brings immigrants to Wellington.

Table 2. Reasons for coming to Wellington

Name	Wellington	No to other areas
Mr. T	I saw an opportunity here, a few Thai restaurant in that year 2006, when I graduated BA from Victoria university, and cost of living here is lower than other places. I like this place, there is not much habitants only 600,000 people, however, my businesses are ok and I can survive. Until now I still expand my business every year. Now I have 6 chain restaurants.	Higher cost
Mr. VP	I came with my grand mom, she lives here, I've got only temporary visa in Vietnam, actually I immigrated from Cambodia	I have no choice
Mr. A	I found job here. I like Wellington. It's calm and good weather	-
Mrs. E	I came here first as a Columbia scholarship student at Victoria University which was provided only in Wellington. Later, I married with a New Zealand guy and worked here teaching at school for 5 years. After that i worked for Thai embassy for 11 years.	Everything is here

c. Motivation to Shift from Home to Wellington

With respect the motivation to shift from home to Wellington, Mr. T. clarifies with his explanation. He said that "I don't like a routine work. After I've obtained Bachelor degree (B . A .) from Victoria University, I went back to Bangkok and worked for 3 months with Dutch bank but I don't like at all. I love freedom, I like western thinking system because I can discuss with adults but you can't do this in Thailand. There is lesser hierarchical system here than Thailand. I feel good and happy here. I'm a hyper-person, so I think I can work better here than my country."Mr. VP says he had no better choice at that time. "Life is get better here than Vietnam, over there I got nothing". Mr.A explained the motivation to shift from home to Wellington in that "I got job here, and later I met my girlfriend, she's the owner of Thai restaurant and then I worked with her". Mrs. E declared "I'm married and follow him to here otherwise I have to separate with my family, then I decide to come".

Table 3. Motivation to shift from home to Wellington

Name of entrepreneur	Reason from home to Wellington
Mr. T.	I don't like a routine work. After I've got BA. from Victoria University, I went back to Bangkok and worked for 3 months with Dutch bank but I don't like at all. I love freedom, I like western thinking system because I can discuss with adults but you can't in Thailand. There is lesser hierarchical system here than Thailand. I feel good and happy here. I'm a hyper-person, so I think I can work better here than my country.
Mr. VP	Life is better here than Vietnam, over there I got nothing.
Mr. A	I got job and met my girlfriend.
Mrs. E	Married and followed husband.

4.1.2 Types and Characteristics of Businesses

Reason for becoming a self-employed business

a. Business Background

All of the entrepreneurs have had experienced prior to running their businesses. "I helped my mom and aunt to run business at Palmerstone North before", noted Mr. T. Also, Mr. VP said "Yes, I had one restaurant in Island bay but it was smaller than this one. I sold that one to buy here from my aunt. Anyway, I had Thai cooking experience in Vietnam. I have had experience in this field for over 20 years. " Mr. A stated "I have had experience in this field for over 20 years". In the same way, Mrs. E said that "I helped my parents run our business when I was in Thailand".

Table 4. Business background

Name of owner	Experience in similar business	No experience & reason to set up
Mr. T	I helped my mom and aunt to run business at Palmerstone North before.	
Mr. VP	Yes, I had one restaurant in Island bay but it was smaller than this one. I sold that one to buy here from my aunt. Anyway, I had Thai cooking experience in VN.	
Mr. A	I have had experience in this field for over 20 years.	
Mrs. E	Yes, when I was in Thailand, I helped my parents run our business	

b. Employment opportunity

For entrepreneurs, experience before running their own business is very important. The target entrepreneurs here have been employed before thinking of their own business, at businesses such as McDonald's, Thai restaurants and other work such as in school as a teacher or work in the Thai embassy. All of them have obtained standard payment according to New Zealand labor law.

Table 5. Employment opportunity

Name of owner	been employed by other		Standard payment	
	yes	no (try to get employment)	yes	no
Mr. T	At McDonald's, Thai restaurant		x	
Mr. VP	Thai restaurant		x	
Mr. A	Thai restaurant		x	
Mrs. E	Wellington school, Thai Embassy		x	

c. Reason to be Entrepreneur

Entrepreneurs like to be free and manage their own time (Thechatakerng 2009; Collin & Moore, 1964). The youngest entrepreneur claimed that "I don't like to work on routine job, I want to be free and do whatever I want to do". Mr. VP clearly explained, "I don't like to work for other". In the same way, Mr. A affirmed that I don't like to be employed by other. I don't like to be forced to work for others. Then, I become entrepreneur; I can do what I want to do." However, Mrs. E has her own reasons related to her health, "I was sick and I couldn't work routine job anymore but I still want to do something to earn money".

Table 6. Reason to be Entrepreneur

Mr. T	I don't like to work on routine job, I want to be free and do whatever I want to do.
Mr. VP	I don't like to work for others.
Mr. A	I don't like to be employed by other. I don't like to be forced to work for others. Then, I become entrepreneur; I can do what I want to do.
Mrs.E	Because I was sick and I couldn't work routine job anymore.

d. Characteristics of Businesses

Immigrant entrepreneurs' businesses were both classified as what we interpreted as a young business, which has been established for 4 years or less, and experienced firms, which have been in operation for 10 years (Thechatakerng & Rialp,

2005). The younger firm in this case belongs to Mr. T, who is only 26 years old, which we also define as a young entrepreneur. His aggressively expanding operation has grown by a new branch every year until now, and he presently has 6 branches since beginning his business. As Thechatkerng (2009) argued, young entrepreneurs like to try new things and hunger for new innovation; they like to penetrate to markets quickly upon seeing an opportunity. In contrast, the experienced entrepreneur would consider chances and take time in making decisions and in expanding a branch. This study found that the immigrant entrepreneurs have small businesses, however when we consider each branch and each firm they are micro businesses that have between 3 and 8 employees. As regards types of business, we found that they are full course Thai restaurants and one Thai fast food restaurant that has already expanded to six chains.

Table 7. Characteristics of Businesses

Name		Mr. T	Mr. VP	Mr. A	Mrs. E
Year established		2008 (4 yrs)		2000 (12 yrs)	2002 (10 yrs)
Type of business		Thai fast food	Thai restaurant full course	Thai restaurant full course	Thai fast food & full course restaurant
Business		Co. ltd.	Ltd. Part		
Employee	Part time	15	6	2	3
	Full time	20	0	2	5
Investment (Nz$)		>150,000	>150,000	>150,000	>50,000-100,000
Chain		6	1	1	2
Generation			1	1	1

e. Nationality of employees

One young immigrant entrepreneur explained that "I accepted every nationality, I gave a chance to everybody who has ID card and legally and want to work hard but the chef must be Thai". Another entrepreneur agreed with the first point of view but said "I'm a chef, I work by myself, I can do because I have so many of Thai kitchen experienced". On the other hand, the eldest entrepreneur noted that "I want all Thai employee because we can communicate and understand each other well". This idea was supported by the other entrepreneur.

Table 8. Nationality of employees

Name of Restaurant	Ethnicity
1	Mix; whoever who has legal ID, but the chef must be Thai
2	Mix, whoever who has legal ID
3	Thai
4	Thai

f. Period of decision making to set up own business

Younger entrepreneurs made a decision in not more than 6 months in establishing their own business, while the elder entrepreneurs spent more time in making a decision; in this case they spent one year.

Table 9. Period of decision making to set up own business

Name of owner	< 1 yr.	1-2 yrs.
Mr. T	3-4 months	
Mr. VP	2 months	
Mr. A		1 yr.
Mrs. E		1 yr.

4.2 Business Performance and Satisfaction

4.2.1 Business Performance

a. Business Performance

In terms of business performance of the entrepreneurs, all of them have earned over NZD 100,000. We interpreted this to signify that their business performances were all "in good situation".

Table 10. Business performance

Name of Busines	Earnings/year (**Nz$**)				
	< 10,000	10,000-30,000	30,000-60,000	60,000-100,000	Over 100,000
1					x
2					x
3	-	-	-	-	-
4					x

b. Satisfaction of outcome from business performance

When we interviewed their satisfaction from their businesses performance, two of them responded with "medium level". Mrs. E said "it should be better"; similarly, Mr. VP Stated "I should do it better than this". Conversely, Mr. T was pleased with his performance, saying "I'm very much satisfied with my business and the growth of my business that I expand every year but this year I expanded 2 branches. I'm still looking for places to expand more [branches]", also Mr.A expressed very much satisfaction in his performance.

Table 11. Satisfaction of outcome from business performance

Name of Business	yes	no	Ps.
1	x		Very much, I'm satisfied with the growth of business and I'm still looking for places to expand.
2	x		Medium
3	x		Very much
4	x		Medium, it should be better than this

5 Conclusion, Implications and Future Research

The paper discovered various determinants of entrepreneurship related to economical, psychological, sociological and demographical aspects of entrepreneurship. *Middleman minority theory, the Blocked mobility theory, Ethnic enclave economy theory,* and *Interactive Theory* are involved. 4 entrepreneurs were interviewed, limited to entrepreneurs from a single sector of industry, i.e. Thai restaurants.

The findings show the various characters of entrepreneurship; for example, immigrant entrepreneurs are of various ages from 26 to 62, they are married, but some single, are educated persons, and they practice Buddhism. The important factors that influence immigrants to be entrepreneurs include freedom and time management. The result also shows that their businesses' performance proved to have done very well, with positive levels of their satisfaction. The results implied that entrepreneurs are driving the new economy (John Wiley & Sons, 2009), as demonstrated in their firms' performance. The study expresses an interesting point in that the young entrepreneur in this paper does not like to be employed by others; he prefers to work by his own account, which stands in contrast with the argument of Small Business Administration (2001) and Verheul et al. (2001) that "younger people are less likely to be self-employed than elder people are". Furthermore, the younger entrepreneur in this study also illustrates his own passion to work on his own as an entrepreneur by expanding new restaurants every year, which is not consistent with the previous explanation of Bosma et al. (2000).

Our results support the finding of Verheul et al. (2001) as well, which reported mixed findings on the relationship between the degree of urbanization and the rate of entrepreneurship. On one hand, a high population density in urban areas is found to stimulate the start-up of new firms. This suggests that individuals living in large cities are more likely to be entrepreneurs than those living in less urbanized places. However, population density and urbanization can lead to the pursuit of economies of scale, which has a negative effect on the rate of entrepreneurship (Bais et al., 1995).

As the study on Thai immigrant entrepreneurs is still limited, this study opens the initial path in this area and can also enhance knowledge for scholars who are interested in this field. However, future research should be focused in various sectors of immigrant entrepreneurs and should not be limited in sample. In addition, the comparative research should endeavor to spotlight the growth of other economies

The information from this study can be advantageous to university, faculty, colleagues, students and policy makers in planning suitable conditions for mutual benefits. Moreover, institutes such as government agencies can be use this information to plan to support immigrant entrepreneurs, as we believe that they assist to drive the country's economy.

References

1. Agrawal, R.K., Chavan, M.: Entrepreneurship development amongst the ethnic community in Australia (1997), `http://www.usasbe.org/knowledge/proceedings/1997/P141Agrawal.PDF` (retrieved June 8, 2005)
2. Collins, J.: Immigrant entrepreneurs in Australia: Regulations and responses. In: Oliveira, C.R., Rath, J. (eds.) Migrações Journal - Special Issue on Immigrant Entrepreneurship, vol. 3, pp. 49–59. ACIDI, Lisbon (2008)
3. Herman, T.R., Smith, R.L.: IMMIGRANT, INC.: Why Immigrant Entrepreneurs Are Driving the New Economy (And How They Will Save the American Worker). John Wiley & Sons, Inc., USA (2009)
4. Jansen, M., de Kok, J., van Spronsen, J., Willemsen, S.: Immigrant entrepreneurship in theNetherlands: Demographic determinants of entrepreneurship of immigrants from non-western countries, Research Report H200304, Scientific Analysis of Entrepreneurship and SMEs (2003)
5. Van Stel, A., Carree, M.: Business ownership and sectoral growth, Research Report H200206. EIM, Zoetermeer (2002)
6. Barrett, G.A., Jones, T.P., McEvoy, D.: Ethnic Minority Business: Theoretical Discourse in Britain and North America. Urban Studies 33(4-5), 783–809 (1996)
7. Bosma, N.: Global Entrepreneurship Monitor. EIM, Zoetermeer (2002)
8. Bosma, N., van Praag, M., de Wit, G.: Determinants of successful entrepreneurship, Research Report 0002. EIM, Zoetermeer (2000)
9. Bosma, N., de Wit, G., Carree, M.: Modelling entrepreneurship: unifying the equilibrium and entry/exit approach. Small Business Economics (2003) (forthcoming)
10. Butler, J.S., Greene, P.G.: Wealth building and entrepreneurship: lessons from Pakistani/Ismali enterprises: University of Texas at Austin & Rutgers University (1997)

11. Chou, L.: Chinese immigrants in New Zealand society: a study of migrant acculturation and the effects of communication and multicultural public relations. Unpublished M.A, Auckland University of Technology, Auckland (2000)
12. Clark, K., Drinkwater, S.: Pushed Out of Pulled In? Self-Employment Amoung Ethnic Minorities in England and Wales. Labour Economics 7(5) (2000)
13. De Raijman, R.B.: Pathways to self-employment and entrepreneurship in an immigrant community in Chicago. The University of Chicago, United States - Illinois (1996)
14. Hiebert, D.: Canada: a false consensus. In: Kloosterman, R., Rath, J. (eds.) Immigrant Entrepreneurs: Venturing Abroad in the Age of Gloablization, pp. 39–60. Berg, New York (2003)
15. Le, A.T.: The determinants of immigrant self-employment in Australia. The International Migration Review 34(1), 183 (2000)
16. Lee, J.S.: Why do Asian immigrants become entrepreneurs? The case of Korean self-employed immigrants in New Zealand, a Master Thesis, Auckland University of Technology (2008)
17. Light, I., Bhachu, P.: Immigration and Entrepreneurship. Culture, Capital and Ethnic Networks. Transaction Publishers, New Brunswick (1993)
18. La Portes, A., Zhou, M.: Self-employment and the earnings of immigrants. American Sociologican Review, 61 (1996)
19. Middleton, J.: The migrant experience: Jobs that shut out migrants. The New Zealand Herald (May 19, 2005)
20. Min, P.G., Bozorgmehr, M.: United States: The entrepreneurial cutting edge. In: Kloosterman, R., Rath, J. (eds.) Immigrant Entrepreneurs: Venturing Abroad in the Age of Gloablization, pp. 17–37. Berg, Oxford (2003)
21. Portes, A., Zhou, M.: Entrepreneurship and Economic Progress in the Nineties: A Comparative Analysis of Immigrants and African Americans, Working Paper Series, Center for Migration and Development, Princeton University (1998)
22. Rath, J.: Immigrant businesses: the economic, political and social environment. Macmillan, Basing-stoke (2000)
23. Rath, J., Kloosterman, R.: Outsiders's business: Research of immigrant entrepreneur-ship in the Netherlands. International Migration Review 34(3) (2000)
24. Statistics New Zealand (2012), http://www.asianz.org.nz/asia-matters
25. Thechatakerng, P.: Determinants of Entrepreneur. In: EDP Workshop. Universitat Autonoma de Barcelona, Barcelona, Spain (2009)
26. Thechatakerng, S., Rialp, J.: When They Go Together: Alliances Implementing by Thai Firms, Paper Presented in EURAM Conference at TUM Business School, Munich, Germany, Formally Published on the Web (2005), http://euram2005.wi.tum.de/index.php/Paper323.pdf?page=downloadPaper_afterconference&form_id=323
27. Valenzuela, A.J.: Working on the margins: immigrant day labor characteristics and prospects for employment (2000)

Application-Aware Storage Strategy for Scientific Data

Runtao Wang[1], Jian Xiao[1,*], Jizhou Sun[1], Ce Yu[1], Chao Sun[1],
Xiaoqian Zhu[2], and Xiangfei Meng[2]

[1] School of Computer Science and Technology, Tianjin University
[2] National Supercomputer Center in Tianjin, China,
Tianjin 300072, China
{yuce,jzsun,xiaojian,schsch321}@tju.edu.cn

Abstract. The explosive growth of modern scientific data opens new challenges for storing and accessing very large (petabytes) scale data. Traditional file systems and databases cannot meet the requirements of managing scientific data. Arrays are considered as a natural data model for scientific data. Some science-oriented systems have been developed for array data model handling. However, a shortcoming of those systems is that most of them use a "no overwrite" storage strategy, which destabilizes the performance of supporting different applications. In this paper, we proposed an application-aware storage strategy which can optimize data layout gradually according to different access patterns. We implemented the strategy based off of SciDB by creating arrays with different indices for specific parts of the dataset. Experiment testing has been conducted to verify the proposed strategy, and the experimental results show that our strategy improves the performance of science-oriented database on supporting various kinds of applications.

Keywords: storage management, scientific data, data layout.

1 Introduction

In the past few decades, scientific data quantities were growing explosively. For example: the Large Hadron Collider will produce approximately 15 petabytes of data annually [6]. Scientific data is different from business data in many aspects, most important of those is the data model. Arrays are the natural data model for a significant subset of science users, specifically astronomy, oceanography, fusion, remote sensing, climate modeling, seismology, biology and genomics [2]. That's the key reason why very few scientific applications make use of relational database systems [4].

There are a number of research efforts on scientific databases (e.g. Sequoia 2000 with Postgres [7], Paradise [8], RasDaMan [11] and extensions to MonetDB [9]), but these systems all still lack important features to meet the needs of increasingly data-rich sciences [2]. There are also array data management systems (one prominent example is SciDB [3], which is an open-source distributed scientific-oriented database

---

* Corresponding author.

V. Khachidze et al. (Eds.): iCETS 2012, CCIS 332, pp. 671–681, 2012.

system). A Standard Science DBMS Benchmark has verified that databases with array data models brought more significant improvements than relational databases [10].

However, an obvious shortcoming is that in order to get better performance, array based systems are often designed to be “write once, read many”, which is influenced by the design of modern distributed computing systems that use a Map/Reduce model [12] [1]. This makes data layout in these systems application-specific, which means that one array can only serve several applications with the same access pattern well, but not for others.

In this paper, we proposed an application-aware scientific data storage strategy to address the application-specific issues. We implemented our strategy based off of SciDB and conducted an experiment with astronomic data by simulating a query sequence with different access patterns. The experimental results show that the scientific databases get improved performance with our strategy when dealing with applications with various kinds of access patterns.

The rest of this paper is organized as follows. In Section 2, we briefly discuss the background and our motivation. Section 3 discusses the design and implementation of our strategy. Experiments and results are presented in Section 4. Section 5 concludes the paper.

2 Background and Motivation

Scientific data differs from business data in many respects. First of all, scientific data are extremely large. It’s easy to generate petabytes of data for a scientific application. Second, scientific data always consist of rectangular arrays obtained from sensor arrays. Third, scientific data often don’t change after they are obtained, and the most important difference is that scientists usually query specific parts of data repeatedly to do specific research.

Those features of scientific data make arrays a natural data model for most science applications. Very few scientists use traditional database system because scientific data doesn’t fit into the relational data model. Scientific applications had struggled with poor performance until the appearance of science-oriented databases.

Science-oriented databases are organized as collections of n-dimensional arrays, and each cell in an array contains a tuple of attributes associated with different attribute names. The values of dimensions are normally integral numbers. The non-integral numbers for dimensions are supported but not suggested for the inefficiency. Values of attributes could be of any type, but numeric values are the most used.

The problem of these database systems is that the indices for an array cannot be changed easily. Once a very large scale array is built, it is actually built for few access patterns which use the indices of it. The open source science-oriented database system SciDB indeed provides a function called “reshape” to reorganize the data layout, but it can only reshape one-dimension array and it has to reorganize the whole given array, which is inefficient and inflexible.

A scientific database system should never limit the kinds of queries; scientific users should be able to query whatever they want. If a user repeatedly queries the database with a new kind of access pattern, persistent low performance is unacceptable.

To address this problem, we proposed an application-aware storage strategy that made science-oriented databases capable of adjusting data layout automatically to meet the requirements of various applications.

3 Design and Implementation

3.1 Terminologies

Array. Array is the data structure into which scientific datasets are loaded. A demonstration of an array in SciDB is described in formula (1).

arrayName<attr:attr_type[, …]>[dim=start:end,chunkSize,overlap[, …]] (1)

As mentioned above, an array consists of dimensions and attributes, each dimension should have an integral range from start to end. An array is divided into chunks according to each dimension's chunkSize which is an integral number as well. Overlap in SciDB is designed for parallelizing applications referring to "boundary problems" such as Gaussian Smoothing [1]. Attributes of an array could be of any data type theoretically, but actually attributes of scientific data from scientific observations are always turned into numeric values for more convenient analyzing. For this reason, we are only concerned about the optimization for numeric data in this paper. Here's an example of an array:

sdss<a:int32, b:float, c:int32>[X=0:9,2,0, Y=0:9,2,0] (2)

The array with definition in formula (2) is shown in Fig. 1.

Y \ X	0	1	2	3	4	5
0	(2, 1.6, 4)	(3, 1.4, 2)	(1, 3.2, 5)	(4, 1.1, 2)	(6, 0.6, 1)	(7, 1.5, 4)
1	(1, 2.2, 3)	(2, 1.1, 2)	(4, 1.8, 2)	(2, 2.4, 1)	(6, 6.6, 0)	(2, 6.1, 3)
2	(0, 0.6, 1)	(1, 2.7, 5)	(9, 2.6, 3)	(5, 2.6, 1)	(1, 1.3, 2)	(5, 2.8, 6)
3	(8, 1.1, 3)	(3, 3.6, 3)	(4, 1.2, 4)	(1, 5.6, 7)	(5, 1.1, 2)	(5, 1.3, 1)
4	(2, 7.1, 3)	(5, 5.1, 3)	(1, 2.6, 4)	(3, 2.6, 6)	(7, 5.6, 7)	(4, 2.6, 5)
5	(7, 2.2, 3)	(9, 1.5, 4)	(4, 2.3, 9)	(9, 2.1, 5)	(8, 4.1, 5)	(8, 4.8, 2)

Fig. 1. An example of an array with two dimensions and three attributes in each cell. Chunks are separated by different colors.

Access Pattern. An access pattern is a list of tuples, each of which consists of predicates on dimensions and attributes of an array. For example, formula (3) and formula (4) shows two query statements in SciDB.

$$\text{between(sdss,1,1,3,3)} \tag{3}$$

$$\text{filter(between(sdss,2,2,5,5), (a > 2 or a < 1) and c < 5)} \tag{4}$$

The access patterns of the two statements are shown in formula (5) and formula (6) respectively.

$$(X > 1 \text{ and } X < 3,\ Y > 1 \text{ and } Y < 3) \tag{5}$$

$$(X > 2 \text{ and } X < 5,\ Y > 2 \text{ and } Y < 5,\ a > 2 \text{ or } a < 1,\ c < 5) \tag{6}$$

The relationship between predicates in one tuple is "and". And one access pattern is the collection of queries with the same subjects.

Original Array. The original array is the first array built for a scientific dataset.

Perfect Array. An array is perfect to an access pattern when the subjects in the access pattern are all dimensions of that array. For example, the array in formula (2) is a perfect array to the access pattern in formula (5).

3.2 Strategy Design

We designed an application-aware storage strategy based on the fact that a portion of scientific data is usually re-used multiple times [1]. When scientists are interested in one part of data, they will query it for many times to do different kinds of researching.

We maintain the access patterns that have been used by users, and the mapping relationship between access patterns and its perfect arrays. Once a query request comes, we estimate its access pattern and decide whether a perfect array of this access pattern exists.

If no perfect array exists for the access pattern, another query statement will be generalized with the same access pattern querying the original array, which is inefficient. After the query results is returned to the user, an asynchronous process will begin. This process's task is creating a perfect array for the new access pattern, and loading data with more wide range than the query request into the new array. We can't assume that user would query data with exactly same range for many times, but query data with similar range is reasonable.

If a perfect array exists and it contains the data that the user wants, the data should be just retrieved from it, which is the most efficient way. Otherwise, the system should retrieve a part of the data from the perfect array and then retrieve other parts from the original array. After retrieving, the system should add some data to the existing perfect array making a broader range of data for the succeeding queries.

Our strategy continually adjusts the data layout according to different access patterns. After several iterations, each access pattern that has been used will has its perfect array, and it's obvious that retrieving data from the perfect array is much more efficient than from the original array.

3.3 Implementation with SciDB

SciDB is a prominent science-oriented distributed data management system developed by leaders of the database research community.

Metabase. We created a metabase to maintain the information that our strategy needs. Three tables in the metabase are shown in Fig. 2.

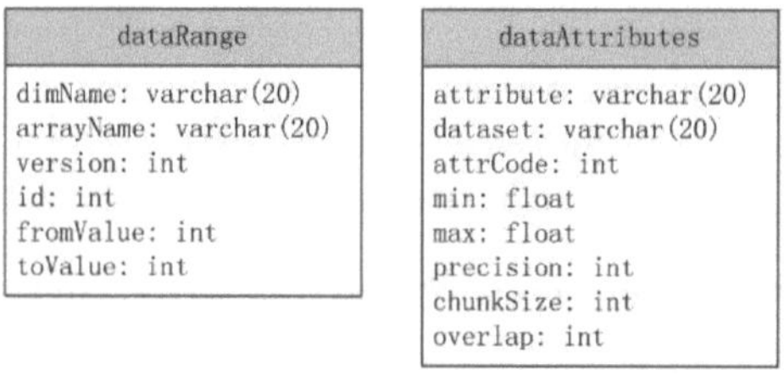

Fig. 2. Three main tables in the metabase: *dataRange, dataAttributes* and *arrayIndex*

Table *dataAttributes* contains information of the original scientific dataset. Names of the attributes and datasets are represented by *attribute* and *dataset*. Each attribute has a code called *attrCode*; the encoding method will be discussed later. The minimum and maximum values are both of float type and recorded in *min* and *max*. When the attribute is used as a dimension of an array, *precision* is used to turn the float number into an integral number, *chunkSize* and *overlap* are used in the definition of the array.

Table *dataRange* maintains the range of data stored in the array by *fromValue* and *toValue* of each dimension. The *dimName* and *arrayName* are corresponding to *attribute* and *dataset* in table *dataAttributes* respectively. The range of *dimName* is the range of a subset of the dataset.

Table *arrayIndex* keeps track of the *indexCode* information for different versions of an array. The *indexCode* is the sum of the array's dimensions' code in table *dataAttribute*.

Encoding Method. Let *i* be the specified order of the dataset's attributes. If the dataset has *N* attributes, then *i* is from 0 to *N*-1, and attribute *i* has code 2^i.

With this encoding method, the *indexCode* of each version of an array is corresponding to a unique binary sequence of length *N*. Fig. 3. illustrates the principle of this encoding method.

attr5	attr4	attr3	attr2	attr1
16	8	4	2	1

array_1<attr2, attr3>[attr1, attr4, attr5] → indexCode = 1 + 8 + 16 = 25 → 11001

array_2<attr1, attr2, attr4>[attr3, attr5] → indexCode = 4 + 16 = 20 → 10100

Fig. 3. The relationship between attribute code and array *indexCode*. Different versions of an array with different dimensions have different *indexCode*, which is corresponding to a unique binary sequence.

Query Client. We've developed a query client on the top of SciDB. We didn't use the query client "iquery" from SciDB because we need a query client that be able to analyze the access patterns of queries and interact with the metabase discussed above. The functionalities of our query client are as follows.

Parsing users' queries. User could give a query including conditions on any attributes of the dataset. The query client is responsible to parse the query, check the correctness and rationality of it, and finally summarize out the access pattern.

Interacting with metabase. Once the access pattern is got, query client should check the metabase to see if the perfect array for that access pattern exists. And it's the duty of the query client to keep the metabase up to date after reorganizing the data.

Fetching and asynchronously reorganizing data. We divide query client situations into three classes.

First of all, if the perfect array for the access pattern exists, and the range of data in the perfect array could meet the user's requirement, the query client should fetch the data from the perfect array and put the result into a file for download.

Second, if the perfect array doesn't exist, the query client should fetch data from the original array. After returning data to the user, the query client should start an asynchronous process, which is responsible for fetching more data, creating a perfect array, reorganizing the fetched data and loading it to the perfect array.

Third and the most complicated situation is that the perfect array exists but with data could not meet the user's requirement. It's reasonable to fetch a part of the data from the perfect array and fetch other parts from the original array, after that, load the other parts into the perfect array.

However, due to the realization of SciDB, data could not be loaded into chunks already with data, and it's inevitable that data in perfect arrays share the same chunk with data in original array. The second best solution was implemented in our query client. Once the third situation occurs, the query client creates a temp perfect array having the same definition with the former perfect array, and loads more data into it. After finishing, it will replace the former perfect array with the temp perfect array. This method may be slightly inefficient, but it could solve the problem that SciDB caused.

Reorganizing more data. As mentioned above, we can't guarantee that the query conditions of different queries are exactly the same, but the appearance of queries with similar query conditions is reasonable. So, we should prepare more data for the perfect array in order to speed up the succeeding queries with the same access pattern. The strategy of reorganizing more data is not unique. It should be decided by different applications.

In our implementation, we've arranged the range of the data in a specific dimension to be reorganized by optional parameters, which means the user can tell the query client the range of the data he may use. But if the user doesn't give the optional parameters, the range of the data is calculated by the largest interval among four values. They are the two ends of user's query interval in this dimension, and the minimum and maximum value of data stored in the perfect array. And if the query interval is an open interval, the two ends of query interval would be the minimum and maximum value of the whole dataset in this dimension.

Let *minValue* and *maxValue* be the minimum and maximum value of the four values discussed above respectively. And let *dataFrom* and *dataTo* be the range of the whole dataset in this dimension. Then, the data range need to be reorganized will be decided by formula (7).

$$\text{Range} = [\ \min(\ \text{minValue} - (\text{maxValue} - \text{minValue}),\ \text{dataFrom}\ ),$$
$$\max(\ \text{maxValue} + (\text{maxValue} - \text{minValue}),\ \text{dataTo}\ )\ ] \quad (7)$$

4 Experimental Evaluation

4.1 Experimental Platform

These experiments were conducted on a SciDB cluster, including 4 nodes. The hardware and software configuration of the nodes are shown in Table 1.

Table 1. Node information of the experimental platform

Options	Configurations
CPU	3.00 GHz Dual-Core Intel Pentium
Memory	2GB
Storage	160GB
Network	Gigabit Ethernet
OS	Ubuntu 11.04, Linux 2.6.38-8-generic
SciDB	11.06

We used the observation catalog data from Sloan Digital Sky Survey (SDSS) [14] to conduct our experiments. The fields we used are shown in Table 2. The size of original data is 289GB, and after converting them to arrays, we got 100GB of compressed data for the original array.

Table 2. SDSS data fields used in the experiments

Field name	Data type	Description
objID	int	Object ID
ra	float	Right ascension
dec	float	Declination
u	float	Magnitude of ultraviolet
g	float	Magnitude of green
r	float	Magnitude of red

The experiments consisted of two parts. The first part was to verify the performance improvement by creating perfect arrays for a specific access pattern. The second part was to verify the efficiency of the application-aware storage strategy.

4.2 Perfect Array Performance Verification

First we conducted an experiment to verify that, when dealing with a specific access pattern, the performance of querying a perfect array is much higher than the performance of querying an original array.

In order to prove our viewpoint, we conducted several queries with the same access pattern but querying a different number of cells from an original array and a perfect array respectively. As Fig. 4 illustrates, the performance of array-based system will have a significant improvement when creating the perfect array for an access pattern. This result makes it worthwhile to develop a strategy that maintains perfect arrays for access patterns as much as possible. The performance after applying our application-aware storage strategy is discussed later.

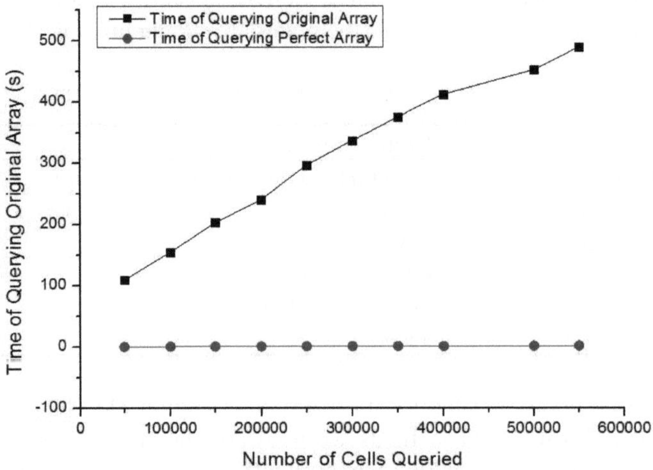

Fig. 4. The query performance of querying original array and perfect array when dealing with a specific access pattern. As the amount of cells queried increased, an approximate linear growth showed up for original array, but a stable high performance for perfect array.

4.3 Application-Aware Storage Strategy Evaluation

In this section, we will discuss the efficiency of the application-aware storage strategy that we've proposed.

To evaluate the performance of our strategy, we extracted 30 query statements from the query log of NAOC's PostgreSQL DBMS and converted them to SciDB style. These statements contain 11 access patterns. Statements with the same access pattern may not be exactly the same, which means that two statements with the same access pattern may query different ranges of data. The classification of these queries is shown in Table 3.

Table 3. Classification of queries

Access Pattern ID	Query IDs
1	1, 4
2	5, 10, 15, 23, 30
3	3, 7, 28
4	12, 18, 26
5	9, 14, 21, 27
6	20, 24
7	25, 29
8	2, 8, 13
9	16, 19
10	6, 17
11	11, 22

We first executed the query list without applying our strategy, which means that every query statement queries the original array in SciDB. The performance was uneven, which was shown in Fig. 5. When the access pattern of the query statement matches the indices of the original array, better performance could be achieved. Otherwise, even a simple query statement might take quite a long time.

We then applied the application-aware storage strategy to SciDB and executed the query list again. There were three situations in the first run after applying our strategy. First, when encountered a new access pattern was never met before, the performance of the system would be much the same as querying an original array, that's because it did query the original array. As shown in Fig. 5, when dealing with queries with ID 1, 5, 6, etc. Second, when dealing with an access pattern that already had a perfect array but without enough data, the performance would have still been the same as querying the original array. Queries with ID 5, 9 and 12, 16 illustrated this situation. Third, when the perfect array existed and had enough data for the access pattern, the system would get a rather high performance. Queries with ID 1, 4 and 9, 14 could help understand this situation better. Although only in the third situation it could get highest performance, the system did perform better in the first run after applying our strategy.

We executed the query list for a second time after applying our strategy to SciDB. And this time the system showed a really high performance score. The result is shown in Fig. 5. This is because after the first run, the system built perfect arrays for all of the queries in the query list, and consequently the query time were all less than 10 seconds, which was as expected.

The experimental results have verified the efficiency of the application-aware storage strategy that we proposed. As our strategy adjusted the data layout automatically, users will find the performance improvement when accessing data for several times with the same access pattern. And we can conclude that this strategy will benefit the science-oriented database system significantly in a long run.

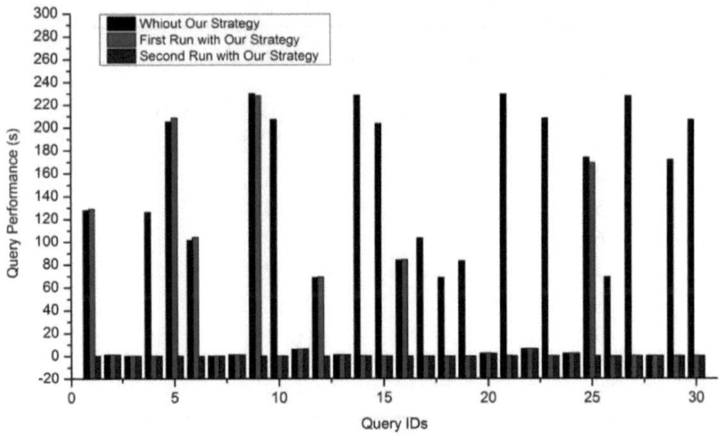

Fig. 5. The query performance before and after applying the application-aware storage strategy. The first run after applying that strategy got some performance improvements. The second run brought significant improvement after all perfect arrays had been built. The third run showed a stable high performance.

5 Conclusion

In this paper, we proposed an application-aware storage strategy for scientific data. When applying the strategy, the data layout will be adjusted automatically according to different access pattern and then better performance will be achieved when the same access pattern comes up again. In order to implement the strategy, a metabase was designed to maintain the information of arrays in the system, and an indexing method was designed to make sure the one-to-one correspondence between an access pattern and its perfect array. We've also designed a method expanding the perfect array to meet succeeding queries. We conducted experimental evaluations and verified the effectiveness and efficiency of the strategy. As a future goal, it is required to support more data types and optimize the implementation of this strategy.

Acknowledgments. The work is sponsored by the National Natural Science Foundation of China(10978016, 61039001), Key Technologies R&D Program of Tianjin, China (11ZKFGX01000, 11ZCKFGX04200), FP7 of European Union (No. 287746).

References

1. Paul, G.B.: Overview of SciDB: large scale array storage, processing and analysis. In: Proceedings of the 2010 International Conference on Management of Data, SIGMOD 2010, pp. 963–968. ACM, New York (2010)

2. Cudre-Mauroux, P., Lim, H., Simakov, J.: A Demonstration of SciDB: A Science-Oriented DBMS. In: 35th International Conference on Very Large Data Bases (VLDB 2009), Lyon, pp. 1534–1537 (2009)
3. Stonebraker, M., Becla, J., DeWitt, D.J., Lim, K.T., Maier, D., Ratzesberger, O., Zdonik, S.: Requirements for science data bases and scidb. In: Conference on Innovative Data Systems Research (CIDR), Monterey (2009)
4. Kesheng, W., Surendra, B., Doron, R., Arie, S.: Scientific data services: a high-performance I/O system with array semantics. In: Proceedings of the First Annual Workshop on High Performance Computing Meets Databases, pp. 9–12. ACM, Washington (2011)
5. Huaiming, S., Yanlong, Y., Yong, C., Xian-He, S.: A cost-intelligent application-specific data layout scheme for parallel file systems. In: Proceedings of the 20th International Symposium on High Performance Distributed Computing, pp. 37–48. ACM, California (2011)
6. European Organization for Nuclear Research, `http://public.web.cern.ch/public/`
7. Stonebraker, M.: A next-generation information system for the study of global change. In: Proc. 13th IEEE Symp. on Mass Storage Systems, Sequoia, pp. 47–53 (1994)
8. Dewitt, P.J., Kabra, N., Luo, P., Patel, M.: Client-Server Paradise. In: Proceedings of the 20th International Conference on Very Large Data Bases, pp. 558–569. Morgan Kaufmann (1994)
9. Ivanova, P., Nes, N., Goncalves, R., Kersten, M.: MonetDB/SQL Meets SkyServer: the Challenges of a Scientific Database. In: Proceedings of the 19th International Conference on Scientific and Statistical Database Management, p. 13. IEEE, Washington (2007)
10. Cudre-Maroux, P.: SS-DB: A Standard Science DBMS Benchmark (submitted for publication)
11. Baumann, P., Dehmel, A., Furtado, P., Ritsch, R., Widmann, N.: The multidimensional database system RasDaMan. In: Proceedings of the 1998 ACM SIGMOD International Conference on Management of Data, pp. 575–577. ACM Press, Washington (1998)
12. Dean, J., Ghemawat, S.: Mapreduce: Simplified data processing on large clusters. In: Proceedings of the 6th Conference on Symposium on Opearting Systems Design & Implementation, pp. 137–150. USENIX Association, San Francisco (2004)
13. National Astronomical Observatories, Chinese Academy of Sciences, `http://www.bao.ac.cn/`
14. Sloan Digital Sky Survey, `http://www.sdss.org/`

CMMI Based Multi-agent Software Process Control and Improvement Model

Jing Cao[1], Zijian Zhang[2], Li Zhang[3], Guozheng Rao[1], and Ruiguang Liu[1]

[1] School of Computer Science and Technology, TianJin University, Tianjin 300072, China
[2] Tianjin Navigation Instrument Research Institute, Tianjin, 300131, China
[3] School of Economics and Management, Tianjin University of Science and Technology, Tianjin300222, China
cj0000@vip.sina.com, zzj1969@yahoo.com.cn, {zhangli,rgz}@tju.edu.cn, tiduslrg@gmail.com

Abstract. Traditional software process models are mostly linear, non-formalized, static, mechanical and passive. A CMMI (Capability Maturity Model Integration) based Multi-Agent dynamic software process control and improved model is presented in this paper to address this issue. The software process elements (e.g. process areas, activities, resources, roles, process area products, etc.) and their relationship are described by the formalized multi-agent. The agent's reasoning and adaptive mechanisms are applied to deal with the changes in the software process. Specific practices, generic practices, subpractices, task planning, resource allocation, product management and process collaborative are organized as self-adaptive process model. Based on this model, on one hand, a CMMI based software measurement process can be tailored for the process goals. On the other hand, the subpractice for software process improvement will be exported based on the software process measure results.

Keywords: CMMI, Multi-Agent, Software Process Control, Software Process Improvement.

1 Introduction

In the late 1980s, software process control and improvement is introduced to software engineering to improve product quality which is learning from the manufacturing control and improvement process. In 1987, the ICSE 9 paper, "Software Processes are Software Too", suggests that software processes are themselves a form of software and that there are considerable benefits that will derive from basing a discipline of software process development on the more traditional discipline of application software development [1]. Since then, a number of software process modeling methods, software process models and specific international standards are made available within software engineering discipline to support Software Process Improvement (SPI) such as finite state automata [2], Petri nets [3], SPICE (Software Process Improvement and Capability Determination) [4], Capability Maturity Model

V. Khachidze et al. (Eds.): iCETS 2012, CCIS 332, pp. 682–695, 2012.

Integration (CMMI), ISO/IEC 15504, ISO/IEC 90003 and ISO/IEC 12207. In 2004, CMMI is integrated from multiple CMM model by the Software Engineering Institute (SEI) of Carnegie Mellon University [5]. Its continuous and multi-levels representation has greater flexibility for the implementation of software process improvement [6]. However, the software process is very different from the traditional manufacturing process. The complexity and uncertainty of the software process is its basic features [7]. Process capability is related with people, the environment, technology and understanding of user needs. The traditional software process models are mostly linear, non-formalized, static, mechanical and passive. Furthermore, all the possible conditions and solutions for them will be described and defined by the software engineer in the traditional software process model previously [8]. When the environment changes, it is not highly adaptive enough to make the appropriate adjustments in response to the changes; rather it must rely on software engineer intervention and modification [9]. As a result, software engineer must spend a great deal of time and effort on the process of change in the software, so the management costs of the software are increased.

The flexibility and the ability of supporting dynamic changes are the basic requirements of a software process model. An effective way to solve the problem is introducing adaptive features to the software process model. The software processes can autonomously change their behavior to adapt to changes in the software process environment and to achieve the goal of software development.

An agent is an autonomous entity which observes through sensors and acts upon an environment using actuators and directs its activity towards achieving goals. It should exhibit the following characteristics:

- accommodate new problem solving rules incrementally
- adapt online and in real time
- be able to analyze itself in terms of behavior, error and success.
- learn and improve through interaction with the environment
- learn quickly from large amounts of data
- have memory-based exemplar storage and retrieval capacities
- have parameters to represent short and long term memory, age, forgetting, etc.

]These characteristic is fit to describe the elements of the software process. The agent is able to simulate the behavior of the software process. Furthermore, Agent with adaptive mechanism can implement the function of mission planning, resource allocation, process management and agent collaborative in the software process.

On the other hand, Agent is supported distributed applications. The software process is built by agents with the capacity of sense, knowledge representation, reasoning and negotiation collaboratively.

This paper aims to introduce CMMI Based software process multi-agent formally. Each software process Agent can determine what it can do by using descriptive knowledge, how to reason by using process knowledge, and how many resources would be needed. The definition provides a working mechanism for the software process Agent.

2 Related Works

In recent years, more and more Agent-based software process models provide a next generation of software process modeling. Multi Agent-based software process model consists of agents cooperating to achieve a common process goal. To succeed the common goals, agents can be working in the form of highly distributed, mobile, autonomous, intelligent and cooperative entities. These models are belong two main types, Agent-enhanced process model and Agent-Based Process Model. Agent-enhanced process model focuses on integration of Agent Technology and the existing software workflow process model. In this model, the formal method for process modeling still is the traditional workflow method. For instance, process changes and distributed collaboration are controlled by the implement of the Agent. The advantage of this process model is the reuse of existing processes and systems. Such solution can achieve the adaptive characteristics of the process on the basis of the retained organization already exists. The disadvantage is that retaining the traditional factors of the process model for the process. It cannot adapt the change of the software within the organization. For example, Agent can collaborate with each other, but within the agent, the organization still does not fit the change. Moreover, such a solution is not uniform. It is necessary to introduce heterogeneous Agents to manage all aspects of the process, which increase the complexity of the problem. In recent years, research on Agent-enhanced software process model has mainly been focused on distributed software process cooperation [10].

Agent-based process models describe the process elements and their relationship with formal Agent. These models introduce the fundamental agent adaptive features. It is based on the idea of the Agent process model produced in the field of artificial intelligence, which aims to establish the Distributed Management Agent-based business model in order to achieve the integration of services and tasks. Multiple kinds of agents are adopted to represent the flexible organization structure of the software development process model and their automation.

Chang-Hyun Jo and their partners propose a new software engineering process based on the BDI agent concept [11]. A systematic and realistic process has been born to construct BDI agent-based is refined and extend substantially Modeling Technique (AMT) and Agent-based Software Development Process (ASP). It is a unique and novel approach of thinking for BDI agent-based modeling. Institute of Software, The Chinese Academy of Sciences conducts research on Organization-Entities capabilities-based software process modeling and presents a corresponding method [12]. The Organization-Entities have definite as Process-Agents with capabilities. The modeling method applies Agent technology to organize the basic process units and to establish the project process system self-adaptively according to the special project goal and constraining environment. ASPECS is an agent-oriented software process for engineering complex systems, which details the entire ASPECS development process and provides a set of methodological guidelines for each process activity [13]. ASPECS uses UML extended as a modeling language. Xinpei Zhao etc. propose an approach for applying agent technology to software process modeling (SPM) and process-centered software engineering environment (PSEE) [14]. Software processes are defined as the collaboration of a group of process agents that know how to manage the software development activities and can act in the way software developers go about planning, enacting and reflecting on their work. Carlos Cares, etc. discuss the convenience of representing the software process using an agent-oriented language to model it and a goal-driven procedure to design it. They propose using i* framework which is both an agent-and a goal-oriented modeling language. Moreover, the agent-oriented concept is introduced in personal software process tool, which provide a visual representation of performance to the user [15].

All the problems with process model based on Agent above are that many key elements of the software process are ignored. Such as the role of the implementation of the process activities and the process of resource allocation are few defined. On the other hand, there are a variety of different functions, heterogeneous Agents in the current process model. It is difficult for the heterogeneous Agents to interact with each other. Therefore, the model is more complex.

3 Multi-agent Software Process Model Based on CMMI

3.1 Software Process Description Model

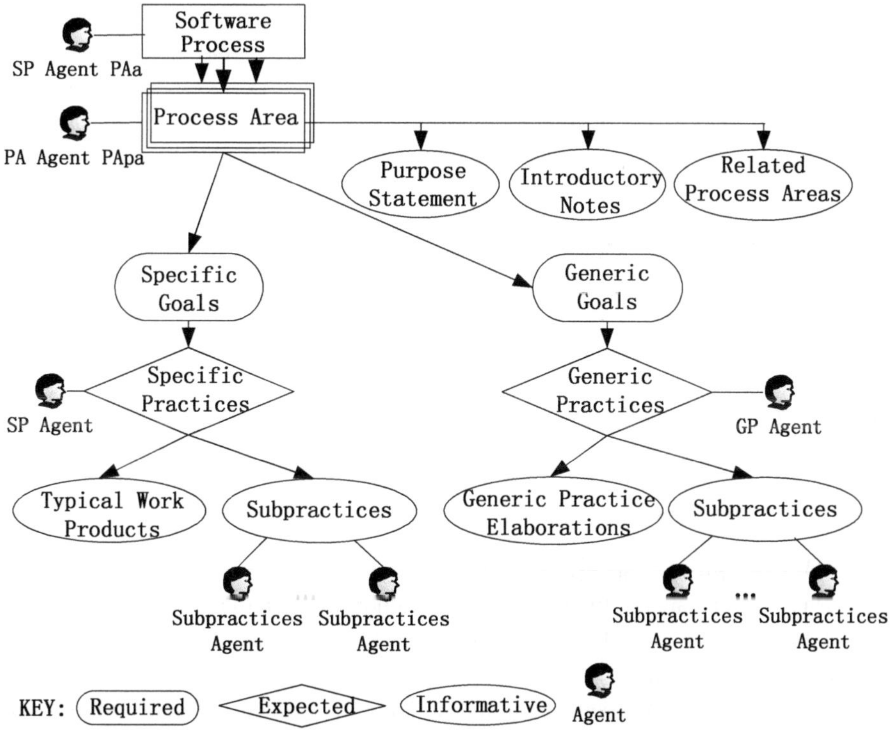

Fig. 1. CMMI based multi-agent software process model

The multi Agent-Based adaptive software process model based on CMMI is shown in Figure 1. There are a set of process agents in the software process including process area agents (PA Agent Pag_i), practices Agents (SP (Specific Goals) Agent) and subpractices Agent. To succeed the special goals, agents can be working in the form of highly distributed, mobile, autonomous, intelligent and cooperative Organizations (e.g. Engineering Process Group, EPG). In fact, in the adaptive software process model, the Agents of the software process are described as the process elements, their relationship and the process knowledge for establishing the relationship between these elements. When the process is implemented, the process agent with specific goals and state of the environment dynamically determines the collaborative relationship with other Agents. And then they will achieve the goal of software development through adjusting the relationship among the agents. While goals and environment are changing, they adjust these relationships under the new conditions to ensure the goal automatically. So the relationship between agents in the adaptive software process is dynamic. The CMMI based multi-agent software process model showed in Figure 1 is static. It only shows a specific goal and process state of the adaptive software process.

Definition 1. (Software Process SP) SP describes what an adaptive software process looks like and can be used to what is the software process elements, it is composed of 4 elements. $SP=(UPA,S,G,PAa)$.

(1) In the PAS part, PAS is a set of software process areas belong to specific software. $UPA=\{PA_1,PA_2,\cdots,PA_l\},l\in N,and,l\leq 25$. PA_l is a software process area in CMMI. It will be defined in Definition 2 formally.
(2) S is a set of process area environment. $S=\{PAs_1,PAs_2,\cdots,PAs_l\},l\in N,and,l\leq 25$, $PAs_j(j\leq l)$ is a process area environment state;
(3) G, softwarc goal, is a set of process area goals (goals set), $G=\{PAgoal_1,PAgoal_2,\cdots,PAgoal_l\},l\in N,and,l\leq 25$.
(4) PAa is an independent and collaborative process area agent.

Definition 2. (Process Area, PA) PA is a cluster of related best practices in an area, which when implemented collectively, satisfy a set of goals considered important for making significant improvement in that area. It can be defined as $PA=(PAid,PAs,PAgoal,PApa),PA\in PAS$, among this.

(1) $PAid$ is software process area ID;
(2) PAs is the states of the practice environment state in the process areas.
(3) $PAgoal$ is the set of a group of process area goals, It will be defined in Definition 3 formally.
(4) $PApa$ is a set of independent and collaborative practice Agents which is aim to specific goals and generic goals. There are two types practice Agents, specific practice Agent and generic practice Agent. It will be defined in Definition 4 formally.

Definition 3. (Process area goal, $PAgoal$) A process area goal is composed of 6 elements. $PAgoal = (g\_id, PAid, g\_cls, T, g\_c, RES)$, among this:

(1) g_id is set of process area goal ID.

(2) $PAid$ is software process area ID;

(3) g_cls is the same goal type. $g\_cls \in g\_clsType$, $g\_clsType = \{specific\_goal, generic\_goal\}$. $specific\_goal$ is the specific goal type according to the specific practice in the process area. $generic\_goal$ is the generic goal type according to the generic practice.

(4) T is 2nd-level indicators set of process area. It can be defined as $T = \{t_1, t_2, \cdots, t_n\}, n \in N$. The "$t$" will be defined in Definition 7 formally.

(5) g_c is the constraint conditions of the practice goal.

(6) RES it is resource constraint set. It can be defined as $RES = \{RES_1, RES_2, \cdots, RES_n\}, n \in N$.

Definition 4. (Practice Agent, $PApa$) $PApa$ is a practice Agent. It is composed of 5 elements. $PApa = (pa\_s, p\_r, p\_res, p\_act, p\_prod)$

(1) pa_s Is the practice environment state, $pa\_s \in PAs$;

(2) p_r is a role (actor) related to corresponding practice Agent.

(3) p_res is the resource constraints of a practice agent. It describes the amount of resources owned by the Agent.

(4) p_act is a set of process practice activities, $p\_act = \{p\_act_1, p\_act_2, \cdots, p\_act_q\}, q \in N$. It will be defined in Definition 5 formally.

(5) p_prod denotes the results (products) of the practice.

Definition 5. (Process practice activities, p_act) p_act is consist of 5 elements. $p\_act = \{s\_CRM, s\_a, s\_res, s\_m, s\_prod\}$, among this:

(1) s_CRM is a subpractice control model of a practice activity. It describes how to control the implementation of the practice activities;

(2) s_a is the subpractice agent set. $s\_a = \{s\_a_1, s\_a_2, \cdots, s\_a_o\}, o \in N$;

(3) s_res is the resource constraints of subpractice activities. $s\_res \subseteq p\_res$

(4) s_m is describes the method to implement the activities subpractice.

(5) s_prod denotes the results (products) of the subpractice.

Definition 6. (get element operation) $\forall X = (C_1, C_2, \cdots, C_u), u \in N$, $X.GetElement(C_i) = C_i.Value$, in short, $X.C_i = C_i.Value$

Definition 7. (2nd-level indicators, t) t is a 2nd-level indicators. It is consist of 3 elements. $t = (T\_id, t\_cls, I)$, among this:

(1) T_id is the id of T defined before.

(2) t_cls denotes the types of the 2nd-level indicators. $t\_cls = \{Speci\_prod,\ Speci\_proc,\ Gener\_sub\}$. $Speci\_prod$ is defined as the type of 2nd-level Specific product indicators. $Speci\_proc$ is defined as the type 2nd-level Specific process indicators. $Gener\_sub$ is defined as the type 2nd-level generic indicators.

(3) I is a set of 3rd-level indicators. It can be defined as $I = \{I_1, I_2, \cdots, I_u\}, u \in N$. The " I " will be defined in Definition 8 formally.

A 2nd-level indicator is related to a set of 3rd-level indicators.

Definition 8. (3rd-level indicators, I) The 3rd-level indicators I should include measurement data, data acquisition methods and activities. So I can be defined as $I = (t\_id, dI(t), AI(t))$, among this:

(1) t_id is the id of t defined before.

(2) $dI(t)$ is the measurement data of I which is related to t.

(3) $AI(t)$ is the data acquisition methods and activities of I which is related to t

In addition, it is easy to measure while I is quantifiable indicators. A 2nd-level indicator is related to one or more 3rd-level indicators. For example, process stability should measure by process cost, schedule, and the rate of the process change. On the other hand, a 3rd-level indicator is related to 2nd-level indicators. For example, code complexity is not only influence the reliability of the product, maintainability and portability.

The 2nd-level indicators can be measured by its related 3rd-level indicators. Similarly, Process area goal can be measured by its related 2nd-level indicators. There are many different algorithms for different software process measurement. So, measurement method can be defined as follow:

Definition 9. (Measurement Method, $Meas$) if $Meas$ is a measurement method, $Meas = (i, f(i))$. i is a set of measurement indicators. $f(i)$ is an indicators comprehensive measurement algorithm. $f \in F$, F is the set of the measurement algorithms. We extract the measurement method from the model. The measurement method is independent. It is loosely coupled between the measurement method and the model, so that, the user can select appropriate algorithms for different types of software.

3.2 Multi-agent Software Process Control and Improvement Algorithms

All the elements for software process area and its relationship defined before are shown in Figure 2. The process goal, characteristics and measurement, etc. indicators of different software process are variable, so in this model, users can define them according to the special software process flexibly.

In Figure 2, every characteristics of the software process area can show part and all the goals of the process. A 2nd-level indicator is related to one or more 3rd-level indicators. The 2nd-level indicators can be measured by its related 3rd-level indicators. Similarly, Process area goal can be measured by its related 2nd-level indicators. So the CMMI based multi-agent software process control and improvement process is a multi-objective decision-making process.

Since $PAgoal = (g\_id, PAid, g\_cls, T, g\_c, RES)$, then, 2nd-level indicator set can get as $T_{PAgoal} = PAgoal.T$.

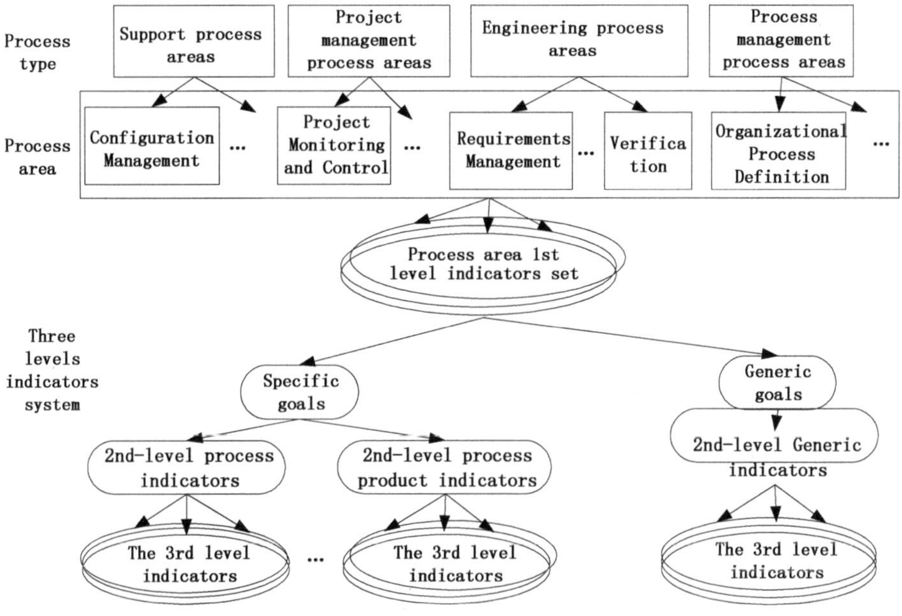

Fig. 2. Relationship of elements for software process area

The reverse mapping relationship between these elements will be discussed as follows, in order to support process improving methods based on the measurement model. According to the above definition, the mapping algorithm between the characteristics and objectives is presented as Algorithm 1.

Algorithm 1. Mapping algorithm from 2nd-level indicators to software process goals:
Input: Any 2nd-level indicators set, $T = \{t_1, t_2, \cdots, t_n\}, n \in N$.

Output: software process goals set $SP\_G = \{(PA_1, S_1, Pgoal_1), (PA_2, S_2, Pgoal_2), \cdots\}$

Steps:

(1) Let $SP\_G = \varnothing$, $UPA = ALL$

(2) Loop 1 :

If $UPA = \varnothing$,then Break

ELSE

$\forall PA_i \in UPA, PAs \in S$

then

$UPA = UPA - PA_i$

$S = S - PAs_i$

According to the Definition 1, $G = \{PAgoal_1, PAgoal_2, \cdots, PAgoal_l\}$

(3) Loop 2 :

If $G = \varnothing$,then Break

ELSE

$\forall PAgoal_j \in G$

then

$G = UPA - PAgoal_j$

According to the Definition 2,

$PAgoal = (g\_id, PAid, g\_cls, T, g\_c, RES)$

According to the **Definition3, 7,**

$T = \{t_1, t_2, \cdots, t_n\}, n \in N$, $t = (T\_id, t\_cls, I)$

If $t \in PAgoal_j.T$

then

$SP\_G = SP\_G + \{(PA_j, S_j, Pgoal_j)\}$

(4) End Loop 2

(5) End Loop 1

In Algorithm 1, we can get process area, environment state and goal of 2nd-level indicator.

Similarly, we can get 3rd-level indicator from 2nd level indicators easily. Since $t = (T\_id, t\_cls, I)$, then, $I = t.I$

Instead, we can get the mapping algorithm from 3rd-level indicators to 2nd level indicators as follow.

Algorithm 2. The mapping algorithm from 3rd-level indicators to 2nd level indicators.

Input: Any 3rd-level indicators I

Output: relationships from 3rd-level indicators to 2nd level indicators, $ItoT$

Steps:

(1) Let $ItoT = \varnothing$, $T = ALL$

(2) Loop :

If $T = \varnothing$,then Break

ELSE

$\forall t_i \in T$

then

$T = T - t_i$

According to the **Definition3, 7,**

$T = \{t_1, t_2, \cdots, t_n\}, n \in N$, $t = (T\_id, t\_cls, I)$

$ItoT = ItoT + t_i$

(5) End Loop

In Algorithm 1, we can get 2nd-level indicators related to 3rd-level indicators.

3.3 Software Process Comprehensive Measurement Model

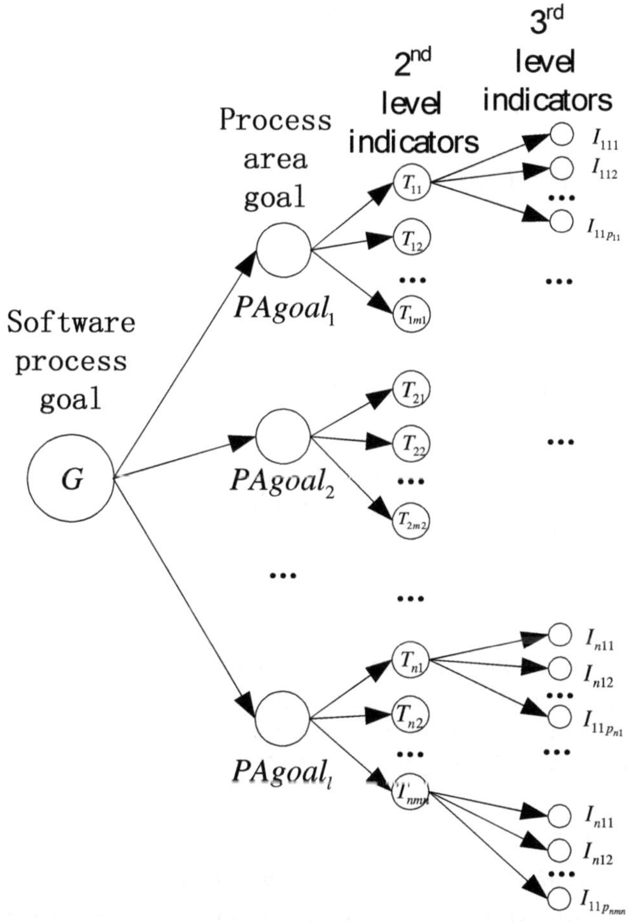

Fig. 3. Software Process Comprehensive Measurement Model

Having defined the basic relationship between the elements, we can define the software process measurement model as follows:

Definition 10. CMMI based Software Process Measurement Model. We set $CMMI\_Model$ is the CMMI based software process measurement model, and $CMMI\_Model = (G, PAgoal, T, I, Meas)$. $G, PAgoal, T, I, Meas$ have defined before, $G = \{PAgoal_1, PAgoal_2, \cdots, PAgoal_l\}$, $PAgoal = (g\_id, PAid, g\_cls, T, g\_c, RES)$, $T = \{t_1, t_2, \cdots, t_n\}, n \in N$, $I = \{I_1, I_2, \cdots, I_u\}, u \in N$, $I = (t\_id, dI(t), AI(t))$, $Meas$ is a measurement method, $Meas = (i, f(i))$.

A software process comprehensive measurement model is shown in Figure 3.
Input: $G, PAgoal, T, I, Meas$ of a software process.
Output: software process comprehensive measurement result.

$$T = \bigcup_{k=1}^{n} Meas_k(I_k)$$

$$PAgoal = \bigcup_{j=1}^{m} Meas_j(T_j)$$

$$G = \bigcup_{i=1}^{l} Meas_i(PAgoal_i)$$

3.4 Software Process Control and Improvement

The measurement results will help to control and improve software process decision support. The software process control and improvement is needed when the measurement results are not well satisfied. The software defect, abnormal state, etc. will be identified based on a comprehensive measure results. The corresponding process goals and process practices can also be exported by Algorithm 1, 2. Then, it will be the guidance on control and improvement.

Algorithm 3. Software Process Control and Improvement (SPCI) algorithm.
Input: software defect, abnormal state, or higher expectations measure results, Result;
Output: need to Control and Improvement software process goals set:

$$SPCI = \{SP\_G_1, SP\_G_2, \cdots, SP\_G_r\}$$

Steps:

(1)Let $SPCI = \varnothing$;

(2)Since $CMMI\_Model = (G, PAgoal, T, I, Meas)$, software defect, abnormal state, or higher expectations measure results can be exported by the measurement process. So the 3rd-level indicators which is needed to improve from the results of measurement will be extracted:

$SPCI\_I = \{I_1, I_2, \cdots, I_r\}$

Loop 1:

If $SPCI\_I = \varnothing$, then Break

ELSE

$\forall I_i \in SPCI\_Iset$

then

$SPCI\_I = SPCI\_I - I_i$

According to **Algorithm 2** $T_{I_i} = ItoT(I_i)$

Loop 2:

If $T_{I_i} = \varnothing$, then Break

ELSE

$\forall t \in T_{I_i}$

then

$T_{I_i} = T_{I_i} - t$

According to **Algorithm 1**

$SP\_G_i = \{(PA_{i1}, S_{i1}, Pgoal_{i1}), \cdots\}$

End If

$SPCI = SPCI \cup SP\_G_i$

(3) End Loop 2

Repeat the Loop 1 (get the another $I_i \in SPCI\_Iset$)

(4) End Loop 1

The process areas, environment state and process area goal needed to control and improve are exported by Algorithm 3 based on the measurement results.

4 Conclusion

Traditional software process models are mostly linear, non-formalized, static, mechanical and passive. Software engineer should describe all the change possibilities before the software process implement. What is more, the solution of problems should be given in advance. When the environment of the software process changes, software process cannot adapt and make adjustments to correspond with these changes. With the complexity of software development process increasing, a distributed, flexible dynamic process model for software development activities, documented, execution, analysis, and evolution in the software process is needed. To address to these problem, a CMMI based Multi-Agent dynamic software process control and improved model is presented. Firstly, process resources and process roles are introduced to the model. The software process has been described as a set of independent software process Agent. Process Agent, in every aspect of the process, determines its behavior, so it should consider whether it has sufficient resources and be able to determine the implementation of its behavior when its corresponding role has the appropriate capacity. The software processes Agents achieve the goal of software development through adaptively adjust their behavior meeting software process environment changes. In the model, Agent package knowledge, activities, resources, environment and activities, role, etc of the process. This kind of model has the characteristics of high cohesion, low coupling, and a favorable system structure.

Acknowledgement. This work is supported by Special Fund for Fast Sharing of Science Paper in Net Era by CSTD (No. 2011117).

References

1. Osterweil, L.J.: Software processes are software too. In: Proc. of the 9th Int'l Conf. on Software Engineering (ICSE 1987), pp. 2–13. IEEE Computer Society Press, Osterweil (1987)
2. Engels, G., Groenewegen, L.: SOCCA: Specification of coordinated and cooperative activities. In: Software Process Modeling and Technology, pp. 71–100. Research Studies Press Ltd., Taunton (1994)
3. Bandinelli, S., Fuggetta, A., Lavazza, L., Loi, M., Picco, G.: Modeling and improving an industrial software process. IEEE Trans. on Software Engineering 21(5), 440–454 (1995)
4. Dorling, A.: SPICE: Software process improvement and capability determination. Software Quality Journal 2(4), 209–224 (1993)
5. SEI. CMMI for Development, Version 1.2-Improving Processes for Better Products. SEI, CMU (2006)
6. García, I., Pacheco, C.: A Web-based Tool for Automatizing the Software Process Improvement Initiatives in Small Software Enterprises. Latin America Transactions, IEEE (Revista IEEE America Latina) 8(6), 685–694 (2010)
7. Alshammari, F.H., Ahmad, R.: The effect of geographical region on the duration of CMMI-based software process improvement initiatives: An empirical study. In: 2010 2nd International Conference on Software Technology and Engineering (ICSTE), vol. 2, pp. V2-97-V2-100. IEEE Press, San Juan (2010)
8. Choi, S., Kim, D.-K., Park, S.: ReMo: A recommendation model for software process improvement. In: 2012 International Conference on Software and System Process (ICSSP), pp. 135–139. IEEE Press, Zurich (2012)
9. Lee, C.S., Wang, M.H.: Ontology-based computational intelligent multi-agent and its application to CMMI assessment. Applied Intelligence 30(2), 203–219 (2009)
10. Zhao, X.P., Li, M.S., Wang, Q., Chan, K., Leung, H.: An Agent-based self-adaptive software process model. Journal of Software 15(3), 348–359 (2004)
11. Jo, C.H., Chen, G., Choi, J.: A new approach to the BDI agent-based modeling. In: The Proceedings of the 2004 ACM symposium on Applied Computing, pp. 1541–1545. ACM, Seoul (2004)
12. Wang, Q., Xiao, J., Li, M., Nisar, M.W., Yuan, R., Zhang, L.: A Process-Agent Construction Method for Software Process Modeling in SoftPM. In: Wang, Q., Pfahl, D., Raffo, D.M., Wernick, P. (eds.) SPW 2006 and ProSim 2006. LNCS, vol. 3966, pp. 204–213. Springer, Heidelberg (2006)

13. Cossentino, M., Gaud, N., Hilaire, V., Galland, S., Koukam, A.: ASPECS: an agent-oriented software process for engineering complex systems. Autonomous Agents and Multi-Agent Systems 20(2), 260–304 (2010)
14. Zhao, X.P., Li, M.S., Wang, Q., Chan, K., Leung, H.: An Agent-based self-adaptive software process model. Journal of Software 15(3), 348–359 (2004)
15. Cares, C., Franch, X., Mayol, E., Alvarez, E.: Goal-Driven agent-oriented software processes. In: The Proceeding of the 32nd EUROMICRO Conference on Software Engineering and Advanced Applications, pp. 336–347. IEEE Press, Cavtat (2006)

The Design and Realization of 3G-Based Vehicular Video Surveillance System

Weimin Ge, Yang Liu, Heng Lv, and Zhan Jin

School of Computer Science and Technology
Tianjin University
Tianjin, China
{gewm,jinzhan}@tju.edu.cn, liuyang_tju@126.com
lv.gobbin@gmail.com

Abstract. The third generation mobile communication system technology has been widely used in various aspects of our daily life. Making use of the 3G networks to remote monitor and managing vehicle video can well adapt to the mobility characteristics of the vehicle network. Moreover, this technology has obvious advantages compared with traditional technologies. We design and implement a vehicular network video surveillance communication system, which consists of two major sub-systems, the streaming media server (SMS) and the central management system (CMS). This system has achieved the characteristics of full functionality and high operating efficiency. In particular, this system has a streaming media cache control algorithms and data distribution strategy to overcome delay and jitter in the video processing. Finally, the test results show that this system meets the application requirements and can provide good performance in network connection, cache control, remote real-time video transmission, and display aspects.

Keywords: 3G, Video Surveillance, Streaming Media Server (SMS), Central Management System (CMS).

1 Introduction

In recent years, along with computer image processing technology and network transmission technology development, video surveillance technology has also been making great progress [1]. Video surveillance system makes full use of modern computer network technology and multimedia information processing technology [2], and is widely used in many security situations because of its convenient and information-rich features. We can find the video surveillance system to be used widely in the military, railway, electricity, telecommunications, transportation, banking and other production and management departments.

However, a variety of monitoring systems have many shortcomings. Some systems' overall function is not fully operable, which is insufficient to well serve our customers and take full advantage of the 3G technology to achieve the desired effect [3]. Some systems' playing terminal inexistence special frame control mechanism on

V. Khachidze et al. (Eds.): iCETS 2012, CCIS 332, pp. 696–707, 2012.

jitter and delay. In practical applications, videos cannot begin playing until all the data has been downloaded; moreover, the real-time performance is poor [4] [5]. Some systems' features are redundant, consuming tremendous time and space resources in order to produce unsatisfactory application effects [6].

The public transport vehicles embedding the 3G video surveillance system are examined in this paper; herewith some improvements are made in response to the existing 3G video surveillance system's inadequacies. The overall system design theme has three modules which not only provide a full range of functions but can overcome delay and jitter. The goal is to design and implement an efficient mobile video surveillance and a real-time network transmission system for vehicles.

This paper studies two modules: 1) SMS and 2) CMS. The first component is an important part of the vehicular video surveillance system, playing a connecting role. The second component is the location of the real-time vehicle information processing. These modules can provide basic management functions for managers. In this paper, we focus on the system's characteristics of fully functional and efficient operation, and describe a streaming media cache control algorithm and a data receiving and distributing strategy. The algorithm and strategy can effectively overcome the video terminal's delay and jitter.

The rest of the paper is organized as follows: the outline design of the vehicle video surveillance system, including the overall operation of the structure, SMS and CMS's functionality partitioning are described in section 2. The key parts of the surveillance system, that is, the specific design of the streaming media cache control algorithms and streaming media controller's video data receiving and distributing strategy are described in section 3. The realization of the video surveillance system's testing and result analysis are described in section 4. Finally, section 5 summarizes our conclusions.

2 System Overview

This section details the design ideas of the 3G-based vehicular video surveillance system. First, we provide an overall architecture diagram. Then, in accordance with the architecture diagram, we divide the SMS and the CMS into several function units. This system's architecture and partitioning strategy are more complete and more efficient than other systems.

2.1 The Overall System Architecture

The surveillance system's service architecture is shown in Fig. 1. SMS, CMS and State message database are deployed on different servers. Although this deployment increases the time of connection with the database, it can better make use of the available resources. Each server can also be made to start its own CMS when there is more than one management system terminal. This architecture may not only be easily extended by adding servers but also has better data redundancy function.

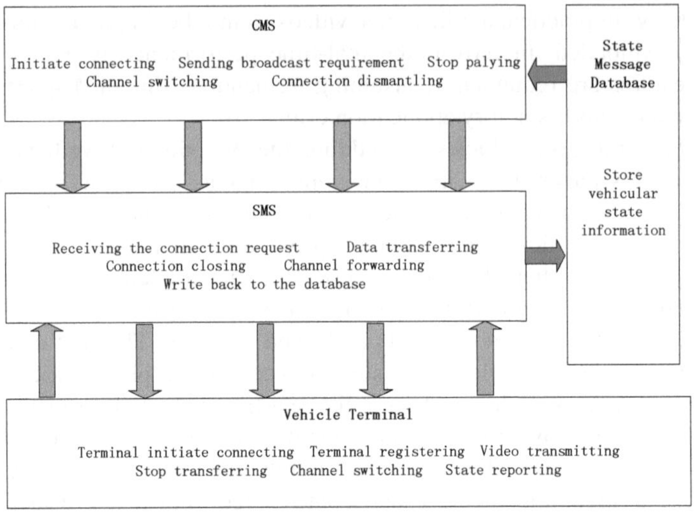

Fig. 1. Overall function operation architecture of the vehicular video surveillance system

2.2 Functions Description of SMS

The 3G-based vehicular video surveillance system and WEB-based streaming media transmission system are different in transmission mode. The former requires dedicated SMS, transport protocols, and multi-level control of the media by a specific server, to ensure that the media signal broadband and network connectivity match. Therefore, the system needs a greater regulation mechanism in order to ensure reliability of the operation.

SMS provides access functions and basic commands for the CMS. It integrates commands parsing of upper and lower as well as distributing and monitoring of videos. Furthermore, the performance of SMS will determine the performance of the video surveillance system. SMS is divided into the following modules, according to function:

1) Vehicle terminal maintenance module: Responsible for maintaining the initial vehicle access and re-connection functions as the interface of the vehicle terminal.
2) Management system maintenance module: Responsible for establishing a CMS's data access connection. Also responsible for maintaining vehicle monitoring and observation table as a registration CMS interface.
3) Forward command module: As a core module in the SMS, this module operates upstream and downstream command messages.
4) Receiving and sending data module: Used for receiving and forwarding data; also responsible for caching and backing up local data.
5) Operation log module: Responsible for logging and displaying functions.

2.3 Functions Description of CMS

CMS is the upper part in the video surveillance system. It includes network data decoding, resource management, media display, user servicing, and other functions.

CMS protects the normal operation of the overall video surveillance system, and provides the management system for managers. CMS is divided into the following modules, according to function:

1) Vehicle state information monitoring module: CMS provides a view of vehicle information; this function does not depend on the connection state.
2) Network data receiving module: Responsible for receiving network video data for CMS.
3) Monitoring video control module: As a core module in the CMS, this module provides the most important video control function for CMS.
4) Logging module: Responsible for logging CMS's important events.

3 System Key Mechanism

This section is the key implementation section in the video surveillance system. This section details the description of the streaming media cache control algorithm and video data receiving and distributing strategy. These two mechanisms are key to overcoming the latency and jitter in the video broadcast terminal.

3.1 Cache Control Algorithm of Streaming Media

This section describes a video data stream cache control algorithm based on the characteristics of the 3G-based video surveillance system. This algorithm has many functions, including buffer vehicle terminal, SMS and CMS mutual communication, and reduced system delay jitter, providing a smooth support service for the monitoring system. The system variables are as follows:

Vehicles terminal video data sent rate R_1;
SMS stream forwarding rate R_2;
SMS remaining cache B;
SMS data forwarding window W;
CMS video playback rate R_3;
CMS receiving cache upper limit B_R;
CMS remaining cache B_L;
CMS minimum cache B_W;

Assuming the upper limit of the cache capacity is infinite, the upper limit of cache size in the CMS should be taken into consideration. SMS in the normal working state is $B >= 0.5W$, and CMS in the normal state is $B_W <= B_L <= B_R$.

3.1.1 Cache Control Algorithm of SMS

```
Initialize variables
while Don't stop receiving and forwarding
  if R1=R2 then/* Forwarding and receiving rate are consistent */
     if W is filled up then
        Forwarding videos
```

```
    end if
end if
if R1<R2 then/* The vehicle terminal has wrong operations when forwarding data*/
    if B<W then/* Cached data is not enough */
        Reduce the forwarding rate/* Look forward to receiving network data and writing cache */
    end if
    if B<0.5W then
        Pause forwarding/* Look forward to receiving network data and writing cache */
    end if
    if W is filled up then
        Forwarding videos/* B continues to decline */
    end if
end if
if R1>R2 then/* The SMS forwarding rate is too low */
    if B>2W then/* Burst transmission of the vehicle terminal*/
        Increase data forwarding rate/* Look forward to restoring buffer to the normal state */
    end if
    if R2=0 then
        Restore initial value of the R2
    end if
    if W is filled up then
        Forwarding videos
    end if
end if
end while
```

According to the algorithm descriptions, the SMS has experienced four major states. The states' flow diagram and conversion conditions are shown in Fig. 2:

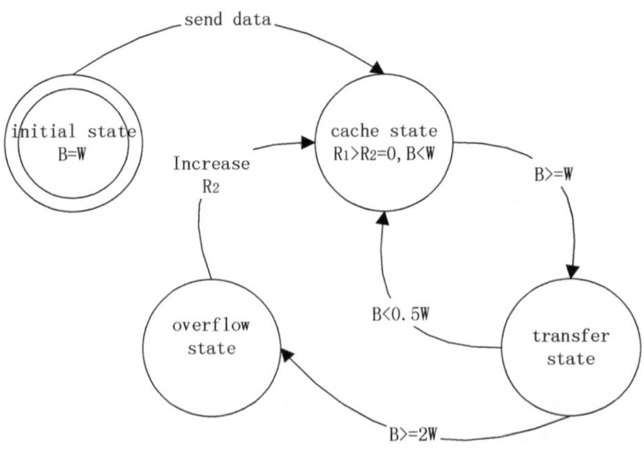

Fig. 2. State transition diagram of SMS

3.1.2 Cache Control Algorithm of CMS

```
Initialize variables
while Don't stop playing
  if R2=R3 then/* Sending and receiving rate are consistent */
    if BW is filled up then
      Playing videos
    end if
  end if
  if R2<R3 then/* Data receiving rate is less than the current video playing rate */
    if BL<BW then/* Playing cache is not enough */
      Pause playing /*Look forward to receiving network data and writing cache
                */
    end if
    if BW is filled up then
      Playing videos/* BL continues to decline */
    end if
  end if
  if R2>R3 then/* Data stream is steady increasing */
    if BR is not enough then
      Copy BL's valid data to the initial position of the cache
      if BR is also not enough then
        Reserve BL's recently 80% data and copy them to the initial
        position of the cache
      end if
    end if
    if R3=0 then
      Restore initial value of the R3
    end if
    if BW is filled up then
      Playing videos/* BL will continue to increase */
    end if
  end if
end while
```

3.2 Receiving and Distributing Strategy of the Video Data

SMS is a transfer station between CMS and vehicle monitoring terminal, which is mainly responsible for the video data receiving and distributing processes. Data receiving and distributing strategies have a direct impact on the video quality of the terminal.

3.2.1 Receiving Processing Strategy of the Video Data

After vehicle terminals are accessed to SMS, SMS divides them into different units according to the vehicle terminal ID, and sets up a dedicated data receiver for them.

When a playing request is made, SMS and data receiver will broadcast a playing command and set a cache location for the vehicle terminal, respectively. Then SMS will start a thread to receive video data stream.

After the cache path is confirmed and the old cache is cleaned up, SMS needs to determine the timestamp, receive the end playing data stream, and write data back to the cache files and the backup files.

When the vehicle signal breaks or CMS makes a request to stop, SMS needs to update the running state, stop data writing, and end the receiving thread. These processes are shown in Fig. 3:

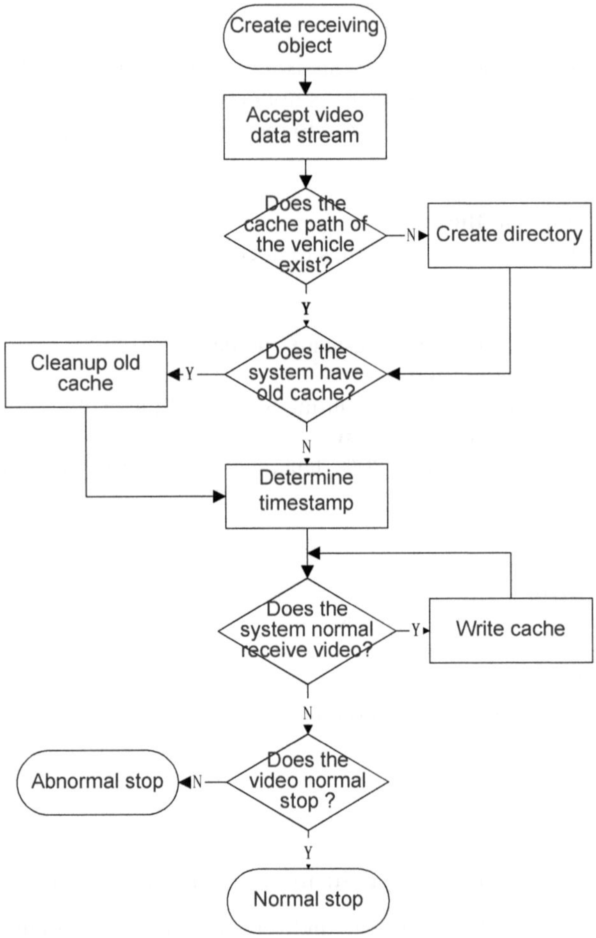

Fig. 3. Receiving processing flow chart of the video data

3.2.2 Distributing Processing Strategy of the Video Data

This strategy is similar to the vehicle terminal strategy. SMS divides CMS threads into different units according to their ID, and provides independent video data resources for each thread.

After the playing request is made and the uploaded video data from the vehicle terminal is confirmed, SMS sets data receiver and playing sources for each terminal. This method will obtain the location and size of the playing data source file. The processes are shown in Fig. 4:

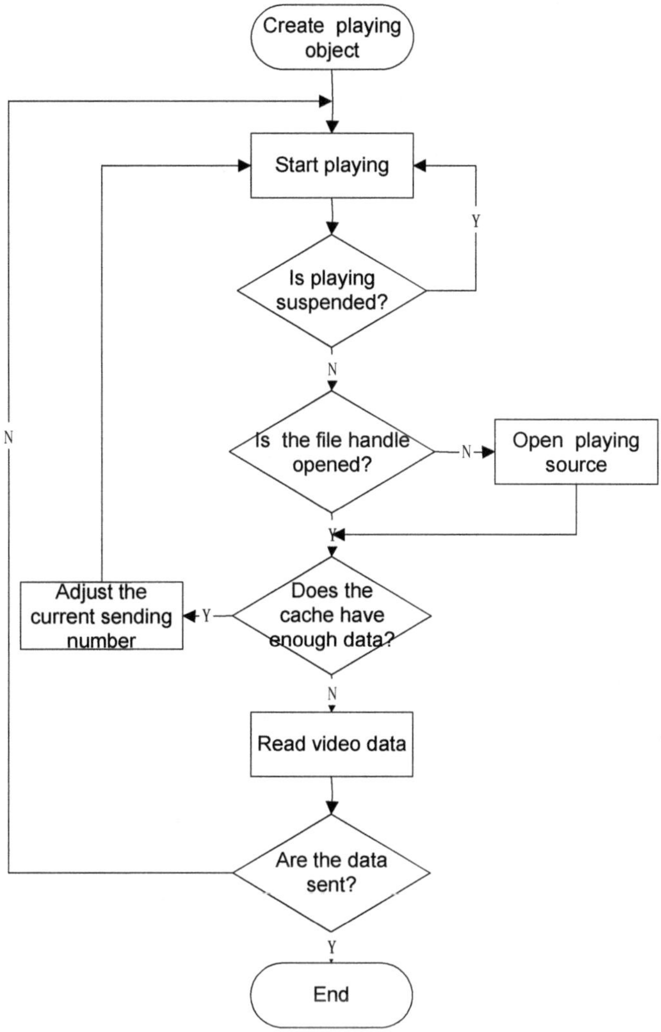

Fig. 4. Distributing processing flow chart of the video data

4 Testing and Result Analysis

In this section, the testing is divided into two components. The first component tests the system's basic operation to verify the advantages of full-featured and efficient operation. The second component tests and analyses the real-time function and fluency of the system to verify the performance of the end-to-end delay jitter.

4.1 CMS and SMS Running Interfaces

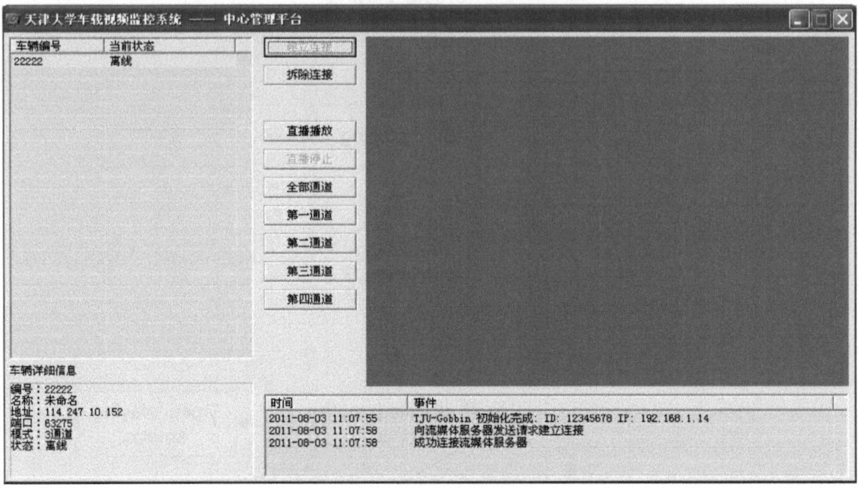

Fig. 5. A screenshot of CMS GUI

Fig. 6. A screenshot of SMS GUI

4.2 The Initial Delay Testing

T_0 represents the moment of the vehicle's terminal sending the first data to the SMS; T_1 represents the moment of the SMS forwarding the first data to the CMS, and T_2 the moment of the CMS successfully playing the video. In particular, D_1 represents the delay between T_0 and T_1. D_2 represents the delay between T_1 and T_2. D represents the total delay, which is the average delay of creating a complete playing link.

In the experiment, the SMS forwarding window W is set to 20KB, the CMS B_R is set to 10MB, and the CMS B_W is set to 20KB. The results of 100 connection tests are shown in Fig. 7:

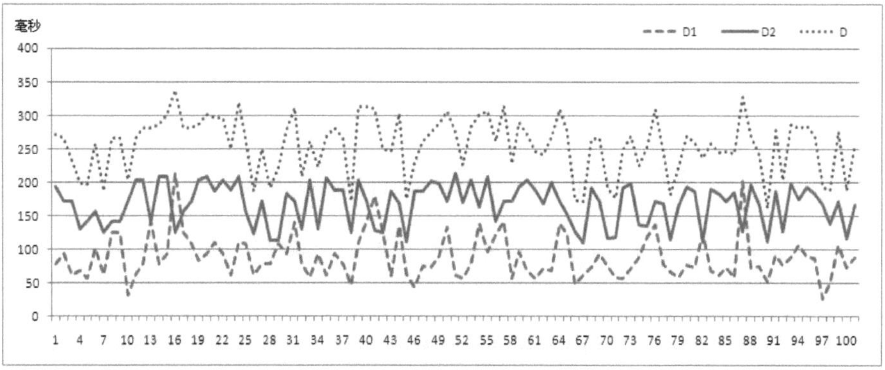

Fig. 7. Initial delay testing results

The initial delay testing results are shown in Fig. 7. The average delay of creating a complete playing link, D, is not more than 260ms. In particular, the vehicle terminal transmits data to the SMS, and the average delay of this transmission, D_1, is not more than 100ms. The SMS transits data to the CMS to create the playing video, and the average delay of this transmission, D_2, is not more than 160ms.

The instability of the 3G network makes D_1 unstable, resulting in the strong jitter in the whole process of the created connection. However, playing jitter can be controlled through the cache control algorithm in the latter process.

The ITU (International Telecommunications Union) suggests that the end-to-end average delay, here noted D_1, does not exceed 150ms; moreover, in practical applications, users only require that the average delay of creating a complete playing link, D, does not exceed 500ms. Therefore, we consider the video transmission delay and the delay of creating a complete link are in the acceptable range: the performance of the real-time can meet the actual needs.

4.3 Inter-Frame Jitter Testing

CMS receives the streaming video and determines the correlation among packets. The data are divided into the basic frame units to record inter-frame time interval. The experiment is divided into three groups. The SMS forwarding window W is set to 0 (not using cache control algorithm), 20KB, and 200KB, respectively. The testing results are shown in Fig. 8:

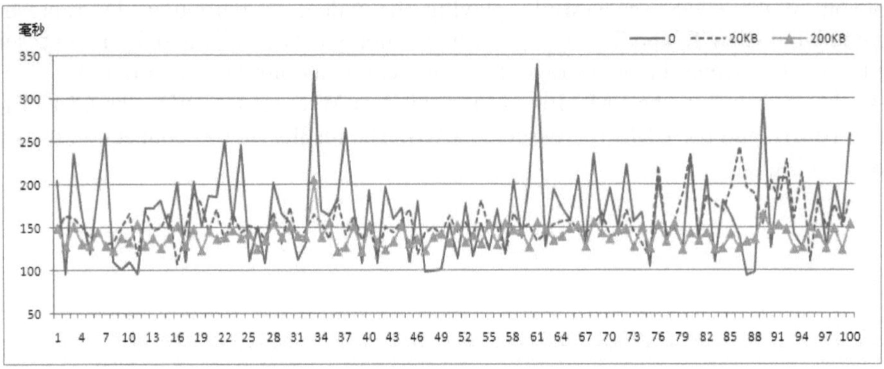

Fig. 8. Inter-frame jitter testing results

Fig. 8 shows the inter-frame jitter testing results. If SMS does not use cache control algorithm, the received frame time interval will fluctuate and big jitters will cause poor continuity. When the forwarding window is equal to the average frame size, the jitter becomes smaller and the continuity becomes stronger. When the forwarding window becomes bigger, the buffer control effect becomes more pronounced and the delay becomes more stable.

In fact, the cache control algorithm has sacrificed real-time to obtain much more stable delay. In practical applications, we need to set the buffer size depending on the network conditions to decrease delay jitter.

5 Conclusion

This paper presents the design and development of the 3G Vehicular Video Surveillance System, which includes a vehicle terminal, a SMS and a CMS. Built with the DirectShow play technology [7] and standard MFC libraries, this video surveillance system can be executed on the Windows platform.

Two major subsystems, SMS and CMS are discussed in detail in this paper. While SMS plays a pivotal role of providing connection and data transmission, CMS provides a central control platform full of management functions for the vehicle managers. A new streaming media cache control algorithm and a video data distribution strategy have been designed for this system, which help secure system functionality and efficiency. It has been demonstrated through various test cases that these two techniques can reduce delay and jitter in situations similar to real-world applications.

Real-time and fluency tests show the sub-systems of the SMS and CMS meet the application requirements and can provide strong support for the 3G vehicle video surveillance system.

References

1. 徐力, 孔岩: 视频监控系统的现状和发展趋势. 信息技术与信息化 04, 60–62 (2005)
2. Lu, S., Jin, Z.-G., Jin, Z., et al.: 3G Wireless Video Surveillance System Designed for Bus and Reliable Network Transmission. Wireless Communications Networking and Mobile Computing, 1–4 (2001)
3. Kankanhalli, M.S.: Multimedia Surveillance and Monitoring. Video and Signal Based Surveillance, 1 (2006)
4. Wu, D., Hou, Y.T., Zhu, W., et al.: Streaming video over the Internet: Approaches and Directions. IEEE Transactions on Circuits and Systems for Video Technology 11(3), 282–300 (2002)
5. 林鹏: 基于流媒体实验室监控系统的设计及实现. 实验室研究与探索 02, 21–22 (2007)
6. Zhang, Y., Wan, X., Fan, Z.: Design of Transmission for Video Monitor System Based on 3G Network. Video Engineering 02, 61–62 (2009)
7. 闻恩友, 赵正德, 杨立朝等: 3G网络的移动视频监控系统. 中国图象图形学报 10, 1987–1990 (2008)

Mobile Clerk Integral System Based on Distributed Performance Evaluation Systems

Qing Xie, Guodong Liu, Zhenghua Shu, Dengji Zhao, and Bingxin Wang

Key Laboratory for Optoelectronics & Communication of Jiangxi Province
Jiangxi Science & Technology Normal University
Nanchang, Jiangxi, China
xqwyy163@163.com

Abstract. Distributed systems are increasingly favored by various industries. This proposed system is designed based on the integral characteristics of the distributed system, and modified existing conventional algorithms. The system integration of rules and the integral main program is completely separated; so that the complex and changing rules is not embedded in the main program, and the rules form the separate module. At the same time, this system retains the advantages of centralized system, so as to achieve the best effect of the system in the field.

Keywords: Distributed systems, integral characteristics, integration rules, centralized system.

1 Introduction

With the improved performance of computer hardware, terminal equipment has the ability to process data, and distributed systems are widely used in various aspects with high-performance applications. Distributed data were used to establish a postal QOS model1and Corba-based distributed system development, so as to gradually replace the centralized system. However, the distributed system is not perfect, for example, it takes the data and stores in the system, rather than storing data in a central system, and therefore it is difficult to make an effective plan to backup the data. Therefore, in comparing the centralized system to distributed systems, their respective advantages are also each other's shortcomings.

In the history of system designing, the main program and the integral form of the rules have always been curable, if the system encounters failures. Or, to modify the rules of the system, one must find the error through seeking from the beginning to the end.

Therefore, based on the two major issues, one must think, whether it is possible to make full use of the distributed systems advantages and disadvantages of centralized systems. To establish a system that is conducive to stability and efficiency, the integral of the rules and procedures must be completely separated, as opposed to changing rules of complex points to cure or embed in the main system. Therefore, we

V. Khachidze et al. (Eds.): iCETS 2012, CCIS 332, pp. 708–714, 2012.

designed the mobile clerk integral system. The system is designed based on the above mentioned advantages. It focuses on centralized management, distributed applications, the characteristics of the management mechanism, and a flexible and unified scoring system.

2 The Concept

The centralized computer network consists of a large central system; the terminal is the client, and all the data is stored in a central system which is managed by the database management system. All the processing is done by the large systems, using the input and output terminal. The terminal itself does not perform any tasks; all of the tasks are processed on the host. The main characteristics of the centralized data storage can make all the data available to store in one place, all over the office of the remote terminal through cable links to the central computer (host).This ensures that each end-use is of the same information source. Backing up data is done easily, because they are stored on the server; therefore only the server is needed to back up the system.

The Centralized system is application to IBM-HP and other major minicomputer. The terminal has no data processing capabilities, operations are performed on the host. As for banking systems, most are centralized systems which include large enterprises, research institutes, military and government, etc. The centralized system has been prevalent in the last century and continues to be used; the software is often very expensive.

As the performance of personal computers have greatly improved and been widespread in use, for the purpose of processing province is distributed to all computers on the network. Distributed systems are composed of a group of autonomous computers, and middleware distributed throughout the network connection, allowing one to connect to others' activities and shared system resources. To the user, the distributed system appears as a whole entity. From simple file sharing to general multi-machine resource sharing, from a single computational model to a variety of multi-level computational models, and from a closed local network to an open global network, the distributed system has evolved into a basic structure of modern computer systems, to support a very wide range of industrial and commercial applications.

Distributed computing and centralized computing are opposing concepts; distributed computing of data can be distributed over a large area. Distributed networks, data storage and processing are carried out on the local workstation. Data output can be printed and may also be saved on a floppy disk. Through the network, data can be accessed more quickly, as well as more conveniently. Because each computer is capable of storing and processing data, it does not require the server to be very powerful; furthermore, the price is not too expensive. This type of network can adapt to various needs of different users, while allowing them to share network data, resources and services.

In comparison to centralized systems, distributed systems have several notable features, including sharing, openness, concurrency, scalability, fault tolerance and transparency.

3 Design and Realization

3.1 System Framework

Along with the expansion of enterprise, the overall framework of the company belongs to the headquarters and branch structure. Therefore, in order to better reflect the characteristics of the distribution of applications, and prominent the system under the framework of the centralized management mode, using the following framework. The market just as a computer system, the parent company is used as the ultimate command and the computer's central system. Each division is used as each transition terminal which processes the data from under all the provinces. The bottom is the source of the data at the bottom terminal.

The headquarters system is at the highest command of the central computer system and consists of various divisions, as the central system consists of various transition terminals to process data from the various cities beneath the headquarters system. To the bottom it is the source of the data, to become the bottom of the terminal. The system was combined to form a highly functioning machine, without individual local systems interfering with one another. The Headquarters system then directly observes the operation of each province or autonomous region and the data processing conditions through the central system platform. This building has become a centralized, distributed application integration system.

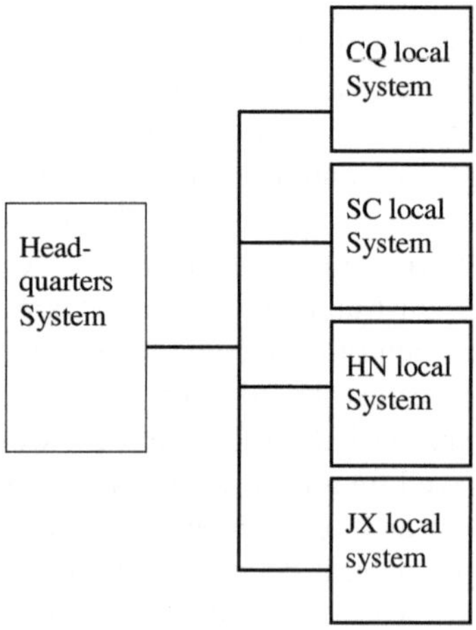

Fig. 1. Diagram of system framework

3.2 System Algorithm

To design the system program, the algorithm will be placed in the main program, to form a complete individual system. The main program is composed of thousands of instructions in a system. Therefore, when the system fails or modifies the rules, it is easy for the program's designers to identify where the problem lies. However, for maintenance personnel, it is difficult to understand the part of the relationship. Therefore, maintenance personnel must find the location of the error by searching from the beginning of instruction to the end, which is not only an overly time-consuming and difficult procedure, if your factory personnel are responsible for maintenance, but it also increases the expenses of the corresponding company.

Therefore, in order to avoid the above situation, the algorithm is improved. The entire system uses the following algorithm, which works with template-based operations. The system integration of rules and the integral main program is completely separated; it is no longer embedded in the complex and changing rules in the main program, but rather forms more than one integral model.

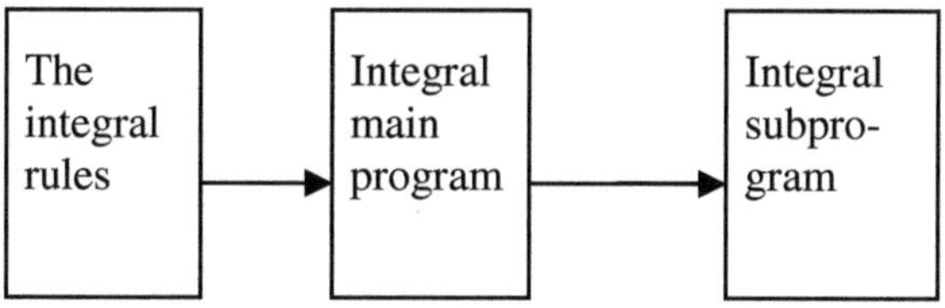

Fig. 2. Diagram of general algorithm

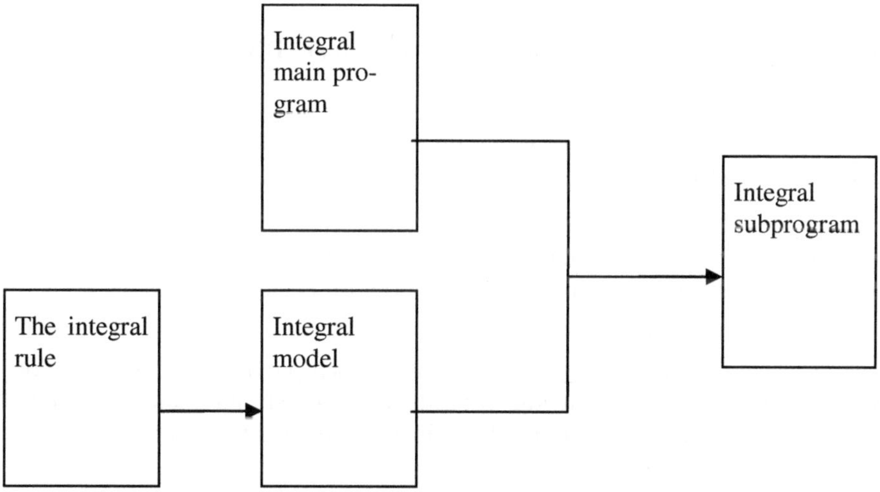

Fig. 3. The improved algorithm

The advantage of this algorithm is that not only does it provide flexible, fast and accurate operation, but it also reduces system maintenance costs and maintenance requirements, reflecting the effective separation of the user-level data and system-level data. According to the actual situation each province develops the personalized rule, and submits to the integral management system. At the same time, provinces management processes the system integration rule table that was submitted, and generates different point's templates, to be stored in the system database.

3.3 The Composition of System Rules and Scripts

Staff integration is divided into service points and other points. The other points include the following: bonus points, point's deductions, and non-BOSS business integration. The integration of business was divided into operations and benefits of integration. The following diagram demonstrates this composition.

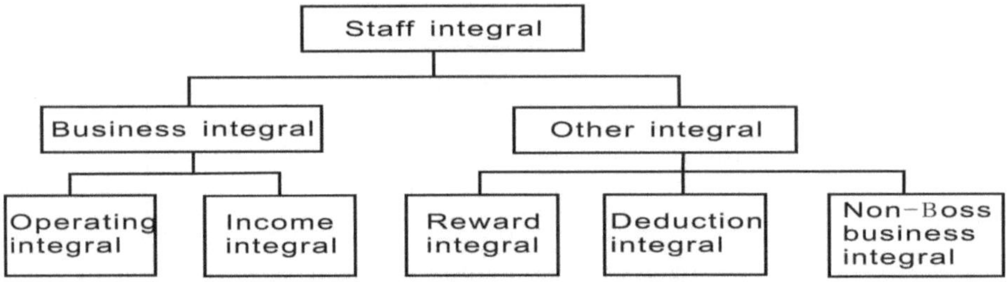

Fig. 4. Diagram of business integration

The Point's Script Figure and the Main Program are Divided into Four Steps:

- First, check the hardware system to run space.

The script checks the hardware system running space to determine whether it is adequate, if it is inadequate, it must free up an appropriate amount of space.

- Second, extract data from the BOSS

When there is enough space, the required data is extracted from the clone libraries in the BOSS system and stored in various categories of temporary tables.

- Third, owner's arithmetic

Each province has its own algorithm, based on each province's actual situation, resulting in the personalized integration needs, and refined into a total algorithm. The integral needs of the individual must be refined into individual algorithms.

- Finally, query the data

The data is inserted into the query table, and stored in a temporary table. Lastly the data is stored in the final query table; including employees of seven business integration subsidiaries, employees of seven major types of business integration, and the business daily staff integral monthly, etc.

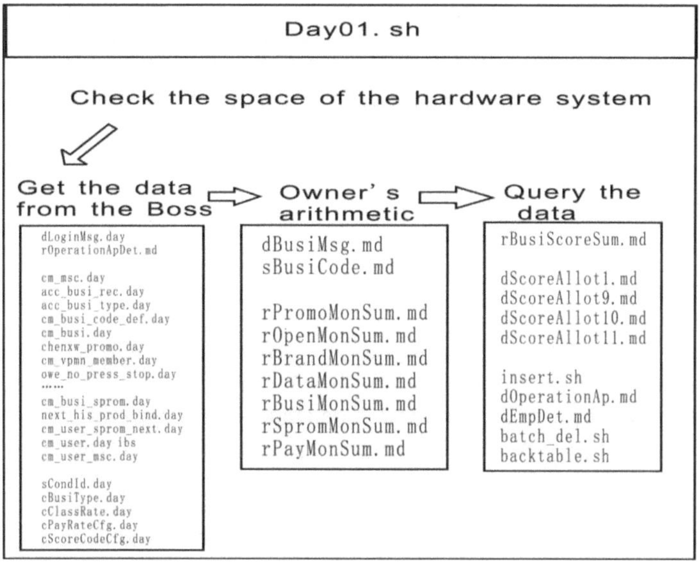

Fig. 5. Basic steps of the main program

3.4 Summary of the Composition System

The integral system is divided into five levels within the framework: the show level, logic level, data level, I/O level, and Outside data level. The show level is the main

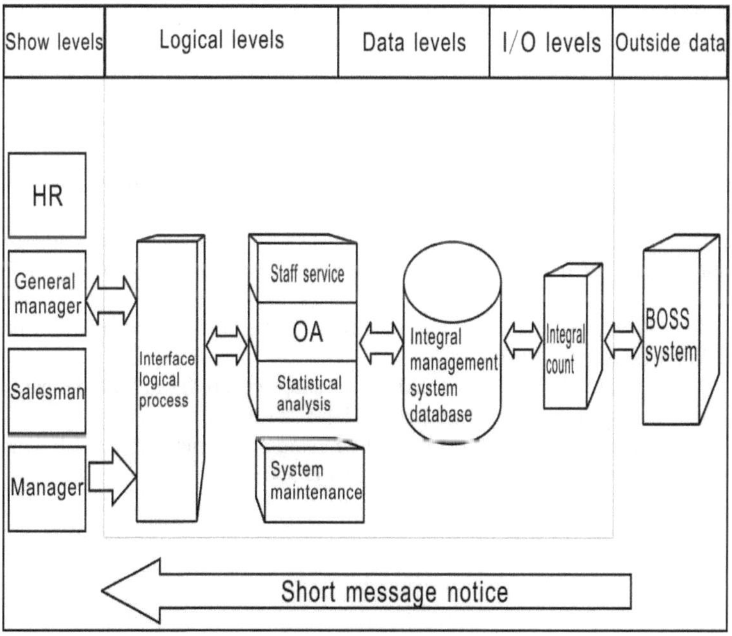

Fig. 6. Diagram of data processing points

office floor, and is mainly reflected in the operator, including human resources department, general manager, salesman, and managers. Logical level is reflected in the web interface system, it mainly includes sections such as staff services, collaboration, statistical analysis, and system maintenance.

The show level is base on logical level operation, and gets data from the data level. At the same time data processing was conducted using integral calculation rules, to query and get the required data.

4 Summary

The system is mainly based on the use of centralized systems and shaped by concepts that may be learned from the use of distributed system, under the guidance of some features. Not only can it be achieved independently in various regions, but also through the use and personal modification templates,, one can create a unique implementation of the same system. The system is highly conducive to the ability of head offices to create timely updates and policy adjustments for different market conditions, while significantly reducing the investment needs of resources and equipment. At present, distributed systems are everywhere (commercial, academic, government departments and family). These distributed systems typically provide shared resources (such as color printers or scanners and other special equipment) and the means to share data, which is extremely important for our information-based economy. Point calculation is an example of a distributed system, which provides computing resources and services that are becoming more and more popular. While the use of distributed systems is more challenging in solving sub-problems through parallel computing to provide higher performance, they provide greater availability of certain components to prevent failure.

References

1. Yue, G., Song, Y., Wang, Y., Liu, J., Gang, Z.G., Ma, X.: Distributed systems QoS model data postal. Computer Engineering, 04 (2010)
2. Cheung, D.W., Lee, S.D., Xiao, Y.Q.: Effect of data skewness and workload balance in parallel data mining. IEEE Transactions on Knowledge and Data Engineering 14(3), 498–514 (2006)
3. Goethals, B.: Survey on Frequent Pattern Mining. Hel-sinki Institute for Information Technology, Technical Report (2003)
4. Hu, K., Cheung, D.W., Xia, S.W.: Effect of adaptive configuration on parallel mining association rules. Journal of Software 11(1), 159–172 (2000)
5. Lu, H., Rudy, S., Liu, H.: Effective data mining using neural networks. IEEE Transaction on Knowledge and Data Engineering 8(6), 975–961 (1996)

A Dynamic Scanning Approach Based on Trie Matching for Clustering XML Data in E-business

Jing Zhang[1], Hanqi Zhu[2], and Gang Sun[3]

[1] School of Management and Economics
[2] College of Precision Instrument and Opto-Electronics Engineering
[3] School of Civil Engineering
Tianjin University, 92 Weijin Road, Nankai District, Tianjin 300072, China
{zjing,hqzhu,sungang}@tju.edu.cn

Abstract. The emergence of e-business has increased interest in XML data transactions. XML clustering techniques have been the key mechanisms to efficiently manage and categorize XML data when e-business transactions occur. Most previous works in the related literature focus on extracting frequent subtrees or common structures from a tree collection, which may incur the serious loss of structure information of the original tree during the extracting process. In this paper, we propose a Dynamic Scanning approach for XML structural clustering based on Trie Matching (DSTM). We initially extracted structure paths from XML documents and then constructed their XML tries. The structural similarity is computed between two XML tries utilizing trie matching method. By dynamically scanning the unassigned XML tries, XML documents are allocated into different clusters according the given structural similarity threshold, and finally our approach discovers the number of clusters on its own, where the complete cluster structure is preserved without any loss of structure information. Further, we develop a heuristic to automatically determine a suitable similarity threshold to achieve good clustering results. To demonstrate the effectiveness and efficiency of DSTM, we conduct extensive experiments on XML documents in e-business. The experimental results show that DSTM is approximately linear to the size of XML documents, is efficient for dynamic and incremental XML documents clustering, and outperforms K-means and the traditional hierarchical clustering methods in efficiency. In conclusion, our approach is scalable, effective and efficient for clustering large amounts of XML documents in e-business.

Keywords: e-business, XML clustering, dynamic scanning, trie matching, structural similarity threshold.

1 Introduction

Due to the inherent flexibility and self-describing nature in data representation, XML[1] (*eXtensible Markup Language*) is becoming a ubiquitous standard for information representation and exchange on the Web. Therefore, the widespread adoption of XML documents has led to massive amounts of XML data, raising many issues regarding methods of data management and e-business in large XML documents repositories.

---

[1] `http://www.w3.org/XML/`

V. Khachidze et al. (Eds.): iCETS 2012, CCIS 332, pp. 715–728, 2012.

Data mining techniques, such as clustering, can facilitate these processing applications by grouping XML documents according to their structural similarity. Clustering of similar XML documents has been seen as potentially one of the most effective solutions to improve document handling by facilitating better e-business transactions, information retrieval, data indexing, data integration and query processing [13].

Clustering techniques have been researched over several years for grouping numerical, symbolic and text data. Clustering of XML data significantly differs from the clustering of flat data and text, and is more complex with a nested structure. Firstly, XML allows embedding the semantic and structural aspects to document contents, resulting in the semi-structured and hierarchical data. An XML document contains tags and text enclosed within those tags. The tag not only describes the element name, including the semantics in the form of text data, but also defines the structure of an XML document showing the relationships between elements. Therefore, the XML clustering algorithms should handle both semantic and structural information in the process. Secondly, the user can define one's own XML documents with great flexibility and few restrictions, in both structure and semantics. Consequently, the heterogeneity in XML documents raises many challenges to detect similarity among the XML documents [9].

Several XML clustering methods have been suggested from different perspectives. Most of the existing methods focus on extracting frequent subtrees [7] or common structures [6] in a tree collection. The main problem with this is that some structural information is lost compared to the original tree during the extracting process, and the minimum support threshold for frequent pattern mining is difficult to determine. Moreover, some other methods compute the pair-wise structure similarity between documents based on the notion of tree editing distance [12]. However, the generation of similarity matrix can be computationally expensive when dealing with large data among diverse documents.

In this paper we propose a Dynamic Scanning approach for XML structural clustering based on the notion of Trie Matching (DSTM). Our approach neither mines frequent patterns in XML document collection, nor computes the pair-wise similarity between two XML documents. We devise a concise but efficient method to represent the structural similarity between two XML documents, based on trie matching. Given a set of XML documents, we initially derive all the paths and their frequencies in each XML document by utilizing VTD-XML parsing technique, and construct its corresponding XML trie. Subsequently, by dynamically scanning all these XML tries, XML documents are allocated into different clusters. A new cluster containing structurally similar XML documents according to the given similarity threshold will be generated when one scan of these XML trie is completed, and finally our method discovers the number of clusters on its own. The experimental results show that our approach is accurate, fast and scalable for grouping collections of large schemaless XML documents.

In this paper, the significant contributions of our approach are the following:

(1). A novel structural similarity representation between two XML documents based on trie matching is presented in our approach and we develop a heuristic to automatically determine a suitable similarity threshold to achieve good clustering results

(2). Unlike frequent subtrees and common structures mining, the complete cluster structure is preserved as a Cluster trie during dynamic scanning algorithm, and meanwhile frequent paths of an XML cluster can be easily obtained by traversing the Cluster trie to efficiently improve the performance of XML retrieval.

(3). Our approach is not sensitive to the order of input data, maintaining a stable and excellent clustering performance toward random input order. Moreover, our approach is substantially computationally efficient for incremental and dynamic clustering. When assigning a new incoming XML document into already discovered clusters, we only calculate the structural similarity between the document and the discovered Cluster Trie, rather than the whole set of documents.

This paper proceeds as follows. Section 2 discusses related work on XML document clustering. A dynamic scanning approach based on trie matching for XML clustering is presented in Section 3. Experimental evaluations are analyzed in Section 4, and finally Section 5 concludes our work.

2 Related Works

At present, a subset of the Web comprising XML documents is developing into a large XML document repository. However, it is known that only 48% of the XML documents contain links to specific schemas [8]. Consequently, integrating the enormous volume of schemaless and semantically different documents to realize a Web Database is a breath-taking task. Therefore, the difficulty of this integration task can be alleviated by utilizing a document clustering technique, and several attempts have been made in prior works.

The majority of previous work focuses on computing pair-wise similarities between XML documents, mainly based on tree edit distance [12], which is a popular measure for comparing trees. While there are algorithms that compute the edit distance between ordered trees in polynomial time, those for unordered trees are known to be NP-complete [15]. Additionally, some active researches [6], [7] proposed common structures or frequent subtrees for clustering XML documents. Recently, Antonellis, Makris and Tsirakis [2] proposed XEdge: Each XML document is represented by a LevelEdge, a structure that summarizes the distinct edges in each level of the document, and documents of similar structures are then grouped based on the LevelEdge. Kutty, Nayak, and Li [7] propose a novel way to represent the common substructures of XML documents using frequent subtrees to represent structural similarity. They focus on generating Closed Frequent Embedded (CFE) subtrees to improve the clustering performance. However, extracting frequent subtrees or common substructures may incur serious loss of structure information which would dramatically influence the quality of clustering results.

Recently, the Initiative for the Evaluation of XML Retrieval (INEX) has brought together a great number of brilliant researchers in the field of XML IR, thereby contributing a large amount of efficient and innovative approaches [1], [5], [10], [11] to clustering XML documents in the context of XML Information Retrieval. In INEX 2009 XML Mining Track [10], Altingovde, Atilgan, and Ulusoy [1] used Cover-Coefficient Based Clustering Methodology (C3M) to cluster XML documents. They adapted term-centric and document-centric index pruning techniques to obtain more compact representations of the documents. Documents are clustered with these reduced representations for various pruning levels, again using C3M algorithm. De Vries, Geva and De Vine [5] utilized the Random Indexing (RI) K-tree to cluster the entire XML documents in INEX 2009 Wikipedia collection. RI is an efficient dimensionality reduction technique that projects points in a high dimensional space onto a randomly selected lower dimensional space and is able to preserve the topology of the points. Pinto et al [11] used a modified version of the Star clustering method, which automatically obtains the number of clusters. In each iteration, this clustering method brings together all items whose similarity value is higher than a given threshold T, which is typically assumed to be the similarity average of the whole document collection and, therefore, the clustering method "discovers" the number of clusters on its own. Our approach is similar to K-Star algorithm, except without iteration and computation of the similarity matrix. By dynamically scanning the XML documents collection based on similarity measures of trie matching, different clusters are discovered and the complete Cluster structure is preserved with high performance in terms of execution time and clustering quality.

3 The DSTM Approach for Clustering XML Documents

3.1 XML Tries Construction

In order to measure structural similarity between two XML documents, an XML trie for the XML document is initially constructed based on the notion of trie. An XML trie resembles the DTD tree representing the structure of an XML document. A standard trie[2], the name of which derives from the word 'retrieval', is commonly designed to store a words dictionary and implement approximate matching algorithm, preserving great advantages over binary search trees (BSTs) and hash tables in looking up and space storing performance.

The structure of an XML document is stored as decomposed paths and their corresponding frequencies. The process of constructing XML trie is to progressively insert nodes by decomposing paths with '/' delimiter and matching element string. Fig 1 illustrates a high-level description of XML trie construction algorithm.

Algorithm: XML_trie_Constrcution

Input: A set of $<path_i, f_i>$ pairs PF
Output: An XML trie
For each $path_i$ in PF
(1). Split $path_i$ into terms array *T*;
(2). If root node is empty
    Set root node key to *T*[0];
(3). Else If orientate successfully next term in *T*
        Go to Step (4);
        Else Insert the term into the hash table field of current node;
(4). Repeat (3) until all terms in *T* are checked;
    Set the frequency of last term node to f_i ;
End for

Fig. 1. XML trie construction algorithm

[2] http://en.wikipedia.org/wiki/trie

Steps (1)-(4) provide the process of inserting paths into an XML trie; this is called *path inserting algorithm* (PIA), which will be applied multiple times in the following methods. The corresponding XML trie for an example XML in Figure 2 is constructed as shown in Fig 3.

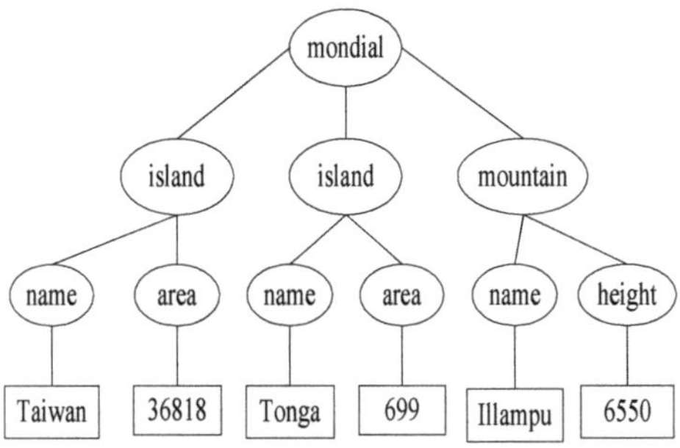

Fig. 2. An example of an XML document tree

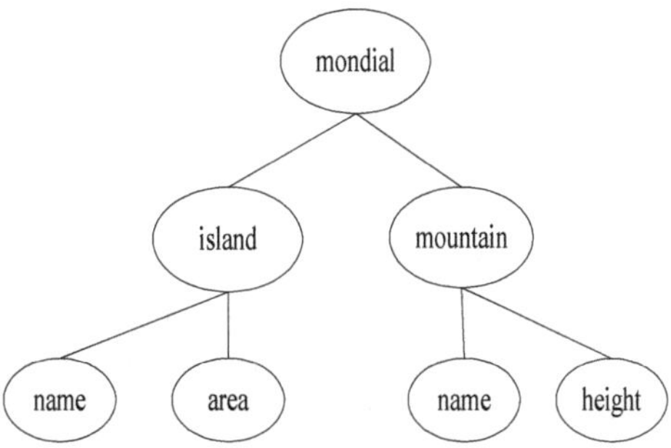

Fig. 3. The XML trie for Fig. 2

3.2 Structural Similarity between Two XML Tries

We develop a new solution for measuring the structural similarity between two XML documents based on their XML tries. Here we provide formal definitions for better understanding and formulating our method.

Definition 1 (Total Length of Trie Paths: TLp). For a given XML trie *T*, let TLp(T)=$\sum_{i=1}^{n} l_i$ denote total length of paths in *T*, where l_i is the length of *i*th path and n is the total number of paths in *T*.

Definition 2 (Length of prefix-matched path: Lpp). Given an XML trie *T* and a path *p*, Lpp(p,T) is denoted as the length of prefix-matched *p* in T.

Example 2. Assume that there exists a path *p* ={mondial/island/country} to be matched in a trie shown in Figure 3. Utilizing matching algorithm similar to *path inserting algorithm* (PIA) described in Figure 1, the prefix-matched path of {mondial/island/country} is {mondial/island} whose Lpp(p,T) is 2.

Definition 3 (Total length of prefix-matched path: TLpp). Considering two XML tries T_1 and T_2, let TLpp(T_1, T_2)= $\sum_{i=1}^{n} Lpp(p_i, T_1)$ be the total length of prefix-matched paths, where n is total number of paths in T_2 and p_i denotes *i*th path in T_2.

With the previous definitions, the structural similarity of two XML tries T_1 and T_2 is defined as follows:

$$\varphi(T_1, T_2) = \varphi(T_2, T_1) = \frac{2\text{TLpp}(T_1, T_2)}{\text{TLp}(T_1) + \text{TLp}(T2)} \qquad (1)$$

For a given $\varphi_{\text{threshold}}$ ranging from 0 to 1, if $\varphi(T_1, T_2) \geq \varphi_{\text{threshold}}$, two XML tries are to be assigned in the same cluster. Otherwise, two XML tries should be allocated into different clusters. The higher the $\varphi_{\text{threshold}}$, the more rigorous the requirements for grouping XML documents into a same cluster, whereas a lower $\varphi_{\text{threshold}}$ leads to loose requirements to assign XML documents into a same cluster.

3.3 DSTM Algorithm

Based on constructed XML tries and structural similarity measures described above, we developed DSTM for clustering XML documents, which is able to automatically identify the number of clusters. Unlike most clustering methods, DSTM requires a given structural similarity threshold $\varphi_{\text{threshold}}$ ranging from 0 to 1, rather than computing a similarity matrix among XML documents. The DSTM algorithm is described in Figure 4.

Algorithm: DSTM

Input: XML documents $D=\{D_1, D_2, \ldots, D_n\}$and their XML tries $T=\{T_1, T_2, \ldots, T_n\}$;
A given similarity threshold $\varphi_{\text{threshold}}$
Output: A clustering solution $C=\{C_1, C_2, \ldots, C_m\}$ and their corresponding cluster trie $CT=\{CT_1, CT_2, \ldots, CT_m\}$
1. Mark the first unassigned document D_i as assigned to form a new cluster C_j.
2. Scan the remaining unassigned document(D_k)
   If $\varphi(T_i, T_k) \geq \varphi_{\text{threshold}}$
      Add D_k into cluster C_j and mark D_k as assigned;
      For each path p_t in T_k
         Insert p_t into T_i; /*using PIA described in Figure 1-4*/
3. Save T_i as the cluster trie(CT_i) of C_j;
4. Repeat step 1 until all XML documents are marked as assigned.

Fig. 4. DSTM clustering algorithm

Step 2 is the core of DSTM clustering algorithm, which involves assigning documents into different clusters and building their corresponding cluster trie utilizing *PIA*. The amount of unassigned documents dynamically decreases in Step 2 by scanning the unassigned documents. Generally, the decreasing rate of unassigned documents is inversely proportional to the given similarity threshold. The smaller the given similarity threshold, the higher the decreasing rate DSTM achieves. When all the documents are marked as assigned, DSTM terminates the clustering process.

The main advantages of DSTM over most clustering algorithms are that DSTM preserves the complete cluster structural information (Cluster trie), and frequent paths of a specific cluster with a given min_support can be efficiently extracted using a DFS algorithm according to their corresponding frequency, recorded in the Cluster trie. In the ideal case, DSTM takes O(n) time to achieve clustering solutions (i.e. all XML documents are allocated into one cluster) by scanning the XML documents collection only once. However, in the worst case DSTM needs to scan the XML documents collection n times to obtain clustering solutions (i.e. all XML documents are allocated into n clusters) in $O(n^2)$. In reality, the number of detected clusters is far less than the number of XML documents. Therefore, the average time complexity of DSTM is O(n*m), approximately linear to the number of XML documents, where m is the number of detected clusters.

4 Experimental Evaluation

In this section, we evaluate the performance of DSTM on several data sets by conducting extensive experiments.

4.1 Datasets

The data sets used in our experiments are the XML files data set from Wisconsin's NIAGARA experimental data[3] and a subset of INEX 2010 IMDB collection[4]. The first data set includes XML documents from various domains of e-business. The majority of these domains contain a number of different documents that have structural and semantic differences. Thus, even though documents are from the same domain, they might be considered not similar enough to be grouped into the same clusters. The second data set is a subset of INEX 2010 IMDB collection from the Internet Movie Database website. Each document belongs to a single category, which is aimed at a clustering benchmark. Table 2 displays detailed statistics of the two data-sets.

Table 1. Statistics of two data sets

Statistics	NIAGARA	IMDB
No. of Doc.	863	7,012
No. of categories	10	5
Mean size of Doc. (bytes)	32,582	4,421
Mean depth of Doc.	8.67	6.72
Number of Nodes/Document	294	112

4.2 Evaluation Methods

To evaluate the performance of DTSM, we adopt the standard criteria namely intra-cluster, inter-cluster similarity [9] and FScore [17]. FScore is an external cluster quality evaluation based on the comparison of solution categories to known external categories, whereas intra-cluster and inter-cluster similarity are internal cluster quality evaluation criteria.

Intra-cluster similarity measures the cohesion of a cluster in terms of how similar the documents are within a cluster. This is computed by calculating the structural similarity between each XML trie within a cluster and the corresponding Cluster trie. The intra-cluster similarity of a given cluster C_i is the average structural similarities between all documents and the cluster, represented as follows:

$$IntraSim(C_i) = \frac{\sum_{j=1}^{n} \varphi(T_j, CT)}{n} \tag{2}$$

[3] http://www.cs.wisc.edu/niagara/data.html

[4] http://www.inex.otago.ac.nz/data/

Where n is the number of documents in C_i, T_j is the XML trie of the jth document in C_i and CT is the Cluster trie of cluster C_i. Therefore, the intra-cluster similarity of a clustering solution $C=\{C_1, C_2, \ldots, C_k\}$ is the average intra-cluster similarities of all clusters taking the numbers of documents within each cluster into consideration:

$$IntraSim = \frac{\sum_{i=1}^{k} n_i * IntraSim(C_i)}{N} \quad (3)$$

Where n_i is the number of documents in C_i, N is the total number of documents collection and k is the number of detected clusters in the solution. Generally, the higher the intra-cluster similarity value, the better the clustering solution is. Particularly, the intra-cluster similarity value is 1 when each cluster contains only one document.

Inter-cluster similarity measures the separation among different clusters. It is computed by calculating the structural similarity between two Cluster tries. The inter-cluster similarity of a clustering solution $C=\{C_1, C_2, \ldots, C_k\}$ is the average of all pair-wise structural similarities of two Cluster tries, formulated as follows:

$$InterSim = \frac{\sum_{i=1}^{k} \sum_{j=i+1}^{k} \varphi(CT_i, CT_j)}{0.5 * k * (k-1)} \quad (4)$$

Where k is the number of discovered clusters in the solution. Commonly, the lower the inter-cluster similarity value, the better the clustering solution is. In particular, the inter-cluster similarity value equals 1 when all the documents are allocated into the same cluster.

FScore is a combination of precision and recall. Precision defines the rate of correct matches in the solution categories, and Recall defines the rate of correct matches in the known categories. Given an XML document category Z_r with the number n^r of similar XML documents, and a cluster C_i with the number n_i of similar documents categorized by the clustering approach, let n_i^r be the number of documents in cluster C_i belonging to Z_r.

Precision (correctness) is denoted as: $P(Z_r, C_i) = n_i^r / n_i$

Recall (accuracy) is denoted as: $R(Z_r, C_i) = n_i^r / n^r$

Therefore, the FScore combining precision and recall with equal weight is defined as:

$$F(Z_r, C_i) = \frac{2P(Z_r, C_i) * R(Z_r, C_i)}{P(Z_r, C_i) + R(Z_r, C_i)} = \frac{2n_i^r}{n_i + n^r} \quad (5)$$

The FScore of a category Z_r is the maximum Fscore value attained in any cluster of the clustering solution. Hence, the Fscore of the overall clustering solution is defined as the sum of each individual categories' Fscore, weighted differently according to the number of documents in the category:

$$Fscore = \frac{\sum_{r=1}^{k} n^r * F(Z_r, C_i)}{N} \quad (6)$$

Where k is the number of discovered clusters and N is the total number of documents collection. A good clustering solution has Fscore value closer to 1.

4.3 Experimental Design

We carried out our experiments on an i3 2.27GHz CPU, 2GB RAM and 500GB hard disk running Windows 7 Home Basic operating system. Experiments were conducted to evaluate the number of detected clusters, response time, and the accuracy of clustering results with increasing similarity thresholds, as well as the scalability of DSTM over other clustering techniques.

The only parameter in our clustering approach is the structural similarity threshold which is crucial to the performance of DSTM. We initially obtained the number of detected clusters and their corresponding response time by ranging the similarity threshold from 0 to 1. Subsequently, the relationship between the number of detected clusters and the response time is compared to validate the analysis of time complexity in Section 4.2. Additionally, we designed the experiment to evaluate the intra-cluster, inter-cluster similarity and Fscore with increasing values of the similarity threshold, aiming to infer the optimal similarity threshold to achieve the best clustering performance taking intra-cluster, inter-cluster similarity and Fscore into consideration.

The dynamic and incremental clustering methods are usually criticized for being sensitive to the order in which the input data appears and, as a result, for only providing the local optimum solutions. In order to verify the scalability and flexibility of DSTM, we evaluated the clustering performance by randomly generating the entry order of input data. Also, experiments are conducted to compare the response time of DSTM using the optimal similarity threshold against K-means and the traditional hierarchical clustering methods by increasing the number of XML documents.

4.4 Results and Analysis

We adjusted the structural similarity threshold (φ) from 0 to 1 on NIAGARA dataset to derive the number of discovered clusters (Nc) and their corresponding response time (t). Table 3 shows that our approach discovered more clusters and took longer response time as the structural similarity increases. Moreover, Figure 5 exhibits an approximately linear relationship between the number of discovered clusters and their response time, which accords with the time complexity analyzed in Section 3.2.

Table 2. Number of clusters and response time with different φ on NIAGARA dataset

φ	0.1	0.2	0.3	0.4	0.5	0.6	0.7	0.8	0.9	1
Nc	9	11	11	11	13	15	18	32	63	161
t(ms)	1992	2053	2070	2086	2095	2181	2370	3471	5329	17064

To run DSTM in NIAGARA and IMDB datasets, we set $\varphi_{threshold}$ to 0.7 which is an empirical value. We analyzed the IntraSim, InterSim and Fscore performance of DSTM on NIAGARA and IMDB datasets with different $\varphi_{threshold}$. Figure 6 reveals that on NIAGARA dataset Fscore, values waved as the structural similarity threshold increases, achieving the optimal value 0.97 when the structural similarity threshold equals 0.7; meanwhile, the IntraSim and InterSim exhibited considerably excellent behavior. Similarly, Score achieved the optimal value 0.71 when the structural similarity threshold was set to 0.9 on IMDB dataset, shown in Figure 7. Therefore, when DSTM was performed with the empirical threshold, it could achieve excellent clustering results in most cases.

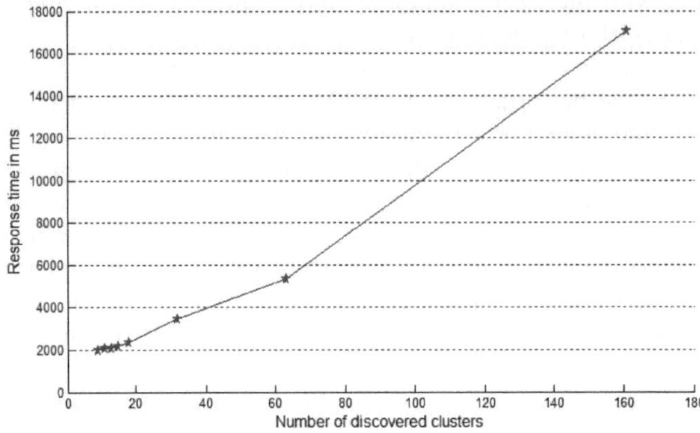

Fig. 5. Relationship between number of discovered clusters and response time

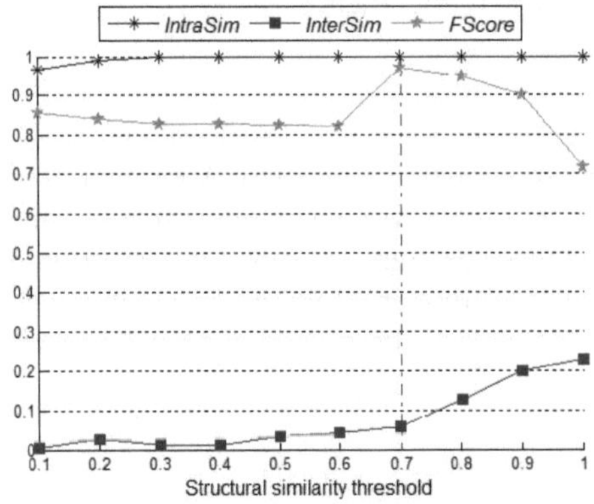

Fig. 6. The IntraSim, InterSim and Fscore performance of DSTM on NIAGARA dataset

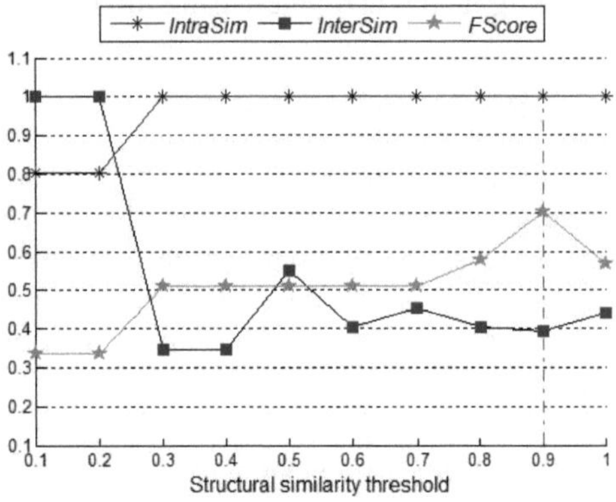

Fig. 7. The IntraSim, InterSim and FScore performance of DSTM on IMDB

Experiments were also evaluated to test the sensitivity of DSTM toward different input order. FScore values of five randomly generated input orders on XML Files dataset are represented in Figure 8. We can see that the overall trends of FScore did not significantly differ with regard to the five randomly generated input orders. When assigning a new incoming XML document into already discovered clusters, we only calculated the structural similarity between the document and discovered Cluster trie rather than the whole set of documents, where the input order of XML documents did not influence the clustering performance. As a result, DSTM was effective for dynamic and incremental documents clustering.

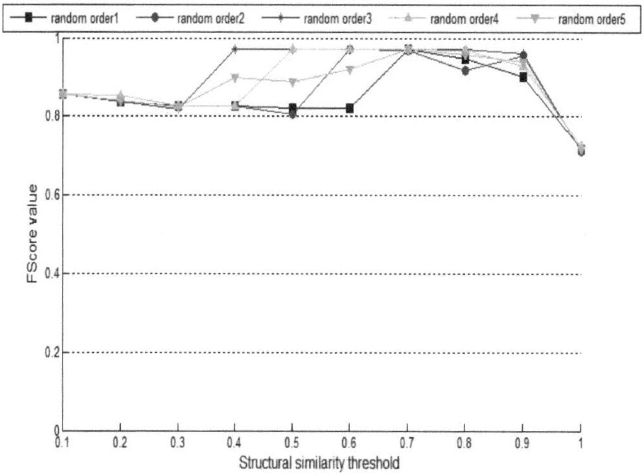

Fig. 8. FScore values of fives random orders of NIAGARA dataset

We also compared the execution time of DSTM against K-means and the traditional hierarchical clustering methods with respect to the increase in the number of NIAGARA documents. The similarity measure based on trie matching was also adopted in K-means and hierarchical clustering methods for fair comparison. Figure 9 illustrats the comparison result that the execution time of hierarchical clustering method dramatically increased as the number of NIAGARA documents increased, and the execution time of K-means increased in a small amount with respect to the number of XML files, due to the iterations and updating computation for the new cluster center. However, there was no significant difference in execution time of DSTM. The pair-wise similarity computation in the traditional hierarchical clustering method was fairly expensive and infeasible for large amounts of data. DSTM dynamically scanned the unassigned documents and generated new clusters with the optimal similarity threshold, outperforming K-means and the traditional hierarchical clustering methods in clustering efficiency.

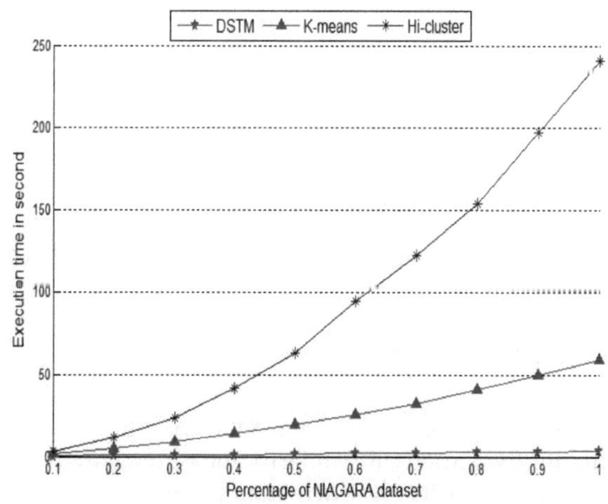

Fig. 9. Scalability performance

4.5 Parameter Discussion

In DSTM, we only need to set the structural similarity threshold $\varphi_{threshold}$ to cluster XML documents. The higher the IntraSim, and FScore value, and the lower the InterSim value, the better the clustering results. As FScore is an external cluster quality evaluation and in most real applications we do not have the known cluster labels, FScore cannot provide any heuristic information. We utilize IntraSim and InterSim values to automatically determine a suitable $\varphi_{threshold}$ with the following method: We first vary $\varphi_{threshold}$ from 0 to 1 and calculate the corresponding IntraSim and InterSim value, where $\varphi_{threshold}$ with high IntraSim and low InterSim Value will output good clustering results. When we obtain a small $\varphi_{threshold}$ range achieving high IntraSim and lower InterSim, we analyze the trend of the number of discovered clusters within this threshold range, and the suitable $\varphi_{threshold}$ would locate the place wherein the number of discovered clusters significantly changes which means the end of stable outputs of clustering results. As for NIAGARA dataset, we first get the $\varphi_{threshold}$ range [0.3, 0.7] shown in Figure 6 and check the number of discovered clusters within [0.3, 0.7], which is displayed in Figure 10, in which case the suitable $\varphi_{threshold}$ should be set to 0.7 because the number of discovered clusters significantly changes in $\varphi_{threshold} = 0.7$. When taking FScore into consideration, the optimal $\varphi_{threshold}$ should be also 0.7, as analyzed in Section 4.3, showing the great effectiveness of our method to automatically determine the suitable $\varphi_{threshold}$.

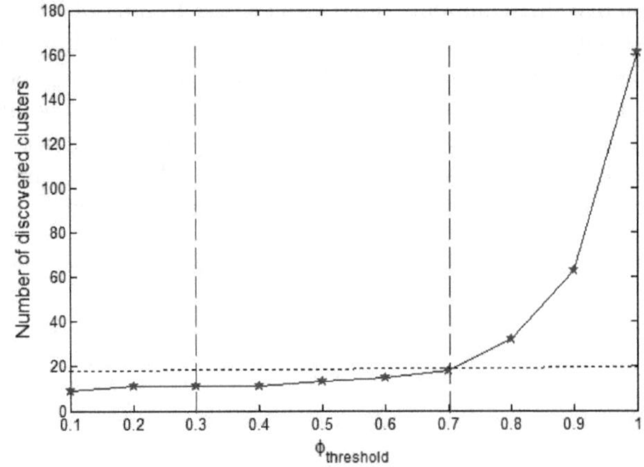

Fig. 10. Illustration of determining suitable $\varphi_{threshold}$ for NIAGARA dataset

5 Conclusions and Future Work

In this paper, we proposed a novel algorithm DSTM for clustering XML documents by their structures utilizing the structural similarity measures based on trie matching. An XML document is represented by its XML trie, which is used to compute structural similarity between other XML tries. By dynamically scanning the unassigned XML tries, XML documents are allocated into different clusters according to the given structural similarity threshold, and finally DSTM discovers the number of clusters on its own. Experimental results indicate that DSTM is scalable, robust, effective and efficient for clustering XML documents in e-business.

DSTM has broad applicability, such as in automatically clustering the incremental Web documents when a new transaction occurs in e-business, e.g. in Amazon, Taobao and 360buy, which will greatly facilitate the analysis and management of XML transaction data in e-business. In the future, we will incorporate semantic meaning of XML tags into DSTM and extend our clustering technique into recommendation systems in e-business.

References

[1] Altingovde, I.S., Atilgan, D., Ulusoy, Ö.: Exploiting Index Pruning Methods for Clustering XML Collections. In: Geva, S., Kamps, J., Trotman, A. (eds.) INEX 2009. LNCS, vol. 6203, pp. 379–386. Springer, Heidelberg (2010)

[2] Antonellis, P., Makris, C., Tsirakis, N.: XEdge: Clustering Homogeneous and Heterogeneous XML Documents Using Edge Summaries. In: Proceedings of the 23rd Annual ACM Symposium on Applied Computing, pp. 1081–1088 (2008)

[3] Costa, G., Manco, G., Ortale, R., Tagarelli, A.: A Tree-Based Approach to Clustering XML Documents by Structure. In: Boulicaut, J.-F., Esposito, F., Giannotti, F., Pedreschi, D. (eds.) PKDD 2004. LNCS (LNAI), vol. 3202, pp. 137–148. Springer, Heidelberg (2004)

[4] Dalamagas, T., Cheng, T., Winkel, K.J., Sellis, T.: A methodology for clustering XML documents by structure. Inform Syst. 31, 187–228 (2006)

[5] De Vries, C.M., Geva, S., De Vine, L.: Clustering with Random Indexing K-tree and XML Structure. In: Geva, S., Kamps, J., Trotman, A. (eds.) INEX 2009. LNCS, vol. 6203, pp. 407–415. Springer, Heidelberg (2010)

[6] Hwang, J.H., Ryu, K.H.: A weighted common structure based clustering technique for XML documents. J. Syst. Software 83, 1267–1274 (2010)

[7] Kutty, S., Nayak, R., Li, Y.Y.: XCFS-a novel approach for clustering XML documents using both the structure and the content (2010)

[8] Mignet, L., Barbosa, D., Veltri, P.: International Conference on World Wide Web Conference, pp. 500–510. ACM (2003)

[9] Nayak, R.: Fast and effective clustering of XML data using structural information. Knowl. Inf. Syst. 14, 197–215 (2008)

[10] Nayak, R., De Vries, C.M., Kutty, S., Geva, S., Denoyer, L., Gallinari, P.: Overview of the INEX 2009 XML Mining Track: Clustering and Classification of XML Documents. In: Geva, S., Kamps, J., Trotman, A. (eds.) INEX 2009. LNCS, vol. 6203, pp. 366–378. Springer, Heidelberg (2010)

[11] Pinto, D., Tovar, M., Vilariño, D., Beltrán, B., Jiménez-Salazar, H., Campos, B.: BUAP: Performance of K-Star at the INEX'09 Clustering Task. In: Geva, S., Kamps, J., Trotman, A. (eds.) INEX 2009. LNCS, vol. 6203, pp. 434–440. Springer, Heidelberg (2010)

[12] Tai, K.C.: The tree-to-tree correction problem. Journal of the ACM (JACM) 26, 433 (1979)

[13] Tran, T., Nayak, R., Bruza, P.D.: Document Clustering Using Incremental and Pairwise Approaches. In: Fuhr, N., Kamps, J., Lalmas, M., Trotman, A. (eds.) INEX 2007. LNCS, vol. 4862, pp. 222–233. Springer, Heidelberg (2008)

[14] Tran, T., Nayak, R., Bruza, P.D.: Combining structure and content similarities for XML document clustering (2010)
[15] Zhang, K., Statman, R., Shasha, D.: On the editing distance between unordered labeled trees. Information Processing Letters 42, 133–139 (1992)
[16] Zhang, L., Li, Z., Chen, Q., Li, N.: Structure and Content Similarity for Clustering XML Documents. In: Shen, H.T., Pei, J., Özsu, M.T., Zou, L., Lu, J., Ling, T.-W., Yu, G., Zhuang, Y., Shao, J. (eds.) WAIM 2010. LNCS, vol. 6185, pp. 116–124. Springer, Heidelberg (2010)
[17] Zhao, Y., Karypis, G.: Criterion functions for document clustering. Citeseer (2005)

Author Index

MIX
Papier aus verantwortungsvollen Quellen
Paper from responsible sources
FSC® C105338

If you have any concerns about our products,
you can contact us on
ProductSafety@springernature.com

In case Publisher is established outside the EU,
the EU authorized representative is:
Springer Nature Customer Service Center GmbH
Europaplatz 3, 69115 Heidelberg, Germany

Printed by Libri Plureos GmbH
in Hamburg, Germany

Communications in Computer and Information Science 332